Welcome to

McGraw-Hill's

SAT

Congratulations! You've chosen the SAT guide from America's leading educational publisher. You probably know us from many of the textbooks you used in school. Now we're ready to help you take the next step — and get into the college or university of your choice.

This book gives you everything you need to succeed on the test. You'll get in-depth instruction and review of every topic tested, tips and strategies for every question type, and plenty of practice exams to boost your test-taking confidence. To get started, go to the following pages where you'll find:

- **How to Use This Book:** Step-by-step instructions to help you get the most out of your test-prep program.

- **Your SAT Action Plan:** Learn how to make the best use of your preparation time.

- **SAT Format Table:** This handy chart shows the test structure at a glance: question types, time limits, and number of questions per section.

- **The 50 Top Strategies for Test Day:** Use this list to check your knowledge, or as a last-minute refresher before the exam.

- **The 9 Core SAT Essay Themes:** Find out the most common SAT essay themes, based on the SATs from the past 5 years.

- **The 5 Top SAT Calculator Tips:** Learn some smart ways that your calculator can help you.

- **Getting the Most from the Free Online Practice Tests:** Log on to the companion website for additional test-taking practice.

ABOUT McGRAW-HILL EDUCATION

This book has been created by a unit of McGraw-Hill Education, a division of The McGraw-Hill Companies. McGraw-Hill Education is a leading global provider of instructional, assessment, and reference materials in both print and digital form. McGraw-Hill Education has offices in 33 countries and publishes in more than 65 languages. With a broad range of products and services — from traditional textbooks to the latest in online and multimedia learning — we engage, stimulate, and empower students and professionals of all ages, helping them meet the increasing challenges of the 21st century knowledge economy.

Learn more. Mc Graw Hill **Do more.**

How to Use This Book

This book is designed for students who want an effective program for the most dramatic SAT score improvements. It is based on the College Hill Method™, the elite training system used by the tutors of College Hill Coaching since 1990. It focuses on what works best in SAT prep: mindful training in the reasoning skills at the core of the SAT, and not just test-taking tricks or mindless drills.

This book provides all the material you need to score well on the SAT. It will teach you the knowledge that is required for this difficult exam, including information about each type of question on the test. It also provides ample practice for you to refine the skills you are learning and then test yourself with full-length practice tests. For best results as you work your way through the book and the accompanying online tests, follow this four-step program:

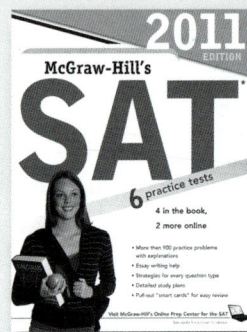

1 Learn About the SAT

Don't skip Chapter 1. In it you'll meet the SAT and learn exactly what academic skills it tests. You'll also find valuable test-taking strategies and information about how the test is scored.

2 Take a Realistic Practice SAT

Take the SAT diagnostic test in Chapter 2 of this book. Take the test strictly timed, in one sitting, and proctored if possible. Then use the answer key to evaluate your results so you can learn your strengths and weaknesses. Fill out the "College Hill SAT Study Plan" at the end of the test to analyze the strategies, concepts, reasoning skills, and vocabulary that you need to learn.

3 Study What You Need to Learn with the Lessons and Exercises

If you miss a question on your practice SAT, read its answer explanation at the end of the test. If it refers to a lesson in chapters 4–15, make that lesson part of your weekly review.

▸ First read each **Lesson** carefully, underlining important ideas or writing notes in the margins.

▸ Then move on to the **Concept Review** worksheet, which reinforces the key ideas in the lesson. Try to answer these questions without peeking back at the lesson. Circle any tough questions as you go so that you can review them later. Check your answers with the Answer Key.

▸ Then move on to the **SAT Practice** worksheet, which gives you questions as they might appear on the SAT. Work through these questions as if you were taking a real SAT.

▸ When you're done, read all of the explanations in the **Answer Key**, even for questions that you got right. Why? Because very often, there are many ways to get a question right, and some may be much more efficient than the one you used!

4 Repeat the Cycle Until You've Surpassed Your SAT Score Goal

Take the practice tests at the back of this book and on the companion website, trying each time to simulate actual testing conditions. After you take each test, fill out the College Hill SAT Study Plan at the end of the test to help you analyze your results. If you are still having problems, go back and review the corresponding lessons in Chapters 4–15. This process is designed to help you focus on the central reasoning skills at the core of the SAT. No quick tricks or simple formulas can do these things for you.

Your SAT Action Plan

To make the best use of your SAT preparation time, you'll need a personalized action plan that's based on you needs and the time you have available. This book has been designed for flexibility; you can work through it from cover to cover or you can move around from one chapter to another in the order you want based on your own priorities and needs. However, before you jump in, maximize the effectiveness of your preparation time by spending a few minutes to develop a realistic action plan. Use the tools provided in these pages to help you focus on the areas where you are weakest, plan your study program, and gain the discipline you need to pace yourself and achieve 5your goals.

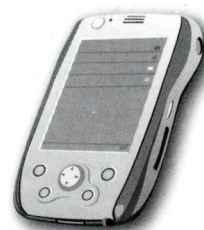

The College Hill SAT Study Plan

Each time you take a practice SAT in this book, on the CD (if you have purchased the book-CD version) or online, take a few minutes to fill out the College Hill Study Plan once you are finished. A copy of the plan is shown on page 4A. Blank Plans appear at the end of each test; for the CD or online tests, make your own copy of the plan. The Plan shows you your progress and provides an action plan for improving your score over the next week. Here's how to fill it in:

Scores

Write your raw and scaled scores in the box at the top, following the directions in the Score Conversion Table at the end of each test. These provide a record of your weekly progress.

Questions About the Test

1 **What were your test conditions?** Did you take your practice SAT as you would take a real SAT? Were you sitting at a desk and at a neutral site? Did you time yourself strictly? Did you take the test all at one sitting? If your conditions were not realistic, make sure that they are more realistic next time. Also, note any conditions that may have affected your performance, like "broken clock," "noisy radiator," "freezing room," or "phone interruption." Learning to deal with distractions and with the length and time limits of the SAT is very important to peak performance.

2 **What was your pre-test routine?** What you do just before the test can be very important to your performance. Having a raging argument with someone, for instance, probably won't help. To perform your best, get at least 8 hours of sleep the night before, get 30 minutes of exercise prior to the SAT, and have a good breakfast. Write down anything significant that you did just prior to the test, like "ran 4 miles," "had oatmeal and orange juice," "was yelled at by Dad," or "did 15 minutes of yoga."

3 **Did you attack the questions you need to attack?** The table on the upper right of the worksheet shows you what percent of questions you should plan to attack, and what percent you should get right, in order to achieve particular score goals. Set an aggressive but realistic score goal for yourself on each section: Critical Reading, Math, and Writing. Then, after taking the test, notice how close you came to the percentages you need on each section. The "attack" percentage is the total number of questions you answered (right or wrong) divided by the total number of

College Hill™ SAT Study Plan

Test # _____	RAW SCORES:	CR _____	M _____	W _____	Essay _____
	SCALED SCORES:	CR _____	M _____	W _____	Essay _____

1. What were your test conditions?

2. What was your pre-test routine?

Goal	Attack	Get	CR pts	M pts	W pts
500	75%	50%	30	25	25
550	80%	60%	37	32	32
600	85%	67%	45	38	38
650	90%	80%	52	44	42
700	100%	90%	59	49	45
750	100%	95%	62	52	47
800	100%	100%	66	54	49

3. Did you attack all of the questions you needed to attack? (See the table above.)

4. Did you rush to complete any section?

5. How many more raw points do you need to make your score goal?   CR _____   M _____   W _____

6. Did you make educated guesses on any questions? If so, how many points did you pick up on these questions?

7. STUDY PLAN: Use the detailed answer key after the test to review the answers to the questions you missed. Below, list the lessons linked to the questions you missed, and list the tough words you missed from the test.

Lessons to Review

_____
_____
_____
_____
_____
_____
_____
_____

Words to Review

_____
_____
_____
_____
_____
_____
_____
_____

questions on that section. (There are 67 total Critical Reading questions, 54 total Math questions, and 49 total Writing questions.) The "get" percentage is the total number of *raw score points* you got on each section divided by the total number of questions on that section. For instance, if you're gunning for a 600 math score, you'll have to get 67%, or about two-thirds, of the available points on that section. Of course, you should attack *more* than 67% of the questions to give yourself room for error, but don't answer too many questions so that you rush and make a lot of careless mistakes. A good compromise is to attack about 85% of the questions and leave the hardest 15% (about 3 of every 20) unanswered, hoping to get 67% of the available points.

Be sure to attack the easy questions first. On every subsection except the Critical Reading passages, the questions start easy and get harder. If your plan involves skipping questions, make sure they are the hard ones at the end, not the easy ones at the beginning. However, don't get bogged down on any question, even one that is supposed to be "easy." Your job is to maximize your points, so if a question seems challenging at first, move on and come back to it later if you have time.

4 **Did you rush to complete any section?** Although it's always better to skip tough SAT questions rather than get bogged down by them, it's also never good to rush. After you complete a practice SAT, ask yourself: did I make any careless errors because I was rushing? Remember: because of the SAT's wrong-answer penalty, skipping a question is better than getting it wrong!

5 **How many more raw points do you need to make your score goal?** Again, the table at the top right of the worksheet provides your guide. Just look up your score goal for each section and find the corresponding raw score needed for that goal, and then subtract your *actual raw score* for each section. This tells you how many more questions you'll need to pick up.

6 **Did you make educated guesses on any questions?** While some students are very reluctant to leave any question unanswered, others have the opposite feeling and think that they should never guess on a question unless they are absolutely certain. But this is a bad strategy too. Educated guessing usually helps your score; if you can eliminate just a couple of wrong answers, take your best guess. When reviewing your test, look at the questions you guessed on, and notice whether you picked up points from them.

7 **Study Plan.** This is the real key to improving your SAT score. Go to the answer explanations and carefully read the explanations for the questions you missed. Then notice the lesson(s) listed after each explanation, and list these lessons on this part of the Study Plan. If you need to improve your reading skills, include "Chapter 4, Critical Reading Skills." If you need to work on sentence completion strategies, include "Chapter 5, Sentence Completion Skills." If the multiple-choice questions on the Writing section are giving you trouble, include "Chapter 14, How to Attack SAT Writing Questions." If you are struggling with the essay, then include "Chapter 12, How to Write a Great Persuasive Essay" or "Chapter 13, SAT Essay Writing Practice." Next, from the sentence completion explanations, list the vocabulary words that gave you trouble and make flashcards (using the method described in Chapter 3) to study in the coming weeks.

College Hill™ SAT Weekly Study Schedule

First Week

Saturday	Sunday	Monday	Tuesday	Wednesday	Thursday	Friday
Take Diagnostic SAT in Chapter 2 (3.5 hours)	Score and review SAT Read Chapter 3: "Building an Impressive Vocabulary" Make 30 new vocabulary cards (1 hour)	Review vocabulary cards Complete 1–2 lessons from Chapter 4: "Critical Reading Skills" Read and analyze op-ed page (0.5–1 hour)	Review vocabulary cards Complete 1–2 lessons from Chapter 4: "Critical Reading Skills" Read and analyze op-ed page (0.5–1 hour)	Review vocabulary cards Complete 1–2 lessons from Chapter 4: "Critical Reading Skills" Read and analyze op-ed page (0.5–1 hour)	Review vocabulary cards Complete 1–2 lessons from Chapter 4: "Critical Reading Skills" Read and analyze op-ed page (0.5–1 hour)	Review vocabulary cards Complete 1–2 lessons from Chapter 4: "Critical Reading Skills" Read and analyze op-ed page (0.5–1 hour)

Second Week

Saturday	Sunday	Monday	Tuesday	Wednesday	Thursday	Friday
Take Practice SAT #1 in Chapter 16 (3.5 hours)	Score and review SAT Complete 1–2 lessons from Chapter 5: "Sentence Completion Skills" Make 30 new vocabulary cards (1 hour)	Review vocabulary cards Complete 1–2 lessons from Chapter 5: "Sentence Completion Skills" Make 30 new vocabulary cards (0.5–1 hour)	Review vocabulary cards Complete 1–2 lessons from Chapter 5: "Sentence Completion Skills" Make 30 new vocabulary cards (0.5–1 hour)	Review vocabulary cards Complete 1–2 lessons from Chapter 5: "Sentence Completion Skills" Make 30 new vocabulary cards (0.5–1 hour)	Review vocabulary cards Complete 1–2 lessons from Chapter 5: "Sentence Completion Skills" Make 30 new vocabulary cards (0.5–1 hour)	Review vocabulary cards Complete 1–2 lessons from Chapter 5: "Sentence Completion Skills" Make 30 new vocabulary cards (0.5–1 hour)

Third Week and Beyond

Saturday	Sunday	Monday	Tuesday	Wednesday	Thursday	Friday
Take Practice SAT (3.5 hours)	Score and review SAT Make SAT Study Plan Make 30 new vocabulary cards Read and analyze op-ed page	Review vocabulary cards Complete 1–2 lessons from SAT Study Plan Read and analyze op-ed page (0.5–1 hour)	Review vocabulary cards Complete 1–2 lessons from SAT Study Plan Read and analyze op-ed page (0.5–1 hour)	Review vocabulary cards Complete 1–2 lessons from SAT Study Plan Read and analyze op-ed page (0.5–1 hour)	Review vocabulary cards Complete 1–2 lessons from SAT Study Plan Read and analyze op-ed page (0.5–1 hour)	Review vocabulary cards Complete 1–2 lessons from SAT Study Plan Read and analyze op-ed page (0.5–1 hour)

Your Weekly SAT Study Schedule

Once you have a plan, it's time to start studying. Be diligent, but don't overwhelm yourself. Your schoolwork should take priority over SAT prep — colleges care a lot about those grades, and for good reason! But if you make a manageable plan to work for at least 30 minutes every weeknight on your SAT review, you will see great results in just a matter of weeks.

Page 6A shows a suggested Weekly SAT Study Schedule. Most students find this schedule both manageable and highly productive. Of course, you will need to adapt it to your own schedule, but remember that it is more productive to do some work every day rather than a lot of work just one day a week.

Notice that this study schedule (which, remember, is only a basic guide) includes two "groundwork" weeks, in which you will work through lessons in those areas that almost every student needs to review: vocabulary skills, reading skills, and persuasive writing skills. As such, the first two weeks of the schedule don't provide much flexibility regarding which lessons to review. However, if you feel that you are exceptionally strong in those areas, feel free to replace those lessons with math (chapters 6–11) or grammar (chapters 14 and 15) lessons from the Study Plan that you complete after your practice tests. From the third week on, your study plan will be completely personalized, based on each week's post-test Study Plan.

Notice also that the plan includes studying 30 new vocabulary words each week and reading the op-ed page of a major national or international newspaper like *The New York Times* or the *Wall Street Journal,* every day. Good newspaper opinion pieces provide excellent all-around SAT preparation: they immerse you in important contemporary issues and ideas, reinforce college-level vocabulary, and serve as (usually) good examples of persuasive prose. One of the best ways to improve your persuasive essay-writing skills is to read lots of good op-ed pieces.

How to Stick to Your Study Plan

- Believe it or not, about 20 minutes of aerobic exercise is a great warm-up before you sit down to do your homework. Exercise doesn't help just your muscles; it also helps your brain. When your brain is well oxygenated, it works more efficiently, so you do your work better and faster. If you don't already have an exercise routine, try to build up to a good 20- to 45-minute aerobic workout — running, rowing, swimming, biking — every day. Your routine will also help you enormously on test day; exercising on the morning of the SAT will help you to relax, focus, and perform!

- If you start to get nervous when you think about the SAT, try learning "focusing" exercises, like deep breathing, meditation, or yoga. Such exercises will also help enormously on test day.

- Prepare your space. Many students waste a lot of study time because they don't prepare their work space properly. Find a quiet, clean place where you can stay focused for a good stretch of time, away from the TV and troublesome siblings. Sit in an upright chair at a table or desk with good lighting. Also, make sure that all the tools you will need are within easy reach: a dictionary, note cards, calculator, and pencils with erasers. Turn off your cell phone and close the door!

- Sit up straight when you work. Don't work on your bed, on the floor, or in a reclining chair. When your body tilts, your brain goes into "sleep mode" and has to work harder to focus.

- Whenever you feel fatigued from studying, take a 10-minute break. Get a quick snack or listen to a couple of your favorite songs.

SAT Format

The table below shows the format of a typical SAT. The order of the 10 sections varies from test to test, except that Section 1 is always the Essay, the 25-minute sections always precede the 20-minute sections, and the 10-minute Writing section is always last.

About the "Experimental" Section: Every official SAT includes one 25-minute "experimental" section, which is used to field-test questions for future SATs, and does not count toward your score. You will not know which section is experimental, however, because it will be inserted randomly into the test and will have the same format as one of the other 25-minute sections; it could be a math, critical reading, or writing section. Each test in this book omits the experimental section, and so contains 9 sections rather than 10.

Section Type	Section	Total Number of Questions	Time Limit (minutes)
Essay	**Essay Section**	1	25
Math	**Long Math Multiple-Choice Section** ▶ 20 Multiple-choice questions	20	25
	Long Math Grid-In Section ▶ 8 Multiple-choice questions ▶ 10 Student-produced Response questions	18	25
	Short Math Section ▶ 16 Multiple-choice questions	16	20
Critical Reading	**Long Critical Reading Section 1** ▶ 8 Sentence Completion questions ▶ 15–17 Critical Reading questions	23–25	25
	Long Critical Reading Section 2 ▶ 5 Sentence Completion questions ▶ 18–20 Critical Reading questions	23–25	25
	Short Critical Reading Section ▶ 6 Sentence Completion questions ▶ 13–14 Critical Reading questions	19–20	20
Writing	**Long Writing Section** ▶ 11 Improving Sentences questions ▶ 18 Error ID questions ▶ 6 Improving Paragraphs questions	35	25
	Short Writing Section ▶ 14 Improving Sentences questions	14	10
Experimental	**Long Math, Critical Reading, or Writing Section** ▶ Same format as one of the 25-minute Math, Critical Reading, or Writing sections	18–35	25

50 Top Strategies for Test Day

When it's almost test day and you've read this book and taken the Practice Tests, make sure you review this page and the pages that follow. Here you'll find 50 essential strategies that can definitely help you earn more points on the SAT. You'll see longer explanations of some of these strategies, along with examples, in the review portions of this book. The purpose of these pages is to provide a handy, all-in-one, last-minute reminder of these valuable concepts. Use this review to check your test readiness and make sure you're prepared to do your best — and get your best score.

General Test-taking Strategies

1   Take control. Not every student will ace the SAT, but any student can take *charge of it*. Go into the test with confidence and the game plan that you've determined from using this book.

2   Lay everything out the night before. Sleep easy the night before the SAT knowing that you're ready to go. Lay out three #2 pencils *with good erasers*, your calculator *with fresh batteries*, your admission ticket, your photo ID, and a snack.

3   Have a good breakfast. Your brain can't work well without fuel.

4   Know where you're going. If you're taking the SAT at an unfamiliar school, acquaint yourself with it before test day. Take a trip there in the days before the test.

5   Dress properly. Dress in light layers so you'll be comfortable whether the testing room is sweltering or frigid. An uncomfortable body makes for a distracted brain.

6   Get a good two nights' sleep. A rested brain is a smarter brain. The nights before the SAT are for sleeping, not for all-nighters. Get a good eight hours each of the two nights before your SAT.

7   Get some exercise. Most teenagers are pretty foggy in the morning, so get a leg up on the competition by waking your brain with exercise. Twenty minutes of cardio will keep you alert.

8   Bring a snack. Your brain burns calories when it's thinking hard. Bring a granola bar, banana, or energy bar to the SAT to refuel during the break.

9   Know what to attack. As you begin each section of your SAT, know how many questions to attack. For instance, if you've got a realistic shot at breaking 700, you should be attacking every question. But if your goal is 600, you can skip about 15% of the questions, and if it's 500, you can skip the toughest 25%. The "College Hill SAT Study Plan" at the end of each practice test in this book provides you with a solid guide for building your game plan.

10   Take a "two-pass" approach. If you've built a smart game plan and practiced with it, you should have enough time to tackle all of your "must answer" questions, then take one more pass through them, checking for common mistakes. Once all of your "must answer" questions have been double-checked, you can approach the hardest questions carefully.

11   Shut out distractions. If you have a game plan and have practiced it, confidently shut out everyone else during the test. Don't speed up just because the girl next to you is racing through her test — ignore her. She's probably rushing because she's nervous. Stick to your game plan. Also, if you are easily distracted by noises around you like tapping pencils, sniffling testers, or clanking radiators, bring a pair of wax earplugs.

12   Watch the clock — but not too much. If you have taken enough practice SATs, you should go into the test with confidence in your ability to pace yourself. But for insurance, bring a *silent* stopwatch (not one that beeps). Check it occasionally to make sure you're on pace.

13 **Work briskly, but not carelessly.** Don't get bogged down on tough questions: if you get stuck on a question, circle it on your test booklet (so you know where it is if you have time to come back to it later) and move on. (Make sure that you skip that space on your answer sheet as well!) On the other hand, rushing is never a good strategy. Optimize your score by working briskly enough to attack all of the questions you need to, but not so quickly that you make careless errors.

14 **Don't worry about answer patterns.** Some SAT takers refuse to make certain patterns on their answer sheet. For instance, they won't mark (C) — even if it's clearly the best answer — if they already have three (C)s in a row. Bad idea. Bottom line: *always* pick what you think is the best answer, regardless of any answer patterns.

The SAT Essay

15 **Be ready for the essay.** On SAT day, you need to go in with a clear understanding of what SAT essay readers are looking for: a clear and consistent thesis, specific and well-explained examples, logical organization, and good language skills.

16 **Put aside 6 minutes to plan.** When the essay section starts, take 6 minutes to think carefully about the question, consider your examples, develop an interesting thesis, and write a quick outline. You should still have plenty of time to write a solid essay, and it will flow much more easily.

17 **Get your examples before your thesis.** Don't put the cart before the horse. Don't pick a thesis until you've considered what the most interesting examples actually *say* about the question. Remember to look at the question from all sides.

18 **Write at least 4 paragraphs.** According to The College Board, a good SAT essay "is well organized and clearly focused, demonstrating clear coherence and smooth progression of ideas." This means that you must use paragraphs effectively. Think of your paragraphs as the "stepping stones" of your argument. Two or three steps isn't much of a journey, is it?

19 **Have at least five "high-yield" sources ready.** Have at least five (but preferably about a dozen) "high yield" examples from literature, history, and personal experience ready to discuss in your essay. Specific and relevant examples earn big points on your essay.

20 **Know the common essay themes.** The SAT essay questions tend to focus on nine basic themes, which are listed on page 13A in this insert. Although there is no guarantee that your essay question will be on this list, there's an excellent chance that it will. Be ready to write on any of these questions, and think carefully about how to use your "high-yield" examples on each one.

21 **Focus like a laser on your thesis.** As you write your essay, never lose sight of your central purpose: to articulate, support, and explain your thesis. For each example you present, explain clearly how it supports your thesis.

22 **Write a real argument.** Every argument has more than one side. Don't just list reasons why your thesis is correct. Also remember to consider any viable counter-arguments to your thesis and explain why they're wrong.

Sentence Completion Questions

23 **Read the whole sentence first.** On sentence completion questions, read the whole sentence, saying "blank" in place of the missing words, and try to understand the logical gist of the sentence. Don't even look at the choices before you understand the whole sentence.

24 **Come up with your own word.** If you understand the sentence and its structure, you should be able to generate your own word or phrase for each blank. Write them down if it helps.

25 Work by process of elimination. Once you have your own word(s) in mind for the sentence, go through the choices and eliminate those that don't convey the same idea in the sentence.

26 Focus on tone. Pay attention to the tone of the words (positive, negative, or neutral) as you try to complete the sentence, and eliminate those choices that give the wrong tone.

27 Analyze for roots and prefixes. If the words in the choices are tough, try to guess their meanings based on their prefixes and roots. Important word roots and prefixes are covered Chapter 3.

Critical Reading Questions

28 Don't psych yourself out on the reading sections. When you get to the critical reading portion of the SAT, don't say, "Oh no, more boring and obscure science passages." Instead, take a positive attitude and tell yourself that you're going to learn something interesting.

29 Focus on the 3 key questions. The key to good reading comprehension is answering three key questions discussed in Chapter 4: What is the purpose? What is the main idea? And what is the overall structure of the passage?

30 Get your own answer first. On the reading questions, don't jump to the choices too quickly. Instead, read each question carefully and think of your own answer first, then find the choice that best matches it. This will help you avoid the "traps."

31 Deal with your "space outs." Many students "space out" on the reading because they get overwhelmed or disoriented when reading about topics like paleontology or primitivism. If it happens to you, don't panic and don't rush. Just continue from where you left off.

32 Be selective on the reading questions. Unlike the other SAT sections, the reading questions don't get progressively harder. Instead, they follow the sequence of the passage: the first questions focus on the beginning of the passage, and the last questions on the end. If you get to a tough reading question, skip it and move on; the next one might be easier.

33 Don't fall for the traps. Always read critical reading questions very carefully. Many choices are "traps:" they make true statements about the passage, but they are not "correct" because they do not answer the question asked. You won't fall for them if you get your own answer first.

34 Know how to attack the "paired passages." On the "paired" passages (Passage 1 vs. Passage 2), it is generally best to read Passage 1 and then go right to the questions that pertain to Passage 1 before moving on to Passage 2. If you try to read the passages back-to-back, it may be harder to recall and distinguish the key information from the two passages. Don't let them run together.

Math Questions

35 Mark up the test. The best test takers do a lot of scratch work on the SAT, particularly on the math section. Write down what you know and show your steps. Mark up diagrams, write equations, and show your work so that you can check it when you come back later.

36 Look for patterns and use them. One important skill the SAT math section tests is "pattern finding." Always pay special attention to simple patterns or repetitions in a problem, because exploiting them is usually the key to the solution.

37 Keep it simple. If you're doing lots of calculations to solve an SAT math problem, you're probably missing a key fact that simplifies the problem. Always look for the easy way.

38 Know the basic formulas. Most of the formulas you will need for the SAT are given to you in the "Reference Information" at the beginning of each math section. Even so, get fluent in them so you can easily recognize when to use them. Also, there are several others that good test-takers need to memorize, like the slope formula (Chapter 10, Lesson 4), the rate formula (Chapter 9, Lesson 4), and the average formula (Chapter 9, Lesson 2).

39 Check your work. There are many ways to make careless mistakes on the SAT math. Give yourself time to go back and check over your arithmetic and algebra, and make sure everything's okay.

40 Consider different approaches. If you're stuck on a math question, try working backwards from the choices, or plugging in numbers for the unknowns.

41 Watch out for key words. Pay special attention to words like *integer, even, odd*, and *consecutive* when they show up, because students commonly overlook them. And make sure you don't confuse *area* with *perimeter*!

42 Don't overuse your calculator. Your calculator can be handy on the SAT, but the best test-takers hardly use it at all. If you're doing a lot of calculator work for a problem, you're probably making it too hard. Keep it simple, and only use the calculator as a check.

43 Re-read the question. Before finalizing your answer, re-read the question to be sure you've answered the right question. If it asks for $5x$, don't give the value for x!

Writing Questions

44 Know the 15 key grammar rules. Go into the SAT writing with a solid understanding of the 15 key grammar rules. If you can't explain parallelism, dangling participles, or pronoun case errors, make sure you study Chapter 15 carefully!

45 Trust your ear (at least at first). If you've read a lot of good prose in your life, you have probably developed a good ear for standard English grammar. On the easy and medium writing questions, then, your ear will be your best guide: bad phrases will "sound" wrong. On harder questions (the last third of them), however, your skill in analyzing sentences will come into play.

46 Know how to analyze the tricky sentences. Chapters 14 and 15 provide tons of exercises to help you to recognize the most relevant grammar mistakes, and to analyze sentences like a pro. Without these skills, you will struggle to figure out the toughest sentences on the writing sections.

47 Don't fear perfection. On SAT writing questions, the "no error" choice should be correct roughly 1/5 of the time over the long term, or roughly 3-4 questions out of the 18 "identifying sentence errors" questions. Bottom line: don't shy away from "no error," but choose it only after careful analysis.

48 Make sure it's a real mistake. On "identifying sentence errors" questions, a word or phrase isn't necessarily wrong just because you might say it differently. For instance, if the word *since* is underlined, don't choose it just because you prefer to say *because* — the words are interchangeable. Make sure that you know how to fix the mistake — and that it's a *real* grammatical or semantic mistake — before choosing it.

49 On "improving paragraphs" questions, pay attention to "in context" questions. You can attack some "improving paragraphs" questions (those at the end of the 25-minute writing section) without having to read the passage in detail. However, if the question uses the phrase "in context," or asks about paragraph transitions or cohesiveness, you must understand the *logical flow* of the passage to get it right. For these questions, read the two previous sentences, and understand the logical gist of the paragraph in question.

50 Read it again to check. Before choosing an answer on a writing question, always re-read the entire sentence, including the correction, to make sure the sentence flows smoothly and logically. If the whole *sentence* doesn't sound better, it's wrong.

The 9 Core SAT Essay Themes

To ace the SAT essay, you have to know what to expect. Although you can't know exactly what question you'll be asked to write on, you can study those that have appeared on previous SATs. To make it easier, we've categorized the nine most common SAT essay themes below, based on the SATs from the past 5 years. We recommend prepping for the SAT essay by writing at least one 4- or 5-paragraph essay, giving specific examples and clear explanations, for each of the sample questions below.

1. Independent Thinking vs. Conformism

Should we learn for ourselves or learn from others? What is the value of creative thinking?

2. Truthfulness

Is honesty always the best policy? Is truth (or the value of truth) relative?

3. Selfishness/Competition vs. Generosity/Cooperation

Can competition or selfishness be good?

4. Change

How and why do people change? Is change good or necessary?

5. Success vs. Failure

What and how can we learn from our failures? What is success, and how can we achieve it?

6. Learning from Different Perspectives

Are our biases harmful? Can we benefit from the perspectives of others?

7. Responsibility

What are our responsibilities to ourselves and to our society?

8. Evaluating Modern History

What do you think of the world today and how it's changing?

9. Decision Making

How can we make sound decisions? What guides our decision-making process?

The 5 Top SAT Calculator Tips

1. Don't Overuse the Calculator

Even though calculators are allowed on the SAT, don't let them think for you. The SAT is a reasoning test, not a calculation test. If you pick up your calculator more than three times per math section, you need to wean yourself off of it and start working on your thinking skills!

Of course, smart calculator use is occasionally helpful, as the following examples show.

2. Know How to MATH▶FRAC

Let's say you're solving an SAT math problem about probabilities and you get 34/85 as an answer, but the choices are

A. 4/17
B. 2/7
C. 2/5
D. 3/7
E. 7/17

Did you mess up? No — you just have to simplify. Here, a TI-83 or similar calculator with ▶FRAC might save you time. Type "34/85" and enter, then press the MATH button and then ▶FRAC. Like magic, it will convert the fraction to lowest terms: 2/5. Sweet!

On "grid in" questions, it's also a good idea to MATH▶FRAC any decimal answer you get to make sure that it gives a fraction that can fit into the grid. If not, you've probably done something wrong!

3. Know How to Get a Remainder

Consider this math question: The tables at a wedding reception are set up to accommodate 212 people. There are 24 tables, some seating 8 people and the rest seating 9 people. How many 9-seat tables are there?

Without getting into the details, the answer is simply the remainder when 212 is divided by 24. You could do this by long division, but you can probably do it faster with a calculator:

Enter the division problem and enter: $212 \div 24 = 8.833333\ldots$
Subtract the integer part: $ANS - 8 = 0.833333\ldots$
Multiply by the original divisor: $ANS \times 24 = 20$
So the answer is 20! Memorize this handy procedure to streamline "remainder" problems.

4. Beware of "Killer Program" Gimmicks

Don't believe your friends who tell you they have a killer "SAT-busting" calculator program. They don't. These are usually gimmicks that waste time rather than save it. Again, if you're depending on your calculator to do anything but check basic calculations, you're thinking about the SAT in the wrong way.

5. Get fresh batteries

Even if you don't use your calculator much, you won't be happy if it dies halfway through the SAT. Put in a set of fresh batteries the night before!

Getting the Most from the Free Online Practice Tests

Visit **MHPracticePlus.com/SAT** for your free access to additional complete SAT practice tests. These are complete interactive exams with automatic timing and scoring, as well as detailed explanations for every question. You'll also see a list of other SAT study resources available from McGraw-Hill.

Accessing the Tests

At the website, click on the words "SAT Center." You'll be taken to a web page that offers full-length practice SATs. Click on any one to begin.

Taking the Tests

Main Menu ● ● ● ● ● ● ● ● ● ● ● ● ●

On the Main Menu, roll your cursor over the Practice Test that you wish to take. You will see a submenu showing the various sections of that test. If you have not taken that section before, you will see a dialogue box that says "To begin this section, click the Start Section button." When you click the button, you will be asked if you wish to take the section timed or untimed. If you choose the timed test mode, a countdown clock will appear at the upper right corner of the screen.

   You will then be shown the View Instructions screen for that test section. These present the directions for each question type. When you close the View Instructions screen, the first question will appear.

Answering Questions ● ● ● ● ● ● ● ● ● ●

To answer questions, click on the answer circle beside the letter of your choice (or enter your answer in the grid provided). At the bottom right corner of the screen you will see a note such as "2 of 20," telling you how many questions are in the section and which question you are answering. After answering each question, click on one of the two arrows at either side of that note to go to the next or previous question.

   At any time, you may roll your cursor over the **Question Status** at the bottom left corner of the screen to see the total number of questions in the section and which ones you have answered or not answered.

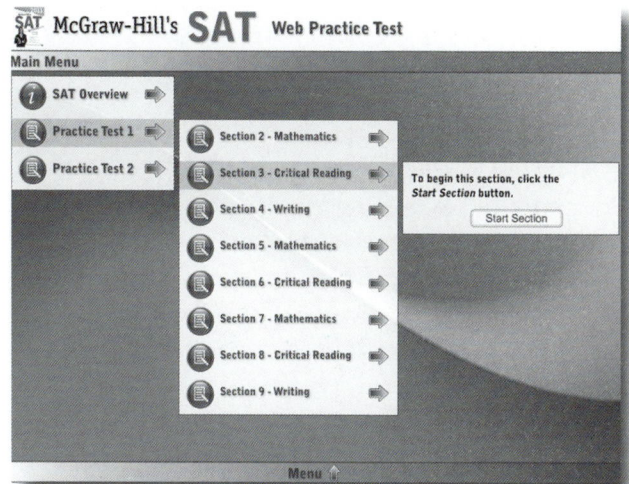

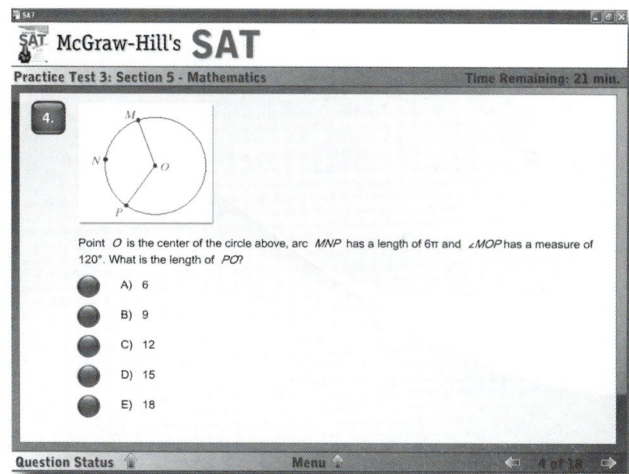

Menu Options ●●●

At the bottom center of the screen you will see a **Menu** button. Roll your cursor over that button to see these choices:

● **Exit Program:** Choose this option if you wish to exit the program entirely. Then, if you wish to resume work on to the same test section, relaunch the program. From the Main Menu, you will have the opportunity to complete the section that you exited or to restart it from the beginning.

● **Score and Exit Section:** You may choose this option at any time while working on a test section. You will get a new dialogue box that will tell how many questions in the section you answered correctly and allow you to review the questions, your answers, the correct responses, and the explanations. See "Scoring the Practice Tests" below for more information.

● **Save and Exit Section:** This option takes you back to the Main Menu. Your work will be saved, and whenever you go back to the Main Menu, you will have the opportunity to complete or restart the section that you exited.

● **View Instructions:** Choose this option if you wish to see again the instructions for the question type(s) in the section in which you are currently working.

Scoring the Practice Tests

After you answer the last question in a section, if you have not answered all of the preceding questions, you will be prompted to roll your cursor over the Question Status button to see which ones you have not answered. You can then return to them and answer them if you wish. Then return to the final question in the section.

You will then be asked if you wish to score and exit the section. If you click "Score and Exit," you will see a new dialogue box that will tell you how many of the questions in the section you answered correctly. You will then be asked, "Would you like to review the section now?" If you click "yes," the questions will appear one by one on the screen as shown at right.

There will be an "X" next to every incorrect answer and a "+" next to every correct answer. For each question, you will also see an inset panel with the explanation ("rationale") for the correct answer. You may then navigate away or close the program.

Later, if you return to the Main Menu and roll your cursor over the section that you completed, you will see a dialogue box that will tell you when you completed the section and how you scored. You can then either review your work on the section, or restart it and take it again.

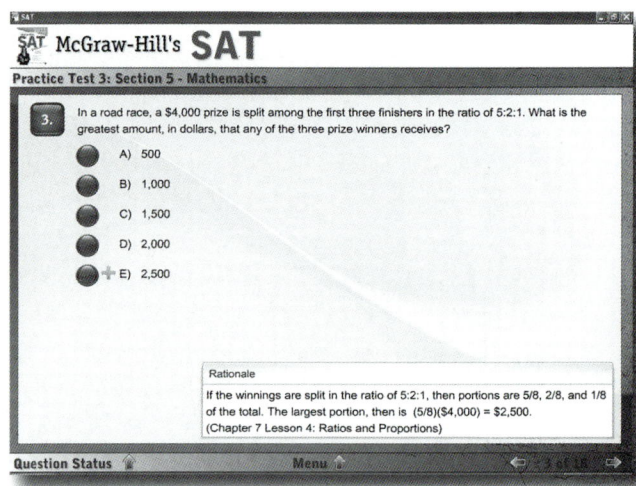

McGRAW-HILL's

SAT

McGRAW-HILL's

SAT

2011 EDITION

CHRISTOPHER BLACK

MARK ANESTIS

and the TUTORS of COLLEGE HILL COACHING™

Mc Graw Hill

NEW YORK / CHICAGO / SAN FRANCISCO / LISBON / LONDON / MADRID / MEXICO CITY
MILAN / NEW DELHI / SAN JUAN / SEOUL / SINGAPORE / SYDNEY / TORONTO

1 2 3 4 5 6 7 8 9 0   WDQ/WDQ   1 5 4 3 2 1 0

Book alone:
ISBN: 978-0-07-174094-4
MHID: 0-07-174094-5
ISSN: 1944-7131

Book/cd set:
ISBN: P/N 978-0-07-174096-8 of set
           978-0-07-174098-2
MHID: P/N 0-07-174096-1 of set
           0-07-174098-8
ISSN: 1944-7140

McGraw-Hill books are available at special quantity discounts to use as premiums and sales promotions, or for use in corporate training programs. To contact a representative please e-mail us at bulksales@mcgraw-hill.com

SAT is a registered trademark of the College Entrance Examination Board, which does not endorse this book.

College Hill Coaching® is a registered trademark under the control of Christopher F. Black.

Visit the College Hill Coaching Web site at www.collegehillcoaching.com.

ACKNOWLEDGMENTS

We would like to gratefully acknowledge the help of those who have contributed to this enormous project and have been committed to its success. This project would not have been the same without the help of so many of our close friends and relatives: Elizabeth Black, the world's greatest teacher of mathematics, for her many years of patience, wisdom, and gracious support; Sarah and Anna Black for their constant inspiration and marvelous good humor; Stephanie Anestis for her invaluable efforts in reading and editing the text and for her incredible love and support; and Robert, Janice, Michael, and Matthew Anestis, who also gave their insight on the work in progress. We would also like to thank Brigid Barry, Aulden Kaye, Peter Obourn, Kristoffer Shields, and the brilliant tutors of College Hill Coaching for their thoughtful and valuable assistance. We appreciate the hard work of those at McGraw-Hill who made this project work and the thoughtful help of our agent, Grace Freedson. Finally, we would like to thank all the students of College Hill Coaching who have contributed to the growth of these materials over the years; their insight and experiences have thoroughly inspired and informed this book.

CONTENTS

McGRAW-HILL's

SAT

CHAPTER 1

CONQUERING THE SAT WITH THE COLLEGE HILL™ METHOD

1   WHAT DOES THE SAT REALLY TEST?

Contrary to popular opinion, the SAT does not merely test how well you can take a multiple-choice test or write a formulaic essay. Also, it is *not* designed to predict your college grades (because grades are too subjective and unstandardized). But neither is it a test of overall intelligence nor of the major subject material you've learned in high school. Instead, it is designed to do what your school grades rarely do directly: assess a very particular set of academic skills that are central to your success as a college student. These skills include thinking under pressure, writing cogently and fluently, understanding complex prose, and tackling a wide range of quantitative problems. Of course, there are many other skills that are important to college success: creativity, organization, social intelligence, perseverance, and so on. But those skills are almost impossible to assess with a multiple-choice test. So, college admissions officers look elsewhere in your application—your essays, your recommendations, your extracurricular activities, and so on—to evaluate those qualities. But don't take the SAT lightly or cynically: critical reading, writing, and math skills are central to success in college and beyond.

2   THE EIGHT KEY REASONING SKILLS

Students who ace the SAT are adept at eight core reasoning skills: mapping problems, analyzing problems, finding patterns, simplifying problems, connecting to knowledge, considering alternatives, thinking logically, and checking their work. If you practice tackling SAT problems with these skills in mind, you will find that you can break through even the toughest questions. Let's look at these skills a little more closely.

Mapping Problems

Mapping a problem is the first step to solving it. Mapping means *orienting* yourself to the problem and *representing* its information. It's called mapping because it is like pulling out a map to start a trip. The map doesn't tell you how to get to your destination (you still have to find the best route), but it orients you to the problem by showing where you are and where you are going, and it represents what you can use to get there.

If you have the wrong map at the start, you'll never solve the problem—on the SAT or anywhere else. Many students struggle on the SAT because they don't realize what it is really testing. For instance, many students try to tackle SAT math questions with rote procedures or heavy calculations rather than looking for the elegant, simple solutions that emerge from seeking patterns and analyzing problems from different angles. They forget to read the math problems carefully, so they miss essential facts and restrictions that make the problems easier to solve. Chapters 6–11 show you how to find *quick, simple,* and *elegant* solutions to SAT math problems. On the critical reading section, students often don't pick up essential information from the passages because they use test-taking tricks rather than solid, active reading skills. Chapter 4 teaches you how to read actively so that you can pick up the essential information and ace *any*

questions that follow. On the essay, many students think they need to plug lots of big words, complicated language, and Shakespearean references into a standard five-paragraph formula. Surprisingly, this approach usually leads to mediocre essays. To practice the *real* skills that the SAT graders are looking for, read Chapters 12 and 13. On the writing section, many students think that they have to apply dozens of obscure grammar "rules" like "never start a sentence with *but* or *because*" or "never use verbs in the passive voice" or "never end a sentence with a preposition." In fact, none of these is a rule of standard English, so don't waste your time looking for these "violations" on the SAT. The SAT writing only tests your understanding of about 15 standard grammar rules, and they're all discussed in detail in Chapter 15.

Analyzing Problems

Once you understand the problem, you must look at its parts and think about how they fit together. This is called *analysis.* To fix a watch, you have to analyze its parts and see how they work together. To solve a tough SAT problem, you have to analyze the parts of a math problem, a sentence, a writing prompt, or a reading passage. Make sure to *mark up the test booklet*—draw on the diagrams, underline the passages, cross out wrong answers, write out your equations, and so on.

On math problems, analyzing means understanding how equations work, what unknowns represent, and how parts of geometric figures relate to one another. Chapter 6, Lesson 2; Chapter 8, Lesson 7; and Chapter 9, Lesson 5 are particularly helpful for honing your analytical math skills. On sentence completion questions, analyzing means understanding the parts of the sentences: the clauses, the parallel elements, the modifying phrases, and so on, as discussed in

Chapter 5. On the essay, analyzing means examining the issue from different angles, carefully defining your terms, and creating a cohesive outline, as discussed in Chapter 12. On the critical reading section, analyzing means seeing how the paragraphs fit together into a coherent whole, as discussed in Chapter 4.

Analysis even helps with your vocabulary. You can tackle tough vocabulary questions much more easily once you learn the common Latin and Greek roots. Knowing the meanings of the *parts* of a new word helps you to make a strong guess about its meaning. Chapter 3 gives you nearly 200 of the most common SAT roots and affixes, with lots of examples of how they are used.

Finding Patterns in the Problem

After analyzing a problem, look for patterns—simple rules that relate the parts. For instance, if a SAT question gives you a sequence like 3, 8, 13, 18, ..., you should recognize a simple pattern—add 5—that lets you keep track of the terms without memorizing every single term. Similarly, formulas such as *distance = rate × time* show important relationships between the parts of a problem: for instance, as the rate increases for traveling a given distance, the time decreases. Mathematical patterns are discussed throughout the math chapters in this book, but especially in Chapter 6, Lesson 3; Chapter 7, Lessons 2 and 4; Chapter 10, Lesson 6; and Chapter 11, Lesson 1.

Language patterns such as *parallel structure* help you to understand complex passages and to write fluently. This simple but ubiquitous language pattern is discussed in Chapter 4 (Lesson 3), Chapter 5 (Lessons 3 and 5), Chapter 12 (Lessons 6 and 7), and Chapter 15 (Lesson 3). Also, good readers and writers always pay attention to *paragraph structure*—how one paragraph links logically with the next. Solid paragraph structure is key to writing high-scoring SAT essays. Chapter 12 (particularly Lessons 6, 7, and 12) gives you lots of practice in structuring a top-scoring essay.

Simplifying the Problem

Another key to SAT success is simplifying tough math problems, tough essay assignments, and tough reading passages. Your working memory holds only between five and nine pieces of information at a time. If you can reduce the amount of information in a problem, you make it easier to solve. If you ever struggle to simplify tough SAT math problems, be sure to review Chapter 6, Lesson 4; Chapter 7, Lessons 1 and 2; Chapter 8, Lessons 2, 3, and 5; and Chapter 10, Lesson 5. Simplification is also enormously important to success on the SAT critical reading and writing sections. Chapter 4 shows you how to summarize complex essays so that they don't overwhelm you. Chapter 15, Lesson 2 shows you how to simplify

sentences so that you can analyze their "core structure" and catch common errors.

Connecting to Knowledge

Even though the SAT mainly tests flexible reasoning skills, you still need to have plenty of memorized facts and procedures—word and root definitions, reading strategies, basic math formulas, and grammar rules—at the tip of your brain.

Don't worry—you don't need to memorize a ton of facts (in fact, every SAT math section gives you most of the common formulas you'll need), and this book will make it as easy as possible. Everything you need to memorize is right here: Chapter 3 provides an organized list of over 2,000 high-frequency SAT words and nearly 200 key word roots; Chapter 4 will hammer home the three "key questions" you must ask to understand any reading passage; Chapters 6–11 discuss all of the major math facts and formulas you'll need (and even a few that go beyond the "reference information" on the test); and Chapter 15 discusses all of the grammar rules you'll be expected to apply on the SAT.

Considering Alternatives

On SAT math problems, students often perform the first procedure that pops into their heads—distributing whenever they see parentheses, solving equations whenever they contain a variable, and so on. Big mistake. The SAT math isn't testing your memorization of rote skills as much as it is testing your mental *flexibility*. Every SAT question is unique, and many can be solved in several different ways. Good test-takers consider their alternatives before diving in.

Some SAT math problems that look like algebra problems can be solved more simply with numerical or geometric methods, and some that look like geometry problems can be solved more simply with algebraic or numerical methods. To find the simplest method, you have to consider your options. Don't assume that someone else's favorite method is always the best one for you. Chapter 6, Lesson 6 discusses multiple approaches to solving SAT math problems, as do Chapter 7, Lesson 1; Chapter 8, Lesson 6; and the many answer explanations for math worksheets throughout the book.

Similarly, many students think there is just a "formula" for writing a good SAT essay with pre-set literary examples, and so don't take advantage of their own unique abilities or the differences from question to question. (As great a book as *Huckleberry Finn* is, it probably won't work so well as the basis of an essay about modern communication technology.) In fact, there are hundreds of different ways to approach any given essay question that will get you a perfect score.

Carefully consider your own unique perspective and knowledge before deciding what point of view to take. Chapter 12 walks you through the writing process so that you can adapt any SAT essay assignment to your personal point of view.

Thinking Logically

Logic is one of the most powerful reasoning tools you can use on the SAT: sentence completion questions ask you to analyze the logical structure of sentences, critical reading questions often ask you to make logical inferences or examine logical assumptions based on the claims made in a passage, and SAT math questions often require you to figure out what *must* be true based on some given assumptions. All of these are exercises in logic.

Chapter 6, Lesson 7 discusses three logical methods for solving tough SAT math problems; Chapter 4, Lesson 7 teaches you to analyze critical reading questions logically; Chapter 5, Lessons 2 and 3 help you to analyze the logical structure of sentences; and Chapter 12, Lesson 7 helps you to strengthen your essay with logic.

Checking Your Work

Everyone makes dumb mistakes now and then. Good students, however, always check their work for errors. Don't wait until you're completely finished with a problem, and don't merely repeat the same steps to check (because you'll probably just repeat the same mistake you made the first time). Instead, as you solve an SAT math problem, ask: *Am I getting closer to my goal? Is there a quicker way to get to my goal? Do I need to find something else before I can get to my goal?* Then, after you've found an answer, ask: *Did I show my steps clearly? Are they correct? Does my solution make sense when I reread the problem? Is there another way I can look at the problem to check my answer?*

On SAT math questions, estimate whenever you can to check your work. If you can make an easy estimate of the answer, then you can eliminate choices that are way off base, as well as check your work when you do it "the long way." This and other math-checking strategies are discussed in Chapter 6, Lesson 8. On sentence completion questions, always reread the sentence one more time with your answer "filled in," and check that it works logically. On the critical reading section, check that your responses make sense, given the overall purpose of the passage. Chapter 4, Lesson 8 discusses some other checking strategies for critical reading. On the writing questions, check that any error you find is *really* one of the legitimate grammatical errors listed in Chapter 15, and not just something that sounds a little strange.

---

3 THE COLLEGE HILL COACHING SAT POWER READING LIST

Students who ace the SAT have one important thing in common: they read a lot. Good reading habits give you an enormous advantage in life and on the SAT. One of the best ways to prepare for the critical reading section of the SAT is to dive into books like those below, which deal with the world of ideas you will explore in a good liberal arts education: philosophy, the arts, history, biography, science, and the humanities. Read books that challenge your thinking and introduce you to new ideas.

The New York Times: www.nytimes.com
> Read the op-ed page every day, the *Science Times* on Tuesdays, and the *Week in Review* on Sundays.

The Atlantic: www.theatlantic.com
> Read the features and the *Atlantic Voices*.

Slate Magazine: www.slate.com
> Read the *News & Politics* section.

BBC News: http://news.bbc.co.uk
> Read the *Features, Views, Analysis* section, and the *Background* links to the right of the feature stories.

Salon: www.salon.com
> Read the *Editor's Picks*.

Internet Resources

Set your homepage to one of the following, and save bookmarks of the others. Some of these sites may require a subscription, but most provide a good deal of their material free of charge.

Narratives

One Hundred Years of Solitude, G. Garcia-Marquez
The Painted Bird, Jerzy Kozinsky
Candide, Voltaire
Macbeth, William Shakespeare
The Wall, John Hersey

Growing Up, Russell Baker
The Best American Short Stories of the Century, John Updike, editor
Baby, It's Cold Inside, S. J. Perelman
Pride and Prejudice, Jane Austen
Frankenstein, Mary Wollstonecraft Shelley
Atlas Shrugged, Ayn Rand
The Color Purple, Alice Walker
The Life of Pi, Yann Martel
Metamorphosis (and other stories), Franz Kafka
Crime and Punishment, Fyodor Dostoyevsky
Narrative of the Life of Frederick Douglass, Frederick Douglass
Animal Farm, George Orwell
Night, Elie Wiesel
Waiting for Godot, Samuel Beckett
Things Fall Apart, Chinua Achebe
Jane Eyre, Charlotte Brontë
The Stranger, Albert Camus
Go Tell It on the Mountain, James Baldwin
Robinson Crusoe, Daniel Defoe
Invisible Man, Ralph Ellison
Heart of Darkness, Joseph Conrad
The Sound and the Fury, William Faulkner
The Great Gatsby, F. Scott Fitzgerald
As I Lay Dying, William Faulkner
Faust, Johann Wolfgang von Goethe
Tom Jones, Henry Fielding

Arguments

Drift and Mastery, Walter Lippmann
The Best American Essays, Robert Atwan, editor
The Norton Reader, Linda H. Peterson, John C. Brereton, and Joan E. Hartman, editors
Walden, Henry David Thoreau
Lanterns and Lances, James Thurber

The Chomsky Reader, Noam Chomsky
The World Is Flat, Thomas L. Friedman
Silent Spring, Rachel Carson
A Room of One's Own, Virginia Woolf
Up from Slavery, Booker T. Washington
Speak, Memory, Vladimir Nabokov
The American Language, H. L. Mencken
Selected Essays, 1917–1932, T.S. Eliot
The Nature and Destiny of Man, Reinhold Niebuhr
Notes of a Native Son, James Baldwin
Aspects of the Novel, E. M. Forster
Patriotic Gore, Edmund Wilson

Analyses

1776, David McCullough
A Brief History of Time, Stephen Hawking
QED, Richard Feynman
The Mismeasure of Man, Stephen J. Gould
The Lives of a Cell, Lewis Thomas
The Republic, Plato
Democracy in America, Alexis de Tocqueville
Civilization and its Discontents, Sigmund Freud
The Language Instinct, Steven Pinker
A People's History of the United States, Howard Zinn
Freakonomics, Steven Leavitt and Stephen Dubner
How the Mind Works, Steven Pinker
Guns, Germs, and Steel, Jared Diamond
The Double Helix, James D. Watson
The Affluent Society, John Kenneth Galbraith
The Ants, Bert Hoelldobler and Edward O. Wilson
The Civil War, Shelby Foote
The Age of Jackson, Arthur Schlesinger, Jr.
Science and Civilization in China, Joseph Needham
The General Theory of Employment, Interest, and Money, John Maynard Keynes

4   FAQS ABOUT THE SAT

How Much Studying Should I Do for the SAT?

We expect our private SAT students to spend about 30 minutes every weeknight doing homework, as well as 4 hours every Saturday morning taking a practice test, for 8 to 10 weeks. This is a lot of work, but it pays off very nicely, if it is done well. Even if you only have a few hours per week to prepare, this book will help you to get the most out of it. At the very least, try your best to set aside 30 minutes at least four times per week to do the work in your weekly "SAT Study Plan,"

and set aside 3.5 hours on the weekend to take a practice SAT.

What Is "Score Choice" and How Do I Use It?

Colleges that accept the SAT Score Choice option allow you to submit certain SAT and SAT Subject Test scores while withholding others. According to the College Board, this option is "designed to reduce student stress and improve the test-day experience." But keep in mind: not every college allows Score

Choice. Some will require you to release all or none of your SAT and SAT Subject Test scores. Check with the colleges to learn their policies on Score Choice. Find out more about SAT Score Choice by visiting www.collegeboard.com.

SAT Score Choice can help you to simplify your testing profile by submitting only the scores you like. For the SAT, you can choose which tests to submit, but not which individual subscores. For instance, if you like the Math and Writing scores from your first SAT, but you like your Critical Reading score from your second SAT, you may not submit just the Critical Reading score from the second test without also submitting the other subscores. In that situation, it is likely best to just submit all of the scores from both tests, because most colleges simply take the top individual subscores from all SATs you submit. They call this "superscoring." (For instance, if your first SAT scores are 570CR 430M 600W and your second SAT scores are 520CR 500M 560W, and you submit both sets to a college, then that college will most likely give you credit for a 570CR 500M 600W SAT score.)

So what's the point of Score Choice if most colleges will just maximize your SAT score for you anyway? Basically, it keeps students from freaking out too much about taking any particular SAT. If you bomb it, no one will have to know!

So here's our advice:

1. Go to the websites of the colleges you like, and find out what their policies are on Score Choice.
2. If your favorite colleges allow Score Choice, you can relax and remind yourself that you don't have to ace any particular SAT.
3. Even if they don't, no worries—they probably "superscore" anyway.
4. Plan to take the SAT at least twice, preferably in your junior year, well before any possible college application deadlines, so that you can maximize your testing profile.
5. Don't—we repeat, don't—release your scores until you're satisfied with your overall score report.

What Do Colleges Do with My SAT Scores?

Your SAT scores show college admissions officers how ready you are to do college work. They know that students with high SAT scores are less likely to struggle with tough math, writing, or reading assignments in college. Recent studies have also shown that SAT scores correlate strongly with post-college success. Students with high SAT scores are more likely to graduate from college, and have successful careers after college.

But let's face it: one reason colleges want you to send them SAT scores is that high scores make *them* look good. The higher the average SAT score of their applicants, the better their rankings and prestige. This is why most colleges cherry pick your top subscores if you submit multiple SAT results. (It's also easy to see why some colleges have adopted "SAT-optional" policies. Although colleges like to *say* it's because they like to look beyond test scores, it's hard to deny that there are other compelling reasons. When a college makes SAT scores optional, only the high-scoring students are likely to submit them, and so the college's average scores automatically increase, thereby improving its national rankings.)

In addition to your SAT scores, most good colleges are interested in your grades, your curriculum, your recommendations, your leadership skills, your extracurricular activities, and your essay. But standardized test scores are becoming more important as colleges become more selective. Without exception, high SAT scores will provide you with an admission advantage regardless of whether your college requires them or not. Some large or specialized schools will weigh test scores heavily. If you have any questions about how heavily a certain college weighs your SAT scores, call the admissions office and ask.

When Should I Take My SATs, and Which Subject Tests Should I Take?

The vast majority of colleges and universities require the SAT or ACT, but some have "SAT-optional" policies. Some schools require no SAT Subject Tests, and some require up to three. If you want to be able to apply to any competitive college in the country, plan to take the SAT twice, as well as a set of SAT Subject Tests, in the spring of your junior year, and retake any of those tests, if necessary, in the fall of your senior year. (Taking the ACT can also be a good insurance policy; you can submit those scores instead if they're much better than your SAT scores.) This way, you will have a full testing profile by the end of your junior year, and you'll have a much clearer picture of where you stand before you start your college applications.

Even if your favorite colleges don't require standardized tests, take them anyway, because if you do well, you can use them to boost your application. Say, for instance, you're an A student, but you got one C– in chemistry class. Submitting a strong SAT Subject Test score in chemistry will show your colleges (even those that don't require the Subject Tests) that you're a better chemistry student than your transcript shows.

And what if you *don't* do well? If a college doesn't require them, don't submit them. Remember, *you* control when and if your SAT scores are submitted to the colleges.

Take any SAT Subject Test when the subject material is fresh in your mind. For most students, this is in June, just as courses are finishing up. However, if you are taking AP exams in May, you might prefer to take the SAT Subject Tests in May, also.

Learn which SAT Subject Tests your colleges require, and try to complete them by June of your junior year. You can take up to three SAT Subject Tests on any test date. Here are the upcoming test dates for 2010–2011:

SAT Test Dates 2010–2011*

Test Dates	Test	Test Dates	Test
October 9, 2010	SAT & Subject Tests	March 12, 2011	SAT only
November 6, 2010	SAT & Subject Tests	May 7, 2011	SAT & Subject Tests
December 4, 2010	SAT & Subject Tests	June 4, 2011	SAT & Subject Tests
January 22, 2011	SAT & Subject Tests		

*These test dates are subject to change. For the latest updates on the test dates and registration deadlines, go to the College Board website, www.collegeboard.com.

How Do I Register for the SATs?

Check the College Board Web site, www.college-board.com, for the most up-to-date information about registration, test sites, deadlines, fees, and procedures for applying for special testing accommodations. You can also pick up a Registration Bulletin in your school's guidance office, which will give you all of the information you need.

What Is a Good SAT Score?

It all depends on what colleges you are applying to. Each of the three SAT sections—Critical Reading, Math, and Writing—is scored on a scale from 200 to 800. The median (50th percentile) score for each section is usually between 490 and 530. At the most competitive colleges, like those in the Ivy League, the average SAT score is above 700 on each section. Of course, only about 5% of students are in that category.

Go to the Web sites of those colleges that interest you (or look up their data in one of those big college guides in your local library) and look for their "quartile SAT scores." These are scores for the 25th percentile, the 50th percentile, and the 75th percentile of incoming freshmen. For instance, if the quartile scores for SAT math for a college are 480-550-650, then 25% of the incoming class scored below 480 on the math SAT, 50% scored below 550, and 75% scored below 650. These numbers give you a good idea of how your scores compare with those of other students who have been admitted.

Should I Guess If I Don't Know the Answer to a Question?

In general, random guessing probably won't help, but educated guessing probably will. If you can eliminate at least two choices, make your best guess. Although wrong answers on multiple-choice questions deduct $1/4$ point from your raw score, there is no penalty on "grid-in" math questions. So, if you have any kind of guess, fill it in.

Can I Get Extra Time on the SAT?

Only if you really need it. Some students with special needs can qualify to take the SAT with accommodations such as extended time. But take note: these are available only to students with professional recommendations. If you're thinking it would just be nice to have extra time to think things over, tough luck. Surprisingly, extra time actually hurts many students, because it causes them to lose focus. If you have been diagnosed as having special testing needs by a qualified psychologist and feel that you would benefit from special accommodations, talk to your guidance counselor about how to register, or go to the College Board Web site.

When Will I Get My Scores?

You can get your SAT scores by phone or on the Web between two and three weeks after you take the test. About ten days after your scores are available online a written report will be mailed to you free of charge. Any schools you send your scores to will receive them by mail at about the same time you do. If a college needs your scores sooner, you can "rush" them for a fee.

Can I Get the Actual Test Back When I Get My Scores?

If you take the SAT in October, January, or May, you can request the Question and Answer Service (QAS) for a fee. The QAS provides you with a copy of the test booklet, a record of your answers, the answer key, scoring instructions, and information about the types and difficulty of each question. You may order this service when you register or up to five months after the date of the test. You may also order a copy of your answer sheet only, for a smaller fee. You can find information about these services in your score report.

Are Some SATs Easier than Others?

No. Some students believe, mistakenly, that the SAT is easier on certain dates than on others. Such misconceptions usually derive from student bias rather than test bias. For instance, many students are nervous and ill-prepared for their first SAT, but mistakenly blame their underperformance on the difficulty of the test. Some students also swear that the SAT scoring curve is tougher when the smarter kids or the professional SAT tutors take it. Wrong. The curve on every SAT is determined ahead of time, based on the "equating" or "experimental" sections of previous exams. These experimental sections help the ETS (Educational Testing Service) to ensure that every SAT is as "difficult" as every other recent SAT. Don't design your testing schedule around your friends' misconceptions about the SAT. Instead, design it around your schedule and Study Plan. Take it when *you* are best prepared to take it.

What About the ACT?

The ACT was developed in the 1960s as an alternative to the SAT for students applying chiefly to Midwestern and Southern vocational, mechanical, and agricultural schools. Today, it is accepted in lieu of the SAT by most colleges. Although it is more of a basic skills test and less of an academic reasoning test than the SAT, you should consider taking the ACT at least as an insurance policy for your college application. If your ACT percentile score is much better than your SAT score, you might want to submit your ACT scores instead of, or in addition to, your SAT scores. You can find out more about the ACT testing program at www.act.org.

What Should I Do in the Two Days Before the SAT?

The most important things to do in the two days before your exam are:

- Get plenty of rest.
- Visualize yourself being successful.
- Get some exercise.
- Don't cram.
- Tell yourself you're ready.

See a funny movie, grab a good dinner, and get a good night's rest. For a truly peaceful slumber, lay out everything you need for test day the night before:

- Admission ticket
- Photo ID
- Several #2 pencils with erasers
- Calculator (with fresh batteries)
- Stopwatch
- A light snack, like a banana or granola bar
- Your brain
- Earplugs (if you need them to shut out distractions)
- Directions to the test site (if you haven't been there before)

What Should I Do the Morning of the SAT?

- Get a good breakfast and some exercise to get the blood and nutrients flowing.
- Dress in layers so that you can stay comfortable whether the furnace (or air conditioner) is broken or working overtime.
- Don't worry about what anyone else is doing; stick to your own game plan. Have confidence that your practice will pay off!
- Don't panic when you get to a tough passage or question. Expect it—this is the SAT! Just do your best and move on if you need to. You can come back later to the hard problems if necessary.
- When you feel yourself getting nervous, take three slow, deep breaths.
- Think positive, and try to have fun!

CHAPTER 2

DIAGNOSTIC SAT

ANSWER SHEET

Last Name:_____   First Name:_____

Date:_____   Testing Location:_____

Directions for Test

- Remove these answer sheets from the book and use them to record your answers to this test.
- This test will require 3 hours and 20 minutes to complete. Take this test in one sitting.
- The time allotment for each section is written clearly at the beginning of each section. This test contains six 25-minute sections, two 20-minute sections, and one 10-minute section.
- This test is 25 minutes shorter than the actual SAT, which will include a 25-minute "experimental" section that does not count toward your score. That section has been omitted from this test.
- You may take one short break during the test, of no more than 10 minutes in length.
- You may only work on one section at any given time.
- You must stop ALL work on a section when time is called.
- If you finish a section before the time has elapsed, check your work on that section. You may NOT work on any other section.
- Do not waste time on questions that seem too difficult for you.
- Use the test book for scratchwork, but you will receive credit only for answers that are marked on the answer sheets.
- You will receive one point for every correct answer.
- You will receive no points for an omitted question.
- For each wrong answer on any multiple-choice question, your score will be reduced by $\frac{1}{4}$ point.
- For each wrong answer on any "numerical grid-in" question, you will receive no deduction.

When you take the real SAT, you will be asked to fill in your personal information in grids as shown below.

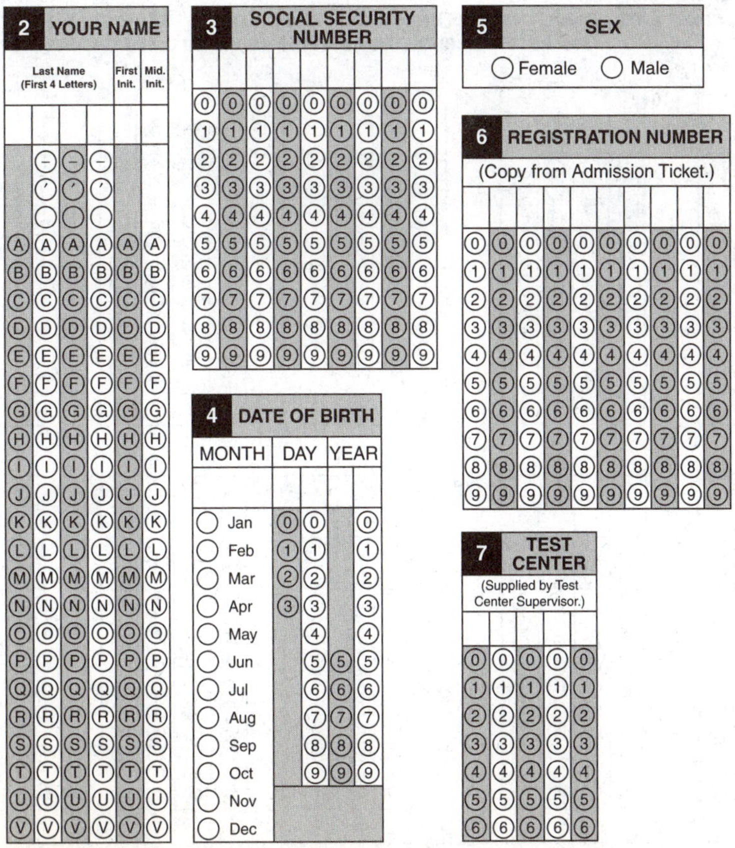

Start with number 1 for each new section. If a section has fewer questions than answer spaces, leave the extra answer spaces blank. Be sure to erase any errors or stray marks completely.

SECTION 2

1 Ⓐ Ⓑ Ⓒ Ⓓ Ⓔ	11 Ⓐ Ⓑ Ⓒ Ⓓ Ⓔ	21 Ⓐ Ⓑ Ⓒ Ⓓ Ⓔ	31 Ⓐ Ⓑ Ⓒ Ⓓ Ⓔ
2 Ⓐ Ⓑ Ⓒ Ⓓ Ⓔ	12 Ⓐ Ⓑ Ⓒ Ⓓ Ⓔ	22 Ⓐ Ⓑ Ⓒ Ⓓ Ⓔ	32 Ⓐ Ⓑ Ⓒ Ⓓ Ⓔ
3 Ⓐ Ⓑ Ⓒ Ⓓ Ⓔ	13 Ⓐ Ⓑ Ⓒ Ⓓ Ⓔ	23 Ⓐ Ⓑ Ⓒ Ⓓ Ⓔ	33 Ⓐ Ⓑ Ⓒ Ⓓ Ⓔ
4 Ⓐ Ⓑ Ⓒ Ⓓ Ⓔ	14 Ⓐ Ⓑ Ⓒ Ⓓ Ⓔ	24 Ⓐ Ⓑ Ⓒ Ⓓ Ⓔ	34 Ⓐ Ⓑ Ⓒ Ⓓ Ⓔ
5 Ⓐ Ⓑ Ⓒ Ⓓ Ⓔ	15 Ⓐ Ⓑ Ⓒ Ⓓ Ⓔ	25 Ⓐ Ⓑ Ⓒ Ⓓ Ⓔ	35 Ⓐ Ⓑ Ⓒ Ⓓ Ⓔ
6 Ⓐ Ⓑ Ⓒ Ⓓ Ⓔ	16 Ⓐ Ⓑ Ⓒ Ⓓ Ⓔ	26 Ⓐ Ⓑ Ⓒ Ⓓ Ⓔ	36 Ⓐ Ⓑ Ⓒ Ⓓ Ⓔ
7 Ⓐ Ⓑ Ⓒ Ⓓ Ⓔ	17 Ⓐ Ⓑ Ⓒ Ⓓ Ⓔ	27 Ⓐ Ⓑ Ⓒ Ⓓ Ⓔ	37 Ⓐ Ⓑ Ⓒ Ⓓ Ⓔ
8 Ⓐ Ⓑ Ⓒ Ⓓ Ⓔ	18 Ⓐ Ⓑ Ⓒ Ⓓ Ⓔ	28 Ⓐ Ⓑ Ⓒ Ⓓ Ⓔ	38 Ⓐ Ⓑ Ⓒ Ⓓ Ⓔ
9 Ⓐ Ⓑ Ⓒ Ⓓ Ⓔ	19 Ⓐ Ⓑ Ⓒ Ⓓ Ⓔ	29 Ⓐ Ⓑ Ⓒ Ⓓ Ⓔ	39 Ⓐ Ⓑ Ⓒ Ⓓ Ⓔ
10 Ⓐ Ⓑ Ⓒ Ⓓ Ⓔ	20 Ⓐ Ⓑ Ⓒ Ⓓ Ⓔ	30 Ⓐ Ⓑ Ⓒ Ⓓ Ⓔ	40 Ⓐ Ⓑ Ⓒ Ⓓ Ⓔ

SECTION 3

1 Ⓐ Ⓑ Ⓒ Ⓓ Ⓔ	11 Ⓐ Ⓑ Ⓒ Ⓓ Ⓔ	21 Ⓐ Ⓑ Ⓒ Ⓓ Ⓔ	31 Ⓐ Ⓑ Ⓒ Ⓓ Ⓔ
2 Ⓐ Ⓑ Ⓒ Ⓓ Ⓔ	12 Ⓐ Ⓑ Ⓒ Ⓓ Ⓔ	22 Ⓐ Ⓑ Ⓒ Ⓓ Ⓔ	32 Ⓐ Ⓑ Ⓒ Ⓓ Ⓔ
3 Ⓐ Ⓑ Ⓒ Ⓓ Ⓔ	13 Ⓐ Ⓑ Ⓒ Ⓓ Ⓔ	23 Ⓐ Ⓑ Ⓒ Ⓓ Ⓔ	33 Ⓐ Ⓑ Ⓒ Ⓓ Ⓔ
4 Ⓐ Ⓑ Ⓒ Ⓓ Ⓔ	14 Ⓐ Ⓑ Ⓒ Ⓓ Ⓔ	24 Ⓐ Ⓑ Ⓒ Ⓓ Ⓔ	34 Ⓐ Ⓑ Ⓒ Ⓓ Ⓔ
5 Ⓐ Ⓑ Ⓒ Ⓓ Ⓔ	15 Ⓐ Ⓑ Ⓒ Ⓓ Ⓔ	25 Ⓐ Ⓑ Ⓒ Ⓓ Ⓔ	35 Ⓐ Ⓑ Ⓒ Ⓓ Ⓔ
6 Ⓐ Ⓑ Ⓒ Ⓓ Ⓔ	16 Ⓐ Ⓑ Ⓒ Ⓓ Ⓔ	26 Ⓐ Ⓑ Ⓒ Ⓓ Ⓔ	36 Ⓐ Ⓑ Ⓒ Ⓓ Ⓔ
7 Ⓐ Ⓑ Ⓒ Ⓓ Ⓔ	17 Ⓐ Ⓑ Ⓒ Ⓓ Ⓔ	27 Ⓐ Ⓑ Ⓒ Ⓓ Ⓔ	37 Ⓐ Ⓑ Ⓒ Ⓓ Ⓔ
8 Ⓐ Ⓑ Ⓒ Ⓓ Ⓔ	18 Ⓐ Ⓑ Ⓒ Ⓓ Ⓔ	28 Ⓐ Ⓑ Ⓒ Ⓓ Ⓔ	38 Ⓐ Ⓑ Ⓒ Ⓓ Ⓔ
9 Ⓐ Ⓑ Ⓒ Ⓓ Ⓔ	19 Ⓐ Ⓑ Ⓒ Ⓓ Ⓔ	29 Ⓐ Ⓑ Ⓒ Ⓓ Ⓔ	39 Ⓐ Ⓑ Ⓒ Ⓓ Ⓔ
10 Ⓐ Ⓑ Ⓒ Ⓓ Ⓔ	20 Ⓐ Ⓑ Ⓒ Ⓓ Ⓔ	30 Ⓐ Ⓑ Ⓒ Ⓓ Ⓔ	40 Ⓐ Ⓑ Ⓒ Ⓓ Ⓔ

CAUTION **Use the answer spaces in the grids below for Section 2 or Section 3 only if you are told to do so in your test book.**

Student-Produced Responses — ONLY ANSWERS ENTERED IN THE CIRCLES IN EACH GRID WILL BE SCORED. YOU WILL NOT RECEIVE CREDIT FOR ANYTHING WRITTEN IN THE BOXES ABOVE THE CIRCLES.

9 10 11 12 13

14 15 16 17 18

Start with number 1 for each new section. If a section has fewer questions than answer spaces, leave the extra answer spaces blank. Be sure to erase any errors or stray marks completely.

SECTION 4

1 Ⓐ Ⓑ Ⓒ Ⓓ Ⓔ	11 Ⓐ Ⓑ Ⓒ Ⓓ Ⓔ	21 Ⓐ Ⓑ Ⓒ Ⓓ Ⓔ	31 Ⓐ Ⓑ Ⓒ Ⓓ Ⓔ
2 Ⓐ Ⓑ Ⓒ Ⓓ Ⓔ	12 Ⓐ Ⓑ Ⓒ Ⓓ Ⓔ	22 Ⓐ Ⓑ Ⓒ Ⓓ Ⓔ	32 Ⓐ Ⓑ Ⓒ Ⓓ Ⓔ
3 Ⓐ Ⓑ Ⓒ Ⓓ Ⓔ	13 Ⓐ Ⓑ Ⓒ Ⓓ Ⓔ	23 Ⓐ Ⓑ Ⓒ Ⓓ Ⓔ	33 Ⓐ Ⓑ Ⓒ Ⓓ Ⓔ
4 Ⓐ Ⓑ Ⓒ Ⓓ Ⓔ	14 Ⓐ Ⓑ Ⓒ Ⓓ Ⓔ	24 Ⓐ Ⓑ Ⓒ Ⓓ Ⓔ	34 Ⓐ Ⓑ Ⓒ Ⓓ Ⓔ
5 Ⓐ Ⓑ Ⓒ Ⓓ Ⓔ	15 Ⓐ Ⓑ Ⓒ Ⓓ Ⓔ	25 Ⓐ Ⓑ Ⓒ Ⓓ Ⓔ	35 Ⓐ Ⓑ Ⓒ Ⓓ Ⓔ
6 Ⓐ Ⓑ Ⓒ Ⓓ Ⓔ	16 Ⓐ Ⓑ Ⓒ Ⓓ Ⓔ	26 Ⓐ Ⓑ Ⓒ Ⓓ Ⓔ	36 Ⓐ Ⓑ Ⓒ Ⓓ Ⓔ
7 Ⓐ Ⓑ Ⓒ Ⓓ Ⓔ	17 Ⓐ Ⓑ Ⓒ Ⓓ Ⓔ	27 Ⓐ Ⓑ Ⓒ Ⓓ Ⓔ	37 Ⓐ Ⓑ Ⓒ Ⓓ Ⓔ
8 Ⓐ Ⓑ Ⓒ Ⓓ Ⓔ	18 Ⓐ Ⓑ Ⓒ Ⓓ Ⓔ	28 Ⓐ Ⓑ Ⓒ Ⓓ Ⓔ	38 Ⓐ Ⓑ Ⓒ Ⓓ Ⓔ
9 Ⓐ Ⓑ Ⓒ Ⓓ Ⓔ	19 Ⓐ Ⓑ Ⓒ Ⓓ Ⓔ	29 Ⓐ Ⓑ Ⓒ Ⓓ Ⓔ	39 Ⓐ Ⓑ Ⓒ Ⓓ Ⓔ
10 Ⓐ Ⓑ Ⓒ Ⓓ Ⓔ	20 Ⓐ Ⓑ Ⓒ Ⓓ Ⓔ	30 Ⓐ Ⓑ Ⓒ Ⓓ Ⓔ	40 Ⓐ Ⓑ Ⓒ Ⓓ Ⓔ

SECTION 5

1 Ⓐ Ⓑ Ⓒ Ⓓ Ⓔ	11 Ⓐ Ⓑ Ⓒ Ⓓ Ⓔ	21 Ⓐ Ⓑ Ⓒ Ⓓ Ⓔ	31 Ⓐ Ⓑ Ⓒ Ⓓ Ⓔ
2 Ⓐ Ⓑ Ⓒ Ⓓ Ⓔ	12 Ⓐ Ⓑ Ⓒ Ⓓ Ⓔ	22 Ⓐ Ⓑ Ⓒ Ⓓ Ⓔ	32 Ⓐ Ⓑ Ⓒ Ⓓ Ⓔ
3 Ⓐ Ⓑ Ⓒ Ⓓ Ⓔ	13 Ⓐ Ⓑ Ⓒ Ⓓ Ⓔ	23 Ⓐ Ⓑ Ⓒ Ⓓ Ⓔ	33 Ⓐ Ⓑ Ⓒ Ⓓ Ⓔ
4 Ⓐ Ⓑ Ⓒ Ⓓ Ⓔ	14 Ⓐ Ⓑ Ⓒ Ⓓ Ⓔ	24 Ⓐ Ⓑ Ⓒ Ⓓ Ⓔ	34 Ⓐ Ⓑ Ⓒ Ⓓ Ⓔ
5 Ⓐ Ⓑ Ⓒ Ⓓ Ⓔ	15 Ⓐ Ⓑ Ⓒ Ⓓ Ⓔ	25 Ⓐ Ⓑ Ⓒ Ⓓ Ⓔ	35 Ⓐ Ⓑ Ⓒ Ⓓ Ⓔ
6 Ⓐ Ⓑ Ⓒ Ⓓ Ⓔ	16 Ⓐ Ⓑ Ⓒ Ⓓ Ⓔ	26 Ⓐ Ⓑ Ⓒ Ⓓ Ⓔ	36 Ⓐ Ⓑ Ⓒ Ⓓ Ⓔ
7 Ⓐ Ⓑ Ⓒ Ⓓ Ⓔ	17 Ⓐ Ⓑ Ⓒ Ⓓ Ⓔ	27 Ⓐ Ⓑ Ⓒ Ⓓ Ⓔ	37 Ⓐ Ⓑ Ⓒ Ⓓ Ⓔ
8 Ⓐ Ⓑ Ⓒ Ⓓ Ⓔ	18 Ⓐ Ⓑ Ⓒ Ⓓ Ⓔ	28 Ⓐ Ⓑ Ⓒ Ⓓ Ⓔ	38 Ⓐ Ⓑ Ⓒ Ⓓ Ⓔ
9 Ⓐ Ⓑ Ⓒ Ⓓ Ⓔ	19 Ⓐ Ⓑ Ⓒ Ⓓ Ⓔ	29 Ⓐ Ⓑ Ⓒ Ⓓ Ⓔ	39 Ⓐ Ⓑ Ⓒ Ⓓ Ⓔ
10 Ⓐ Ⓑ Ⓒ Ⓓ Ⓔ	20 Ⓐ Ⓑ Ⓒ Ⓓ Ⓔ	30 Ⓐ Ⓑ Ⓒ Ⓓ Ⓔ	40 Ⓐ Ⓑ Ⓒ Ⓓ Ⓔ

CAUTION Use the answer spaces in the grids below for Section 4 or Section 5 only if you are told to do so in your test book.

Student-Produced Responses ONLY ANSWERS ENTERED IN THE CIRCLES IN EACH GRID WILL BE SCORED. YOU WILL NOT RECEIVE CREDIT FOR ANYTHING WRITTEN IN THE BOXES ABOVE THE CIRCLES.

9   10   11   12   13

14   15   16   17   18

Start with number 1 for each new section. If a section has fewer questions than answer spaces, leave the extra answer spaces blank. Be sure to erase any errors or stray marks completely.

SECTION 6

1 Ⓐ Ⓑ Ⓒ Ⓓ Ⓔ	11 Ⓐ Ⓑ Ⓒ Ⓓ Ⓔ	21 Ⓐ Ⓑ Ⓒ Ⓓ Ⓔ	31 Ⓐ Ⓑ Ⓒ Ⓓ Ⓔ
2 Ⓐ Ⓑ Ⓒ Ⓓ Ⓔ	12 Ⓐ Ⓑ Ⓒ Ⓓ Ⓔ	22 Ⓐ Ⓑ Ⓒ Ⓓ Ⓔ	32 Ⓐ Ⓑ Ⓒ Ⓓ Ⓔ
3 Ⓐ Ⓑ Ⓒ Ⓓ Ⓔ	13 Ⓐ Ⓑ Ⓒ Ⓓ Ⓔ	23 Ⓐ Ⓑ Ⓒ Ⓓ Ⓔ	33 Ⓐ Ⓑ Ⓒ Ⓓ Ⓔ
4 Ⓐ Ⓑ Ⓒ Ⓓ Ⓔ	14 Ⓐ Ⓑ Ⓒ Ⓓ Ⓔ	24 Ⓐ Ⓑ Ⓒ Ⓓ Ⓔ	34 Ⓐ Ⓑ Ⓒ Ⓓ Ⓔ
5 Ⓐ Ⓑ Ⓒ Ⓓ Ⓔ	15 Ⓐ Ⓑ Ⓒ Ⓓ Ⓔ	25 Ⓐ Ⓑ Ⓒ Ⓓ Ⓔ	35 Ⓐ Ⓑ Ⓒ Ⓓ Ⓔ
6 Ⓐ Ⓑ Ⓒ Ⓓ Ⓔ	16 Ⓐ Ⓑ Ⓒ Ⓓ Ⓔ	26 Ⓐ Ⓑ Ⓒ Ⓓ Ⓔ	36 Ⓐ Ⓑ Ⓒ Ⓓ Ⓔ
7 Ⓐ Ⓑ Ⓒ Ⓓ Ⓔ	17 Ⓐ Ⓑ Ⓒ Ⓓ Ⓔ	27 Ⓐ Ⓑ Ⓒ Ⓓ Ⓔ	37 Ⓐ Ⓑ Ⓒ Ⓓ Ⓔ
8 Ⓐ Ⓑ Ⓒ Ⓓ Ⓔ	18 Ⓐ Ⓑ Ⓒ Ⓓ Ⓔ	28 Ⓐ Ⓑ Ⓒ Ⓓ Ⓔ	38 Ⓐ Ⓑ Ⓒ Ⓓ Ⓔ
9 Ⓐ Ⓑ Ⓒ Ⓓ Ⓔ	19 Ⓐ Ⓑ Ⓒ Ⓓ Ⓔ	29 Ⓐ Ⓑ Ⓒ Ⓓ Ⓔ	39 Ⓐ Ⓑ Ⓒ Ⓓ Ⓔ
10 Ⓐ Ⓑ Ⓒ Ⓓ Ⓔ	20 Ⓐ Ⓑ Ⓒ Ⓓ Ⓔ	30 Ⓐ Ⓑ Ⓒ Ⓓ Ⓔ	40 Ⓐ Ⓑ Ⓒ Ⓓ Ⓔ

SECTION 7

1 Ⓐ Ⓑ Ⓒ Ⓓ Ⓔ	11 Ⓐ Ⓑ Ⓒ Ⓓ Ⓔ	21 Ⓐ Ⓑ Ⓒ Ⓓ Ⓔ	31 Ⓐ Ⓑ Ⓒ Ⓓ Ⓔ
2 Ⓐ Ⓑ Ⓒ Ⓓ Ⓔ	12 Ⓐ Ⓑ Ⓒ Ⓓ Ⓔ	22 Ⓐ Ⓑ Ⓒ Ⓓ Ⓔ	32 Ⓐ Ⓑ Ⓒ Ⓓ Ⓔ
3 Ⓐ Ⓑ Ⓒ Ⓓ Ⓔ	13 Ⓐ Ⓑ Ⓒ Ⓓ Ⓔ	23 Ⓐ Ⓑ Ⓒ Ⓓ Ⓔ	33 Ⓐ Ⓑ Ⓒ Ⓓ Ⓔ
4 Ⓐ Ⓑ Ⓒ Ⓓ Ⓔ	14 Ⓐ Ⓑ Ⓒ Ⓓ Ⓔ	24 Ⓐ Ⓑ Ⓒ Ⓓ Ⓔ	34 Ⓐ Ⓑ Ⓒ Ⓓ Ⓔ
5 Ⓐ Ⓑ Ⓒ Ⓓ Ⓔ	15 Ⓐ Ⓑ Ⓒ Ⓓ Ⓔ	25 Ⓐ Ⓑ Ⓒ Ⓓ Ⓔ	35 Ⓐ Ⓑ Ⓒ Ⓓ Ⓔ
6 Ⓐ Ⓑ Ⓒ Ⓓ Ⓔ	16 Ⓐ Ⓑ Ⓒ Ⓓ Ⓔ	26 Ⓐ Ⓑ Ⓒ Ⓓ Ⓔ	36 Ⓐ Ⓑ Ⓒ Ⓓ Ⓔ
7 Ⓐ Ⓑ Ⓒ Ⓓ Ⓔ	17 Ⓐ Ⓑ Ⓒ Ⓓ Ⓔ	27 Ⓐ Ⓑ Ⓒ Ⓓ Ⓔ	37 Ⓐ Ⓑ Ⓒ Ⓓ Ⓔ
8 Ⓐ Ⓑ Ⓒ Ⓓ Ⓔ	18 Ⓐ Ⓑ Ⓒ Ⓓ Ⓔ	28 Ⓐ Ⓑ Ⓒ Ⓓ Ⓔ	38 Ⓐ Ⓑ Ⓒ Ⓓ Ⓔ
9 Ⓐ Ⓑ Ⓒ Ⓓ Ⓔ	19 Ⓐ Ⓑ Ⓒ Ⓓ Ⓔ	29 Ⓐ Ⓑ Ⓒ Ⓓ Ⓔ	39 Ⓐ Ⓑ Ⓒ Ⓓ Ⓔ
10 Ⓐ Ⓑ Ⓒ Ⓓ Ⓔ	20 Ⓐ Ⓑ Ⓒ Ⓓ Ⓔ	30 Ⓐ Ⓑ Ⓒ Ⓓ Ⓔ	40 Ⓐ Ⓑ Ⓒ Ⓓ Ⓔ

CAUTION Use the answer spaces in the grids below for Section 6 or Section 7 only if you are told to do so in your test book.

Student-Produced Responses ONLY ANSWERS ENTERED IN THE CIRCLES IN EACH GRID WILL BE SCORED. YOU WILL NOT RECEIVE CREDIT FOR ANYTHING WRITTEN IN THE BOXES ABOVE THE CIRCLES.

9   10   11   12   13

14   15   16   17   18

PLEASE DO NOT WRITE IN THIS AREA

Start with number 1 for each new section. If a section has fewer questions than answer spaces, leave the extra answer spaces blank. Be sure to erase any errors or stray marks completely.

SECTION 8

1 Ⓐ Ⓑ Ⓒ Ⓓ Ⓔ	11 Ⓐ Ⓑ Ⓒ Ⓓ Ⓔ	21 Ⓐ Ⓑ Ⓒ Ⓓ Ⓔ	31 Ⓐ Ⓑ Ⓒ Ⓓ Ⓔ
2 Ⓐ Ⓑ Ⓒ Ⓓ Ⓔ	12 Ⓐ Ⓑ Ⓒ Ⓓ Ⓔ	22 Ⓐ Ⓑ Ⓒ Ⓓ Ⓔ	32 Ⓐ Ⓑ Ⓒ Ⓓ Ⓔ
3 Ⓐ Ⓑ Ⓒ Ⓓ Ⓔ	13 Ⓐ Ⓑ Ⓒ Ⓓ Ⓔ	23 Ⓐ Ⓑ Ⓒ Ⓓ Ⓔ	33 Ⓐ Ⓑ Ⓒ Ⓓ Ⓔ
4 Ⓐ Ⓑ Ⓒ Ⓓ Ⓔ	14 Ⓐ Ⓑ Ⓒ Ⓓ Ⓔ	24 Ⓐ Ⓑ Ⓒ Ⓓ Ⓔ	34 Ⓐ Ⓑ Ⓒ Ⓓ Ⓔ
5 Ⓐ Ⓑ Ⓒ Ⓓ Ⓔ	15 Ⓐ Ⓑ Ⓒ Ⓓ Ⓔ	25 Ⓐ Ⓑ Ⓒ Ⓓ Ⓔ	35 Ⓐ Ⓑ Ⓒ Ⓓ Ⓔ
6 Ⓐ Ⓑ Ⓒ Ⓓ Ⓔ	16 Ⓐ Ⓑ Ⓒ Ⓓ Ⓔ	26 Ⓐ Ⓑ Ⓒ Ⓓ Ⓔ	36 Ⓐ Ⓑ Ⓒ Ⓓ Ⓔ
7 Ⓐ Ⓑ Ⓒ Ⓓ Ⓔ	17 Ⓐ Ⓑ Ⓒ Ⓓ Ⓔ	27 Ⓐ Ⓑ Ⓒ Ⓓ Ⓔ	37 Ⓐ Ⓑ Ⓒ Ⓓ Ⓔ
8 Ⓐ Ⓑ Ⓒ Ⓓ Ⓔ	18 Ⓐ Ⓑ Ⓒ Ⓓ Ⓔ	28 Ⓐ Ⓑ Ⓒ Ⓓ Ⓔ	38 Ⓐ Ⓑ Ⓒ Ⓓ Ⓔ
9 Ⓐ Ⓑ Ⓒ Ⓓ Ⓔ	19 Ⓐ Ⓑ Ⓒ Ⓓ Ⓔ	29 Ⓐ Ⓑ Ⓒ Ⓓ Ⓔ	39 Ⓐ Ⓑ Ⓒ Ⓓ Ⓔ
10 Ⓐ Ⓑ Ⓒ Ⓓ Ⓔ	20 Ⓐ Ⓑ Ⓒ Ⓓ Ⓔ	30 Ⓐ Ⓑ Ⓒ Ⓓ Ⓔ	40 Ⓐ Ⓑ Ⓒ Ⓓ Ⓔ

SECTION 9

1 Ⓐ Ⓑ Ⓒ Ⓓ Ⓔ	11 Ⓐ Ⓑ Ⓒ Ⓓ Ⓔ	21 Ⓐ Ⓑ Ⓒ Ⓓ Ⓔ	31 Ⓐ Ⓑ Ⓒ Ⓓ Ⓔ
2 Ⓐ Ⓑ Ⓒ Ⓓ Ⓔ	12 Ⓐ Ⓑ Ⓒ Ⓓ Ⓔ	22 Ⓐ Ⓑ Ⓒ Ⓓ Ⓔ	32 Ⓐ Ⓑ Ⓒ Ⓓ Ⓔ
3 Ⓐ Ⓑ Ⓒ Ⓓ Ⓔ	13 Ⓐ Ⓑ Ⓒ Ⓓ Ⓔ	23 Ⓐ Ⓑ Ⓒ Ⓓ Ⓔ	33 Ⓐ Ⓑ Ⓒ Ⓓ Ⓔ
4 Ⓐ Ⓑ Ⓒ Ⓓ Ⓔ	14 Ⓐ Ⓑ Ⓒ Ⓓ Ⓔ	24 Ⓐ Ⓑ Ⓒ Ⓓ Ⓔ	34 Ⓐ Ⓑ Ⓒ Ⓓ Ⓔ
5 Ⓐ Ⓑ Ⓒ Ⓓ Ⓔ	15 Ⓐ Ⓑ Ⓒ Ⓓ Ⓔ	25 Ⓐ Ⓑ Ⓒ Ⓓ Ⓔ	35 Ⓐ Ⓑ Ⓒ Ⓓ Ⓔ
6 Ⓐ Ⓑ Ⓒ Ⓓ Ⓔ	16 Ⓐ Ⓑ Ⓒ Ⓓ Ⓔ	26 Ⓐ Ⓑ Ⓒ Ⓓ Ⓔ	36 Ⓐ Ⓑ Ⓒ Ⓓ Ⓔ
7 Ⓐ Ⓑ Ⓒ Ⓓ Ⓔ	17 Ⓐ Ⓑ Ⓒ Ⓓ Ⓔ	27 Ⓐ Ⓑ Ⓒ Ⓓ Ⓔ	37 Ⓐ Ⓑ Ⓒ Ⓓ Ⓔ
8 Ⓐ Ⓑ Ⓒ Ⓓ Ⓔ	18 Ⓐ Ⓑ Ⓒ Ⓓ Ⓔ	28 Ⓐ Ⓑ Ⓒ Ⓓ Ⓔ	38 Ⓐ Ⓑ Ⓒ Ⓓ Ⓔ
9 Ⓐ Ⓑ Ⓒ Ⓓ Ⓔ	19 Ⓐ Ⓑ Ⓒ Ⓓ Ⓔ	29 Ⓐ Ⓑ Ⓒ Ⓓ Ⓔ	39 Ⓐ Ⓑ Ⓒ Ⓓ Ⓔ
10 Ⓐ Ⓑ Ⓒ Ⓓ Ⓔ	20 Ⓐ Ⓑ Ⓒ Ⓓ Ⓔ	30 Ⓐ Ⓑ Ⓒ Ⓓ Ⓔ	40 Ⓐ Ⓑ Ⓒ Ⓓ Ⓔ

1   ESSAY   ESSAY   1

ESSAY
Time—25 minutes

Write your essay on separate sheets of standard lined paper.

The essay gives you an opportunity to show how effectively you can develop and express ideas. You should, therefore, take care to develop your point of view, present your ideas logically and clearly, and use language precisely.

Your essay must be written on the lines provided on your answer sheet—you will receive no other paper on which to write. You will have enough space if you write on every line, avoid wide margins, and keep your handwriting to a reasonable size. Remember that people who are not familiar with your handwriting will read what you write. Try to write or print so that what you are writing is legible to those readers.

Important Reminders:

- **A pencil is required for the essay.** An essay written in ink will receive a score of zero.
- **Do not write your essay in your test book.** You will receive credit only for what you write on your answer sheet.
- **An off-topic essay will receive a score of zero.**

You have 25 minutes to write an essay on the topic assigned below.

Consider carefully the issue discussed in the following passage, then write an essay that answers the question posed in the assignment.

> In a culture obsessed with superficial appearances, our leaders should be those who can see beyond the surface. Judging a book by its cover is the job of the consumer, but reading the book—pondering its contents and perhaps seeking to write new chapters—is the job of a leader.

Assignment: **How important is it to look beyond superficial appearances?** Write an essay in which you answer this question and discuss your point of view on this issue. Support your position logically with examples from literature, the arts, history, politics, science and technology, current events, or your experience or observation.

If you finish before time is called, you may check your work on this section only.
Do not turn to any other section in the test.

2   **2**   **2**   **2**   **2**   **2**

SECTION 2
Time—25 minutes
20 questions

Turn to Section 2 of your answer sheet to answer the questions in this section.

Directions: For this section, solve each problem and decide which is the best of the choices given. Fill in the corresponding circle on the answer sheet. You may use any available space for scratchwork.

Notes

1. The use of a calculator is permitted.

2. All numbers used are real numbers.

3. Figures that accompany problems in this test are intended to provide information useful in solving the problems. They are drawn as accurately as possible EXCEPT when it is stated in a specific problem that the figure is not drawn to scale. All figures lie in a plane unless otherwise indicated.

4. Unless otherwise specified, the domain of any function f is assumed to be the set of all real numbers x for which $f(x)$ is a real number.

Reference Information

$A = \pi r^2$ $A = \ell w$ $A = \frac{1}{2} bh$ $V = \ell wh$ $V = \pi r^2 h$ $c^2 = a^2 + b^2$ Special right triangles
$C = 2\pi r$

The number of degrees of arc in a circle is 360.
The sum of the measures in degrees of the angles of a triangle is 180.

---

1. If $2m + k = 12$ and $k = 10$, what is the value of m?

(A) 0
(B) $\frac{3}{4}$
(C) 1
(D) 2
(E) 4

2. The average (arithmetic mean) of three numbers is 50. If two of the numbers are 35 and 50, what is the third number?

(A) 45
(B) 50
(C) 55
(D) 60
(E) 65

$$\begin{array}{r} A5 \\ A3 \\ A5 \\ +\ 2A \\ \hline 157 \end{array}$$

3. In the correctly worked addition problem above, each A represents the same digit. What is the value of A?

(A) 1
(B) 2
(C) 3
(D) 4
(E) 6

GO ON TO THE NEXT PAGE

4. What number is the same percent of 225 as 9 is of 25?

    (A) 27
    (B) 45
    (C) 54
    (D) 64
    (E) 81

5. If $2^{x-1} = 32$, what is the value of x?

    (A)   4
    (B)   6
    (C)   9
    (D) 16
    (E) 17

VOTING RESULTS FOR REFERENDUM

	Yes	No	Total
Men	26		
Women			76
Total	59		137

6. The table above, representing the results of a vote taken by the Zoning Commission on a recent referendum, is only partially completed. Based on the table, how many women on the Commission voted no?

    (A) 43
    (B) 48
    (C) 57
    (D) 61
    (E) 78

7. Kenny and Mike each begin with the same number of baseball cards. After Mike gives Kenny 12 cards, Kenny has twice as many as Mike. How many cards do they have all together?

    (A) 36
    (B) 48
    (C) 60
    (D) 72
    (E) 84

8. A bag of Texas Tillie's Trail Mix contains x ounces of walnuts, 15 ounces of peanuts, and 20 ounces of pecans. Which of the following expressions gives the fraction of the mix that is walnuts?

    (A) $\dfrac{x}{35}$

    (B) $\dfrac{35}{x}$

    (C) $\dfrac{x}{35+x}$

    (D) $\dfrac{35+x}{x}$

    (E) $\dfrac{35-x}{35+x}$

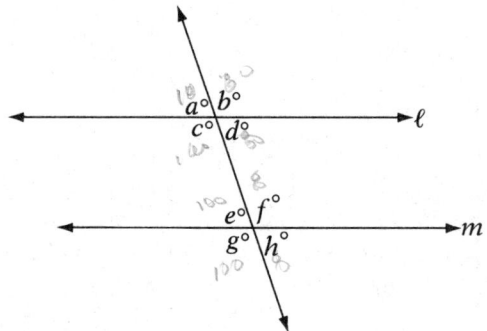

9. In the diagram above, if $\ell \parallel m$, which of the following is equivalent to $a + d + f + g$?

    (A) $2c + 2f$
    (B) $b + c + e + h$
    (C) $2d + 2e$
    (D) $a + d + e + h$
    (E) $2b + 2g$

10. For which of the following ordered pairs (x, y) is $2x + 3y > 6$ and $x - y > 6$?

    (A) $(7, -1)$
    (B) $(7, 1)$
    (C) $(4, -3)$
    (D) $(3, 3)$
    (E) $(-3, 4)$

GO ON TO THE NEXT PAGE

2   2   2   2   2   2

---

11. When n is divided by 12, the remainder is 6. What is the remainder when n is divided by 6?

(A) 0
(B) 1
(C) 2
(D) 3
(E) 4

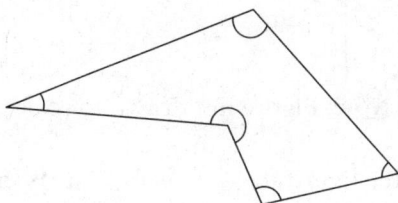

12. The figure above shows a polygon with five sides. What is the average (arithmetic mean) of the measures, in degrees, of the five angles shown?

(A)   85°
(B)   108°
(C)   120°
(D)   324°
(E)   540°

---

13. At a pet store, if d represents the number of dogs and c represents the number of cats, then which of the following is equivalent to the statement "The number of dogs is 3 fewer than 4 times the number of cats?"

(A) $4d + 3 = c$
(B) $4d - 3 = c$
(C) $d = 4c + 3$
(D) $d = 4c - 3$
(E) $4d - 3c = 0$

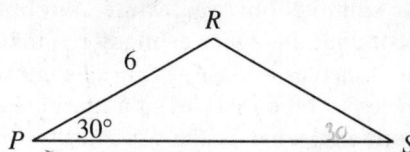

14. In the figure above, if $PR = RS$, what is the area of triangle PRS?

(A) $9\sqrt{2}$
(B) $9\sqrt{3}$
(C) $18\sqrt{2}$
(D) $18\sqrt{3}$
(E) $36\sqrt{3}$

---

15. A $50,000 prize is divided among four winners in a ratio of 4:3:2:1. What is the greatest amount of money that any winner receives?

(A) $5,000
(B) $10,000
(C) $12,500
(D) $20,000
(E) $40,000

---

16. For all non-zero integers a and b, let

$$a\{b\} = \frac{a^2}{b^2}.$$

If $m\{n\} = 9$, which of the following must be true?

    I. $m > n$
    II. $m^2 - n^2 = 8n^2$
    III. $\dfrac{m}{3n}$ is an integer.

(A) II only
(B) I and II only
(C) II and III only
(D) I and III only
(E) I, II, and III

GO ON TO THE NEXT PAGE

2   2   2   2   2   **2**

17. A jar contains only red, white, and blue marbles. It contains twice as many red marbles as white marbles and three times as many white marbles as blue marbles. If a marble is drawn at random, what is the probability that it is white?

(A) $\dfrac{1}{10}$

(B) $\dfrac{1}{6}$

(C) $\dfrac{3}{10}$

(D) $\dfrac{1}{3}$

(E) $\dfrac{3}{5}$

18. A certain class has 6 girls and 5 boys. Four of these students are to line up in the front of the room, with two girls on either end and two boys in between. How many such arrangements are possible?

(A) 20
(B) 200
(C) 462
(D) 600
(E) 900

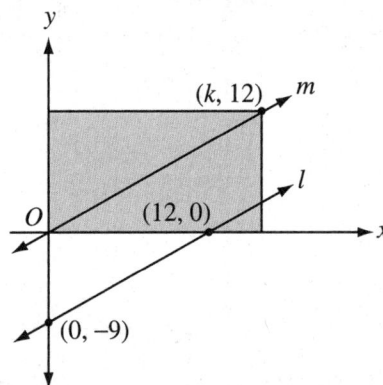

Note: Figure not drawn to scale.

19. In the figure above, if $m \parallel l$, what is the area of the shaded rectangle?

(A) 96
(B) 108
(C) 144
(D) 192
(E) 204

20. A rectangular solid is a centimeters long, b centimeters wide, and c centimeters high. Its volume is v cubic centimeters and its surface area is s square centimeters. If a, b, c, v, and s are all integers, and v is odd, which of the following must be true?

    I. $a + b + c$ is odd.

    II. $a = \dfrac{v}{bc}$

    III. s is even.

(A) I only
(B) I and II only
(C) I and III only
(D) II and III only
(E) I, II, and III

STOP

If you finish before time is called, you may check your work on this section only. Do not turn to any other section of the test.

3   **3**   **3**   **3**   **3**   **3**

SECTION 3
Time—25 minutes
24 questions

Turn to Section 3 of your answer sheet to answer the questions in this section.

Directions: For each question in this section, select the best answer from among the choices given and fill in the corresponding circle on the answer sheet.

Each sentence below has one or two blanks, each blank indicating that something has been omitted. Beneath the sentence are five words or sets of words labeled A through E. Choose the word or set of words that, when inserted in the sentence, best fits the meaning of the sentence as a whole.

EXAMPLE:

Rather than accepting the theory unquestion-ingly, Deborah regarded it with _____.

(A) mirth
(B) sadness
(C) responsibility
(D) ignorance
(E) skepticism

ⓐ ⓑ ⓒ ⓓ ●

---

1. They enjoyed each other's company enor-mously, but they rarely agreed on any issue; in fact, one could be sure that on any important topic their opinions would -------.

(A) diverge
(B) coincide
(C) retreat
(D) assemble
(E) truncate

2. Once accepted as an incontrovertible truth, the theory that nine planets revolve around our sun is now regarded by astronomers as ------.

(A) enacted
(B) irrefutable
(C) universal
(D) dubious
(E) conclusive

3. Having lost his wife and three children to untimely deaths, Rembrandt entered his dark period in 1642, when his immersion in painting often seemed his only ------- from abject -------.

(A) salvation . . prudence
(B) remorse . . adulation
(C) solace . . melancholy
(D) elation . . poverty
(E) departure . . cheerfulness

4. Many proponents of the new curriculum con-sidered its omission of Romance literature to be -------, while the more conservative educators considered such a removal -------.

(A) repugnant . . premature
(B) innocuous . . deplorable
(C) reprehensible . . benevolent
(D) malicious . . disgraceful
(E) auspicious . . encouraging

GO ON TO THE NEXT PAGE ⟩

5. As the expedition leader quickly realized, the recently accelerated program to acclimate the climbers to high altitudes was ------; as a result, several team members were soon ------ by the lack of oxygen.

(A) illusory . . initiated
(B) excessive . . mitigated
(C) appropriate . . confused
(D) ineffective . . enervated
(E) venerable . . absolved

6. Although the mainstream of most societies reviles the ------, nearly every culture reserves at least some small place for those who question its treasured norms and mores.

(A) charlatan
(B) surrogate
(C) philanthropist
(D) pragmatist
(E) iconoclast

7. Steven Pinker is far from ------ about the heated controversy of whether the human mind is a *tabula rasa;* he stands ------ in the negative camp.

(A) ambivalent . . unequivocally
(B) apathetic . . furtively
(C) impartial . . reluctantly
(D) adamant . . vehemently
(E) subjective . . stubbornly

8. Although Ivan Illich was dismissed as a ------ by many of his contemporaries, many modern thinkers now regard his revolutionary insights on the dehumanization of society as ------.

(A) pedant . . derivative
(B) neophyte . . vociferous
(C) radical . . visionary
(D) partisan . . conciliatory
(E) hermit . . simplistic

The passages below are followed by questions based on their content. Answer the questions on the basis of what is <u>stated</u> or <u>implied</u> in the passage and in any introductory material that may be provided.

Questions 9–12 are based on the following passages.

PASSAGE 1

In many instances, the study of life on Earth
ultimately involves the study of the molecules
Line of which living organisms are composed.
How does photosynthesis convert the energy
5   of sunlight into the energy of sugar molecules? What is the structure of the cell mem-
brane, and how does it function in controlling
the movement of materials into and out of the
cell? How do muscles contract? How do the
10   nerve cells in your brain communicate with
one another? What causes cancer? To understand the answers to these questions, you
must first learn about energy and matter, the
properties of atoms, and how atoms interact
15   with one another to form molecules.

PASSAGE 2

For centuries the idea that photosynthesis
supports the earth's biosystem had been fundamental to our understanding of life on
Earth. If the sun went out, we assumed, life
20   would soon follow. Yet in the 1970s, scientists
discovered organisms thriving in deep-sea
hydrothermal vents far from any light energy
required for photosynthesis. These organisms
relied on bacteria that harvest energy not from
25   light but from the chemical bonds in sulfides
and other molecules that poured from the heat
vents. This process is called chemosynthesis.
Other organisms eat these bacteria or house
the living bacteria in their tissues. Such rela-
30   tionships mirror the myriad complex relationships we see in the photosynthetic food chain,
in which bacteria are either consumed or
co-opted by organisms to aid in breaking
down or synthesizing chemicals that the
35   organisms' own tissues cannot.

GO ON TO THE NEXT PAGE ⇨

3   3   3   3   3   3

9. Both passages focus primarily on

   (A) how groups of cells form tissues
   (B) the origin of life on Earth
   (C) biochemical processes
   (D) the importance of the sun to life on Earth
   (E) unusual life forms

10. The questions listed in lines 4–11 of Passage 1 are presented as those that

    (A) biologists have yet to explore in great depth
    (B) inspire controversy within the scientific community
    (C) necessarily concern those who are interested in a deep understanding of biology
    (D) are difficult to investigate with current methods and technology
    (E) researchers have considered to be less important than ecological questions

11. Which of the five questions posed in Passage 1 is most relevant to the discussion in Passage 2?

    (A) How does photosynthesis convert the energy of sunlight into the energy of sugar molecules?
    (B) What is the structure of the cell membrane, and how does it function in controlling the movement of materials into and out of the cell?
    (C) How do muscles contract?
    (D) How do the nerve cells in your brain communicate with one another?
    (E) What causes cancer?

12. Which of the following concepts is mentioned in Passage 2 but NOT in Passage 1?

    (A) the structure of cells
    (B) the conversion of light energy to food energy
    (C) disease
    (D) relationships among separate organisms
    (E) bonds within molecules

GO ON TO THE NEXT PAGE

Questions 13–18 are based on the following passage.

The following is an excerpt from a popular book on "innumeracy," the common inability of people to deal rationally with numbers.

Without some appreciation of common large numbers, it's impossible to react with the
Line proper skepticism to terrifying reports that more than a million American kids are kid-
5   napped each year, or with the proper sobriety to a warhead carrying a megaton of explosive power—the equivalent of a million tons (or two billion pounds) of TNT.

And if you don't have some feeling for proba-
10 bilities, automobile accidents might seem a rel- atively minor problem of local travel, whereas being killed by terrorists might seem to be a major risk when going overseas. As often observed, however, the 45,000 people killed
15 annually on American roads are approximately equal in number to all American dead in the Vietnam War. On the other hand, the seventeen Americans killed by terrorists in 1985 were among the 28 million of us who traveled
20 abroad that year—that's one chance in 1.6 mil- lion of becoming a victim. Compare that with these annual rates in the United States: one chance in 68,000 of choking to death; one chance in 75,000 of dying in a bicycle crash;
25 one chance in 20,000 of drowning; and one chance in only 5,300 of dying in a car crash.

Confronted with these large numbers and with the correspondingly small probabilities associated with them, the innumerate will
30 inevitably respond with the non sequitur,[1] "Yes, but what if you're that one," and then nod knowingly, as if they've demolished your argument with penetrating insight. This ten- dency to personalize is a characteristic of
35 many who suffer from innumeracy. Equally typical is a tendency to equate the risk from some obscure and exotic malady with the chances of suffering from heart and circulatory disease, from which about 12,000 Americans die each week.
40 There's a joke I like that's marginally rele- vant. An old married couple in their nineties contact a divorce lawyer, who pleads with them to stay together. "Why get divorced now after seventy years of marriage?" The little old

45 lady finally pipes up in a creaky voice: "We wanted to wait until the children were dead."

A feeling for what quantities or time spans are appropriate in various contexts is essential to getting the joke. Slipping between millions
50 and billions or between billions and trillions should in this sense be equally funny, but it isn't, because we too often lack an intuitive grasp for these numbers.

A recent study by Drs. Kronlund and
55 Phillips of the University of Washington showed that most doctors' assessments of the risks of various operations, procedures, and medications (even in their own specialties) were way off the mark, often by several orders
60 of magnitude. I once had a conversation with a doctor who, within approximately 20 min- utes, stated that a certain procedure he was contemplating (a) had a one-chance-in-a- million risk associated with it; (b) was 99
65 percent safe; and (c) usually went quite well. Given the fact that so many doctors seem to believe that there must be at least eleven people in the waiting room if they're to avoid being idle, I'm not surprised at this new
70 evidence of their innumeracy.

---

[1]A non sequitur is a statement that does not follow logically from previous statements.

GO ON TO THE NEXT PAGE ➡

3   3   3   3   3   3

13. Which of the following can be inferred to be the author's view of the "reports that more than a million American kids are kidnapped each year" (lines 4–5)?

 (A) They are typical examples of American journalism.
 (B) They are evidence of a terrible problem that must be addressed.
 (C) They are probably untrue.
 (D) They properly use a number to convey a simple fact.
 (E) They demonstrate an American obsession with statistics.

14. What fact is the list of probabilities cited in lines 21–26 intended to illustrate?

 (A) that probability can be used in many different ways in everyday life
 (B) that terrorism is far less a threat to Americans than many other common dangers
 (C) that the world is filled with many dangers
 (D) that a knowledge of probability can help Americans decide where to travel most safely abroad
 (E) that bicycles are nearly as dangerous as cars

15. Which of the following is *not* an element of the discussion in this passage?

 (A) a personal recollection
 (B) a verifiable statistic
 (C) a reference to an authoritative study
 (D) a discussion of a common misconception
 (E) a refutation of a scientific theory

16. What is the author's view of the "penetrating insight" mentioned in line 33?

 (A) It is the result of careful analysis.
 (B) It is illogical.
 (C) It demolishes a statistical argument.
 (D) It does not sufficiently personalize the situation being discussed.
 (E) It is not found enough in everyday discussions.

17. In what way does the author suggest that the joke described in lines 41–46 is like "slipping between millions and billions" (lines 49–50)?

 (A) They both involve a lack of appreciation for particular quantities.
 (B) They both describe mistakes the elderly are likely to make.
 (C) They both illustrate a common scenario.
 (D) They both reveal the value of understanding probabilities.
 (E) They both illustrate humor in mathematics.

18. The author mentions the time span of "approximately 20 minutes" (lines 61–62) in order to emphasize

 (A) the doctor's inability to appreciate relevant time spans
 (B) the comparison with the elderly couple in the preceding joke
 (C) the frequency with which the doctor contradicted himself
 (D) the common need to approximate rather than use precise numbers
 (E) how quickly he was able to get an appointment

GO ON TO THE NEXT PAGE ▷

Questions 19–24 are based on the following passage.

The following is an excerpt from a memoir of Richard Feynman, a Nobel Prize–winning physicist, in which he describes the experience of having an artist friend named Jerry teach him to draw.

I promised to work, but still bet that he couldn't teach me to draw. I wanted very much to
Line learn to draw, for a reason that I kept to
    myself: I wanted to convey an emotion I have
5　about the beauty of the world. It's difficult to
    describe because it's an emotion. It's analo-
    gous to the feeling one has in religion that has
    to do with a god that controls everything in
    the universe: there's a generality aspect that
10　you feel when you think about how things
    that appear so different and behave so differ-
    ently are all run "behind the scenes" by the
    same organization, the same physical laws.
    It's an appreciation of the mathematical
15　beauty of nature, of how she works inside; a
    realization that the phenomena we see result
    from the complexity of the inner workings
    between atoms; a feeling of how dramatic and
    wonderful it is. It's a feeling of awe—of scien-
20　tific awe—which I felt could be communicated
    through a drawing to someone who had also
    had this emotion. It could remind him, for a
    moment, of this feeling about the glories of
    the universe.
25　Jerry turned out to be a very good teacher. He
    told me first to go home and draw anything.
    So I tried to draw a shoe; then I tried to draw
    a flower in a pot. It was a mess!
    The next time we met I showed him my
30　attempts: "Oh, look!" he said. "You see, around
    in back here, the line of the flower pot doesn't
    touch the leaf." (I had meant the line to come
    up to the leaf.) "That's very good. It's a way of
    showing depth. That's very clever of you."
35　　"And the fact that you don't make all the
    lines the same thickness (which I *didn't* mean
    to do) is good. A drawing with all the lines the
    same thickness is dull." It continued like that:
    everything that I thought was a mistake, he
40　used to teach me something in a positive way.
    He never said it was wrong; he never put me
    down. So I kept on trying, and I gradually got
    a little bit better, but I was never satisfied.

19. In line 13, the word "organization" most nearly means

(A) corporation
(B) rules of physics
(C) social group
(D) arrangement of objects
(E) system of emotional expression

20. Which of the following experiences is closest to what the author describes as "dramatic and wonderful" (lines 18–19)?

(A) proving a physical law
(B) creating a beautiful sculpture
(C) appreciating the power of physical laws in nature
(D) teaching another person how to play an instrument
(E) seeing a masterful painting for the first time

21. What assumption does the author make about the appreciation of art?

(A) It comes only through the experience of creating art.
(B) It is enhanced by having experiences similar to those that inspired the artist.
(C) It is not as important as the appreciation of science.
(D) It is difficult for a scientist.
(E) It requires an understanding of the historical period in which the piece was created.

Excerpted from "Surely You're Joking Mr. Feynman!": Adventures of A Curious Character by Richard Feynman as told to Ralph Leighton. Copyright © 1985 by Richard P. Feynman and Ralph Leighton. Reprinted with permission of W.W. Norton & Company, Inc.

GO ON TO THE NEXT PAGE ⟶

3 3 3 3 3 3

22. If Jerry is really a "very good teacher" (line 25) in the way that the author suggests, what would he most likely have done if the author had drawn the flower pot with lines of all the same thickness?

(A) Jerry would have shown the author how to vary the thickness of his lines.
(B) Jerry would have shown the author examples of how line thickness affects the quality of a drawing.
(C) Jerry would have mentioned that the drawing was dull, but could be made more lively with color.
(D) Jerry would have found something positive elsewhere in the drawing.
(E) Jerry would have made the author re-do the drawing.

23. The author suggests that the "way of showing depth" (lines 33–34) is actually

(A) unintentional
(B) unattractive
(C) difficult to accomplish
(D) not characteristic of true art
(E) a reflection of the author's theory of nature

24. In what way was the author "never satisfied" (line 43)?

(A) He was never able to fully appreciate great art.
(B) He was never able to draw a realistic flower pot.
(C) He was not able to replicate his teacher's talent for emphasizing the positive in his students.
(D) He never fully appreciated the talent of his teacher.
(E) He was never able to convey adequately his feelings about the beauty of the world.

STOP

If you finish before time is called, you may check your work on this section only. Do not turn to any other section of the test.

4   4   4   4   4   4

SECTION 4
Time—25 minutes
35 questions

Turn to Section 4 of your answer sheet to answer the questions in this section.

Directions: For each question in this section, select the best answer from among the choices given and fill in the corresponding circle on the answer sheet.

The following sentences test correctness and effectiveness of expression. Part of each sentence or the entire sentence is underlined; beneath each sentence are five ways of phrasing the underlined material. Choice A repeats the original phrasing; the other four choices are different. Select the choice that completes the sentence most effectively.

In making your selection, follow the requirements of standard written English; that is, pay attention to grammar, choice of words, sentence construction, and punctuation. Your selection should result in the most effective sentence—clear and precise, without awkwardness or ambiguity.

EXAMPLE:

The children <u>couldn't hardly believe their eyes</u>.

(A) couldn't hardly believe their eyes
(B) could hardly believe their eyes
(C) would not hardly believe their eyes
(D) couldn't nearly believe their eyes
(E) couldn't hardly believe his or her eyes

Ⓐ ● Ⓒ Ⓓ Ⓔ

1. The anthology contains mostly the work of modern poets, but <u>which includes a few significant older works as well</u>.

   (A) which includes a few significant older works as well
   (B) it includes a few significant older works as well
   (C) also it contains a few significant older works as well
   (D) as well, it also includes a few significant older works
   (E) which also include a few significant older works

2. The coach worked long and hard into the night <u>for preparing the team's strategy</u> for the next game.

   (A) for preparing the team's strategy
   (B) in preparing the team's strategy
   (C) for the preparation of the team's strategy
   (D) in order for proper preparation of the team's strategy
   (E) to prepare the team's strategy

3. Although usually unflappable even in front of a crowd, <u>Carla's anxiety overwhelmed her</u> during the recital.

   (A) Carla's anxiety overwhelmed her
   (B) her anxiety overwhelmed Carla completely
   (C) Carla being overwhelmed by anxiety
   (D) Carla was overwhelmed by anxiety
   (E) nevertheless Carla's anxiety was overwhelming

GO ON TO THE NEXT PAGE ⟹

4   4   4   4   4   4

---

4. Those students who sit through her lectures <u>day after day, having been numbed into thinking</u> that history could never be even remotely interesting.

   (A)   day after day, having been numbed into thinking

   (B)   day after day being numbed into thinking

   (C)   day after day have been numbed into thinking

   (D)   day after day of being numbed into thinking

   (E)   day after day of having been numbed into thinking

5. Swimming in the deepest part of the lake, <u>the current pushed Justine farther from shore</u>.

   (A)   the current pushed Justine farther from shore

   (B)   Justine by the current was pushed farther from shore

   (C)   Justine was pushed farther from shore by the current

   (D)   the current's push made sure that Justine moved farther from shore

   (E)   the push of the current moved Justine farther from shore

6. Writing a good twenty-page research paper is more difficult than <u>when you have to write</u> two good ten-page papers.

   (A)   when you have to write

   (B)   when one must write

   (C)   the writing of

   (D)   writing

   (E)   one's writing of

7. <u>If we had not stopped for gas</u>, we probably would have arrived in time for the movie.

   (A)   If we had not stopped for gas

   (B)   If we would not have stopped for gas

   (C)   If we didn't have stopped for gas

   (D)   Because we had stopped for gas

   (E)   If not for having been stopped for gas

8. The spectators watched <u>agape, they could not believe</u> what they were seeing on the playing field.

   (A)   agape, they could not believe

   (B)   agape having not believed

   (C)   agape, for the reason that they could not believe

   (D)   agape: they could not believe

   (E)   agape, therefore they could not believe

9. The evidence for clairvoyance has never been <u>persuasive, and many people continue to believe</u> that it is a widespread phenomenon.

   (A)   persuasive, and many people continue to believe

   (B)   persuasive; nevertheless, many people continue to believe

   (C)   persuasive, so many people continue to believe

   (D)   persuasive: and people continue to believe anyway

   (E)   persuasive, which is why people continue to believe

10. The strange theories that explain the atom <u>reveals how deeply the common and the bizarre are entwined</u> in the physical world.

   (A)   reveals how deeply the common and the bizarre are entwined

   (B)   reveal how common the entwining of the bizarre is

   (C)   reveals the deep bizarre common entwining

   (D)   reveal how the common and the bizarre are so entwined deeply

   (E)   reveal how deeply the common and the bizarre are entwined

11. The transportation board announced <u>their anonymous approval</u> of the new contract at the press conference that afternoon.

   (A)   their anonymous approval

   (B)   its anonymous approval

   (C)   their unanimous approval

   (D)   its unanimous approval

   (E)   about its unanimous approval

GO ON TO THE NEXT PAGE ⟹

The following sentences test your ability to recognize grammar and usage errors. Each sentence contains either a single error or no error at all. No sentence contains more than one error. The error, if there is one, is underlined and lettered. If the sentence contains an error, select the one underlined part that must be changed to make the sentence correct. If the sentence is correct, select choice E. In choosing answers, follow the requirements of standard written English.

EXAMPLE:

By the time they reached the halfway point
            A
in the race, most of the runners hadn't hardly
   B   C   D
begun to hit their stride. No error
                            E

Ⓐ Ⓑ Ⓒ ● Ⓔ

12. The reporters failed to notice the discrepancies
                                        A
    in the report that the Congressman presented,

    because his staff and him had successfully
           B   C
    diverted the media's attention to other issues.
                                    D
    No error
    E

13. The Warren family, whose ancestors

    founded the town over three hundred years
    A   B
    ago, have ran the general store for seven
         C   D
    generations. No error
                  E

14. Surprisingly absent from the game were the
    A   B
    crowd's customary taunting of the opposing
            C   D
    players. No error
              E

15. Much of the class time was dedicated to
    A   B
    discussing those theories that seemed to be
                                   C
    most commonly misconstrued

    by the students.   No error
    D   E

16. The refraction of light as it passes from air
                            A
    into a denser medium like water or glass
                   B
    often produce interesting kaleidoscopic
          C
    effects.   No error
    D   E

17. The spate of recent exhibitions

    featuring the work of Merce Cunningham
    A
    demonstrates that audiences continue to be
    B   C
    receptive for his postmodernist choreography.
    D
    No error
    E

4   4   4   4   4   4

18. Having invested so much effort in getting

her team <u>so far</u> <u>in the tournament</u>,
      A   B
Coach Moran could hardly be blamed for

reacting so <u>emotional</u> <u>to the foul</u> called on
         C   D
her player in the waning seconds of the

game. <u>No error</u>
     E

19. To its most eminent proponents, anarchism

<u>implies</u> not a desire for lawlessness or
 A
chaos, but <u>rather it is</u> a respect <u>for the ability of</u>
        B   C
individuals <u>to manage</u> their own affairs
        D
justly without the intervention of a

government. <u>No error</u>
        E

20. The senate adopted new rules to prevent

representatives <u>from serving</u> on a committee
          A
<u>while at the same time</u> maintaining an
     B
interest <u>in any company</u> that conducts
        C
business that is <u>affected</u> by that committee's
         D
decisions. <u>No error</u>
     E

21. The labor coalition, <u>which consists</u> of
           A
representatives from all of the skilled labor

unions, <u>have expressed</u> concern <u>about</u> the
     B   C
new hiring policies <u>enacted by</u> the board.
             D
<u>No error</u>
  E

22. Most cognitive scientists <u>now believe</u> that
               A
the way the human brain <u>stores information</u>
             B
is <u>different</u> in many significant ways from
    C
<u>a computer hard drive</u>. <u>No error</u>
    D   E

23. The museum, which <u>has sponsored</u> free
            A
programs in the arts for city children since

the late 1960s, was <u>cited</u> <u>by the mayor</u> for
          B   C
<u>their</u> many civic contributions. <u>No error</u>
  D   E

24. <u>When given the choice</u>, Harlow's monkeys
    A
clearly preferred the warmer, cloth-covered

surrogate mother <u>more than</u> the wire
           B
surrogate, <u>even when</u> the latter was able
       C
<u>to provide</u> them with nourishment.
  D
<u>No error</u>
 E

25. Although both films <u>accurately depict</u> the
          A
horrors <u>of fighting</u> on the front lines, *Saving*
      B
Private Ryan is by <u>far</u> the <u>most</u> graphic.
         C   D
<u>No error</u>
 E

GO ON TO THE NEXT PAGE ⟹

26. The debate team, <u>which</u> included
                    A
    <u>Emma and I,</u> <u>was</u> stuck on the bus for
      B   C
    <u>more than two</u> hours. <u>No error</u>
         D   E

27. By the time he <u>reached</u> the island, David
                  A
    had already <u>swam</u> further than <u>anyone</u>
             B   C
    else ever <u>had</u>. <u>No error</u>
           D   E

28. <u>Far from</u> being a liberal fanatic, Davis
       A
    actually <u>espouses</u> very conservative
            B
    <u>views on</u> social and <u>economic</u> issues.
       C   D
    <u>No error</u>
      E

29. <u>For building</u> vocabulary skills, students
        A
    should <u>try to</u> speak and write new words in
          B
    <u>appropriate contexts</u>, rather <u>than</u> merely
       C   D
    memorizing definitions. <u>No error</u>
                    E

GO ON TO THE NEXT PAGE ⟹

4   4   4   4   4   4

Directions: The following passage is an early draft of an essay. Some parts of the passage need to be rewritten.

Read the passage and select the best answers for the questions that follow. Some questions are about particular sentences or parts of sentences and ask you to improve sentence structure or word choice. Other questions ask you to consider organization and development. In choosing answers, follow the requirements of standard written English.

Questions 30–35 are based on the following passage.

(1) Maria Montessori, who was born in 1870, was a remarkable woman for her time. (2) She surprised her parents by telling them that she wanted to study engineering when she was young, a position that they thought was unladylike. (3) She later decided to switch to medicine and became the first female physician in Italy. (4) As a doctor, the treatment of children who they said were "deficient" bothered her. (5) She realized that isolating them and depriving them of stimulation was doing them a lot of harm.

(6) In 1907 Maria opened her Casa dei Bambini, or "Children's House," a daycare center where impoverished children could receive a stimulating learning environment. (7) She believed that there are specific time schedules where children's minds are ready to learn particular things at their own pace, and these periods are different for every child. (8) She decided it was important to help each child through his or her own curriculum rather than a standardized one for everybody. (9) What was most amazing, the children who used to be aggressive and unmanageable became very proud of their accomplishments and eager to learn more when they were taught skills that gave them control and independence. (10) There were fifty students in her first class.

(11) One of the things that Dr. Montessori did that might be the most important is not just treat children as small adults, but as people with their own special needs. (12) She designed special furniture, toys, and learning aids that were appropriate for their size and abilities.

(13) Her philosophy has had a profound effect on education throughout the world. (14) Today, even the most traditional and regimented schools acknowledge many contributions of Maria Montessori.

30. Which of the following is the best revision of sentence 2 (reproduced below)?

She surprised her parents by telling them that she wanted to study engineering when she was young, a position that they thought was unladylike.

(A) When she was young, she surprised her parents by telling them that she wanted to study the unladylike position of engineering, they thought.
(B) When she was young, she surprised her parents by telling them that she wanted to study engineering, a subject they thought was unladylike.
(C) She surprised her parents by telling them that she wanted to study engineering, a subject that they thought was unladylike when she was young.
(D) She surprised her parents by telling them that she wanted to study the unladylike, so her parents thought, subject of engineering when she was young.
(E) She surprised her parents when she was young by telling them, who thought it was unladylike, that she wanted to study engineering.

31. Which of the following is the best way to revise the underlined portion of sentence 4 (reproduced below)?

As a doctor, the treatment of children who they said were "deficient" bothered her.

(A) she was bothered by the treatment of children who were said to be "deficient."
(B) the way children were treated who they said were "deficient" bothered her.
(C) the treatment bothered her of children who they said were "deficient."
(D) she was bothered by those children they said were "deficient" and the way they were treated.
(E) she was bothered by the children treated who were said to be "deficient."

GO ON TO THE NEXT PAGE

32. The unity of the second paragraph can best be improved by deleting which of the following sentences?

(A) sentence 6
(B) sentence 7
(C) sentence 8
(D) sentence 9
(E) sentence 10

33. Where is the best place to insert the following sentence?

It was developed according to her theories about learning.

(A) after sentence 6
(B) after sentence 7
(C) after sentence 8
(D) after sentence 9
(E) after sentence 10

34. Which of the following is the best revision of sentence 7 (reproduced below)?

She believed that there are specific time schedules where children's minds are ready to learn particular things at their own pace, and these periods are different for every child.

(A) She believed that there are specific time schedules, and these schedules are different for every child, where children's minds are ready at their own pace to learn particular things.

(B) She believed that there are different time periods for every child where their minds are ready to learn particular things at their own pace.

(C) She believed different children at their own pace each have their own time schedules where they are ready to learn particular things.

(D) She believed that each child's mind has its own unique pace and schedule for learning.

(E) She believed that there are specific schedules that are different for every child's mind that make them able to learn at their own pace.

35. Which is the best sentence to insert between sentence 8 and sentence 9?

(A) Her need to blaze trails persisted well into her old age.

(B) It wasn't long until Dr. Montessori was recognized for her efforts.

(C) This focus on the individual child produced amazing results.

(D) She soon opened many of these schools throughout Italy.

(E) Even though she was a physician by training, she earned eminence as a teacher.

STOP

If you finish before time is called, you may check your work on this section only. Do not turn to any other section of the test.

5   **5**   **5**   **5**   **5**   **5**

SECTION 5
Time—25 minutes
18 questions

Turn to Section 5 of your answer sheet to answer the questions in this section.

Directions: This section contains two types of questions. You have 25 minutes to complete both types. For questions 1–8, solve each problem and decide which is the best of the choices given. Fill in the corresponding circle on the answer sheet. You may use any available space for scratchwork.

Notes

1. The use of a calculator is permitted.

2. All numbers used are real numbers.

3. Figures that accompany problems in this test are intended to provide information useful in solving the problems. They are drawn as accurately as possible EXCEPT when it is stated in a specific problem that the figure is not drawn to scale. All figures lie in a plane unless otherwise indicated.

4. Unless otherwise specified, the domain of any function f is assumed to be the set of all real numbers x for which $f(x)$ is a real number.

Reference Information

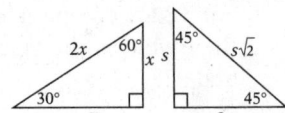

$A = \pi r^2$
$C = 2\pi r$

$A = \ell w$

$A = \frac{1}{2} bh$

$V = \ell wh$

$V = \pi r^2 h$

$c^2 = a^2 + b^2$

Special right triangles

The number of degrees of arc in a circle is 360.
The sum of the measures in degrees of the angles of a triangle is 180.

---

1. If $5y - 2 = 3y + 7$, what is the value of y?

   (A) 3.0
   (B) 4.5
   (C) 6.0
   (D) 7.5
   (E) 9.0

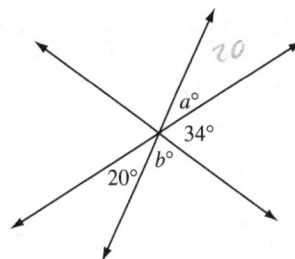

2. In the figure above, three lines intersect in a single point. What is the value of $a + b$?

   (A) 20
   (B) 54
   (C) 126
   (D) 146
   (E) 252

GO ON TO THE NEXT PAGE ▷

3. If $(2x)(3x) = \left(\dfrac{2}{8}\right)\left(\dfrac{3}{2}\right)$, and $x > 0$, what is the value of x?

(A) $\dfrac{1}{16}$

(B) $\dfrac{1}{8}$

(C) $\dfrac{1}{4}$

(D) $\dfrac{1}{3}$

(E) $\dfrac{1}{2}$

4. Two positive integers are "compatible" if their greatest common factor is a prime number. For instance, 15 and 25 are compatible because their greatest common factor is 5, which is prime. If m and 98 are compatible, and m is an odd number, then what is the greatest common factor of m and 98?

(A) 2
(B) 5
(C) 7
(D) 14
(E) 49

5. For how many integer values of k is $|k - 0.5| < 10$?

(A) 17
(B) 18
(C) 19
(D) 20
(E) 21

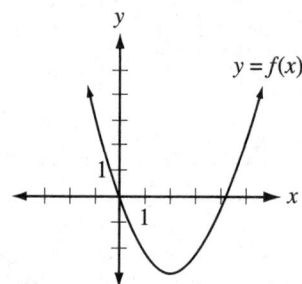

6. The figure above shows the graph of a quadratic function f that has a minimum value when $x = 2$. If $f(5) = f(k)$, then which of the following could be the value of k?

(A) −1
(B) 1
(C) 2
(D) 3
(E) 4

7. If m and n are integers and $1 < m^3 = n^2 < 100$, what is the value of $m + n$?

(A) 4
(B) 8
(C) 12
(D) 16
(E) 32

8. Amanda travels to work from home in 60 minutes. If, on her way home, she increases her average speed by 20% and she travels by the exact same route, how many minutes will it take her to get home?

(A) 48
(B) 50
(C) 54
(D) 60
(E) 64

GO ON TO THE NEXT PAGE

5   5   5   5   5   5

Directions: For Student-Produced Response questions 9–18, use the grids at the bottom of the answer sheet page on which you have answered questions 1–8.

Each of the remaining 10 questions requires you to solve the problem and enter your answer by marking the circles in the special grid, as shown in the examples below. You may use any available space for scratchwork.

Answer: $\frac{7}{12}$

Answer: 2.5

Answer: 201
Either position is correct.

Write answer in boxes.

Fraction line

Decimal point

Grid in result.

Note: You may start your answers in any column, space permitting. Columns not needed should be left blank.

- Mark no more than one circle in any column.

- Because the answer sheet will be machine-scored, **you will receive credit only if the circles are filled in correctly.**

- Although not required, it is suggested that you write your answer in the boxes at the top of the columns to help you fill in the circles accurately.

- Some problems may have more than one correct answer. In such cases, grid only one answer.

- No question has a negative answer.

- **Mixed numbers** such as $3\frac{1}{2}$ must be gridded as 3.5 or 7/2. (If $\boxed{3\,1\,/\,2}$ is gridded, it will be interpreted as , $\frac{31}{2}$ not $3\frac{1}{2}$.)

- **Decimal Answers:** If you obtain a decimal answer with more digits than the grid can accommodate, it may be either rounded or truncated, but it must fill the entire grid. For example, if you obtain an answer such as 0.6666..., you should record your result as .666 or .667. **A less accurate value such as .66 or .67 will be scored as incorrect.**

Acceptable ways to grid $2/3$ are:

5   **5**   5   5   **5**   **5**

9. What is 0.5% of 80?

10. If d is the middle number of three consecutive odd integers whose sum is s, what is the value of d divided by s?

11. If $\dfrac{4}{9}$ of c^2 is 24, what is $\dfrac{5}{9}$ of c^2?

12. The measures of the four angles in a quadrilateral have a ratio of $3:4:5:6$. What is the measure, in degrees, of the smallest of these angles?

13. If $5a + 6b = 13$ and $4a + 5b = 9$, then what is the value of $7a + 7b$?

14. If $m = 3$, what is the value

    of $\dfrac{\dfrac{1}{m+1} + \dfrac{1}{m-1}}{\dfrac{1}{m^2 - 1}}$?

15. If x and y are positive integers such that $x^2 + y^2 = 41$, then what is the value of $(x + y)^2$?

16. A jar contains fifteen marbles, five of which are white and the rest black. What is the *least* number of white marbles that must be added to the jar so that at least three-fifths of the marbles will be white?

NUMBER OF BOOKS READ
DURING SUMMER VACATION

Number of Books Read	Number of Students
1	4
2	6
3	5
4	3
More than 4	2

17. The table above shows the number of books 20 students read over their summer vacation. What is the median number of books read by these students?

18. In one basketball game, Tamara made 50% of her shots, and in the next game, she made 60% of her shots. In the two games, she made 52% of her shots altogether. If she took a shots in the first game and b shots in the second game, what is the value of $\dfrac{a}{b}$?

STOP

If you finish before time is called, you may check your work on this section only. Do not turn to any other section of the test.

6   6   6   6   6   6

SECTION 6
Time—25 minutes
24 questions

Turn to Section 6 of your answer sheet to answer the questions in this section.

Directions: For each question in this section, select the best answer from among the choices given and fill in the corresponding circle on the answer sheet.

Each sentence below has one or two blanks, each blank indicating that something has been omitted. Beneath the sentence are five words or sets of words labeled A through E. Choose the word or set of words that, when inserted in the sentence, best fits the meaning of the sentence as a whole.

EXAMPLE:

Rather than accepting the theory unquestioningly, Deborah regarded it with ------.

(A) mirth
(B) sadness
(C) responsibility
(D) ignorance
(E) skepticism

(A) (B) (C) (D) ●

---

1. Rather than giving Sandra thoughtful and useful advice, her father admonished her with hollow clichés and ------- platitudes.

    (A) irate
    (B) inane
    (C) homogeneous
    (D) flamboyant
    (E) altruistic

2. Maintaining a courageous ------- even while in prison, Nelson Mandela spent years trying to convince others that his fight against apartheid was not -------.

    (A) optimism . . worthwhile
    (B) will . . treacherous
    (C) hope . . futile
    (D) fortitude . . premeditated
    (E) instability . . porous

3. The ------- of the construction near the building rendered the school far less ------- to learning; the teachers could hardly hear themselves talk.

    (A) din . . conducive
    (B) efficiency . . accustomed
    (C) noise . . averse
    (D) precision . . discernible
    (E) racket . . irascible

4. Although no real problem in physics can be solved -------, an approximate solution by a simplified method is sufficient so long as the complicating factors are -------.

    (A) precisely . . large
    (B) completely . . difficult
    (C) exactly . . negligible
    (D) plausibly . . minimal
    (E) ethically . . nonexistent

GO ON TO THE NEXT PAGE

6   **6**   **6**   **6**   **6**   **6**

5. The ------- of a civil war depends on the factions' access to martial resources; the conflict may drag on for years or even decades so long as each side has sufficient ------- to continue fighting.

(A) violence . . mediation
(B) popularity . . opposition
(C) length . . reluctance
(D) duration . . means
(E) value . . skill

The passages below are followed by questions based on their content. Answer the questions on the basis of what is stated or implied in the passage and in any introductory material that may be provided.

Questions 6 and 7 are based on the following passage.

Jung was never dogmatic as to a single "cause" of schizophrenia,[1] although he inclined to the
Line belief that a psychological, rather than a physical, origin was probable. He was also modest
5 in his therapeutic claims, recognizing that only a limited number of cases responded to analysis, and that partial alleviation was more common than cure. Jung considered that there were many schizophrenics who never came near a
10 mental hospital. If such people consulted him, he was cautious and sometimes dismissed them without attempting psychoanalysis. Jung was one of the first to recognize that a psychotic episode could be precipitated by psychoanalysis.

[1]Schizophrenia is a type of mental illness characterized by a withdrawal from reality and, occasionally, by delusions and mood disorders.

6. According to the passage, with which of the following statements would Jung most likely agree?

(A) Schizophrenia is much more common than most psychologists acknowledge.
(B) Schizophrenia has a single common cause.
(C) Psychoanalysis is not helpful to all mentally ill patients.
(D) Schizophrenia might be caused by physical trauma.
(E) Psychoanalysis, in the right measure, can cure all schizophrenic patients.

7. As it is used in line 14, "precipitated by" most nearly means

(A) hastened by
(B) cured by
(C) responsive to
(D) made more efficient by
(E) composed of

Questions 8 and 9 are based on the following passage.

The tragic (and the dramatic)—it is said— are *universal*. At a distance of centuries we
Line still grieve at the tribulations of Oedipus and Orestes, and even without sharing the ideology
5 of Homais we are distressed by the tragedy of Emma Bovary. The comic, on the other hand, seems bound to its time, society, cultural anthropology. We understand the drama of the protagonist of *Rashomon*, but we don't under-
10 stand when and why the Japanese laugh. It is an effort to find Aristophanes comic, and it takes more culture to laugh at Rabelais than it does to weep at the death of the paladin Orlando.

GO ON TO THE NEXT PAGE

6 6 6 6 6 6

8. Which of the following would the author consider most difficult for a modern American to find humorous?

   (A) a farcical musical about animals who talk
   (B) a comic film about gangsters set in Chicago
   (C) a satirical poem written in 16th-century China
   (D) a situation comedy based on the life of a plumber
   (E) a funny movie with a tragic ending

9. The "effort" (line 11) to which the author refers is a task that requires which of the following?

   (A) great planning
   (B) the work of more than one person
   (C) overcoming cultural obstacles
   (D) a great many natural resources
   (E) emotional fortitude

Questions 10–16 are based on the following passage.

The following is an excerpt from a book on the writing process in which the author describes an interview he gave by telephone to a radio show to promote a writer's conference.

The appointed evening arrived, and my phone rang, and the host came on and greeted me with
Line the strenuous joviality of his trade. He said he had three lovely ladies in the studio with him
5 and he was eager to find out what we all thought of the present state of literature and what advice we had for all his listeners who were members of the literati and had literary ambitions themselves. This hearty introduction dropped
10 like a stone in our midst, and none of the three lovely ladies said anything in response, which I thought was the proper response.

The silence lengthened, and finally I said, "I think we should banish all further mention of
15 the words 'literature' and 'literary' and 'literati.'" I knew that the host had been briefed about what kind of writers we were and what we wanted to discuss. But he had no other frame of reference. "Tell me," he said, "what insights
20 do you have about the literary experience in America today?" Silence also greeted this question. Finally I said, "We're here to talk about the craft of writing."

He didn't know what to make of that, and he
25 began to involve the names of authors like Ernest Hemingway and Saul Bellow and William Styron, whom we surely regarded as literary giants. We said those writers didn't happen to be our models, and we mentioned people like
30 Lewis Thomas and Joan Didion and Garry Wills. He had never heard of them. One of them mentioned Tom Wolfe's *The Right Stuff*, and he hadn't heard of that. We explained that these were writers we admired for their ability to
35 harness the issues and concerns of the day.

"But don't you want to write anything literary?" our host said. The three women said they felt they were already doing satisfying work. That brought the program to another halt, and
40 the host began to accept phone calls from his listeners, all of whom were interested in the craft of writing and wanted to know how we went about it. "And yet, in the stillness of the night," the host said to several callers, "don't you ever dream of
45 writing the great American novel?" They didn't. They had no such dreams—in the stillness of the night or any other time. It was one of the all-time lousy radio talk shows.

The story sums up a situation that any partic-
50 ular practitioner of nonfiction will recognize. Those of us who are trying to write well about the world we live in, or to teach students to write well about the world *they* live in, are caught in a time warp, where literature by definition still
55 consists of forms that were certified as "literary" in the 19th century: novels and short stories and poems. But in fact the great preponderance of what writers now write and sell, what book and magazine publishers publish and what readers
60 demand is nonfiction.

GO ON TO THE NEXT PAGE ⟩

6   6   6   6   6   6

10. In the first paragraph, the author suggests that he regards the host's introduction to be

   (A) insincere
   (B) inappropriate
   (C) erudite
   (D) flattering
   (E) incoherent

11. Throughout the passage, the author uses the term "literary" to mean

   (A) well-written
   (B) with regard to love stories
   (C) pertaining to the writing of fiction and poetry
   (D) concerning contemporary issues
   (E) persuasive

12. What is the main substance of the misunderstanding between the interviewer and the interviewees?

   (A) The interviewer believed that the writers had written books that they actually had not.
   (B) The interviewer lacked a frame of reference on writing beyond literary fiction.
   (C) The interviewees wanted to be more critical of classic authors, while the interviewer wanted to praise them.
   (D) The interviewer wanted to discuss current issues, while the writers wanted to discuss 19th-century literary forms.
   (E) The interviewer disagreed with the writers on the merits of *The Right Stuff*.

13. The authors in lines 30–31 are mentioned as examples of

   (A) the most popular authors of the time
   (B) authors who had set the trend for the "literary" style of that era
   (C) authors who had influenced the work of the writers being interviewed
   (D) authors whose works followed in the manner of Hemingway, Bellow, and Styron
   (E) authors who wrote experimental fiction

14. In context, the word "harness" (line 35) most nearly means

   (A) dominate
   (B) make easier to understand
   (C) influence the direction of
   (D) witness
   (E) reinforce

15. If the callers shared the sensibilities of the interviewees, then by saying that they had "no such dreams" (line 46), the callers were most likely suggesting that they

   (A) did not wish to pursue literary fame in such a competitive environment
   (B) had disdain for those who wrote fiction for profit
   (C) knew that the public did not care for writers like Thomas, Didion, and Wills
   (D) had been discouraged by their negative experiences with publishers in the literary world
   (E) were happy doing what they were doing

16. In context, the word "preponderance" (line 57) most nearly means

   (A) evidence
   (B) domination
   (C) majority
   (D) heaviness
   (E) quality

GO ON TO THE NEXT PAGE

6   6   6   6   6   6

Questions 17–24 are based on the following passage.

The following is from a book on the history of Western philosophy by Bertrand Russell, in which he discusses ancient Greek philosophy.

To understand the views of Aristotle, as of most Greeks, on physics, it is necessary to apprehend
Line his imaginative background. Every philosopher, in addition to the formal system which he offers
5 to the world, has another much simpler system of which he may be quite unaware. If he is aware of it, he probably realizes that it won't quite do; he therefore conceals it, and sets forth something more sophisticated, which he believes because it
10 is like his crude system, but which he asks others to accept because he thinks he has made it such as cannot be disproved. The sophistication comes in by way of refutation of refutations, but this alone will never give a positive result: it
15 shows, at best, that a theory *may* be true, not that it *must* be. The positive result, however little the philosopher may realize it, is due to his imaginative preconceptions, or to what Santayana calls "animal faith."
20   In relation to physics, Aristotle's imaginative background was very different from that of a modern student. Nowadays, students begin with mechanics, which, by its very name, suggests machines. They are accustomed to auto-
25 mobiles and airplanes; they do not, even in the dimmest recesses of their subconscious imagi- nation, think that an automobile contains some sort of horse inside, or that an airplane flies because its wings are those of a bird possessing
30 magical powers. Animals have lost their impor- tance in our imaginative pictures of the world, in which humans stand comparatively alone as masters of a mainly lifeless and largely sub- servient material environment.
35   To the ancient Greek, attempting to give a scientific account of motion, the purely mechanical view hardly suggested itself, except in the case of a few men of genius such as Democritus and Archimedes. Two sets of

40 phenomena seemed important: the movements of animals, and the movements of the heavenly bodies. To the modern man of science, the body of an animal is a very elaborate machine, with an enormously complex physico-chemical
45 structure; every new discovery consists in diminishing the apparent gulf between animals and machines. To the Greek, it seemed more natural to assimilate apparently lifeless motions to those of animals. A child still distinguishes
50 live animals from other things by the fact that animals can move themselves; to many Greeks, and especially to Aristotle, this peculiarity sug- gested itself as the basis of a general theory of physics.
55   But how about the heavenly bodies? They dif- fer from animals by the regularity of their move- ments, but this may be only due to their superior perfection. Every Greek philosopher, whatever he may have come to think in adult life, had
60 been taught in childhood to regard the sun and moon as gods; Anaxagoras was prosecuted for impiety because he thought that they were not alive. It was natural that a philosopher who could no longer regard the heavenly bodies
65 themselves as divine should think of them as moved by the will of a Divine Being who had a Hellenic love of order and geometric simplicity. Thus the ultimate source of all movement is Will: on earth the capricious Will of human
70 beings, but in heaven the unchanging Will of the Supreme Artificer.

GO ON TO THE NEXT PAGE

17. Which of the following best summarizes the overall purpose of this passage?

(A) to compare Aristotle's philosophy with those of Democritus and Archimedes
(B) to describe the preconceptions behind Aristotle's physical theories
(C) to uncover the flaws in ancient Greek astronomy
(D) to show how Aristotle's theories facilitated the development of modern technology
(E) to contrast the modern conception of the animal with that of the ancient Greeks

18. According to the passage, in what way have animals "lost their importance" (lines 30–31)?

(A) Humans no longer treat animals as respectfully as they once did.
(B) Humans no longer need animals to do hard labor.
(C) Few religions today require animal sacrifices.
(D) Modern writers rarely write stories or fables with animals as main characters.
(E) Animals no longer inspire modern physical theories.

19. Which of the following is most similar to the "imaginative preconceptions" (lines 17–18) of Aristotle?

(A) the belief that animals are inferior to humans
(B) the belief that all scientific problems can be solved through rigorous philosophical analysis
(C) the belief that computers have minds and souls like humans or animals
(D) the belief that the body of an animal is a complicated machine
(E) the belief that the sun and moon are not alive

20. What does the author imply about the "men of genius" (line 38)?

(A) They believed that physics is essentially the study of the mechanics of motion rather than spirits or wills.
(B) They were able to precisely determine the orbits of the planets.
(C) They regarded the sun and moon as gods.
(D) They alone saw the similarity between the motion of animals and the motion of heavenly bodies.
(E) They regarded all movement as being produced by a Divine Being.

21. According to the passage, modern scientists diminish "the apparent gulf between animals and machines" (lines 46–47) by

(A) using machines to train animals
(B) studying the motivations of animals
(C) working to make machines function more like animals
(D) using technology to improve the lives of animals
(E) uncovering the mechanical laws behind biology

22. In line 48, the word "assimilate" most nearly means

(A) compare
(B) repeat
(C) attach
(D) refer
(E) elevate

GO ON TO THE NEXT PAGE ⟩

6   6   6   6   6   6

---

23. In the final paragraph, which of the following does the author imply about Greek philosophers?

  (A) Some of them were not rigorous in demonstrating their theories through experiment.
  (B) They were more concerned with popularizing their theories than proving them.
  (C) Some of them departed dramatically from their childhood teachings.
  (D) They all regarded the planetary bodies as divine.
  (E) Most of them disagreed strongly with Aristotle.

24. The "Hellenic love of order and geometric simplicity" (line 67) attributed to the "Divine Being" (line 66) can be inferred to involve which of the following?

  I. a need to simplify mathematical equations
  II. a desire to make astronomical objects move in elegant paths
  III. a need to unify the laws of motion with a single theory

  (A) I only
  (B) II only
  (C) I and II only
  (D) II and III only
  (E) I, II, and III

STOP

If you finish before time is called, you may check your work on this section only. Do not turn to any other section of the test.

SECTION 7
Time—20 minutes
16 questions

Turn to Section 7 of your answer sheet to answer the questions in this section.

Directions: For this section, solve each problem and decide which is the best of the choices given. Fill in the corresponding circle on the answer sheet. You may use any available space for scratchwork.

Notes

1. The use of a calculator is permitted.

2. All numbers used are real numbers.

3. Figures that accompany problems in this test are intended to provide information useful in solving the problems. They are drawn as accurately as possible EXCEPT when it is stated in a specific problem that the figure is not drawn to scale. All figures lie in a plane unless otherwise indicated.

4. Unless otherwise specified, the domain of any function f is assumed to be the set of all real numbers x for which $f(x)$ is a real number.

Reference Information

$A = \pi r^2$
$C = 2\pi r$

$A = \ell w$

$A = \frac{1}{2} bh$

$V = \ell wh$

$V = \pi r^2 h$

$c^2 = a^2 + b^2$

Special right triangles

The number of degrees of arc in a circle is 360.
The sum of the measures in degrees of the angles of a triangle is 180.

---

1. The number that is $\frac{2}{3}$ of 60 is what fraction of 80?

   (A) $\frac{1}{6}$

   (B) $\frac{1}{3}$

   (C) $\frac{1}{2}$

   (D) $\frac{3}{4}$

   (E) $\frac{8}{9}$

2. If $4x + 2y = 8$, then $x + \frac{1}{2}y =$

   (A) 0.25
   (B) 0.5
   (C) 1
   (D) 2
   (E) 4

GO ON TO THE NEXT PAGE

3. 29 apples, 21 pears, and 64 oranges are to be distributed among three baskets, with each basket getting an equal number of apples, each basket getting an equal number of pears, and each basket getting an equal number of oranges. If as much of the fruit as possible is distributed in this way, what fruit will remain undistributed?

(A) 2 apples, 2 pears, and 1 orange
(B) 2 apples, 1 pear, and 1 orange
(C) 2 apples and 1 orange
(D) 1 pear and 1 orange
(E) 1 apple only

4. For all values of x and y, let x & y be defined by the equation x & $y = x(x - 1) + y(y - 1)$. What is the value of 1 & 2?

(A) 1
(B) 2
(C) 3
(D) 4
(E) 5

5. In $\triangle ABC$, $AB = 15$ and $BC = 9$. Which of the following could *not* be the length of AC?

(A) 5
(B) 7
(C) 9
(D) 16
(E) 22

6. What is the surface area of a cube that has a volume of 64 cubic centimeters?

(A) 64 square centimeters
(B) 96 square centimeters
(C) 256 square centimeters
(D) 288 square centimeters
(E) 384 square centimeters

7. The average (arithmetic mean) of x, 2, 6, and 10 is 8. What is the <u>median</u> of x, 2, 6, and 10?

(A) 4
(B) 6
(C) 7
(D) 8
(E) 9

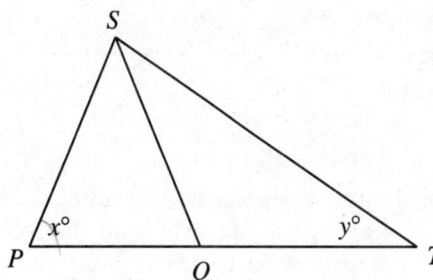

Note: Figure not drawn to scale.

8. In the figure above, $PS = SQ$ and $SQ = QT$. Which of the following expresses y in terms of x?

(A) $\dfrac{x}{2}$

(B) $90 - x$

(C) $90 - \dfrac{x}{2}$

(D) $180 - 2x$

(E) $180 - x$

GO ON TO THE NEXT PAGE

7   **7**   **7**   **7**   **7**   **7**

-4 -3 -2 -1 0 1 2 3 4

9. The graph above represents the set of all possible solutions to which of the following statements?

(A) $|x - 1| > 1$
(B) $|x + 1| < 1$
(C) $|x - 1| < 1$
(D) $|x + 1| > 1$
(E) $|x + 1| > -1$

$$a > b$$
$$b < c$$
$$a = 2c$$

10. If a, b, and c represent different integers in the statements above, which of the following statements must be true?

    I. $a > c$
   II. $2c > b$
  III. $ac > b^2$

(A)   I only
(B)   II only
(C)   I and II only
(D)   II and III only
(E)   I, II, and III

11. How many different positive three-digit integers begin with an odd digit and end with an even digit?

(A)   125
(B)   180
(C)   200
(D)   225
(E)   250

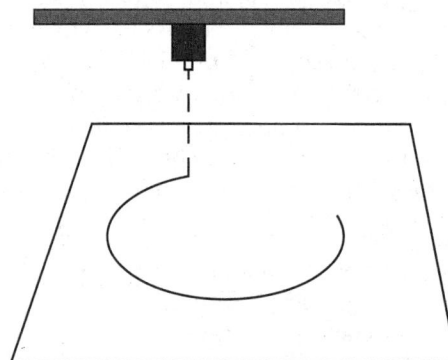

12. A machine uses a laser beam to cut circles from a sheet of plastic, as shown in the figure above. The beam cuts at the rate of 3 cm per second. If circle A has an area of 64π square centimeters and circle B has an area of 16π square centimeters, how many more seconds will it take the machine to cut circle A than circle B?

(A) 2π seconds
(B) $\dfrac{8\pi}{3}$ seconds
(C) $\dfrac{16\pi}{3}$ seconds
(D) 8π seconds
(E) $\dfrac{48\pi}{3}$ seconds

GO ON TO THE NEXT PAGE ⟩

7   **7**   7   7   **7**   **7**

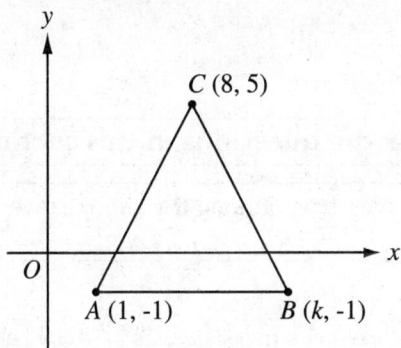

Note: Figure not drawn to scale.

13. In the figure above, the slope of *AC* is the opposite of the slope of *CB*. What is the value of *k*?

(A) 9
(B) 10
(C) 12
(D) 14
(E) 15

14. If *m* is the product of all of the integers from 1 to 10, inclusive, and 2^n is a factor of *m*, then what is the greatest possible value of *n*?

(A) 2
(B) 4
(C) 8
(D) 16
(E) 32

15. An equilateral triangle with area $36\sqrt{3}$ square centimeters is divided into two triangles by the bisector of one of its angles. What is the sum of the perimeters of these two triangles?

(A) $18 + 6\sqrt{3}$

(B) $18 + 9\sqrt{3}$

(C) $36 + 6\sqrt{3}$

(D) $36 + 12\sqrt{3}$

(E)

16. A culture of bacteria doubles in population every 2 hours. A sample of 100 bacteria grows to 1,000 bacteria by 4:00 p.m. At what time were there 250 bacteria in this sample?

(A) 11:30 am
(B) 12 noon
(C) 12:30 pm
(D) 1:00 pm
(E) 2:00 pm

STOP

If you finish before time is called, you may check your work on this section only. Do not turn to any other section of the test.

SECTION 8
Time—20 minutes
19 questions

Turn to Section 8 of your answer sheet to answer the questions in this section.

Directions: For each question in this section, select the best answer from among the choices given and fill in the corresponding circle on the answer sheet.

Each sentence below has one or two blanks, each blank indicating that something has been omitted. Beneath the sentence are five words or sets of words labeled A through E. Choose the word or set of words that, when inserted in the sentence, best fits the meaning of the sentence as a whole.

EXAMPLE:

Rather than accepting the theory unquestioningly, Deborah regarded it with ......

(A) mirth
(B) sadness
(C) responsibility
(D) ignorance
(E) skepticism

Ⓐ Ⓑ Ⓒ Ⓓ ●

---

1. To Clara's relief, the biopsy revealed that the tumor on her skin was -------.

   (A) malignant
   (B) irreverent
   (C) serene
   (D) benign
   (E) mortal

2. The speaker's message was ------- by jargon that rendered it decipherable only to those few audience members familiar with her particular area of expertise.

   (A) elated
   (B) revealed
   (C) obscured
   (D) enlightened
   (E) consoled

3. To those consumers who are more influenced by style than by performance, the ------- value of the sports car outweighs its functional flaws.

   (A) utilitarian
   (B) pragmatic
   (C) approximate
   (D) aesthetic
   (E) inexplicable

4. A student becomes a thinker only when he or she realizes that most so-called facts are merely ------- claims, each serving its purpose only temporarily.

   (A) provisional
   (B) polemical
   (C) authoritative
   (D) dramatic
   (E) pedantic

GO ON TO THE NEXT PAGE ▷

8   **8**   **8**   **8**   **8**   **8**

5. Traditionally, the role had been played demurely to provide a foil for the bolder personalities in the play, but Ms. Linney has decided to ------- convention and emphasize her character's -------.

   (A)   respect . . bluster
   (B)   abandon . . solitude
   (C)   forgo . . coyness
   (D)   uphold . . bombast
   (E)   eschew . . impudence

6. Despite the attempts of popular analysts to depict the stock market as driven by predictable financial principles, an increasing number of investors believe that the price of any security is -------.

   (A)   invaluable
   (B)   complacent
   (C)   capricious
   (D)   responsive
   (E)   obscure

The passages below are followed by questions based on their content; questions following a pair of related passages may also be based on the relationship between the paired passages. Answer the questions on the basis of what is stated or implied in the passage and in any introductory material that may be provided.

Questions 7–19 are based on the following passages.

Since 1996, when scientists at the Roslin Institute in England cloned a sheep from the cells of another adult sheep, many inside and outside the scientific community have debated the ethics of cloning the cells of human beings. The following passages are excerpts of arguments on this issue.

PASSAGE 1

With the specter of human cloning looming on the horizon, the dominant ethical question is:
Line what is a human being? Until now, our respect for human life has rested fundamentally on the

5 deep understanding that human life is perhaps the ultimate gift of nature or God. This gift is made even more profound by the fact that we ourselves are not only its recipients but also its conduits: we receive life and we help create it.
10 But our participation in the creation of life must never be misconstrued as control. Rather, we must be humbled by the power of the life force at the moment of conception.

The idea of "outsourcing" the creation of
15 human life, of relegating it to a laboratory, of reducing the anticipation of childbirth to a trip to the mall or a selection from a catalog, leaves us with a profoundly hollow feeling. The mystery is replaced by design; the surrender to
20 nature is replaced by arrogant control. Should we turn our noses up at one who would offer us the most precious gift in the universe, only to say: "Sorry, but I think I can do better?"

Cloning is the engineering of human life. We
25 have for the first time the ability to determine the exact genetic makeup of a human being, to thwart the essential random (or seemingly random) processes that form the basis of natural selection, to employ unnatural selection. A child
30 can be created that is no longer a unique creation but the end product of an assembly line, with carefully designed and tested features. Are the astonishing products of natural selection that we find around us somehow deficient? Are
35 we so full of hubris[1] as to think we have a better way than nature or God?

If human cloning becomes acceptable, we will have created a new society in which the essence of human life is marginalized. Industries will
40 arise that turn human procreation into a profitable free-market enterprise. The executive boards of these companies, rather than nature or God, will decide the course of human evolution, with more concern for quarterly profit reports
45 than for the fate of humanity.

_____
[1] Excessive pride or arrogance

GO ON TO THE NEXT PAGE ➡

8   **8**   **8**   **8**   **8**   **8**

These are not idle concerns. Even as we ponder the ethical implications of human cloning,
50 companies are forging ahead with the cloning of human stem cells for seemingly beneficial purposes, marching steadily toward a Brave New World[2] in which humanity will be forever different from what it is today.

PASSAGE 2

55 The irrational fears about human cloning that abound from all parts of the political spectrum should not surprise anyone who knows a little bit about the history of technology. Hardly anything significant has been invented that no
60 segment of the population has denounced as evil: factories, trains, automobiles, telephones, televisions, computers. Not even medicine has been spared this vituperation, despite its obvious benefits to humanity. Before the merits of
65 surgery became obvious, it was unimaginable that slicing the flesh of a human being could do more harm than good.

At first glance, it might seem that cloning is a whole new ballgame. After all, cloning is "the en-
70 gineering of human life," isn't it? It is the mass production of designer babies. It is the end of evolution, or at least the beginning of its corporate management. It is certainly a slap in the face of God. Or is it?
75 One of scariest things to the opponents of cloning is the prospect of human beings having identical genetic codes. As cloning foe Jeremy Rifkin has said: "It's a horrendous crime to make a Xerox of someone. You're putting a
80 human into a genetic straitjacket." Logically, then, Mr. Rifkin must be repulsed by natural-born identical multiples: there is no scientific way to distinguish the DNA of one's identical twin from that of one's clone. Perhaps the whole
85 system of natural human procreation is suspect, if it is capable of occasionally churning out such monstrosities.

We need nothing more than the most rudimentary common sense to see how vacuous
90 such an argument is. We all know identical twins who have their own unique thoughts, talents, experiences, and beliefs. They are not horrendous monsters. Human beings are more than merely their DNA; they are the products of
95 the continual and inscrutably complex interactions of environment and biology. Human clones would be no different.

The most common objection we hear from the anti-cloning lobby is that those who would
100 clone human beings are "playing God," and trespassing into territory that can only bring the wrath of nature or its creator. Most of these arguments are basically theological, and rest on the most effective tool of human control ever in-
105 vented: fear of God. We can easily get people to hate something by calling it "unnatural." But this argument is even more easily demolished than the previous one, because it falls so easily in line with so many obviously silly claims. This
110 argument rests on the assumption that human ingenuity has essentially no value, that improving on nature is the height of hubris. This is the reasoning of the Dark Ages. Nature presents vegetables and meats only in raw form, so isn't the
115 cooking of food a human transgression against nature? Nature gives us feet, not wheels, so aren't bicycles evil? If we were to abandon all of the "unnatural" practices and products from our lives, we would be shivering in caves eating
120 uncooked leaves and bugs.

Maybe human procreation is a different arena, however, more sacred than all of the others. But then, why have the technologies of fertility enhancement, in vitro fertilization, embryo
125 transfer, and birth control become so widely accepted? They are telling examples: each of these procreational technologies had legions of vocal opponents—*at first*—but over time the protests mellowed as people realized that the sky
130 wouldn't fall after all. Familiarity dissipates fear.

What most opponents of genetic technology don't realize is that their supposedly "moral" objections are impeding true moral progress. With genetic engineering and stem cell research,
135 scientists finally have within their grasp technologies that can produce ample food for a starving world and cure devastating illnesses. Only ignorant superstition stands in their way.

[2]A futuristic novel by Aldous Huxley that describes the mass production of genetically identical human babies

GO ON TO THE NEXT PAGE ⇒

8   8   8   8   8   8

7. The "control" mentioned in line 11 is control over

    (A) the effects of cloning
    (B) the development of genetic technologies
    (C) the process of conception
    (D) the moral debate about cloning
    (E) activities in a laboratory

8. Which of the following best describes the attitude of the author of Passage 1 toward "outsourcing" (line 14)?

    (A) reluctant approval
    (B) disdain
    (C) strong support
    (D) ironic detachment
    (E) ambivalence

9. The statement "sorry, but I think I can do better" (line 23) is intended to represent a comment from

    (A) a religious person to a nonreligious person
    (B) an opponent of cloning to a scientist
    (C) a voter to a politician
    (D) the author to the reader
    (E) an advocate of cloning to nature or God

10. The parenthetical comment in lines 27–28 is intended to account for the possibility that

    (A) life might be designed by a power beyond humanity
    (B) cloning technologies might become uncontrollable
    (C) two human beings might have the same genetic makeup by chance alone
    (D) some scientific theories might not be reliable
    (E) cloning technology might not succeed

11. Passage 1 mentions which of the following as elements of "unnatural selection" (line 29)?

    I.   mechanical procedures
    II. random processes
    III. selection of characteristics

    (A) I only
    (B) III only
    (C) I and II only
    (D) I and III only
    (E) I, II, and III

12. In the first paragraph of Passage 2, the author suggests that the opponents of human cloning, as a group, are all of the following EXCEPT

    (A) very religious
    (B) unreasonable about the implications of cloning
    (C) from widely varied political orientations
    (D) ignorant of scientific history
    (E) fearful of new ideas

13. Surgery is mentioned in lines 62–65 as an example of

    (A) a practice that requires a great deal of education
    (B) something that most people still fear
    (C) a medical technology that was once denounced
    (D) a viable alternative to genetic technologies
    (E) a skill in need of more practitioners

GO ON TO THE NEXT PAGE

8   **8**   **8**   **8**   **8**   **8**

14. The author of Passage 2 quotes Jeremy Rifkin (lines 76–78) in order to

(A) illustrate the dangers of cloning
(B) show a well-reasoned perspective
(C) indicate an illogical claim
(D) represent the views of medical professionals
(E) show how others support the author's thesis

15. The author of Passage 2 mentions that identical human twins "have their own unique thoughts" (line 89) in order to suggest that those twins

(A) would likely oppose human cloning
(B) are not simply the product of their DNA
(C) are among the most vocal advocates of cloning
(D) are able to provide alternatives to procreational technologies
(E) are less likely to be swayed by illogical theories

16. Passage 2 suggests that those individuals who had previously denounced "procreational technologies" (line 125) have since come to accept them because those individuals

(A) became more familiar with the technologies
(B) realized that the technologies were indeed "natural"
(C) understood the theories behind the technologies
(D) realized that the technologies were inexpensive
(E) themselves needed to use those technologies

17. The tone of the last paragraph of Passage 2 is best described as

(A) indignant
(B) analytical
(C) resigned
(D) humorous
(E) whimsical

18. Which of the following best describes the relationship between the pair of questions presented in Passage 1 ("Are the astonishing products . . . nature or God?" [lines 32–36]) and the pair of questions presented in Passage 2 ("Nature presents . . . evil?" [lines 111–115])?

(A) The first two are not intended to be answered, while the second two are.
(B) The first two are scientific questions, while the second two are moral questions.
(C) Both pairs of questions indicate points of view criticized by their respective authors.
(D) The first two are intended as questions from cloning opponents, while the second two are intended as questions from cloning advocates.
(E) The first two are common questions, the second two are asked only by experts.

19. The last paragraphs of both passages indicate that both authors share what assumption?

(A) Cloning needs more scientific study.
(B) Genetic engineering will have profound global effects.
(C) Cloning will marginalize human life.
(D) Procreational technology can benefit the poor.
(E) Scientists are ill-suited to make moral decisions.

◆ **STOP**

If you finish before time is called, you may check your work on this section only. Do not turn to any other section of the test.

9　　9　　9　　9　　9　　9

SECTION 9
Time—10 minutes
14 questions

Turn to Section 9 of your answer sheet to answer the questions in this section.

Directions: For each question in this section, select the best answer from among the choices given and fill in the corresponding circle on the answer sheet.

The following sentences test correctness and effectiveness of expression. Part of each sentence or the entire sentence is underlined; beneath each sentence are five ways of phrasing the underlined material. Choice A repeats the original phrasing; the other four choices are different. Select the choice that completes the sentence most effectively.

In making your selection, follow the requirements of standard written English; that is, pay attention to grammar, choice of words, sentence construction, and punctuation. Your selection should result in the most effective sentence—clear and precise, without awkwardness or ambiguity.

EXAMPLE:

The children couldn't hardly believe their eyes.

(A) couldn't hardly believe their eyes
(B) could hardly believe their eyes
(C) would not hardly believe their eyes
(D) couldn't nearly believe their eyes
(E) couldn't hardly believe his or her eyes

Ⓐ ● Ⓒ Ⓓ Ⓔ

---

1. One way to improve the effectiveness of the treatment is <u>by moving the source of radiation more closely</u> to the patient.

   (A) by moving the source of radiation more closely
   (B) to move the source of radiation more closely
   (C) to move the source of radiation closer
   (D) in moving the source of radiation closer
   (E) to move more closely the source of radiation

2. <u>Until becoming more affordable by standardizing its technology</u>, cell phones were quite rare.

   (A) Until becoming more affordable by standardizing its technology
   (B) Having become more affordable through standardizing their technology
   (C) Becoming more affordable through standardized technology
   (D) Until they became more affordable in standardized technology
   (E) Until standardized technology made them more affordable

GO ON TO THE NEXT PAGE ⟩

9   9   9   9   9   9

3. The airline industry has adopted new pricing <u>procedures; seeming to benefit both the consumers as well as</u> the companies.

   (A) procedures; seeming to benefit both the consumers as well as
   (B) procedures; seemingly benefitting both the consumers and
   (C) procedures seemingly in benefit of both the consumers as well as
   (D) procedures that seem benefitting of both the consumers and
   (E) procedures that seem to benefit both the consumers and

4. The thirty-foot-high stone <u>wall, built over the course of eighty years, once protecting</u> the city from invaders.

   (A) wall, built over the course of eighty years, once protecting
   (B) wall, built over the course of eighty years, once protected
   (C) wall was built over the course of eighty years, which protected
   (D) wall was built over the course of eighty years in protecting
   (E) wall, built over the course of eighty years; it once protected

5. A concise and informative guide for writers, <u>William Zinsser's *On Writing Well* has sold nearly one million copies.</u>

   (A) William Zinsser's *On Writing Well* has sold nearly one million copies
   (B) nearly one million copies of William Zinsser's *On Writing Well* have been sold
   (C) William Zinsser wrote *On Writing Well*, which has sold nearly one million copies
   (D) William Zinsser's *On Writing Well* having sold nearly one million copies
   (E) *On Writing Well* has sold nearly one million copies by William Zinsser

6. When you submit personal information to a Web site, <u>one should make sure</u> that it won't be used for unauthorized purposes.

   (A) one should make sure
   (B) and make sure
   (C) then make sure
   (D) be sure of
   (E) make sure

7. Although passenger pigeons once filled the skies over Michigan, <u>relentless hunting eliminated their entire population by 1901</u>.

   (A) relentless hunting eliminated their entire population by 1901
   (B) it was relentless hunting eliminating their entire population by 1901
   (C) its entire population was eliminated by relentless hunting by 1901
   (D) by 1901 it was relentless hunting eliminating their entire population
   (E) relentless hunting having eliminated their entire population by 1901

8. The failure of the relief effort was more a result of <u>poor coordination than because of blatant corruption</u>.

   (A) poor coordination than because of blatant corruption
   (B) coordination being poor than by blatant corruption
   (C) poor coordination than by blatant corruption
   (D) poor coordination than of blatant corruption
   (E) coordination being poor than corruption being blatant

GO ON TO THE NEXT PAGE ⟹

9   9   9   9   9   9

9. Until revealing that she had been working at a design firm, few of her friends realized that Amanda was interested in art.

   (A) Until revealing that she had been working
   (B) Having revealed that she had been working
   (C) Until she revealed that she had been working
   (D) Being that she revealed she had worked
   (E) Until she revealed about her working

10. Inspired by reading about the great explorers, it was Gerald's decision to sail around the world.

   (A) it was Gerald's decision to sail around the world
   (B) Gerald decided to sail around the world
   (C) the decision was made by Gerald to sail around the world
   (D) sailing around the world was what Gerald decided to do
   (E) Gerald having decided to sail around the world

11. The results of the election were so close that the club had it decided that they would have co-presidents.

   (A) had it decided that they would have co-presidents
   (B) decided to have co-presidents
   (C) would have decided to have co-presidents
   (D) decided they would have co-presidents
   (E) had decided that they would have co-presidents

12. Writing skills are waning because the widespread use of e-mail and instant messaging discourages students from developing their ideas and supporting those ideas logically.

   (A) messaging discourages students from developing their ideas and supporting
   (B) messaging discourage students to develop their ideas and support
   (C) messaging, which discourages students from developing their ideas and supporting
   (D) messaging discouraging students from developing their ideas and supporting
   (E) messaging discouraging students to develop their ideas and support

13. To acknowledge opposing viewpoints does not mean subverting your own thesis, and in fact usually creates a more cogent essay.

   (A) To acknowledge
   (B) In acknowledging
   (C) Acknowledging
   (D) While acknowledging
   (E) For the acknowledgment of

14. To get the full benefit of any medication, avoid problems, and for the reduction of possible side effects, discuss your prescription with your doctor.

   (A) for the reduction of possible side effects
   (B) for reducing possible side effects
   (C) reducing possible side effects
   (D) also to reduce possible side effects
   (E) reduce possible side effects

STOP

If you finish before time is called, you may check your work on this section only. Do not turn to any other section of the test.

ANSWER KEY

Critical Reading

Section 3

	COR. ANS.	DIFF. LEV.		COR. ANS.	DIFF. LEV.
1.	A	1	13.	C	2
2.	D	1	14.	B	3
3.	C	2	15.	E	3
4.	B	3	16.	B	4
5.	D	4	17.	A	4
6.	E	4	18.	C	3
7.	A	4	19.	B	3
8.	C	5	20.	C	4
9.	C	2	21.	B	3
10.	C	3	22.	D	2
11.	A	3	23.	A	3
12.	D	4	24.	E	5

Number correct _____

Number incorrect _____

Section 6

	COR. ANS.	DIFF. LEV.		COR. ANS.	DIFF. LEV.
1.	B	2	13.	C	3
2.	C	2	14.	B	4
3.	A	3	15.	E	3
4.	C	3	16.	C	4
5.	D	4	17.	B	4
6.	C	3	18.	E	5
7.	A	3	19.	C	3
8.	C	2	20.	A	3
9.	C	3	21.	E	4
10.	B	2	22.	A	3
11.	C	4	23.	C	4
12.	B	5	24.	B	4

Number correct _____

Number incorrect _____

Section 8

	COR. ANS.	DIFF. LEV.		COR. ANS.	DIFF. LEV.
1.	D	1	11.	D	4
2.	C	2	12.	A	2
3.	D	3	13.	C	2
4.	A	4	14.	C	4
5.	E	5	15.	B	4
6.	C	5	16.	A	3
7.	C	2	17.	A	3
8.	B	4	18.	C	3
9.	E	4	19.	B	4
10.	A	3			

Number correct _____

Number incorrect _____

Math

Section 2

	COR. ANS.	DIFF. LEV.		COR. ANS.	DIFF. LEV.
1.	C	1	11.	A	3
2.	E	1	12.	B	3
3.	D	3	13.	D	3
4.	E	2	14.	B	4
5.	B	2	15.	D	3
6.	A	2	16.	C	4
7.	D	3	17.	C	4
8.	C	2	18.	D	4
9.	B	3	19.	D	5
10.	A	3	20.	E	5

Number correct _____

Number incorrect _____

Section 5

Multiple-Choice Questions

	COR. ANS.	DIFF. LEV.
1.	B	1
2.	D	2
3.	C	3
4.	C	3
5.	D	3
6.	A	4
7.	C	4
8.	B	5

Number correct _____

Number incorrect _____

Student-produced Response questions

	COR. ANS.	DIFF. LEV.
9.	0.4	1
10.	.333 or 1/3	2
11.	30	3
12.	60	3
13.	28	3
14.	6	4
15.	81	3
16.	10	4
17.	2.5	4
18.	4	5

Number correct _____
(9–18)

Section 7

	COR. ANS.	DIFF. LEV.		COR. ANS.	DIFF. LEV.
1.	C	2	9.	D	4
2.	D	2	10.	B	4
3.	C	2	11.	E	3
4.	B	3	12.	B	4
5.	A	3	13.	E	3
6.	B	3	14.	C	4
7.	D	3	15.	D	5
8.	A	3	16.	B	5

Number correct _____

Number incorrect _____

Writing

Section 4

	COR. ANS.	DIFF. LEV.		COR. ANS.	DIFF. LEV.		COR. ANS.	DIFF. LEV.		COR. ANS.	DIFF. LEV.
1.	B	1	11.	D	4	21.	B	3	31.	A	3
2.	E	1	12.	B	1	22.	D	4	32.	E	3
3.	D	2	13.	C	1	23.	D	3	33.	A	3
4.	C	3	14.	B	2	24.	B	4	34.	D	3
5.	C	4	15.	E	3	25.	D	3	35.	C	3
6.	D	2	16.	C	3	26.	B	3			
7.	A	3	17.	D	2	27.	B	4			
8.	D	4	18.	C	3	28.	E	4			
9.	B	4	19.	B	3	29.	A	5			
10.	E	3	20.	B	3	30.	B	3			

Number correct _____

Number incorrect _____

Section 9

	COR. ANS.	DIFF. LEV.		COR. ANS.	DIFF. LEV.
1.	C	1	11.	B	3
2.	E	2	12.	A	4
3.	E	2	13.	C	4
4.	B	2	14.	E	3
5.	A	2			
6.	E	2			
7.	A	3			
8.	D	3			
9.	C	3			
10.	B	3			

Number correct _____

Number incorrect _____

NOTE: Difficulty levels are estimates of question difficulty that range from 1 (easiest) to 5 (hardest).

SCORE CONVERSION TABLE

How to score your test

Use the answer key on the previous page to determine your raw score on each section. **Your raw score on each section except Section 5 is simply the number of correct answers minus ¼ of the number of wrong answers. On Section 5, your raw score is the sum of the number of correct answers for questions 1–8 minus ¼ of the number of wrong answers for questions 1–8 plus the total number of correct answers for questions 9–18.** Next, add the raw scores from Sections 3, 6, and 8 to get your Critical Reading raw score, add the raw scores from Sections 2, 5, and 7 to get your Math raw score, and add the raw scores from Sections 4 and 9 to get your Writing raw score. Write the three raw scores here:

Raw Critical Reading score: _____ Raw Math score: _____ Raw Writing score: _____

Use the table below to convert these to scaled scores.

Scaled scores: Critical Reading: _____ Math: _____ Writing: _____

Raw Score	Critical Reading Scaled Score	Math Scaled Score	Writing Scaled Score	Raw Score	Critical Reading Scaled Score	Math Scaled Score	Writing Scaled Score
67	800			32	520	570	610
66	800			31	510	560	600
65	790			30	510	550	580
64	780			29	500	540	570
63	770			28	490	530	560
62	750			27	490	520	550
61	740			26	480	510	540
60	730			25	480	500	530
59	720			24	470	490	520
58	700			23	460	480	510
57	690			22	460	480	500
56	680			21	450	470	490
55	670			20	440	460	480
54	660	800		19	440	450	470
53	650	800		18	430	450	460
52	650	780		17	420	440	450
51	640	760		16	420	430	440
50	630	740		15	410	420	440
49	620	730	800	14	400	410	430
48	620	710	800	13	400	410	420
47	610	710	800	12	390	400	410
46	600	700	790	11	380	390	400
45	600	690	780	10	370	380	390
44	590	680	760	9	360	370	380
43	590	670	740	8	350	360	380
42	580	660	730	7	340	350	370
41	570	650	710	6	330	340	360
40	570	640	700	5	320	330	350
39	560	630	690	4	310	320	340
38	550	620	670	3	300	310	320
37	550	620	660	2	280	290	310
36	540	610	650	1	270	280	300
35	540	600	640	0	250	260	280
34	530	590	630	−1	230	240	270
33	520	580	620	−2 or less	210	220	250

SCORE CONVERSION TABLE FOR WRITING COMPOSITE
[ESSAY + MULTIPLE CHOICE]

Calculate your writing raw score as you did on the previous page, and grade your essay from a 1 to a 6 according to the standards that follow in the detailed answer key.

Essay score: _____   Raw Writing score: _____

Use the table below to convert these to scaled scores.

Scaled score: Writing: _____

Raw Score	Essay Score 0	Essay Score 1	Essay Score 2	Essay Score 3	Essay Score 4	Essay Score 5	Essay Score 6
−2 or less	200	230	250	280	310	340	370
−1	210	240	260	290	320	360	380
0	230	260	280	300	340	370	400
1	240	270	290	320	350	380	410
2	250	280	300	330	360	390	420
3	260	290	310	340	370	400	430
4	270	300	320	350	380	410	440
5	280	310	330	360	390	420	450
6	290	320	340	360	400	430	460
7	290	330	340	370	410	440	470
8	300	330	350	380	410	450	470
9	310	340	360	390	420	450	480
10	320	350	370	390	430	460	490
11	320	360	370	400	440	470	500
12	330	360	380	410	440	470	500
13	340	370	390	420	450	480	510
14	350	380	390	420	460	490	520
15	350	380	400	430	460	500	530
16	360	390	410	440	470	500	530
17	370	400	420	440	480	510	540
18	380	410	420	450	490	520	550
19	380	410	430	460	490	530	560
20	390	420	440	470	500	530	560
21	400	430	450	480	510	540	570
22	410	440	460	480	520	550	580
23	420	450	470	490	530	560	590
24	420	460	470	500	540	570	600
25	430	460	480	510	540	580	610
26	440	470	490	520	550	590	610
27	450	480	500	530	560	590	620
28	460	490	510	540	570	600	630
29	470	500	520	550	580	610	640
30	480	510	530	560	590	620	650
31	490	520	540	560	600	630	660
32	500	530	550	570	610	640	670
33	510	540	550	580	620	650	680
34	510	550	560	590	630	660	690
35	520	560	570	600	640	670	700
36	530	560	580	610	650	680	710
37	540	570	590	620	660	690	720
38	550	580	600	630	670	700	730
39	560	600	610	640	680	710	740
40	580	610	620	650	690	720	750
41	590	620	640	660	700	730	760
42	600	630	650	680	710	740	770
43	610	640	660	690	720	750	780
44	620	660	670	700	740	770	800
45	640	670	690	720	750	780	800
46	650	690	700	730	770	800	800
47	670	700	720	750	780	800	800
48	680	720	730	760	800	800	800
49	680	720	730	760	800	800	800

College Hill™ SAT Study Plan

See page 3A–5A for instructions.

Test # _____   RAW SCORES: CR _____ M _____ W _____ Essay _____

                     SCALED SCORES: CR _____ M _____ W _____ Essay _____

1. What were your test conditions?
2. What was your pre-test routine?

Goal	Attack	Get	CR pts	M pts	W pts
500	75%	50%	30	25	25
550	80%	60%	37	32	32
600	85%	67%	45	38	38
650	90%	80%	52	44	42
700	100%	90%	59	49	45
750	100%	95%	62	52	47
800	100%	100%	66	54	49

3. Did you attack all of the questions you needed to attack? (See the table above.)

4. Did you rush to complete any section?

5. How many more raw points do you need to make your score goal?   CR _____ M _____ W _____

6. Did you make educated guesses on any questions? If so, how many points did you pick up on these questions?

7. STUDY PLAN: Use the detailed answer key after the test to review the answers to the questions you missed. Below, list the lessons linked to the questions you missed, and list the tough words you missed from the test.

Lessons to Review   **Words to Review**

_____   _____
_____   _____
_____   _____
_____   _____
_____   _____
_____   _____
_____   _____
_____   _____

Detailed Answer Key

Section I

Consider carefully the issue discussed in the following passage, then write an essay that answers the question posed in the assignment.

> In a culture obsessed with superficial appearances, our leaders should be those who can see beyond the surface. Judging a book by its cover is the job of the plebeian or the consumer, but reading the book—pondering its contents and perhaps seeking to write new chapters—is the job of a leader.

Assignment: **How important is it to look beyond superficial appearances?** Write an essay in which you answer this question and discuss your point of view on this issue. Support your position logically with examples from literature, the arts, history, politics, science and technology, current events, or your experience or observation.

The following essay received 6 points out of a possible 6, meaning that it demonstrates *clear and consistent competence* in that it

- develops an insightful point of view on the topic
- demonstrates exemplary critical thinking
- uses effective examples, reasons, and other evidence to support its thesis
- is consistently focused, coherent, and well organized
- demonstrates skillful and effective use of language and sentence structure
- is largely (but not necessarily completely) free of grammatical and usage errors

The creature that Victor Frankenstein created was horrible to all who saw it, including Victor himself. Huge, misshapen and awkward, the creature was not even considered human. Indeed, the creature began to fulfill the only role that humans allowed him to occupy: the role of a bloodthirsty monster. Yet what Mary Shelley's *Frankenstein* shows us is not so much how rare and horrible it is to alter the natural order, but how tragically simple it is to create a monster. Victor Frankenstein created a monster not by contravening nature, as many would believe, but by judging the creature by his outward appearance and treating him like an unworthy freak.

How simple it is to hate others, to consider them less than human, based on superficial analysis. Hatred is the desperate accomplice of fear. In recent years, too many of us Americans—denizens of the land of the free and home of the brave—have become imprisoned by our hatred and cowed by our fear of the unknown. Our leaders are too often complicit in rousing this fear and fueling this hate, and in mistaking a quick trigger finger for bravery in the face of threat. They become quick to imprison or kill people who scare us at first, rather than acknowledge that they are humans with rights. They see the populace cringing at foreigners because foreigners attacked us

in 2001. They can't see past their irrational fear to the enormous need to reach out to disenfranchised and subjugated cultures and listen to their concerns. If only Victor Frankenstein had tried to learn what his creature would need once it was given life.

Our leaders are often the blindest of all because, to survive, they must not edify but pander. They see the populace cringing in fear at the prospect of human cloning because they imagine Frankenstein's monster. They can't see past their irrational fear to the huge potential medical benefits of stem cell research. They refuse to see that clones are indistinguishable from twins, and that twins are not horrible monstrosities. We can't really expect politicians or the media—who pander to popularity polls and big corporate donations—to see the world for what it truly is. They judge the world book by its cover, as did the angry villagers of Ingolstadt.

Our current situation will get better only once a critical mass of the American population begins to see that we are creating monsters everywhere by our irrational fear of the new and the foreign. We value instant polls of superficial and uninformed opinions more than careful thought and deep analysis. Perhaps it's time to open the book and read it carefully rather than just glancing at the cover.

> The following essay received 4 points out of a possible 6, meaning that it demonstrates *adequate competence* in that it
>
> - develops a point of view on the topic
> - demonstrates some critical thinking, but perhaps not consistently
> - uses some examples, reasons, and other evidence to support its thesis, but perhaps not adequately
> - shows a general organization and focus, but shows occasional lapses in this regard
> - demonstrates adequate but occasionally inconsistent facility with language
> - contains occasional errors in grammar, usage, and mechanics

Whoever said you can't judge a book by its cover probably never had to drive on the highway behind a Hummer. Americans are obsessed with making a first impression, usually an impression of aggression and wealth. Certainly, first impressions about human beings are usually wrong, but American culture is, unfortunately, being increasingly defined by consumer items that give an aggressive first impression and last impression. These items, unlike human beings, are designed carefully, and their first impressions are intended to convey the entire product.

A good example of this is the Super Bowl. It has become a flashy, decadent display of consumption rather than what it should be, a display of athletic prowess. Our obsession with consumer goods that make us seem more attractive or stronger and more powerful have made it clear that we're not concerned with substance as much as appearances. Every commercial shouts at you that first appearances are everything. Our schools are filled with people who think that the most important things in their lives are what shoes they wear or what cell phone they use.

Popular psychologists like Dr. Phil appear on television and tell us how important it is for us to be ourselves and not let other people tell us who we are, and then a string of commercials comes on telling you how a beer or car or deodorant makes you look more attractive. Which message do we really hear?

> The following essay received 2 points out of a possible 6, meaning that it demonstrates *some incompetence* in that it
>
> - has a seriously limited point of view
> - demonstrates weak critical thinking
> - uses inappropriate or insufficient examples, reasons, and other evidence to support its thesis
> - is poorly focused and organized and has serious problems with coherence
> - demonstrates frequent problems with language and sentence structure
> - contains errors in grammar and usage that seriously obscure the author's meaning

I think that definitely you can't judge a book by its cover. Like my friend Cal is a really good wrestler and he even got into the state finals for his weight class. Everybody thinks he's a total jock but not a lot of people know also that he works really hard every day after practice at his uncle's garage and a lot of people think he's as good as a lot of other mechanics. He's a lot smarter than people give him credit for and he get's really good grades in math.

As a matter of fact he's in the honors level of math and will probably take calculus next year, so he's not just a jock or even just a great mechanic. When you look at him, especially when he's got his game face on just before a match, you would hardly believe that he could be a good student.

The next time you see an athlete, don't assume that he is just a dumb jock. Professional athletes have sometimes become senators and business leaders, so sometimes they have minds as well as muscles.

Section 2

1. **C**   Substitute $k = 10$ into $2m + k = 12$ to get
$$2m + 10 = 12$$
$$\text{Subtract 10: } 2m = 2$$
$$\text{Divide by 2: } m = 1$$
(Chapter 8, Lesson 1: Solving Equations)

---

2. **E**   If the average of three numbers is 50, then their sum must be $3(50) = 150$. If two of the numbers are 35 and 50, then the third is $150 - 35 - 50 = 65$
(Chapter 9, Lesson 2: Mean/Median/Mode Problems)

---

3. **D**   Since the ones column has only one A, it is easy to figure out its value from there. The only value for A that yields a 7 in the ones column is 4.
(Chapter 9, Lesson 3: Numerical Reasoning Problems)

---

4. **E**   The problem is best solved with a proportion: $\dfrac{9}{25} = \dfrac{x}{225}$. Cross-multiply: $25x = 2025$
$$\text{Divide by 25: } x = 81$$
(Chapter 7, Lesson 4: Ratios and Proportions)

---

5. **B**   Since $32 = 2^5$, we can substitute: $2^{x-1} = 32$
$$2^{x-1} = 2^5$$
$$x - 1 = 5$$
$$\text{Add 1: } x = 6$$
(Chapter 8, Lesson 3: Working with Exponents)

---

6. **A**   Since there were 59 yes votes, 26 of which were from men, $59 - 26 = 33$ of them were from women. Since there were 76 women in total, 33 of whom voted yes, $76 - 33 = 43$ of them must have voted no.
(Chapter 11, Lesson 5: Data Analysis)

---

7. **D**   They both start with x cards. After Mike gives Kenny 12 cards, Mike has $x - 12$ and Kenny has $x + 12$ cards. If Kenny has twice as many as Mike, then
$$x + 12 = 2(x - 12)$$
$$\text{Distribute: } x + 12 = 2x - 24$$
$$\text{Add 24: } x + 36 = 2x$$
$$\text{Subtract x: } 36 = x$$
Since they each had 36 cards to start, they had a total of $36 + 36 = 72$.
(Chapter 8, Lesson 7: Word Problems)

---

8. **C**   The fraction that is walnuts equals the amount of walnuts divided by the total amount: $\dfrac{x}{(x + 15 + 20)}$
$$\text{Simplify: } \dfrac{x}{(x + 35)}$$
(Chapter 7, Lesson 4: Ratios and Proportions)

---

9. **B**   You might simplify this problem by plugging in possible values for the angle measures, remembering the parallel lines theorem. Your diagram might look like this:

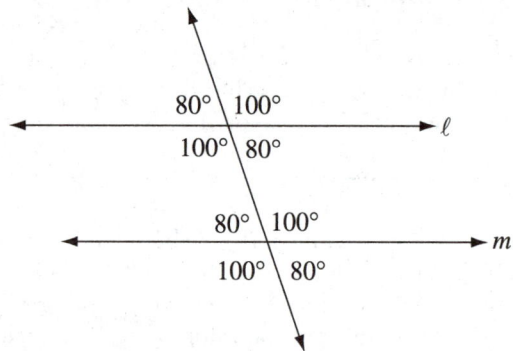

This example shows that $a + d + f + g = 360°$, and the only other sum among the choices that equals $360°$ is (B).
(Chapter 10, Lesson 1: Lines and Angles)

---

10. **A**   Either plug in the ordered pairs to check, or draw a graph, as long as you can do it quickly. Notice that the point $(7, -1)$ satisfies both inequalities: $2(7) + 3(-1) > 6$ and $7 - (-1) > 6$.
(Chapter 8, Lesson 6: Inequalities, Absolute Value, and Plugging In)

---

11. **A**   If n has a remainder of 6 when it is divided by 12, it must be 6 more than a multiple of 12. Pick any one you like: 18, for example. When 18 is divided by 6, the remainder is 0.
(Chapter 7, Lesson 7: Divisibility)

---

12. **B**   Any five-sided polygon can be divided into three triangles like so:

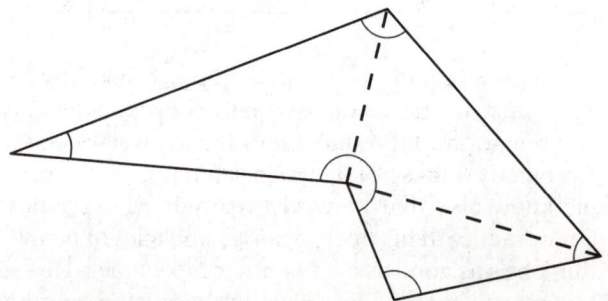

Since the sum of the angles in a triangle is 180°, the sum of the angles in this figure is $3(180) = 540°$. The average measure of the five angles, then, is $540/5 = 108°$.
(Chapter 10, Lesson 2: Triangles)

13. **D**   Remember that the word "is" can be interpreted as the equals sign (=). Therefore, "The number of dogs is 3 fewer than 4 times the number of cats" can be translated into $d = 4c - 3$.
(Chapter 8, Lesson 7: Word Problems)

14. **B**   Mark up the diagram with the information given:

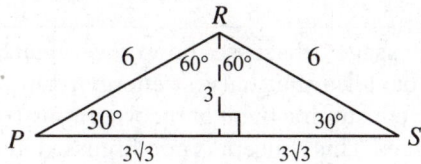

To find the area of the triangle, you need to use the formula *area = base × height*/2. Since the height divides the triangle into two 30° – 60° – 90° triangles, the other sides have lengths shown. The base of the triangle is $6(\sqrt{3})$ and the height is 3, so the area is $\frac{6(\sqrt{3})(3)}{2} = 9\sqrt{3}$.
(Chapter 10, Lesson 3: The Pythagorean Theorem)

15. **D**   The sum of the parts is $4 + 3 + 2 + 1 = 10$.
Therefore, the parts are $\frac{4}{10}, \frac{3}{10}, \frac{2}{10}$, and $\frac{1}{10}$ of the whole. The largest share, then, is $(\$50,000)(4/10) = \$20,000$.
(Chapter 7, Lesson 4: Ratios and Proportions)

16. **C**   Use the definition to translate the equation:
$$m\{n\} = 9$$
Translate: $m^2/n^2 = 9$
Now think about what values of m and n will work. Notice that 3 and 1 will work, but so will –3 and –1. Now plug these into the statements, and see if any are false. Since –3 is not greater than –1, statement I can be eliminated, and so can answers (B), (D), and (E). Notice that this means you don't have to check statement II, because it's in both remaining answers. Statement III must be true because if $\frac{m^2}{n^2} = 9$, then $\frac{m}{n}$ must equal 3 or –3.
Therefore, $\frac{m}{3n}$ equals 1 or –1, so it is an integer.
(Chapter 6, Lesson 7: Thinking Logically and Checking)
(Chapter 9, Lesson 1: New Symbol or Term Problems)

17. **C**   Let's say there are x blue marbles in the jar. This means there are $3x$ white marbles, and $2(3x) = 6x$ red marbles, for a total of $10x$ marbles. Since $3x$ are white, the probability of picking a white is $3x/10x = 3/10$.
(Chapter 9, Lesson 6: Probability Problems)

18. **D**   Think about how many options you have to fill each place, from left to right. Since the first person must be a girl, you have 6 options. Since the next must be a boy, you have 5 options. Since the next must be a boy, you have 4 options (one is already up there). Since the next must be a girl, you have 5 options left. This means that the total number of possible arrangements is $(6)(5)(4)(5) = 600$.
(Chapter 9, Lesson 5: Counting Problems)

19. **D**   If the two lines are parallel, then they have the same slope. The slope of l is $\frac{9}{12} = \frac{3}{4}$, so the slope of m must be $\frac{3}{4}$ as well. Therefore $\frac{12}{k} = \frac{3}{4}$
   Cross-multiply: $3k = 48$
   Divide by 3: $k = 16$
Therefore, the rectangle has a width of 16 and a height of 12, so its area is $(16)(12) = 192$.
(Chapter 10, Lesson 4: Coordinate Geometry)

20. **E**   If v is the volume of the solid, then $abc = v$. Solving this equation for a gives $a = \frac{v}{bc}$, so statement II must be true. Now go to the answer choices, and notice that you can eliminate any choice without II, namely (A) and (C). Also notice from the original equation that v could not be odd if any of the integers a, b, or c were even, therefore they must all be odd. This implies that $a + b + c$ is odd, so statement I must be true. This eliminates choice (D). To check statement III, you need an expression for the surface area of the solid, which is $2(ab) + 2(bc) + 2(ac) = 2(ab + bc + ac)$. Since this is a multiple of 2, it is even, so statement III is also true.
(Chapter 9, Lesson 3: Numerical Reasoning Problems)
(Chapter 10, Lesson 7: Volumes and 3-D Geometry)

Section 3

1. **A**   The fact that they *rarely agreed* implies that their opinions would often *differ*.
diverge = differ or move apart; *coincide* = fit together or occur simultaneously; *retreat* = move away; *assemble* = put together; *truncate* = cut short

2. **D**   The sentence implies a contrast between what *once was* and what *is now*. If it is no longer an *incontrovertible* (irrefutable) *truth*, it must now be *in doubt*.
enacted = put into effect officially; *irrefutable* = impossible to disprove; *universal* = true at all places and times; *dubious* = doubtful; *conclusive* = acting as final proof

3. **C** One who has encountered such tragedy would be expected to look to his painting as a *departure* from such *abject* (wretched) *sorrow*.
prudence = conservative wisdom; *remorse* = regret; *adulation* = admiration; *solace* = peaceful respite; *melancholy* = sadness; *elation* = extreme happiness

4. **B** *Proponents of a new curriculum* are people who support the change, while *conservative educators* are those who want to keep things the same.
repugnant = disgusting; *innocuous* = harmless; *deplorable* = regrettable; *reprehensible* = worthy of scorn; *benevolent* = kind; *malicious* = evil; *auspicious* = favorable

5. **D** What effect should a *lack of oxygen* have on climbers? It should be expected to *weaken* them. But this implies that the expedition leader's plan to acclimate them (get them used to the environment) was a *failure*.
illusory = like an illusion; *initiated* = started; *mitigated* = soothed or made better; *enervated* = weakened; *venerable* = worthy of honor; *absolved* = forgiven

6. **E** One who *questions norms* (conventions) *and mores* (moral standards) is a *rebel* of sorts.
charlatan = a fake; *surrogate* = one who stands in place of another; *philanthropist* = one who gives to charity; *pragmatist* = one concerned with practical matters; *iconoclast* = one who destroys sacred objects or traditions

7. **A** If he *stands in the negative camp*, then he must have a firm opinion about the issue.
ambivalent = having conflicting opinions on an issue; *unequivocally* = without doubt; *apathetic* = lacking concern; *furtively* = secretly; *impartial* = fair and unbiased; *adamant* = stubborn; *vehemently* = passionately; *subjective* = being a matter of opinion

8. **C** If he was *dismissed* by his contemporaries, they must have thought negatively of him. The *although* implies a contrast, so modern thinkers must now think positively of him.
pedant = a know-it-all; *derivative* = deriving from the work of others; *neophyte* = beginner; *vociferous* = loudly opinionated; *radical* = one with an extreme opinion; *visionary* = able to envision the future; *partisan* = marked by party loyalty; *conciliatory* = bringing people together; *hermit* = one who prefers to live alone

9. **C** Passage 1 focuses on *the study of molecules of which living organisms are composed.* Passage 2 discusses the ways in which organisms harvest energy through chemical processes like photosynthesis and chemosynthesis, which are biochemical processes.

10. **C** The main point of the paragraph is in the first sentence: the *study of life on Earth ultimately involves the study of molecules.* The questions that follow are therefore questions about molecules that concern those who study life on Earth, that is, biologists.

11. **A** Passage 2 focuses on organisms that harvest energy in a way that is analogous to, but different from, photosynthesis. The process of converting energy into food for the organism, then, is a relevant topic for Passage 2.

12. **D** Passage 2 discusses how *other organisms* utilize the bacteria that harvest energy from sulfides, either by consuming them or incorporating them into their tissues. This concept is not discussed in Passage 1. Both passages discuss the *conversion of light energy to food energy, and bonds within molecules*. Only Passage 1 discusses the *structure of cells and disease,* specifically cancer.

13. **C** The author indicates that one should react with *proper skepticism* to those reports, thereby implying that they are *probably untrue*.

14. **B** The author asks (in line 21) the reader to *compare* the probability of being a victim of terrorism to the list of probabilities that follow, which are much greater, thereby implying that terrorism is not much of a threat.

15. **E** The personal recollection begins on line 60: *I once had a conversation.* . . . The verifiable statistics abound in paragraphs 1, 2, and 3. The authoritative study is mentioned in lines 54–60. Common misconceptions are mentioned multiple times, as in lines 12–13: *being killed by terrorists might seem to be a major risk.*

16. **B** The author says that this *penetrating insight* is really a *non sequitur,* that is, something that doesn't follow logically. Therefore it is not a penetrating insight at all.

17. **A** The author says that a *feeling for what quantities or time spans are appropriate in various contexts is essential to getting the joke* (lines 47–49), thereby implying that the couple, like those who slip *between millions and billions,* lack an appreciation for particular quantities.

18. **C** In the span of *approximately 20 minutes* the doctor said three different things about the procedure, so he contradicted himself frequently.

19. **B** The passage refines the usage of the word by saying *the same organization, the same physical laws,* thereby suggesting that the author meant *rules of physics* when he said *organization.*

20. C In lines 16–19, the author describes the *realization that the phenomena we see result from the complexity of the inner workings between atoms* as being *dramatic and wonderful.*

21. B In lines 20–22, the author says that his feeling of awe *could be communicated through a drawing to someone who had also had this emotion,* thereby suggesting that appreciating such art depends on having a similar experience as the artist.

22. D The author says that Jerry is a *very good teacher* in that *everything that I thought was a mistake, he used to teach me something in a positive way. He never said it was wrong; he never put me down.* We can infer, then, that Jerry would have done something positive and affirming.

23. A The parenthetical comment that precedes this sentence indicates that the fact that the line did not touch the flower pot was unintentional.

24. E The main point of the passage is that the author wanted to learn to draw to convey the awe he felt about the workings of nature and the physical world. So when he finishes by saying *I was never satisfied,* we know that he was *never able to convey adequately his feelings about the beauty of the world.*

Section 4

1. B The pronoun *which* is out of place because it is assumed to refer to the preceding noun *poets.* If the pronoun is eliminated, the meaning is clearer and the two clauses are **parallel.**
(Chapter 15, Lesson 5 and Lesson 15)

2. E This is an awkward usage of the gerund *preparing.* To convey purpose, the infinitive *to prepare* is much more effective.
(Chapter 15, Lesson 3)

3. D This contains a **dangling modifier.** The modifying phrase that begins the sentence describes *Carla* rather than *Carla's anxiety.*
(Chapter 15, Lesson 7 and Lesson 8)

4. C This is a sentence fragment without a verb. Choice (C) completes the thought and makes a complete sentence.

5. C The participle *swimming* **dangles** in this sentence. *Justine* should follow the **participial phrase** because she is the one swimming, not *the current.*
(Chapter 15, Lesson 7)

6. D The comparison is not **parallel.** The sentence should say that *writing* one thing is *more difficult than **writing*** something else.
(Chapter 15, Lesson 3)

7. A This sentence is correct.

8. D This is a **run-on sentence,** or a **comma splice.** Two sentences cannot be "spliced" together with only a comma; you must use a conjunction, a semicolon, or a colon. Since the second clause explains the idea in the first clause, a colon is most appropriate.
(Chapter 15, Lesson 15)

9. B The two clauses are not properly coordinated. Since the second clearly contradicts the first, a contrasting conjunction like *but* or a contrasting coordinating adverb like *nevertheless* should be used.
(Chapter 15, Lesson 15)

10. E The verb *reveals* does not agree with the subject *theories* and should be *reveal* instead.
(Chapter 15, Lesson 1 and Lesson 2)

11. D The pronoun *their* does not agree in number with its antecedent *board* and should be changed to *its.*
(Chapter 15, Lesson 5)

12. B The phrase *his staff and him* serves as the subject of the verb *had diverted,* and so it must be in the subjective case: *his staff and he.*
(Chapter 15, Lesson 6)

13. C This is incorrect **past participle** form; the **present perfect** form of *to run* is *have run.*
(Chapter 15, Lesson 9 and Lesson 13)

14. B The subject of the verb *were* is *taunting.* (This is an **inverted sentence** because the subject comes after the verb.) Since *taunting* is singular, the verb should be *was.*
(Chapter 15, Lesson 1)

15. E The sentence is correct.

16. C The verb *produce* does not agree with its subject *refraction.* It should be changed to *produces.*
(Chapter 15, Lesson 1)

17. D The phrase *receptive for* is not idiomatic. The standard idiom is *receptive to.*
(Chapter 15, Lesson 10)

18. **C**   This word answers the question *how did she react?* Therefore it modifies a verb and should be in the form of an **adverb:** *emotionally.*
(Chapter 15, Lesson 12)

19. **B**   This phrase is part of a **parallel construction:** *"not A but B."* The construction is parallel only if this phrase is eliminated.
(Chapter 15, Lesson 3)

20. **B**   This phrase is **redundant.** The word *while* means *at the same time,* so the second phrase should be eliminated.
(Chapter 15, Lesson 12)

21. **B**   The verb *have expressed* does not agree with its subject *coalition,* and should be changed to *has expressed.*
(Chapter 15, Lesson 1 and Lesson 2)

22. **D**   This is an **illogical comparison.** A *way* cannot be compared to a *hard drive.* The phrase should be *the way a computer hard drive stores information.*
(Chapter 15, Lesson 4)

23. **D**   The pronoun *their* does not agree with its **antecedent** *museum,* and should be changed to *its.*
(Chapter 15, Lesson 5)

24. **B**   This is an **idiom error.** The correct form of this comparison is *"prefer A to B"* not *"prefer A more than B."*
(Chapter 15, Lesson 3 and Lesson 10)

25. **D**   Since only two films are being compared, the comparative adjective *more* is required.
(Chapter 15, Lesson 4: Comparison Problems)

26. **B**   The phrase *Emma and I* is the object of the verb *included* and therefore should take the objective case *Emma and me.*
(Chapter 15, Lesson 6: Pronoun Case)

27. **B**   The past perfect tense requires the past participle *swum.*
(Chapter 15, Lesson 9: Tricky Tenses)

28. **E**   The sentence is correct as written.

29. **A**   The participle *building* dangles in the original sentence. It should be changed to the infinitive *to build* so that it properly modifies the verb *try.*
(Chapter 15, Lesson 7: Dangling and Misplaced Participles)

30. **B**   The modifying phrases are awkwardly placed. Modifiers should obey the **law of proximity** and be as close as possible to the words they modify.
(Chapter 15, Lesson 8)

31. **A**   The modifying phrase at the beginning is **dangling.** Since *she* is *a doctor, she* should follow the opening phrase. (D) and (E) do not work because they improperly imply that she was bothered by the *children* rather than their *treatment.* You might notice that the correct choice contains verbs in the passive voice. Although you should minimize the use of the passive voice, it is not always incorrect.
(Chapter 12, Lesson 10: Write Forcefully)
(Chapter 15, Lesson 7 and Lesson 8)

32. **E**   This paragraph discusses Montessori's methods and results in the *Casa dei Bambini,* and so the trivial and unrelated fact that *there were fifty students in her first class* is out of place.

33. **A**   The pronoun *it* refers to Montessori's day care center, and so this sentence should follow the one that mentions the day care center, but precede the sentence that discusses her *theories* in detail.

34. **D**   Revision (D) is the most concise and effective of the choices.

35. **C**   Sentences 8 and 9 discuss Montessori's philosophy and its effectiveness. Sentence 8 indicates that Montessori *decided it was important to help each child through his or her own curriculum,* which is clearly a *focus on the individual child.*

Section 5

1. **B** $5y - 2 = 3y + 7$
   Subtract 3y: $2y - 2 = 7$
   Add 2: $2y = 9$
   Divide by 2: $y = 4.5$
(Chapter 8, Lesson 1: Solving Equations)

2. **D**   Since vertical angles are equal, $a = 20$. Since angles that form a straight line have a sum of 180°, $20 + b + 34 = 180$. Therefore $b = 126$. So $a + b = 20 + 126 = 146$.
(Chapter 10, Lesson 1: Lines and Angles)

3. **C** $(2x)(3x) = (2/8)(3/2)$
   Simplify: $6x^2 = 6/16$
   Divide by 6: $x^2 = 1/16$
   Take the square root: $x = 1/4$
(Chapter 7, Lesson 3: Fractions)

4. C Since the prime factorization of 98 is $2 \times 7 \times 7$, and since the greatest common factor of m and 98 is a prime number, that greatest common factor must be 2 or 7. Since it is not even, it must be 7.
(Chapter 7, Lesson 7: Divisibility)
(Chapter 8, Lesson 5: Factoring)
(Chapter 9, Lesson 1: New Symbol or Term Problems)

5. D $|k - 0.5| < 10$
Translate: $-10 < k - 0.5 < 10$
Add 0.5: $-9.5 < k < 10.5$
The smallest possible integer value for k is -9 and the greatest is 10. The total number of integers between -9 and 10, inclusive, is $10 - (-9) + 1 = 20$.
(Chapter 6, Lesson 2: Analyzing Problems)
(Chapter 8, Lesson 6: Inequalities, Absolute Value, and Plugging In)

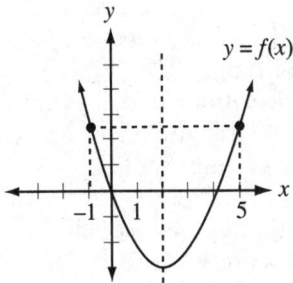

6. A Since f is a quadratic function, its graph is a parabola with a vertical axis of symmetry through its vertex, which in this case is the line $x = 2$. This means that, for any given point on the graph, its reflection over $x = 2$ is also on the graph. Notice from the given graph that the value of $f(5)$ is about 2.5, as shown above. If we reflect this point, $(5, 2.5)$ over the axis of symmetry, we get the point $(-1, 2.5)$. In other words, $f(5) = f(-1)$, so $k = -1$.

7. C It helps to know the perfect squares and the perfect cubes. The first seven perfect squares greater than 1 are 4, 9, 16, 25, 36, 49, and 64. The first three perfect cubes are 8, 27, and 64. Clearly, the only integer between 1 and 100 that is both a perfect cube and a perfect square is $64 = 4^3 = 8^2$. Therefore $m = 4$ and $n = 8$, so $m + n = 4 + 8 = 12$.
(Chapter 8, Lesson 4: Working with Roots)

8. B This is a rate problem, so remember the basic rate formula: *distance = rate × time*. Start by picking a value for the distance from Amanda's home to work. No matter what distance you choose, the final answer will be the same, so choose a distance that's easy to calculate with, like 50 miles. If it takes her 60 minutes (1 hour) to get to work, she must be going 50 miles/hour. If she increases her speed by 20% for the trip home, then her speed coming home is (1.20)(50 miles/hour) = 60 miles/hour. To travel 50 miles at 60 miles/hour will take her (50 miles)/(60 mph) = 5/6 hour, which is 5/6(60 minutes) = 50 minutes.
(Chapter 9, Lesson 4: Rate Problems)

9. 0.4 Remember that "percent" means "divided by 100," so 0.5 percent of 80 means $0.5 \div 100 \times 80 = 0.4$
(Chapter 7, Lesson 5: Percents)

10. .333 or 1/3 Just pick three consecutive odd integers, like 1, 3, and 5. Since d is the middle of these, $d = 3$. Since s is the sum of these, $s = 1 + 3 + 5 = 9$. So d divided by s is 3/9 or 1/3.
(Chapter 9, Lesson 3: Numerical Reasoning Problems)

11. 30   4/9 of c^2 is 24
Translate: $(4/9)(c^2) = 24$
Multiply by 5/4: $(5/4)(4/9)(c^2) = (5/4)(24)$
Simplify: $(5/9)(c^2) = 30$
(Chapter 6, Lesson 4: Simplifying Problems)
(Chapter 8, Lesson 1: Solving Equations)

12. 60 The sum of the four angles in a quadrilateral is 360°. The sum of the parts in the ratio is $3 + 4 + 5 + 6 = 18$. Therefore the angles are 3/18, 4/18, 5/18, and 6/18 of the whole, which is 360°. So the smallest angle measures $(3/18)(360°) = 60°$.
(Chapter 10, Lesson 2: Triangles)
(Chapter 7, Lesson 4: Ratios and Proportions)

13. 28   Subtract the equations: $5a + 6b = 13$
$\underline{- (4a + 5b = 9)}$
$a + b = 4$
Multiply by 7: $7a + 7b = 28$
(Chapter 6, Lesson 4: Simplifying Problems)
(Chapter 8, Lesson 2: Systems)

14. 6 Simply substituting $m = 3$ in the equation gives $\dfrac{\frac{1}{4} + \frac{1}{2}}{\frac{1}{8}}$. The quickest way to simplify this expression is to multiply both the numerator and the denominator by the common denominator, 8. This gives $\dfrac{2 + 4}{1} = 6$.

If you happen to be an algebra jock, you might notice that you can simplify the original expression by multiplying numerator and denominator by the common denominator $m^2 - 1$, which is equivalent to $(m - 1)(m + 1)$. This simplifies the complex expression to just $2m$, which equals 6 when $m = 3$.

15. 81 By guessing and checking positive integers, you should be able to see that the only positive integers that satisfy the equation are 5 and 4. Therefore $(x + y)^2 = (5 + 4)^2 = 81$.
(Chapter 9, Lesson 3: Numerical Reasoning Problems)

16. 10 Five out of the 15 marbles are white. If x more white marbles are added, the probability of choosing a white marble is $\frac{(5+x)}{(15+x)}$. This fraction must be at least $\frac{3}{5}$, so

$$\frac{(5+x)}{(15+x)} \geq 3/5$$

Cross-multiply: $25 + 5x \geq 45 + 3x$
Subtract $3x$: $25 + 2x \geq 45$
Subtract 25: $2x \geq 20$
Divide by 2: $x \geq 10.$

(Chapter 9, Lesson 6: Probability Problems)

NUMBER OF BOOKS READ
DURING SUMMER VACATION

Number of Books Read	Number of Students
1	4
2	6
3	5
4	3
More than 4	2

17. 2.5 Notice that the question asks for the *median* of these numbers, not for their *average* or *mode*. The median is the "middle" number when the numbers are listed in order, or the average of the *two* middle numbers if there are an even number of numbers. According to the table, there are 20 numbers representing the number of books each child has read:

1, 1, 1, 1, 2, 2, 2, 2, 2, 2, 3, 3, 3, 3, 3, 4, 4, 4, 5+, 5+

We don't know the final two numbers in the list, only that they are integers greater than 4. That's okay: to find the median, we don't need these last two numbers; we only need to find the average of the two middle numbers (the 10th and 11th), which are 2 and 3. Therefore the median is 2.5.

18. 4 If she took a shots in her first game and made 50% of them, then she made $.5a$ shots in the first game. Similarly, she made $.6b$ shots in the second game. If she made 52% of her shots altogether, then

$$\frac{.5a + .6b}{a + b} = .52$$

Cross-multiply: $.5a + .6b = .52a + .52b$
Subtract $.5a$ and $.52b$: $.08b = .02a$
Divide by $0.02b$: $4 = \frac{a}{b}$

(Chapter 7, Lesson 4: Ratios and Proportions)
(Chapter 7, Lesson 5: Percents)

Section 6

1. B Sandra's father's words were not *thoughtful* or *useful*, but rather they were *hollow clichés*. They were *overused* and *thoughtless*.
irate = angry; *inane* = pointless; *homogeneous* = the same throughout; *flamboyant* = lively; *altruistic* = selfless

2. C If he was *courageous* in prison, he must not have given up his fight.
treacherous = deceitful; *futile* = having no hope of success; *fortitude* = strength; *premeditated* = planned in advance; *porous* = full of holes

3. A Since the teachers couldn't hear themselves talk, the construction must have been noisy, and therefore was not very *constructive* to learning (no pun intended).
din = noise; *conducive* = helpful, constructive; *averse* = opposed to; *discernible* = detectable; *irascible* = easily angered

4. C The sentence implies that solutions to physics problems are *approximate*, so they cannot be *exact*. The approximate solution would be sufficient as long as the complicating factors are *small*.
negligible = not significant; *plausibly* = with a good likelihood of success; *ethically* = with regard to moral standards

5. D *Martial resources* are those resources that sustain an army's ability to fight; they are the *means* to continue fighting. If the factions both have *access* to these resources, the fight is likely to drag on.
mediation = attempt to resolve a conflict

6. C Since Jung was *modest in his therapeutic claims* (lines 4–5) and *cautious* (line 11) when consulted by schizophrenics, we can conclude that he did not yet believe that his therapy worked for all mentally ill patients.

7. A The sentence indicates that psychoanalysis could *bring about* a psychotic episode.

8. C The passage says that the *comic . . . seems bound to its time, society, cultural anthropology* (lines 7–8). This implies that it's harder to find something humorous if it is from another culture or time. Choice (C) is the most foreign to modern Americans.

9. C Because the passage says that it is harder to understand the comedy of other societies and eras because of cultural obstacles, the *effort* is in overcoming these obstacles.

10. B The author states that the host's introduction *dropped like a stone in our midst* (lines 9–10), and that no response at all to this introduction was *the proper response* (line 12). The rest of the essay makes clear that the author considers the host's comments, particularly with its focus on *literature,* to be inappropriate.

11. C The author defines the term somewhat in lines 55–57 by listing the forms to which the term *literary* is applied: *novels and short stories and poems.* Throughout the passage, the author distinguishes *literary* works from works of nonfiction, which can be very well written.

12. B The interviewer asked the writers about the *"literary experience"* (line 20) of the day, and then whether they *"write anything literary"* (lines 36–37), when in fact they did not write literature at all, but rather nonfiction.

13. C Those writers are mentioned as *our models* by the author, suggesting that the author and the other writers have been influenced by them.

14. B In saying that writers were admired for *their ability to harness the issues,* the author is saying that they make them easy to understand for their readers.

15. E The writers being interviewed had said that *they felt they were already doing satisfactory work* (lines 37–38). The callers implied that they felt the same way.

16. C The phrase *the great preponderance of what writers now write and sell* refers to the *majority* of what they write and sell.

17. B The first sentence indicates the purpose of this passage: *To understand . . . Aristotle . . . it is necessary to apprehend his imaginative background* (lines 1–3), in other words, to understand the preconceptions behind his theories.

18. E This paragraph discusses the ancient Greek idea that mechanical devices are somehow imbued with the spirit of animals with similar abilities, for instance, an airplane having the spirit of a bird. The comment that *animals have lost their importance in our imaginative pictures of the world* indicates that modern thinkers no longer suppose any link between the life-spirit of animals and the behavior of machines.

19. C The *imaginative preconceptions* of Aristotle are explained in the second and third paragraphs, where it says that *to the Greek, it seemed more natural to assimilate apparently lifeless motions to those of animals* (lines 47–49).

20. A The passage says that *the . . . mechanical view hardly suggested itself, except in the case of a few men of genius* (lines 36–38). So these men of genius had the *mechanical view.*

21. E The passage says that *to the modern man of science, the body of an animal is a very elaborate machine* (lines 42–43). The difference between animals and machines is diminished with discoveries about the *physico-chemical structure* (lines 44–45) of animals, or the mechanical and chemical nature of biology.

22. A In saying that, to the ancient Greek, *it seemed more natural to assimilate apparently lifeless motions to those of animals* (lines 47–49), the author is saying that Greeks were inclined to compare the motions of lifeless things to the motions of living things, and that these comparisons were *the basis of a general theory of physics* (lines 53–54).

23. C The passage says that *Every Greek philosopher . . . had been taught in childhood to regard the sun and moon as gods* (lines 58–61), and then that *Anaxagoras was prosecuted for impiety because he thought that they were not alive* (lines 61–63). This implies that he departed dramatically from his childhood teachings.

24. B The *Hellenic love of order and geometric simplicity* (line 67) is attributed to the Divine Being who moves the heavenly bodies. These heavenly bodies were said to move with *regularity* (line 56) and *superior perfection* (lines 57–58). Therefore, it can be inferred that this *love of order and geometric simplicity* pertains to the movement of the heavenly bodies.

Section 7

1. C $\frac{2}{3}$ of 60 is 40, and $\frac{40}{80} = 50\%$.

(Chapter 7, Lesson 3: Fractions)

2. D
$$4x + 2y = 8$$

Divide by 4: $x + \frac{1}{2}y = 2$

(Chapter 6, Lesson 4: Simplifying Problems)

3. C   This question is asking what the remainder is when 29, 21, and 64 are each divided by 3. When 29 is divided by 3 the remainder is 2; when 21 is divided by 3 the remainder is 0; and when 64 is divided by 3 the remainder is 1.
(Chapter 7, Lesson 7: Divisibility)

4. B   1 & 2
   Substitute using definition: $1(1-1) + 2(2-1)$
   Simplify: $0 + 2 = 2$
(Chapter 9, Lesson 1: New Symbol or Term Problems)

5. A   In a triangle, any side must have a length that is less than the sum of the two other lengths but greater than the difference of the two other lengths. Therefore, the third side must have a length between $15 - 9 = 6$ and $15 + 9 = 24$, so a length of 5 is impossible.
(Chapter 10, Lesson 2: Triangles)

6. B   The volume of a cube is equal to s^3, where s is the length of one edge. If $s^3 = 64$, then $s = 4$, and so each square face has an area of $s^2 = 4^2 = 16$. Since a cube has six faces, the total surface area is $6(16) = 96$.
(Chapter 10, Lesson 7: Volumes and 3-D Geometry)

7. D $\dfrac{(x+2+6+10)}{4} = 8$, so $x + 2 + 6 + 10 = 32$

                              Simplify: $x + 18 = 32$
                              Subtract 18: $x = 14$
So the numbers are 2, 6, 10, and 14. The median is the average of the two middle numbers: $\dfrac{(6+10)}{2} = 8$.
(Chapter 9, Lesson 2: Mean/Median/Mode Problems)

8. A   Indicate the congruent sides with tick marks: in a triangle, the angles across from equal sides are equal; indicate this in the diagram. Your angles should be marked as shown. Since the angles in a triangle have a sum of 180°, $y + y + 180 - x = 180$
              Subtract 180: $2y - x = 0$
              Add x: $2y = x$
              Divide by 2: $y = \dfrac{x}{2}$

(Chapter 10, Lesson 2: Triangles)

9. D   Notice that the graph is of all the points that are more than one unit away from –1. The distance from a point to –1 is $|x - (-1)|$, or $|x + 1|$; if this distance is greater than one, then $|x + 1| > 1$.
(Chapter 8, Lesson 6: Inequalities, Absolute Value, and Plugging In)

10. B   "Must be true" kinds of questions are often best answered by process of elimination with examples.

Begin with a simple set of values, for instance $a = 0$, $b = -1$, and $c = 0$. Notice that these values satisfy all of the given information. This example clearly shows that statement I need not be true, because 0 is not greater than 0, and that statement III need not be true, because $(0)(0)$ is not greater than $(-1)^2$. This leaves only statement II as a possibility, so the answer must be (B).
(Chapter 6, Lesson 7: Thinking Logically and Checking)
(Chapter 9, Lesson 3: Numerical Reasoning Problems)

11. E   You have five choices for the first digit: 1, 3, 5, 7, and 9; ten choices for the middle digit (any digit will do), and five choices for the last digit: 0, 2, 4, 6, and 8. So the total number of possibilities is $5 \times 10 \times 5 = 250$.
(Chapter 9, Lesson 5: Counting Problems)

12. B   To find how many more seconds it will take the machine to cut circle A than circle B, you can find the length of time it takes to cut each circle and subtract them. The laser cuts the circumference of each circle, so you must find that first. Circle A has an area of 64π. Since the area of a circle is πr^2, the radius of the circle is 8. Since the area of circle B is 16π, its radius is 4. The circumference of a circle is $2\pi r$, so the circumference of A is $2\pi(8) = 16\pi$ and the circumference of B is $2\pi(4) = 8\pi$. The difference of their radii is $16\pi - 8\pi = 8\pi$. The time it takes to cut that length is given by the formula *time = distance/rate*.

$$\frac{(8\pi \text{ cm})}{(3 \text{ cm/second})} = \frac{8\pi}{3} \text{ sec}$$

(Chapter 10, Lesson 8: Circles)
(Chapter 9, Lesson 4: Rate Problems)

13. E   The slope of AC is *rise/run* = $\dfrac{(5-(-1))}{(8-1)} = 6/7$.

Therefore the slope of CB is $-6/7$. Using the slope formula: $\dfrac{(5-(-1))}{(8-k)} = -6/7$

              Simplify: $\dfrac{6}{(8-k)} = -6/7$
      Cross-multiply: $-6(8-k) = 42$
          Divide by 6: $-8 + k = 7$
                Add 8: $k = 15$
(Chapter 10, Lesson 4: Coordinate Geometry)

14. C $m = 1 \times 2 \times 3 \times 4 \times 5 \times 6 \times 7 \times 8 \times 9 \times 10$. You can factor even further in terms of primes: $m = 1 \times 2 \times 3 \times (2 \times 2) \times 5 \times (2 \times 3) \times 7 \times (2 \times 2 \times 2) \times (3 \times 3) \times (2 \times 5)$. This shows that there are a maximum of eight factors of 2, so the greatest power of 2 that is a factor of m is 2^8.

15. **D**   First draw a diagram to see how the area of an equilateral triangle is related to the lengths of the sides:

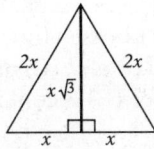

Notice that the height (which is also the bisector of the "top" angle) divides the triangle into two 30°-60°-90° triangles, with sides as shown. The area of a triangle is *base × height*/2, which in this case is $\dfrac{(2x)\left(x\sqrt{3}\right)}{2} = x^2\sqrt{3}$. Since the area is given as $36\sqrt{3}$, x must equal 6. Substituting this into the diagram, each smaller triangle has sides of length 6, $6\sqrt{3}$, and 12. Therefore the sum of the perimeters of the two triangles is $36 + 12\sqrt{3}$.
(Chapter 10, Lesson 2: Triangles)
(Chapter 10, Lesson 3: The Pythagorean Theorem)
(Chapter 10, Lesson 5: Areas and Perimeters)

16. **B**   At 4:00 pm, there are 1,000 bacteria. Since the population doubles every two hours, there must have been half as many two hours ago. So at 2:00 pm there were 500 bacteria, and at 12:00 noon there were 250 bacteria. (Notice that the fact that there were 100 bacteria to start is irrelevant.)
(Chapter 9, Lesson 4: Rate Problems)

Section 8

1. **D**   If she was relieved, the tumor must not have been dangerous.
malignant = dangerous; *irreverent* = disrespectful; *serene* = calm; *benign* = harmless; *mortal* = capable of dying

2. **C**   If the jargon rendered the speech *decipherable only to* a few audience members, then it rendered the speech *undecipherable* to the rest of the audience. Therefore the message was *obscured*.

3. **D**   If one prefers *style* to *performance*, then the *cosmetic* appeal of the car would be most important.
utilitarian = concerned with practical uses; *pragmatic* = concerned with function; *aesthetic* = pertaining to beauty

4. **A**   If something *serves its purpose only temporarily*, then it is by definition *provisional*.
provisional = serving a temporary purpose; *polemical* = relating to a controversial intellectual position; *pedantic* = acting like a know-it-all

5. **E**   A *foil* is a character that provides a dramatic contrast to the personality of another character. The

but in the sentence indicates that Ms. Linney is *going against the tradition,* and does not portray her character *demurely* (modestly).
bluster = brashness; *forgo* = abandon an inclination or plan; *coyness* = shyness; *bombast* = pompous speech; *eschew* = abandon; *impudence* = impertinence, rudeness

6. **C**   *Despite* implies an ironic situation. If analysts have tried to depict the stock market as *driven by predictable principles,* it would be ironic if people believed that it was not predictable at all.
invaluable = very valuable; *complacent* = self-satisfied; *capricious* = arbitrary, whimsical; *responsive* = tending to respond quickly; *obscure* = not widely known

7. **C**   The *control* is mentioned in the context of *the creation of life* (line 10). This is the *process of conception.*

8. **B**   The author says that this *"outsourcing" . . . leaves us with a profoundly hollow feeling* (lines 14–18). This indicates a *disdain.*

9. **E**   This statement is from those who *turn [their] noses up at one who would offer us the most precious gift in the universe,* that is, the advocates of cloning are turning up their noses at nature or God.

10. **A**   The parenthetical comment suggests that the *essential random . . . processes that form the basis of natural selection* may be only *seemingly* random. This suggests that these processes may be planned rather than random.

11. **D**   The *"unnatural selection"* is described as involving *an assembly line* (lines 29–31), which is a type of *mechanical procedure,* and *carefully designed and tested features* (line 32), which implies a *selection of characteristics.* The *random processes* (lines 27–28) are attributed to *natural* selection.

12. **A**   The passage implies that those who know *a little bit about the history of technology* (lines 55–56) would not have such *irrational fears about human cloning* (line 53). Therefore you can eliminate choice (D). The fact that these *fears* are called *irrational* eliminates choices (B) and (E). Since these fears are said to *abound from all parts of the political spectrum* (line 54), you can eliminate choice (C). The passage never mentions that the opponents are *very religious,* so the answer is (A).

13. **C**   Surgery is mentioned in line 63 as something *significant* (line 57) that was once *denounced* (line 58).

14. **C**   After quoting Mr. Rifkin, the author then goes on to describe the illogic behind the quote.

15. B The passage mentions that human twins *"have their own unique thoughts"* in order to refute the claim that identical genes put *a human into a genetic strait-jacket* (lines 77–78).

16. A The passage says that *familiarity* [with procreational technologies] *dissipates fear* (line 128), implying that these technologies become more acceptable as they become more familiar.

17. A This paragraph says that *ignorant superstition* (line 136) stands in the way of *technologies that can produce ample food for a starving world and cure devastating illnesses* (lines 133–135). This indicates anger at an unjust situation.

18. C In each case, the questions represent the perspective that the author argues against.

19. B The first passage says that cloning technologies will make the world *forever different from what it is today* (lines 51–52), and the second says that these technologies *can produce ample food for a starving world and cure devastating illnesses* (lines 134–135).

Section 9

1. C The infinitive *to move* more effectively conveys purpose than does the phrase *by moving*. Also, the modifier *more closely* has the incorrect form. It should be in adjectival form *closer*, because it modifies the noun *source*.
(Chapter 15, Lesson 12: Other Modifier Problems)

2. E The original sentence illogically suggests that cell phones standardized their own technology. The only choice that logically coordinates the ideas is choice (E).
(Chapter 15, Lesson 15: Coordinating Ideas)

3. E The colon is misused in the original sentence, since it does not introduce a list of examples or an independent explanatory clause. Choice (B) has the same problem. Choices (C) and (D) use improper idioms. Only choice (E) conveys the idea clearly and idiomatically.
(Chapter 15, Lesson 15: Coordinating Ideas)

4. B The original phrasing is a sentence fragment; it contains no verb. Choices (B), (C), and (D) correct this mistake, but (C) and (D) do not clearly convey what protected the city. Only choice (B) conveys the idea logically.
(Chapter 12, Lesson 7: Write Logically)

5. A The original sentence is correct. The phrase preceding the comma is an appositive modifying *On*

Writing Well. Therefore, (B) and (C) cause this modifier to be misplaced. Choice (D) is a fragment and (E) misplaces the modifier *by William Zinsser*.

6. E The original phrase shifts the pronoun from *you* to *one*. Choices (B) and (C) are illogical, and (D) is unidiomatic. Choice (E) is concise and avoids these problems.

7. A The original sentence conveys the idea clearly and effectively. Choices (B) and (C) misuse the singular pronoun *it* to refer to the plural noun *pigeons*. Choice (D) is awkward, and (E) produces a fragment.

8. D Choice (D) is the only choice that makes the comparison idiomatic, logical, and parallel.
(Chapter 15, Lesson 3: Parallelism)

9. C In the original sentence, the participle *revealing* is misplaced, since it does not modify the closest noun *friends*. Choice (B) repeats this error, and choices (D) and (E) are unidiomatic. The only choice that fixes this problem and conveys the logical sequence of ideas is choice (C).
(Chapter 15, Lesson 7: Dangling and Misplaced Participles)

10. B The participle *inspired* is left dangling in the original sentence. Its subject, *Gerald*, must follow the comma. Since choice (E) produces a sentence fragment, the best choice is (B).
(Chapter 15, Lesson 7: Dangling and Misplaced Participles)

11. B The original phrasing does not clearly convey who *decided*. Also, the noun *club* is singular, so the plural pronoun *they* is inappropriate. Choice (B) concisely and clearly fixes these problems.
(Chapter 15, Lesson 5: Pronoun-Antecedent Disagreement)

12. A The original phrasing is clear, logical, and effective.

13. C Since this sentence is giving general advice about a general practice, the gerund *acknowledging* is more effective than the infinitive *to acknowledge*. Further, the gerund is parallel with the gerund *subverting* with which it is compared.
(Chapter 15, Lesson 3: Parallelism)

14. E The sentence is not parallel. The first two items in the list establish the pattern: *get . . . avoid. . . .* So the last item should be *reduce. . . .*
(Chapter 15, Lesson 3: Parallelism)

CHAPTER 3

BUILDING AN IMPRESSIVE VOCABULARY

1. The College Hill Method for SAT Word Power

2. The 2,000 Key SAT Words and 200 Key SAT Roots: Vocabulary Units 1–7

1   THE COLLEGE HILL METHOD FOR SAT WORD POWER

A strong vocabulary is essential to achieving a top SAT critical reading score. But building a solid vocabulary doesn't mean just memorizing thousands of flashcards. In fact, the way most students use flashcards is not only dull, but utterly ineffective. Believe it or not, you've been using a much better system for years. If you're a normal 16-year-old, you have about a 40,000-word vocabulary. Did you memorize all those words with flashcards? No. You didn't "study" them at all. You just absorbed them by trying to understand and communicate with the people around you.

When you take words out of the context of real communication, your brain's "vocabulary machine" doesn't work very well. So don't just study flashcards to memorize word meanings in isolation. Instead, follow these rules while using the College Hill flashcard system (which is discussed below) to study the words in the lessons in this chapter.

Surround Yourself with Good Language

When you were a baby, you were surrounded by people with much stronger vocabularies than yours, so your vocabulary grew very quickly. As you got older, however, your vocabulary grew to match that of the people you hung out with, so its growth slowed. How do you rev it up again? Talk to smart adults. Hang around friends with good vocabularies. Read college-level books. Watch documentaries on television rather than mindless game shows, soap operas, and reality shows. Listen to National Public Radio. Read The *New York Times* Op-Ed page and Sunday Magazine. Read articles and stories from *Harper's*, *Atlantic Monthly*, *New Yorker*, *The Nation*, and *Scientific American*.

Use Your New Vocabulary with Friends and Family

To build your vocabulary, you have to try out your new words. If you feel self-conscious about trying out new words (and most teens do), find a close friend or relative to practice vocabulary with—maybe a friend who's also prepping for the SAT. On the next couple of pages we'll give you lots of good strategies for building vocabulary with a friend.

Analyze Words as You Read and Speak

As you run across new words, think about their roots, their synonyms, and their antonyms. The 49 lessons in this chapter include 200 of the key roots, prefixes, and suffixes, as well as lists of synonyms and antonyms for each word. Reinforce your new words by breaking them into their roots, prefixes, and suffixes and connecting them to other words that share them. For instance,

if you want to learn the word *magnanimity*, you should notice that it has three parts: *magna* (great) + *anima* (spirit or life) + *-ity* (suffix indicating a quality). It means generosity, and you should see why from its roots.

Use the Patterns of Words in Sentences

When you run across a new word in a sentence, make a guess about its meaning based on how it's used. Consider this sentence: *Even her favorite toy could not placate the screaming child*. Even if you have never seen the word *placate* before, you should be able to tell from the sentence that it is a *verb*. Even more, you can tell that it's something a favorite toy might do to a screaming child (even though it wasn't successful in this case). Since screaming children need to be calmed down, and since toys often can do that, it's a good bet that *placate* means something like "calm down."

Simplify Your Task by Connecting Words in Groups

Memorizing is always easier when you can group the information into chunks. Most words are related to other words with the same basic meaning (*synonyms*), the opposite meaning (*antonyms*), or the same root (*cognates*). The lessons in this chapter help you to group words in many ways: into *theme groups* (such as "words about talking"), *synonym groups*, *antonym groups*, and *cognate groups*.

Connect New Words to Your Own Experience or Knowledge

To learn a new word, you must connect it to something you understand. Word meanings aren't isolated facts to memorize. Think about how to *use* your new words. For instance, when learning the word *enervate* (to weaken or decrease in strength or vitality), think about what *enervates* you (a 4-hour standardized test, perhaps?) or about examples of *enervation* in books you've read (such as the *enervation* of Moby Dick as Captain Ahab hunts him down). Visualize them and say them out loud: "The SAT can be an *enervating* experience," and "Moby Dick was *enervated* by the incessant chase and his many harpoon wounds."

Consider Alternative Strategies Such as the ALIVE Visual Mnemonic System

Some words are hard to memorize because they have obscure meanings or are hard to connect to other words. For such words, College Hill Coaching's ALIVE visual mnemonic system is a great tool. Here's how it works:

1. *Break down the sounds of the word, and turn those sounds into a picture.* Let's say that you're trying to learn the word *polemic*. First, break down its syllables. It sounds like *pole* and *lemon*, so imagine a lemon on the end of a pole. (You might break it down differently, for instance, as *pole* and *Mick*. That's fine, as long as you turn it into a picture!)

2. *Imagine a picture for the meaning of the word.* *Polemic* means "a strong verbal or written attack," so you might visualize someone arguing loudly with a politician at a debate. Try to picture someone you actually know, if possible, someone with strong opinions.

3. *Put the two pictures together into one.* See the debater hitting the politician with the lemon on the end of the pole. The crazier the picture, the better!

4. *Make your image come ALIVE.* As you visualize your picture, make it come ALIVE—*active, linking, illogical, vivid,* and *exaggerated.* Here's how:

   - Give the picture *action* by making it move like a wacky animated cartoon.
   - Make sure the picture *links* two things: the *sound* of the word and the *meaning* of the word.
   - Make the picture bizarre and *illogical* so that it's more memorable.
   - Make it so *vivid* that you see it in 3-D, in color, and in rich detail.
   - Work on *exaggerating* the picture so that the meaning of the word "pops out."

Keep a Vocabulary Notebook

Keep a small notebook handy when you're reading. When you run across a new or interesting word, jot it down so that you can look it up later and make a flashcard for it using the system described below. Have a good collegiate dictionary handy, too—one with a pronunciation guide and etymology for each word.

Study with the College Hill Coaching Flashcard System—10 Minutes a Day

Flashcards are enormously helpful for building vocabulary, but only if you use them the right way. Get in the habit of making and studying 30 to 40 flashcards *per week* of SAT words from this chapter, your practice tests, or your reading. But don't just make plain old flashcards. College Hill flashcards are far more effective. Each one looks like the figures at the top of this page.

When you've made a card for any word from the lessons in this chapter, check it off the list. Keep your cards handy in a plastic recipe box, and study them daily for at least 10 minutes. *Don't* just study these cards to memorize definitions by rote. *Instead,* shuffle through the following seven study methods on a regular basis.

> Although some appreciate flattery, I think that such OBSEQUIOUS behavior is revolting.

Front: Write a meaningful sentence using the word. Write the word in CAPITALS and underline any roots.

> Overly submissive
> (to + follow)
>
>   O

Back: Write the definition of the word, then, in parentheses, the definition of any roots or affixes. Beneath, write the first letter of the word.

- *Study Method 1.* Your friend reads you the word, and then you create a new sentence using that word. The sentence must show that you understand the meaning of the word. For instance, "The boy was obsequious" doesn't really show that you know what *obsequious* means.
- *Study Method 2.* Your friend reads you the word, and then you give its roots and, for each root, as many words as you can that share that root.
- *Study Method 3.* Your friend reads the definition from the back of the card and gives you the first letter of the word, and then you give the word.
- *Study Method 4.* Your friend reads the word, and then you describe three different situations in which the word would be appropriate.
- *Study Method 5.* Your friend reads the word, and then you teach your friend any clever ALIVE mnemonics you have created for the word.
- *Study Method 6.* Your friend reads the sentence, and then you give the definition of the word.
- *Study Method 7.* Post a bunch of flashcards around your room where you'll see them every day. Think of appropriate places to post them, such as *narcissist* on the mirror, *lethargic* on the bed, and so on.

Check Your Understanding with the Review Exercises

At the end of each vocabulary unit in this chapter is a set of exercises to check your understanding of the words you've studied. Do them faithfully at the end of each seven-lesson unit. They provide great reinforcement and help you to see which words you may need to go back and review.

Vocabulary Unit I

Vocabulary Lesson 1: Get to the Point!

Today's roots:	co-, con-	together, with	brev	brief
	cis	cut	cur	run, course

❑ *concise* (adj)   brief and to the point (*con-* altogether + *cis* cut)

Ricky, try to be a bit more **concise** in this paper; the assignment was for a three-page paper; yours was 106.
Synonyms: *succinct, terse*   Antonyms: *prolix, discursive, protracted, circumlocutory, verbose*

❑ *laconic* (adj)   disposed to using few words (from Latin term for Spartans, who spoke little)

I've known Lucy for ten years, but she's so **laconic** that I hardly know anything about her past.
Synonyms: *taciturn, reticent*   Antonyms: *garrulous, loquacious*

❑ *succinct* (adj)   spoken or written in a clear and precise manner

Because commercial time during the Super Bowl runs over $3 million per minute, it's good to be **succinct.**
Synonyms: *terse, concise*   Antonyms: *prolix, discursive, protracted, circumlocutory, verbose*

❑ *brusque* (adj)   rudely abrupt

My girlfriend tends to be **brusque** when she's mad; she just tells me to "talk to the hand."
Synonyms: *curt, abrupt, petulant*

❑ *abridge* (v)   to shorten a written text

The dictionary was 1,400 pages long before it was **abridged** by the publishers to 850 pages.
Synonym: *abbreviate*   Antonyms: *augment, amplify, protract*

❑ *brevity* (n)   quality of succinct expression (*brev-* brief + *-ity* quality of)

Speeches at the Academy Awards are not known for their **brevity;** they often go on long past their allotted time.
Synonyms: *conciseness, pithiness, succinctness, laconism*

❑ *conspire* (v)   to plan together secretly to commit an illegal act (*con-* together + *-spire* breathe)
Synonyms: *collude, collaborate*

❑ *concur* (v)   to agree (*con-* together + *-cur* run)
Synonyms: *accord, harmonize, cohere*

❑ *concord* (n)   a state of harmony (*con-* together + *-cord* heart)
Synonyms: *unanimity, consensus*

❑ *congenital* (adj)   existing at birth (*con-* together + *gen* born)
Synonyms: *innate, inborn*

❑ *schism* (n)   a division into political or religious factions (*cis* cut)
Synonyms: *faction, rift, divergence*

❑ *incisive* (adj)   having or indicating keen insight (*in-* in + *cis* cut)
Synonyms: *acute, keen, astute, canny, perspicacious, judicious, shrewd*

Vocabulary Lesson 2: Think Before You Judge

Today's roots:	*jud*	judge	*leg*	law
	jur	oath, law	*scrut*	to examine

❑ *judicious* (adj)   showing sound judgment; prudent (*jud-* judge + *-ious* full of)

After much thought, I decided that the most **judicious** thing to do was to avoid the swamp full of alligators.
Synonyms: *prudent, sensible, circumspect, sagacious*   Antonyms: *improvident, rash*

❑ *adjudicate* (v)   to hear and judge a case (*jud-* judge + *-ate* to do)

Sometimes when my two children fight, I feel like I'm **adjudicating** a capital crime rather than settling a quarrel.

❑ *astute* (adj)   shrewd; keen

The young Sherlock Holmes was quite the **astute** investigator; he always unraveled even the toughest mysteries.
Synonyms: *sagacious, shrewd, incisive, canny, perspicacious*   Antonyms: *vacuous, vapid, obtuse*

❑ *scrutinize* (v)   to examine carefully (*scruta* examine + *-ize* to do)

Before buying an apple, **scrutinize** it to be sure that it has no bruises.
Synonyms: *analyze, peruse*

❑ *pragmatic* (adj)   concerned with practical outcomes

The architects chose a solarium design that was less aesthetic than pragmatic: it was not beautiful, but it kept heating and lighting costs down.

❑ *perjure* (v)   to lie under oath (*per-* through + *jur* oath)

The mobster told blatant lies while on the stand, **perjuring** himself to keep his partners out of jail.
Synonym: *prevaricate*

❑ *prudent* (adj)   using good judgment (*prudentia* knowledge)

It would not be **prudent** to sneak out of your room again tonight; your parents will ground you if they catch you!
Synonyms: *judicious, sensible*   Antonyms: *improvident, rash*

❑ *jurisprudence* (n)   the science or philosophy of law (*jur-* law + *prudentia* knowledge)

❑ *jurisdiction* (n)   the sphere of authority or control (*jur-* law + *dictio* declaration)
Synonym: *domain*

❑ *adjure* (v)   to command solemnly, as under oath (*ad-* to + *jur* oath)
Synonyms: *enjoin, entreat, beseech*

❑ *adjudge* (v)   to determine based upon law (*ad-* to + *jud* judge)
Synonym: *adjudicate*

❑ *acumen* (n)   keenness of judgment (*acus* sharp)
Synonyms: *discernment, perspicacity, shrewdness*

❑ *inscrutable* (adj)   beyond comprehension or examination (*in-* not + *scruta* examine)
Synonyms: *enigmatic, recondite, abstruse*

❑ *allegation* (n)   a formal accusation (*ad-* to + *legare* dispute)
Synonyms: *contention, assertion, charge*

Vocabulary Lesson 3: Let's Talk About It

| Today's roots: | *locu, loqu*   talk | *circum*   around |
| | *verb*   word | *e-, ex-*   out |

❑ **eloquent** (adj)   well spoken (*e-* out + *loqu* talk)

She is an **eloquent** spokeswoman for animal rights; she conveys her ideas with great ease and fluidity.
Synonyms: *articulate, fluent*   Antonym: *inarticulate*

❑ **loquacious** (adj)   very talkative (*loqu-* talk + *-ious* full of)

That guy never stops talking; now I understand why they call him "**Loquacious** Larry"!
Synonyms: *garrulous, voluble*   Antonyms: *laconic, taciturn, reticent*

❑ **circumlocution** (n)   evasive speech; talking around the subject (*circum-* around + *loqu* talk)

The politician had perfected the art of **circumlocution;** he knew exactly how to avoid answering direct questions.
Synonym: *evasion*

❑ **colloquial** (adj)   conversational; using everyday language (*co-* together + *loqu* talk)

I like Professor Thompson because she is so **colloquial;** yesterday she said my thesis idea was "really cool."

❑ **grandiloquent** (adj)   speaking in a pompous manner (*grand-* great + *loqu* talk + *-ent* adjective)

His speech was pompous and **grandiloquent;** it seemed he was just trying to use as many big words as possible.
Synonyms: *pontifical, portentous*

❑ **elocution** (n)   expressive delivery of public speech (*e-* out + *loqu* talk + *-tion* noun)

James is adept at **elocution;** his expressions and mannerisms add a new level of meaning to his words.

❑ **garrulous** (adj)   talkative

Karl is always ready to talk about any subject, no matter how trivial, but at parties he is even more garrulous.
Synonyms: *loquacious, voluble*

❑ **pontificate** (v)   to speak pompously (*pontifex* high priest)

Synonyms: *declaim, sermonize, dogmatize*

❑ **verbose** (adj)   wordy (*verb-* word + *-ose* full of)

Synonyms: *prolix, discursive, digressive*

❑ **verbatim** (adv)   word for word (*verb-* word)

I followed the recipe **verbatim.**

❑ **ineffable** (adj)   unable to be expressed in words (in- not + effari utter)

Try as he might to express his love in a poem, his feelings seemed **ineffable.**

❑ **tangential** (adj)   only superficially relevant; off-topic

Synonyms: *irrelevant, incidental, immaterial*

❑ **tout** (v)   to promote or praise energetically

Synonyms: *acclaim, herald, laud*

❑ **anecdote** (n)   a short and often humorous story
Don't confuse with *antidote* (n), a remedy.

❑ **discursive** (adj)   straying from the topic (*dis-* away + *curs* course)

Synonyms: *digressive, desultory*

Vocabulary Lesson 4: "Good, Thanks"

Today's roots:	ben, bene, bon good	eu good
	grat to please, thank	vole wish

- ❏ **benefactor** (n) one who supports or helps another (*bene-* good + *fact* to make)

  Mr. King is the **benefactor** who generously donated the money for the new children's wing in the hospital.
  Synonyms: *philanthropist, patron*   Antonyms: *malefactor, nemesis, antagonist, adversary*

- ❏ **benign** (adj) harmless (*bene* good)

  She was relieved to find out that her tumor was **benign.**
  Synonym: *innocuous*   Antonyms: *malignant, virulent*

- ❏ **benevolent** (adj) kind; considerate (*bene-* good + *vole* wish)

  The **benevolent** Cub Scout did his good deed for the day when he helped a motorist change a tire.
  Synonyms: *gracious, altruistic, magnanimous*   Antonyms: *malevolent, malicious, inimical, pernicious*

- ❏ **benediction** (n) an expression of good wishes (*bene-* good + *dictus* declaration)

  At the reception, the father of the bride offered a **benediction,** wishing the couple never-ending love and happiness.
  Synonyms: *blessing, sanction*   Antonyms: *curse, malediction, execration*

- ❏ **euphemism** (n) the substitution of an inoffensive term for an offensive one (*eu-* good + *pheme* speech)

  A good journalist avoids the **euphemisms** of war, like "ordnance" for bombs and "collateral damage" for casualties.

- ❏ **eulogy** (n) a praising tribute (*eu-* good + *logia* discourse) (Although associated with funerals, "eulogy" has a positive tone.)

  His touching **eulogy** for his fallen friend left all the mourners weeping.
  Synonyms: *encomium, laudation, extolment, paean*   Antonyms: *denunciation, execration, censure*

- ❏ **ingratiate** (v) to put oneself in good favor with another (*in-* in + *grat* to please)

  When starting at a new school, Mary sought to **ingratiate** herself with her classmates by being excessively nice.
  Synonyms: *flatter, wheedle, toady, cajole*

- ❏ **beneficiary** (n) one who receives benefits (*bene-* good + *fic* to make)

  Synonyms: *heir, recipient, legatee*

- ❏ **gratuity** (n) a small payment in gratitude (*grat-* thank)
  Don't confuse with **gratuitous** (adj) unnecessary

- ❏ **gratis** (adj) free of charge (*grat-* thank)
  He let me borrow his car **gratis.**

- ❏ **gratify** (v) to please (*grat-* please)
  Synonyms: *appease, mollify, indulge*

- ❏ **euphoria** (n) a feeling of extreme happiness (*eu-* good)
  Synonyms: *elation, rapture, jubilation, ecstasy*

- ❏ **euphonious** (n) sweet sounding (*eu-* good + *phon* sound)
  Synonyms: *mellifluous, dulcet, lyrical*

Vocabulary Lesson 5: Changes

Today's roots:	*rupt*	break	*morph*	form, shape
	mut	change	*meta*	change, beyond

❑ **immutable** (adj)   unchangeable (*im-* not + *mut* change)

Emily is an **immutable** vegetarian. No matter how hard we try, we cannot get her to eat meat.
Synonyms: *permanent, inveterate*   Antonyms: *mutable, protean, vacillating, mercurial*

❑ **metamorphosis** (n)   a transformation (*meta-* change + *morph* form)

The old house underwent a **metamorphosis** from a rundown shack into a beautiful cottage.
Synonyms: *transformation, mutation, transmogrification*

❑ **rupture** (v)   to break open (*rupt-* break)

When the vat of smelly liquid **ruptured,** we picked up our feet to avoid getting the stuff on our shoes.
Synonyms: *burst, fissure, cleave*

❑ **transmute** (v)   to transform (*trans-* across + *mut* change)

Harry Potter was able to **transmute** a feather into a frog using a spell he learned in incantations class.
Synonyms: *metamorphose, alter, transmogrify*

❑ **amorphous** (adj)   lacking shape; changeable in form (*a-* without + *morph* shape)

Rather than marching in precise formation, the battalion broke down into an **amorphous** mass of charging soldiers.
Synonyms: *shapeless, nebulous, vague, nondescript*   Antonym: *crystalline*

❑ **mercurial** (adj)   erratic; subject to wild changes in character (from the speedy god Mercury)

Molly is the most **mercurial** person in the office; we can never tell if she'll be the evil Molly or the sympathetic Molly.
Synonyms: *fickle, capricious, vacillating*   Antonyms: *immutable, stable*

❑ **protean** (adj)   capable of assuming different forms (from the form-changing sea god Proteus)

He has changed his position on issues so many times that he is considered the most **protean** member of Congress.
Synonyms: *polymorphous, labile*   Antonyms: *immutable, stable*

❑ **mutate** (v)   to change form (*mut-* change)

Synonyms: *transform, transmogrify*

❑ **fickle** (adj)   likely to change opinion unpredictably

Synonyms: *capricious, vacillating, mercurial*

❑ **fluctuate** (v)   to vary irregularly (*flux* flow)

Synonyms: *vacillate, waver*

❑ **vacillate** (v)   to change one's mind repeatedly

Synonyms: *fluctuate, waver*

❑ **revamp** (v)   to revise; to renovate (*re-* again)

Synonyms: *refurbish, renovate*

❑ **amend** (v)   to improve; to remove the faults of

Synonyms: *rectify, redress, ameliorate, mitigate*

Vocabulary Lesson 6: One Boring World

Today's roots:	*vac* empty	*uni* one
	mund world	*anima* spirit, mind

❑ **hackneyed** (adj)   overused; trite

This film was a **hackneyed** remake with a storyline that has been done a hundred times.
Synonyms: *trite, prosaic, banal*   Antonyms: *original, novel*

❑ **mundane** (adj)   ordinary; typical (*mund-* world)

Having worked for years behind a desk, she wanted to leave the **mundane** world behind for exotic adventures abroad.
Synonyms: *routine, workaday, banal*   Antonyms: *singular, extraordinary, sublime*

❑ **vacuous** (adj)   lacking substance (*vac-* empty)

His latest book is widely criticized as **vacuous** and unintelligent.
Synonyms: *inane, asinine, fatuous*   Antonyms: *profound, thoughtful, deep*

❑ **prosaic** (adj)   unimaginative; ordinary

I don't understand why his oration was selected as the best; it was so **prosaic** that I nearly fell asleep.
Synonyms: *mundane, pedestrian*   Antonyms: *innovative, quixotic, whimsical*

❑ **insipid** (adj)   uninteresting; dull; without flavor (*in-* not + *sapere* taste)

Christine is the life of the party, but Tom is as **insipid** as they come; hardly anyone wants to talk with him.
Synonyms: *bland, nondescript, vapid*   Antonyms: *engaging, enchanting, piquant*

❑ **banal** (adj)   ordinary; trivial

That show used to be my favorite, but its story lines became so **banal** that I could no longer stand it.
Synonyms: *hackneyed, trite*   Antonyms: *extraordinary, singular, sublime*

❑ **pedestrian** (adj)   commonplace; ordinary

Synonyms: *prosaic, banal, vapid*

❑ **dormant** (adj)   inactive; sleeping (*dormire* sleep)

Synonyms: *inert, fallow*

❑ **unanimous** (adj)   in full agreement (*un-* one + *anima* mind)

Synonyms: *concordant, concerted*

❑ **uniform** (adj)   unvarying; always the same (*un-* one + *forma* form)

Synonym: *homogeneous*

❑ **equanimity** (n)   the quality of being even-tempered (*equa-* same + *anima* mind)

Synonyms: *composure, imperturbability, aplomb*

❑ **magnanimous** (adj)   noble of heart; generous; forgiving (*magna-* great + *anima* mind)

Synonyms: *philanthropic, altruistic, merciful*

Vocabulary Lesson 7: The Humours

| Today's roots: | *sanguis* blood | *melan* black |
| | *choler* bile | *anima* spirit, mind |

In medieval Europe, it was widely believed that one's health and disposition were largely determined by the balance of four bodily liquids called "humours": blood (*sang*), phlegm, black bile (*melancholer*), and yellow bile (*choler*).

❏ **sanguine** (adj)   cheerfully optimistic (*sanguis* blood)

After acing his final, David was **sanguine** about his prospects for a good overall course grade.
Synonyms: *blithe, buoyant*   Antonyms: *morose, forlorn, melancholy, sullen*

❏ **phlegmatic** (adj)   sluggish

His prolonged illness turned Julio from a spry, happy bon vivant into a morose and **phlegmatic** bore.
Synonyms: *languorous, lethargic, somnolent, torpid*   Antonyms: *vigorous, vibrant, hale, spry*

❏ **melancholy** (adj)   sad, depressed (*melan-* black + *choler* bile)

She has been so **melancholy** ever since she broke up with her boyfriend; sometimes she is even too depressed to talk with her friends.
Synonyms: *morose, despondent, disconsolate, sullen*   Antonyms: *blithe, buoyant, sanguine*

❏ **choleric** (adj)   easily angered (*choler-* bile + *-ic* characterized by)

Gena's mom is really nice but her dad is **choleric;** he freaks out about the smallest things.
Synonyms: *irascible, fractious, bilious, splenetic*

❏ **recalcitrant** (adj)   stubbornly resistant to authority (*re-* back + *calcitrare* kick)

Christine is a talented volleyball player, but she's so **recalcitrant** that our coach often keeps her on the bench.
Synonyms: *refractory, intractable*   Antonyms: *compliant, docile, tractable, obsequious, obeisant*

❏ **lethargic** (adj)   sluggish; dully apathetic

After three weeks of factoring polynomials, my entire class became **lethargic;** we were bored to death!
Synonyms: *languorous, phlegmatic, torpid*   Antonyms: *vigorous, vibrant, hale, spry*

❏ **splenetic** (adj)   irritable; easily angered (*splen-* spleen)

Synonyms: *bilious, choleric*

❏ **querulous** (adj)   disposed to complaining

Synonyms: *peevish, captious, carping, caviling*

❏ **dolorous** (adj)   marked by or expressive of sorrow or pain (*dolor-* pain)

Synonyms: *lugubrious, doleful*

❏ **animosity** (n)   hostility; ill-will (*animosus* bold)

Synonyms: *malevolence, antagonism, invidiousness*

❏ **pusillanimous** (adj)   cowardly (*pusillus-* weak + *anima* spirit)

Synonyms: *timorous, craven, dastardly*

❏ **lassitude** (n)   feeling of weakness or listlessness

Synonyms: *lethargy, languor, torpor, stupor*

Vocabulary Unit I Exercise Set I

1. Julia is amazingly ------ for a 5-year-old: She adeptly persuaded her reluctant parents to let her stay up to watch another thirty minutes of television.
   (A) concise
   (B) astute
   (C) verbose
   (D) recalcitrant
   (E) capricious

2. He recited the President's speech back to me ------; it was almost as if he had written it himself.
   (A) loquaciously
   (B) insipidly
   (C) verbatim
   (D) curtly
   (E) diffidently

3. Those not used to Larry's ------ speaking style found him to be ------ and did not like him at first.
   (A) monosyllabic . . incisive
   (B) surly . . congenial
   (C) laconic . . brusque
   (D) circumlocutory . . direct
   (E) garrulous . . phlegmatic

4. During his first year at boarding school, Ricardo underwent ------ from a shy and reserved young boy to a garrulous and extroverted teenager.
   (A) a schism
   (B) an adjudication
   (C) a benediction
   (D) a soliloquy
   (E) a metamorphosis

5. Janice is so ------ that she ------ over even the simplest decision.
   (A) shrewd . . perjures
   (B) magnanimous . . denigrates
   (C) pusillanimous . . admonishes
   (D) surreptitious . . purges
   (E) fickle . . vacillates

6. Despite having always been ------ at heart, Paula found herself ------ about the near future at work.
   (A) pessimistic . . sanguine
   (B) lethargic . . placid
   (C) morose . . querulous
   (D) prudent . . verbose
   (E) succinct . . terse

7. Kemal was the ------ of his father's generosity while at the supermarket because he got to eat an ice cream treat on the way home.
   (A) beneficiary
   (B) benefactor
   (C) benediction
   (D) patron
   (E) sanction

8. Because we are short on time, ------ would be appreciated; we need to leave in five minutes to catch the last bus of the night.
   (A) circumlocution
   (B) allegation
   (C) pontification
   (D) brevity
   (E) lassitude

9. The audience found the presentation to be ------ and vacuous; it was unimaginative and lacking substance.
   (A) dormant
   (B) unanimous
   (C) amorphous
   (D) dolorous
   (E) prosaic

10. The play was a blend of the mirthful and the ------; many scenes were ------, while others made me cry like a baby.
    (A) melancholy . . hilarious
    (B) reprehensible . . wistful
    (C) somber . . bitter
    (D) humorous . . jocular
    (E) despicable . . whimsical

_____ _____
_____ _____
_____ _____
_____ _____

HIT LIST

Vocabulary Unit I Exercise Set II

Write the meaning next to each root, and then write as many words as you can that contain the root.

1. ANIMA _____

6. CIRCUM _____

11. JUD_____

2. VAC _____

7. EX-, E_____

12. CIS_____

3. BENE _____

8. LEG_____

13. CO-_____

4. EU _____

9. JUR_____

14. VOL_____

5. LOQU _____

10. VERB_____

15. GRAT_____

Vocabulary Unit I Exercise Set III

1.　Should a talk show host be *laconic*?　　Y　N

2.　Is wearing a seat belt *prudent*?　　Y　N

3.　Should a politician be *perspicacious*?　　Y　N

4.　Is something *innocuous* harmful?　　Y　N

5.　Is a *beneficiary* one who gives?　　Y　N

Write the word with the given meaning.

6.　to change form　　m_____

7.　lacking substance　　v_____

8.　even-temperedness　　e_____

9.　commonplace　　p_____

10.　overused　　h_____

11.　sluggish　　p_____

12.　resistant to authority　　r_____

13.　disposed to complain　　q_____

14.　rudely abrupt　　b_____

15.　talkative　　g_____

16.　a political split　　s_____

17.　keenly perceptive　　p_____

18.　with sound judgment　　j_____

19.　to examine carefully　　s_____

20.　keenness of judgment　　a_____

21.　evasive speech　　c_____

22.　short humorous story　　a_____

23.　change one's mind often　v_____

24.　able to change form　　p_____

25.　feeling of weakness　　l_____

Write the correct form of the italicized word.

26.　the state of feeling *lethargic*

_____

27.　the quality of being *pusillanimous*

_____

28.　having the quality of a *euphemism*

_____

29.　the act of *adjudicating*

_____

30.　the act of *perjuring*

_____

Write the word with the given root.

31.　beyond comprehension (*scrut*)

_____

32.　existing at birth (*con*)

_____

33.　kind-hearted (*anim*)

_____

34.　to command solemnly (*jur*)

_____

35.　speaking in a pompous manner (*loqu*)

_____

36.　a praising tribute (*eu*)

_____

37.　harmless (*ben*)

_____

38.　inoffensive term substituted for an offensive one (*eu*)

_____

39.　to please (*grat*)

_____

40.　expressive delivery of public speech (*loqu*)

_____

41.　sphere of legal authority (*jur*)

_____

Unit I Exercise Set I Answer Key

1. **B** The colon (:) introduces an explanation. *Adeptly* means *with great skill*. A 5-year-old would have to be pretty *sharp* to persuade reluctant parents.
　concise = brief and to the point
　astute = shrewd, keen
　verbose = wordy
　recalcitrant = stubborn
　capricious = whimsical

2. **C** The information after the semicolon (;) describes the word in the blank. If he reads it as if he had written it himself, it implies that he knows it very well, and perhaps can read it word for word.
　loquaciously = in a talkative manner
　insipidly = in a painfully dull way
　verbatim = word for word
　curtly = in an abrupt manner, rudely
　diffidently = timidly, lacking confidence

3. **C** They did not like him at first, so the second blank is a negative word. The first blank should describe a speaking style that would cause someone to think that he is described by the second word.
　monosyllabic = one syllable; *incisive* = cogent
　surly = rude; *congenial* = friendly
　laconic = terse; *brusque* = rude, unfriendly
　circumlocutory = talkative
　garrulous = talkative; *phlegmatic* = sluggish

4. **E** Ricardo clearly changed from a shy person to a talkative extrovert. The word that fits the blank should mean *change*.
　schism = rift, large gap
　adjudication = judgment
　benediction = blessing
　soliloquy = speech to one's self
　metamorphosis = major change in form

5. **E** The second word is a verb that should complement the first word. Only E presents a pair that makes sense. Fickle people *do* tend to vacillate.
　shrewd = clever; *perjure* = to lie under oath
　magnanimous = generous; *denigrate* = to slander
　pusillanimous = cowardly; *admonish* = to scold
　surreptitious = sneaky; *purge* = to clear away
　fickle = erratic; *vacillate* = to go back and forth

6. **A** *Despite* indicates a contrast. So look for two words that are nearly opposite.
　pessimistic = negative; *sanguine* = optimistic
　lethargic = sluggish; *placid* = calm
　morose = sullen, gloomy; *querulous* = complaining
　prudent = wise, provident; *verbose* = wordy
　succinct = concise, to the point; *terse* = concise

7. **A** The recipient of generosity is a *beneficiary*.
　beneficiary = one who receives benefits
　benefactor = one who supports or helps another
　benediction = a blessing
　patron = a customer, someone who protects
　sanction = approval, permission

8. **D** A person short on time would likely appreciate something that is quick, which makes *brevity* a good choice.
　circumlocution = speaking in circles
　allegation = accusation
　pontification = speaking in a pompous manner
　brevity = briefness
　lassitude = fatigue, torpor

9. **E** The presentation was *vacuous*, which means lacking substance. This implies that the two clauses in the sentence are parallel, so the missing word must be similar to *unimaginative*.
　dormant = inactive
　unanimous = everyone agrees
　amorphous = lacking shape
　dolorous = causing pain or sorrow
　prosaic = dull, unimaginative

10. **A** Use the parallelism in the sentence. The two adjectives in the first clause are parallel to the two ideas in the second clause. The first word describes something that makes one cry, and the second word describes *mirthful* scenes. Two simple words to complete the sentence would be *depressing* and *funny*.
　melancholy = sadness; *hilarious* = funny
　reprehensible = blameworthy; *wistful* = sad
　somber = gloomy; *bitter* = unhappy
　humorous = funny; *jocular* = joking
　despicable = mean; *whimsical* = impulsive

Unit I Exercise Sets II and III Answer Key

Exercise Set II

1. ANIMA: spirit, life, mind
   unanimous, magnanimous, animosity, animation, animal, inanimate

2. VAC: empty
   vacate, evacuate, vacuum, vacuous, vacation, vacant

3. BENE: good
   benevolent, beneficiary, bonus, bona fide, benediction

4. EU: good
   euphemism, eulogy, euphony, euphoria, eugenics

5. LOQU: talk
   loquacious, eloquent, ventriloquist, elocution, circumlocution

6. CIRCUM: around
   circumference, circumnavigate, circumlocute, circuit, circuitous

7. EX-, E-: out
   emit, extract, exclaim, exit, egregious, enormous

8. LEG: law
   allege, legal, legitimate, legislate

9. JUR: oath, law
   jurisdiction, abjure, adjure, jury, jurisprudence

10. VERB: word
    verbatim, verbose, verbal, verbalize, proverb

11. JUD: judge
    adjudicate, judicious, adjudge, judiciary

12. CIS: cut
    incisive, scissors, concise, schism, decide, suicide

13. CO-: together, with
    cooperate, connect, correlate, committee, collect, conspire

14. VOLE: wish
    voluntary, benevolent, malevolent, volition

15. GRAT: please, thank
    gratify, ingratiate, ingrate, congratulate, gratuity

Exercise Set III

1. N
2. Y
3. Y
4. N
5. N
6. mutate
7. vacuous
8. equanimity
9. pedestrian
10. hackneyed
11. phlegmatic
12. recalcitrant
13. querulous
14. brusque
15. garrulous
16. schism
17. perspicacious
18. judicious
19. scrutinize
20. acumen
21. circumlocution
22. anecdote
23. vacillate
24. protean
25. lassitude
26. lethargy
27. pusillanimity
28. euphemistic
29. adjudication
30. perjury
31. inscrutable
32. congenital
33. magnanimous
34. adjure
35. grandiloquent
36. eulogy
37. benign
38. euphemism
39. gratify
40. elocution
41. jurisdiction

Vocabulary Unit 2

Vocabulary Lesson 8: Sneaky Sneaky

Today's roots:	*duplit* twofold	*pseudo* fake
	nym name	*rapere* to seize

❑ **spurious** (adj)   fake; counterfeit

The head of the FBI cursed the **spurious** tip that incorrectly led them to an abandoned warehouse.
Synonyms: *fictitious, dubious, fabricated*   Antonyms: *authentic, substantiated*

❑ **guile** (n)   trickery; deceit

The Big Bad Wolf deceived Little Red Riding Hood with **guile** and cunning.
Synonyms: *cleverness, cunning, duplicity*   Antonyms: *candor, straightforwardness*

❑ **beguile** (v)   to deceive with charm

The con artist **beguiled** me out of my money, convincing me to play his game over and over.
Synonyms: *charm, entrance, captivate*   Antonym: *disenchant*

❑ **strategem** (n)   a deceitful scheme (*strategos* army general)

The teenager devised an elaborate **strategem** to escape his parents' curfew.
Synonyms: *ploy, gimmick, ruse, subterfuge*

❑ **surreptitious** (adj)   deceptive; sneaky (*sub-* secretly + *rapere* seize)

The **surreptitious** movements of the lion lured the gazelle into a trap.
Synonyms: *covert, furtive, stealthy*   Antonyms: *honest, trustworthy, overt*

❑ **clandestine** (adj)   secret; hidden

The **clandestine** military facility in the capital city was unknown even to the President of the United States.
Synonyms: *stealthy, surreptitious, covert*   Antonyms: *forthright, straightforward, candid*

❑ **stealth** (n)   sneakiness; ability to avoid detection

The "**stealth** bomber" is so effective because it is undetectable by most radars.
Synonyms: *furtiveness, covertness*   Antonyms: *perceptible, observable*

❑ **duplicity** (n)   deceit; hypocritical deception (*duplit* twofold)

Synonyms: *chicanery, improbity*

❑ **specious** (adj)   false, but plausible (*specere* to look at)

Synonyms: *ostensible, sophistic*

❑ **furtive** (adj)   secretive; sneaky <a **furtive** plan to steal the diamond>

Synonyms: *stealthy, cloaked, guileful*

❑ **pseudonym** (n)   pen name (*pseudo-* fake + *onoma* name)

Synonyms: *alias, anonym*

❑ **fallacious** (adj)   deceptive; false (*fallacia* deceit + *-ious* full of)

Synonyms: *delusory, erroneous*

❑ **rapacious** (adj)   greedy; ravenous (*rapere* seize + *-ious* full of)

Synonyms: *ravenous, covetous*

Vocabulary Lesson 9: Time Is of the Essence

Today's roots:	*trans* across, through	*fluere* to flow
	chronos time	*tempus* time

□ *transient* (adj)   fleeting; short-lived (*transire* to go across)

We never understand the **transient** nature of childhood until we wake up one day and realize we're all grown up.
Synonyms: *ephemeral, evanescent, deciduous, transitory*   Antonyms: *permanent, interminable*

□ *ephemeral* (adj)   short-lived (*hemera* day)

Critics wrote off the band as a fad, their success as an **ephemeral** phenomenon.
Synonyms: *transient, evanescent, fleeting*   Antonyms: *permanent, everlasting, interminable*

□ *sporadic* (adj)   irregular or unpredictable; infrequent (*sporas* scattered)

He has experienced **sporadic** success as an actor, with occasional big roles amid many unmemorable parts.
Synonyms: *intermittent, episodic, mercurial*   Antonyms: *frequent, regular, permanent*

□ *capricious* (adj)   whimsical; impulsive

My English teacher runs her class **capriciously,** flitting from idea to idea with no reason or direction.
Synonyms: *fickle, volatile, mercurial, erratic*

□ *evanescent* (adj)   likely to vanish (*vanescere* to disappear)

The aurora borealis is beautiful but **evanescent,** a curtain of cascading light that can disappear in a heartbeat.
Synonyms: *transient, ephemeral, transitory*   Antonyms: *perpetual, enduring*

□ *extemporaneous* (adj)   done with little or no practice (*ex tempore* of time)

The speech was all the more remarkable because Dr. Sherman gave it **extemporaneously,** filling in for the scheduled speaker at the last moment.
Synonym: *impromptu*

□ *anachronism* (n)   something out of place in time (*ana-* backward + *chronos* time)

Her old-fashioned perspective on motherhood makes her an **anachronism** among her friends.
Synonyms: *archaism, incongruity, asynchronism*

□ *transitory* (adj)   lasting for a short time (*transitus* gone across)

Synonyms: *transient, fleeting*

□ *expedite* (v)   to speed up (*ex-* out + *pedis* foot)

Synonyms: *hasten, quicken, facilitate*

□ *influx* (n)   a flowing in (*in-* in + *fluere* to flow)

The country of Chad has seen a massive **influx** of refugees from the fighting in neighboring Sudan.

□ *superfluous* (adj)   beyond what is necessary or sufficient (*super-* over + *fluere* to flow)

□ *contemporaneous* (adj)   existing or occurring at about the same time (*con-* together + *tempore* time)

□ *interminable* (adj)   never ending (*in-* not + *term* end)

Synonyms: *incessant, unremitting*

□ *protracted* (adj)   prolonged; extended in time (*pro-* forward + *tract* pull)

Synonym: *drawn out*

Vocabulary Lesson 10: If You Can't Say Anything Nice . . .

Today's roots:	*dia* thoroughly, through	*de-* down
	dictus declared, word	*pugn* to fight

❑ **censure** (n)   official condemnation; harsh criticism (*censor* Roman supervisor for morals)

Congress voted to declare **censure** on the representative who took money and gifts from a lobbyist.
Synonyms: *castigation, derision, rebuke*   Antonyms: *laudation, endorsement*

❑ **calumny** (n)   slander; false accusation

Too many tabloids know that **calumny** about celebrities is more profitable than the truth.
Synonyms: *libel, denigration, defamation*   Antonyms: *acclaim, extolment, approbation*

❑ **diatribe** (n)   malicious criticism or abuse (*dia-* through + *tribein* to rub)

A good debate must avoid vicious personal **diatribe,** and focus on a respectful discussion of issues.
Synonyms: *castigation, derision, harangue*   Antonyms: *laudation, extolment, honor*

❑ **caustic** (adj)   corrosive; sarcastic

James immediately regretted making such a **caustic** remark; he could tell his words truly hurt Vanessa.
Synonyms: *abrasive, acrimonious*   Antonyms: *mitigating, conciliatory, mollifying*

❑ **repudiate** (v)   to cast off publicly (*repudium* divorce)

The consumers **repudiated** the shoe company for using sweatshops, and began buying from its competitor.
Synonyms: *disavow, abjure, forswear*   Antonym: *condone*

❑ **derogatory** (adj)   disparaging; belittling (*de-* down, away)

Derogatory remarks are not allowed in class; discussions should criticize ideas, not people.
Synonyms: *pejorative, derisive, disparaging*

❑ **admonish** (v)   to reprimand mildly (*ad-* to + *monere* to warn)

The boy was **admonished** by his mom for spilling his soda on the brand-new rug.
Synonyms: *rebuke, reprove*   Antonyms: *laud, revere, endorse*

❑ **disparage** (v)   to belittle; to demean (*dis-* apart + *parage* rank, peer)

Synonyms: *deprecate, discredit*

❑ **impugn** (v)   to attack as untrue; to refute by argument (*in-* against + *pugn* to fight)

❑ **malediction** (n)   a curse (*mal-* bad + *dictus* declared)

Synonyms: *anathema, execration*

❑ **denigrate** (v)   to attack the character of; to disparage

Synonyms: *slander, decry*

❑ **harangue** (n)   a long, critical, and pompous speech

Synonyms: *diatribe, discourse*

❑ **pejorative** (adj)   tending to make worse (*pejor* worse)

The senator suggested that discussing the issue dispassionately would be more productive than slinging pejorative personal comments.
Synonym: *disparaging*

❑ **slander** (n)   false comments that injure another's reputation (*scandalum* scandal)

Vocabulary Lesson 11: Holy Cow

Today's roots:	*sacer* sacred	*venus* respect, love
	sanctus holy	*vereri* respect

❑ *sanctimonious* (adj)   falsely pious or self-righteous (*sanctus* holy)

I prefer ministers who are real people, not **sanctimonious** know-it-all preachers.
Synonyms: *holier-than-thou, self-righteous, unctuous*   Antonyms: *sincere, unaffected, guileless*

❑ *sacrosanct* (adj)   profoundly sacred (*sacer* sacred + *sanctus* holy)

To Hindus, the cow is a **sacrosanct** creature to be treated with the utmost respect.
Synonyms: *inviolable, consecrated, divine, revered*   Antonym: *unholy*

❑ *sanctuary* (n)   a place of refuge; a sacred place (*sanctus* holy)

The Notre Dame cathedral is a **sanctuary** to all; anyone in need of a safe place to rest is welcome.
Synonyms: *shrine, asylum*

❑ *sacrilegious* (adj)   grossly irreverent; disrespectful of something sacred (*sacer* sacred)

To Hindus, to whom cows are sacred, the mass slaughter of cattle is considered **sacrilegious.**
Synonyms: *blasphemous, desecrating, impious*   Antonyms: *reverent, pious*

❑ *revere* (v)   to regard with honor and devotion (*re-* intensive + *vereri* respect)

Every genre of music has its stars, whom fans **revere** like gods.
Synonyms: *venerate, idolize, esteem*   Antonyms: *condemn, loathe*

❑ *pious* (adj)   showing religious reverence

Cotton Mather, being a devoted Puritan, considered it his **pious** duty to hang anyone in Salem accused of witchcraft.
Synonyms: *devout, reverential*   Antonyms: *irreverent, blasphemous*

❑ *deference* (n)   respect for the wishes of others (*de-* away + *ferre* carry)

It is important to show **deference** to your elders and treat them with respect.
Synonyms: *courtesy, reverence*   Antonyms: *irreverence, impertinence*

❑ *sacrament* (n)   a formal religious act or oath (*sacer* sacred)

Synonyms: *rite, liturgy*

❑ *venerable* (adj)   worthy of respect (*venus* respect)

Synonyms: *revered, honorable*

❑ *venerate* (v)   to regard with reverence or respect (*venus* respect)

Synonyms: *revere, extol*

❑ *consecrate* (v)   to declare to be holy (*sacer* sacred)

The marriage was **consecrated** by both a priest and an imam.
Synonyms: *venerate, bless*

❑ *talisman* (n)   an object with magical powers (*telos* result)

Synonyms: *charm, amulet*

❑ *lionize* (v)   to treat as a celebrity

Synonyms: *glorify, exalt, panegyrize, apotheosize, deify*

Vocabulary Lesson 12: Power It Up!

Today's roots:	*potens*	strong	*in-, im-*	not
	domit	lord	*efficere*	to effect

❏ *formidable* (adj)   awesome; hard to overcome; dreadful (*formido* fear)

The Yankees are a **formidable** team; we'll be lucky to win a single game against them this year.
Synonyms: *indomitable, redoubtable*   Antonyms: *anemic, ineffectual*

❏ *potent* (adj)   strong and effective (*potens* strong)

Although the drug is clearly the most **potent** treatment for depression, it also has the strongest side effects.
Synonyms: *efficacious, forceful*   Antonyms: *impotent, enervated, feckless*

❏ *bulwark* (n)   a strong defense

The newly constructed dam is in place as a **bulwark** against future flooding.
Synonyms: *bastion, redoubt, rampart*

❏ *indomitable* (adj)   unable to be conquered (*in-* not + *domit* lord)

The **indomitable** castle has been under the control of the Spaniards for 6,000 years, despite repeated attacks.
Synonyms: *impregnable, invincible*

❏ *redoubtable* (adj)   arousing fear; formidable; awesome (*re-* intensive + *douter* to doubt)

The mob boss is a **redoubtable** figure who makes his enemies cower in fear.
Synonyms: *formidable, intimidating*

❏ *robust* (adj)   full of vigor

The **robust** young men were able to run miles at a time through the rugged terrain without breaking a sweat.
Synonyms: *brawny, athletic, potent*   Antonyms: *weak, delicate*

❏ *impervious* (adj)   incapable of being penetrated or affected (*im-* not + *per-* through + *via* road)

Bulletproof vests are almost always **impervious** to bullets.
Synonyms: *impenetrable, impregnable*   Antonyms: *permeable, penetrable*

❏ *efficacious* (adj)   capable of producing a desired effect (*efficere* to effect)

Synonym: *proficient*

❏ *stalwart* (n)   physically or morally strong person; strong supporter

Synonyms: *mainstay, partisan*

❏ *impotent* (adj)   lacking strength or power (*im-* not + *potens* strong)

Synonyms: *enervated, effete*

❏ *predominant* (adj)   most important (*pre-* before + *domit* lord)

Synonyms: *paramount, preeminent*

❏ *impregnable* (adj)   unable to be entered by force (*im-* not + *prehendere* grasp)

The castle was an **impregnable** fortress.
Synonyms: *impenetrable, invincible, indomitable*

❏ *brawn* (n)   muscular strength

Our best wrestler was all **brawn** and no brains.
Synonyms: *robustness, vigor*

❏ *bastion* (n)   stronghold, fortress

The college is a **bastion** of liberalism.
Synonym: *bulwark*

Vocabulary Lesson 13: Come Together

Today's roots:	co-, com-, con- together	vocare to call
	syn- same, together	legere choose

❑ *coalesce* (v)   to blend or fuse together (*co-* together)

Raindrops are usually formed when water vapor **coalesces** on microscopic particles in the atmosphere.
Synonyms: *amalgamate, consolidate, fuse*   Antonyms: *disperse, diverge, dissipate*

❑ *anthology* (n)   a collection of works

The Beatles' **Anthology** is one of the best-selling greatest hits albums of all time.
Synonyms: *compilation, compendium, treasury*

❑ *convoke* (v)   to call together (*con-* together + *vocare* call)

The village elders **convoked** the citizens to discuss the sale of the ceremonial land.
Synonyms: *assemble, summon*   Antonyms: *dismiss, disperse*

❑ *synchronize* (v)   to arrange events to occur simultaneously (*syn-* same + *chron* time)

Nothing is harder for a dance teacher than trying to **synchronize** ten eight-year-old ballerinas.
Synonym: *coordinate*

❑ *synthesis* (n)   a fusion; a bringing together (*syn-* together + *tithenai* to put)

The **synthesis** of DNA occurs when many ribonucleic acids are joined together into one long double helix.
Synonyms: *amalgam, composite, fusion*   Antonyms: *division, disjuncture*

❑ *eclectic* (adj)   made up of parts from many different sources (*ec-* out + *legere* to choose)

Rob Mathes' **eclectic** compositions reveal a subtle yet effective blend of blues, gospel, classical, and jazz styles.
Synonyms: *multifaceted, multifarious, manifold, diverse, synthesized*

❑ *yoke* (v)   to join different things

Politicians often **yoke** unpopular legislation to popular bills so that they can sneak them through Congress.
Synonym: *couple*

❑ *amalgam* (n)   a combination of different substances into one mass

Synonyms: *composite, hybrid*

❑ *amass* (v)   to gather; to pile up

We **amassed** a huge collection of CDs.
Synonyms: *stockpile, accrue*

❑ *invoke* (v)   to call on for help or inspiration (*in-* in + *vocare* call)

The judge invoked an obscure, seldom-used statute in order to keep the defendant in jail.

❑ *compatible* (adj)   capable of living together harmoniously

The two were very **compatible** roommates.
Synonym: *agreeable*

❑ *contemporary* (adj)   living or occurring during the same time period (*con-* together + *tempore* time)

❑ *predilection* (n)   disposition in favor of something (*pre-* before + *legere* to choose)

Scott has a strong **predilection** for chocolate.
Synonyms: *inclination, bent, proclivity, propensity, penchant*

Vocabulary Lesson 14: Cruel and Unusual

| Today's roots: | vilis worthless | de- down |
| | super- above, beyond | -less without |

❑ **ruthless** (adj)   cruel; merciless (*rue* regret + *-less* without)

Torquemada is widely regarded as the most **ruthless** interrogator of the Spanish Inquisition.
Synonyms: *brutal, callous*   Antonyms: *civilized, humane, merciful*

❑ **contempt** (n)   scorn; disrespect

Many eminent and successful scientists often show **contempt** for novel theories that question their own.
Synonyms: *disdain, scorn*   Antonyms: *respect, honor, reverence*

❑ **callous** (adj)   hardened; insensitive

Because they see so much suffering daily, emergency room doctors often struggle to avoid becoming **callous.**
Synonyms: *insensitive, dispassionate*   Antonyms: *compassionate, empathetic, sympathetic*

❑ **sadistic** (adj)   taking pleasure in the pain of others (from the *Marquis de Sade*)

The **sadistic** youngster smiled as he watched his classmate get hit in the head with a dodgeball.
Synonyms: *barbarous, savage, ruthless*   Antonyms: *civilized, humane*

❑ **supercilious** (adj)   full of haughty arrogance (*super-* above + *cilium* eyebrow)

Although he seems **supercilious** when you first meet him, Joe is actually a modest and down-to-earth guy.
Synonyms: *haughty, cavalier*   Antonyms: *diffident, unassuming, humble*

❑ **idiosyncrasy** (n)   a peculiar trait or habit (*idio* peculiar)

My history teacher has the **idiosyncrasy** of always squinting just before she asks a question of the class.
Synonyms: *quirk, affectation, eccentricity, singularity*

❑ **anomaly** (n)   unusual event (*an-* not + *homos* same)

The ninety-degree day in Siberia was an **anomaly;** the temperature had gone that high only once before.
Synonyms: *aberration, irregularity*   Antonym: *regularity*

❑ **incongruous** (adj)   inappropriate; not in keeping with a pattern (*in-* not + *congru* agree)

❑ **fetter** (v)   to tie up; to chain
Synonyms: *shackle, hamper*

❑ **notorious** (adj)   famous for bad things (*notus* known)
Synonyms: *infamous, disreputable*

❑ **decry** (v)   to speak out against (*de-* down + *crier* cry)
Synonyms: *vilify, condemn*

❑ **vilify** (v)   to slander; to defame (*vilis* worthless)
Synonyms: *denigrate, malign, libel, calumniate*

❑ **heinous** (adj)   cruel and unusual (*haine* hatred)
Synonyms: *atrocious, monstrous*

❑ **revile** (v)   to denounce abusively (*vilis* worthless)
Benedict Arnold has long been **reviled** as a traitor

Vocabulary Unit 2 Exercise Set I

Time—8 minutes
For each question, select the best answer among the choices given. Note any vocabulary words to review on the Hit List below.

1. The emotional outburst was quite unusual for Peter; he is typically one of the most ------ individuals you could ever meet.
   (A) stoic
   (B) demonstrative
   (C) extroverted
   (D) irascible
   (E) inimical

2. Ayn Rand, whose writing is considered by some awkward and contrived, is nevertheless ------ by many as ------ of individualism and objectivism, the cornerstones of her philosophy.
   (A) lionized . . a stalwart
   (B) repudiated . . a protagonist
   (C) censured . . an advocate
   (D) praised . . an antagonist
   (E) extolled . . a skeptic

3. Fearing ------ from officials in their home country, the dissidents sought ------ in the American embassy.
   (A) veneration . . solitude
   (B) oppression . . sanctuary
   (C) impotence . . asylum
   (D) calumny . . disparagement
   (E) judiciousness . . salvation

4. Because female authors were not treated as equals in the 19th century, many women used ------ in an effort to disguise themselves as males.
   (A) influxes
   (B) anachronisms
   (C) pseudonyms
   (D) diatribes
   (E) amalgams

5. The newly implemented tax cut was not as ------ as its supporters had hoped in ------ the economy by spurring investment and growth.
   (A) formidable . . enervating
   (B) efficacious . . invigorating
   (C) delicate . . stimulating
   (D) ruthless . . lauding
   (E) incongruous . . encouraging

6. After many said that her last novel was too ------, she included a bizarre and shocking ending to her newest book in an effort to ------ her critics.
   (A) banal . . support
   (B) elegant . . pacify
   (C) spurious . . silence
   (D) mundane . . appease
   (E) contrived . . endorse

7. When unhappy, Richard quickly becomes ------, picking fights with anyone around him.
   (A) sadistic
   (B) pious
   (C) capricious
   (D) belligerent
   (E) fallacious

8. Although sparrows appear to be weak and harmless, they can actually be quite ------ when their nest is threatened.
   (A) redoubtable
   (B) furtive
   (C) evanescent
   (D) fickle
   (E) laconic

9. Many societies detest ------, and as a result the ------ among them are often treated as outcasts.
   (A) compatibility . . antagonistic
   (B) idiosyncrasy . . callous
   (C) duplicity . . perfidious
   (D) superficiality . . profound
   (E) potency . . sacrosanct

10. The ------ remarks made by the press hurt Kendra's feelings, but she vowed to ignore the ------ and continue toward her goal.
    (A) derogatory . . consecrations
    (B) inimical . . conciliations
    (C) sanctimonious . . predilections
    (D) venerable . . harangues
    (E) caustic . . denigrations

_____

_____

_____

_____

_____

_____

_____

_____

_____

_____

HIT LIST

Vocabulary Unit 2 Exercise Set II

Write the meaning next to each root, and then write as many words as you can that contain the root.

1. NYM_____

6. TRANS_____

11. TEMPUS_____

2. FLUERE_____

7. SACER_____

12. SANCTUS_____

3. CHRONOS_____

8. VERERI_____

13. POTENS_____

4. SYN-_____

9. VOCARE_____

14. DOMIT_____

5. IN-, IM-_____

10. VILIS_____

15. DE-_____

Vocabulary Unit 2 Exercise Set III

1. Should a good boxer be *redoubtable?*   Y N
2. Is a *stalwart* weak?   Y N
3. Can a mountain be *evanescent?*   Y N
4. Do *compatible* things work together well?   Y N
5. Is a *diffident* person haughty?   Y N

Write the word with the given meaning.

6. slander; false accusation c_____
7. reprimand mildly   a_____
8. irregular; infrequent   s_____
9. extended in time   p_____
10. trickery; deceit   g_____
11. sneaky   s_____
12. greedy; ravenous   r_____
13. to regard with honor   r_____
14. magical object   t_____
15. falsely pious   s_____
16. a strong defense   b_____
17. unconquerable   i_____
18. to slander; defame   v_____
19. scorn; disrespect   c_____
20. deceitful scheme   s_____
21. out of place in time   a_____
22. place of refuge   s_____
23. full of vigor   r_____
24. collection of works   a_____
25. call on for inspiration   i_____

Write the correct form of the italicized word.

26. like an *anomaly*

_____

27. showing *contempt*

_____

28. having the quality of an *anachronism*

_____

29. to give *censure*

_____

30. having the tendency to *evanesce*

_____

Write the word with the given meaning and root.

31. deceit (*duplit*)

_____

32. fake name (*nym*)

_____

33. disparaging (*de-*)

_____

34. to attack as untrue (*pugn*)

_____

35. falsely pious (*sanct*)

_____

36. regard with respect (*venus*)

_____

37. most important (*domit*)

_____

38. weak (*potens*)

_____

39. blend or fuse together (*co-*)

_____

40. full of haughty arrogance (*super-*)

_____

41. to denounce abusively (*vilis*)

_____

Unit 2 Exercise Set I Answer Key

1. **A** The sentence indicates that showing emotion is *unusual* for Peter. Look for a word that means *unemotional* to fill the blank.
   stoic = unaffected by pleasure or pain
   demonstrative = effusive, emotional
   extroverted = outgoing, gregarious
   irascible = easily angered
   inimical = unfriendly, harmful

2. **A** *Nevertheless* indicates that the blank should contrast *awkward and contrived*. A contrasting response would be *praise*. And if *individualism and objectivism* are the *cornerstones of her philosophy,* she must agree with them.
   lionized = worshipped; *stalwart* = unwavering person
   repudiated = cast off; *protagonist* = main character
   censured = condemned; *advocate* = supporter
   praised = commended; *antagonist* = opposed
   extolled = praised highly; *skeptic* = doubter

3. **B** The sentence indicates that they *fear* the first word and if they fear something, they should seek *comfort* of some sort.
   veneration = reverence; *solitude* = loneliness
   oppression = holding back; *sanctuary* = place of refuge
   impotence = lack of power; *asylum* = a safe place
   calumny = slander; *disparagement* = belittlement
   judiciousness = wisdom; *salvation* = being saved

4. **C** The word in the blank is something that they would use to disguise themselves as men. The only word that fits this description is *pseudonyms*.
   influxes = inward flows
   anachronisms = things out of place in time
   pseudonyms = false names
   diatribes = prolonged speeches
   amalgams = mixtures

5. **B** Supporters of the tax cut would obviously hope that it would do well and cause good things. So you want a positive word in the first blank. The supporters hoped it would "spur investment and growth" which shows they thought it would strengthen the economy.
   formidable = imposing; *enervating* = weakening
   efficacious = effective; *invigorating* = strengthening

delicate = fragile; *stimulating* = causing activity
ruthless = cruel; *lauding* = praising
incongruous = not matching; *encouraging* = inspiring

6. **D** The second part of the sentence implies that the critics deemed her first novel to be lacking a *bizarre and shocking* ending. She would include a shocking ending to *silence* these critics. Two simple words to complete the sentence would be *predictable* and *quiet*.
   banal = trivial; *support* = to hold up
   elegant = refined; *pacify* = to soothe
   spurious = fake; *silence* = to quiet
   mundane = ordinary; *appease* = to quiet
   contrived = obvious; *endorse* = support

7. **D** As is often the case, the information after the semicolon tells us everything we need to know. When Richard is unhappy, he *picks fights*.
   sadistic = enjoying the pain of others
   pious = holy
   capricious = acting on impulse
   belligerent = warlike, prone to fighting
   fallacious = false

8. **A** *Although* shows a classic contrast. Sparrows appear to be *weak and harmless,* but when something important to them is threatened, they become the opposite of *weak and harmless*.
   redoubtable = formidable, intimidating
   furtive = sneaky
   evanescent = ephemeral, short-lived
   fickle = prone to change one's mind
   laconic = not inclined to speaking much

9. **C** If society *detests* it, the first word must indicate something negative. The *as a result* shows a cause and effect, so you'd expect the second word to describe a person who has the characteristic in the first blank.
   compatibility = ability to go together; *antagonistic* = hostile
   idiosyncrasy = odd behavior; *callous* = hardened
   duplicity = deceptiveness; *perfidious* = untrustworthy
   superficial = lacking substance; *profound* = deep
   potency = strength, power; *sacrosanct* = sacred

10. **E** The first word indicates something that would hurt one's feelings. The second word must be a noun to describe such remarks.

    derogatory = insulting; *consecrations* = blessings

    inimical = unfriendly; *conciliations* = actions or remarks that regain trust or friendship

sanctimonious = smug;

        predilections = inclinations

venerable = worthy of respect;

        harangues = tirades

caustic = harmful; *denigrations* = slander

Unit 2 Exercise Sets II and III Answer Key

Exercise Set II

1. NYM: name
   *pseudonym, anonymous,
   synonym, antonym*

2. FLUERE: flow
   *fluent, superfluous,
   confluence, effluvium*

3. CHRONOS: time
   *synchronize, chronology,
   anachronism, chronicle*

4. SYN-: same
   *synonym, sympathy,
   synchronize, synthesis*

5. IN-, IM-: not
   *intolerant, immoral,
   immodest, inconceivable*

6. TRANS: across
   *transparent, transmit,
   translate, transition*

7. SACER: sacred
   *sacrilegious, sacrament,
   sacrosanct, consecrate*

8. VERERI: respect
   *revere, reverent, irreverent,
   reverend*

9. VOCARE: to call
   *invoke, provoke, vocation,
   voice, revoke*

10. VILIS: worthless
    vilify, revile, villain, evil

11. TEMPUS: time
    *extemporaneous, temporary,
    contemporary*

12. SANCTUS: holy
    *sanctify, sanctuary,
    sacrosanct, sanctimonious*

13. POTENS: strong
    *potent, impotent, potential,
    despot*

14. DOMIT: lord
    *dominion, indomitable,
    domesticate, dominate*

15. DE-: down
    *descend, demoralize, demote,
    deride, decline*

Exercise Set III

1. Y
2. N
3. N
4. Y
5. N
6. calumny
7. admonish
8. sporadic
9. protracted
10. guile
11. surreptitious
12. rapacious
13. revere
14. talisman

15. sanctimonious
16. bulwark
17. indomitable
18. vilify
19. contempt
20. stratagem
21. anachronistic
22. sanctuary
23. robust
24. anthology
25. invoke
26. anomalous
27. contemptuous
28. anachronistic

29. censure
30. evanescent
31. duplicity
32. pseudonym
33. derogatory
34. impugn
35. sanctimonious
36. venerate
37. predominant
38. impotent
39. coalesce
40. supercilious
41. revile

Vocabulary Unit 3

Vocabulary Lesson 15: Weak and Weaker

Today's roots:	*batre* to beat	*troph* nourishment
	sequi follow	*pli* fold

❑ **atrophy** (v)   to weaken from disuse (*a-* without + *troph* nourishment)

After surgery, extended bed rest often causes muscles to **atrophy** unless it is accompanied by physical therapy.
Synonyms: *degenerate, deteriorate*   Antonyms: *thrive, flourish*

❑ **abate** (v)   to subside; to decrease in intensity (*ad-* to + *batre* to beat)

The crews had to wait until the storm **abated** before they could begin to assess the damage to the coastal town.
Synonyms: *wane, diminish*   Antonyms: *expand, amplify*

❑ **porous** (adj)   filled with many holes (*porus* opening)

The teenager's story was a **porous** one that her parents could easily see through.
Synonyms: *penetrable, pervious*   Antonyms: *impervious, impenetrable, impregnable*

❑ **wane** (v)   to grow smaller or less intense

As the brightness of the moon **wanes** over the next few nights, it will become easier to see the surrounding stars.
Synonyms: *abate, ebb*   Antonyms: *wax, intensify*

❑ **lassitude** (n)   a feeling of weakness (*lassus* weary)

Although she tried valiantly to play through her illness, Danielle's **lassitude** overtook her in the second half.
Synonyms: *listlessness, weariness*   Antonyms: *vitality, vigor*

❑ **undermine** (v)   to weaken or diminish something

The continual setbacks to the project over many weeks **undermined** the morale of the workers.
Synonyms: *undercut, attenuate*   Antonyms: *fortify, strengthen*

❑ **obsequious** (adj)   overly submissive (*ob-* to + *sequi* follow)

Synonyms: *fawning, compliant*

❑ **attrition** (n)   a wearing away of strength or morale

Synonyms: *debilitation, weakening*

❑ **enervate** (v)   to weaken someone's vitality

Synonym: *debilitate*

❑ **vulnerable** (adj)   prone to attack or harm

Synonyms: *assailable, susceptible*

❑ **ebb** (v)   to decrease or decline slowly

Synonyms: *wane, abate*

❑ **compliant** (adj)   submissive (*pli* fold)

Synonyms: *yielding, conciliatory*

❑ **debilitate** (v)   to sap the strength of (*de-* away + *bilis* strength)

Synonyms: *cripple, enervate*

Vocabulary Lesson 16: Chillin'

Today's roots:	*status* position, standing	*quies* rest
	plac to please	*serenus* calm

❏ *placid* (adj)   calm (*plac* to please)

A relaxing day at the spa always makes me feel more **placid.**
Synonyms: *serene, tranquil*   Antonyms: *frenzied, frenetic*

❏ *inert* (adj)   sluggish; inactive (*in-* not + *ertem* active)

After his final exams, Ricky sat **inert** on his couch for two days watching soap operas and game shows.
Synonyms: *quiescent, torpid, phlegmatic*   Antonyms: *alert, lively*

❏ *listless* (adj)   sluggish; without energy (*-less* without)

I always feel **listless** on rainy days; sometimes I don't even want to get out of bed.
Synonyms: *enervated, inert, phlegmatic, lethargic*   Antonyms: *lively, robust*

❏ *quiescent* (adj)   resting; quiet (*quies* rest)

During the **quiescent** phase of cell division, the cell does not split or grow.
Synonym: *inactive*   Antonyms: *dynamic, active*

❏ *serene* (adj)   tranquil; calm; placid (*serenus* peaceful, calm)

There was not a single wave on the surface of the **serene** lake.
Synonyms: *quiescent, sedate*   Antonyms: *frenzied, turbulent*

❏ *static* (adj)   stationary (*status* standing)

The patient's vitals have been **static** for an hour. We hope this means he can be moved from intensive care.
Synonyms: *stagnant, inert*   Antonyms: *itinerant, peripatetic*

❏ *lethargic* (adj)   lazy; sluggish

The flu left me feeling **lethargic** even two days after my fever had broken.
Synonyms: *phlegmatic, dormant, enervated, listless*

❏ *moratorium* (n)   postponement
Synonyms: *deferral, delay*

❏ *stagnate* (v)   to become inactive; to become stale (*status* standing)
Synonym: *idle*

❏ *torpor* (n)   lethargy; apathy
Synonyms: *inertness, lassitude*

❏ *respite* (n)   rest; time of relief; pause (*respit* delay)
Synonyms: *hiatus, moratorium*

❏ *hiatus* (n)   a break in the continuity of something
Synonyms: *respite, discontinuity*

❏ *torpid* (adj)   hibernating; dormant (*torpere* be numb)
Synonyms: *inert, idle*

Vocabulary Lesson 17: Wanna Fight?

| Today's roots: | *bellum* war | *pro-* forward, forth |
| | *pugnare* fight | *ire* anger |

❑ *belligerent* (adj)   warlike; quarrelsome (*bellum* war)

My brother is a **belligerent** guy; he picks his fair share of bar fights.
Synonyms: *antagonistic, cantankerous, contentious*   Antonyms: *passive, peaceful*

❑ *irascible* (adj)   easily angered (*ire* anger)

Adam's **irascible** nature landed him in anger management therapy; he overreacts to the smallest things.
Synonyms: *choleric, splenetic, petulant*   Antonym: *even-tempered*

❑ *volatile* (adj)   explosive; tending to evaporate quickly (*vola* to fly)

The situation in the Middle East is a **volatile** one that must be handled with care.
Synonyms: *unsettled, temperamental*   Antonym: *stable*

❑ *rebuttal* (n)   refutation; opposing response to an argument (*re-* back)

After the opponent made his remarks, the debate team captain approached the podium to deliver her **rebuttal.**
Synonyms: *repartee, rejoinder*   Antonym: *agreement*

❑ *refute* (v)   to disprove; to rebut forcefully (*refutare* to drive back)

The judge found no evidence to **refute** your claim that the car is yours, so you get to keep it for now.
Synonyms: *contradict, rebut*   Antonyms: *support, endorse*

❑ *incite* (v)   to urge into action (*citare* to cause to move)

The rebels **incited** a revolt in the small city by convincing the citizens that their mayor was a crook.
Synonyms: *coax, cajole, instigate*   Antonym: *dissuade*

❑ *pugnacious* (adj)   quarrelsome; warlike (*pugnare* fight)

The **pugnacious** punk was happiest when his fists were pounding someone else's chin.
Synonyms: *truculent, belligerent*   Antonyms: *pacific, passive*

❑ *bellicose* (adj)   warlike in manner (*bellum* war)

Synonyms: *pugnacious, belligerent*

❑ *harass* (v)   to bother; to annoy

Synonyms: *irritate, torment*

❑ *assail* (v)   to attack or assault (*ad-* at + *salire* leap)

Synonym: *berate*

❑ *tumultuous* (adj)   violently agitated

Synonyms: *hectic, unruly*

❑ *instigate* (v)   to goad; to urge on

Synonyms: *incite, foment, coax, cajole*

❑ *provocative* (adj)   tending to aggravate or stimulate (*pro-* forth + *vocare* to call)

Synonyms: *goading, alluring*

❑ *propensity* (n)   a natural inclination; a tendency (*pro-* forth)

Vocabulary Lesson 18: Bad and Ugly

Today's roots:	*acri*	bitter	*caco*	ugly
	noi	harm	*phon*	sound

❑ **acrimony** (n)   bitterness of feeling; harsh words (*acri* bitter + *monia* action or condition)

Her toast was inappropriately **acrimonious,** and we could all tell that she had not forgiven her friend.
Synonyms: *belligerence, rancor*   Antonym: *civility*

❑ **appalling** (adj)   shocking; causing dismay (*palir* to grow pale)

The way he yells at his wife is **appalling;** he treats her as if she were his servant.
Synonyms: *astounding, offensive*   Antonyms: *benevolent, virtuous*

❑ **cacophony** (n)   discord; harsh sounds (*cacos* ugly + *phon* sound)

How can this **cacophony** coming out of my son's room be today's popular music?
Synonyms: *disharmony, dissonance*   Antonym: *harmony*

❑ **abysmal** (adj)   extremely bad; wretched

The food at this hospital is **abysmal!** Is this bread or cardboard?
Synonyms: *deplorable, pathetic*   Antonyms: *commendable, laudable*

❑ **acrid** (adj)   harsh smelling or tasting (*acri* bitter)

Don't inhale too much of this chemical; it is known to be quite **acrid** and can make you pass out.
Synonyms: *astringent, pungent*   Antonyms: *savory, sweet*

❑ **blatant** (adj)   very conspicuous; annoyingly loud

The blaring of loud music despite my repeated requests for silence shows your **blatant** disregard for my needs.
Synonyms: *flagrant, impudent*   Antonym: *unobtrusive*

❑ **deplorable** (adj)   worthy of reproach or censure (*plorare* to cry out in sorrow)

Although they claimed to love animals, the conditions at their run-down shelter were **deplorable.**
Synonyms: *disgraceful, egregious*   Antonyms: *commendable, laudable*

❑ **egregious** (adj)   conspicuously bad; flagrant (*e-* out + *greg* herd)

Synonyms: *atrocious, deplorable*

❑ **lurid** (adj)   shocking; sensational

Synonyms: *graphic, vivid*

❑ **noisome** (adj)   offensive to the senses or the health (*noi* harm)

Synonyms: *loathsome, detestable*

❑ **flagrant** (adj)   offensively bad; reprehensible

Synonyms: *egregious, blatant*

❑ **heinous** (adj)   cruel; shockingly evil (*haine* hatred + *-ous* full of)

Synonyms: *atrocious, monstrous*

❑ **astringent** (adj)   caustic; pungent

Synonyms: *acrid, harsh*

Vocabulary Lesson 19: Moving Right Along

| **Today's roots:** | *ambulare*   walk | *flux*   flow |
| | *pel, pul*   force, drive | *peri-*   around |

❑ *ambulatory* (adj)   capable of moving around (*ambulare* walk)

He must stay in bed for a week, and once he is **ambulatory** he will need crutches.
Synonyms: *mobile, peripatetic*   ·   Antonyms: *static, immobile*

❑ *deviate* (v)   to swerve or deflect (*de-* away + *via* path)

The tire sitting in the left lane of the highway caused the driver to **deviate** from her path.
Synonyms: *digress, veer*   Antonym: *conform*

❑ *influx* (n)   a flowing in (*in-* in + *flux* flow)

The school saw quite an **influx** of new applicants once it increased the number of scholarships.
Synonyms: *inundation, inpouring, immigration*   Antonyms: *efflux, emigration*

❑ *meander* (v)   to wander aimlessly (from *Maiandros,* a Greek river known for its winding path)

The confused lost child **meandered** through the streets with no apparent destination.
Synonyms: *roam, drift*

❑ *peripatetic* (adj)   traveling from place to place (*peri-* around + *patein* to walk)

The nomads were a **peripatetic** clan; they never stayed in the same place very long.
Synonyms: *itinerant, ambulant*   Antonyms: *stationary, static*

❑ *impel* (v)   to put into motion; to urge (*pel* force)

The zoo visitors were **impelled** into action by the announcement that a lion was loose.
Synonyms: *goad, spur*   Antonyms: *impede, dissuade*

❑ *expedite* (v)   to speed up the progress of (*ex-* out + *pes* foot: to free from entanglement)

The project was **expedited** once the CEO decided that its outcome reflected on him personally.
Synonyms: *facilitate, hasten, precipitate, advance*   Antonyms: *impede, hinder*

❑ *itinerant* (adj)   traveling from place to place

Synonyms: *peripatetic, ambulant*

❑ *nomadic* (adj)   wandering without a permanent home

Synonyms: *migratory, drifting*

❑ *peripheral* (adj)   located on the outer boundary (*peri-* around)

Synonym: *bordering*

❑ *compel* (v)   to urge into action by force (*com-* together + *pel* force)

Synonyms: *impel, coerce*

❑ *vagrant* (adj)   wandering from place to place (*vagus* wandering)

Synonyms: *nomadic, peripatetic*

❑ *perambulate* (v)   to move about (*per-* through + *ambulare* walk)

Synonyms: *wander, drift*

Vocabulary Lesson 20: Going, Going, Gone!

Today's roots:	*purgare*	cleanse	*re-*	back
	deplare	to empty	*ab-*	away

❑ **raze** (v)   to destroy completely

The massive level-five hurricane **razed** the entire port city, crushing everything in its path.
Synonyms: *obliterate, decimate*   Antonym: *preserve*

❑ **jettison** (v)   to throw overboard

The killer **jettisoned** the murder weapon into the lake as he sailed to his hideout in the cove.
Synonyms: *heave, dump*   Antonym: *retain*

❑ **abort** (v)   to terminate prematurely

The soldiers **aborted** their mission when they learned their cover was blown and it was no longer safe.
Synonyms: *scratch, cancel*   Antonyms: *execute, continue*

❑ **purge** (v)   to cleanse of something unwanted (*purgare* to cleanse)

It is satisfying to **purge** your email inbox of unwanted junk messages.
Synonyms: *remove, expunge*   Antonyms: *amass, collect*

❑ **forgo** (v)   to give something up (*for-* away + *go* go)

The woman decided to leave the hospital early and **forgo** further treatment on her injured hip.
Synonyms: *abandon, forsake*   Antonyms: *maintain, participate*

❑ **deplete** (v)   to decrease the supply of (*deplare* to empty)

The run on gasoline **depleted** the gas station of its fuel reserves, and it was forced to shut down.
Synonyms: *exhaust, diminish*   Antonyms: *replenish, restock*

❑ **dearth** (n)   lack; scarcity (*dear* greatly valued)

There has been a **dearth** of good will between the teams ever since the bench-clearing brawl.
Synonyms: *paucity, scarcity, want, deficiency*   Antonyms: *abundance, plenitude, bounty*

❑ **rescind** (v)   to take back; to cancel (*re-* back + *scindere* cut)

Synonyms: *annul, void*

❑ **efface** (v)   to erase by rubbing (*e-* out + *face* appearance)

Synonyms: *omit, cancel*

❑ **abdicate** (v)   to give up power (*ab-* away + *dicare* proclaim)

Synonyms: *relinquish, renounce*

❑ **renounce** (v)   to give up in a formal announcement

Synonyms: *abdicate, resign*

❑ **nullify** (v)   to make invalid (*nullus* none)

Synonyms: *cancel, void*

❑ **relinquish** (v)   to abandon or give up (*re-* back + *linquere* to leave)

Synonyms: *abdicate, vacate*

❑ **cathartic** (adj)   having a purging effect; inducing the release of emotional tension

Forgiving his father turned out to be a very **cathartic** experience for Kenneth.

Vocabulary Lesson 21: Mr. Nice Guy

Today's roots:	*amicus*	friend	*anthro*	humankind
	munus	gift, money, sharing	*phila*	brotherly love

❑ *altruism* (n)   selflessness (*alter* other)

Tom's **altruism** pushes him to spend thirty hours per week working with the needy.
Synonyms: *humaneness, benevolence*   Antonyms: *egoism, malevolence*

❑ *amiable* (adj)   friendly; agreeable (*amicus* friend)

Mr. Richards is such an **amiable** guy, always smiling and laughing as he interacts with his customers.
Synonyms: *affable, amicable*   Antonyms: *surly, disdainful*

❑ *philanthropist* (n)   one who does good; lover of humankind (*phila-* love + *anthro* humankind)

It is amazing that a penny-pincher like Paul is a **philanthropist** who has donated millions to charity.
Synonyms: *altruist, humanitarian*   Antonyms: *misanthrope, antagonist*

❑ *congenial* (adj)   friendly; pleasant (*con-* with + *genialis* pleasant)

After months of imagining her in-laws as monsters, Julia was surprised at how **congenial** they actually were.
Synonyms: *amicable, affable*   Antonyms: *hostile, surly*

❑ *munificent* (adj)   generous (*munus* sharing)

Donating that outfit to charity is quite a **munificent** gesture, considering that it is your favorite.
Synonyms: *beneficent, magnanimous*   Antonyms: *greedy, egoistic*

❑ *decorum* (n)   propriety; good manners (*decorus* proper)

While eating at the country club, you must behave with the utmost **decorum** and mind your manners.
Synonym: *etiquette*   Antonym: *impropriety*

❑ *amity* (n)   friendship (*amicus* friend)

Synonyms: *benevolence, amicableness*

❑ *decorous* (adj)   exhibiting good taste in behavior or appearance (*decorus* proper)

Synonyms: *civilized, dignified*

❑ *affable* (adj)   friendly; kind (*affabilis* easy to converse with)

Synonyms: *amiable, amicable*

❑ *gregarious* (adj)   sociable (*greg* flock)

Synonym: *friendly*

❑ *amicable* (adj)   polite and friendly (*amicus* friend)

Synonyms: *amiable, affable*

❑ *magnanimous* (adj)   generous; big-hearted (*magna-* great + *animus* spirit)

Synonyms: *altruistic, munificent*

❑ *geniality* (n)   cheerfulness (*genialis* pleasant)

Synonyms: *affability, amiability*

Vocabulary Unit 3 Exercise Set I

Time—8 minutes
For each question, select the best answer among the choices given. Note any vocabulary words to review on the Hit List below.

1. Stephen's job as censor for the magazine was to ------ any material that might be objectionable to its readers.
   (A) abridge
   (B) amass
   (C) refute
   (D) expurgate
   (E) enervate

2. As more travelers have decided to ------ their garbage as they sail, the lake has become quite polluted.
   (A) pilfer
   (B) jettison
   (C) yoke
   (D) assail
   (E) impel

3. The movie critic refused to take back his ------ remarks because he thoroughly intended to ------ the director's abilities.
   (A) caustic . . compliment
   (B) derogatory . . revere
   (C) sanctimonious . . reveal
   (D) laconic . . lionize
   (E) scathing . . disparage

4. The ------ young salesman made his living wandering from town to town.
   (A) bellicose
   (B) inert
   (C) lethargic
   (D) acrid
   (E) peripatetic

5. Normally a ------ person, when stuck in horrible traffic on the highway Peter becomes even more ------, often provoking fisticuffs with other drivers.
   (A) congenial . . rapacious
   (B) contentious . . belligerent
   (C) listless . . dolorous
   (D) choleric . . serene
   (E) sanguine . . pugnacious

6. The normally ------ daytime television show had one surprisingly ------ episode and got yanked off the air.
   (A) decorous . . provocative
   (B) compliant . . obsequious
   (C) vulnerable . . porous
   (D) volatile . . tumultuous
   (E) deplorable . . altruistic

7. Coming off of the worst recession in the country's 250-year history, the sudden ------ of money was a welcome sight to the rulers of the destitute nation.
   (A) depletion
   (B) influx
   (C) transgression
   (D) fluctuation
   (E) bulwark

8. The ------ from the construction work on the busy street below made it very difficult for me to concentrate with the window open.
   (A) torpor
   (B) cacophony
   (C) euphoria
   (D) anomaly
   (E) sacrament

9. As if he knew I was exhausted and in need of ------ from his interminable mischief, the puppy went to his bed and took a nap.
   (A) an elocution
   (B) a euphemism
   (C) a respite
   (D) a rebuttal
   (E) a testimony

10. Although it was nice to be ------ again after being bedridden for four weeks, the muscular ------ that resulted from my immobilization was going to take a lot of work to fix.
    (A) itinerant . . deterioration
    (B) amiable . . bastion
    (C) ambulatory . . atrophy
    (D) amorphous . . attrition
    (E) pedestrian . . acrimony

HIT LIST

_____   _____
_____   _____
_____   _____
_____   _____
_____   _____

Vocabulary Unit 3 Exercise Set II

Write the meaning next to each root, then write as many words as you can that contain the root.

1. A-_____

2. AN-_____

3. PERI-_____

4. AB-_____

5. ACRI_____

6. BELLUM-_____

7. AM-, AMICUS_____

8. ANTHRO_____

9. MUNUS_____

10. TROPH_____

11. PRO-_____

12. PHON_____

13. PURG_____

14. PEL_____

15. SEQUI_____

Vocabulary Unit 3 Exercise Set III

1. Is a *heinous* act cruel?   Y N
2. Is a *gregarious* person friendly?   Y N
3. Is an *obsequious* person disobedient?   Y N
4. Is something *abysmal* good?   Y N
5. Is a *philanthropist* generous?   Y N

Write the word with the given meaning.

6. traveling from place to place   i_____
7. hibernating, dormant   t_____
8. good manners   d_____
9. to destroy completely   r_____
10. to decrease the supply of   d_____
11. filled with many holes   p_____
12. capable of moving around   a_____
13. selflessness   a_____
14. to urge into action   i_____
15. to intentionally weaken   u_____
16. offensive to the senses   n_____
17. prone to attack   v_____
18. stationary   s_____
19. to terminate prematurely   a_____
20. to put in motion   i_____
21. politely friendly   a_____
22. warlike   p_____
23. to throw overboard   j_____
24. worthy of reproach   d_____
25. a break   h_____

Write the correct form of the italicized word.

26. characterized by *torpor*

_____

27. the act of *abdicating*

_____

28. the quality of being *volatile*

_____

29. how someone who displays *altruism* behaves

_____

30. the quality of being *pugnacious*

_____

Write the word with the given root.

31. lazy, sluggish (*argos*)

_____

32. to erase (*fac*)

_____

33. to weaken from disuse (*a-*)

_____

34. postponement (*mora*)

_____

35. generous (*muni*)

_____

36. quarrelsome (*belli*)

_____

37. overly submissive (*sequi*)

_____

38. to swerve (*via*)

_____

39. easily angered (*irasci*)

_____

40. sociable (*greg*)

_____

41. harsh words (*acri*)

_____

Unit 3 Exercise Set I Answer Key

1. **D** A *censor* is one who removes objectionable material.
   abridge = to shorten
   amass = to accumulate or collect
   refute = to disprove
   expurgate = to remove inappropriate material
   enervate = to weaken

2. **B** The waters are becoming more polluted, which indicates that people are probably putting their garbage into the lake.
   pilfer = to steal
   jettison = to throw overboard
   yoke = to tie together
   assail = to attack
   impel = to provoke

3. **E** The critic *thoroughly intended* to say what he said. But if they were things he was expected to *take back,* they must have been pretty negative. The second word should be negative as well.
   caustic = harmful; *compliment* = to praise
   derogatory = offensive; *revere* = to respect
   sanctimonious = smug
   laconic = terse; *lionize* = to worship
   scathing = harsh; *disparage* = to put down

4. **E** This person makes his living *wandering from town to town.*
   bellicose = warlike
   inert = inactive
   lethargic = sluggish
   acrid = harsh
   peripatetic = traveling from place to place

5. **B** Peter sometimes picks fights (*fisticuffs*). The second word should be slightly stronger than the first.
   congenial = friendly; *rapacious* = ravenous
   contentious = inclined to argue; *belligerent* = warlike
   listless = lethargic; *dolorous* = painful
   choleric = easily angered; *serene* = peaceful
   sanguine = optimistic; *pugnacious* = combative

6. **A** It got yanked off the air, so the show must have done something bad. The word *surprisingly* indicates a contrast, so the first word is positive.
   decorous = proper; *provocative* = risqué
   compliant = obedient; *obsequious* = submissive
   vulnerable = susceptible; *porous* = full of holes
   volatile = explosive; *tumultuous* = turbulent
   deplorable = very bad; *altruistic* = selfless

7. **B** The nation is *destitute,* and therefore needs money to pour in.
   depletion = draining
   influx = inward flow
   transgression = violation
   fluctuation = shift back and forth
   bulwark = a defensive wall

8. **B** It is difficult to concentrate and the street is busy with construction; there must be lot of noise down there.
   torpor = sluggishness
   cacophony = harsh noise
   euphoria = elation, ecstasy
   anomaly = an abnormality
   sacrament = a formal religious act

9. **C** The owner of the puppy is exhausted and therefore in need of rest. *Interminable* means *never-ending.* The puppy's nap would provide the owner with a nice break from the mischief.
   an elocution = an expressive delivery of a speech
   a euphemism = an inoffensive expression substituted for an offensive one
   a respite = a rest
   a rebuttal = a retort
   a testimony = an account, evidence

10. **C** The first word describes one who is no longer bedridden. The second word describes a problem from being bedridden. *Atrophy* works because it is the result of disuse.
    itinerant = wandering; *deterioration* = degeneration
    amiable = friendly; *bastion* = a fortified area
    ambulatory = able to move; *atrophy* = withering
    amorphous = lacking shape; *attrition* = erosion
    pedestrian = common; *acrimony* = harsh words
    (*pedestrian* can also mean "on the move")

Unit 3 Exercise Sets II and III Answer Key

Exercise Set II

1. A-: without
   atheist, atrophy, apathy, asexual, amorphous, abyss

2. AN-: without
   anarchy, anecdote, anaerobic, analgesic, anemia, anesthesia, anonymous

3. PERI-: around
   peripatetic, perambulate, pericardium, period, perimeter, peripheral, peristalsis, periscope

4. AB-: away
   abdicate, abscond, abduct, aberration, absolve, abject, abscess, abomination

5. ACRI: bitter
   acrimony, acrid, acrimonious

6. BELLUM-: war
   belligerent, bellicose, rebel, rebellion

7. AM-, AMICUS: friend
   amiable, amicable, enemy, inimical, amity

8. ANTHRO-: mankind
   anthropology, anthropocentric, philanthropist, misanthrope

9. MUNUS: gift
   munificent, immunity, remuneration

10. TROPH: nourishment
    atrophy, phototroph, heterotroph, autotroph, dystrophy

11. PRO-: forward, forth
    procrastinate, prolific, prophesy, propagate, propensity, profound, provoke, provocative

12. PHON: sound
    cacophony, phonetic, symphony, euphonious

13. PURG-: to clean
    expurgate, purge, purgatory, spurge

14. PEL: to push
    compel, impel, expel, propulsion

15. SEQUI: to follow
    obsequious, prosecute, pursue, segue, subsequent

Exercise Set III

1. Y
2. Y
3. N
4. N
5. Y
6. itinerant
7. torpid
8. decorum
9. raze
10. deplete
11. porous
12. ambulatory
13. altruism
14. incite
15. undermine
16. noisome
17. vulnerable
18. static
19. abort
20. impel
21. amicable
22. pugnacious
23. jettison
24. deplorable
25. hiatus
26. torpid
27. abdication
28. volatility
29. altruistically
30. pugnacity
31. lethargic
32. efface
33. atrophy
34. moratorium
35. munificent
36. belligerent
37. obsequious
38. deviate
39. irascible
40. gregarious
41. acrimony

Vocabulary Unit 4

Vocabulary Lesson 22: Show Off!

Today's roots:	*ped, paedere* instruct	*grandis* great, big
	ostentare to display	*pomp* splendor

❑ *pedantic* (adj)   showy about knowledge (*paedere* to instruct)

Kim's **pedantic** teaching style bothers her students; she uses bizarre vocabulary words nobody understands.
Synonyms: *didactic, egotistic*

❑ *grandiose* (adj)   pretentious; ridiculously exaggerated (*grandis* great)

The castle's foyer was the most **grandiose** of its kind, adorned with crystal chandeliers and gilded banisters.
Synonyms: *ostentatious, flamboyant, lofty*   Antonym: *humble*

❑ *bombastic* (adj)   pompous; using inflated language

The **bombastic** language in the mayor's campaign speech made her seem arrogant and disconnected from the public.
Synonyms: *grandiose, overblown*   Antonyms: *understated, reserved*

❑ *braggart* (n)   one who boasts; a showoff (*braguer* to show off)

No one likes a braggart; it's better to be modest and humble about your successes.
Synonym: *egotist*

❑ *ostentatious* (adj)   showy; pretentious (*ostentare* to display + *-ious* full of)

That solid gold statue is the most **ostentatious** display of wealth I have ever seen.
Synonyms: *gaudy, grandiose, garish*   Antonyms: *understated, reserved*

❑ *pompous* (adj)   possessing excessive self-esteem; pretentious (*pomp* splendor + *-ous* full of)

His **pompous,** holier-than-thou attitude annoyed all of his classmates.
Synonyms: *conceited, self-centered, pontifical*   Antonyms: *modest, self-effacing, humble*

❑ *swagger* (v)   to walk or strut in an arrogant manner

Having beat their crosstown rivals handily, the players **swaggered** back to the locker room.
Synonyms: *brag, strut*

❑ *lofty* (adj)   haughty; overly proud

Synonyms: *cavalier, pretentious*

❑ *garish* (adj)   flashy; loud

Synonyms: *ornate, ostentatious, gaudy*

❑ *ornate* (adj)   overly decorated (*ornatus* to adorn)

Synonyms: *ostentatious, opulent, gaudy*

❑ *opulence* (adj)   luxuriousness (*opulentus* wealthy)

Synonyms: *grandeur, affluence*

❑ *pretentious* (adj)   ostentatious

Synonyms: *gaudy, grandiose, garish*

❑ *baroque* (adj)   extravagantly ornate and convoluted in style

Synonyms: *flamboyant, florid*

Vocabulary Lesson 23: Like a Pit Bull

| **Today's roots:** | *tract* pull | *tenax* holding fast |
| | *ob-* against | *per-* very |

- ❏ *dogged* (adj)   determined; unwilling to give up

  Outmanned and overmatched, the **dogged** fighters nevertheless refused to surrender the Alamo.
  Synonyms: *tenacious, inexorable*   Antonyms: *yielding, irresolute*

- ❏ *inexorable* (adj)   relentless (*in-* not + *exorabilis* able to be swayed)

  Inexorable in his wooing, Jason vowed to send Kathy roses every day until she accepted his prom invitation.
  Synonyms: *obstinate, dogged*   Antonyms: *yielding, irresolute*

- ❏ *obstinate* (adj)   stubborn (*obstinatus* to stand stubbornly)

  No matter what she tried, she could not make her **obstinate** husband change his mind.
  Synonyms: *adamant, relentless, obdurate*   Antonyms: *acquiescent, obsequious*

- ❏ *intransigent* (adj)   uncompromising (*in-* not + *transigente* compromising)

  Pat's **intransigent** nature showed itself when he adamantly refused to shift his appointment from 5:00 to 5:05.
  Synonyms: *obstinate, intractable*   Antonyms: *concordant, accommodating, complaisant*

- ❏ *contentious* (adj)   quarrelsome (*contendere* to strive after + *-ious* full of)

  Julia sighed as her excessively **contentious** husband started another unnecessary argument with their waiter.
  Synonyms: *pugnacious, belligerent*   Antonyms: *passive, conciliatory*

- ❏ *pertinacity* (n)   stubbornness (*per-* very + *tenax* holding fast)

  Kyle showed incredible **pertinacity** after breaking his leg, making it back in time for the championship game.
  Synonyms: *doggedness, steadfastness*

- ❏ *steadfast* (adj)   unchanging; unswerving (*stede* stand + *foest* firmly fixed)

  Despite many hardships, the team was **steadfast** in its pursuit of the summit.
  Synonyms: *obdurate, inexorable*   Antonyms: *fickle, vacillatory*

- ❏ *recalcitrant* (adj)   stubbornly rebellious

  Synonyms: *defiant, stubborn, wayward*

- ❏ *tenacious* (adj)   holding firmly; persistent (*tenax* holding fast)

  Synonyms: *persistent, steadfast, resolute*

- ❏ *disputatious* (adj)   inclined to arguing (*disputare* to argue)

  Synonyms: *contentious, litigious, polemical*

- ❏ *obdurate* (adj)   intractable; not easily persuaded (*obdurare* to harden)

  Synonyms: *inexorable, dogged*

- ❏ *intractable* (adj)   hard to manage; stubborn (*in-* not + *tract* pull)

  Synonyms: *obstinate, headstrong*

- ❏ *adamant* (adj)   refusing to yield (*adamas* unbreakable)

  Synonyms: *inexorable, obdurate*

- ❏ *litigious* (adj) prone to bringing lawsuits (*lis-* lawsuit + *agere* to drive)

  Synonym: *contentious*

Vocabulary Lesson 24: You're Good at That!

Today's roots:	*apt* fit	*summus* highest
	para- beyond	*dexter* skillful

❑ *adroit* (adj)   dexterous; skillful

An **adroit** con man, Clarence knew how to fool even the most skeptical eye.
Synonyms: *deft, proficient*   Antonyms: *clumsy, inept*

❑ *unerring* (adj)   committing no mistakes; perfect (*un-* not + *err* to make a mistake)

Her **unerring** sense of direction always puts her in the right place even if she has never been there before.
Synonym: *infallible*   Antonym: *inferior*

❑ *adept* (adj)   highly skilled

Roberto, an **adept** mathematician, completed the outrageously difficult calculus final in just 25 minutes.
Synonyms: *dexterous, adroit*   Antonyms: *incompetent, clumsy*

❑ *aptitude* (n)   a natural ability; intelligence (*apt* fit)

Kenneth showed a great **aptitude** for computers as a child, designing complex programs at the age of ten.
Synonyms: *competence, expertise*   Antonyms: *ineptitude, incompetence*

❑ *paragon* (n)   a model of excellence; perfection (*para-* beyond)

The head of several charities, Susan is the **paragon** of philanthropy.
Synonyms: *prototype; epitome*

❑ *deft* (adj)   adroit, skillful

The graceful ballerina kept from tripping on stage by **deftly** avoiding the poorly placed electrical wires.
Synonyms: *proficient, adroit*   Antonyms: *clumsy, inept, awkward*

❑ *preeminent* (adj)   outstanding

A **preeminent** psychologist, Dr. Carter is often asked to lend his expertise on difficult cases.
Synonyms: *unsurpassed, paramount*   Antonym: *inferior*

❑ *expertise* (n)   knowledge or skill in a particular area

Synonyms: *prowess, savvy, bailiwick*

❑ *discerning* (adj)   showing good judgment or keen insight (*dis-* off + *cernere* distinguish)

Synonyms: *astute, judicious, sage*

❑ *agility* (n)   nimbleness (*agilis* to move)

Synonyms: *spryness, litheness*

❑ *consummate* (adj)   perfect in every respect (*con-* with + *summus* highest)

Synonym: *impeccable*

❑ *dexterous* (adj)   skillful with the hands (*dexter* skillful + *-ous* full of)

Synonyms: *adroit, adept*

❑ *impeccable* (adj)   flawless (*im-* not + *peccare* to sin)

Synonyms: *immaculate, infallible, transcendent*

❑ *precocious* (adj)   unusually advanced or mature in development (especially in mental attitude)

Vocabulary Lesson 25: Bad and Worse

Today's roots:	*mal*	bad, evil	*vol*	wish
	mis	bad, wretched, hatred	*anthro*	humankind

❑ **nefarious** (adj)   wicked; sinful (*ne-* not + *fas* lawful)

Cinderella's **nefarious** stepsisters took joy in making her do their daily chores.
Synonyms: *infamous, odious*

❑ **repugnant** (adj)   offensive; repulsive (*re-* back + *pugnare* to fight)

Christopher's mother found his superstition of not bathing after games **repugnant.**
Synonyms: *abhorrent, vile, abominable*   Antonyms: *alluring, admirable*

❑ **infamous** (adj)   famous for bad deeds; notorious (*in-* not + *famosus* celebrated)

The **infamous** "El Héctor" was remembered for the way he tortured the poor villagers of Santa Potula.
Synonyms: *contemptible, ignominious*   Antonym: *noble*

❑ **odious** (adj)   worthy of dislike; arousing feelings of dislike (*odiosus* hateful)

Jimmy was no longer afraid to go to school once the **odious** bully was suspended.
Synonyms: *abhorrent, loathsome, repugnant*   Antonyms: *delightful, laudable*

❑ **malevolent** (adj)   wishing harm to others; evil (*mal-* evil + *vol* wish)

The **malevolent** dictator smiled as he ordered his soldiers to burn down the church.
Synonym: *sinister*   Antonym: *benevolent*

❑ **malefactor** (n)   an evildoer (*mal-* evil + *facere* to perform)

Superman has found and stopped many a **malefactor** before the crime could actually be committed.
Synonyms: *scamp, delinquent*   Antonym: *benefactor*

❑ **abominable** (adj)   loathsome; unpleasant

His **abominable** behavior at the game included excessive drinking, loud swearing, and the removal of his clothes.
Synonyms: *contemptible, vile*   Antonyms: *delightful, laudable*

❑ **avarice** (n)   extreme greed
Synonyms: *miserliness, penuriousness*

❑ **bigotry** (n)   intolerance toward those who are different

❑ **hypocrite** (n)   one who says one thing but does another (*hypokrites* Gr pretender)

❑ **miserly** (adj)   lacking generosity (*mis-* wretched)
Synonyms: *avaricious, penurious*

❑ **inimical** (adj)   unfriendly (*in-* not + *amicus* friend)
Synonyms: *antagonistic, hostile*

❑ **curmudgeon** (n)   a cranky person

❑ **misanthrope** (n)   one who hates humankind (*mis-* hatred + *anthro* humankind)

❑ **perfidy** (n)   deliberate breach of trust; treachery

Vocabulary Lesson 26: Ripped Off

| Today's roots: | *sub-, subter-* under, secretly | *fugere* to flee |
| | *larecin* theft | *machina* device |

❏ *charlatan* (n)   a fraud; a quack (*chiarlatino* a quack)

June's family warned her that Chaz was a **charlatan** only pretending to be a successful lawyer.
Synonyms: *imposter, con man, swindler*

❏ *ruse* (n)   a crafty scheme

The clever criminal came up with a flawless **ruse** to steal the money from the bank.
Synonyms: *strategem, machination*

❏ *subterfuge* (n)   a scheme; an attempt to deceive (*subter* secretly + *fugere* to flee)

It takes real **subterfuge** to sneak anything past Principal Guber; it's like he is able to see your every move.
Synonyms: *surreptitiousness, strategem, ploy*   Antonyms: *forthrightness, candor*

❏ *dupe* (n)   one who is easily deceived

The con artist has a knack for picking the perfect **dupe,** someone who will easily fall for his scam.
Synonyms: *chump, pushover*

❏ *pilfer* (v)   to steal

The looters **pilfered** countless items from the electronics store during the riot.
Synonyms: *embezzle, filch*

❏ *swindle* (v)   to cheat

The street hustler **swindled** the unsuspecting man, tricking him into buying a fake designer watch.
Synonyms: *bamboozle, hoodwink*

❏ *gullible* (adj)   easily deceived

The **gullible** teenager was easily tricked by her friends into believing that one of them was a secret agent.
Synonym: *naive*   Antonym: *astute*

❏ *embezzle* (v)   to steal money from one's employer

Synonyms: *loot, pilfer*

❏ *machination* (n)   a crafty scheme (*machina* device)

Synonyms: *strategem, ruse*

❏ *bilk* (v)   to cheat, to swindle

Synonyms: *hoodwink, defraud, cheat, fleece*

❏ *larceny* (n)   theft (*larecin* Fr theft)

Synonym: *thievery*

❏ *filch* (v)   to steal

Synonyms: *pilfer, embezzle*

❏ *fleece* (v)   to defraud of money, to swindle

Synonyms: *swindle, bilk, hoodwink, defraud*

Vocabulary Lesson 27: Good Guys and Bad Guys

Today's roots:	*archos*	leader, government	*theos*	god
	a-, an-	without	*pacis*	peace

❑ *hedonist* (n)   a pleasure seeker (*hedone* pleasure)

The '60s are often considered the age of the **hedonist,** a time when everyone felt they had the right to have fun.
Synonyms: *epicurean, epicure, sybarite, bon vivant*

❑ *ascetic* (n)   one who lives a holy life of self-denial (*asketes* monk)

Tim has spent years at a time as an **ascetic,** each time giving away all he owns and living on rice and prayer.
Synonym: *monk*

❑ *anarchist* (n)   one who opposes all political authority (*an-* without + *archos* leader)

Before the coup d'état, the dictator claimed to be an **anarchist;** that all changed once he was given power.
Synonyms: *insurgent, rebel*

❑ *pacifist* (n)   an individual who is opposed to violence (*pacis* peace + *facere* to make)

Forever a **pacifist,** Julie organized a rally protesting the war in the Middle East.
Synonym: *peace-seeker*   Antonyms: *warmonger, combatant*

❑ *atheist* (n)   one who does not believe that God exists (*a-* without + *theos* god)

Although she is an **atheist** and does not worship the Buddha, Cathy meditates with her Buddhist friends.

❑ *nihilist* (n)   one who rejects moral distinctions and knowable "truths"

Because she is a **nihilist,** Carrie likes to contend that the world may be a figment of her imagination.

❑ *despot* (n)   a tyrant; one who rules oppressively (*despotes* Gk absolute ruler)

The **despot** rules with reckless abandon, doing only what he wants, with no concern for the citizens.
Synonyms: *tyrant, oppressor*

❑ *narcissist* (n)   one in love with his/her own image (from Narcissus, who fell in love with himself)

❑ *zealot* (n)   one who engages passionately in a cause

Synonyms: *enthusiast, fanatic, devotee*

❑ *sybarite* (n)   an individual who seeks luxury

Synonym: *hedonist*

❑ *pessimist* (n)   an individual who focuses on the negative side of a situation (*pessimus* worst)

Synonyms: *alarmist, Cassandra, defeatist*

❑ *optimist* (n)   one who focuses on the positive side of a situation (*optimus* best)

Synonyms: *idealist, Pollyanna, Pangloss, Candide*

❑ *fanatic* (n)   one who shows extreme enthusiasm for a cause (*fanaticus* enthusiastic)

Synonyms: *extremist, radical, zealot, enthusiast*

Vocabulary Lesson 28: That's Better

Today's roots:	*culpa* blame	*placare* to please
	ex-, e- out	*mollis* soft

❑ *vindicate* (v)   to clear from blame

The adroit defense lawyer was able to **vindicate** her client of all charges, and he was set free.
Synonyms: *exonerate, absolve*   Antonym: *convict*

❑ *assuage* (v)   to soothe anger or pain; to satisfy a hunger (*suavis* agreeable, sweet)

If your dog gets stung by a bee, place a wet washcloth on the area to **assuage** the pain.
Synonyms: *pacify, appease, quench, allay*   Antonyms: *provoke, vex, exacerbate*

❑ *mollify* (v)   to soothe the anger of (*mollis* soft)

The waiter attempted to **mollify** the angry customer by offering him a free dessert with his dinner.
Synonyms: *assuage, appease, placate, conciliate*   Antonyms: *rile, provoke*

❑ *exonerate* (v)   to clear from accusation (*ex-* out + *onus* burden)

When the principal found the spray paint in Rex's locker, Timmy was **exonerated** of all graffiti charges.
Synonyms: *acquit, exculpate, absolve*   Antonym: *incriminate*

❑ *placate* (v)   to soothe; to mollify (*placare* to please)

The mother attempted to **placate** her crying baby by handing him his favorite teddy bear.
Synonyms: *pacify, assuage, conciliate, appease*   Antonyms: *enrage, provoke*

❑ *exculpate* (v)   to free from blame (*ex-* out + *culpa* blame)

Although the DNA evidence did not identify the killer, it did **exculpate** the police's primary suspect.
Synonyms: *acquit, disculpate, exonerate*   Antonyms: *impeach, convict*

❑ *anesthetic* (n)   something that reduces sensation (*an-* without + *aisthesis* Gk feeling)

Before closing the cut, the doctor administered an **anesthetic** to numb the area around the wound.
Synonym: *palliative*

❑ *pacify* (v)   to soothe the agitation or anger of (*pacis* peace)

Synonyms: *appease, conciliate*

❑ *invigorate* (v)   to energize (*in-* in + *vigor* liveliness + *-ate* to do)

Synonyms: *stimulate, rejuvenate*

❑ *alleviate* (v)   to relieve (think of "Aleve" to relieve body aches)

Synonyms: *assuage, allay*

❑ *emollient* (n)   a substance that softens (*mollis* soft)

❑ *absolve* (v)   to pardon (*ab-* from + *solvere* to loosen)

Synonyms: *exculpate, acquit*

❑ *placid* (adj)   peaceful; calm (*placare* to please)

Synonyms: *serene, tranquil*

❑ *mitigate* (v)   to make less severe; to lessen the force of

Vocabulary Unit 4 Exercise Set I

Time—8 minutes
For each question, select the best answer among the choices given. Note any vocabulary words to review on the Hit List below.

1. The ------ soldiers were commended for their refusal to surrender even when survival seemed to be an impossibility.
   (A) bombastic
   (B) dogged
   (C) disputatious
   (D) infamous
   (E) dexterous

2. Five months after the surgical procedure, the patient requested a stronger pain medication to help ------ the daily discomfort she felt in her shoulder.
   (A) exonerate
   (B) alleviate
   (C) invigorate
   (D) perambulate
   (E) scrutinize

3. The ------ golden statues added to the front of the house were excessively ------ even for the pretentious family that lived there.
   (A) ornate . . ostentatious
   (B) opulent . . nefarious
   (C) insipid . . pompous
   (D) splenetic . . grandiose
   (E) gaudy . . mercurial

4. In an effort to ------ his bitter opponents, the President passed a law they had been pushing unsuccessfully for years.
   (A) consummate
   (B) mollify
   (C) vindicate
   (D) purge
   (E) invoke

5. Sally's ------ made her a ------ for many a con artist.
   (A) loftiness . . chump
   (B) infallibility . . curmudgeon
   (C) pacifism . . charlatan
   (D) placidity . . ruse
   (E) gullibility . . dupe

6. Despite having ruled the nation for thirty years as ------ and ------ dictator, the prime minister was remembered for his munificence during the food shortage of 1987.
   (A) an abominable . . beneficent
   (B) a repugnant . . magnanimous
   (C) an obstinate . . lithe
   (D) a steadfast . . benevolent
   (E) an odious . . malevolent

7. The deft way in which the lawyer was able to deflect the negative testimony to his favor showed why he is the ------ of prosecution.
   (A) paragon
   (B) conviction
   (C) braggart
   (D) machination
   (E) misanthrope

8. The resort island is a fantasy vacation spot for a ------; one has rarely seen so much luxury and splendor in one place.
   (A) sybarite
   (B) zealot
   (C) nihilist
   (D) narcissist
   (E) ascetic

9. When a basketball player commits ------ foul in a flagrant attempt to hurt a player, the referee calls a "technical foul" and the team that is fouled receives two foul shots and retains possession of the ball.
   (A) a preeminent
   (B) a peripheral
   (C) a masochistic
   (D) an inexorable
   (E) an egregious

10. The young scamp has always shown ------ for larceny, having successfully ------ his first purse at the young age of six.
    (A) an equanimity . . filched
    (B) a bigotry . . bilked
    (C) an aptitude . . pilfered
    (D) a predilection . . exculpated
    (E) an agility . . razed

HIT LIST

Vocabulary Unit 4 Exercise Set II

Write the meaning next to each root, and then write as many words as you can that contain the root.

1. GRANDIS_____

2. SUB-_____

3. SUAVIS_____

4. PACIS_____

5. SUMMUS_____

6. APT_____

7. PUGNARE_____

8. MIS_____

9. DEXTER_____

10. TRACT_____

11. CULPA_____

12. MOLLIS_____

13. THEOS_____

14. PLACARE_____

15. PED_____

Vocabulary Unit 4 Exercise Set III

1. Is an *ostentatious* person humble?   Y N

2. Is a *deft* person good at what she does?   Y N

3. Is a *recalcitrant* person *obsequious*?   Y N

4. Does an *anarchist* resist authority?   Y N

5. Is an *infamous* person known for   Y N
   kind things?

Write the word with the given meaning.

6. a fraud   c_____

7. showy about knowledge   p_____

8. a pleasure seeker   h_____

9. nimbleness   a_____

10. famous for bad deeds   i_____

11. to steal   p_____

12. luxuriousness   o_____

13. to clear from blame   v_____

14. worthy of dislike   o_____

15. to clear from blame   e_____

16. unswerving   s_____

17. a substance that softens   e_____

18. a crafty scheme   m_____

19. using inflated language   b_____

20. a resentful person   c_____

21. a tyrant   d_____

22. skillful   a_____

23. determined   d_____

24. relentless   i_____

25. one who seeks luxury   s_____

Write the correct form of the italicized word.

26. the quality of being *recalcitrant*

_____

27. characterized by *agility*

_____

28. characteristic of *hypocrites*

_____

29. That which an *anarchist* seeks

_____

30. To achieve *vindication*

_____

Write the word with the given root.

31. wishing harm to others (*vol*)

_____

32. stubbornness (*per*)

_____

33. natural ability (*apt*)

_____

34. a scheme (*subter*)

_____

35. to soothe (*suavis*)

_____

36. difficult to manipulate (*tract*)

_____

37. to soothe (*mollis*)

_____

38. wicked (*fas*)

_____

39. to free from blame (*culp*)

_____

40. model of excellence (*para*)

_____

41. lacking generosity (*mis*)

_____

Unit 4 Exercise Set I Answer Key

1. **B** If the soldiers are being *commended,* they must have done something good, which means that the missing word is positive. The phrase *refusal to surrender* tells us that *dogged* is the best choice.

   bombastic = pompous
   dogged = refusing to surrender
   disputatious = argumentative
   infamous = famous for evil acts
   dexterous = skillful with the hands

2. **B** The patient is having a lot of pain and discomfort and wants to get rid of it. *Alleviate* is a perfect fit.

   exonerate = to clear of blame
   alleviate = to lessen
   invigorate = to give strength to
   perambulate = to move around
   scrutinize = to examine closely

3. **A** The phrase *even for the pretentious family* leads us to believe that these statues must be quite pretentious. You want to pick words that relate to pretentiousness and luxury for both blanks.

   ornate = overly decorated; *ostentatious* = showy
   opulent = luxurious; *nefarious* = wicked
   insipid = dull; *pompous* = arrogant
   splenetic = irritable; *grandiose* = pretentious
   gaudy = showy; *mercurial* = changing

4. **B** The opponents are *bitter,* which means that they are quite unhappy about something. They have been trying to get a particular law passed, and finally this President helps them pass the law. You want a word that means to *soothe* or *please.*

   consummate = to make perfect
   mollify = to soothe the anger of
   vindicate = to clear from blame
   purge = to get rid of
   invoke = to call into being

5. **E** Con artists like to take advantage of people. Both words should describe a person who is easily taken advantage of. *Gullible* and *dupe* fit the best.

   loftiness = excessive pride; *chump* = a pushover
   infallibility = perfection; *curmudgeon* = resentful person
   pacifism = love of peace; *charlatan* = a fraud
   placidity = calm; *ruse* = a crafty scheme
   gullibility = easily fooled; *dupe* = a pushover

6. **E** *Despite* implies that the second half of the sentence should provide a contrast to the first. The leader is remembered for his munificence, or generosity, which is a positive quality. Therefore the two words should be negative.

   abominable = terrible; *beneficent* = doing good, kind
   repugnant = offensive; *magnanimous* = generous
   obstinate = stubborn; *lithe* = agile
   steadfast = determined; *benevolent* = kind
   odious = worthy of hate; *malevolent* = evil

7. **A** The lawyer *deftly* (skillfully) turns something that is negative into his advantage. This must mean that he is quite good at what he does. The word choice that best fits this is *paragon.*

   paragon = the model of perfection
   conviction = strongly held belief
   braggart = one who boasts
   machination = a crafty scheme
   misanthrope = a hater of humankind

8. **A** The sentence tells us that the resort island is filled with *luxury and splendor.* Who would love that? A *sybarite.*

   sybarite = an individual who seeks luxury
   zealot = one who engages passionately in a cause
   nihilist = one who does not believe anything can truly exist
   narcissist = a person in love with his or her own image
   ascetic = a person who lives a life of self-denial

9. **E** The technical foul is called when a player creates a foul that is obvious and *flagrant. Egregious* is a perfect choice.

   preeminent = outstanding
   peripheral = on the side
   masochistic = enjoying one's own pain
   inexorable = relentless
   egregious = flagrant, blatant

10. **C** A scamp is a mischievous person with a tendency toward crime. The word *having* indicates that the second word should support the first.

    equanimity = calmness; *filched* = stole
    bigotry = intolerance towards others; *bilked* = stole
    aptitude = talent; *pilfered* = stole
    predilection = preference; *exculpated* = freed from blame
    agility = swiftness; *razed* = completely destroyed

Unit 4 Exercise Sets II and III Answer Key

Exercise Set II

1. **GRANDIS:** great, big
   grandeur, grandparent, grandiose, grandiloquent

2. **SUB:** under, secretly
   subtle, subcutaneous, subliminal, subterfuge, subservient, subconscious

3. **SUAVIS:** agreeable, sweet
   assuage, suave, sweet

4. **PACIS:** peace
   pacifist, peace, pacify, pacific

5. **SUMMUS:** highest
   summit, consummate, sum

6. **APT:** fit
   inept, aptitude, apt, adapt

7. **PUGNARE:** to fight
   pugnacity, impugn, pugnacious, repugnant

8. **MIS:** bad, wretched, hatred
   miserly, miserable, misanthrope, miser, misery, misogyny

9. **DEXTER:** skillful
   dexterity, dexterous, ambidextrous

10. **TRACT:** to pull
    subtract, abstract, attract, distract, contract, traction, intractable, tractor

11. **CULPA:** blame
    exculpate, inculpate, disculpate, culprit, culpable

12. **MOLLIS:** soft
    emollient, mollify

13. **THEOS:** god
    atheist, theology, enthusiasm, pantheist, theocracy, monotheism

14. **PLACARE:** to please
    placate, placid, placebo, complacent, complaisant, plea, please, displease

15. **PED:** instruct
    pedagogue, pedantic, pedant

Exercise Set III

1. N
2. Y
3. N
4. Y
5. N
6. charlatan
7. pedantic
8. hedonist
9. agility
10. infamous
11. pilfer
12. opulence
13. vindicate
14. odious
15. exonerate or exculpate
16. steadfast
17. emollient
18. machination
19. bombastic
20. curmudgeon
21. despot
22. adroit or adept
23. dogged
24. inexorable
25. sybarite
26. recalcitrance
27. agile
28. hypocritical
29. anarchy
30. vindicate
31. malevolent
32. pertinacity
33. aptitude
34. subterfuge
35. assuage
36. intractable
37. mollify
38. nefarious
39. exculpate
40. paragon
41. miserly

Vocabulary Unit 5

Vocabulary Lesson 29: Make Me!

Today's roots:	*ligare*	to bind	*vocare*	to call
	ducere	to lead	*pro-*	forth

❑ *cajole* (v)　to persuade by using flattery

The clever eight-year-old girl successfully **cajoled** her parents into taking her to Disney World.
Synonyms: *coax, wheedle, deceive*

❑ *exhort* (v)　to urge strongly　(*ex-* thoroughly + *hortari* to urge)

The doctor **exhorted** his patient to stop smoking by explaining how dangerous a habit it really was.
Synonyms: *provoke, instigate, rouse*　　Antonyms: *inhibit, discourage*

❑ *coerce* (v)　to persuade through the use of force

The bully **coerced** the smaller boy into handing over his lunch money with threats of wedgies and deadarms.
Synonyms: *compel, intimidate*

❑ *induce* (v)　to cause　(*in-* in + *ducere* to lead)

After thirty-six hours of labor, the doctors decided to **induce** the baby's birth with medication.
Synonyms: *sway, incite, impel*　　Antonyms: *curb, stall*

❑ *coax* (v)　to persuade by using flattery

The charming man used well-placed compliments to **coax** the pretty waitress into meeting him for a drink.
Synonyms: *cajole, wheedle*

❑ *provoke* (v)　to stir up; to excite　(*pro-* forth + *vocare* to call)

Eric **provoked** his older brother into fighting by whacking him on the head with his action figure.
Synonyms: *irritate, rile, incite*　　Antonyms: *placate, assuage*

❑ *obligatory* (adj)　required　(*ob-* to + *ligare* to bind)

The **obligatory** jumps in the skating competition must be performed or the competitor loses points.
Synonyms: *mandatory, compulsory*　　Antonyms: *optional, elective*

❑ *wheedle* (v)　to influence by flattery

Synonyms: *coax, cajole*

❑ *goad* (v)　to urge into action

Synonyms: *spur, incite, catalyze*

❑ *begrudge* (v)　to give in to something reluctantly

Synonyms: *concede, acquiesce*

❑ *spur* (v)　to goad into action

Synonyms: *provoke, goad, incite*

❑ *prerequisite* (n)　a requirement (don't confuse with *perquisite:* a perk)

Synonym: *obligation*

❑ *resigned* (adj)　accepting of one's fate

Synonyms: *begrudging, acquiescent*

Vocabulary Lesson 30: Come to Your Senses!

Today's roots:	*audire* to hear	*palpare* to touch
	gustare to taste	*cernere* to separate

❑ **tactile** (adj)   able to be sensed by touch (*tactilis* to touch)

The petting zoo provides a fun **tactile** experience for children, allowing them to touch dozens of animals.
Synonym: *palpable*

❑ **olfactory** (adj)   relating to the sense of smell (*olere a* to smell of + *facere* to make)

For those with a strong **olfactory** sense, the spray of a skunk is extremely pungent.

❑ **gustatory** (adj)   relating to the sense of taste (*gustare* to taste)

The meal was a **gustatory** extravaganza; her taste buds were exploding from all the savory spices.

❑ **auditory** (adj)   relating to the sense of hearing (*audire* to hear)

Kris's **auditory** deterioration prevented him from appreciating the subtle tonality of the music.
Synonym: *aural*

❑ **discern** (v)   to perceive as separate; to sense keenly (*dis-* away + *cernere* distinguish, separate)

The fog made it difficult for me to **discern** how many people stood at the far end of the parking lot.
Synonyms: *perceive, distinguish, ascertain*

❑ **pungent** (adj)   having a sharp or irritating odor (*pungere* to sting)

Many find garlic breath to be so **pungent** that they avoid cooking with the herb entirely.
Synonyms: *piquant, zesty*

❑ **palpable** (adj)   detectable by touch (*palpare* to touch)

As the tightrope walker attempted to regain his balance, the tension in the audience was nearly **palpable.**
Synonyms: *tangible, tactile*

❑ **ascertain** (v)   to learn for certain

Synonym: *discern*

❑ **savory** (adj)   pleasant tasting; appetizing

Synonym: *palatable*

❑ **putrid** (adj)   rotten; having a foul odor (*putris* rotten)

Synonyms: *rancid, decayed*

❑ **myopic** (adj)   short-sightedness

Synonyms: *narrow-minded, injudicious, undiscerning*

❑ **perceive** (v)   to become aware

Synonyms: *discern, ascertain*

❑ **aural** (adj)   relating to the sense of hearing (*auris* ear)

Synonym: *auditory*

❑ **tangible** (adj)   detectable by touch; substantial (*tangere* to touch)

Synonyms: *palpable, concrete*

Vocabulary Lesson 31: Stop It!

Today's roots:	*ab-, abs-* from	*terrere* to frighten
	tenere hold	*suadere* to urge

❑ *thwart* (v) to stop something before it is able to succeed

Thanks to inside information, the police department was able to **thwart** the bank robbery before it even began.
Synonyms: *circumvent, stymie, foil*   Antonym: *abet*

❑ *abstain* (v) to refrain from action (*abs-* from + *tenere* to hold)

An alcoholic for twenty years, Robert was unable to **abstain** from drinking when offered a beer.
Synonyms: *forgo, eschew*   Antonym: *indulge*

❑ *deterrent* (n) something that acts to discourage (*de-* away + *terrere* to frighten)

The picture of the vicious lion baring his teeth was an effective **deterrent** against kids' reaching into the cage.
Synonyms: *hindrance, impediment*   Antonym: *incentive*

❑ *impede* (v) to slow the progress of, to block

The orange cones did not do much to **impede** the progress of the cars; they just drove right over them.
Synonyms: *hinder, obstruct*   Antonyms: *assist, expedite*

❑ *hinder* (v) to slow the progress of

The weed-killer sprayed on the garden successfully **hindered** the growth of the unwanted plants.
Synonyms: *impede, obstruct, thwart*   Antonyms: *promote, facilitate*

❑ *curtail* (v) to make less (*curtus* short)

In an effort to lose weight, Mark tried to **curtail** his ice cream consumption.
Synonym: *diminish*   Antonyms: *extend, boost*

❑ *impediment* (n) something that works to impede progress; a hindrance

Louise had a speech **impediment** that caused her to stutter, but that did not keep her from being a DJ.
Synonyms: *impedance, encumbrance, hindrance*   Antonym: *aid*

❑ *stymie* (v) to present an obstacle to

Synonyms: *hinder, impede*

❑ *dissuade* (v) to persuade not to do something (*dis-* against + *suadere* to urge)

Synonyms: *deter, divert*

❑ *refrain* (v) to hold back from doing (*re-* back + *frenare* to restrain)

Synonyms: *halt, inhibit*

❑ *abstinence* (n) the voluntary avoidance of something (*abs-* from + *tenere* to hold)

❑ *tentative* (adj) uncertain

The **tentative** schedule was not set in stone.
Synonyms: *cautious, diffident*

❑ *hamper* (v) to restrict the progress of

Synonyms: *impede, hinder*

❑ *abstemious* (adj) sparing or moderate in consumption

Vocabulary Lesson 32: Must Be the Money

Today's roots:	*pecunia* money	*parsi* to save
	pro- ahead	*indu* within

❑ **destitute** (adj)   completely penniless (*destitutus* abandoned)

The stock market collapse of 2000–2002 left many an adept investor **destitute.**
Synonyms: *impoverished, penniless*   Antonyms: *affluent, wealthy*

❑ **frugal** (adj)   economical; good with money (*frux* fruit, profit)

A **frugal** shopper does not make a purchase before checking many other places for a lower price.
Synonyms: *thrifty, parsimonious*   Antonyms: *squandering, prodigal*

❑ **remuneration** (n)   payment for services (*re-* back + *munerari* to give)

The job is tedious, but the **remuneration** is worthwhile—over fifty dollars per hour!
Synonyms: *income, earnings*

❑ **impecunious** (adj)   without money (*im-* not + *pecunia* money)

You would never guess that Marisa was so **impecunious** if you watched her spend money at the mall.
Synonyms: *destitute, penurious*   Antonyms: *affluent, wealthy*

❑ **improvident** (adj)   failing to provide for the future (*im-* not + *pro-* ahead + *videre* to see)

Despite once being a millionaire, Claudio was now broke due to his **improvident** spending decisions.
Synonyms: *prodigal, negligent, spendthrifty*   Antonyms: *thrifty, frugal*

❑ **parsimony** (n)   excessive thriftiness (*parsi-* to spare, save + *monium* an action, a condition)

Al's **parsimoniousness** reached an extreme when he hand-delivered a bill rather than spending money on a stamp.
Synonyms: *miserliness, stinginess*   Antonyms: *magnanimity, munificence*

❑ **venal** (adj)   able to be bribed (*venalis* that is for sale)

The local outlaws knew that the **venal** sheriff could be paid to let them escape.
Synonym: *corruptible*

❑ **thrifty** (adj)   economical; good with money

Synonyms: *frugal, provident, parsimonious*

❑ **pauper** (n)   an extremely poor individual (*pau* little + *parere* to get)

Synonym: *mendicant*

❑ **mercenary** (n)   one who gives his services to the highest bidder (*merces* pay, reward)

❑ **perquisite** (n)   payment or privilege received in addition to wages (**perk** for short)

Debra enjoyed the perquisites of being the newspaper's culture editor, such as free tickets to the opera and ballet.

❑ **insolvent** (adj)   bankrupt (*in-* not + *solvent* able to pay what one owes)

Synonym: *broke*

❑ **indigent** (adj)   impoverished, poor (*indu-* within + *egere* to need, want)

Synonym: *destitute*

❑ **pecuniary** (adj)   pertaining to money (*pecunia* money)

Vocabulary Lesson 33: Saw That Coming

Today's roots:	*pro-, pre-, fore-* before	*scientia* knowledge
	monere to warn	*por-* forward

❑ *prophecy* (n)   a prediction of the future (*pro-* before + *phanai* to speak)

The **prophecy** told of a boy who would soon be born to save the human race from extinction.
Synonyms: *divination, prognostication*

❑ *harbinger* (n)   a precursor

Many consider the robin to be a **harbinger** of spring.
Synonyms: *omen, forerunner*

❑ *augur* (v)   to predict the future (an *augur* in ancient Rome was an official who foretold events)

The "psychic network" claims to **augur** what is to come for its callers, but most believe it to be a hoax.
Synonyms: *prophesy, divine*

❑ *premonition* (n)   a forewarning (*pre-* before + *monere* to warn)

The traveler had a **premonition** of the upcoming disaster and refused to board the plane.
Synonyms: *presentiment, hunch*

❑ *portend* (v)   to give advance warning (*por-* forward + *tendere* to extend)

The weather service looks for atmospheric signs that **portend** violent storms.
Synonyms: *foretell, foreshadow*

❑ *prescient* (adj)   having knowledge of future events (*pre-* before + *scientia* knowledge)

The seemingly **prescient** gambler made a fortune at the racetrack, always knowing which horse would win.
Synonym: *clairvoyant*

❑ *omen* (n)   a sign of something to come

The nervous bride took the death of the minister who was to marry them as an **omen** that her marriage was doomed.
Synonyms: *portent, prognostication*

❑ *foresight* (n)   the ability to see things coming (*fore-* before)

Synonyms: *anticipation, forethought*

❑ *clairvoyant* (n)   one with great foresight (*clair-* clear + *voyant* seeing)

Synonyms: *visionary, psychic*

❑ *portent* (n)   an omen of a future event (*por-* forward + *tendere* to extend)

Synonym: *omen*

❑ *preempt* (v)   to block by acting first (*pre-* before)

Synonym: *anticipate*

❑ *premeditate* (v)   to plan ahead of time (*pre-* before + *meditari* to consider)

Synonym: *plot*

❑ *prophetic* (adj)   able to tell the future (*pro-* before + *phanai* to speak)

Synonym: *prescient*

❑ *bode* (v)   to be an omen for something

A red sky at dawn **bodes** ill for sailors.
Synonym: *portend*

Vocabulary Lesson 34: Old and Worn Out

Today's roots:	*arch*	ancient	*per-*	through
	ante-	before	*ob-*	away, against

❑ **archaic** (adj)   ancient (*arch* ancient)

The boat's **archaic** navigation system confused the young sailor, who knew how to read only the newer consoles.
Synonyms: *primitive, antiquated*   Antonyms: *modern, novel*

❑ **relic** (n)   an object from an ancient time (*re-* back + *linquere* to leave)

The **relic** found at the ancient burial site once served as a water pitcher for an Aztec family.
Synonyms: *artifact, remnant*

❑ **decrepit** (adj)   worn out from old age or use (*de-* down + *crepare* to break, to crack)

The **decrepit** swing set in the schoolyard had been used by four generations of children.
Synonyms: *feeble, battered, threadbare*

❑ **antiquated** (adj)   obsolete; outdated (*antiquus* ancient)

The computer technology in rural Italy is quite **antiquated;** even Internet access is rare.
Synonyms: *archaic, primitive*   Antonyms: *modern, novel*

❑ **antediluvian** (adj)   very old (*ante-* before + *diluvim* a flood, in reference to the Biblical flood)

The piece of pottery they found was an **antediluvian** bowl that was made over 4,000 years ago.
Synonyms: *primeval, archaic*   Antonyms: *modern, novel*

❑ **defunct** (adj)   no longer in existence (*defunctus* dead, off-duty)

Telegrams as a means of communication are **defunct;** the existence of email and telephones made them obsolete.
Synonyms: *dead, extinct*   Antonym: *extant*

❑ **perpetuate** (v)   to keep from dying out (*per-* through + *petere* to seek, go to)

The myth that cigarettes don't harm you has been **perpetuated** by the cigarette companies.
Synonyms: *immortalize, commemorate*

❑ **outmoded** (v)   out of fashion; obsolete

Synonyms: *anachronistic, obsolete*

❑ **artifact** (n)   an object of historical interest (*arte-* skill + *factum* thing made)

Synonyms: *relic, remnant*

❑ **obsolete** (adj)   outmoded (*ob-* away + *solere* to be used)

Synonyms: *anachronistic, antiquated*

❑ **dilapidated** (adj)   worn out

Synonyms: *decrepit, feeble*

❑ **threadbare** (adj)   shabby; worn down such that the threads show

Synonyms: *dilapidated, decrepit*

❑ **archive** (n)   a collection of historically interesting material (*arch* ancient)

Vocabulary Lesson 35: Feelings

Today's roots:	*pathos* emotion	*anti-* against
	con- with	*syn-, sym-* together

❑ **apathy** (n)   lack of feeling; lack of interest (*a-* without + *pathos* emotion)

Mark was **apathetic** about Stephanie's desire to keep her laptop clean; he put his fingerprints all over the screen.
Synonyms: *indifference, torpor*   Antonym: *intensity*

❑ **apprehensive** (adj)   anxious about what is to come

It is normal to feel **apprehensive** on the morning of your driver's test; it is a nerve-wracking experience.
Synonyms: *uneasy, concerned*   Antonyms: *fearless, intrepid, dauntless*

❑ **contrite** (adj)   repentant (*con-* with + *terere* to wear down)

The **contrite** murder suspect scored points with the judge, who appreciated her remorseful attitude.
Synonym: *remorseful*   Antonyms: *unrepentant, inveterate*

❑ **lament** (v)   to mourn, to show sorrow (*lamentum* a wailing)

The fans **lamented** the passing of John Lennon; they cried as if they had lost a brother.
Synonyms: *bemoan, grieve*   Antonym: *celebrate*

❑ **console** (v)   to comfort (*con-* with + *solari* to comfort)

There were many family members on hand to **console** the grieving widow at her husband's funeral.
Synonyms: *soothe, calm*   Antonyms: *enrage, provoke*

❑ **impassive** (adj)   lacking emotion (*im-* not + *passivus* capable of feeling)

Joy's **impassiveness** about her grades upset her parents; they wanted her to care more about her work.
Synonyms: *indifferent, apathetic*   Antonyms: *intense, demonstrative*

❑ **ignominy** (n)   humiliation; shame

Football is so important in our town that dropping a pass in the end zone is more ignominious than going to prison.
Synonyms: *disgrace, dishonor*   Antonyms: *gratification, dignity*

❑ **pathos** (n)   pity; feeling of sorrow (*pathos* emotion)

Synonyms: *anguish, woe*

❑ **empathy** (n)   the ability to identify with another's feelings (*em-* in + *pathos* feeling)

❑ **penitent** (adj)   feeling remorse for one's actions

Synonyms: *repentant, contrite*

❑ **ambivalent** (adj)   having mixed feelings toward something (*ambi-* both)

Synonyms: *conflicted, irresolute*

❑ **poignant** (adj)   causing a sharp emotional response (*poindre* to prick)

Synonyms: *stirring, moving*

❑ **remorse** (n)   regret for past deeds (*re-* again + *mordere* to bite)

Synonyms: *anguish, contrition*

❑ **antipathy** (n)   strong feelings against something (*anti-* against + *pathos* feeling)

Vocabulary Unit 5 Exercise Set I

Time—8 minutes
For each question, select the best answer among the choices given. Note any vocabulary words to review on the Hit List below.

1. Elizabeth's assistant was ------ with his words and spoke only when it was absolutely necessary.
   (A) improvident
   (B) parsimonious
   (C) antiquated
   (D) clairvoyant
   (E) sympathetic

2. The salary Julia received for her job was unsatisfactory, but the ------ were phenomenal: a dental plan, five weeks of vacation, and a company car.
   (A) perquisites
   (B) harbingers
   (C) mercenaries
   (D) impediments
   (E) resolutions

3. In spite of his aggressive attempts to ------ us into doing something against the law, we were able to ------ from partaking in the illicit act.
   (A) goad . . refrain
   (B) cajole . . stagnate
   (C) coax . . rebound
   (D) impede . . abstain
   (E) dissuade . . recuperate

4. Because the team had been eliminated from the playoffs, they played with ------ in their final five games, losing by an average of forty points per game.
   (A) fortitude
   (B) apathy
   (C) dread
   (D) vigor
   (E) resolution

5. The wise old man who lived at the top of the mountain is visited often by villagers looking for him to use his ------ powers to ------ their future.
   (A) olfactory . . augur
   (B) tactile . . portend
   (C) prescient . . divine
   (D) prophetic . . console
   (E) clairvoyant . . perjure

6. A departure from the bland food and mundane atmosphere that characterized our recent dining experiences, Chez Henri provided ------ cuisine and ------ ambience.
   (A) pungent . . a hedonistic
   (B) savory . . a transcendent
   (C) piquant . . an artificial
   (D) obsolete . . a supreme
   (E) palatable . . an imperious

7. Management's decision to raise the salaries of the workers was more pragmatic than ------; the executives didn't want so much to be generous as to keep the assembly lines moving.
   (A) magnanimous
   (B) mellifluous
   (C) rigid
   (D) masochistic
   (E) frugal

8. After giving birth to her first child, the woman was finally able to ------ with her mother about the pain and discomfort that come with childbirth.
   (A) empathize
   (B) collaborate
   (C) perpetuate
   (D) premeditate
   (E) associate

9. The defendant's contrite behavior was not an act; he truly felt great ------ for the crime of which he was accused.
   (A) apprehension
   (B) indigence
   (C) foresight
   (D) bliss
   (E) remorse

10. Even though she was unable to walk without a limp, she did not allow this ------ to ------ her ability to run short sprints for the track team.
    (A) deterrent . . spur
    (B) barrier . . impel
    (C) abstinence . . thwart
    (D) impediment . . hamper
    (E) pathos . . hinder

HIT LIST
_____
_____
_____
_____
_____

_____
_____
_____
_____
_____

Vocabulary Unit 5 Exercise Set II

Write the meaning next to each root, and then write as many words as you can that contain the root.

1. PATHOS_____
   _____
   _____
   _____
   _____

2. DUCERE_____
   _____
   _____
   _____
   _____

3. TERRERE_____
   _____
   _____
   _____
   _____

4. ANTI-_____
   _____
   _____
   _____
   _____

5. AUDIRE_____
   _____
   _____
   _____
   _____

6. FORE-_____
   _____
   _____
   _____
   _____

7. SCIENTIA_____
   _____
   _____
   _____
   _____

8. VOCARE_____
   _____
   _____
   _____
   _____

9. POR-_____
   _____
   _____
   _____
   _____

10. SUADERE_____
    _____
    _____
    _____
    _____

11. MONERE_____
    _____
    _____
    _____
    _____

12. TENERE_____
    _____
    _____
    _____
    _____

13. PALPARE_____
    _____
    _____
    _____
    _____

14. INDU_____
    _____
    _____
    _____
    _____

15. CERNERE_____
    _____
    _____
    _____
    _____

Vocabulary Unit 5 Exercise Set III

1. Can you be *parsimonious* with words?   Y N
2. Is an *omen* necessarily bad?   Y N
3. Does something *savory* taste good?   Y N
4. Is something *obsolete* new?   Y N
5. Does someone *thrifty* waste money?   Y N

Write the word with the given meaning.

6. lacking emotion   i_____
7. repentant   c_____
8. to foretell   p_____
9. without money   i_____
10. outmoded   o_____
11. capable of being felt   p_____
12. to make less   c_____
13. to cause by persuasion   i_____
14. ancient   a_____
15. a forewarning   p_____
16. relating to taste   g_____
17. to refrain from action   a_____
18. to persuade with flattery   c_____
19. deeply emotional   p_____
20. economical   t_____
21. to urge strongly   e_____
22. humiliation   i_____
23. payment   r_____
24. able to be bribed   v_____
25. to stop before it begins   t_____

Write the correct form of the italicized word.

26. showing *apathy*

   _____

27. to act as a *deterrent*

   _____

28. the act of *abstaining*

   _____

29. the act of touching something that is *palpable*

   _____

30. the act of *cajoling*

   _____

Write the word with the given root.

31. to urge into motion (*citare*)

   _____

32. a prediction of the future (*pro-*)

   _____

33. lacking feeling (*a-*)

   _____

34. relating to smell (*olere*)

   _____

35. extremely poor individual (*pau*)

   _____

36. to comfort (*solari*)

   _____

37. economical (*frux*)

   _____

38. to stir up (*vocare*)

   _____

39. worn out (*crepare*)

   _____

40. to make less (*curtus*)

   _____

41. regret (*mordere*)

   _____

Unit 5 Exercise Set I Answer Key

1. **B**   If the assistant *only spoke when it was absolutely necessary*, then he was *frugal* or *sparing* with his words.
   improvident = not economical
   parsimonious = excessively thrifty
   antiquated = very old
   clairvoyant = having great foresight
   sympathetic = feeling pity

2. **A**   The *but* indicates a contrast. Extra benefits like a dental plan, a vacation, and a car are called *perks* or *perquisites*.
   perquisite = a perk, a dividend
   harbinger = a sign of something to come
   mercenary = one who works for the highest bidder
   impediment = an obstruction
   resolution = firm determination

3. **A**   The phrase *in spite* indicates a contrast in the second half of the sentence. If he was *aggressive* in getting us to do something *illicit* (illegal), the contrast suggests that we didn't give in. Words like *persuade* and *stay away* would work.
   goad = to urge; *refrain* = to hold back from doing
   cajole = to persuade; *stagnate* = to remain still
   coax = to persuade; *rebound* = to bounce back
   impede = to block; *abstain* = to avoid something
   dissuade = to deter; *recuperate* = to recover

4. **B**   The sentence implies that the team has nothing left to play for. The fact that they also consistently lose by forty points indicates that they are playing with a *lack of heart*.
   fortitude = strength of mind; strength to endure
   apathy = lack of concern or effort
   dread = profound fear; anxious anticipation
   vigor = physical energy or strength
   resolution = firm determination

5. **C**   The word *future* is the key context clue. What can one do to the future? A *wise* man in particular might be able to *predict* it.
   olfactory = related to smell; *augur* = to predict the future
   tactile = touchable; *portend* = to predict the future
   prescient = clairvoyant; *divine* = to predict the future
   prophetic = prescient; *console* = to comfort
   clairvoyant = able to predict future; *perjure* = to lie under oath

6. **B**   The word *departure* indicates a contrast, and the parallelism between the clauses sets up the contrast. The two words must be the opposite of *bland* and *mundane*, respectively.
   pungent = strong; *hedonistic* = pleasure-seeking
   savory = delicious; *transcendent* = inspiring
   piquant = spicy; *artificial* = not genuine
   obsolete = outmoded; *supreme* = great
   palatable = edible; *imperious* = overbearing

7. **A**   The second clause logically extends the idea of the first. The decision was done for *pragmatic* (practical) reasons rather than out of generosity to the employees. Look for a word that means *generous*.
   magnanimous = generous
   mellifluous = smooth-flowing
   rigid = inflexible
   masochistic = enjoying one's own pain
   frugal = thrifty; disinclined to waste money

8. **A**   The woman now knows first hand about the pain and discomfort associated with childbirth. Because she has now experienced what her mother went through, she can now *empathize* with her about the sensations.
   empathize = to identify with another's feelings
   collaborate = work together
   perpetuate = cause to continue
   premeditate = plan in advance

9. **E**   If the *contrite behavior was not an act*, then the defendant must truly feel regret for what was done.
   apprehension = nervousness
   indigence = neediness
   foresight = ability to see things coming
   bliss = extreme happiness
   remorse = regret

10. **D**   *Even though* indicates an unexpected twist. The inability to walk without a limp is certainly a nuisance. It would make sense that the first word should mean *hindrance* and the second word should mean *prevent*.
   deterrent = something that discourages; *spur* = to goad into action
   barrier = a block; *impel* = to urge
   abstinence = avoidance; *thwart* = to stop
   impediment = barrier; *hamper* = to hinder
   pathos = sorrow; *hinder* = to obstruct

Unit 5 Exercise Sets II and III Answer Key

Exercise Set II

1. PATHOS: emotion
   apathy, sympathy, empathy, osteopathy, pathogen, pathetic, psychopath

2. DUCERE: to lead
   induce, conduction, conducive, produce, deduce

3. TERRERE: to frighten
   deter, deterrent, terrible, terrify, terror, terrific

4. ANTI-: against
   antipathy, antibiotic, antonym, antiseptic, antagonist, antisocial

5. AUDIRE: to hear
   audition, auditorium, auditory, inaudible, audible

6. FORE-: before
   foremost, foretell, forethought, forehand, forecast, forebear, foresight

7. SCIENTIA: knowledge
   scientist, omniscient, prescient, conscientious

8. VOCARE: to call
   vocabulary, convocation, provoke, revoke, convoke, vocation, invoke, advocate, equivocate

9. POR-: forward
   portent, portend, portray

10. SUADERE: to urge
    sway, persuasion, persuade, dissuade

11. MONERE: to warn
    premonition, summon, admonish, monitor

12. TENERE: to hold
    sustain, abstain, contain, detain, entertain, tenable, tenacity, pertinacity, retain, obtain, pertain

13. PALPARE: to touch
    palpate, palpable, palpatation

14. INDU: in, within
    indigenous, industrial, indigent, industry

15. CERNERE: to separate
    discern, certain, concern, excrement, secretary

Exercise Set III

1. Y
2. N
3. Y
4. N
5. N
6. impassive
7. contrite
8. portend
9. insolvent, impecunious
10. obsolete
11. palpable
12. curtail
13. impel, induce
14. archaic
15. premonition
16. gustatory
17. abstain
18. cajole
19. poignant
20. thrifty
21. exhort
22. ignominy
23. remuneration
24. venal
25. thwart
26. apathetic
27. deter
28. abstinence
29. palpation
30. cajolery
31. incite
32. prophecy
33. apathetic
34. olfactory
35. pauper
36. console
37. frugal
38. provoke
39. decrepit
40. curtail
41. remorse

Vocabulary Unit 6

Vocabulary Lesson 36: What the Heck?

Today's roots:	*gradi*	to step, to go	*equi*	equal
	crypto	secret	*dis-*	apart

❑ **ambiguous** (adj)   unclear in meaning (*ambigere* to wander)

The teacher's **ambiguous** instructions left us with no idea of what we were supposed to do.
Synonyms: *vague, obscure*   Antonyms: *apparent, lucid*

❑ **obscure** (adj)   not easily understood; indistinct (*obscurus* darkness)

The comedian's jokes contained **obscure** references that left the audience confused and silent.
Synonyms: *vague, enigmatic, cryptic*   Antonyms: *evident, lucid*

❑ **equivocal** (adj)   deliberately ambiguous or misleading (*equi-* same + *vocare* to call)

The defendant's **equivocal** answers made it hard for the prosecutor to prove his case.
Synonyms: *evasive, indirect*   Antonyms: *straightforward, forthright, candid*

❑ **convoluted** (adj)   intricate and hard to follow (*con-* together + *volvere* to roll)

The instructions in this manual are so **convoluted** that I don't even know where to begin.
Synonyms: *cryptic, inscrutable, incomprehensible*   Antonyms: *coherent, intelligible*

❑ **cryptic** (adj)   enigmatic; mysterious (*crypto* concealed, secret)

The soldier's **cryptic** reply over the radio to his captain suggested that something was amiss.
Synonyms: *cryptic, obscure, incomprehensible*   Antonyms: *coherent, intelligible*

❑ **unfathomable** (adj)   impossible to comprehend (*un-* not + *fathom* to grasp)

The idea that time slows as our speed increases is **unfathomable** to most of us.
Synonyms: *baffling, impenetrable, inscrutable*   Antonyms: *coherent, intelligible*

❑ **nebulous** (adj)   vague; indefinite (*nebula* mist)

Bill's memory of the car accident was **nebulous;** he remembered only bits and pieces of the ordeal.
Synonyms: *hazy, unclear*   Antonym: *lucid*

❑ **enigma** (n)   a mystery or riddle (*oenigma* riddle)

Synonyms: *conundrum, riddle*

❑ **esoteric** (adj)   difficult to understand (Gr *esoterikos* belonging to an inner circle)

❑ **ramble** (v)   to wander aimlessly, either verbally or physically

Synonyms: *stray, babble*

❑ **desultory** (adj)   aimless; prone to random digressions (*desultorious* skipping about)

❑ **digress** (v)   to go off topic (*dis-* away + *gradi* to step, to go)

Synonyms: *diverge, deviate, ramble*

❑ **profound** (adj)   deep; insightful (*pro-* forth + *fundus* bottom)

Synonyms: *philosophical, sagacious*

Vocabulary Lesson 37: True or False?

Today's roots:	*verax* true	*candere* to shine
	genuinus natural	*apo-* away

❑ *candor* (n)   honesty; straightforwardness (*candere* to shine)

I appreciated my doctor's **candor;** I prefer a straightforward approach when discussing my health.
Synonyms: *forthrightness, frankness*   Antonyms: *disingenuousness, fraudulence, equivocation*

❑ *affect* (v)   to put on airs; to behave unnaturally

Hoping to fit in while in London, Jules **affected** a British accent.
Synonyms: *feign, impersonate*

❑ *veracity* (n)   truthfulness (*verax* true)

Since we can't test the **veracity** of his statements, we will never know for sure if he was telling the truth.
Synonyms: *sincerity, candor*   Antonyms: *fallacy, falsehood*

❑ *debunk* (v)   to expose something as fraudulent   (*bunkum* nonsense)

The DA knew that the cop was crooked and made it his mission to **debunk** the officer's claims.
Synonyms: *uncover, reveal*   Antonyms: *conceal, camouflage*

❑ *apocryphal* (adj)   of doubtful authenticity (*apo-* away + *kryptein* hide)

Before they found out it was a fake, the **apocryphal** Van Gogh painting sold for over a million dollars.
Synonyms: *counterfeit, forged*   Antonym: *authentic*

❑ *forthright* (adj)   honest; straightforward

The student's **forthright** admission of guilt was appreciated by the principal, who reduced his suspension.
Synonyms: *candid, frank*   Antonyms: *deceitful, treacherous*

❑ *disingenuous* (adj)   insincere; crafty (*dis-* away from + *genuinus* natural)

Daphne's expression of remorse was clearly **disingenuous,** because she did not feel any regret for her actions.
Synonyms: *deceitful, treacherous*   Antonyms: *forthright, candid*

❑ *candid* (adj)   straightforward; honest (*candere* to shine)

Synonyms: *frank, forthright*

❑ *dubious* (adj)   doubtful (*dubium* doubt)

Synonyms: *suspect, questionable*

❑ *prevaricate* (v)   to lie (*pre-* before + *varicare* to straddle)

Synonyms: *equivocate, fabricate*

❑ *verisimilitude* (n)   the quality of appearing to be true (*verax-* true + *similis* like)

❑ *outspoken* (adj)   candid and unsparing in speech

Synonyms: *forthright, frank*

❑ *fraudulent* (adj)   deceitful (*fraus* deceit)

Synonyms: *duplicitous; crooked*

❑ *facade* (n)   outward appearance; a false front (*faccia* face)

Synonyms: *superficiality, frontispiece*

Vocabulary Lesson 38: Arts and Entertainment

Today's roots:	*curare* to take care of	*levis* light in weight
	jocus joke	*para-* beside, beyond

❑ *mirth* (n)   merriment; laughter

The little boy could not contain his **mirth** when playing with the bubbles.
Synonyms: *jollity, levity, gaiety*   Antonyms: *melancholy, dejection, despondency*

❑ *aesthetic* (adj)   relating to beauty or a theory of beauty (*aisthetikos* Gr perception)

The beautiful colors that emerged from the crystal when struck by the sunlight were **aesthetically** pleasing.

❑ *satire* (n)   a mocking literary or dramatic work (*satira* a poetic medley)

Animal Farm by George Orwell is a **satire** that mocks socialism.
Synonyms: *burlesque, parody, lampoon, travesty, spoof*

❑ *curator* (n)   the individual in charge of a museum (*curare* to take care of)

The **curator** in charge of the Louvre in Paris controls the Mona Lisa, perhaps the world's most famous painting.

❑ *witticism* (n)   a clever or funny remark

Will Rogers was famous for his **witticisms** about American life.
Synonyms: *epigram, bon mot, quip, badinage*

❑ *jocular* (adj)   done in a joking way (*jocus* joke)

Jeff's **jocular** tone relaxed the visitors trapped in the elevator; he even made a few people laugh.
Synonyms: *facetious, waggish, salty*   Antonyms: *despondent, somber, morose, plaintive, lugubrious*

❑ *malapropism* (n)   the outrageous misuse of a word

Saying "for all intensive purposes" instead of "for all intents and purposes" is a classic example of a **malapropism.**
Synonyms: *misusage, solecism, catachresis*

❑ *levity* (n)   a lack of seriousness (*levis* light in weight)

Synonyms: *frivolity, flippancy*

❑ *bard* (n)   a skilled poet

Synonyms: *sonneteer, versifier*

❑ *parody* (n)   a spoof (*para-* beside + *ode* song)

Synonyms: *burlesque, lampoon, travesty, satire*

❑ *epic* (n)   a lengthy poem that celebrates the life of a hero (Gr *epos* word, story)

❑ *aesthete* (n)   a person interested in the pursuit of beauty (Gr *aisthetikos* sensitive)

❑ *dilettante* (n)   one who dabbles in an art (*dilettare* to delight)

Synonym: *amateur*

❑ *lampoon* (v)   to make fun of

Synonyms: *satirize, mock, parody*

Vocabulary Lesson 39: You're in Trouble

Today's roots:	*culpa* blame	*censura* judgment
	dictare to declare	*probus* honest, worthy

❑ *chastise* (v)   to punish or criticize (*castus* pure)

The congressman was **chastised** in the media for his ties to big business.
Synonyms: *condemn, rebuke*   Antonyms: *applaud, hail*

❑ *reprove* (v)   to scold (*re-* not + *probus* worthy)

The teacher **reproved** her students strongly for talking during her lecture.
Synonyms: *rebuke, berate, reprimand*   Antonyms: *hail, compliment, acclaim*

❑ *reprehensible* (adj)   worthy of blame or censure

The woman could not believe that her son would do something so **reprehensible** as torturing small animals.
Synonyms: *culpable, disgraceful, censurable*   Antonym: *laudable*

❑ *culpable* (adj)   deserving blame (*culpa* blame)

Although the DNA evidence clearly proved he was **culpable,** the defendant continued to claim innocence.
Synonyms: *guilty, blameworthy*   Antonyms: *innocent, blameless, sinless*

❑ *indict* (v)   to accuse of an offense (*dictare* to declare)

The mob boss was **indicted** on ten counts of money laundering.
Synonyms: *accuse, impeach*   Antonyms: *acquit, exonerate*

❑ *reproach* (v)   to blame; to express disapproval

After hitting the softball through the window, Ella was **reproached** by her mother for being so careless.
Synonyms: *censure, condemn, rebuke*   Antonyms: *compliment, commend*

❑ *rebuke* (v)   to scold (*re-* back + *buke* to strike)

Because Belinda was **rebuked** the last time she left her toys out, she cleaned up thoroughly to avoid another scolding.
Synonyms: *reprove, reproach, reprehend, reprimand, chide*

❑ *castigate* (v)   to punish severely

Synonyms: *reprimand, berate, chastise*

❑ *impeach* (v)   to accuse of wrongdoing (*im-* in + *pedica* shackle)

Synonyms: *indict, charge*

❑ *irreproachable* (adj)   beyond blame

Synonyms: *innocent, impeccable*

❑ *berate* (v)   to punish severely (*be-* thoroughly + *rate* to scold)

Synonyms: *reprimand, castigate, chastise*

❑ *culprit* (n)   one guilty of a crime (*culpa* blame)

Synonyms: *offender, criminal*

❑ *acquit* (v)   to clear of a charge (*a-* to + *quite* free)

Synonyms: *vindicate, exonerate*

❑ *reprimand* (v)   to scold (*reprimare* to reprove)

Synonyms: *reprove, castigate, censure*

Vocabulary Lesson 40: Working Hard

Today's roots:	*fatigare*	tire	*sedere*	to sit
	metus	fear	*integer*	whole

❑ *diligence* (n)   hard work and dedication (*diligentia* attentiveness)

Ty's **diligence** paid off when his boss gave him a promotion and a raise.
Synonyms: *assiduousness, industry, perseverance*   Antonyms: *laziness, indolence*

❑ *scrupulous* (adj)   careful, ethical (*scruples* ethical standards)

Always a **scrupulous** student, Simone made sure she got her assignments in on time.
Synonyms: *conscientious, honorable, meticulous*   Antonyms: *immoral, wanton*

❑ *meticulous* (adj)   attentive to detail (*metus* fear)

The accountant was incredibly **meticulous;** no detail ever slipped by her.
Synonyms: *thorough, painstaking*   Antonyms: *lackadaisical, cavalier*

❑ *indefatigable* (adj)   untiring (*in-* not + *fatigare* to tire)

Despite working 100 hours per week, the lawyer was **indefatigable,** remaining energetic about his job.
Synonyms: *tireless, unremitting, dogged*   Antonyms: *listless, lethargic*

❑ *spartan* (adj)   full of self-discipline (from Sparta whose army was known for its discipline and valor)

Alissa's **spartan** regimen included learning fifty new vocabulary words each week.
Synonyms: *ascetic, rigorous*   Antonyms: *cavalier, lackadaisical*

❑ *painstaking* (adj)   meticulous; paying great attention to detail

After eleven **painstaking** hours in the operating room, the surgeon declared the brain surgery a complete success.
Synonyms: *thorough, meticulous*   Antonyms: *lackadaisical, cavalier*

❑ *assiduous* (adj)   hard working (*sedere* to sit)

My parents are always telling me that my grades would improve if I were more **assiduous** in my studies.
Synonyms: *diligent, industrious*   Antonyms: *indolent, slothful*

❑ *prolific* (adj)   extremely productive (*pro-* forth + *facere* to make)

Synonyms: *productive, abundant*

❑ *integrity* (n)   honesty and virtue (*integer* whole)

Synonym: *purity*

❑ *enterprising* (adj)   full of initiative and imagination (*entreprendre* to undertake)

❑ *entrepreneur* (n)   a self-made businessman (*entreprendre* to undertake)

Synonyms: *magnate, industrialist*

❑ *industrious* (adj)   hard-working; diligent

Synonym: *assiduous*

❑ *resolute* (adj)   determined; willing to push on

Synonyms: *dogged, steadfast, tenacious*

Vocabulary Lesson 41: The Faithful and the Unfaithful

| Today's roots: | *orthos* | straight, strict | *sub-* | under |
| | *surgere* | to rise | *klan* | to break |

❏ **conform** (v)   to do what one is expected to do (*com-* together + *formare* to form)

His desire to avoid punishment at all costs causes him to **conform** to his parents' many rules.
Synonyms: *comply, obey*   Antonyms: *defy, rebel*

❏ **orthodoxy** (n)   strict adherence to tradition (*orthos-* straight, strict + *doxa* opinion)

The Amish are well known for their **orthodoxy;** tradition is very important to their culture.
Synonyms: *conventionality, traditionalism*   Antonyms: *heresy, apostasy*

❏ **iconoclast** (n)   one who challenges tradition (*eikon* Gr image + *klan* to break)

Always an **iconoclast,** Michael did everything in his power to do the opposite of what was expected.
Synonyms: *heretic, apostate, rebel, nonconformist, infidel*   Antonyms: *conformist, traditionalist*

❏ **heresy** (n)   opinion or action that violates traditional belief

In many villages in colonial New England, to question religious doctrine was considered **heresy.**
Synonyms: *iconoclasm, apostasy*   Antonyms: *sycophancy, toadyism, compliance, submission, obsequy*

❏ **insurgent** (adj)   rebellious (*in-* against + *surgere* to rise)

The villagers became more **insurgent** each day that the army remained in their midst.
Synonyms: *insubordinate, mutinous*   Antonym: *conformist, yes-man, toady, sycophant*

❏ **convention** (n)   a practice that comports with the norms of a society

Ms. Frazier's teaching style went against **convention** and thus angered the conservative school board.
Synonyms: *protocol, practice*   Antonym: *irregularity*

❏ **insubordination** (n)   refusal to submit to authority (*in-* against + *sub-* under + *ordinare* arrange)

By punishing all **insubordination,** the commander showed his troops that no disobedience would be tolerated.
Synonyms: *agitation, subversion, rebellion*   Antonym: *pacification*

❏ **renegade** (n)   an outlaw (*negare* to deny)

Synonyms: *defector, traitor*

❏ **insurrection** (n)   an uprising (*in-* against + *surgere* to rise)

Synonyms: *coup, mutiny, rebellion*

❏ **dissident** (n)   one who strongly opposes accepted opinion (*dis-* apart + *sedere* to sit)

Synonym: *rebel*

❏ **mutiny** (n)   a rebellion

Synonyms: *revolt, riot, uprising*

❏ **servile** (adj)   overly submissive (*servus* slave)

Synonym: *obsequious*

❏ **heretic** (n)   one who dissents

Synonyms: *rebel, iconoclast*

❏ **apostasy** (n)   abandonment of a belief (*apo-* away from + *stanai* to stand)

Synonym: *heresy*

Vocabulary Lesson 42: How Rude!

Today's roots:	*pudere*	to cause shame	*trux*	fierce
	solere	accustomed	*haut*	high

❑ *insolent* (adj)　rudely disrespectful (*in-* not + *solere* accustomed)

The despot punished the rebel's **insolence** with a lengthy prison sentence.
Synonyms: *impudent, impertinent*　　　Antonyms: *courteous, deferential, decorous*

❑ *affront* (n)　an insult (*afronter* Fr to confront)

When he found out that his dad had let him win, Frank took it as an **affront** to his tennis skills.
Synonyms: *slur, barb, aspersion, obloquy*　　　Antonyms: *tribute, exaltation, veneration*

❑ *haughty* (adj)　overly proud (*haut* high)

The **haughty** young goalie felt that he had no equal in the league.
Synonyms: *conceited, supercilious, cavalier, arrogant*　　　Antonyms: *modest, diffident*

❑ *crass* (adj)　unrefined

Luke's **crass** behavior at the dinner table horrified the princess, who had never seen such poor manners.
Synonyms: *boorish, oafish, philistine*　　　Antonyms: *decorous, civilized, refined*

❑ *impudent* (adj)　rudely bold (*im-* not + *pudere* to cause shame)

The young soldier's **impudence** would be punished; it is not wise to undermine the authority of a superior officer.
Synonyms: *insolent, impertinent, audacious*　　　Antonyms: *courteous, civilized*

❑ *boorish* (adj)　crude, barbaric (unrelated to *boar*, a wild pig, but *piggish* is a close synonym)

The **boorish** barbarians ripped at the meat with their bare hands and spit bones out onto the table.
Synonyms: *crass, oafish, barbaric, philistine*　　　Antonyms: *decorous, polite*

❑ *irreverence* (n)　disrespect (*ir-* not + *vereri* to respect)

The **irreverence** with which he mocked his teachers showed he had no respect for their authority.
Synonyms: *impertinence, flippancy*　　　Antonym: *deference*

❑ *flippant* (adj)　disrespectfully jocular; using humor inappropriately

Synonyms: *irreverent, impertinent*

❑ *brazen* (adj)　bold and insolent

The thieves pulled off a **brazen** midday heist
Synonym: *impudent*

❑ *truculent* (adj)　cruel and aggressive　(*trux* fierce)

Synonyms: *obstreperous, bellicose*

❑ *effrontery* (n)　boldness, brashness

Synonyms: *insolence, impudence*

❑ *impertinent* (adj)　inappropriately bold　(*im-* not + *pertinere* to concern)

Synonyms: *impudent, brazen*

❑ *glacial* (adj)　having a cold personality　(like a *glacier*)

Synonym: *frigid*

❑ *rebuff* (v)　to refuse in an abrupt or rude manner

Synonyms: *reject, snub*

Vocabulary Unit 6 Exercise Set I

1. Those used to his frequent equivocation in describing his business dealings were shocked by his ------ description of his latest acquisition.
   (A) forthright
   (B) apocryphal
   (C) esoteric
   (D) boorish
   (E) indefatigable

2. Heidi's sudden indolence was ------ to her colleagues; until recently she had been an assiduous and exemplary employee.
   (A) an insurrection
   (B) a satire
   (C) an enigma
   (D) an indiscretion
   (E) an indictment

3. Decades after being appointed ------ of the renowned museum, Charles confessed to be only ------ who scarcely appreciated the significance of the great works he oversaw.
   (A) curator . . a dilettante
   (B) lampoon . . a dabbler
   (C) entrepreneur . . an amateur
   (D) fanatic . . a nihilist
   (E) philanthropist . . an ascetic

4. The film is a collection of lowbrow ------ that lampoon some of the more popular movies of recent years.
   (A) parodies
   (B) epics
   (C) anthologies
   (D) strategems
   (E) bards

5. The villager's ------ behavior was ------ to the queen, who was not used to being treated with such effrontery.
   (A) tenacious . . a malapropism
   (B) crass . . a witticism
   (C) jocular . . a moratorium
   (D) downtrodden . . an insult
   (E) insolent . . an affront

6. The press lambasted the congresswoman for her part in the scandal, but she knew that since she was not ------, the ------ was unfair.
   (A) seditious . . digression
   (B) guilty . . candor
   (C) veracious . . prevarication
   (D) jocular . . castigation
   (E) culpable . . censure

7. Helga was so ------ that she didn't even make eye contact with us as we greeted her at her door.
   (A) garrulous
   (B) glacial
   (C) loquacious
   (D) rapacious
   (E) industrious

8. The other medical residents were tired of Dr. Bob's ------; every other word out of his mouth was an obsequious compliment to a high-ranking doctor or hospital official.
   (A) belligerence
   (B) eloquence
   (C) munificence
   (D) xenophobia
   (E) sycophancy

9. Tom's ------ ideas contrasted sharply with the conventional views held by the strongly orthodox community.
   (A) truculent
   (B) diligent
   (C) iconoclastic
   (D) scrupulous
   (E) candid

10. They expected the funeral to be a sedate and somber affair, but were shocked by the grieving husband's ------.
    (A) orthodoxy
    (B) mirth
    (C) irrelevance
    (D) simplicity
    (E) decorum

HIT LIST

Vocabulary Unit 6 Exercise Set II

Write the meaning next to each root, then write as many words as you can that contain the root.

1. CANDERE_____
   _____
   _____
   _____
   _____

2. LEVIS_____
   _____
   _____
   _____
   _____

3. JOCUS_____
   _____
   _____
   _____
   _____

4. VERAX_____
   _____
   _____
   _____
   _____

5. APO-_____
   _____
   _____
   _____
   _____

6. EQUI_____
   _____
   _____
   _____
   _____

7. BUNKUM_____
   _____
   _____
   _____
   _____

8. DICTARE_____
   _____
   _____
   _____
   _____

9. FATIGARE_____
   _____
   _____
   _____
   _____

10. PARA-_____
    _____
    _____
    _____
    _____

11. CRYPTO_____
    _____
    _____
    _____
    _____

12. ORTHOS_____
    _____
    _____
    _____
    _____

13. CURARE_____
    _____
    _____
    _____
    _____

14. SURGERE_____
    _____
    _____
    _____
    _____

15. DOXA_____
    _____
    _____
    _____
    _____

Vocabulary Unit 6 Exercise Set III

1. Is it honest to *equivocate*?   Y N
2. Can a task be *painstaking*?   Y N
3. Does a reprehensible person   Y N
   deserve *censure?*
4. Is a *dilettante* very skilled and   Y N
   experienced?
5. Does an *iconoclast conform?*   Y N

Write the word with the given meaning.

6. merriment   m_____
7. vague   n_____
8. honest   f_____
9. hard work   d_____
10. strong disapproval c_____
11. unclear   a_____
12. to do what is expected c_____
13. to reprimand   r_____
14. candid   o_____
15. rebellious   i_____
16. incomprehensible   u_____
17. skilled poet   b_____
18. insubordination   s_____
19. clever remark   w_____
20. doubtful   d_____
21. barbaric   b_____
22. overly submissive   s_____
23. lie   p_____
24. rudely disrespectful i_____
25. insult   a_____

Write the correct form of the italicized word.

26. a person who is *culpable*

   _____

27. having the quality of *heresy*

   _____

28. the quality of being *diligent*

   _____

29. having the qualities of an *iconoclast*

   _____

30. the act of *castigating*

   _____

Write the word with the given root.

31. deserving blame (*culpa*)

   _____

32. deliberately ambiguous (*vocare*)

   _____

33. to punish (*rate*)

   _____

34. deep, insightful (*pro-*)

   _____

35. done in a joking way (*jocus*)

   _____

36. attentive to detail (*metus*)

   _____

37. truthfulness (*verax*)

   _____

38. untiring (*fatiga*)

   _____

39. honesty (*candere*)

   _____

40. overly proud (*haut*)

   _____

41. of doubtful authenticity (*apo-*)

   _____

Unit 6 Exercise Set I Answer Key

1. **A** Those used to his *equivocation* (failure to be straightforward) would be shocked by *straightforwardness*.
   forthright = honest, straightforward
   apocryphal = of doubtful authenticity
   esoteric = difficult to understand
   boorish = rude
   indefatigable = untiring

2. **C** Heidi had been *assiduous* (hard-working) and *exemplary* (worthy of imitation). Sudden *indolence* (laziness) would be surprising and puzzling, to say the least.
   insurrection = rebellion
   satire = mocking work of literature or drama
   enigma = puzzle
   indictment = accusation

3. **A** One who lacks a sophisticated appreciation of art is a *dilettante*. One who oversees a museum is a *curator*.
   curator = person in charge of a museum;
       dilettante = dabbler in the arts
   lampoon = satirical work; *dabbler* = amateur
   entrepreneur = businessman; *amateur* = novice
   fanatic = passionate supporter; *nihilist* = one
       who denies moral absolutes
   philanthropist = benefactor; *ascetic* = monk

4. **A** Something that *lampoons* (makes fun of) something is a *satire*, *spoof*, or *parody*.
   parody = a spoof that makes fun of something
   epic = a heroic poem
   anthology = a collection of works
   strategem = a deceitful scheme
   bard = a poet

5. **E** The queen is not used to being treated with *effrontery* (rude boldness). This implies that the villager's behavior is probably *rude* and that such behavior would *bother* the queen.
   tenacious = intense; *malapropism* = incorrect
       use of a word
   crass = rude; *witticism* = funny remark
   jocular = joking; *moratorium* = rest, a break
   downtrodden = made submissive by constant
       harsh treatment; *insult* = rude
       remark
   insolent = rude; *affront* = insult

6. **E** The congresswoman is getting *lambasted* (harshly criticized) in the press. She feels that this *criticism* is unfair, so she must feel that she is not *guilty*.
   seditious = insubordinate; *digression* = aside
   guilty = blameworthy; *candor* = honesty
   veracious = truthful; *prevarication* = lies
   jocular = joking; *castigation* = punishment
   culpable = guilty; *censure* = criticism

7. **B** Helga did not make eye contact with her guests, a decidedly unfriendly thing to do.
   garrulous = friendly, talkative
   glacial = cold, unfriendly
   loquacious = talkative
   rapacious = ravenous
   industrious = hard-working

8. **E** The semicolon joins two clauses that support each other. *Obsequious* compliments are those that try to curry favor with others. He must be a *flatterer*.
   belligerence = inclination to picking fights
   eloquence = skill in speech
   munificence = generosity
   xenophobia = fear of foreigners
   sycophancy = excessive flattery

9. **C** Tom's ideas contrasted sharply with the *conventional* (typical) views held by the strongly *orthodox* (traditional) community. He must be a *nonconformist* who eschews tradition.
   truculent = cruel
   diligent = hard-working
   iconoclastic = resistant to tradition
   scrupulous = ethical, meticulous
   candid = honest

10. **B** The fact that they are *shocked* implies that the funeral was not so *sedate and somber*. It must have been *happier* than they expected.
   orthodoxy = strict adherence to dogma
   mirth = merriment
   irrelevance = lack of importance
   decorum = appropriateness of behavior

Unit 6 Exercise Sets II and III Answer Key

Exercise Set II

1. CANDERE: to shine
   candid, candor, incandescent, candle

2. LEVIS: light in weight
   levity, relieve, elevate, elevator, levitate, alleviate, oblivion

3. JOCUS: joke
   jocular, jocund, joker, jocose, juggler, joke

4. VERAX: true
   verisimilitude, veracity, verify, very

5. APO-: away
   apocalypse, aphorism, apostate, apoplexy, apostle, apothecary, apocryphal, apology

6. EQUI: equal
   equinox, equivalent, equanimity, equipotential, equality, inequality, equitable, equator, equalize

7. BUNKUM: nonsense
   bunk, debunk

8. DICTARE: to declare
   dictate, indict, diction, dictum, dictionary

9. FATIGARE: tire
   indefatigable, fatigued

10. PARA-: beyond, beside
    paraphrase, parasite, paramedic, paranoia, parallel, paramount, paradigm

11. CRYPTO: secret
    cryptic, crypt, cryptogram, cryptography

12. ORTHOS: straight, strict
    orthography, orthodox, unorthodox, orthopedic, orthodontics, orthodoxy

13. CURARE: to take care of
    procure, curator, curate, pedicure, manicure

14. SURGERE: to rise
    resurrection, resurgent, insurgent, insurrection, surge

15. DOXA: opinion
    orthodox, paradox, heterodox

Exercise Set III

1. N
2. Y
3. Y
4. N
5. N
6. mirth
7. nebulous
8. forthright
9. diligence
10. censure
11. ambiguous
12. conform
13. rebuke or reprove
14. outspoken
15. insurgent
16. unfathomable
17. bard
18. sedition
19. witticism
20. dubious
21. boorish
22. servile
23. prevaricate
24. insolent
25. affront
26. culprit
27. heretical
28. diligence
29. iconoclastic
30. castigation
31. culpable
32. equivocal
33. berate
34. profound
35. jocular
36. meticulous
37. veracity
38. indefatigable
39. candor
40. haughty
41. apocryphal

Vocabulary Unit 7

Vocabulary Lesson 43: Earth, Moon, and Sky

Today's roots:	*astrum*	star	*luna*	moon
	naus	ship	*celum*	sky

❏ **arid** (adj)   extremely dry (*arere* to be dry)

Some regions of Africa have become so **arid** that entire lakes have evaporated.
Synonyms: *barren, parched*   Antonyms: *fecund, fertile*

❏ **astral** (adj)   relating to the stars (*astrum* star)

The supernova is perhaps the most dramatic of **astral** events.
Synonyms: *celestial, cosmic*

❏ **nautical** (adj)   pertaining to sailing (*naus* ship)

The southern tip of Africa poses many **nautical** challenges to even the most adept and experienced sailor.
Synonyms: *marine, maritime*

❏ **lunar** (adj)   relating to the moon (*luna* moon)

The **lunar** vehicle can traverse some of the rockiest and most forbidding terrain on the moon.

❏ **fecund** (adj)   fertile; fruitful (*fecundus* fruitful)

Over the summer, our **fecund** vegetable garden provided us with an endless supply of wonderful salads.
Synonyms: *prolific, abundant*   Antonyms: *barren, infertile, sterile*

❏ **fallow** (adj)   unused; plowed but not cultivated

The **fallow** land would be replanted in two years, once all the nutrients had been restored.
Synonyms: *dormant, inactive, uncultivated*

❏ **cosmic** (adj)   relating to the universe (*kosmos* Gr universe, order)

The enormous and unprecedented meteor shower was being hailed as the **cosmic** event of the century.
Synonyms: *astral, celestial, astronomical*

❏ **celestial** (adj)   relating to the sky (*celum* sky, heaven)

Synonyms: *heavenly, astral*

❏ **arable** (adj)   able to be cultivated (*arare* to plow)

Synonyms: *fertile, fruitful*

❏ **desiccated** (adj)   completely dried out

Synonyms: *arid, parched*

❏ **quagmire** (n)   swampy land; difficult situation (*quag* bog)

Synonyms: *marsh, swamp, bog*

❏ **bucolic** (adj)   characteristic of the countryside

Synonyms: *rustic, sylvan, rural, pastoral*

❏ **cultivate** (v)   to nurture; to grow crops (*cultivus* tilled)

Synonyms: *farm, till, sow*

Vocabulary Lesson 44: More or Less

Today's roots:	*facere*	to do	*plere*	to fill
	copia	abundance	*macer*	thin

- ❑ **paucity** (adj)   lack; scarcity (*paucus* few, little)

  I love good food, so I'm frustrated by the **paucity** of good restaurants in town.
  Synonyms: *dearth, scantiness*   Antonyms: *abundance, plenitude, copiousness*

- ❑ **surfeit** (n)   an excessive amount (*sur-* over + *facere* to do)

  The **surfeit** of food on the table for Thanksgiving dinner left us all with bulging stomachs.
  Synonyms: *glut, plethora, overabundance*   Antonyms: *deficiency, dearth, paucity*

- ❑ **copious** (adj)   abundant (*copia* abundance)

  The **copious** mistakes in Robert's final paper showed his lack of effort.
  Synonyms: *ample, bountiful*   Antonyms: *scanty, sparse, deficient*

- ❑ **barren** (adj)   infertile

  The **barren** land was so devoid of life that it was difficult to find even a weed.
  Synonyms: *sterile, desolate*   Antonyms: *fecund, fertile*

- ❑ **capacious** (adj)   having lots of room (*capax* able to hold a lot)

  The **capacious** auditorium had enough seats for all 5,000 students with room to spare.
  Synonyms: *spacious, voluminous*   Antonyms: *exiguous, scanty*

- ❑ **scanty** (adj)   meager; barely enough

  The **scanty** portions the soldiers received left them hungry and weak.
  Synonyms: *inadequate, meager, deficient*   Antonyms: *sufficient, adequate*

- ❑ **replete** (adj)   completely filled (*re-* again + *plere* to fill)

  The old storage facility was **replete** with decrepit furniture that had far outlived its usefulness.
  Synonyms: *crammed, stuffed*   Antonyms: *vacant, barren*

- ❑ **sparse** (adj)   thinly dispersed or scattered (sparsus scattered)

  Synonyms: scant, scanty, paltry

- ❑ **voluminous** (adj)   having great size (*volumen* roll of writing)

  Synonyms: *cavernous, capacious, plentiful*

- ❑ **desolate** (adj)   deserted (*de-* completely + *solus* alone)

  Synonyms: *uninhabited, barren*

- ❑ **diminutive** (adj)   tiny (*de-* completely + *minuere* to make small)

  Synonyms: *undersized, miniature*

- ❑ **meager** (adj)   inadequate (*macer* thin)

  Synonyms: *measly, paltry*

- ❑ **rarefy** (v)   to make less dense or less plentiful (*rarus* rare + *facere* to make)

- ❑ **rife** (adj)   plentiful

  Synonyms: *abundant, rampant, widespread*

Vocabulary Lesson 45: Tough Times

| Today's roots: | *logia* speaking | *dolus* grief |
| | *epi-* over | *emia* blood |

❏ **tribulation** (n) a cause of great trouble or suffering (*tribulare* oppress)

Being a pop star is not as glamorous as it seems; it often involves many unforeseen **tribulations**.
Synonyms: *adversity, travail, woe, anguish*

❏ **despondent** (adj) lacking hope (*de-* without + *sperare* hope)

With their team trailing by ten runs in the ninth inning, the fans became **despondent.**
Synonyms: *dejected, depressed, disheartened, desperate*   Antonyms: *ecstatic, elated, euphoric*

❏ **doleful** (adj) filled with grief (*dolus* grief + *-ful* full of)

The funeral for the child was a **doleful** affair; it is always so sad to see someone die at such a young age.
Synonyms: *crestfallen, depressed, woeful*   Antonyms: *ecstatic, elated, euphoric*

❏ **anemic** (adj) feeble; characterized by oxygen deficiency in the blood (*a-* without + *emia* blood)

Our offense was so **anemic** that we didn't hit the ball out of the infield the whole game.
Synonyms: *pallid, weak, feeble*   Antonyms: *robust, vigorous, hale*

❏ **malady** (n) a disease (*mal* bad)

The flu is a common **malady** that strikes millions of people each year.
Synonyms: *affliction, ailment, disorder*

❏ **anguish** (n) extreme suffering

The **anguish** Walter felt when his dog died was unbearable; he could hardly stop crying for a week.
Synonyms: *agony, grief, misery*   Antonyms: *ecstasy, elation, euphoria*

❏ **dirge** (n) a funeral song

You may think all **dirges** are depressing until you've been to a New Orleans jazz funeral.
Synonyms: *requiem, elegy*

❏ **blight** (n) a diseased condition

Synonyms: *curse, affliction*

❏ **affliction** (n) a disorder causing suffering (*ad-* to + *fligere* to strike)

Synonyms: *adversity, hardship*

❏ **elegy** (n) a poem or song relating to death (*legos* Gr poem of lament)

Synonyms: *dirge, requiem*

❏ **epitaph** (n) an inscription found on a gravestone (*epi-* Gr over + *taphos* tomb)

❏ **doldrums** (n) the blues; persistent unhappiness (*dolus* grief)

Synonyms: *depression, melancholy*

❏ **adversity** (n) hardship

He fought back from **adversity** to win the title.
Synonym: *affliction*

Vocabulary Lesson 46: Good Learnin'

| Today's roots: | *arkhaios* ancient | *demos* people |
| | *logos* study, word, speech | *genea* descent |

❑ *etymology* (n)   the study of the origin of words (*etymon-* Gr true sense + *logos* word)

A good understanding of **etymology** can help you succeed on the SAT I.

❑ *archaeology* (n)   the study of past cultures (*arkhaios* Gr ancient + *logia* study)

There are many fascinating **archaeological** sites right in the center of Athens.

❑ *anthropology* (n)   the study of human cultures (*anthros-* humankind + *logia* study)

Anthropologists are fascinated by the similarities between tribal rituals and modern social conventions.

❑ *ethics* (n)   the study of and philosophy of moral choice (*ethos-* character)

The more deeply one studies **ethics,** the less one is able to think in terms of moral absolutes.

❑ *semantics* (n)   the study of the meanings of words and symbols (*sema-* sign)

It's amazing that the noun *pedestrian* and the adjective *pedestrian* can be so different **semantically.**

❑ *theology* (n)   the study of religion (*theos-* god + *logia* study)

While in Catholic school, we had many **theological** discussions about the role of God in daily life.

❑ *pathology* (n)   the study of disease (*pathos* suffering + *logia* study)

The tissue sample was sent to the **pathology** lab to determine if there was any disease in the liver.

❑ *sociology* (n)   the study of human social behavior and social institutions (*socius-* fellow + *logia* study)

I was amazed to learn in **sociology** class that mandatory schooling until age sixteen is a fairly recent practice.

❑ *entomology* (n)   the study of insects (*entomon-* insect + *logia* study)

Anna spends so much time burrowing in the yard that she may know more about bugs than most **entomologists.**

❑ *genealogy* (n)   the study of ancestry (*genea* descent + *logia* study)

Sarah was so fascinated by **genealogy** that she compiled a three-volume guide to her family ancestry.

❑ *demographics* (n)   the study of statistics relating to human populations (*demos-* people + *graphein* to write)

The **demographics** reveal that Democratic candidates typically perform better in urban areas than in rural areas.

❑ *oncology* (n)   the study of tumors (*onco-* tumor + *logia* study)

When my doctor discovered a tumor near my kidney, he referred me to the best **oncologist** on the staff.

❑ *paleontology* (n)   the study of fossils and ancient life (*palai* long ago + *logia* study)

I like to dig in my backyard and pretend I'm a **paleontologist** making an important fossil discovery.

❑ *neurology* (n)   the study of the human brain and nervous system (*neuron* Gr nerve)

I love studying the brain, but I don't want to cut it up; I think I prefer **neurology** to neurosurgery.

Vocabulary Lesson 47: All Alone

Today's roots:	*claudere* to close	*solus* alone
	insula island	*se-* apart

❑ *hermit* (n)   one who prefers to live alone (*ermita* Gr a person of solitude)

The **hermit** lived alone in a shack in the middle of the woods, more than ten miles from the nearest road.
Synonyms: *recluse, loner, eremite*   Antonyms: *socialite, extrovert*

❑ *ostracize* (v)   to exclude from a group

Her comments to the others were so self-centered and cruel that she was **ostracized** for months.
Synonyms: *exile, banish*   Antonyms: *welcome, accept*

❑ *exile* (n)   a banishment (*ex-* away)

After the dictator was overthrown, he lived a life of **exile** far away from his native country.
Synonyms: *banishment, ostracism, deportation, expulsion*   Antonyms: *inclusion, welcome*

❑ *expel* (v)   to force to leave (*ex-* away + *pellere* to push)

The student who slashed the bus tires was **expelled** and won't be seen back here again.
Synonyms: *discharge, evict*   Antonyms: *invite, admit*

❑ *recluse* (n)   one who likes to live alone (*re-* away + *claudere* to close)

In *To Kill a Mockingbird*, the **recluse** Boo Radley is endlessly fascinating to Scout.
Synonyms: *hermit, loner*

❑ *isolate* (v)   to place something apart from everything else (*insula* island)

The patient with tuberculosis was **isolated** from the other patients so he could not infect them.
Synonyms: *detach, segregate*   Antonyms: *include, embrace*

❑ *solitude* (n)   isolation; the quality of being alone (*solus* alone)

Before the two cosmonauts joined him, the lone astronaut on the space station had spent five months in **solitude.**
Synonyms: *seclusion, solitariness, detachment*   Antonyms: *camaraderie, companionship*

❑ *banish* (v)   to force to leave an area

Synonyms: *exile, ostracize, evict*

❑ *outcast* (n)   an individual who has been excluded from a group

Synonyms: *castaway, pariah*

❑ *seclusion* (n)   privacy (*se-* apart + *claudere* to close)

Synonyms: *isolation, solitude*

❑ *pariah* (n)   an individual who has been excluded from a group

Synonyms: *outcast, exile*

❑ *relegate* (v)   to banish, to demote in rank (*re-* back + *legare* to send)

Synonyms: *ostracize, exile*

❑ *quarantine* (n)   a period of isolation for someone infected with a contagion (*quaranta* forty [days])

Vocabulary Lesson 48: Go Forth

> **Today's roots:** *supare* scatter   *satur* full
>   *vergere, vert* to turn   *undare* to flow

☐ *disseminate* (v) to spread information (*dis-* away + *seminare* to sow)

The members of the band **disseminated** flyers that advertised their debut concert this coming weekend.
Synonyms: *circulate, publicize, distribute*   Antonym: *suppress*

☐ *diverge* (v) to go apart (*dis-* away + *vergere* to turn)

After traveling together for nearly 100 miles, the two cars finally **diverged.**
Synonyms: *divide, branch*   Antonyms: *converge, merge*

☐ *proliferate* (v) to grow rapidly; to produce offspring at a rapid pace (*proles* offspring)

The bacteria **proliferated** at an alarming rate, multiplying tenfold in just 30 minutes.
Synonyms: *expand, multiply*   Antonyms: *wither, shrink*

☐ *amass* (v) to accumulate; to gather together

Over the years, Rick has **amassed** quite a collection of CDs, accumulating over 1,000 of them.
Synonyms: *collect, gather, hoard*   Antonyms: *distribute, disperse*

☐ *distend* (v) to swell; to increase in size (*dis-* apart + *tendere* to stretch)

Malnutrition can cause the abdominal cavity to **distend** and produce a bloated look.
Synonyms: *expand, dilate*   Antonym: *constrict*

☐ *propagate* (v) to cause to multiply; to publicize; to travel through a medium (*pro-* forth)

Plants of all sizes and shapes **propagate** by forming seeds, which develop into new seedlings.
Synonyms: *procreate, breed*

☐ *inundate* (v) to flood (*in-* into + *undare* to flow)

After days without work, the lawyer was astonished to suddenly find himself **inundated** with paperwork.
Synonyms: *engulf, overwhelm, swamp, deluge*

☐ *diffuse* (v) to spread out, as a gas (*dis-* apart + *fundere* to pour)

Synonyms: *circulate, disseminate*

☐ *germinate* (v) to sprout; to grow (*germen* sprout)

Synonyms: *bud, burgeon, develop*

☐ *disperse* (v) to spread apart (*dis-* apart + *spargere* to scatter)

Synonyms: *diffuse, disseminate*

☐ *rampant* (adj) growing out of control (*ramper* to climb)

Synonyms: *rife, predominant, prevalent*

☐ *dissipate* (v) to scatter (*dis-* apart + *supare* to scatter)

Synonyms: *dispel, disperse*

☐ *saturate* (v) to fill completely, as with a liquid or solute (*satur* full)

Synonyms: *soak, imbue*

Vocabulary Lesson 49: Even More

Today's roots:	*ad-* to	*scribere* to write
	post- after	*augere* to increase

❑ **annex** (v)   to attach; to acquire land to expand an existing country (*ad-* to + *nectare* to attach)
   When Hitler **annexed** Poland, the dictator's imperialist designs should have been clear.
   Synonyms: *acquire, appropriate, append*   Antonyms: *disengage, dissociate*

❑ **addendum** (n)   something added; a supplement to a book (*ad-* onto)
   After he completed the story, the author wrote an **addendum** explaining why he finished it the way he did.
   Synonyms: *appendix, supplement*

❑ **postscript** (n)   a message added after the completion of a letter (P.S.) (*post-* after + *scriber* to write)
   After my wife signed the postcard, she remembered something else she wanted to say and wrote a **postscript.**

❑ **epilogue** (n)   an extra chapter added onto the end of a novel (*epi-* Gr in addition + *logia* words)
   In the **epilogue,** the author described what the characters of the novel did 15 years after the main narrative.
   Synonyms: *afterword, postlude*   Antonyms: *prelude, forward, preface, prologue*

❑ **append** (v)   to affix something; to add on (*ad-* to + *pendere* to hang)
   The publishers **appended** an index to the end of the text to help the reader find things more easily.
   Synonym: *annex*

❑ **adjunct** (adj)   added in a subordinate capacity (*ad-* to + *jungere* to attach)
   Although principally a biologist, Dr. Carter was also an **adjunct** professor in the zoology department.
   Synonyms: *subordinate, subsidiary*

❑ **augment** (v)   to add onto; to make greater (*augere* to increase)
   One important way to **augment** your SAT score is to study vocabulary.
   Synonyms: *enlarge, enhance, amplify, boost, strengthen*   Antonym: *diminish*

❑ **cession** (n)   the act of surrendering or yielding (*cessare* to yield)
   Synonyms: *capitulation, relinquishment*

❑ **affix** (v)   to attach (*ad-* to + *figere* to fasten)
   Synonyms: *annex, append*

❑ **appropriate** (v)   to take another's work or possessions as one's own (*ad-* to + *proprius* one's own)

❑ **encore** (n)   an extra performance at the end of a show (*encore* Fr again)
   Synonym: *curtain call*

❑ **appendix** (n)   supplementary material at the end of a text (*ad-* to + *pendere* to hang)
   Synonym: *addendum*

❑ **supplement** (v)   to add something to complete or strengthen a whole (*supplere* to complete)

❑ **circumscribed** (adj)   having distinct boundaries or limits (*circum-* around + *scribere* to write)

Vocabulary Unit 7 Exercise Set I

Time—8 minutes
For each question, select the best answer among the choices given. Note any vocabulary words to review on the Hit List below.

1. While most people would probably be ------ in her position, Stacey somehow managed to remain upbeat and was convinced that things would get better.
   (A) elated
   (B) diminutive
   (C) defamed
   (D) anemic
   (E) despondent

2. Seemingly without scruples, the professor ------ the work of his graduate students and published papers on topics he himself had not even researched.
   (A) isolated
   (B) relegated
   (C) appropriated
   (D) annexed
   (E) eulogized

3. It is shocking that someone who was once so ------ by the public can so quickly become ------ after just one social blunder.
   (A) belittled . . a malady
   (B) disparaged . . a pariah
   (C) saturated . . an exile
   (D) lionized . . an outcast
   (E) ostracized . . a recluse

4. The dearth of ------ land in this region of the country makes it very difficult to maintain plentiful harvests.
   (A) desiccated
   (B) arable
   (C) fallow
   (D) celestial
   (E) arid

5. The entrance of the cavern was so ------ that the indigenous tribes took advantage of its ------ shelter to keep entire clans dry during the heavy rain season.
   (A) voluminous . . capacious
   (B) enormous . . scanty
   (C) cavernous . . meager
   (D) fecund . . spacious
   (E) astral . . copious

6. Although many consider "Deadman's Run" to be the most ------ ski trail on the mountain, Tommy was able to maneuver through the course without ------ after having just learned to ski.
   (A) simple . . trouble
   (B) difficult . . speed
   (C) arduous . . exertion
   (D) pedestrian . . concern
   (E) pragmatic . . practical

7. Zach's knowledge of ------ helped him to identify and avoid the rare and poisonous African spitting beetle.
   (A) entomology
   (B) etymology
   (C) ethics
   (D) pathology
   (E) sociology

8. The spy was immediately ------ back to his country after he was caught attempting to pilfer information from the CIA database.
   (A) quarantined
   (B) secluded
   (C) disseminated
   (D) distended
   (E) deported

9. It is hard to imagine that this barren desert with little to no plant life was once ------ with farms and wildlife.
   (A) doleful
   (B) replete
   (C) germinated
   (D) rarefied
   (E) afflicted

10. After finishing a good novel, I'm always eager to see if an ------ follows to tell me what happened to the main characters after the conclusion of the narrative.
    (A) elegy
    (B) epitaph
    (C) epilogue
    (D) encore
    (E) eulogy

HIT LIST

_____   _____
_____   _____
_____   _____
_____   _____
_____   _____

Vocabulary Unit 7 Exercise Set II

Write the meaning next to each root, and then write as many words as you can that contain the root.

1. EPI-_____

_____

_____

_____

_____

2. AD-_____

_____

_____

_____

_____

3. SCRIBERE_____

_____

_____

_____

_____

4. COPIA_____

_____

_____

_____

_____

5. LUNA_____

_____

_____

_____

_____

6. ASTRUM_____

_____

_____

_____

_____

7. PLERE_____

_____

_____

_____

_____

8. SOLUS_____

_____

_____

_____

_____

9. GENEA_____

_____

_____

_____

_____

10. POST-_____

_____

_____

_____

_____

11. ARKHAIOS_____

_____

_____

_____

_____

12. DEMOS_____

_____

_____

_____

_____

13. VERT_____

_____

_____

_____

_____

14. LOGOS_____

_____

_____

_____

_____

15. CLAUDERE_____

_____

_____

_____

_____

Vocabulary Unit 7 Exercise Set III

1. Can a person be *capacious?*   Y N
2. Is a *pariah* popular?   Y N
3. Can a person be *fecund?*   Y N
4. Is it fun to be *despondent?*   Y N
5. Do people *germinate?*   Y N

Write the word with the given meaning.

6. a disease   m_____
7. study of cultures   a_____
8. to shun   o_____
9. relating to the stars   a_____
10. study of ancestry   g_____
11. relating to the universe   c_____
12. abundant   c_____
13. one who lives alone   r_____
14. lacking hope   d_____
15. to accumulate   a_____
16. able to be cultivated   a_____
17. an extra chapter   e_____
18. inadequate   m_____
19. to flood   i_____
20. unused, uncultivated   f_____
21. to fill completely   s_____
22. study of populations   d_____
23. an extra performance   e_____
24. excessive amount   s_____
25. extreme suffering   a_____

Write the correct form of the italicized word.

26. having *anemia*

_____

27. one who studies *sociology*

_____

28. the act of *ceding*

_____

29. in *solitude*

_____

30. the act of *proliferating*

_____

Write the word with the given root.

31. relating to the sky (*celum*)

_____

32. to swell (*dis-*)

_____

33. a poem (*legos*)

_____

34. an inscription (*taphos*)

_____

35. study of insects (*entomon*)

_____

36. a scarcity (*paucus*)

_____

37. tiny (*minuere*)

_____

38. banishment (*ex-*)

_____

39. high praise (*eu*)

_____

40. to multiply (*pro-*)

_____

41. to make greater (*aug*)

_____

Unit 7 Exercise Set I Answer Key

1. **E** *While* indicates a contrast. If she is *upbeat and optimistic*, it must be that most people would be the opposite: *depressed.*
   elated = extremely happy
   diminutive = tiny
   defamed = slandered
   anemic = weak
   despondent = lacking hope

2. **C** The professor lacks *scruples* (moral standards), so he must have done something bad to the work of his students. If he is publishing papers on topics that he has not researched, he is probably stealing the work.
   isolated = secluded
   relegated = banished
   appropriated = taken as his own
   annexed = added on to
   eulogized = praised

3. **D** The fact that it is *shocking* implies that the two words should contrast with each other.
   belittle = to put down; *malady* = illness
   disparage = to put down; *pariah* = outcast
   saturate = to fill completely; *exile* = outcast
   lionize = to worship; *outcast* = someone excluded
   ostracize = to exclude; *recluse* = loner

4. **B** If it is *difficult to maintain plentiful harvests,* it must be because there is too little *usable* land.
   desiccated = dry
   arable = fertile
   fallow = unused
   celestial = relating to the sky
   arid = dry

5. **A** An entrance that can accommodate *entire clans* must be pretty *large.*
   voluminous = large; *capacious* = having lots of room
   enormous = huge; *scanty* = inadequate
   cavernous = large; *meager* = inadequate
   fecund = fertile; *spacious* = full of room
   astral = pertaining to stars; *copious* = abundant

6. **C** *Although* indicates contrast. Although many think it's *hard,* Tommy must not have had difficulty with it.
   arduous = difficult, strenuous; *exertion* = effort, strain
   pedestrian = ordinary, mundane
   pragmatic = practical, concerned with results

7. **A** Zach had knowledge of insects that allowed him to identify the creature. *Entomology* is the study of insects.
   entomology = study of insects
   etymology = study of the origin of words
   ethics = study of moral choices
   pathology = study of disease
   sociology = study of social institutions

8. **E** If a country catches a spy *pilfering* (stealing) information, they will send the spy back to his country of origin.
   quarantined = isolated
   secluded = left alone
   disseminated = spread out
   distended = swollen
   deported = banished

9. **B** If the desert is now *barren* (infertile), it would be hard to imagine it *filled* with farms and wildlife.
   doleful = filled with grief
   replete = filled
   germinated = sprouted
   rarefied = thinned out
   afflicted = suffering

10. **C** The section of a novel that follows the main story is called an *epilogue.*
    elegy = song or poem about death
    epitaph = inscription found on a tombstone
    epilogue = extra chapter added at end of novel
    encore = an extra performance at the end of a show
    eulogy = high praise, speech given at funeral

Unit 7 Exercise Sets II and III Answer Key

Exercise Set II

1. **EPI-**: over
   ephemeral, epitaph, epicenter, epidemic, epidermis, epilepsy, epitome

2. **AD-**: to, towards
   add, annex, adduct, adjure, adhere

3. **SCRIBERE**: to write
   inscribe, circumscribe, conscription, description, inscription, subscription

4. **COPIA**: abundance
   cornucopia, copious, copy

5. **LUNA**: moon
   lunacy, lunar, lunatic, lunate

6. **ASTRUM**: star
   astral, astronomy, astrology, disaster, astronaut

7. **PLERE**: to fill
   accomplish, complement, deplete, manipulate, replete, supplement

8. **SOLUS**: alone
   sole, soliloquy, solitaire, solitary, solitude, solo

9. **GENEA**: descent
   generation, genealogy, congenital

10. **POST-**: after
    posterior, posterity, posthumous, postpone, postscript

11. **ARKHAIOS**: ancient
    archaic, archaeology, archives

12. **DEMOS**: people
    demographics, democracy, epidemic, pandemic

13. **VERT**: to turn
    diverge, divert, revert, pervert, convert

14. **LOGOS**: study of
    psychology, anthropology, oncology, geology

15. **CLAUDERE**: to close
    claustrophobia, conclude, exclude, recluse, seclude

Exercise Set III

1. N
2. N
3. Y
4. N
5. N
6. malady
7. anthropology
8. ostracize
9. astral
10. genealogy
11. cosmic
12. copious
13. recluse
14. despondent
15. amass
16. arable
17. epilogue
18. meager
19. inundate
20. fallow
21. saturate
22. demographics
23. encore
24. surfeit
25. anguish
26. anemic
27. sociologist
28. cession
29. solitary
30. proliferation
31. celestial
32. distend
33. elegy
34. epitaph
35. entomology
36. paucity
37. diminutive
38. exile
39. eulogy
40. propagate
41. augment

CHAPTER 4

CRITICAL READING SKILLS

Lesson 1:
What SAT Critical Reading Is All About

If you want to ace the SAT Critical Reading (CR) section, you need to know more than just a bunch of vocabulary words and a few test-taking tricks. You need solid analytical and critical reading skills to help you tackle any difficult hunk of prose the SAT can throw at you. The most important of these skills is "active reading," which means reading with key questions in mind.

The Three Key Questions

To ace SAT Critical Reading questions, read each passage with these questions at the front of your mind:

1. What is the *purpose* of this passage?
2. What is the *central idea* of this passage?
3. What is the *general structure* of this passage?

SAT CR questions focus on these questions, so you should, too. Here's a quick explanation of each of the three questions you should keep in mind:

1. The *purpose* of the passage can be either

   - to examine a topic objectively,
   - to prove a point, or
   - to tell a story.

2. The *central idea* of the passage is the single idea that provides the focus of the entire passage.
3. The *general structure* of the passage is the way the paragraphs work together to convey the central idea.

Later we'll discuss and practice strategies for finding all these things.

Put the Horse before the Cart—and the Passage before the Questions

A favorite trick of "test crackers" is to read the Critical Reading questions first, answering those that don't require much reading, and then to scan using the line references to get the rest of the answers. This sounds like a great trick because it's so simple. In fact, this trick usually hurts most test takers by forcing them to focus on details rather than the all-important "big picture." If you want a score higher than 500 (and if you don't want to struggle with your reading assignments when you get to college) learn how to analyze passages for the big picture.

Don't read the questions first. Read the *passage* first (including the introduction), but read *actively* and *briskly* to answer the three key questions. You often can answer the first two questions after just reading the introduction and the first paragraph or two! At that point, read the remaining paragraphs just to note how they support the central idea. *The big picture is what counts!* If you practice, you will learn to read SAT passages briskly and confidently.

These Aren't Your English Teacher's Questions

SAT Critical Reading questions aren't the same questions your English teachers ask. English teachers like to ask you to explore symbolism, read between the lines, and interpret passages *subjectively*. But SAT questions must be *objective*—they must have answers that don't depend on your point of view (otherwise, everyone would be arguing constantly about the answers). The SAT only asks questions about what the passage *literally means* and *logically implies*, not what the passage *might suggest*.

SAT Critical Reading questions can't ask you to draw on outside knowledge. Again, all the information you need to answer the question is *in the passage*. Therefore, you should be able to *underline it*. You won't be asked to make creative connections, read between the lines, or explore your feelings about a passage. All you have to do is say what the passage, *literally means* or *logically implies*.

Get Psyched Up, Not Psyched Out

Don't psyche yourself out on the Critical Reading section by thinking, "Oh, great—another boring, pointless reading passage!" This guarantees failure by creating a self-fulfilling prophecy. If you *expect* the passage to be boring and pointless, you won't look for the interesting points, and you'll miss the key ideas!

How well you read depends enormously on your attitude. SAT Critical Reading passages are chosen because they discuss ideas that college professors teach in class. Tell yourself, "I'm going to learn something interesting and valuable from this passage!" This will help you to read *actively*—with relevant questions in mind—rather than *passively*, hoping to soak up information just by decoding the words.

Concept Review 1: Mapping What the SAT Critical Reading Is All About

1. What three key questions should be at the front of your mind as you read?

2. Why is it better to read the passage before reading the questions?

3. What is "active reading," and why is it better than "passive reading"?

4. What does "objective" mean?

5. Why do SAT Critical Reading questions have to be "objective"?

6. What kind of reading questions do English teachers ask that the SAT can't?

SAT Practice 1:
Mapping What the SAT Critical Reading Is All About

The following is an essay regarding current knowledge of subatomic physics.

A tantalizing paradox peers out from every basic physics textbook, but rarely do students
Line notice it or teachers exploit it. Despite the vast knowledge that scientists have accumulated
5   about the subatomic realm, including astonishingly accurate equations for predicting the behavior of barely detectable particles, an obvious conundrum persists that they are only recently beginning to understand: protons
10   stick together in atomic nuclei.

All first-year physics students learn that the atomic nucleus contains neutrons, which have no charge, and protons, which are positively charged. They also learn that while opposite
15   charges attract, all like charges repel each other, just like the north poles of two magnets. So what keeps all of those positively charged protons bound together in a nucleus? Physicists have long postulated that there must be
20   another special force, called the nuclear force, that counteracts the electrical repulsion between protons. But where does it come from?

One theory, proposed by Nobel laureate Hideki Yukawa in the 1930s, held that the nu-
25   clear force is conveyed by a particle called a pion, which, he claimed, is exchanged among the neutrons and protons in the nucleus. Forty years later, physicists discovered that pions, not to mention the protons and neu-
30   trons themselves, are actually composed of yet smaller particles called "quarks," which are held together by aptly named "gluons." The force conveyed by gluons is called the "strong" force. Although experiments had clearly
35   demonstrated that these gluons are responsible for the force that binds quarks within protons and neutrons, nothing suggested that gluons are exchanged between protons and neutrons. Nevertheless, by the early 1980s,
40   most physicists became convinced that some combination of gluons and quarks, perhaps the pion, must be responsible for the nuclear force.

Professor Yukawa's theory, however, was dealt a blow by a series of experiments that
45   were conducted at Los Alamos National Laboratory in the early 1990s. These experiments

demonstrated that pions carry the nuclear force only over distances greater than half a fermi—the radius of a proton—yet the
50   distance between bound protons is far less than that. The pion seemed to be a giant plumber's wrench trying to do a tweezer's job.

In the years since, physicists have refined Yukawa's theory to suggest that closely
55   bound protons or neutrons are held by a "residual" force left over from the strong forces binding quarks together into protons and neutrons, so that pions don't need to be exchanged. If the protons and neutrons are
60   far enough apart within the nucleus, however, perhaps pions do the job.

1.   Which of the following best summarizes the "paradox" mentioned in line 1?

   (A) Teachers don't utilize educational materials effectively.
   (B) A law of physics appears to be violated.
   (C) Scientists continue to test hypotheses that they suspect are false.
   (D) Hideki Yukawa's theory is incorrect.
   (E) Scientists are increasingly reluctant to explore the difficult field of nuclear physics.

2.   In lines 3–4, the author uses the term "vast knowledge" in order to

   (A) emphasize the daunting task faced by science teachers
   (B) empathize with overburdened students
   (C) draw a contrast to an area of relative ignorance
   (D) praise the productivity of physicists relative to other scientists
   (E) acknowledge the difficulty of writing physics textbooks

3. In lines 35–36, the phrase "responsible for" most nearly means

   (A) guardians of
   (B) indebted to
   (C) representative of
   (D) capable of conveying
   (E) responsive to

4. According to the passage, the nuclear force cannot be completely explained in terms of the exchange of pions because pions

   (A) are not composed of quarks
   (B) have little or no effect on the distances between nuclear particles
   (C) repel each other
   (D) cannot coexist with the gluons that convey the "strong" force
   (E) are positively charged

5. Which of the following best describes the purpose of the fifth paragraph (lines 53–61)?

   (A) It resolves a problem indicated in the previous paragraph.
   (B) It provides an example of a concept introduced in the previous paragraph.
   (C) It presents a counterexample to a misconception described in the previous paragraph.
   (D) It provides an example similar to the one presented in the previous paragraph.
   (E) It logically analyzes a claim made in the previous paragraph.

6. Which of the following best describes the organization of this passage as a whole?

   (A) presentation of a theory followed by refutation
   (B) description of a problem followed by a history of attempts to solve it
   (C) statement of fact followed by logical analysis
   (D) description of a scientific discovery followed by a discussion of its implications
   (E) analysis of a theory and suggestions on how it should be taught

Answer Key 1:
Mapping What the SAT Critical Reading Is All About

Concept Review 1

1. What is the purpose of this passage? What is the central idea of this passage? What is the general structure of this passage?

2. It's better to read the passage first, before reading the questions, because you get the most points on the questions only when you get the "big picture" of the passage. The "read the questions first" strategy only distracts you from getting the big picture.

3. Active reading means reading with the three key questions in mind. "Passive" reading (which is reading without questions in mind and merely "hoping" to absorb information) is utterly ineffective on the SAT. Top scorers must read actively.

4. "Objective" means based on clear evidence and facts, not on your opinion or conjecture.

5. SAT Critical Reading questions must be objective—that is, based only on the clear, literal evidence in the passage—because if they weren't, there would be no consistent way to score the test. People would be arguing incessantly about the answers to the questions.

6. English teachers ask lots of interesting questions that could never be asked on the SAT because they are too subjective, such as "What personal experiences does this story remind you of?" or "What kind of job would Hamlet have if he were alive today?" or "What could water represent in this story?" Contrary to what some claim, SAT Critical Reading questions are certainly not "worse" than English teachers' questions just because they are less creative. Indeed, you can't begin to interpret a passage subjectively *until* you first interpret it objectively. You have to understand what the passage says before you can get creative.

SAT Practice 1

1. **B** The paradox is that "protons stick together" (lines 9–10) even though a law of physics suggests that they should repel each other.

2. **C** The passage states that "Despite the vast knowledge that scientists have accumulated" (lines 3–4), "an obvious conundrum persists" (lines 7–8). Therefore, the phrase "vast knowledge" is being used to contrast the "conundrum," which is a vexing problem yet to be solved.

3. **D** The passage states that gluons "are responsible for the force that binds quarks within protons and neutrons" (lines 35–37). In other words, they *convey* the force that binds the particles.

4. **B** The passage states that "pions carry the nuclear force only over distances greater than half a fermi—the radius of a proton—yet the distance between bound protons is far less than that" (lines 47–51). This indicates that pions do not bind protons because they are ineffective in the small distances between bound nuclear particles.

5. **A** The fifth paragraph describes how "physicists have refined Yukawa's theory" (lines 53–54) in order to resolve the problem described in the fourth paragraph, namely, the fact that pions are not effective in the distances within nuclei.

6. **B** This is essentially the third key question: What is the overall structure of the passage? The passage begins by describing a "conundrum" (line 8), then describing attempts to resolve it. The passage ends, however, without a definitive solution: Scientists still don't know precisely what holds an atomic nucleus together. Thus the passage is a description of a problem followed by a history of attempts to solve it.

Lesson 2:
Analyzing the Purpose and Central Idea

Finding the Purpose

About 20–30% of SAT CR questions are "purpose" questions, such as "The overall purpose of this passage is to . . . ." or "The author refers to the 'mountaintop' in line 6 in order to emphasize. . . ." These questions ask *why* the author wrote the passage or used a particular word, phrase, or reference. You will always be prepared for these questions if you focus on overall purpose as you read.

SAT CR passages are drawn from a wide range of disciplines, but every passage has only one of three possible purposes:

- *To examine a concept objectively.* A passage that examines a concept is an *analysis*. It is strictly informative, like a newspaper article or a textbook passage. Think of it as a response to an essay question. It is *objective*—sticking to facts rather than opinions.
- *To prove a point.* A passage that proves a point is an *argument*. It presents the author's point of view on a topic and explains why it is better than another point of view. It is *subjective*—a matter of opinion rather than fact.
- *To tell a story.* A passage that tells a story is a *narrative*—a piece of fiction, a biography, or a memoir. It describes how a character changes in order to deal with a conflict or problem.

To understand a passage, begin by asking, "Is this passage an *analysis*, an *argument*, or a *narrative*? Is its main purpose *to inform to persuade*, or *to inform*?" Knowing this makes answering many SAT questions easier.

Often, the introduction to the passage gives you clues about the purpose. Look for key words such as these:

- Analysis key words: *examine, analyze, scientific, historical, explore*
- Argument key words: *comment, argue, opinion, perspective, point of view, position*
- Narrative key words: *biography, story, autobiography, memoir, novel, fiction, account*

Finding the Central Idea

Often, the first question after an SAT passage is a "central idea" question such as "With which of the following statements would the author most likely agree?" or "This passage is primarily concerned with. . . ." Knowing the central idea is critical to answering these questions. When you are given two "paired" passages, it is particularly important to know how their central ideas compare and contrast.

Although SAT passages contain lots of ideas, each has only one *central idea*. Find it. Every different type of prose has a different type of central idea.

- Every analysis focuses on a *question* that might interest a college professor. It might answer a question such as "What methods do scientists use to measure the location and intensity of earthquakes?" or "What were the social conditions of women in 19th-century England?"
- Every argument focuses on a *thesis*—the point the writer is trying to make. An argument takes a side and makes an evaluation. It argues *against* something substantial and doesn't merely support a claim that everyone already agrees with. Too many students forget this. When reading an argument, ask "What substantial idea is this author arguing *against*?"
- Every narrative focuses on a *conflict*—the problem that the main character must deal with. There is no story without conflict—conflict drives the story. Basically, every story consists of (1) the *introduction* of the conflict, (2) the *development* of the conflict, and (3) the *resolution* of the conflict. Understanding a story begins with understanding this structure.

Once you discover the purpose of the passage, find its central idea—the question, the thesis, or the conflict. Underline it in the passage or jot it down in the margin. To make sure that you really have the central idea, check that it is supported by *every* paragraph. Often, students mistakenly think that the first idea in the passage must be the central idea. Not necessarily. For instance, an author may describe an *opposing* viewpoint before presenting his or her own, so his or her central idea doesn't appear until the second or third paragraph.

Concept Review 2:
Analyzing the Purpose and Central Idea

1. Name the three kinds of prose, and describe the purpose of each.

2. For each type of prose, name four "key words" in the introduction that indicate that particular type of prose:

   a. Narrative

   b. Argument

   c. Analysis

3. What is the function of the "central idea" of a piece of prose?

4. The central idea of a narrative is the

5. The central idea of an argument is the

6. The central idea of an analysis is the

7. How do you know whether you've found the central idea of a passage?

8. After reading the passage on the next page, write what type of prose it is and its central idea.

SAT Practice 2:
Analyzing the Purpose and the Central Idea

The following passage was written in 1911 by Wassily Kandinsky, a renowned abstract painter. Here he discusses the relationship between Primitivism, an artistic movement that seeks to move away from technology and the divisions of modern society, and Materialism, which denies that there is a spiritual component of reality.

Every work of art is the child of its age and, in many cases, the mother of our emotions. It
Line follows that each period of culture produces an art of its own which can never be repeated.
5 Efforts to revive the art-principles of the past will at best produce an art that is still-born. It is impossible for us to live and feel as did the ancient Greeks. In the same way those who strive to follow the Greek methods in sculp-
10 ture achieve only a similarity of form, the work remaining soulless for all time. Such imitation is mere aping. Externally the monkey completely resembles the human being; he will sit holding a book in front of his nose,
15 and turn over the pages with a thoughtful aspect, but his actions have for him no real meaning.
    There is, however, in art another kind of external similarity which is founded on a fun-
20 damental truth. When there is a similarity of inner tendency in the whole moral and spiritual atmosphere, a similarity of ideals, at first closely pursued but later lost to sight, a similarity in the inner feeling of any one period to
25 that of another, the logical result will be a revival of the external forms which served to express those inner feelings in an earlier age. An example of this today is our sympathy, our spiritual relationship, with the Primitives.
30 Like ourselves, these artists sought to express in their work only internal truths, renouncing in consequence all considerations of external form.
    This all-important spark of inner life today
35 is at present only a spark. Our minds, which are even now only just awakening after years of materialism, are infected with the despair of unbelief, of lack of purpose and ideal. The nightmare of materialism, which has turned
40 the life of the universe into an evil, useless game, is not yet past; it holds the awakening soul still in its grip. Only a feeble light glimmers like a tiny star in a vast gulf of darkness. This

feeble light is but a presentiment, and
45 the soul, when it sees it, trembles in doubt whether the light is not a dream, and the gulf of darkness reality. This doubt and the still-harsh tyranny of the materialistic philosophy divide our soul sharply from that of the Primi-
50 tives. Our soul rings cracked when we seem to play upon it, as does a costly vase, long buried in the earth, which is found to have a flaw when it is dug up once more. For this reason, the Primitive phase, through which we are
55 now passing, with its temporary similarity of form, can only be of short duration.

1. Which of the following is the best title for this passage?

    (A) The Art of the Early 20th Century
    (B) The Dangers of Materialism
    (C) Obstacles to the Revival of Primitive Art
    (D) The Similarities in Artistic Movements
    (E) The Lack of Purpose in Art

2. In context, the word "aspect" (line 16) most nearly means

    (A) meaningful perspective
    (B) facial expression
    (C) configuration
    (D) contemplation
    (E) minor part

3. Which of the following is an example of the "fundamental truth" mentioned in lines 19–20?

    (A) the inability of great artists like Vincent Van Gogh to achieve fame in their lifetimes
    (B) the tendency of artists from all cultures to eschew social conventions
    (C) the failure to reproduce artwork that was created in the fourth century BC.
    (D) the ability of apes to create paintings that resemble abstract works by humans
    (E) the similarity between two paintings created a century apart, each in the midst of a great class war

4. In saying that the soul "trembles in doubt" (line 45) when it sees the "feeble light" (line 44), the author suggests that

    (A) artists have doubts about whether the era of materialism is truly past
    (B) the public is unsure that its hunger for art will be met
    (C) artists do not know from where their next inspiration will come
    (D) the Primitives found mysterious lights more frightening than modern people do
    (E) artists usually do not work well under the harsh light of scrutiny

5. How would the author characterize the effect of materialism on the artist's soul?

    (A) supportive
    (B) confusing
    (C) calming
    (D) oppressive
    (E) inspirational

6. According to the metaphor in the final paragraph, the "costly vase" (line 51) represents

    (A) a materialistic aspiration
    (B) a meticulously crafted piece of modern art
    (C) an irretrievable frame of mind
    (D) a cynical attempt at forgery
    (E) a lack of purpose

Answer Key 2:
Analyzing the Purpose and Central Idea

Concept Review 2

1. Narrative: to tell a story; argument: to persuade; analysis: to inform.
2. a. Narrative: *biography, story, autobiography, memoir, novel, fiction, account*
   b. Argument: *comment, argue, opinion, perspective, point of view, position*
   c. Analysis: *examine, analyze, scientific, historical, explore*
3. The central idea is the idea that *focuses, organizes,* and *unifies* the passage. Every paragraph must contribute to the central idea.
4. the conflict
5. the thesis
6. the question being analyzed
7. The central idea must "carry through" the entire passage, so to check that you've found the central idea, make sure that every paragraph contributes to that central idea. If not, then reread the paragraph until it "fits" with the central idea, or reconsider what the central idea is.
8. This passage is an argument; the author is presenting a subjective theory about art and artistic movements. Its central idea, or thesis, is summarized in lines 3–4: *each period of culture produces an art of its own which can never be repeated.*

SAT Practice 2

1. **C** The title should capture the central idea of the passage, which is the thesis that it is difficult to rekindle primitive art because all art is "a child of its age" (line 1) and because modern materialism is interfering with primitive impulses. The best title, then, is (C) Obstacles to the Revival of Primitive Art.

2. **B** The passage says that a monkey can look at a book with a "thoughtful aspect" but really have no understanding of the book. Since the monkey does not understand the book, choices (A) and (D) are illogical. The sentence is saying that the monkey only *looks* thoughtful, so choice (B) is the only sensible one.

3. **E** The "fundamental truth" described in the second paragraph is that a "revival of external forms" (line 26), that is, art forms that resemble those of the past, can occur only when there is "a similarity of inner tendency in the whole moral and spiritual atmosphere" (lines 20–22). The only example given that suggests that fact is (E).

4. **A** In these lines, the author is using a metaphor to describe how "our minds" and "the soul," by which he means the artistic, spiritual mind, are affected by the materialism of the age. Artistic inspiration is described as a "spark," and materialism as a "nightmare" and a "vast gulf of darkness." The soul "trembles" because it doubts that the light is "not a dream," meaning that the light might be a dream and the darkness reality. Therefore the author suggests that materialism might still hold the artistic soul in its grip.

5. **D** The metaphor in the final paragraph makes it clear that materialism "holds the awakening soul in its grip" (lines 41–42). This is not a nurturing grip, because the soul "trembles" (line 45) before the "nightmare of materialism" (line 39). Therefore, according to the author, materialism oppresses the artistic soul.

6. **C** The "costly vase" is described as something that has been "long buried in the earth, which is found to have a flaw when it is dug up once more" (lines 51–53). This vase is compared to "our soul" (line 50), which is described as having a "sympathy" (line 28) and "spiritual relationship" (line 29) with the primitives. Therefore, the costly vase clearly represents the irretrievable idea of primitivism.

Lesson 3:
Finding Patterns in the Structure of the Passage

Finding the Structure of the Passage

Many SAT CR questions are *structure* questions such as "Which of the following best describes the overall structure of this passage?" or "What is the relationship between the third paragraph and the fourth paragraph?" They ask you to focus on the relationships between paragraphs and how they work together to convey the central idea. After you've found the purpose and central idea of the passage, ask "What does each paragraph or section do to support the central idea?"

A good piece of prose is like a good painting: It has an effective *structure*—the parts work together to create an overall effect. The basic unit of structure in a passage is the paragraph. To give another analogy, a paragraph is like a stepping-stone on a journey. Good writers make sure that each paragraph takes the reader further on the journey. No paragraph should deviate from the goal of developing the central idea.

The Structure of an Analysis

Most analytical essays have three basic parts: the introduction, the development, and the conclusion. The first paragraph of an analytical essay usually introduces the topic. A good introduction shows why the topic is worth exploring and draws the reader in by revealing interesting facts. It might describe an interesting phenomenon, a theory, or concept. If it describes a phenomenon, then the next paragraphs might give examples of it, present a theory to explain it, or describe its discovery. The passage also may describe a problem or debate related to that phenomenon.

There are many ways to structure an analysis, so pay attention. As you read, focus on the role each paragraph is playing and what devices the author uses to support the central idea. SAT questions often ask about devices, as in "The author's reference to the 'maze' (line 32) serves the same illustrative purpose as which of the following?"

The Structure of an Argument

There are many ways to prove a point. For instance, if you want to persuade your readers to support gun control, you might tell a tragic story of a gun-related death, cite government statistics about gun violence, refer to a study about the behavior of people when they have guns versus when they don't, or discuss the effectiveness or ineffectiveness of past gun policies and education programs. Each of these is a different *rhetorical device* for persuading the reader. Noticing the choices a writer makes when constructing an argument makes you not only a better reader but also a better writer.

When reading an argument, pay attention to the rhetorical devices the author uses with a critical eye. Are they convincing to you? Are the examples strong? Is the reasoning sound? Asking these questions helps you to read more actively. Furthermore, reading critically prepares you to answer higher-order questions such as "Which of the following, if true, would suggest a basic flaw in the author's reasoning?" or "Which of the following elements is NOT used in this passage?"

The Structure of a Narrative

As we discussed in the last lesson, every narrative has the same basic skeleton: The conflict is introduced, then developed, and then resolved. This is helpful to remember because paragraphs don't work the same way in narratives as they do in other kinds of prose. For instance, in an essay, a new paragraph signals the start of a new idea, but in a narrative, it also may signal a new line of dialogue or a new scene.

To understand the structure of a narrative, continually ask "How does this dialogue or description introduce, explain, develop, or resolve the conflict?" For instance, a description of a fight between friends *establishes* a conflict. A paragraph about a character's inner thoughts about the fight *develops* the conflict. And a dialogue in which the friends make up *resolves* the conflict. Look for such key points in every narrative you read.

Concept Review 3:
Finding Patterns in the Structure of the Passage

1. What is the "structure" of a passage?

2. What is the basic unit of structure in a passage?

3. What are the three basic parts of most analyses?

4. What are the three basic parts of most narratives?

5. Name four kinds of rhetorical devices that an argument might use.

SAT Practice 3:
Finding Patterns in the Structure of the Passage

The following passage, from a text on the principles of zoology, discusses theories of biogenesis, the process by which life forms are created.

From ancient times, people commonly believed that life arose repeatedly by sponta-
Line neous generation from nonliving material in addition to parental reproduction. For exam-
5   ple, frogs appeared to arise from damp earth, mice from putrefied matter, insects from dew, and maggots from decaying meat. Warmth, moisture, sunlight, and even starlight often were mentioned as factors that
10 encouraged spontaneous generation of living organisms.
    Among the accounts of early efforts to syn-thesize organisms in the laboratory is a recipe for making mice, given by the Belgian plant
15 nutritionist Jean Baptiste van Helmont (1648). "If you press a piece of underwear soiled with sweat together with some wheat in an open jar, after about 21 days the odor changes and the ferment. . . . changes the
20 wheat into mice. But what is more remarkable is that the mice which came out of the wheat and underwear were not small mice, not even miniature adults or aborted mice, but adult mice emerge!"
25 In 1861, the great French scientist Louis Pasteur convinced scientists that living organisms cannot arise spontaneously from nonliving matter. In his famous experi-ments, Pasteur introduced fermentable
30 material into a flask with a long s-shaped neck that was open to air. The flask and its contents were then boiled for a long time to kill any microorganisms that might be pre-sent. Afterward the flask was cooled and left
35 undisturbed. No fermentation occurred because all organisms that entered the open end were deposited in the neck and did not reach the fermentable material. When the neck of the flask was removed, micro-
40 organisms in the air promptly entered the fermentable material and proliferated. Pasteur concluded that life could not originate in the absence of previously existing organisms and their reproductive
45 elements, such as eggs and spores. Announc-ing his results to the French Academy, Pasteur proclaimed, "Never will the doctrine

of spontaneous generation arise from this mortal blow."
50 All living organisms share a common ances-tor, most likely a population of colonial microorganisms that lived almost 4 billion years ago. This common ancestor was itself the product of a long period of prebiotic
55 assembly of nonliving matter, including organic molecules and water, to form self-replicating units. All living organisms retain a fundamental chemical composition inherited from their ancient common
60 ancestor.

1. Throughout the passage, the word "spontaneous" can best be taken to mean

    (A) without reproductive elements
    (B) in a medium
    (C) unthinking
    (D) free-spirited
    (E) adult

2. In Pasteur's experiment, why was the neck of the flask removed?

    (A) to allow the air to escape
    (B) to provide access to microorganisms
    (C) to kill any microorganisms that may be present
    (D) to permit the heating of the flask
    (E) to introduce fermentable material

3. In line 49, the word "mortal" most nearly means

    (A) human
    (B) impermanent
    (C) fatal
    (D) earthly
    (E) malicious

4. If both Pasteur's conclusion that "life could not originate in the absence of . . . eggs and spores" (lines 42–45) and the statement, "This common ancestor . . . units" (lines 53–57) are true, then which of the following statements also must be true about "prebiotic assembly" (lines 54–55)?

(A) It is not a "spontaneous" process.
(B) It does not depend on sunlight.
(C) It produces molecules unlike those in current life forms.
(D) It occurs in the absence of water.
(E) It occurs very quickly.

5. The author of this passage would likely agree with all of the following statements EXCEPT

(A) Jean Baptiste van Helmont's efforts to synthesize organisms were poorly controlled.
(B) Life on earth began about 4 billion years ago.
(C) Nonliving matter cannot form units that can reproduce themselves.
(D) The chemical makeup of organisms must be fundamentally similar to that of their parents.
(E) Carefully controlled experiments can disprove even widely held biological theories.

6. The theory of biogenesis described in lines 50–60 shares what common element with the theory of spontaneous generation described in lines 1–11?

(A) a single common ancestor
(B) water as an essential reactant
(C) the process of fermentation
(D) sexual reproduction
(E) decaying organisms

Answer Key 3:
Finding Patterns in the Structure of the Passage

Concept Review 3

1. The structure of the passage is the way that individual paragraphs work together to convey the central idea of the passage.
2. The paragraph
3. The introduction, the development, and the conclusion

4. The introduction of the conflict, the development of the conflict, and the resolution of the conflict
5. Studies, authoritative quotes, anecdotes, statistics, logical analysis, examples, etc.

SAT Practice 3

1. **A** The theory of "spontaneous generation" is described as one in which life arises from substances that do not contain the reproductive elements of that life form.
2. **B** The important difference between the flask with the neck intact and the flask with the neck removed was the presence of microorganisms in the fermentable material. When the neck was removed, "microorganisms in the air promptly entered the fermentable material and proliferated."
3. **C** The experiment, Pasteur claimed, "killed" the theory of spontaneous generation, so it dealt a *fatal* blow.
4. **A** The "prebiotic assembly" is said to occur over a "long period." This must not be an example of "spontaneous generation," that is, generation of life over a short period of time from nonliving material, because the theory of spontaneous generation has been disproven.

5. **C** The author clearly believes that van Helmont's study was poorly controlled and that controlled experiments can disprove widely held theories because van Helmont's theory was refuted when Pasteur imposed tighter controls. He also states that all living organisms derived from an ancestor "that lived almost 4 billion years ago" (lines 52–53) and that they "retain a fundamental chemical composition inherited from their ancient common ancestor" (lines 58–60). However, the author would not agree that "nonliving matter cannot form units that can reproduce themselves" because he describes just such matter in lines 53–57.
6. **B** The theory of spontaneous generation described in lines 1–11 mentions "damp earth," "dew," and "moisture" as "factors that encouraged spontaneous generation." The theory of biogenesis described in lines 50–60 states that water is an essential element of prebiotic assembly.

Lesson 4: Simplifying the Passage

Simplify by Paraphrasing

When you read, your brain is not a CD burner: It doesn't just record all the information for perfect recall. You need to train your brain to process the information into simpler forms. This is called *paraphrasing*, summarizing paragraphs and passages in a few tidy words.

Good readers constantly paraphrase paragraphs as they read. Don't worry—it doesn't waste time. With practice, paraphrasing will actually *save* you time on the reading section. Having the key ideas fresh in your mind helps you to zero in on the right answers.

> As you read SAT passages, practice paraphrasing each paragraph. You may want to write each summary in the margin. Be as concise as possible, but capture the key idea. For instance, "This paragraph is about dolphins and their intelligence" is a poor summary because it doesn't capture the key idea, just the topic. A better summary is "Dolphins have communication skills that other mammals lack." If it's relevant, make a quick note of how the paragraph relates to the previous paragraph. Does it provide an example of a concept described previously? Does it describe a situation that contrasts with the previous one?

Simplify, but Don't Oversimplify

Avoid test-taking tricks that *oversimplify* SAT CR questions. Two of the most popular tricks in SAT courses and books are the "chuck the extremes" trick and the "don't dis the minorities" trick. As with many simplistic shortcuts, they don't work so well. They assume that the right answers to SAT questions are never "extreme," particularly if they pertain to reading passages about minorities or women. So, they say, just eliminate any choices that take an extremely positive or negative tone, and eliminate all answers with a *negative* tone if the passage pertains to a minority or minority group "because the SAT will never disparage minorities."

The problem is that the SAT always knows how to thwart these shortcuts, to force students to *read* to get the right answer, rather than just apply a test-taking trick. For instance, the "minority" passage on the May 2006 SAT was a story about two Asian-American poets. Here are two of the questions:

The tone of the characterizations quoted in lines 11–12 is best described as

(A) morose
(B) curious
(C) sardonic
(D) threatening
(E) incredulous

The tone of the statement in line 20 is best described as

(A) impatient
(B) apologetic
(C) reflective
(D) anxious
(E) unconvinced

Nationwide, thousands of students who had taken SAT courses were confident that they could "crack" these questions. Because the passage concerns American minorities, the tone of the correct answers must be positive, right? In question 12, the only choice with a positive tone is (B), and in question 13, the only one is (C). Easy!

But wrong. Even a cursory reading would reveal the correct answers to be (C) *sardonic* and (E) *unconvinced*, respectively. Pretty negative, huh? Of course, SAT passages are *not* disparaging of minority groups, but this fact is not so easy to translate into a quick-and-easy test-taking trick as some would like you to believe.

Simplify by Visualizing

Visualization increases your brain's ability to absorb information. After all, "a picture is worth a thousand words," right? Visualizing as you read increases your interest as well as your retention. Visualizing a narrative is relatively simple because narratives contain characters and action. But how do you visualize an analysis or argument?

> - When reading an analysis, visualize the subject matter as best you can. For instance, if it's about life in 15th–century Italy, picture a map of Italy, and visualize the people in dress of the times. If it's about the discovery of a quasar, visualize the pulsing star and the astronomers gazing at it through telescopes, and perhaps visualize a timeline of the discoveries.
> - When you read an argument, visualize a battle with the author's thesis on one side battling the opposing thesis. It's very important to "see" the two sides. The explanations and examples are like "weapons" against the enemy.

Concept Review 4: Simplifying the Passage

1. What should you visualize when reading a narrative?

2. What should you visualize when reading an argument?

3. What should you visualize when reading an analysis?

4. What questions should you answer at the end of each paragraph?

Practice paraphrasing by writing a quick summary after each paragraph.

5. *When examined closely, "raising standards" does not often have the effect of improving education, despite all the rhetoric. When this game—and it is largely a game—is played right, the statistics improve, and its proponents claim victory. But we can do all sorts of horrible things to students in order to improve educational statistics: kick out slow learners, encourage cheating, employ superficial tests that are easily coached but reflect no real academic skill, and so on. We think that by saying we're "raising standards," we are challenging our children more intensely, and thereby producing smarter and more mature kids. For the most part, it's a con game, and we're all being taken in.*

   _____

   _____

   _____

6. *Art historians and aestheticians have long been confounded by Dadaism's complexities and seeming paradoxes. Few seem able to express its real meaning. Dadaism imbues art with the outrageous and the whimsical, but it is a mistake to think that it is mere child's play. It is a profound expression of art as life in the moment. Its works have sadly been lost on a public that expects erudition, archetypes, and allusions in its art, rather than the exuberance of life that art should be.*

   _____

   _____

   _____

SAT Practice 4: Simplifying the Passage

The following passage discusses the philosophi-
cal distinction between two methods of explain-
ing scientific phenomena.

As our theories about the world around us have
evolved and have become more useful, they
Line have become, almost without exception, less
teleological and more mechanistic. A teleolog-
5 ical explanation of a phenomenon describes
causes and effects in terms of desires or purposes: something happens simply because it
serves a certain purpose, because it is "supposed" to happen, or because someone or
10 something "wants" it to happen. A ball falls to
earth because, as it is in the air, it perceives that
its more proper place is on the ground, and not
because anything pushes it. Teleological
explanations never survive as useful theories
15 because they are backward: they place the
cause after the effect.

A mechanistic explanation, on the other
hand, requires that any discussion of causes
and effects be restricted by the known laws of
20 how physical objects and substances interact
as time moves *forward*. This is the language of
the scientist. No right-minded chemist would
say that trinitrotoluene explodes because it
"wants to." It does so because the presence of
25 heat and oxygen releases the potential energy
stored in its bonds.

Early scientific theories were almost exclusively teleological. If you could drive Socrates
around in an SUV, he would be far more
30 likely to ask you about your vehicle's nature, or
its desires, or its soul than about how the engine
worked, how the odometer received its information, or how the different buttons on the CD
player produced their effects. It would
35 seem to him that he was in the belly of a metal-
lic animal, or at least a possessed machine.

Teleological explanations are convenient for
explaining what people do, because most of us
understand the concepts of "wants" and
40 "needs" far more deeply than we understand
the mind's mechanisms for processing information. If you only have three minutes to
explain to your friend why you are not going to
a party, you don't very well have the knowledge,
45 not to mention the time or desire, to explain
how your cerebral cortex processed the
information and concepts associated with the

decision to stay home. You just give a reason why you don't want to, and your friend
understands.
50 This convenience persuades us that teleological explanations are the best for analyzing
human behavior. Furthermore, we resist
mechanistic explanations of behavior because
55 they seem to deny another preciously guarded
concept: free will. If our decision to stay home
from a party could be explained in the same
way that the action of an internal combustion
engine can be explained, then doesn't that
60 reduce us all to mindless machines?

No: the mind's understanding of the mind
will always leave room for "free will," whatever that really means. Full understanding of
a phenomenon depends on the mind's ability
65 to detach from and observe it, and the mind
can never fully detach from itself. This com-
plication may imply that a full understanding
of the human mind is impossible, but it does
not imply that we must be satisfied with mere
70 teleology. Perhaps this will require an entirely
new conception of psychology, but if psychology is to remain relevant, we have no other
choice.

1. Which of the following is the best title for this
   passage?

   (A) Why Mechanism Should Replace Teleology
   (B) The Science of the Ancient Greeks
   (C) The Psychology of Wants and Needs
   (D) The Causes of Scientific Ignorance
   (E) Obstacles to a Full Understanding of the
       Mind

2. Which of the following is an example of a "teleological" explanation?

   (A) water evaporates because it absorbs heat
   (B) an engine works because it burns fuel
   (C) a bird sings because it likes the sound
   (D) a dog yelps because it perceives pain
   (E) a ball falls because a gravitational field
       pulls it

3. The reference to Socrates (lines 28–36) emphasizes the fact that he was

   (A) more influential than other Greek philosophers
   (B) fearful of complicated machines
   (C) concerned more with ethics than with physics
   (D) aware of the mechanistic laws of physics
   (E) inclined to explain phenomena in terms of purposes

4. In line 36, the word "possessed" most nearly means

   (A) owned
   (B) willful
   (C) purchased
   (D) determined
   (E) spontaneous

5. The fourth paragraph (lines 37–49) suggests that teleological explanations persist chiefly because they

   (A) are easier to use
   (B) are more logically consistent
   (C) agree with physical laws
   (D) deny free will
   (E) explain physical phenomena accurately

6. Which of the following best describes the characterizations of the "machine" in line 36 and the "machines" in line 60?

   (A) The "machine" is modern, but the "machines" are ancient.
   (B) The "machine" obeys mechanistic physical laws, but the "machines" do not.
   (C) The "machine" cannot be explained teleologically, but the "machines" can.
   (D) The "machine" is simple, but the "machines" are not.
   (E) The "machine" is thought to have a soul, but the "machines" have had their souls diminished.

Answer Key 4: Simplifying the Passage

Concept Review 4

1. Visualize the characters and the action in vivid detail. Pay close attention to the conflict or problem in the story.
2. Visualize a physical battle between the opposing viewpoints in the argument. Imagine each rhetorical device as a weapon against the enemy.
3. Visualize the subject matter as best you can. If it is a historical analysis, try to visualize a map of the region being discussed, and visualize the people in dress of the times. If it is about animals, try to imagine watching a documentary about those animals as the "narrator" speaks.
4. What is the main idea of the paragraph? How does it relate to the previous paragraph? How does it support the central idea of the passage?
5. "Raising standards" can have many negative effects like cheating, unfairness, and superficial learning.
6. Dadaism is not silly or irrelevant; it is the expression of life in the moment.

SAT Practice 4

1. **A**   The passage compares mechanistic explanations to teleological ones and explains why mechanistic ones are "more useful." Choices (B), (C), and (D) describe tasks that go far beyond what this passage accomplishes, and choice (E) describes an idea that is mentioned only in the last paragraph.

2. **C**   "Teleological" explanations are those that "describe causes and effects in terms of desires or purposes." Saying that a bird sings because it "likes the sound" implies that the bird's action is caused by a desire.

3. **E**   Socrates is said to "be far more likely to ask you about your vehicle's nature, or its desires, or its soul than about how the engine worked." This underscores the author's belief that Socrates explained things in terms of their "purposes."

4. **B**   Socrates, the author tells us, would believe that the SUV possessed a soul, so the "possessed machine" is one with a living spirit and will.

5. **A**   The fourth paragraph tells us that teleological explanations "are convenient," and goes on to explain why people continue to use them.

6. **E**   The "possessed machine" in line 36 is the SUV that Socrates would believe has a soul. The "mindless machines" of line 60 represent the conception of human beings that many would have if human behavior were explained "mechanistically," thereby removing (they would think) our free will and soul.

Lesson 5:
Connecting the Questions to the Passage

Think of Your Own Answer First

After answering the three key questions for yourself, attack the SAT questions by following these steps:

1. Read each question carefully, *covering up the answer choices for now.*
2. Translate it into a "stand-alone" question, if possible.
3. Formulate your own answer to the translated question.
4. Choose the best match among the choices.

This strategy takes advantage of the work you've done answering the key questions, and keeps you from getting "talked into" wrong answers that only *look* good.

For instance, a question such as "The passage suggests that most people do not notice bias in the media because . . ." can be translated into the open-ended question. "Why [according to this author] don't people notice bias in the media?" Answer this question on your own, then find the best match among the choices.

Know the 6 Question Types

1. *Purpose* questions ask why the author wrote the passage or used some particular word or lines, as in "The reference to the 'tragedy' (line 16) primarily serves to. . . ." These questions usually contain key phrases such as "in order to" or "primarily serves to." *To tackle these questions, first remind yourself of the purpose of the whole passage, and then of the paragraph, then of any line references.*

2. *Central idea* questions ask you to summarize the central idea or make an inference based on the author's position, as in "Which of the following is the best title of this passage?" or "With which of the following statements would the author most likely agree?" *To tackle these questions, remind yourself of the central idea before checking the choices.*

3. *Secondary idea* questions ask you to identify the main ideas of individual paragraphs rather than of the passage as a whole, as in "The 'problems' mentioned in line 56 are those of . . ." or "The third paragraph suggests. . . ." *To tackle these questions, reread the specified lines—sticking to the specified*

lines and perhaps the sentence before—and summarize them before checking the choices.

4. *Tone* questions ask you about the attitude of the author or the tone of particular characterizations. *To tackle tone questions, pay attention when the author is being funny, critical, condescending, or objective.*

5. *Word or phrase in context* questions ask you what a particular word or phrase means in the context of a sentence. *To tackle these questions, reread the specific sentence, translate the given word into your own word, and compare this to the choices.*

6. *Structure or device* questions ask you about the relationship between paragraphs or the author's use of such devices as *anecdotes, authoritative references, statistics, metaphors, counterexamples, and such. To tackle these questions, pay particular attention to such devices as you read analyses or arguments.*

Check the Line References

Always carefully reread any words or lines the question refers to, with the question type in mind. For instance, if the question is a "purpose" question—using a phrase such as "in order to"—reread the words or lines asking, "What purpose does this word, phrase, or reference have in this discussion?" If it is a "secondary idea" question—using a word such as "suggests," "represents," or "means"—reread the words or lines asking, "What does the author mean by that?"

Use the "Sandwich Strategy" to Find the Answer

Unlike questions on other SAT sections, CR questions do *not* go in order of increasing difficulty. Rather, they *follow the order of the passage*. Generally, the first questions are about the beginning of the passage, and the last questions are about the end of the passage. Use the "sandwich strategy" to answer questions without line references. For instance, if question 23 does not contain a line reference, but question 22 refers to line 15 and question 24 refers to line 25, then the answer to question 23 is probably "sandwiched" between lines 15 and 25!

Concept Review 5:
Connecting the Questions to the Passage

1. What are the four steps to effectively attacking SAT CR questions?

2. What does it mean to translate SAT CR questions into "stand-alone" questions?

3. Why is it important to translate SAT CR questions into "stand-alone" questions whenever possible?

4. Translate each of the following questions into a "stand-alone" open-ended essay question:

    a. "The author's attitude toward the opposition (line 42) is one of . . ."
    b. "The garden has become important to the author because . . ."
    c. "The last paragraph suggests that Davis is motivated by . . ."
    d. "The author refers to the freedom of estuary birds in lines 1–2 in order to emphasize the fact that . . ."
    e. "The author uses the term solid (line 16) primarily in order to . . ."

5. What is the "sandwich strategy"?

6. How should you attack a question that contains the phrase "in order to"?

SAT Practice 5:
Connecting the Questions to the Passage

The following is an excerpt from a recent book by two science writers on the evolution of human intelligence.

Where can freedom be found? Perhaps in a flock of estuary birds? Flying together at high
Line speeds, thousands of birds maneuver with precise coordination. The flock flies this way
5   and then that. It turns as if a wave has passed through it. These "maneuver waves" start slowly in a few individuals but quickly spread. Unless the individual birds reacted together, the flock would disperse, exposing isolated
10   birds to predators. Sometimes it is "smart," in a survival sense, to give up your freedom and fit in with a group.
     Once started, a wave travels through a flock at about 70 birds a second. Surprisingly, this
15   is much faster than a single bird's reaction time. Thus, individual birds cannot have seen their neighbors and said to themselves, "Hey, they've changed direction—I'd better copy them." Something else besides copying is
20   synchronizing the birds. Somehow they see themselves, if only for a short time, as part of a whole. They see the wave maneuver and time their own change of flight with it.
     Individuals cease to be individuals in many
25   ways—not just when flying together. Humans can react physically as a group; a wave of legs passes down a chorus line at roughly 10 dancers every second. As with birds taking off, this is too fast for movements made in reaction
30   to neighbors. A similar thing, no doubt at a deeper level, organizes a jazz jam or a basket-ball team. This suggests that people are good—surprisingly good—at synthesizing their actions into a larger whole. Soldiers
35   marching in step with each other are not doing so as individuals.
     We all have a sense of "we" that identifies with "our" group and favors "us" against out-siders. We have our fraternities, sororities,
40   and other old boy and girl networks. We seek out people who share the same club, school tie, or accent. Much of this activity is harm-less, but our loyalties also have their darker side. When loyal group members are found to
45   be doing wrong—committing sexual or physi-cal abuse, faking data, or taking bribes—other

group members protect them. The bonds among group members may make them treat the whistle-blower, not the wrongdoer, as the
50   criminal. They do this especially if the whistle-blower is a member of their in-group—one does not squeal, tell tales, or inform on one's comrades.
     Social psychologists find that we easily
55   become prejudiced. It takes the smallest hint that you belong to one group and other people to another for you to favor "your own" group. The reason you belong to one group rather than another may be no more than a prefer-
60   ence for abstract artists, Paul Klee rather than Wassily Kandinsky. You need not even meet and interact with the members of your own group, but prejudice will nonetheless rear its ugly head. It may be our football team, school,
65   town or nation, or the color of our skin. Once fully identified with that "we," people become sensitive to the needs of their group and callous toward other groups. Outsiders cease to matter. The stronger our identification with
70   the "we," the blinder we become to the humanity we share with "them." Out of this psychology comes the nasty side of history and the human race: the world of "ethnic cleansing," genocide, racial prejudice, and
75   global terrorism. Thus, we may be born alone, but we quickly learn to identify ourselves with a group, leading, in some cases, to barbaric consequences.

1. The primary purpose of this passage is to

(A) examine a problem
(B) compare human behavior with bird behavior
(C) disprove a theory
(D) suggest an alternative
(E) analyze a phenomenon

John R. Skoyles and Dorion Sagan, *Up from Dragons.* © 2002 McGraw-Hill. Reprinted by permission of The McGraw-Hill Companies.

2. The passage refers to the "freedom" of estuary birds in lines 1–2 in order to emphasize the fact that

(A) birds are more physically free than humans
(B) something is not as it appears
(C) scientists do not yet understand how birds move in flocks
(D) the coordination of birds in flight is distinctly different from the coordination of human political movements
(E) birds do not appreciate the complexity of their actions

3. By saying that soldiers do not march "as individuals" (line 36), the authors suggest that the soldiers

(A) are compelled to march through coercion
(B) must obey the orders of their superiors
(C) react as a part of an organized whole
(D) lack leadership skills
(E) are reluctant

4. Klee and Kandinsky (lines 60–61) are mentioned as examples of

(A) artists whose works are closely related
(B) people who do not act as individuals
(C) men whose followers may form distinct groups
(D) those who belong to a privileged group
(E) individuals who express prejudice

5. On the whole, the authors' attitude toward group behavior is one of

(A) ambivalence
(B) disdain
(C) admiration
(D) skepticism
(E) fear

6. The "psychology" mentioned in line 72 is closest to the mindset of

(A) an orchestra conductor working to perfect a performance
(B) a scientist studying the nature of cooperation
(C) a football player trying to become a productive member of a team
(D) an artist seeking isolation in which to work
(E) an ideologue trying to inspire hatred of an enemy

Answer Key 5:
Connecting the Questions to the Passage

Concept Review 5

1. (1) Read each question carefully, covering up the answer choices for now, (2) translate it into a "stand-alone" question, if possible, (3) formulate your own answer to the translated question, and (4) choose the best match among the choices.

2. A "stand-alone" question is one that can be answered without needing to look at multiple choices. It should be phrased like an open-ended essay question, such as "What is the tone of line 35?" rather than "The tone of line 35 is best characterized as. . . ."

3. Translating and answering the question as a "stand-alone" question helps you to avoid the most common "traps" in SAT Critical Reading questions. Many of the choices will sound good because they are "true" in some sense but in fact do not answer the question. (More on this in Lesson 8.)

4. a. What is the author's attitude toward the "opposition" in line 42?
   b. Why has the garden become important to the author?
   c. What motivates Davis, according to the last paragraph?
   d. What is the author trying to emphasize by mentioning the freedom of estuary birds in lines 1–2?
   e. Why does the author use the term "solid" in line 16?

5. The "sandwich strategy" shows you where to look when a Critical Reading question does not contain a line reference. Because the questions follow the order of the passage, the answer usually can be found between the line reference in the previous question and the line reference in the next question.

6. The phrase "in order to" indicates that the question is asking you to determine the purpose of the passage as a whole or the purpose of some part of the passage. To tackle purpose questions, first remind yourself of the purpose of the passage *overall*, then of the purpose of the specific paragraph, and then of the purpose of the specific word or reference.

SAT I Practice 5

1. **E** This passage analyzes (examines closely) the phenomenon of group behavior, first in terms of birds flying together, then in terms of human beings acting as teams, and then in terms of human group identification. This passage is not focused on a "problem" because group behavior is often depicted as a positive thing, particularly in the first three paragraphs, so choice (A) is incorrect. Since the passage discusses birds only in the first couple of paragraphs, (B) must be incorrect. Also, since no alternative to a situation or refutation of a theory is presented, (C) and (D) cannot be right.

2. **B** The authors begin with a question: "Where can freedom be found?" and a rhetorical answer: "Perhaps in a flock of estuary birds?" This leads us to believe that the author might use the example of birds flying as an example of "freedom." However, the paragraph (and the passage as a whole) goes on to suggest that bird flight is not as "free" as it seems and often typifies group behavior.

3. **C** The example of the marching soldiers follows the examples of the estuary birds, the chorus line, the jazz band, and the basketball team. All of these examples reinforce the common theme of group behavior being an organized whole.

4. **C** The sentence says that "The reason you belong to one group rather than another may be no more than a preference for abstract artists, Paul Klee rather than Wassily Kandinsky." This means that those who like the art of Klee might form a distinct group from those who like Kandinsky.

5. **A** The authors indicate the positive benefits of group behavior in the first three paragraphs, then its "darker side" in the last two paragraphs. This is an example of *ambivalence*, in which the authors are not saying that group behavior is always good or always bad.

6. **E** According to the passage, the "psychology" mentioned in line 72 is the mind-set by which people become blind "to the humanity we share with 'them'" (lines 70–71) and which leads to scourges such as "'ethnic cleansing,' genocide, racial prejudice, and global terrorism" (lines 73–75). Therefore, it is closest to the mind-set of *an ideologue trying to inspire hatred of an enemy.*

Lesson 6:
Finding Alternatives in Attacking the Questions

"Whole-Passage Attack" versus "Paragraph Attack"

Although many students do best by reading the whole passage before attacking the questions, some prefer to attack the questions sooner. This approach, called the "paragraph attack," takes advantage of the ordering of SAT CR questions. In this mode of attack, you read the first paragraph or two, and then answer the questions that pertain to just those paragraphs (skipping any "big picture" questions for now). When you reach a question that refers to a portion of the passage that you haven't read, go back and read the next paragraph or two, and so on. Always read and summarize whole paragraphs at a time before going to the questions. Don't stop in the middle of a paragraph.

> Experiment with the "whole-passage attack" and the "paragraph attack" strategies as you practice, and decide which works better for you.

Attacking Paired Passages

Every SAT contains "paired" passages—one pair of long passages and one pair of short passages—that share a common theme but are written by different authors. They are followed by normal CR questions and then questions comparing or contrasting the ideas and tone of the two passages. For these passages, you'll want to change your attack strategy slightly.

> Here's how to attack paired passages:
>
> - First, read Passage 1 with the key questions in mind, paying particular attention to tone.
> - After summarizing, attack the questions that pertain only to Passage 1.
> - Next, read Passage 2, again paying attention to tone. Ask, "How do the perspective and tone of this passage differ from those of Passage 1? How are they similar?"
> - Then attack the questions that pertain to Passage 2 and the comparison questions.
> - Do *not* read the passages back-to-back because then you will be more likely to confuse the ideas in the passages.

Attacking SAT Passages from Hell

Hopefully, if you've practiced the College Hill Method for attacking the SAT CR, you've learned that you can attack even tough reading passages about, say, ancient Greek metaphysics. But what if you're faced with a real SAT passage from hell? What if you just can't get through the language or concepts in a really tough SAT passage? Don't panic. Just change your mode of attack.

> If a particular passage seems completely incomprehensible, first see if there is another passage to attack on that section, and move on to that one. If not, just go to the questions that require little reading: the "word in context" questions and the "secondary idea" questions. Usually these don't require you to understand the "big picture," so they are easier to attack.

The Need for Speed

The SAT isn't a speed-reading test, so don't rush through the passages. With practice in the College Hill Method, your reading will become brisker and more efficient on its own. But what if you still struggle to finish the SAT CR sections on time? Here's our approach:

- Step 1: Don't panic. Your efficiency will improve as you practice with the College Hill Method, and the problem may well take care of itself. But what if you still struggle with time after weeks of practice?

- Step 2: Use your finger to "push" your eyes more quickly over the words. Move your finger smoothly over the words, and focus your eyes right next to your finger. With just a little practice, you may be amazed at how much faster you can read without losing comprehension. Practice this strategy *continuously* with *everything* you read for two weeks—use it when you're reading the newspaper, your homework assignments, magazines, *everything*. But what if even this doesn't work well enough?

- Step 3: Get tested to see if you can take the SAT with extended time. If you have a diagnosable learning disability that slows down your reading, you may well qualify for extra time on the SAT. Talk to your guidance counselor about getting tested, and do it at least a few months before taking the SAT.

Concept Review 6:
Finding Alternatives in Attacking the Questions

1. Briefly describe the difference between the "whole-passage attack" and the "paragraph attack."

2. How should your attack strategy shift when reading paired passages?

3. How should your attack strategy shift when reading an extremely difficult passage?

4. What strategies should you try if you have trouble finishing the CR sections in time?

SAT Practice 6:
Finding Alternatives in Attacking the Questions

PASSAGE 1

We have five senses in which we glory, senses that constitute the sensible world for us. But
Line there are other senses, equally vital, but unrecognized and unlauded. These senses,
5 unconscious, automatic, had to be discovered. What the Victorians vaguely called "muscle sense"—the awareness of the relative position of trunk and limbs, was only really defined, and named "proprioception," in the 1890s.
10 And the complex mechanisms and controls by which our bodies are properly aligned and balanced in space have only been defined in the 20th century and still hold many mysteries. Perhaps it will only be in this space age,
15 with the paradoxical license and hazards of gravity-free life, that we will truly appreciate our inner ears, our vestibules, and all the other obscure receptors and reflexes that govern our body orientation. For normal man, in
20 normal situations, they simply do not exist.

PASSAGE 2

A person can "know" something and apply that knowledge but also can "know" something
Line without applying that knowledge. There is a difference between doing wrong when one
25 knows but does not reflect on that knowledge and doing wrong when one knows *and* reflects. Wrongdoing does not seem strange in the former case, but it does in the latter. When a person has knowledge but does not
30 apply it, "having" has an unconventional meaning. In fact, in one sense he has knowledge and in another sense he does not, as in sleep or madness or intoxication. This is the condition of people under the influence of

35 passion, for fits of anger and craving for sensual pleasures and some such things do unmistakenly produce a change in bodily condition and in some instances actually cause madness.

1. The last sentence of Passage 1 ("For normal man . . . do not exist,' lines 19–20) suggests that

   (A) certain modern discoveries have hindered our understanding of our bodily senses
   (B) biological knowledge has grown rapidly in recent decades
   (C) we must work hard to maintain the pace of technological progress
   (D) recent studies of proprioception have been misleading
   (E) most people do not appreciate the function of certain physical senses

2. According to Passage 2, wrongdoing "does not seem strange" (line 27) when the wrongdoer

   (A) applies moral knowledge to the situation
   (B) is attacking a person incapable of self-defense
   (C) is in full control of his or her faculties of reason
   (D) fails to think about what is right and wrong before committing the act
   (E) is doing something that he or she believes is right

3. Unlike Passage 2, Passage 1 is primarily concerned with

    (A) the nature of bodily senses
    (B) knowledge that helps us to decide between right and wrong
    (C) technological innovations in science
    (D) the importance of controlling our consciousness
    (E) the biological systems involved in emotion

4. The authors of both passages would most likely agree that

    (A) it is immoral to ignore knowledge gained from our senses
    (B) emotions often interfere with rational thought
    (C) certain kinds of ignorance are essential to human survival
    (D) people are not always conscious of the information that their minds process
    (E) moral knowledge is gained directly through the physical senses

Answer Key 6:
Finding Alternatives in Attacking the Questions

Concept Review 6

1. The "whole-passage attack" involves reading the entire passage—but with a focus on just answering the three key questions, not on absorbing every detail—before attacking the questions. Many students prefer this method because they prefer to stay "in the flow" of the passage and to absorb information in large chunks. The "paragraph attack" involves reading the introduction and first paragraph or two and then answering the questions that pertain only to the parts you've read, skipping any "big picture" questions for now. Then go on to the next paragraph or two, and answer those questions, and so on. Remember only to read *whole* paragraphs. Don't stop in the middle of a paragraph. (And be sure to go back and answer those "big picture" questions.)

2. First read Passage 1, paying particular attention to tone. After Passage 1, attack the questions that pertain only to Passage 1. Next, read Passage 2, again paying attention to tone. Ask, "How do the perspective and tone of this passage differ from those of Passage 1? How are they similar?" Then attack the questions that pertain to Passage 2 and the comparison questions. Do *not* read the passages back-to-back because then you will be more likely to confuse the ideas in the passages.

3. Hopefully, the SAT "passages from hell" won't seem so hellish with some practice with the College Hill Method. But if you've read through a passage and its language or concepts seem incomprehensible, just (1) move on to an easier passage, if it's available, or, if not, (2) attack the questions that require relatively little reading, namely, the "word in context" questions and the "secondary idea" questions.

4. First, don't panic. Most students struggle a bit with the time limit in their first few practice tests. Often, with a bit of patient practice, the problem will resolve itself. If it doesn't, then practice "eye-finger" coordination, using your finger to sweep through the passage smoothly and at a quicker pace than your eyes are inclined to go. Practice this *continually* with *everything* you read for several weeks. As a last resort, talk to your guidance counselor to see if you qualify to take the SAT with extended time.

SAT Practice 6

1. **E** The central idea of this passage is that "there are other senses [that are] unrecognized and . . . unconscious [and] automatic" (lines 3–5). Thus, when the final sentence states that for "normal man . . . they simply do not exist" (lines 19–20), it suggests that most people do not appreciate the functioning of certain physical senses.

2. **D** The passage states that a wrongdoing "does not seem strange in the former case" (lines 27–28), which is the case in which one knows something but does not reflect on that knowledge. In the case of a wrongdoing, this is a knowledge of right and wrong. The author is suggesting that wrongdoing only makes sense when the wrongdoer either does not know right from wrong or does not reflect on that knowledge.

3. **A** Passage 1 is primarily concerned with "unconscious" and "automatic" bodily senses, specifically the "awareness of the relative position of trunk and limbs" (lines 7–8) and the "controls by which our bodies are properly aligned and balanced" (lines 10–12). Passage 2 is concerned with moral knowledge but not knowledge that comes directly from the bodily senses. Although Passage 1 does mention "the space age" (line 14) in passing, it is certainly not primarily concerned with technological advances.

4. **D** Both authors would clearly agree that people are not always conscious of the information their minds process. Passage 1 states that there are "senses [that are] unconscious [and] automatic" (lines 4–5), and Passage 2 states that in certain cases a person "has knowledge and [yet] in another sense he does not, as in sleep or madness or intoxication" (lines 31–33).

Lesson 7:
Thinking Logically About the Questions

Using Logic on the Questions

Straightforward logic can help enormously on the toughest SAT CR questions. For instance, if one answer choice implies another answer choice, it cannot be correct without *both* answers being correct; therefore, it must be wrong. Okay, maybe that was a little confusing. Let's look at an example:

What is the author's attitude toward the "transgressions" mentioned in line 12?

(A) dismissiveness
(B) vehement opposition
(C) ambivalence
(D) disapproval
(E) resignation

Even if you didn't read the passage, you should know that the answer couldn't possibly be (B). Why? Because (B) implies (D). If someone is *vehemently opposed* to something, he or she sure as heck *disapproves* of it too, right? So, if (B) were right, (D) would have to be right, too. But there can't be two right answers! So (B) is out.

Okay, we kind of cheated there, in order to illustrate a concept (just like those physics problems that ignore friction even though it's always there). In fact, questions that can be solved without reading the passage almost never appear on the SAT (although crack-the-test folks want you to believe it's chock full of them). But logical thinking is still extremely helpful. It's just that on the *real test,* you have to pair it with a solid understanding of the passage.

Meet Logic's Best Bud, Common Sense

> Logic shows you what *must be true*, given a set of assumptions. Common sense shows you what *is probably true*, given a set of assumptions. Using basic principles of common sense pays off on the Critical Reading questions.

Let's go back to the question above. Your common sense tells you that writers write about things they care about. And even if they're only writing on assignment and *don't* really care about the subject, they at least have to *pretend* that they care about the subject. So decent writers almost never write with a *dismissive* tone toward their subjects. So choice (A) *dismissiveness* is

probably not the right answer. But don't be too hasty—it's *remotely* possible that the author is really saying, "These transgressions are what other people focus on, but they really don't matter." Just *check the passage quickly* to see if this is the case—but chances are, anyone who writes about transgressions isn't indifferent about them.

So logical elimination, *with quick passage checks,* can help a lot. So now you're left with choices (C) *ambivalence,* (D) *disapproval,* and (E) *resignation.* The answer is (C) if the author thinks the transgressions are *both good and bad* (remember *ambivalent* means "having conflicting feelings," not "unclear and vague"—that's *ambiguous*), (D) if he criticizes it consistently, and (E) if he thinks they're bad, but he can't do anything about them.

What Can You Do in 500 Words?

Can you "delineate *(describe precisely)* the history of European political reform" in 500 words? I sure can't, and neither can anyone who writes SAT passages. But someone sure can "suggest a few political reforms" in 500 words. So, when answering purpose questions, use common sense to eliminate unreasonable or petty purposes.

Which of the following best expresses the purpose of the passage as a whole?

(A) to describe the relationship between literature and history *(too big a task—eliminate)*
(B) to belittle modern literary critics *(possible, but that seems petty—eliminate)*
(C) to refute a misconception *(very possible and worthwhile—keep)*
(D) to delineate a new mode of literary analysis *(too big a task—eliminate)*
(E) to suggest several remedies for a problem *(very possible and worthwhile—keep)*

> When answering general purpose questions, use your common sense when thinking about the scope of a 500-word essay. It can't be trivial or petty, but it also can't do too much.

Concept Review 7:
Thinking Logically About the Questions

1. If the answer to a CR question is either "extremely enthusiastic" or "positive," which must be the correct answer and why?

2. Why is it nearly impossible for an author's attitude on a topic to be "indifferent?"

Using only logic and common sense, make your best guess on the following questions:

3. The first paragraph implies that art is primarily the product of

    (A) desire for wealth
    (B) anxiety
    (C) exact imitation
    (D) reason
    (E) intuition

4. With which of the following statements would the author most likely agree?

    (A) Voters always choose incapable political candidates.
    (B) Voters should be more educated about candidates.
    (C) Political candidates rarely campaign effectively.
    (D) Politicans do not represent their constituents well.
    (E) Voters are not interested in critical political issues.

5. Which of the following best expresses the purpose of this passage?

    (A) to dissuade students from studying political science
    (B) to describe the evolution of ethics in American history
    (C) to attack the credibility of politicians
    (D) to refute a misconception
    (E) to prescribe a solution to a problem

SAT Practice 7:
Thinking Logically About the Questions

The following is an excerpt from John Adams' A Dissertation on the Canon and Feudal Law, *written in 1765. John Adams (1735–1826) was the first vice-president of the United States and the second president of the United States.*

Liberty cannot be preserved without a general knowledge among the people, who have a
Line right, from the frame of their nature, to knowledge, as their great Creator, who does
5 nothing in vain, has given them understandings, and a desire to know; but besides this, they have a right, an indisputable, unalienable, indefeasible, divine right to that most dreaded and envied kind of knowledge; I
10 mean, of the characters and conduct of their rulers. Rulers are no more than attorneys, agents, and trustees, for the people; and if the cause, the interest and trust, is insidiously betrayed, or wantonly trifled away, the people
15 have a right to revoke the authority that they themselves have deputed, and to constitute abler and better agents, attorneys and trustees. And the preservation of the means of knowledge among the lowest ranks is of more im-
20 portance to the public than all the property of all the rich men in the country. It is even of more consequence to the rich themselves, and to their posterity. The only question is whether it is a public emolument;[1] and if it is,
25 the rich ought undoubtedly to contribute, in the same proportion as to all other public burdens—that is, in proportion to their wealth, which is secured by public expenses. But none of the means of information are more sacred, or
30 have been cherished with more tenderness and care by the settlers of America, than the press. Care has been taken that the art of printing should be encouraged, and that it should be easy and cheap and safe for any person to
35 communicate his thoughts to the public. . . .
　　Let us dare to read, think, speak and write. Let every order and degree among the people rouse their attention and animate their resolution. Let them all become attentive to the
40 grounds and principles of government, ecclesiastical[2] and civil. Let us study the law of nature; search into the spirit of the British Constitution; read the histories of ancient ages; contemplate the great examples of

45 Greece and Rome; set before us the conduct of our own British ancestors, who have defended for us the inherent rights of mankind against foreign and domestic tyrants and usurpers, against arbitrary kings and cruel
50 priests; in short, against the gates of earth and hell. Let us read and recollect and impress upon our souls the views and ends of our own more immediate forefathers in exchanging their native country for a dreary, inhospitable
55 wilderness. Let us examine the nature of that power, and the cruelty of that oppression, which drove them from their homes. Recollect their amazing fortitude, their bitter sufferings—the hunger, the nakedness, the cold,
60 which they patiently endured—the severe labors of clearing their grounds, building their houses, raising their provisions, amidst dangers from wild beasts and savage men, before they had time or money or materials for com-
65 merce. Recollect the civil and religious principles and hopes and expectations which constantly supported and carried them through all hardships with patience and resignation. Let us recollect it was liberty, the hope
70 of liberty for themselves and us and ours, which conquered all the discouragements, dangers and trials. In such researches as these let us all in our several departments cheerfully engage—but especially the proper patrons and
75 supporters of law, learning, and religion!

[1]Benefit
[2]Related to church matters

1. The "right" in line 7 is the right of the people to

    (A) pursue happiness
    (B) read what they wish
    (C) know about their leaders
    (D) set up printing presses
    (E) run for public office

2. In context, the word "constitute" (line 16) most nearly means

    (A) consist of
    (B) produce
    (C) remove
    (D) install
    (E) enjoy

3. It can be inferred from the passage that "our own more immediate forefathers" (lines 52–53) endured all of the following EXCEPT

    (A) political oppression
    (B) difficult terrain
    (C) arduous labor
    (D) hopelessness
    (E) physical deprivation

4. As it is described in line 56, the "power" is

    (A) a personal skill
    (B) a national virtue
    (C) a despotic agent
    (D) a mysterious spirit
    (E) a fearsome mirage

5. The tone of the second paragraph (lines 36–75) is best described as

    (A) prescriptive
    (B) critical
    (C) objective
    (D) melancholy
    (E) joyous

6. Which of the following best describes the relationship between the first paragraph (lines 1–35) and the second paragraph (lines 36–75)?

    (A) The first describes a current state of affairs, while the second describes a situation in the past.
    (B) The first describes a right, while the second gives recommendations for exercising that right.
    (C) The first describes a problem, while the second describes a way to remedy that problem.
    (D) The first describes a theory, while the second describes the evidence for that theory.
    (E) The first addresses the leaders of a country, while the second addresses its citizens.

7. According to the passage, citizens should

    I.   understand the precepts by which governments and churches are run
    II. take up arms for their country in the name of liberty
    III. appreciate the sacrifices of their forefathers
    IV. study to partake in their government as elected officials

    (A) I and III only
    (B) I, II, and III only
    (C) I, II, and IV only
    (D) I, III, and IV only
    (E) II, III, and IV only

Answer Key 7:
Thinking Logically About the Questions

Concept Review 7

1. The answer must be "positive" because it includes "extremely enthusiastic." In other words, anyone who is "extremely enthusiastic" is necessarily also "positive." Therefore, "extremely enthusiastic" cannot be correct without "positive" also being correct, but this contradicts the fact that there is only one correct answer.

2. Because writers generally write about things that interest them. And even when they write about things that *don't* interest them (as when they are given an assignment), they still at least *pretend* to be interested, so they do not write with a tone of indifference.

3. Best choice: **E** What would a reasonable person say about where art *primarily* comes from? You don't need special knowledge here, just common sense.
   (A) desire for wealth *(Are most artists money-grubbers? Probably not.)*
   (B) anxiety *(Are most artists anxious? Could be, but that's mean.)*
   (C) exact imitation *(Do most artists make exact copies? No.)*
   (D) reason *(Do most artists paint logically? Probably not.)*
   (E) intuition *(Do most artists rely on feelings and hunches? Seems reasonable.)*

4. Best choice: **B** Focus on the exclusivity of the answers:
   (A) Voters always choose incapable political candidates. *("Always" is exclusive; statement is mean.)*
   (B) Voters should be more educated about candidates. *(Reasonable and inclusive.)*
   (C) Political candidates rarely campaign effectively. *("Rarely" is somewhat exclusive; statement is harsh.)*
   (D) Politicans do not represent their constituents well. *("Do not" is exclusive; statement is mean.)*
   (E) Voters are not interested in critical political issues. *(Since this answer would imply that (B) is also true, it must be wrong.)*

5. Best choice: **D** or **E** Think about what can reasonably be accomplished in 400–800 words.
   (A) to dissuade students from studying political science *(Reasonable but harsh and petty.)*
   (B) to describe the evolution of ethics in American history *(Far too big a task.)*
   (C) to attack the credibility of politicians *(Reasonable but harsh.)*
   (D) to refute a misconception *(Reasonable.)*
   (E) to prescribe a solution to a problem *(Reasonable.)*

SAT Practice 7

1. **C** The "right" is described as the right to "knowledge . . . of the characters and conduct of their rulers."

2. **D** The sentence says that "the people have a right to revoke the authority that they themselves have deputed, and to *constitute* abler and better agents. . . ." This means that they can remove the leaders who don't lead well and replace them with those who do. So *constitute* means something like *replace them with*, or choice (D) *install*.

3. **D** The passage explains that "our own more immediate forefathers" experienced
   (A) political oppression: "that oppression . . . which drove them from their homes" (lines 56–57)
   (B) difficult terrain: "inhospitable wilderness" (lines 54–55)
   (C) arduous labor: "severe labors" (lines 60–61)
   (E) physical deprivation: "the hunger, the nakedness, the cold" (line 59)

However, lines 69–71 say that it was "the hope of liberty . . . which conquered all the discouragements. . . ."

4. **C** The "power" is described as that "which drove them from their homes." So it is a despotic agent.

5. **A** Most sentences begin with "Let us . . . ," which indicates that he is strongly suggesting what his fellow citizens should do. He is *prescribing* action.

6. **B** The first paragraph describes the "right . . . to knowledge," while the second describes what kind of knowledge the citizens should acquire.

7. **A** The passage does not advocate taking up arms or running for office. It does, however, say that citizens should "become attentive to the grounds and principles of government, ecclesiastical (church-related), and civil" (lines 39–41) and reflect on their forefathers' "amazing fortitude [and] bitter sufferings" (lines 58–59).

Lesson 8:
Checking That You've Nailed the Answer

Avoid the Choices That Are True but Wrong

Too often students make the mistake of choosing an answer that *makes a true statement* but *does not answer the question correctly*. How can that be? Imagine that you've read a passage written by an art critic praising a museum that has been harshly criticized by others. The passage acknowledges certain flaws in the planning and design of the building but on the whole praises the building for its innovations. Then you read a question like this:

The author uses the term "monstrosity" (line 4) primarily in order to

(A) justify the building of the museum
(B) characterize the opinion of certain critics
(C) express his dismay about certain decisions made by the planners
(D) disparage the work of certain architects
(E) praise the museum for its innovative design

Looking back to line 4, you read: "They could not understand how such a monstrosity could have been erected under their noses." When you look at the passage as a whole, you see that the author does, in different places, "justify the building of the museum" (choice (A)), "characterize the opinion of certain critics" (choice (B)), "express his dismay about certain decisions made by the planners" (choice (C)), and "praise the museum for its innovative design" (choice (E)). These are all basically "true" statements. So how do you pick the right answer? Read the question *carefully*. It asks why the author uses the term "monstrosity." Does the author think the museum is a monstrosity? No, because the passage as a whole *praises* the museum. The sentence in line 4 says that *they*—other critics—thought it was a monstrosity. Therefore, this word is being used to (B) *characterize the opinion of certain critics*.

> Some choices may make statements that are *true* without being the *correct* answer to the question. Read the question very carefully to be sure you've answered what it asks. Carefully note the question type, as discussed in Lesson 5.

Underline Your Evidence

> It's worth repeating: To check your answers, *underline your evidence* in the passage. This forces you to focus on what is *in the passage* and not what is just *in your head*. The right answers are always right there in the passage, if you look for them. You *never* need to draw on outside knowledge or read between the lines.

Keep Your Eyes on the Prize

Always check your progress in terms of your score goal. Unless you've got a realistic shot at an 800, you don't need to get every question right. Don't get bogged down on tough questions. If you can't decide between two answers, make your best guess and move on. Keep in mind that to break 500, you need only to get about half of the questions right, and to break 600, you need to get only about two-thirds of the questions right. To break 700, though, you'll need to get more than 86% of the questions right.

> In addition to checking individual answers, check that you've carefully attacked at least the number of questions that you should according to your "SAT Study Plan."

Learn to Deal with "Space-Outs"

Nearly everyone "spaces out" from time to time when they read. Have you ever suddenly realized that you've "read" three paragraphs but nothing has sunk in? This is costly *only if you panic* and let it distract you for the rest of the test.

> If you space out a little on the SAT reading, relax. It happens to everyone, and you'll be fine if you don't panic. Just calmly go back to where you left off, and reread normally. To minimize space-outs, just focus on answering the three key questions and summarizing each paragraph. When your brain has a conscious task, it doesn't space out.

Concept Review 8:
Checking That You've Nailed the Answer

1. What does it mean for an answer to be "true" but "wrong"?

2. How do you avoid choices that are "true" but "wrong"?

3. Why is it helpful to underline evidence for your answers in the passage?

4. What is your score goal on the SAT CR section, and what percentage of the questions should you attack in order to get that score?

5. How should you deal with "space-outs" on the CR section?

SAT Practice 8:
Checking That You've Nailed the Answer

The following passage is taken from a book written in 2002 about the evolution of human intelligence.

We are a bright species. We have gone into space and walked on the moon. Yet you would
Line never have guessed that if you traveled back to between 100,000 and 40,000 years ago. At that
5   time our ancestors and Neanderthals coex- isted. Neanderthals were like us but physically stronger, with large bones and teeth, protrud- ing brows and face, and hardly a chin. Perhaps what we lacked in brawn we made up for
10   in brains. But for most of our history, our species was not bright enough to act very dif- ferently from the Neanderthals, let alone be more successful than they were. Only around 40,000 to 32,000 years ago, in Western Asia
15   and Europe, did Neanderthal people disap- pear, to be replaced by our species.
        Why did we coexist with Neanderthals for 60,000 years—a far longer case of hominids living side by side than any other in human
20   history? And why did we eventually win out? Brains alone cannot provide the answer, as Ne- anderthals may in fact have had the larger ones. Perhaps they lacked the long vocal cham- ber needed for speech. Equal certainty
25   exists among those who study the base of their skulls that they did and that they did not. If they did lack one, then this could be the expla- nation, but maybe not, since even without a voice box, gestures can communicate, as can
30   be seen among the deaf. Indeed, hunters find advantages in using sign language (speech sounds would warn off potential prey), and not just while hunting but in everyday life. Anthropologists find that hunter-gatherers use
35   sophisticated sign languages to complement their speech. Sign language might even have other advantages—evidence even suggests that it is easier to learn than speech: deaf children start to pick up signs earlier than hearing
40   ones learn to speak. So "spoken speech" is not in all ways superior to "signed speech." It is not something that can explain our replace- ment of the Neanderthals.
        The reason we—anatomically modern
45   humans—won out lies, we suspect, not in being brighter or better able to speak but in our very physical frailty and our resulting need to exploit

our minds. Neanderthals, stronger than us, did not need to take this route. They could
50   survive with their physical strength rather than tapping into the potential of their brains. An analogy is with countries: the richest ones, such as Switzerland, Finland, Singapore, and Japan, are not blessed with, but rather lack
55   natural resources. Without them, they have been forced to use their brains to innovate, providing products and services ranging from mobile phones to diplomacy.

1. The main purpose of the second paragraph (lines 17–43) is to

    (A) make a suggestion
    (B) examine some claims
    (C) explain a situation
    (D) present information objectively
    (E) tell a story

2. In line 20, the phrase "win out" most nearly means

    (A) become justified
    (B) defeat their foes by force
    (C) come to dominate
    (D) become politically successful
    (E) become more popular

3. The evidence in lines 34–36 ("Anthropologists find . . . speech") is presented primarily in order to

    (A) refute the misconception that hunter- gatherers were not good communicators
    (B) explain how modern humans replaced the Neanderthals
    (C) support the claim that hunter-gatherers have larger brains than Neanderthals
    (D) suggest that long vocal chambers may not provide an advantage to a particular species
    (E) show why some humans prefer gestures to spoken language

4. The "physical frailty" in line 47 is

    (A) the reason our ancestors struggled to survive
    (B) the result of a harsh physical environment
    (C) an ironic advantage to modern humans
    (D) something the Neanderthals exploited
    (E) a trait that arose late in human history

5. In line 58, "mobile phones" and "diplomacy" are mentioned as examples of

    (A) innovations that are used worldwide
    (B) different ways of communicating
    (C) luxuries that are denied to the physically frail
    (D) inventions that Neanderthals could never use
    (E) products or services that require intellectual rather than natural resources

Answer Key 8:
Checking That You've Nailed the Answer

Concept Review 8

1. An answer is "true" but "wrong" if it reflects a point that is made in the passage but does not answer the question that is asked. Such answers are very common on SAT Critical Reading questions.
2. You can avoid the trap of choosing a "true" but "wrong" answer by reading the question very carefully and focusing on the specific line references it mentions and on the question it asks.
3. Underlining the evidence in the passage helps you to focus on what is in the passage rather than what is in your head.

4. The percentage of questions that should be attacked to get particular score goals are as follows: 500 = 75%, 550 = 80%, 600 = 85%, 650 = 90%, 700 and above = 100%.
5. First, don't panic. When you notice that you have spaced out, calmly come back to the point where you left off and continue to read. The key to *avoiding* "space-outs" in the first place is to focus on answering the three key questions and summarizing each paragraph.

SAT Practice 8

1. **B** Words and phrases such as "perhaps" (line 23), "if" (line 26), and "maybe not" (line 28) indicate that the second paragraph is examining hypotheses.
2. **C** The passage explores the question of how modern humans came to "win out" (line 20) over the Neanderthals, that is, how they came to thrive while the Neanderthals died out, or how they came to dominate them.
3. **D** The sentence "Anthropologists find . . . speech" (lines 34–36) is used to support the later claim that "'spoken speech' is not in all ways superior to 'signed speech'" (lines 40–41), which would cast doubt on the advantages of the "long vocal chamber needed for speech" (lines 23–24).

4. **C** According to the final paragraph, the relative "physical frailty" (line 47) of modern humans compared to Neanderthals created a need for modern humans to "tapping . . . into the potential of their brains" (line 51), which led to their dominance over the Neanderthals.
5. **E** The "mobile phones" and "diplomacy" in line 58 are examples of how countries that "lack natural resources" (lines 54–55) can still "use their brains to innovate" (line 56).

CHAPTER 5

SENTENCE COMPLETION SKILLS

Lesson 1: Verbal Inference

What Are Sentence Completion Questions?

> Every SAT will contain about 20 Sentence Completion questions as part of the Critical Reading portion of the test. These questions test your *verbal inference skills*. Your verbal inference skills are the skills you use to figure out the meaning and usage of an unfamiliar word when you read or hear it in a sentence.

Consider the following sentence:

As part of our game, we ran twice around the cregiendo until we became so trepindant that we collapsed in a heap on the porch.

Is the word *cregiendo* a noun, a verb, or an adjective? How about *trepindant*? Since they are nonsense words, you could not have known the answer to those questions before reading this sentence. After reading it, though, you should have some idea about what cregiendo and trepindant might mean. *Cregiendo* must be a noun because it's the *thing* we ran around, and *trepindant* must be an adjective because it describes us after we ran around the *cregiendo*. With your vast verbal inference skills, you've probably figured out more than just the part of speech of *cregiendo* and *trepindant*. Try these questions:

1. A *cregiendo* is about as big as (A) a spider (B) a pillow (C) a car (D) a house (E) a village.
2. Can a *cregiendo* be *trepindant*?

Even the world's smartest and most powerful computers find these kinds of questions very, very tough. It's easier to program a computer to become a chess grandmaster or to predict hurricanes than to answer such "common-sense" questions. Common sense seems simple, but this simplicity is deceptive. So revel in your brilliance!

Look at Question 1: A *cregiendo* is something that kids can run around, but running around it twice causes you to collapse. Your common sense tells you that such a thing would be roughly as big as a house. A village is way too big to run around in a game, and the other things are much too small to exhaust you.

Now look at Question 2: Since we became *trepindant* after running around the *cregiendo*, the word *trepindant* describes human beings, and perhaps other animals that can run, rather than, say, rocks. It also seems to describe a *temporary state* rather than a permanent trait, since we weren't *trepindant* before we started running around. What would make us collapse in a heap? Exhaustion, of course. So *trepindant* probably means *exhausted*, which big objects like *cregiendos* could never be.

Attacking the Questions

> Attack Sentence Completion questions systematically: (1) *Read the entire sentence*, saying "blank" in place of the missing words. (2) *Think about the logic* of the sentence. (3) *Complete the sentence with your own words.* (4) *Scan through the choices and look for a match.* (It probably won't be an exact match; pick the closest choice.)

Example:
Although these animals migrate, they are not ------; they remain loyal to their established ranges and seldom stray into new areas.

(A) predators   (B) burrowers
(C) grazers   (D) scavengers
(E) wanderers

Don't worry about the choices yet, just read the sentence. These animals *seldom stray*, so they must not be *wanderers*. It's possible that they are not *predators*, or *burrowers*, or *grazers*, or *scavengers* also, but the sentence doesn't provide any information about those traits. Your choice should be (E).

Check Your Work

> Always reread the sentence with your selected response to check it. Too many students forget this simple step. Rereading helps you to avoid overlooking anything important. Check that the *logic* and the *tone* make sense.

Concept Review 1: Verbal Inference

1. What is "verbal inference"?

2. What should you do before trying to complete a Sentence Completion question?

Read the following sentences, think about them, then answer the questions about the nonsense words.

Far from being an arnacular pastime, numismatics, or the study of currency, can purnade our appreciation of the history and economic development of a nation.

3. *Arnacular* is (A) a verb (B) a noun (C) an adjective (D) an adverb (E) a preposition (F) a pronoun.

4. Can a person be *arnacular*?

5. *Arnacular* most nearly means (A) invalid (B) obsessive (C) aimless (D) interesting (E) foreign (F) dangerous.

6. *Purnade* is (A) a verb (B) a noun (C) an adjective (D) an adverb (E) a preposition (F) a pronoun.

7. Is *purnading our appreciation* of something probably a good thing or a bad thing?

8. *Purnade* most nearly means (A) undermine (B) complicate (C) heighten (D) clarify (E) ignore (F) adore.

Car buyers, when given a choice of engines, will typically choose the most powerful and gas-guzzling option, refuting the popular belief that fellinance is the primary concern of consumers.

9. *Fellinance* is (A) a verb (B) a noun (C) an adjective (D) an adverb (E) a preposition (F) a pronoun.

10. Are all car engines *fellinant*?

11. Is *fellinance* more likely to be associated with a small sedan or a large pickup truck?

12. *Fellinance* most nearly means (A) longevity (B) continuity (C) propriety (D) efficiency (E) luxury.

SAT Practice 1: Verbal Inference

1. Although he clearly was obsessed with the ------ of moral perfection, he was also aware of its potential ------: self-righteousness, arrogance, and condescension.
   (A) pursuit . . pitfalls
   (B) likelihood . . dangers
   (C) contemplation . . insights
   (D) morality . . tenets
   (E) sanctity . . inequities

2. Whereas Gerald was always the frivolous one, Bernard felt compelled to compensate for his brother's indiscretions by exercising profound moral ------.
   (A) hysteria
   (B) embarrassment
   (C) prudence
   (D) acceptance
   (E) equivocation

3. In need of a ------ from persecution, many young refugees wandered far from their homeland seeking ------ communities in which to settle.
   (A) nightmare . . just
   (B) haven . . tolerant
   (C) plight . . magnanimous
   (D) pledge . . malevolent
   (E) sanctuary . . invidious

4. The synthesized voices from today's computerized machines are a far cry from the ------ sounds of older machines; rather, they sound almost like real human speech.
   (A) melancholy
   (B) cordial
   (C) fervid
   (D) inflammatory
   (E) mechanical

5. Even in communities that value ------, investment in technologically advanced industries can be an important source of ------.
   (A) progress . . prestige
   (B) liberty . . concern
   (C) competition . . decay
   (D) tradition . . income
   (E) profits . . dismay

6. Some contend that the quatrains of Nostradamus ------ events that would not take place for centuries, including ------ like wars, conflagrations, and earthquakes.
   (A) foreboded . . cataclysms
   (B) mitigated . . marvels
   (C) impersonated . . myths
   (D) transcended . . auguries
   (E) disrupted . . coincidences

7. While the script for the movie consummately depicted the wit and charm of Oscar Wilde, the incompetent actor portraying him mutilated the most ------ lines.
   (A) tactless
   (B) sober
   (C) ingenious
   (D) unintelligible
   (E) unnecessary

8. Rather than ------ the attitude of the entire community from that of a few individuals, she was willing to concede that there were many conflicting opinions on the matter.
   (A) distinguishing
   (B) concealing
   (C) protecting
   (D) inferring
   (E) expelling

9. For all Nick's ------ at the office, his close friends knew that this trait ------ his true contemplative and introspective nature.
   (A) bluster . . belied
   (B) pomposity . . determined
   (C) sarcasm . . revealed
   (D) presumptuousness . . emphasized
   (E) shallowness . . bolstered

Answer Key 1: Verbal Inference

Concept Review 1

1. The ability to determine the tone, meaning, and usage of unknown words when they are read or heard in context.

2. Read the entire sentence, saying "blank" when you encounter a missing word; think about the overall meaning of the sentence; and try to complete it with your own words before checking the choices.

3. (C) an adjective

4. Probably. Words that describe pastimes, like *fun*, *popular*, or *dangerous*, can often be used to describe people.

5. (C) aimless

6. (A) a verb

7. Probably good, because *studying* usually *helps* you to appreciate things, rather than the opposite.

8. (C) heighten

9. (B) a noun

10. No. Since buyers can choose between engines with *fellinance* or without it, it must not be universal.

11. A small sedan. Since *fellinance* is not a quality of *powerful and gas-guzzling* engines, it is more likely a quality of smaller engines.

12. (D) efficiency

SAT Practice 1

1. **A** The colon introduces examples. What are *self-righteousness, arrogance,* and *condescension* examples of? Certainly not something good! So *insights* and *tenets* (core beliefs) don't make sense. The *likelihood of perfection* doesn't have *dangers*, the *sanctity of perfection* doesn't have *inequities* (unequal treatments), but the *pursuit of perfection* can certainly have *pitfalls* (negative consequences) like those listed.
contemplation = deep thought; *sanctity* = holiness

2. **C** *Whereas* indicates a contrast. *Frivolous* means lacking soberness or seriousness. The missing word has to indicate a quality that a serious person would have, like *prudence* (conservative wisdom).
hysteria = irrational and excessive emotion; *equivocation* = failure to commit to a position

3. **B** *Refugees* are people in search of safety, usually from war. They wouldn't seek *malevolent* (ill-wishing) or *invidious* (causing resentment) communities. They are not in need of a *nightmare* or a *plight* (difficult situation). The only choice that makes sense indicates that they are seeking a *haven* (safe place) from persecution in a *tolerant* community.
just = proper and righteous; *magnanimous* = generous; *pledge* = oath; *sanctuary* = safe place

4. **E** *Today's computerized machines* make sounds that are *almost like real human speech*, so they must be *a far cry* from artificial-sounding speech, or *mechanical* speech.
melancholy = depressed; *cordial* = friendly; *fervid* = passionate; *inflammatory* = tending to incite anger

5. **D** *Even in* indicates irony (a reversal of expectations). If *technologically advanced industries* bring something *important*, that will certainly not be *concern, decay,* or *dismay*. Since technological advances are far from traditional, it would be ironic that a *traditional* community would value *technology*.
prestige = public esteem; *liberty* = freedom

6. **A** If the events *would not take place for centuries*, he must have *predicted* them. *Wars, conflagrations, and earthquakes* are types of *cataclysms* (events that cause widespread destruction).
foreboded = predicted; *mitigated* = improved a situation; *transcended* = rose above; *auguries* = predictions

7. **C** If the script *consummately* (with superior skill) depicted wit and charm, it must be very good. An *incompetent* (unskilled) actor would *mutilate* the *ingenious* (brilliant) lines.
tactless = inconsiderate; *sober* = serious; *unintelligible* = hard to understand

8. **D** If you aren't *willing to concede that there were many conflicting opinions*, then you must believe that everyone shares the same opinion. Therefore, you would not have to ask everyone's opinion, but could *infer* (make a generalization about) everyone's attitude from those of just a few individuals.
distinguishing = recognizing as distinct; *expelling* = throwing out

9. **A** Here the phrase *for all* is an idiom meaning *despite*, so it indicates irony. If Nick's true nature is *contemplative and introspective*, it would be ironic if he were outgoing and *blustery* in the office. This trait would *misrepresent* or *belie* his true nature.
pomposity = haughtiness; *sarcasm* = bitter insulting attitude; *presumptuousness* = overconfidence; *bolstered* = supported

Lesson 2: The Four Logical Relationships

Logic Is as Important as an Enormous Vocabulary

The Sentence Completion questions on the SAT are logical questions. That is, they are asking you to find the best word or phrase to complete each thought logically. They are not asking you to find the "most interesting" or the "most complicated" word or phrase. *Each question will include only one choice that will complete the sentence in a way that makes logical sense. The other choices will be illogical or incomplete in one way or another.*

Example:
What Mr. Harrison's writing lacked in clarity it made up for in -------, for it contained enough information for a clever craftsman to re-create his invention down to the most minute detail.

At first reading, it may seem as if there are many different ways of completing the sentence. That is, there are many ways that a piece of writing might make up for a lack of clarity: it might be clever, or funny, or useful, or thought-provoking. But when you look at the sentence as a whole, there is only one logical way to complete the sentence. The second part of the sentence is key: it says that his writing contains *enough information for a clever craftsman to re-create his invention down to the most minute detail.* In other words, it provides a lot of *detail*. This must be what makes up for its lack of clarity! So while there are many "good" ways to complete the sentence, only a word like *meticulousness, comprehensiveness, completeness, detail*, etc., will make the sentence logically complete.

The Logical Structure of a Sentence

Every sentence in a Sentence Completion question has a logical structure that shows the logical relationship among the ideas in the sentence. That scheme will always include one or more of the four basic logical relationships.

Contrast
e.g. *Although we waited over two hours for a table, it seemed like only a few minutes.*

Support
e.g. *We loved staying at the cottage; the sounds of the ocean calmed us and the sea air invigorated us.*

Cause and Effect
e.g. *We were irritated by the noise, so we moved to the next room.*

Definition or Explanation
e.g. *Joel was a nihilist, someone who doesn't believe that any truth is absolute.*

Many sentences include more than one logical structure. Think carefully about each sentence and make sure you see all of the logical relationships.

Example:
The motion of the region's glaciers is both ------ and ------: they seem not to be moving at all, yet they transform the landscape more profoundly than any other force of nature.

When you first read the phrase *both ------ and ------*, it may seem that the two missing words must be similar, because they are joined with *and* rather than *but* or *yet*. But you must get the overall logical structure first. The colon indicates that the two statements support each other, and the use of *yet* in the second statement shows a contrast between the two ideas within the second statement. Therefore, the first missing word should mean *seemingly motionless*, and the second word should mean something like *having a profound effect. Imperceptible* and *dramatic* work nicely.

Concept Review 2:
The Four Logical Relationships

1. What are the four basic logical relationships a sentence may include?

After each sentence, describe its "logical structure" by circling each logical relationship—contrast, support, cause and effect, or definition—that you can find within the sentence. (Remember that a sentence may show more than one relationship.)

2. Although he clearly was obsessed with the ------ of moral integrity, he was also aware of its potential -------: self-righteousness, arrogance, and condescension.

        support   contrast   cause and effect   definition

3. Few of us appreciated our group leader's ------; we were too intelligent and had too much self-esteem to be persuaded by her constant use of insult and humiliation.

        support   contrast   cause and effect   definition

4. In need of a ------ from persecution, many young refugees wandered far from their homeland seeking ------ communities in which to settle.

        support   contrast   cause and effect   definition

5. Because the population of bacteria soon ------ the food supply, their once rapid proliferation soon slows, and may even stop altogether.

        support   contrast   cause and effect   definition

6. Deer in the wild often seem ------ to the concept of death; they are utterly unaware of any danger even when they notice their friends nearby dropping one by one.

        support   contrast   cause and effect   definition

7. Some contend that the quatrains of Nostradamus ------ events that would not take place for centuries, including ------ like wars, conflagrations, and earthquakes.

        support   contrast   cause and effect   definition

8. While the script for the movie consummately depicted the wit and charm of Oscar Wilde, the incompetent actor portraying him mutilated the most ------ lines.

        support   contrast   cause and effect   definition

9. The herd of lemmings always acted ------, thus ensuring that either they all survived or they all perished.

        support   contrast   cause and effect   definition

10. By ------ his announcement of the new promotions, Carl felt that he could maintain his employees' eagerness with the element of anticipation.

        support   contrast   cause and effect   definition

SAT Practice 2: The Four Logical Relationships

1. Possessing seemingly boundless energy, DeVare fights for the causes she supports with a ------ that would leave others ------ at the end of the workday.
   (A) grace . . scandalized
   (B) commitment . . uncertain
   (C) loyalty . . contrite
   (D) vigor . . exhausted
   (E) sincerity . . disillusioned

2. The members of the committee saw Vance's reign as chairman becoming more and more ------; his decisions seemed based more on personal whim than on the opinions of his fellow members.
   (A) inclusive
   (B) abstract
   (C) irresistible
   (D) illusory
   (E) arbitrary

3. The boundary between Canada and the United States is more a political than a cultural ------; the people on both sides ------ a great deal in terms of artistic sensibilities.
   (A) demarcation . . share
   (B) partition . . estrange
   (C) event . . partake
   (D) affiliation . . admit
   (E) division . . conflict

4. Some criminal investigators believe that polygraphs reliably ------ deception by recording ------ reactions in a subject such as slight changes in breathing rate or perspiration elicited by a set of questions.
   (A) judge . . imaginative
   (B) detect . . physiological
   (C) predict . . imperceptible
   (D) subvert . . simulated
   (E) induce . . verifiable

5. The author intentionally combines the vernacular of the Bronx with pretentious academic jargon, creating a uniquely ------ style that makes her novel particularly difficult to translate into other languages.
   (A) mundane
   (B) taciturn
   (C) alliterative
   (D) idiosyncratic
   (E) orthodox

6. The fact that polar bears are tremendously strong indicates the degree of ------ they must have in their aggressive play, for they never hurt each other.
   (A) intensity
   (B) stamina
   (C) concentration
   (D) instinct
   (E) restraint

7. Long an advocate of deterrence, General Wallace had hoped that the ------ display of force would ------ further military action.
   (A) formidable . . obviate
   (B) subtle . . require
   (C) impressive . . generate
   (D) unnecessary . . prevent
   (E) unbridled . . sustain

8. Disillusioned and ------, the impoverished young writer was ready to ------ the artistic life for a real job.
   (A) capable . . abandon
   (B) complacent . . invoke
   (C) dejected . . forsake
   (D) gracious . . deny
   (E) crushed . . capture

9. The meal of raw eggs and vegetables, while ------, in fact ------ all requisite nutrition to the young athlete in training.
   (A) meager . . denied
   (B) sumptuous . . supplied
   (C) spartan . . provided
   (D) doleful . . restored
   (E) appropriate . . allowed

Answer Key 2: The Four Logical Relationships

Concept Review 2

1. support, contrast, cause and effect, and definition
2. support (*colon* indicates examples), contrast (*although*)
3. support (*semicolon* indicates development), definition (missing word means *constant use of insult and humiliation*)
4. support (------ *communities* must provide ------ *from persecution*), cause and effect (the *need* caused their *search*)

5. cause and effect (*because*)
6. definition (missing word means *utterly unaware*)
7. support (*examples* are given)
8. support (the *script* was *consummate* so the *lines* must have been good, too), contrast (*while*)
9. cause and effect (*thus*)
10. cause and effect (*by . . .*)

SAT Practice 2

1. **D** *Boundless energy* is the **definition** of *vigor*. This is the kind of thing that would **cause** someone to be *exhausted* at the end of the day.
   grace = elegance; *scandalized* = shamed publicly; *contrite* = filled with regret; *vigor* = great energy; *disillusioned* = with lowered esteem for another

2. **E** This sentence contains a **definition.** The missing word means *based more on personal whim than on the opinions of his fellow members.* This is what *arbitrary* means.
   inclusive = including; *abstract* = not concrete; *illusory* = based on or characteristic of illusion; *arbitrary* = based on whim or random power

3. **A** The semicolon indicates **support.** The phrase *more . . . than . . .* indicates a **contrast.** The word *boundary* is the **definition** of the first missing word.
   demarcation = boundary; *estrange* = cause to grow apart; *partake* = participate; *affiliation* = close association

4. **B** *Such as* indicates **support** through example. *Breathing rate* and *perspiration* are examples of *physiological* reactions. (They aren't *imperceptible* because they're being recorded!) The word *by* indicates a **cause and effect** relationship. The recording of such reactions would not *induce* (cause) deception, but might just *detect* it.
   imperceptible = incapable of being detected; *subvert* = undermine; *simulated* = artificial; *induce* = cause; *verifiable* = capable of being proven true

5. **D** The sentence shows a **cause and effect:** something about the novel *makes* it (causes it to be) *difficult to translate.* The description makes it sound *quirky*, which would indeed make it hard to translate.

   mundane = ordinary; *taciturn* = not talkative; *alliterative* = tending to use words that begin with the same sound; *idiosyncratic* = quirky; *orthodox* = adhering strictly to teachings

6. **E** This sentence shows a **cause and effect.** Some quality of the bears causes them not to hurt each other, even in *aggressive play*. Particularly since they are so **strong,** they would have to have a lot of *restraint*.
   stamina = endurance; *concentration* = focus; *instinct* = inborn ability; *restraint* = ability to hold back

7. **A** This sentence **supports** the main idea with a description of the General's beliefs. *Deterrence* is the belief that a strong offensive capability will *deter* (prevent) attack from one's enemies, that is, that a *formidable* (awesome) display of force would *obviate* (render unnecessary through foresight) further military action.
   subtle = hard to detect; *unbridled* = lacking restraint

8. **C** This sentence **supports** the main idea with a description of the writer's mood. If a writer is *disillusioned* and *impoverished*, she would probably not want to stay in that situation for much longer. She would want to *give up* the artistic life. The first word should be a negative adjective that describes the life she wants to give up.
   complacent = self-satisfied; *invoke* = call in; *dejected* = sad; *forsake* = abandon; *gracious* = full of grace

9. **C** The word *while* and the phrase *in fact* indicate a **contrast.** A meal of raw eggs and vegetables sounds pretty *minimal*, but it must *provide all requisite* (necessary) nutrition to the young athlete.
   meager = minimal; *sumptuous* = bountiful; *spartan* = minimal, stark; *doleful* = sad

Lesson 3: Structural Keys

The Structural Key Words

Structural key words are the words or phrases that show the logical relationship between the statements in the sentence. Certain logical relationships require key words: for instance, it's almost impossible to say that one thing **caused** another thing without using a word like *because, therefore, thus, in order to,* or *consequently*.

> As you read the sentences, underline or circle any structural key words you see. Completing the sentence logically requires you to think about these key words first.

Here is a partial list of some structural key words:

Contrast	*but*	*however*	*in contrast*	*nevertheless*
	whereas	*although*	*instead of*	*rather*
	despite	*unusual*	*unexpected*	*surprising*
	abnormal	*anomalous*	*curious*	*illogical*
Cause and Effect	*because*	*thus*	*consequently*	*therefore*
	so that	*in order to*	*if . . . then*	*since*
Support	*furthermore*	*likewise*	*moreover*	*also*
	besides	*additionally*	*similarly*	*like*
	for instance	*that is*	*for example*	

Semicolons and Colons

Some punctuation marks can also help you determine the logical relation between parts of a sentence. Semicolons and colons, for instance, indicate a "supporting" relationship between statements. A semicolon (;) between two statements indicates that the second statement *extends* or *develops* the previous statement. A colon (:) between two statements indicates that the second statement *explains* the previous one.

Example:
   The string arrangements by Rob Mathes are unobtrusive yet ------; the violins rise ------, but soon they reach deeply into the piece and transform it into a lyrically rich and moving experience.
   (A) carefree . . stiffly   (B) reserved . . involuntarily   (C) profound . . subtly
   (D) detached . . carefully   (E) hesitant . . methodically

The semicolon indicates that the second statement develops the first, repeating the same general idea but with more detail. The two clauses are parallel, that is, they have similar grammatical structures. The first says: *These are A yet B; they do C but then D.* The structure indicates that A and C go together, and B and D go together. If the arrangements are *unobtrusive* then they rise *subtly,* and if they *reach deeply into the piece and transform it,* they must be *profound.*

Example:
   Newton inferred that the law of gravity was ------: even the gravitational pull of an ant on Earth will ------ a star millions of light-years away.

   (A) universal . . influence   (B) inconsequential . . accelerate   (C) intense . . support
   (D) minute . . affect   (E) complete . . replace

The colon after the first statement indicates that the second statement explains the first, in this case by giving an example. To understand the sentence as a whole, it's probably best to try to understand the second statement first and then ask: "What general idea does that example explain?" The second part says that *the gravitational pull of an ant will ------ a star* far away. Well, a scientist like Isaac Newton wouldn't be so silly as to say that an ant's gravity could *support* or *replace* a star, so it must *influence, accelerate,* or *affect* it. If this is true, then even small gravitational effects must travel a long, long, long, long way. This is the important point of the example, so Newton's theory must have been that gravity is *universal.*

Concept Review 3: Structural Keys

1. Name as many structural key words or phrases as you can that indicate a contrast of ideas.

2. Name as many words or phrases as you can that indicate a cause-and-effect relationship.

3. What do colons and semicolons indicate about the statements they join, and what does a colon do that a semicolon does not do?

Circle each structural key word, phrase, or punctuation mark in each sentence, and indicate above the word, phrase, or mark whether it shows *support, contrast, cause and effect,* or *definition.*

4. Although the words coming from his mouth were refined and deferential, his eyes betrayed a subtle ------ for his subject.

5. In order to be newsworthy, a story should be ------; that is, it should not merely warm over old facts the reader has heard many times before.

6. The building should be ------ not only for its long-recognized architectural merit but also for its ------ in the history of Black American theater.

7. Because the President was used to receiving the support of his advisers, he was ------ when he discovered that their views on the handling of the crisis were ------ with his own.

8. Some criminal investigators believe that polygraphs will reliably ------ deception by recording ------ reactions such as slight changes in breathing rate or perspiration rate elicited by a set of questions.

SAT Practice 3: Structural Keys

1. The ------ of the neighborhood is revealed by subtle practices, like the fact that so many people in the community use the same hand gestures when speaking.
   - (A) diversity
   - (B) adaptability
   - (C) modernization
   - (D) cohesiveness
   - (E) creativity

2. During the day, crabs move slowly and ------, but at night, they roam ------ across sandy sea bottoms, climbing reefs or foraging for kelp.
   - (A) frantically . . wildly
   - (B) cautiously . . freely
   - (C) gradually . . sluggishly
   - (D) deliberately . . carefully
   - (E) rashly . . rapidly

3. Because the President was used to receiving the support of his advisers, he was ------ when he discovered that their views on the handling of the crisis were ------ with his own.
   - (A) stunned . . irreconcilable
   - (B) relieved . . inconsistent
   - (C) amused . . consonant
   - (D) oblivious . . compatible
   - (E) sorry . . commensurate

4. The building should be ------ not only for its long-recognized architectural merit but also for its ------ in the history of Black American theater.
   - (A) designed . . role
   - (B) commissioned . . usefulness
   - (C) preserved . . importance
   - (D) demolished . . future
   - (E) constructed . . place

5. The lecture on number theory and its applications might have been particularly trying for the nonspecialists in the audience had the professor not ------ it with humorous asides.
   - (A) exhorted
   - (B) leavened
   - (C) intercepted
   - (D) countermanded
   - (E) rebuffed

6. His ------ maintained that Mr. Frank was constantly at odds with the corporate officers; yet the truth was that his ideas were not at all ------ with the officers' reasonable goals.
   - (A) detractors . . in accord
   - (B) supporters . . at variance
   - (C) advocates . . harmonious
   - (D) disparagers . . incompatible
   - (E) apologists . . in conflict

7. In spite of the ------ of Larry's speech, most of the audience was ------ well before he had finished.
   - (A) conciseness . . cheering
   - (B) humor . . intrigued
   - (C) appropriateness . . enrapt
   - (D) brevity . . asleep
   - (E) cleverness . . reluctant

8. If a child is ------ by arbitrary parental restrictions and denied the opportunity to exercise personal responsibility, at adolescence the child is likely to engage in dangerous and self-destructive behavior.
   - (A) nurtured
   - (B) appeased
   - (C) confined
   - (D) fascinated
   - (E) liberated

9. Although the government has frequently ------ some parental responsibilities, at heart it must still be parents, not agencies, who are ------ to care for children.
   - (A) obscured . . assumed
   - (B) precluded . . adjured
   - (C) exulted . . incompetent
   - (D) disavowed . . impelled
   - (E) usurped . . obligated

Answer Key 3: Structural Keys

Concept Review 3

1. *but, however, in contrast, nevertheless, whereas, although*, etc.

2. *because, therefore, thus, by*, etc.

3. Colons indicate that an explanation or a list of examples will follow; semicolons indicate that the statement that follows will extend or develop the previous one.

4. *Although* (contrast)

5. *In order to* (cause and effect); semicolon (support); *that is* (definition)

6. *not only . . . but also* (support)

7. *Because* (cause and effect); *discovered* (contrast)

8. *by* (cause and effect); *such as* (support)

SAT Practice 3

1. **D** The word *like* indicates examples. What are common hand gestures examples of? The unity or sameness of the community.
   diversity = variety; *adaptability* = ability to fit in; *cohesiveness* = unity

2. **B** The *but* indicates contrast. The first missing word must fit well with *slowly*.
   frantically = wildly; *sluggishly* = slowly; *rashly* = hastily

3. **A** *Because* indicates cause and effect. The word *discover* indicates surprise. If the President *was used to receiving the support of his advisers*, then it would be surprising to discover that they didn't agree with him on something.
   irreconcilable = unable to be made to agree; *consonant* = in agreement with; *oblivious* = unaware; *compatible* = fitting well together; *commensurate* = in proportion to

4. **C** *Not only . . . but also . . .* indicates a supportive relationship between the ideas.
   commissioned = paid for an artistic work to be created; *demolished* = destroyed

5. **B** It *might have been trying* (difficult to tolerate) *had the professor not ------ it with humorous asides.* What do humorous asides do to make something easier to tolerate? They *lighten* it up.
   exhorted = urged strongly; *leavened* = lightened with humor; *intercepted* = caught in transit; *countermanded* = cancelled; *rebuffed* = refused abruptly

6. **D** It's not particularly good to be *constantly at odds with the corporate officers,* so this is something that *critics* would say of him. The word *yet* indicates a contrast. If the officers' goals were *reasonable,* then one would likely *not disagree* with them.

detractors = critics; *accord* = agreement; *variance* = disagreement; *advocates* = supporters; *harmonious* = in pleasant agreement; *disparagers* = critics; *incompatible* = difficult to reconcile; *apologists* = those who make supportive arguments

7. **D** *In spite of* shows irony. It would certainly be ironic if the speech were short and yet still put people to sleep.
   conciseness = brevity; *enrapt* = enthralled; *brevity* = briefness

8. **C** *Parental restrictions* by definition are things that *confine; nurtured* = cared for; *appeased* = made less angry; *liberated* = freed

9. **E** *Although* indicates contrast. The sentence makes it clear that although government has *overtaken* some parental responsibilities, still, parents, not agencies, *should* care for children.
   obscured = made less clear; *precluded* = prevented; *adjured* = commanded solemnly; *exulted* = rejoiced; *disavowed* = renounced; *impelled* = urged to action; *usurped* = took over; *obligated* = morally compelled

Lesson 4: Simplifying the Sentence

Simplify

Some sentences are hard to interpret. But don't give up immediately just because you can't think of a good way to complete the sentence right away. When that happens, try to simplify your task using one of these strategies.

Process of Elimination

If you understand any part of the sentence, see if that understanding can help you to rule out any choices.

Example:

Statistics are often ------ information, but this is an ------ impression, because they must, by definition, obscure data by reducing many values to a single number.

(A) equated with . . erroneous
(B) mistaken for . . aesthetic
(C) superior to . . inaccurate
(D) relegated to . . insidious
(E) substituted for . . interesting

This sentence may be tough to understand at the first reading (or two). But you may know that statistics can't be *relegated to* (assigned to the lower status of) information, because data *is* information. If you just focus on the relationship between *statistics* and *information,* you can probably eliminate choices (C), (D), and (E). From there, you can try out the remaining choices and see that (A) works best.

If a sentence does contain two blanks, it is usually easier to complete the second blank first. Why? Because by the time you get to the second blank, you will have read more context clues. Of course, the example we just used is an exception, but you will find that usually the second blank is easier to complete than the first.

Focus on Tone

If you can't find the right word or words to complete the sentence, try to at least determine the tone of the word, that is, whether it's positive, negative, or neutral. Then eliminate any choices that don't have the right tone.

Example:

Without David's ------, the dispute between the parties might never have been resolved so tactfully.

(A) conciliation   (B) antagonism
(C) embarrassment   (D) indelicacy
(E) ridicule

The right word might not come right to mind, but it *should* be pretty clear that whatever David used was a *good* thing, because it helped resolve the dispute *tactfully.* Therefore, if you notice any words that are negative or neutral, you can eliminate them! The beauty of this strategy is that you don't have to know all of the words: just go to the ones you do know, and eliminate them if they're not the right tone. (The answer, by the way, is (A).)

Paraphrase

You may also often find it helpful to paraphrase the sentence, that is, restate it in your own words. This helps you to focus on the logic of the sentence as a whole, without getting stuck on *any particular* words or phrases. Just read the sentence completely, then try to restate the idea in the simplest terms possible. When you read the sentence again, you will probably find it easier to complete it, or at least to eliminate wrong choices.

Don't Be Afraid to Cut and Paste

Remember that you don't have to find the perfect word to fill the blank; you simply want to capture the right idea. Often, you will find it easy to just pick a word (or a form of a word) from elsewhere in the sentence.

Example:

Her account was so sterile that it made all of the other ------ seem ------ by contrast.

To complete the sentence, just reuse the words: *accounts* and *unsterile* sound a bit redundant, but they do the job!

Concept Review 4: Simplifying the Sentence

1. Why is it important to pay attention to tone?

2. What does *paraphrase* mean?

Place a + (positive), – (negative), or = (neutral) next to each word based on its tone.

3. lurid

4. purchase

5. euphoria

6. innocuous

7. pretentious

8. overwhelm

9. rejuvenate

10. modify

11. insidious

Place a +, –, or = in each blank to indicate whether the word should be positive, negative, or neutral in tone, then use the tone to determine and check the answer.

12. A ------ politician, Congresswoman Andrews worked hard and made so few mistakes that her opponents seemed to be ------ by contrast.

    (A) shrewd . . sages   (B) slothful . . drones   (C) canny . . blunderers
    (D) dynamic . . firebrands   (E) conscientious . . geniuses

13. His inability to relate to the latest trends in art led him to fear that his critical faculties had ------ during his long hiatus.

    (A) diversified   (B) atrophied   (C) converted   (D) enhanced   (E) multiplied

14. To her chagrin, Ellen soon learned that she could not hide her ------; her friends at the party could see the signs of weariness on her face.

    (A) amusement   (B) incoherence   (C) gratitude   (D) sorrow   (E) exhaustion

15. McLanham's ------ prose, particularly when compared to that of his more flamboyant ------, illustrates how artists of the same era can reflect startlingly different perspectives on the same reality.

    (A) stark . . contemporaries   (B) spartan . . enemies   (C) imprecise . . role models
    (D) flowery . . friends   (E) well-crafted . . teachers

SAT Practice 4: Simplifying the Sentence

1. In genetic research, ------ mice are often essential because their ------ allows scientists to pose questions answerable only if all the mice in a group have similar hereditary traits.
   (A) sedated . . temperament
   (B) cloned . . unpredictability
   (C) adaptable . . vigor
   (D) inbred . . uniformity
   (E) adult . . familiarity

2. Historians generally ------ the film, not only for its excessive sentimentality and unrealistic dialogue, but because it did not ------ a true understanding of the problems of the era.
   (A) advocated . . exhibit
   (B) challenged . . hinder
   (C) panned . . demonstrate
   (D) exalted . . ascertain
   (E) censured . . eliminate

3. The fact that even the most traditional European languages have ------ such words as "e-mail" seems to indicate that no language is impervious to foreign influences.
   (A) originated
   (B) prohibited
   (C) invalidated
   (D) recounted
   (E) incorporated

4. Although many have ------ the theoretical undergirdings of her research, her experimental protocols have always been beyond reproach.
   (A) lingered over
   (B) disputed
   (C) presumed
   (D) interpreted
   (E) publicized

5. Director T. C. Kehrwuld, whose mastery of stark objectivity in film has long been recognized by critics, has released another cinematic masterpiece which, while bound to satisfy those same critics, may be too ------ for public acceptance.
   (A) flamboyant
   (B) maudlin
   (C) ecstatic
   (D) austere
   (E) humane

6. The humanists in the class emphasized the ------ of scientific discovery, asserting that although the world could have formulated calculus without Newton, it would never have produced the Hammerklavier Sonata without Beethoven.
   (A) monotony
   (B) triviality
   (C) symmetry
   (D) impersonality
   (E) intricacy

7. Even Emily, who had to be ------ to participate at first, eventually confessed that she ------ a great deal from the workshop.
   (A) cajoled . . benefitted
   (B) inclined . . intuited
   (C) restrained . . resented
   (D) persuaded . . obscured
   (E) discouraged . . recalled

8. Although his manner was didactic and imperious, this fact was generally ------ and occasionally even ------ as qualities befitting a man of his stature.
   (A) encouraged . . dismissed
   (B) overlooked . . ignored
   (C) discussed . . denounced
   (D) criticized . . glorified
   (E) tolerated . . applauded

9. The novel's realistic depiction of social injustice in early-nineteenth-century America was an unmistakable ------ of the new republic's ------ to its democratic ideals.
   (A) denunciation . . infidelity
   (B) disavowal . . reversion
   (C) trivialization . . devotion
   (D) revelation . . gratitude
   (E) commendation . . allegiance

Answer Key 4: Simplifying the Sentence

Concept Review 4

1. Because it is often easier to attend to tone than to meaning, and it can be used to eliminate inappropriate choices.
2. To restate in your own, simpler terms.
3. lurid (–)
4. purchase (=)
5. euphoria (+)
6. innocuous (+)
7. pretentious (–)
8. overwhelm (=)
9. rejuvenate (+)
10. modify (=)
11. insidious (–)
12. **C** A (+) politician, Congresswoman Andrews worked hard and made so few mistakes that her opponents seemed to be (–) by contrast.
    shrewd = smart; *sages* = wise people; *slothful* = lazy; *drones* = mindless laborers; *canny* = smart; *blunderers* = people prone to mistakes; *dynamic* = energetic; *firebrands* = troublemakers; *conscientious* = attentive

13. **B** His inability to relate to the latest trends in art led him to fear that his critical faculties had (–) during his long hiatus.
    diversified = made more various; *atrophied* = weakened from disuse; *converted* = changed; *enhanced* = made more valuable, effective, or beautiful
14. **E** To her chagrin, Ellen soon learned that she could not hide her (–); her friends at the party could see the signs of weariness on her face.
    incoherence = confusion
15. **A** McLanham's (=) prose, particularly when compared to that of his more flamboyant (=), illustrates how artists of the same era can reflect startlingly different perspectives on the same reality.
    stark = plain; *contemporaries* = peers; *spartan* = stark

SAT Practice 4

1. **D** If mice all have similar traits, they are *uniform*, probably because they are very closely related. They must be *clones* or *close family members*.
   sedated = put to sleep; *temperament* = disposition; *vigor* = energetic health; *inbred* = bred with family members; *uniformity* = lack of variation
2. **C** If the film has *excessive sentimentality and unrealistic dialogue*, historians must not like it. They would *criticize* the film. It must not have *shown* a *true understanding of the problems of the era*.
   advocated = spoke in favor of; *exhibit* = display; *hinder* = impede; *panned* = criticized harshly; *exalted* = praised highly; *ascertain* = determined the truth of; *censured* = criticized
3. **E** If this fact indicates *that no language is impervious to foreign influences*, it must reveal a strong influence from foreign sources. *Incorporating such words as "e-mail"* would show that influence.
   originated = started; *invalidated* = made worthless; *recounted* = retold; *incorporated* = assumed into a whole
4. **B** *Although* indicates contrast. Although her *protocols have always been beyond reproach*, many must have *questioned* the undergirdings of her research.
   lingered over = considered carefully; *disputed* = called into question; *presumed* = assumed to be true
5. **D** *Stark objectivity* in film means plain, unadorned perspective. *Stark* and *austere* are synonyms.
   flamboyant = ornate; *maudlin* = depressed; *ecstatic* = very happy; *humane* = compassionate
6. **D** To say that *the world could have formulated calculus without Newton* is to suggest that scientific discovery does not depend on the creativity of particular individuals.
   monotony = tedium; *triviality* = ordinariness; *impersonality* = detachment from personal qualities; *intricacy* = complicatedness
7. **A** If Emily only *eventually* confessed about the workshop, she must have *had to be forced to participate* at first, but then she must have gotten a lot out of it.
   cajoled = coaxed persistently; *intuited* = determined by a hunch; *restrained* = held back; *obscured* = made unclear

8. **E** If being *didactic* (preachy) *and imperious* (overbearing) were thought *befitting* (appropriate), they must have been *accepted*.

9. **A** What is the relationship between a *depiction of social injustice* in a society and that society's *democratic ideals?* Such a depiction would certainly call those ideals into question, perhaps even *denounce* them.

denunciation = harsh criticism; *infidelity* = unfaithfulness; *disavowal* = swearing off; *reversion* = return to a previous state; *devotion* = strong commitment; *revelation* = revealing experience; *commendation* = praise; *allegiance* = faithfulness

Lesson 5: Using Context Intelligently

Parallelism

Parallelism is often an essential element of the logical structure of a sentence. Noticing parallel structures often makes completing sentences much simpler. What is parallelism? Well, it's discussed in a bit more detail in Chapter 15, Lesson 3, entitled "Parallelism." In short, it is the similarity among phrases that are *listing* things or *comparing* things.

For instance, consider the sentence

Rather than being dull and arcane, her lecture on galaxy formation was ------ and ------.

This contains two ideas that are parallel: *dull and arcane,* and ------ *and* ------. By the *law of parallelism,* the first missing word is an adjective that contrasts with *dull,* and the second is an adjective that contrasts with *arcane* (obscure and hard to understand). The missing words should contrast with the *tone and meaning* of the first two adjectives, preferably *in order.* So a nice, tidy, logical way to complete the sentence would be:

Rather than being dull and arcane, her lecture on galaxy formation was exciting and easy to understand.

Modifiers

The modifiers (that is, adjectives and adverbs) in Sentence Completion questions are not chosen casually. *Modifiers usually play key roles in the logical structure of the sentence.* If you read a sentence a couple of times, and its main idea isn't perfectly clear, try reading it through once more, this time focusing primarily on the adjectives and adverbs.

Example:
The training center, clean and regimented, is ------ to those seeking the ------ once associated with boxing.

(A) surprising . . austerity
(B) disappointing . . seediness
(C) convincing . . chaos
(D) refreshing . . camaraderie
(E) inspiring . . ambition

At first, you might focus on the modifiers *clean* and *regimented.* These could be positive descriptions, so such a training center might *impress* people who seek *cleanliness and order.* But no choice really fits this reading. The real key word is hard to miss: *once.* This word implies that people are seeking something that was *once* part of boxing but *is not any more.* Therefore, they would be disappointed by its absence, and so they must have been seeking something that is the *opposite* of *clean and regimented,* like *seedy and undisciplined.* (It may seem strange, but some people like that kind of stuff!)

Context and Common Sense

Your common sense is one of your best tools on Sentence Completion questions. For instance, if a sentence refers to a *scientist,* it's not just for decoration. Think: what do scientists do or think that makes them different from nonscientists? Or how about *teachers,* or *politicians,* or *advocates,* or *critics,* etc.? Of course, the sentences won't always show people acting in typical ways, but they generally require you to understand how these folks *typically* act or think.

Example:
An inveterate procrastinator, Pat could always be counted on to ------ any assignment he is given.

The only real context clue we have here is the fact that Pat is a procrastinator. If you know what a procrastinator does, then you know how to complete the sentence. Procrastinators *postpone* things.

Practice Your Verbal Inference Skills

Just like every other reading skill, verbal inference skills can be improved best by reading. *Read books and articles with challenging vocabulary so that you can practice "figuring out" the meaning of unfamiliar words.* Some students think it's best to look up new vocabulary words as soon as they encounter them. Rather, it's better to make an educated guess about the meaning before you look it up. Of course, once you do look it up, you should make a flashcard using the College Hill flashcard system described in Chapter 3, and practice it so that you never forget it.

Concept Review 5: Using Context Intelligently

1. What is parallelism, and how can it help you to complete sentences?

2. What is a modifier?

3. What should you do when you encounter an unfamiliar word in your reading?

Each of the three following sentences contains some of the same information, but in very different *logical contexts*. Complete each sentence with your own word or phrase according to the logical context.

4. Britain can hardly be considered _____, despite the fact that it is separated from the European continent both physically and linguistically.

5. Even while it maintains a deep respect, even reverence, for its history, Britain can hardly be considered _____.

6. Britain can hardly be considered _____, having been reduced to a mere shadow of the vast dominion it once was.

Complete the following sentences with your own words or phrases, utilizing any parallelism in each sentence.

7. The speakers ran the gamut from the eloquent to the bumbling; some were _____ while others spoke with profound _____.

8. I did not want to sit through another lecture that was rambling and mind-numbing; rather, I was hoping for one that was _____ and _____.

SAT Practice 5: Using Context Intelligently

1. Most art critics regard her early style as pedestrian and conventional, utterly devoid of technical or artistic ------.
   - (A) lucidity
   - (B) analysis
   - (C) articulation
   - (D) mediocrity
   - (E) innovation

2. Historical buildings in many developing towns, rather than being razed, are now being ------.
   - (A) constructed
   - (B) renovated
   - (C) described
   - (D) condemned
   - (E) designed

3. Some linguists claim that French is characterized by brevity of expression and therefore may be the most ------ of all languages.
   - (A) beautiful
   - (B) vivid
   - (C) concise
   - (D) accessible
   - (E) concrete

4. The melée that punctuated the meeting between the rival factions was not entirely ------; the groups have long ------ each other on many important issues.
   - (A) surprising . . supported
   - (B) unusual . . copied
   - (C) explicit . . evaluated
   - (D) unanticipated . . opposed
   - (E) expected . . encountered

5. Having been devastated by the earthquake, the freeway was virtually ------ to all but the most rugged of vehicles.
   - (A) destroyed
   - (B) impassable
   - (C) improper
   - (D) winding
   - (E) unnecessary

6. Those who assume that they can easily be ------ chefs in the classic tradition are almost as ------ as those who think they can write a novel if they simply sit down and type.
   - (A) amateur . . candid
   - (B) renowned . . skeptical
   - (C) superb . . timid
   - (D) clumsy . . pessimistic
   - (E) competent . . naive

7. Many opponents of psychoanalysis contend that since its assumptions cannot be tested with scientific rigor, it is properly characterized as merely ------ system rather than a reliable therapeutic method.
   - (A) a concise
   - (B) a courageous
   - (C) a necessary
   - (D) an intuitive
   - (E) an ornamental

8. Paranoia, extreme competitiveness, and many other ------ of the modern rat race, despite what many cutthroat executives are saying, are hardly ------ to long-term success in the business world.
   - (A) by-products . . conducive
   - (B) responsibilities . . detrimental
   - (C) ornaments . . helpful
   - (D) establishments . . reliable
   - (E) inequities . . charitable

9. Under certain conditions, the virus can mutate into ------ strain, transforming what was once simply ------ into a menacing poison.
   - (A) a new . . an epidemic
   - (B) a deficient . . a derivative
   - (C) an erratic . . a rudiment
   - (D) a virulent . . a nuisance
   - (E) an advanced . . a disease

Answer Key 5: Using Context Intelligently

Concept Review 5

1. Parallelism is the grammatical and logical consistency in phrases that list or compare things in a sentence.
2. A modifier is a word or phrase that describes another word. A word that modifies a noun is called an *adjective*, and a word that modifies a verb, an adjective, or another adverb is an *adverb*.
3. Try to infer its meaning from its usage in the sentence, then look it up in the dictionary to see if you are correct, then make a flashcard for the word using the College Hill system described in Chapter 3.
4. Britain can hardly be considered *an island*, despite the fact that it is separated from the European continent both physically and linguistically.
5. Even while it maintains a deep respect, even reverence, for its history, Britain can hardly be considered *archaic*.
6. Britain can hardly be considered *an empire*, having been reduced to a mere shadow of the vast dominion it once was.
7. The speakers ran the gamut from the eloquent to the bumbling; some were *articulate* while others spoke with profound *ineptitude*. (You may have used different words, but be sure that the first word is *positive* in tone and corresponds roughly to *articulate* and that the second word is negative and corresponds roughly to *ineptitude* in meaning.)
8. I did not want to sit through another lecture that was rambling and mind-numbing; rather, I was hoping for one that was *focused* and *engaging*. (You may have used different words, but be sure that both words are *positive* in tone and that the first corresponds roughly to *focused* and that the second word corresponds roughly to *engaging* in meaning.)

SAT Practice 5

1. **E** Something *pedestrian and conventional* is ordinary and uses methods that have been used many times before. Therefore it is not *new*.
   lucidity = clarity; *analysis* = examination of parts; *articulation* = expression; *mediocrity* = averageness; *innovation* = novelty, creativity
2. **B** To *raze* something is to destroy it completely. If a historical building is not *razed*, it is preserved or, even better, made new again.
   renovated = made new again
3. **C** *Brevity of expression* is *conciseness*.
   vivid = full of lively forms or colors; *concise* = to the point; *accessible* = easily understood; *concrete* = perceived through the senses
4. **D** A *melée* is a fight. If the groups were fighting, they probably have *disagreed with* each other. Therefore the melée was not *unexpected*.
5. **B** A highway that has *been devastated by the earthquake* would be *hard to travel through*.
   impassable = unable to be travelled through
6. **E** Those who *think they can write a novel if they simply sit down and type* are probably unaware of how challenging such a task is. They are *naive*.
   amateur = nonprofessional; *candid* = frank and honest; *renowned* = reputable, well-known; *skeptical* = inclined to doubting; *superb* = exceptional; *timid* = shy; *naive* = lacking a sophisticated understanding
7. **D** If something cannot be *tested with scientific rigor* and is not a *reliable method*, it must be without a reasonable, scientific basis.
   intuitive = based on hunches rather than reason; *ornamental* = decorative
8. **A** *Despite* indicates contrast. *Paranoia* and *extreme competitiveness* are certainly bad things. Of course, *cutthroat executives* would claim that they help, but they can't really be *helpful* to *success in the business world*.
   by-products = results of a process; *conducive* = helpful; *detrimental* = harmful; *inequities* = unfair situations
9. **D** If something is *transformed* into a *menacing poison*, then it must not have been so bad before. Perhaps it was only a little bit *troublesome*.
   epidemic = a broad outbreak; *derivative* = repetitive of previous works; *rudiment* = basic element; *virulent* = dangerous; *nuisance* = annoyance

Lesson 6: The Toughest Sentences

Tough Sentences

Some sentences are tough not because they have tough vocabulary, but because they have a complicated or ambiguous logical structure.

Negatives

Negatives can easily complicate a sentence and are easily overlooked. Watch carefully for negative words like *not, hardly, rarely, lacking,* etc., because they are as important as the key words! When you encounter a sentence with negatives, it may help to paraphrase the sentence more "positively."

Example:

Their approach was not unlike that of the Neo-Darwinians, whose lack of respect for quasi-scientific methods was far from unknown in the University community.

This sentence is easier to work with if it is first paraphrased without so many negatives:

Their approach was like that of the Neo-Darwinians, whose support for the scientific method was well known in the University community.

Ambiguous Sentences

Some sentences are tough to work with because they are ambiguous; that is, they have more than one possible interpretation, usually one positive and one negative. Since there are usually only two possibilities, just try them both.

Example:

The recent trend of using ------ dialogue in films can be traced to directors who have ------ the natural half-sentences and interrupted thoughts that characterize genuine human speech.

(A) halting . . embraced
(B) formal . . assumed
(C) imperfect . . eschewed
(D) stilted . . adopted
(E) passionate . . endured

There are two ways to complete this sentence. Modern film directors might *like* or *dislike* the *natural half-sentences and interrupted thoughts that characterize genuine human speech.* If they like them, they would use them; choice (A) supports this reading. If they don't like them, they would prefer more *formal* dialogue. Choice (B) gives *formal* and (D) gives *stilted*, which convey that idea. But if the directors use *formal* language, they wouldn't *assume* imperfect dialogue, so (B) is out. Likewise, if they used *stilted* (formal) dialogue, they wouldn't *adopt* imperfect dialogue. So (A) is the correct response.

Abstract vs. Concrete

Concrete nouns, which usually represent *people* and *objects*, are typically easier to understand than abstract nouns, which typically represent *quantities, qualities,* or *ideas.* When we focus on the concrete nouns in a sentence more than the abstract ones, we can misread the sentence. Pay special attention to abstract nouns in sentences.

Example:

The dissent regarding the new restrictions on student parking was ------ those who wanted to be able to drive freely to school.

(A) spearheaded by
(B) surprising to
(C) troublesome to
(D) disputed by
(E) disregarded by

This sentence is not about the *parking restrictions*, but rather about the *dissent*. It's easy to misread if you don't focus on the word *dissent*. (We overlook it because it's so abstract.) If you wanted to drive freely to school, how would you feel about the *dissent regarding parking restrictions*? You'd probably be one of the people dissenting! You may even *initiate* the dissent, which is why (A) is the best choice.

Concept Review 6: The Toughest Sentences

1. What, other than tough vocabulary, can make a sentence hard to understand?

2. What are abstract nouns, and why should you pay close attention to them in sentences?

3. Circle the abstract nouns and draw boxes around the concrete nouns in the sentence below.

   The lack of interest among the voters ensured that the referendum about the new playground could sneak through, even though it contained some objectionable clauses.

Paraphrase the following sentences to minimize negatives.

4. *It is not uncommon to find people who refuse to deny that ghosts exist.*

5. *The council did not fail to block a single motion.*

Complete the following ambiguous sentences in two ways, with different tones.

6. Despite the _____ of the climb, the explorers were beginning to believe that the trek would soon become _____.

   Despite the _____ of the climb, the explorers were beginning to believe that the trek would soon become _____.

7. Far from being _____ on the issue of gun control, Will has _____ on the issue for many years.

   Far from being _____ on the issue of gun control, Will has _____ on the issue for many years.

SAT Practice 6: The Toughest Sentences

1. The country's confidence, formerly sustained by an ------ sense of power, was replaced by an equally exaggerated sense of ------ following the hasty evacuation of its troops from three foreign capitals.
    (A) inflated . . weakness
    (B) overwhelming . . inviolability
    (C) erratic . . hysteria
    (D) unquestioned . . omnipotence
    (E) arbitrary . . resolution

2. According to their detractors, the leaders of the Union for Progressive Politics do not truly ------ change, but simply rehash old and discredited theories of political philosophy.
    (A) admonish
    (B) censor
    (C) advocate
    (D) caricature
    (E) hinder

3. Dr. Cuthbert often ------ his former associates for not continuing to support him; apparently he harbored great animosity because of their ------ of him.
    (A) disparaged . . endorsement
    (B) excoriated . . abandonment
    (C) exonerated . . denunciation
    (D) extolled . . betrayal
    (E) venerated . . dismissal

4. Despite her gregariousness, Andrea seems to have been a woman who cherished her ------ highly.
    (A) colleagues
    (B) friendships
    (C) privacy
    (D) integrity
    (E) humility

5. It is extremely rare to see a politician ------ any opinion that is widely unpopular; it seems that, for them, public censure is more ------ even than death.
    (A) conform to . . desirable
    (B) tolerate . . exciting
    (C) reject . . feared
    (D) espouse . . painful
    (E) manipulate . . natural

6. The cogency and animation he showed in private belied his reputation for a notably ------ style of lecturing.
    (A) tepid
    (B) incisive
    (C) versatile
    (D) infrequent
    (E) fluent

7. The haiku, with its ------, its reduction of natural and everyday events to their mere essence, seems to economically depict the ------ of even the simplest human experience.
    (A) casualness . . destructiveness
    (B) optimism . . barrenness
    (C) capriciousness . . rigidity
    (D) digressiveness . . precariousness
    (E) conciseness . . poignancy

8. Sadly, most people who say they want change in public schools will struggle to resist it, or at least ------ its effects on them.
    (A) initiate
    (B) distort
    (C) palliate
    (D) defend
    (E) enhance

9. Despite the ------ literature debunking the theory of ESP, a critical and rational awareness of the subject continues to ------ most of the public.
    (A) vivid . . pervade
    (B) voluminous . . elude
    (C) provocative . . captivate
    (D) ambiguous . . perplex
    (E) incomprehensible . . escape

Answer Key 6: The Toughest Sentences

Concept Review 6

1. Complicated or ambiguous logical structure.
2. Abstract nouns are nouns that represent ideas, quantities, or qualities; that is, they represent things that cannot be directly perceived.
3. *The lack (abstract noun) of interest (abstract noun) among the voters (concrete noun) ensured that the referendum (abstract noun) about the new playground (concrete noun) could sneak through, even though it contained some objectionable clauses (abstract noun).*
4. *It is common to find people who believe in ghosts.*
5. *The council blocked every motion.*

6. Despite the *ease* of the climb, the explorers were beginning to believe that the trek would soon become *treacherous.* (or some similar words)
   Despite the *arduousness* of the climb, the explorers were beginning to believe that the trek would soon become *easier.* (or some similar words)
7. Far from being *passive* on the issue of gun control, Will has *pontificated* on the issue for many years. (or some similar words)
   Far from being *consistent* on the issue of gun control, Will has *equivocated* on the issue for many years. (or some similar words)

SAT Practice 6

1. **A** What would follow a *hasty evacuation* of a country's troops? A feeling of being overwhelmed and defeated, most likely. This feeling of *weakness,* we are told, is just as *exaggerated* as the sense of power just prior to the withdrawal.
   inviolability = invincibility; *erratic* = irregular; *hysteria* = irrational and exaggerated emotion; *omnipotence* = supreme power; *arbitrary* = based on whim and random power; *resolution* = determination

2. **C** If their *detractors* (critics) believe that they only *rehash old and discredited theories,* then they are suggesting that they do not really *speak out for change.*
   admonish = reprimand; *censor* = eliminate objectionable material; *advocate* = speak in favor of; *caricature* = exaggerate comically; *hinder* = get in the way of

3. **B** If his associates did not continue to support him, they must have *abandoned* him. If he harbored *animosity* for them, he must have *criticized* them.
   disparaged = criticized harshly; *endorsement* = show of support; *excoriated* = criticized harshly; *exonerated* = proved innocent; *denunciation* = condemnation; *extolled* = praised highly; *venerated* = honored

4. **C** *Despite* indicates contrast. *Gregariousness* is sociability. Its opposite is *solitude, reclusiveness,* or *privacy.*

5. **D** If *public censure* is like *death,* politicians must not like it. They must never *openly adopt* a widely unpopular opinion.

conform = do what is expected; *espouse* = adopt publicly; *manipulate* = take control of

6. **A** *Cogency* is *persuasiveness* and *animation* is *liveliness.* To *belie* is to *misrepresent,* so he must **not** have a reputation for being lively and persuasive, so people must think he's dull.
   tepid = dull, lukewarm; *incisive* = keen and thoughtful; *versatile* = well-rounded; *fluent* = smooth, flowing

7. **E** The first word must mean something like *reduction to its essence,* and the second word must mean something like *essence.*
   barrenness = starkness; *capriciousness* = whimsy, randomness; *digressiveness* = tendency to go off topic; *precariousness* = danger; *conciseness* = brevity; *poignancy* = sharpness of feeling

8. **C** If they *resist* it, then they want to prevent its effects on him, or at least *minimize* its effects on them.
   initiate = begin; *distort* = twist; *palliate* = make less severe; *enhance* = make better

9. **B** *Despite* indicates irony. If there is *literature debunking the theory of ESP,* it would be ironic if the public *failed to develop* a critical and rational awareness of the subject. What would make it even more ironic is if the literature were *plentiful.*
   vivid = full of vibrant imagery; *pervade* = fill completely; *voluminous* = plentiful; *elude* = escape capture or understanding; *provocative* = tending to elicit strong reactions; *captivate* = capture; *ambiguous* = unclear; *perplex* = confuse; *incomprehensible* = beyond understanding

CHAPTER 6

WHAT THE SAT MATH IS *REALLY* TESTING

1. Mapping Problems

2. Analyzing Problems

3. Finding Patterns

4. Simplifying Problems

5. Connecting to Knowledge

6. Finding Alternatives

7. Thinking Logically

8. Checking Your Work

Lesson 1: Mapping Problems

What Is Mapping?

Mapping a problem means *orienting* yourself to the problem and *representing* its information. It's like pulling out a map before you start a trip. The map shows you where you're going but not how to get there. On some tough SAT math problems, half the battle is "mapping"—orienting yourself to the problem and figuring out what it's asking.

Tips for mapping tough SAT math problems:

- Write out any *diagrams*, *equations*, or *tables* that represent the key information in the problem. You don't get neatness points on the SAT—good test-takers scribble all over the test booklet. Writing things down helps you to keep track of the information as well as your thought process.
- Notice any restrictions on the unknowns. For instance, do they have to be *integers* or *positive* numbers or *multiples* of some number? Are they measures of *angles* or *segments* or *areas* in a figure? Underline key restrictions.
- Know the definitions of special terms such as *primes*, *integers*, *factors*, *multiples*, *perimeter*, and so on, and underline these terms when you see them.
- Notice whether any unknowns can take *any* values that you choose or have only *one particular* value that you have to find. You can solve many complicated-looking problems by just choosing values for the unknowns!
- Read carefully and notice *exactly* what the problem is asking for. Does it ask you to solve an equation? Find the value of an expression? Find an area? Underline what the problem is asking you to find so that you don't lose track of it.
- Notice whether the question is multiple-choice, and if so, notice the range of the answer choices. If the answers are far apart, you might be able to just *estimate* an answer to zero in on the right choice. Also, notice how the choices are expressed. Are they *fractions*, *decimals*, *radicals*, *algebraic expressions*? Noticing this often helps you to see what you have to do to get the answer.

Watch for the Common Mix-Ups

Even the best students sometimes miss questions because they misinterpret key terms in the problem. You can avoid this by underlining these key terms and thinking about the terms they are commonly confused with.

- A *perimeter* is the distance around a figure. Don't confuse it with *area*, which is the number of square units that fit inside a figure.
- The *circumference formula* for a circle is $c = 2\pi r$. Don't confuse it with the *area formula* of a circle, which is $a = \pi r^2$. To avoid confusing them, remember that area is always measured in *square units*, so its formula contains the "square."
- An *odd number* is any integer not divisible by 2. Don't confuse it with a *negative number*, which is any number less than 0. These two are commonly confused because both of these words have a "bad" tone.
- An *even number* is any integer divisible by 2. Don't confuse it with an *integer* in general, which is any positive or negative whole number. These two are commonly confused because when we talk of a number dividing another "evenly," we really mean that it goes in an *integer* number of times, not necessarily an *even* number of times.
- A *product* is the result of a multiplication. Don't confuse it with a *sum*, which is the result of addition.

Don't Rush—Avoid Quick Gimmicks

Always read the whole problem carefully before deciding how to solve it. SAT math questions—especially medium and hard-level ones—are designed to trap students who don't read carefully or who pigeon-hole questions too quickly. Getting an answer quickly doesn't help if it's the wrong answer.

Concept Review I: Mapping Problems

1. Describe what it means to "map" a problem.

2. Why is it important to consider the choices (in a multiple-choice question) as part of the problem?

Define the following terms, and indicate what terms they are sometimes confused with.

3. *Odd* means   and is sometimes confused with

4. *Even* means   and is sometimes confused with

5. *Perimeter* means   and is sometimes confused with

6. *Integers* are   and are sometimes confused with

Equations or inequalities are powerful "mapping" tools. Translate the following statements into equations or inequalities. Be sure to specify the meanings of any unknowns you may use.

7. The sum of two consecutive odd numbers is 28.

8. Ellen is twice as old as Maria.

9. Last year, Jennifer was twice as old as Brian is now.

SAT Practice 1: Mapping Problems

Map each of the following problems before solving it. Use the space for scratchwork, and underline any key words in the problem. Then solve each problem.

Do Your Scratchwork Here

1. The product of five consecutive even integers is 0. What is the greatest possible value of any one of these integers?

2. The perimeter of a rectangle is 28 inches, and its area is x square inches. If x is an even integer, what is the greatest possible value of x?

3. Carlos begins with twice as much money as David. After Carlos gives $12 to David, Carlos still has $10 more than David. How much money did they have <u>combined</u> at the start?

   (A) $32
   (B) $66
   (C) $68
   (D) $92
   (E) $102

4. Corinne travels from home to work at an average speed of 50 miles per hour, and returns home by the same route at 60 miles per hour. It takes her 10 more <u>minutes</u> to get to work than it takes her to get home. How many miles is it from Corinne's home to work?

   (A) 25
   (B) 35
   (C) 50
   (D) 75
   (E) 90

Answer Key I: Mapping Problems

Concept Review I

1. To map means to represent the general problem situation and goal, either mentally or on paper.

2. Because the choices tell you the range of values to consider, as well as the form of the numbers (integers, fractions, etc.) and format (factored, decimal, etc.).

3. *Odd* means *an integer not divisible by 2* and is sometimes confused with *negative* because of the "negative" tone of both words.

4. *Even* means *an integer divisible by 2* and is sometimes confused with *positive* because of the "positive" tone of both words.

5. *Perimeter* means *distance around a figure* and is sometimes confused with *area*, which is the *number of square units that fit inside a figure*.

6. *Integers* are *whole numbers and negative whole numbers* and are sometimes confused with *counting numbers, which are the **positive** integers: 1, 2, 3, 4, . . .*

7. Let n be the smaller of the two numbers. Then the next odd number is $n + 2$, so an equation that says that the sum of two consecutive odd numbers is 28 is $n + n + 2 = 28$.

8. Let e stand for Ellen's current age and m stand for Maria's current age. An equation that says that Ellen is twice as old as Maria is $e = 2m$.

9. Let j stand for Jennifer's age now and b stand for Brian's age now. Last year, Jennifer was $j - 1$ years old, so an equation that says that last year Jennifer was twice as old as Brian is now is $j - 1 = 2b$.

SAT Practice I

1. **8** If the product of a set of integers is 0, then one of the numbers must be 0. To maximize the value of any one of them, let 0 be the smallest of the integers. If they are **consecutive even** integers, they must be 0, 2, 4, 6, and 8. If your answer was 4, then you overlooked the fact that the numbers are **even.**

2. **48** Your first tool in mapping a geometry problem is a good diagram. This one has no diagram, so you must draw your own. Draw a rectangle, labeling its width w and its length l:

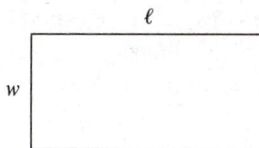

Since the perimeter of the rectangle is 28 inches, you can set up an equation: $2w + 2l = 28$. Divide both sides of the equation by 2 to get $w + l = 14$. Since the area is x, you can set up the equation $lw = x$. If x is even, then l and w can't both be odd. (Can you see how we know that?) You should be able to see that the possible values for w and l are 2 and 12, 4 and 10, and 6 and 8. (Check them and see.) This means that x can have values of $2 \times 12 = 24$, $4 \times 10 = 40$, or $6 \times 8 = 48$. The greatest of these, of course, is 48.

3. **E** Let c be the number of dollars Carlos had to start and d be the number of dollars David had to start. The question asks for the value of $c + d$. If Carlos begins with twice as much money as David, then $c = 2d$. After Carlos gives $12 to David, he has $c - 12$ dollars, and David has $d + 12$ dollars. If Carlos still has $10 more than David, then $c - 12 = (d + 12) + 10$.

Simplify: $\qquad\qquad\qquad c - 12 = d + 22$

Add 12: $\qquad\qquad\qquad\quad c = d + 34$

Substitute $c = 2d$: $\qquad\quad 2d = d + 34$

Subtract d: $\qquad\qquad\qquad\quad d = 34$

Plug back in: $\qquad\qquad\quad c = 2(34) = 68$

So $c + d = 34 + 68 = 102$.

4. **C** To "map" this problem, you must know that distance = speed × time. You must find the number of miles from Corinne's home to work, so call that d. If she travels from home to work at an average speed of 50 miles per hour, then it must take her $d/50$ hours, or $60 \times d/50 = 6d/5$ minutes. If she returns home at 60 miles per hour, it must take her $d/60$ hours, or $60 \times d/60 = d$ minutes. If it takes her 10 more minutes to get to work than it takes her to get home, then:

$$\frac{6d}{5} - d = 10$$

Simplify: $\qquad\qquad\qquad \dfrac{d}{5} = 10$

Multiply by 5: $\qquad\qquad\quad d = 50$

Lesson 2: Analyzing Problems

Break Complicated Problems into Simple Ones

Analyzing is key to solving many SAT math problems. Analyzing a problem means simply looking at its parts and seeing how they relate. Often, a complicated problem can be greatly simplified by looking at its individual parts. If you're given a geometry diagram, mark up the angles and the sides when you can find them. If you're given algebraic expressions, notice how they relate to one another.

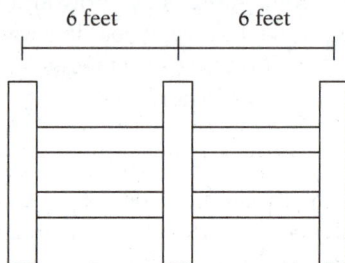

For a certain fence, vertical posts must be placed 6 feet apart with supports in between, as shown above. How many vertical posts are needed for a fence 120 feet in length?

You may want to divide 120 by 6 and get 20, which seems reasonable. But how can you check this without drawing a fence with 20 posts? Just change the question to a much simpler one to check the relationship between length and posts. How many posts are needed for a 12-foot fence? The figure above provides the answer. Obviously, it's 3. But $12 \div 6$ isn't 3; it's 2. What gives? If you think about it, you will see that dividing only gives the number of *spaces* between the posts, but there is always one more post than spaces. So a 120-foot fence requires $20 + 1 = 21$ vertical posts.

Look for Simple Relationships

Once you see the parts of a problem, look for simple relationships between them. Simple relationships usually lead to simple solutions.

If $2x^2 + 5y = 15$, then what is the value of $12x^2 + 30y$?

Don't worry about solving for x and y. You only need to see the simple relationship between the expressions. The expression you're looking for, $12x^2 + 30y$, is 6 times the expression you're given, $2x^2 + 5y$. So, by substitution, $12x^2 + 30y$ must equal 6 times 15, or 90.

If You Can't Find What You Want, Find What You Can!

If you can't find what you want right away, just look at the parts of the problem one at a time, and *find what you can*. Often, going step by step and noticing the relationships among the parts will lead you eventually to the answer you need.

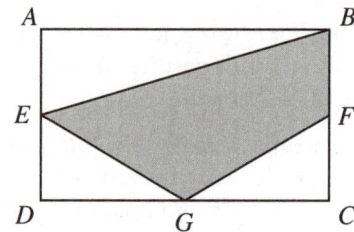

In the figure above, *ABCD* is a rectangle with area 60, and $AB = 10$. If E, F, and G are the midpoints of their respective sides, what is the area of the shaded region?

This looks complicated at first, but it becomes much simpler when you analyze the diagram. You probably know that the formula for the area of a rectangle is $a = bh$, but the shaded region is not a rectangle. So how do you find its area? Analyze the diagram using the given information. First, write the fact that $AB = 10$ into the diagram. Since the area of the rectangle is 60 and its base is 10, its height must be 6. Then, knowing that E, F, and G are midpoints, you can mark up the diagram like this:

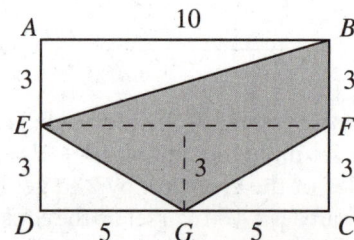

Notice that the dotted lines divide the shaded region into three right triangles, which are easy to work with. The two bottom triangles have base 5 and height 3 (flip them up if it helps you to see), and the top triangle has base 10 and height 3. Since the formula for the area of a triangle is $a = \frac{1}{2}bh$, the areas of the triangles are 7.5, 7.5, and 15, for a total area of 30.

Concept Review 2: Analyzing Problems

1. What does it mean to analyze a problem?

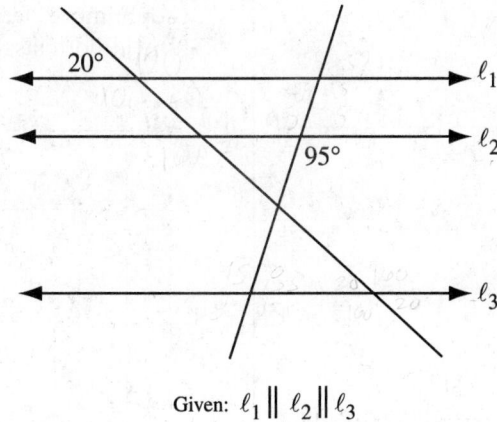

Given: $\ell_1 \parallel \ell_2 \parallel \ell_3$

2. Analyze the diagram above by indicating the measures of as many angles as possible.

3. If $20,000 is divided among three people in the ratio of 2:3:5, how much does each person get?

4. If $(x)(x-1)(x-2)$ is negative and x is greater than 0, then what can be concluded about $x - 1$ and $x - 2$?

SAT Practice 2: Analyzing Problems

1. How many odd integers are there between 1 and 99, not including 1 and 99?

    (A) 46
    (B) 47
    (C) 48
    (D) 49
    (E) 50

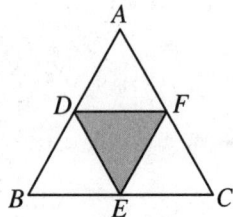

2. In the figure above, equilateral triangle ABC has an area of 20, and points D, E, and F are the midpoints of their respective sides. What is the area of the shaded region?

3. In the sophomore class at Hillside High School, the ratio of boys to girls is 2 to 3. The junior class contains as many boys as the sophomore class does, and the ratio of boys to girls in the junior class is 5 to 4. If there are 200 students in the sophomore class, how many students are there in the junior class?

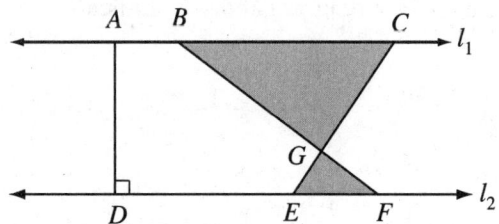

Note: Figure not drawn to scale.

4. In the figure above, $\ell_1 \parallel \ell_2$, $AD = 8$, $EF = 4$, $GF = 3$, and $BG = 9$. What is the total area of the shaded regions?

    (A) 32
    (B) 36
    (C) 40
    (D) 42
    (E) 44

Answer Key 2: Analyzing Problems

Concept Review 2

1. To analyze a problem means to look at its parts and find how they relate to each other.

2. Your diagram should look like this:

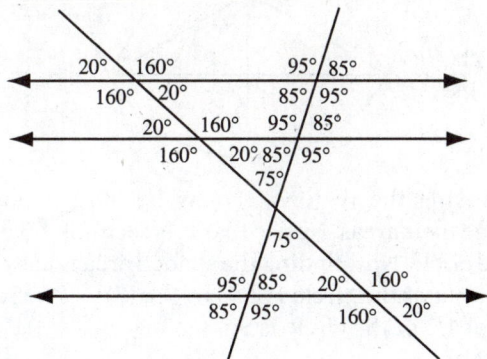

3. If the total is divided in the ratio of 2:3:5, then it is divided into 2 + 3 + 5 = 10 parts. The individual parts, then, are 2/10, 3/10, and 5/10 of the total. Multiplying these fractions by $20,000 gives parts of $4,000, $6,000, and $10,000.

4. If $(x)(x - 1)(x - 2)$ is negative, and x is greater than 0, then $(x - 1)(x - 2)$ must be negative, which means that one of the factors is positive and the other negative. Since $x - 2$ is less than $x - 1$, $x - 2$ must be negative and $x - 1$ must be positive.

SAT Practice 2

1. **C** You might start by noticing that every other number is odd, so that if we have an even number of consecutive integers, half of them will always be odd. But this one is a little trickier. Start by solving a simpler problem: How many odd numbers are between 1 and 100, inclusive? Simple: there are 100 consecutive integers, so 50 of them must be odd. Now all we have to do is remove 1, 99, and 100. That removes 2 odd numbers, so there must be 48 left.

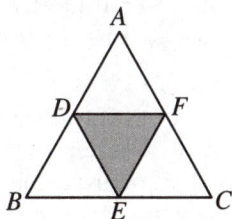

2. **5** Don't worry about finding the base and height of the triangle and using the formula *area = (base × height)/2*. This is needlessly complicated. Just notice that the four smaller triangles are all equal in size, so the shaded region is just 1/4 of the big triangle. Its area, then, is 20/4 = 5.

3. **144** If the ratio of boys to girls in the sophomore class is 2 to 3, then 2/5 are boys and 3/5 are girls. If the class has 200 students, then 80 are boys and 120 are girls. If the junior class has as many boys as the sophomore class, then it has 80 boys, too. If the ratio of boys to girls in the junior class is 5 to 4, then there must be $5n$ boys and $4n$ girls. Since $5n = 80$, n must be 16. Therefore, there are 80 boys and 4(16) = 64 girls, for a total of 144 students in the junior class.

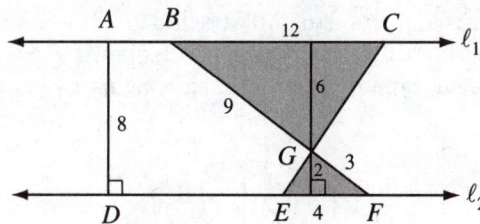

4. **C** Write what you know into the diagram. Because the lines are parallel, $\angle GEF$ is congruent to $\angle GCB$, and the two triangles are similar. (To review similarity, see Lesson 6 in Chapter 10.) This means that the corresponding sides are proportional. Since *GF* and *BG* are corresponding sides, the ratio of corresponding sides is 3/9, or 1/3. Therefore, *EF* is 1/3 of *BC*, so *BC* = 12. To find the areas of the triangles, you need the heights of the triangles. The sum of the two heights must be 8, and they must be in a ratio of 1:3. You can guess and check that they are 2 and 6, or you can find them algebraically: if the height of the smaller triangle is h, then the height of the larger is $8 - h$.

$$\frac{h}{8-h} = \frac{1}{3}$$

Cross-multiply: $3h = 8 - h$
Add h: $4h = 8$
Divide by 4: $h = 2$

So the shaded area is $(4)(2)/2 + (12)(6)/2 = 4 + 36 = 40$.

Lesson 3: Finding Patterns

Repeating Patterns

> Finding patterns means looking for simple rules that relate the parts of a problem. One key to simplifying many SAT math problems is exploiting repetition. If something repeats, you usually can *cancel* or *substitute* to simplify.

If $5x^2 + 7x + 12 = 4x^2 + 7x + 12$, then what is the value of x?

This question is much simpler than it looks at first because of the repetition in the equation. If you subtract the repetitive terms from both sides of the equation, it reduces to $5x^2 = 4x^2$. Subtracting $4x^2$ from both sides then gives $x^2 = 0$, so $x = 0$.

Patterns in Geometric Figures

> Sometimes you need to play around with the parts of a problem until you find the patterns or relationships. For instance, it often helps to treat geometric figures like jigsaw puzzle pieces.

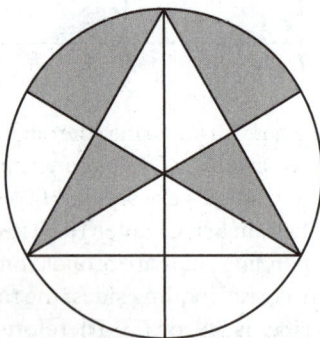

The figure above shows a circle with radius 3 in which an equilateral triangle has been inscribed. Three diameters have been drawn, each of which intersects a vertex of the triangle. What is the sum of the areas of the shaded regions?

This figure looks very complicated at first. But look closer and notice the *symmetry* in the figure. Notice that the three diameters divide the circle into six congruent parts. Since a circle has 360°, each of the central angles in the circle is $360° \div 6 = 60°$. Then notice that the two shaded triangles fit perfectly with the other two shaded regions to form a sector such as this:

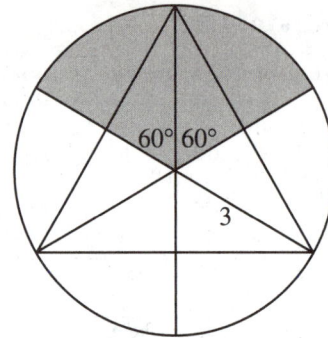

Moving the regions is okay because it doesn't change their areas. Notice that this sector is 1/3 of the entire circle. Now finding the shaded area is easy. The total area of the circle is $a = \pi r^2 = \pi(3)^2 = 9\pi$. So the area of 1/3 of the circle is $9\pi/3 = 3\pi$.

Patterns in Sequences

> Some SAT questions will ask you to analyze a sequence. When given a sequence question, write out the terms of the sequence until you notice the pattern. Then use whole-number division with remainders to find what the question asks for.

$$1, 0, -1, 1, 0, -1, 1, 0, -1, \ldots$$

If the sequence above continues according to the pattern shown, what will be the 200th term of the sequence?

Well, at least you know it's either 1, 0, or −1, right? Of course, you want a better than a one-in-three guess, so you need to analyze the sequence more deeply. The sequence repeats every 3 terms. In 200 terms, then the pattern repeats itself $200 \div 3 = 66$ times with a remainder of 2. This means that the 200th term is the same as the second term, which is 0.

What is the units digit of 27^{40}?

The units digit is the "ones" digit or the last digit. You can't find it with your calculator because when 27^{40} is expressed as a decimal, it has 58 digits, and your calculator can only show the first 12 or so. To find the units digit, you need to think of 27^{40} as a term in the sequence $27^1, 27^2, 27^3, 27^4, \ldots$. If you look at these terms in decimal form, you will notice that the units digits follow a pattern: 7, 9, 3, 1, 7, 9, 3, 1, ... The sequence has a repeating pattern of four terms. Every fourth term is 1, so the 40th term is also 1. Therefore, the units digit of 27^{40} is 1.

Concept Review 3: Finding Patterns

Solve the following problems by taking advantage of repetition.

1. If 5 less than 28% of x^2 is 10, then what is 15 less than 28% of x^2?

2. If m is the sum of all multiples of 3 between 1 and 100, and n is the sum of all multiples of 3 between 5 and 95, what is $m - n$?

3. How much greater is the combined surface area of two cylinders each with a height of 4 cm and a radius of 2 cm than the surface area of a single cylinder with a height of 8 cm and a radius of 2 cm?

Solve each of the following problems by analyzing a sequence.

4. What is the units digit of 4^{134}?

5. The first two terms of a sequence are 1 and 2. If every term after the second term is the sum of the previous two, then how many of the first 100 terms are odd?

SAT Practice 3: Finding Patterns

1. If $\dfrac{3}{y} + \dfrac{x}{2} = 10$, then $\dfrac{6}{y} + x =$

(A)   5
(B)   15
(C)   20
(D)   40
(E)   60

2. Every term of a sequence, except the first, is 6 less than the square of the previous term. If the first term is 3, what is the fifth term of this sequence?

(A)   3
(B)   15
(C)   19
(D)   30
(E)   43

$$-4, 0, 4, -4, 0, 4, -4, 0, 4, \ldots$$

3. If the sequence above continues according to the pattern shown, what is the sum of the first 200 terms of the sequence?

(A)   −800
(B)   −268
(C)   −4
(D)   0
(E)   268

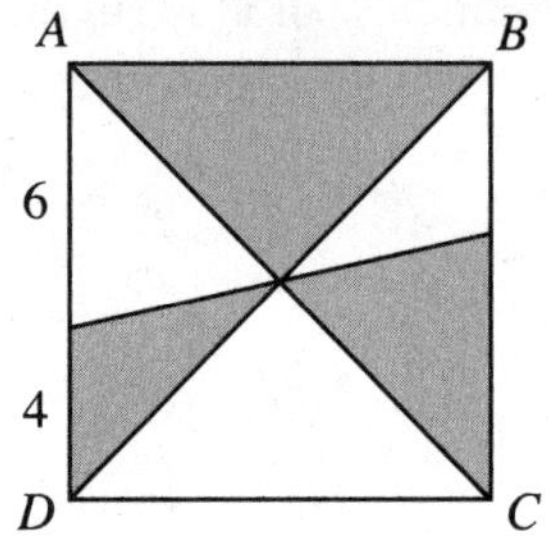

4. The figure above shows a square with three line segments drawn through the center. What is the total area of the shaded regions?

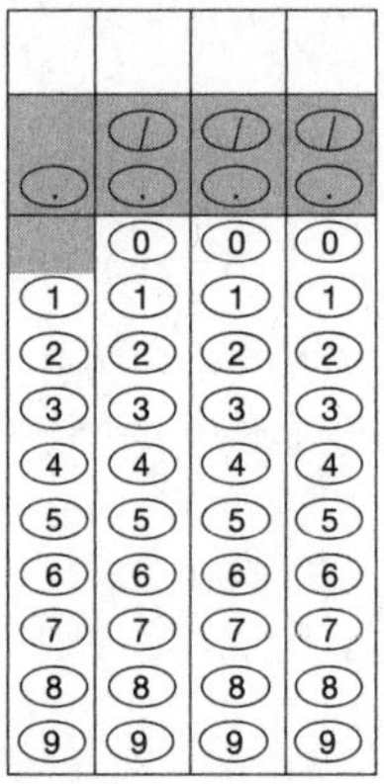

5. What is the units digit of 3^{40}?

(A)   1
(B)   3
(C)   6
(D)   7
(E)   9

Answer Key 3: Finding Patterns

Concept Review 3

1. Don't worry about the percent or about finding x.
   Translate: 5 less than 28% of x^2 is 10 means
   $$.28(x^2) - 5 = 10$$
   Subtract 10: $.28(x^2) - 15 = 0$
   So 15 less than 28% of x^2 is 0.

2. $m = 3 + 6 + 9 + \ldots + 93 + 96 + 99$
   $n = 6 + 9 + \ldots + 93$
   When you subtract n from m, all the terms cancel
   except $3 + 96 + 99 = 198$.

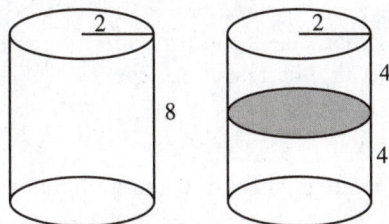

3. Don't calculate the total surface area. Instead, just notice that the two small cylinders, stacked together, are the same size as the large cylinder. But remember that you are comparing **surface areas,** not **volumes.** The surface areas are almost the same, except that the smaller cylinders have two extra bases. Each base has an area of $\pi(2)^2 = 4\pi$, so the surface area of the smaller cylinders is $2(4\pi) = 8\pi$ greater than that of the larger cylinder.

4. Your calculator is no help on this one because 4^{134} is so huge. Instead, think of 4^{134} as a term in the sequence $4^1, 4^2, 4^3, 4^4, \ldots$. What is the units digit of 4^{134}? If you write out the first few terms, you will see a clear pattern to the units digits: 4, 16, 64, 256, ... Clearly, every odd term ends in a 4 and every even term ends in a 6. So 4^{134} must end in a 6.

5. The first few terms are 1, 2, 3, 5, 8, 13, 21, ... Since we are concerned only about the "evenness" and "oddness" of the numbers, think of the sequence as odd, even, odd, odd, even, odd, odd, even, ... Notice that the sequence repeats every three terms: (odd, even, odd), (odd, even, odd), (odd, even, odd), ... In the first 100 terms, this pattern repeats 100/3 = 33⅓ times. Since each pattern contains 2 odd numbers, the first 33 repetitions contain 66 odd numbers and account for the first 99 terms. The last term must also be odd because each pattern starts with an odd number. Therefore, the total number of odds is 66 + 1 = 67.

SAT Practice 3

1. **C** $\dfrac{6}{y} + x = 2\left(\dfrac{3}{y} + \dfrac{x}{2}\right) = 2(10) = 20$

2. **A** If every term is 6 less than the square of the previous term, then the second term must be $(3)^2 - 6 = 9 - 6 = 3$. The third term, then, is also $(3)^2 - 6 = 3$, and so on. Every term, then, must be 3, including the fifth.

3. **C** The sequence repeats every three terms: $(-4, 0, 4), (-4, 0, 4), (-4, 0, 4), \ldots$. Each one of the groups has a sum of 0. Since 200/3 = 67⅔, the first 200 terms contain 67 repetitions of this pattern, plus two extra terms. The 67 repetitions will have a sum of 67(0) = 0, but the last two terms must be –4 and 0, giving a total sum of –4.

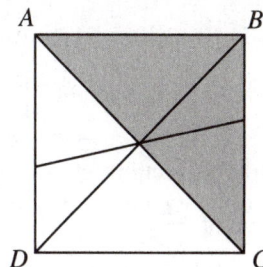

4. **50** Move the shaded regions around, as shown above, to see that they are really half of the square. Since the area of the square is (10)(10) = 100, the area of the shaded region must be half of that, or 50.

5. **A** The number 3^{40} is so big that your calculator is useless for telling you what the last digit is. Instead, think of 3^{40} as being an element in the sequence $3^1, 3^2, 3^3, 3^4, \ldots$. If you write out the first six terms or so, you will see that there is a clear pattern to the units digits: 3, 9, 27, 81, 243, 729, ... So the pattern in the units digits is 3, 9, 7, 1, 3, 9, 7, 1, ... The sequence repeats every four terms. Since 40 is a multiple of 4, the 40th term is the same as the 4th and the 8th and the 12th terms, so the 40th term is 1.

Lesson 4: Simplifying Problems

Beeline, Substitute, Combine, and Cancel

> When a problem seems overwhelming, try one of these four simplification strategies: *beelining, substituting, combining,* and *canceling.*

Look for the Beeline—The Direct Route

> Many SAT problems have "beelines"—direct paths from the given information to the answer. We sometimes miss the "beeline" because we get trapped in a knee-jerk response—for instance, automatically solving every equation or using the Pythagorean theorem on every right triangle. Avoid the knee-jerk response. Instead, step back and look for the "beeline."

If $\dfrac{3a}{2b} = \dfrac{1}{4}$ and $\dfrac{b}{5c} = 3$, what is the value of $\dfrac{a}{10c}$?

This problem looks tough because of all the unknowns. You might do the knee-jerk thing and try to solve for a, b, and c. Whoa, there! Step back. The question doesn't ask for a, b, and c. It asks for a fraction that you can get much more directly. Notice that just multiplying the two given fractions gets you almost there:

$\dfrac{3a}{2b} \times \dfrac{b}{5c} = \dfrac{3a}{10c}$. This is close to what you want—all

you have to do is divide by 3 to get $\dfrac{a}{10c}$. Substituting

the given values of the fractions gives you $\dfrac{1}{4} \times 3 \div 3 = \dfrac{1}{4}$,

which is the value of $\dfrac{a}{10c}$.

Simplify by Substituting

> The simplest rule in algebra is also the most powerful: *Anything can be substituted for its equal.* When you notice a complicated expression on the SAT, just notice if it equals something simpler, and substitute!

If $3x^2 + 5x + y = 8$ and $x \neq 0$, then what is the value

of $\dfrac{16-2y}{3x^2+5x}$?

Again, take a deep breath. Both the equation and the fraction look complicated, but you can simplify by

just remembering that *anything can be substituted for its equal.* Notice that $3x^2 + 5x$ appears in both the equation and the fraction. What does it equal? Subtract y from both sides of the equation to get $3x^2 + 5x = 8 - y$. If you substitute $8 - y$ for $3x^2 + 5x$ in the fraction, you get

$\dfrac{16-2y}{8-y} = \dfrac{2(8-y)}{8-y} = 2$. Nice!

Simplify by Combining or Canceling

> Many algebraic expressions can be simplified by combining or canceling terms. Always keep your eye out for *like terms* that can be combined or canceled and for *common factors in fractions* that can be canceled.

If m and n are positive integers such that $m > n$ and

$\dfrac{m^2 - n^2}{2m - 2n} = \dfrac{9}{2}$, what is the value of $m + n$?

To simplify this one, it helps to know a basic factoring formula from Chapter 8, Lesson 5: $m^2 - n^2 = (m - n)(m + n)$. If you factor the numerator and denominator of the fraction, a common factor reveals itself, and it

can be canceled: $\dfrac{m^2 - n^2}{2m - 2n} = \dfrac{(m-n)(m+n)}{2(m-n)} = \dfrac{m+n}{2}$.

Since $\dfrac{m + n}{2} = \dfrac{9}{2}$, $m + n$ must equal 9.

If $f(x) = 2x^2 - 5x + 3$ and $g(x) = 2x^2 + 5x + 3$, then for how many values of x does $f(x) = g(x)$?

(A) 0
(B) 1
(C) 2
(D) 3
(E) 4

Remember the simple rule that *anything can be substituted for its equal,* and then cancel to simplify. Since $f(x) = g(x)$, you can say that $2x^2 - 5x + 3 = 2x^2 + 5x + 3$.

Subtract $2x^2$ and 3: $-5x = 5x$

Add $5x$: $0 = 10x$

Divide by 10: $0 = x$

So the answer is (A) 0, right? Wrong! Remember that the question asks *for how many values of x* are the function values equal. Since we only got one solution for x, the answer is (B) 1.

Concept Review 4: Simplifying Problems

Simplify the following expressions.

1. $-2n - (6 - 5n) - n$

2. $\dfrac{2x^2 - 18}{x^2 + 2x - 3}$

3. $\dfrac{2}{x} + \dfrac{1}{2}$

4. $\dfrac{6x^3 + 4x^2 + 10x}{2x}$

5. $x\sqrt{x^6}$

Solve the following problems with substitution.

6. If $y = 1 - x$ and $2y + x = 5$, then what is the value of x?

7. If $3 + m + n = n^2 + m^2$, what is the value of $\dfrac{(n^2 - n) + (m^2 - m)}{6}$?

8. For all real numbers x, let $<x> = (1 - x)^2$. What is the value of $<<4>>$?

SAT Practice 4: Simplifying Problems

1. If $3y - 4z = 6$ and $2y + z = 10$, then $y - 5z =$

   (A) 12
   (B)   6
   (C)   4
   (D)   0
   (E) −4

2. If $a + b = 3$, $a + c = 5$, and $b + c = -6$, then $a + b + c =$

   (A)   4
   (B)   2
   (C)   1
   (D)   0
   (E) −1

3. If $\dfrac{a+b}{b} = 3$ and $\dfrac{a+c}{c} = 5$, what is the value of $\dfrac{b}{c}$?

   (A) $\dfrac{1}{2}$

   (B) $\dfrac{3}{5}$

   (C) $\dfrac{5}{3}$

   (D) 2

   (E) 8

Questions 4 and 5 pertain to the following definition:

For all non-zero real numbers k, let $^\wedge k = 1 - \dfrac{1}{k}$.

4. Which of the following is equivalent to $^\wedge 3 - {}^\wedge 2$?

   (A) $^\wedge \dfrac{1}{6}$

   (B) $^\wedge \dfrac{5}{6}$

   (C) $^\wedge 1$

   (D) $^\wedge \dfrac{6}{5}$

   (E) $^\wedge 2$

5. Other than 0, what is the only value of k for which $^{\wedge\wedge}k$ is undefined?

Answer Key 4: Simplifying Problems

Concept Review 4

1. $-2n - (6 - 5n) - n = -2n - 6 + 5n - n = 2n - 6$

2. $\dfrac{2x^2 - 18}{x^2 + 2x - 3} = \dfrac{2(x-3)(x+3)}{(x+3)(x-1)} = \dfrac{2(x-3)}{(x-1)}$

3. $\dfrac{2}{x} + \dfrac{1}{2} = \dfrac{4}{2x} + \dfrac{x}{2x} = \dfrac{4+x}{2x}$

4. $\dfrac{6x^3 + 4x^2 + 10x}{2x} = \dfrac{6x^3}{2x} + \dfrac{4x^2}{2x} + \dfrac{10x}{2x} = 3x^2 + 2x + 5$

5. $x\sqrt{x^6} = x \times x^3 = x^4$

6. Substitute $y = 1 - x$ into $2y + x = 5$ to get
$$2(1 - x) + x = 5$$

Distribute:	$2 - 2x + x = 5$
Simplify:	$2 - x = 5$
Subtract 2:	$-x = 3$
Multiply by -1:	$x = -3$

7.
$$3 + m + n = n^2 + m^2$$
Subtract n and m: $\qquad 3 = (n^2 - n) + (m^2 - m)$

Substitute: $\qquad \dfrac{(n^2 - n) + (m^2 - m)}{6} = \dfrac{3}{6} = \dfrac{1}{2}$

8.
	$<<4>>$
Substitute for $<4>$:	$= <(1 - 4)^2>$
Simplify:	$= <(-3)^2>$
Simplify:	$= <9>$
Substitute for $<9>$:	$= (1 - 9)^2$
Simplify:	$= (-8)^2$
Simplify:	$= 64$

SAT Practice 4

1. **E** Subtract the equations:
$$\begin{aligned} 3y - 4z &= 6 \\ -(2y + z &= 10) \\ \hline y - 5z &= -4 \end{aligned}$$

2. **C** Add the equations:
$$(a + b) + (a + c) + (b + c) = 3 + 5 + -6$$
Simplify: $\qquad 2a + 2b + 2c = 2$
Divide by 2: $\qquad a + b + c = 1$

3. **D** Start by simplifying the expressions:
$$\dfrac{a + b}{b} = \dfrac{a}{b} + \dfrac{b}{b} = \dfrac{a}{b} + 1$$

$$\dfrac{a + c}{b} = \dfrac{a}{c} + \dfrac{c}{c} = \dfrac{a}{c} + 1$$

Substituting into the original equations gives
$$\dfrac{a}{b} + 1 = 3 \quad \text{and} \quad \dfrac{a}{c} + 1 = 5$$

Subtract 1: $\quad \dfrac{a}{b} = 2 \quad \text{and} \quad \dfrac{a}{c} = 4$

Divide the fraction: $\quad \dfrac{\frac{a}{c}}{\frac{a}{b}} = \dfrac{4}{2}$

Simplify: $\qquad \dfrac{a}{c} \times \dfrac{b}{a} = 2$

Simplify: $\qquad \dfrac{b}{c} = 2$

4. **D** Begin by simplifying $^3 - {}^2$ by substitution:
$$^3 - {}^2 = (1 - 1/3) - (1 - 1/2) = 2/3 - 1/2 = 1/6$$

But be careful not to pick (A) $^1/6$ because
$$^1/6 = 1 - 6 = -5$$

Notice that the choices must be evaluated first before we can see which one equals 1/6. Notice that choice (D) is $^6/5 = 1 - 5/6 = 1/6$.

5. **I** Begin by simplifying $^\wedge{}^\wedge k$ by substitution:
$$^\wedge{}^\wedge k = {}^\wedge\left(1 - \dfrac{1}{k}\right) = 1 - \dfrac{1}{1 - \frac{1}{k}}$$

Yikes! That doesn't look simple! But think about it: why is it that k can't be 0? Because division by 0 is undefined, and k is in a denominator. But notice that $1 - \dfrac{1}{k}$ is also in a denominator, so $1 - \dfrac{1}{k}$ can't be 0, either!

Solving: $\qquad 1 - \dfrac{1}{k} \neq 0$

Add $\dfrac{1}{k}$: $\qquad 1 \neq \dfrac{1}{k}$

Multiply by k: $\qquad k \neq 1$

Then check by noticing that $^\wedge{}^\wedge 1$ is undefined:
$^\wedge{}^\wedge 1 = {}^\wedge(1 - 1/1) = {}^\wedge 0 = 1 - 1/0$, and $1/0$ is undefined.

Lesson 5: Connecting to Knowledge

Know What You Need

Some SAT math questions require you to use special formulas or know the definitions of special terms. Fortunately, you won't need to memorize very many formulas (none of that trig stuff, for instance), and some of the most important ones are given to you right on the test!

Reference Information

Every SAT math section gives you this *reference information.* Check it out and use it when you need it.

$$A = \pi r^2$$
$$C = 2\pi r$$

$$A = \ell w$$

$$A = \tfrac{1}{2} bh$$

$$V = \ell w h$$

$$V = \pi r^2 h$$

$$c^2 = a^2 + b^2$$

Special right triangles

The arc of a circle measures 360°.
Every straight angle measures 180°.
The sum of the measures of the angles in a triangle is 180°.

Memorize the Key Formulas They DON'T Give You

It's awfully nice of the SAT to give you those formulas, but those are not quite *all* you'll need. Fortunately, we can fit the other key formulas on a single page. Here they are:

Rate formula (Chapter 9, Lesson 4):

Distance (or work) = rate × time

Average (arithmetic mean) *formulas* (Chapter 9 Lesson 2):

$$Average = \frac{sum}{number\ of\ things}$$

Sum = average × number of things

Slope formula (Chapter 10, Lesson 4):

$$Slope = \frac{rise}{run} = \frac{y_2 - y_1}{x_2 - x_1}$$

Midpoint formula (Chapter 10, Lesson 4):

$$Midpoint = \left(\frac{x_1 + x_2}{2}, \frac{y_1 + y_2}{2} \right)$$

Percent change formula (Chapter 7, Lesson 5):

$$Percent\ change = \frac{final - starting}{starting} \times 100\%$$

Memorize the Key Definitions

You'll also want to memorize the definitions of some key terms that show up often:

Mode = the number that appears the most frequently in a set. Remember that *mode* and *most* both begin with *mo* (Chapter 9, Lesson 2).

Median = the "middle number" of a set of numbers when they are listed in order. If there are an even number of numbers, the median is the average of the *two* middle numbers (Chapter 9, Lesson 2).

Remainder = the *whole number* left over when one *whole number* has been divided into another *whole number* a *whole number* of times (Chapter 7, Lesson 7).

Absolute value = the distance a number is from 0 on the number line (Chapter 8, Lesson 6).

Prime number = an integer greater than 1 that is divisible *only* by itself and 1 (Chapter 7, Lesson 7).

Factor = a number or expression that is part of a product. (*Product* = result of a multiplication.)

Concept Review 5: Connecting to Knowledge

Write out each formula, theorem, definition, or property.

1. The Pythagorean theorem

2. The zero product property

3. The parallel lines theorem

4. The rate formula

5. The average (arithmetic mean) formula

6. The definition of the median

7. The definition of the mode

8. The circumference formula

9. The circle area formula

10. The triangle area formula

SAT Practice 5: Connecting to Knowledge

1. If x is the average (arithmetic mean) of k and 10, and y is the average (arithmetic mean) of k and 4, what is the average of x and y, in terms of k?

    (A) $\dfrac{k+14}{4}$ (B) $\dfrac{k+14}{2}$ (C) $\dfrac{k+7}{2}$

    (D) $7k$ (E) $14k$

    Key formula(s):

2. If, on average, x cars pass a certain point on a highway in y hours, then, at this rate, how many cars should be expected to pass the same point in z hours?

    (A) xyz (B) $\dfrac{xy}{z}$ (C) $\dfrac{z}{xy}$

    (D) $\dfrac{xz}{y}$ (E) $\dfrac{x}{yz}$

    Key formula(s):

h feet

8 feet

3 feet

4 feet

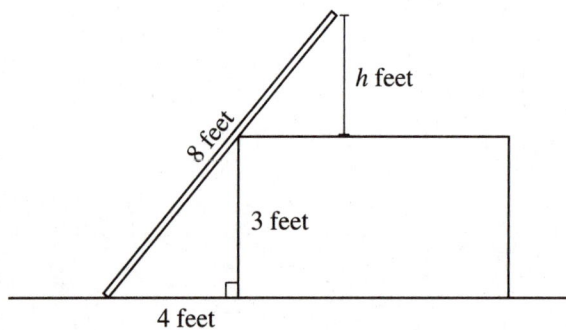

Note: Figure not drawn to scale.

3. A straight 8-foot board is resting on a rectangular box that is 3 feet high, as shown in the diagram above. Both the box and the board are resting on a horizontal surface, and one end of the board rests on the ground 4 feet from the edge of the box. If h represents the height, in feet, of the other end of the board from the top of the box, what is h?

    Key formula(s):

Answer Key 5: Connecting to Knowledge

Concept Review 5

1. The Pythagorean theorem: In a right triangle, if c is the length of the hypotenuse and a and b are the lengths of the two legs, then $c^2 = a^2 + b^2$ (Chapter 10, Lesson 3).

2. The zero product property: If a set of numbers has a product of zero, then at least one of the numbers is zero. Conversely, if zero is multiplied by any number, the result is zero (Chapter 8, Lesson 5).

3. The parallel lines theorem: If a line cuts through two parallel lines, then all acute angles formed are congruent, all obtuse angles formed are congruent, and any acute angle is supplementary to any obtuse angle (Chapter 10, Lesson 1).

4. The rate formula: *distance (or work) = rate × time* (Chapter 9, Lesson 4).

5. The average (arithmetic mean) formula: *Average = sum ÷ number of things* (Chapter 9, Lesson 2).

6. The definition of the median: The "middle number" of a set of numbers when they are listed in order. If there are an odd number of numbers, the median is the "middle number," and if there are an even number of numbers, it is the average of the two middle numbers (Chapter 9, Lesson 2).

7. The definition of the mode: The number that appears the most frequently in a set (Chapter 9, Lesson 2).

8. The circumference formula: *Circumference = $2\pi r$* (Chapter 10, Lesson 5).

9. The circle area formula: *Area = πr^2* (Chapter 10, Lesson 5).

10. The triangle area formula: *Area = base × height/2* (Chapter 10, Lesson 5).

SAT Practice 5

1. **C**   Key formula: *Average = sum ÷ number of things.*

   So if x is the average of k and 10, then $x = \dfrac{k+10}{2}$.

   And if y is the average of k and 4, then $y = \dfrac{k+4}{2}$.

   The average of x and y, then, is

   $$\dfrac{\dfrac{k+10}{2}+\dfrac{k+4}{2}}{2} = \dfrac{k+10}{4}+\dfrac{k+4}{4} = \dfrac{2k+14}{4} = \dfrac{k+7}{2}$$

2. **D**   Key formulas: *Number of cars = rate × time*, and

   $rate = \dfrac{number\ of\ cars}{time}$. Since x is the number of cars and y is the time in hours, the rate is x/y cars per hour. Using the first formula, then, the number of cars that would pass in z hours is

   $$\left(x/y \text{ cars per hour}\right)\left(z \text{ hours}\right) = \dfrac{xz}{y}$$

   You should notice, too, that simply plugging in values for x, y, and z can make the problem easier to think about. Say, for instance, that $x = 10$ cars pass every $y = 2$ hours. In $z = 4$ hours, then, it should be clear that 20 cars should pass by. Plugging these numbers into the choices, you will see that (D) is the only one that gives an answer of 20.

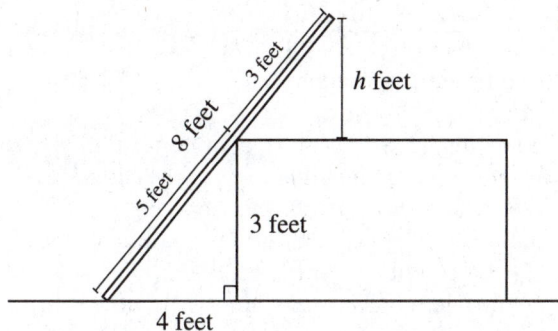

3. **1.8**   Key formula: The Pythagorean theorem: $c^2 = a^2 + b^2$. Key theorem: In similar triangles, corresponding sides are proportional. Notice that the figure has two right triangles, and they are similar. The hypotenuse of the bottom triangle is 5 because $3^2 + 4^2 = 5^2$. Therefore, the hypotenuse of the top triangle is $8 - 5 = 3$. Since the two triangles are similar, the corresponding sides are proportional:

   $$\dfrac{3}{5} = \dfrac{h}{3}$$

   Cross-multiply: $5h = 9$
   Divide by 5: $h = 1.8$

Lesson 6: Finding Alternatives

Keep Your Options Open

There are often many good ways to solve an SAT math problem. Consider different strategies. This gives you a way to check your work. If two different methods give you the same answer, you're probably right!

Numerical Analysis—Plugging In

Let's come back to the problem we saw in Lesson 4:

If $3x^2 + 5x + y = 8$ and $x \neq 0$, then what is the value of $\dfrac{16 - 2y}{3x^2 + 5x}$?

Back in Lesson 4 we solved this using substitution, an *algebraic method*. Now we'll use a *numerical method*. Notice that the equation contains two unknowns. This means that we can probably find solutions by *guessing and checking*. Notice that the equation works if $x = 0$ and $y = 8$. But—darn it—the problem says $x \neq 0$! No worries—notice that $x = 1$ and $y = 0$ also work. (Check and see.) Now all we have to do is plug those numbers in for x and y: $\dfrac{16 - 2y}{3x^2 + 5x} = \dfrac{16 - 2(0)}{3(1)^2 + 5(1)} = \dfrac{16}{8} = 2$. Same answer, whole different approach!

"Plugging in" works in two common situations: *when you have more unknowns than equations* and *when the answer choices contain unknowns*. Always check that your numbers satisfy the conditions of the problem. Then solve the problem *numerically*, and write down the answer. If the answer choices contain unknowns, plug the values into every choice and eliminate those that don't give the right answer. If more than one choice gives the right answer, plug in again with different numbers.

If $3m = mn + 1$, then what is the value of m in terms of n?

(A) $n + 1$
(B) $n - 2$
(C) $\dfrac{1}{3 - n}$
(D) $\dfrac{1}{3 + n}$
(E) $\dfrac{2}{3 + n}$

Because the choices contain unknowns, you can plug in. Pick a simple number for m to start, such as 1. Plugging into the equation gives $3 = n + 1$, which has the

solution $n = 2$. Now notice that the question asks for m, which is 1. Write that down and circle it. Now substitute 2 for n in the choices and see what you get:

(A) 3
(B) 0
(C) 1
(D) 1/5
(E) 2/5

Only (C) gives the right answer.

Algebraic Analysis

You can also solve the problem above algebraically:

	$3m = mn + 1$
Subtract mn:	$3m - mn = 1$
Factor:	$m(3 - n) = 1$
Divide by $(3 - n)$:	$m = \dfrac{1}{3 - n}$

Testing the Choices

Some SAT math questions can be solved just by "testing" the choices. Since numerical choices are usually given in order, start by testing choice (C). If (C) is too big, then (D) and (E) are too big, also, leaving you with just (A) and (B). This means that you have only one more test to do, at most, until you find the answer.

If $3(2)^{n+1} - 3(2)^n = 24$, what is the value of n?

(A) 2
(B) 3
(C) 4
(D) 5
(E) 6

Here you can take an *algebraic* or a *numerical* approach. That is, you can solve the equation for n or you can "test" the choices to see if they work. For this lesson, we'll try the "testing" strategy. Since the choices are given in ascending order, we'll start with the middle number, (4). Substituting 4 for n gives us $3(2)^5 - 3(2)^4$ on the left side, which equals 48, not 24. (It's okay to use your calculator!) Since that doesn't work, we can eliminate choice (C). But since it's clearly too *big*, we can also rule out choices (D) and (E). That's why we start with (C)—even if it doesn't work, we still narrow down our choices as much as possible. Now just test either (A) or (B). Notice that (B) gives us $3(2)^4 - 3(2)^3$, which equals 24, the right answer.

Now try solving the problem algebraically, and see if it's any easier!

Concept Review 6: Finding Alternatives

1. When can a multiple-choice problem be solved by just "testing the choices"?

2. When solving by testing the choices, why is it often best to start with choice (C)?

3. When testing the choices, when is it not necessarily best to start with choice (C)?

4. When can you simplify a multiple-choice question by plugging in values?

5. What are the four steps to solving by plugging in values?

6. Why is it best to understand more than one way to solve a problem?

SAT Practice 6: Finding Alternatives

Try to find at least two different ways of solving each of the following problems, and check that both methods give you the same answer.

---

1. If $m = 2x - 5$ and $n = x + 7$, which of the following expresses x in terms of m and n?

(A) $\dfrac{m-n+2}{2}$

(B) $m - n + 2$

(C) $\dfrac{m-n+12}{2}$

(D) $m - n + 12$

(E) $2(m - n + 12)$

---

2. Three squares have sides with lengths a, b, and c. If b is 20% greater than a and c is 25% greater than b, then by what percent is the area of the largest square greater than the area of the smallest square?

(A) 20%
(B) 50%
(C) 75%
(D) 125%
(E) 225%

---

3. Jim and Ellen together weigh 290 pounds. Ellen and Ria together weigh 230 pounds. All three together weigh 400 pounds. What is Ellen's weight?

(A) 110 lbs
(B) 120 lbs
(C) 130 lbs
(D) 140 lbs
(E) 170 lbs

---

4. A painter used one-fourth of her paint on one room and one-third of her paint on a second room. If she had 10 gallons of paint left after painting the second room, how many gallons did she have when she began?

(A) 19
(B) 24
(C) 28
(D) 30
(E) 50

---

5. If $r = \dfrac{s}{5}$ and $4r = 7t$, what is the value of s in terms of t?

(A) $35t$

(B) $\dfrac{35t}{4}$

(C) $35t - 4$

(D) $31t$

(E) $70t$

Answer Key 6: Finding Alternatives

Concept Review 6

1. There are many situations in which this is possible, but perhaps the most common is where you're asked to find the solution of an equation, and the choices are ordinary numbers.

2. Because the answer choices are usually presented in numerical order. If choice (C) doesn't work, you may be able to tell whether it is too big or too small, and thereby eliminate two other answers as well. This way, you will only need to "test" one more choice to get the answer.

3. When it is not easy to tell whether the choice is "too big or too small," or when there is no pattern to the choices.

4. Usually, when the answer choices contain unknowns or represent ratios of unknowns; also when the problem contains more unknowns than equations.

5. (1) Check that the values satisfy any given equations or other restrictions, (2) write down the values you are plugging in for each unknown, (3) solve the problem *numerically* and write down this number, and (4) plug in the values to *every* choice and eliminate those that don't give the right answer. If more than one choice gives the right answer, plug in different numbers.

6. Because the two methods can provide a "check" against one another: if they both give the same answer, you are almost certainly right!

SAT Practice 6

1. Method 1: The problem asks you to solve for x in terms of m and n. Notice that every choice contains the expression $m - n$.

   By substitution: $m - n = (2x - 5) - (x + 7)$
   Simplify: $m - n = x - 12$
   Add 12: $m - n + 12 = x$

   So the answer is (D).

   Method 2: Just plug in simple values for the unknowns. If $x = 1$, then $m = (2)(1) - 5 = -3$ and $n = (1) + 7 = 8$. Since the problem asks for x, write down its value, 1, and circle it. Then plug in $m = -3$ and $n = 8$ to every choice, and simplify:

   (A) -4.5 (B) -9 (C) 0.5 (D) 1 (E) 2

   So the answer is (D).

2. Method 1: Plug in numbers. Let a be 100. If b is 20% greater than a, then $b = 120$. If c is 25% greater than b, then $c = 150$. The area of the largest square, then, is $(150)^2 = 22,500$, and the area of the smallest square is $(100)^2 = 10,000$. The percent difference is $(22,500 - 10,000)/10,000 = 1.25 = 125\%$ (D).

   Method 2: Use algebra. $b = 1.2a$ and $c = (1.25)(1.2a) = 1.5a$. So the area of the smallest square is a^2 and the area of the largest square is $(1.5a)^2 = 2.25a^2$. Since $2.25a^2 - a^2 = 1.25a^2$, the area of the bigger square is 125% larger.

3. Method 1: Test the choices, starting with (C). If Ellen weighs 130 pounds, then Jim weighs $290 - 130 = 160$ pounds and Ria weighs $230 - 130 = 100$ pounds. All together, their weight would be $130 + 160 + 100 = 390$ pounds. Close, but too small. This means that our guess for Ellen's weight is too *big* (because increasing Ellen's weight decreases *both* Jim and Ria's weight by the same amount, for a net *decrease*). This lets us eliminate choices (C), (D), and (E). Since our guess wasn't far off, it makes sense to

   test choice (B) next. If Ellen weighs 120 pounds, then Jim weighs $290 - 120 = 170$ pounds and Ria weighs $230 - 120 = 110$ pounds. In total, they weigh $120 + 170 + 110 = 400$ pounds. Bingo! The answer is (B).

   Method 2: Use algebra. Let e = Ellen's weight, j = Jim's weight, and r = Ria's weight. Translate the problem into equations:
   $$e + j = 290$$
   $$e + r = 230$$
   $$e + j + r = 400$$
   Add first two equations: $2e + j + r = 520$
   Subtract third equation: $-(e + j + r = 400)$
   $$e = 120$$

4. Method 1: Use algebra. Let x be the number of gallons of paint that she starts with. Translate the problem into an equation: $x - (1/4)x - (1/3)x = 10$
   Simplify: $(5/12)x = 10$
   Multiply by 12/5: $x = 24$

   The answer is (B).

   Method 2: Test the choices. Look at the problem carefully. She uses one-fourth of her paint, then one-third of her paint, and is left with 10 gallons of paint, a *whole number*. This suggests that she started with a quantity that is divisible by 3 and 4. Since 24 is divisible by 3 and 4, it's a good choice to test. One-fourth of 24 is 6, and one-third of 24 is 8. This means she would be left with $24 - 6 - 8 = 10$. Bingo!

5. Method 1: Plug in. Let $s = 35$, so $r = 35/5 = 7$ and $t = 4$. (Check that they "fit.") Since the question asks for the value of s, write down 35 and circle it. Plugging these values into the choices gives

   (A) 140 (B) 35 (C) 136 (D) 124 (E) 280

   The answer is (B).

   Method 2: Use algebra. Solve the first equation for s: $s = 5r$. Then solve the second equation for r: $r = (7/4)t$. Then substitute: $s = 5(7/4)t = 35t/4$.

Lesson 7: Thinking Logically

Numerical and Algebraic Proof

Logical proofs aren't just for geometry class. They apply to arithmetic and algebra, too. In arithmetic, you often need to apply the laws of arithmetic (such as *odd × even = even, negative ÷ positive = negative*—see Chapter 9, Lesson 3) to *prove* what you're looking for. When you solve an algebraic equation, you use logical laws of equality (such as the *addition law of equality*) to *prove* the equation you want.

"Must Be True" Questions

Logic is especially useful in solving SAT "must be true" questions. You know them and hate them—they usually have those roman numerals I, II, and III. To prove that a statement "must be true," apply the laws of equality or the laws of arithmetic. To prove that a statement *doesn't* have to be true, just find one *counterexample*, a valid example for which the statement is false.

If a and b are positive integers such that $a < b$ and $ab - a = 6$, which of the following must be true?

I. $\dfrac{b}{a}$ is an integer.

II. b is an even number.

III. ab is 6 greater than a.

(A) I only
(B) I and II only
(C) I and III only
(D) II and III only
(E) I, II, and III

This requires both numerical and algebraic logic. First, let's see how far we can get trying to solve the equation for a and b.

$$ab - a = 6$$

Factor out the a: $a(b - 1) = 6$

Okay, we've got a problem. We have two unknowns but only one equation, which means we can't solve it uniquely. Fortunately, we know that a and b must be positive integers, so the equation basically says that the product of two positive integers, a and

$b - 1$, is 6. The only positive integer pairs with a product of 6 are 2×3 and 1×6, so one possibility is that $a = 2$ and $b = 4$. This gives $a(b - 1) = 2(4 - 1) = 2(3) = 6$, and it satisfies the condition that $a < b$. Now check the statements. Statement I is true here because $4/2 = 2$, which is an integer. Statement II is also true here because 4 is an even number. Statement III is also true because $2 \times 4 = 8$, which is 6 greater than 2. So the answer is (E) I, II and III, right?

Wrong. Remember that the question asks what *must* be true, not just what *can* be true. We've only shown that the statements *can* be true. We can prove that statement I *must* be true by testing all the possible cases. Since there is only one other possible solution that satisfies the conditions: $a = 1$ and $b = 7$, and since $7/1 = 7$ is an integer, we can say with confidence that statement I *must be true*. But statement II *doesn't* have to be true because b can equal 7, which is not even. We have found a counterexample. Next, we can prove that statement III must be true by checking both cases: 2×4 is 6 greater than 2, and 1×7 is 6 greater than 1. (We can prove it *algebraically* too! If we add a to both sides of the original equation, we get $ab = a + 6$, which proves that ab is 6 greater than a.)

Process of Elimination (POE)

On multiple-choice questions (and especially "must be true" questions), it helps to cross off wrong answers right away. Sometimes POE simplifies the problem dramatically.

What if, in the preceding question, the first solution we found was $a = 1$ and $b = 7$. For this solution, statements I and III are true, but statement II is not. Therefore, we could eliminate those choices containing II—(B), (D), and (E). Since the two remaining choices contain statement I, it must be true—we don't even need to prove it!

Concept Review 7: Thinking Logically

1. What is a proof, and why is understanding proofs helpful on the SAT?

2. How can POE help on the SAT?

3. What is the difference between *geometric*, *algebraic*, and *numerical* proofs?

4. Name two *geometric theorems* that are useful on the SAT.

5. Name two *algebraic theorems* that are useful on the SAT.

6. Name two *numerical theorems* that are useful on the SAT.

SAT Practice 7: Thinking Logically

Use logical methods to solve each of the following SAT questions.

1. If $a > b$ and $b(b - a) > 0$, which of the following must be true?

        I. $b < 0$
       II. $a < 0$
      III. $ab < 0$

(A) I only
(B) II only
(C) I and II only
(D) I and III only
(E) I, II, and III

A, B, C, and D are the consecutive vertices of a quadrilateral.
$\angle ABC$ and $\angle BCD$ are right angles.

2. If the two statements above are true, then which of the following also must be true?

(A) $ABCD$ is a rectangle.

(B) $\overline{AB}$ is parallel to $\overline{DC}$.

(C) $\overline{BC}$ is parallel to $\overline{AD}$.

(D) Triangle ACD is a right triangle.

(E) Triangle ABD is a right triangle.

---

3. The statement $a \Leftrightarrow b$ is defined to be true if and only if $\dfrac{a}{5} > \dfrac{b}{3}$. Which of the following is true?

(A) $3 \Leftrightarrow 5$
(B) $5 \Leftrightarrow 3$
(C) $4 \Leftrightarrow 2$
(D) $6 \Leftrightarrow 4$
(E) $7 \Leftrightarrow 5$

---

4. If $(m + 1)(n + 1) = 1$, which of the following can be true?

        I. m and n are both positive.
       II. m and n are both negative.
      III. m is positive and n is negative.

(A) II only
(B) III only
(C) I and II only
(D) I and III only
(E) II and III only

---

5. If p is a prime number greater than 5 and q is an odd number greater than 5, which of the following must be true?

        I. $p + q$ is *not* a prime number.
       II. pq has at least three positive integer factors greater than 1.

      III. $\dfrac{q}{p}$ is *not* an integer.

(A) I only
(B) I and II only
(C) I and III only
(D) II and III only
(E) I, II, and III

Answer Key 7: Thinking Logically

Concept Review 7

1. A proof is a sequence of logical statements that begins with a set of assumptions and proceeds to a desired conclusion. You construct a logical proof every time you solve an equation or determine a geometric or arithmetic fact.

2. The process of elimination (POE) is the process of eliminating wrong answers. Sometimes it is easier to show that one choice is wrong than it is to show that another is right, so POE may provide a quicker path to the right answer.

3. Geometric proofs depend on geometric facts such as "angles in a triangle have a sum of 180°," algebraic proofs use laws of equality such as "any number can be added to both sides of an equation," and numerical proofs use facts such as "an odd number plus an odd number always equals an even number."

4. The most important geometric theorems for the SAT are given in Chapter 10. They include parallel lines theorems such as "if two parallel lines are cut by a transversal, then alternate interior angles are congruent" and triangle theorems such as "if two sides of a triangle are congruent, then the angles opposite those sides are also congruent."

5. The most important algebraic theorems are the laws of equality, such as "you can subtract any number from both sides of an equation."

6. The most important numerical theorems are discussed in Chapter 9, Lesson 3, and Chapter 7, Lesson 7. They include "*odd × odd = odd*" and "*positive × negative = negative*."

SAT Practice 7

1. **A** Since a is greater than b, $b - a$ must be a negative number. Since $b(b - a)$ must be positive, but $b - a$ is negative, b also must be negative because *negative × negative = positive*, but *positive × negative = negative*. This proves that statement I must be true. However, statement II does not have to be true because a counterexample is $a = 1$ and $b = -1$. Notice that this satisfies the conditions that $a > b$ and that $b(b - a) > 0$. Statement III also isn't necessarily true because a counterexample is $a = -1$ and $b = -2$. Notice that this also satisfies the conditions that $a > b$ and $b(b - a) > 0$ but contradicts the statement that $ab < 0$.

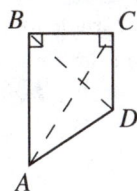

2. **B** First draw a diagram that illustrates the given conditions, such as the one above. This diagram shows that the only true statement among the choices is (B). This fact follows from the fact that "if a line (BC), crosses two other lines (AB and DC) in a plane so that same-side interior angles are supplementary, then the two lines are parallel."

3. **C** First, translate each choice according to the definition of the bizarre new symbol. This gives us (A) 3/5 > 5/3, (B) 5/5 > 3/3, (C) 4/5 > 2/3, (D) 6/5 > 4/3, and (E) 7/5 > 5/3. The only true statement among these is (C).

4. **E** The question asks whether the statements *can* be true, not whether they *must* be true. The equation says that two numbers have a product of 1. You might remember that such numbers are *reciprocals*, so we want to find values such that $m + 1$ and $n + 1$ are reciprocals of each other. One pair of reciprocals is 2 and $^1/_2$, which we can get if $m = 1$ and $n = -^1/_2$. Therefore, statement III can be true, and we can eliminate choices (A) and (C). Next, think of negative reciprocals, such as -2 and $-^1/_2$, which we can get if $m = -3$ and $n = -^1/_2$. Therefore, statement II can be true, and we can eliminate choices (B) and (D), leaving only (E), the correct answer. Statement I can't be true because if m and n are both positive, then both $m + 1$ and $n + 1$ are greater than 1. But, if a number is greater than 1, its reciprocal must be *less than 1*.

5. **A** You might start by just choosing values for p and q that satisfy the conditions, such as $p = 7$ and $q = 9$. When you plug these values in, all three statements are true. Bummer, because this neither proves any statement true nor proves any statement false. Are there any *interesting* possible values for p and q that might disprove one or more of the statements? Notice that nothing says that p and q must be *different*, so choose $p = 7$ and $q = 7$. Now $pq = 49$, which only has 1, 7, and 49 as factors. Therefore, it does *not* have at least three positive integer factors greater than 1, and statement II is not necessarily true. Also, $q/p = 1$, which is an integer, so statement III is not necessarily true. So we can eliminate any choices with II or III, leaving only choice (A).

Lesson 8: Checking Your Work

Check the Question

> Always quickly reread the question before marking your answer to make sure that you've answered the *right* question and to make sure that your solution makes sense in the context of the question.

A bin contains 20 basketballs and soccer balls. If there are 8 more basketballs than soccer balls in the bin, how many soccer balls are in the bin?

    (A)   4
    (B)   6
    (C)   8
    (D)   10
    (E)   12

Many students think that since there are 8 more basketballs than soccer balls, they should just subtract 8 from the total to get the number of soccer balls, getting $20 - 8 = 12$ soccer balls. The answer is (E), right?

Wrong. If there are 12 soccer balls, then there must be 8 basketballs, for a total of 20. But the question says that there are 8 *more* basketballs than soccer balls, and 8 sure isn't more than 12! So now what? Eliminate choice (E) first of all. Since there are fewer basketballs than soccer balls, soccer balls must make up fewer than half the balls, so there must be fewer than 10 soccer balls, eliminating choice (D). Checking the remaining choices shows (B) 6 works because if there are 6 soccer balls, there are 14 basketballs, and 14 is 8 greater than 6!

The "direct" method for solving is to subtract 8 from 20 and then *divide the result by 2* to get the number of soccer balls.

Check Your Algebra

> When solving an equation, check two things: first your *answer*, and then your *steps*. If the answer works when you plug it back into the equation, there's no need to check the steps. If it doesn't, then check your steps. When solving equations, *write out every step*, and make sure that each one is logical. You're likely to make mistakes if you skip steps or do them too quickly in your head.

If $\dfrac{2x}{x-2} = \dfrac{x^2}{x-2}$, then what is the value of x?

    (A)   0
    (B)   1
    (C)   2
    (D)   3
    (E)   4

You might notice that since both fractions have the same numerator, the equation can be simplified and solved without much trouble.

$$\frac{2x}{x-2} = \frac{x^2}{x-2}$$

Multiply by $x - 2$: $2x = x^2$
Divide by x: $2 = x$

Piece of cake. The answer is (C), right? Wrong. Notice that substituting $x = 2$ into the original equation gives you $4/0 = 4/0$. Although this seems true at first, it's not, because $4/0$ isn't a number! (Just ask your calculator.) What now? The check suggests a solution: you can just test the choices. Plugging in the other choices for x shows that only (A) 0 produces a true equation: $0/-2 = 0/-2$.

What went wrong the first time? Check the steps. Our second step was to *divide by x*. We're allowed to divide both sides of an equation by any number *except* 0 because division by 0 is undefined. That's where we went wrong: *We didn't check division by 0.* Notice that division by 0 also explains why $x = 2$ doesn't work in the original equation.

Check by Estimating

> Estimation is one of the simplest and most effective checking strategies you can use on the SAT. Getting an *approximate* answer can help you to narrow down the choices quickly.

If Carla drives at 40 miles per hour for n miles and then drives at 60 miles per hour for another n miles, what is her average speed, in miles per hour, for the entire trip?

    (A)   42
    (B)   48
    (C)   50
    (D)   52
    (E)   54

Many students average 40 and 60 and get 50. But this is wrong because Carla is not spending *equal times* at 40 and 60 miles an hour. Since 40 mph is slower than 60 mph, she spends *more time* at that speed. So her average speed is closer to 40 than 60. This eliminates choices (C), (D), and (E). The correct answer is (B). (For more on rate problems, see Chapter 9, Lesson 4.)

Concept Review 8: Checking Your Work

1. What are the best strategies for avoiding mistakes when solving an equation?

2. When should you estimate on an SAT math question?

3. Why should you estimate on certain SAT math questions?

4. What is the last thing to check before marking an answer to an SAT math question?

5. What steps "aren't allowed" when solving equations?

SAT Practice 8: Checking Your Work

Check your work carefully before choosing your answer to the following questions.

---

1. If $3x - 5 = 20$, what is the value of $3x + 5$?

---

2. If $s^2 - 1 = 2s - 1$, which of the following gives all possible values of s^2?

    (A) 2 only
    (B) 4 only
    (C) 0 and 2 only
    (D) 0 and 4 only
    (E) All even integers

---

3. Last year, Tom was twice as old as Julio. This year, the sum of their ages is 65. How old is Tom now?

    (A) 22
    (B) 32
    (C) 41
    (D) 42
    (E) 43

---

4. If the 30 students in Ms. Harkin's class scored an average of 80% on their final exams, and if the 20 students in Ms. Johnson's class scored an average of 70% on their final exams, what was the average score for the two classes combined?

    (A) 74%
    (B) 75%
    (C) 76%
    (D) 77%
    (E) 78%

---

5. What is the least positive integer m such that $168m$ is the square of an integer?

Answer Key 8: Checking Your Work

Concept Review 8

1. Check your answer by plugging it back into the *original* equation and checking your steps. Write out each step, one beneath the other, so that checking your logic and arithmetic is easier.

2. Estimate only when it is easy to do. If the answer choices are numerically far apart, estimation can help you to eliminate obviously wrong answers.

3. If you can quickly "ballpark" a numerical answer and rule out those choices that are "out of the ball-

park," you can often avoid doing complicated calculations or algebra.

4. Reread the question and make sure that you've answered the *right question*, and make sure that your answer makes sense in the context of the question.

5. Dividing by 0 and taking the square root of an expression that can be negative are not allowed because they are undefined.

SAT Review 8

1. **30** The simplest way to solve this problem is to add 10 to both sides of the equation, which gives $3x + 5 = 30$. However, many students do the "knee-jerk" of solving for x and become prone to silly arithmetic mistakes. If you *did* solve for x, you should have checked your answer by plugging it back in to the original equation.

2. **D** Did you say (C)? Then you misread the question. Always reread before marking your answer. It asks for the value of s^2, not s. Although s can be 0 or 2, s^2 is either 0 or 4. Did you say (A) or (B)? Then you may have made this common mistake:

$$s^2 - 1 = 2s - 1$$
Add 1: $$s^2 = 2s$$
Divide by s: $$s = 2$$

What went wrong? In the second step, we divided by s *without checking whether it could equal 0*. (Remember that division by 0 is undefined and usually causes trouble.) Indeed, plugging in shows that $s = 0$ is in fact a solution. The correct method is

$$s^2 - 1 = 2s - 1$$
Add 1: $$s^2 = 2s$$
Subtract $2s$: $$s^2 - 2s = 0$$
Factor: $$s(s - 2) = 0$$
Use 0 product property: $$s = 0 \text{ or } 2$$

3. **E** You might start by approximating. Since the sum of their ages is about 60, and since Tom is about twice as old as Julio, Tom is about 40 and Julio is about 20. This rules out (A) and (B). From here, you may just want to "test" the remaining choices until you find what works. If you prefer algebra, you may want to let t equal Tom's age now and j equal Julio's age now. You are told that $t + j = 65$ and that $2(j - 1) = t - 1$. Since you only need the value of t, solve the first equation for j, getting $j = 65 - t$, and substitute this into the second equation. This gives

$$2(65 - t - 1) = t - 1$$
Simplify: $$2(64 - t) = t - 1$$
Distribute: $$128 - 2t = t - 1$$
Add $2t$ and 1: $$129 = 3t$$
Divide by 3: $$43 = t$$

Therefore, Tom is now 43 and Julio is now $65 - 43 = 22$. Notice that last year they were 42 and 21, respectively, and 42 is twice as old as 21.

4. **E** Since more students averaged 80% than 70%, the overall average should be closer to 80%. This rules out (A) and (B). To get the precise answer, let x be the overall average. There are two ways to calculate the

sum of all the scores: $(30)(80) + (20)(70)$ and $(50)(x)$. Since these must be equal,

$$2,400 + 1,400 = 50x$$

Simplify: $\quad\quad\quad\quad 3,800 = 50x$

Divide by 50: $\quad\quad\quad\quad\quad 76 = x$

5. **42** Do the prime factorization of 168: $2^3 \times 3 \times 7$. Since, in a perfect square, all prime factors "pair up," we need to multiply at least one more factor of 2, one more factor of 3, and one more factor of 7 to make a perfect square: $2^4 \times 3^2 \times 7^2 = 7,056 = 84^2$. (Notice that now every factor appears an even number of times.) Therefore, $k = 2 \times 3 \times 7 = 42$.

CHAPTER 7

ESSENTIAL PRE-ALGEBRA SKILLS

1. Numbers and Operations

2. Laws of Arithmetic

3. Fractions

4. Ratios and Proportions

5. Percents

6. Negatives

7. Divisibility

Lesson 1: Numbers and Operations

Integers and Real Numbers

On the SAT, you only need to deal with two kinds of numbers: *integers* (the positive and negative whole numbers, . . . , −3, −2, −1, 0, 1, 2, 3, . . .) and *real numbers* (all the numbers on the number line, *including integers*, but also including all fractions and decimals). You don't have to know about wacky numbers such as *irrationals* or *imaginaries*.

> The SAT only uses *real numbers*. It will never (1) divide a number by 0 or (2) take the square root of a negative number because both these operations fail to produce a real number. Make sure that you understand why both these operations are said to be "undefined."

> Don't assume that a number in an SAT problem is an *integer* unless you are specifically told that it is. For instance, if a question mentions the fact that $x > 3$, don't automatically assume that x is 4 or greater. If the problem doesn't say that x must be an integer, then x might be 3.01 or 3.6 or the like.

The Operations

The only operations you will have to use on the SAT are the basics: *adding, subtracting, multiplying, dividing, raising to powers,* and *taking roots.* Don't worry about "bad boys" such as *sines, tangents,* or *logarithms*—they won't show up. (Yay!)

> Don't confuse the key words for the basic operations: *Sum* means the result of addition, *difference* means the result of subtraction, *product* means the result of multiplication, and *quotient* means the result of division.

The Inverse Operations

Every operation has an *inverse*, that is, another operation that "undoes" it. For instance, subtracting 5 is the inverse of adding 5, and dividing by −3.2 is the inverse of multiplying by −3.2. If you perform an operation and then perform its inverse, you are back to where you started. For instance, $135 \times 4.5 \div 4.5 = 135$. No need to calculate!

> Using inverse operations helps you to solve equations. For example,
>
> $$3x - 7 = 38$$
> To "undo" −7, add 7 to both sides: $3x = 45$
> To "undo" × 3, divide both sides by 3: $x = 15$

Alternative Ways to Do Operations

> Every operation can be done in two ways, and one way is almost always easier than the other. For instance, subtracting a number is the same thing as *adding the opposite number.* So subtracting −5 is the same as adding 5. Also, dividing by a number is exactly the same thing as *multiplying by its reciprocal.* So dividing by 2/3 is the same as multiplying by 3/2. When doing arithmetic, always think about your options, and do the operation that is easier! For instance, if you are asked to do $45 \div -1/2$, you should realize that it is the same as 45×-2, which is easier to do in your head.

The Order of Operations

> Don't forget the order of operations: P-E-MD-AS. When evaluating, first do what's grouped in *parentheses* (or above or below fraction bars or within radicals), then do *exponents* (or roots) from left to right, then *multiplication* or *division* from left to right, and then do *addition* or *subtraction* from left to right. What is $4 - 6 \div 2 \times 3$? If you said 3, you mistakenly did the multiplication before the division. (Instead, do them left to right). If you said −3 or −1/3, you mistakenly subtracted before taking care of the multiplication and division. If you said −5, pat yourself on the back!
>
> When using your calculator, be careful to use parentheses when raising negatives to powers. For instance, if you want to raise −2 to the 4th power, type "(−2)^4," and not just "−2^4," because the calculator will interpret the latter as −1(2)^4, and give an answer of −16, rather than the proper answer of 16.

Concept Review 1: Numbers and Operations

1. What is the greatest integer less than –9.5?   1. _____

2. Express the answer to Question 1 as a fraction *in two different ways*.   2. _____

3. When is taking the square root of a number *not* the inverse of squaring a number? Be specific.

   _____

   _____

4. Four consecutive even integers have a sum of 76. What is the greatest of these numbers?   4. _____

5. If –2 < x < 2, how many possible values may *x* have?   5. _____

6. The result of an addition is called a _____.

7. The result of a subtraction is called a _____.

8. The result of a multiplication is called a _____.

9. What is the difference between the product of 12 and 3 and their sum?   9. _____

What is the *alternative* way to express each of the following operations?

10. – (6) _____   11. ÷ (4) _____   12. $\times -\dfrac{5}{3}$ _____   13. $+\dfrac{6}{7}$ _____

What is the *inverse* of each of the following operations?

14. – (6) _____   15. ÷ (4) _____   16. $\times -\dfrac{5}{3}$ _____   17. $+\dfrac{6}{7}$ _____

Simplify *without* a calculator:

18. $4 - 6 \div 2 \times 3 + 1 - (2 + 1)^2 =$ _____   19. $9 - \left(\sqrt{25} - \sqrt{16} \div 2\right)^2 =$ _____

20. $\dfrac{1}{2}\left(6^1 + 2^2\right)^2 =$ _____   21. $\left(1 - \left(2 - \left(1 - 2\right)^2\right) - 2\right) - 2 =$ _____

22. Circle the *real numbers* and underline the *integers*: 3.75 1.333... $\sqrt{25}$ $\sqrt{-7}$ $-\dfrac{2}{5}$ $\dfrac{56}{7}$ 0

23. The *real* order of operations is _____.

24. Which two symbols (besides parentheses) are "grouping" symbols? _____

25. If $\dfrac{x}{5}, \dfrac{x}{6}, \dfrac{x}{8}$, and $\dfrac{x}{12}$ are all positive integers, what is the least possible value of *x*?   25. _____

26. List the three operations that must be performed on each side of this equation (in order!) to solve for *x*:

   $3x^2 + 7 = 34$ Step 1 _____   Step 2 _____   Step 3 _____   x = _____

SAT Practice 1: Numbers and Operations

1. Which of the following is NOT equal to $\frac{1}{3}$ of an integer?

(A) $\frac{1}{3}$ (B) 1 (C) $\frac{5}{2}$ (D) $\frac{16}{2}$ (E) 10

2. Which of the following can be expressed as the product of two consecutive even integers?

(A) 22 (B) 36 (C) 48 (D) 60 (E) 72

3. $(1-(1-(1-3)))-(1-(1-(1-2)))=$

(A) −3 (B) −2 (C) −1 (D) 2 (E) 3

4. If $\sqrt{k}-3=8$, what is the value of k?

(A) 11 (B) 64 (C) 67 (D) 121 (E) 132

5. In the country of Etiquette, if 2 is a company and 3 is a crowd, then how many are 4 crowds and 2½ companies?

(A) 14 (B) 17 (C) 23 (D) 28½ (E) 29

6. For what integer value of x is $3x + 7 > 13$ and $x - 5 < -1$?

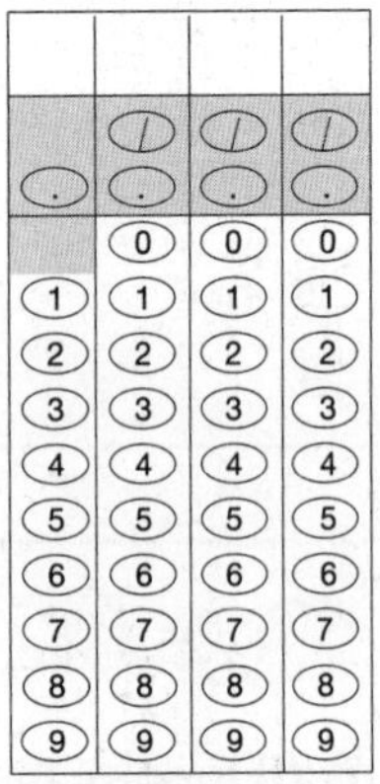

7. For all real numbers x, let ⌈x be defined as the least integer greater than x.

⌈−5.6 =

(A) −6 (B) −5.7 (C) −5.5 (D) −5 (E) 1

8. Dividing any positive number by ¾ and then multiplying by −2 is equivalent to

(A) multiplying by $-\frac{8}{3}$
(B) dividing by $\frac{3}{2}$
(C) multiplying by $-\frac{3}{2}$
(D) dividing by $\frac{3}{8}$
(E) multiplying by $-\frac{3}{8}$

9. When 14 is taken from 6 times a number, 40 is left. What is half the number?

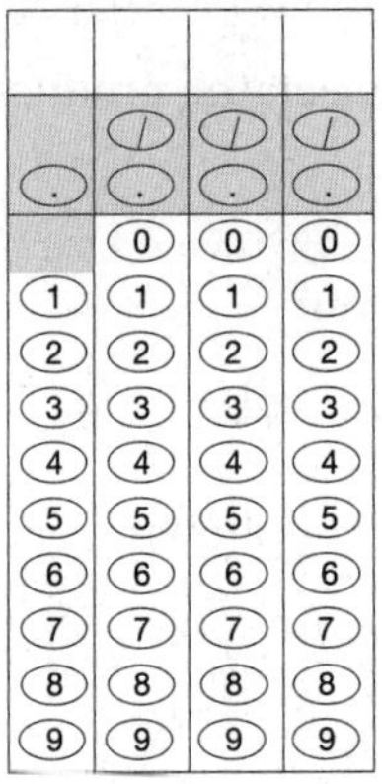

10. If the smallest positive four-digit integer without repeated digits is subtracted from the greatest four-digit integer without repeated digits, the result is

(A) 8,642 (B) 1,111 (C) 8,853
(D) 2,468 (E) 8,888

11. If $x > 1$, the value of which of the following expressions increases as x increases?

I. $\frac{1}{x^2}$

II. $\sqrt{x}$

III. $10-\frac{1}{x}$

(A) II only (B) III only
(C) I and II only (D) II and III only
(E) I, II, and III

Answer Key 1: Numbers and Operations

Concept Review 1

1. –10 (Remember: "greatest" means farthest to the right on the number line.)
2. –10/1, –20/2, –30/3, etc. (Fractions can be integers.)
3. If the original number is negative, then taking a square root doesn't "undo" squaring the number. Imagine that the original number is –3. The square of –3 is 9, but the square root of 9 is 3. This is the *absolute value* of the original number, but not the original number itself.
4. 22 (16 + 18 + 20 + 22 = 76. Just divide 76 by 4 to get the "middle" of the set = 19.)
5. Infinitely many (If you said 3, don't assume that unknowns are integers!)
6. sum
7. difference
8. product
9. 21 ((12 × 3) – (12 + 3) = 36 – 15 = 21)
10. + (–6) 11. × (1/4) 12. ÷ (–3/5) 13. × (7/6)
14. + (6) 15. × (4) 16. ÷ (–5/3) 17. × (6/7)
18. –13 (If you said –5, remember to do multiplication/division from left to right.)
19. 0
20. 50
21. –4
22. Circle all numbers except $\sqrt{-7}$ and underline only 0, $\sqrt{25}$ (= 5), and 56/7 (= 8).
23. PG-ER-MD-AS (Parentheses/grouping (left to right), exponents/roots (left to right), multiplication/division (left to right), addition/subtraction (left to right))
24. Fraction bars (group the numerator and denominator), and radicals (group what's inside)
25. 120 (It is the least common multiple of 5, 6, 8, and 12.)
26. Step 1: subtract 7; step 2: divide by 3; step 3: take the square root; $x = 3$ or -3 (not just 3!)

SAT Practice 1

1. **C** $\frac{5}{2}$ is not $\frac{1}{3}$ of an integer because $\frac{5}{2} \times 3 = \frac{15}{2} = 7.5$, which is not an integer.
2. **C** $48 = 6 \times 8$
3. **C** $(1-(1-(1-3)))-(1-(1-(1-2)))$
$= (1-(1-(-2)))-(1-(1-(-1)))$
$= (1-3)-(1-2)$
$= -2-(-1)$
$= -2+1$
$= -1$
4. **D** $\sqrt{k} - 3 = 8$
Add 3: $\sqrt{k} = 11$
Square: $k = 121$
5. **B** $(4 \times 3) + (2\frac{1}{2} \times 2) = 12 + 5 = 17$
6. **3** $3x + 7 > 13$ and $x - 5 < -1$
$3x > 6$ and $x < 4$
$x > 2$ and $x < 4$
7. **D** –5 is the least (farthest to the left on the number line) of all the integers that are greater than (to the right on the number line of) –5.6.
8. **A** Dividing by $\frac{3}{4}$ is equivalent to multiplying by $\frac{4}{3}$:
$x \div \frac{3}{4} \times -2$
$= x \times \frac{4}{3} \times -2$
$= x \times -\frac{8}{3}$
9. **4.5** $6x - 14 = 40$
Add 14: $6x = 54$
Divide by 6: $x = 9$
(Don't forget to find *half* the number!)
10. **C** 9,876 – 1,023 = 8,853
Don't forget that 0 is a digit, but it can't be the first digit of a four-digit integer.
11. **D** You might "plug in" increasing values of x to see whether the expressions increase or decrease. 1 and 4 are convenient values to try. Also, if you can graph $y = 1/x^2$, $y = \sqrt{x}$, and $y = 10 - \frac{1}{x}$ quickly, you might notice that $y = \sqrt{x}$, and $y = 10 - 1/x$ "go up" as you move to the right of 1 on the x-axis.

Lesson 2: Laws of Arithmetic

The Laws of Arithmetic

When evaluating expressions, you don't always have to follow the order of operations strictly. Sometimes you can play around with the expression first. You can **commute** (with addition or multiplication), **associate** (with addition or multiplication), or **distribute** (multiplication or division over addition or subtraction). Know your options!

> When simplifying an expression, consider whether the laws of arithmetic help to make it easier.

Example:

$57(71) + 57(29)$ is much easier to simplify if, rather than using the order of operations, you use the "distributive law" and think of it as $57(71 + 29) = 57(100) = 5,700$.

The Commutative and Associative Laws

> Whenever you add or multiply terms, the order of the terms doesn't matter, so pick a convenient arrangement. To commute means to move around. (Just think about what commuters do!)

Example:

$1 + 2 + 3 + 4 + 5 + 6 + 7 + 8 + 9 =$
$1 + 9 + 2 + 8 + 3 + 7 + 4 + 6 + 5$

(Think about why the second arrangement is more convenient than the first!)

> Whenever you add or multiply, the grouping of the terms doesn't matter, so pick a convenient grouping. To associate means to group together. (Just think about what an association is!)

Example:

$(32 \times 4) \times (25 \times 10) \times (10 \times 2) =$
$32 \times (4 \times 25) \times (10 \times 10) \times 2$

(Why is the second grouping more convenient than the first?)

> Whenever you subtract or divide, the grouping of the terms does matter. Subtraction and division are neither commutative nor associative.

Example:

$15 - 7 - 2 \neq 7 - 15 - 2$ (So you can't "commute" the numbers in a difference until you convert it to addition: $15 + -7 + -2 = -7 + 15 + -2$.)

$24 \div 3 \div 2 \neq 3 \div 2 \div 24$ (So you can't "commute" the numbers in a quotient until you convert it to multiplication:

$24 \times \frac{1}{3} \times \frac{1}{2} = \frac{1}{3} \times \frac{1}{2} \times 24$.)

The Distributive Law

> When a grouped sum or difference is multiplied or divided by something, you can do the multiplication or division first (instead of doing what's inside parentheses, as the order of operations says) as long as you "distribute." Test these equations by plugging in numbers to see how they work:

Example:

$a(b + c) = ab + ac$

$\frac{(b + c)}{a} = \frac{b}{a} + \frac{c}{a}$

> Distribution is never something that you have to do. Think of it as a tool, rather than a requirement. Use it when it simplifies your task. For instance, $13(832 + 168)$ is actually much easier to do if you don't distribute: $13(832 + 168) = 13(1,000) = 13,000$. Notice how annoying it would be if you distributed.

> Use the distributive law "backwards" whenever you factor polynomials, add fractions, or combine "like" terms.

Example:

$9x^2 - 12x = 3x(3x - 4)$
$\frac{3}{b} + \frac{a}{b} = \frac{3 + a}{b}$ $5\sqrt{7} - 2\sqrt{7} = 3\sqrt{7}$

> Follow the rules when you distribute! Avoid these common mistakes:

Example:

$(3 + 4)^2$ is not $3^2 + 4^2$
(Tempting, isn't it? Check it and see!)
$3(4 \times 5)$ is not $3(4) \times 3(5)$

Concept Review 2: Laws of Arithmetic

Simplify the following expressions, and indicate what law(s) of arithmetic you use to do it. Write *D* for distribution, *CA* for commutative law of addition, *CM* for commutative law of multiplication, *AA* for associative law of addition, and *AM* for associative law of multiplication.

1. $3 + x + 9$ _____

2. $-2x(x - 3)$ _____

3. $(5m^2n)(2mn^3)$ _____

4. $5 + (7 + 2y) + 5y$ _____

Look carefully at the following equations. If the equation is always *true*, write the law of arithmetic that justifies it (D, CA, CM, AA, or AM). If it is *false*, rewrite the right side of the equation to make it true.

5. $\dfrac{2x}{y} + \dfrac{3x}{2y} = \dfrac{5x}{3y}$

5. _____

6. $15(67) + 15(33) = 15(100)$

6. _____

7. $(a + b)^2 = a^2 + b^2$

7. _____

8. $5c(c \times 3x) = 5c^2 \times 15cx$

8. _____

9. $3(2^6 + 3^4) = 6^6 + 9^4$

9. _____

10. $\dfrac{6 + y}{3y} = \dfrac{2}{y} + \dfrac{1}{3}$

10. _____

Rewrite the expression $3x^2 + 12x^3$ according to the following laws:

11. distributive law: 12. commutative law of addition: 13. commutative law of multiplication:

_____ _____ _____

Do the following calculations *mentally* (no calculator!) by using the appropriate laws of arithmetic:

14. $25 + 48 + 75 + 60 + 52 + 40 =$ _____

15. $(4y)(6y)(25)(y^2)(5) =$ _____

16. $19(550) + 19(450) =$ _____

17. $(25 \times 5x)(4x \times 20) =$ _____

If *a* and *b* are not 0:

18. What's the relationship between $a \div b$ and $b \div a$?

18. _____

19. What's the relationship between $a \times b$ and $b \times a$?

19. _____

20. What's the relationship between $a - b$ and $b - a$?

20. _____

21. The distributive law says that only _____ or _____ can be distributed over grouped _____ or _____.

22. Which operations are not commutative?

22. _____

23. Are powers commutative? That is, is $(x^m)^n$ always equal to $(x^n)^m$?

23. _____

SAT Practice 2: Laws of Arithmetic

1. The difference of two integers is 4 and their sum is 14. What is their product?

(A) 18   (B) 24   (C) 36
(D) 45   (E) 56

2. For all real numbers x and y, $4x(x) - 3xy(2x) =$

(A) $12x^2y(x - 2x)$
(B) $2x^2(2 - 3y)$
(C) $xy(-x)$
(D) $2x^2(2 + 3y)$
(E) $4x^2(x - 3y)$

3. If $3x^2 + 2x = 40$, then $15x^2 + 10x =$

(A) 120   (B) 200   (C) 280
(D) 570   (E) 578

4. The expression $-2(x + 2) + x(x + 2)$ is equivalent to which of the following expressions?

    I. $x^2 - 4$
    II. $(x - 2)(x + 2)$
    III. $x^2 - 4x - 4$

(A) none   (B) II only
(C) I and II only   (D) II and III only
(E) I, II, and III

5. If $(x + y) + 1 = 1 - (1 - x)$, what is the value of y?

(A) -2
(B) -1
(C) 0
(D) 1
(E) 3

6. For all real numbers x, $1 - (1 - (1 - x) - 1) =$

(A) x
(B) $x - 1$
(C) $x - 2$
(D) $1 - x$
(E) $2 - x$

7. If $a = 60(99)^{99} + 30(99)^{99}$, $b = 99^{100}$, and $c = 90(90)^{99}$, then which of the following expresses the correct ordering of a, b, and c?

(A) $c < a < b$
(B) $b < c < a$
(C) $a < b < c$
(D) $c < b < a$
(E) $b < a < c$

8. Which of the following is equivalent to $5x(2x \times 3) - 5x^2$ for all x?

(A) $5x^2 + 15x$
(B) $5x^2 \times 15x$
(C) $10x^2 \times 15x - 5x^2$
(D) $145x$
(E) $25x^2$

9. Which of the following statements must be true for all values of x, y, and z?

    I. $(x + y) + z = (z + y) + x$
    II. $(x - y) - z = (z - y) - x$
    III. $(x \times y) \times z = (z \times y) \times x$

(A) I only
(B) I and II only
(C) I and III only
(D) II and III only
(E) I, II, and III

10. The symbol $\lozenge$ represents one of the fundamental arithmetic operators: $+$, $-$, $\times$, or $\div$. If $(x \lozenge y) \times (y \lozenge x) = 1$ for all positive values of x and y, then $\lozenge$ can represent

(A) $+$ only
(B) $\times$ only
(C) $+$ or $\times$ only
(D) $-$ only
(E) $\div$ only

Answer Key 2: Laws of Arithmetic

Concept Review 2

1. $x + 12$ (commutative law of arithmetic)

2. $-2x^2 + 6x$ (distributive law)

3. $10m^3n^4$ (commutative law of multiplication and associative law of multiplication)

4. $7y + 12$ (associative law of arithmetic and commutative law of arithmetic)

5. false: $\dfrac{7x}{2y}$ (Find a common denominator, then add numerators.)

6. true: distributive law

7. false: $a^2 + 2ab + b^2$ (Don't ever distribute a power over addition. Expand and "FOIL" (First + Outside + Inside + Last).)

8. false: $15c^2x$ (Don't ever distribute multiplication over multiplication. Use the associative and commutative laws of multiplication.)

9. false: $3(2)^6 + 3^5$ (You can distribute, but don't multiply before doing the powers!)

10. true: distributive law (Remember you can distribute division over addition!)

11. $3x^2(1 + 4x)$

12. $12x^3 + 3x^2$

13. $x^3 \times 12 + x^2 \times 3$

14. 300 (Reorder: $(25 + 75) + (48 + 52) + (60 + 40)$)

15. $3{,}000y^4$ (Reorder: $(4 \times 25)(6 \times 5)(y \times y \times y^2)$)

16. 19,000 (Use the distributive law.)

17. $10{,}000x^2$ (You can't "FOIL" here! Reorder: $(4 \times 25)(5 \times 20)(x)(x) = (100)(100)(x^2)$)

18. They're reciprocals. (Their product is 1.)

19. They're the same.

20. They're opposites. (Their sum is 0.)

21. multiplication or division over addition or subtraction

22. subtraction and division

23. yes

SAT Practice 2

1. **D** $m - n = 4$
   $\underline{m + n = 14}$
   $2m\quad = 18$
   $m = 9 \qquad n = 5 \qquad 9 \times 5 = 45$

2. **B** $4x(x) - 3xy(2x) =$
   $4x^2 - 6x^2y = 2x^2(2 - 3y)$

3. **B** Don't solve for x. It's too hard, and it's unnecessary.
   $15x^2 + 10x = 5(3x^2 + 2x) = 5(40) = 200$

4. **C** $-2(x + 2) + x(x + 2)$

   $= (-2 + x)(x + 2)$ Distributive law
   $= (x - 2)(x + 2)$ Commutative law of addition
   $= x^2 - 4$ Distributive law ("FOILing")

5. **B** $(x + y) + 1 = 1 - (1 - x)$
   associate: $x + y + 1 = 1 - (1 - x)$
   distribute: $x + y + 1 = 1 - 1 + x$
   simplify: $x + y + 1 = x$
   subtract x: $y + 1 = 0$
   subtract 1: $y = -1$

6. **E** $1 - (1 - (1 - x) - 1)$
   distribute: $= 1 - (1 - 1 + x - 1)$
   distribute: $= 1 - 1 + 1 - x + 1$
   commute: $= 1 - 1 + 1 + 1 - x$
   simplify: $= 2 - x$

7. **A** Each number has 100 factors, to make them simpler to compare:
   $a = 60(99)^{99} + 30(99)^{99}$ $= 90(99)^{99}$
   $b = 99^{100}$ $= 99(99)^{99}$
   $c = 90(90)^{99}$ $= 90(90)^{99}$

8. **E** $5x(2x \times 3) - 5x^2$
   parentheses: $= 5x(6x) - 5x^2$
   multiplication: $= 30x^2 - 5x^2$
   subtraction: $= 25x^2$

9. **C** Just remember that only addition and multiplication are commutative and associative. If you're not convinced, you might plug in 1, 2, and 3 for x, y, and z, and notice that equation II is not true.

10. **E** $(x \div y) \times (y \div x)$

   $= \dfrac{x}{y} \times \dfrac{y}{x}$

   $= \dfrac{xy}{xy}$

   $= 1$

Lesson 3: Fractions

Adding and Subtracting Fractions

Just as 2 apples + 3 apples = 5 apples, so 2 sevenths + 3 sevenths = 5 sevenths! So it's easy to add fractions if the denominators are the same. But if the denominators are different, just "convert" them so that they *are* the same.

> When "converting" a fraction, always multiply (or divide) the numerator and denominator by the same number.

Example:

$$\frac{2}{5} = \frac{2 \times 5}{5 \times 5} = \frac{10}{25} \qquad \frac{12}{18} = \frac{12 \div 6}{18 \div 6} = \frac{2}{3}$$

> If the denominator of one fraction is a multiple of the other denominator, "convert" only the fraction with the smaller denominator.

Example:

$$\frac{5}{18} + \frac{4}{9} = \frac{5}{18} + \frac{4 \times 2}{9 \times 2} = \frac{5}{18} + \frac{8}{18} = \frac{13}{18}$$

> One easy way to add fractions is with "zip-zap-zup": cross-multiply for the numerators, and multiply denominators for the new denominator. You may have to simplify as the last step.

Example:

$$\frac{x}{3} + \frac{2}{5} = \frac{5x}{3} \times \frac{6}{5} = \frac{5x}{15} + \frac{6}{15} = \frac{5x+6}{15}$$

$$\frac{5}{6} + \frac{7}{8} = \frac{40}{6} \times \frac{42}{8} = \frac{40}{48} + \frac{42}{48} = \frac{82}{48} = \frac{41}{24}$$

Multiplying and Dividing Fractions

> To multiply two fractions, just multiply straight across. *Don't* cross-multiply (we'll discuss that in the next lesson), and *don't* worry about getting a common denominator (that's just for adding and subtracting).

Example:

$$\frac{y}{5} \times \frac{3}{x} = \frac{y \times 3}{5 \times x} = \frac{3y}{5x}$$

> To multiply a fraction and an integer, just multiply the integer to the numerator (because an integer such as 5 can be thought of as 5/1).

Example:

$$\frac{4}{7} \times 5 = \frac{4}{7} \times \frac{5}{1} = \frac{4 \times 5}{7} = \frac{20}{7}$$

To divide a number by a fraction, remember that *dividing by a number is the same as multiplying by its reciprocal*. So just "flip" the second fraction and multiply.

Example:

$$\frac{3m}{7} \div \frac{5}{2m} = \frac{3m}{7} \times \frac{2m}{5} = \frac{6m^2}{35}$$

Simplifying Fractions

> Always try to simplify complicated-looking fractions. To simplify, *just multiply or divide top and bottom by a convenient number or expression*. If the numerator and the denominator have a common factor, *divide* top and bottom by that common factor. If there are fractions within the fraction, *multiply* top and bottom by the common denominator of the "little" fractions.

Example:

$$\frac{4x+2}{2} = \frac{2(2x+1)}{2} = 2x+1$$

$$\frac{\frac{2}{5} + \frac{2}{3}}{\frac{1}{4}} = \frac{60 \times \left(\frac{2}{5} + \frac{2}{3}\right)}{60 \times \left(\frac{1}{4}\right)} = \frac{24 + 40}{15} = \frac{64}{15}$$

(Notice that, in the second example, 60 is the common multiple of all of the "little denominators": 5, 3, and 4.)

> Be careful when "canceling" in fractions. Don't "cancel" anything that is not a common *factor*. To avoid the common canceling mistakes, be sure to *factor before canceling*.

Example:

Wrong: $\dfrac{x^2 \cancel{-1}}{x \cancel{-1}} = \dfrac{x^2}{x} = x$

Right: $\dfrac{x^2-1}{x-1} = \dfrac{(x+1)\cancel{(x-1)}}{\cancel{(x-1)}} = x+1$

Concept Review 3: Fractions

Simplify the following expressions:

1. $\dfrac{1}{7} + \dfrac{2}{5} =$ _____

2. $\dfrac{\dfrac{5}{2}}{\dfrac{3}{8}} =$ _____

3. $\dfrac{56}{21} =$ _____

4. $\dfrac{2}{9} \div \dfrac{5}{4} =$ _____

5. $\dfrac{4}{7} + \dfrac{2}{3x} =$ _____

6. $\dfrac{3x}{\dfrac{2}{9z}} =$ _____

7. $\dfrac{12m+4}{8m+4} =$ _____

8. $-\dfrac{2}{9x^2} \div \dfrac{4}{3x} =$ _____

9. $\dfrac{1}{2} + \dfrac{1}{3} + \dfrac{1}{4} =$ _____

10. $\dfrac{3}{4} - \dfrac{x}{2} =$ _____

11. $\dfrac{x^2-25}{x-5} =$ _____

12. $\dfrac{6n+9}{12n} =$ _____

Convert each expression to a fraction:

13. $25\% =$ _____

14. $0.20 =$ _____

15. $10\% =$ _____

16. $0.333\ldots =$ _____

17. How do you divide a number by a fraction?

_____

18. How do you add two fractions by "zip-zap-zup"?

_____

19. What can be canceled to simplify a fraction?

_____

20. How do you convert a fraction to a decimal?

_____

21. If a class contains 12 boys and 15 girls, then what fraction of the class is boys?   21. _____

22. If 2/3 of a class is girls, and there are 9 boys in the class, what is the total number of students in the class?   22. _____

23. If m and n are positive, and $m < n$, then what is true about $\dfrac{m}{n}$?   23. _____

SAT Practice 3: Fractions

1. If 4 quarts of apple juice are mixed with 5 quarts of cranberry juice and 3 quarts of grape juice, what part of the total mixture is apple juice?

(A) $\dfrac{1}{6}$ (B) $\dfrac{1}{4}$ (C) $\dfrac{1}{3}$

(D) $\dfrac{4}{9}$ (E) $\dfrac{2}{3}$

2. For what value of y does $\dfrac{1}{y} = -3$?

(A) -3 (B) $-\dfrac{1}{3}$ (C) $\dfrac{1}{3}$

(D) 3 (E) 6

3. Which of the following is greatest?

(A) $\dfrac{2}{3} \times 1$ (B) $1 - \dfrac{2}{3}$ (C) $1 \div \dfrac{2}{3}$

(D) $\dfrac{2}{3} \div \dfrac{2}{3}$ (E) $\dfrac{2}{3} \div 1$

4. If $\dfrac{\frac{1}{2}}{x} = 5$, then $x =$

(A) $\dfrac{1}{10}$ (B) $\dfrac{1}{5}$ (C) $\dfrac{2}{5}$

(D) $\dfrac{5}{2}$ (E) 10

5. If $\dfrac{1}{2} + \dfrac{1}{m} = \dfrac{5}{6}$, then $m =$

(A) $\dfrac{1}{3}$ (B) $\dfrac{2}{5}$ (C) $\dfrac{2}{3}$

(D) 3 (E) 5

6. If $x \neq y$ and $x + y = 0$, then $\dfrac{x}{y} =$

(A) -1 (B) 0 (C) $\frac{1}{2}$
(D) 1 (E) 2

7. If $\dfrac{m}{4} + \dfrac{n}{2} = \dfrac{7}{8}$, then $m + 2n =$

(A) $\dfrac{7}{4}$ (B) $\dfrac{7}{2}$ (C) 5 (D) 7 (E) 14

8. If $z \neq 0$, which of the following is equivalent to $\dfrac{1}{z + \frac{1}{z}}$?

(A) 1 (B) $\dfrac{1}{2z}$ (C) $\dfrac{2}{z}$

(D) $\dfrac{z}{z+1}$ (E) $\dfrac{z}{z^2 + 1}$

9. Five-eighths of Ms. Talbott's students are boys, and two-thirds of the girls do not have dark hair. What fraction of Ms. Talbott's students are girls with dark hair?

(A) $\dfrac{1}{24}$ (B) $\dfrac{1}{10}$ (C) $\dfrac{1}{8}$

(D) $\dfrac{1}{4}$ (E) $\dfrac{1}{3}$

10. If $\dfrac{2}{3} + \dfrac{6}{7} - \dfrac{1}{6} = \dfrac{2}{3} - \dfrac{1}{6} + \dfrac{1}{x}$, then $x =$

11. If $n > 1$, and $\dfrac{nx}{m + x} = 1$, then $x =$

(A) $\dfrac{m}{n-1}$ (B) $\dfrac{m}{n+1}$ (C) $\dfrac{m+1}{n}$

(D) $\dfrac{m+1}{n-1}$ (E) $\dfrac{m+1}{n+1}$

Answer Key 3: Fractions

Concept Review 3

1. 19/35 (Use zip-zap-zup: it's better than using your calculator!)

2. 20/3 (Change to $5/2 \times 8/3$.)

3. 8/3 (Divide numerator and denominator by their common factor: 7.)

4. 8/45 (Change to $2/9 \times 4/5$.)

5. $(12x + 14)/21x$ (Use zip-zap-zup.)

6. $4x/3z$ (Change to $3x/2 \times 8/9z$ and simplify.)

7. $(3m + 1)/(2m + 1)$ (Factor and cancel 4 from the numerator and denominator.)

8. $-1/(6x)$ (Change to $-2/(9x^2) \times 3x/4$ and simplify.)

9. 13/12 (Change to $6/12 + 4/12 + 3/12$.)

10. $(3 - 2x)/4$ (Use zip-zap-zup and simplify.)

11. $x + 5$ (As long as $x \neq 5$.) (Factor as $\dfrac{(x-5)(x+5)}{(x-5)}$ and cancel the common factor. For factoring review, see Chapter 8, Lesson 5.)

12. $(2n + 3)/4n$ (Divide numerator and denominator by the common factor: 3. Don't forget to "distribute" the division in the numerator!)

13. ¼ 14. ⅕ 15. ¹⁄₁₀ 16. ⅓
(Knowing how to "convert" numbers back and forth from percents to decimals to fractions can be very helpful in simplifying problems!)

17. Multiply by the reciprocal of the fraction.

18. "Cross-multiply" to get the new numerators, and multiply the denominators to get the new denominator, then just add (or subtract) the numerators.

19. Only common *factors*. (Factors = terms in *products*.)

20. Just divide the numbers by hand or on a calculator.

21. 4/9 (Not 4/5! Remember the fraction is a part of the *whole*, which is 27 students, 12/27 = 4/9.)

22. 27 (If 2/3 are girls, 1/3 are boys: $t/3 = 9$, so $t = 27$.)

23. It must have a value between 0 and 1 ("bottom-heavy").

SAT Practice 3

1. **C** $4/(4+5+3) = 4/12 = 1/3$

2. **B**
$$\frac{1}{y} = -3$$
Multiply by y: $1 = -3y$
Divide by -3: $-\dfrac{1}{3} = y$

3. **C** $\dfrac{2}{3} \times 1 \qquad\qquad = 0.666\ldots$

$1 - \dfrac{2}{3} = \dfrac{3}{3} - \dfrac{2}{3} = \dfrac{1}{3} \quad = 0.333\ldots$

$1 \div \dfrac{2}{3} = 1 \times \dfrac{3}{2} \qquad = 1.5$

$\dfrac{2}{3} \div \dfrac{2}{3} = \dfrac{2}{3} \times \dfrac{3}{2} = \dfrac{6}{6} \quad = 1$

$\dfrac{2}{3} \div 1 = \dfrac{2}{3} \times 1 \qquad = 0.666\ldots$

4. **A** $\dfrac{\frac{1}{2}}{x} = 5$ Multiply by x: $\dfrac{1}{2} = 5x$

Multiply by $\dfrac{1}{5}$: $\dfrac{1}{10} = x$

5. **D** $\dfrac{1}{2} + \dfrac{1}{m} = \dfrac{5}{6}$ Multiply by $6m$: $3m + 6 = 5m$
Subtract $3m$: $6 = 2m$
Divide by 2: $3 = m$

6. **A**   The quotient of opposites is always -1. (Try $x = 2$ and $y = -2$ or any other solution.)

7. **B**   To turn $\dfrac{m}{4} + \dfrac{n}{2}$ into $m + 2n$, we only need to multiply by 4!
$$m + 2n = 4\left(\frac{m}{4} + \frac{n}{2}\right) = 4\left(\frac{7}{8}\right) = \frac{28}{8} = \frac{7}{2}$$

8. **E**   You can solve this by "plugging in" a number for z or by simplifying algebraically. To plug in, pick $z = 2$ and notice that the expression equals ⅖ or 4. Substituting $z = 2$ into the choices shows that only (E) is .4.

Alternatively, you can simplify by just multiplying numerator and denominator by z:
$$\frac{1}{z + \dfrac{1}{z}} = \frac{z \times 1}{z\left(z + \dfrac{1}{z}\right)} = \frac{z}{z^2 \times 1}$$

9. **C**   ⅝ are boys, so ⅜ must be girls. Of the girls, ⅔ do not have dark hair, so ⅓ do. Therefore, ⅓ of ⅜ of the class are girls with dark hair. ⅓ × ⅜ = ⅛.

10. **7/6 or 1.16 or 1.17**   Begin by subtracting 2/3 from both sides and adding −1/6 to both sides, to simplify. This gives $\dfrac{6}{7} = \dfrac{1}{x}$. Just "reciprocate" both sides or cross-multiply.

11. **A** $\dfrac{nx}{m+x} = 1$ Multiply by $m + x$: $nx = m + x$

Subtract x: $nx - x = m$

Factor: $x(n-1) = m$

Divide by $(n-1)$: $x = \dfrac{m}{n-1}$

Lesson 4: Ratios and Proportions

Working with Ratios

When you see a ratio—such as 5:6—don't let it confuse you. If it is *not* a part-to-part ratio, then just think of it as a fraction. For instance, 5:6 = 5/6. If it *is* a part-to-part ratio, just divide each number by the sum to find the fraction of each part to the whole. For instance, if the ratio of boys to girls in a class is 5:6, then the sum is 5 + 6 = 11, so the boys make up 5/11 of the whole class, and the girls make up 6/11 of the whole class. (Notice that these fractions must add up to 1!)

Example:

If a $200 prize is divided up among three people in a 1:4:5 ratio, then how much does each person receive? The total of the parts is 1 + 4 + 5 = 10. Therefore, the three people receive 1/10, 4/10, and 5/10 of the prize, respectively. So one person gets (1/10) × $200 = $20, another gets (4/10) × $200 = $80, and the other gets (5/10) × $200 = $100.

Working with Proportions

A *proportion* is just an equation that says that two fractions are equal, as in 3/5 = 9/15. Two ways to simplify proportions are with the *law of cross-multiplication* and with the *law of cross-swapping*. The law of cross-multiplication says that if two fractions are equal, then their "cross-products" also must be equal. The law of cross-swapping says that if two fractions are equal, then "cross-swapping" terms will create another true proportion.

Example:

If we know that $\dfrac{x}{4} = \dfrac{3}{7}$, then by the law of cross-multiplication, we know that $7x = 12$, and by the law of cross-swapping, that $\dfrac{x}{3} = \dfrac{4}{7}$.

In a word problem, the phrase "at this rate" means that you can set up a proportion to solve the problem. A *rate* is just a *ratio* of some quantity to time. For instance, your *reading rate* is in *words per minute*; that is, it is the ratio of the number of words you read divided by the number of minutes it takes you to read them. (The word *per* acts like the : in the ratio.) IMPORTANT: When setting up the proportion, check that the units "match up"—that the numerators share the same unit and the denominators share the same unit.

Example:

A bird can fly 420 miles in one day if it flies continuously. At this rate, how many miles can the bird fly in 14 hours?

To solve this, we can set up a proportion that says that the two rates are the same.

$$\frac{420 \text{ miles}}{24 \text{ hours}} = \frac{x \text{ miles}}{14 \text{ hours}}$$

Notice that the units "match up"—miles in the numerator and hours in the denominator. Now we can cross-multiply to get $420 \times 14 = 24x$ and divide by 24 to get $x = 245$ miles.

Similarity

Two triangles are *similar* (have the same shape) if their corresponding angles all *have* the same measure. If two triangles are similar, then their corresponding sides are proportional.

Example:

In the figure above,

$$\frac{m}{k} = \frac{n}{l} \text{ or } \frac{m}{n} = \frac{k}{l}$$

When setting up proportions of sides in similar figures, double-check that the corresponding sides "match up" in the proportion. For instance, notice how the terms "match up" in the proportions above.

Concept Review 4: Ratios and Proportions

1. A speed is a ratio of _____ to _____.   2. An average is a ratio of _____ to _____.

3. Define a proportion:

_____

_____

4. Write the law of cross-multiplication as an "If . . . then . . ." statement:

If _____

then _____

5. Write three equations that are equivalent to $\dfrac{2}{x} = \dfrac{y}{3}$.   5. a)_____

     b)_____

     c)_____

6. Three people split a $24,000 prize in a ratio of 2:3:5. What is the value of each portion?   6. a)_____

     b)_____

     c)_____

7. A machine, working at a constant rate, manufactures 25 bottles every 6 minutes. At this rate, how many *hours* will it take to produce 1,000 bottles?   7. _____

8. If m meteorites enter the Earth's atmosphere every x days ($m > 0$), then, at this rate, how many meteors will enter the Earth's atmosphere in mx days?   8. _____

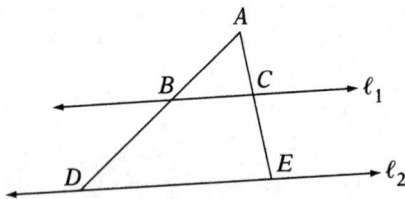

9. In the diagram above, $\ell_1 \parallel \ell_2$, $AC = 4$, $BC = 5$, and $CE = 6$. What is DE?   9. _____

10. There are 12 boys and g girls in Class A, and there are 27 girls and b boys in Class B. In each class, the ratio of boys to girls is the same. If $b = g$, then how many students are in Class A?   10. _____

SAT Practice 4: Ratios and Proportions

1. If x is the product of .03 and .2, then x is equivalent to the ratio of 6 to what number?

2. Jar A contains six red marbles and no green marbles. Jar B contains two red marbles and four green marbles. How many green marbles must be moved from Jar B to Jar A so that the ratio of green marbles to red marbles is the same for both jars?

(A) 0   (B) 1   (C) 2   (D) 3   (E) 4

3. 90 students are at a meeting. The ratio of girls to boys at the meeting is 2 to 3. How many girls are at the meeting?

(A) 30   (B) 36   (C) 40
(D) 54   (E) 60

4. If $\dfrac{x}{y+1} = \dfrac{3}{5}$, then $5x + 1 =$

(A) $3y + 1$ (B) $3y + 2$ (C) $3y + 3$
(D) $3y + 4$ (E) $3y + 5$

5. On a map that is drawn to scale, two towns that are x miles apart are represented as being 4 inches apart. If two other towns are $x + 2$ miles apart, how many inches apart would they be on the same map?

(A) $4(x + 2)$ (B) 6   (C) $\dfrac{4x}{x+2}$

(D) $\dfrac{4(x+2)}{x}$ (E) $\dfrac{6}{x}$

6. If 3,600 baseball caps are distributed to 4 stores in the ratio of 1:2:3:4, what is the maximum number of caps that any one store receives?

(A) 360   (B) 720   (C) 1,080
(D) 1,440   (E) 14,400

7. David's motorcycle uses $\dfrac{2}{5}$ of a gallon of gasoline to travel 8 miles. At this rate, how many miles will it travel on 5 gallons of gasoline?

8. On a blueprint that is drawn to scale, the drawing of a rectangular patio has dimensions 5 cm by 7.5 cm. If the longer side of the actual patio measures 21 feet, what is the area, in square feet, of the actual patio?

(A) 157.5
(B) 294.0
(C) 356.5
(D) 441.0
(E) 640.5

9. To make a certain purple dye, red dye and blue dye are mixed in a ratio of 3:4. To make a certain orange dye, red dye and yellow dye are mixed in a ratio of 3:2. If equal amounts of the purple and orange dye are mixed, what fraction of the new mixture is red dye?

(A) $\dfrac{9}{20}$ (B) $\dfrac{1}{2}$ (C) $\dfrac{18}{35}$

(D) $\dfrac{27}{40}$ (E) $\dfrac{1}{1}$

Answer Key 4: Ratios and Proportions

Concept Review 4

1. distance to time

2. a sum to the number of terms in the sum

3. A proportion is a statement that two fractions or ratios are equal to each other.

4. If two fractions are equal, then the two "cross-products" must also be equal.

5. a) $6 = xy$ b) $\dfrac{3}{x} = \dfrac{y}{2}$ c) $\dfrac{2}{y} = \dfrac{x}{3}$

6. $4,800, $7,200, and $12,000. The sum of the parts is $2 + 3 + 5 = 10$, so the parts are 2/10, 3/10, and 5/10 of the whole.

7. 4.
$$\frac{25 \text{ bottles}}{6 \text{ minutes}} = \frac{1,000 \text{ bottles}}{x \text{ minutes}}$$

Cross-multiply: $25x = 6,000$
Divide by 25: $x = 240$ minutes

Convert to hours: $240 \text{ mins} \times \left(\dfrac{1 \text{ hour}}{60 \text{ mins}}\right) = 4 \text{ hrs}$

8. m^2. "At this rate . . ." implies a proportion:

$$\frac{m \text{ meteorites}}{x \text{ days}} = \frac{? \text{ meteorites}}{mx \text{ days}}$$

Cross-multiply: $m^2x = ?x$
Divide by x: $m^2 = ?$

9. 12.5. Because $\ell_1 \parallel \ell_2$; $\triangle ABC$ is similar to $\triangle ADE$.
Thus, $\dfrac{AC}{AE} = \dfrac{BC}{DE}$. Substituting x for DE gives

$$\frac{4}{4+6} = \frac{5}{x}.$$

Cross-multiply: $4x = 50$
Divide by 4: $x = 12.5$

10. 30. Since the ratios are the same, $\dfrac{12}{g} = \dfrac{b}{27}$.

Cross-multiply: $bg = 324$
Substitute b for g: $b^2 = 324$
Take the square root: $b = 18$
So the number of students in Class A $= 12 + 18 = 30$.

SAT Practice 4

1. **1,000.** $.03 \times .2 = 6/x$
Simplify: $.006 = 6/x$
Multiply by x: $.006x = 6$
Divide by .006: $x = 1,000$

2. **D**   Moving three green marbles from Jar B to Jar A leaves three green marbles and six red marbles in Jar A and one green marble and two red marbles in Jar B. 3:6 = 1:2.

3. **B**   2:3 is a "part to part" ratio, with a sum of 5. Therefore 2/5 of the students are girls and 3/5 are boys. 2/5 of 90 = 36.

4. **D**   Cross-multiply: $5(x) = 3(y + 1)$
Simplify: $5x = 3y + 3$
Add 1: $5x + 1 = 3y + 4$

5. **D**   Since the map is "to scale," the corresponding measures are proportional:

$$\frac{x}{4} = \frac{x+2}{?}$$

Cross-multiply: $?x = 4(x + 2)$

Divide by x: $? = \dfrac{4(x+2)}{x}$

6. **D**   The ratio is a "ratio of parts" with a sum of $1 + 2 + 3 + 4 = 10$. The largest part, then, is 4/10 of the whole. 4/10 of 3,600 $= .4 \times 3,600 = 1,440$.

7. **100.**   "At this rate" implies a proportion:

$$\frac{\frac{2}{5} \text{ gallon}}{8 \text{ miles}} = \frac{5 \text{ gallons}}{x \text{ miles}}$$

Cross-multiply: $\dfrac{2}{5}x = 40$

Multiply by $\dfrac{5}{2}$: $x = \dfrac{5}{2} \times 40 = \dfrac{200}{2} = 100$ miles

8. **B**

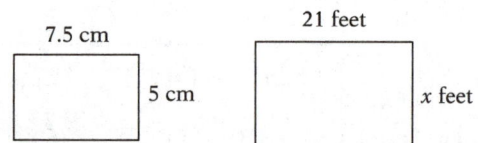

Set up the proportion: $\dfrac{7.5}{5} = \dfrac{21}{x}$

Cross-multiply: $7.5x = 105$
Divide by 7.5: $x = 14$ feet
Find the area: Area $= 21 \times 14 = 294 \text{ ft}^2$

9. **C**   Each ratio is a "ratio of parts." In the purple dye, the red dye is 3/(3 + 4), or 3/7, of the total, and in the orange dye, the red dye is 3/(3 + 2), or 3/5, of the total. If the mixture is half purple and half orange, the fraction of red is

$$\frac{1}{2}\left(\frac{3}{7}\right) + \frac{1}{2}\left(\frac{3}{5}\right) = \frac{3}{14} + \frac{3}{10} = \frac{72}{140} = \frac{18}{35}$$

Lesson 5: Percents

Word Problems with Percents

The word *percent* simply means *divided by 100*. Word problems are easy to solve once you know how to translate sentences into equations. Use this key:

percent	means	÷100
is	means	=
of	means	×
what	means	x, y, n, etc.

Example:

What number is 5 percent of 36?
Use the translation key to translate the question into

$$x = \frac{5}{100} \times 36$$

Then simplify to get $x = 1.8$.

Example:

28 is what percent of 70?
Use the translation key to translate the question into

$$28 = \frac{x}{100} \times 70$$

Then simplify to get $28 = .7x$ and divide by .7 to get $x = 40$.

To convert a percent into a decimal, just remember that percent means *divided by 100* and that dividing by 100 just means moving the decimal two places to the left.

Example:

$35.7\% = 35.7 \div 100 = .357 \qquad .04\% = .04 \div 100 = .0004$

Finding "Percent Change"

Some word problems ask you to find the "percent change" in a quantity, that is, by what percent the quantity increased or decreased. A percent change is always the percent that the *change* is of the *original amount*. To solve these, use the formula

Percent change =

$$\frac{\text{final amount} - \text{starting amount}}{\text{starting amount}} \times 100\%$$

Example:

If the population of Bradford increased from 30,000 to 40,000, what was the percent increase? According to the formula, the percent change is

$$\frac{40,000 - 30,000}{30,000} \times 100\% = 33\frac{1}{3}\%$$

Increasing or Decreasing by Percents

When most people want to leave a 20% tip at a restaurant, they do *two* calculations: First, they calculate 20% of the bill, and then they add the result to the original bill. But there's a simpler, *one-step method*: Just multiply the bill by 1.20! This idea can be enormously helpful on tough percent problems. Here's the idea:

When increasing or decreasing a quantity by a given percent, use the one-step shortcut: Just multiply the quantity by the *final percentage*. For instance, if you decrease a quantity by 10%, your final percentage is 100% − 10% = 90%, so just multiply by 0.9. If you increase a quantity by 10%, your final percentage is 100% + 10% = 110%, so just multiply by 1.1.

Example:

If the price of a shirt is $60 but there is a 20% off sale and a 6% tax, what is the final price?

Just multiply $60 by .80 and by 1.06: $60 × .80 × 1.06 = $50.88

Here's a cool fact that simplifies some percent problems: *a% of b is always equal to b% of a.* So, for instance, if you can't find 36% of 25 in your head, just remember that it's equal to 25% of 36! That means 1/4 of 36, which is 9.

Concept Review 5: Percents

1. Complete the translation key:

Word(s) in problem	Symbol in equation
what, what number, how much	
of	
	=
percent	

2. Write the formula for "percent change":

3. To increase a quantity by 30%, multiply it by _____   4. To decrease a quantity by 19%, multiply it by _____

5. To increase a quantity by 120%, multiply it by _____   6. To decrease a quantity by 120%, multiply it by _____

Translate the following word problems and solve them.

7. 5 is what percent of 26?   Translation: _____   Solution: _____

8. 35% of what number is 28?   Translation: _____   Solution: _____

9. 60 is 15% of what number?   Translation: _____   Solution: _____

10. What percent is 35 of 20?   Translation: _____   Solution: _____

11. What percent greater than 1,200 is 1,500?   11. _____

12. If the price of a sweater is marked down from $80 to $68, what is the percent markdown? 12. _____

13. The population of a city increases from 32,000 to 44,800. What is the percent increase?   13. _____

14. What number is 30% greater than 20?   14. _____

15. Increasing a number by 20%, then decreasing the new number by 20%, is the same as multiplying the original by _____.

16. Why don't the changes in problem 15 "cancel out"?

_____

17. If the sides of a square are decreased by 5%, by what percent is the area of the   17. _____
square decreased?

18. 28% of 50 is the same as _____percent of _____, which equals _____.

19. 48% of 25 is the same as _____percent of _____, which equals _____.

SAT Practice 5: Percents

1. David has a total of $3,500 in monthly expenses. He spends $2,200 per month on rent and utilities, $600 per month on clothing and food, and the rest on miscellaneous expenses. On a pie graph of his monthly expenses, what would be the degree measure of the central angle of the sector representing miscellaneous expenses?

    (A) 45°   (B) 50°   (C) 70°
    (D) 72°   (E) 75°

2. In one year, the price of one share of ABC stock increased by 20% in Quarter I, increased by 25% in Quarter II, decreased by 20% in Quarter III, and increased by 10% in Quarter IV. By what percent did the price of the stock increase for the whole year? (Ignore the % symbol when gridding.)

3. On a two-part test, Barbara answered 60% of the questions correctly on Part I and 90% correctly on Part II. If there were 40 questions on Part I and 80 questions on Part II, and if each question on both parts was worth 1 point, what was her score, as a percent of the total?

    (A) 48%   (B) 75%   (C) 80%
    (D) 82%   (E) 96%

4. If x is $\frac{2}{3}$% of 90, then $1 - x =$

    (A) −59   (B) −5   (C) 0
    (D) 0.4   (E) 0.94

5. The cost of a pack of batteries, after a 5% tax, is $8.40. What was the price before tax?

    (A) $5.60
    (B) $7.98
    (C) $8.00
    (D) $8.35
    (E) $8.82

6. If the population of Town B is 50% greater than the population of Town A, and the population of Town C is 20% greater than the population of Town A, then what percent greater is the population of Town B than the population of Town C?

    (A) 20%   (B) 25%   (C) 30%
    (D) 35%   (E) 40%

7. If the length of a rectangle is increased by 20% and the width is increased by 30%, then by what percent is the area of the rectangle increased?

    (A) 10%   (B) 50%
    (C) 56%   (D) 65%
    (E) It cannot be determined from the given information.

8. If 12 ounces of a 30% salt solution are mixed with 24 ounces of a 60% salt solution, what is the percent concentration of salt in the mixture?

    (A) 45%   (B) 48%   (C) 50%
    (D) 52%   (E) 56%

9. The freshman class at Hillside High School has 45 more girls than boys. If the class has n boys, then what percent of the freshman class are girls?

    (A) $\dfrac{n}{n+45}\%$ (B) $\dfrac{n+45}{2n+45}\%$

    (C) $\dfrac{100n}{2n+45}\%$ (D) $\dfrac{100(n+45)}{2n+45}\%$

    (E) $\dfrac{100(n+45)}{n+45}\%$

Answer Key 5: Percents

Concept Review 5

1. x, y, or any unknown; $\times$; *is*; $\div 100$

2. $\dfrac{\text{final amount} - \text{starting amount}}{\text{starting amount}} \times 100\%$

3. 1.30   4. 0.81   5. 2.20   6. -20

7. $5 = \dfrac{x}{100} \times 26$ $x = 19.23\%$

8. $.35x = 28$ $x = 80$

9. $60 = .15x$ $x = 400$

10. 175%. Rephrase: *What percent of 20 is 35?* (or remember *is over of* equals the *percent*)

$$\dfrac{x}{100} \times 20 = 35 \quad \text{or} \quad \dfrac{35}{20} = \dfrac{x}{100}$$

$$3{,}500 = 20x \quad x = 175(\%)$$

11. 25%. Use the "percent change" formula:

$$\dfrac{1{,}500 - 1{,}200}{1{,}200} \times 100\% = \dfrac{300}{1{,}200} \times 100\% = 25\%$$

12. $-15\%. \dfrac{168 - 80}{80} \times 100\% = \dfrac{-12}{80} \times 100\% = -15\%$

13. 40%.

$$\dfrac{44{,}800 - 32{,}000}{32{,}000} \times 100\% = \dfrac{12{,}800}{32{,}000} \times 100\% = 40\%$$

14. 26. To increase a number by 30%, multiply by 1.30: $20 \times 1.30 = 26$.

15. 0.96. $x(1.20)(.80) = 0.96x$

16. Because the two percentages are "of" different numbers.

17. 9.75%. Assume the original square has sides of length x and area x^2. The new square, then, has sides of $.95x$ and area of $.9025x^2$.

$$\dfrac{.9025x^2 - x^2}{x^2} \times 100\% = \dfrac{-.0975x^2}{x^2} \times 100\% = -9.75\%$$

18. 50% of 28, which equals 14

19. 25% of 48, which equals 12

SAT Practice 5

1. **D** Miscellaneous expenses = \$3,500 − \$2,200 − \$600 = \$700. As a percent of the total, 700/3,500 = 20%. The total number of degrees in a pie graph is 360°, so the sector angle = 20% of 360° = $.20 \times 360 = 72°$.

2. **32%** Assume the starting price is x. The final price is $x(1.20)(1.25)(.80)(1.10) = 1.32x$, which represents a 32% increase. Notice that you can't just "add up" the percent changes, as we saw in Question 16 of the Concept Review.

3. **C** The total number of points is 40 + 80 = 120. The number of points she earned is $.60(40) + .90(80) = 24 + 72 = 96$. 96/120 = .80 = 80%.

4. **D** If you chose (A), remember: 2/3% is NOT the same thing as 2/3! Don't forget that % means ÷ 100.
$x = 2/3\%$ of $90 = (2/3) \div 100 \times 90 = 0.6$
$1 - 0.6 = 0.4$

5. **C** If you chose (B), remember that the tax is 5% of the starting amount, not the final amount. The final price must be 5% higher than the starting price. If the starting price is x, then $\$8.40 = 1.05x$. Dividing by 1.05, $x = \$8.00$.

6. **B** Let a = population of Town A, b = population of Town B, and c = population of Town C. Since b is 50% greater than a, $b = 1.50a$. Since c is 20% greater than a, $c = 1.20a$.

$$\dfrac{1.5a - 1.2a}{1.2a} \times 100\% = \dfrac{.3a}{1.2a} \times 100\% = 25\%$$

You can also set $a = 100$, so $b = 150$ and $c = 120$.

7. **C** If the rectangle has length a and width b, then its area is ab. The "new" rectangle, then, has length $1.2a$ and width $1.3b$ and so has an area of $1.56ab$, which represents an increase of 56%.

8. **C** The total amount of salt is $.30(12) + .60(24) = 3.6 + 14.4 = 18$ ounces. The total amount of solution is 36 ounces, and 18/36 = 50%. Or you might notice that 24 is twice as much as 12, so the concentration of the mixture is the average of "two 60s and one 30."
$(60\% + 60\% + 30\%)/3 = 50\%$

9. **D** The number of girls is $n + 45$, so the total number of students is $2n + 45$. So the percentage of girls is

$$\dfrac{100(n + 45)}{2n + 45}\%$$

Lesson 6: Negatives

Visualize the Number Line

Visualize the number line when comparing, adding, or subtracting numbers. *Greater than* always means *to the right on the number line* and *less than* means *to the left on the number line*. A negative number is *greater* than another if it is *closer to 0*.

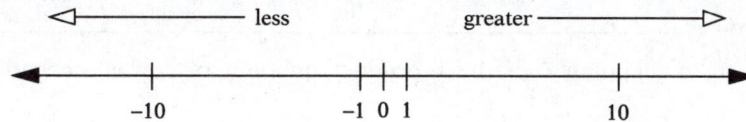

Example:

Which is greater, –2/5 or –7/5? Answer: Visualize the number line. Although 2/5 is less than 7/5, on the negative side this relationship is "flipped." –2/5 is closer to 0 than –7/5 is, so –2/5 is greater.

Adding and Subtracting with Negatives

To add, visualize the number line. To add a positive, jump to the right. To add a negative, jump to the left.

Example:

To add –5 + –12, start at –5 and move 12 spaces to the *left* (negative), to land on –17.

(Or you could start at –12 and jump 5 spaces to the left!)

To subtract, you can change the subtraction to addition by changing the sign of the second number.

Example:

To subtract –5 – (–12), change it to addition by changing the sign of the second number: –5 + 12 = 12 – 5 = 7.

To subtract, you can also "swap" the numbers and change the sign of the result, because $a - b$ is the opposite of $b - a$.

Example:

$$4 - 18 = -(18 - 4) = -14$$

Remember these helpful facts about subtracting:
- $a - b$ is *positive* if a is greater than b and *negative* if b is greater than a (regardless of the signs).
- $a - b$ is always the *opposite* of $b - a$.

Products, Quotients, and Powers of Negatives

Any product, quotient, or power is *negative* if it has an *odd* number of negatives and *positive* if it has an *even* number of negatives.

Example:

$-12 \times 5 \times 7$ is negative: it has an odd number (1) of negatives.

$\dfrac{(-4x)(-3x)}{(-2x)(-6x^3)}$ is positive: it has an even number (4) of negatives.

$(-3)^{12}(5)^7(-2)^5$ is negative: it has an odd number $(12 + 5 = 17)$ of negatives.

Inequalities and Negatives

Any inequality must be "flipped" whenever you multiply or divide both sides by a negative.

Example:

Solve $-3x > 6y - 3$ for x.

To isolate x, you must divide both sides by -3. But, since this changes the sign of both sides, you must "flip" the inequality, so the solution is $x < -2y + 1$.

Concept Review 6: Negatives

Write the correct inequality (< or >) in each space.

1. $-\dfrac{3}{5}$ ____ $-\dfrac{2}{5}$ 2. -10 ____ -25 3. $-\dfrac{4}{7}$ ____ $-\dfrac{2}{5}$ 4. $\dfrac{3}{5}$ ____ $-\dfrac{2}{5}$

5. When does the expression $-x$ represent a *positive* number? _____

6. An inequality must be "flipped" whenever _____.

7. When is $x - y$ negative? _____

8. What is the simple way to tell quickly whether a product, quotient, or power is negative?

_____

_____

9. If $(x - y)(y - x) = -10$, then $(x - y)^2 =$ ____. (Think before doing any algebra!)

Simplify the following expressions *without* a calculator.

10. If $x \neq 2$, then $\dfrac{9x - 18}{18 - 9x} =$ ____.

11. $-13y^2 - (-4y^2) =$ ____

12. $\dfrac{2}{-3} - \dfrac{-2}{-5} =$ ____

13. $\dfrac{(-5)^3 (-1)^{16}}{(2)^4 (5)^3} =$ ____

14. $-15 - (-9) =$ ____

15. $-5(-x)^6 \times -7x^{11} =$ ____

16. If $a(2 - x) > b(2 - x)$, then

$a > b$ only if _____

$a < b$ only if _____

Solve the following inequalities for x:

17. $-4x + 20 > 16$ 17. _____

18. $4x - 20 \geq 16$ 18. _____

19. $-20 - 4x < 16$ 19. _____

20. $-4x - 20 > -16$ 20. _____

SAT Practice 6: Negatives

1. For all real numbers b, $-(-b - b - b - b) =$

(A) $-4b$ (B) $4b$ (C) b^4

(D) $-b^4$ (E) $4b^4$

---

2. If $k = (m - 1)(m - 2)(m - 3)$, then for which of the following values of m is k greater than 0?

(A) -2.47
(B) -1.47
(C) 0.47
(D) 1.47
(E) 2.47

---

3. For all real numbers w, $-w^2 - (-w)^2 =$

(A) $-w^4$
(B) $-2w^2$
(C) 0
(D) $2w^2$
(E) w^4

---

4. If $\dfrac{m}{n} > 1$, which of the following must be true?

     I. $m > n$

     II. $\dfrac{m}{n} > 0$

     III. $m > 1$

(A) I only
(B) II only
(C) III only
(D) I and II only
(E) I and III only

---

5. If $x = -y$ and $x \neq 0$, then which of the following must be true?

     I. $x^2y^3 < 0$
     II. $(x + y)^2 = 0$
     III. $\dfrac{x}{y} < 0$

(A) III only
(B) I and II only
(C) II and III only
(D) I and III only
(E) I, II, and III

---

6. If $mn^4p^5 > 0$ and $m < 0$, then which of the following expressions must be negative?

(A) mn
(B) m^2
(C) p^5
(D) mp
(E) np

---

7. If $0 < a < b < c < d < e < f$ and
$(a - b)(c - d)\,(e - f)(x) = (b - a)(d - c)(f - e)$,
then $x =$

(A) -4
(B) -3
(C) -2
(D) -1
(E) 0

---

8. If the sum of the integers from 15 to 50, inclusive, is equal to the sum of the integers from n to 50, inclusive, and $n < 15$, then $n =$

(A) -50
(B) -49
(C) -35
(D) -15
(E) -14

---

9. If $-2x < -7$ and $y < 2.5$, then which of the following must be true?

     I. $xy > 0$
     II. $x - y > 0$
     III. $x > 3$

(A) II only
(B) I and II only
(C) II and III only
(D) I and III only
(E) I, II, and III

---

10. A sequence of numbers begins with the numbers $-1, 1, 1, \ldots$, and each term afterward is the product of the preceding three terms. How many of the first 57 terms of this sequence are negative?

(A) 19   (B) 20   (C) 28

(D) 29   (E) 30

Answer Key 6: Negatives

Concept Review 6

1. <   2. >   3. <   4. >

5. Whenever x is negative.

6. You multiply or divide by a negative on both sides.

7. Whenever y is greater than x (regardless of sign).

8. If the number of negatives in the term is odd, then the result is negative. If the number of negatives in the term is even, then the result is positive. Remember to add the exponents of all the negative numbers in the term.

9. 10. Notice that $y - x$ is the opposite of $x - y$. So $(x - y)(x - y)$ is the opposite of $(x - y)(y - x)$.

10. −1. Notice that $9x - 18$ and $18 - 9x$ must be opposites, and the quotient of non-zero opposites is always −1. ($-5/5 = -1$, $20/-20 = -1$, etc.)

11. $-9y^2$.

	$-13y^2 - (-4y^2)$
Change to addition:	$-13y^2 + 4y^2$
Commute:	$4y^2 + -13y^2$
Change to subtraction:	$4y^2 - 13y^2$
Swap and negate:	$-(13y^2 - 4y^2) = -9y^2$

12. −16/15. $\dfrac{2}{-3} - \dfrac{-2}{-5}$

Simplify fractions: $-\dfrac{2}{3} - \dfrac{2}{5}$

Factor out −1: $-\left(\dfrac{2}{3} + \dfrac{2}{5}\right)$

Zip-zap-zup: $-\dfrac{10 + 6}{15} = -\dfrac{16}{15}$

13. −1/16.   Since there are an odd number (19) of negatives, the result is negative. Notice, too, that the powers of 5 cancel out.

14. −6   15. $35x^{17}$

16. $a > b$ only if $x < 2$ (and so $2 - x$ is positive). $a < b$ only if $x > 2$ (and so $2 - x$ is negative).

17. $x < 1$ 18. $x \geq 9$

19. $x > -9$ 20. $x < -1$

SAT Practice 6

1. **B**

	$-(-b - b - b - b)$
Convert to addition:	$-(-b + -b + -b + -b)$
Distribute −1:	$(b + b + b + b)$
Simplify:	$4b$

2. **D**   Notice that $m - 1 > m - 2 > m - 3$. If the product is positive, then all three terms must be positive or one must be positive and the other two negative. They would all be positive only if $m > 3$, but no choice fits. If two terms are negative and one positive, then, by checking, $1 < m < 2$.

3. **B**   Don't forget the order of operations: powers before subtraction!

	$-w^2 - (-w)^2$
Simplify power:	$-w^2 - w^2$
Change to addition:	$-w^2 + -w^2$
Simplify:	$-2w^2$

4. **B**   If m/n is positive, then m and n must have the same sign. Using $m = -2$ and $n = -1$ disproves statements I and III. Statement II must be true because m and n must have the same sign.

5. **C**   The example $x = -1$ and $y = 1$ disproves statement I. Substituting $-y$ for x (because an expression can always be substituted for its equal) and simplifying in statements II and III proves that both are true.

6. **C**   Since m is negative, n^4p^5 must be negative because the whole product is positive. n can be either positive or negative; n^4 will be positive in either case. Therefore, p^5 must be negative.

7. **D**   Since $x - y$ is always the opposite of $y - x$, $(a - b)(c - d)(e - f)(x) = (b - a)(d - c)(f - e)$.
Substitute: $= -(a - b) \times -(c - d) \times -(e - f)$
Simplify: $= -(a - b)(c - d)(e - f)$
By comparing the two sides, x must equal −1.

8. **E**   If the two sums are equal, then the sum of the integers from n to 14, which are not included in the first sum, must "cancel out." That can only happen if n is −14.

9. **C**   Simplify the first inequality by dividing both sides by −2. (Don't forget to "flip" the inequality!) This gives $x > 3.5$. The example of $x = 4$ and $y = -1$ disproves statement I. Since x must be greater than y, statement II must be true. Since x is greater than 3.5, it must certainly be greater than 3, so statement III must be true.

10. **D**   The sequence follows the pattern $(-1, 1, 1, -1)$, $(-1, 1, 1, -1)$, $(-1, 1, 1, -1)$, ... Since the pattern is four terms long, it repeats $57 \div 4 = 14$ times, with a remainder of 1 (the remainder shows that it includes the first term of the 15th repetition), which means it includes $14(2) + 1 = 29$ negatives.

Lesson 7: Divisibility

Divisibility

There are five different ways of saying that one integer, a, is a multiple of another integer, b. Understand each phrasing.

- a is divisible by b.
- a is a multiple of b.
- b is a factor (divisor) of a.
- When a is divided by b, the remainder is 0.
- a/b is an integer.

Example:

42 is a multiple of 7, so

- 42 is divisible by 7.
- 42 is a multiple of 7.
- 7 is a factor (divisor) of 42.
- When 42 is divided by 7, the remainder is 0.
- 42/7 is an integer (6).

To see if integer a is divisible by integer b, divide a by b on your calculator and see whether the result is an integer. Or use one of the quick checks below.

- Multiples of 3 have digits that add up to a multiple of 3.

Example:

345 is a multiple of 3 because $3 + 4 + 5 = 12$, which is a multiple of 3.

- Multiples of 5 end in 0 or 5.
- Multiples of 6 end in an even digit, and their digits add up to a multiple of 3.
- Multiples of 9 have digits that add up to a multiple of 9.

Example:

882 is a multiple of 9 because $882 \div 9 = 98$, which is an integer, and because its digit sum $(8 + 8 + 2 = 18)$ is a multiple of 9.

- If an integer is a multiple of 10, it ends in 0.

Remainders

A remainder is a whole number "left over" when one whole number is divided by another whole number a whole number of times.

Think about giving balloons to kids: you can only have a whole number of balloons, a whole number of kids, and you can't give any kid a fraction of a balloon. If you try to divide 34 balloons among 4 kids, each kid can get 8 balloons, but then you will have 2 balloons "left over." This is your remainder.

To find a remainder with a calculator, divide the two whole numbers on your calculator, then multiply the "decimal part" of the result by the divisor.

Example:

What is the remainder when 34 is divided by 5?
$34 \div 5 = 6.8$ and $.8 \times 5 = 4$

Remainders can be very useful in solving SAT "pattern" problems.

Example:

What is the 50th term in this sequence? 7, 9, 3, 1, 7, 9, 3, 1, . . .

The pattern repeats every four terms. The remainder when 50 is divided by 4 is 2, so the 50th term is the same as the 2nd term, which is 9.

Primes, Evens, and Odds

- A **prime number** is any integer greater than 1 that is divisible only by 1 and itself (like 2, 3, 5, 7, 11, 13, 17, . . .).
- An **even number** is any multiple of 2. It can always be expressed as $2n$, where n is some integer. e.g., $28 = 2(14)$
- An **odd number** is any integer that is not a multiple of 2. Any odd number can be expressed as $2n + 1$, where n is some integer. e.g., $37 = 2(18) + 1$.

Be careful not to confuse *odd* with *negative* (and *even* with *positive*). Students commonly do this because *odd* and *negative* are "bad" words and *even* and *positive* are "good" words. To avoid this mistake, pay special attention to the words *odd, even, negative,* and *positive* by underlining them when you see them in problems.

Concept Review 7: Divisibility

1. What is a prime number? _____

2. What is a remainder? _____
_____

3. An odd number is _____
and can always be expressed as _____.

4. What can you do to avoid confusing *odd* with *negative* or *even* with *positive*? _____
_____

5. How do you find a remainder with your calculator? _____
_____

6. If an integer is divisible by k, 12, and 35, and k is a prime number greater than 7, then the integer must also be divisible by which of the following? (Circle all that apply.)

   $3k$ $5k^2$ 10   24 $28k$ $k+12$ 2 $35k$

7. When a whole number is divided by 7, what are the possible remainders? _____

8. What is the 100th term of this sequence? 3, 5, 7, 3, 5, 7, . . .   8. _____

9. What is the remainder when 357 is divided by 4?   9. _____

10. When x apples are divided equally among 7 baskets, one apple remains.   10. _____
When those apples are divided equally among 9 baskets, one apple remains.
If x is greater than 1 but less than 100, what is x?

$$1, 2, 2, 1, . . .$$

11. In the sequence above, every term from the third onward is the quotient   11. _____
of the previous term divided by the next previous term. For instance, the
7th term is equal to the quotient of the 6th term divided by the 5th term.
What is the 65th term of this sequence?

12. When an odd number is divided by 2, the remainder is always _____.

13. How many multiples of 6 between 1 and 100 are also multiples of 9?   13. _____

14. How many multiples of 6 between 1 and 100 are also prime?   14. _____

15. If z is an integer, which of the following must be odd? (Circle all that apply.)

   $5z$ $4z-1$ $7z+2$ z^2 z^2+1 z^3 $\dfrac{z}{2}$ z^2+z+1

16. If a divided by b leaves a remainder of r, then a must be _____ greater than a multiple of _____.

SAT Practice 7: Divisibility

1. When an integer n is divided by 10, the remainder is 7. What is the remainder when n is divided by 5?

2. When 8 is divided by 12, the remainder is

   (A) $\dfrac{1}{3}$ (B) $\dfrac{2}{3}$ (C) 4

   (D) 8   (E) 12

3. If p is odd and q is even, then which of the following must be an odd number?

   I. $p^2 + q^2$

   II. $\dfrac{p^2}{q^2}$

   III. $p^2 q^2$

   (A) none   (B) I only
   (C) I and II only   (D) I and III only
   (E) I, II, and III

4.   1, 3, 5, 7, 9, 1, 3, 5, 7, 9, 1, ...

   If the sequence above follows the pattern shown, what is the 103rd term of the sequence?

   (A) 1   (B) 3   (C) 5
   (D) 7   (E) 9

5. $\begin{array}{r} 0 \text{ remainder } 3 \\ a\overline{)b} \end{array}$

   In the division problem shown above, if a and b are positive, which of the following must be true?

   (A) $a = 3$ (B) $a = 3b$ (C) $b = 0$
   (D) $b = 3$ (E) $b = 3a$

6. Which of the following is a counterexample to the statement: *All prime numbers are odd?*

   (A) 2   (B) 3   (C) 9
   (D) 11   (E) 12

7. If $\dfrac{k}{7}$ and $\dfrac{k}{12}$ are both positive integers, then which of the following must also be an integer?

   (A) $\dfrac{k}{42}$ (B) $\dfrac{k}{24}$ (C) $\dfrac{k}{19}$

   (D) $\dfrac{k}{15}$ (E) $\dfrac{k}{10}$

8. If $a, b, c, d,$ and e are consecutive integers, then which of the following statements must be true?

   I. This set contains 3 odd numbers.
   II. This set contains a number divisible by 5.
   III. $bc + 1$ is odd.

   (A) I only   (B) II only
   (C) I and II only   (D) II and III only
   (E) I, II, and III

9. m and n are positive integers. If m is divided by n, the quotient is 7 with a remainder of 4. Which of the following expresses m in terms of n?

   (A) $4n - 7$ (B) $7n - 4$ (C) $4n + 7$

   (D) $\dfrac{n}{7} + 4$ (E) $7n + 4$

10. If a and b are positive integers and $\dfrac{a}{b} = 2.5$, then which of the following must be true?

    I. $(a + b)$ is odd
    II. $(a + b)$ is a multiple of 7

    III. $\dfrac{5b}{a}$ is an integer

    (A) II only   (B) I and III only
    (C) I and II only   (D) II and III only
    (E) I, II, and III

Answer Key 7: Divisibility

Concept Review 7

1. Any integer greater than 1 that is divisible only by 1 and itself.

2. The whole number "left over" when one whole number is divided by another whole number a whole number of times.

3. Any integer that is not divisible by 2. $2n + 1$.

4. Underline and think about those words when you see them in problems.

5. Divide the two integers, then multiply the decimal part of the result by the divisor (the number you divided by).

6. The least common multiple of k, 12, and 35 is $420k$, which is divisible by $3k$, 10, $28k$, 2, and $35k$.

7. 0, 1, 2, 3, 4, 5, and 6.

8. 3.   The pattern is 3 terms long, and 3 divided by 100 has a remainder of 1, so the 100th term is the same as the 1st.

9. 1.

10. 64. The number must be 1 greater than both a multiple of 7 and a multiple of 9. The only multiple

of 7 and 9 that is between 1 and 100 is 63, and $63 + 1 = 64$.

11. 1/2. The sequence is
1, 2, 2, 1, 1/2, 1/2, 1, 2, 2, 1, 1/2, 1/2, . . . , so the pattern is 6 terms long. 65 divided by 6 leaves a remainder of 5, so the 65th term is the same as the 5th, which is 1/2.

12. 1.

13. 5. The least common multiple of 6 and 9 is 18, and $100 \div 18 = 5.555 . . .$, which means that there are 5 multiples of 18 between 1 and 100.

14. None.   Prime numbers are divisible only by themselves and 1, but any multiple of 6 must also be divisible by 2 and 3.

15. $4z - 1$ and $z^2 + z + 1$ are the only expressions that must be odd. Since 4 is even, $4z$ is even, so $4z - 1$ must be odd. $z^2 + z + 1 = z(z + 1) + 1$, and since either z or $z + 1$ must be even, $z(z + 1)$ is even and $z(z + 1) + 1$ is odd.

16. If a divided by b leaves a remainder of r, then a must be r greater than a multiple of b.

SAT Practice 7

1. **2**   Since n leaves a remainder of 7 when divided by 10, it must be 7 more than a multiple of 10, like 7, 17, 27, etc. When any of these is divided by 5, the remainder is 2.

2. **D**   Don't confuse remainder with quotient. Remember to think of balloons and kids. If you had 8 balloons to divide among 12 kids, you'd have to keep all 8 balloons because there aren't enough to go around fairly. Also, you can use the calculator method, and divide 8 by 12, then multiply the decimal part of the result by 12.

3. **B**   Using $p = 1$ and $q = 2$ rules out II (1/4 is not an integer, let alone an odd number) and III (4 is even). $p^2 + q^2$ will always be odd, because the square of an odd is always odd and the square of an even is always even, and an odd plus an even is always odd.

4. **C**   The sequence that repeats is 5 terms long. 103 divided by 5 leaves a remainder of 3, so the 103rd term is the same as the 3rd term, which is 5.

5. **D**   For the statement to be correct, $b = a(0) + 3$, so $b = 3$.

6. **A**   A counterexample to the statement *All prime numbers are odd* would be a prime number that is not odd. The only even prime number is 2.

7. **A**   If $k/7$ and $k/12$ are both positive integers, then k must be a common multiple of 7 and 12. The least common multiple of 7 and 12 is 84. If we substitute 84 for k, (A) is the only choice that yields an integer.

8. **D**   Using the example of 2, 3, 4, 5, 6 disproves statement I. Since multiples of 5 occur every 5 consecutive integers, II must be true (remember that 0 is a multiple of every integer, including 5). Since bc will always be an even times an odd or an odd times an even, the result must always be even, so $bc + 1$ must be odd.

9. **E**   You might simplify this problem by picking values for m and n that work, like 46 and 6. (When 46 is divided by 6, the quotient is 7 with a remainder of 4.) If we substitute 6 for n, choice (E) is the only one that yields 46.

10. **D**   Using $a = 10$ and $b = 4$ disproves statement I. If a/b equals 5/2 and a and b are both integers, then $a = 5k$ and $b = 2k$, where k is an integer. Therefore $a + b = 7k$, so II is true. Also, since a/b equals 5/2, $b/a = 2/5$, so $5b/a = 10/5 = 2$, which is an integer, so III is true.

CHAPTER 8

ESSENTIAL ALGEBRA I SKILLS

Lesson 1: Solving Equations

Equations as Balanced Scales

Algebra is really common sense once you start thinking of every equation as a balanced scale. The terms on either side of the equals sign must be "balanced," just like the weights on a scale.

> The laws of equations come from the common-sense rules for keeping a scale balanced. Imagine that you are the keeper of a scale, and you must keep it balanced. What would you do if someone took weights from one side of the scale? You'd remove an equal weight from the other side, of course. This is a law of equality: anything you do to one side of the equation, you must do to the other to maintain the balance.

Example:

If $12x - 8 = 28$, then what is the value of $3x - 2$?

Don't worry about solving for x, because that's not what the question is asking for. Notice that the expression you are given, $12x - 8$, is 4 times the expression you are looking for, $3x - 2$. So to turn the given expression into the one you want, divide by 4. Of course, you must do the same to the other side to keep the balance:

$$\frac{12x - 8}{4} = \frac{28}{4} \longrightarrow 3x - 2 = 7$$

Solving as Unwrapping

Solving simple algebraic equations is basically the same thing as unwrapping a present. (And it's just as fun, too, right? Okay, maybe not.) Wrapping a present involves a sequence of steps: 1. Put the gift in the box. 2. Close the box. 3. Wrap the paper around the box. 4. Put the bow on. Here's the important part: unwrapping the present just means **inverting** those steps and **reversing** their order: 1. **Take off** the bow. 2. **Unwrap** the paper. 3. **Open** the box. 4. **Take out** the gift.

Example:

Solve for x: $5x^2 - 9 = 31$

The problem is that x is not alone on the left side; it is "wrapped up" like a gift. How is it wrapped? Think of the order of operations for turning x into $5x^2 - 9$:

1. Square it: x^2
2. Multiply by 5: $5x^2$
3. Subtract 9: $5x^2 - 9$

So to "unwrap" it, you **reverse** and **invert** the steps:

1. Add 9: $(5x^2 - 9) + 9 = 5x^2$
2. Divide by 5: $5x^2/5 = x^2$
3. Find the square roots (both of them!): $\pm\sqrt{x^2} = \pm|x|$

If you perform these steps to both sides, $5x^2 - 9 = 31$ transforms into $x = \pm\sqrt{8}$.

Watch Your Steps

To solve that last equation, we had to perform three operations. Many equations, as you probably know, require more steps to solve. It is very important that you keep track of your steps so that you can check your work if you need to. In other words, the equation we just solved should really look like this on your scratch paper:

$$5x^2 - 9 = 31$$

Step 1 (Add 9) :
$$\frac{+9 \quad +9}{5x^2 = 40}$$

Step 2 (Divide by 5):
$$\frac{5x^2}{5} = \frac{40}{5}$$

Step 3 (Simplify):
$$x^2 = 8$$

Step 4 (Square root):
$$x = \pm\sqrt{8}$$

Check by Plugging Back In

> Always check your answer by plugging it back into the original equation to see if it works. Remember that solving an equation means simply finding the value of each unknown that makes the equation true.

Example:

Are $\pm\sqrt{8}$ solutions to $5x^2 - 9 = 31$? Plug them in:

$$5\left(\pm\sqrt{8}\right)^2 - 9 = 5(8) - 9 = 40 - 9 = 31 \text{ (Yes!)}$$

There's a lot of detail to learn and understand to do well on the SAT. For more tools and resources that will help, visit our Online Practice Plus at www.MHPracticePlus.com/SATmath.

Concept Review 1: Solving Equations

1. Explain the laws of equality.

2. Are there any operations you can perform to both sides of an equation that will *not yield* a true equation? Explain.

Show your steps and check your work in solving the following equations.

3. $9x - 12 + 5x = 3x$

4. $(x - 4)^2 = 5$

5. $\dfrac{2x^2}{3} = x^2$

6. $\dfrac{x+2}{3} = \dfrac{x-5}{2}$

Solve the following equations for the given expression by performing *one operation* on both sides.

7. If $\dfrac{5x}{2} + 3 = 7$, then $10x + 12 =$ _____   Operation: _____   Solution: _____

8. If $18y + 12 = 7$, then $6y + 4 =$ _____   Operation: _____   Solution: _____

SAT Practice 1: Solving Equations

1. If $5d + 12 = 24$, then $5d - 12 =$

   (A) -24 (B) -12 (C) 0
   (D) 12 (E) 24

2. What number decreased by 7 equals 5 times the number?

   (A) $-\dfrac{7}{4}$ (B) $-\dfrac{7}{5}$ (C) $-\dfrac{5}{7}$

   (D) $-\dfrac{4}{7}$ (E) $\dfrac{4}{7}$

3. If $\dfrac{2y^2}{5} = y^2$, then $y + 5 =$

4. If $2x^2 - 5x = 9$, then $12x^2 - 30x =$

   (A) -54 (B) -6 (C) 18
   (D) 36 (E) 54

$$(p + 2)^2 = (p - 5)^2$$

5. The equation above is true for which of the following values of p?

   (A) -2 and 5
   (B) 2 and -5
   (C) 0 and 1
   (D) 1.5 only
   (E) 3.5 only

6. If $\dfrac{5}{x} + \dfrac{7}{5} = 1$, what is the value of x?

   (A) $-\dfrac{25}{2}$ (B) -7 (C) $-\dfrac{24}{7}$

   (D) $-\dfrac{7}{5}$ (E) 7

7. The product of x and y is 36. If both x and y are integers, then what is the least possible value of $x - y$?

   (A) -37 (B) -36 (C) -35
   (D) -9 (E) -6

8. The graph of $y = f(x)$ contains the points $(-1, 7)$ and $(1, 3)$. Which of the following could be $f(x)$?

   I. $f(x) = |5x - 2|$
   II. $f(x) = x^2 - 2x + 4$
   III. $f(x) = -2x + 5$

   (A) I only   (B) I and II only
   (C) I and III only   (D) II and III only
   (E) I, II, and III

9. If $20 - \sqrt{x} = 11$, which of the following gives all possible values of x?

   (A) 9 only   (B) -9 and 9
   (C) 81 only   (D) 81 and -81
   (E) 961

10. For all positive values of m and n,
    if $\dfrac{3x}{m - nx} = 2$, then $x =$

    (A) $\dfrac{2m - 2n}{3}$ (B) $\dfrac{2m - 3}{2n}$

    (C) $\dfrac{3 + 2n}{2m}$ (D) $\dfrac{2m}{3 + 2n}$

    (E) $\dfrac{3}{2m - 2n}$

Answer Key 1: Solving Equations

Concept Review 1

1. The laws of equality say that whatever you do to one side of an equation you must do to the other side, to maintain the balance.

2. Yes. Dividing by 0 and taking the square root of a negative number are "undefined" operations in the real numbers. Be careful, then, when dividing both sides of an equation by an unknown, to check that the unknown could not possibly be 0.

3. $9x - 12 + 5x = 3x$

   Commutative law: $14x - 12 = 3x$
   Add 12, subtract $3x$: $11x = 12$
   Divide by 11: $x = 12/11$

4. $(x - 4)^2 = 5$

   Take square root: $x - 4 = \pm\sqrt{5}$

   Add 4: $x = 4 \pm \sqrt{5}$

5. $\dfrac{2x^2}{3} = x^2$

   Multiply by 3: $2x^2 = 3x^2$
   Subtract $2x^2$: $0 = x^2$
   Take square root: $0 = x$

6. $\dfrac{x+2}{3} = \dfrac{x-5}{2}$

   Cross-multiply: $2x + 4 = 3x - 15$
   Subtract $2x$: $4 = x - 15$
   Add 15: $19 = x$

7. Operation: Multiply both sides by 4
   Solution: $10x + 12 = 28$

8. Operation: Divide both sides by 3
   Solution: $6y + 4 = 7/3$

SAT Practice 1

1. **C** $5d + 12 = 24$
   Subtract 24: $5d - 12 = 0$

2. **A** Translate into an equation: $x - 7 = 5x$
   Subtract x: $-7 = 4x$
   Divide by 4: $-7/4 = x$
   You can also "test" the choices and see which one works, but that's probably more time-consuming.

3. **5** It's easiest to solve the equation for y, then add 5

$$\frac{2y^2}{5} = y^2$$

   Multiply by 5: $2y^2 = 5y^2$
   Subtract $2y^2$: $0 = 3y^2$
   Divide by 3: $0 = y^2$
   Take the square root: $0 = y$
   Add 5: $5 = y + 5$

4. **E** $2x^2 - 5x = 9$
   Multiply by 6: $12x^2 - 30x = 54$

5. **D** Plugging in and checking is perhaps easiest here, but you could do the algebra too:

$$(p + 2)^2 = (p - 5)^2$$

   FOIL: $p^2 + 4p + 4 = p^2 - 10p + 25$
   Subtract p^2: $4p + 4 = -10p + 25$
   Subtract 4: $4p = -10p + 21$
   Add $10p$: $14p = 21$
   Divide by 14: $p = 1.5$

6. **A** $\dfrac{5}{x} + \dfrac{7}{5} = 1$

   Multiply by $5x$: $25 + 7x = 5x$
   Subtract $7x$: $25 = -2x$
   Divide by -2: $-25/2 = x$

7. **C** Guess and check here. If $x = -36$ and $y = -1$, or $x = 1$ and $y = 36$, then $x - y = -35$.

8. **E** Just plug in the points $(-1, 7)$ and $(1, 3)$ to the equations, and confirm that the points "satisfy" all three equations.

9. **C** $20 - \sqrt{x} = 11$
   Subtract 20: $-\sqrt{x} = -9$
   Multiply by -1: $\sqrt{x} = 9$
   Square both sides: $x = 81$

10. **D** $\dfrac{3x}{m - nx} = 2$

   Multiply by $m - nx$: $3x = 2(m - nx)$
   Distribute on right: $3x = 2m - 2nx$
   Add $2nx$: $3x + 2nx = 2m$
   Factor left side: $x(3 + 2n) = 2m$

   Divide by $(3 + 2n)$: $x = \dfrac{2m}{3 + 2n}$

Lesson 2: Systems

Systems

A system is simply a set of equations that are true at the same time, such as these:

$$3x - 2y = 12$$
$$x + 3y = 15$$

Although many values for x and y "satisfy" the first equation, like (4, 0) and (2, –3) (plug them in and check!), there is only one solution that works in *both* equations: (6, 3). (Plug this into both equations and check!)

The Law of Substitution

The **law of substitution** simply says that if two things are equal, you can always substitute one for the other.

Example:

$$\begin{cases} 3x + y^2 = 7 \\ y = x + 1 \end{cases}$$

The easiest way to solve this is to *substitute* the second equation (which is already "solved" for y) into the first, so that you *eliminate* one of the unknowns. Since $y = x + 1$, you can replace the y in the first equation with $x + 1$ and get

$$3x + (x + 1)^2 = 7$$

FOIL the squared binomial: $\quad 3x + x^2 + 2x + 1 = 7$
Combine like terms: $\qquad\qquad x^2 + 5x + 1 = 7$
Subtract 7: $\qquad\qquad\qquad x^2 + 5x - 6 = 0$
Factor the left side: $\qquad\quad (x + 6)(x - 1) = 0$
Apply the Zero Product Property: $\quad x = -6$ or $x = 1$
Plug values back into 2nd equation:

$$y = (-6) + 1 = -5$$
$$\text{or } y = (1) + 1 = 2$$

Solutions: (–6, –5) and (1, 2) (Check!)

Combining Equations

If the two equations in the system are alike enough, you can sometimes solve them more easily by combining equations. The idea is simple: if you add or subtract the corresponding sides of two true equations together, the result should also be a true equation, because you are adding equal things to both sides. This strategy can be simpler than substitution.

Example:

$$\begin{cases} 2x - 5y = 7 \\ 3x + 5y = 23 \end{cases}$$

Adding the corresponding sides will eliminate the y's from the system

Add equations: $\quad 5x = 30$
Divide by 5: $\qquad x = 6$

Plug this back in and solve for y:

$$2(6) - 5y = 7$$
Simplify: $\qquad 12 - 5y = 7$
Subtract 12: $\qquad -5y = -5$
Divide by 5: $\qquad y = 1$

Special Kinds of "Solving"

Sometimes a question gives you a system, but rather than asking you to solve for each unknown, it simply asks you to evaluate another expression. Look carefully at what the question asks you to evaluate, and see whether there is a simple way of combining the equations (adding, subtracting, multiplying, dividing) to find the expression.

Example:

If $3x - 6y = 10$ and $4x + 2y = 2$, what is the value of $7x - 4y$?

Don't solve for x and y! Just notice that $7x - 4y$ equals $(3x - 6y) + (4x + 2y) = 10 + 2 = 12$.

"Letter-Heavy" Systems

An equation with more than one unknown, or a system with more unknowns than equations, is "letter-heavy." Simple equations and systems usually have just one solution, but these "letter-heavy" equations and systems usually have more than one solution, and you can often easily find solutions simply by "plugging in" values.

Example:

If $2m + 5n = 10$ and $m \neq 0$, then what is the value of $\dfrac{4m}{10 - 5n}$?

You can "guess and check" a solution to the equation pretty easily. Notice that $m = -5$, $n = 4$ works. If you plug these values into the expression you're evaluating, you'll see it simplifies to 2.

Concept Review 2: Systems

1. What is a system?

2. What are two algebraic methods for solving systems?

3. How do you check the solution of a system?

Solve the following systems by substitution, and check your solution.

4. $3x - 4y = 2$
    $x = y - 2$

5. $x^2 - 2y = 10$
    $y = 3x - 9$

6. $5m + 5 = 3n$

   $m = \dfrac{2}{5}n$

Solve the following systems by combination, and check your solution.

7. $a - b = 5$
    $a + b = 12$

8. $-3x - 5y = 20$
    $-3x - 4y = 14$

9. $\dfrac{x}{3} - \dfrac{y}{3} = -9$

   $\dfrac{x}{4} + \dfrac{y}{3} = 2$

Give three different solutions to each of the following "letter-heavy" systems.

10. $2x + 5y = 40$

11. $-2a + 5b + c = 10$
     $a + b = 7$

$x = $ _____ $y = $ _____

$x = $ _____ $y = $ _____

$x = $ _____ $y = $ _____

$a = $ _____ $b = $ _____ $c = $ _____

$a = $ _____ $b = $ _____ $c = $ _____

$a = $ _____ $b = $ _____ $c = $ _____

SAT Practice 2: Systems

1. If $3x + 2y = 72$ and $y = 3x$, then $x =$

   (A) 6
   (B) 7
   (C) 8
   (D) 9
   (E) 10

2. The difference of two numbers is 4 and their sum is −7. What is their product?

   (A) −33.0
   (B) −28.0
   (C) −10.25
   (D) 8.25
   (E) 10.5

3. If $4m - 7n = 10$ and $2m + 2n = 4$, what is the value of $2m - 9n$?

4. If $9p = 3a + 1$ and $7p = 2a - 3$, then which of the following expresses p in terms of a?

   (A) $\dfrac{3a+1}{7}$ (B) $\dfrac{2a-3}{9}$ (C) $\dfrac{2a}{63}$

   (D) $\dfrac{7a}{9}$ (E) $\dfrac{a+4}{2}$

5. The cost of one hamburger and two large sodas is $5.40. The cost of three hamburgers and one large soda is $8.70. What is the cost of one hamburger?

   (A) $1.50   (B) $1.95   (C) $2.40
   (D) $2.50   (E) $2.75

6. If $m^6 = \dfrac{3}{y}$ and $m^5 = \dfrac{y^2}{6}$, then which of the following expresses m in terms of y?

   (A) $\dfrac{18}{y^3}$

   (B) $\dfrac{y^3}{18}$

   (C) $\dfrac{y}{2}$

   (D) $\dfrac{2}{y}$

   (E) $\dfrac{18 - y^3}{6y}$

7. The sum of two numbers is 5 and their difference is 2. Which of the following could be the difference of their squares?

   (A) −17
   (B) −3
   (C) 3
   (D) 10
   (E) 21

8. If $7x + 2y - 6z = 12$, and if x, y, and z are positive, then what is the value of $\dfrac{2+z}{7x+2y}$?

   (A) 1/12
   (B) 1/6
   (C) 1/4
   (D) 5/12
   (E) 7/12

9. If $\dfrac{a}{2b} = \dfrac{3}{5}$ and $\dfrac{4b}{3c} = \dfrac{1}{7}$, then $\dfrac{a}{c} =$

   (A) $\dfrac{2}{35}$ (B) $\dfrac{9}{70}$ (C) $\dfrac{8}{35}$

   (D) $\dfrac{17}{70}$ (E) $\dfrac{9}{35}$

Answer Key 2: Systems

Concept Review 2

1. Any set of equations that are true at the same time.

2. Substitution and combination.

3. Plug the solutions back into the equations and check that both equations are true.

4. $(-10, -8)$ Substitute: $3(y - 2) - 4y = 2$
           Distribute: $3y - 6 - 4y = 2$
           Combine: $-y - 6 = 2$
           Add 6: $-y = 8$
           Multiply by -1: $y = -8$
Plug in and solve for x: $x = y - 2 = (-8) - 2 = -10$

5. $(4, 3)$ and $(2, -3)$ Substitute: $x^2 - 2(3x - 9) = 10$
                      Distribute: $x^2 - 6x + 18 = 10$
                      Subtract 10: $x^2 - 6x + 8 = 0$
                      Factor: $(x - 4)(x - 2) = 0$
(Look over Lesson 5 if that step was tough!)
           Zero Product Property: $x = 4$ or $x = 2$

Plug in and solve for y: $y = 3x - 9 = 3(4) - 9 = 3$
                       or $= 3(2) - 9 = -3$
So the solutions are $x = 4$ and $y = 3$ or
                 $x = 2$ and $y = -3$.

6. $(2, 5)$ Substitute: $5\left(\dfrac{2}{5}n\right) + 5 = 3n$
          Simplify: $2n + 5 = 3n$
          Subtract $2n$: $5 = n$

   Plug in to find m: $m = \dfrac{2}{5}(5) = 2$

7. $(8.5, 3.5)$ $a - b = 5$
                          $\underline{+a + b = 12}$
      Add the equations: $2a = 17$
      Divide by 2: $a = 8.5$
Plug in to find b: $(8.5) - b = 5$
      Subtract 8.5: $-b = -3.5$
      Multiply by -1: $b = 3.5$

8. $(10/3, -6)$ $-3x - 5y = 20$
                       $\underline{-(-3x - 4y = 14)}$
      Subtract the equations: $-y = 6$
      Multiply by -1: $y = -6$
Plug in to find x: $-3x - 5(-6) = 20$
      Simplify: $-3x + 30 = 20$
      Subtract 30: $-3x = -10$
      Divide by -3: $x = 10/3$

9. $(-12, 15)$ Add the equations to get $\dfrac{x}{3} + \dfrac{x}{4} = -7$

      Combine fractions: $\dfrac{7x}{12} = -7$
      Multiply by 12: $7x = -84$
      Divide by 7: $x = -12$
Plug in and solve for y: $y = 15$

10. There are many solutions. Here are a few:
$(0, 8); (20, 0); (10, 4); (5, 6)$

11. There are many solutions. Here are a few:
$(1, 6, 0); (3, 4, -4); (2, 5, 31); (7, 0, 24)$

SAT Practice 2

1. **C**   Substitute: $3x + 2(3x) = 72$
     Simplify: $9x = 72$
     Divide by 9: $x = 8$

2. **D**   Translate into equations: $x - y = 4$
                            $\underline{x + y = -7}$
     Add the equations: $2x = -3$
     Divide by 2: $x = -1.5$
     Substitute: $-1.5 + y = -7$
     Add 1.5: $y = -5.5$
               $(-1.5)(-5.5) = 8.25$

3. **6**   Subtract them:
        $2m - 9n = (4m - 7n) - (2m + 2n)$
                $= 10 - 4 = 6$

4. **E**   Subtracting gives $2p = a + 4$
     Divide by 2: $p = (a + 4)/2$

5. **C**   Translate: $h + 2s = 5.40$
                      $3h + s = 8.70$
    Multiply 2nd eq. by 2: $6h + 2s = 17.40$
                      $\underline{-(h + 2s = 5.40)}$
    Subtract 1st equation: $5h = 12.00$
    Divide by 5: $h = 2.40$

6. **A**   Divide the first equation by the second:

$$\frac{m^6}{m^5} = \frac{3}{y} \div \frac{y^2}{6}$$

    Simplify: $m = \dfrac{3}{y} \times \dfrac{6}{y^2} = \dfrac{18}{y^3}$

7. **D**   Translate: $x + y = 5$ and $x - y = 2$

Although you could solve this system by combining, it's easier to remember the "difference of squares" factoring formula:
$x^2 - y^2 = (x + y)(x - y) = (5)(2) = 10$

8. **B** This is "letter-heavy," so you can guess and check a solution, like (2, 11, 4), and evaluate the expression: $\dfrac{2+(4)}{7(2)+2(11)} = \dfrac{6}{36} = \dfrac{1}{6}$. Or you can also just add $6z$ to both sides of the equation to get $7x + 2y = 12 + 6z$, then substitute:

$$\frac{2+z}{7x+2y} = \frac{2+z}{(12+6z)} = \frac{2+z}{6(2+z)} = \frac{1}{6}$$

9. **B** Multiply the equations:

$$\left(\frac{a}{2b}\right)\left(\frac{4b}{3c}\right) = \frac{2a}{3c} = \left(\frac{3}{5}\right)\left(\frac{1}{7}\right) = \frac{3}{35}$$

Multiply by $\dfrac{3}{2}$: $\dfrac{a}{c} = \dfrac{3}{35}\left(\dfrac{3}{2}\right) = \dfrac{9}{70}$

Lesson 3: Working with Exponentials

What Are Exponentials?

An **exponential** is simply any term with these three parts:

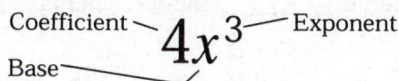

$$\text{Coefficient} \diagdown \underset{\overset{\diagup}{\text{Base}}}{4x^3} \diagup \text{Exponent}$$

If a term seems not to have a coefficient or exponent, the coefficient or exponent is always assumed to be 1!

Examples:

$2x$ means $2x^1$ y^3 means $1y^3$

Expand to Understand

Good students memorize the rules for working with exponentials, but great students understand where the rules come from. They come from simply expanding the exponentials and then collecting or cancelling the factors.

Example:

What is $(x^5)^2$ in simplest terms? Do you *add* exponents to get x^7? *Multiply* to get x^{10}? *Power* to get x^{25}?

The answer is clear when you expand the exponential. Just remember that *raising to the nth power* simply means *multiplying by itself n times.* So $(x^5)^2 = (x^5)(x^5) = (x\cdot x\cdot x\cdot x\cdot x)(x\cdot x\cdot x\cdot x\cdot x) = x^{10}$. Doing this helps you to see and understand the rule of "multiplying the powers."

Adding and Subtracting Exponentials

When adding or subtracting exponentials, you can combine only like terms, that is, terms with the same base and the same exponent. When adding or subtracting like exponentials, remember to leave the bases and exponents alone.

Example:

$5x^3 + 6x^3 + 4x^2 = (5x^3 + 6x^3) + 4x^2 = x^3(5 + 6) + 4x^2 = 11x^3 + 4x^2$

Notice that combining like terms always involves the Law of Distribution (Chapter 7, Lesson 2).

Multiplying and Dividing Exponentials

You can simplify a **product** or **quotient** of exponentials when the bases are the same or the exponents are the same.

If the bases are the same, add the exponents (when multiplying) or subtract the exponents (when dividing) and leave the bases alone.

$$(5m^5)(12m^2) = (5)(m)(m)(m)(m)(m)(12)(m)(m)$$
$$= (5)(12)(m)(m)(m)(m)(m)(m)(m)$$
$$= 60m^7$$

$$\frac{6p^7}{3p^4} = \frac{6(p)(p)(p)(\cancel{p})(\cancel{p})(\cancel{p})(\cancel{p})}{3(\cancel{p})(\cancel{p})(\cancel{p})(\cancel{p})} = 2p^3$$

If the exponents are the same, multiply (or divide) the bases and leave the exponents alone.

Example:

$$(3m^4)(7n^4) = (3)(m)(m)(m)(m)(7)(n)(n)(n)(n)$$
$$= (3)(7)(mn)(mn)(mn)(mn)$$
$$= 21(mn)^4$$

$$\frac{5(12)^5}{(3)^5} = \frac{5(12)(12)(12)(12)(12)}{(3)(3)(3)(3)(3)}$$

$$= 5\left(\frac{12}{3}\right)\left(\frac{12}{3}\right)\left(\frac{12}{3}\right)\left(\frac{12}{3}\right)\left(\frac{12}{3}\right)$$

$$= 5(4)^5$$

Raising Exponentials to Powers

When raising an exponential to a power, multiply the exponents, but don't forget to raise the coefficient to the power and leave the base alone.

Example:

$$(3y^4)^3 = (3y^4)(3y^4)(3y^4)$$
$$= (3y\cdot y\cdot y\cdot y)(3y\cdot y\cdot y\cdot y)(3y\cdot y\cdot y\cdot y)$$
$$= (3)(3)(3)(y\cdot y\cdot y\cdot y)(y\cdot y\cdot y\cdot y)(y\cdot y\cdot y\cdot y)$$
$$= 27y^{12}$$

Concept Review 3: Working with Exponentials

1. The three parts of an exponential are the _____, _____, and _____.

2. When multiplying two exponentials *with the same base,* you should _____ the coefficients, _____ the bases, and _____ the exponents.

3. When dividing two exponentials *with the same exponent,* you should _____ the coefficients, _____ the bases, and _____ the exponents.

4. When multiplying two exponentials *with the same exponent,* you should _____ the coefficients, _____ the bases, and _____ the exponents.

5. When dividing two exponentials *with the same base,* you should _____ the coefficients, _____ the bases, and _____ the exponents.

6. To raise an exponential to a power, you should _____ the coefficient, _____ the base, and _____ the exponents.

Complete the tables:

	coefficient	base	exponent
7. -4^x			
9. xy^{-4}			

	coefficient	base	exponent
8. $(xy)^{-4}$			
10. $(3x)^9$			

Simplify, if possible.

11. $x^2y - 9x^2y =$ _____

12. $4x^3 + 2x^5 + 2x^3 =$ _____

13. $[(2)^{85} + (3)^{85}] + [(2)^{85} - (3)^{85}] =$ _____

14. $(3)^{2y}(5)^{2y} =$ _____

15. $6(29)^{32} \div 2(29)^{12} =$ _____

16. $18(6x)^m \div 9(2x)^m =$ _____

17. $(2x)^{m+1}(2x^2)^m =$ _____

18. $(3x^3(8)^2)^3 =$ _____

19. $(x^3 + y^5)^2 =$ _____

SAT Practice 3: Working with Exponentials

1. If $g = -4.1$, then $\dfrac{-3g^2}{(-3g)^2} =$

   (A) -1

   (B) $-\dfrac{1}{3}$

   (C) $-\dfrac{1}{9}$

   (D) $\dfrac{1}{3}$

   (E) 1

2. If $(200)(4{,}000) = 8 \times 10^m$, then $m =$

   (A) 2
   (B) 3
   (C) 4
   (D) 5
   (E) 6

3. If $2a^2 + 3a - 5a^2 = 9$, then $a - a^2 =$

   (A) 1
   (B) 3
   (C) 6
   (D) 9
   (E) 12

4. If $2^x = 10$, then $2^{2x} =$

   (A) 20
   (B) 40
   (C) 80
   (D) 100
   (E) 200

5. If $5^x = y$ and x is positive, which of the following equals $5y^2$ in terms of x?

   (A) 5^{2x}
   (B) 5^{2x+1}
   (C) 25^{2x}
   (D) 125^{2x}
   (E) 125^{2x+1}

6. If $9^x = 25$, then $3^{x-1} =$

7. If $p = \dfrac{3n}{m^3}$, then what is the effect on the value of p when n is multiplied by 4 and m is doubled?

   (A) p is unchanged.
   (B) p is halved.
   (C) p is doubled.
   (D) p is multiplied by 4.
   (E) p is multiplied by 8.

8. For all real numbers n, $\dfrac{2^n \times 2^n}{2^n \times 2} =$

   (A) 2

   (B) 2^n

   (C) 2^{n-1}

   (D) $\dfrac{n^2}{n+1}$

   (E) $\dfrac{2n}{n+1}$

9. If m is a positive integer, then which of the following is equivalent to $3^m + 3^m + 3^m$?

   (A) 3^{m+1}
   (B) 3^{3m}
   (C) 3^{3m+1}
   (D) 9^m
   (E) 9^{3m}

Answer Key 3: Working with Exponentials

Concept Review 3

1. coefficient, base, and exponent

2. *multiply* the coefficients, *keep* the bases, and *add* the exponents.

3. *divide* the coefficients, *divide* the bases, and *keep* the exponents.

4. *multiply* the coefficients, *multiply* the bases, and *keep* the exponents.

5. *divide* the coefficients, *keep* the bases, and *subtract* the exponents.

6. *raise* the coefficient (to the power), *keep* the base, and *multiply* the exponents.

7. -4^x coefficient: -1; base: 4; exponent: x

8. $(xy)^{-4}$ coefficient: 1; base: xy; exponent: -4

9. xy^{-4} coefficient: x; base: y; exponent: -4

10. $(3x)^9$ coefficient: 1; base: $3x$; exponent: 9

11. $x^2y - 9x^2y = -8x^2y$

12. $4x^3 + 2x^5 + 2x^3 = (4x^3 + 2x^3) + 2x^5 = 6x^3 + 2x^5$

13. $[(2)^{85} + (3)^{85}] + [(2)^{85} - (3)^{85}] = 2(2)^{85} = (2)^{86}$

14. $(3)^{2y}(5)^{2y} = (15)^{2y}$

15. $6(29)^{32} \div 2(29)^{12} = (6/2)(29)^{32-12} = 3(29)^{20}$

16. $18(6x)^m \div 9(2x)^m = (18/9)(6x/2x)^m = 2(3)^m$

17. $(2x)^{m+1}(2x^2)^m = (2^{m+1})(x^{m+1})(2^m)(x^{2m}) = (2^{2m+1})(x^{3m+1})$

18. $(3x^3(8)^2)^3 = (3)^3(x^3)^3((8)^2)^3 = 27x^9(8)^6$

19. $(x^3 + y^5)^2 = (x^3 + y^5)(x^3 + y^5) = (x^3)^2 + 2x^3y^5 + (y^5)^2 = x^6 + 2x^3y^5 + y^{10}$

SAT Practice 3

1. **B** You don't need to plug in $g = -4.1$. Just simplify:

If $g \neq 0$, $\dfrac{-3g^2}{(-3g)^2} = \dfrac{-3g^2}{9g^2} = -\dfrac{1}{3}$

2. **D** $(200)(4,000) = 800,000 = 8 \times 10^5$

3. **B**

	$2a^2 + 3a - 5a^2 = 9$
Regroup:	$3a + (2a^2 - 5a^2) = 9$
Simplify:	$3a - 3a^2 = 9$
Factor:	$3(a - a^2) = 9$
Divide by 3:	$a - a^2 = 3$

4. **D**

	$2^x = 10$
Square both sides:	$(2^x)^2 = 10^2$
Simplify:	$2^{2x} = 100$

5. **B**

	$5^x = y$
Square both sides:	$(5^x)^2 = y^2$
Simplify:	$5^{2x} = y^2$
Multiply by 5:	$5(5^{2x}) = 5y^2$
"Missing" exponents = 1:	$5^1(5^{2x}) = 5y^2$
Simplify:	$5^{2x+1} = 5y^2$

6. **5/3 or 1.66 or 1.67**

	$9^x = 25$
Take square root:	$\sqrt{9^x} = \sqrt{9}^x = \sqrt{25}$
Simplify:	$3^x = 5$
Divide by 3:	$3^x \div 3^1 = 5/3$
Simplify:	$3^{x-1} = 5/3 = 1.66$

7. **B** Begin by assuming $n = m = 1$.

Then $p = \dfrac{3n}{m^3} = \dfrac{3(1)}{(1)^3} = 3$.

If n is multiplied by 4 and m is doubled, then $n = 4$ and $m = 2$, so $p = \dfrac{3n}{m^3} = \dfrac{3(4)}{(2)^3} = \dfrac{12}{8} = \dfrac{3}{2}$, which is half of the original value.

8. **C** (Remember that $2^n \times 2^n$ equals 2^{2n}, or 4^n, but *not* 4^{2n}!)

$$\dfrac{2^n \times 2^n}{2^n \times 2}$$

Cancel common factor 2^n: $\dfrac{2^n}{2}$

Simplify: 2^{n-1}

9. **A** $3^m + 3^m + 3^m = 3(3^m) = 3^1(3^m) = 3^{m+1}$

Lesson 4: Working with Roots

What Are Roots?

The Latin word *radix* means *root* (remember that *radishes* grow underground), so the word *radical* means *the root of a number* (or *a person who seeks to change a system "from the roots up"*). What does the root of a plant have to do with the root of a number?

Think of a square with an area of 9 square units sitting on the ground:

The bottom of the square is "rooted" to the ground, and it has a length of 3. So we say that 3 is the *square root* of 9!

> The square root of a number is what you must square to get the number.

All positive numbers have two square roots. For instance, the square roots of 9 are 3 and –3.

The radical symbol, $\sqrt{}$, however, means only the **non-negative** square root. So although the square root of 9 equals either 3 or –3, $\sqrt{9}$ equals only 3.

The number inside a radical is called a **radicand.**

Example:

If x^2 is equal to 9 or 16, then what is the least possible value of x^3?

x is the square root of 9 or 16, so it could be –3, 3, –4, or 4. Therefore, x^3 could be –27, 27, –64, or 64. The least of these, of course, is –64.

> Remember that $\sqrt{x^2}$ does not always equal x. It does, however, always equal $|x|$.

Example:

Simplify $\sqrt{\left(\dfrac{3x+1}{y}\right)^2}$.

Don't worry about squaring first, just remember the rule above. It simplifies to

$\left|\dfrac{3x+1}{y}\right|.$

Working with Roots

> Memorize the list of *perfect squares*: 4, 9, 16, 25, 36, 49, 64, 81, 100. This will make working with roots easier.

> To simplify a square root expression, factor any perfect squares from the radicand and simplify.

Example:

Simplify $3\sqrt{27}$.

$$3\sqrt{27} = 3\sqrt{9 \times 3} = 3\sqrt{9} \times \sqrt{3} = 3 \times 3 \times \sqrt{3} = 9\sqrt{3}$$

Simplify $\sqrt{m^2 + 10m + 25}$.

$$\sqrt{m^2 + 10m + 25} = \sqrt{(m+5)^2} = |m+5|$$

> When adding or subtracting roots, treat them like exponentials: combine only like terms— those with the same radicand.

Example:

Simplify $3\sqrt{7} + 5\sqrt{2} + 13\sqrt{7}$.

$$3\sqrt{7} + 5\sqrt{2} + 13\sqrt{7} = \left(3\sqrt{7} + 13\sqrt{7}\right) + 5\sqrt{2} = 16\sqrt{7} + 5\sqrt{2}$$

> When multiplying or dividing roots, multiply or divide the coefficients and radicands separately.

Example:

Simplify $\dfrac{8\sqrt{6}}{2\sqrt{2}}$.

$$\frac{8\sqrt{6}}{2\sqrt{2}} = \frac{8}{2}\sqrt{\frac{6}{2}} = 4\sqrt{3}$$

Simplify $5\sqrt{3x} \times 2\sqrt{5x^2}$.

$$5\sqrt{3x} \times 2\sqrt{5x^2} = (5 \times 2)\sqrt{3x \times 5x^2} = 10\sqrt{15x^3}$$

> You can also use the commutative and associative laws when simplifying expressions with radicals.

Example:

Simplify $\left(2\sqrt{5}\right)^3$.

$$\left(2\sqrt{5}\right)^3 = 2\sqrt{5} \times 2\sqrt{5} \times 2\sqrt{5} = (2 \times 2 \times 2)\left(\sqrt{5} \times \sqrt{5}\right) \times \sqrt{5}$$

$$= 8 \times 5 \times \sqrt{5} = 40\sqrt{5}$$

Concept Review 4: Working with Roots

1. List the first 10 perfect square integers greater than 1: _____

2. How can you tell whether two radicals are "like" terms?

3. An exponential is a perfect square only if its coefficient is _____ and its exponent is _____.

For questions 4–7, state whether each equation is true (T) or false (F). If it is false, rewrite the expression on the right side to correct it.

4. $2\left(3 \times \sqrt{x}\right) = 6\sqrt{2x}$ _____

5. $3\sqrt{2} + 5\sqrt{8} = 13\sqrt{2}$ _____

6. $\left(\sqrt{3x}\right)^5 = 9x^2\sqrt{3x}$ _____

7. $\sqrt{81x^2} = 9x$ _____

8. If $x^2 = 25$, then $x =$ _____ or _____.

9. If $x^2 = \sqrt{64^4}$ then $x =$ _____.

Simplify the following expressions, if possible.

10. $5\sqrt{7} - 8\sqrt{7} =$ _____

11. $\dfrac{6mn\sqrt{10m}}{3n\sqrt{5}} =$ _____

12. $\left(g\sqrt{5}\right)\left(g\sqrt{5}\right) =$ _____

13. $\left(2\sqrt{3}\right)^3 =$ _____

14. $5\sqrt{12} - 4\sqrt{27} =$ _____

15. $5\sqrt{52} =$ _____

16. $\sqrt{6} + \sqrt{3} =$ _____

17. $\left(3\sqrt{5}\right)\left(7\sqrt{2}\right) =$ _____

18. $\left(1 + \sqrt{2}\right)^2 =$ _____

19. $\dfrac{2\sqrt{2} + 4\sqrt{18}}{\sqrt{2}} =$ _____

SAT Practice 4: Working with Roots

1. The square root of a certain positive number is twice the number itself. What is the number?

   (A) $\dfrac{1}{8}$ (B) $\dfrac{1}{4}$ (C) $\dfrac{3}{8}$

   (D) $\dfrac{1}{2}$ (E) 1

2. If $\dfrac{1}{2}x < \sqrt{x} < x$, what is one possible value of x?

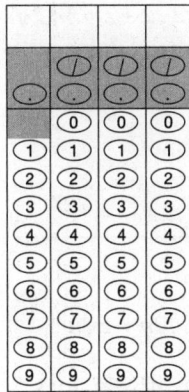

3. If $a^2 + 1 = 10$ and $b^2 - 1 = 15$, what is the greatest possible value of $a - b$?

   (A) −3   (B) −1   (C) 3
   (D) 5   (E) 7

4. If $3y = \sqrt{\dfrac{2}{y}}$, then $y^3 =$

   (A) $\dfrac{2}{9}$ (B) $\dfrac{4}{9}$ (C) $\dfrac{2}{3}$

   (D) $\dfrac{4}{3}$ (E) 18

5. If $x^2 = 4$, $y^2 = 9$, and $(x - 2)(y + 3) \neq 0$, then $x^3 + y^3 =$

   (A) −35   (B) −19   (C) 0
   (D) 19   (E) 35

6. If m and n are both positive, then which of the following is equivalent to $\dfrac{2m\sqrt{18n}}{m\sqrt{2}}$?

   (A) $3m\sqrt{n}$

   (B) $6m\sqrt{n}$

   (C) $4\sqrt{n}$

   (D) $6\sqrt{n}$

   (E) $8\sqrt{n}$

7. A rectangle has sides of length $\sqrt{a}$ cm and $\sqrt{b}$ cm. What is the length of a diagonal of the rectangle?

   (A) $\sqrt{a} + \sqrt{b}$ cm

   (B) $a + b$ cm

   (C) $\sqrt{a+b}$ cm

   (D) $\sqrt{a^2 + b^2}$ cm

   (E) $\sqrt{ab}$ cm

8. The area of square A is 10 times the area of square B. What is the ratio of the perimeter of square A to the perimeter of square B?

   (A) $\sqrt{10}:4$ (B) $\sqrt{10}:2$

   (C) $\sqrt{10}:1$ (D) $4\sqrt{10}:1$

   (E) 40:1

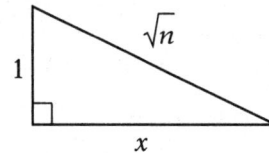

9. In the figure above, if n is a real number greater than 1, what is the value of x in terms of n?

   (A) $\sqrt{n^2 - 1}$

   (B) $\sqrt{n-1}$

   (C) $\sqrt{n+1}$

   (D) $n - 1$

   (E) $n + 1$

Answer Key 4: Working with Roots

Concept Review 4

1. 4, 9, 16, 25, 36, 49, 64, 81, 100, 121

2. They are "like" if their radicands (what's inside the radical) are the same.

3. An exponential is a perfect square only if its co-efficient is *a perfect square* and its exponent is *even*.

4. false: $2(3 \times \sqrt{x}) = 2 \times 3 \times \sqrt{x} = 6\sqrt{x}$

5. true: $3\sqrt{2} + 5\sqrt{8} = 3\sqrt{2} + 10\sqrt{2} = 13\sqrt{2}$

6. true: $\left(\sqrt{3x}\right)^5 = \left(\sqrt{3x}\right)^4 \left(\sqrt{3x}\right) = 9x^2\sqrt{3x}$

7. false if x is negative: $\sqrt{81x^2} = 9|x|$

8. 5 or –5

9. 64 or –64

10. $5\sqrt{7} - 8\sqrt{7} = -3\sqrt{7}$ (Law of Distribution)

11. $\dfrac{6mn\sqrt{10m}}{3n\sqrt{5}} = 2m\sqrt{2m}$

12. $\left(g\sqrt{5}\right)\left(g\sqrt{5}\right) = 5g^2$

13. $\left(2\sqrt{3}\right)^3 = 24\sqrt{3}$

14. $5\sqrt{12} - 4\sqrt{27} =$
    $5\sqrt{4} \times \sqrt{3} - 4\sqrt{9} \times \sqrt{3} = 10\sqrt{3} - 12\sqrt{3} = -2\sqrt{3}$

15. $5\sqrt{52} = 5\sqrt{4} \times \sqrt{13} = 10\sqrt{13}$

16. $\sqrt{6} + \sqrt{3}$ can't be simplified (unlike terms).

17. $\left(3\sqrt{5}\right)\left(7\sqrt{2}\right) = 21\sqrt{10}$

18. $\left(1 + \sqrt{2}\right)^2 = \left(1 + \sqrt{2}\right)\left(1 + \sqrt{2}\right) = 1 + 2\sqrt{2} + 2 = 3 + 2\sqrt{2}$

19. $\dfrac{2\sqrt{2} + 4\sqrt{18}}{\sqrt{2}} = 2 + 4\sqrt{9} = 2 + 4 \times 3 = 2 + 12 = 14$

SAT Practice 4

1. **B** The square root of ¼ is ½, because (½)² = ¼. Twice ¼ is also ½, because 2(¼) = ½. You can also set it up algebraically: $\sqrt{x} = 2x$

   Square both sides: $x = 4x^2$
   Divide by x (it's okay; x is positive): $1 = 4x$
   Divide by 4: $¼ = x$

2. Any number between 1 and 4 (but not 1 or 4). Guess and check is probably the most efficient method here. Notice that $\sqrt{x} < x$ only if $x > 1$, and $\frac{1}{2}x < \sqrt{x}$ only if $x < 4$.

3. **E** $a^2 = 9$, so $a = 3$ or –3. $b^2 = 16$, so $b = 4$ or –4. The greatest value of $a - b$, then, is $3 - (-4) = 7$.

4. **A** $3y = \sqrt{\dfrac{2}{y}}$

   Square both sides: $9y^2 = \dfrac{2}{y}$
   Multiply by y: $9y^3 = 2$
   Divide by 9: $y^3 = 2/9$

5. **D** If $x^2 = 4$, then $x = 2$ or –2, and if $y^2 = 9$, then $y = 3$ or –3. But if $(x - 2)(y + 3) \neq 0$, then x cannot be 2 and y cannot be –3. Therefore, $x = -2$ and $y = 3$. $(-2)^3 + 3^3 = -8 + 27 = 19$

6. **D** $\dfrac{2m\sqrt{18n}}{m\sqrt{2}} = \left(\dfrac{2m}{m}\right)\sqrt{\dfrac{18n}{2}} = 2\sqrt{9n} = 6\sqrt{n}$

   Also, you can plug in easy positive values for m and n like 1 and 2, evaluate the expression on your calculator, and check it against the choices.

7. **C** The diagonal is the hypotenuse of a right triangle, so we can find its length with the Pythagorean theorem: $\left(\sqrt{a}\right)^2 + \left(\sqrt{b}\right)^2 = d^2$

   Simplify: $a + b = d^2$
   Take the square root: $\sqrt{a + b} = d$

   Or you can plug in numbers for a and b, like 9 and 16, before you use the Pythagorean theorem.

8. **C** Assume that the squares have areas of 10 and 1. The lengths of their sides, then, are $\sqrt{10}$ and 1, respectively, and the perimeters are $4\sqrt{10}$ and 4. $4\sqrt{10} : 4 = \sqrt{10} : 1$

9. **B** Use the Pythagorean theorem:

   $1^2 + x^2 = \left(\sqrt{n}\right)^2$

   Simplify: $1 + x^2 = n$
   Subtract 1: $x^2 = n - 1$

   Take the square root: $x = \sqrt{n - 1}$ (Or plug in!)

Lesson 5: Factoring

Factoring

To factor means to write as a product (that is, a multiplication). All of the terms in a product are called factors (divisors) of the product.

Example:

There are many ways to factor 12: 12×1, 6×2, 3×4, or $2 \times 2 \times 3$.

Therefore, 1, 2, 3, 4, 6, and 12 are the *factors* of 12.

Know how to factor a number into prime factors, and how to use those factors to find greatest common factors and least common multiples.

Example:

Two bells, A and B, ring simultaneously, then bell A rings every 168 seconds and bell B rings every 360 seconds. What is the minimum number of seconds between simultaneous rings?

This question is asking for the least common multiple of 168 and 360. The prime factorization of 168 is $2 \times 2 \times 2 \times 3 \times 7$ and the prime factorization of 360 is $2 \times 2 \times 2 \times 3 \times 3 \times 5$. A common multiple must have all of the factors that each of these numbers has, and the smallest of these is $2 \times 2 \times 2 \times 3 \times 3 \times 5 \times 7 = 2,520$. So they ring together every 2,520 seconds.

When factoring polynomials, think of "distribution in reverse." This means that you can check your factoring by distributing, or FOILing, the factors to make sure that the result is the original expression. For instance, to factor $3x^2 - 18x$, just think: what common factor must be "distributed" to what other factor to get this expression? Answer: $3x(x - 6)$ (Check by distributing.) To factor $z^2 + 5z - 6$, just think: what two binomials must be multiplied (by FOILing) to get this expression? Answer: $(z - 1)(z + 6)$ (Check by FOILing.)

The Law of FOIL:

$$(a + b)(c + d) = (a)(c + d) + (b)(c + d) \quad \text{(distribution)}$$
$$= ac + ad + bc + bd \quad \text{(distribution)}$$
$$\text{First} + \text{Outside} + \text{Inside} + \text{Last}$$

Example:

Factor $3x^2 - 18x$.

Common factor is $3x$: $3x^2 - 18x = 3x(x - 6)$ (check by distributing)

Factor $z^2 + 5z - 6$.

$z^2 + 5z - 6 = (z - 1)(z + 6)$ (check by FOILing)

Factoring Formulas

To factor polynomials, it often helps to know some common factoring formulas:

Difference of squares: $\quad x^2 - b^2 = (x + b)(x - b)$

Perfect square trinomials:
$$x^2 + 2xb + b^2 = (x + b)(x + b)$$
$$x^2 - 2xb + b^2 = (x - b)(x - b)$$

Simple trinomials:
$$x^2 + (a + b)x + ab = (x + a)(x + b)$$

Example:

Factor $x^2 - 36$.

This is a "difference of squares":
$x^2 - 36 = (x - 6)(x + 6)$.

Factor $x^2 - 5x - 14$.

This is a simple trinomial. Look for two numbers that have a sum of -5 and a product of -14. With a little guessing and checking, you'll see that -7 and 2 work. So $x^2 - 5x - 14 = (x - 7)(x + 2)$.

The Zero Product Property

Factoring is a great tool for solving equations if it's used with the zero product property, which says that if the product of a set of numbers is 0, then at least one of the numbers in the set must be 0.

Example:

Solve $x^2 - 5x - 14 = 0$.

Factor: $(x - 7)(x + 2) = 0$

Since their product is 0, either $x - 7 = 0$ or $x + 2 = 0$, so $x = 7$ or -2.

The only product property is the zero product property.

Example:

$(x - 1)(x + 2) = 1$ *does not* imply that $x - 1 = 1$. This would mean that $x = 2$, which clearly doesn't work!

Concept Review 5: Factoring

1. What does it mean to factor a number or expression?

    _____

2. Write the four basic factoring formulas for quadratics.   _____

    _____

    _____

    _____

3. What is the zero product property?

    _____

4. Write the prime factorization of 108.   4. _____

5. Find the least common multiple of $21mn$ and $75n^2$.   5. _____

6. Find the greatest common factor of $108x^6$ and $90x^4$.   6. _____

Factor and check by FOILing: FOIL:

7. $1 - 49x^4$ _____   10. $\left(y + \sqrt{3}\right)\left(y - \sqrt{3}\right)$ _____

8. $m^2 + 7m + 12$ _____   11. $\left(\dfrac{x}{2} + \dfrac{1}{3}\right)\left(\dfrac{x}{5} + \dfrac{1}{2}\right)$ _____

9. $16x^2 - 40x + 25$ _____   12. $\left(3x - 2\sqrt{5}\right)^2$ _____

Solve by factoring and using the zero product property. (Hint: each equation has two solutions.)

13. $4x^2 = 12x$ $x =$ _____ or _____   14. $x^2 - 8x = 33$ $x =$ _____ or _____

15. If $3xz - 3yz = 60$ and $z = 5$, then $x - y =$ _____

SAT Practice 5: Factoring

1. Chime A and chime B ring simultaneously at noon. Afterwards, chime A rings every 72 minutes and chime B rings every 54 minutes. What time is it when they next ring simultaneously?

   (A) 3:18 pm   (B) 3:24 pm
   (C) 3:36 pm   (D) 3:54 pm
   (E) 4:16 pm

2. For all real numbers x and y, if $xy = 7$, then $(x - y)^2 - (x + y)^2 =$

   (A) y^2 (B) 0   (C) -7
   (D) -14 (E) -28

3. If for all real values of x,
   $(x + a)(x + 1) = x^2 + 6x + a$, then $a =$

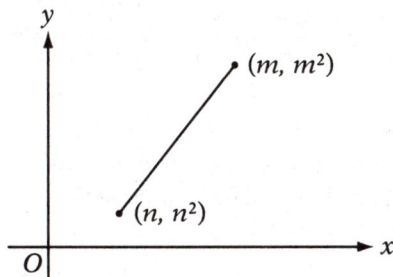

4. In the figure above, if $m \neq n$, what is the slope of the line segment?

   (A) $m + n$ (B) $m - n$

   (C) $\dfrac{m^2 - m}{n^2 - n}$ (D) $\dfrac{1}{m+n}$

   (E) $\dfrac{1}{m-n}$

5. If $a^2 + b^2 = 8$ and $ab = -2$, then $(a + b)^2 =$

   (A) 4   (B) 6   (C) 8
   (D) 9   (E) 16

6. If $f^2 - g^2 = -10$ and $f + g = 2$, then what is the value of $f - g$?

   (A) -20 (B) -12 (C) -8
   (D) -5 (E) 0

7. If $x > 0$, then

   $$\frac{x^2 - 1}{x + 1} + \frac{(x+1)^2 - 1}{x + 2} + \frac{(x+2)^2 - 1}{x + 3} =$$

   (A) $(x + 1)^2$
   (B) $(x - 1)^2$
   (C) $3x - 1$
   (D) $3x$
   (E) $3(x + 1)^2$

8. If $y = 3p$ and $p \neq 2$, then $\dfrac{y^2 - 36}{(y - 6)^2} =$

   (A) 1   (B) $\dfrac{p + 2}{p - 2}$ (C) $\dfrac{3p + 2}{3p - 2}$

   (D) $\dfrac{3p + 2}{3p}$ (E) $\dfrac{9p^2 + 36}{9p^2 - 36}$

9. If $n - \dfrac{1}{n} = x$, then what is $n^2 + \dfrac{1}{n^2}$ in terms of x?

   (A) $x^2 - 2$
   (B) $x^2 - 1$
   (C) x^2
   (D) $x^2 + 1$
   (E) $x^2 + 2$

Answer Key 5: Factoring

Concept Review 5

1. To write it as a product (result of multiplication).

2.
$$x^2 - b^2 = (x + b)(x - b)$$
$$x^2 + 2xb + b^2 = (x + b)(x + b)$$
$$x^2 - 2xb + b^2 = (x - b)(x - b)$$
$$x^2 + (a + b)x + ab = (x + a)(x + b)$$

3. If the product of a set of numbers is 0, then at least one of the numbers must be 0.

4. $108 = (2)(2)(3)(3)(3)$

5. $21mn = (3)(7)(m)(n)$ and $75n^2 = (3)(5)(5)(n)(n)$, so the least common multiple is
$(3)(5)(5)(7)(m)(n)(n) = 525mn^2$.

6. $108x^6 = (2)(2)(3)(3)(3)(x)(x)(x)(x)(x)(x)$ and $90x^4 = (2)(3)(3)(5)(x)(x)(x)(x)$, so the greatest common factor is $(2)(3)(x)(x)(x)(x)(x) = 6x^4$.

7. $1 - 49x^4 = (1 - 7x^2)(1 + 7x^2)$

8. $m^2 + 7m + 12 = (m + 4)(m + 3)$

9. $16x^2 - 40x + 25 = (4x - 5)(4x - 5) = (4x - 5)^2$

10. $\left(y + \sqrt{3}\right)\left(y - \sqrt{3}\right) = y^2 - y\sqrt{3} + y\sqrt{3} - \sqrt{3}^2 = y^2 - 3$

11. $\left(\dfrac{x}{2} + \dfrac{1}{3}\right)\left(\dfrac{x}{5} + \dfrac{1}{2}\right) = \left(\dfrac{x}{2}\right)\left(\dfrac{x}{5}\right) + \left(\dfrac{x}{2}\right)\left(\dfrac{1}{2}\right)$
$$+ \left(\dfrac{1}{3}\right)\left(\dfrac{x}{5}\right) + \left(\dfrac{1}{3}\right)\left(\dfrac{1}{2}\right)$$
$$= \dfrac{x^2}{10} + \dfrac{x}{4} + \dfrac{x}{15} + \dfrac{1}{6}$$
$$= \dfrac{x^2}{10} + \dfrac{19x}{60} + \dfrac{1}{6}$$

12. $\left(3x - 2\sqrt{5}\right)^2 =$
$$\left(3x\right)\left(3x\right) - \left(3x\right)\left(2\sqrt{5}\right) - \left(3x\right)\left(2\sqrt{5}\right) + \left(2\sqrt{5}\right)\left(2\sqrt{5}\right)$$
$$= 9x^2 - 12x\sqrt{5} + 20$$

13.
	$4x^2 = 12x$
Subtract 12x:	$4x^2 - 12x = 0$
Factor:	$4x(x - 3) = 0$
Use zero product property:	$x = 0$ or 3

14.
	$x^2 - 8x = 33$
Subtract 33:	$x^2 - 8x - 33 = 0$
Factor:	$(x - 11)(x + 3) = 0$
Use zero product property:	$x = 11$ or -3

15.
	$3xz - 3yz = 60$
Factor:	$3z(x - y) = 60$
Substitute $z = 5$:	$15(x - y) = 60$
Divide by 15:	$(x - y) = 4$

SAT Practice 5

1. **C** $72 = (2)(2)(2)(3)(3)$ and $54 = (2)(3)(3)(3)$, so the least common multiple is $(2)(2)(2)(3)(3)(3) = 216$. 216 minutes is 3 hours 36 minutes.

2. **E**   You can solve this one simply by plugging in $x = 7$ and $y = 1$ and evaluating $(7 - 1)^2 - (7 + 1)^2 = 36 - 64 = -28$. Or you could do the algebra: $(x - y)^2 - (x + y)^2$
   FOIL: $(x^2 - 2xy + y^2) - (x^2 + 2xy + y^2)$
   Simplify: $-4xy$
   Substitute $xy = 7$: $-4(7) = -28$

3. **5** $(x + a)(x + 1) = x^2 + 6x + a$
   FOIL: $x^2 + x + ax + a = x^2 + 6x + a$
   Subtract x^2 and a: $x + ax = 6x$
   Factor: $x(1 + a) = 6x$
   Divide by x: $1 + a = 6$
   Subtract 1: $a = 5$

4. **A**   The slope is "the rise over the run," which is the difference of the y's divided by the difference of the x's:
$$\frac{m^2 - n^2}{m - n} = \frac{(m + n)(m - n)}{(m - n)} = m + n$$

   Or you can just choose values for m and n, like 2 and 1, and evaluate the slope numerically. The slope between $(1, 1)$ and $(2, 4)$ is 3, and the expression in (A) is the only one that gives a value of 3.

5. **A** $(a + b)^2 = (a + b)(a + b) = a^2 + 2ab + b^2$
   Commute: $= a^2 + b^2 + 2ab$
   Substitute $ab = -2$
   and $a^2 + b^2 = 8$: $= (8) + 2(-2)$
                        $= 4$

6. **D**   Factor: $f^2 - g^2 = (f + g)(f - g)$
   Substitute $f^2 - g^2 = -10$
   and $f + g = 2$: $-10 = 2(f - g)$
   Divide by 2: $-5 = f - g$

7. **D**   Plugging in $x = 1$ gives you $0 + 1 + 2 = 3$, and (D) is the only choice that yields 3. Or:

$$\frac{x^2-1}{x+1}+\frac{(x+1)^2-1}{x+2}+\frac{(x+2)^2-1}{x+3}$$

$$=\frac{\cancel{(x+1)}(x-1)}{\cancel{x+1}}+\frac{(x+1+1)(x+1-1)}{x+2}$$

$$+\frac{(x+2+1)(x+2-1)}{x+3}$$

$$=(x-1)+(x)+(x+1)=3x$$

8. **B** $\dfrac{y^2-36}{(y-6)^2}=\dfrac{\cancel{(y-6)}(y+6)}{\cancel{(y-6)}(y-6)}=\dfrac{(y+6)}{(y-6)}$

Substitute $y = 3p$: $\dfrac{(3p+6)}{(3p-6)}=\dfrac{3(p+2)}{3(p-2)}=\dfrac{p+2}{p-2}$

9. **E** $$n-\frac{1}{n}=x$$

Square both sides:

$$\left(n-\frac{1}{n}\right)^2=n^2-2+\frac{1}{n^2}=\left(x\right)^2$$

Add 2: $$n^2+\frac{1}{n^2}=x^2+2$$

Lesson 6:
Inequalities, Absolute Values, and Plugging In

Inequalities as Unbalanced Scales

Inequalities are just unbalanced scales. Nearly all of the laws of equality pertain to inequalities, with one exception. When solving inequalities, keep the direction of the inequality (remember that "the alligator < always eats the bigger number") unless you divide or multiply by a negative, in which case you "switch" the inequality.

Example:
Solve $x^2 > 6x$ for x.

You might be tempted to divide both sides by x and get $x > 6$, but this incorrectly assumes that x is positive. *If x is positive, then $x > 6$, but if x is negative, then $x < 6$. (Switch the inequality when you divide by a negative!) But of course *any* negative number is less than 6, so the solution is either $x > 6$ or $x < 0$. (Plug in numbers to verify!)

Absolute Values as Distances

The absolute value of x, written as $|x|$, means the distance from x to 0 on the number line. Since distances are never negative, neither are absolute values. For instance, since –4 is four units away from 0, we say $|-4| = 4$.

The distance between numbers is found from their difference. For instance, the distance between 5 and –2 on the number line is $5 - (-2) = 7$. But differences can be negative, and distances can't! That's where absolute values come in. Mathematically, the distance between a and b is $|a - b|$.

Example:
Graph the solution of $|x + 2| \geq 3$.

You can think about this in two ways. First think about distances. $|x + 2|$ is the same as $|x - (-2)|$, which is the distance between x and –2. So if this distance must be greater than or equal to 3, you can just visualize those numbers that are at least 3 units away from –2:

Or you can do it more "algebraically" if you prefer. The only numbers that have an absolute value greater than or equal to 3 are numbers greater than or equal to 3 or less than or equal to –3, right? Therefore, saying $|x + 2| \geq 3$ is the same as saying $x + 2 \geq 3$ or $x + 2 \leq -3$. Subtracting 2 from both sides of both inequalities gives $x \geq 1$ or $x \leq -5$, which confirms the answer by the other method.

Plugging In

After solving each of the examples above, you should, as with all equations and inequalities, *plug in* your solution to confirm that it works in the equation or inequality. But plugging in can also be a good way of solving multiple-choice problems that ask you to find an expression with variables rather than a numerical solution.

If a multiple-choice question has choices that contain unknowns, you can often simplify the problem by just plugging in values for the unknowns. But think first: in some situations, plugging in is not the simplest method.

Example:
If $y = r - 6$ and $z = r + 5$, which of the following expresses r in terms of y and z?

(A) $y + z - 1$

(B) $y + z$

(C) $y + z + 1$

(D) $\dfrac{y + z - 1}{2}$

(E) $\dfrac{y + z + 1}{2}$

If you pick r to be 6—it can be whatever you want, so pick an easy number!—then y is $6 - 6 = 0$ and z is $6 + 5 = 11$. The question is asking for an expression for r, so look for 6 among the choices. Plugging in your values gives (A) 10 (B) 11 (C) 12 (D) 5 (E) 6. Always evaluate *all* the choices because you must work by *process of elimination*. Only (E) gives 6, so it must be the right answer!

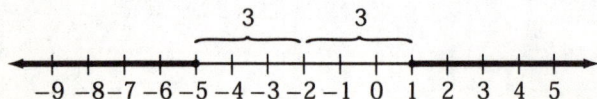

Concept Review 6:
Inequalities, Absolute Values, and Plugging In

Express each of the following statements as equations or inequalities using absolute values.

1. The distance from y to 3 is less than 5.   _____

2. The distance from a to 2 is equal to the distance from b to –2.   _____

3. The distance from x to –1 is no greater than 10.   _____

4. The distance from a to b is no more than twice the distance from a to c. _____

Graph the solution to each of the following inequalities on the given number line. Check your answer by testing points.

5. $|x - 3| < 2$ 6. $y^2 \geq 4$ 7. $6x > 2x^2$

$\longleftrightarrow$ $\longleftrightarrow$ $\longleftrightarrow$

8. $-3x \geq 12$ 9. $5 - x^2 < 5$ 10. $x + 3 < x - 1$

$\longleftrightarrow$ $\longleftrightarrow$ $\longleftrightarrow$

Solve the following problem by plugging in, then see if you can solve it "algebraically."

11. If $a = 2b - c$ and $5b = a + 1$, then which of the following expressions is equivalent to a?

   (A) $3b + c - 1$ (B) $3b - c + 1$ (C) $\dfrac{7b - c + 1}{2}$ (D) $\dfrac{7b - c - 1}{2}$ (E) $\dfrac{7b + c - 1}{2}$

SAT Practice 6:
Inequalities, Absolute Values, and Plugging In

1. If $2 - 4x < 20$, then which of the following could NOT be the value of x?

    (A) -5 (B) -4 (C) -3
    (D) -2 (E) -1

2. If $x < 0$, $xy > 0$, and $xyz > 0$, then which of the following expressions must be positive?

    (A) x^2yz (B) xy^2z (C) xyz^2
    (D) xy^2 (E) xz^2

3. Which of the following is equivalent to the statement $|x - 2| < 1$?

    (A) $x < 3$ (B) $x < -1$
    (C) $1 < x < 3$ (D) $-1 < x < 3$
    (E) $-3 < x < -1$

4. If $|m| > -2$, then which of the following represents all possible values of m?

    (A) $m > -2$ (B) $m > 2$
    (C) $m > 2$ or $m < -2$ (D) $-2 < m < 2$
    (E) all real numbers

5. If $r = 5w = 7a$ and $r \neq 0$, then what is the value of $r - w$ in terms of a?

    (A) $28a$ (B) $\dfrac{28a}{5}$ (C) $3a$

    (D) $\dfrac{7a}{5}$ (E) $\dfrac{a}{7}$

6. If x is the average (arithmetic mean) of k and 10 and y is the average (arithmetic mean) of k and 4, what is the average of x and y, in terms of k?

    (A) $\dfrac{k+14}{4}$ (B) $\dfrac{k+14}{2}$

    (C) $\dfrac{k+7}{2}$ (D) $7k$ (E) $14k$

7. If $m = 2x - 5$ and $n = x + 7$, which of the following expresses x in terms of m and n?

    (A) $m - n + 2$ (B) $m - n + 12$

    (C) $2(m - n + 12)$ (D) $\dfrac{m-n+2}{2}$

    (E) $\dfrac{m-n+12}{2}$

8. What is the only integer n such that

    $20 - 2n > 5$ and $\dfrac{2n}{3} > 4$?

9. If $b = 2a - 4$ and $c = a + 2$, then which of the following expresses a in terms of b and c?

    I. $b - c + 6$

    II. $\dfrac{b+c+2}{3}$

    III. $2c - b - 8$

    (A) I only   (B) II only
    (C) I and II only   (D) I and III only
    (E) I, II, and III

10. Which of the following is equivalent to the statement "The distance from 1 to x is greater than the distance from 3 to x?"

    I. $|x - 1| > |x - 3|$
    II. $x > 3$ or $x < 1$
    III. $x > 2$

    (A) I only   (B) I and II only
    (C) II and III only   (D) I and III only
    (E) I, II, and III

Answer Key 6:
Inequalities, Absolute Values, and Plugging In

Concept Review 6

1. $|y - 3| < 5$

2. $|a - 2| = |b + 2|$

3. $|x + 1| \leq 10$

4. $|a - b| \leq 2|a - c|$

5. $|x - 3| < 2$

6.
$$y^2 \geq 4$$
Take the square root: $\qquad\qquad |y| \geq 2$
Interpret without absolute value: $y \leq -2$ or $y \geq 2$
Graph:

-4 -3 -2 -1 0 1 2 3 4

7.
$$6x > 2x^2$$
Divide by x with conditions: if $x > 0$, then $6 > 2x$
$\qquad\qquad\qquad\qquad\qquad$ if $x < 0$, then $6 < 2x$
Simplify: if $x > 0$, then $3 > x$, so $0 < x < 3$
$\qquad\quad$ if $x < 0$, then $3 < x$ (no solution)
Graph:

-4 -3 -2 -1 0 1 2 3 4

8.
$$-3x \geq 12$$
Divide by -3: $\qquad\qquad x \leq -4$
Graph:

-8 -7 -6 -5 -4 -3 -2 -1 0

9.
$$5 - x^2 < 5$$
Subtract 5: $\qquad\qquad\qquad\qquad -x^2 < 0$
Multiply by -1 (and "switch"): $\qquad x^2 > 0$
Take the square root: $\qquad\qquad |x| > 0$
Interpret: $\qquad\qquad x > 0$ or $x < 0$
Graph:

-4 -3 -2 -1 0 1 2 3 4

10.
$$x + 3 < x - 1$$
Subtract x: $\qquad\qquad\qquad 3 < -1$
But this is impossible, so there's no solution!

11. **(D)** If you plug in $a = 4$, then $b = 1$ and $c = -2$. Since you're looking for an expression that equals a, plug these into the choices and see which one gives $a = 4$:

(A) $3(1) + (-2) - 1 = 0$

(B) $3(1) - (-2) + 1 = 6$

(C) $(7(1) - (-2) + 1)/2 = 5$

(D) $(7(1) - (-2) - 1)/2 = 4$

(E) $(7(1) + (-2) - 1)/2 = 2$

Since (D) is the only choice that gives 4, it is the right choice. To solve it algebraically, solve each equation for a:

$$a = 2b - c$$
$$a = 5b - 1$$
Add the equations: $\qquad 2a = 7b - c - 1$
Divide by 2: $\qquad\qquad a = (7b - c - 1)/2$

SAT Practice 6

1. **A** $2 - 4(-5) = 2 + 20 = 22$, which is not less than 20.

2. **C** To satisfy the inequalities, x must be negative, y must be negative, and z must be positive. You might choose $x = -1$, $y = -1$, and $z = 1$ to confirm that (C) is the only one that gives a positive value.

3. **C**
$$|x - 2| < 1$$
Translate without absolute value: $-1 < x - 2 < 1$
Add 2: $\qquad\qquad\qquad\qquad 1 < x < 3$

4. **E** All absolute values are greater than or equal to zero, so any value of m would satisfy $|m| > -2$.

5. **B** You can solve by plugging in for the unknowns, but be careful to choose values that work in the equation. The simplest values that work are $r = 35$, $w = 7$, and $a = 5$. In this case, $r - w = 35 - 7 = 28$. If you plug $a = 5$ into the choices, (B) is the only one that equals 28.

Or you can solve algebraically by expressing r and w in terms of a. $r = 7a$ and $w = \frac{7}{5}a$, so

$$r - w = 7a - \frac{7}{5}a = \frac{35}{5}a - \frac{7}{5}a = \frac{28a}{5}.$$

6. **C** You might plug in $k = 2$. Since x is the average of k and 10, $x = (2 + 10)/2 = 6$. Since y is the average of k and 4, $y = (2 + 4)/2 = 3$. The average of x and y, then, is $(6 + 3)/2 = 4.5$. If you then plug $k = 2$ into the choices, (C) is the only choice that equals 4.5.

7. **B** Plug in $x = 3$. Then $m = 2(3) - 5 = 1$ and $n = (3) + 7 = 10$. The question asks for an expression that equals x, so look for 3 in the choices when you plug in $m = 1$ and $n = 10$. The only choice that gives you 3 is (B).

8. **7** $20 - 2n > 5$
   Subtract 20: $-2n > -15$
   Divide by -2: $n < 7.5$ (Don't forget the switch!)

The greatest integer n could be, then, is 7. Notice that 7 also satisfies the other inequality: $2(7)/3 = 4.666$, which of course is greater than 4.

9. **C** Plugging in isn't good enough here, because more than one expression may be correct. The best method is substitution, using $b = 2a - 4$ and $c = a + 2$:

   I. $b - c + 6 = (2a - 4) - (a + 2) + 6 = a$ (Yes!)

   II. $\dfrac{b + c + 2}{3} = \dfrac{(2a - 4) + (a + 2) + 2}{3} = \dfrac{3a}{3} = a$
   (Yes!)

   III. $2c - b - 8 = 2(a + 2) - (2a - 4) - 8 = 0$
   (No.)

10. **D** The distance from 1 to x is $|x - 1|$ and the distance from 3 to x is $|x - 3|$, so I is clearly correct. To see why III is true, notice that 2 is the only number equidistant from 1 and 3, so all numbers that are farther from 1 than from 3 are greater than 2.

Lesson 7: Word Problems

How to Attack Word Problems

Don't be afraid of word problems—they're easier than they look. In word problems, the facts about the unknowns are written as sentences instead of equations. So all you have to do is name the unknowns and translate the sentences into equations. Then it's all algebra.

Step 1: Read the problem carefully, and try to get "the big picture." Note carefully what the question asks you to find.

Step 2: Ask: what are the unknowns? Call them x or n or some other convenient letter. Don't go overboard. The fewer the unknowns, the simpler the problem. For instance, if the problem says, "Dave weighs twice as much as Eric," rather than saying $d = 2e$ (which uses two unknowns), it might be simpler to say that Eric weighs x pounds and Dave weighs $2x$ pounds (which only uses one unknown).

Step 3: Translate any key sentence in the question into an equation. *If your goal is to solve for each unknown, you'll need the same number of equations as you have unknowns.* Use this handy translation key to translate sentences into equations:

percent	means	$\div 100$
of	means	*times*
what	means	x
is	means	*equals*
per	means	$\div$
x less than y	means	$y - x$
decreased by	means	$-$
is at least	means	$\geq$
is no greater than	means	$\leq$

Step 4: Solve the equation or system. *Check the question to make sure that you're solving for the right thing.* Review Lessons 1 and 2 in this chapter if you need tips for solving equations and systems.

Step 5: Check that your solution makes sense in the context of the problem.

Example:

Ellen is twice as old as Julia. Five years ago, Ellen was three times as old as Julia. How old is Julia now?

Let's say that this is a grid-in question, so you can't just test the choices. Guessing and checking might work, but it also may take a while before you guess the right answer. Algebra is quicker and more reliable. First, think about the unknowns. The one you really care about is Julia's *current* age, so let's call it j. We don't know Ellen's current age either, so let's call it e. That's two unknowns, so we'll need two equations. The first sentence, *Ellen is twice as old as Julia*, can be translated as $e = 2j$. The next sentence, *Five years ago, Ellen was three times as old as Julia*, is a bit trickier to translate. Five years ago, Ellen was $e - 5$ years old, and Julia was $j - 5$ years old. So the statement translates into $e - 5 = 3(j - 5)$. Now solve the system:

$$e - 5 = 3(j - 5)$$

Distribute:	$e - 5 = 3j - 15$
Add 5:	$e = 3j - 10$
Substitute $e = 2j$:	$2j = 3j - 10$
Subtract $2j$:	$0 = j - 10$
Add 10:	$10 = j$

Now reread the problem and make sure that the answer makes sense. If Julia is 10, Ellen must be 20 because she's twice as old. Five years ago, they were 5 and 15, and 15 is three times 5! It works!

Concept Review 7: Word Problems

For each of the following statements, specify and name the unknowns and translate the statement into an equation.

1. Mike is twice as old as Dave was 5 years ago.

2. The population of town A is 40% greater than the population of town B.

3. After 2/3 of the marbles are removed from a jar, 5 more than 1/6 of the marbles remain.

4. In a jar, there are 4 more than twice as many blue marbles as red marbles.

Solve the following word problems.

5. Three candy bars and two lollipops cost $2.20, and four candy bars and two lollipops cost $2.80. What is the cost of one lollipop?

6. At a football stadium, 2/3 of the seats were filled at the beginning of a game. At halftime, 1,000 people left the stadium, leaving 3/7 of the seats filled. What is the total number of seats in the stadium?

7. If the average of m and n is one-half of the average of s and t, then what is s in terms of m, n, and t?

8. A blue chip is worth 2 dollars more than a red chip, and a red chip is worth 2 dollars more than a green chip. If 5 green chips are worth m dollars, give an expression that represents the price, in dollars, of 10 blue chips and 5 red chips.

SAT Practice 7: Word Problems

1. When x is subtracted from 24 and this difference is divided by x, the result is 3. What is x?

(A) 4
(B) 5
(C) 6
(D) 8
(E) 12

2. Three years ago, Nora was half as old as Mary is now. If Mary is four years older than Nora, how old is Mary now?

3. If the ratio of p to q is 9:7 and the ratio of q to r is 14:3, then what is the ratio of p to r?

(A) 1:6
(B) 27:98
(C) 2:5
(D) 5:2
(E) 6:1

4. Joan originally had twice as many books as Emily. After she gave Emily 5 books, Joan still had 10 more than Emily. How many books did Joan have originally?

5. The cost of living in a certain city rose 20% between 1960 and 1970, and rose 50% between 1960 and 1980. By what percent did the cost of living increase between 1970 and 1980?

(A) 15%
(B) 20%
(C) 25%
(D) 30%
(E) 35%

6. The Mavericks baseball team has a won-lost ratio of 7 to 5. If the team played a total of 48 games and no game ended in a tie, how many more games have the Mavericks won than they have lost?

7. When the Apex Pet Store first opened, the ratio of cats to dogs was 4 to 5. Since then, the number of cats has doubled, while the number of dogs has increased by 12. If the ratio of dogs to cats is now 1 to 1, how many cats did the store have when it opened?

8. Hillside High School has 504 students. One-quarter of the students are sophomores, and 3/7 of the sophomores are boys. If one-third of the sophomore girls take French, how many sophomore girls do *not* take French?

(A)   24
(B)   36
(C)   48
(D)   72
(E)   126

9. A jar contains only red, green, and blue marbles. If it is three times as likely that you randomly pick a red marble as a green marble, and five times as likely that you pick a green one as a blue one, which of the following could be the number of marbles in the jar?

(A)   38
(B)   39
(C)   40
(D)   41
(E)   42

Answer Key 7: Word Problems

Concept Review 7

1. m = Mike's current age, d = Dave's current age; $m = 2(d - 5)$

2. a = the population of town A, b = the population of town B; $a = 1.4b$

3. n = number of marbles in the jar; $n - (2/3)n = 5 + (1/6)n$

4. b = number of blue marbles, r = number of red marbles; $b = 4 + 2r$

5. c = cost of one candy bar, l = cost of one lollipop; $3c + 2l = 2.20$, and $4c + 2l = 2.80$.

Subtract:	$4c + 2l = 2.80$
	$- (3c + 2l = 2.20)$
	$c = .60$
Plug in to find l:	$3(.60) + 2l = 2.20$
Simplify:	$1.80 + 2l = 2.20$
Subtract 1.80:	$2l = .40$
Divide by 2:	$l = .20$

6. n = number of seats in the stadium;

$$(2/3)n - 1{,}000 = (3/7)n$$

Subtract $(2/3)n$:	$-1{,}000 = -(5/21)n$
Multiply by $-(21/5)$:	$4{,}200 = n$

7. $$\frac{m+n}{2} = \frac{1}{2}\left(\frac{s+t}{2}\right)$$

Simplify:	$\dfrac{m+n}{2} = \left(\dfrac{s+t}{4}\right)$
Multiply by 4:	$2m + 2n = s + t$
Subtract t:	$2m + 2n - t = s$

8. b = value of blue chip, r = value of red chip, g = value of green chip; $b = 2 + r$, $r = 2 + g$, and $5g = m$, so

Cost of 10 blue and 5 red chips:	$10b + 5r$
Substitute $b = 2 + r$:	$10(2 + r) + 5r$
Simplify:	$20 + 15r$
Substitute $r = 2 + g$:	$20 + 15(2 + g)$
Simplify:	$50 + 15g$
Substitute $g = m/5$:	$50 + 3m$

SAT Practice 7

1. **C** You could test the choices here, or do the algebra:

$$\frac{24 - x}{x} = 3$$

Multiply by x:	$24 - x = 3x$
Add x:	$24 = 4x$
Divide by 4:	$6 = x$

2. n = Nora's current age, m = Mary's current age.

Interpret first sentence:	$n - 3 = (1/2)m$
Interpret second sentence:	$m = n + 4$
Subtract 4:	$m - 4 = n$
Substitute $n = m - 4$:	$m - 4 - 3 = (1/2)m$
Simplify:	$m - 7 = (1/2)m$
Subtract m:	$-7 = -(1/2)m$
Multiply by -2:	$14 = m$

3. **E** $p/q = 9/7$, $q/r = 14/3$.

Multiply: $\left(\dfrac{p}{q}\right)\left(\dfrac{q}{r}\right) = \dfrac{p}{r} = \left(\dfrac{9}{7}\right)\left(\dfrac{14}{3}\right) = \dfrac{6}{1}$

4. **40** J = number of books Joan had **originally.** E = number of books Emily had originally. $J = 2E$. After the exchange, Emily has $E + 5$ and Joan has $J - 5$ books, so $J - 5 = 10 + (E + 5)$.

Simplify:	$J - 5 = E + 15$
Subtract 15:	$J - 20 = E$
Substitute into first equation:	$J = 2(J - 20)$
Solve for J:	$J = 40$

(Reread and check)

5. **C** Let x be the cost of living in 1960. In 1970, the cost of living was $1.2x$, and in 1980 it was $1.5x$. Use the percent change formula: $(1.5x - 1.2x)/1.2x = .25 = 25\%$.

6. **8** Let w = the number of games won and l = the number of games lost. $w/l = 7/5$ and $w + l = 48$.

Multiply by l:	$w = (7/5)l$
Substitute into 2nd eq.:	$(7/5)l + l = 48$
Simplify:	$(12/5)l = 48$
Multiply by 5/12:	$l = 20$
Plug in to find w:	$w + 20 = 48$
Subtract 20:	$w = 28$

How many more games won than lost?

$$w - l = 28 - 20 = 8$$

7. **16** Let c = number of cats originally, d = number of dogs originally. $c/d = 4/5$. Now the number of cats is $2c$ and the number of dogs is $d + 12$. If the ratio of dogs to cats is now 1 to 1, $2c = d + 12$.

Cross-multiply:	$5c = 4d$
Divide by 4:	$(5/4)c = d$
Substitute:	$2c = (5/4)c + 12$
Subtract $(5/4)c$:	$(3/4)c = 12$
Multiply by 4/3:	$c = 16$ (Reread and check)

8. **C** Number of sophomores = $(1/4)(504) = 126$. If 3/7 of the sophomores are boys, 4/7 are girls: $(4/7)(126) = 72$. If 1/3 of the sophomore girls take French, 2/3 do not: $(2/3)(72) = 48$.

9. **E** r, g, and b are the numbers of red, green, and blue marbles. $r = 3g$ and $g = 5b$. Total marbles = $r + g + b$.

Substitute $r = 3g$:	$3g + g + b = 4g + b$
Substitute $g = 5b$:	$4(5b) + b = 21b$

So the total must be a multiple of 21, and $42 = 2(21)$.

CHAPTER 9

SPECIAL MATH PROBLEMS

1. New Symbol or Term Problems

2. Mean/Median/Mode Problems

3. Numerical Reasoning Problems

4. Rate Problems

5. Counting Problems

6. Probability Problems

Lesson 1: New Symbol or Term Problems

New Symbol or Term Problems

Don't be intimidated by SAT questions with strange symbols, like Δ, φ, or ¥, or new terms that you haven't seen before. These crazy symbols or terms are just made up on the spot, and the problems will always explain what they mean. Just read the definition of the new symbol or term carefully and use it to "translate" the expressions with the new symbol or term.

Example:

Let the "kernel" of a number be defined as the square of its greatest prime factor. For instance, the kernel of 18 is 9, because the greatest prime factor of 18 is 3 (prime factorization: $18 = 2 \times 3 \times 3$), and 3^2 equals 9.

Question 1: What is the kernel of 39?

Don't worry about the fact that you haven't heard of a "kernel" before. Just read the definition carefully. By the definition, the kernel of 39 is the square of its greatest prime factor. So just find the greatest prime factor and square it. First, factor 39 into 3×13, so its greatest prime factor is 13, and $13^2 = 169$.

Question 2: What is the greatest integer less than 20 that has a kernel of 4?

This requires a bit more thinking. If a number has a kernel of 4, then 4 must be the square of its greatest prime factor, so its greatest prime factor must be 2. The only numbers that have a greatest prime factor of 2 are the powers of 2. The greatest power of 2 that is less than 20 is $2^4 = 16$.

Example:

For all real numbers a and b, let the expression $a \mathbin{¿} b$ be defined by the equation $a \mathbin{¿} b = 10a + b$.

Question 3: What is $5 \mathbin{¿} 10$?

Just substitute 5 for a and 10 for b in the given equation: $5 \mathbin{¿} 10 = 10(5) + 10 = 60$.

Question 4: If $2.5 \mathbin{¿} x = 50$, what is the value of x?

Just translate the left side of the equation:
$$2.5 \mathbin{¿} x = 10(2.5) + x = 50$$
Then solve for x:
$$25 + x = 50$$
$$x = 25$$

Question 5: What is $1.5 \mathbin{¿} (1.5 \mathbin{¿} 1.5)$?

According to the order of operations, evaluate what is in parentheses first:

	$1.5 \mathbin{¿} (1.5 \mathbin{¿} 1.5)$
Substitute:	$1.5 \mathbin{¿} (10(1.5) + 1.5)$
Simplify:	$1.5 \mathbin{¿} (16.5)$
Substitute again:	$10(1.5) + 16.5$
Simplify:	$15 + 16.5 = 31.5$

Concept Review 1:
New Symbol or Term Problems

For questions 1–6, translate each expression into its simplest terms, using the definition of the new symbol.

The following definition pertains to questions 1–3:
   For any real number x, let §x be defined as the greatest integer less than or equal to x.

1. §–4.5   =   _____

2. §–1.5 + §1.5   =   _____

3. §$\sqrt{15}$ + §$\sqrt{17}$ =   _____

The following definition pertains to questions 4–6:
   If q is any positive real number and n is an integer, let q @ n be defined by the equation $q @ n = \sqrt{q}^{\,n+1}$.

4. 8 @ 3   =   _____

5. 9 @ (k – 1)   =   _____

6. x^2 @ 0   =   _____

7. If q is any positive real number and n is an integer, let q @ n be defined by the equation $q @ n = \sqrt{q}^{\,n+1}$.

   If y @ 2 = 64, what is the value of y?

8. For any integer n and real number x, let x ^ n be defined by the equation x ^ $n = nx^{n-1}$. If y ^ 4 = –32, what is the value of y?

9. For any integer n, let Ωn be defined as the sum of the distinct prime factors of n. For instance, $\Omega 36 = 5$, because 2 and 3 are the only prime factors of 36 and 2 + 3 = 5. What is the smallest value of w for which $\Omega w = 12$?

SAT Practice 1: New Symbol or Term Problems

1. For all real numbers d, e, and f, let $d * e * f = de + ef + df$. If $2 * 3 * x = 12$, then $x =$

   (A) $\dfrac{5}{6}$

   (B) $\dfrac{6}{5}$

   (C) $\dfrac{8}{5}$

   (D) 2

   (E) 6

2. If $b \neq 0$, let $a \# b = \dfrac{a^2}{b^2}$. If $x \# y = 1$, then which of the following statements must be true?

   (A) $x = y$
   (B) $x = |y|$
   (C) $x = -y$
   (D) $x^2 - y^2 = 0$
   (E) x and y are both positive

3. On a digital clock, a time like 6:06 is called a "double" time because the number representing the hour is the same as the number representing the minute. Other such "doubles" are 8:08 and 9:09. What is the *smallest* time period between any two such doubles?

   (A) 11 mins.   (B) 49 mins.
   (C) 60 mins.   (D) 61 mins.
   (E) 101 mins.

4. Two numbers are "complementary" if their reciprocals have a sum of 1. For instance, 5 and $\dfrac{5}{4}$ are complementary because $\dfrac{1}{5} + \dfrac{4}{5} = 1$.

   If x and y are complementary, and if $x = \dfrac{2}{3}$, what is y?

   (A) -2 (B) $-\dfrac{1}{2}$ (C) $-\dfrac{1}{3}$

   (D) $\dfrac{1}{3}$ (E) 3

5. For $x \neq 0$, let $\$x = \dfrac{1}{x}$. What is the value of $\$\$5$?

6. For all nonnegative real numbers x, let $\Diamond x$ be defined by the equation $\Diamond x = \dfrac{\sqrt{x}}{4}$. For what value of x does $\Diamond x = 1.5$?

   (A) 0.3   (B) 6   (C) 12
   (D) 14   (E) 36

7. For any integer n, let $[n]$ be defined as the sum of the digits of n. For instance, $[341] = 3 + 4 + 1 = 8$. If a is an integer greater than 0 but less than 1,000, which of the following must be true?

   I. $[10a] < [a] + 1$
   II. $[[a]] < 20$
   III. If a is even, then $[a]$ is even

   (A) none
   (B) II only
   (C) I and II only
   (D) II and III only
   (E) I, II, and III

8. For all integers, n, let $n\& = \begin{cases} 2n & \text{if } n \text{ is even} \\ n-3 & \text{if } n \text{ is odd} \end{cases}$

   What is the value of $13\&\&$?

   (A) 10   (B) 13   (C) 20
   (D) 23   (E) 26

Answer Key 1: New Symbol or Term Problems

Concept Review 1

1. $\S -4.5 = -5$

2. $\S -1.5 + \S 1.5 = -2 + 1 = -1$

3. $\S \sqrt{15} + \sqrt{17} = 3 + 4 = 7$

4. $8 @ 3 = \left(\sqrt{8}\right)^4 = 64$

5. $9 @ (k-1) = \left(\sqrt{9}\right)^{k-1+1} = 3^k$

6. $x^2 @ 0 = \left(\sqrt{x^2}\right)^{0+1} = |x|$

7.
$$y @ 2 = \left(\sqrt{y}\right)^{2+1} = 64$$

Simplify: $\qquad\qquad \left(\sqrt{y}\right)^3 = 64$

Take the cube root: $\qquad \sqrt{y} = 4$

Square: $\qquad\qquad\qquad y = 16$

8.
$$y^{\wedge}4 = -32$$

Translate: $\qquad\qquad\qquad 4y^{4-1} = -32$

Simplify and divide by 4: $\qquad y^3 = -8$

Take the cube root: $\qquad\qquad y = -2$

9. If $\Omega w = 12$, then w must be a number whose distinct prime factors add up to 12. The prime numbers less than 12 are 2, 3, 5, 7, and 11. Which of these have a sum of 12? (Remember you can't repeat any, because it says the numbers have to be *distinct*.) A little trial and error shows that the only possibilities are 5 and 7, or 2, 3, and 7. The smallest numbers with these factors are $5 \times 7 = 35$ and $2 \times 3 \times 7 = 42$. Since the question asks for the *least* such number, the answer is 35.

SAT Practice 1

1. **B**
   $\qquad\qquad\qquad\qquad\qquad\qquad 2 * 3 * x = 12$
   Translate: $\qquad (2)(3) + (3)(x) + (2)(x) = 12$
   Simplify: $\qquad\qquad\qquad\qquad 6 + 5x = 12$
   Subtract 6: $\qquad\qquad\qquad\qquad 5x = 6$
   Divide by 5: $\qquad\qquad\qquad\qquad x = 6/5$

2. **D** If $x \# y = 1$, then $(x^2/y^2) = 1$, which means $x^2 = y^2$. Notice that $x = -1$ and $y = 1$ is one possible solution, which means that
   (A) $x = y$
   (B) $x = |y|$
   (E) x and y are both positive
      is *not* necessarily true. Another simple solution is $x = 1$ and $y = 1$, which means that
   (C) $x = -y$
      is not necessarily true, leaving only
   (D) as an answer.

3. **B** All of the consecutive "double times" are 1 hour and 1 minute apart except for 12:12 and 1:01, which are only 49 minutes apart.

4. **A** If $\frac{2}{3}$ and y are complementary, then the sum of their reciprocals is 1: $\qquad \frac{3}{2} + 1/y = 1$
   Subtract $\frac{3}{2}$: $\qquad\qquad\qquad 1/y = -1/2$
   Take the reciprocal of both sides: $\qquad y = -2$

5. **5** The "double" symbol means you simply perform the operation twice. Start with 5, then $\$5 = 1/5$. Therefore, $\$\$5 = \$(1/5) = 1/(1/5) = 5$.

6. **E**
   $$\Diamond x = \frac{\sqrt{x}}{4} = 1.5$$
   Multiply by 4: $\qquad\qquad \sqrt{x} = 6$
   Square both sides: $\qquad\qquad x = 36$
   Plug in $x = 36$ to the original and see that it works.

7. **C** If a is 12, which is even, then $[12] = 1 + 2 = 3$ is odd, which means that statement III is not necessarily true. (Notice that this eliminates choices (D) and (E).) Statement I is true because $[10a]$ will always equal $[a]$ because $10a$ has the same digits as a, but with an extra 0 at the end, which contributes nothing to the sum of digits. Therefore, $[10a] < [a] + 1$ is always true. Notice that this leaves only choice (C) as a possibility. To check statement II, though (just to be sure!), notice that the biggest sum of digits that you can get if a is less than 1,000 is from 999. $[999] = 9 + 9 + 9 = 27$; therefore, $[[999]] = [27] = 2 + 7 = 9$. It's possible to get a *slightly* bigger value for $[[a]]$ if a is, say, 991: $[[991]] = [19] = 10$, but you can see that $[[a]]$ will never approach 20.

8. **C** Since 13 is odd, $13\& = 13 - 3 = 10$. Therefore, $13\&\& = 10\&$. Since 10 is even, $10\& = 2(10) = 20$.

Lesson 2: Mean/Median/Mode Problems

Average (Arithmetic Mean) Problems

Just about every SAT will include at least one question about *averages,* otherwise known as arithmetic means. These won't be simplistic questions like "What is the average of this set of numbers?" You will have to really understand the concept of averages beyond the basic formula.

You probably know the procedure for finding an average of a set of numbers: add them up and divide by how many numbers you have. For instance, the average of 3, 7, and 8 is $(3 + 7 + 8)/3 = 6$. You can describe this procedure with the "average formula":

$$\text{Average} = \frac{\text{sum}}{\text{how many numbers}}$$

Since this is an algebraic equation, you can manipulate it just like any other equation, and get two more formulas:

$$\text{Sum} = \text{average} \times \text{how many numbers}$$

$$\text{How many numbers} = \frac{\text{sum}}{\text{average}}$$

All three of these formulas can be summarized in one handy little "pyramid":

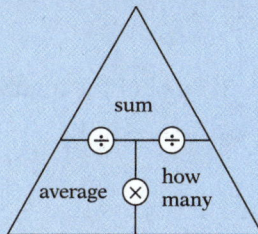

This is a great tool for setting up tough problems. To find any one of the three quantities, you simply need to find the other two, and then perform the operation between them. For instance, if the problem says, "The average (arithmetic mean) of five numbers is 30," just write 30 in the "average" place and 5 in the "how many" place. Notice that there is a multiplication sign between them, so multiply $30 \times 5 = 150$ to find the third quantity: their sum.

Medians

A *median* is something that splits a set into two equal parts. Just think of the median of a highway:

it splits the highway exactly in half. *The median of a set of numbers, then, is the middle number when they are listed in increasing order.* For instance, the median of {−3, 7, 65} is 7, because the set has just as many numbers bigger than 7 as less than 7. If you have an even number of numbers, like {2, 4, 7, 9}, then the set doesn't have one "middle" number, so the median is the average of the two middle numbers. (So the median of {2, 4, 7, 9} is $(4+7)/2 = 5.5$.)

When you take standardized tests like the SAT, your score report often gives your score as a percentile, which shows the percentage of students whose scores were lower than yours. If your percentile score is 50%, this means that you scored at the *median* of all the scores: just as many (50%) of the students scored below your score as above your score.

The average (arithmetic mean) and the median are not always equal, but they are equal whenever the numbers are spaced symmetrically around a single number.

Example:
Consider any set of numbers that is evenly spaced, like 4, 9, 14, 19, and 24:

Notice that these numbers are spaced symmetrically about the number 14. This implies that the mean and the median both equal 14. This can be helpful to know, because finding the median of a set is often much easier than calculating the mean.

Modes

Occasionally the SAT may ask you about the *mode* of a set of numbers. *A mode is the number that appears the most frequently in a set.* (Just remember: MOde = MOst.) It's easy to see that not every set of numbers has a mode. For instance, the mode of {−3, 4, 4, 1, 12} is 4, but {4, 9, 14, 19, 24} doesn't have a mode.

Concept Review 2:
Mean/Median/Mode Problems

1. Draw the "average pyramid."

2. Explain how to use the average pyramid to solve a problem involving averages.

3. Define a median.

4. Define a mode.

5. In what situations is the mean of a set of numbers the same as its median?

6. The average (arithmetic mean) of four numbers is 15. If one of the numbers is 18, what is the average of the remaining three numbers?

7. The average (arithmetic mean) of five different positive integers is 25. If none of the numbers is less than 10, then what is the greatest possible value of one of these numbers?

8. Ms. Appel's class, which has twenty students, scored an average of 90% on a test. Mr. Bandera's class, which has 30 students, scored an average of 80% on the same test. What was the combined average score for the two classes?

SAT Practice 2: Mean/Median/Mode Problems

1. If $y = 2x + 1$, what is the average (arithmetic mean) of $2x$, $2x$, y, and $3y$, in terms of x?

   (A) $2x$ (B) $2x + 1$ (C) $3x$
   (D) $3x + 1$ (E) $3x + 2$

2. The average (arithmetic mean) of seven integers is 11. If each of these integers is less than 20, then what is the least possible value of any one of these integers?

   (A) -113 (B) -77 (C) -37
   (D) -22 (E) 0

3. The median of 8, 6, 1, and k is 5. What is k?

4. The average (arithmetic mean) of two numbers is z. If one of the two numbers is x, what is the value of the other number in terms of x and z?

   (A) $z - x$ (B) $x - z$ (C) $2z - x$
   (D) $x - 2z$ (E) $\dfrac{x + z}{2}$

5. A set of n numbers has an average (arithmetic mean) of $3k$ and a sum of $12m$, where k and m are positive. What is the value of n in terms of k and m?

   (A) $\dfrac{4m}{k}$ (B) $\dfrac{4k}{m}$ (C) $\dfrac{k}{4m}$

   (D) $\dfrac{m}{4k}$ (E) $36km$

6. The average (arithmetic mean) of 5, 8, 2, and k is 0. What is the median of this set?

   (A) 0 (B) 3.5 (C) 3.75
   (D) 5 (E) 5.5

Roll	Frequency
1	5
2	3
3	3
4	3
5	3
6	3

7. A die is rolled 20 times, and the outcomes are as tabulated above. If the average (arithmetic mean) of all the rolls is a, the median of all the rolls is b, and the mode of all the rolls is c, then which of the following must be true?

   I. $a = b$ II. $b > c$ III. $c = 5$

   (A) I only   (B) II only
   (C) I and II only   (D) II and III only
   (E) I, II, and III

8. If a 30% salt solution is added to a 50% salt solution, which of the following could be the concentration of the resulting mixture?

   I.   40%
   II. 45%
   III. 50%

   (A) I only   (B) I and II only
   (C) I and III only   (D) II and III only
   (E) I, II, and III

9. Set A consists of five numbers with a median of m. If Set B consists of the five numbers that are two greater than each of the numbers in Set A, which of the following must be true?

   I.   The median of Set B is greater than m.
   II. The average (arithmetic mean) of Set B is greater than m.
   III. The greatest possible difference between two numbers in Set B is greater than the greatest possible difference between two numbers in Set A.

   (A) I only   (B) I and II only
   (C) I and III only   (D) II and III only
   (E) I, II, and III

Answer Key 2: Mean/Median/Mode Problems

Concept Review 2

1. It should look like this:

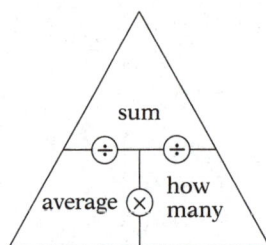

2. When two of the three values are given in a problem, write them in the pyramid and perform the operation between them. The result is the other value in the pyramid.

3. A median is the "middle" number when the numbers are listed in order. If there are an even number of numbers in the set, it is the average of the two middle numbers.

4. The number that appears the most frequently in a set.

5. When the numbers are evenly spaced, the mean is always equal to the median. This is true more generally if the numbers are distributed "symmetrically" about the mean, as in $[-10, -7, 0, 7, 10]$.

6. If the average of four numbers is 15, then their sum must be $(4)(15) = 60$. If one of the numbers is 18, then the sum of the other three is $60 - 18 = 42$. So the average of the other three is $42/3 = 14$.

7. You need to read this problem super-carefully. If the average of the five numbers is 25, then their sum is $(5)(25) = 125$. If none of the numbers is less than 10, and since they are all *different integers,* the least that four of them can be is 10, 11, 12, and 13. Therefore, if x is the largest possible number in the set,

$$x + 10 + 11 + 12 + 13 = 125$$
Simplify: $\qquad\qquad\qquad\qquad x + 46 = 125$
Subtract 46: $\qquad\qquad\qquad\qquad\quad x = 79$

8. If the 20 students in Ms. Appel's class averaged 90%, then they must have scored a total of $(20)(90) = 1{,}800$ points. Similarly, Mr. Bandera's class scored a total of $(30)(80) = 2{,}400$. The combined average is just the sum of all the scores divided by the number of scores: $(1{,}800 + 2{,}400)/50 = 84$.

Notice, too, that you can get a good estimate by just noticing that *if* there were an equal number of students in each class, the overall average would simply be the average of 80 and 90, which is 85. But since there are more students in Mr. Bandera's class, the average must be weighted more heavily toward 80.

SAT Practice 2

1. **D** The average of $2x$, $2x$, y, and $3y$ is $(2x + 2x + y + 3y)/4 = (4x + 4y)/4 = x + y$. Substituting $2x + 1$ for y gives $x + (2x + 1) = 3x + 1$.

2. **C** If the average of seven integers is 11, their sum is $(7)(11) = 77$. If each of these integers is less than 20, then the greatest any can be is 19. The question doesn't say that the integers must be different, so if x is the least possible of these integers, $x + 19 + 19 + 19 + 19 + 19 + 19 = 77$.

Simplify: $\qquad\qquad\qquad x + 114 = 77$
Subtract 114: $\qquad\qquad\qquad\quad x = -37$

3. **4** The median is the average of the two middle numbers. A little trial and error shows that 1, 4, 6, and 8 have a median of 5, so k must be 4.

4. **C** Call the number you are looking for y. The average of x and y is z, so set up the equation and solve:

$$(x + y)/2 = z$$
Multiply by 2: $\qquad\qquad\qquad x + y = 2z$
Subtract x: $\qquad\qquad\qquad\qquad\quad y = 2z - x$

5. **A** Just fill in the pyramid: $n = 12m/3k = 4m/k$.

6. **B** The average is 0, so $(5 + 8 + 2 + k) = 0$. Solving for k gives us $k = -15$. So we put the numbers in order: $-15, 2, 5, 8$. Since there are an even number of numbers, the median is the average of the two middle numbers: $(2+5)/2 = 3.5$.

7. **B** The most frequent number is 1, so $c = 1$. This means that statement III is untrue, and you can eliminate choices (D) and (E). To find the median, you need to find the average of the 10th and 11th numbers, when you arrange them in order. Since

both of these are 3, $b = 3$. Therefore, statement II is true, and you can eliminate choice (A). To find the average, just divide the sum by 20: $((1)(5) + (2)(3) + (3)(3) + (4)(3) + (5)(3) + (6)(3))/20 = 3.25$, so $a = 3.25$. Therefore, statement I is not true, so the answer is (B).

8. **B** When a 30% solution and a 50% solution are combined, the concentration must be anywhere between 30% and 50%, depending on how much of each you added. It can't be 50%, though, because the 30% solution dilutes it.

9. **A** If Set A were {0, 0, 10, 10, 10}, then its median, m, would be 10. Set B would be {2, 2, 12, 12, 12}. Inspection of Set B shows that it is a counterexample to statements II and III, leaving (A) as a possible answer.

Lesson 3: Numerical Reasoning Problems

Arithmetic Reasoning

> Some of the most common problems on the SAT are *numerical reasoning* problems, which ask you to think about what happens to numbers when you perform basic operations on them. You just need to know the common numerical and arithmetic rules and think logically.

Example:

If $a + b$ is negative, which of the following CANNOT be negative?

(A) ab (B) ab^2 (C) a^2b
(D) a^2b^2 (E) $a - b$

Start by thinking about what *might* be true about a and b and what *must* be true about a and b. First think of possible values for a and b. –2 and 1 work, because $a + b = -2 + 1 = -1$. Notice that this proves that (A), (B), and (E) are incorrect, because they can be negative: (A) $ab = (-2)(1) = -2$, (B) $ab^2 = (-2)(1)^2 = -2$, and (E) $a - b = (-2) - (1) = -3$. But (C) $a^2b = (-2)^2(1) = 4$ is *positive*, so does that mean the answer is (C)? Not so fast! Your job is *not* to find which one *can be positive*, but rather which *cannot be negative*. Notice that (C) can be negative if a and b are, say, 1 and –2 (notice that $a + b$ is still negative, so those values work): (C) $a^2b = (1)^2(-2) = -2$. Therefore, by process of elimination, the answer is (D).

This question is much easier if you remember a simple fact: If x is a real number, then x^2 is never negative. If you don't know this already, play around with possible values of x until you see why this is true. Then look at choice (D) a^2b^2. a^2 can't be negative, and neither can b^2, so a^2b^2 can't be negative.

Example:

If $m < n < p < r$, $mnpr = 0$, and $m + n + p + r = 0$, then which of the following must be true?

    I. If m and n are negative, then $p = 0$.
   II. $np = 0$
  III. $m + r = 0$

(A) I only   (B) II only
(C) I and II only   (D) I and III only
(E) I, II, and III

The first statement, $m < n < p < r$, tells you that the alphabetical order is also the numerical order of the numbers. The second statement, $mnpr = 0$, tells you that one of the numbers must be 0. (This is the zero product property!) The third statement, $m + n + p + r = 0$, tells you that you must have at least one positive and one negative, and all the numbers must "cancel out." This means that m can't be 0 because then none of the numbers would be negative, and r can't be 0, because then none of the numbers would be positive. Thus, either n or p is 0. This means that both I and II are necessarily true, so you can eliminate choices (A), (B), and (D). The example $m = -3$, $n = 0$, $p = 1$, $r = 2$ shows that statement III is not necessarily true, so the answer is (C).

Digit Problems

> You may see a question on the SAT like the one below, where letters represent *digits*. Remember that *digits can only take the values 0, 1, 2, 3, 4, 5, 6, 7, 8, and 9*. Also remember that you may have to consider "carried" digits when looking at a sum or product. Lastly, you may find it best to work from left to right rather than right to left.

Example:

$$\begin{array}{r} 1BA \\ + 8B \\ \hline 211 \end{array}$$

If A and B represent distinct digits in this addition problem, what is the value of $A - B$?

(A) –9   (B) –7   (C) 2
(D) 7   (E) 9

Look at the left (hundreds) column first. Since the sum has a 2 in the hundreds place, there must be a carry of 1 from the tens place. Therefore, $B + 8 +$ (carry from ones column, if any) = 11. This means $B = 2$ or 3. Trying each one shows that only $B = 2$ and $A = 9$ works, giving $129 + 82 = 211$. Therefore $A - B = 9 - 2 = 7$, so the answer is (D).

Concept Review 3:
Numerical Reasoning Problems

1. If neither a nor b is 0, what is the relationship between $a \div b$ and $b \div a$?

2. What is the relationship between $a - b$ and $b - a$?

Complete the following "parity rules."

3. Odd × even = _____

4. Even × even = _____

5. Odd × odd = _____

6. Even + even = _____

7. Odd + even = _____

8. Odd + odd = _____

Complete the following "sign rules."

9. If n is odd, $(-1)^n =$ _____.

10. If n is even, $(-1)^n =$ _____.

11. If $x + y = 0$ and $x \neq 0$, then $x/y =$ _____.

12. Dividing by x is the same as multiplying by _____.

13. Subtracting $(x + 1)$ is the same as adding _____.

14. When a number is multiplied by its reciprocal, the result is _____.

15. When a number and its opposite are added, the result is _____.

16. When a number (other than 0) is divided by its opposite, the result is _____.

17. If a positive number is multiplied by a number greater than 1, what happens to it? _____

18. If a positive number is multiplied by a number between 0 and 1, what happens to it? _____

19. If a negative number is multiplied by a number greater than 1, what happens to it? _____

20. Is x always bigger than $-x$? Explain.

21. Is x^2 always bigger than x? Explain.

22. Is x^3 always bigger than x^2? Explain.

23. If x is between 0 and 1, then $1/x$ is _____.

24. If $a > b > 0$, then $\dfrac{a}{b}$ is _____.

25. If $b > a > 0$, then $\dfrac{a}{b}$ is _____.

SAT Practice 3: Numerical Reasoning Problems

1. If m and n are both odd integers, which of the following must be true?

        I. $m^2 + n^2$ is even
       II. $m^2 + n^2$ is divisible by 4
     III. $(m + n)^2$ is divisible by 4

(A) none
(B) I only
(C) I and II only
(D) I and III only
(E) I, II, and III

2.
$$\begin{array}{r} 6AA \\ \times\ 8 \\ \hline 50B4 \end{array}$$

If A and B represent distinct digits in this correctly worked multiplication problem, what is the value of B?

(A) 2   (B) 3   (C) 5
(D) 6   (E) 8

3. If j is the number of integers between 1 and 500 that are divisible by 9 and k is the number of integers between 1 and 500 that are divisible by 7, what is $j + k$?

(A) 126   (B) 127   (C) 128
(D) 129   (E) 130

4. If 60 is written as the product of four integers, each greater than 1, then what is the sum of those integers?

5. If n is an integer and 2^n is a factor of $1 \times 2 \times 3 \times 4 \times 5 \times 6 \times 7 \times 8 \times 9$, what is the greatest possible value of n?

(A) 5   (B) 6   (C) 7
(D) 8   (E) 9

6. If $p + pq$ is 4 times $p - pq$, and $pq \neq 0$, which of the following has exactly one possible value?

(A) p
(B) q
(C) pq
(D) $p + pq$
(E) $p - pq$

7. If a, b, c, d, and e are whole numbers and $a(b(c + d) + e)$ is odd, then which of the following CANNOT be even?

(A) a
(B) b
(C) c
(D) d
(E) e

$$a + b + c = 7$$
$$c + d + e = 9$$

8. If each letter in the sums above represents a different positive integer, then $c =$

(A) 1   (B) 2   (C) 3
(D) 4   (E) 5

$$\begin{array}{r} ABB \\ +9B7 \\ \hline AA7C \end{array}$$

9. If A, B, and C are distinct digits in the correctly worked addition problem above, what is the value of $A + B + C$?

(A) 4   (B) 9   (C) 14
(D) 16   (E) 17

Answer Key 3: Numerical Reasoning Problems

Concept Review 3

1. They are reciprocals, so their product is 1.

2. They are opposites, so their sum is 0.

3. Odd × even = even

4. Even × even = even

5. Odd × odd = odd

6. Even + even = even

7. Odd + even = odd

8. Odd + odd = even

9. If n is odd, $(-1)^n = -1$.

10. If n is even, $(-1)^n = 1$.

11. If $x + y = 0$ and $x \neq 0$, then $x/y = -1$.

12. Dividing by x is the same as multiplying by $1/x$.

13. Subtracting $(x + 1)$ is the same as adding $-x - 1$.

14. When a number is multiplied by its reciprocal, the result is 1.

15. When a number and its opposite are added, the result is 0.

16. When a number (other than 0) is divided by its opposite, the result is –1.

17. It gets bigger.

18. It gets smaller.

19. It gets smaller (more negative).

20. No. If x is 0, then $-x$ is equal to x, and if x is negative, then $-x$ is greater than x.

21. No. If x is between 0 and 1, then x^2 is smaller than x. And if x is 0 or 1, then they are the same. If x is negative, then x^2 is positive, and therefore greater than x.

22. No. If x is between 0 and 1, then x^3 is smaller than x^2. And if x is 0 or 1, then they are the same. If x is negative, then x^2 is positive, and therefore greater than x^3.

23. greater than 1.

24. greater than 1.

25. between 0 and 1.

SAT Practice 3

1. **D**   Start with the simplest odd values for m and n: $m = n = 1$. (There's no reason why m and n can't equal the same number!) Notice that $m^2 + n^2 = 1^2 + 1^2 = 2$, which isn't divisible by 4, so statement II is not necessarily true, and you can eliminate choices (C) and (E). Next, notice that m^2 and n^2 must both be odd, so $m^2 + n^2$ must be even, so statement I is necessarily true, and you can eliminate choice (A). $(m + n)^2$ must be a multiple of 4 because $m + n$ must be even (odd + odd = even), so it is a multiple of 2. When it is squared, it becomes a multiple of 4. So III is true, and the answer is (D).

2. **D**   Trial and error should show that A = 3. If A is less than 3, the product is too small. If A is greater than 3, the product is too large. Since 633 × 8 = 5,064, B = 6.

3. **A** $500 \div 9 = 55.55$, so there are 55 multiples of 9 between 1 and 500. $500 \div 7 = 71.43$, so there are 71 multiples of 7 between 1 and 500. So $j + k = 55 + 71 = 126$.

4. **12**   Trial and error shows that the only way to write 60 as the product of four integers, each greater than 1, is 2 × 2 × 3 × 5. Their sum is $2 + 2 + 3 + 5 = 12$.

5. **C**   Do the prime factorization:

    $1 \times 2 \times 3 \times 4 \times 5 \times 6 \times 7 \times 8 \times 9 = 1 \times 2 \times 3 \times (2 \times 2)$
    $\times 5 \times (2 \times 3) \times 7 \times (2 \times 2 \times 2) \times (3 \times 3)$

Since there are seven factors of 2, the greatest power of 2 that is a factor is 2^7.

6. **B**
	$p + pq = 4(p - pq)$
Distribute:	$p + pq = 4p - 4pq$
Divide by p:	$1 + q = 4 - 4q$

    (This is okay as long as p is anything but 0.)
Add $4q$:	$1 + 5q = 4$
Subtract 1:	$5q = 3$
Divide by 5:	$q = 3/5$

    Because p can have many possible values but q can only equal 3/5, (B) q is the only expression that has only one possible value.

7. **A** a cannot be even, because an even number times any other integer yields an even number, but $a(b(c + d) + e)$ is odd.

8. **A**   The only three different positive integers that have a sum of 7 are 1, 2, and 4. The only three different positive integers that have a sum of 9 are 1, 3, and 5 or 1, 2, and 6. But $1 + 2 + 6$ doesn't work, since that would have *two* numbers in common with the first set, but it may only have one (C). Since (C) is the only number they may have in common, it must be 1.

9. **C**   The only solution is $188 + 987 = 1,175$, so $A + B + C = 1 + 8 + 5 = 14$.

Lesson 4: Rate Problems

What Are Rates?

The word *rate* comes from the same Latin root as the word *ratio*. All rates are ratios. The most common type of rate is *speed*, which is a *ratio with respect to time*, as in *miles per hour* or *words per minute*, but some rates don't involve time at all, as in *miles per gallon*. Rate units always have *per* in their names: *miles per gallon*, *meters per second*, etc. *Per*, remember, means *divided by*, and is like the colon (:) or fraction bar in a ratio.

The Rate Pyramid

The name of any rate is equivalent to its formula.
For instance, speed is miles per hour

can be translated as $\text{Speed} = \dfrac{\text{number of miles}}{\text{number of hours}}$

or

$\text{Speed} = \dfrac{\text{distance}}{\text{time}}$

Since this formula is similar to the "average" formula, you can make a *rate pyramid*.

This can be a great tool for solving rate problems. If a problem gives you two of the quantities, just put them in their places in the pyramid, and do the operation between them to find the missing quantity.

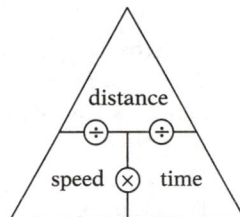

Example:

How long will it take a car to travel 20 miles at 60 miles per hour?

Simply fill the quantities into the pyramid: 20 miles goes in the distance spot, and 60 miles an hour goes in the speed spot. Now what? Just do the division the way the diagram says: 20 miles ÷ 60 miles per hour = 1/3 hour.

Watch Your Units

Whenever you work with formulas, you can check your work by paying attention to units. For instance, the problem above asks *how long*, so the calculation has to produce a *time* unit. Check the units in the calculation:

$$\dfrac{\text{miles}}{\dfrac{\text{miles}}{\text{hours}}} = \text{miles} \times \dfrac{\text{hours}}{\text{miles}} = \text{hours}$$

Two-Part Rate Problems

Rate problems are tougher when they involve two parts. When a problem involves, say, two people working together at different rates and times, or a two-part trip, you have to analyze the problem more carefully.

Example:

Toni bicycles to work at a rate of 20 miles per hour, then takes the bus home *along the same route* at a rate of 40 miles per hour. What is her average speed for the entire trip?

At first glance, it might seem that you can just average the two rates: (20 + 40)/2 = 30 miles per hour, since she is traveling the same distance at each of the two speeds. But this won't work, because she isn't spending the same **time** at each speed, and that is what's important. But if that's true, you might notice that she spends **twice** as much time going 20 miles per hour as 40 miles per hour (since it's half as fast), so instead of taking the average of 20 and 40, you can take the average of **two** 20s and a 40:

(20 + 20 + 40)/3 = 26.67 miles per hour. Simple! But if that doesn't make sense to you, think of it this way: Imagine, for simplicity's sake, that her trip to work is 40 miles. (It doesn't matter what number you pick, and 40 is an easy number to work with here.) Now the average speed is simply the total distance divided by the total time (as the pyramid says). The total distance, there and back, is 80 miles. The total time is in two parts. Getting to work takes her 40 miles ÷ 20 miles per hour = 2 hours. Getting home takes her 40 miles ÷ 40 miles per hour = 1 hour. So the **total** time of the trip is 3 hours. The average speed, then, must be 80 miles ÷ 3 hours = 26.67 miles per hour!

Concept Review 4: Rate Problems

For each of the following rates, write the formula of the rate and the corresponding "rate pyramid."

1. Speed is miles per hour.

2. Efficiency is miles per gallon of fuel.

3. Typing speed is pages per minute.

Find the missing quantity, including the units, in each of these rate situations.

4. A train travels for 375 miles at 75 mph.

5. A car that gets 28 miles per gallon uses 4.5 gallons of fuel.

6. Harold can type 600 words in 5 minutes.

7. A landscaper who cuts 1.6 acres of grass per hour cuts an 8-acre lot.

8. A train leaves New York at 1:00 pm, going 50 mph, bound for Philadelphia, which is 90 miles away. If it makes no stops, at what time should it be expected to arrive?

9. Anne can paint a room in 2 hours, and Barbara can paint a room in 3 hours. When they work together, their work rate is the sum of their rates working separately. How long should it take them to paint a room if they work together?

SAT Practice 4: Rate Problems

1. Janice and Edward are editors at a newspaper. Janice can edit 700 words per minute and Edward can edit 500 words per minute. If each page of text contains 800 words, how many pages can they edit, working together, in 20 minutes?

2. Two cars leave the same point simultaneously, going in the same direction along a straight, flat road, one at 35 mph and one at 50 mph. After how many <u>minutes</u> will the cars be 5 miles apart?

3. What is the average speed, in miles per hour, of a sprinter who runs ¼ mile in 45 seconds? (1 hour = 60 minutes)

(A) 11.25 mph   (B) 13.5 mph
(C) 20 mph   (D) 22 mph
(E) 25 mph

4. A car travels d miles in t hours and arrives at its destination 3 hours late. At what average speed, in miles per hour, should the car have gone in order to have arrived on time?

(A) $t - 3$ (B) $\dfrac{t-3}{d}$ (C) $\dfrac{d}{t-3}$

(D) $\dfrac{d}{t} - 3$ (E) $\dfrac{t}{d-3}$

5. If $x > 1$, how many hours does it take a train traveling at $x - 1$ miles per hour to travel $x^2 - 1$ miles?

(A) $\dfrac{1}{x-1}$ (B) $\dfrac{1}{x+1}$ (C) x

(D) $x - 1$ (E) $x + 1$

6. In three separate 1-mile races, Ellen finishes with times of x minutes, y minutes, and z minutes. What was her average speed, in miles per *hour*, for all three races? (1 hour = 60 minutes)

(A) $\dfrac{x+y+z}{3}$ (B) $\dfrac{3}{x+y+z}$

(C) $\dfrac{x+y+z}{180}$ (D) $\dfrac{180}{x+y+z}$

(E) $\dfrac{x+y+z}{20}$

7. A hare runs at a constant rate of a mph, a tortoise runs at a constant rate of b mph, and $0 < b < a$. If they race each other for d miles, how many more hours, in terms of a, b, and d, will it take the tortoise to finish than the hare?

(A) $\dfrac{a+b}{2d}$ (B) $\dfrac{d}{b} - \dfrac{d}{a}$

(C) $\dfrac{b}{d} - \dfrac{a}{d}$ (D) $ad - bd$ (E) $a - b$

8. Sylvia drives 315 miles and arrives at her destination in 9 hours. If she had driven at an average rate that was 10 mph faster than her actual rate, how many hours sooner would she have arrived?

(A) 1.75   (B) 2.00   (C) 2.25
(D) 2.50   (E) 2.75

Answer Key 4: Rate Problems

Concept Review 4

1. Speed = #miles ÷ #hours

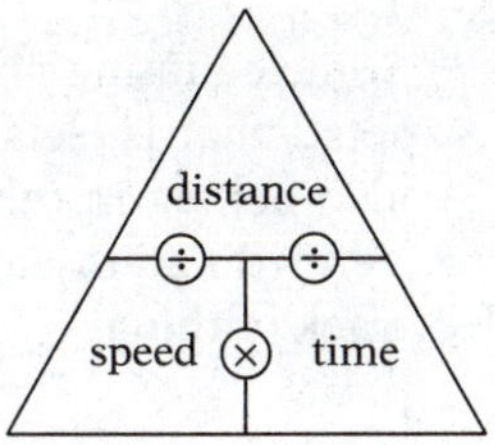

2. Efficiency = #miles ÷ #gallons

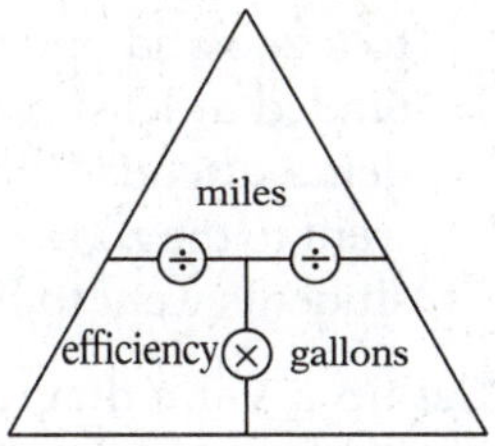

3. Typing speed = #pages ÷ #minutes

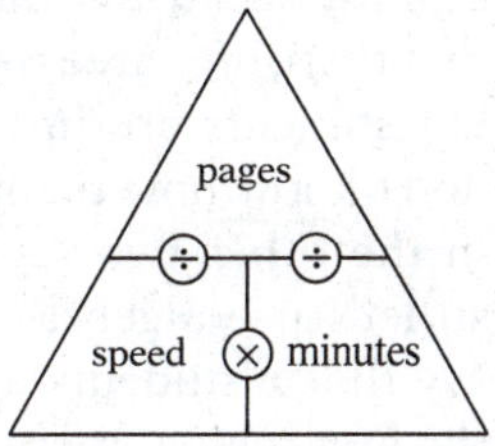

4. 375 miles ÷ 75 mph = 5 hours for the trip.
5. 28 miles per gallon × 4.5 gallons = 126 miles the car can go before it runs out of fuel.
6. 600 words ÷ 5 minutes = 120 words per minute is Harold's typing speed.
7. 8 acres ÷ 1.6 acres per hour = 5 hours for the job.
8. 90 miles ÷ 50 mph = 1.8 hours, or 1 hour 48 minutes for the entire trip. At 1 hour and 48 minutes after 1:00 pm, it is 2:48 pm.
9. Anne can paint one room in 2 hours, so her rate is $\frac{1}{2}$ room per hour. Barbara can paint one room in 3 hours, so her rate is $\frac{1}{3}$ room per hour. When they work together, their rate is $\frac{1}{2} + \frac{1}{3} = \frac{5}{6}$ room per hour. So to paint one room would take one room ÷ $\frac{5}{6}$ room per hour = $\frac{6}{5}$ hours, or 1.2 hours, or 1 hour 12 minutes.

SAT Practice 4

1. **30** Working together, they edit 700 + 500 = 1,200 words per minute. Since each page is 800 words, that's 1,200 words per minute ÷ 800 words per page = 1.5 pages per minute. In 20 minutes, then, they can edit 1.5 × 20 = 30 pages.
2. **20** Since the two cars are traveling in the same direction, their relative speed (that is, the speed at which they are moving away from each other) is 50 – 35 = 15 mph. In other words, they will be 15 miles farther apart each hour. Therefore, the time it takes them to get 5 miles apart is 5 miles ÷ 15 miles per hour = 1/3 hour, which is equivalent to 20 minutes.
3. **C** Since there are (60)(60) = 3,600 seconds in an hour, 45 seconds = 45/3,600 hour. Speed = distance ÷ time = 1/4 mile ÷ 45/3,600 hour = 3,600/180 = 20 miles per hour.
4. **C** To arrive on time, the car must take $t - 3$ hours for the whole trip. To travel d miles in $t - 3$ hours, the car must go $d/(t - 3)$ miles per hour.
5. **E** According to the rate pyramid, time = distance ÷ speed = $(x^2 - 1)$ miles ÷ $(x - 1)$ miles per hour = $\frac{x^2-1}{x-1} = \frac{(x-1)(x+1)}{x-1} = x+1$ hours. Or you can pick a simple value for x, like 2, and solve numerically.
6. **D** Speed = miles ÷ hours. Her total time for the three races is $x + y + z$ minutes, which we must convert to hours by multiplying by the conversion factor (1 hour/60 minutes), which gives us $(x + y + z)/60$ hours. Since her total distance is 3 miles, her overall speed is 3 miles ÷ $(x + y + z)/60$ hours = $180/(x + y + z)$ miles per hour.
7. **B** If the hare's rate is a mph, then he covers d miles in d/a hours. Similarly, the tortoise covers d miles in d/b hours. The difference in their finishing times, then, is $d/b - d/a$.
8. **B** Sylvia's speed is 315 miles ÷ 9 hours = 35 mph. If she were to go 10 mph faster, then her speed would be 45 mph, so her time would be 315 miles ÷ 45 mph = 7 hours, which is 2 hours sooner.

Lesson 5: Counting Problems

The Fundamental Counting Principle

Some SAT questions ask you to count things. Sometimes it's easy enough to just write out the things in a list and count them by hand. Other times, though, there will be too many, and it will help to use the Fundamental Counting Principle.

> To use the **Fundamental Counting Principle** (FCP), you have to think of the things you're counting as coming from a sequence of choices. The Fundamental Counting Principle says that the number of ways an event can happen is equal to the product of the choices that must be made to "build" the event.

Example:

How many ways can five people be arranged in a line?

You might consider calling the five people *A, B, C, D,* and *E,* and listing the number of arrangements. After a while, though, you'll see that this is going to take a lot of time, because there are a lot of possibilities. (Not to mention that it's really easy to miss some of them.) Instead, think of "building" the line with a sequence of choices: first pick the first person, then pick the second person, etc. There are five choices to make, so we'll have to multiply five numbers. Clearly, there are five people to choose from for the first person in line. Once you do this, though, there are only four people left for the second spot, then three for the third spot, etc. By the Fundamental Counting Principle, then, the number of possible arrangements is $5 \times 4 \times 3 \times 2 \times 1 = 120$.

Example:

How many odd integers greater than 500 and less than 1,000 have an even digit in the tens place?

This seems a lot harder than it is. Again, think of "building" the numbers in question. All integers between 500 and 1,000 have three digits, so building the number involves choosing three digits, so we will multiply three numbers to get our answer. If each number is between 500 and 1,000, then there are only five choices for the first digit: 5, 6, 7, 8, or 9. If the tens digit must be even, we have five choices again: 2, 4, 6, 8, or 0. If the entire number is odd, then we have five choices for the last digit as well: 1, 3, 5, 7, or 9. Therefore, the total number of such integers is $5 \times 5 \times 5 = 125$.

Using Venn Diagrams to Keep Track of Sets

> Some counting problems involve "overlapping sets," that is, sets that contain elements that also belong in other sets. In these situations, Venn diagrams are very helpful for keeping track of things.

Example:

A class of 29 students sponsored two field trips: one to a zoo and one to a museum. Every student attended at least one of the field trips, and 10 students attended both. If twice as many students went to the zoo as went to the museum, how many students went to the zoo?

Set up a Venn diagram of the situation. We represent the two sets—those who went to the museum and those who went to the zoo—as two overlapping circles, because some students went to both. Notice that there are three regions to consider. We know that ten students are in the overlapping region, but we don't know how many are in the other two regions, so let's use algebra. Let's say that x students are in the first region, representing those who went to the museum but not to the zoo. This means that $x + 10$ students must have gone to the museum altogether. Since twice as many students went to the zoo, the total number in the zoo circle must be $2(x + 10) = 2x + 20$. Since 10 of these are already accounted for in the overlapping region, there must be $2x + 20 - 10 = 2x + 10$ in the third region. So now the diagram should look like this:

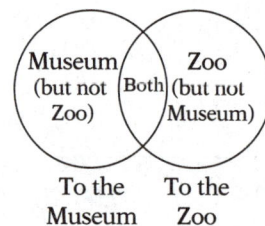

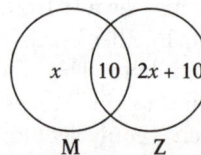

The total number of students is 29, so

$$(x) + (10) + (2x + 10) = 29$$

Simplify: $\qquad\qquad\qquad\qquad 3x + 20 = 29$

Solve: $\qquad\qquad\qquad\qquad\qquad\quad x = 3$

So the number of students who went to the zoo is $2(3) + 20 = 26$.

Concept Review 5: Counting Problems

1. What is the fundamental counting principle?

2. How many different four-letter arrangements of the letters LMNO can be made if no letter can be repeated? Answer this first by listing all of the possible arrangements, then by using the Fundamental Counting Principle, and check that the two answers agree.

3. If the first digit of a 3-digit area code cannot be 0 and the second digit is either 0 or 1, then how many different area codes are possible?

4. A baseball team has six players, each of whom can play in any of the three outfield positions: left field, center field, and right field. How many possible different arrangements of these players can the team place in the outfield? (This one is a bit harder to do by listing!)

5. Among a set of 40 sophomores, 20 students take French and 27 students take Spanish. If all of the students take either French or Spanish, how many students take both French *and* Spanish?

6. A box contains buttons, each of which is either blue or green and has either two or four holes. If there are four times as many blue buttons as green buttons and six times as many four-holed buttons as two-holed buttons, what is the *least* number of buttons that could be in the box?

SAT Practice 5: Counting Problems

1. A pizzeria offers three different sizes of pizza, two different kinds of crust, and eight different choices for toppings. How many different one-topping pizzas are there to choose from?

(A) 13   (B) 16   (C) 24
(D) 48   (E) 60

0, 2, 4, 6, 8

2. How many different integers between 30 and 70 contain only digits from the list above?

(A) 7   (B) 10   (C) 15
(D) 20   (E) 25

---

3. In how many ways can you arrange four different paintings in a line on a wall?

(A) 12   (B) 24   (C) 36
(D) 48   (E) 64

---

4. At Lincoln County High School, 36 students are taking either calculus or physics or both, and 10 students are taking both calculus and physics. If there are 31 students in the calculus class, how many students are there in the physics class?

(A) 5   (B) 8   (C) 11
(D) 15   (E) 21

---

5. Dave's stickball team has six players. How many different six-player batting lineups can they make if Dave must bat second and either Zack or Paul must bat first?

(A) 48   (B) 96   (C) 192
(D) 256   (E) 720

---

6. Maria gave David x cards, gave Tina two more cards than she gave David, and gave Samuel five fewer cards than she gave Tina. In terms of x, how many cards did Maria give Tina, David, and Samuel all together?

(A) $3x + 9$ (B) $3x - 1$
(C) $3x - 3$ (D) $x - 3$
(E) $x - 1$

---

7. From a collection of six paintings, four are to be chosen to hang on a wall. How many different arrangements are possible if every painting is different?

(A) 24   (B) 120   (C) 360
(D) 720   (E) 1,296

---

8. Every marble in a jar has either a dot, a stripe, or both. The ratio of striped marbles to non-striped marbles is 3:1, and the ratio of dotted marbles to nondotted marbles is 2:3. If six marbles have both a dot and a stripe, how many marbles are there all together?

(A) 16   (B) 18   (C) 20
(D) 36   (E) 40

---

9. An ant must walk from one vertex of a cube to the "opposite" vertex (that is, the vertex that is farthest from the starting vertex) and back again to its starting position. It may only walk along the edges of the cube. For the entire trip, its path must traverse exactly six edges, and it *may* travel on the same edge twice. How many different six-edge paths can the ant choose from?

Answer Key 5: Counting Problems

Concept Review 5

1. The number of ways an event can happen is equal to the product of the choices that must be made to "build" the event.

2. Try listing all the "words" that start with L, then all that start with M, and so on:

LMNO	MLNO	NLMO	OLMN
LMON	MLON	NLOM	OLNM
LNMO	MNLO	NMLO	OMLN
LNOM	MNOL	NMOL	OMNL
LOMN	MOLN	NOLM	ONML
LONM	MONL	NOML	ONLM

Whew! 24 in total. Annoying, but not impossible. Using the FCP makes it a lot easier: $4 \times 3 \times 2 \times 1 = 24$. That's it!

3. There are too many possibilities to list, but the FCP makes it easy: We have 9 choices for the first digit, 2 choices for the second digit, and 10 choices for the last digit, and $9 \times 2 \times 10 = 180$.

4. "Build" the outfield from left to right. You have 6 players to choose from for left field, but then just 5 for center field and 4 for right field. $6 \times 5 \times 4 = 120$.

5. Since $20 + 27 - 40 = 7$, there must be 7 students who take both. This Venn diagram shows how it works out:

13 (7) 20
F S

6. This one's tough. Say there are g green buttons. If there are four times as many blue buttons as green buttons, then there are $4g$ blue buttons, so $g + 4g = 5g$ buttons in total. So the total number of buttons must be a multiple of 5. Similarly, if there are n two-holed buttons, there must be $6n$ four-holed buttons, so the total number of buttons is $n + 6n = 7n$, so the total number of buttons is also a multiple of 7. The least common multiple of 5 and 7 is 35, so there are 35 buttons: 5 two-holed and 30 four-holed, and 7 green and 28 blue.

SAT Practice 5

1. **D** Use the FCP: $3 \times 2 \times 8 = 48$.

2. **B** "Build" the number: If it's between 30 and 70, it must be a two-digit number that begins with 4 or 6. That's two choices. The second digit can be anything in the list, so that's 5 choices. $2 \times 5 = 10$

3. **B** Since there are four spaces, there are four decisions to make, so four numbers to multiply. You can choose from four paintings for the first spot, then three paintings for the second spot, etc. $4 \times 3 \times 2 \times 1 = 24$

4. **D** If there are 31 students in calculus but 10 of these are also taking physics, then $31 - 10 = 21$ students are taking only calculus. If there are 36 students taking either physics or calculus, but only 31 are taking calculus, then $36 - 31 = 5$ students are taking only physics. Therefore, the Venn diagram should look like this:

As you can see, $5 + 10 = 15$ students are taking physics.

5 (10) 21
P C

5. **A** "Build" the lineup. You have six spots to fill, and thus six decisions to make and six numbers to multiply. You only have two choices for the first spot (Zack or Paul) and one choice for the second spot (Dave), then you have four players left to fill the other slots, so you have four choices for the third spot, then three for the fourth spot, etc. $2 \times 1 \times 4 \times 3 \times 2 \times 1 = 48$

6. **B** David gets x cards. Tina gets two more cards than David, which is $x + 2$. Samuel gets five fewer cards than Tina, which is $x + 2 - 5 = x - 3$. So all together, $x + x + 2 + x - 3 = 3x - 1$.

7. **C** You have six choices for the first spot, then five for the second, then four for the third and three for the fourth. $6 \times 5 \times 4 \times 3 = 360$

8. **E** Set up the Venn diagram: Since the ratio of striped marbles to nonstriped marbles is 3:1, $x + 6 = 3y$, and since the ratio of dotted marbles to nondotted marbles is 2:3, $y + 6 = 2/3x$ and therefore $y = 2/3x - 6$. Substituting, we get $x + 6 = 3(2/3x - 6)$ or $x + 6 = 2x - 18$, so $x = 24$. Plug this back in to get $y = 2/3(24) - 6 = 10$. Total = $24 + 6 + 10 = 40$.

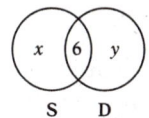

x (6) y
S D

9. **36** Draw the cube. To get from any vertex to its opposite vertex, the ant has $3 \times 2 \times 1$ possible paths. To see why, trace a path and notice it has three choices for the first edge, then two for the second, then only one option for the third. Since it must return to the opposite vertex, it has $3 \times 2 \times 1$ different paths it can take back. $3 \times 2 \times 1 \times 3 \times 2 \times 1 = 36$

Lesson 6: Probability Problems

Probability

A probability is a number between 0 and 1 that represents the likelihood of an event. An event with a probability of 0 is impossible, and an event with a probability of 1 is certain. Most probabilities, of course, are somewhere in between 0 and 1. For instance, the probability of rolling a 5 on a fair die is ⅙. It's best to think of a probability as a part-to-whole ratio. There are six possible outcomes when you roll a die (the whole), but only one of them is 5 (the part). Thus, the probability of rolling a 5 is ⅙.

Example:
What is the probability of rolling a sum of 5 on two dice?

Here is a table showing all the possible sums on a roll of two dice:

Die 1

	1	2	3	4	5	6
1	2	3	4	5	6	7
2	3	4	5	6	7	8
3	4	5	6	7	8	9
4	5	6	7	8	9	10
5	6	7	8	9	10	11
6	7	8	9	10	11	12

Die 2

Clearly, there are four ways of getting a sum of 5 out of a possible 36, so the probability is ⁴⁄₃₆, or ⅑.

Geometrical Probability

An SAT question may ask you to find the probability that something hits a certain region, like a dart hitting a dartboard. In these situations, the probability is just the ratio of the particular area to the entire area.

Example:
A landing target for skydivers consists of two concentric circles. The smaller circle has a radius of 3 meters, and the larger one has a radius of 6 meters. If a skydiver hits the target, what is the probability that she hits the smaller circle?

It might help to sketch the target:

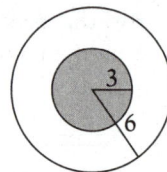

If she hits the target, then she hits an area that is $\pi(6)^2 = 36\pi$ square meters in area. The smaller circle, though, is only $\pi(3)^2 = 9\pi$ square meters in area, so the probability that she lands within the smaller region should be just $9\pi/36\pi = 1/4$.

Concept Review 6: Probability Problems

1. The probability of an impossible event is _____.

2. The probability of an event that is certain is _____.

3. If a jar contains 3 red marbles, 4 white marbles, and 5 blue marbles, then what is the probability of randomly choosing

    a red marble?   _____

    a white marble?   _____

    a blue marble?   _____

4. A jar contains 5 red marbles and 10 white marbles.

    What is the probability of drawing a red marble? _____

    If 3 more red marbles are added, then what is the probability of drawing a red marble? _____

5. A jar contains 24 red and blue marbles. If the probability of selecting a red marble at random is ⅜, then how many red marbles must be added so that the probability of randomly selecting a red marble becomes ½?

6. A jar contains only black, white, and red marbles. The probability of choosing a white marble is ⅗. If there are 4 times as many red marbles as black marbles, what is the least possible number of marbles in the jar?

SAT Practice 6: Probability Problems

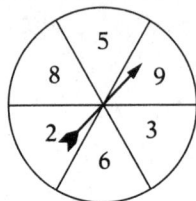

1. The figure above shows a spinner in the middle of a disc divided into six equal parts, each labeled with a number. What is the probability that the spinner will land on a number that is either even or greater than 5?

(A) $\frac{1}{6}$ (B) $\frac{1}{3}$ (C) $\frac{1}{2}$

(D) $\frac{2}{3}$ (E) $\frac{5}{6}$

2. A jar contains 10 blue marbles, 8 green marbles, and 14 red marbles. How many green marbles must be added so that the probability of choosing a green marble at random is $\frac{3}{4}$?

(A) 16 (B) 32 (C) 40
(D) 64 (E) 72

3. A fair six-sided die has faces bearing the numbers 1, 2, 3, 4, 5, and 6. When the die is thrown, the numbers on the five visible faces are added. What is the probability that this sum is greater than 18?

(A) $\frac{1}{6}$ (B) $\frac{1}{3}$ (C) $\frac{1}{2}$

(D) $\frac{2}{3}$ (E) $\frac{5}{6}$

4. A target consists of three concentric circles, with radii of 1 meter, 2 meters, and 3 meters. If an arrow that hits the target hits any point on the target with equal probability, what is the probability that an arrow that hits the target falls in the outermost region (between the second and third circles)?

(A) $\frac{1}{9}$ (B) $\frac{1}{3}$ (C) $\frac{\pi}{9}$

(D) $\frac{4}{9}$ (E) $\frac{5}{9}$

5. The probability of a meteor shower occurring in the skies above a particular island on any given night is $\frac{2}{25}$. Independently, the probability that any given night will be cloudless is $\frac{1}{4}$. What is the probability that, on any given night, there will be a meteor shower *and* it will be cloudless?

(A) $\frac{1}{50}$ (B) $\frac{3}{100}$ (C) $\frac{17}{200}$

(D) $\frac{4}{25}$ (E) $\frac{8}{25}$

6. A basket contains red, green, and yellow balls, all of equal size. The probability of choosing a green ball at random is $\frac{4}{7}$. If there are 3 times as many red balls as yellow balls, what is the probability of choosing a yellow ball at random?

7. A certain disease occurs in 1 person out of every 101 people. A test for the disease is 100% accurate for patients with the disease and 99% accurate for patients without it. That is, it gives a "false positive" 1% of the time even if the person tested doesn't have the disease. If you take this test and it returns a positive result, what is the probability that you have the disease?

(A) 1 (B) .99 (C) .95
(D) .50 (E) .01

Answer Key 6: Probability Problems

Concept Review 6

1. 0

2. 1

3. red marble: $3/12$, or $1/4$
   white marble: $4/12$, or $1/3$
   blue marble: $5/12$

4. What is the probability of drawing a red marble?
   $5/15$, or $1/3$
   If 3 more red marbles are added, what is the probability of drawing a red marble? $8/18$, or $4/9$

5. If the jar contains 24 red and blue marbles and the
   probability of selecting a red marble at random is $3/8$,
   there must be $(3/8)(24) = 9$ red marbles, and $24 - 9 = 15$
   blue marbles. If the probability of drawing a red
   marble is to be $1/2$, there must be as many red as blue
   marbles, so you must add $15 - 9 = 6$ marbles.

6. Let's say that the probability of drawing a black
   marble is x. Since there are 4 times as many red
   marbles as black marbles, the probability of
   drawing a red marble must be $4x$. The probability of choosing a white marble is $2/3$. Since we are
   certain to pick one of these colors, the sum of all
   of these probabilities must be 1: $x + 4x + 2/3 = 1$
      Simplify: $5x + 2/3 = 1$
      Subtract $2/3$: $5x = 1/3$
      Divide by 5: $x = 1/15$
   Therefore, $1/15$ of the marbles are black, $4/15$ of the
   marbles are red, and $2/3$ of the marbles are white.
   The least common denominator of these fractions
   is 15, which means that 15 is the least possible
   number of marbles. In that case, there are 1 black
   marble, 4 red marbles, and 10 white marbles.

SAT Practice 6

1. **D** Put an "x" through any number that is *either*
   even *or* greater than 5, or both. This gives us 8, 9,
   2, and 6, which is 4 out of the 6 spaces, giving a
   probability of $4/6$, or $2/3$.

2. **D** If the probability of choosing a green marble is
   to be $3/4$, then $3/4$ of the marbles should be green and
   $1/4$ not green. There are 10 blue and 14 red, for a total
   of 24 "not green" marbles, and this will not change,
   since you are adding only green marbles. If this is $1/4$
   of the total, then there must be $4(24) = 96$ marbles
   total after you add the extra green marbles. The jar
   now contains $10 + 8 + 14 = 32$ marbles, so you must
   add $96 - 32 = 64$ green marbles.

3. **B** The six sides of a die add up to $1 + 2 + 3 + 4 +$
   $5 + 6 = 21$. The sum of any five faces can be greater than
   18 only if the "down" face is 1 or 2 (so that the sum of
   the other faces is either $21 - 1 = 20$ or $21 - 2 = 19$. This
   is 2 possibilities out of 6 for a probability of $2/6$, or $1/3$.

4. **E** Sketch the target:

   You want to know the probability of the arrow hitting the
   outermost ring, which is the
   ratio of the area of the ring to
   the entire area of the target.
   The area of the whole target is $\pi(3)^2 = 9\pi$. The area
   of the outermost ring is $9\pi - \pi(2)^2$ (subtract the area
   of the middle circle from the area of the big circle)
   $= 9\pi - 4\pi = 5\pi$. So the probability is $5\pi/9\pi = 5/9$.

5. **A** Consider a stretch of 100 consecutive nights.
   If the probability of a meteor shower is $2/25$, then we
   should expect a meteor shower on $(2/25)(100) = 8$ of
   those nights. If only $1/4$ of the nights are cloudless,
   though, then $(1/4)(8) = 2$ of the nights with a meteor
   shower, on average, should be cloudless. This
   gives a probability of $2/100$, or $1/50$. Mathematically,
   we can just multiply the two probabilities (as long
   as they are independent) to get the *joint* probability: $(2/25)(1/4) = 1/50$.

6. **$3/28$** Call the probability of choosing a yellow ball x.
   If there are three times as many red balls as yellow
   balls, the probability of choosing a red ball must
   be $3x$. The probability of choosing a green ball is
   $1/7$. These probabilities must have a sum of 1:
                                     $x + 3x + 1/7 = 1$
   Simplify: $4x + 1/7 = 1$
   Subtract $1/7$: $4x = 6/7$
   Divide by 4: $x = 3/28$

7. **D** Most people would say that this probability is
   quite high, because the test is so reliable. But intuition is often wrong. Imagine that you test 101 people. Of these, on average, one will have the disease,
   and 100 will not. Since the test is 100% accurate
   for those who have the disease, that person will test
   positive. Of the 100 who do not have the disease,
   99 will test negative, but one will test positive, because of the 1% "false positive" rate. So of those
   two who test positive, only one will have the disease; thus, the probability is $1/2$.

CHAPTER 10

ESSENTIAL GEOMETRY SKILLS

1. Lines and Angles

2. Triangles

3. The Pythagorean Theorem

4. Coordinate Geometry

5. Areas and Perimeters

6. Similar Figures

7. Volumes and 3-D Geometry

8. Circles

Lesson 1: Lines and Angles

When Two Lines Cross

When two lines cross, four angles are formed. *"Vertical" angles are equal, and look like this:*

vertical
angles

Don't be fooled by diagrams that look like vertical angles, but aren't. Vertical angles are formed by two and only two crossed lines:

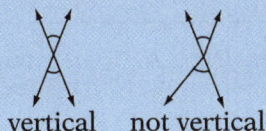

vertical   not vertical

When two pairs of vertical angles are formed, four pairs of adjacent angles (side-by-side) are also formed. *Adjacent angles add up to 180°:*

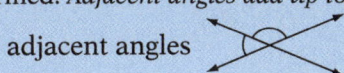

adjacent angles

When a Line Crosses Parallel Lines

Imagine taking two crossed lines, making a "copy" of them, and sliding the copy down one of the lines so that together they look like this:

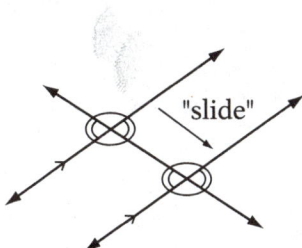

"slide"

This produces a pair of parallel lines crossed by a third line.

When two parallel lines are crossed by another line, all acute angles are equal, and all obtuse angles are equal. Also, every acute angle is supplementary to every obtuse angle (that is, they add upto 180°).

To show that two lines are parallel, use the arrow marks ">" like those in the figure in the previous column. To show that two angles are equal, use the arc marks ")" like those in the figure in the previous column.

Don't be fooled by diagrams that only look as if they have two parallel lines crossed by another line. Don't *assume* that two lines are parallel just because they *look* parallel. It must be *given* that they are parallel.

To help yourself to see the relationships between angles in parallel line systems, you might try looking for these special "letters":

Angles that make Z's are equal:

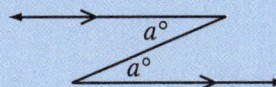

$a°$
$a°$

Angles that make C's or U's are supplementary (they have a sum of 180°):

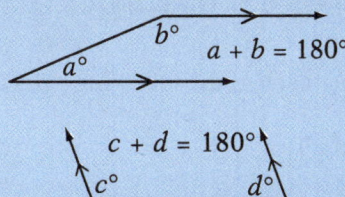

$b°$
$a°$ $a + b = 180°$

$c + d = 180°$
$c°$ $d°$

Angles that make F's are equal:

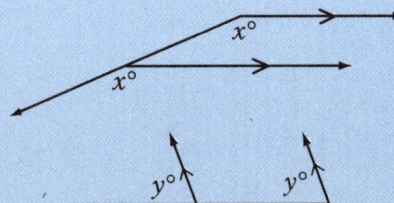

$x°$
$x°$

$y°$ $y°$

Concept Review 1: Lines and Angles

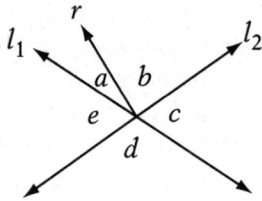

l_1 and l_2 are lines and r is a ray.

Questions 1 and 2 refer to the diagram above.

1. List all of the different pairs of angles that are congruent (equal).

2. List all of the different sets of angles that have a sum of 180°.

Mark the figure to show the following information: $AD \parallel HN$, $AI \parallel BM$, and $HD \parallel JL$. Then list the angles in the figure that have the given characteristic:

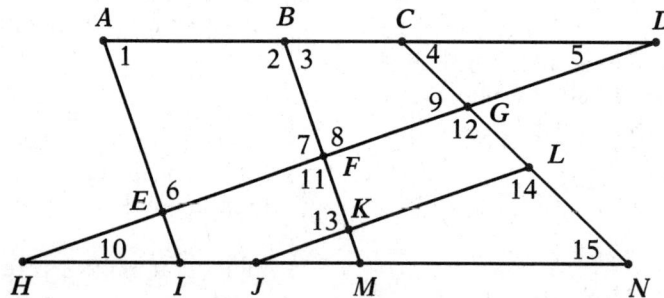

3. One angle equal to ∠10

4. Two angles supplementary to ∠6

5. Two angles supplementary to ∠9

6. One angle equal to ∠15

7. Three angles supplementary to ∠13

State whether each of the following pairs is *supplementary* (has a sum of 180°), *equal*, or *neither*.

8. ∠13 and ∠7

9. ∠13 and ∠6

10. ∠2 and ∠9

11. ∠14 and ∠9

12. ∠7 and ∠3

13. ∠1 and ∠2

14. ∠6 and ∠7

SAT Practice 1: Lines and Angles

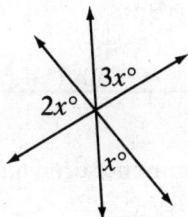

Note: Figure not drawn to scale.

1. The figure above shows the intersection of three lines. $x =$

   (A) 16
   (B) 20
   (C) 30
   (D) 60
   (E) 90

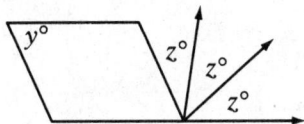

2. The figure above shows a parallelogram with one side extended. If $z = 40$, then $y =$

   (A) 40
   (B) 60
   (C) 80
   (D) 110
   (E) 120

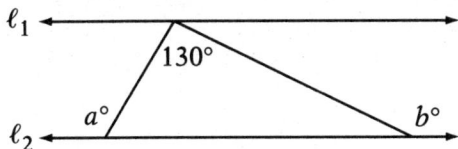

Note: Figure not drawn to scale.

3. In the figure above, if $\ell_1 \| \ell_2$, then $a + b =$

   (A) 130
   (B) 270
   (C) 280
   (D) 290
   (E) 310

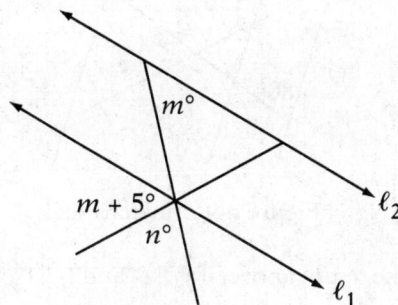

4. In the figure above, if $l_1 \| l_2$, then what is the value of n in terms of m?

   (A) $355 - 2m$
   (B) $185 - 2m$
   (C) $175 - 2m$
   (D) $95 - 2m$
   (E) $85 - 2m$

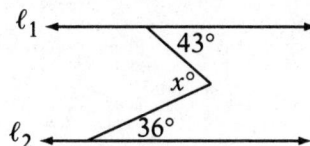

5. In the figure above, if $l_1 \| l_2$, then $x =$

   (A) 43
   (B) 69
   (C) 79
   (D) 101
   (E) 111

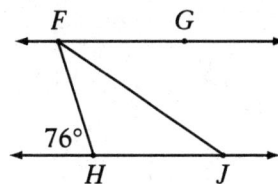

6. In the figure above, if $\overleftrightarrow{FG} \| \overleftrightarrow{HJ}$ and $\overline{FJ}$ bisects $\angle HFG$, what is the measure of $\angle FJH$?

   (A) 14
   (B) 38
   (C) 40
   (D) 56
   (E) 76

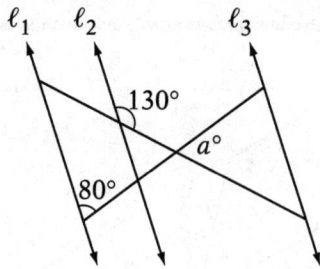

Note: Figure not drawn to scale.

7. In the figure above, if $\ell_1 \parallel \ell_2$ and $\ell_2 \parallel \ell_3$, then $a =$

    (A) 50
    (B) 55
    (C) 60
    (D) 65
    (E) 70

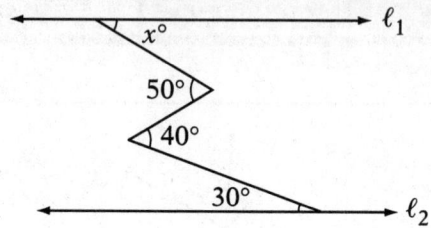

Note: Figure not drawn to scale.

8. In the diagram above, if $\ell_1 \parallel \ell_2$, then $x =$

    (A) 65
    (B) 60
    (C) 50
    (D) 45
    (E) 40

Answer Key 1: Lines and Angles

Concept Review 1

1. Only c and e are congruent.

2. $a + b + c = 180°$, $c + d = 180°$, $d + e = 180°$, $e + a + b = 180°$

3. $\angle 5$

4. $\angle 7$ and $\angle 13$

5. $\angle 12$ and $\angle 14$

6. $\angle 4$

7. $\angle 11$, $\angle 8$, and $\angle 6$

8. equal

9. supplementary

10. neither

11. supplementary

12. neither

13. supplementary

14. supplementary

SAT Practice 1

1. **C** Draw in the three angles that are "vertical," and therefore congruent, to the angles that are shown. Then choose any three adjacent angles, and notice that they form a straight angle. Therefore, $x + 2x + 3x = 180$. So $6x = 180$ and $x = 30$.

2. **B** The opposite angles in a parallelogram must be equal, and any two "consecutive angles" as you move around the figure must be supplementary. (Notice that consecutive angles form C's or U's. If you're not sure why this theorem is true, sketch a few sample parallelograms and work out the angles.) The angle opposite the $y°$ must also measure $y°$, and when this is added to the three $z°$ angles, they form a straight angle. Therefore, $y + 40 + 40 + 40 = 180$ and $y = 60$.

3. **E** In the triangle, the angles must have a sum of 180°. (See the next lesson for a simple proof.) Therefore, the other two angles in the triangle must have a sum of 50°. Pick values for these two angles that add up to 50°, and write them in. It doesn't matter how you do it: 25° and 25°, 20° and 30°, 40° and 10°, as long as they add up to 50°. You can then find the values of a and b by noticing that they form straight angles with the interior angles. So if the interior angles are 25° and 25°, then a and b must both be 155.

4. **C** Notice that the $m°$ angle has a "corresponding" angle below that has the same measure. (Notice that they form an F.) Then $(m + 5) + n + m = 180$.

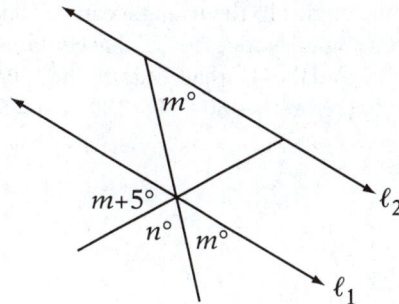

Simplify: $2m + 5 + n = 180$
Subtract $(5 + 2m)$: $n = 175 - 2m$

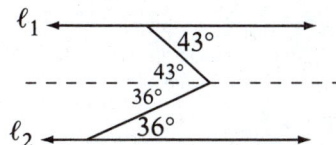

5. **C** Draw an extra line through the vertex of the angle that is parallel to the other two. Notice that this forms two "Z" pairs. Therefore, $x = 36 + 43 = 79$.

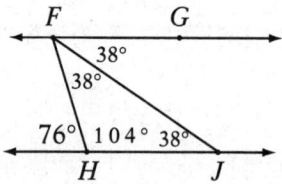

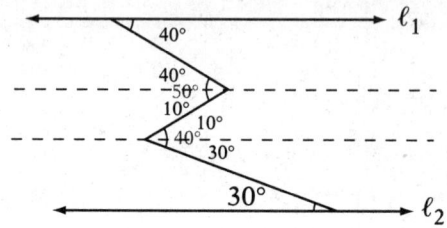

6. **B**   There are many relationships here to take advantage of. Notice that $\angle HFG$ and the 76° angle form a "Z," so $\angle HFG = 76°$. Remember that "bisect" means to divide into two equal parts, so $\angle HFJ = \angle JFG = 38°$. Then notice that $\angle JFG$ and $\angle FJH$ form a "Z," so $\angle FJH = 38°$.

8. **E**   Draw two more parallel lines and work with the Z's. Your figure should look like the one above.

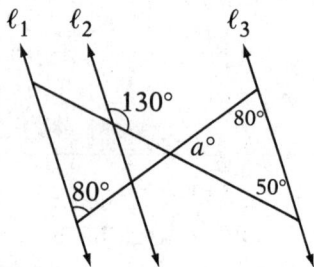

7. **A**   Consider the triangle with the $a°$ angle. The other two angles in the triangle can be found from the given angles. Notice the "Z" that contains the two 80° angles and the "U" that contains the 130° and 50° angles. Therefore, $a + 80 + 50 = 180$, so $a = 50$.

Lesson 2: Triangles

Angles in Polygons

Remembering what you learned about parallel lines in the last lesson, consider this diagram:

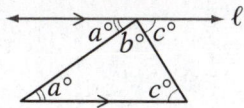

We drew line ℓ so that it is parallel to the opposite side of the triangle. Do you see the two Z's? The angles marked a are equal, and so are the angles marked c. We also know that angles that make up a straight line have a sum of 180°, so $a + b + c = 180$. The angles inside the triangle are also a, b, and c.

> Therefore, *the sum of angles in a triangle is always 180°.*

Every polygon with n sides can be divided into $n - 2$ triangles that share their vertices (corners) with the polygon:

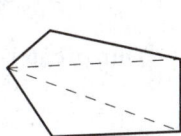 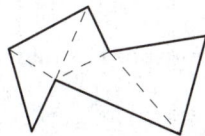

5 sides, 3 triangles = 3(180°) = 540°   7 sides, 5 triangles = 5(180°) = 900°

> Therefore, *the sum of the angles in any polygon with n sides is 180(n − 2)°.*

Angle-Side Relationships in Triangles

A triangle is like an alligator mouth with a stick in it: The wider the mouth, the bigger the stick, right?

> Therefore, the largest angle of a triangle is always across from the longest side, and vice versa. Likewise, the smallest angle is always across from the shortest side.

Example:
In the figure below, 72 > 70, so $a > b$.

a / b

70° 72°

An isosceles triangle

> An isosceles triangle is a triangle with two equal sides. If two sides in a triangle are equal, then the angles across from those sides are equal, too, and vice versa.

The Triangle Inequality

Look closely at the figure below. The shortest path from point A to point B is the line segment connecting them. Therefore, unless point C is "on the way" from A to B, that is, unless it's on $\overline{AB}$, the distance from A to B through C must be longer than the direct route. In other words:

> The sum of any two sides of a triangle is always greater than the third side. This means that the length of any side of a triangle must be between the sum and the difference of the other two sides.

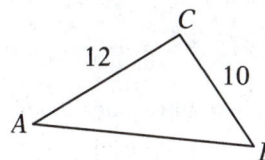

$12 - 10 < AB < 12 + 10$
$2 < AB < 22$

The External Angle Theorem

> The extended side of a triangle forms an external angle with the adjacent side. The external angle of a triangle is equal to the sum of the two "remote interior" angles. Notice that this follows from our angle theorems:

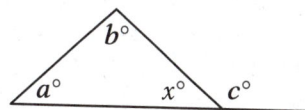

$a + b + x = 180$ and $c + x = 180$;
therefore, $a + b = c$

Concept Review 2: Triangles

1. The sum of the measures of the angles in a quadrilateral is _____.

2. The sum of the measures of the interior angles in an octagon is _____.

3. In $\triangle ABC$, if the measure of $\angle A$ is 65° and the measure of $\angle B$ is 60°, then which side is longest? _____.

4. The angles in an equilateral triangle must have a measure of _____.

5. Can an isosceles triangle include angles of 35° and 60°? Why or why not?

6. Draw a diagram to illustrate the external angle theorem.

7. If a triangle has sides of lengths 20 and 15, then the third side must be less than _____ but greater than _____.

8. Is it possible for a triangle to have sides of lengths 5, 8, and 14? Why or why not?

9. If an isosceles triangle includes an angle of 25°, the other two angles could have measures of _____ and _____ or _____ and _____.

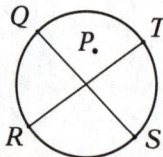

10. In the figure above, $\overline{QS}$ and $\overline{RT}$ are diameters of the circle and P is *not* the center. Complete the statement below with >, <, or =.

$PQ + PR + PS + PT$ _____ $QS + RT$
(not shown)

SAT Practice 2: Triangles

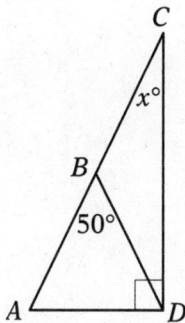

1. In the figure above, if $AB = BD$, then $x =$

    (A) 25
    (B) 30
    (C) 35
    (D) 50
    (E) 65

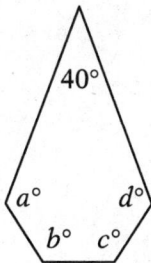

2. In the figure above, $a + b + c + d =$

3. The three sides of a triangle have lengths of 9, 16, and k. Which of the following could equal k?

    I. 6
    II. 16
    III. 25

    (A) I only
    (B) II only
    (C) I and II only
    (D) II and III only
    (E) I, II, and III

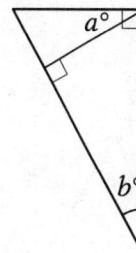

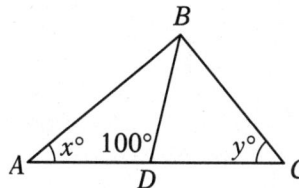

Note: Figure not drawn to scale.

4. Which of the following statements about a and b in the figure above must be true?

    I. $a = b$
    II. $a + b = 90$
    III. $a < 60$

    (A) I only
    (B) II only
    (C) I and II only
    (D) II and III only
    (E) I, II, and III

5. In the figure above, if $AD = DB = DC$, then $x + y =$

    (A) 70
    (B) 80
    (C) 90
    (D) 100
    (E) 120

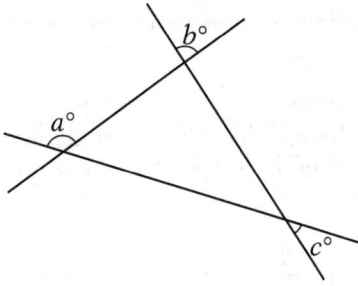

6. In the figure above, which of the following expresses *a* in terms of *b* and *c*?

(A) $180 - (b + c)$
(B) $180 - (b - c)$
(C) $90 - (b + c)$
(D) $90 - (b - c)$
(E) $b + c$

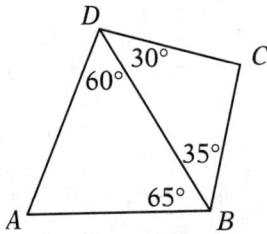

Note: Figure not drawn to scale.

7. Which of the following represents the correct ordering of the lengths of the five segments in the figure above?

(A) $AD > AB > DB > BC > DC$
(B) $AD > DB > AB > DC > BC$
(C) $AD > DB > AB > BC > DC$
(D) $AD > AB > DB > DC > BC$
(E) $AD > DB > DC > AB > BC$

8. A triangle has two sides of lengths 4 centimeters and 6 centimeters. Its area is *n* square centimeters, where *n* is a prime number. What is the greatest possible value of *n*?

(A) 11
(B) 12
(C) 19
(D) 23
(E) 24

Answer Key 2: Triangles

Concept Review 2

1. 360°

2. 1,080°

3. Draw a diagram. If the measure of ∠A is 65° and the measure of ∠B is 60°, then the measure of ∠C must be 55°, because the angles must have a sum of 180°. Since ∠A is the largest angle, the side opposite it, $\overline{BC}$, must be the longest side.

4. 60°. Since all the sides are equal, all the angles are, too.

5. No, because an isosceles triangle must have two equal angles, and the sum of all three must be 180°. Since $35 + 35 + 60 \neq 180$, and $35 + 60 + 60 \neq 180$, the triangle is impossible.

6. Your diagram should look something like this:

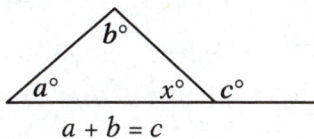

$a + b = c$

7. If a triangle has sides of lengths 20 and 15, then the third side must be less than 35 (their sum) but greater than 5 (their difference).

8. No. The sum of the two shorter sides of a triangle is always greater than the third side, but $5 + 8$ is not greater than 14. So the triangle is impossible.

9. 25° and 130° or 77.5° and 77.5°

10. Draw in the line segments PQ, PR, PS, and PT. Notice that this forms two triangles, ΔPQS and ΔPRT. Since any two sides of a triangle must have a sum greater than the third side, $PQ + PS > QS$, and $PR + PT > RT$. Therefore, $PQ + PR + PS + PT > QS + RT$.

SAT Practice 2

1. **A** If $AB = BD$, then, by the Isosceles Triangle theorem, ∠BAD and ∠BDA must be equal. To find their measure, subtract 50° from 180° and divide by 2. This gives 65°. Mark up the diagram with this information. Since the angles in the big triangle have a sum of 180°, $65 + 90 + x = 180$, so $x = 25$.

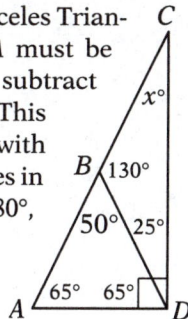

2. **500** Drawing two diagonals shows that the figure can be divided into three triangles. (Remember that an n-sided figure can be divided into $n - 2$ triangles.) Therefore, the sum of all the angles is $3 \times 180° = 540°$. Subtracting 40° leaves 500°.

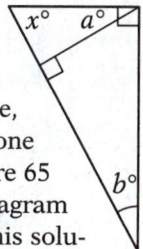

3. **B** The third side of any triangle must have a length that is between the sum and the difference of the other two sides. Since $16 - 9 = 7$ and $16 + 9 = 25$, the third side must be between (but not including) 7 and 25.

4. **A** Since the big triangle is a right triangle, $b + x$ must equal 90. The two small triangles are also right triangles, so $a + x$ is also 90. Therefore, $a = b$ and statement I is true. In one "solution" of this triangle, a and b are 65 and x is 25. (Put the values into the diagram and check that everything "fits.") This solution proves that statements II and III are not necessarily true.

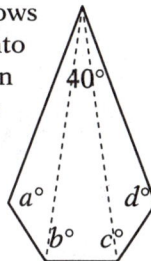

5. **C** If $AD = DB$, then, by the Isosceles Triangle theorem, the angles opposite those sides must be equal. You should mark the other angle with an x also, as shown here. Similarly, if $DB = DC$, then the angles opposite those sides must be equal also, and they should both be marked y. Now consider the big triangle. Since its angles must have a sum of 180, $2x + 2y = 180$. Dividing both sides by 2 gives $x + y = 90$. (Notice that the fact that ∠ADB measures 100° doesn't make any difference!)

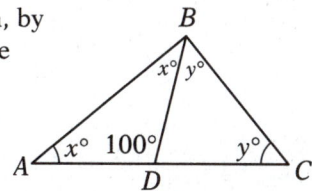

6. **E**   Label the two angles that are "vertical" to those marked b and c. Notice that the angle marked a is an "external" angle. By the External Angle theorem, $a = b + c$.

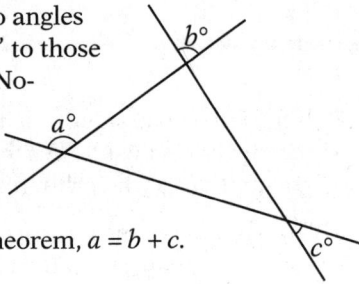

7. **D**   Write in the missing angle measures by using the fact that the sum of angles in a triangle is 180°. Then use the fact that the biggest side of a triangle is always across from the biggest angle to order the sides of each triangle.

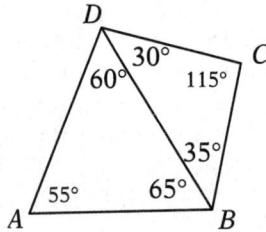

8. **A**   Consider the side of length 4 to be the base, and "attach" the side of length 6. Notice that the triangle has the greatest possible height when the two sides form a right angle. Therefore, the greatest possible area of such a triangle is (1/2)(4)(6) = 12, and the minimum possible area is 0. The greatest prime number less than 12 is 11.

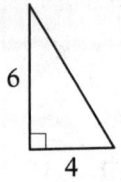

Lesson 3: The Pythagorean Theorem

The Pythagorean Theorem

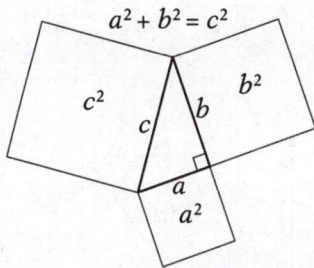

The *Pythagorean theorem* says that in any *right triangle, the sum of the squares of the two shorter sides is equal to the square of the longest side*. If you know two sides of any right triangle, the Pythagorean theorem can always be used to find the third side.

Example:

In the figure below, what is x?

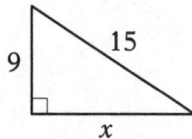

Pythagorean theorem:	$9^2 + x^2 = 15^2$
Simplify:	$81 + x^2 = 225$
Subtract 81:	$x^2 = 144$
Take the square root:	$x = 12$

You can also use the modified Pythagorean theorem to find whether a triangle is acute or obtuse.

If $(side_1)^2 + (side_2)^2 < (\text{longest side})^2$, the triangle is **obtuse.** (If the stick gets bigger, the alligator's mouth gets wider!)

If $(side_1)^2 + (side_2)^2 > (\text{longest side})^2$, the triangle is **acute.** (If the stick gets smaller, the alligator's mouth gets smaller!)

Special Right Triangles

Certain special right triangles show up frequently on the SAT. If you see that a triangle fits one of these patterns, it may save you the trouble of using the Pythagorean Theorem. But be careful: you must know two of three "parts" of the triangle in order to assume the third part.

3-4-5 triangles   More accurately, these can be called $3x$-$4x$-$5x$ triangles because the multiples of 3-4-5 also make right triangles. Notice that the sides satisfy the Pythagorean theorem.

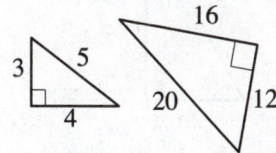

5-12-13 triangles   Likewise, these can be called $5x$-$12x$-$13x$ triangles because the *multiples* of 5-12-13 also make right triangles. Notice that the sides satisfy the Pythagorean theorem.

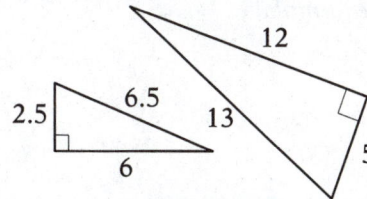

45°-45°-90° triangles   These triangles can be thought of as *squares cut on the diagonal.* This shows why the angles and sides are related the way they are. Notice that the sides satisfy the Pythagorean theorem.

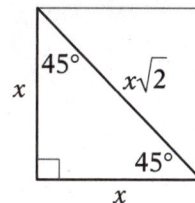

30°-60°-90° triangles These triangles can be thought of as *equilateral triangles cut in half*. This shows why the angles and sides are related the way they are. Notice that the sides satisfy the Pythagorean theorem.

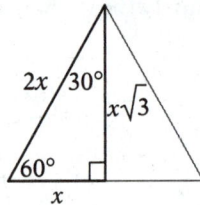

The Distance Formula:

$$d^2 = (x_2 - x_1)^2 + (y_2 - y_1)^2$$

so

$$d = \sqrt{\left(x_2 - x_1\right)^2 + \left(y_2 - y_1\right)^2}$$

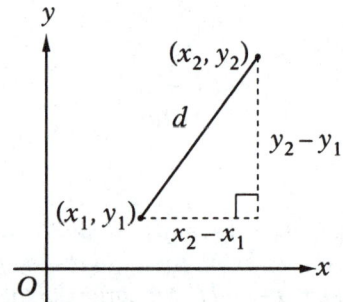

The Distance Formula

Say you want to find the distance between two points (x_1, y_1) and (x_2, y_2). Look carefully at this diagram and notice that you can find it with the Pythagorean theorem. Just think of the distance between the points as the hypotenuse of a right triangle, and the Pythagorean theorem becomes—lo and behold— the *distance formula*!

Concept Review 3: The Pythagorean Theorem

1. Draw an example of each of the four "special" right triangles.

Use the modified Pythagorean theorem and the triangle inequality to find whether a triangle with the given side lengths is acute, obtuse, right, or impossible.

2. 5, 6, 9

3. 2, 12, 12

4. 6, 8, 11

5. 2, 2, 12

6. 3, 4, 7

7. 1.5, 2, 2.5

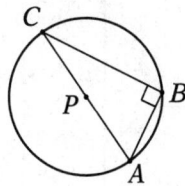

8. The circle above has its center at P and an area of 16π. If $AP = AB$, what is the area of $\triangle ABC$? _____

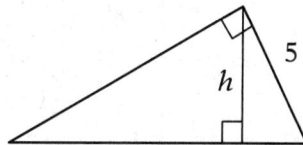

9. The area of the triangle above is 30. What is the value of h? _____

10. What is the height of an equilateral triangle with sides of length $6\sqrt{3}$ cm? _____

11. Point P is at $(0, 0)$, point M is at $(4, 0)$, and point N is at $(9, 12)$. _____
    What is the perimeter of $\triangle MNP$?

SAT Practice 3: The Pythagorean Theorem

1. The length and width of a rectangle are in the ratio of 5:12. If the rectangle has an area of 240 square centimeters, what is the length, in centimeters, of its diagonal?

(A) 26
(B) 28
(C) 30
(D) 32
(E) 34

2. A spider on a flat horizontal surface walks 10 inches east, then 6 inches south, then 4 inches west, then 2 inches south. At this point, how many inches is the spider from its starting point?

(A) 8
(B) 10
(C) 12
(D) 16
(E) 18

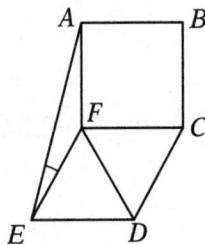

3. In the figure above, *ABCF* is a square and Δ*EFD* and Δ*FCD* are equilateral. What is the measure of ∠*AEF*?

(A) 15°
(B) 20°
(C) 25°
(D) 30°
(E) 35°

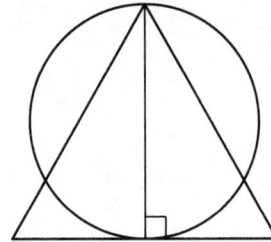

4. In the figure above, an equilateral triangle is drawn with an altitude that is also the diameter of the circle. If the perimeter of the triangle is 36, what is the circumference of the circle?

(A) $6\sqrt{2}\pi$

(B) $6\sqrt{3}\pi$

(C) $12\sqrt{2}\pi$

(D) $12\sqrt{3}\pi$

(E) 36π

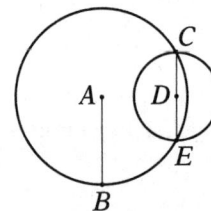

5. In the figure above, *A* and *D* are the centers of the two circles, which intersect at points *C* and *E*. $\overline{CE}$ is a diameter of circle *D*. If *AB* = *CE* = 10, what is *AD*?

(A) 5

(B) $5\sqrt{2}$

(C) $5\sqrt{3}$

(D) $10\sqrt{2}$

(E) $10\sqrt{3}$

6. Point H has coordinates $(2, 1)$, and point J has coordinates $(11, 13)$. If $\overline{HK}$ is parallel to the x-axis and $\overline{JK}$ is parallel to the y-axis, what is the perimeter of $\triangle HJK$?

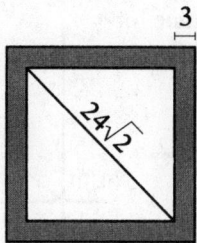

7. A square garden with a diagonal of length $24\sqrt{2}$ meters is surrounded by a walkway 3 meters wide. What is the area, in square meters, of the walkway?

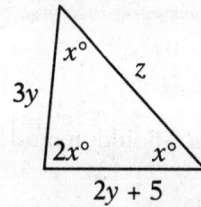

Note: Figure not drawn to scale.

8. In the figure above, what is the value of z?

(A)   15

(B) $15\sqrt{2}$

(C) $15\sqrt{3}$

(D) $30\sqrt{2}$

(E) $30\sqrt{3}$

Answer Key 3: The Pythagorean Theorem

Concept Review 3

1. Your diagram should include one each of a 3x-4x-5x, a 5x-12x-13x, a 30°-60°-90°, and a 45°-45°-90° triangle.

2. Obtuse: $5^2 + 6^2 = 61 < 9^2 = 81$

3. Acute: $2^2 + 12^2 = 148 > 12^2 = 144$

4. Obtuse: $6^2 + 8^2 = 100 < 11^2 = 121$

5. Impossible: $2 + 2$ isn't greater than 12

6. Impossible: $3 + 4$ isn't greater than 7

7. Right: $1.5^2 + 2^2 = 6.25 = 2.5^2$

8. Since the area of a circle is $\pi r^2 = 16\pi$, $r = 4$. Put the information into the diagram. Use the Pythagorean theorem or notice that, since the hypotenuse is twice the shorter side, it is a 30°-60°-90° triangle. Either way, $CB = 4\sqrt{3}$, so the area of the triangle is $(bh)/2 = (4)(4\sqrt{3})/2 = 8\sqrt{3}$.

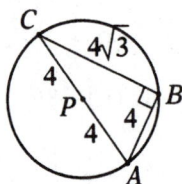

9. At first, consider the shorter leg as the base. In this case, the other leg is the height. Since the area is $(bh)/2 = 30$, the other leg must be 12. This is a 5-12-13 triangle, so the hypotenuse is 13. Now consider the hypotenuse as the base. Since $13h/2 = 30$, $h = 60/13 = 4.615$.

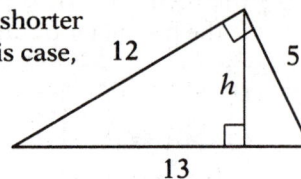

10. Your diagram should look like this: The height is $(3\sqrt{3})(\sqrt{3}) = 9$.

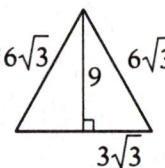

11. Sketch the diagram. Use the Pythagorean theorem or distance formula to find the lengths. The perimeter is $4 + 13 + 15 = 32$.

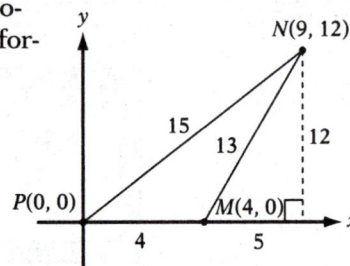

SAT Practice 3

1. **A** Draw the rectangle. If the length and width are in the ratio of 5:12, then they can be expressed as 5x and 12x. The area, then, is $(5x)(12x) = 60x^2 = 240$. So $x = 2$, and the length and width are 10 and 24. Find the diagonal with the Pythagorean theorem: $10^2 + 24^2 = a^2$, so $100 + 576 = 676 = a^2$ and $d = 26$. (Notice that this is a 5-12-13 triangle times 2!)

2. **B** Draw a diagram like this. The distance from the starting point to the finishing point is the hypotenuse of a right triangle with legs of 6 and 8. Therefore, the distance is found with Pythagoras: $6^2 + 8^2 = 36 + 64 = 100 = d^2$, so $d = 10$. (Notice that this is a 3-4-5 triangle times 2!)

3. **A** Draw in the angle measures. All angles in a square are 90° and all angles in an equilateral triangle are 60°. Since all of the angles around point F add up to 360°, $\angle EFA = 360 - 60 - 60 - 90 = 150°$. Since $EF = AF$, ΔEFA is isosceles, so $\angle AEF = (180 - 150)/2 = 15°$.

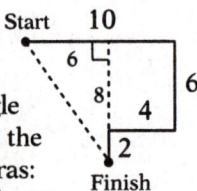

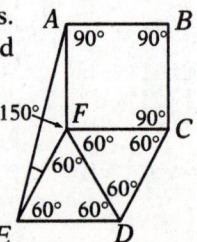

4. **B** If the perimeter of the triangle is 36, each side must have a length of 12. Since the altitude forms two 30°-60°-90° triangles, the altitude must have length $6\sqrt{3}$. This is also the diameter of the circle. The circumference of a circle is π times the diameter: $6\sqrt{3}\pi$.

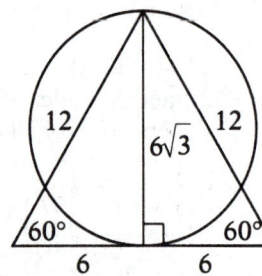

5. **C** Draw in AE and AC. Since all radii of a circle are equal, their measures are both 10 as well. Therefore ΔACE is equilateral, and AD divides it into two 30°-60°-90° triangles. You can use the Pythagorean theorem, or just use the 30°-60°-90° relationships to see that $AD = 5\sqrt{3}$.

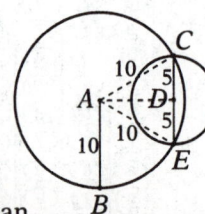

6. **36** Sketch a diagram. Point K has coordinates (11, 1). ΔHJK is a right triangle, so it satisfies the Pythagorean theorem. Your diagram should look like this one. The perimeter is $9 + 12 + 15 = 36$.

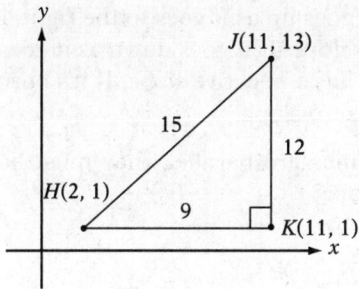

7. **324** Since the garden is a square, the diagonal divides it into 45°-45°-90° triangles. Therefore the sides have a length of 24. The outer edge of the walkway is therefore $24 + 3 + 3 = 30$. The area of the walkway is the difference of the areas of the squares: $30^2 - 24^2 = 324$.

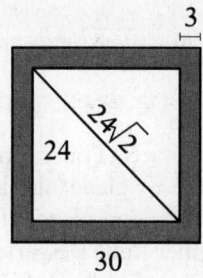

8. **B** The sum of the angles is 180°, so $x + x + 2x = 4x = 180$, and $x = 45$. Therefore the triangle is a 45°-45°-90° triangle. Since it is isosceles, $3y = 2y + 5$, and therefore $y = 5$. The three sides, then, have lengths of 15, 15, and $15\sqrt{2}$.

Lesson 4: Coordinate Geometry

Plotting Points

Some SAT questions may ask you to work with points on the *x-y* plane (also known as the coordinate plane or the Cartesian plane, after the mathematician and philosopher René Descartes). When plotting points, remember these four basic facts to avoid the common mistakes:

- The coordinates of a point are always given alphabetically: the *x*-coordinate first, then the *y*-coordinate.
- The *x*-axis is always horizontal and the *y*-axis is always vertical.
- On the *x*-axis, the positive direction is to the right of the origin (where the *x* and *y* axes meet, point (0,0)).
- On the *y*-axis, the positive direction is up from the origin (where the *x* and *y* axes meet, point (0,0)).

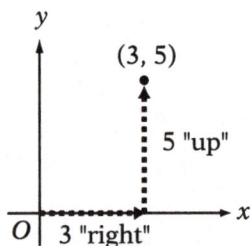

Working with Slopes

Every line has a slope, which is the distance you move up or down as you move one unit to the right along the line. Imagine walking between any two points on the line. As you move, you go a certain distance "up or down." This distance is called the rise. You also go a certain distance "left or right." This distance is called the run.

The slope is simply the rise divided by the run.

$$\text{Slope} = \frac{rise}{run} = \frac{y_2 - y_1}{x_2 - x_1}$$

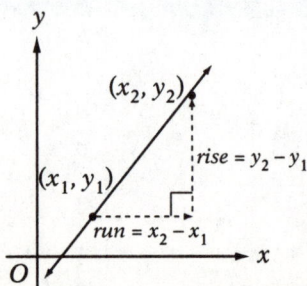

You should be able to tell at a glance whether a slope has a *positive*, *negative*, or *zero* slope. If the line goes up as it goes to the right, it has a positive slope. If it goes down as it goes to the right, it has a negative slope. If it's horizontal, it has a zero slope.

If two lines are parallel, they must have the same slope.

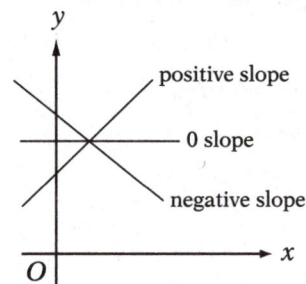

Finding Midpoints

The midpoint of a line segment is the point that divides the segment into two equal parts.

Think of the midpoint as the average of the two endpoints.

$$\text{Midpoint} = \left(\frac{x_1 + x_2}{2}, \frac{y_1 + y_2}{2} \right)$$

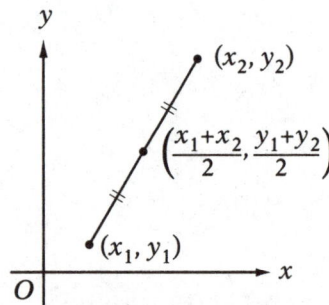

Concept Review 4: Coordinate Geometry

Questions 1–10 refer to the figure below.
Horizontal and vertical lines are spaced 1 unit apart.

1. What are the coordinates
   of point A?   _____

2. What are the coordinates of the
   midpoint of $\overline{AB}$?   _____

3. What is the slope of $\overline{AB}$? _____

4. Draw a line through B that is parallel to the
   y-axis and label it ℓ_1.

5. What do all points on ℓ_1 have
   in common?   _____

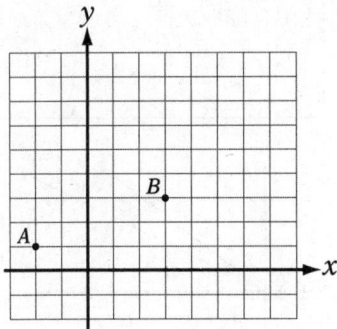

6. Draw a line through B that is parallel to the x-axis
   and label it l_2.

7. Draw the line $y = -1$ and label it ℓ_3.

8. If point A is reflected over ℓ_2, what are the coordinates of its image?   _____

9. If line segment $\overline{AB}$ is rotated 90° clockwise about
   point B, what are the coordinates of the image of
   point A?   _____

10. If point B is the midpoint of line segment $\overline{AC}$,
    what are the coordinates of point C? _____

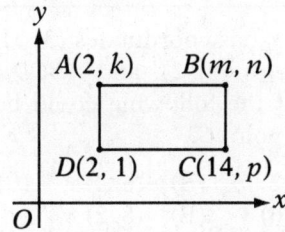

Rectangle $ABCD$ has an area of 108.

Note: Figure not drawn to scale.

Questions 11–15 pertain to the figure above.

11. $k =$ _____ $m =$ _____ $n =$ _____ $p =$ _____

12. What is the ratio of AC to
    the perimeter of $ABCD$?   _____

13. What is the slope of $\overline{DB}$? _____

14. At what point do $\overline{AC}$ and
    $\overline{DB}$ intersect?   _____

15. If B is the midpoint of
    segment $\overline{DF}$, what are the
    coordinates of point F?   _____

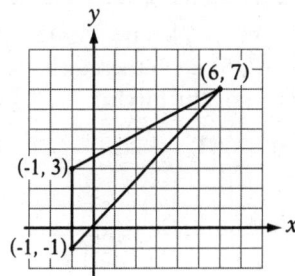

Questions 16–18 pertain to the figure above.

16. What is the area of the
    triangle above?   _____

17. If the triangle above were reflected over the line
    $x = 3$, what would be the least x-coordinate of any
    point on the triangle?   _____

18. If the triangle above were reflected over the line
    $y = 1$, what would the area of the
    new triangle be?   _____

SAT Practice 4: Coordinate Geometry

1. If point A has coordinates (3, 5), point B has coordinates (3, 2), and $ABCD$ is a square, which of the following could be the coordinates of point C?

(A) (4, 2)   (B) (6, 2)   (C) (6, 6)
(D) (4, 6)   (E) (8, 2)

2. If ℓ_1 is a horizontal line passing through (1, 8) and ℓ_2 is a vertical line passing through (−3, 4), then at what point do ℓ_1 and ℓ_2 intersect?

(A) (−3, 8)   (B) (1, 4)   (C) (−1, 6)
(D) (−2, 12)   (E) (0, 0)

3. The point (−3, 4) is on a circle with its center at the origin. Which of the following points must also be on the circle?

  I. (0, −5)
  II. (−4, −3)
  III. (3, 4)

(A) I only   (B) II only
(C) I and II only   (D) II and III only
(E) I, II, and III

4. If the point (3, −7) is the center of a circle and the point (8, 5) is on the circle, what is the circumference of the circle?

(A) 13π (B) 15π (C) 18π
(D) 25π (E) 26π

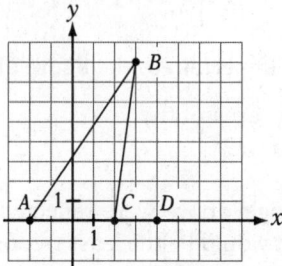

5. In the figure above, point E is to be drawn so that $\triangle CDE$ has the same area as $\triangle ABC$. Which of the following could be the coordinates of E?

(A) (16, 5)   (B) (3, 8)   (C) (5, 12)
(D) (2, 16)   (E) (4, 24)

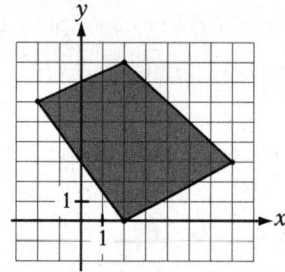

6. What is the area, in square units, of the shaded region in the figure above?

(A) 32
(B) 33
(C) 34
(D) 35
(E) 36

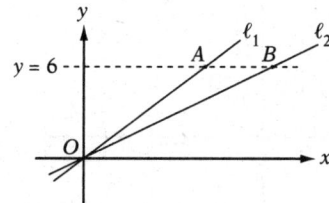

Note: Figure not drawn to scale.

7. Points A and B lie on the line $y = 6$, as shown above. Lines ℓ_1 and ℓ_2 pass through the origin, and ℓ_1 has a slope of ½. If the distance from A to B is 4, what is the slope of line ℓ_2?

Answer Key 4: Coordinate Geometry

Concept Review 4

1. (–2, 1)

2. (0.5, 2)

3. 2/5

4. Your line should be vertical (straight up and down) and pass through B.

5. The x-coordinate of all the points is 3, so ℓ_1 can be described by the equation $x = 3$.

6. ℓ_2 should be horizontal (straight across) and pass through B.

7. ℓ_3 should be a horizontal (straight across) line one unit below the x-axis.

8. (–2, 5)

9. (1, 8) (Notice that the new segment must be the same length as AB, but its slope is the negative reciprocal of AB's slope, that is, –5/2.)

10. (8, 5)

11. The area of the rectangle is 108, and its length DC is 14 – 2 = 12. So its height is 108/12 = 9. Therefore, $k – 1 = 9$, and $k = 10$.

    $m = 14$

    $n = 10$

    $p = 1$

12. AC is the hypotenuse of a right triangle with legs of 9 and 12. This is a 3-4-5 triangle times 3—a 9-12-15 triangle—so AC is 15. The perimeter of the rectangle is 9 + 12 + 9 + 12 = 42. So the ratio of the diagonal to the perimeter is 15/42 = 5/14.

13. The slope of DB is 3/4, or .75.

14. AC and DB intersect at the midpoint of each segment. The midpoint of AC is ((14 + 2)/2, (10 + 1)/2) = (8, 5.5).

15. (26, 19)

16. Use the left side of the triangle as the base. This way, the base is vertical and the height is horizontal, so the lengths are easier to find. The base is 4 units and the height is 7 units, so the area is $(4 \times 7)/2 = 14$.

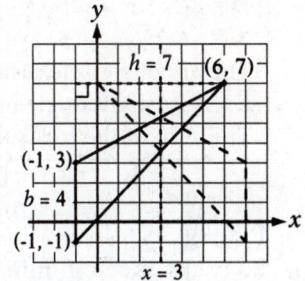

17. The reflection of the triangle over the line $x = 3$ is shown above. The "leftmost" point has an x-coordinate of 0.

18. No matter how the triangle is reflected, the area remains the same. The area is still 14.

SAT Practice 4

1. **B** The vertices of a square must always be listed in consecutive order, so point C must follow consecutively after B and can be in either position shown in the figure at right. Therefore, C can be at (0, 2) or (6, 2).

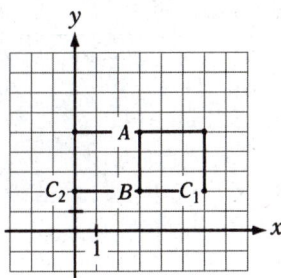

2. **A** The horizontal line passing through (1, 8) is the line $y = 8$, and the vertical line passing through (–3, 4) is the line $x = –3$. So they intersect at (–3, 8).

3. **E** The distance from (0, 0) to (–3, 4) is 5, which is the radius of the circle. Therefore, any point that is 5 units from the origin is also on the circle. Each of the given points is also 5 units from the origin.

4. **E** The distance from (3, –7) to (8, 5) is

    $\sqrt{(8-3)^2 + (5-(-7))^2} = \sqrt{5^2 + 12^2} = 13$.

    The circumference is $2\pi r = 26\pi$.

5. **D** $\triangle ABC$ has a base of 4 and height of 8, so its area is $(4 \times 8)/2 = 16$. Since the base of $\triangle CDE$ is 2, its height must be 16 if it is to have the same area as $\triangle ABC$. The y-coordinate of E, then, must be 16 or –16.

6. **E** Draw a rectangle around the quadrilateral as in the figure at right. The rectangle has an area of $9 \times 8 = 72$. If we "remove" the areas of the four right triangles from the corners, the area of the shaded region will remain.

    $72 – 4 – 12 – 12.5 – 7.5 = 36$

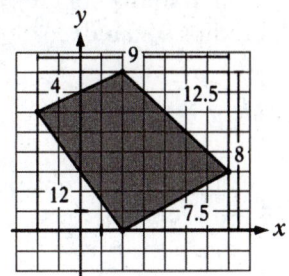

7. **⅜** The y-coordinate of point A is 6, which means the "rise" from O to A is 6. Since the slope of ℓ_1 is ½, the "run" must be 12. The "run" from O to B is 12 + 4 = 16, and the "rise" is 6, so the slope of ℓ_2 is 6/16 = 3/8.

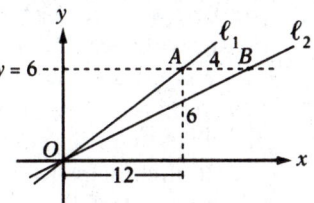

Lesson 5: Areas and Perimeters

The Formulas

The only area or perimeter formulas you will need for the SAT will be given at the beginning of each section:

Reference Information

$A = \pi r^2$
$C = 2\pi r$　　$A = \ell w$　　$A = \frac{1}{2}bh$　　$V = \ell wh$　　$V = \pi r^2 h$　　$c^2 = a^2 + b^2$　　Special right triangles

The arc of a circle measures 360°.
Every straight angle measures 180°.
The sum of the measures of the angles in a triangle is 180°.

Finding the area of an obtuse triangle can be tricky. Keep in mind that *any* side can be the base—rotate the triangle if it helps. Also remember that an altitude *might* be outside the triangle, as in the diagram below.

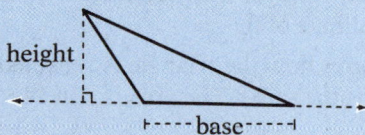

Don't confuse the area formula for a circle (πr^2) with the circumference formula ($2\pi r$). Just remember that areas are measured in *square* units, so the area formula is the one with the radius squared.

Using Diagrams

If a geometry problem *doesn't* include a figure, draw one, because seeing the relationships among the parts is essential to solving geometry problems! If it *does* include a figure, mark it up with any information you find!

You can use the diagram to estimate angle measures and lengths, unless it is labeled "Note: Figure not drawn to scale," which means that the figure is drawn inaccurately, or in only one of many different possible ways. In this case, it often helps to redraw the figure. If it's drawn inaccurately, redraw it accurately, and see whether anything important changes. If it can be drawn in different ways, redraw it so that it is as different as possible from the original, but all of the given information is maintained.

Strange Shapes

Don't panic when you see a strange-looking shape on an SAT. Just notice how the shape relates to simple shapes.

Example:

In the figure below, the shaded region is constructed of only horizontal and vertical sides. That is, all angles are right angles. What is the perimeter of the shaded region?

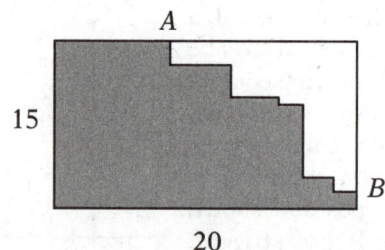

Compare the shaded region to the rectangle, but keep in mind that the question asks about the perimeter, not the area! Even though the *area* of the shaded region is clearly less than the *area* of the rectangle, their *perimeters* must be the same! How do we know? Consider the two different paths from *A* to *B*. Notice that all the horizontal segments of the "jagged" path add up in length to the horizontal part of the "simple" path along the rectangle. The same is true of the vertical parts. So the perimeter is 15 + 20 + 15 + 20 = 70.

Example:

If the circle with center C has an area of 16π, what is the area of the shaded region?

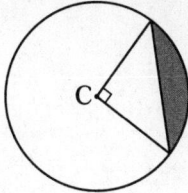

Piece together the strange shape from simple shapes. Notice that the shaded region is simply a quarter of the circle minus the triangle. If the area of the circle is 16π, then a quarter of the circle has an area of 4π. Since $\pi r^2 = 16\pi$, the radius must be 4. Therefore, the base and height of the triangle are both 4, and the area of the triangle is (4×4)/2 = 8. Therefore, the area of the shaded region is 4π − 8.

Concept Review 5: Areas and Perimeters

Draw a diagram in the space below for the following situation:
The length and width of rectangle *ABCD* are integers. The area of *ABCD* is 32. Diagonal *AC* is extended to point *F* such that *C* is the midpoint of *AF*.

1. If the area of *ABCD* is 32, what is the area of Δ*FDB*?

2. What is the ratio of the area of Δ*FCB* to the area of Δ*FAD*?

Questions 3 and 4 pertain to the diagram below, in which P is the center of the semicircle.

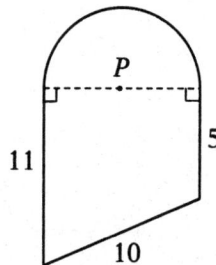

3. What is the area of the figure above?

4. What is the perimeter of the figure above?

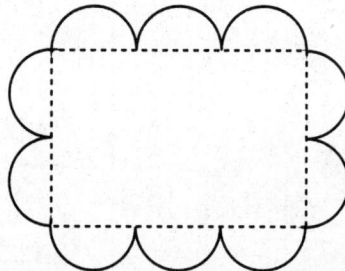

5. The figure above consists of a rectangle and a curved path which is made up of 10 semicircles of equal diameter. If the total length of this curved path is 40π, then the area of the rectangle is
    (A) 40   (B) 80   (C) 96   (D) 192   (E) 384

SAT Practice 5: Areas and Perimeters

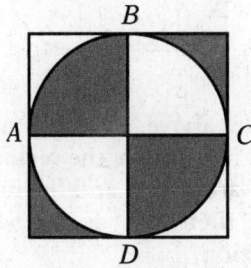

1. In the figure above, a circle is inscribed in a square and intersects the square at points A, B, C, and D. If $AC = 12$, what is the total area of the shaded regions?

    (A) 18
    (B) 36
    (C) 18π
    (D) 24π
    (E) 72

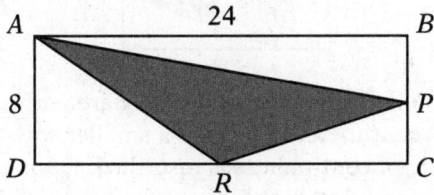

2. In the figure above, $ABCD$ is a rectangle and P and R are midpoints of their respective sides. What is the area of $\triangle APR$?

    (A) 54
    (B) 68
    (C) 72
    (D) 78
    (E) 96

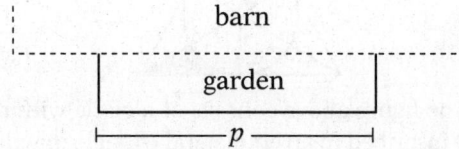

3. A fence encloses three sides of a rectangular garden that is bordered on the other side by a barn, as shown in the figure above. If the total length of the fence is 44 meters and p is the length, in meters, of the fence parallel to the barn wall, then which of the following expresses the area of the garden?

    (A) $22p - p^2$

    (B) $\dfrac{44p - p^2}{2}$

    (C) $22p$

    (D) $\dfrac{22p - p^2}{2}$

    (E) $44p - p^2$

4. What is the maximum number of pieces that can be cut from a paper circle with four straight cuts if none of the pieces are moved or folded between cuts?

    (A) 7
    (B) 8
    (C) 9
    (D) 10
    (E) 11

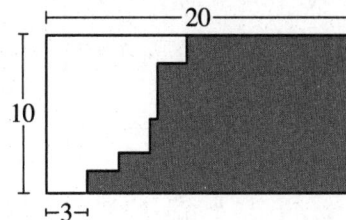

5. In the figure above, all angles shown are right angles. What is the perimeter of the shaded region?

    (A) 51
    (B) 54
    (C) 57
    (D) 60
    (E) 63

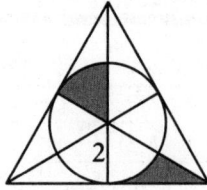

6. The figure above consists of a circle with radius 2 inscribed in an equilateral triangle in which all three interior angle bisectors are drawn. What is the total area of the shaded regions?

(A) $2\sqrt{3}$

(B) $\dfrac{2\pi + 2}{3}$

(C) $\dfrac{2\pi - 2}{3}$

(D) $2\pi + 2$

(E) $\pi + 2$

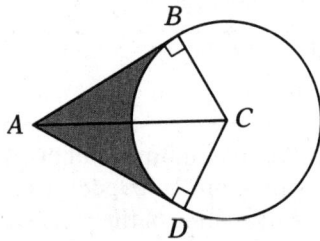

7. In the figure above, C is the center of the circle, $AC = 12$, and $\angle BAD = 60°$. What is the *perimeter* of the shaded region?

(A) $12 + 4\pi$

(B) $6\sqrt{3} + 4\pi$

(C) $6\sqrt{3} + 3\pi$

(D) $12\sqrt{3} + 3\pi$

(E) $12\sqrt{3} + 4\pi$

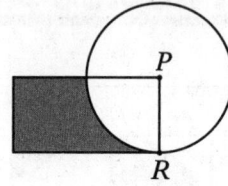

8. In the figure above, PR is the radius of the circle as well as a side of the rectangle. If the circle has an area of 4π and the rectangle has an area of 8, then what is the *perimeter* of the shaded region?

(A) $\pi + 8$
(B) $\pi + 10$
(C) $\pi + 12$
(D) $2\pi + 8$
(E) $2\pi + 12$

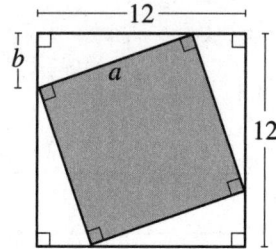

9. The figure above shows a square with sides of 12 centimeters in which a smaller square with sides a centimeters is inscribed. If a is an integer and $2 \le b \le 5$, then what is one possible value for the area of the shaded square?

Answer Key 5: Areas and Perimeters

Concept Review 5

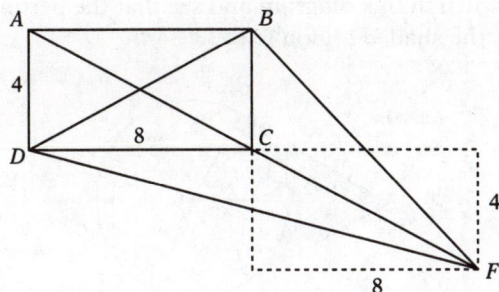

Your diagram should look something like the one above, although the rectangle can also have dimensions of 1 and 32 or 2 and 16.

1. Think of the area of ΔFDB as the sum of the areas of ΔDCB, ΔFDC, and ΔFCB. Each of these triangles has an area that is half of the rectangle, because each one has the same base and height as the rectangle. (If you have a tough time seeing this, think of BC as the base of ΔFCB and CD as the base of ΔFDC. Since these triangles are obtuse, their heights are "outside" the triangles.) Therefore, the area of ΔFDB is 16 + 16 + 16 = 48.

2. We just found that ΔFCB has an area of 16. The area of ΔFAD is the area of ΔFCD + the area of

ΔADC, which is 16 + 16 = 32. Therefore, the ratio is 1:2.

3. Draw the extra segment as shown and determine its length from the Pythagorean theorem. (It's a 3-4-5 right triangle times 2!) The area of the semicircle is 16π/2 = 8π, the area of the rectangle is 40, and the area of the triangle is 24, for a total area of 64 + 8π.

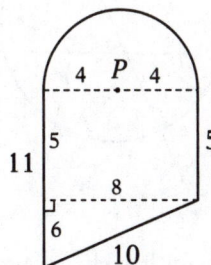

4. The perimeter of the semicircle is 4π, so the perimeter of the whole figure is 26 + 4π.

5. **E** Each semicircle has a perimeter of 4π, which means the circumference of a "whole" circle would be 8π and therefore the diameter of each circle is 8. Therefore, the height of the rectangle is 16 and the length is 24. 24 × 16 = 384

SAT Practice 5

1. **E** Move the shaded pieces around to see that they make up half of the square. The area of the square is 12 × 12 = 144, so the shaded region has area 144/2 = 72.

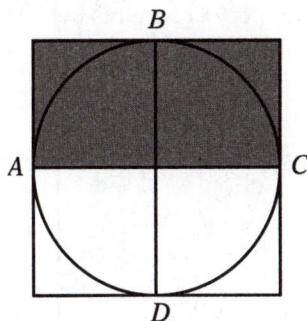

2. **C** Find the area indirectly by subtracting the three right triangles from the rectangle. The rectangle has area 8 × 24 = 192, so the triangle has area 192 − 48 − 48 − 24 = 72.

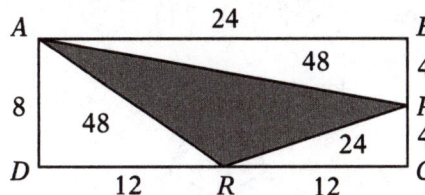

3. **B** The length of the garden is p. The width is half of $44 - p$. Therefore, the area is $p((44 - p)/2) = (44p - p^2)/2$.

4. **E** You get the maximum number of pieces (11) by making sure that each cut intersects every other previous cut in a new spot. Your diagram should look something like this, with six points of intersection in the circle.

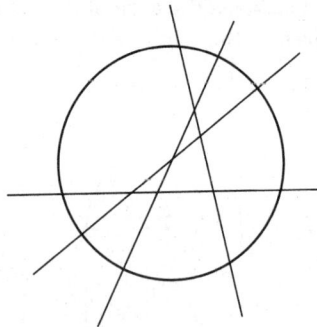

5. **B** Draw the extra line shown here to see that the shaded region has a perimeter equal to a 10-by-17 rectangle. Therefore its perimeter is $10 + 17 + 10 + 17 = 54$.

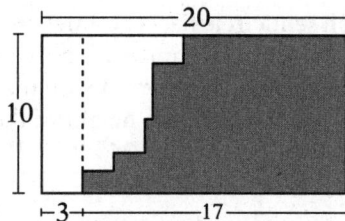

6. **A** Move the pieces together to see that they form a right triangle. Since all of the interior angles of an equilateral triangle are 60° and the bisectors divide them in half, the triangle is a 30°-60°-90° triangle, so its base must be $2\sqrt{3}$, and the area is $\left((2\sqrt{3})(2)\right)/2 = 2\sqrt{3}$.

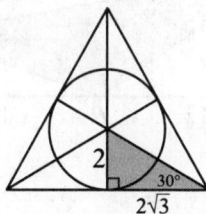

7. **E** The two right triangles have two pairs of equal sides (the two radii and the shared hypotenuse), so they must be congruent triangles. Arc BD is ⅓ of the circle, with circumference 12π. Therefore, you should be able to determine the measures shown in this diagram and see that the perimeter of the shaded region is $12\sqrt{3} + 4\pi$.

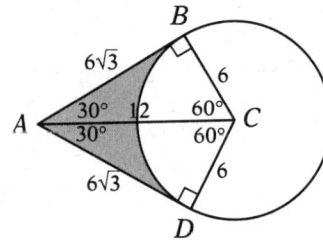

8. **A** If the circle has an area of 4π, its radius is 2. If the rectangle has an area of 8, its length must be 4. The arc portion of the shaded region is ¼ of the circle with circumference 4π, so the perimeter is $2 + 2 + 4 + \pi = 8 + \pi$.

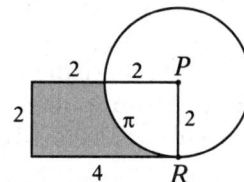

9. **81 or 100** Consider the right triangle in the upper-left corner of the diagram. Notice that it has a hypotenuse of a and legs of length b and $12 - b$. The question is asking for the area of the shaded square, which is a^2. By the Pythagorean theorem, $a^2 = b^2 + (12 - b)^2 = 2b^2 - 24b + 144$. Since $2 \leq b \leq 5$, the maximum possible value of a^2 is $2(2)^2 - 24(2) + 144 = 104$, and the minimum possible value of a^2 is $2(5)^2 - 24(5) + 144 = 74$. Since a must be an integer, a^2 must be a perfect square, and the only perfect squares between 74 and 104 are 81 and 100.

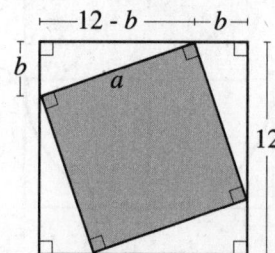

Lesson 6: Similar Figures

Similar Figures

When you think of *similar* you probably think of "almost the same, but not quite." In mathematics, however, the word *similar* has a much more specific, technical meaning. Two figures are similar if they are the same shape, but not necessarily the same size. For instance, all circles are similar to each other, and all squares are similar to each other: there is only one "shape" for a circle, and only one "shape" for a square. But there are many different shapes that a rectangle may have, so two rectangles aren't necessarily similar.

If two shapes are similar, then all corresponding angles are equal and all corresponding lengths are proportional.

Use proportions to find the lengths of unknown sides in similar figures.

Example:

What is *x* in the figure at left below?

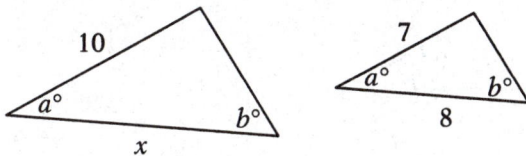

The two triangles are similar because all of their corresponding angles are equal. (Even though only two pairs of angles are **given** as equal, we know that the other pair are also equal, because the angles in a triangle must add up to 180°.) So we can set up a proportion of corresponding sides:

$$\frac{10}{7} = \frac{x}{8} \qquad \text{Cross-multiply: } 7x = 80$$

$$\text{Divide by 7: } x = 80/7 = 11.43$$

Two triangles are similar if any of the following is true:

- Two pairs of corresponding angles are equal. (If two pairs are equal, the third pair must be equal, too.)
- Two pairs of corresponding sides are proportional and the angles between them are equal.
- All three pairs of corresponding sides are proportional.

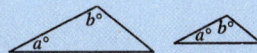

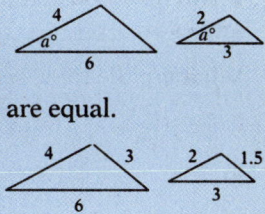

Ratios of Areas

Consider two squares: one with a side length of 2 and the other with a side length of 3. Clearly, their sides are in the ratio of 2:3. What about their areas? That's easy: their areas are $2^2 = 4$ and $3^2 = 9$, so the areas are in a ratio of 4:9. This demonstrates a fact that is true of all similar figures:

If corresponding lengths of two similar figures have a ratio of *a*:*b*, then the areas of the two figures have a ratio of a^2:b^2.

Example:

A garden that is 30 feet long has an area of 600 square feet. A blueprint of the garden that is drawn to scale depicts the garden as being 3 inches long. What is the area of the blueprint drawing of the garden?

It is tempting to want to say 60 square inches because 30:600 = 3:60. But be careful: the ratio of areas is the square of the ratio of lengths! You can draw a diagram, assuming the garden to be a rectangle. (The shape of the garden doesn't matter: it's convenient to draw the garden as a rectangle, but it doesn't have to be.) Or you can simply set up the proportion using the formula:

$$\frac{x}{600} = \frac{3^2}{30^2} = \frac{9}{900}$$

Cross-multiply: $\qquad 900x = 5,400$
Divide by 900: $\qquad x = 6$

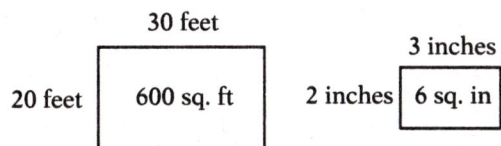

Concept Review 6: Similar Figures

1. If two figures are similar, then their corresponding sides are _____ and their corresponding angles are _____.

2. What are the three sets of conditions of which any one is sufficient to show that two triangles are similar?

   a.

   b.

   c.

3. The hypotenuses of two similar right triangles are 4 centimeters and 6 centimeters long, respectively. If the area of the larger triangle is 27, what is the area of the smaller one?

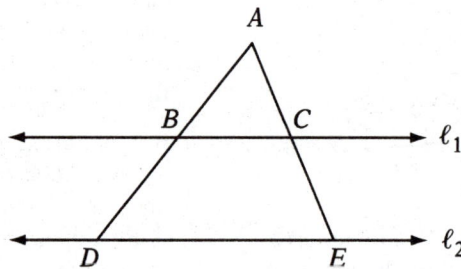

Note: Figure not drawn to scale.

4. In the figure above, $\ell_1 \parallel \ell_2$, $AC = 4$, $BC = 5$, and $CE = 6$. What is the length of DE?

5. In a 5- × 8-inch rectangular photograph, the image of a tree is 3 inches high. The photograph is then magnified until its area is 1,000 square inches. What is the height of the tree image in the larger photograph?

SAT Practice 6: Similar Figures

1. The ratio of the areas of two squares is 4:1. If the perimeter of the smaller square is 20, what is the perimeter of the larger square?

   (A) 5
   (B) 10
   (C) 20
   (D) 40
   (E) 80

2. A scale drawing of a rectangular patio measures 5 centimeters by 7 centimeters. If the longer side of the actual patio is 21 feet, what is the area, in square feet, of the actual patio?

   (A) 72
   (B) 315
   (C) 356
   (D) 441
   (E) 617

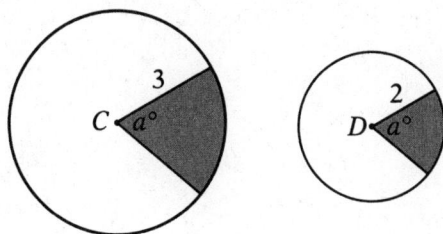

Note: Figure not drawn to scale.

3. In the figure above, C and D are the centers of the two circles with radii of 3 and 2, respectively. If the larger shaded region has an area of 9, what is the area of the smaller shaded region?

   (A) 4
   (B) 5
   (C) 6
   (D) 7
   (E) 8

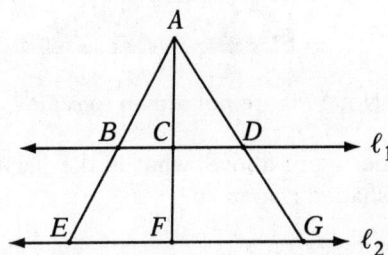

4. In the figure above, $\ell_1 \parallel \ell_2$. If $EF = x$, and $EG = y$, then which of the following represents the ratio of CD to BC?

   (A) $1 - \dfrac{y}{x}$

   (B) $1 + \dfrac{y}{x}$

   (C) $\dfrac{y}{x} - 1$

   (D) $1 - \dfrac{x}{y}$

   (E) $1 + \dfrac{x}{y}$

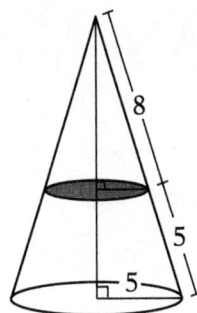

5. A circular cone with a base of radius 5 has been cut as shown in the figure above. What is the height of the smaller cone?

   (A) $\dfrac{8}{13}$

   (B) $\dfrac{96}{13}$

   (C) $\dfrac{96}{12}$

   (D) $\dfrac{96}{5}$

   (E) $\dfrac{104}{5}$

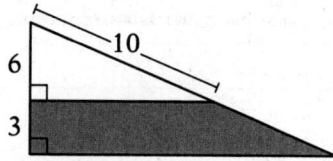

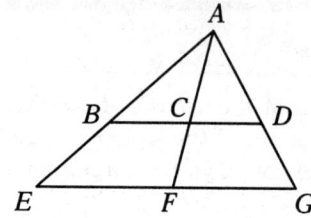

Note: Figure not drawn to scale.

6. In the figure above, what is the perimeter of the shaded trapezoid?

Note: Figure not drawn to scale.

7. In the figure above, $\overline{BD}$ is parallel to $\overline{EG}$, $AD = 6$, $DG = 4$, and $\triangle AEF$ has an area of 75. What is the area of $\triangle ABC$?

(A) 27
(B) 36
(C) 45
(D) 54
(E) 63

Answer Key 6: Similar Figures

Concept Review 6

1. If two figures are similar, then their corresponding sides are *proportional* and their corresponding angles are *equal (or congruent)*.

2. a. two pairs of corresponding angles are equal
   b. two pairs of corresponding sides are proportional and the included angles are equal
   c. all three pairs of corresponding sides are proportional

3. The ratio of the sides is 4:6 or 2:3. The ratio of the areas is the square of the ratio of sides, which is 4:9. If x is the area of the smaller triangle, then $x/27 = 4/9$. Solving for x gives $x = 12$.

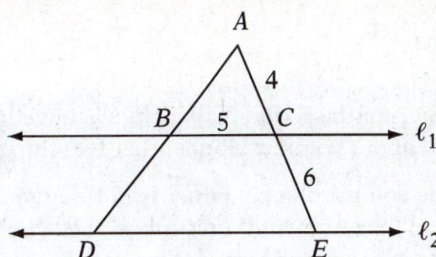

4. If $\ell_1 \parallel \ell_2$, then the two triangles must be similar. Since corresponding sides are proportional, $AC/AE = BC/DE$.
Substituting, this gives $4/10 = 5/DE$.
Cross-multiply: $4DE = 50$
Divide by 4: $DE = 12.5$

5. A 5- × 8-inch rectangle has an area of 40 square inches. The ratio of areas, then, is 40:1,000, or 1:25. This is the square of the ratio of lengths, so the ratio of lengths must be 1:5. If x is the length of the larger tree image, then $3/x = 1/5$. Cross-multiplying gives $x = 15$, so the tree is 15 inches high in the larger photograph.

SAT Practice 6

1. **D** If the ratio of the areas is 4:1, then the ratio of corresponding lengths is the square root: 2:1. If the perimeter of the smaller square is 20, then the perimeter of the larger one is twice as big.

2. **B** Find the width of the patio with a proportion:

$$5/7 = x/21$$
Cross-multiply: $7x = 105$
Divide by 7: $x = 15$

So the patio is a 15- × 21-foot rectangle, which has an area of $15 \times 21 = 315$ square feet.

3. **A** The two regions are similar, because the central angles are the same. The ratio of their corresponding lengths is 3:2, so the ratio of their areas is 9:4. Since the larger area is 9, the smaller area must be 4.

4. **C** If EF has length x and EG has length y, then FG must have length $y - x$, as shown. Since the two lines are parallel, $\triangle ABC$ is similar to $\triangle AEF$ and $\triangle ACD$ is similar to $\triangle AFG$. Therefore $AC/CF = BC/x$ and $AC/CF = CD/(y - x)$. So $BC/x = CD/(y - x)$, and therefore $CD/BC = (y - x)/x = y/x - 1$.

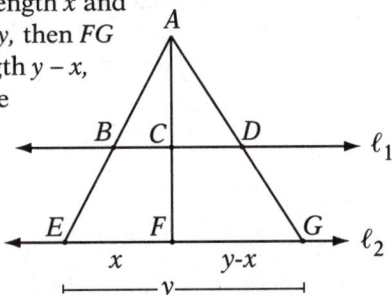

5. **B** The height of the larger cone can be found with the Pythagorean theorem to be 12. (It's the old 5-12-13 right triangle!) Since the two triangles are similar, $x/12 = 8/13$. Multiplying by 12 gives $x = 96/13$.

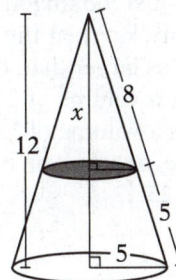

6. **28** The two triangles are similar because their corresponding angles are equal. Since they are right triangles, the missing sides can be found with the Pythagorean theorem. Your diagram should look like the one above. The perimeter is $3 + 8 + 5 + 12 = 28$.

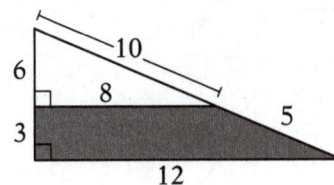

7. **A** Since the lines are parallel, $\triangle ABC$ is similar to $\triangle AEF$ and $\triangle ACD$ is similar to $\triangle AFG$. Therefore, $AD/AG = AC/AF = 6/10 = 3/5$. The ratio of areas between $\triangle ABC$ and $\triangle AEF$ is the square of the ratio of sides, which is $(3/5)^2 = 9/25$. Since $\triangle AEF$ has an area of 75, (the area of $\triangle ABC$)/75 = 9/25. So $\triangle ABC$ has an area of 27.

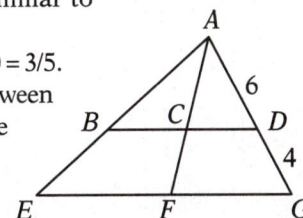

Lesson 7: Volumes and 3-D Geometry

Volume

The SAT math section may include a question or two about volumes. Remember two things:

- The volume of a container is nothing more than the number of "unit cubes" it can hold.
- The only volume formulas you will need are given to you in the "Reference Information" on every math section.

Example:

How many rectangular bricks measuring 2 inches by 3 inches by 4 inches must be stacked together (without mortar or any other material) to create a solid rectangular box that measures 15 inches by 30 inches by 60 inches?

Don't be too concerned with **how** the bricks could be stacked to make the box; there are many possible arrangements, but the arrangement doesn't affect the answer. All you need to know is that it can be done. If so, just looking at the volumes is enough: if you use n bricks, then the box must have a volume that is n times larger than the volume of one brick. Each brick has a volume of $2 \times 3 \times 4 = 24$ cubic inches. The box has a volume of $15 \times 30 \times 60 = 27{,}000$ square inches. The number of bricks, then, must be $27{,}000/24 = 1{,}125$.

3-D Distances

If you are trying to find the length of a line segment in three dimensions, look for a right triangle that has that segment as its hypotenuse.

Example:

The figure at right shows a cube with edges of length 4. If point C is the midpoint of edge BD, what is the length of $\overline{AC}$?

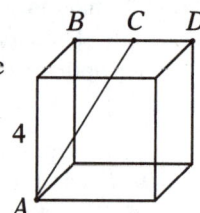

Draw segment $\overline{CE}$ to see that $\overline{AC}$ is the hypotenuse of right triangle $\triangle AEC$.

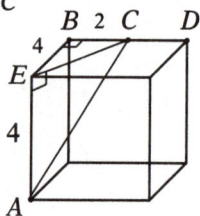

Leg $\overline{AE}$ has a length of 4, and leg $\overline{EC}$ is the hypotenuse of right triangle $\triangle EBC$, with legs of length 2 and 4. Therefore,

$$EC = \sqrt{2^2 + 4^2} = \sqrt{4 + 16} = \sqrt{20}$$

so $AC = \sqrt{\left(\sqrt{20}\right)^2 + 4^2} = \sqrt{20 + 16} = \sqrt{36} = 6.$

One possible shortcut for finding lengths in three dimensions is the three-dimensional distance formula:

$$d = \sqrt{\left(x_2 - x_1\right)^2 + \left(y_2 - y_1\right)^2 + \left(z_2 - z_1\right)^2}$$

If you think of point A in the cube above as being the origin $(0, 0, 0)$, then point C can be considered to be $(4, 4, 2)$. The distance from A to C, then, is

$$\sqrt{\left(4 - 0\right)^2 + \left(4 - 0\right)^2 + \left(2 - 0\right)^2} = \sqrt{16 + 16 + 4} = \sqrt{36} = 6.$$

Concept Review 7: Volumes and 3-D Geometry

1. What is the definition of volume?

2. Write the formula for the volume of a rectangular box.

3. Write the 3-D distance formula.

4. Graph the points $A(-2, 3, 1)$ and $B(2, 1, -2)$ on an x-y-z graph.

5. What is the distance from point A to point B in the figure above?

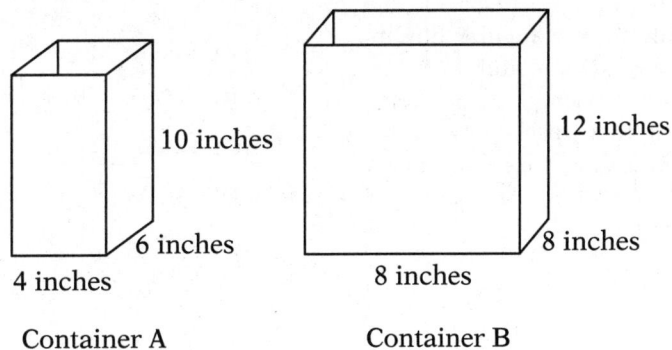

Container A   Container B

6. The two containers with rectangular sides in the figure above have the interior dimensions shown. Both containers rest on a flat, horizontal surface. Container A is filled completely with water, and then this water is poured, without spilling, into Container B. When all of the liquid is poured from Container A into Container B, what is the depth of the water in Container B?

SAT Practice 7: Volumes and 3-D Geometry

1. The length, width, and height of a rectangular box, in centimeters, are a, b, and c, where a, b, and c are all integers. The total surface area of the box, in square centimeters, is s, and the volume of the box, in cubic centimeters, is v. Which of the following must be true?

I. v is an integer.
II. s is an even integer.
III.   The greatest distance between any two vertices of the box is $\sqrt{a^2+b^2+c^2}$.

(A) I only
(B) I and II only
(C) I and III only
(D) II and III only
(E) I, II, and III

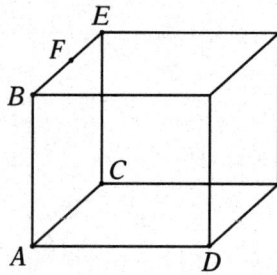

2. The figure above shows a rectangular box in which $AB = 6$, $AC = 5$, $AD = 8$, and F is the midpoint of $\overline{BE}$. What is the length of the shortest path from A to F that travels only on the edges of the box and does *not* pass through either point B or point C?

(A) 27.5
(B) 28.5
(C) 29.5
(D) 30
(E) 30.5

3. A pool-filling service charges $2.00 per cubic meter of water for the first 300 cubic meters and $1.50 per cubic meter of water after that. At this rate, how much would it cost to have the service fill a rectangular pool of uniform depth that is 2 meters deep, 20 meters long, and 15 meters wide?

(A) $450
(B) $650
(C) $800
(D) $1,050
(E) $1,200

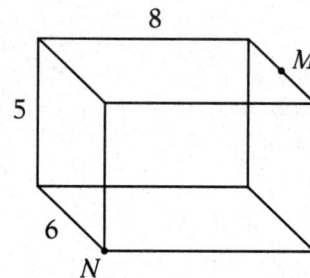

4. In the figure above, a rectangular box has the dimensions shown. N is a vertex of the box, and M is the midpoint of an edge of the box. What is the length of $\overline{NM}$?

(A) $\sqrt{63}$
(B) $\sqrt{77}$
(C) $\sqrt{98}$
(D) $\sqrt{108}$
(E) $\sqrt{125}$

5. A cereal company sells oatmeal in two sizes of cylindrical containers. The smaller container holds 10 ounces of oatmeal. If the larger container has twice the radius of the smaller container and 1.5 times the height, how many ounces of oatmeal does the larger container hold? (The volume of a cylinder is given by the formula $V = \pi r^2 h$.)

(A) 30
(B) 45
(C) 60
(D) 75
(E) 90

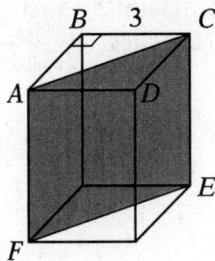

6. The figure above shows a rectangular solid with a volume of 72 cubic units. Base *ABCD* has an area of 12 square units. What is the area of rectangle *ACEF*?

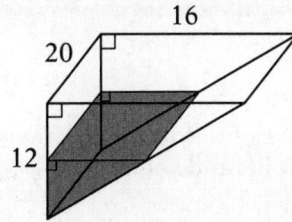

7. The figure above shows a wedge-shaped holding tank that is partially filled with water. If the tank is 1/16 full, what is the depth of the water at the deepest part?

(A) 3
(B) 2
(C) 1.5
(D) 1
(E) 0.75

Answer Key 7: Volumes and 3-D Geometry

Concept Review 7

1. The volume of a solid is the number of "unit cubes" that fit inside of it.

2. $V = lwh$

3. $d = \sqrt{(x_2 - x_1)^2 + (y_2 - y_1)^2 + (z_2 - z_1)^2}$

4. Your graph should look like this one:

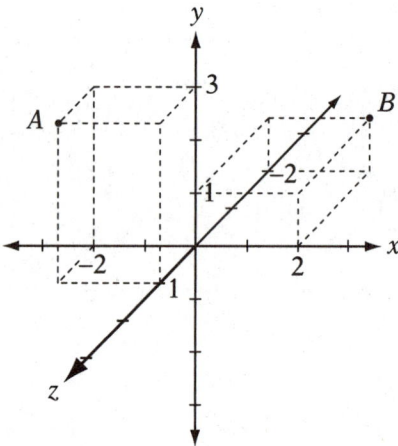

5. Using the 3-D distance formula,

$$d = \sqrt{(2-(-2))^2 + (1-3)^2 + (-2-1)^2}$$

$$= \sqrt{(4)^2 + (-2)^2 + (-3)^2}$$

$$= \sqrt{16 + 4 + 9} = \sqrt{29}$$

6. Since the water is poured without spilling, the volume of water must remain the same. Container A has a volume of $4 \times 6 \times 10 = 240$ cubic inches. Since Container B is larger, the water won't fill it completely, but will fill it only to a depth of h inches. The volume of the water can then be calculated as $8 \times 8 \times h = 64h$ cubic inches. Since the volume must remain the same, $64h = 240$, so $h = 3.75$ inches.

SAT Practice 7

1. **E** $v = abc$, so if a, b, and c are integers, v must be an integer also and statement I is true. The total surface area of the box, s, is $2ab + 2bc + 2ac = 2(ab + bc + ac)$, which is a multiple of 2 and therefore even. So statement II is true. Statement III is true by the 3-D distance formula.

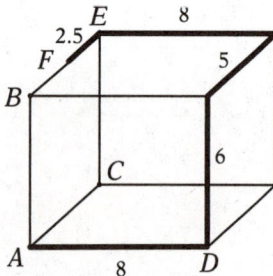

2. **C** The path shown above is the shortest under the circumstances. The length of the path is

$8 + 6 + 5 + 8 + 2.5 = 29.5$.

3. **D** The volume of the pool is $2 \times 20 \times 15 = 600$ cubic meters. The first 300 cubic meters cost $300 \times 2 = \$600$, and the other 300 cubic meters cost $300 \times 1.50 = \$450$, for a total of $\$1,050$.

4. **C** Draw segment $\overline{NP}$ as shown. It is the hypotenuse of a right triangle, so you can find its length with the Pythagorean theorem:

$$NP = \sqrt{8^2 + 5^2} = \sqrt{64 + 25} = \sqrt{89}$$

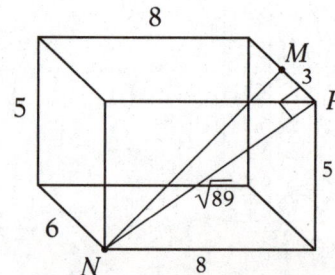

$\overline{NM}$ is the hypotenuse of right triangle $\triangle NPM$, so

$$NM = \sqrt{\left(\sqrt{89}\right)^2 + 3^2} = \sqrt{89 + 9} = \sqrt{98}.$$

5. **C** If the volume of the smaller container is $V = \pi r^2 h$, then the volume of the larger container is $\pi(2r)^2(1.5h) = 6\pi r^2 h = 6v$. So the larger container holds six times as much oatmeal as the smaller one. The smaller container holds 10 ounces of oatmeal, so the larger one holds $10 \times 6 = 60$ ounces.

6. **30** Mark up the diagram as shown. If the base has an area of 12, AB must be 4. If the volume of the box is 72, then the height must be $72/12 = 6$. AC must be 5, because it's the hypotenuse of a 3-4-5 triangle. So the rectangle has an area of $5 \times 6 = 30$.

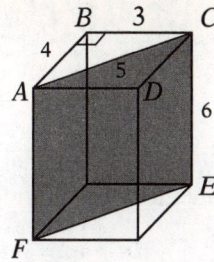

7. **A** If the volume of the water is 1/16 the volume of the tank, the smaller triangle must have an area 1/16 that of the larger triangle. The two are similar, so the ratio of the lengths must be 1/4, because $1/16 = (1/4)^2$. Therefore, the depth of water is 1/4 the depth of the tank: $12/4 = 3$.

Lesson 8: Circles

Circle Basics

Okay, we all know a circle when we see one, but it often helps to know the mathematical definition of a circle.

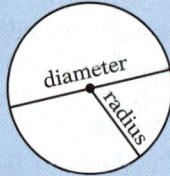

- A circle is all of the points in a plane that are a certain distance *r* from the center.

- The *radius* is the distance from the center to any point on the circle.

Radius means *ray* in Latin; a radius comes from the center of the circle like *a ray of light from the sun*.

- The *diameter* is twice the radius: *d* = 2*r*.

Dia- means *through* in Latin, so the diameter is a segment that goes *all the way through the* circle.

The Circumference and Area

It's easy to confuse the circumference formula with the **area** formula, because both formulas contain the same symbols arranged differently: *circumference* = 2π*r* and *area* = π*r*². There are two simple ways to avoid that mistake:

- Remember that the formulas for circumference and area are given in the reference information at the beginning of every math section.
- Remember that area is always measured in square units, so the area formula is the one with the "square:" *area* = π*r*².

Tangents

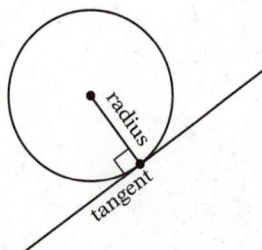

A *tangent is a line that touches (or intersects) the circle at only one point*. Think of a plate balancing on its side on a table: the table is like a tangent line to the plate.

> A tangent line is always perpendicular to the radius drawn to the point of tangency.

Just think of a bicycle tire (the circle) on the road (the tangent): notice that the center of the wheel must be "directly above" where the tire touches the road, so the radius and tangent must be perpendicular.

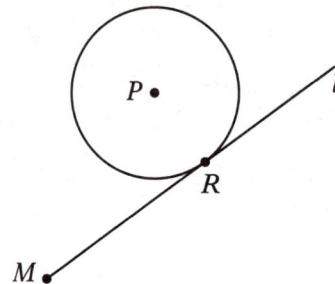

Example:

In the diagram above, point *M* is 7 units away from the center of circle *P*. If line *l* is tangent to the circle and *MR* = 5, what is the area of the circle?

First, connect the dots. Draw *MP* and *PR* to make a triangle.

Since *PR* is a radius and *MR* is a tangent, they are perpendicular.

Since you know two sides of a right triangle, you can use the Pythagorean theorem to find the third side: $5^2 + (PR)^2 = 7^2$
Simplify: $25 + (PR)^2 = 49$
Subtract 25: $(PR)^2 = 24$

$(PR)^2$ is the radius squared. Since the area of the circle is π*r*², it is **24π**.

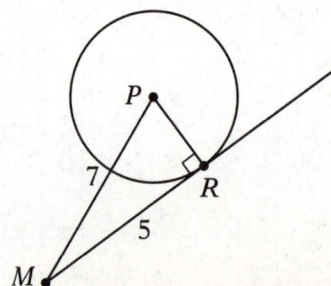

Concept Review 8: Circles

1. What is the formula for the circumference of a circle?

2. What is the formula for the area of a circle?

3. What is a tangent line?

4. What is the relationship between a tangent to a circle and the radius to the point of tangency?

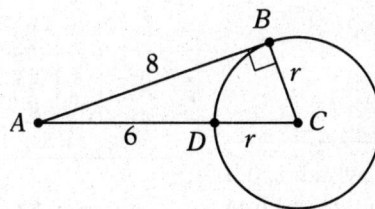

5. In the figure above, $\overline{AB}$ is a tangent to circle C, $AB = 8$, and $AD = 6$. What is the circumference of circle C?

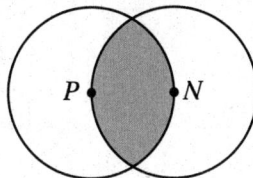

6. In the figure above, P and N are the centers of the circles and are 6 centimeters apart. What is the area of the shaded region?

SAT Practice 8: Circles

1. Two circles, *A* and *B*, lie in the same plane. If the center of circle *B* lies on circle *A*, then in how many points could circle *A* and circle *B* intersect?

    I. 0
    II. 1
    III. 2

(A) I only
(B) III only
(C) I and III only
(D) II and III only
(E) I, II, and III

2. What is the area, in square centimeters, of a circle with a circumference of 16π centimeters?

(A) 8π
(B) 16π
(C) 32π
(D) 64π
(E) 256π

3. Point *B* lies 10 units from point *A*, which is the center of the circle of radius 6. If a tangent line is drawn from *B* to the circle, what is the distance from *B* to the point of tangency?

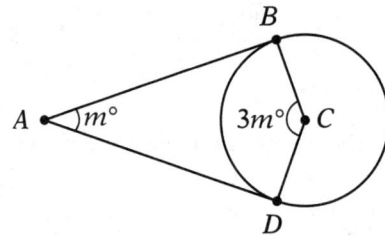

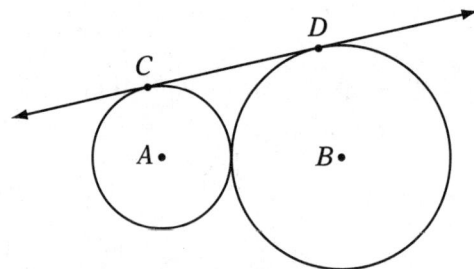

Note: Figure not drawn to scale.

4. In the figure above, $\overline{AB}$ and $\overline{AD}$ are tangents to circle *C*. What is the value of *m*?

Note: Figure not drawn to scale.

5. In the figure above, circle *A* intersects circle *B* in exactly one point, $\overline{CD}$ is tangent to both circles, circle *A* has a radius of 2, and circle *B* has a radius of 8. What is the length of $\overline{CD}$?

Answer Key 8: Circles

Concept Review 8

1. circumference = $2\pi r$

2. area = πr^2

3. A tangent line is a line that intersects a circle at only one point.

4. Any tangent to a circle is perpendicular to the radius drawn to the point of tangency.

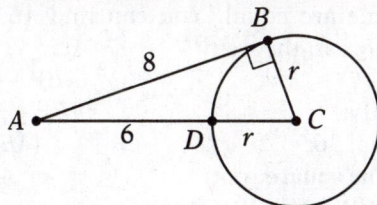

5. Draw $\overline{BC}$ to make a right triangle, and call the length of the radius r. Then you can use the Pythagorean theorem to find r:

$$8^2 + r^2 = (r + 6)^2$$

FOIL:	$64 + r^2 = r^2 + 12r + 36$
Subtract r^2:	$64 = 12r + 36$
Subtract 36:	$28 = 12r$
Divide by 12:	$7/3 = r$

The circumference is $2\pi r$, which is $2\pi(7/3) = 14\pi/3$.

6. Draw the segments shown here. Since PN is a radius of both circles, the radii of both circles have the same length. Notice that PN, PR, RN, PT, and NT are all radii, so they are all the same length; thus, $\triangle PNT$ and $\triangle PRN$ are equilateral triangles and their angles are all 60°. Now you can find the area of the left half of the shaded region. This is the area of the sector minus the area of $\triangle RNT$. Since $\angle RNT$ is 120°, the sector is 120/360, or ⅓, of the circle. The circle has area 36π, so the sector has area 12π. $\triangle RNT$ consists of two 30°-60°-90° triangles, with sides as marked, so its area is

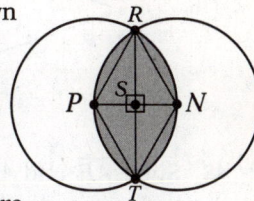

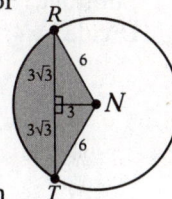

$(1/2)(6\sqrt{3})(3) = 9\sqrt{3}$. Therefore, half of the original shaded region is $12\pi - 9\sqrt{3}$, and the whole is $24\pi - 18\sqrt{3}$.

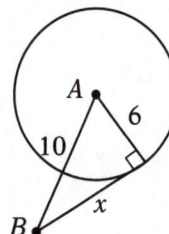

SAT Practice 8

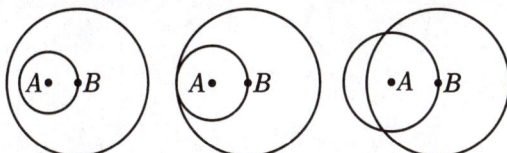

1. **E** The figure above demonstrates all three possibilities.

2. **D** The circumference $= 2\pi r = 16\pi$. Dividing by 2π gives $r = 8$. Area $= \pi r^2 = \pi(8)^2 = 64\pi$.

3. **8** Draw a figure as shown, including the tangent segment and the radius extended to the point of tangency. You can find x with the Pythagorean theorem:

	$6^2 + x^2 = 10^2$
Simplify:	$36 + x^2 = 100$
Subtract 36:	$x^2 = 64$
Take the square root:	$x = 8$

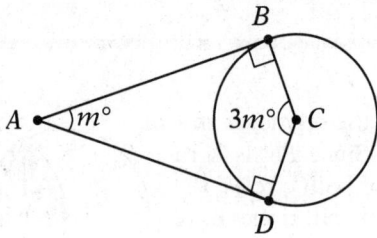

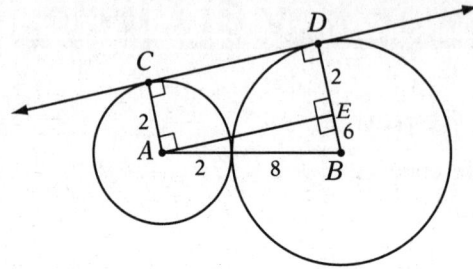

4. **45** Since $\overline{AB}$ and $\overline{AD}$ are tangents to the circle, they are perpendicular to their respective radii, as shown. The sum of the angles in a quadrilateral is 360°, so

$$m + 3m + 90 + 90 = 360$$

Simplify:	$4m + 180 = 360$
Subtract 180:	$4m = 180$
Divide by 4:	$m = 45$

5. **8** Draw the segments shown. Choose point E to make rectangle $ACDE$ and right triangle AEB. Notice that $CD = AE$, because opposite sides of a rectangle are equal. You can find AE with the Pythagorean theorem:

$$(AE)^2 + 6^2 = 10^2$$

Simplify:	$(AE)^2 + 36 = 100$
Subtract 36:	$(AE)^2 = 64$
Take the square root:	$AE = 8$

Since $CD = AE$, $CD = 8$.

CHAPTER 11

ESSENTIAL ALGEBRA 2 SKILLS

1. Sequences

2. Functions

3. Transformations

4. Variation

5. Data Analysis

6. Negative and Fractional Exponents

Lesson 1: Sequences

Analyzing Sequences

A *sequence* is just a list of numbers, each of which is called a *term*. An SAT math question might ask you to use a sequential pattern to solve a problem, such as "How many odd numbers are in the first 100 terms of the sequence 1, 2, 3, 1, 2, 3, . . . ?"

An SAT sequence question usually gives you the first few terms of a sequence or the rule for generating the sequence, and then asks you either to *find a specific term* in the sequence (as in "What is the 59th term of this sequence?") or to *analyze a subset of the sequence* (as in "What is the sum of the first 36 terms of this sequence?"). To tackle sequence problems:

1. Use the pattern or rule to write out the first six to eight terms of the sequence.

2. Try to identify the pattern in the sequence. Notice in particular when the sequence begins to repeat itself, if it does.

3. Use this pattern, together with whole-number division (Chapter 7, Lesson 7), if it's helpful, to solve the problem.

Example:

$$-1, 2, -2, . . .$$

The first three terms of a sequence are shown above. Each term after the second term is found by dividing the preceding term by the term before that. For example, the third term is found by dividing the second term, 2, by the first term, −1. What is the value of the 218th term of this sequence?

Don't panic. You won't have to write out 218 terms! Just write out the first eight or so until you notice that the sequence begins to repeat. The fourth term is $-2 \div 2 = -1$, the fifth term is $-1 \div -2 = 1/2$, and so on. This gives the sequence $-1, 2, -2, -1, \frac{1}{2}, -\frac{1}{2}$, $-1, 2, ...$

Notice that the first two terms of the sequence, −1 and 2, have come back again! This means that the first six terms in the sequence, the underlined ones, will just repeat over and over again. Therefore, in the first 218 terms, this six-term pattern will repeat $218 \div 6 = 36\frac{2}{3}$ times, or 36 with a remainder of 2. So, the 218th term will be the same as the second term in the sequence, which is 2.

Example:

$$-1, 1, 0, -1, 1, 0, . . .$$

If the sequence above repeats as shown, what is the sum of the first 43 terms of this sequence?

Since the sequence clearly repeats every three terms, then in 43 terms this pattern will repeat $43 \div 3$ = 14 (with remainder 1) times. Each full repetition of the pattern −1, 1, 0 has a sum of 0, so the first 14 repetitions have a sum of 0. This accounts for the sum of the first 14 × 3 = 42 terms. But you can't forget the "remainder" term! Since that 43rd term is −1, the sum of the first 43 terms is −1.

You won't need to use the formulas for "arithmetic sequences" or "geometric sequences" that you may have learned in algebra class. Instead, SAT "sequence" questions simply require that you figure out the pattern in the sequence.

Concept Review 1: Sequences

1. What is a sequence?

2. If the pattern of a sequence repeats every six terms, how do you determine the 115th term of the sequence?

3. If the pattern of a number sequence repeats every four terms, how do you find the sum of the first 32 terms of the sequence?

4. If a number sequence repeats every five terms, how do you determine how many of the first 36 terms are negative?

5. What is the 30th term of the following sequence?

    $\frac{1}{9}, \frac{1}{3}, 1, 3, 9, \ldots$

6. The first term in a sequence is 4, and each subsequent term is eight more than twice the preceding term. What is the value of the sixth term?

7. The word SCORE is written 200 times in a row on a piece of paper. How many of the first 143 letters are vowels?

8. The third term of a sequence is x. If each term in the sequence except the first is found by subtracting 3 from the previous term and dividing that difference by 2, what is the first term of the sequence in terms of x?

9. A 60-digit number is created by writing all the positive integers in succession beginning with 1. What is the 44th digit of the number?

SAT Practice 1: Sequences

1. The first term in a sequence is x. Each subsequent term is 3 less than twice the preceding term. What is the fifth term in the sequence?

   (A) $8x - 21$
   (B) $8x - 15$
   (C) $16x - 39$
   (D) $16x - 45$
   (E) $32x - 93$

$$\tfrac{1}{8}, \tfrac{1}{4}, \tfrac{1}{2}, \ldots$$

2. In the sequence above, each term after the first is equal to the previous term times a constant. What is the value of the 13th term?

   (A) 2^7
   (B) 2^8
   (C) 2^9
   (D) 2^{10}
   (E) 2^{11}

3. The first term in a sequence is 400. Every subsequent term is 20 less than half of the immediately preceding term. What is the fourth term in the sequence?

4. In the number $0.\overline{148285}$, the digits 148285 repeat indefinitely. How many of the first 500 digits after the decimal point are odd?

   (A) 83
   (B) 166
   (C) 167
   (D) 168
   (E) 332

$$5, 6, 5, 6, 6, 5, 6, 6, 6, 5, 6, 6, 6, 6, 5, \ldots$$

5. In the sequence above, the first 5 is followed by one 6, the second 5 is followed by two 6s, and so on. If the sequence continues in this manner, how many 6s are there between the 44th and 47th appearances of the number 5?

   (A) 91
   (B) 135
   (C) 138
   (D) 182
   (E) 230

6. The first term in a sequence is -5, and each subsequent term is 6 more than the immediately preceding term. What is the value of the 104th term?

   (A) 607
   (B) 613
   (C) 618
   (D) 619
   (E) 625

7. What is the units digit of 3^{36}?

   (A) 0
   (B) 1
   (C) 3
   (D) 7
   (E) 9

$$210, 70, \ldots$$

8. After the first term in the sequence above, each odd-numbered term can be found by multiplying the preceding term by three, and each even-numbered term can be found by multiplying the previous term by 1/3. What is the value of the 24th term?

9. The first two terms of a sequence are 640 and 160. Each term after the first is equal to one-fourth of the previous term. What is the value of the sixth term?

$$6, 4, \ldots$$

10. After the first two terms in the sequence above, each odd-numbered term can be found by dividing the previous term by 2. For example, the third term is equal to $4 \div 2 = 2$. Each even-numbered term can be found by adding 8 to the previous term. For example, the fourth term is equal to $2 + 8 = 10$. How many terms are there before the first noninteger term?

(A) 3
(B) 4
(C) 5
(D) 6
(E) 7

$$-2, 4, -8, \ldots$$

11. The first three terms of a sequence are given above. If each subsequent term is the product of the preceding two terms, how many of the first 90 terms are negative?

(A) 16
(B) 30
(C) 45
(D) 60
(E) 66

Answer Key 1: Sequences

Concept Review 1

1. A sequence is simply a list of numbers, each of which is called a "term."

2. If the sequence repeats every six terms, you can find the 115th term by finding the remainder when 115 is divided by 6. Since $115 \div 6$ equals 19 with a remainder of 1, the 115th term will be the same as the first term.

3. Begin by finding the sum of the repeating pattern. Next, determine how many times the pattern occurs in the first 32 terms: $32 \div 4 = 8$ times. Then multiply the sum of the pattern by 8 to obtain the sum.

4. Count the number of negative terms in each repetition of the pattern, then find how many times the pattern repeats in the first 36 terms. Since $36 \div 5 = 7$ with a remainder of 1, the pattern repeats 7 times and is 1 term into the eighth repetition. Multiply the number of negative terms per repetition by 7, and if the first term of the sequence is negative, add 1 to the total.

5. This is a geometric sequence. Each term is the previous one times 3 ($1 \times 3 = 3$; $3 \times 3 = 9$, etc.). The first term of the sequence is 3^{-2}, and the 30th term is $3^{-2} \times 3^{29} = 3^{27}$.

6. The first term is 4. Second: $4(2) + 8 = 16$. Third: $16(2) + 8 = 40$. Fourth: $40(2) + 8 = 88$. Fifth: $88(2) + 8 = 184$. Sixth: $184(2) + 8 = 376$.

7. The pattern repeats every five terms, and each repetition contains two vowels. Since $143 \div 5 = 28$ with a remainder of 3, the first 143 letters contain $28 \times 2 = 56$ vowels plus the one vowel in the first three letters of the word SCORE, for a total of $56 + 1 = 57$.

8. Work backwards: x was found by subtracting 3 from the second term and dividing by 2. Therefore, multiply x by 2 and add 3 to get the second term: $2x + 3$. Repeat to find the first term: $2(2x + 3) + 3 = 4x + 9$.

9. The integers 1 through 9 represent the first 9 digits, and 10 through 19 represent the next 20 digits. Each integer thereafter contains 2 digits. 26 represents the 42nd and 43rd digits, so 2 is the 44th digit.

SAT Practice 1

1. **D** The first term of the sequence is x. The second term is $2(x) - 3 = 2x - 3$. The third term is $2(2x - 3) - 3 = 4x - 6 - 3 = 4x - 9$. The fourth term is $2(4x - 9) - 3 = 8x - 18 - 3 = 8x - 21$. The fifth term is $2(8x - 21) - 3 = 16x - 42 - 3 = 16x - 45$.

2. **C** Each term in the sequence is the previous term times 2. The first term, $\frac{1}{8}$, is equal to 2^{-3}. To find the value of the 13th term, multiply the first term by 2 twelve times or by 2^{12} to get your answer.

   $2^{-3} \times 2^{12} = 2^{-3+12} = 2^9$

3. **15** The first term is 400, after which each term is 20 less than 1/2 the previous term. The second term is $\frac{1}{2}(400) - 20 = 180$. The third term is $\frac{1}{2}(180) - 20 = 70$. The fourth term is $\frac{1}{2}(70) - 20 = 15$.

4. **C** The sequence contains a repeating six-term pattern: 148285. To find out how many times the pattern repeats in the first 500 terms, divide 500 by 6: $500 \div 6 = 83\frac{1}{3}$. By the 500th term, the pattern has repeated 83 full times and is $\frac{1}{3}$ of the way through the 84th repetition. Each repetition of the pattern contains two odd digits, so in the 83

   full repetitions there are $83 \times 2 = 166$ odd digits. In the first $\frac{1}{3}$ of the pattern there is one odd digit. Therefore there are $166 + 1 = 167$ odd digits.

5. **B** There will be $44 + 45 + 46 = 135$ 6s between the 44th and 47th appearances of 5.

6. **B** In this arithmetic sequence you must add 6 to each term. To get from the 1st to the 104th term you will add 103 terms, or 103 6s. The value of the 104th term is thus $-5 + (103)(6) = 613$.

7. **B** $3^1 = 3$; $3^2 = 9$; $3^3 = 27$; $3^4 = 81$; $3^5 = 243$; $3^6 = 729$. The units digits repeat in the pattern 3, 9, 7, 1, 3, 9, 7, 1, . . ., and $36 \div 4 =$ nine full repetitions. Since it goes in evenly, it must fall on the last term of the pattern, which is 1.

8. **70** The pattern alternates back and forth between 210 and 70. Each odd-numbered term is 210 and each even-numbered term is 70, so the 24th term is 70.

9. **5/8 or .625** The first term of the sequence is 640. Each term thereafter is 1/4 of the immediately preceding term. The first six terms are 640, 160, 40, 10, 2.5, .625 (.625 = 5/8).

10. **D** The third term of the sequence is $4 \div 2 = 2$. The fourth term is $2 + 8 = 10$. The fifth term is $10 \div 2 = 5$. The sixth term is $5 + 8 = 13$. The seventh term is $13 \div 2 = 6.5$, which is the first noninteger term.

11. **D** In this problem, only the signs of the terms matter. The first term is negative and the second is positive. The third term is $(-)(+) = -$. The fourth term is $(+)(-) = -$. The fifth term is $(-)(-) = +$. The sixth term is $(-)(+) = -$. The first six terms of the sequence are: $-, +, -, -, +, -$. The pattern $-, +, -$ repeats every three terms. In the first 90 terms, the pattern repeats $90 \div 3 = 30$ times. Each repetition contains two negative numbers, so in 30 full repetitions there are $30 \times 2 = 60$ negative numbers.

Lesson 2: Functions

What Is a Function?

A *function* is any set of instructions for turning an input number (usually called x) into an output number (usually called y). For instance, $f(x) = 3x + 2$ is a function that takes any input x and multiplies it by 3 and then adds 2. The result is the output, which we call $f(x)$ or y.

If $f(x) = 3x + 2$, what is $f(2h)$?

In the expression $f(2h)$, the $2h$ represents the input to the function f. So just substitute $2h$ for x in the equation and simplify: $f(2h) = 3(2h) + 2 = 6h + 2$.

Functions as Equations, Tables, or Graphs

The SAT usually represents a function in one of three ways: as an equation, as a table of inputs and outputs, or as a graph on the xy-plane. Make sure that you can work with all three representations. For instance, know how to use a table to verify an equation or a graph, or how to use an equation to create or verify a graph.

Linear Functions

A linear function is any function whose graph is a line. The equations of linear functions always have the form $f(x) = mx + b$, where m is the slope of the line, and b is where the line intersects the y-axis. (For more on slopes, see Chapter 10, Lesson 4.)

The function $f(x) = 3x + 2$ is linear with a slope of 3 and a y-intercept of 2. It can also be represented with a table of x and y (or $f(x)$) values that work in the equation:

x	$f(x)$
−2	−4
−1	−1
0	2
1	5
2	8
3	11
4	14

Notice several important things about this table. First, as in every linear function, when the x values are "evenly spaced," the y values are also "evenly spaced." In this table, whenever the x value increases by 1, the y value increases by 3, which is the slope of the line and the coefficient of x in the equation. Notice

also that the y-intercept is the output to the function when the input is 0.

Now we can take this table of values and plot each ordered pair as a point on the xy-plane, and the result is the graph of a line:

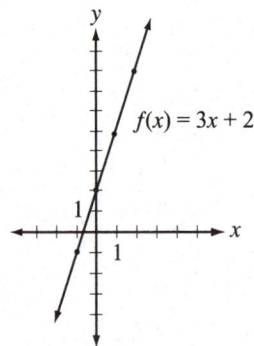

Quadratic Functions

The graph of a quadratic function is always a parabola with a vertical axis of symmetry. The equations of quadratic functions always have the form $f(x) = ax^2 + bx + c$, where c is the y-intercept. When a (the coefficient of x^2) is positive, the parabola is "open up," and when a is negative, it is "open down."

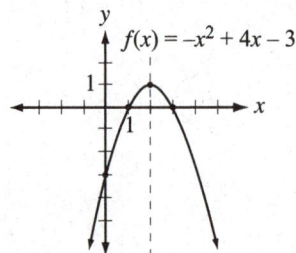

The graph above represents the function $y = -x^2 + 4x - 3$. Notice that it is an "open down" parabola with an axis of symmetry through its vertex at $x = 2$.

The figure above shows the graph of the function f in the xy-plane. If $f(0) = f(b)$, which of the following could be the value of b?

(A) −3　(B) −2　(C) 2　(D) 3　(E) 4

Although this can be solved algebraically, you should be able to solve this problem more simply just by inspecting the graph, which clearly shows that $f(0) = -3$. (You can plug $x = 0$ into the equation to verify.) Since this point is two units from the axis of symmetry, its reflection is two units on the *other* side of the axis, which is the point $(4, -3)$.

Concept Review 2: Functions

1. What is a function?

2. What are the three basic ways of representing a function?

3. What is the general form of the equation of a linear function, and what does the equation tell you about the graph?

4. How can you determine the slope of a linear function from a table of its inputs and outputs?

5. How can you determine the slope of a linear function from its graph?

6. What is the general form of the equation of a quadratic function?

7. What kind of symmetry does the graph of a quadratic function have?

SAT Practice 2: Functions

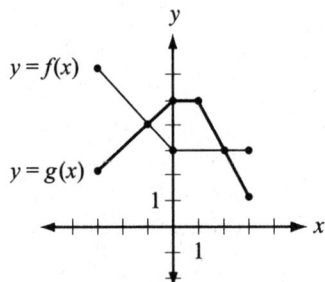

1. The graphs of functions f and g for values of x between -3 and 3 are shown above. Which of the following describes the set of all x for which $g(x) \geq f(x)$?

(A) $x \geq -3$
(B) $-3 \leq x \leq -1$ or $2 \leq x \leq 3$
(C) $-1 \leq x \leq 2$
(D) $1 \leq x \leq 6$
(E) $3 \leq x \leq 5$

2. If $f(x) = x + 2$ and $f(g(1)) = 6$, which of the following could be $g(x)$?

(A) $3x$
(B) $x + 3$
(C) $x - 3$
(D) $2x + 1$
(E) $2x - 1$

3. What is the least possible value of $(x + 2)^2$ if $-3 \leq x \leq 0$?

(A) -3
(B) -2
(C) -1
(D) 0
(E) 1

x	2	3	4
$f(x)$	a	8	b

4. The table above gives the value of the linear function f for several values of x. What is the value of $a + b$?

(A) 8
(B) 12
(C) 16
(D) 24
(E) It cannot be determined from the information given.

5. The graph on the xy-plane of the quadratic function g is a parabola with vertex at $(3, -2)$. If $g(0) = 0$, then which of the following must also equal 0?

(A) $g(2)$
(B) $g(3)$
(C) $g(4)$
(D) $g(6)$
(E) $g(7)$

6. In the xy-plane, the graph of the function h is a line. If $h(-1) = 4$ and $h(5) = 1$, what is the value of $h(0)$?

(A) 2.0
(B) 2.2
(C) 3.3
(D) 3.5
(E) 3.7

Answer Key 2: Functions

Concept Review 2

1. A set of instructions for turning an input number (usually called x) into an output number (usually called y).

2. As an equation (as in $f(x) = 2x$), as a table of input and output values, and as a graph in the xy-plane.

3. $f(x) = mx + b$, where m is the slope of the line and b is its y-intercept.

4. If the table provides two ordered pairs, (x_1, y_1) and (x_2, y_2), the slope can be calculated with $\frac{y_2 - y_1}{x_2 - x_1}$. (Also see Chapter 10, Lesson 4.)

5. Choose any two points on the graph and call their coordinates (x_1, y_1) and (x_2, y_2). Then calculate the slope with $\frac{y_2 - y_1}{x_2 - x_1}$.

6. $f(x) = ax^2 + bx + c$, where c is the y-intercept.

7. It is a parabola that has a vertical line of symmetry through its vertex.

SAT Practice 2

1. **C** In this graph, saying that $g(x) \geq f(x)$ is the same as saying that the g function "meets or is above" the f function. This is true between the points where they meet, at $x = -1$ and $x = 2$.

2. **B** Since $f(x) = x + 2$, $f(g(1))$ must equal $g(1) + 2$. Therefore $g(1) + 2 = 6$ and $g(1) = 4$. So $g(x)$ must be a function that gives an output of 4 when its input is 1. The only expression among the choices that equals 4 when $x = 1$ is (B) $x + 3$.

3. **D** This question asks you to analyze the "outputs" to the function $y = (x + 2)^2$ given a set of "inputs." Don't just assume that the least input, -3, gives the least output, $(-3 + 2)^2 = 1$. In fact, that's not the least output. Just think about the arithmetic: $(x + 2)^2$ is the square of a number. What is the least possible square of a real number? It must be 0, because 0^2 equals 0, but the square of any other real number is positive. Can $x + 2$ in this problem equal 0? Certainly, if $x = -2$, which is in fact one of the allowed values of x. Another way to solve the problem is to notice that the function $y = (x + 2)^2$ is quadratic, so its graph is a parabola. Choose values of x between -3 and 0 to make a quick sketch of this function to see that its vertex is at $(-2, 0)$.

4. **C** Since f is a linear function, it has the form $f(x) = mx + b$. The table shows that an input of 3 gives an output of 8, so $3m + b = 8$. Now, if you want, you can just "guess and check" values for m and b that work, for instance, $m = 2$ and $b = 2$. This gives the equation $f(x) = 2x + 2$. To find the missing outputs in the table, just substitute $x = 2$ and then $x = 4$: $f(2) = 2(2) + 2 = 6$ and $f(4) = 2(4) + 2 = 10$. Therefore, $a + b = 6 + 10 = 16$. But how do we know that $a + b$

will **always** equal 16? Because the slope m of any linear function represents the amount that y increases (or decreases) whenever x increases by 1. Since the table shows x values that increase by 1, a must equal $8 - m$, and b must equal $8 + m$. Therefore $a + b = (8 - m) + (8 + m) = 16$.

5. **D** Don't worry about actually finding the equation for $g(x)$. Since g is a quadratic function, it has a vertical line of symmetry through its vertex, the line $x = 3$. Since $g(0) = 0$, the graph also passes through the origin. Draw a quick sketch of a parabola that passes through the origin and $(3, -2)$ and has an axis of symmetry at $x = 3$:

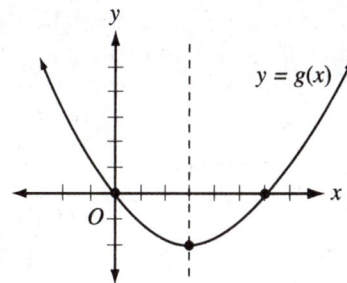

The graph shows that the point $(0, 0)$, when reflected over the line $x = 3$, gives the point $(6, 0)$. Therefore $g(6)$ is also equal to 0.

6. **D** The problem provides two ordered pairs that lie on the line: $(-1, 4)$ and $(5, 1)$. Therefore, the slope of this line is $(4 - 1)/(-1 - 5) = -3/6 = -1/2$. Therefore, for every one step that the line takes to the right (the x direction), the y value *decreases* by $1/2$. Since 0 is one unit to the right of -1 on the x-axis, $h(0)$ must be $1/2$ less than $h(-1)$, or $4 - 1/2 = 3.5$.

Lesson 3: Transformations

Functions with similar equations tend to have similar shapes. For instance, functions of the quadratic form $f(x) = ax^2 + bx + c$ have graphs that look like *parabolas*. You also should know how specific changes to the function equation produce specific changes to the graph. Learn how to recognize basic *transformations* of functions: *shifts* and *reflections*.

> To learn how changes in function equations produce changes in their graphs, study the graphs below until you understand how graphs change with changes to their equations.

Horizontal Shifts

> The graph of $y = f(x + k)$ is simply the graph of $y = f(x)$ shifted k units to the left. Similarly, the graph of $y = f(x - k)$ is the graph of $y = f(x)$ shifted k units to the right. The graphs below show why.

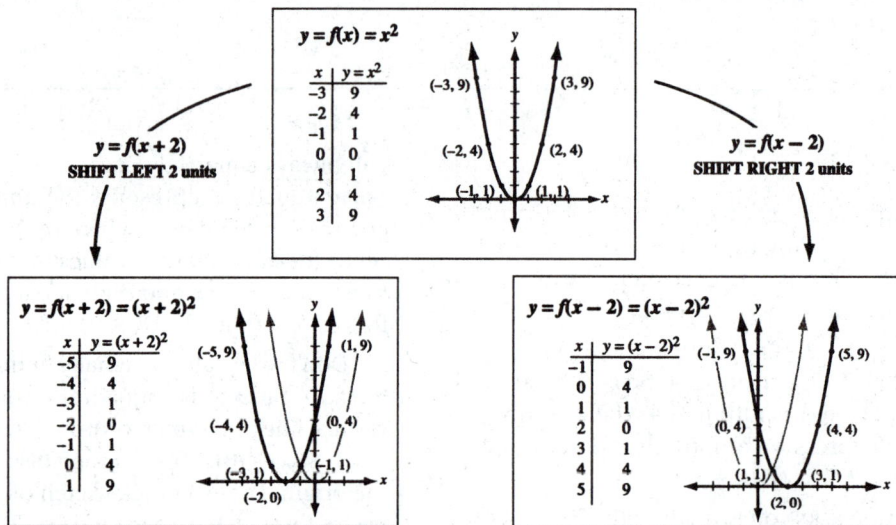

$y = f(x) = x^2$

x	$y = x^2$
-3	9
-2	4
-1	1
0	0
1	1
2	4
3	9

(−3, 9)   (3, 9)
(−2, 4)   (2, 4)
(−1, 1)   (1, 1)

$y = f(x + 2)$
SHIFT LEFT 2 units

$y = f(x - 2)$
SHIFT RIGHT 2 units

$y = f(x + 2) = (x + 2)^2$

x	$y = (x+2)^2$
-5	9
-4	4
-3	1
-2	0
-1	1
0	4
1	9

(−5, 9)   (1, 9)
(−4, 4)   (0, 4)
(−3, 1)   (−1, 1)
(−2, 0)

$y = f(x - 2) = (x - 2)^2$

x	$y = (x-2)^2$
-1	9
0	4
1	1
2	0
3	1
4	4
5	9

(−1, 9)   (5, 9)
(0, 4)   (4, 4)
(1, 1)   (3, 1)
(2, 0)

Vertical Shifts

> The graph of $y = f(x) + k$ is simply the graph of $y = f(x)$ shifted k units up. Similarly, the graph of $y = f(x) - k$ is the graph of $y = f(x)$ shifted k units downward. The graphs below show why.

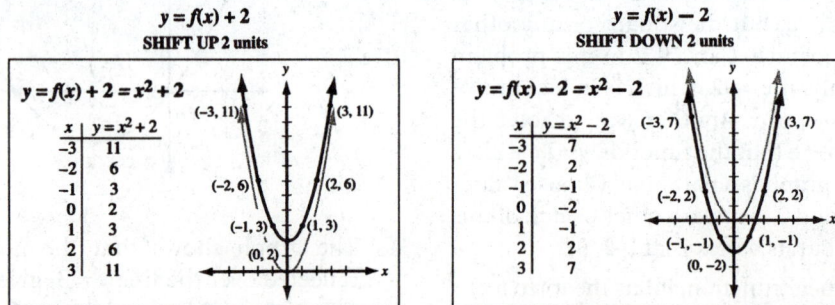

$y = f(x) + 2$
SHIFT UP 2 units

$y = f(x) - 2$
SHIFT DOWN 2 units

$y = f(x) + 2 = x^2 + 2$

x	$y = x^2+2$
-3	11
-2	6
-1	3
0	2
1	3
2	6
3	11

(−3, 11)   (3, 11)
(−2, 6)   (2, 6)
(−1, 3)   (1, 3)
(0, 2)

$y = f(x) - 2 = x^2 - 2$

x	$y = x^2-2$
-3	7
-2	2
-1	-1
0	-2
1	-1
2	2
3	7

(−3, 7)   (3, 7)
(−2, 2)   (2, 2)
(−1, −1)   (1, −1)
(0, −2)

Reflections

When the point (3, 4) is reflected over the y-axis, it becomes $(-3, 4)$. That is, the x coordinate is negated. When it is reflected over the x-axis, it becomes $(3, -4)$. That is, the y coordinate is negated. (Graph it and see.) Likewise, if the graph of $y = f(x)$ is reflected over the x-axis, it becomes $y = -f(x)$.

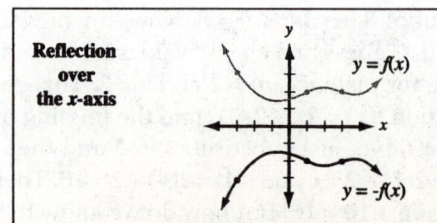

Reflection over the x-axis

$y = f(x)$

$y = -f(x)$

Concept Review 3: Transformations

1. What equation describes the function $y = f(x)$ after it has been shifted to the right five units?

2. What equation describes the function $y = x^2 - 5$ after it has been reflected over the x-axis?

3. How does the graph of $y = -4f(x)$ compare with the graph of $y = f(x)$?

4. What specific features do the graphs of $y = f(x)$ and $y = f(x + 15)$ have in common?

5. What specific features do the graphs of $y = f(x)$ and $y = 6f(x)$ have in common?

6. The quadratic function h is given by $h(x) = ax^2 + bx + c$, where a is a negative constant and c is a positive constant. Which of the following could be the graph of $y = h(x)$?

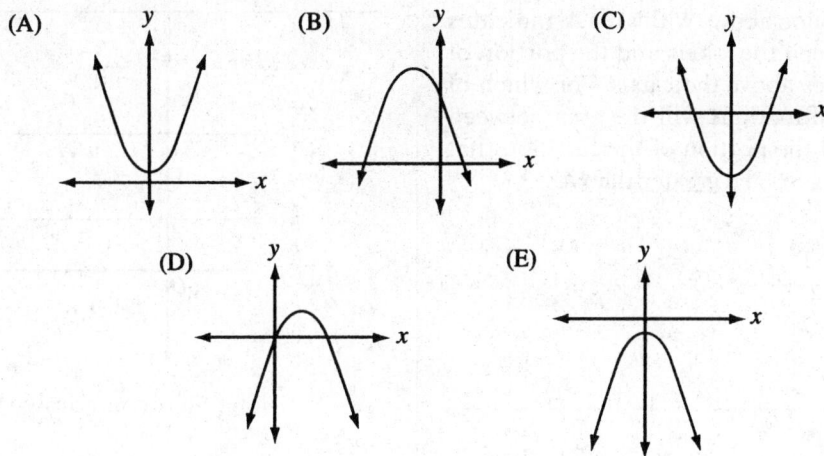

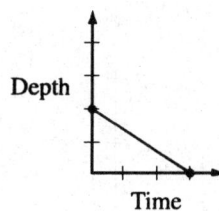

(A) (B) (C)

(D) (E)

Depth

Time

7. The figure above is a graph showing the depth of water in a rectangular tank that is being drained at a constant rate over time. Which of the following represents the graph of the situation in which the tank starts with twice as much water, and the water drains out at twice the rate?

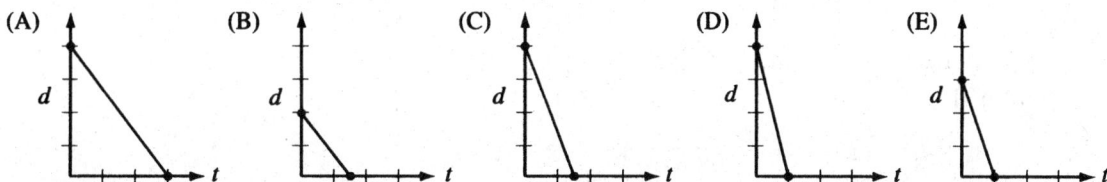

(A) (B) (C) (D) (E)

SAT Practice 3: Transformations

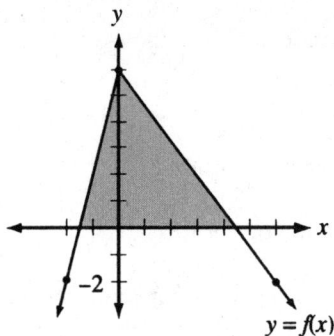

y = f(x)

1. The shaded region above, with area *A*, indicates the area between the *x*-axis and the portion of *y* = *f*(*x*) that lies above the *x*-axis. For which of the following functions will the area between the *x*-axis and the portion of the function that lies above the *x*-axis be <u>greater</u> than *A*?

(A) *y* = ½*f*(*x*)
(B) *y* = *f*(*x* − 2)
(C) *y* = *f*(*x* + 2)
(D) *y* = *f*(*x*) + 2
(E) *y* = *f*(*x*) − 2

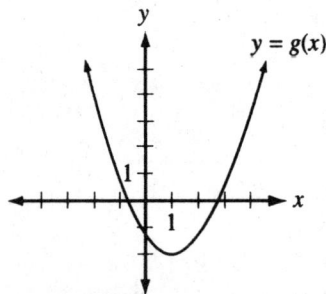

y = g(x)

2. The figure above shows the graph of the function *y* = *g*(*x*), which has a minimum value at the point (1, −2). What is the <u>maximum</u> value of the function *h*(*x*) = −3*g*(*x*) − 1?

(A) 7
(B) 6
(C) 5
(D) 4
(E) It cannot be determined from the information given.

3. A point is reflected first over the line *y* = *x*, then over the *x*-axis, and then over the *y*-axis. The resulting point has the coordinates (3, 4). What were the coordinates of the original point?

(A) (3, 4)
(B) (−3, −4)
(C) (3, −4)
(D) (−4, −3)
(E) (4, 3)

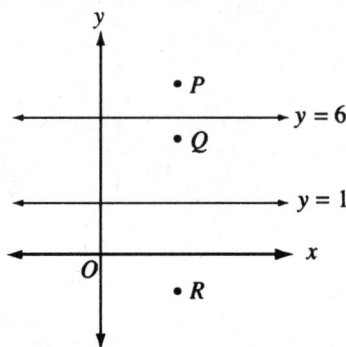

Note: Figure not drawn to scale.

4. In the figure above, point *Q* is the reflection of point *P* over the line *y* = 6, and point *R* is the reflection of point *Q* over the line *y* = 1. What is the length of line segment *PR*?

(A) 10
(B) 11
(C) 12
(D) 13
(E) 14

5. If the functions $f(x)$, $g(x)$, and $h(x)$ are defined
    by the equations $f(x) = x + 1$, $g(x) = -x$, and
    $h(x) = x^2$, then which of the following represents
    the graph of $y = g(f(h(x)))$?

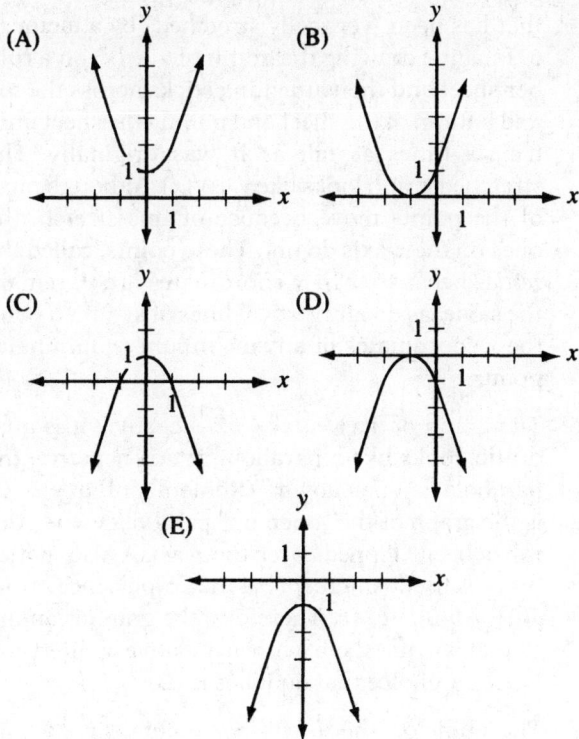

(A)

(B)

(C)

(D)

(E)

Answer Key 3: Transformations

Concept Review 3

1. $y = f(x - 5)$. Although the -5 seems to suggest a shift to the left (because when we subtract 5 from a number, we move five units to the left on the number line), this change actually shifts the graph to the *right*. To see why, look back at the first two examples in Lesson 3, and pay particular attention to how the changed equations produce the individual points on the graph and how these points compare with the points on the original graph. It also may help to pick a simple function, such as $y = x^2$, graph it by hand (by choosing values for x, calculating the corresponding values for y, and plotting the ordered pairs), and then graph $y = (x - 5)^2$ in the same way to see how the graphs compare.

2. $y = -x^2 + 5$. Since the point $(x, -y)$ is the reflection of (x, y) over the x-axis, reflecting any function over the x-axis simply means multiplying y by -1. This "negates" every term in the function.

3. It is the original graph after it has been "flipped" vertically and "stretched" vertically. The graph of $y = -4f(x)$ is a "vertically stretched" version of $y = f(x)$ that also has been reflected over the x-axis. Every point on $y = -4f(x)$ is four times farther from the x-axis as its corresponding point on $y - f(x)$ and is also on the opposite side of the x-axis.

4. Overall shape and maximum and minimum values. The graph of $y = f(x + 15)$ is simply the graph of $y = f(x)$ shifted to the left 15 units. It maintains the shape of the original graph and has the same maximum and minimum values. (That is, if the greatest value of y on $y = f(x)$ is 10, then the greatest value of y on $y = f(x + 15)$ is also 10.)

5. Zeroes, vertical lines of symmetry, and x coordinates of maximum and minimum values. The graph of $y = 6f(x)$ is simply the graph of $y = f(x)$ that has been "vertically stretched" by a factor of 6. Imagine drawing the graph of $y = f(x)$ on a rubber sheet and then attaching sticks across the top and bottom of the sheet and pulling the sheet until it's six times as tall as it was originally. The stretched graph looks like $y = 6f(x)$. Although most of the points move because of this stretch, the ones on the x-axis do not. These points, called the *zeroes* because their y coordinates are 0, remain the same, as do any vertical lines of symmetry and the x coordinates of any maximum or minimum points.

6. The graph of $h(x) = ax^2 + bx + c$, since it is quadratic, looks like a parabola. If a is negative, the parabola is "open down." (Remember that $y = -x^2$ is the graph of the "open up" parabola $y = x^2$ after it has been "flipped" over the x-axis.) Also, notice that c is the "y-intercept" of the graph, since $h(0) = a(0)^2 + b(0) + c = c$. Therefore, the graph is an upside-down parabola with a positive y-intercept. The only choice that qualifies is (B).

7. The point on the d-axis represents the starting depth of the water. If the tank begins with twice as much water, the starting point, or "d-intercept," must be twice that of the original graph. Also, if the water drains out at twice the rate, the line must be twice as steep. Since twice as much water drains out at twice the rate, the tank should empty in the same amount of time it took the original tank to drain. The only graph that depicts this situation is (A).

SAT Practice 3

1. **D** The transformation in (D) is a shift of the original function upward two units. This creates a triangular region above the x-axis with a greater height and base than those of the original graph, and therefore creates a greater overall area. The transformation in (A) will create a triangle with area $^1/_2 A$, the transformations in (B) and (C) are horizontal shifts, and so will not change the area. The downward shift in (E) will reduce the height and base, and therefore the total area.

2. **C** The function $h(x)$ is equivalent to the function $g(x)$ after it has been reflected over the x-axis, vertically stretched by a factor of 3, and shifted downward one unit. After these transformations, the vertex of the parabola will be at $(1, 5)$, so the maximum value is $y = 5$.

3. **D** Call the original point (a, b). Its reflection over the line $y = x$ is (b, a). (Draw a graph to see.) The reflection of this point over the x-axis is $(b, -a)$, and the reflection of this point over the y-axis is $(-b, -a)$. If the final point is $(3, 4)$, then the original point was $(-4, -3)$.

4. **A**   A point and its reflection over a line are both equidistant to that line. Imagine that point Q has a y coordinate of 4 (any value between 1 and 6 will do). This implies that point Q is two units from the line $y = 6$, and therefore, point P also must be two units from the line $y = 6$ and must have a y coordinate of 8. Point Q also must be three units from the line $y = 1$, so point R also must be three units from the line $y = 1$ and must have a y coordinate of -2. Therefore, the length of PR is $8 - (-2) = 10$.

5. **E**   You can determine the equation defining the function through substitution: $y = g(f(h(x))) = g(f(x^2)) = g(x^2 + 1)) = -x^2 - 1$, which describes an "open-down" parabola with vertex at $(0, -1)$. Notice that this sequence of transformations takes the standard parabola $y = x^2$ and shifts it up one unit and then reflects the new graph over the x-axis.

Lesson 4: Variation

Direct Variation

> The statement "y varies directly as x" means that the variables are related by the equation $y = kx$, where k is a non-zero constant. This equation implies that x and y go up and down *proportionally*. For instance, whenever x is multiplied by 3, y is also *multiplied* by 3.

x	$y = .5x$	$y = 1x$	$y = 2x$
1	.5	1	2
2	1.0	2	4
3	1.5	3	6
4	2.0	4	8

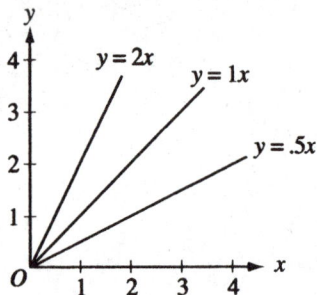

The table and graph above show three examples of direct variation functions. Notice that (1) every graph passes through the origin, (2) as k increases, so does the slope of the graph, and (3) for any given k, whenever x is doubled (or tripled or halved), so is the corresponding value of y.

Example:

If x varies directly as y and $x = 20$ when $y = 60$, then what is the value of x when $y = 150$?

First find the value of the constant k by substituting the values of x and y into the equation $y = kx$.

$$y = kx$$

Substitute: $60 = k(20)$

Divide by 20: $3 = k$

Now we know that the equation is $y = 3x$.

Substitute $y = 150$: $150 = 3x$

Divide by 3: $50 = x$

Inverse Variation

> The statement "y varies inversely as x" means that the variables are related by the equations

$y = \dfrac{k}{x}$ or $xy = k$, where k is a non-zero constant.

> These equations imply that x and y go up and down *inversely*. For instance, whenever x is multiplied by 3, y is *divided* by 3.

x	$y = 1/x$
.25	4
.5	2
1	1
2	.5
4	.25

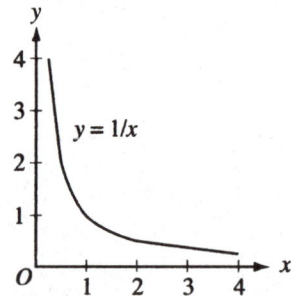

The table and graph above show an example of an inverse variation function. Notice that (1) the graph never touches the x-or y-axis, (2) as x increases, y decreases, and (3) for every point on the graph, the product of x and y is always the constant k, in this case $k = 1$.

Example:

If x varies inversely as y and $x = 40$ when $y = 10$, then what is the value of x when $y = 25$?

First find the value of the constant k by substituting the values of x and y into the equation $xy = k$.

$$xy = k$$

Substitute: $(40)(10) = k$

Simplify: $400 = k$

Now we know that the equation is $xy = 400$.

Substitute $y = 25$: $x(25) = 400$

Divide by 25: $x = 16$

Joint and Power Variation

> A variable can vary with more than one other variable or with powers of a variable. For instance, the statement "y varies directly as x and inversely as w" means that $y = \dfrac{kx}{w}$, and "y varies inversely as the square of x" means that $y = \dfrac{k}{x^2}$.

Concept Review 4: Variation

1. What equation is equivalent to the statement *y varies directly as the square of x*?

2. If *y* varies inversely as *x*, then the _____ of *x* and *y* is a constant.

3. If *y* varies directly as *x*, then the _____ of *x* and *y* is a constant.

4. Describe the features of the graph of a direct variation function.

5. If *w* varies directly as v^3 and *w* = 16 when *v* = 2 , what is the value of *w* when *v* = 3?

6. If *y* varies inversely as the square of *x*, then what will be the effect on *y* if the value of *x* is doubled?

7. The variable *a* varies inversely as *b*. If *b* = 0.5 when *a* = 32, then for how many ordered pairs (*a* , *b*) are both *a* and *b* <u>positive integers</u>?

8. If *x* varies directly as the square root of *y* and directly as *z*, and if *x* = 16 when *y* = 64 and *z* = 2, what is the value of *z* when *y* = 36 and *x* = 60?

SAT Practice 4: Variation

1. If p varies inversely as q and $p = 4$ when $q = 6$, then which of the following represents another possible solution for p and q?

   (A) $p = 8$ and $q = 12$
   (B) $p = 8$ and $q = 10$
   (C) $p = 10$ and $q = 12$
   (D) $p = 12$ and $q = 1$
   (E) $p = 12$ and $q = 2$

m	n
1	4
2	1
4	.25

2. Which of the following describes one possible relationship between the values of m and n shown in the table above?

   (A) n varies directly as m
   (B) n varies inversely as m
   (C) n varies directly as the square of m
   (D) n varies inversely as the square of m
   (E) n varies directly as the square root of m

3. If the function f is defined by the equation $f(x, y) = x^2y^3$ and $f(a, b) = 10$, what is the value of $f(2a, 2b)$?

   (A)   50
   (B)   100
   (C)   160
   (D)   320
   (E)   640

4. At a fixed temperature, the volume of a sample of gas varies inversely as the pressure of the gas. If the pressure of a sample of gas at a fixed temperature is increased by 50%, by what percent is the volume <u>decreased</u>?

   (A)   25%
   (B) $33\frac{1}{3}\%$
   (C)   50%
   (D)   75%
   (E)   100%

5. The force of gravity between two stars varies inversely as the square of the distance between the stars. If the force of gravity between two stars that are four light-years apart is 64 exanewtons (1 exanewton = 10^{18} newtons), what would the force between these stars be if they were eight light-years apart?

   (A)   256 exanewtons
   (B)   128 exanewtons
   (C)   32 exanewtons
   (D)   16 exanewtons
   (E)   8 exanewtons

6. If the variable a varies directly as b and inversely as c, and if $a = 10x + 5$ when $c = 2$ and $b = 10$, then what is the value of a when $b = 4$ and $c = 2x + 1$?

7. If the variable y varies inversely as the square of x, and if $x > 0$, then which of the following operations will <u>double</u> the value of y?

    (A) multiplying x by 2
    (B) dividing x by 2
    (C) multiplying x by $\sqrt{2}$
    (D) dividing x by $\sqrt{2}$
    (E) dividing x by 4

8. If $y = 1$ when $x = 8$ and $y = 4$ when $x = 2$, which of the following could express the relationship between x and y?

    I. y varies inversely as x
    II. y varies directly as the square of x
    III. y varies directly as x

    (A) none
    (B) I only
    (C) I and II only
    (D) I and III only
    (E) I, II, and III

Answer Key 4: Variation

Concept Review 4

1. $y = kx^2$

2. product

3. quotient or ratio

4. It is a straight line passing through the origin with a slope equal to k, the constant of proportionality. For every point on the line, the ratio of the y coordinate to the x coordinate is equal to k.

5. Write the general variation equation: $w = kv^3$

Substitute $w = 16$ and $v = 2$:	$(16) = k(2)^3$
Simplify:	$16 = 8k$
Divide by 8:	$2 = k$
Write the specific variation equation: $w = 2v^3$	
Substitute $v = 3$:	$w = 2(3)^3$
Simplify:	$w = 54$

6. Write the variation equation: $y = k/x^2$ or $x^2y = k$

   Choose any values for x and y: $x^2y = (1)^2(3) = 3 = k$

   Write the specific variation equation: $x^2y = 3$

   Double the original value of x: $(2)^2y = 3$

   Simplify: $4y = 3$

   Solve for y: $y = 3/4$

So what was the effect on y when you doubled the value of x? It went from 3 to 3/4, therefore, it was divided by 4 or multiplied by 1/4.

7. If a varies inversely as b, then $ab = k$, where k is a constant. If $b = 0.5$ when $a = 32$, then $k = (0.5)(32) = 16$. Therefore, in any ordered pair solution (a, b), the product of a and b must be 16. The only solutions in which a and b are both positive integers are $(1, 16)$, $(2, 8)$, $(4, 4)$, $(8, 2)$, and $(16, 1)$, for a total of five ordered pairs.

8. If x varies directly as the square root of y and directly as z, then $x = kz\sqrt{y}$. First, substitute the values $x = 16$, $y = 64$, and $z = 2$ to find k:

$$16 = k(2)(\sqrt{64})$$

Simplify:	$16 = 16k$
Divide by 16:	$1 = k$
Substitute $y = 36$ and $x = 60$:	$60 = 1z\sqrt{36}$
Simplify:	$60 = 6z$
Divide by 6:	$10 = z$

SAT Practice 4

1. **E**   Recall from the lesson that whenever two variables vary inversely, they have a constant product. The product of 4 and 6 is 24, so every other correct solution for p and q must have a product of 24 also. Choice (E) is the only one that gives values that have a product of 24.

2. **D**   It helps first to notice from the table that as m increases, n decreases, so any variation relationship must be an *inverse* variation. Therefore, only choices (B) and (D) are possibilities. If n varied inversely as m, then the two variables would always have the same product, but this is not the case: $1 \times 4 = 4$, $2 \times 1 = 2$, and $4 \times .25 = 1$. However, if n varied inversely as the *square* of m, then n and m^2 would always have the same product. This is true: $1^2 \times 4 = 4$, $2^2 \times 1 = 4$, and $4^2 \times .25 = 4$. Therefore, the correct answer is (D).

3. **D**   You are given that $f(a, b) = a^2b^3 = 10$. Using the definition, $f(2a, 2b) = (2a)^2(2b)^3 = (4a^2)(8b^3) = 32a^2b^3$. Substituting $a^2b^3 = 10$, you get $32a^2b^3 = 32(10) = 320$.

4. **B**   It's probably easiest to set up the equation, then choose simple values for the volume and pressure, and then "experiment." Since the volume varies inversely as the pressure, the product of the volume and the pressure is a constant: $vp = k$. Now choose simple values for v and p, such as 2 and 4: $vp = (2)(4) = 8 = k$. Therefore, in this case, the product of the volume and the pressure is always 8. If the pressure is increased 50%, then it grows to $1.5(4) = 6$. Now solve for the corresponding value of v:

$$v(6) = 8$$

Divide by 6: $$v = \frac{4}{3}$$

Therefore, the volume has decreased from 2 to $\frac{4}{3}$. To calculate the percent decrease, use the "percent change" formula from Chapter 7, Lesson 5:

Percent change =

$$\frac{\frac{4}{3} - 2}{2} \times 100\% = \frac{-\frac{2}{3}}{2} \times 100\% = -\frac{1}{3} \times 100\% = 33\frac{1}{3}\%$$

5. **D** If the force varies inversely as the square of the distance, then the product of the force and the square of the distance is a constant. For these particular stars, the force times the square of the distance is $(4)^2(64) = 1024$. If they were eight light-years apart, then the force would satisfy the equation $(8)^2(f) = 1024$, so $f = 16$.

6. **4** Set up the variation equation:
$$a = kb/c$$

Substitute: $10x + 5 = k(10)/2$

Simplify: $10x + 5 = 5k$

Divide by 5: $2x + 1 = k$

Substitute new values: $a = (2x + 1)(4)/(2x + 1)$

Simplify: $a = 4$

7. **D** If y varies inversely as the square of x, then their product x^2y is a constant. To keep it simple, pick x and y to be 1, so the product $(1)^2(1) = 1$. To find the value of x that would double y, simply double y and solve for x.
If $x^2(2) = 1$, then $x = 1/\sqrt{2}$. This is the original value of x divided by $\sqrt{2}$.

8. **B** Since y increases as x decreases, any variation must be an *inverse* variation. Since the product of x and y is a constant ($1 \times 8 = 4 \times 2 = 8$), y varies inversely as x.

Lesson 5: Data Analysis

Scatterplots and Lines of Best Fit

A *scatterplot* is a collection of points plotted on a graph that is used to visualize the relationship between two variables. A *line of best fit* is a straight line that best "hugs" the data of a scatterplot. This line usually divides the points roughly in half. This line can be used to make predictions about how one of the variables will change when the other is changed.

> The SAT may ask you to describe the basic features of a line of best fit for a set of data, but it won't ask you to find this equation *exactly*. You can usually just eyeball it: draw a line that fits the data and cuts the points roughly in half, and then notice whether the slope of the line is positive, negative, or 0, and then notice roughly where its *y*-intercept is.

CORRELATION OF READING AND
MATH SCORES FOR MS. SMITH'S
20 STUDENTS

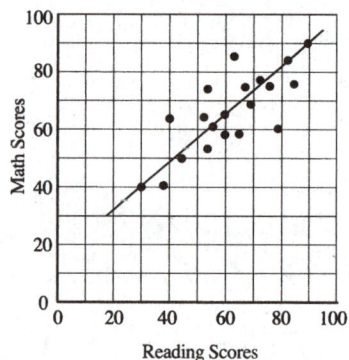

Example:

What is the approximate slope of the line of best fit in the scatterplot above?

To estimate the slope of a line of best fit, pick two points on your line of best fit and use the slope equation (from Chapter 10, Lesson 4) to solve for *m*. It appears that the line of best fit connects the points (30, 40) and (90, 90), so $m = \dfrac{90-40}{90-30} = \dfrac{50}{60} = \dfrac{5}{6}$.

Tables, Charts, and Graphs

> A *table* is a set of data arranged in rows and columns. If an SAT question includes a table, *always read the table carefully first*, paying special attention to the axis labels, and try to understand what the table represents before tackling the question. If you are given *two* tables, make sure you understand how the two tables are related.

ELECTRONICS IN THE SMITH
AND CARSON HOUSEHOLDS

	Smiths	Carsons
Computers	2	3
Telephones	*n*	4
Televisions	2	2

TELEPHONES IN THE SMITH
AND CARSON HOUSEHOLDS

	Cell phone	Other
Smiths	*m*	2
Carsons	1	3

Example:

If the Smiths own as many pieces of electronic equipment as the Carsons do, how many cell phones do the Smiths own?

Start with the first table. The Carsons own 3 + 4 + 2 = 9 pieces of equipment. If the Smiths own the same number of pieces, they must own 9 − 4 = 5 telephones. Now go to the "Telephones" table. Since the Smiths have five telephones and two are not cell phones, they must own 5 − 2 = 3 cell phones.

> As with tables, always carefully read the labels of *pie charts* to understand what the data represent before tackling the question. In a pie chart, a sector containing *x*% of the data has a central angle of (*x*/100)(360°).

THE FAVORITE COLOR OF
4,000 KINDERGARTEN
STUDENTS

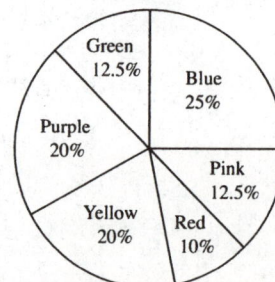

Example:

In the pie chart above, what is the angle measure of the sector represented by the color purple?

Purple accounts for 20% of the circle, and 20% of 360° = (0.2)(360°) = 72°.

Concept Review 5: Data Analysis

1. What is a line of best fit?

2. How is a line of best fit created?

3. How do you estimate the slope of a best fit line?

4. When given percentages in a pie chart, how do you determine how many degrees each sector represents?

Questions 5 and 6 refer to the bar graph at right:

5. The largest percent increase in number of accidents occurred between which two days of the week?

6. Approximately what percentage of the accidents occurred on Friday, Saturday, or Sunday?

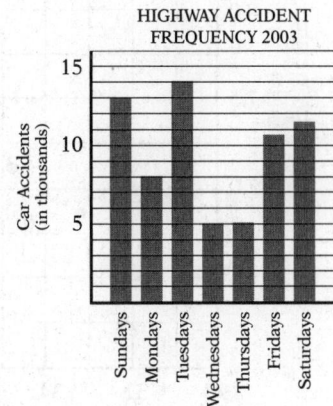

HIGHWAY ACCIDENT FREQUENCY 2003

Questions 7–9 refer to the pie chart at right:

7. The pie chart shows the results of a survey that asked 4,000 kindergarten students their favorite color. How many more students said yellow was their favorite color than said blue was their favorite color?

8. What is the degree measure of the sector of the circle that represents red?

9. Using the data in the pie chart, how many students would have to change their answer to blue in order for blue to account for 50% of the data?

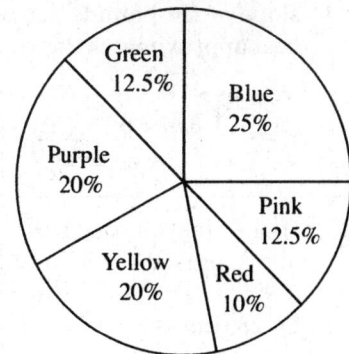

THE FAVORITE COLOR OF 4,000 KINDERGARTEN STUDENTS

Questions 10 and 11 refer to the tables at right:

10. According to the tables, which school ordered the most amusement park tickets?

11. If all the students who went to Coaster Heaven from New Haven Public and Hamden High bought 5-day passes, how much more money did Hamden High spend than New Haven Public did at Coaster Heaven?

NUMBER OF PARK TICKETS ORDERED

	Adventure City	Galaxy Island	Coaster Heaven
Hamden High	36	28	81
New Haven Public	64	23	64
Waterbury High	53	31	51

PRICE OF ADMISSION

	1-day Pass	2-day Pass	5-day Pass
Adventure City	$40	$75	$150
Galaxy Island	$45	$85	$175
Coaster Heaven	$50	$94	$200

SAT Practice 5: Data Analysis

Questions 1 and 2 refer to the following information:

RELATIONSHIP BETWEEN
GESTATION AND AVERAGE BIRTH
WEIGHT

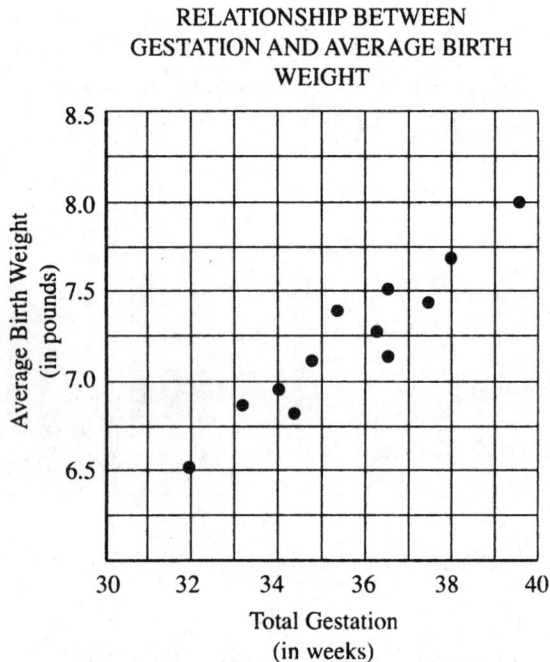

1. Which of the following best approximates the slope m (in pounds per week) of the line that best approximates these data?

   (A) $m > 1$ (B) $0 < m < 1$ (C) $m = 1$
   (D) $-1 < m < 0$ (E) $m < -1$

2. If the line of best fit for the data presented above passed through the points (32, 6.5) and (39.5, 8.0), it can be estimated that a baby born at 28 weeks would most nearly weigh how many pounds?

   (A) 5.3   (B) 5.5   (C) 5.7
   (D) 5.9   (E) 6.1

MONTHLY TICKET SALES
AT WACKY WATER PARK

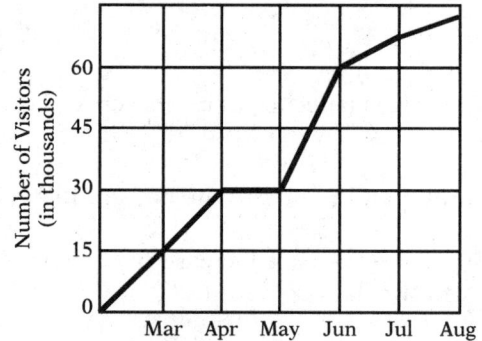

3. According to the graph above, Wacky Water Park experienced its largest increase in park attendance between which two consecutive months?

   (A) March and April   (B) April and May
   (C) May and June   (D) June and July
   (E) July and August

COST/REVENUE ANALYSIS FOR
THE TRINKET FACTORY

	Revenue per Unit	Cost per Unit
Widgets	$w	$4
Gadgets	$x	$3
Tinkers	$6	$y

4. The table above shows the per unit revenue and cost of three products at the Trinket Factory. If profit equals revenue minus cost, how much profit do they make if they produce and sell two of each item?

   (A) $2w + 2x - 2y - 2$ (B) $2y - 2x - 2w - 2$
   (C) $w + x - y - 1$ (D) $x + 2w + y - 7$
   (E) $2x + 2y - 2w + 2$

Questions 5 and 6 refer to the following tables:

Cost of food		
	Sandwich	Sandwich and Fries
Turkey	$ 4.50	$ 5.50
Ham	$ 5.00	$ 6.00
Veggie	$ 3.75	$ 4.75

Number of sandwiches ordered at a local deli			
	Turkey	Ham	Veggie
Boys	75	80	22
Girls	40	35	64

5. Based on the tables above, if every boy bought a sandwich without fries and every girl bought a sandwich with fries, how much more money did the boys spend at the deli than the girls?

6. If the girls who bought turkey sandwiches have $206 in total to spend on their lunches, what is the greatest number of turkey sandwiches with fries they could buy without exceeding their budget?

(A)   23
(B)   24
(C)   25
(D)   26
(E)   27

Answer Key 5: Data Analysis

Concept Review 5

1. A best fit line is a straight line that "hugs" the data most closely on a scatterplot.

2. It can be created by connecting the "outermost" points on the plot or by drawing a line that best "hugs" the points and divides them in half. Try to ignore any outliers that don't fit with the rest of the data.

3. For the SAT, you just need to be able to tell if a slope is positive or negative, or perhaps greater or less than 1. Positive slopes go up to the right, and negative slopes go down to the right. If the slope is positive and the "rise" is greater than the "run," the slope is greater than 1; if the rise is less than the run, the slope is less than 1.

4. If you know what percent of the data are in a sector of the pie chart, multiply the percentage by 360° to obtain the degree measure of that sector (e.g., a sector that represents 40% of the circle would be $(.40)(360°) = 144°$).

5. The biggest percent change occurs between Thursday and Fridays.
   Percent change = $(100\%)(10.5 - 5)/(5) = 110\%$.

6. There were a total of $13 + 7 + 14 + 5 + 5 + 10.5 + 11.5 = 66,000$ accidents; 35,000 of them occurred on Friday, Saturday, or Sunday. $35/66 = 53\%$

7. 25% of the kids said blue was their favorite color. 25% of $4,000 = 0.25 \times 4,000 = 1,000$. 20% of the kids said yellow was their favorite color. 20% of $4,000 = 0.20 \times 4,000 = 800$. $1,000 - 800 = 200$ kids.

8. The color red represents 10% of the circle, which is 10% of 360°. $\dfrac{10(360)}{100} = 36°$

9. There are currently $(.25)(4,000) = 1,000$ votes for blue. In order for blue to be 50% of the circle, it would need $(.50)(4,000) = 2,000$ votes. Therefore, 1,000 votes must change.

10. Hamden High ordered $36 + 28 + 81 = 145$ tickets. New Haven Public ordered $64 + 23 + 64 = 151$. Waterbury High ordered $53 + 31 + 51 = 135$.

11. 81 Hamden High students bought 5-day passes at $200.00/pass, spending $(81)(200) = \$16,200$. 64 students at New Haven Public bought 5-day passes at $200/pass, spending $(64)(200) = \$12,800$. The difference is $\$16,200 - \$12,800 = \$3,400$.

SAT Practice 5

1. **B** A line connecting $(32, 6.5)$ and $(39.5, 8.0)$ is a good line of fit, and has a slope of $1.5/7.5 = 0.2$, which is between 0 and 1.

2. **C** If the slope is about 0.2, you can use the slope equation to solve: $\dfrac{(y_2 - y_1)}{(x_2 - x_1)} = 0.2$

   Plug in values: $\dfrac{(6.5 - y_1)}{(32 - 28)} = 0.2$

   Simplify: $\dfrac{(6.5 - y_1)}{(4)} = 0.2$

   Multiply by 4: $(6.5 - y_1) = 0.8$
   Subtract 6.5: $-y_1 = -5.7$
   Divide by −1: $y_1 = 5.7$

3. **C** From March to April: $30 - 15 = 15,000$
   From April to May: $30 - 30 = 0$
   From May to June: $60 - 30 = 30,000$
   From June to July: $65 - 60 = 5,000$
   From July to August: $69 - 65 = 4,000$

4. **A** The revenue generated from two widgets, two gadgets, and two tinkers is $\$2w$, $\$2x$, and $\$2(6)$, respectively. The cost of producing two widgets, two gadgets, and two tinkers is \$8, \$6, and $\$2y$, respectively. Therefore, the total profit can be found by subtracting the cost from the revenue: $(2w + 2x + 12) - (8 + 6 + 2y) = 2w + 2x - 2y - 2$.

5. **86** The boys bought only sandwiches and spent $(\$4.50)(75) + (\$5.00)(80) + \$3.75(22) = \$820.00$. If the girls bought only sandwiches with fries, then they spent $(\$5.50)(40) + (\$6.00)(35) + \$4.75(64) = \$734.00$. $\$820.00 - \$734.00 = \$86.00$

6. **D** If $x =$ sandwiches: $x(4.5) + (40 - x)(5.5) = 206$
   Distribute: $4.5x + 220 - 5.5x = 206$
   Combine like terms: $-1.0x = -14$
   Divide by −1: $x = 14$
   There were $(40 - x) = 40 - 14 = 26$ meals with fries.

Lesson 6: Negative and Fractional Exponents

Exponents Review

In Chapter 8, Lesson 3, we discussed the practical definition of exponentials:

> The expression x^n means x multiplied by itself n times.

This is a useful definition when you need to evaluate something like 4^3: you simply multiply $4 \times 4 \times 4$ and get 64. But what about expressions like 4^0 or 4^{-3} or $4^{1/2}$? How do you multiply 4 by itself 0 times, or -3 times, or half of a time? It doesn't make much sense to think of it that way. So to understand such expressions, you must expand your understanding of exponents.

Zero and Negative Exponents

Using what you have learned in Lesson 1 of this chapter, what are the next three terms of this sequence?

$$81, 27, 9, 3, \underline{\hspace{1cm}}, \underline{\hspace{1cm}}, \underline{\hspace{1cm}}$$

The rule seems to be "divide by 3," so the next three terms are 1, $\frac{1}{3}$, and $\frac{1}{9}$.

Now, what are the next three terms of this sequence?

$$3^4, 3^3, 3^2, 3^1, \underline{\hspace{1cm}}, \underline{\hspace{1cm}}, \underline{\hspace{1cm}}$$

Here, the rule seems to be "reduce the power by 1," so that the next three terms are 3^0, 3^{-1}, and 3^{-2}.

Notice that the two sequences are exactly the same, that is, $3^4 = 81$, $3^3 = 27$, $3^2 = 9$, and $3^1 = 3$. This means that the pattern can help us to understand zero and negative exponents: $3^0 = 1$, $3^{-1} = \frac{1}{3}$, and $3^{-2} = \frac{1}{9}$. Now, here's the million-dollar question:

Without a calculator, how do you write 3^{-7} without a negative exponent?

If you follow the pattern you should see that

$$3^{-7} = \frac{1}{3^7} \quad \text{and, in general:}$$

> $$x^0 = 1 \text{ and } x^{-n} = \frac{1}{x^n}$$

> Notice that raising a positive number to a negative power *does not* produce a negative result. For instance 3^{-2} does not equal -9; it equals $\frac{1}{9}$.

Fractional Exponents

What if a number is raised to a *fractional* exponent? For instance, what does $8^{1/3}$ mean? To understand expressions like this, you have to use the basic rules of exponents from Chapter 8, Lesson 3. Specifically, you need to remember that $x^n \times x^m = x^{m+n}$.

$(8^{1/3})^3 = 8^{1/3} \times 8^{1/3} \times 8^{1/3}$. Using the rule above, $8^{1/3} \times 8^{1/3} \times 8^{1/3} = 8^{1/3 + 1/3 + 1/3} = 8^1 = 8$. In other words, when you raise $8^{1/3}$ to the 3rd power, the result is 8. This means that $8^{1/3}$ is the same as the cube root of 8, and, in general:

> The expression $x^{1/n}$ means $\sqrt[n]{x}$, or the nth root of x. For example, $\sqrt{a}$ can be written as $a^{1/2}$.

Example:

What is the value of $16^{3/4}$?

The first step is to see that $16^{3/4}$ is the same as $(16^{1/4})^3$ (because $(16^{1/4})^3 = 16^{1/4} \times 16^{1/4} \times 16^{1/4} = 16^{3/4}$). Using the definition above, $16^{1/4}$ is the 4th root of 16, which is 2 (because $2^4 = 16$). So $(16^{1/4})^3 = 2^3 = 8$.

> The expression $x^{m/n}$ means the nth root of x raised to the mth power. For instance, $4^{3/2}$ means the square root of 4 raised to the third power, or $2^3 = 8$.

Concept Review 6:
Negative and Fractional Exponents

Evaluate the following expressions without a calculator.

1. 5^{-2}

2. $9^{1/2}$

3. 2^{-5}

4. $25^{-1/2}$

5. $4^{3/2}$

6. $\left(\dfrac{16}{25}\right)^{-3/2}$

Simplify the following expressions, eliminating any negative or fractional exponents.

7. $x^{1/3}$

8. $(4g)^{1/2}$

9. $4x^{-2}$

10. $(4y)^{-2}$

11. $(9m)^{3/2}$

12. $(27b)^{1/3}/(9b)^{-1/2}$

13. If $x^{3/4} = 27$, what is the value of x?

14. If $b^{-1/2} = 4$, what is the value of b?

15. If $(2^m)^{-6} = 16$, what is the value of 2^{3m}?

SAT Practice 6:
Negative and Fractional Exponents

---

1. If $4^n = 20$, then what is the value of 4^{-n}?

2. If $5^4 \times m = 5^2$, then $m =$

  (A) -5^2

  (B) 5^{-2}

  (C) $\frac{1}{5}$

  (D) $5^{1/2}$

  (E) $\frac{1}{2}$

---

3. If $2^m \times 2^m \times 2^m \times 2^m = 2$, then $m =$

---

4. For all values of n, $\dfrac{3 \times 3^{2n}}{9^n} =$

  (A)   3

  (B) $\left(\dfrac{2}{3}\right)^n$

  (C) 3^n

  (D) 9^2

  (E) 9^n

---

5. If x is a positive number, then $\dfrac{x^{3/2} \times x^{1/2}}{x^{-(1/2)}} =$

  (A) $x^{3/4}$

  (B) $x^{-(1/4)}$

  (C) $x^{3/4}$

  (D) $\sqrt{x}^{\,3}$

  (E) $\sqrt{x}^{\,5}$

---

6. If $x = a^5 = b^3$ and x is positive, then $ab =$

  (A) $x^{1/5}$

  (B) $x^{1/8}$

  (C) $x^{8/15}$

  (D) x^8

  (E) x^{15}

Answer Key 6:
Negative and Fractional Exponents

Concept Review 6

1. $5^{-2} = 1/(5^2) = 1/25$

2. $9^{1/2} = \sqrt{9} = 3$

3. $2^{-5} = 1/(2^5) = 1/32$

4. $25^{-1/2} = 1/(25^{1/2}) = 1/\sqrt{25} = 1/5$

5. $4^{3/2} = (4^{1/2})^3 = (\sqrt{4})^3 = 2^3 = 8$

6. $(16/25)^{-3/2} = 1/(16/25)^{3/2} = (25/16)^{3/2} = ((25/16)^{1/2})^3$

   $= \left(\sqrt{\dfrac{25}{16}}\right)^3 = \left(\dfrac{5}{4}\right)^3 = \dfrac{125}{64}$

7. $x^{1/3} = \sqrt[3]{x}$

8. $(4g)^{1/2} = \sqrt{4g} = 2\sqrt{g}$

9. $4x^{-2} = 4/x^2$

10. $(4y)^{-2} = 1/(4y)^2 = 1/(16y^2)$

11. $(9m)^{3/2} = \left((9m)^{1/2}\right)^3 = (3\sqrt{m})^3 = 27m\sqrt{m}$

12. $(27b)^{1/3}/(9b)^{-1/2} = (27b)^{1/3} \times (9b)^{1/2} = 3b^{1/3} \times 3b^{1/2}$

    $= 9b^{1/6} = 9\sqrt[6]{b}$

13. $x^{3/4} = 27$
    Raise both sides to the
       4/3 power: $(x^{3/4})^{4/3} = 27^{4/3}$
    Simplify: $x^1 = (27^{1/3})^4$
    Simplify: $x = 3^4$
    Simplify: $x = 81$

14. $b^{-1/2} = 4$
    Raise both sides to the
       −2 power: $(b^{-1/2})^{-2} = 4^{-2}$
    Simplify: $b^1 = 1/(4^2)$
    Simplify: $b = 1/16$

15. $(2^m)^{-6} = 16$
    Simplify: $2^{-6m} = 16$
    Raise to the −1/2 power: $2^{3m} = 16^{-1/2}$
    Simplify: $2^{3m} = 1/\sqrt{16}$
    Simplify: $2^{3m} = 1/4$

SAT Practice 6

1. **1/20 or 0.05** $4^n = 1/4^n = 1/20$

2. **B** $5^4 \times m = 5^2$
   Divide by 5^4: $m = 5^2/5^4$
   Simplify (subtract exponents): $m = 5^{-2}$

3. **1/4 or 0.25** $2^m \times 2^m \times 2^m \times 2^m = 2$
   Simplify (add exponents): $2^{4m} = 2$
   Exponents must be equal: $4m = 1$
   Divide by 4: $m = 1/4$

4. **A**
                                        $\dfrac{3 \times 3^{2n}}{9^n}$

   Write as powers of 3: $\dfrac{3^1 \times 3^{2n}}{(3^2)^n}$

   Simplify denominator: $\dfrac{3^1 \times 3^{2n}}{3^{2n}}$

   Divide numerator and
      denominator by 3^{2n}: $3^1/1 = 3$

   Perhaps a simpler method is to simply pick n to be 0 (because n can be any number). This gives $(3 \times 3^0)/9^0 = (3 \times 1)/1 = 3$. The only choice that equals 3 when $n = 0$ is (A).

5. **E**
                                        $\dfrac{x^{\frac{3}{2}} \times x^{\frac{1}{2}}}{x^{-\frac{1}{2}}} =$

   Simplify numerator (add exponents): $\dfrac{x^{4/2}}{x^{-1/2}}$

   Simplify quotient
   (subtract exponents): $x^{4/2 - (-1/2)}$
   Simplify exponent: $x^{5/2}$

   Rewrite as a root: $\sqrt{x}^5$

6. **C** $x = a^5 = b^3$
   Solve for a (raise to the 1/5): $x^{1/5} = a$
   Solve for b (raise to the 1/3): $x^{1/3} = b$
   Multiply a and b: $ab = x^{1/5} \times x^{1/3}$
   Simplify (add exponents): $ab = x^{1/5 + 1/3}$
   Simplify: $ab = x^{8/15}$

   (Remember the quick way to add fractions: "zip-zap-zup" from Chapter 7, Lesson 3.)

CHAPTER 12

WRITING A GREAT ESSAY

1.   Map the SAT Essay Assignment

2.   Analyze the Assignment Closely

3.   Brainstorm Your Alternatives Creatively

4.   Connect to Your Knowledge with "Source Summaries"

5.   Write a Strong and Creative Thesis

6.   Organize Your Thoughts

7.   Write Logically

8.   Write Clearly

9.   Write Concisely

10.   Write Forcefully

11.   Write Masterfully

12.   Finish with a Bang

Lesson 1: Map the SAT Essay Assignment

The Assignment

Your essay assignment will look something like this:

Consider carefully the issue discussed in the following passage, and then write an essay that answers the question posed in the assignment.

Our leaders love to tell us that only victory will do, as if they are imparting great wisdom. They seek to defeat the enemy, to achieve the goal. Yet many times a loss, particularly one that is hard fought, is more valuable than victory. We cannot live a life full of only victories, nor should we. The quality of our lives depends as much on how we manage our losses as on how we achieve our victories.

Assignment: Can a loss ever be more valuable than a victory? Write an essay in which you answer this question and discuss your point of view on this issue. Support your position logically with examples from literature, the arts, history, politics, science and technology, current events, or your experience or observation.

The essay assignment asks you to formulate a point of view regarding a particular aspect of human values or behavior. It does not require you to recall any *specific* knowledge from your studies, although you should try to connect your thesis with your studies. There is never a "right" or "wrong" answer to the question; that is, your actual position does not affect your score. More important (contrary to what a lot of SAT-prep folks claim), the graders are not looking for essays that fit a particular formula. You can use narration, exposition, persuasion, or argument as long as it is focused on developing an interesting point of view that answers the question.

Know What They're Looking For

Two English teachers who have been trained by the Educational Testing Service (ETS) will read and score your essay from 1 (poor) to 6 (outstanding). They are trained to look for five things:

Interesting, relevant, and consistent point of view. Do you take a thoughtful and interesting position on the issue? Do you answer the question as it is presented? Do you maintain a consistent point of view?

Good reasoning. Do you define any necessary terms to make your reasoning clear? Do you explain the reasons for and implications of your thesis? Do you acknowledge and address possible objections to your thesis without sacrificing its integrity?

Solid support. Do you give relevant and *specific* examples to support your thesis? Do you explain how these examples support your thesis?

Logical organization. Does every paragraph relate clearly to your thesis? Do you provide logical transitions between paragraphs? Do you have a clear introduction and conclusion? Does the conclusion provide thoughtful commentary rather than mere repetition of the thesis?

Effective use of language. Do you use effective and appropriate vocabulary? Do you vary sentence length and structure effectively? Do you avoid needless repetition? Do you use parallelism, metaphor, personification, or other rhetorical devices to good effect? Do you use strong verbs? Do you avoid needlessly abstract language? Do you avoid cliché?

The readers will not mark you down for minor spelling or grammar mistakes, and they won't mark you up just for using big words. Focus on *good reasoning.* If you can take an interesting position, explore its implications, discuss relevant examples that support it, and maintain your focus, you will get a very good score.

How Long Should It Be?

Quality is much more important than quantity, but it's hard to get a great score with fewer than four paragraphs. This is so because the readers are looking for *structure* and *development,* which require good use of paragraphs. Think of your paragraphs as "stepping-stones" on a journey. Only two or three stepping-stones don't make for much of a journey. Plan to write four well-defined paragraphs—five if you have enough time.

Practice 1: Map the SAT Essay Assignment

SAT Essay Grading Review

1. What does it mean for an essay to have good substance?

2. What does it mean for an essay to have strong organization?

3. What does it mean for an essay to be clear?

4. What does it mean for an essay to have an effective and interesting style?

5. How long should your SAT essay be?

Check your answers with the answer key at the end of the chapter.

Lesson 2: Analyze the Assignment Closely

Focus on the Key Terms in the Question

Always take a minute to read the assignment question very carefully. Focus on the *question* first, not the quotation. Usually this question asks you to consider the relationship between two concepts. For instance, the assignment in Lesson 1 asks you to consider the "value" of "losing." Circle these words in the question, and begin by *defining* them: What is *losing*, really, and what does it mean for an experience to have *value*? This focus helps you to establish your point of view. Does losing only apply to contests? Can you win a game but lose in a bigger sense? Is the thrill of victory the only value in winning, or are there more important values associated with competition?

Answer the Question

One of the most common mistakes that students make on the SAT essay is simply not focusing on the question. Rather than taking a stance that answers the question, they talk about how silly or difficult taking a stance is. Don't do it! Your job is to *take a stance*. If you're asked, "Can a loss ever be more valuable than a victory?" *don't* spend all your time talking about how hard it is sometimes to achieve victory. That would miss the point. Your job is to discuss *loss* and whether or not it can be *valuable*.

Below are some examples of SAT essay questions and approaches that students could take that are *off* the mark (that is, they don't answer the question) and others that are *on* the mark. Read these carefully and think about why the second set of responses is better than the first set.

Assignment	OFF the mark	ON the mark
Who is your hero and why?	Discuss your belief that pro athletes shouldn't be heroes and that we don't value true heroism anymore.	Pick a person you admire; define what a hero is to you and show how he or she exemplifies heroic qualities.
Has technology mostly benefited humankind or harmed it?	Discuss how internet companies have made so much money on IPOs, and explain why technology stocks are a good investment.	Discuss the cost vs. benefits of technology through many eras with three examples.
Vince Lombardi said, "Winning isn't everything; it's the only thing." Do you agree or disagree?	Describe how important the arts and music are to a good education, and argue that they are more important than sports.	Describe an experience with an out-of-control father at a soccer match to show how focusing on winning alone harms kids.
"Every cloud has a silver lining." Agree or disagree?	Explain how "clouds" represent difficult times. Show how some people, for instance the poor, have more "clouds" than do other people, and this isn't fair.	Describe a difficult situation in your life that made you stronger for having endured it.

Practice 2: Analyze the Assignment Closely

Defining Terms Practice

Below are some examples of common terms that may show up on an SAT writing assignment and that you should define if you use them in an essay. Avoid a simplistic "dictionary" definition. Think carefully about each one, and then write a simple but useful definition of each term in your own words. Include a well-chosen example if it helps to illustrate your definition.

1. Democracy

2. Courage

3. Adventure

4. Liberty

5. Political power

6. Discipline

Lesson 3:
Brainstorm Your Alternatives Creatively

Take 6 to 8

Good writers always brainstorm creatively before writing, even when they have strict time limits. If you brainstorm and organize well, the rest of the essay will flow smoothly and easily. If you don't take the time to brainstorm and organize, your essay will flounder.

- Always set aside 6 to 8 minutes to analyze the question, brainstorm possible examples, write a thesis, and write a quick outline. Don't worry—you won't waste time. Doing these right will *save* you lots of time in writing the essay. The writing will flow easily once you've laid the groundwork.
- When brainstorming, turn off your internal "critic." Don't dismiss ideas right away. Think about them for a bit, and you may find that the ideas you were going to throw away are the best ones after all!
- Brainstorm on paper, not just in your head. The SAT will give you room to scribble notes. Use it. Write down thoughts, connect them, cross them out, underline them—do whatever your creative brain tells you to do.

Be Unique

Don't take the first thesis that pops into your head. Chances are that the first thesis you think of will be the same thing that pops into thousands of other heads. Instead, focus on *finding a unique perspective*. You can hone your perspective by first thinking of the most interesting examples.

Think of Examples Before You Make Your Thesis

Don't write your thesis until you've brainstormed several interesting examples. Since your thesis rests on your discussion of your examples, think about interesting examples first.

After you have analyzed the assignment and defined your terms, ask, "What is the most interesting example I can think of that helps to answer this question?" Show off what you know and how creative a thinker you are. Think of examples from your reading, your studies, and your life. Think of examples that other students won't think of, but make sure that they are on the mark and that you can discuss them with authority.

Go Off the Beaten Path

Avoid a run-of-the-mill point of view. If you're asked, "Can a loss ever be more valuable than a victory?" try to avoid clichés such as "losing the championship game" or "getting a D on a test" *unless* you can analyze them with unique insights. Instead, go off the beaten path, and try to think of more *interesting* examples of loss, such as the Green Party's loss in the 2000 presidential election, or America's loss in the race to put a human being into space, or Captain Ahab's failure to capture *Moby Dick*. Make the readers notice your unique and well-informed mind.

Going off the beaten path will keep you on your toes and force you to write a better essay. If you take an "easy" position, you will fall into lazy writing habits such as cliché, redundancy, and vagueness.

Practice 3:
Brainstorm Your Alternatives Creatively

Brainstorming Practice

Give yourself 6 minutes for each exercise below. Use the space below each question to practice brainstorming. Write down all the words, ideas, associations, people, events, books, etc. that pertain to the issue implied by the question. *Don't censor or criticize any idea; just get it down on the paper*. Then, in the last few minutes, try to organize your thoughts into ideas for individual paragraphs. Try to find one idea for each of four paragraphs. (Don't write the paragraphs, though.)

1. Should safety always be first?

2. Is the pen always mightier than the sword?

Show this work to your teacher or tutor. Discuss ways of efficiently releasing your creativity and connecting to your academic knowledge.

Lesson 4: Connect to Your Knowledge with "Source Summaries"

Prepare by Writing Out "Source Summaries"

Good writers support their claims with good examples. Well-chosen and well-analyzed examples often mean the difference between a mediocre essay and a great one. If you ever have trouble thinking of good examples, spend some time in the months before the SAT writing out "source summaries" such as those below. These help you to connect to good examples from your studies and experience—novels, historical events, people, cultural movements, and so on.

A *source summary* is simply a summary of the key ideas about a topic: *themes, theses,* and *details,* that you can use in your essay. Look carefully at the two examples below. Notice that each focuses only on the information that you would use in an essay on the given theme. It includes the important details you need to mention in order to sound like you know what you're talking about.

Sample Source Summaries

Book, Person, or Event   *Jane Eyre* by Charlotte Bronte

Themes	Theses	Details
Feminism	*Women are more constrained by society than men are.*	*Jane complains about what society expects of her, and that men aren't held to such high moral standards.*
Social status	*In 19th-century England, one's status in society had to do with breeding rather than ability.*	*Jane is disgusted by how she is treated by Rochester's houseguests.*
Love	*Love is blind and often irrational.*	*Rochester marries Jane while literally blind. Jane overlooks Rochester's previous marriage.*
Independence	*Independence can open one to new experiences, but can also lead to tragic isolation and inability to connect emotionally with others.*	*Orphaned as a child, Jane learns that she must fend for herself, and that others don't necessarily have her best interests in mind. She doubts Rochester's love for her at first, and takes an assumed name to avoid revealing herself to Reverend St. John Rivers.*

Book, Person, or Event   *D-Day* or *Operation Overlord* June 6, 1944, Normandy, France

Themes	Theses	Details
Strategic planning	*Intelligent planning pays off.*	*Operation Overlord was a monumental achievement. Thousands of soldiers had to keep it secret. Not since 1688 had an invading army crossed the English Channel. Over 800 planes brought paratroopers, and another 300 dropped 13,000 bombs. Within weeks, 20,000 tons of supplies per day were being brought ashore.*
Loss	*Great achievements require great losses.*	*By nightfall, 100,000 soldiers had landed, but over 9,000 were dead or wounded.*
Bravery	*To accomplish great things, we must conquer our fears.*	*Many went ashore knowing that they would die. From D-Day until Christmas 1944, Allied soldiers captured German prisoners at the rate of 1,000 per day.*

Practice 4:
Connect to Your Knowledge with "Source Summaries"

Source Summaries Make copies of this sheet and summarize the major books, people, and events you have recently studied. Try to make a source summary for at least ten different topics of study.

Book, person, or event ————————————————————

| Themes | Theses | Details |

Book, person, or event ————————————————————

| Themes | Theses | Details |

Book, person, or event ————————————————————

| Themes | Theses | Details |

Discuss these examples with your teacher or tutor to see if your analyses are "on the mark."

Lesson 5: Write a Strong and Creative Thesis

The Importance of a Good Thesis

> After a few minutes of brainstorming, write "THESIS:" on your scratch paper, and then write the strongest, most creative one-sentence thesis that you can support. The thesis should capture the essence of the essay in one well-crafted sentence. This sentence should be concise, interesting, specific, and informative.

Good short essays revolve around a good thesis. If your thesis is weak or dull, your essay will be weak or dull. Once you have brainstormed about the topic and examples, focus on a strong, creative thesis.

Below are some examples of weak theses and strong theses. The weak theses may be true, but they show little insight into the topic and are run-of-the-mill observations. The strong theses are more thoughtful and creative and have a wider scope.

Assignment	Weak Thesis	Strong Thesis
Has technology been good or bad for humankind?	• Good, because it has given us computers, video games, and DVDs. • Bad, because kids spend too much time online and playing video games.	• Good, because it has given us tools for exploring the universe and uncovering its secrets. • Bad, because it impedes genuine social interaction and separates us from nature.
Vince Lombardi said, "Winning isn't everything; it's the only thing." Do you agree or disagree?	• Agree: we should always strive to win, because that's what sports are all about. • Disagree: we focus too much on winning and not enough on sportsmanship.	• Agree: we love sports because our genes, which we inherit from our hunter ancestors, compel us to. • Disagree: winning is only a very small part of a successful and happy life, and here are some things that make us happier than winning.
"Every cloud has a silver lining." Agree or disagree?	• Agree, because I once had a bad experience that had a good side. • Disagree, because there are some experiences that are just tragic.	• Agree, because every trial can strengthen a person for having endured it, as these examples from literature show. • Disagree, because interpreting every tragedy in a Panglossian way prevents us from solving important problems like the following.

Play "Devil's Advocate"

> Every good thesis must argue *against* something as well as argue *for* something. A good thesis should acknowledge the common objections to it and address them thoughtfully. As you compose your thesis, *play "devil's advocate."*

Don't worry—playing "devil's advocate" doesn't mean selling your soul to the devil for a good essay grade. It simply means *addressing objections to your argument to strengthen it.* If you want to persuade a good reader, you must address common objections to your thesis. For instance, if your thesis is "Competition for grades creates a bad learning environment," a reader might object: "But competition motivates students to do their best, much as it motivates athletes." Your argument will not be complete until you address this objection. So you might address it this way in your essay:

Although many will say that competition motivates students to do their best, much as it motivates athletes, such objections misrepresent real learning. A decent artist is not motivated to create great art by the mere thought of "defeating" other artists, but to express a capacity that makes her more in tune with nature and with her own humanity. Similarly, some children do not learn merely to get better grades than other kids (if they did, then how would they learn to speak, to walk, to tell jokes, and the myriad other things they learn outside of school?), but to make themselves more competent and happier human beings.

Practice 5: Write a Strong and Creative Thesis

Strong and Creative Thesis Practice

Look again at the questions from Practice 3. Now that you have brainstormed about these questions, and understand the difference between a weak thesis and a *strong thesis*, write a strong thesis, in one sentence, to answer the two questions.

1. Should safety always be first?

2. Is the pen always mightier than the sword?

Devil's Advocate Practice

To play devil's advocate and write a strong thesis, you must be able to look at opposing sides of an issue. After each of the following questions, write two thesis statements, one for the "pro" position and one for the "con" position.

3. Should criminal trials be televised?

    Yes, because:

    No, because:

4. Is jealousy ever a good thing?

    Yes, because:

    No, because:

5. Does wealth make people happier?

    Yes, because:

    No, because:

Discuss your answers with your teacher or tutor, focusing on whether your responses are creative and forceful.

Lesson 6: Organize Your Thoughts

Write a Quick Four- or Five-Point Outline

Once you have written a strong and creative thesis and brainstormed a good example or two, you are almost ready to write. Your last step should be to quickly organize the other three or four paragraphs. This outline should be very brief: Simply write one short sentence that captures the gist of each paragraph.

Writing a quick outline helps you to avoid one of the most common writing problems: redundancy. Students who do not plan their paragraphs usually end up repeating themselves too much; their essays don't "go anywhere." Good organization helps you to develop your thoughts. Once you've stated your thesis and example, what then? You have many options: you can explain your example in more detail, you can give another example, you can address an objection, and so on.

Understand the Function of Paragraphs

Think of paragraphs as "minichapters" of your essay. Each one must be complete in itself, but must also be part of a whole. When you start a new paragraph, you signal that you are doing something new: giving a new example, analyzing a new idea, presenting a counter-argument, or the like. Your paragraphs give your essay *structure*. (For more on structure, see Chapter 4,

Lesson 3.) You might like a standard "top-down" (thesis at the beginning) structure:

Paragraph 1: State thesis and summarize reasons or examples.

Paragraph 2: Explain first reason or example.

Paragraph 3: Explain second reason or example.

Paragraph 4: Conclude with an extension or clarification of your thesis.

This is a simplification of the standard "five-paragraph" essay structure. We have simplified it to four paragraphs, because five paragraphs may be too much to write in 25 minutes, and because most essays that get perfect scores have only four paragraphs. Writing more than four paragraphs is usually too hard, and writing fewer than four paragraphs indicates weak development.

You might also want to use a "bottom-up" (thesis near the end) structure like this:

Paragraph 1: Begin with a quick story that introduces the topic.

Paragraph 2: Analyze the significance of the story.

Paragraph 3: State and explain your thesis that follows from the story.

Paragraph 4: Generalize from this thesis and connect it to a broader scope of ideas.

There is no one "right" structure; choose the structure that works best with your ideas, your examples, and your style.

Practice 6: Organize Your Thoughts

Organization Review

1.   What is the difference between a "top-down" essay structure and a "bottom-up" essay structure?

2.   What should a good outline consist of?

Check your answers with the answer key at the end of the chapter.

Organization Practice

Spend a few minutes reading and brainstorming about each of the questions below. Then write a brief four-point outline with thesis, development, and conclusion. Capture just the essence of your argument, and *be brief*.

3.   Is honesty always the best policy?

    1. THESIS:

    2.

    3.

    4. CONCLUSION:

4.   What is an example of true courage?

    1. THESIS:

    2.

    3.

    4. CONCLUSION:

Discuss your outlines with your teacher or tutor, focusing on whether your outlines show good development.

Lesson 7: Write Logically

Be Specific

> Your argument is much more effective when you discuss *real and specific examples rather than hypothetical and general ones.* You can generalize in your thesis and conclusion, but be specific everywhere else.

Consider this paragraph:

Although our Constitution provides us with the right to bear arms, this right should not be a universal one. That's not what the Second Amendment was intended for. A lot of times it's not appropriate and just plain dangerous or foolish. This is obvious to anyone who reads newspapers or watches the TV news and knows about what is going on in the world.

The argument isn't effective because it gives no specifics. Consider this improvement:

Although our Constitution provides us with the right to bear arms, this right was intended only to protect citizens from the tyranny of government, and not to arm citizens against one another. In many places, for instance in schools and other public places, the right to bear arms does not enhance public safety. Even the popular argument that it makes our homes safer is absurd. Rather, it merely increases the likelihood that a problematic situation like an argument will turn deadly, as it did last month when an eight-year-old boy shot his six-year-old sister to death in New Jersey.

This revision is more forceful because it turns the generalizations into specifics, and gives concrete examples.

Help Your Reader with Logical Transitions

> Provide your readers with "guideposts" to help them understand the logical relationships between your ideas. These guideposts, which usually come at the beginning of a paragraph or a sentence, are called *transitions.* They include words like *however* (to indicate a contrast), *therefore* (to indicate a result), *furthermore* (to indicate an extension of an argument), *first, second,* or *third* (to indicate a sequence of examples or reasons), *nevertheless* (to indicate irony), and so on.

Consider the following paragraphs:

Every first-year chemistry or physics student learns that opposite charges attract and like charges repel. If we try to force two positive charges together, they will fly apart as soon as we release them. Similarly, if we try to hold a positive charge apart from a negative charge, they will fly together as soon as we release them.

The nucleus of an atom consists of a collection of positively charged protons and uncharged neutrons squashed together in a very small space. Negatively charged electrons remain in "shells" that never touch the nucleus.

You should notice that the facts in these paragraphs don't "fit" logically. If like charges fly apart, then how on earth could they remain together in a nucleus? Also, if unlike charges fall toward each other, why don't the negative electrons fall into the positive nucleus? However, the second paragraph provides no logical "guideposts" to indicate this surprising relationship between these ideas. A good writer should acknowledge the contrasts between the ideas of the first paragraph and the ideas of the second paragraph with *logical transitions.* Notice how this revision provides the necessary transitions:

Every first-year chemistry or physics student learns that opposite charges attract and like charges repel. If we try to force two positive charges together, they will fly apart as soon as we release them. Similarly, if we try to hold a positive charge apart from a negative charge, they will fly together as soon as we release them.

However, science students are also told that the nucleus of an atom consists of a collection of positively charged protons and uncharged neutrons squashed together in a very small space. They are also told that negatively charged electrons remain in "shells" that never touch the nucleus. How can this be?

You need to think carefully about the logic of individual sentences, as well.

Not logical: *The bill was in committee, and the opposition of several senators killed it because of the unpopular amendments that they attached to it.*

Better: *Several senators who opposed the bill killed it in committee by attaching unpopular amendments to it.*

Practice 7: Write Logically

Logical Transition Practice

Rewrite the second sentence of each of the following pairs so that it includes a logical transition from the previous one.

1. *We knew that the game would be hard fought. We never thought it would last 8 hours and 20 innings.*

2. *There were thousands of visitors in town for the game. It was almost impossible to find a hotel room.*

3. *The theory of evolution has had a profound effect on scientific thought. It has influenced many artists and writers.*

4. *We knew that punishing the culprits would do no good. We took no action against them.*

5. *Perfect games are rare. In the last two years, only one was bowled in the entire state.*

6. *There were several reasons for the delay. The bus driver had the wrong directions.*

Check your answers with the answer key at the end of the chapter.

Lesson 8: Write Clearly

Use Natural Language

> Good writing follows more rules than conversational speech does, but this doesn't mean that good writing is stiff and unnatural. Convoluted and abstract language doesn't make "better" writing. *Although you should avoid wordiness and egregious grammatical errors, natural language is always better than overly formal language.*

This sentence is far too stiff and unnatural:

An individual person's lack of tolerance and inability to appreciate and even enjoy different aspects in other individuals is a concept that negatively affects the ability of a community to avoid hatred and establish the environment in which we would like to bring our children up.

It is much more effective when phrased more naturally and concisely:

We create a much more peaceful society when we learn to appreciate the differences in others.

Use Personal and Concrete Nouns

Is the following sentence easy to understand?

My concerns in general center on numerous omissions of relevant facts and quotes, which had the effect of diminishing the extent of the apparent support of free expression, and the force of the moral arguments for free expression, and of enhancing the support of those who are vigilant against dangerous speech, and obscuring the more extreme arguments made on their behalf.

No. Why not? Just look at the nouns:

My <u>concerns</u> in general center on numerous <u>omissions</u> of relevant <u>facts</u> and <u>quotes</u>, which had the <u>effect</u> of <u>diminishing</u> the <u>extent</u> of the apparent <u>support</u> of free <u>expression</u>, and the <u>force</u> of the moral <u>arguments</u> for free <u>expression</u>, and of <u>enhancing</u> the <u>support</u> of those who are vigilant against dangerous <u>speech</u>, and <u>obscuring</u> the more extreme <u>arguments</u> made on their <u>behalf</u>.

These nouns are all *impersonal* and *abstract*, so they are hard to relate to. *Personal nouns* refer to the things in your readers' common experience, things that they personally understand. *Concrete nouns* refer to things that can be *seen, heard, smelled, tasted,* or *touched.* Of course, if you are talking about ideas, you will need to use abstract nouns, but don't use any more than are necessary. Not many people can keep track of 18 abstract and impersonal nouns in a single sentence. Here's a good revision:

Some <u>people</u> have left out relevant <u>facts</u> in this <u>discussion</u>, and have therefore minimized how much <u>people</u> support free <u>expression</u> and maximized how much <u>people</u> want to eliminate offensive <u>speech</u>. <u>They</u> have also ignored or obscured the crazy and illogical <u>arguments</u> against offensive <u>speech</u>. In fact, the majority of <u>Americans</u> support free <u>expression</u>, and regard it as a moral <u>necessity</u>.

Without question, this conveys the author's ideas much more clearly and effectively.

> Minimize abstract and impersonal nouns. When they pile up, your thoughts become hard to follow.

Eliminate Jargon

> *Jargon* such as *win-win scenario, thinking outside the box, bulletizing the issues, targeting a goal, bottom line, downside, facilitate, prioritize, optimize, time frame, mutually beneficial, parameter, utilize,* etc. annoys good readers, particularly when simpler, more common words suffice.

Jargony: *If we think outside the box and prioritize our concerns, I'm sure we can facilitate a win-win scenario for all parties.*

Better: *If we think creatively and set our priorities, I'm sure we can find a solution that everyone will like.*

Practice 8: Write Clearly

Clarification Practice

Rewrite the following sentences to eliminate stiffness, vagueness, and jargon.

1. *The concept of competition is an essential element with regard to the ability of society to encourage people to achieve excellence.*

2. *The consideration of all ideas of our employees is done by our management with the thinking that only the most quality concepts will elevate to the forefront.*

3. *A concern in the general population with regard to the ability of the government to optimize the positive use of federal funds has accelerated in recent times.*

4. *When one is placing the emphasis on the deterioration of the individual concern for others and personal moral responsibility, the role of social institutions is ignored.*

Check your answers with the answer key at the end of the chapter.

Lesson 9: Write Concisely

Eliminate Wordiness

The fewer words you can use to convey an idea, the better. You won't impress readers by making them work hard or by confusing them. When you use wordy or unnatural language, a good reader will think that you don't have command over your words, or that you're stalling because you don't have anything interesting to say.

Wordy: *Courage is a value that is very difficult to be found in and among individuals in the world today, even though it is clearly something that nearly everyone of every persuasion and creed finds to be an extremely important and valuable element of human morality.*

Better: *Courage today is rare, and so all the more precious.*

Avoid wordy phrases like those below. Use the concise versions.

Wordy	Concise	Wordy	Concise
has a reaction	*reacts*	*in the event that*	*if*
has a dependence on	*depends*	*regardless of the fact that*	*although*
provides enforcement	*enforces*	*in our world today*	*today*
is in violation of	*violates*	*in this day and age*	*today*
has knowledge of	*knows*	*being that*	*because*
achieves the maximization of	*maximizes*	*due to the fact that*	*because*
provides opposition to	*opposes*	*at this point in time*	*now*
is reflective of	*reflects*	*at the present moment*	*now*
give consideration to	*consider*	*are aware of the fact*	*know*
lend assistance to	*assist*	*make contact with*	*contact*

Watch Your Prepositional Phrases

Sometimes even good writers can get ambushed by prepositional phrases. Like most things, prepositional phrases are fine in moderation. But too many—particularly when they are strung together—make a sentence wordy and unclear.

Wordy: *Few people in the media recognize their responsibility to the public for writing fair and unbiased pieces for the sake of expanding their readers' trust in their representations of the world around them. (seven prepositional phrases)*

Better: *Few journalists understand that they must sustain scrupulous impartiality in order to maintain the trust of their readers. (one prepositional phrase)*

Avoid Redundancy

Eliminate any word or phrase that conveys an idea already stated or implied in the sentence.

Redundant: *We are now serving breakfast **at this time.***
Better: *We are now serving breakfast.*

Redundant: *The best elements of her previous works were combined **together** in this symphony.*
Right: *The best elements of her previous works were combined in this symphony.*

Redundant: *They could always rely on him to tell the **honest** truth.*
Right: *They could always rely on him to tell the truth.*

Practice 9: Write Concisely

Redundancy Sweeping Practice

Eliminate any redundancies in the following sentences.

1. *An effective and good manager must need to rely on sound, solid management principles as well as past experience.*

2. *Both parents as well as students should have input into the new testing plan.*

3. *Many cleaning substances should not be combined together, because violent reactions could result.*

4. *Even if each and every citizen contributed to the effort, it would still take several years to complete.*

5. *The food and blankets dropped for the suffering refugees were far from sufficient enough to ward off the hunger and cold.*

6. *We watched the jet until it disappeared from view.*

Tightening-Up Practice

Rewrite the following sentences to eliminate wordiness.

7. *In this day and age, all too many people have a dependence on television as their exclusive source of information.*

8. *Few people are aware of the fact that such gambling is in violation of federal law.*

9. *Due to the fact that corporations endeavor to achieve the maximization of profit, they rarely put their focus on environmental needs.*

10. *In the event that your boss expresses opposition to your proposal at the meeting, consider having a head-to-head conversation with her about it personally.*

11. *It is certainly clear that too few people give consideration to the fact that economic strength is often reflective of the hopes of consumers.*

Check your answers with the answer key at the end of the chapter.

Lesson 10: Write Forcefully

Eliminate Weak Verbs—Uncover the "Lurking Verbs"

Take an essay you've written recently and circle all of the verbs. How many are forms of the verb *to be*, like *is*, *are*, *was*, and *were*? Probably too many. *To be* is the most overused verb in the English language, and it is also the *weakest*. Other weak verbs are *to exist* and *to have*. Too many of these verbs in your writing make it weak and lifeless. If your writing contains too many weak verbs, find the stronger lurking verbs in the sentence, and rewrite it. Lurking verbs are words in the sentence that aren't verbs but should be, because they convey the idea or action of the sentence more effectively.

Weak: *The mice **have** a tendency to overeat when they are in the absence of this hormone.*

Stronger: *The mice **tend** to overeat when they **lack** this hormone.*

The original verbs, *have* and *are*, are weak. More effective verbs are "lurking" as nouns in the first sentence: *tendency* and *absence* seem to carry the main ideas, but they are nouns. Notice how much more forceful the revision is because these ideas were transformed into verbs.

Weak: *We **will not be** tolerant of anyone who is disrespectful of the opposing players.*

Stronger: *We won't **tolerate** anyone who **disrespects** the opposing players.*

Use Clear and Active Verbs

Consider this example of a weak and unclear sentence:

The most aggressive of the new companies, whose priorities are characterized by their capital commitment to market share and name recognition, will be seen as the "players" in their niche, and may see an extension of share overvaluation, despite weak product development or business models.

Why is this sentence so weak and vague? It's filled with jargon, abstract nouns, and weak and passive verbs. Here's a much more effective revision:

Investors like aggressive companies that are committed to making themselves well known and to building their share of the market. As a result, investors put a lot of money into these companies, thereby overvaluing them, even though the companies often have weak products or business models.

We've cut out the jargon, used more concrete nouns, included more logical connections, and found stronger verbs. We also replaced the **passive verb** with an **active verb**. A passive verb places the noun performing the action after the verb, as in *The ball was hit by the boy*, or eliminates the noun performing the action altogether, as in *The ball was hit*. In the original sentence, the verb is in the passive voice and doesn't convey a clear thought: *The companies will be seen as "players."* Seen by whom? It doesn't say, so the sentence is unclear. Notice that the revision makes this clear: *Investors like companies*. This tells us what's happening, and who's doing it.

Use the passive voice sparingly: don't say *The ball was hit by the boy* when you can say *The boy hit the ball*. The passive voice often makes a sentence needlessly wordy and vague.

Eliminate Clichés

Phrases like *give it 110%, go for the gold, rip it to shreds, in the lap of luxury, keep at arm's length, pick up the pieces, cross that bridge when we come to it, go to town*, and so on are **clichés**. A **cliché** is an overused phrase. Whenever you use a cliché in your writing, a good reader will think you are being lazy, or that you cannot think of an original way to convey your idea. Instead, use your own, original words to convey your thoughts.

Clichéd: *Believe me, I felt like a fish out of water giving that speech, but I sucked it up and gave it a go.*

Better: *Although the prospect of speaking in front of the class intimidated me, I tried to focus on my words rather than my fear.*

Practice 10: Write Forcefully

Cliché Sweeping Practice

Rewrite each sentence to eliminate any clichés.

1. *Many people these days are fond of saying that the youth of this day and age are lazy as dogs.*

2. *They say that kids are nothing but couch potatoes who sit like bumps on a log playing video games or watching MTV.*

3. *For all intents and purposes, this assumption is dead wrong.*

4. *As a matter of fact, many of my friends are thinking more about careers that will change the world as we know it rather than careers that will just chase the almighty dollar.*

Verb Strengthening Practice

Rewrite the following sentences to strengthen the verbs. Uncover any good "lurking" verbs.

5. *This action is in violation of the company's own contract.*

6. *The village was affected to a devastating degree by the earthquake.*

7. *My failure on the test was reflective of the fact that I didn't study.*

8. *The movie was considered by the critics to be dull and hackneyed.*

9. *The bold maneuver was made by the army under the cover of night.*

10. *Outside the office were a dozen chairs filling the hallway.*

Check your answers with the answer key at the end of the chapter.

Lesson 11: Write Masterfully

Vary Your Sentence Length Wisely

Consider the following paragraph:

Many people buy into the cliché "guns don't kill people; people kill people." On its surface, this statement seems obviously true. However, some deep thought and analysis about this statement, its assumptions and implications, shows clearly that it is mistaken.

Not bad, but consider the following revision:

Many people buy into the cliché "guns don't kill people; people kill people." On its surface, this statement seems obviously true. It's not.

Why is the last sentence of the revision more effective than the last sentence of the first paragraph? Because it's short. When it follows a series of lengthy, informative sentences, a short sentence hits the reader like a slap in the face and drives home an important point.

> Good writers always think about the length of their sentences. Long sentences may be necessary for explaining complex ideas, but very short sentences are often best for emphasizing important points.

Eliminate Sentences to Nowhere

> Eliminate sentences that state the obvious, are hopelessly vague, or don't move your thesis forward. Sometimes a sentence that seemed profound when you first wrote it may turn out to be nonsensical or unintelligible. Every sentence should convey a fresh and interesting idea that moves your argument forward. Any sentence that fails to do that should be eliminated.

If you must eliminate a sentence from your essay, cross it out neatly. Don't worry about erasing it completely, and don't be concerned about the essay's looking "perfect." The readers understand that you would have been more neat if you had had the time, and won't penalize you for eliminating an unnecessary sentence.

Example:

Life is characterized by the ups and downs one experiences while living from day to day.

The writer probably thought that this sentence was profound when she wrote it. But it really doesn't say anything at all. Saying that *life has ups and downs* is just stating the obvious. No rational person would disagree with that. The writer should eliminate this sentence.

Example:

Every country seeks a constant prosperity in its growth.

This sentence is so vague and uninteresting that it's hardly worth saving. How can a country *seek* anything? Maybe the people can, but not the country. Saying that people seek prosperity is a pretty uninteresting observation. Do they really seek *constant prosperity*? What does that even mean? And what the heck is *prosperity in their growth*? Clearly, this is a sentence to nowhere.

Choose Your Words Carefully

> Good writers have good vocabularies. They know that one well-chosen "bargain" word is often worth six modifiers.

Weak diction: *I walked through the finish line as if my legs were ridiculously heavy, and sat down exhausted.*

Strong diction: *I lumbered through the finish line and collapsed.*

> Don't use overblown vocabulary unnecessarily. Fancy words are often distracting.

Overblown diction: *An astute scribe shall always eschew superfluous grandiloquence.*

Effective diction: *Good writers use big words only when necessary.*

Practice 11: Write Masterfully

Sentence Variation Practice

Cross out the sentence in each paragraph that is too long. Then rewrite the sentence to increase its impact.

1. *Many neoconservatives love to claim that lowering taxes actually raises government revenue. Any rational examination of this claim shows clearly that it is wrong, or at least not as simple as they are claiming. In fact, the government's tax revenue depends on many things other than the tax rate.*

2. *My mother sat me down and explained to me how important it is to spend money wisely. After listening to her carefully, I understood the point she was trying to make. I began keeping better track of my accounts and became a wiser consumer.*

Bargain Word Practice

Find a single word or shorter phrase to capture the idea in bold.

3. *David **looked very closely at** his test results.*

4. *The girls in the car **talked on and on about meaningless things** for hours.*

5. *The coach **gave us a long, harsh, and critical speech** about our lack of effort in the first half.*

Toning Down Practice

Tone down the fancy vocabulary in the sentences below.

6. *When a practitioner of medicine suggests an appropriate remedy for a malady, it is best that the person to whom it was offered utilizes it strictly according to the instructions.*

7. *Plebeians execrate prevaricators, while aristocrats lionize them.*

Check your answers with the answer key at the end of the chapter.

Lesson 12: Finish with a Bang

What a Good Conclusion Does

Your conclusion should do one of the following:

- *Make a broader connection to your thesis.* Discuss an implication of your thesis by connecting it to your own life, society at large, a particular problem, the future, etc.
- *Offer a solution.* If your essay describes a problem, offer some ideas of how to fix it.
- *Refine or clarify your thesis.* Address objections to your point of view, or clarify important points.

Don't Just Summarize

A conclusion provides closure to the essay and should leave the reader with something to think about. A conclusion should not be just a "recap" of your essay. Don't merely restate your thesis in different words. A good conclusion must present a *new* idea. Read good essays in magazines like the *New Yorker* and the *Atlantic Monthly*, and in the *New York Times* Op-Ed page, and you will see that good writers never say "In conclusion, . . ." or "As I have proven in this essay, . . ." So you shouldn't say that, either.

Don't Tell Us What You're Doing— Just Do It

Many writers are distractingly self-conscious. They say things like *It is my opinion that drugs are dangerous* instead of *Drugs are dangerous*. All competent readers know that your essay presents your opinion. You don't need to tell them that you're giving your opinion; just give it.

Weak and self-conscious:

I believe that bullies are often people who don't like themselves. It's just my opinion, of course, but those who have to pick on the weak can't really feel good about themselves, as I can demonstrate with a few examples.

Stronger:

Bullies are often people who don't like themselves. Those who have to pick on the weak can't really feel good about themselves.

Similarly, don't tell your readers that you are concluding your essay. Just conclude. Don't say *In conclusion, . . .* or *As my examples clearly prove. . . .*

Example:

As I said in the beginning, every cloud has a silver lining, and this has been shown in this essay with the examples of some wars and individual diseases. Both of these are bad things overall which sometimes can have good things come out of them. This shows that. . . .

This conclusion seems to be saying: "Well, I guess it's time for the conclusion. In case you weren't paying attention, here's what I just finished saying." This is not what a conclusion should do; it should present new and interesting thoughts connected to the thesis. This conclusion merely repeats the thesis and doesn't give the readers anything new to think about. In fact, it insults the readers by assuming that they can't remember what they just read. Compare it to this revision:

Of course, wars are among the most tragic of all human events. If wars can have beneficial outcomes, then surely we can see the good in lesser tragedies. Perhaps if we could take such a positive perspective on our everyday problems, we would live happier lives.

This conclusion is more effective because it extends the thesis to a wider sphere, offers a suggestion, and leaves the readers thinking without insulting them.

Practice 12: Finish with a Bang

Conclusion Review

1. What are the three things that a good conclusion can do?

2. What does it mean for your writing to be self-conscious?

Self-Consciousness Sweeping Practice

Rewrite the following sentences to make them less self-conscious.

3. *I think that classes should not start until 9:00 am, because I believe students need more rest than they are getting.*

4. *As I have shown with these examples, there are many factors to consider when choosing a college.*

5. *It is my opinion that more money should be spent, in my school and schools like it, on music programs.*

6. *These examples abundantly demonstrate that goals are important in life, as I said earlier.*

Check your answers with the answer key at the end of the chapter.

Chapter 12 Answer Key

Practice 1

1. It means that you respond with a thoughtful and interesting thesis and provide relevant, specific examples and clear, logical explanations.

2. It means that you use paragraphs to develop, support, and explain your thesis, and that you conclude effectively.

3. It means that you avoid needless jargon, wordiness, cliché, or abstraction, and define terms as necessary.

4. It means that you vary your sentence structure appropriately, are concise, and choose your words wisely.

5. Four or five paragraphs.

Practice 6

1. A "top-down" essay states the thesis at the beginning, and a "bottom-up" essay states it near the end of the essay.

2. Four brief sentences: the thesis, the topic sentence of paragraph 2, the topic sentence of paragraph 3, and the concluding idea.

Practice 7

1. *We knew that the game would be hard fought.* **However,** *we never thought it would last 8 hours and 20 innings.*

2. *There were thousands of visitors in town for the game.* **Therefore,** *it was almost impossible to find a hotel room.*

3. *The theory of evolution has had a profound effect on scientific thought.* **Furthermore,** *it has influenced many artists and writers.*

4. *We knew that punishing the culprits would do no good.* **Therefore,** *we took no action against them.*

5. *Perfect games are rare.* **In fact,** *in the last two years, only one was bowled in the entire state.*

6. *There were several reasons for the delay.* **First,** *the bus driver had the wrong directions.*

Practice 8

1. *Competition encourages excellence.*

2. *Our managers consider all ideas from our employees, and use the best ones.*

3. *People are increasingly concerned that the government is wasting money.*

4. *When we focus exclusively on personal moral responsibility, we ignore the importance of social institutions.*

Practice 9

1. *An effective manager must rely on sound management principles as well as past experience.*

2. *Parents and students should have input into the new testing plan.*

3. *Many cleaning substances should not be combined, because violent reactions could result.*

4. *Even if every citizen contributed to the effort, it would still take several years to complete.*

5. *The food and blankets dropped for the refugees was far from sufficient to ward off the hunger and cold.*

6. *We watched the jet until it disappeared.*

7. *Today, too many people depend on television as their exclusive source of information.*

8. *Few people know that such gambling violates federal law.*

9. *Because corporations try to maximize profit, they rarely focus on environmental needs.*

10. *If your boss opposes your proposal at the meeting, consider talking to her about it.*

11. *Too few people realize that economic strength often reflects the hopes of consumers.*

Chapter 12 Answer Key

Practice 10

1. *Many people today think that young people are lazy.*

2. *They say that they spend too much time playing video games or watching MTV.*

3. *They are wrong.*

4. *In fact, many of my friends are choosing careers that help others rather than make themselves rich.*

5. *This action violates the company's own contract.*

6. *The earthquake devastated the village.*

7. *I failed the test because I hadn't studied.*

8. *The critics complained that the movie was dull and hackneyed.*

9. *The army maneuvered boldly under the cover of night.*

10. *A dozen chairs filled the hallway outside the office.*

Practice 11

1. *Many neoconservatives love to claim that lowering taxes actually raises government revenue. **They are wrong. It's not that simple.** In fact, the government's tax revenue depends on many things other than the tax rate.*

2. *My mother sat me down and explained to me how important it is to spend money wisely. **I got the message.** I began keeping better track of my accounts and became a wiser consumer.*

3. *David **scrutinized** his test results.*

4. *The girls in the car **babbled** for hours.*

5. *The coach **harangued us** about our lack of effort in the first half.*

6. *When a doctor prescribes something for you, follow the directions carefully.*

7. *Ordinary people hate liars, but noblemen love them.*

Practice 12

1. Make a broader connection to the thesis; offer a solution; refine or clarify the thesis.

2. It means that you are telling your reader that you are doing something rather than simply doing it.

3. *Classes should not start until 9:00 am, because students need more rest than they are getting.*

4. *There are many factors to consider when choosing a college.*

5. *More money should be spent on school music programs.*

6. *Goals are important in life.*

## CHAPTER 13

ESSAY WRITING PRACTICE

20 Practice SAT Essay Assignments

Practice Essay 1

Time—25 minutes

Directions for Writing the Essay

Plan and write an essay that answers the question below. Do NOT write on another topic. An essay on another topic will receive a score of 0.

Two readers will grade your essay based on how well you develop your point of view, organize and explain your ideas, use specific and relevant examples to support your thesis, and use clear and effective language. How well you write is much more important than how much you write, but to cover the topic adequately you should plan to write several paragraphs.

Your essay must be written only on the lines provided on your answer sheet. You will have enough space if you write on every line, avoid wide margins, and keep your handwriting to a reasonable size. Your essay will be read by people who are not familiar with your handwriting, so write legibly.

You may use this sheet for notes and outlining, but these will not be graded as part of your essay.

Consider carefully the issue discussed in the following passage, then write an essay that answers the question posed in the assignment.

> Without a clear goal to focus our energy and drive us to grow, we cease to be truly alive. We are inert particles floating on the sea of life. This is true of not only ourselves, but our institutions—our families, our corporations, and our societies. The moment we cease to grow, we begin to die.

Assignment: **Is growth necessary to a happy and productive life?** Write an essay in which you answer this question and discuss your point of view on this issue. You may discuss personal or institutional growth. Support your position logically with examples from literature, the arts, history, politics, science and technology, current events, or your experience or observation.

Note: Write your practice essay on two pages of standard lined paper.

Practice Essay 2

Time—25 minutes

Directions for Writing the Essay

Plan and write an essay that answers the question below. Do NOT write on another topic. An essay on another topic will receive a score of 0.

Two readers will grade your essay based on how well you develop your point of view, organize and explain your ideas, use specific and relevant examples to support your thesis, and use clear and effective language. How well you write is much more important than how much you write, but to cover the topic adequately you should plan to write several paragraphs.

Your essay must be written only on the lines provided on your answer sheet. You will have enough space if you write on every line, avoid wide margins, and keep your handwriting to a reasonable size. Your essay will be read by people who are not familiar with your handwriting, so write legibly.

You may use this sheet for notes and outlining, but these will not be graded as part of your essay.

Consider carefully the issue discussed in the following passage, then write an essay that answers the question posed in the assignment.

> Our leaders love to tell us that only victory will do, as if they are imparting great wisdom. They seek only to defeat the enemy, to achieve the goal. Yet many times a loss, particularly one that is hard fought, is more valuable than victory. We cannot live a life full of only victories, nor should we. The quality of our lives depends as much on how we manage our losses as on how we achieve our victories.

Assignment: **Can a loss ever be more valuable than a victory?** Write an essay in which you answer this question and discuss your point of view on this issue. Support your position logically with examples from literature, the arts, history, politics, science and technology, current events, or your experience or observation.

Note: Write your practice essay on two pages of standard lined paper.

Practice Essay 3

Time—25 minutes

Directions for Writing the Essay

Plan and write an essay that answers the question below. Do NOT write on another topic. An essay on another topic will receive a score of 0.

Two readers will grade your essay based on how well you develop your point of view, organize and explain your ideas, use specific and relevant examples to support your thesis, and use clear and effective language. How well you write is much more important than how much you write, but to cover the topic adequately you should plan to write several paragraphs.

Your essay must be written only on the lines provided on your answer sheet. You will have enough space if you write on every line, avoid wide margins, and keep your handwriting to a reasonable size. Your essay will be read by people who are not familiar with your handwriting, so write legibly.

You may use this sheet for notes and outlining, but these will not be graded as part of your essay.

Consider carefully the issue discussed in the following passage, then write an essay that answers the question posed in the assignment.

> Adventure seekers who merely crave the mitigating rush of adrenaline that accompanies risky feats do not demonstrate true courage. Courage is not fearlessness but the willingness to face our unmitigated fears and vulnerabilities, particularly those fears that make us think less of ourselves.

Assignment: **Does true courage always require putting something that is very important to us at risk?** Write an essay in which you answer this question and explain the reasons for your choice. You may choose an example from literature, the arts, history, politics, science and technology, current events, or your experience or observation.

<u>Note:</u> Write your practice essay on two pages of standard lined paper.

Practice Essay 4

Time—25 minutes

Directions for Writing the Essay

Plan and write an essay that answers the question below. Do NOT write on another topic. An essay on another topic will receive a score of 0.

Two readers will grade your essay based on how well you develop your point of view, organize and explain your ideas, use specific and relevant examples to support your thesis, and use clear and effective language. How well you write is much more important than how much you write, but to cover the topic adequately you should plan to write several paragraphs.

Your essay must be written only on the lines provided on your answer sheet. You will have enough space if you write on every line, avoid wide margins, and keep your handwriting to a reasonable size. Your essay will be read by people who are not familiar with your handwriting, so write legibly.

You may use this sheet for notes and outlining, but these will not be graded as part of your essay.

Consider carefully the issue discussed in the following passage, then write an essay that answers the question posed in the assignment.

> Communicating technology was supposed to turn the world into a "global village," enhancing our relationships with others and our understanding of other cultures. Yet I fear it has rendered us more polarized and less articulate. Instant communication allows us to proclaim what is on our minds before we've analyzed it, substantiated it, or rendered it coherent, let alone eloquent.

Assignment: **Do modern means of communication make our society better or worse?** Write an essay in which you answer this question and explain your point of view on this issue. Support your position logically with examples from your reading, current events, or your experience or observation.

Note: Write your practice essay on two pages of standard lined paper.

Practice Essay 5

Time—25 minutes

Directions for Writing the Essay

Plan and write an essay that answers the question below. Do NOT write on another topic. An essay on another topic will receive a score of 0.

Two readers will grade your essay based on how well you develop your point of view, organize and explain your ideas, use specific and relevant examples to support your thesis, and use clear and effective language. How well you write is much more important than how much you write, but to cover the topic adequately you should plan to write several paragraphs.

Your essay must be written only on the lines provided on your answer sheet. You will have enough space if you write on every line, avoid wide margins, and keep your handwriting to a reasonable size. Your essay will be read by people who are not familiar with your handwriting, so write legibly.

You may use this sheet for notes and outlining, but these will not be graded as part of your essay.

Consider carefully the issue discussed in the following passage, then write an essay that answers the question posed in the assignment.

> Being truly human as a member of a society means seeing injustice and working to fix it. The human mind can not only perceive the immediate world and act instinctively, but also visualize a better future and endeavor to realize it.

Assignment: **What is one great injustice in the world, and how should it be addressed?** Write an essay in which you answer this question and explain the reasons for your choice. You may draw inspiration and support from literature, the arts, history, politics, science and technology, current events, or your experience or observation.

<u>Note:</u> Write your practice essay on two pages of standard lined paper.

Practice Essay 6

Time—25 minutes

Directions for Writing the Essay

Plan and write an essay that answers the question below. Do NOT write on another topic. An essay on another topic will receive a score of 0.

Two readers will grade your essay based on how well you develop your point of view, organize and explain your ideas, use specific and relevant examples to support your thesis, and use clear and effective language. How well you write is much more important than how much you write, but to cover the topic adequately you should plan to write several paragraphs.

Your essay must be written only on the lines provided on your answer sheet. You will have enough space if you write on every line, avoid wide margins, and keep your handwriting to a reasonable size. Your essay will be read by people who are not familiar with your handwriting, so write legibly.

You may use this sheet for notes and outlining, but these will not be graded as part of your essay.

Consider carefully the issue discussed in the following passage, then write an essay that answers the question posed in the assignment.

> Acquiring knowledge is like scaling a mountain. The proper attitude in reaching a summit, however, is to marvel not so much at one's achievement as at the glorious view of the unknown beyond. A well-educated person is known not so much for the questions he or she can answer as for the questions he or she can ask.

Assignment: **What is one great question that every educated person should ask?** Write an essay in which you indicate what this question should be and explain the reasons for your choice. You may draw inspiration and support from literature, the arts, history, politics, science and technology, current events, or your experience or observation.

Note: Write your practice essay on two pages of standard lined paper.

Practice Essay 7

Time—25 minutes

Directions for Writing the Essay

Plan and write an essay that answers the question below. Do NOT write on another topic. An essay on another topic will receive a score of 0.

Two readers will grade your essay based on how well you develop your point of view, organize and explain your ideas, use specific and relevant examples to support your thesis, and use clear and effective language. How well you write is much more important than how much you write, but to cover the topic adequately you should plan to write several paragraphs.

Your essay must be written only on the lines provided on your answer sheet. You will have enough space if you write on every line, avoid wide margins, and keep your handwriting to a reasonable size. Your essay will be read by people who are not familiar with your handwriting, so write legibly.

You may use this sheet for notes and outlining, but these will not be graded as part of your essay.

Consider carefully the issue discussed in the following passage, then write an essay that answers the question posed in the assignment.

> Some people spend their lives waiting for the one great challenge that will define them. Every society needs such people, who forge into the unknown and lay new foundations. But society also depends very much on those who meet the small challenges, like feeding mouths and minds and hearts.

Assignment: **Are we defined more by great challenges in our lives or by small, everyday challenges?** Write an essay in which you answer this question and discuss your point of view on this issue. Support your position logically with examples from literature, the arts, history, politics, science and technology, current events, or your experience or observation.

Note: Write your practice essay on two pages of standard lined paper.

Practice Essay 8

Time—25 minutes

Directions for Writing the Essay

Plan and write an essay that answers the question below. Do NOT write on another topic. An essay on another topic will receive a score of 0.

Two readers will grade your essay based on how well you develop your point of view, organize and explain your ideas, use specific and relevant examples to support your thesis, and use clear and effective language. How well you write is much more important than how much you write, but to cover the topic adequately you should plan to write several paragraphs.

Your essay must be written only on the lines provided on your answer sheet. You will have enough space if you write on every line, avoid wide margins, and keep your handwriting to a reasonable size. Your essay will be read by people who are not familiar with your handwriting, so write legibly.

You may use this sheet for notes and outlining, but these will not be graded as part of your essay.

Consider carefully the issue discussed in the following passage, then write an essay that answers the question posed in the assignment.

> Freedom requires the eradication of repression from tyrants and from want, but eliminating these is not enough. We must also eliminate the means by which we oppress ourselves, through our peeves, our addictions, and in our insecurities. This may involve strengthening the restraints within ourselves.

Assignment: **Does freedom require eliminating restraints on behavior, or does it require creating or strengthening certain restraints?** Write an essay in which you answer this question and discuss your point of view on this issue. Support your position logically with examples from literature, the arts, history, politics, science and technology, current events, or your experience or observation.

<u>Note:</u> Write your practice essay on two pages of standard lined paper.

Practice Essay 9

Time—25 minutes

Directions for Writing the Essay

Plan and write an essay that answers the question below. Do NOT write on another topic. An essay on another topic will receive a score of 0.

Two readers will grade your essay based on how well you develop your point of view, organize and explain your ideas, use specific and relevant examples to support your thesis, and use clear and effective language. How well you write is much more important than how much you write, but to cover the topic adequately you should plan to write several paragraphs.

Your essay must be written only on the lines provided on your answer sheet. You will have enough space if you write on every line, avoid wide margins, and keep your handwriting to a reasonable size. Your essay will be read by people who are not familiar with your handwriting, so write legibly.

You may use this sheet for notes and outlining, but these will not be graded as part of your essay.

Consider carefully the issue discussed in the following passage, then write an essay that answers the question posed in the assignment.

> We employ many devices to maintain or create peace among countries—trade agreements, cultural exchanges, treaties. But nothing unites humanity as well as a common foe. Mutual fear of nature or of foreign ideologies is perhaps the greatest diplomacy we know.

Assignment: **What is the most significant means of bringing people together in peace?** Write an essay in which you answer this question and discuss your point of view on this issue. Support your position logically with examples from literature, the arts, history, politics, science and technology, current events, or your experience or observation.

Note: Write your practice essay on two pages of standard lined paper.

Practice Essay 10

Time—25 minutes

Directions for Writing the Essay

Plan and write an essay that answers the question below. Do NOT write on another topic. An essay on another topic will receive a score of 0.

Two readers will grade your essay based on how well you develop your point of view, organize and explain your ideas, use specific and relevant examples to support your thesis, and use clear and effective language. How well you write is much more important than how much you write, but to cover the topic adequately you should plan to write several paragraphs.

Your essay must be written only on the lines provided on your answer sheet. You will have enough space if you write on every line, avoid wide margins, and keep your handwriting to a reasonable size. Your essay will be read by people who are not familiar with your handwriting, so write legibly.

You may use this sheet for notes and outlining, but these will not be graded as part of your essay.

Consider carefully the issue discussed in the following passage, then write an essay that answers the question posed in the assignment.

> We love best not what gives the greatest pleasure, but what comes through the greatest effort, because this effort provides meaning. A plastic medallion received after completing a marathon is not just a $2.00 trinket, but the representation of months of effort and sacrifice. The best things in life are not free, but come at the expense of hard work.

Assignment: **Do we love things most that come at a great cost, or are the best things in life truly free?** Write an essay in which you answer this question and discuss your point of view on this issue. Support your position logically with examples from literature, the arts, history, politics, science and technology, current events, or your experience or observation.

Note: Write your practice essay on two pages of standard lined paper.

Practice Essay 11

Time—25 minutes

Directions for Writing the Essay

Plan and write an essay that answers the question below. Do NOT write on another topic. An essay on another topic will receive a score of 0.

Two readers will grade your essay based on how well you develop your point of view, organize and explain your ideas, use specific and relevant examples to support your thesis, and use clear and effective language. How well you write is much more important than how much you write, but to cover the topic adequately you should plan to write several paragraphs.

Your essay must be written only on the lines provided on your answer sheet. You will have enough space if you write on every line, avoid wide margins, and keep your handwriting to a reasonable size. Your essay will be read by people who are not familiar with your handwriting, so write legibly.

You may use this sheet for notes and outlining, but these will not be graded as part of your essay.

Consider carefully the issue discussed in the following passage, then write an essay that answers the question posed in the assignment.

> Defeating an enemy by force always has profound, and usually unforeseen, consequences. Destroying another requires destroying a part of one's own humanity, and strengthening resentment in others. It is better to understand one's enemy, to learn the subtler but more ennobling art of persuasion and coexistence.

Assignment: **Is it more important to defeat your enemy or to understand your enemy?** Write an essay in which you answer this question and discuss your point of view on this issue. Support your position logically with examples from literature, the arts, history, politics, science and technology, current events, or your experience or observation.

Note: Write your practice essay on two pages of standard lined paper.

Practice Essay 12

Time—25 minutes

Directions for Writing the Essay

Plan and write an essay that answers the question below. Do NOT write on another topic. An essay on another topic will receive a score of 0.

Two readers will grade your essay based on how well you develop your point of view, organize and explain your ideas, use specific and relevant examples to support your thesis, and use clear and effective language. How well you write is much more important than how much you write, but to cover the topic adequately you should plan to write several paragraphs.

Your essay must be written only on the lines provided on your answer sheet. You will have enough space if you write on every line, avoid wide margins, and keep your handwriting to a reasonable size. Your essay will be read by people who are not familiar with your handwriting, so write legibly.

You may use this sheet for notes and outlining, but these will not be graded as part of your essay.

Consider carefully the issue discussed in the following passage, then write an essay that answers the question posed in the assignment.

> A person's greatness derives from the many small moral choices one makes moment by moment. To be born into great wealth, power, or ability is not to be great at all. Rather, greatness only comes from the continual choice to use that endowment wisely, to struggle with the needs of humanity as a member of its family.

Assignment: **Are human beings more the products of their endowments, or of their choices?** Write an essay in which you answer this question and discuss your point of view on this issue. Support your position logically with examples from literature, the arts, history, politics, science and technology, current events, or your experience or observation.

<u>Note:</u> Write your practice essay on two pages of standard lined paper.

Practice Essay 13

Time—25 minutes

Directions for Writing the Essay

Plan and write an essay that answers the question below. Do NOT write on another topic. An essay on another topic will receive a score of 0.

Two readers will grade your essay based on how well you develop your point of view, organize and explain your ideas, use specific and relevant examples to support your thesis, and use clear and effective language. How well you write is much more important than how much you write, but to cover the topic adequately you should plan to write several paragraphs.

Your essay must be written only on the lines provided on your answer sheet. You will have enough space if you write on every line, avoid wide margins, and keep your handwriting to a reasonable size. Your essay will be read by people who are not familiar with your handwriting, so write legibly.

You may use this sheet for notes and outlining, but these will not be graded as part of your essay.

Consider carefully the issue discussed in the following passage, then write an essay that answers the question posed in the assignment.

> We tend to think that rewarding people for doing good things is always better than punishing them for doing bad things. We often fail, however, to realize that rewards can be oppressive, too. Giving someone a prize for doing something he or she would do anyway often makes that person feel manipulated. What's worse, competition for prizes, which invariably occurs when rewards are doled out systematically, often breeds resentment and division rather than cooperation.

Assignment: **Are reward systems, like grades, prizes, and work bonuses, effective means of controlling human behavior?** Write an essay in which you answer this question and discuss your point of view on this issue. Support your position logically with examples from literature, the arts, history, politics, science and technology, current events, or your experience or observation.

Note: Write your practice essay on two pages of standard lined paper.

Practice Essay 14

Time—25 minutes

Directions for Writing the Essay

Plan and write an essay that answers the question below. Do NOT write on another topic. An essay on another topic will receive a score of 0.

Two readers will grade your essay based on how well you develop your point of view, organize and explain your ideas, use specific and relevant examples to support your thesis, and use clear and effective language. How well you write is much more important than how much you write, but to cover the topic adequately you should plan to write several paragraphs.

Your essay must be written only on the lines provided on your answer sheet. You will have enough space if you write on every line, avoid wide margins, and keep your handwriting to a reasonable size. Your essay will be read by people who are not familiar with your handwriting, so write legibly.

You may use this sheet for notes and outlining, but these will not be graded as part of your essay.

Consider carefully the issue discussed in the following passage, then write an essay that answers the question posed in the assignment.

> History books record the deeds of the great inventors, warriors, explorers, and artists, but the real fabric of society is determined by consumers and ordinary workers—not those who make, but those who use; not those who find, but those who settle; not those who fight, but those who repair the damage.

Assignment: **Which is more important to a society: the demands of consumers or the dreams of artists, discoverers, and inventors?** Write an essay in which you answer this question and discuss your point of view on this issue. Support your position logically with examples from literature, the arts, history, politics, science and technology, current events, or your experience or observation.

<u>Note</u>: Write your practice essay on two pages of standard lined paper.

Practice Essay 15

Time—25 minutes

Directions for Writing the Essay

Plan and write an essay that answers the question below. Do NOT write on another topic. An essay on another topic will receive a score of 0.

Two readers will grade your essay based on how well you develop your point of view, organize and explain your ideas, use specific and relevant examples to support your thesis, and use clear and effective language. How well you write is much more important than how much you write, but to cover the topic adequately you should plan to write several paragraphs.

Your essay must be written only on the lines provided on your answer sheet. You will have enough space if you write on every line, avoid wide margins, and keep your handwriting to a reasonable size. Your essay will be read by people who are not familiar with your handwriting, so write legibly.

You may use this sheet for notes and outlining, but these will not be graded as part of your essay.

Consider carefully the issue discussed in the following passage, then write an essay that answers the question posed in the assignment.

> Paradise is not to be found in a life of plenty and ease, free from all suffering. Without challenges to meet, pain to which we can compare delight, and barriers to surmount, paradise would be tedium. Give me the pain and inspiration of struggle over the perfection of your heaven.

Assignment: **Is it better to seek difficult challenges, or to seek relief from difficult challenges?** Write an essay in which you answer this question and discuss your point of view on this issue. Support your position logically with examples from literature, the arts, history, politics, science and technology, current events, or your experience or observation.

Note: Write your practice essay on two pages of standard lined paper.

Practice Essay 16

Time—25 minutes

Directions for Writing the Essay

Plan and write an essay that answers the question below. Do NOT write on another topic. An essay on another topic will receive a score of 0.

Two readers will grade your essay based on how well you develop your point of view, organize and explain your ideas, use specific and relevant examples to support your thesis, and use clear and effective language. How well you write is much more important than how much you write, but to cover the topic adequately you should plan to write several paragraphs.

Your essay must be written only on the lines provided on your answer sheet. You will have enough space if you write on every line, avoid wide margins, and keep your handwriting to a reasonable size. Your essay will be read by people who are not familiar with your handwriting, so write legibly.

You may use this sheet for notes and outlining, but these will not be graded as part of your essay.

Consider carefully the issue discussed in the following passage, then write an essay that answers the question posed in the assignment.

> Oscar Wilde once said that the only thing worse than being talked about was *not* being talked about. Today it seems we have taken this witticism to its logical extreme. Some people make their lives as "personalities" whose only job is to get their names in the media. They lack any discernible talents except self-promotion.

Assignment: **Is fame a good thing or a bad thing?** Write an essay in which you answer this question and discuss your point of view on this issue. Support your position logically with examples from literature, the arts, history, politics, science and technology, current events, or your experience or observation.

<u>Note:</u> Write your practice essay on two pages of standard lined paper.

Practice Essay 17

Time—25 minutes

Directions for Writing the Essay

Plan and write an essay that answers the question below. Do NOT write on another topic. An essay on another topic will receive a score of 0.

Two readers will grade your essay based on how well you develop your point of view, organize and explain your ideas, use specific and relevant examples to support your thesis, and use clear and effective language. How well you write is much more important than how much you write, but to cover the topic adequately you should plan to write several paragraphs.

Your essay must be written only on the lines provided on your answer sheet. You will have enough space if you write on every line, avoid wide margins, and keep your handwriting to a reasonable size. Your essay will be read by people who are not familiar with your handwriting, so write legibly.

You may use this sheet for notes and outlining, but these will not be graded as part of your essay.

Consider carefully the issue discussed in the following passage, then write an essay that answers the question posed in the assignment.

> History books are inclined to focus on power gained through military or political conquest, but power is maintained most efficiently by ideology—control over the symbols of a society and over the framework of debate. This way, popular opinion is controlled without raising popular anger or resentment.

Assignment: **How do people gain power over others?** Write an essay in which you answer this question and discuss your point of view on this issue. Support your position logically with examples from literature, the arts, history, politics, science and technology, current events, or your experience or observation.

<u>Note</u>: Write your practice essay on two pages of standard lined paper.

Practice Essay 18

Time—25 minutes

Directions for Writing the Essay

Plan and write an essay that answers the question below. Do NOT write on another topic. An essay on another topic will receive a score of 0.

Two readers will grade your essay based on how well you develop your point of view, organize and explain your ideas, use specific and relevant examples to support your thesis, and use clear and effective language. How well you write is much more important than how much you write, but to cover the topic adequately you should plan to write several paragraphs.

Your essay must be written only on the lines provided on your answer sheet. You will have enough space if you write on every line, avoid wide margins, and keep your handwriting to a reasonable size. Your essay will be read by people who are not familiar with your handwriting, so write legibly.

You may use this sheet for notes and outlining, but these will not be graded as part of your essay.

Consider carefully the issue discussed in the following passage, then write an essay that answers the question posed in the assignment.

> We can hardly become complete human beings without identifying with at least one social group—family, social clique, political party, ethnic group, nation, or religion. Yet, by distinguishing "us" from "them," these group identities are also the source of great injustices like prejudice and war.

Assignment: **Is group identity a good thing or a bad thing?** Write an essay in which you answer this question and discuss your point of view on this issue. Support your position logically with examples from literature, the arts, history, politics, science and technology, current events, or your experience or observation.

Note: Write your practice essay on two pages of standard lined paper.

Practice Essay 19

Time—25 minutes

Directions for Writing the Essay

Plan and write an essay that answers the question below. Do NOT write on another topic. An essay on another topic will receive a score of 0.

Two readers will grade your essay based on how well you develop your point of view, organize and explain your ideas, use specific and relevant examples to support your thesis, and use clear and effective language. How well you write is much more important than how much you write, but to cover the topic adequately you should plan to write several paragraphs.

Your essay must be written only on the lines provided on your answer sheet. You will have enough space if you write on every line, avoid wide margins, and keep your handwriting to a reasonable size. Your essay will be read by people who are not familiar with your handwriting, so write legibly.

You may use this sheet for notes and outlining, but these will not be graded as part of your essay.

Consider carefully the issue discussed in the following passage, then write an essay that answers the question posed in the assignment.

> I have been gravely disappointed with the . . . moderate who is more devoted to "order" than to justice; who prefers a negative peace which is the absence of tension to a positive peace which is the presence of justice . . . Shallow understanding from people of good will is more frustrating than absolute misunderstanding from people of ill will. Lukewarm acceptance is much more bewildering than outright rejection.
>
> Excerpted from Martin Luther King, Jr., *Letter from a Birmingham Jail*

Assignment: **Are there certain kinds of peace that are unacceptable?** Write an essay in which you answer this question and discuss your point of view on this issue. Support your position logically with examples from literature, the arts, history, politics, science and technology, current events, or your experience or observation.

Note: Write your practice essay on two pages of standard lined paper.

Practice Essay 20

Time—25 minutes

Directions for Writing the Essay

Plan and write an essay that answers the question below. Do NOT write on another topic. An essay on another topic will receive a score of 0.

Two readers will grade your essay based on how well you develop your point of view, organize and explain your ideas, use specific and relevant examples to support your thesis, and use clear and effective language. How well you write is much more important than how much you write, but to cover the topic adequately you should plan to write several paragraphs.

Your essay must be written only on the lines provided on your answer sheet. You will have enough space if you write on every line, avoid wide margins, and keep your handwriting to a reasonable size. Your essay will be read by people who are not familiar with your handwriting, so write legibly.

You may use this sheet for notes and outlining, but these will not be graded as part of your essay.

Consider carefully the issue discussed in the following passage, then write an essay that answers the question posed in the assignment.

> Human beings can attain a worthy and harmonious life if only they are able to rid themselves, within the limits of human nature, of the striving for the wish fulfillment of material kinds. The goal is to raise the spiritual values of society.
>
> Albert Einstein

Assignment: **Is the desire for "wish fulfillment of material kinds" a good or a bad thing?** Write an essay in which you answer this question and discuss your point of view on this issue. Support your position logically with examples from literature, the arts, history, politics, science and technology, current events, or your experience or observation.

Note: Write your practice essay on two pages of standard lined paper.

Sample Essays: Practice Essay 1

Consider carefully the issue discussed in the following passage, then write an essay that answers the question posed in the assignment.

> Without a clear goal to focus our energy and drive us to grow, we cease to be truly alive. We are inert particles floating on the sea of life. This is true of not only ourselves, but our institutions—our families, our corporations, and our societies. The moment we cease to grow, we begin to die.

Assignment: **Is growth necessary to a happy and productive life?** Write an essay in which you answer this question and discuss your point of view on this issue. You may discuss personal or institutional growth. Support your position logically with examples from literature, the arts, history, politics, science and technology, current events, or your experience or observation.

Sample 1: 6 points out of 6

Ever since the Enlightenment, Western thought has been dominated by the idea that humans are endowed with "natural rights," which include not only the right to free speech and the pursuit of happiness, but the right to dominate the natural world and even other "less civilized" societies. The growth of an individual or a society, we believe, is limited only by one's imagination. But not only is eternal growth an illusion, to pursue it is a danger.

Today, our media trumpet the benefits of "growth." A company cannot be satisfied with providing a consistent product or service over time; it must keep growing and expanding, preferably swallowing up competitors to produce more and more value for investors. A school cannot be satisfied with consistently meeting the diverse needs of its students; it must graduate a higher and higher percentage of its students, who must get higher and higher test scores, and get into better and better colleges. But such "growth" only serves the psychological needs of deluded consumers; it provides no real value. CEOs feel compelled to "cook the books" and educators likewise feel compelled to "manipulate" test scores or cheat outright so that the illusion of "growth" can be maintained.

As a society, we must learn to see that the only worthwhile growth in society is that which enhances personal growth. Better profits mean nothing unless they are from a company that helps people to experience life more fully, and not merely give them tasty snack foods or mindless entertainment to consume. Higher test scores mean nothing unless they reflect students who are better problem solvers and more empathetic and happier human beings.

Growth is not a universal good. Just because a statistic is going up doesn't mean the world is getting better. Our statistics-obsessed society has to learn to appreciate the quality of life around us more than the quantities that summarize and, sometimes, eviscerate it.

Evaluation: *Although not exceptionally long, this essay accomplishes a great deal in four paragraphs. It effectively supports the insightful thesis that "not only is eternal growth an illusion, but to pursue it is a danger." The examples of humanity's domination of nature, corporate growth, and higher test scores are very effective, although some could be examined in greater detail. The author also demonstrates a strong facility with language, using terms such as "eviscerate" and "empathetic" to good effect while maintaining a clear style throughout. It is well organized and persuasive.*

Sample 2: 5 points out of 6

My keyboard felt like a world unto itself. The ghosts of Muddy Waters and Stevie Ray Vaughan and Dave Brubeck and Gustav Mahler and, I admit it, even Raffi, were an ether that engulfed the keyboard and infused my fingers, arms and body, so that I had no choice but to play, to give a sound dimension to this world. Sometimes the music that came out was just an etude that I had practiced for Mrs. Parker years before, but sometimes, magically, it was a completely new form that seemed conjured from that ether like a genie from a bottle.

Sometimes my buddy Paul would pick up on the vibe and we'd jam for hours. Our band, the Badunks, was my whole world. But two years later, that all changed. The spark wasn't there any more between Paul and me, and as soon as we stopped growing musically, Badunk began to die.

I think about those years a lot now, and I guess it was inevitable. Paul is a smart guy and, unlike me, he was inspired by history and physics and started to groove on DBQs and equations instead of NRBQ and The Persuasions. We both got girlfriends, and you know how love isn't nearly as inspirational when it's no longer just out of reach. We just weren't able to find the time to jam together, to write together, to just talk music together. Even though Paul and I are still best friends, I feel like I've lost my real best friend—music.

I guess music is a person. You have to nurture it if you want it to stick around. If you don't give it what it needs, which is your whole commitment, your whole soul, then it begins to wither into those dried-up jingles you hear on shampoo or dog food commercials.

Evaluation: *This essay uses a consistent first-person narrative to support the point of view that, without growth, musical inspiration begins to die. It explores a single example in depth, but it does so with a clear sense of organization and a well-developed style. The author uses imagery and metaphor very effectively. Although not written in the traditional five-paragraph expository form, its overall effect is persuasive and insightful. It does not get the highest possible score because it does not discuss the concept of "growth" beyond the author's personal musical experience.*

Sample Essays: Practice Essay 2

Consider carefully the issue discussed in the following passage, then write an essay that answers the question posed in the assignment.

> Our leaders love to tell us that only victory will do, as if they are imparting great wisdom. They seek only to defeat the enemy, to achieve the goal. Yet many times a loss, particularly one that is hard fought, is more valuable than victory. We cannot live a life full of only victories, nor should we. The quality of our lives depends as much on how we manage our losses as on how we achieve our victories.

Assignment: **Can a loss ever be more valuable than a victory?** Write an essay in which you answer this question and discuss your point of view on this issue. Support your position logically with examples from literature, the arts, history, politics, science and technology, current events, or your experience or observation.

Sample 1: 6 points out of 6

My father always says, "It's not whether you win or lose, it's how you play the game." I can understand his point; playing hard and fair is its own reward. We become stronger by learning how to lose gracefully. But sometimes it *is* whether you win or lose. Sometimes, nothing but victory will do.

There are hundreds, maybe thousands, of stories of people who tried to invent flying machines. Nearly all of them are relegated to oblivion or, at best, quaint mentions in arcane history books or old film clips accompanied by a silly trombone. But we all know the Wright Brothers. They're emblazoned on every license plate in North Carolina. We know them for one reason only: they succeeded. They got a big hunk of wood and metal to fly. If their struggles led only to another hapless nose-dive off a cliff, their workshop would long ago have been forgotten and replaced by a Piggly Wiggly.

Without question, World War II was hard fought by America, as much as we tried to avoid getting involved. In the end, we lost well over a quarter of a million American lives to the struggle. Would it have been worth it had we not defeated Hitler, Mussolini and Hirohito? We could hardly claim any benefit if we had lost, and allowed hundreds of thousands of more "undesirables" to be incinerated by Hitler and his henchmen.

Sometimes, a loss, hard fought, is more valuable than an easy victory. But whether this is true depends on the worthiness of the goal. If we are true explorers, true noble warriors, true visionaries, then it is our responsibility to envision goals that are worth every sacrifice to achieve.

Evaluation: *This essay presents well-reasoned and cogent support for the view that "sometimes nothing but victory will do" although at other times "a loss, hard fought, is more valuable than an easy victory." In taking such a nuanced position, the author is obligated to articulate the distinctions between those times when victory is necessary and those when a loss can be acceptable. The author accomplishes this by discussing "the worthiness of the goal" and the fact that we can "become stronger by learning how to lose gracefully" and by giving examples of goals well worth achieving. The examples of the advent of human flight and the American victory in World War II are relevant and well presented.*

Sample 2: 5 points out of 6

I studied my hindquarters off for that test. I had two Starbucks mocha javas (don't tell my mom) to help me stay up until 2:00 am studying for the darn physics test (circular motion and gravitation—yuk) and I still got a C–! For months afterward, I swore that physics was the most ridiculous subject ever. But something about that C– really got to me. I started to wonder why some people would spend their lives studying this subject that seemed so difficult to understand.

I took it as a personal challenge. I guess I felt a lot like an athlete feels when he loses a playoff game, but knows that, if he had just worked harder, he could have won the whole championship. So I started to look into physics. I picked up a book called "Surely You're Joking, Mr. Feynman" about a Noble Prize–winning physicist and how he saw the world. I was hooked. Richard Feynman convinced me that trying to solve the great riddles of physics could be profoundly rewarding, and even fun.

It helped a great deal, too, I think, that I was now confronting physics on my own terms. I wasn't reading this book because it was assigned, but because I wanted to read it (and because my dad said it was hilarious). And I wasn't thinking about physics because I had a test to study for, but because the problems were interesting to think about.

If I had gotten an A on that physics test, instead of a C–, I probably would not have gotten mad enough to venture into the world of physics on my own. I would not have immersed myself in the relativistic twin paradox, or the question of how black holes are formed. I could have done the opposite, as my friends have done, and just shunned science for the rest of my life. I'm glad I didn't. Sometimes losing can be more valuable than victory, if losing opens new doors.

Evaluation: *This essay provides a creative first-person narrative supporting the view that "sometimes a loss, hard fought, is more valuable than an easy victory." It uses colloquial language, but with a consistent and focused point of view. The narrative remains focused on examining the author's "loss" in a particularly difficult science class and how she refocused herself as a result. Although connections to other such "losses" would have strengthened the essay, the overall effect is very strong. It does not receive the highest possible score, however, because it does not explore the general implications of its thesis, and so its conclusion is somewhat incomplete.*

Sample Essays: Practice Essay 3

Consider carefully the issue discussed in the following passage, then write an essay that answers the question posed in the assignment.

> Adventure seekers who merely crave the mitigating rush of adrenaline that accompanies risky feats do not demonstrate true courage. Courage is not fearlessness but the willingness to face our unmitigated fears and vulnerabilities, particularly those fears that make us think less of ourselves.

Assignment: **Does true courage always require putting something that is very important to us at risk?** Write an essay in which you answer this question and explain the reasons for your choice. You may choose an example from literature, the arts, history, politics, science and technology, current events, or your experience or observation.

Sample: 6 points out of 6

Real courage always involves putting something important at risk. Although we often think about what brave people have to gain, like firefighters saving the lives of others, or civil rights advocates working to gain freedoms, what makes these people courageous is not the value of what they are fighting for, but rather with the risks that they are taking with things that are very valuable to them. This can be seen in literature in the character Pip in *Great Expectations* and also in modern soldiers, who take risks that go far beyond potential bodily harm, sacrificing their own freedoms for ours.

Philip Pirrip, or Pip, the hero of *Great Expectations* by Charles Dickens, meets a wild-looking escaped prisoner on the moors and helps the prisoner by giving him food. The prisoner promises to repay Pip's kindness. After growing wealthy in the colonies, the prisoner does return under an assumed name and serves as Pip's anonymous benefactor. When Pip finds out the truth, he resolves that he will help his benefactor, now named Provis, despite the fact that Pip could be put in jail for helping a prisoner. Pip shows true courage by putting his own freedom, as well as his hard-fought position as a gentleman, on the line. It is the same persistent courage that he demonstrated in enduring for years the cruelty of Miss Havisham and the beautiful Estella, whom he finally won over decades later, and in persisting with his support of the pauper Joe Gargery.

To many people, soldiers are overused as examples of courage. Obviously, they face death or injury in battle, but they make another sacrifice we usually don't think about. They know that a strong nation needs a unified army. So when soldiers fight for their country, they must withhold their free speech and refrain from criticizing their superiors. They give up a freedom that they are fighting to maintain for us: the freedom to speak their mind.

Sometimes, when soldiers return from the battlefield they do criticize the president or the strategy of the war. But while they are in uniform, they hold their tongues for the greater good. Today many service men and women serving in Iraq have serious moral and strategic doubts about the execution of the war. But they (at least most of them) do not speak out, not because they are afraid, but because they are courageous enough to sacrifice their own right to free speech for the good of the nation, at least temporarily.

When we do something scary, like skydive out of an airplane, we risk a very tiny chance of falling to our deaths. But when we land, we realize that we have not really lost anything, and actually have gained an exhilarating experience. Real courage involves real sacrifice of something important, like your self-importance, your freedom, or your life.

Evaluation: *This excellent essay provides a persuasive argument that "real courage always involves putting something at risk" and provides two strong examples of such courage in contrast with mere "thrill seeking." The courage of Pip is described from a unique perspective, supporting the idea that he sacrificed his own self-importance for the sake of love and duty. The example of soldiers, also, provides a unique insight into a courageous sacrifice that is not frequently acknowledged. The essay is very well organized, although the transitions could be smoother. The author employs effective diction (execution, exhilarating, benefactor), with only occasional lapses into cliché (hold their tongues, greater good).*

Sample Essays: Practice Essay 4

Consider carefully the issue discussed in the following passage, then write an essay that answers the question posed in the assignment.

> Communicating technology was supposed to turn the world into a "global village," enhancing our relationships with others and our understanding of other cultures. Yet I fear it has rendered us more polarized and less articulate. Instant communication allows us to proclaim what is on our minds before we've analyzed it, substantiated it, or rendered it coherent, let alone eloquent.

Assignment: **Do modern means of communication make our society better or worse?** Write an essay in which you answer this question and explain your point of view on this issue. Support your position logically with examples from your reading, current events, or your experience or observation.

Sample: 6 points out of 6

Communication technology has made the world a "global village," enhancing our understanding of other cultures as never before. Technology has made this possible by granting instant access to a variety of international popular cultures. The internet has allowed people worldwide to sample music, read literature and peruse news items from other cultures, exposing them to artistic ideas and perspectives previously too obscure to find by chance. Before such advances in technology, cross-cultural understanding was more difficult to achieve.

As recently as the early 1990s, a college student might need to spend days in the library, or take an expensive trip, to begin to understand another culture. Not everyone had access to these resources and, as such, the gap was often too vast to bridge. Although technology has not made multi-national enlightenment universal, it has allowed millions to take a more active role in the world around them. MP3s have played a pivotal part in this transition from ignorance to semi-enlightenment. By exposing listeners to artists such as Ireland's Damien Rice, the Internet took control out of the hands of record companies, allowing consumers to decide what should be in demand. People were given insight into a world beyond their own.

We are a global village in more than just music and pop culture. The internet has greatly enhanced our understanding of people in foreign lands—their concerns, their religious views, their political status—and we have become more aware of how similar we are even though we may be thousands of miles apart. Without communication technology, many people have no access to the world outside of their own towns and, as such, have no opportunity to explore other cultures by themselves.

Because of communication technology, the world is now, literally, at our fingertips. With the proper amount of initiative and curiosity, anyone can now delve into the volumes of information available on topics previously locked away in library towers and distant cities. While the internet does not offer the personal feel of a firsthand encounter, it still manages to bring the world together and provide limitless amounts of information. Communication technology has enhanced the average understanding of the world as a whole, creating a less ignorant and provincial lifestyle for millions of people worldwide.

Evaluation: *This well-reasoned and traditionally organized essay supports the point of view that "communication technology has . . . [enhanced] our understanding of other cultures as never before." It discusses not only the issue of communication but also those of research, entertainment, social development, and political awareness. It avoids the redundancy so common to such discussions by examining the aspects and implications of its claims. The author uses vocabulary effectively and shows facility with sentence variation.*

Sample Essays: Practice Essay 5

Consider carefully the issue discussed in the following passage, then write an essay that answers the question posed in the assignment.

> Being truly human as a member of a society means seeing injustice and working to fix it. The human mind can not only perceive the immediate world and act instinctively, but also visualize a better future and endeavor to realize it.

Assignment: **What is one great injustice in the world, and how should it be addressed?** Write an essay in which you answer this question and explain the reasons for your choice. You may draw inspiration and support from literature, the arts, history, politics, science and technology, current events, or your experience or observation.

Sample: 6 points out of 6

One great injustice that has not been adequately addressed is the perception that depression is a sign of weakness. The human mind is a complex puzzle. Psychological theories, diagnoses and treatments are constantly changing and may never be fully understood. Unfortunately, people tend to dismiss theories that don't provide simple answers.

At best, psychologists can create a rough map of tendencies and patterns, connecting them as often as possible to findings in neurology and thus lending them a sense of scientific validity. Diagnosing a complex disease like depression involves examining a wide constellation of symptoms over a long period of time. This doesn't satisfy skeptics. Someone with the flu will show clear symptoms like fever, nausea, and congestion. A depressed person will have less measurable symptoms like lethargy, emotional polarity or apathy. Skeptics tend to view these as simply a lack of will. They do not understand that depression is an illness just like influenza or cancer. Someone with a tumor can't just think happy thoughts and pretend it is not there. The same can be said about clinical depression.

People suffering from depression are unfairly stigmatized. They resist seeking help and so lead lives filled with unnecessary pain. Those lucky enough to find help are often ashamed to tell their peers. Friends often misconstrue symptoms of depression as personal slights: Why didn't she call me? Why is he not fun anymore? Bonds are thus broken due to miscommunication.

Depression alters one's life at least as dramatically as more "accepted" illnesses do. People suffering from depression need others to understand the limitations depression imposes. They need to be allowed to heal. Advances in anti-depressants and mood stabilizers can help ease these adjustments, but social pressure makes it nearly impossible for the victims of depression to live in a suitable environment.

Emotional disorders are a remarkably sad facet of life. To lose control over one's emotions is to lose track of hope. A world that denies one's suffering makes this situation even worse. The key to resolving this problem is education. People of all ages need to understand how prevalent depression is and that it is not a cause for embarrassment. Hopefully, we will one day live in a world where emotional disorders will be treated with the same tolerance and compassion as "traditional" illnesses.

Evaluation: *This is a thoughtful and well-articulated essay supporting the thesis that "the perception that depression is a sign of weakness" is a great injustice. It effectively analyzes the social perception of clinical depression, clearly articulates opposing views on the matter, and explains the reasoning supporting the author's viewpoint. The author does a very good job of engaging the reader and remains focused on portraying this misperception as a great injustice, yet concludes on a hopeful note.*

Sample Essays: Practice Essay 6

Consider carefully the issue discussed in the following passage, then write an essay that answers the question posed in the assignment.

> Acquiring knowledge is like scaling a mountain. The proper attitude in reaching a summit, however, is to marvel not so much at one's achievement as at the glorious view of the unknown beyond. A well-educated person is known not so much for the questions he or she can answer as for the questions he or she can ask.

Assignment: **What is one great question that every educated person should ask?** Write an essay in which you indicate what this question should be and explain the reasons for your choice. You may draw inspiration and support from literature, the arts, history, politics, science and technology, current events, or your experience or observation.

- -

Sample: 6 points out of 6

A well-educated person is known more for the questions he or she asks than for the questions he or she can answer. One great question that I think every educated person should ask is whether the news they read and hear is based on objective facts or subjective views. Within moments, any important news story will be studied, filmed, and disseminated for an entire world to see. Televisions broadcast this information for global audiences and, instantaneously, a world opinion is formed. But does this presentation resemble more closely an objective analysis or a "spun" interpretation of an image-conscious presenter?

Most people think of "news" as the factual story of what is going on in the world. Few would say that the news is a script produced by businessmen seeking ratings and profits, although this is an uncontroversial fact that's hard to deny. Most people either accept what they see in the media as facts or cynically dismiss everything they hear as propaganda. Hiding somewhere in between these two extremes is perspective, the ability to independently judge what is factual and, from that, to create a unique and personal view.

We are continually bombarded with flashy images, scandalous revelations, and sound bites devoid of context. Journalists interpret and explain the news for us, encouraging us to sit quietly rather than think. An educated person must view this programming with a skeptical eye. Every story is tainted by subjectivity, no matter how distant the producer. The educated viewer, however, must be disciplined enough to recognize how the corporate media "spins" the news. By analyzing the differences among storytellers, the viewer can better understand what is real and what is merely opinion.

Information can be potent. Truthful information, in particular, has the power to unite or fracture, to enlighten or confirm previously held beliefs. Unfortunately, truth is slippery, easily lost in the swirling winds of global communication. Educated people must pursue the truth by asking questions and resisting the urge to accept every image flashed before them. Education teaches us to analyze situations from multiple angles whenever possible. Those who have embraced the moral value of critical thinking will apply that ideal to the world around them, treating every bit of news only as a piece of information open to debate and intense analysis.

Evaluation: *This essay provides an excellent examination of the issue of motives and professionalism in journalism to support the idea that every educated person should ask the question, "Is the news objective?" It examines common perceptions of the journalistic media and argues for "perspective" on the part of an educated observer. It is well organized and persuasive, although it could have been made more effective with a discussion of more specific examples.*

Sample Essays: Practice Essay 7

Consider carefully the issue discussed in the following passage, then write an essay that answers the question posed in the assignment.

> Some people spend their lives waiting for the one great challenge that will define them. Every society needs such people, who forge into the unknown and lay new foundations. But society also depends very much on those who meet the small challenges, like feeding mouths and minds and hearts.

Assignment: **Are we defined more by great challenges in our lives or by small, everyday challenges?** Write an essay in which you answer this question and discuss your point of view on this issue. Support your position logically with examples from literature, the arts, history, politics, science and technology, current events, or your experience or observation.

Sample: 5 points out of 6

Whether a challenge is "great" or "small" depends on your attitude and position in life. A problem that seems inconsequential to a parent might be a very important transition for the child. Regardless, I think that what defines people is how they deal with things that they themselves don't actually regard as a big deal. For instance, how a person acknowledges others or solves little everyday problems. Anyone can rise to a big occasion, but it takes a big person to rise to little occasions.

When I think of people I want to emulate, I think of a person who is defined by little challenges: my mom. There is no more considerate person in the world. Even though she is often stressed out from her job and from raising two kids, she always finds time to do something nice for someone every day. Sometimes she will bake a cake and send it over to our elderly neighbor, just because she wants an excuse to go over and say hello and because she knows how a good sweet can brighten someone's day. My mom also writes beautiful thank you notes on nice stationery after every event she attends to thank the host or hostess. She could send a quick e-mail, but she knows that the little extra effort is worth it.

When you pay attention to the little things, they can become big things. For instance, when diplomats or heads of state show kindness and respect to their counterparts, they help to solve the bigger problems like war and trade disagreements. Sometimes I am amazed when I hear a president or a prime minister speaking disrespectfully of another nation's leader. A wise leader always shows kindness and respect to other leaders, even those he or she disagrees with, because, at least, those leaders represent many other decent people. Wars and conflicts are often the result of fears that arise because leaders don't perform the common courtesies that they could use to put their opponent's minds at ease.

When I think about little everyday kindnesses, I also think about "Catcher in the Rye" by J. D. Salinger. Holden Caulfield, the protagonist, is boy who thinks that all of the adults and most of the kids around him at his prep school are "phonies," but in reality Holden is simply too immature to build meaningful relationships with others. He doesn't yet understand the importance of being kind to others, at least not until he takes his little sister to the zoo. Then he realizes that he really can care for something, and he nearly cries just watching her ride the carousel.

Holden learned that the only way to be happy is to care about something or someone, and to respect that thing or person. I wish that more people could learn that lesson, and just show a little bit of kindness to the people they meet every day.

Evaluation: *This very competent essay argues persuasively that "it takes a big person to rise to little occasions." The examples of the author's mother, world leaders, and Holden Caulfield support the author's thesis that even small actions that show consideration for others can be very important not only in resolving disputes but also in maintaining a sense of self-worth. The essay is generally well-organized and coherent, although the conclusion is underdeveloped and the example of Holden Caulfield could be more substantially explained. The author uses language competently, and varies sentence structure effectively.*

Sample Essays: Practice Essay 8

Consider carefully the issue discussed in the following passage, then write an essay that answers the question posed in the assignment.

> Freedom requires the eradication of repression from tyrants and from want, but eliminating these is not enough. We must also eliminate the means by which we oppress ourselves, through our peeves, our addictions, and in our insecurities. This may involve strengthening the restraints within ourselves.

Assignment: **Does freedom require eliminating restraints on behavior, or does it require creating or strengthening certain restraints?** Write an essay in which you answer this question and discuss your point of view on this issue. Support your position logically with examples from literature, the arts, history, politics, science and technology, current events, or your experience or observation.

Sample: 6 points out of 6

In the United States today, the issue of freedom is being discussed as a matter of both foreign and domestic policy. Should we export our freedoms and our democracy to other countries? Should we give up some of our freedoms to make sure that we are safe from terrorism? What is freedom anyway, and what is it worth? Many people who say they are patriots simply say "freedom isn't free" and leave it at that. Actually, real freedom isn't just the right to do whatever we want, and we don't get it just by conquering other people. Freedom is the ability to control our selfish instincts so that we can stop being controlled by them. Ironically, freedom requires constraints.

The reason we are trying to export democracy to Iraq today, some say, is because we will be safer if the Middle East embraces some of our values. But we can't jam our values down their throats, especially values like freedom of choice and speech. Also, we haven't shown that we are restrained enough to be worthy of those freedoms ourselves. Some mercenary contractors have shot up Iraqi civilians because they felt a slight threat. Similarly, our administration does not seem to be able to hold back from any fight because it is filled with people who need to be perceived as tough. But they aren't free because they are still controlled by their fear, and therefore they are prisoners.

In his book, "Night," Elie Wiesel talks about being in a concentration camp in Nazi Germany where he was deprived of almost all of his freedoms. He is whipped for just talking to a girl, is forced to do hard labor and sees people all around him being led to the gas chambers. It was in these horrible conditions that Elie discovered that his most important freedom was his freedom of thought that the Nazis couldn't take away from him. While his body was imprisoned, he found the freedom of his soul.

When people hold protests for freedoms, like the Civil Rights marchers in the 60's or the Women's Rights suffragettes, they are not simply trying to assert their rights. They are also trying to show that they are constrained enough to be worthy of their rights. Civil Rights marchers were well-known for their noble restraint from violence, which helped them to rise above those ignorant citizens who wanted to harm or kill them to prevent them from achieving equality. Through intelligent restraint, both the Civil Rights and the Women's Rights movements have made great strides.

We can't live in freedom if we are controlled by our selfishness and our fears of others who are different from us. Freedom isn't about conquering others, it is about conquering our own worst qualities. Because if we don't, then they will conquer us.

Evaluation: *This excellent essay provides well-reasoned and well-organized support for the thesis that "freedom is about conquering our own worst qualities." The examples of American policy in the Middle East, the Civil and Women's Rights movements, and Elie Wiesel's* Night *provide substantial support to the idea that freedom has more to do with self-control than with physical freedom or conquering one's oppressors. The author's use of language is competent and effective, despite a few slightly awkward sentences.*

Sample Essays: Practice Essay 9

Consider carefully the issue discussed in the following passage, then write an essay that answers the question posed in the assignment.

> We employ many devices to maintain or create peace among countries—trade agreements, cultural exchanges, treaties. But nothing unites humanity as well as a common foe. Mutual fear of nature or of foreign ideologies is perhaps the greatest diplomacy we know.

Assignment: **What is the most significant means of bringing people together in peace?** Write an essay in which you answer this question and discuss your point of view on this issue. Support your position logically with examples from literature, the arts, history, politics, science and technology, current events, or your experience or observation.

Sample: 5 points out of 6

Nothing unifies humanity as well as a common foe. This thought can be said to explain the triumph of the Allied forces in WWII, the French and American Revolution, and other great triumphs in western history. However, this uplifting thought has a dark corollary, because the common foe is usually another segment of humanity.

The great modern historian, T. Ruiz, at UCLA writes and lectures extensively on the middle ages. He explains western history not as a progression from barbarism to high civilization, but as a continuing series of clashes of man against man, advancing only in the increasing number of victims resulting from more powerful weaponry. In all these clashes the victors (who after all write the history of the event) see and explain their success as due to unified humanity against the common foe.

To take a sweeping view of western history after the fall of the Roman Empire, we see a European Society for hundreds of years without borders, without governments, without kings, without commerce, without land ownership, somewhat of an empty slate by modern political and economic terms. As the world changed from a medieval world to a modern world, we can observe some changes which came about by the unification against a common foe. The rise of the nation state was made possible by the emergence of the "king" who united his subjects by invention of a common foe (e.g. "France"). Witchcraft, antisemitism and other concepts of "otherness," can be argued to be offshoots of the movement toward nation states. And these evils are caused by the invention of a common foe.

The nation state, antisemitism, witchcraft all came about as inventions of the modern era. The Crusades, to expel the Arabs from Europe, the fallout from which we are still experiencing, is perhaps nothing but a political example of the successful search for a common enemy. Political, of course, because they occurred in the era when the king realized that religion was too important to be left to the Pope.

As history marches on, we have the modern success of genocide as the ultimate success possible from the unification against the common enemy. The lesson perhaps is that when humanity unifies against a common enemy, make sure you're not the enemy.

Evaluation: *This essay effectively argues for the perspective that "nothing unifies humanity as well as a common foe." The author demonstrates a solid understanding of Europe after the fall of the Roman Empire and gives many examples of "common foes." The author shows a strong facility with language and uses appropriate historical vocabulary. The essay does not receive the highest possible score, however, because it focuses too much on conflict rather than peace, as the question suggests.*

Sample Essays: Practice Essay 10

Consider carefully the issue discussed in the following passage, then write an essay that answers the question posed in the assignment.

> We love best not what gives the greatest pleasure, but what comes through the greatest effort, because this effort provides meaning. A plastic medallion received after completing a marathon is not just a $2.00 trinket, but the representation of months of effort and sacrifice. The best things in life are not free, but come at the expense of hard work.

Assignment: **Do we love things most that come at a great cost, or are the best things in life truly free?** Write an essay in which you answer this question and discuss your point of view on this issue. Support your position logically with examples from literature, the arts, history, politics, science and technology, current events, or your experience or observation.

Sample: 4 points out of 6

We love best not that which gives great pleasure, but what comes through great effort. What do we mean by "love"? For one may love one's mother, chocolate and fine art, all in different ways and all of which usually come with little effort. But perhaps love means "value," as in one loves freedom and one loves life. It is often observed that those who have had to fight for freedom love it more, and those who have recovered from near death accidents or disease have a greater love of freedom and life.

It is an American phenomenon that freedoms are valued so highly because so many Americans have suffered religious or political persecution and suffered great hardship to escape to this country. However, there are many things one loves which are not achieved through great effort, and there are many things achieved through great effort that one comes to hate. The Rubaiyat of Omar Khayyam expresses a way to achieve love, contentment and happiness without effort. It suggests the less effort the better. John Ruskin said, "Life without work is guilt, life without art is brutality," suggesting that effort and love are two separate things.

The Calvinists, and the Protestant ethic, suggest that the only thing worth achieving is achieved through hard work. Or perhaps, they suggest that hard work in itself gives satisfaction. Although something achieved through effort is valued (loved) more highly than the same thing received as a gift, many things are loved intensely without regard to the effort expended.

Although some have discarded the Cartesian duality of mind and body, perhaps it is a real separation. Great effort satisfies the body primarily. The body loves to work. Love, on the other hand, satisfies the mind or the soul.

As Ruskin suggests, if I work hard to achieve a pot of gold, I may find love of riches does not satisfy, but if I work hard to create a work of art, and craft a beautiful shaped and molded chair, I may find that I love this chair more than any other in the world.

Evaluation: *This essay presents a thoughtful point of view but fails to take a clear stance on whether what we love most are things that are free or that come at a great cost. It goes back and forth so often that the reader feels as if she is watching a tennis match. Still, there are things that the author does well, such as discussing intriguing examples of Calvinism and freedom and citing interesting authorities such as Omar Khayam and John Ruskin. The author demonstrates a good facility with language but does not adequately focus the essay to achieve one of the highest scores.*

CHAPTER 14

HOW TO ATTACK SAT WRITING QUESTIONS

Lesson 1:
Mapping: What Do the Writing Questions Want from You?

The Writing portion of the SAT consists of the 25-minute essay and two multiple-choice grammar sections. The grammar questions ask you to spot and correct basic grammar and usage errors such as subject-verb disagreement (as in *There is (are) more than thirty students in the class*), pronoun-antecedent disagreement (as in *The club requires their (its) members to pay dues*), weak parallelism (as in *She likes to hike, fish, and enjoys cooking (cook)*), tense problems (as in *The store changed (has changed) ownership several times over the last decade*), and so on. All these errors are discussed in much more detail in Chapter 15.

Don't worry—here are three pieces of really good news about the SAT Writing:

1. You don't have to memorize hundreds of grammar rules to ace the SAT Writing, just the 15 basic ideas discussed in Chapter 15. Not so bad, right?
2. You don't have to name a single grammar rule. You just have to notice mistakes and fix them. Of course, if you keep making mistakes because your "ear" doesn't catch them, you should learn the rules in Chapter 15 so that you can spot mistakes more easily. However, the SAT itself won't require you to label a mistake as, for instance, a "dangling participle."
3. You don't have to worry about those "grammar rules from nowhere" that your middle-school English teacher might have gotten hung up on, such as the ones listed below.

Five So-Called "Rules" NOT to Worry About on the SAT Writing

1. **Never start a sentence with *because*.** Although about 95% of all middle school students have been told this by one or another of their English teachers, guess what? It's not a rule! As long as every other part of the sentence is okay, it's perfectly fine to start a sentence with *because*, even on the SAT Writing.

2. **Use *which* only for noninclusive modifiers and *that* only for inclusive modifiers.** If you actually know this rule, God bless you. You know more than most English teachers. The simple fact is that the SAT folks don't give a flying prune whether or not you know your *that* from your *which*. The SAT Writing sentences will always use *that* and *which* correctly. Don't waste time worrying about them.

3. **Only use *whom* rather than *who* when the objective case is required.** Again, if you know this rule, props to you. The fact is that the whole issue of *who* versus *whom* is a bit tricky even for folks who spend their whole lives talking about grammar. It's not quite as clear cut as the *him* versus *he* rule. The SAT Writing sentences will always use *who* and *whom* correctly. Don't waste time worrying about them.

4. **The disappearing *thats*.** Don't worry about *thats*. Some students see a sentence such as "The boys found the soccer ball they had lost" and want to stick a *that* in it: The boys found the soccer ball *that* they had lost. Basically, it's okay either way. Don't spend any time worrying about missing *thats*.

5. **Don't split infinitives.** The SAT hasn't included a split infinitive in decades, and it's unlikely to start now. Infinitives are the basic forms of verbs with *to*, such as *to run* and *to be*. They are split whenever someone sticks a modifier between the two words. The classic example is the old *Star Trek* prologue where Captain Kirk says that his mission is "*to boldly go* where no man has gone before." Split infinitives drive some English teachers crazy, but the SAT is cool about them.

Lesson 2:
Attacking "Improving Sentences" Questions

Mapping: What are "Improving Sentences" Questions?

Every SAT Writing section begins with "improving sentences" questions, each of which gives you a sentence and asks you to figure out whether an underlined portion has an error in grammar, usage, or awkwardness. If it does, you must choose the best correction from the choices. If the sentence is okay, choose (A), which leaves the sentence as it is.

The children <u>couldn't hardly believe their eyes</u>.

(A) couldn't hardly believe their eyes
(B) would not hardly believe their eyes
(C) could hardly believe their eyes
(D) couldn't nearly believe their eyes
(E) could hardly believe his or her eyes

The original sentence contains a double negative, *couldn't hardly*. The right answer has to fix this mistake without breaking any other rules of grammar. Choices (C) and (E) both fix the double negative, but choice (E) introduces a new problem: *His or her* is a singular phrase, but the noun it refers to, *children*, is plural. Therefore, the correct answer is (C).

> "Improving sentences" questions require you to *fix* grammatical mistakes rather than merely *find* them. So the best way to attack them is to *look actively for errors and correct them* before looking at the choices.

The College Hill Method for Attacking "Improving Sentences" Questions

1. Read the *entire* sentence naturally. If you have a good grammar "ear," let it tell you if anything in the underlined part sounds wrong. Don't overanalyze the sentence when you first read it. If you have read a lot of well-written prose, you will have developed a good "ear" for grammatical mistakes. Trust it. If you haven't read much good prose, your ear won't help as much, so you'll have to really memorize the rules in Chapter 15 (and start reading good books *now*).
2. If the underlined part has an obvious error, try to fix it so that you have a good idea of what to look for among the choices. Then eliminate choice (A) as well as any other choices that repeat the same error. Remember—the error must violate one of the grammar rules discussed in Chapter 15.

3. If the underlined portion does NOT contain an error, be inclined to choose (A), but test any choices that are *shorter* than (A) to see if they convey the idea as clearly as the original. If you find a shorter option that is just as clear and logical as the original, choose the shorter one.
4. Reread the sentence with your choice, and make sure that the sentence works as a whole and that it does not contain any other errors. Remember that a sentence may have more than one mistake that needs to be fixed!

Check: Only Worry About the "Standard" Errors Listed in Chapter 15

> When your ear catches a possible error, take one more step to check it. Make sure that any error is a "standard" error in grammar or usage and not just a matter of personal preference. Don't assume that a sentence contains an error just because you might have phrased it differently. Instead, try to identify the error as a violation of one of the "standard" errors discussed in Chapter 15.

The captains were given awards despite the team's loss, <u>for they had sacrificed a great deal for the sake of the team</u>.

(A) for they had sacrificed a great deal for the sake of the team
(B) in the sense of sacrificing a great deal for the sake of the team
(C) but had sacrificed a great deal for the sake of the team
(D) their sacrifice for the sake of the team being the reason for them
(E) nevertheless, they sacrificed a great deal for the sake of the team

The original sentence may sound a bit odd, so you may think that it has an error. But after you read the choices, it should be clear that no other choice is clearer or more logical. In fact, the original sentence is best. It sounds odd because it uses the word *for* in a slightly strange (but acceptable) way. Although *for* is usually used as a preposition, it is here used as a conjunction similar to *because* or *since*.

Consider Alternatives: There Are Often Several Ways to Fix a Mistake, So Be Flexible

The coaches weren't as interested in winning games during <u>spring training, they considered it</u> as an opportunity to experiment with different permutations of players.

(A) spring training, they considered it
(B) spring training; but they considered it
(C) spring training, but
(D) spring training as they were in using it
(E) spring training they were in using it

You might notice that the original sentence is a "run on" (see Chapter 15, Lesson 15) because it joins two independent clauses with only a comma. Usually, run-ons can be fixed by replacing the comma with a semicolon, colon, or conjunction. So you might go through the choices and eliminate those that also don't contain a semicolon, colon, or conjunction, leaving you with (B) and (C), but these don't work. Choice (B) incorrectly combines the semicolon and the conjunction, and choice (C) is illogical. Choice (D) is the correct answer because it is the only one that logically completes the *as* comparison.

Simplify and Check: All Else Being Equal, Shorter Is Better

> If you've developed a good ear by reading a lot of good prose, trust it. If a sentence sounds okay, it probably is, and you should be inclined to choose (A). But some writing problems are hard to identify. For instance, some needlessly wordy phrases don't sound so bad at first. Even if a sentence sounds okay, always read any choices that are *shorter* than the original. If a choice says the same thing in fewer words, it's probably better.

Several reviewers suggested that the article was not only frequently inaccurate, <u>but additionally it was needlessly obtuse and, ultimately, it was insubstantial</u>.

(A) but additionally it was needlessly obtuse and, ultimately, it was insubstantial
(B) but it was also needlessly obtuse and it was ultimately also insubstantial
(C) but they also commented on the needless obtuseness and also the ultimate insubstantiality
(D) although it was also needlessly obtuse and ultimately insubstantial
(E) but also needlessly obtuse and ultimately insubstantial

What's wrong with the original sentence? You might have a tough time identifying the grammatical problem, but notice that it is wordy and awkward. Don't pick (A) immediately just because no mistake jumps out. Notice that (B), (D), and (E) are more concise than the original. The most concise is (E), which is the correct answer. (In fact, the grammatical problem is *weak parallelism*, which is discussed in Chapter 15, Lesson 3.)

Check: Check for Dangling Modifiers

Every "improving sentences" section is likely to have one or more *dangling modifier* questions (Chapter 15, Lessons 7 and 8). Make sure that you know how to handle them by applying this simple rule:

> Any modifying phrase must be as close as possible to the word it modifies.

<u>Chosen from the best players from around the county</u>, the coaches found the recruits to be very easy to work with.

(A) Chosen from the best players from around the county
(B) Being chosen from the best players from throughout the county
(C) Having chosen the best players from around the county
(D) Being the best players from throughout the entire county
(E) The best players having been chosen by them from throughout the county

The underlined phrase is a participial phrase based on the participle *chosen*. *Who* was chosen? The *recruits*, not the *coaches*. Since *coaches* is closer to the modifying phrase than *recruits* is, the modifier is misplaced (see Chapter 15, Lessons 7 and 8). Notice that choice (C) changes the participle from *chosen* to *having chosen* so that it modifies *coaches*, the noun that follows. This choice makes it clear that the *coaches* have chosen the best players.

Analyze: Inspect the Sentence for "Extra" Problems

> Remember that the sentence may have more than one problem. Always reread the sentence with your choice to make sure that there are no "extra" problems.

The entire editorial staff worked <u>diligent for completing</u> the article in time for the midnight deadline.

(A) diligent for completing
(B) diligent in order to complete
(C) diligently for completing
(D) diligent to complete
(E) diligently to complete

The most obvious problem is that *diligent*, an adjective, should be changed to *diligently*, an adverb, because it modifies the verb *worked*. But don't jump right to choice (C) because the sentence also contains an error in *idiom* (Chapter 15, Lesson 10). The correct answer is (E) because it corrects both the modifier problem and the idiom problem.

SAT Practice 2:
Attacking "Improving Sentences" Questions

Each of the sentences below contains one underlined portion. The portion may contain one or more errors in grammar, usage, construction, precision, diction (choice of words), or idiom. Some of the sentences are correct.

Consider the meaning of the original sentence, and choose the answer that best expresses that meaning. If the original sentence is best, choose (A), because it repeats the original phrasing. Choose the phrasing that creates the clearest, most precise, and most effective sentence.

EXAMPLE: EXAMPLE ANSWER:

The children couldn't hardly believe their eyes.   (C)

(A) couldn't hardly believe their eyes
(B) would not hardly believe their eyes
(C) could hardly believe their eyes
(D) couldn't nearly believe their eyes
(E) couldn't hardly believe his or her eyes

1. Being highly efficient and with plentiful fuel, physicists consider nuclear fusion to represent a profoundly promising source of energy.

(A) Being highly efficient and with plentiful fuel, physicists consider nuclear fusion to represent
(B) Being so efficient and its sources so plentiful, physicists consider nuclear fusion to be
(C) Because nuclear fusion is so efficient and its fuel so plentiful, physicists consider it to be
(D) Being an efficient and plentiful energy source, nuclear fusion is what physicists considered as being
(E) For an energy source that physicists consider efficient and plentiful, nuclear fusion is

2. Committed to improving student achievement, the use of standardized tests in the elementary grades by the administration has increased dramatically.

(A) the use of standardized tests in the elementary grades by the administration has increased dramatically
(B) standardized tests have been used by the administration increasingly in the elementary grades
(C) the administration has used standardized tests increasingly in the elementary grades
(D) the use of standardized tests by the administration has increased dramatically in the elementary grades
(E) the administration have used more standardized tests in the elementary grades

3. More and more athletes are turning to yoga as a means of increasing flexibility, refining balance, to control their energy, and they can use it to enhance their awareness of their bodies.

(A) increasing flexibility, refining balance, to control their energy, and they can use it to enhance their awareness of their bodies
(B) increasing their flexibility, refining their balance, controlling their energy, and enhancing their body awareness
(C) increasing one's flexibility, balance, energy, and body awareness
(D) to increase flexibility, to refine balance, to control energy and the enhancement of the awareness of one's body
(E) increasing the flexibility and the balance and controlling the energy and the awareness of the body

4. Many of the rights granted by the Constitution were not regarded by the founding fathers as self-evident at all, but rather the subject of often vicious debate.

(A) as self-evident at all, but rather
(B) so much as self-evident at all as they were more
(C) so self-evidently as they were
(D) as self-evident as
(E) as being self-evident, but nevertheless were

Answer Key 2:
Attacking "Improving Sentences" Questions

1. **C** The original sentence is awkward and contains a dangling participle (Chapter 15, Lesson 7). *Being* is the participle, but the noun that it modifies does not follow the participial phrase. Furthermore, the logic of the sentence is unclear. Choice (C) shows the essential cause-and-effect relationship.

2. **C** The original sentence contains a *dangling participle* (Chapter 15, Lesson 7). *Committed* is the participle, and the participial phrase must be followed by the noun it modifies. *Who is committed?* Certainly not *the use of standardized tests,* but rather *the administration.* Notice that choice (E) is incorrect because it contains subject-verb disagreement (Chapter 15, Lesson 1).

3. **B** The original sentence violates the Law of Parallelism (Chapter 15, Lesson 3). In a list, all items should, as far as possible, have the same grammatical form. Choice (C) is parallel and concise, but it changes the meaning of the sentence from the original, and uses the pronoun *one's* inappropriately.

4. **A** The original sentence is best.

Lesson 3:
Attacking "Error ID" Questions

Mapping: What Are "Error ID" Questions?

The next questions on the SAT Writing are the "error ID" questions, which give you a sentence with four underlined parts and ask you whether any of the underlined parts contains a mistake. If one of them does, simply choose the underlined portion that contains the mistake. If the sentence is okay, choose (E).

> Any sentence error must be fixable by replacing *only* the underlined portion. Every other part must remain unchanged, and no parts can be *moved*. If you think that a word or phrase should be moved to another part of the sentence, you're wrong.

The team <u>diligently</u> practiced and <u>prepared</u> a clever
      A   B
game plan, but <u>they</u> never got the opportunity to use
           C
the <u>most ingenious plays</u> in the game. <u>No error</u>
     D   E

You might prefer to say that the team *practiced diligently* rather than that the team *diligently practiced*, but, choosing (A) would be incorrect because this "correction" would involve moving a word to a nonunderlined part of the sentence rather than just replacing it. Remember, *every other part of the sentence must remain unchanged*. In fact, either phrasing is fine: The adverb can come before or after the verb. There is a grammatical mistake here, though—do you see it? The definite pronoun *they* is plural, but its antecedent is *team*, which is singular. So choice (C) is the correct response, and should be replaced by *it*.

Analyze but Don't Overanalyze: Listen for the Clunker

> Attack each "error ID" question by *first reading the whole sentence normally and listening for the "clunker."* Don't overanalyze each underlined part just yet—just trust your ear for now. If your ear is well trained, then when something sounds bad, it probably is. As the questions get tougher, your ear may get less reliable, but it should get you through a lot of the easier questions. For the tougher ones, you'll really need to know the rules in Chapter 15.

Check That It's a Real Mistake

> If something sounds bad, make sure that the error is *completely underlined*. (If it's not, then it's not really an error.) Next, think about how the error could be fixed. If you just want to replace a word or phrase with something that means the same thing—such as replacing *put* with *placed*—it's not really an error, just a matter of preference. If you know the grammar rules in Chapter 15, do your best to identify the violation. If you can identify it, you'll be sure you're right.

<u>Had the speeches been</u> any longer, the assembly
        A
<u>would have needed to be</u> extended <u>into</u> the next
         B   C
<u>class period</u>. <u>No error</u>
    D   E

The first phrase, *Had the speeches been,* may sound strange to your ear. You may prefer to say *If the speeches had been. . . .* But both phrases are fine; the original doesn't violate any rule of grammar. Similarly, instead of *would have needed to be,* you might prefer to say *would have had to be.* But this, again, is just a matter of preference. The original does not violate any grammatical rule. *Every grammatical rule that you need to know for the SAT is discussed in detail in Chapter 15.* For this question, the correct response is (E), no error.

Alternative Mode of Attack: The Process of Elimination

What if your ear doesn't catch a mistake? The sentence could be correct, or perhaps it contains a subtle error. In these cases, most students feel more confident working by process of elimination. Cross out any underlined parts that are clearly okay. If you can get it down to just two choices, it's better to guess than to leave it blank.

Alternative Mode of Attack: The Systematic Approach

If you're not sure whether a sentence has an error, you might want to take a systematic approach. Until you get very good at it, this strategy is a bit more time consuming and requires that you really know the grammar rules discussed in Chapter 15, so it's best to save it for the tougher questions. With this strategy, you look at each underlined part, check whether it contains a *verb*, *pronoun*, *preposition*, or *modifier*, and decide whether it is part of a *list* or *comparison*.

If it contains a verb:

- Does it agree with its subject in person and number? If not, it contains *subject-verb disagreement* (Chapter 15, Lessons 1 and 2).
- Does it convey the right *time* or *extent*? If not, it contains a *tense error* (Chapter 15, Lesson 9).
- Does it properly convey *doubt* or *factuality*? If not, it contains an *error in mood* (Chapter 15, Lesson 14).
- If it's a past participle, is it in the correct form? If not, it is an *irregular verb error* (Chapter 15, Lesson 13).

If it contains a pronoun:

- Is it clear what the pronoun refers to? If not, it has an *unclear antecedent* (Chapter 15, Lesson 5).
- Does it agree in number and person with the noun it replaces? If not, it contains a *pronoun-antecedent disagreement* (Chapter 15, Lesson 5).
- Is it in the proper case, that is, subjective (*I, he, she, we, they*), objective (*me, him, her, us, them*), or possessive (*my, your, his, her, our, their*)? If not, it contains a *case error* (Chapter 15, Lesson 6).

If it contains a preposition:

- Does the preposition "go with" the word or phrase it is near? If not, it contains an *idiom error* (Chapter 15, Lesson 10).

If it contains an adjective or adverb:

- Is it near the word it modifies? If not, it is a *misplaced or dangling modifier* (Chapter 15, Lessons 6, 7, and 8).
- Is it in the correct form? If not, it is probably an *adverb-adjective error* or *comparative form error* (Chapter 15, Lesson 12).
- Does it add meaning to the sentence? If not, it is a *redundancy* (Chapter 15, Lesson 12).

If it is part of a comparison:

- Are the things being compared of the same kind? If not, it is an *illogical comparison* (Chapter 15, Lesson 4).
- Does it properly convey whether two or more than two items are being compared? If not, it is a comparison *number error* (Chapter 15, Lesson 4).
- Does it use *fewer/less*, *number/amount*, or *many/much* correctly? If not, it contains a *countability error* (Chapter 15, Lesson 4).
- Are the things being compared in the same grammatical form? If not, it contains a *parallelism error* (Chapter 15, Lesson 3).

If it is part of a list:

- Does it have the same form as the other item(s) in the list? If not, it contains a *parallelism error* (Chapter 15, Lesson 3).

If a word seems misspelled or unusual:

- Does the word have the right meaning for this context? If not, it is a *diction error* (Chapter 15, Lesson 11).

Check: Don't Fear Perfection

Don't be afraid to pick (E) "No error" if a sentence seems okay, but don't go overboard, either. On recent SATs, there have been anywhere from 2 to 7 "No errors" among the 18 "error ID" questions. The ETS tries to distribute the five answer choices (A-E) evenly in the answer key, so choice (E) should be right about one-fifth of the time, on an average.

SAT Practice 3: Attacking "Error ID" Questions

The following sentences may contain errors in grammar, usage, diction (choice of words), or idiom. Some of the sentences are correct. No sentence contains more than one error.

If the sentence contains an error, it is underlined and lettered. The parts that are not underlined are correct.

If there is an error, select the part that must be changed to correct the sentence.

If there is no error, choose (E).

EXAMPLE: EXAMPLE ANSWER:

By the time <u>they reached</u> the halfway point
                        A   (D)

<u>in the race</u>, most <u>of the runners</u> <u>hadn't hardly</u>
        B   C   D

begun to hit their stride.   <u>No error</u>
                                                    E

---

1. The abundance <u>of</u> recent <u>business failures</u>
                              A   B

    <u>have intimidated</u> many <u>prospective</u>
              C   D

    entrepreneurs.   <u>No error</u>
                                    E

2. When scientists <u>theorize</u> about the traits that
                                  A

    all humans have come to share, they must be

    keenly aware <u>of the fact</u> that these traits
                            B

    <u>are evolving</u> over <u>thousands of generations</u>.
              C   D

    <u>No error</u>
        E

3. The entire industry has steadfastly maintained

    <u>their</u> position <u>that</u> tobacco <u>is not addictive</u>
        A   B   C

    and that smoking <u>is an inalienable right</u>
                                      D

    of consumers.   <u>No error</u>
                                    E

4. <u>In bestowing</u> the award, the critics' guild
          A

    praised the head writer, <u>saying that</u> her writing
                                          B

    for the television series continued to be

    consistently more <u>intelligent and provocative</u>
                                        C

    than <u>anything on the air</u>.   <u>No error</u>
                    D   E

5. The <u>challenge</u> of Everest, its conquerors claim,
              A

    is far more the <u>lack of oxygen</u> at its rarefied
                              B

    heights <u>than even</u> the <u>precarious</u> ice falls or
                      C   D

    precipitous ascents.   <u>No error</u>
                                        E

6. Those who talk more <u>respectful</u>
                                        A

    <u>to their employers</u> are <u>more likely</u> to have their
              B   C

    <u>grievances</u> addressed.   <u>No error</u>
          D   E

Answer Key 3:
Attacking "Error ID" Questions

1. **C** The subject is *abundance*, which is singular, so the verb should be *has intimidated* (Chapter 15, Lesson 1).

2. **C** The phrase *over thousands of generations* indicates that the evolution occurred over an extended time in the past. This means that the verb should be in the **present perfect** form: *have evolved* (Chapter 15, Lesson 9).

3. **A** *Their* is a plural pronoun, but it refers to *industry*, which is singular, so the pronoun should be *its* (Chapter 15, Lesson 5).

4. **D** Since the sentence indicates that the show *continued to be*, it must have been still on the air. Since it could not be better written than itself, choice (D) should be replaced by *anything else on the air* (Chapter 15, Lesson 9).

5. **E** The sentence is correct.

6. **A** This word is modifying the verb *talk*, so it should be in the form of an *adverb: respectfully* (Chapter 15, Lesson 12).

Lesson 4:
Attacking "Improving Paragraphs" Questions

Mapping: What Are "Improving Paragraphs" Questions?

The last type of question on the SAT Writing is the "improving paragraphs" question. "Improving paragraphs" questions give you a draft of a short essay that needs revision. You are then asked questions about how to improve it.

How to Attack "Improving Paragraphs" Questions

> You can answer many "improving paragraphs" questions without even reading the passage, and you may want to answer those "isolated sentences" questions first. Some of the questions, however, require you to understand the general purpose of the passage and the individual paragraphs. These questions often contain the phrase *in context* or ask you to insert, remove, or combine sentences to make the passage clearer, more concise, or more coherent. Before answering these questions, you may want to read quickly through the passage to get the general purpose and central idea.

"Isolated Sentence" Questions

Some "improving paragraphs" questions are very much like "improving sentences" questions. These questions don't contain the words *in context* and just ask you to improve a single sentence in isolation. These "isolated sentence" questions may differ from "improving sentences" questions only in that there may not be a "no error" choice.

Which of the following is the best way to revise sentence 7 (reproduced below)?

If the students would of known in advance about the shortage, they could have prevented the crisis.

(A) If the students would have known in advance
(B) It being that the students might have known in advance
(C) If the students had known in advance
(D) Being known in advance
(E) If it had been that the students knew in advance

In this case the correct choice is (C) because it is the only one in standard subjunctive form.

"Sentence in Context" Questions

"Sentence in context" questions usually contain the phrase *in context*. They ask you to improve sentences by taking the previous sentences into account. Often the given sentences contain *pronouns* (such as *it* or *they*) that refer to things in previous sentences or *transitional adverbs* (such as *therefore, yet, nonetheless, although,* or *furthermore*) that serve as logical connections among ideas.

> When answering "sentence in context" questions, always read the previous sentence or two before thinking about how to improve the given sentence. In the given sentence, pay special attention to pronouns (such as *it* or *they*) and transitional adverbs (such as *therefore, yet, nonetheless, although,* or *furthermore*), and notice how they relate to ideas in the previous sentences.

In context, which of the following is the best version of sentence 12 (reproduced below)?

The racers were shivering as the race began.

(A) (As it is now)
(B) Nevertheless, the racers were shivering
(C) Furthermore, the racers were shivering
(D) Therefore, the racers were shivering
(E) All the while, the racers were shivering

Since the question contains the phrase *in context*, the correct answer depends on what immediately precedes sentence 12 in the passage. For instance, if the previous sentence were *The race organizers had arranged for large, powerful heaters to be placed at the starting line*, then (B) would provide the most logical transition. If, however, the previous sentence were *The temperature had plummeted 20 degrees in the hours before the race was to start*, then (D) would make the most sense.

"Insert, Remove, or Combine" Questions

Some "improving paragraphs" questions ask you to consider inserting, removing, or combining sentences to make the passage clearer, more concise, or more coherent. They ask questions such as *Where is the most logical place to insert the following sentence?* Or *Which of the following is the best sentence to insert after sentence 4?*

> When answering "insert, remove, or combine" questions, remember that every sentence in a paragraph must support the same central idea. If a sentence doesn't follow the flow, it has to go.

SAT Practice 4:
Attacking "Improving Paragraphs" Questions

Below is a draft of an essay that needs improvement. Some sentences may contain grammatical errors, and the paragraphs may need to be altered to improve their logic, clarity, and cohesiveness. Read the passage and answer the questions that follow.

(1) John D. Rockefeller, Jr., was born in 1854 as the only son of America's richest man and first billionaire. (2) Intensely shy as a child and young man, he came out of his shell at Brown University, where he was elected president of the junior class and senior manager of the football team. (3) After graduating from Brown, John had the opportunity to follow his father into the oil business and add to the family fortune. (4) He soon discovered that wealth, rather than being something to hoard, was "an instrumentality of constructive social living." (5) Because of the hard-nosed business practices of John's father, John D. Rockefeller, Sr., the name Rockefeller had become synonymous with greed and trade-busting. (6) The younger John decided that he could make this better.

(7) Perhaps no American has ever done more in the area of philanthropy than John D. Rockefeller, Jr. (8) He created charitable foundations like the Rockefeller Foundation, the Rockefeller Institute, and the General Education Board. (9) He sponsored the construction of Rockefeller Center in New York City, financed the reconstruction of Colonial Williamsburg, which stands to this day as an invaluable historical treasure, and donated the land in New York City for the United Nations complex.

(10) The scope of Rockefeller's conservation efforts, also, was profound. (11) He donated thousands of acres of land to national parks like Acadia, Shenandoah, the Great Smoky Mountains, and the Grand Tetons. (12) He also financed the construction of museums in Yellowstone, the Grand Canyon, and Mesa Verde.

(13) John D. Rockefeller, Jr., is considered the father of philanthropy in the United States never before or since has any one person made such an impact on public institutions. (14) Although always willing to support a good cause, Rockefeller never sought accolades for himself. (15) He was offered dozens of honorary degrees from prestigious universities, and declined all but one, from his alma mater.

1. In context, which of the following is the best revision of the underlined portion of sentence 4 (reproduced below)?

   He soon discovered that wealth, rather than being something to hoard, was "an instrumentality of constructive social living."

   (A) However, he soon discovered
   (B) Furthermore, he soon discovered
   (C) He would only have soon discovered
   (D) Therefore, he soon discovered
   (E) When he soon discovered

2. Where is the most logical place to insert the following sentence?

   John's discovery of philanthropy could hardly have come at a better time for the Rockefellers.

   (A) After sentence 1
   (B) After sentence 3
   (C) After sentence 4
   (D) Before sentence 7, to begin the second paragraph
   (E) After sentence 8

3. Which of the following revisions of sentence 6 (reproduced below) best improves its clarity in the context of the first paragraph?

   The younger John decided that he could make this better.

   (A) The younger John, the son of John D. Rockefeller, Sr., decided that he could make this better.
   (B) The younger John decided that he could restore the prestige of his family name.
   (C) The younger John, who was affectionately called "Johnny D," decided that he could make this better.
   (D) This was something that the younger John himself thought he could improve greatly.
   (E) But this was something that young John knew he could do something about the problem of his family honor.

Answer Key 4:
Attacking "Improving Paragraphs" Questions

1. **A** Sentence 3 indicates that John could have added to the family fortune. Sentence 4 indicates that he did not, but rather used the money for philanthropic purposes. This contrast of ideas should be accompanied by a contrasting transition, as provided by the word *however*.

2. **C** Because sentence 4 introduces John's "discovery of philanthropy," and because sentence 5 explains why it "could hardly have come at a better time," the sentence belongs most logically between sentence 4 and sentence 5.

3. **B** The original sentence is unclear because the word *this* does not have a clear antecedent; that is, it is unclear what *this* refers to. A reader could probably figure out that it refers to the problem with the Rockefeller reputation, discussed in the previous sentence, but sentence 5 does not actually contain the words *the problem with the Rockefeller reputation*, so the reference is unclear. Choice (B) is the only sentence that clarifies that reference.

CHAPTER 15

ESSENTIAL GRAMMAR SKILLS

1. Subject-Verb Disagreement

2. Trimming Sentences

3. Parallelism

4. Comparison Problems

5. Pronoun-Antecedent Disagreement

6. Pronoun Case

7. Dangling and Misplaced Participles

8. Other Misplaced Modifiers

9. Tricky Tenses

10. Idiom Errors

11. Diction Errors

12. Other Modifier Problems

13. Irregular Verbs

14. The Subjunctive Mood

15. Coordinating Ideas

Lesson 1: Subject-Verb Disagreement

Finding Verbs

The verb is the most important part of a sentence, but verbs aren't always easy to spot. Consider the word *swim* in the sentences *The ducks swim in the pond* and *The ducks love to swim*. In the first sentence, *swim* is the verb. In the second sentence, *swim* is part of a noun phrase. (*To swim* is the *thing* that the ducks *love*.) So how do we spot verbs?

A verb is what conveys the essential meaning of a clause (a string of words that convey an idea). Every idea requires a verb. The sentence *The ducks swim in the pond* says that *Something swims somewhere*, so the verb is *swim*. The sentence *The ducks love to swim* says that *Something loves something*, so the verb is *love*. Every verb requires a subject, that is, what *does* the verb. In both sentences, the subject is *ducks*. A verb may also require an *object*, that is, what *receives* the verb. In *The ducks love to swim*, the object is *to swim*, because that is the *thing* that is *loved*.

Example:

When David approached third base, the coach waved him home.

This sentence contains two related ideas, so it contains two clauses, and therefore two verbs:

Clause 1: *When David **approached** third base*
Verb: *approached*   Subject: *David*
Object: *third base*

Clause 2: *the coach **waved** him home*
Verb: *waved*   Subject: *the coach*
Object: *him*

Subject-Verb Disagreement (SVD)

Every verb must agree in number (singular or plural) *with its subject. Subject-verb disagreement* is one of the most common errors tested for on the SAT. If you are a native speaker of English, the best way to check for subject-verb disagreement is to find the subject and verb (ignoring all the intervening words) and *say them together*.

Example:

The people, who are easily persuaded by corporate-sponsored media, spends very little time analyzing issues.

The subject of the verb *spends* is *people*. But *people spends* sounds wrong, because *spends* is the

"third person singular" form—as in *he spends*—but *people* is plural, so the phrase should be *people spend*.

Tricky Plurals and Singulars

These rules will help you to check whether a verb agrees in "number" with its subject:

Phrases like *Sam and Bob* are *plural*, but phrases like *Sam, in addition to Bob*, are *singular*. Phrases that start *as well as . . . , together with . . . , along with . . . ,* or *in addition to . . .* are *interrupters*, which are not part of the main subject.

These words are *singular*: *each, anyone, anybody, anything, another, neither, either, every, everyone, someone, no one, somebody, everything, little,* and *much*. To check for SVD, you can replace any of them with **it**.

These words are *plural*: *phenomena* (singular: *phenomenon*), *media* (singular: *medium*), *data* (singular: *datum*), and *criteria* (singular: *criterion*). To check for SVD, you can replace any of them with **they**.

All of the following can be either *singular or plural*, according to the noun that follows the *of: none (of), any (of), some (of), most (of), more (of),* and *all (of).*

Verbs that follow subjects of the form *either A or B* and *neither A nor B* must *agree with B*, the noun closer to the verb.

Inverted Sentences

Usually the subject comes *before* the verb, but *inverted* clauses have the subject *after* the verb. For instance, sentences that start *There is . . .* or *There are . . .* are inverted. To check subject-verb agreement in these sentences, first "uninvert" them.

Example:

There are many flies in the barn. (inverted)
$\quad$ V $\qquad$ S
Many flies are in the barn. (uninverted)
$\quad$ S $\quad$ V

Concept Review 1: Subject-Verb Disagreement

Next to each noun or noun phrase, write "S" if it is singular or "P" if it is plural.

1. *Neither rain nor snow* _____
2. *Crowd of rowdy fans* _____
3. *Media* _____
4. *Criterion* _____
5. *One or two* _____
6. *Everything* _____
7. *Either of the candidates* _____
8. *Phenomena* _____

Circle the subject in each sentence, and choose the correct verb.

9. *Neither of the cars (is/are) equipped with antilock brakes.*
10. *The flock of geese (was/were) startled by the shotgun blast.*
11. *The data on my computer (was/were) completely erased when the power failed.*
12. *Mathematics and history (is/are) my favorite subjects.*
13. *None of the roast (was/were) eaten.*
14. *All of the games (was/were) played on real grass fields.*
15. *Pride and Prejudice (is/are) my favorite Jane Austen novel.*
16. *Neither of the twins (is/are) allergic to penicillin.*
17. *Much of what I hear in those lectures (goes/go) in one ear and out the other.*
18. *Amy, along with Jamie and Jen, (is/are) applying to Mount Holyoke.*
19. *None of the books (was/were) considered fit for public consumption.*
20. *All of the eggplant (was/were) used to make the sauce.*
21. *Amid the lilies and wildflowers (was/were) one solitary rose.*
22. *Either Ben or his brothers (is/are) in charge of bringing the drinks.*
23. *There (is/are) hardly even a speck of dirt left on the carpet.*
24. *"Stop right there!" (shouts/shout) the Bailey brothers, who are standing in front of me.*
25. *Either the Donovans or Dave (is/are) going to bring the plates.*
26. *There (is/are) at least a hundred people here.*

"Uninvert" the following sentences so that the verb follows the subject, then choose the correct verb form.

27. *There (is/are), in my opinion, far too many smokers in this restaurant.*

   _____

28. *Over that hill (is/are) thousands of bison.*

   _____

29. *Riding on the bus among the children (was/were) over a dozen commuters.*

   _____

30. *Never before (has/have) there been such voices heard here.*

   _____

31. *Absent from the article (was/were) any mention of the director's previous Broadway failures.*

   _____

Worksheet 1: Subject-Verb Disagreement

Label each verb in the following sentences with a "V" and each subject with an "S." If any verbs are incorrect, cross them out and write the correct form in the blank.

1. We were horrified to discover that there was more than three mice living in the attic.   _____

2. Either the president or one of her aides are going to coordinate the project.   _____

3. There is nearly always two or three guards posted at each entrance.   _____

4. Every player on both the Falcons and the Rockets were at the party after the game.   _____

5. There has been a theater and a toy store in the mall ever since it opened.   _____

6. Either Eric or his brother is hosting the party this year.   _____

7. There is no fewer than six crayons in this box.   _____

8. The therapy can resume as planned because neither of the twins are allergic to penicillin.   _____

9. The proceeds from the sale of every auctioned item goes to charity.   _____

10. Economics, particularly with its dependence on the behavior of consumers and producers, has always struck me as more of a human science than a mathematical one.   _____

11. There is more than three years remaining on her contract.   _____

12. Neither of the girls were frightened by the wild animals that scurried incessantly past their tent.   _____

13. The technology behind high-definition television, DVDs, and CDs have transformed nearly every aspect of the home entertainment industry.   _____

14. Every player on both teams were concerned about the goalie's injury.   _____

15. The company's sponsorship of charitable foundations and mentorship programs have garnered many commendations from philanthropic organizations.   _____

16. Neither the children nor their parents utters a word when Mrs. Denny tells her stories.   _____

17. How important is your strength training and your diet to your daily regimen?   _____

Answer Key 1: Subject-Verb Disagreement

Concept Review 1

1. *S*
2. *S*
3. *P*
4. *S*
5. *P*
6. *S*
7. *S*
8. *P*
9. s: *neither*, v: *is*
10. s: *flock*, v: *was*
11. s: *data*, v: *were* (*data* is plural)
12. s: *mathematics and history*, v: *are*
13. s: *none* (*roast*), v: *was*
14. s: *all* (*games*), v: *were*
15. s: *Pride and Prejudice*, v: *is*
16. s: *neither*, v: *is*
17. s: *much*, v: *goes*
18. s: *Amy*, v: *is*
19. s: *none* (*books*), v: *were*
20. s: *all* (*eggplant*), v: *was*
21. s: *rose*, v: *was*
22. s: *brothers*, v: *are*
23. s: *speck*, v: *is*
24. s: *Bailey brothers*, v: *shout*
25. s: *Dave*, v: *is*
26. s: *people*, v: *are*
27. Far too many smokers, in my opinion, are in this restaurant.
28. Thousands of bison are over that hill.
29. Among the children, over a dozen commuters were riding on the bus.
30. Such voices have never before been heard here.
31. Any mention of the director's previous Broadway failures was absent from the article.

Worksheet 1

1. s: *we*, v: *were* (correct); s: *mice*, v: *was* (change to *were*)
2. s: *one*, v: *are* (change to *is*)
3. s: *guards*, v: *is* (change to *are*)
4. s: *every player*, v: *were* (change to *was*)
5. s: *a theater and a toy store*, v: *has been* (change to *have been*)
6. s: *his brother*, v: *is* (correct)
7. s: *crayons*, v: *is* (change to *are*)
8. s: *therapy*, v: *can resume* (correct); s: *neither*, v: *are* (change to *is*)
9. s: *proceeds*, v: *goes* (change to *go*)
10. s: *economics*, v: *has struck* (correct)
11. s: *years*, v: *is* (change to *are*)
12. s: *neither*, v: *were* (change to *was*)
13. s: *technology*, v: *have transformed* (change to *has transformed*)
14. s: *every player*, v: *were* (change to *was*)
15. s: *sponsorship*, v: *have garnered* (change to *has garnered*)
16. s: *their parents*, v: *utters* (change to *utter*); s: *Mrs. Denny*, v: *tells*
17. s: *your strength training and your diet*, v: *is* (change to *are*)

Lesson 2: Trimming Sentences

Why Trim?

Spotting SVD errors is often easier when you "trim" the sentence, that is, eliminate nonessential modifiers to leave the "core" of the sentence. What remains after you "trim" a sentence should still be a grammatically correct and complete sentence.

How to "Trim" a Sentence

Step 1: Cross out all nonessential prepositional phrases.
e.g., *The bird* ~~in the cage~~ *began singing*.

A **preposition** is a word that shows relative position or direction. It can complete one of the following sentences:

The squirrel ran _____ the tree.
Democracy is government _____ the people.

Examples include *to, from, of, for, by, in, before, with, beyond,* and *up*.

A *prepositional phrase* is the preposition and the noun phrase that follows, including its modifiers.

e.g., *from sea to shining sea*
in the beginning with hat in hand

Step 2: Cross out all interrupting phrases.
e.g., *The committee,* ~~*ignoring tradition,*~~ *will approve the measure.*

An *interrupting phrase* is a modifying phrase that interrupts the flow of the sentence. Interrupters are generally separated from the main sentence by commas or dashes.

Step 3: Cross out all other nonessential modifiers and modifying phrases.
e.g., ~~*Having traveled so far,*~~ *the* ~~baseball~~ *team hardly wanted to forfeit the* ~~championship~~ *game.*

Modifiers are *adjectives* and *adverbs*, as well as modifying phrases like *participial phrases* (see Lesson 7). Most modifiers are not essential to a sentence, but some are. Use your best judgment. One kind of essential adjective is a *predicate adjective*, that is, an adjective that is linked to the subject by a linking verb, as in *Martha is* smart.

Trimming a sentence helps you to spot SVD more easily.

Original: *My chief concern with this budget and the other proposals on the table are the cuts in school funds.*

Trimmed: *My concern are the cuts.*

Revised: *My concern is the cuts.*

Who Kicked Whom?

When you write, trim your sentences to play the "Who kicked whom?" exercise. Look at the subject-verb-object ("Who kicked whom?") core, and see if it clearly and forcefully conveys the thought you want to convey.

Original: *The lack of economic programs and no big country's being ready to join it symbolized the problems the League of Nations had in getting established.*

Trimmed: *The lack and no country's being ready symbolized the problems.*

Yikes! That doesn't make a shred of sense; rewrite it.

Revised: *Two problems plagued the establishment of the League of Nations: its lack of viable economic programs and its lack of support from the larger countries.*

Concept Review 2: Trimming Sentences

1. What are the three types of words or phrases that can be eliminated when "trimming" a sentence?

   _____

2. Why is it sometimes helpful to "trim" a sentence?

   _____

   _____

3. Circle all of the prepositions in the list below.

   of   beyond   for   and   with   the   an   without   some   along   below

4. What is a prepositional phrase?

   _____

5. Write four examples of prepositional phrases.

   _____

   _____

Write the trimmed version of each sentence on the line below it, correcting any verb problems.

6. *The team of advisors, arriving ahead of schedule, were met at the airport by the Assistant Prime Minister.*

   _____

7. *The flock of birds that darted over the lake were suddenly an opalescent silver.*

   _____

8. *Carmen, along with her three sisters, are unlikely to be swayed by arguments supporting David's position.*

   _____

Write the trimmed version of each sentence on the line below it, then rewrite the sentence to make it clearer and more forceful, changing the subject and verb entirely, if necessary.

9. *Nearly inevitably, advancements, or those being popularly regarded as such, have to do with modifications, not overhaul.*

   Trimmed: _____

   Revised: _____

10. *The development of the new country's governmental system was affected in a negative regard by the rebels' lack of cohesiveness.*

    Trimmed: _____

    Revised: _____

Worksheet 2: Trimming Sentences

Write the "trimmed" version of each sentence, circling the verbs and subjects and correcting any agreement errors.

1. *Juggling the demands of both school and my social agenda often seem too much to bear.*

   _____

2. *Others on the committee, like the chairwoman Amanda Sanders, is concerned about the lack of attention given to school safety.*

   _____

3. *The waiters' professional demeanor—particularly their keen knowledge, their attention to detail, and their cordiality—are what makes dining there such a sublime culinary experience.*

   _____

   _____

4. *The system by which candidates for local political offices are selected is archaic and, many contend, unfair.*

   _____

5. *The abundance of companies that fail in their first year of business contribute to an intimidating economic climate.*

   _____

6. *When scientists theorize about the traits that all humans have come to share, they must be keenly aware of the fact that these traits have evolved over millions of generations.*

   _____

   _____

7. *The entire industry of tobacco companies and distributors has steadfastly maintained their position that tobacco is not addictive and that smoking is an inalienable right of consumers.*

   _____

   _____

8. *The challenge of Mount Everest, its conquerors claim, is far more the lack of oxygen at its rarefied heights than even the precarious ice falls or precipitous ascents.*

   _____

9. *One in every three Americans agree strongly with the statement: "Anyone who would run for political office is not worth voting for."*

   _____

10. *The fact that humans have committed so many atrocities have forced some historians to adopt a cynical perspective on human nature.*

    _____

    _____

Answer Key 2: Trimming Sentences

Concept Review 2

1. Prepositional phrases, interrupting phrases, and nonessential modifiers

2. Trimming reveals subject-verb disagreement errors and reveals how clear and forceful the sentence is.

3. Prepositions: *of, beyond, for, with, without, along, below.*

4. A prepositional phrase is a preposition and the noun or noun phrase that follows it.

5. Examples might include *in the tree, without hesitation, beyond gimmicks,* and *over two million hungry customers.*

6. *The team were* (change to *was*) *met.*

7. *The flock were* (change to *was*) *silver.*

8. *Carmen are* (change to *is*) *unlikely to be swayed.*

9. Trimmed: *Advancements have to do with modifications.*

   The verb *(have to do with)* is weak, vague, and inactive, and the subject *(advancements)* and object *(modification)* are abstract and vague. To improve the sentence, think about the *intended* meaning of the sentence, and use stronger and less abstract terms. Here's a good revision:

   Typically, societies progress by making small modifications to their institutions, not by overhauling them completely.

10. Trimmed: *The development was affected.*

    The verb *(was affected)* is weak, passive, and vague. Here's a good revision:

    The incohesiveness of the rebels hindered the development of the new government.

Worksheet 2

1. *Juggling the demands seem* (change to *seems*) *too much to bear.*

2. *Others is* (change to *are*) *concerned.*

3. *The demeanor are* (change to *is*) *what makes dining there a sublime experience.*

4. *The system is archaic and unfair.* (correct)

5. *The abundance contribute* (change to *contributes*) *to an intimidating climate.*

6. *They must be keenly aware that these traits have evolved over millions of generations.* (correct)

7. *The industry has maintained their* (change to *its*) *position that tobacco is not addictive and that smoking is an inalienable right.*

8. *The challenge is far more the lack of oxygen than the precarious ice falls or precipitous ascents.* (correct)

9. *One agree* (change to *agrees*) *with the statement: "Anyone who would run for political office is not worth voting for."*

10. *The fact have forced* (change to *has forced*) *some.*

Lesson 3: Parallelism

The Law of Parallelism

> When you *compare* or list items in a sentence, the items should have the *same grammatical form*. That is, if the first item is an infinitive (or a gerund, or an adjective, etc.), the other item(s) should be, too.

Wrong: *She hated **to take** charge, **draw** attention to herself, and **she hated seeming** like a know-it-all.*

The three items have different forms. The sentence sounds best if they are all *gerunds*.

Right: *She hated **taking** charge, **drawing** attention to herself, and **seeming** like a know-it-all.*

Wrong: *Believe it or not, I like **to read** more than I like **going** to parties.*

The first item is an *infinitive*, but the second is a *gerund*. Make them the same form.

Right: *Believe it or not, I like **to read** more than I like **to go** to parties.*

Also right: *Believe it or not, I like **reading** more than I like **going** to parties.*

Parallel Constructions

> In all constructions like the following, the words or phrases that replace *A* and *B* must be parallel.

A is like B	*A more than B*	*prefer A to B*
neither A nor B	*either A or B*	*both A and B*
the more A,	*the better A,*	*not only A,*
the less B	*the better B*	*but also B*
not A but B	*less A than B*	*more A than B*

Infinitives vs. Gerunds

Infinitives are verblike phrases like *to run, to see,* and *to think,* which usually act as *nouns*.

Gerunds are also verblike words, like *running, seeing,* and *thinking,* and they also often act as *nouns*.

I like pizza.   I like to swim.   I like swimming.

What kind of word is *pizza*? Obviously a noun. But notice that in the sentences above, *to swim* (infinitive) and *swimming* (gerund) are playing the same role as *pizza* did in the first sentence. So they must be nouns too!

> Usually, gerunds and infinitives are interchangeable. But in some situations, one is preferable to the other.

- The gerund often indicates a *general class* of activity, while the infinitive indicates a *specific* activity.

  Good: ***Kayaking*** *(not to kayak) is a healthful sport, but can sometimes be dangerous.*

  Good: *Curtis and Dan want **to kayak** (not kayaking) this afternoon.*

- The infinitive indicates a stronger *connection between subject and action* than does the gerund.

  Unclear: *Cara has always loved **dancing**.*

  Does Cara simply like to watch dancing, or does she herself do the dancing?

  Clearer: *Cara has always loved **to dance**.*

  This sentence clearly indicates that Cara herself dances.

- The infinitive often indicates *purpose or intention* better than does the gerund.

  Awkward: *We have supplied cars **for transporting** the guests back to their hotel rooms.*

  Better: *We have supplied cars **to transport** the guests back to their hotel rooms.*

Concept Review 3: Parallelism

1. In what situations do you have to obey the law of parallelism?

In each of the sentences below, circle the words or phrases that are parallel, then write the *form* of those words or phrases (adjectives, prepositional phrases, gerunds, infinitives, nouns, etc.) in the blank.

2. *You can register for the test by mail, by phone, or on the Web.*   _____

3. *Having good study practices is even more important than working hard.*   _____

4. *The more you get to know her, the more you will like her.*   _____

5. *The produce is not only exceptionally fresh but also reasonably priced.*   _____

6. *The show is less a concert than it is a 3-hour nightmare.*   _____

Complete each of the sentences below with the appropriate word or phrase—infinitive or gerund—using the given verb.

7. *(exercise) _____ is essential, but so is (eat) _____ intelligently.*

8. *The purpose of this trip is (show) _____ you what life was like in the 18th century.*

9. *I have always loved (dance) _____, although my condition has always prevented me from doing it myself.*

10. *Is it better (study) _____ a little each night, or a lot the night before?*

11. *The director called a meeting (discuss) _____ the coordination of the marketing phase.*

Correct any infinitive/gerund problems in the sentences below.

12. *The defendant was unwilling to give up his right of having his lawyer present at all questioning.*

13. *I would not dream to try out for the team until I have learned to throw a football.*

14. *Even the reinforced concrete breakwater could not prevent the water to inundate the village.*

15. *Within the next three weeks, we plan having all of the work on the roof completed.*

Fix the parallelism errors in the following sentences.

16. *I like working with Miss Bennett because she is very supportive and has a lot of knowledge.*

   _____

17. *I can't decide whether I should give Maria the tickets or Caitlyn.*

   _____

18. *The movie was both beautifully directed and the acting was a joy to watch.*

   _____

Worksheet 3: Parallelism

In the following sentences, circle all parts that should be parallel, and correct any problems.

1. *Personal digital assistants can be not only practical, but also entertain for hours on end.*

   _____

2. *Filling out applications for summer jobs is about as much fun as when you take the SAT.*

   _____

3. *My lab partners were more concerned about getting the lab done quickly than about what grade they might get.*

   _____

4. *To say she is excitable is like saying Bill Gates is well off.*

   _____

5. *The sheer magnitude of the structure was awesome, but I thought the aesthetics were less than appealing.*

   _____

6. *The elegance of a proof lies more in its conciseness and clarity than in how clever it is.*

   _____

7. *I bought my tickets, reserved the hotel room, and I planned the itinerary myself.*

   _____

8. *We had to build our own shelters, orient ourselves without instruments, and we even had to hunt and gather our own food.*

   _____

9. *The rebels were neither disciplined nor did they have any overall strategy.*

   _____

10. *She was concerned not only with getting good grades, but also wanted to understand the material.*

    _____

11. *Patients with chronic fatigue syndrome tend to exhibit lethargy, a reduced affect, and they often feel depressed.*

    _____

12. *Taxpayers often prefer to pay high property taxes to the paying of high sales taxes.*

    _____

13. *Riding that roller coaster was like a trip over a waterfall in a barrel.*

    _____

14. *As a teacher, she loved to inspire creativity in her students, even more than she loved receiving accolades.*

    _____

Answer Key 3: Parallelism

Concept Review 3

1. when comparing or listing things in a sentence

2. *by mail; by phone; on the web* prepositional phrases

3. *having; working* gerunds

4. *you get to know her; you will like her* clauses

5. *exceptionally fresh; reasonably priced* adverb-adjectives

6. *concert; 3-hour nightmare* nouns

7. *Exercising is essential, but so is eating intelligently.*

8. *The purpose of this trip is to show you what life was like in the 18th century.* The infinitive shows purpose more effectively than the gerund does.

9. *I have always loved dancing, although my condition has always prevented me from doing it myself.* Since the speaker cannot dance, the infinitive is inappropriate.

10. *Is it better to study a little each night, or a lot the night before?* The infinitive shows a clearer link between the action and a particular subject.

11. *The director called a meeting to discuss the coordination of the marketing phase.* The infinitive shows purpose more effectively than the gerund does.

12. *The defendant was unwilling to give up his right to have his lawyer present at all questioning.*

13. *I would not dream of trying out for the team until I have learned to throw a football.*

14. *Even the reinforced concrete breakwater could not prevent the water from inundating the village.*

15. *Within the next three weeks, we plan to have all of the work on the roof completed.*

16. *I like working with Miss Bennett because she is very supportive and knowledgeable.*

17. *I can't decide whether I should give the tickets to Maria or Caitlyn.*

18. *The movie's directing was beautiful and the acting was a joy to watch.*

Worksheet 3

1. *Personal digital assistants can be not only practical, but also entertaining for hours on end.*

2. *Filling out applications for summer jobs is about as much fun as taking the SAT.*

3. *My lab partners were more concerned about getting the lab done quickly than about getting a good grade.*

4. *Saying she is excitable is like saying Bill Gates is well off.*

5. *The sheer magnitude of the structure was awesome, but (omit I thought) the aesthetics were less than appealing.*

6. *The elegance of a proof lies more in its conciseness and clarity than in its cleverness.*

7. *I bought my tickets, reserved the hotel room, and (omit I) planned the itinerary myself.*

8. *We had to build our own shelters, orient ourselves without instruments, and even hunt and gather our own food.*

9. *The rebels lacked both discipline and overall strategy.*

10. *She was concerned not only with getting good grades, but also with understanding the material.*

11. *Patients with CFS tend to exhibit lethargy, a reduced affect, and often depression.*

12. *Taxpayers often prefer paying high property taxes to paying high sales taxes.*

13. *Riding that roller coaster was like taking a trip over a waterfall in a barrel.*

14. *As a teacher, she loved inspiring creativity in her students, even more than (omit she loved) receiving accolades.*

Lesson 4: Comparison Problems

Illogical Comparisons

Any items being compared in a sentence must be logically comparable, that is, in the same general category. Always compare *apples* to *apples*, not *apples* to *car batteries*! Also, comparisons must obey the law of parallelism.

Wrong: *Her chances of getting an A aren't much better than the lottery.*
Chances and *the lottery* aren't comparable things! We must compare *chances* to *chances*.

Right: *Her chances of getting an A aren't much better than her chances of winning the lottery.*

It is always illogical to say that something is different from itself. Watch out for sneaky contrasts like this:

Wrong: *She has played in more concerts than any cellist in her school.*
Of course, she hasn't played in more concerts than herself!

Right: *She has played in more concerts than any other cellist in her school.*

Fewer/Less, Number/Amount, and Many/Much

Use the words *fewer, number,* or *many* only in reference to *countable* things (like *cars, dollars,* and *popsicles*) and *less, amount,* or *much* only in reference to *uncountable* things (like *traffic, money,* and *food*). It is a common mistake to use *less* when you should use *fewer*.

Wrong: *There have been a lot less fans at the games ever since the owners raised ticket prices.*
Since fans can be counted, *less* doesn't work. Use *fewer* instead.

Right: *There have been a lot fewer fans at the games ever since the owners raised ticket prices.*

Wrong: *The team owners showed concern about the increasing amount of dangerously rowdy fans.*

Right: *The team owners showed concern about the increasing number of dangerously rowdy fans.*

Between/Among, More/Most, and -er/-est

Use *between, more,* and any *-er* adjectives only when comparing *exactly two things*. Use *among, most,* and *-est* adjectives when comparing *more than two things*.

Wrong: *The two superpowers seemed to be in a constant battle to see who was strongest.*

Right: *The two superpowers seemed to be in a constant battle to see who was stronger.*

Wrong: *Of the dozens of students in the club, Deborah was the more popular.*

Right: *Of the dozens of students in the club, Deborah was the most popular.*

Number Shift

Things that you compare should, if possible, agree in number. Be sure they are *both plural* or *both singular.*

Wrong: *They were both hoping to be a winner.*

Right: *They were both hoping to be winners.*

Wrong: *The sailors' main point of reference was the two lighthouse beacons.*

Right: *The sailors' main points of reference were the two lighthouse beacons.*

Concept Review 4: Comparison Problems

1. How do you know whether to use *fewer* or *less* in a comparison?

2. How do you know whether to use *more* or *most* in a comparison?

In each sentence, underline any items that are being compared or equated. Below the sentence, state whether the comparison is *logical* or *illogical*. If it is illogical or contains another error in comparison, correct the sentence.

3. *The critics' guild praised the show, saying that it was consistently more intelligent and provocative than anything on the air.*

   _____

4. *Team unity and commitment to practice were regarded by the players as the key to their success.*

   _____

5. *Mathematics lessons in Japanese classrooms, unlike American classrooms, are often focused on solving a single complex problem rather than many simplistic problems.*

   _____

6. *Increasingly, modern singers, like Gregorian chanters, are becoming adept at melisma, the singing of many notes on a single syllable.*

   _____

7. *The electric-combustion engines of the new hybrid cars burn much more cleanly and efficiently than conventional cars.*

   _____

8. *To the critics of the time, the surrealists were as inscrutable, if not more so, than the dadaists.*

   _____

9. *In modern warfare, unlike the past, combatants rarely meet face to face, and are detected as often by video as by sight.*

   _____

10. *Most people vastly prefer turning the pages of a real book to scrolling through the screens of an electronic novel.*

    _____

Worksheet 4: Comparison Problems

Correct any errors in the comparisons in the following sentences.

1. *I prefer a lot of modern poetry to Shakespeare.*

   _____

2. *Her suitcase would not close because she had packed too much of her towels into it.*

   _____

3. *The year-end bonus was equally divided between Parker, Herriot, and me.*

   _____

4. *Many students wanted to be a lifeguard at the club.*

   _____

5. *The toughest thing about her class is you have to do tons of homework every night.*

   _____

6. *Mr. Forstadt's comments, like so many coaches, didn't spare the players' feelings in the least.*

   _____

7. *After several days in the woods, we became concerned that we had packed a lot less meals than we would need.*

   _____

8. *Even in the 21st century, women throughout the globe are treated like a slave, or, worse yet, like a nonperson.*

   _____

9. *I've always preferred observational humor to those quirky prop comedians.*

   _____

10. *It was remarkable that the children had donated so much toys to others who were barely needier than they.*

    _____

11. *The formal structure of the sonnet imposes far more discipline on the mind of the poet than formless free verse.*

    _____

12. *The theories of true anarchists, unlike modern antistatists, do not promote social chaos, but rather organization without authority.*

    _____

13. *Those passengers with a disability will be permitted to board the plane first.*

    _____

14. *The reason we lost the game is because our captain had torn his ACL.*

    _____

15. *Voter apathy and cold weather were a reason that turnout was so poor at this year's election.*

    _____

16. *Having studied Faulkner and Hemingway, I've come to believe that Hemingway is the best writer, although Faulkner tells the best stories.*

    _____

Answer Key 4: Comparison Problems

Concept Review 4

1. *Fewer* is used to compare <u>countable</u> things, while *less* is used to compare <u>uncountable</u> things.

2. *More* is used only when comparing <u>exactly two</u> things, while *most* is used when comparing <u>more than two</u>.

3. *The show* is compared to *anything on the air.* Illogical: *the show* can only be better than *anything <u>else</u> on the air.*

4. *Team unity and commitment* are equated with *the key.* Illogical: they are the <u>keys</u> to their success.

5. *Mathematics lessons* are compared to *American classrooms.* Illogical: they should be compared to *<u>the lessons in</u> American classrooms.*

6. *Modern singers* are compared to *Gregorian chanters.* Logical and correct.

7. *The engines* are compared to *conventional cars.* Illogical: they should be compared to *<u>those in</u> conventional cars.*

8. *The surrealists* are compared to *the dadaists.* Logical, but grammatically incorrect: *the surrealists were regarded as being as inscrutable <u>as the dadaists, if not more so</u>.*

9. *In modern warfare* is compared to *the past.* Illogical: *In modern warfare, unlike <u>warfare in</u> the past . . .*

10. *Turning* is compared to *scrolling.* Logical and correct.

Worksheet 4

1. *I prefer a lot of modern poetry to <u>the poetry of Shakespeare</u>.*

2. *Her suitcase would not close because she had packed too <u>many</u> of her towels into it.*

3. *The year-end bonus was equally divided <u>among</u> Parker, Harriot, and me.*

4. *Many students wanted to be <u>lifeguards</u> at the club.*

5. *The toughest thing about her class is <u>having</u> to do tons of homework every night.*

6. *Mr. Forstadt's comments, like <u>those of</u> so many coaches, didn't spare the players' feelings in the least.*

7. *After several days in the woods, we became concerned that we had packed a lot <u>fewer</u> meals than we would need.*

8. *Even in the 21st century, women throughout the globe are treated like <u>slaves</u>, or, worse yet, like <u>nonpersons</u>.*

9. *I've always preferred observational humor to <u>quirky prop comedy</u>.*

10. *It was remarkable that the children had donated so <u>many</u> toys to others who were barely needier than they.*

11. *The formal structure of the sonnet imposes far more discipline on the mind of the poet than <u>does the formlessness of</u> free verse.*

12. *The theories of the original anarchists, unlike <u>those of</u> modern antistatists, do not promote social chaos, but rather organization without authority.*

13. *Those passengers with <u>disabilities</u> will be permitted to board the plane first* or *<u>Any passenger</u> with a disability will be permitted to board the plane first.*

14. *The reason we lost the game is <u>that</u> our captain had torn his ACL.*

15. *Voter apathy and cold weather were <u>the reasons</u> that turnout was so poor at this year's election.*

16. *Having studied Faulkner and Hemingway, I've come to believe that Hemingway is the <u>better</u> writer, although Faulkner tells the <u>better</u> stories.*

Lesson 5: Pronoun-Antecedent Disagreement

Pronouns

A *pronoun* is a word (such as *it, he, she, what,* or *that*) that substitutes for a noun. A pronoun is either *definite* (like *it, you, she,* and *I*) and refers to a specified thing (or person or place or idea) or *indefinite* (like *anyone, neither,* and *those*), and does *not* refer to a specific thing (or person or place or idea).

Definite Pronouns and Antecedents

Every definite pronoun refers to (or takes the place of) a noun in the sentence, called the pronoun *antecedent*. The pronoun must agree in number (singular or plural) and kind (personal or impersonal) with its antecedent.

Wrong: *Everyone should brush **their** teeth three times a day.*
Because *everyone* is singular, *their* is the wrong pronoun.

Right: *Everyone should brush **his** or **her** teeth three times a day.*

Wrong: *David was the one **that** first spotted the error.*
The pronoun *that* is impersonal, but of course, *David* is a person.

Right: *David was the one **who** first spotted the error.*

The antecedent of a definite pronoun should be clear, not ambiguous.

Wrong: *Roger told Mike that **he** was going to start the next game.*
Who was going to start? Roger or Mike?

Right: *Mike learned that he was going to start the next game when Roger told him so.*

Interrogative Pronouns

An *interrogative pronoun* (like *what, where, why,* and *when*) usually asks a question or refers to an unknown, as in **Where** *are my keys?* But sometimes it can be used as a definite pronoun. When it is, remember two points:

Use *what* only to refer to a *thing*, *where* to refer to a *place*, *when* to refer to a *time*, *why* to refer to a *reason*, *who* to refer to a *person*, and *how* to refer to an *explanation*.

Wrong: *An anachronism is **when** something doesn't fit in with its time period.*
An anachronism isn't a time, is it? It's a thing.

Right: *An anachronism is something **that** doesn't fit in with its time period.*

When following a comma, an interrogative pronoun usually takes the *immediately preceding* noun as its antecedent.

Wrong: *The actors will design their own sets, **who** are participating in the workshop.*
This is awkward because the *sets* are not what the pronoun *who* is logically referring to.

Right: *The actors **who** are participating in the workshop will design their own sets.*

Pronoun Consistency

Be consistent with any pronouns you use to refer to the same thing more than once in a sentence.

Wrong: *Even when **one** is dieting, **you** should always try to get enough vitamins.*
It sounds like we can't make up our minds about whom we're talking to!

Right: *Even when **one** is dieting, **one** should always try to get enough vitamins.*

Concept Review 5: Pronoun-Antecedent Disagreement

1. Name three definite pronouns: _____

2. Name three indefinite pronouns: _____

3. Every _____ pronoun requires a specific antecedent.

4. What is an antecedent?

   _____

   _____

After each interrogative pronoun, write what kind of noun it must represent.

5. *what*   _____

6. *where*   _____

7. *how*   _____

8. *when*   _____

9. *why*   _____

10. *who*   _____

Circle all pronouns in the following sentences, and make any corrections that may be necessary.

11. *There are too many legal situations where misrepresentation seems to be standard practice.*

   _____

12. *If a student wants to memorize the meaning of a word, you should begin by understanding the concept it represents.*

   _____

13. *Caroline passed the phone to Julia, but she couldn't bring herself to speak.*

   _____

14. *Neither of the dogs wanted to give up their territory to the other.*

   _____

15. *David volunteered to be a ticket taker, not wanting to be the one that cleaned the aisles after the show.*

   _____

16. *They lost the game, which is why they didn't celebrate afterwards.*

   _____

Worksheet 5:
Pronoun-Antecedent Disagreement

Correct any pronoun errors in each of the following sentences.

1. *Although the British parliament conducts debates under very formal and decorous rules, they can often produce very animated arguments.*

2. *Brown has always been committed to assisting their students by providing him or her with any necessary financial aid.*

3. *The media ignored the reports, probably because it believed they were not what the public was ready to hear.*

4. *The agency decided that they would give control of the project exclusively to Fiona and me.*

5. *Each of the girls wanted their idea for the logo design to be considered.*

6. *No one who has been through the first week of boot camp ever believes that they will make it through the entire six weeks.*

7. *Although you shouldn't read carelessly, one doesn't need to read slowly, either.*

8. *Neither gentleman thought that their team could win the championship.*

9. *Students sometimes aren't ready to handle the extra work when his or her courses become more demanding.*

10. *Many modern novels are concerned with situations where love goes unrequited.*

11. *Everybody is expected to do their share.*

12. *The entire team turned out to be robots who had been programmed to play lacrosse.*

13. *The radio station's board of directors drafted a proposal modifying their advertising policies.*

14. *The museum received so many donations that they actually had to return over a million dollars to the benefactors.*

15. *They usually give the most points to the skater that makes the fewest mistakes.*

16. *I like movies where the guy gets the girl.*

17. *Each swimmer will have a lane to themselves.*

18. *Who was the one that made the error in the third inning?*

Answer Key 5: Pronoun-Antecedent Disagreement

Concept Review 5

1. *I, you, she, he, it, they, we, us, them, etc.*

2. *anyone, everybody, each, either, one*

3. definite

4. An antecedent is the noun that a definite pronoun refers to.

5. a thing

6. a place

7. an explanation

8. a time

9. a reason

10. a person

11. pronouns: *there, where. There are too many legal situations in which misrepresentation seems to be standard practice.* (*Situations* aren't places, they're things.)

12. pronouns: *you, it. If a student wants to memorize the meaning of a word, he or she should begin by understanding the concept it represents.* (Agreement)

13. pronouns: *she, herself. Caroline passed the phone to Julia, but Julia couldn't bring herself to speak.* (Ambiguous antecedent)

14. pronouns: *neither, their. Neither of the dogs wanted to give up its territory to the other.* (*Neither* is singular.)

15. pronouns: *one, that. David volunteered to be a ticket taker, not wanting to be the one who cleaned the aisles after the show.* (David's a who.)

16. pronouns: *they, which, why, they.* (The sentence is correct because *which* refers to the clause *they lost the game.*)

Worksheet 5

1. *Although the British parliament conducts debate under very formal and decorous rules, it can often produce very animated arguments.*

2. *Brown has always been committed to assisting its students by providing them with any necessary financial aid.*

3. *The media ignored the reports, probably because they believed that those reports were not what the public was ready to hear.*

4. *The agency decided that it would give control of the project exclusively to Fiona and me.*

5. *Each of the girls wanted her idea for the logo design to be considered.*

6. *No one who has been through the first week of boot camp ever believes that he or she will make it through the entire six weeks.*

7. *Although you shouldn't read carelessly, you don't need to read slowly, either.*

8. *Neither gentleman thought that his team could win the championship.*

9. *Students sometimes aren't ready to handle the extra work when their courses become more demanding.*

10. *Many modern novels are concerned with situations in which love goes unrequited.*

11. *Everybody is expected to do his or her share.*

12. *The entire team turned out to be robots that had been programmed to play lacrosse.*

13. *The radio station's board of directors drafted a proposal modifying its advertising policies.*

14. *The museum received so many donations that it actually had to return over a million dollars to the benefactors.*

15. *They usually give the most points to the skater who makes the fewest mistakes.*

16. *I like movies in which the guy gets the girl.*

17. *Each swimmer will have a lane to herself (or himself).*

18. *Who was the one who made the error in the third inning?*

Lesson 6: Pronoun Case

Pronoun Cases

Every pronoun has a *case*, which indicates its relationship to a verb or noun. There are four common cases.

Subjective (or *nominative*) pronouns (*I, you, he, she, we, they, who,* etc.) are used primarily as subjects of verbs.

Objective pronouns (*me, you, him, her, them, whom,* etc.) are used primarily as *objects of verbs*.

Possessive pronouns (*my/mine, her/hers, their/theirs, whose,* etc.) show *attribution* or *ownership*.

Reflexive pronouns (*myself, yourself, himself, herself, themselves,* etc.) show an *object equated with the subject* or show *emphasis*.

Subjective Pronouns

Subjective pronouns are used only as *subjects* of verbs or *as predicate nominatives*.

Subject of real verb:	*Jenna and I were the only two at the meeting.*
Subject of implied verb:	*My brother is taller than I (am).*

Although the verb isn't written, its meaning is implied.

Predicate nominative:	*The winner of the prize was she.*

A *predicate nominative* is a pronoun or noun "linked" to the subject by a linking verb. It takes the *subjective case*.

Example:

Matthew	*is*	*the new captain of the team*.
subject	verb	predicate nominative

The mountain	*became*	*a violent volcano*.
subject	verb	predicate nominative

Objective Pronouns

Objective pronouns are used as *objects of verbs* or as *objects of prepositions*.

Object of verb:	*My father struggled to raise my brother and me.*
Object of preposition:	*This should be a great opportunity for you and her.*

When you have a compound phrase like *Tom and me* and *the coach and them*, deciding the case of the pronoun is easier if you leave out the other part of the phrase.

Sheila and (her or she?) took the cab uptown. —— **She** *took the cab uptown* not **Her** *took the cab uptown.*

It was made for you and (me or I?) —— *It was made for* **me** *not It was made for* **I**.

Possessive Pronouns

Don't use the *objective case* when you should use the *possessive case* before a gerund.

Wrong:	*I resent you taking the car without asking.*
Right:	*I resent your taking the car without asking.*

The object of the verb *resent* is *taking*: the *taking* is what *I resent,* so using the objective pronoun *you* only confuses things. Since it's not *you whom I resent,* the possessive case *your* makes sense.

Reflexive Pronouns

Reflexive pronouns are used in only two ways: to show that a subject and object are the same, as in "I pinched *myself* to make sure I wasn't dreaming," or to emphasize a noun or pronoun, as in "I *myself* would never say such a thing." Never use a reflexive pronoun where an objective pronoun is required. Wrong: The crowd applauded Carl and *myself*. Right: The crowd applauded Carl and *me*.

Concept Review 6: Pronoun Case

1. Name four subjective pronouns: _____

2. Subjective pronouns are used as _____

   or _____

3. Name four objective pronouns: _____

4. Objective pronouns are used as _____

   or _____

5. Name four possessive pronouns: _____

6. Name four reflexive pronouns: _____

7. Reflexive pronouns are used to _____

   or _____

Choose the correct pronoun in each sentence below.

8. *The climb was much easier for them than it was for Jeff and (I/me/myself).*

9. *The other contestants did not seem as confident as (he/him).*

10. *Within a week, George and (me/I) will have completed the project.*

11. *(Us/We) detectives are always careful to follow every lead.*

12. *Every student should make (his or her/their) own study plan.*

13. *They never seem to listen to the opinions of (us/we) students as they should.*

Worksheet 6: Pronoun Case

Choose the correct pronoun in each sentence below.

1. *The university presented the honor to David and (he/him).*

2. *After the game, we all agreed that no one had played harder than (he/him).*

3. *Justine and (me/I) have always been closest friends.*

4. *There is no point in (our/us) delaying the tests any longer.*

5. *I shall grant immortality to (he/him) who can pull the sword from the stone.*

6. *It seems quite clear that you and (I/me) will have to work together to solve this problem.*

7. *It might be hard for (him and me/he and I) to agree.*

8. *The other cheerleaders and (her/she) needed to practice on the weekend.*

9. *The tabloid media were thrilled about (him/his) making such a fool of himself in public.*

10. *(We/Us) and the other members debated the issue for over 2 hours.*

11. *The owners of the club offered my wife and (me/I) a free bottle of wine with dinner.*

12. *No other runner on the team could outrun (myself/me).*

13. *The teachers were getting tired of (him/his) constantly falling asleep in class.*

14. *The ballpark always held a special attraction for Dave and (I/me).*

15. *Our friends gave a party for Ingrid and (I/me/myself).*

16. *In anticipation of the trip, I bought (me/myself) a nice new suitcase.*

Answer Key 6: Pronoun Case

Concept Review 6

1. *I, he, she, you, we, they, who*

2. *subjects of verbs* or *predicate nominatives*

3. *me, him, her, you, us, them, whom*

4. *objects of verbs* or *objects of prepositions*

5. *my, mine, her, hers, his, your, yours, their, theirs, our, ours*

6. *myself, yourself, himself, herself, ourselves, themselves*

7. *show that the object of the verb is the same as the subject* or *emphasize an adjacent noun or pronoun*

8. *The climb was much easier for them than it was for Jeff and <u>me</u>.* (object of a preposition)

9. *The other contestants did not seem as confident as <u>he</u> (did).* (subject of an implied verb)

10. *Within a week, George and <u>I</u> will have completed the project.* (subject of a verb)

11. *<u>We</u> detectives are always careful to follow every lead.* (subject of a verb)

12. *Every student should make <u>his or her</u> own study plan.* (possessive modifier of noun; must agree with singular antecedent)

13. *They never seem to listen to the opinions of <u>us</u> students as they should.* (object of a preposition)

Worksheet 6

1. *The university presented the honor to David and <u>him</u>.* (object of a preposition)

2. *After the game, we all agreed that no one had played harder than <u>he</u>.* (*than he did*: subject of an implied verb)

3. *Justine and <u>I</u> have always been closest friends.* (subject)

4. *There is no point in <u>our</u> delaying the tests any longer.* (*Delaying* is the object of the preposition, so the pronoun should not be objective.)

5. *I shall grant immortality to <u>him</u> who can pull the sword from the stone.* (object of a preposition)

6. *It seems quite clear that you and <u>I</u> will have to work together to solve this problem.* (subject)

7. *It might be hard for <u>him and me</u> to agree.* (object of a preposition)

8. *The other cheerleaders and <u>she</u> needed to practice on the weekend.* (subject)

9. *The tabloid media were thrilled about <u>his</u> making such a fool of himself in public.* (*Making* is the object of the preposition.)

10. *<u>We</u> and the other members debated the issue for over 2 hours.* (subject)

11. *The owners of the club offered my wife and <u>me</u> a free bottle of wine with dinner.* (object of a verb)

12. *No other runner on the team could outrun <u>me</u>.* (object of a verb)

13. *The teachers were getting tired of <u>his</u> constantly falling asleep in class.* (*Falling* is the object, so the pronoun should not be in the objective case.)

14. *The ballpark always held a special attraction for Dave and <u>me</u>.* (object of a preposition)

15. *Our friends gave a party for Ingrid and <u>me</u>.* (object of a preposition)

16. *In anticipation of the trip, I bought <u>myself</u> a nice new suitcase.* (The object and subject represent the same person, so the object should be in the reflexive case.)

Lesson 7: Dangling and Misplaced Participles

What Is a Participle?

> There are two kinds of *participles:*
>
> *Present participles* always end in *-ing* (e.g., *colliding, writing, swimming, eating, fighting*).
>
> *Past participles* often end in *-ed* or *-en*, but not always (e.g., *collided, written, swum, eaten, fought*).

A participle is a verb form used when the verb is *a phrase with a helping verb*, as in the following sentences:

> *I **was** <u>walking</u> through the lobby.*
> *We **had been** <u>talking</u> for over an hour.*
>
> *I **have** not yet <u>begun</u> to fight.*
> *The chairs **were** <u>pushed</u> against the wall.*

Participles as Verbs or Adjectives

A participle can be used as a *verb part* (with a helping verb), as in *He is **writing** his term paper* or *They have **taken** the car.* It can also be used as an *adjective*, as in *Don't trust a **smiling** salesman* or *I like **frozen** treats.*

> Don't confuse *present participles* with *gerunds.* They look the same, but they play very different roles. Present participles act as *verb parts* or *adjectives* (as above), but gerunds act as *nouns*, as in ***Writing** is harder than it looks.* (*Writing* is the subject of the verb *is*, so it is a noun and a gerund.)

Dangling and Misplaced Participial Phrases

> A *participial phrase* is a modifying phrase that includes a participle. Such a phrase always describes something, so it acts like an adjective or adverb. It is usually separated from the main part of the sentence by one or more commas.
>
> ***Eating ravenously,** the vultures remained on the carcass until it was picked clean.*
>
> *The runners, **exhausted from the final sprint,** stumbled over the finish line.*

> If a participial phrase starts a sentence, the word it modifies must follow immediately after the comma.

Wrong:　　*After **having studied** all night, the professor postponed the test until Friday.*

The participial phrase modifies a noun. Who had studied all night? Certainly not *the professor,* so the modifying phrase *dangles.*

One way to correct a dangling participle is simply to place the correct noun next to the participial phrase:

Better:　　*After **having studied** all night, I was frustrated to learn that the professor had postponed the test until Friday.* (*I* answers the question: *who had studied?*)

Another way is to incorporate a subject into the participial phrase, turning it into a dependent clause:

Better:　　*After **I had studied** all night, the professor postponed the test until Friday.*

> Every participial phrase *should be as close as possible to the word it modifies.* If a modifier sounds as if it modifies the wrong thing, it is "misplaced" and must be moved.

Wrong:　　*Bob found his watch **walking to the bathroom.***

Was the watch *walking?* Of course not, so the participial phrase is misplaced.

Better:　　***Walking to the bathroom,** Bob found his watch.*

Also good:　*Bob found his watch as he was **walking to the bathroom.***

Wrong:　　*It was difficult for William to hear the announcements **waiting for the train.***

Were the *announcements* waiting for the train? Of course not.

Better:　　***While waiting for the train,** William found it difficult to hear the announcements.*

Concept Review 7: Dangling and Misplaced Participles

1. If a participial phrase followed by a comma begins a sentence, it must be followed by

_____

Give the past and present participle forms of each of the following verbs.

2. *push*   past participle _____   present participle _____

3. *run*   past participle _____   present participle _____

4. *take*   past participle _____   present participle _____

Identify the underlined word as a *gerund* or a *present participle*.

5. *I've loved <u>singing</u> ever since I was a little girl.*   5. _____

6. *I doubt that they would be <u>working</u> this late at night.*   6. _____

7. *<u>Calling</u> me a bum was a very mean thing to do.*   7. _____

Circle the participle in each sentence, then write whether it is an *adjective* or a *verb participle*.

8. *We saw the meteorite as it was falling from the sky.*   8. _____

9. *We saw the falling meteorite.*   9. _____

10. *The urn was tarnished and chipped.*   10. _____

11. *The urn was chipped at the auction.*   11. _____

12. *The evidence was damaging to the defense.*   12. _____

13. *I could never have run so fast without those shoes.*   13. _____

Circle the participle in each sentence, then rewrite the sentence so that the participle does not "dangle."

14. *Looking at your essay, it seems to me that you need to be more specific.*

_____

15. *Turning the corner, the stadium came into our view.*

_____

16. *Although exhausted after the night's work, Martha's creative instincts compelled her to keep writing.*

_____

17. *Without waiting for an answer, David's eagerness got the better of him, and he left in a flash.*

_____

18. *Thinking her friends were right behind her, it was frightening for Alison to discover that they were gone.*

_____

Worksheet 7:
Dangling and Misplaced Participles

Circle the participles in the following sentences, then rewrite the sentences, if necessary, to correct any "dangling" participles.

1. *Although angered by the irrationality of his opponent, Senator Sanchez's plan was to address each point calmly.*

   _____

2. *Watching from the bridge, the fireworks bloomed spectacularly over the water.*

   _____

3. *Without admitting her transgression, the club found it hard to forgive Megan.*

   _____

4. *Although mildly discolored by the harsh sunlight, the sofa has retained much of its original beauty.*

   _____

5. *Exhausted from the day's climbing, the looming storm forced the hikers to pitch an early camp.*

   _____

6. *Having studied for hours, it was very disappointing that I did so poorly on the exam.*

   _____

7. *Without being aware of it, termites can infest your home if you don't take the proper precautions.*

   _____

8. *Before working at the bank, no one thought I could hold such a responsible position.*

   _____

9. *Lacking any real sailing skills, David's concern was mainly with keeping the ship afloat.*

   _____

10. *Not wanting to be fooled again, she had her husband followed by a private investigator.*

    _____

Answer Key 7: Dangling and Misplaced Participles

Concept Review 7

1. the noun phrase that it modifies

2. past participle *pushed*, present participle *pushing*

3. past participle *run* (not *ran*), present participle *running*

4. past participle *taken* (not *took*), present participle *taking*

5. gerund (It's the object of the verb *loved*.)

6. present participle (The verb is *would be working*.)

7. gerund (It's the subject of the verb *was*.)

8. participle: *falling*, verb participle

9. participle: *falling*, adjective

10. participles: *tarnished* and *chipped*, adjectives

11. participle: *chipped*, verb participle

12. participle: *damaging*, adjective

13. participle: *run*, verb participle

Each revised sentence below represents only one possible revision to correct the dangling participle. We have chosen what seems to be the clearest and most concise of the possibilities.

14. participle: *looking*. It seems to me, <u>*as I look at your essay,*</u> *that you need to be more specific.*

15. participle: *turning*. <u>*As we turned*</u> *the corner, the stadium came into view.*

16. participle: *exhausted*. *Although* <u>*Martha was*</u> *exhausted after the night's work,* <u>*her*</u> *creative instincts compelled her to keep writing.*

17. *David's eagerness got the better of him,* <u>*and without waiting for an answer*</u>*, he left in a flash.*

18. *Thinking her friends were right behind her,* <u>*Alison was frightened*</u> *to discover that they were gone.*

Worksheet 7

Each revised sentence below represents only one possible revision to correct the dangling participle. We have chosen what seems to be the clearest and most concise of the possibilities.

1. participle: *angered*. *Although angered by the irrationality of his opponent,* <u>*Senator Sanchez planned*</u> *to address each point calmly.*

2. participle: *watching*. <u>*As we watched*</u> *from the bridge, the fireworks bloomed spectacularly over the water.*

3. participle: *admitting*. <u>*Because Megan would not admit*</u> *her transgression, the club found it hard to forgive* <u>*her*</u>*.*

4. participle: *discolored*. *Although mildly discolored by the harsh sunlight, the sofa has retained much of its original beauty.* (Correct)

5. participle: *exhausted*. <u>*The looming storm forced the hikers, exhausted from the day's climbing, to pitch an early camp.*</u>

6. participle: *having*. *Having studied for hours,* <u>*I was very*</u> *disappointed to do so poorly on the exam.*

7. participle: *being*. *Without* <u>*your*</u> *being aware of it, termites can infest your home if you don't take the proper precautions.*

8. participle: *working*. *Before* <u>*I started*</u> *working at the bank, no one thought I could hold such a responsible position.*

9. participle: *lacking*. *Lacking any real sailing skills,* <u>*David was mainly concerned*</u> *with keeping the ship afloat.*

10. participle: *wanting*. *Not wanting to be fooled again, she had her husband followed by a private investigator.* (Correct)

Lesson 8: Other Misplaced Modifiers

The Law of Proximity

> Any modifier *should be as close as possible to the word it modifies*.

Of course, there are many other kinds of modifying phrases besides participial phrases, and you should familiarize yourself with them.

Misplaced Prepositional Phrases

Prepositional phrases are modifying phrases. They are sometimes *adjectives*, which means they modify nouns:

Example:

*The dog **in the car** was barking.* (The prepositional phrase answers the question *which **dog?***)

They may also be *adverbs*, which means they modify verbs, adjectives, or other adverbs:

Example:

*David walked **into the pole.*** (The prepositional phrase answers the question *where did David walk?*)

> Like any modifying phrase, a prepositional phrase can be misplaced.

Wrong: ***As a physician,** it was difficult for me to see such suffering.*

The prepositional phrase *as a physician* answers the question *what is my role?* So it modifies *I*, not *it*:

Right: ***As a physician,** I found it difficult to see such suffering.*

Misplaced Appositives

An appositive is a noun phrase that accompanies and expands another noun, as in

*Franklin, **the only one of us who owned a car,** agreed to drive us all to the game.*

> An appositive must always be adjacent to the noun it modifies.

Wrong: ***A splendid example of late synthetic cubism,** Picasso painted* Three Musicians *in the summer of 1924.*

Of course, Picasso is not an example of synthetic cubism, so the appositive is dangling.

Better: ***A splendid example of late synthetic cubism,*** Three Musicians *was painted by Picasso in the summer of 1924.*

Better: *Picasso painted* Three Musicians, ***a splendid example of late synthetic cubism,*** *in the summer of 1924.*

Misplaced Infinitives

Recall, from Lesson 3, that an *infinitive* is the basic *to _____* form of a verb that usually serves as a noun, as in *I love to shop*. Infinitives can also serve as adjectives:

Example:

*We have a lot more math problems **to do.*** (It answers the question *what kind of **problems** are they?*)

They can also serve as *adverbs*:

Example:

*We are working **to earn** money for the trip.* (It answers the question *why are we **working?***)

> Because infinitives are often modifiers, they can be misplaced.

Wrong: ***To get** our attention, we saw Mr. Genovese take out a giant boa constrictor.*

To get answers the question *why did he **take** it out?* So *take* should be the closest verb to the phrase. We can rearrange the sentence in a couple of ways to fix this.

Right: ***To get** our attention, Mr. Genovese took out a giant boa constrictor.*

Right: *We saw Mr. Genovese take out a giant boa constrictor **to get** our attention.*

Concept Review 8: Other Misplaced Modifiers

Label each underlined phrase as a participial phrase (PART), a prepositional phrase (PREP), an appositive (APP), or an infinitive phrase (INF). Although the SAT will NOT ask you to use these terms to label phrases, this exercise will help you to spot modifier errors more easily.

1. *My friend <u>the lawyer</u> told me that I should never sign any contract <u>without first reading it carefully</u>.*

2. *We should go <u>to the meeting</u> <u>to see whether they need our help</u> <u>with the planning</u>.*

3. *<u>Despite spraining her ankle</u>, our first mate was able to navigate our schooner <u>into port</u>.*

4. *Four score and seven years ago our fathers brought forth <u>on this continent</u>, a new nation, <u>conceived in liberty</u>, and <u>dedicated to the proposition that all men are created equal</u>.*

5. *Now we are engaged <u>in a great civil war</u>, <u>testing whether that nation or any nation so conceived and so dedicated, can long endure</u>.*

6. *We have come <u>to dedicate a portion</u> <u>of that field</u> as a final resting place <u>for those who here gave their lives</u> that that nation might live.*

7. *It is for us <u>the living</u>, rather, <u>to be dedicated here</u> <u>to the unfinished work</u> which they who fought here have thus far so nobly advanced.*

8. *It is rather <u>for us</u> <u>to be here</u> <u>dedicated to the great task</u> <u>remaining before us</u>—that <u>from these honored dead</u> we take increased devotion <u>to that cause</u> <u>for which</u> they gave the last full measure of devotion—that we here highly resolve that these dead shall not have died in vain—that this nation, <u>under God</u>, shall have a new birth of freedom—and that government <u>of the people</u>, <u>by the people</u>, <u>for the people</u>, shall not perish from the earth.*

9. *We <u>the people</u>, in order <u>to form a more perfect union</u>, establish justice, ensure domestic tranquility, provide <u>for the common defense</u>, promote the general welfare and secure the blessings of liberty to ourselves and our posterity, do ordain and establish this Constitution <u>for the United States of America</u>.*

Worksheet 8: Other Misplaced Modifiers

In each of the following sentences, underline and label all participial phrases (PART), prepositional phrases (PREP), appositives (APP), and infinitive phrases (INF), and rewrite any sentence to fix any misplaced modifiers.

1. *Without so much as a blink, the gleaming sword was unsheathed by the warrior.*

   _____

2. *To maintain good health, physicians suggest that both vigorous exercise and good eating habits are required.*

   _____

3. *We found my lost earring walking through the parking lot.*

   _____

4. *Having run for over 4 hours, the finish line was still 10 miles ahead of her.*

   _____

5. *Even with a sprained ankle, the coach forced Adam back into the game.*

   _____

6. *To find a good restaurant, there are many good online guides to help you.*

   _____

7. *In search of a good calculator, not a single store in the mall could help me.*

   _____

8. *A dutiful wife and mother, we were surprised to hear Carol complaining about domestic life.*

   _____

9. *To get a good jump out of the starting blocks, most sprinters say that good body positioning is essential.*

   _____

10. *Among the most sought-after collectibles on the market, we found the antique toys at a garage sale.*

   _____

Answer Key 8: Other Misplaced Modifiers

Concept Review 8

1. *the lawyer* (APP)
   without first reading it carefully (PREP)

2. *to the meeting* (PREP)
   to see whether they need our help (INF)
   with the planning (PREP)

3. *Despite spraining her ankle* (PREP containing a PART)
   into port (PREP)

4. *on this continent* (PREP)
   conceived in liberty (PART containing a PREP)
   dedicated to the proposition that all men are created equal (PART containing a PREP)

5. *in a great civil war* (PREP)
   testing whether that nation . . . (PART)

6. *to dedicate a portion* (INF)
   of that field (PREP)
   for those who here gave their lives (PREP)

7. *the living* (APP)
   to be dedicated here (INF containing a PART)
   to the unfinished work (PREP)

8. *for us* (PREP)
   to be here (INF)
   dedicated to the great task (PART containing a PREP)
   remaining before us (PART containing a PREP)
   from these honored dead (PREP)
   to that cause (PREP)
   for which (PREP)
   under God (PREP)
   of the people (PREP)
   by the people (PREP)
   for the people (PREP)

9. *the people* (APP)
   to form a more perfect union (INF)
   for the common defense (PREP)
   of the United States of America (PREP)

Worksheet 8

Each of these answers provides only one possible correction. On some sentences, other corrections are possible.

1. *Without so much as a blink* (PREP), *the gleaming sword was unsheathed by the warrior* (PREP).

   Correction: *Without so much as a blink, the warrior unsheathed the gleaming sword.*

2. *To maintain good health* (INF), *physicians suggest that both vigorous exercise and good eating habits are required.*

   Correction: *Physicians suggest that both vigorous exercise and good eating habits are required to maintain good health.*

3. *We found my lost earring walking through the parking lot* (PART containing a PREP).

   Correction: *Walking through the parking lot, we found my lost earring.*

4. *Having run for over 4 hours* (PART containing a PREP), *the finish line was still 10 miles ahead of her* (PREP).

   Correction: *Although she had run for over 4 hours, the finish line was still 10 miles ahead of her.*

5. *Even with a sprained ankle* (PREP), *the coach forced Adam back into the game* (PREP).

   Correction: *Even though Adam had a sprained ankle, the coach forced him back into the game.*

6. *To find a good restaurant* (INF), *there are many good online guides to help you* (INF).

   Correction: *There are many good online guides to help you find a good restaurant.*

7. *In search of a good calculator* (PREP), *not a single store in the mall* (PREP) *could help me.*

   Correction: *Not a single store in the mall could help me find a good calculator.*

8. *A dutiful wife and mother* (APP), *we were surprised to hear Carol complaining about domestic life* (PREP).

   Correction: *We were surprised to hear Carol, a dutiful wife and mother, complaining about domestic life.*

9. *To get a good jump* (INF) *out of the starting blocks* (PREP), *most sprinters say that good body positioning is essential.*

   Correction: *Most sprinters say that good body positioning is essential for getting a good jump out of the starting blocks.*

10. *Among the most sought-after collectibles* (PREP) *on the market* (PREP), *we found the antique toys at a garage sale* (PREP).

    Correction: *We found the antique toys, which are among the most sought-after collectibles on the market, at a garage sale.*

Lesson 9: Tricky Tenses

Verb Tenses

The *tense* of a verb is what indicates its place and extent in time. There are two common situations in which tenses can be tricky: those with "perfect" verbs and those with "timeless" verbs.

"Perfect" Verbs

You use the *perfect tenses* whenever you need to indicate that some event is *completed* before some other point in time. (Here, the word *perfect* means *complete*, not *flawless*.) They are usually *relative* tenses, that is, they show a particular relationship to another verb or reference to time within the sentence. All perfect tenses use the helping verb *to* **have**, as in *we* **had walked**, *we* **have walked**, and *we* **will have walked**.

> The *past perfect tense* shows that an event had been completed before another point in the past. You can think of it as the "past past" tense.

Example:

> *By the time we* **arrived** *at the reception, Glen* **had** *already* **given** *the toast.*

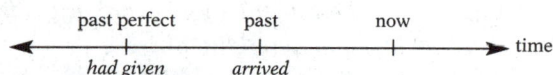

```
        past perfect      past        now
    ◄───────┼──────────────┼───────────┼──────► time
         had given       arrived
```

> When a sentence contains two past-tense verbs, check whether one event was completed before the other. If so, the earlier event should be given the past perfect tense.

> The *present perfect tense*, unlike the other perfect tenses, usually does not show completion, but that an event either *extends from the past to the present* or *occurs at an extended or unspecified time in the past.* You can think of it as the "past plus present" tense or the "unspecific past."

Example:

> *She has been so nice to me.*
> (This means *she was nice to me* and also *she still is nice to me.* It combines past and present.)

Example:

> *We* **have taken** *only two tests this semester.*
> (The taking of the tests did not happen at one specific time, but over an extended time in the past.)

> The *future perfect tense* shows that something will have been completed before some time in the future.

Example:

> *By* **Friday,** *we* **will have completed** *the entire project.*

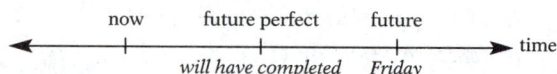

```
            now       future perfect    future
    ◄────────┼──────────────┼─────────────┼──────► time
                      will have completed  Friday
```

> Participles must be "perfect," too, when they indicate an action completed before another action.

Example:

> **Having walked** *all night, we were desperate to find rest at dawn.*
> (The *walking* was *completed* by dawn, so the participle is "past perfect.")

"Timeless" Verbs

> When you need to discuss a theory, an artistic work, or a general nonhistorical fact, the verb that describes it is "timeless" and should take the *present tense* by default.

Wrong: *The ancient Greek philosopher Zeno believed that all motion was an illusion.*

Right: *The ancient Greek philosopher Zeno believed that all motion is an illusion.*
The *believing* is in the past, since Zeno's long gone, but the theory is timeless.

Concept Review 9: Tricky Tenses

1. When are the perfect tenses used?

2. What kinds of ideas are conveyed by "timeless" present-tense verbs?

Circle the correct verb in each of the following sentences.

3. *Glen (came/has come) to work exhausted this morning because he (stayed/had stayed) up all last night.*

4. *Already, and without (spending/having spent) so much as an hour on research, Dale (wrote/has written) the first draft of her essay.*

5. *(Developing/Having developed) the first compressed-air automobile, he (hoped/had hoped) to reveal it to the world at the exposition.*

6. *Shakespeare's tragedies (were/are) concerned with the deepest aspects of the human condition.*

The meaning of the following sentence is ambiguous.

> *His legs ached because he ran farther than he ever had [run] before.*

Rewrite it using the correct tenses to indicate that

7. The aching started *before* he finished running: _____

8. The aching started *after* he finished running: _____

Fix any tense problems in the following sentences.

9. *Right after school, we had gone to Mario's for a pizza and a few Cokes.*

   _____

10. *Finding no evidence against the accused, the detective had to release him.*

    _____

11. *Being captured by the rebels, David soon began to fear he would never escape.*

    _____

12. *When I got home, I wrote an essay on the baseball game that I saw that afternoon.*

    _____

Worksheet 9: Tricky Tenses

Correct any tense errors in the following sentences.

1. *By the time the committee had adjourned, it voted on all four key proposals.*

_____

2. *In the evening, we had a nice meal with the same group of people we skied with that afternoon.*

_____

3. *By the time I am done with finals, I will write four major papers.*

_____

4. *Being nominated for office, Ellen felt that she had to run an honest campaign.*

_____

5. *It surprised us to learn that Venus was almost the same size as Earth.*

_____

6. *Reading* The Sun Also Rises, *I feel as if I've learned a great deal about bullfighting.*

_____

7. *Most Oscar nominees claimed that they were happy simply to be nominated.*

_____

8. *When the epidemic struck Rwanda, the entire population had suffered.*

_____

9. *I have never felt so free as when I am running.*

_____

10. *Centuries ago, physicians had believed that illnesses were caused by imbalances in bodily fluids.*

_____

11. *David has been the president of the club ever since it was founded.*

_____

12. *Over the last several years, real estate values increased by over 20%.*

_____

13. *Students often worry excessively about grades and will forget about actually understanding the concepts.*

_____

14. *We need not bother to patch the hull now that the entire boat had been inundated.*

_____

15. *By the time we arrived at the tent where the reception would be held, the caterers set up all the chairs.*

_____

16. *We will have been in this house for three years in February.*

_____

Answer Key 9: Tricky Tenses

Concept Review 9

1. when showing that an event was completed before another event, or, in the case of the present perfect tense, when showing that an event occurs over an extended time in the past or extends from the past to the present

2. theories, general nonhistorical facts, and works of art

3. *Glen __came__ to work exhausted this morning because he __had stayed__ up all last night.* (The *staying up* was completed before he *came to work*.)

4. *Already, and without __having spent__ so much as an hour on research, Dale __has written__ the first draft of her essay.* (The word *already* establishes the current time as a reference point. Since the verbs indicate actions completed prior to now, they take the present perfect tense.)

5. *__Having developed__ the first compressed-air automobile, he __hoped__ to reveal it to the world at the exposition.* (He must have *developed* it before he could *hope to reveal it*.)

6. *Shakespeare's tragedies __are__ concerned with the deepest aspects of the human condition.* (His works are still available to us, so they get the present tense.)

7. *His legs ached because he __was running__ farther than he ever had before.*

8. *His legs ached because he __had run__ farther than he ever had before.*

9. *Right after school, we __went__ to Mario's for a pizza and a few Cokes.* (No need for past perfect.)

10. *__Having found__ no evidence against the accused, the detective had to release him.* (The search for evidence was completed before the release.)

11. *__Having been__ captured by the rebels, David soon began to fear he would never escape.* (The capture occurred before his fear set in.)

12. *When I got home, I wrote an essay on the baseball game that I __had seen__ that afternoon.* (The *writing* happened after the *seeing*.)

Worksheet 9

1. *By the time the committee __adjourned__, it __had voted__ on all four key proposals.* (The voting was completed before the adjournment, so it should take the perfect tense.)

2. *In the evening, we had a nice meal with the same group of people we __had skied__ with that afternoon.* (The skiing was completed before the meal, so it should take the perfect tense.)

3. *By the time I am done with finals, I __will have written__ four major papers.* (The writing will be completed before the finals.)

4. *__Having been nominated__ for office, Ellen felt that she had to run an honest campaign.* (The *nomination* must be completed before the *running* can start.)

5. *It surprised us to learn that Venus __is__ almost the same size as Earth.* (Facts take the present tense.)

6. *__Having read__ The Sun Also Rises, I feel as if I've learned a great deal about bullfighting.* (Since the learning occurred over an extended time in the past, the present perfect tense is appropriate; since the *reading* was prior to or simultaneous with the *learning*, it must also be in the perfect form.)

7. *Most Oscar nominees claimed that they were happy simply to __have been nominated__.* (The *nominating* must have been completed if they are happy about the outcome.)

8. *When the epidemic struck Rwanda, the entire population __suffered__.* (Since the *suffering* occurred when the epidemic *struck*, the two verbs should have the same tense.)

9. *I __never feel__ so free as when I am running.* (This expresses a general fact, so it is "timeless.")

10. *Centuries ago, physicians __believed__ that illnesses were caused by imbalances in bodily fluids.* (Since this expresses a theory that has been disproven, it is not "timeless," but relegated to the past.)

11. *David has been the president of the club ever since it was founded.* (Correct)

12. *Over the last several years, real estate values __have increased__ by over 20%.* (The increase occurred over an extended time in the past.)

13. *Students often worry excessively about grades and __forget__ about actually understanding the concepts.* (Tense consistency requires the present tense.)

14. *We need not bother to patch the hull now that the entire boat __has been__ inundated.* (The present perfect is needed to show the connection to the present, which is implied by the present-tense verb *bother*.)

15. *By the time we arrived at the tent where the reception would be held, the caterers __had set up__ all the chairs.* (The *setting up* was completed before we *arrived*.)

16. *We will have been in this house for three years in February.* (Correct)

Lesson 10: Idiom Errors

What Is an Idiom?

Idioms are common phrases with quirky, nonliteral meanings. Most idioms, like *carry through, across the board, come on strong, get your feet wet, bang for the buck, all ears, pull your leg, eat crow,* etc., are so ingrained in our language that we hardly notice that their meanings are so nonliteral. We appreciate our idioms when we hear someone speak who has just learned English, since the idioms take the longest to learn.

Watch Your Prepositions

The SAT won't expect you to memorize the thousands of idioms in the English language, but it does expect you to recognize *preposition errors*. Remember from Lesson 2 that prepositions are words like *to, from, of, for, by, in, before, with, beyond,* and *up* that show relative position or direction. Certain idiomatic phrases, like *arguing with*, require a particular preposition. (That is, saying something like *She was arguing **against** her brother* is not a proper idiom.) The choice of preposition is not usually a matter of logic, as in the sentence

> *The house was on fire, so the firefighters put it out.*

This sentence contains two prepositions, *on* and *out*, but neither is used literally or logically: the house wasn't really "on" a fire, and the firemen didn't put the fire "out." But if you tried to make the sentence literal and logical, it would sound ridiculous or overly stilted:

> *The house was aflame, so the firefighters extinguished the blaze.*

So idioms are an important part of clear and effective language.

> When you notice a preposition in a sentence, always ask: "Is that preposition necessary, and if so, is it the correct preposition for that particular phrase?"

Wrong: *We were no longer satisfied **at** the level **of** service we were receiving.*
The prepositions are *at* and *of.* The idiom *level of service* is correct, but the idiom *satisfied at* is not. The correct idiom is *satisfied with.*

Right: *We were no longer satisfied **with** the level of service we were receiving.*

ESP: Eliminate Superfluous Prepositions

> Casual speech often uses extra prepositions. When you write, however, try to eliminate unnecessary prepositions. Notice that in phrases like the following, the preposition is unnecessary and thus "nonstandard."

Examples:

The pole did not extend ~~out~~ far enough.

Since my injury, it hurts to climb ~~up~~ the stairs.

Although clearly angry, the students were not yet ready to fight ~~against~~ the ruling.

We were unsuccessful in our attempt to extract ~~out~~ the chemical from the venom.

The illness can make one dizzy and prone to falling ~~down~~.

If you don't hurry, you'll miss ~~out on~~ all the fun!

There were plenty of volunteers to help ~~out~~ with the race.

Before we prepare the steaks, we should fry ~~up~~ some peppers.

Her speed and strength helped her to dominate ~~over~~ her opponents.

Concept Review 10: Idiom Errors

Choose the correct preposition or phrase (if any) to complete each of the following sentences. If no word or phrase is required, circle the dash (—).

1. *I prefer spaghetti (to/over/more than/—) linguine.*

2. *The students were protesting (against/over/—) the decision to cut financial aid.*

3. *We are all concerned (about/with/—) your decision to drop out of school.*

4. *It took nearly an hour to open (up/—) the trunk.*

5. *Eleanor has always been concerned (with/about/—) feminist issues.*

6. *We all agreed (on/with/about/—) the decision to go skiing rather than hiking.*

7. *She would not agree (to/on/with/about) the plea bargain.*

8. *We found dozens of old photographs hidden (in/—) between the pages.*

9. *Good study habits are necessary (to/for/in) academic success.*

10. *The new house color is not very different (from/than/to/—) the old one.*

11. *His girlfriend was angry (with/at/—) him for not calling sooner.*

12. *It will be many years before we fill (up/—) all the pages in this photo album.*

13. *They were both angry (about/at/with) the boys' behavior.*

14. *You should plan (to come/on coming) before 6:00 pm.*

15. *Matt was kicked off (of/—) the team for drinking at a party.*

16. *We will make sure that your contract complies (with/to/—) the laws of your state.*

17. *After the operation, Denise was no longer capable (of playing/to play) the violin.*

Worksheet 10: Idiom Errors

Consider the idiom in each sentence and fill in the correct preposition, if one is required.

1. *The interview provided insight _____ what great directors think about.*

2. *We were very angry _____ him for ignoring our phone calls.*

3. *Her tests include questions that seem very different _____ those that we see in the homework.*

4. *My mother preferred my singing _____ my practicing guitar.*

5. *Detective Simone ran in pursuit _____ the perpetrators.*

6. *We had to shoo the cat off _____ the car.*

7. *When she arrived on campus, she felt truly independent _____ her parents for the first time.*

8. *They scoured the bedroom in search _____ the missing bracelet.*

9. *We were very angry _____ the exorbitant price of gasoline at the corner gas station.*

10. *Although they were friends, they always seemed to be arguing _____ each other.*

11. *I am concerned _____ your failure to pass the last few quizzes.*

12. *We all agreed _____ the color scheme for the wedding.*

13. *Tony had to climb _____ the ladder to get to the top bunk.*

14. *As a public defender, he was very concerned _____ the legal issue of search and seizure.*

15. *It was hard not to agree _____ her offer of a free movie ticket.*

16. *The vaccine was intended to protect everyone working on the project _____ disease.*

17. *I could hardly pay attention in class because I was daydreaming _____ the prom.*

18. *Allison and her sister both excel _____ dance and music.*

19. *I could never dream _____ confronting the coach with such a trivial concern.*

20. *I arrived at the meeting too late to raise my objection _____ the proposal.*

21. *The third edition of this book really doesn't differ very much at all _____ the first two.*

22. *I beg to differ _____ you, but your story does not fit my recollection at all.*

23. *If we don't act soon, we may miss _____ the opportunity to lock in the lowest rates.*

Answer Key 10: Idiom Errors

Concept Review 10

1. I prefer spaghetti <u>to</u> linguine.

2. The students were protesting (none needed) the decision to cut financial aid.

3. We are all concerned <u>about</u> your decision to drop out of school. (Concerned about means worried about.)

4. It took nearly an hour to open (none needed) the trunk.

5. Eleanor has always been concerned <u>with</u> feminist issues. (Concerned with means occupied with or involved in.)

6. We all agreed <u>on</u> the decision to go skiing rather than hiking. (You agree on mutual decisions or plans.)

7. She would not agree <u>to</u> the plea bargain. (You agree to offers.)

8. We found dozens of old photographs hidden (none needed) between the pages.

9. Good study habits are necessary <u>to</u> (or sometimes <u>for</u>) academic success.

10. The new house color is not very different <u>from</u> the old one. (Use than only with **comparatives** like bigger; different is not a comparative.)

11. His girlfriend was angry <u>with</u> him for not calling sooner. (You get angry with people.)

12. It will be many years before we fill (none needed) all the pages in this photo album.

13. They were both angry <u>about</u> the boys' behavior. (You get angry about situations.)

14. You should plan <u>to come</u> before 6:00 pm. (Plan to means make a plan to, but plan on means rely on.)

15. Matt was kicked off (none needed) the team for drinking at a party.

16. We will make sure that your contract complies <u>with</u> the laws of your state.

17. After the operation, Denise was no longer capable <u>of playing</u> the violin.

Worksheet 10

1. The interview provided insight <u>into</u> what great directors think about.

2. We were very angry <u>with</u> him for ignoring our phone calls.

3. Her tests include questions that seem very different <u>from</u> those that we see in the homework.

4. My mother preferred my singing <u>to</u> my practicing guitar.

5. Detective Simone ran in pursuit <u>of</u> the perpetrators.

6. We had to shoo the cat off (none needed) the car.

7. When she arrived on campus, she felt truly independent <u>of</u> her parents for the first time.

8. They scoured the bedroom in search <u>of</u> the missing bracelet.

9. We were very angry <u>about</u> the exorbitant price of gasoline at the corner gas station.

10. Although they were friends, they always seemed to be arguing <u>with</u> each other.

11. I am concerned <u>about</u> your failure to pass the last few quizzes.

12. We all agreed <u>on</u> the color scheme for the wedding.

13. Tony had to climb (none needed) the ladder to get to the top bunk.

14. As a public defender, he was very concerned <u>with</u> the legal issue of search and seizure.

15. It was hard not to agree <u>to</u> her offer of a free movie ticket.

16. The vaccine was intended to protect everyone working on the project <u>from</u> disease.

17. I could hardly pay attention in class because I was daydreaming <u>about</u> the prom.

18. Allison and her sister both excel <u>in</u> dance and music.

19. I could never dream <u>of</u> confronting the coach with such a trivial concern.

20. I arrived at the meeting too late to raise my objection <u>to</u> the proposal.

21. The third edition of this book really doesn't differ very much at all <u>from</u> the first two.

22. I beg to differ <u>with</u> you, but your story does not fit my recollection at all.

23. If we don't act soon, we may miss (none needed) the opportunity to lock in the lowest rates.

Lesson 11: Diction Errors

What Are Diction Errors?

Diction errors are "wrong word" errors. If an SAT sentence contains a word that sounds *almost* right but not quite, it may well be a diction error. Study this list of words so that you can spot common diction errors.

Commonly Confused Words

accept/except: To *accept* something means to *agree to take it.* <*accept* an offer> To *except* something is to *exclude it.*

adapt/adopt/adept: To *adapt* something means to *make it suitable for a particular purpose* (from *apt*, which means *appropriate* or *suitable*). To *adopt* means to *choose as one's own.* Someone *adept* is *highly skilled.* <an *adept* player>

affect/effect: To *affect* means to *influence.* <It *affected* me deeply.> An *effect* is a *result or consequence.* <It had a good *effect.*> They are easily confused because to *affect* means to *have an effect* on something.

allude/elude/allusion/illusion: To *allude to* something means to *make a subtle or indirect reference* to it. To *elude* something means to *escape from it.* An *allusion* is a *subtle reference,* but an *illusion* is a *deception* or *misconception.*

ambivalent/ambiguous: When you're *ambivalent* you *have conflicting feelings* about something. <I feel *ambivalent* about the party.> Something *ambiguous* is *unclear* or *having more than one interpretation.* <an *ambiguous* signal>

cite/site/sight: To *cite* means to *mention as a source of information* or to *commend for meritorious action.* <*cite* an article in her essay> A *site* is a *place where a planned activity occurs.* To *sight* means to *see at a specific location.*

compliment/complement: A *compliment* is a *praising personal comment.* A *complement* is something that *completes or makes a whole.* (Notice the **ple** in complement and complete.)

council/counsel: A *council* is a *committee.* <the executive **council**> To *counsel* is to *give advice.* <He **counseled** me.>

discrete/discreet: *Discrete* means *distinct.* <A watch contains dozens of *discrete* parts.> Someone *discreet* is *prudently modest.* <Act **discreetly.**>

elicit/illicit: To *elicit* means to *bring out or to call forth.* <The joke **elicited** laughter.> *Illicit* means *unlawful.*

eminent/imminent: Someone *eminent* is *prominently distinguished.* <an **eminent** historian> Something *imminent* is *about to occur.* <**imminent** doom>

flaunt/flout: To *flaunt* something means to *show it off.* <**flaunt** your talents> To *flout* something means to *show contempt for it.* <**flout** the rules>

gambit/gamut: A *gambit* is a *careful strategy* or an *opening move.* The *gamut* is the *complete range.* <run the **gamut**>

imply/infer: To *imply* means to *suggest* or *hint at,* but to *infer* means to *draw a conclusion from evidence.*

its/it's, their/they're, whose/who's, your/you're: Apostrophes can show possession (as in *David's bike*) or indicate missing letters in a contraction (as in *can't* as a contraction of *cannot*). In each of the confusing word pairs above, apostrophes indicate **contraction,** not possession: *it's* = *it is* or *it has,* *they're* = *they are,* *you're* = *you are,* and *who's* = *who is* or *who has.* The possessives are the ones without apostrophes.

morale/moral: *Morale* (n: mor-AL) is *shared enthusiasm for and dedication to a goal.* <The team's **morale** was very high after the win.> A *moral* (n: MOR-al) is a *lesson or principle about good behavior.* <The story had a nice **moral.**>

phase/faze: A *phase* is a *stage in a process.* <third **phase** of the project> The idiom to *phase out* means to *eliminate in stages.* To *faze* someone means to *disturb his or her composure.* <I was a bit **fazed** by the interruption.>

precede/proceed/proceeds: To *precede* something means to *come before it* (*pre-* before). To *proceed* means to *go on, usually after a pause* (*pro-* forward). *Proceeds* are *funds received from a venture.* <**proceeds** from the raffle>

principal/principle: A *principal* is your *pal*—the *head of a school.* It's also the *initial investment in an interest-bearing account.* (Money in the bank can be a pretty good *pal,* too, eh?) A *principle* is a *guiding rule.*

reticent/reluctant: Someone *reticent* is *reserved* or *reluctant to talk freely.* Don't use it to mean *reluctant.*

Concept Review 11: Diction Errors

Circle any diction errors in each of the following sentences, and write the correct word(s) in the blank.

1. *Although most of the manuscripts were signed by their authors, some were written unanimously.* _____

2. *It was hard for the comic to illicit even the slightest laugh from the crowd.* _____

3. *She seems to have a hard time excepting compliments.* _____

4. *We needed to adopt the old engine to fit the new go-cart.* _____

5. *I like all flavors of ice cream accept mocha.* _____

6. *The imminent congresswoman was re-elected easily.* _____

7. *While his activities were clearly immoral, they were not elicit.* _____

8. *The committee decided to adapt the new rules regarding membership.* _____

9. *She thought it wise to be discrete about her previous relationship with the defendant.* _____

10. *The counsel will decide how to finance the new city park.* _____

11. *Rather than cooperating with the rest of the team, Richard is always trying to flaunt the rules.* _____

12. *His knowledge of sports runs the gambit from table tennis to arena football.* _____

13. *The jury should not imply guilt from the defendant's refusal to answer these questions.* _____

14. *We were amazed at how adapt a juggler Carl was.* _____

15. *Rather than eliminate the department all at once, they decided to faze it out gradually.* _____

16. *Dogs barking can often signal eminent danger.* _____

17. *Training a dog is easy, once you've got it's attention.* _____

18. *She was sending mixed signals, so it was ambivalent whether she really wanted to go.* _____

19. *After our vacation, we decided to precede with the plan.* _____

20. *They don't seem to tolerate anyone who does not abide by their principals.* _____

21. *I was trying to infer that I should be considered for the new position.* _____

22. *I always felt reticent to talk in class.* _____

23. *Deanne was not even phased by the fire alarm.* _____

24. *The vitamins didn't have as great an affect as I thought they would.* _____

25. *She was the principle benefactor of the new hospital ward.* _____

26. *The police officer was sighted for her efforts in the hostage rescue.* _____

27. *She made an illusion to the fact that she was once a beauty queen.* _____

28. *Even the most trivial news seems to effect the stock price immediately.* _____

29. *David felt ambiguous about testifying against his partner.* _____

30. *The moral of the troops was at an all-time low during the Christmas season.* _____

31. *That scarf really compliments your outfit.* _____

32. *The meaning of that poem alludes me.* _____

33. *Her study of gorillas has been sited in several major books.* _____

Worksheet 11: Diction Errors

Circle any diction errors in each of the following sentences, and write the correct word(s) in the blank.

1. *The reason we canceled the trip is because Wynona couldn't come on that weekend.* _____

2. *Most of the meeting was spent honing in on the final plans for building the float.* _____

3. *Matt was finally kicked off the starting squad for flaunting the team rules.* _____

4. *I tried to stay awake for the lecture, but I was so disinterested that I dozed off before the professor was half finished.* _____

5. *Ms. Davis said that we should always try and speak as if we were trying to hold a conversation with a person in the very back of the auditorium.* _____

6. *Jennifer was very reticent to speak about the incident, even many years after it occurred.* _____

7. *The article mentioned the low voter turnout in order to infer that the senator may not have been elected by a true majority.* _____

8. *Even the ten-run deficit didn't seem to phase the manager; he refused to waver in his optimism.* _____

9. *We decided that it was prudent to wait until the debris was cleared before we preceded.* _____

10. *Although the police initially had many solid leads, the suspect alluded them for several months.* _____

11. *It may be years before we understand how pollution from the new power plant might effect the regional environment.* _____

12. *The new online store's musical offerings run the gambit from arias to zydeco.* _____

13. *Heather was the principle author of the study that was recently published in a prominent scientific magazine.* _____

14. *We were thrilled to get such an imminent expert on world affairs to speak at our colloquium on such short notice.* _____

15. *All of the invited guests accept Anthony arrived promptly.* _____

16. *Mrs. Sullivan went on all period about the illusions to Victorian society in Alice in Wonderland.* _____

17. *For nearly the entire semester, I felt so inhabited that I never so much as razed my hand in class.* _____

18. *Since they did not have a plan for the project, they decided to refer their approval until later.* _____

19. *Try as they might, the hikers could not find the anecdote to the snake venom.* _____

20. *The acid solution was so potent that we had to delude it with water before we could use it safely.* _____

21. *The symbols on the cave walls are ambivalent; scientists have been debating their meaning for decades.* _____

22. *Despite the setbacks with the caterers, the Breedens managed to give a splendidly eloquent party.* _____

23. *As someone committed to fairness in education, she could not accept the iniquity of the admissions policy.* _____

Answer Key 11: Diction Errors

Concept Review 11

1. *Although most of the manuscripts were signed by their authors, some were written underlined anonymously.*
2. *It was hard for the comic to elicit even the slightest laugh from the crowd.*
3. *She seems to have a hard time accepting compliments.*
4. *We needed to adapt the old engine to fit the new go-cart.*
5. *I like all flavors of ice cream except mocha.*
6. *The eminent congresswoman was re-elected easily.*
7. *While his activities were clearly immoral, they were not illicit.*
8. *The committee decided to adopt the new rules regarding membership.*
9. *She thought it wise to be discreet about her previous relationship with the defendant.*
10. *The council will decide how to finance the new city park.*
11. *Rather than cooperating with the rest of the team, Richard is always trying to flout the rules.*
12. *His knowledge of sports runs the gamut from table tennis to arena football.*
13. *The jury should not infer guilt from the defendant's refusal to answer these questions.*
14. *We were amazed at how adept a juggler Carl was.*
15. *Rather than eliminate the department all at once, they decided to phase it out gradually.*
16. *Dogs barking can often signal imminent danger.*
17. *Training a dog is easy, once you've got its attention.*
18. *She was sending mixed signals, so it was ambiguous whether she really wanted to go.*
19. *After our vacation, we decided to proceed with the plan.*
20. *They don't seem to tolerate anyone who does not abide by their principles.*
21. *I was trying to imply that I should be considered for the new position.*
22. *I always felt reluctant to talk in class.*
23. *Deanne was not even fazed by the fire alarm.*
24. *The vitamins didn't have as great an effect as I thought they would.*
25. *She was the principal benefactor of the new hospital ward.*
26. *The police officer was cited for her efforts in the hostage rescue.*
27. *She made an allusion to the fact that she was once a beauty queen.*
28. *Even the most trivial news seems to affect the stock price immediately.*
29. *David felt ambivalent about testifying against his partner.*
30. *The morale of the troops was at an all-time low during the Christmas season.*
31. *That scarf really complements your outfit.*
32. *The meaning of that poem eludes me.*
33. *Her study of gorillas has been cited in several major books.*

Worksheet 11

1. *The reason we canceled the trip is that. . . . (The reason is a thing.)*
2. *Most of the meeting was spent homing in on. . . .*
3. *Matt was finally kicked off the starting squad for flouting. . . .*
4. *I tried to stay awake for the lecture, but I was so uninterested. . . . (Disinterested means impartial.)*
5. *Ms. Davis said that we should always try to. . . .*
6. *Jennifer was very reluctant to speak. . . .*
7. *The article mentioned the low voter turnout in order to imply. . . .*
8. *Even the ten-run deficit didn't seem to faze the manager. . . .*
9. *We decided that it was prudent to wait until the debris was cleared before we proceeded.*
10. *Although the police initially had many solid leads, the suspect eluded them for several months.*
11. *It may be years before we understand how pollution from the new power plant might affect the regional environment.*
12. *The new online store's musical offerings run the gamut from arias to zydeco.*
13. *Heather was the principal author of the study. . . .*
14. *We were thrilled to get such an eminent expert. . . .*
15. *All of the invited guests except Anthony arrived promptly.*
16. *Mrs. Sullivan went on all period about the allusions. . . .*
17. *For nearly the entire semester, I felt so inhibited that I never so much as raised my hand in class.*
18. *Since they did not have a plan for the project, they decided to defer their approval until later.*
19. *Try as they might, the hikers could not find the antidote. . . .*
20. *The acid solution was so potent that we had to dilute it with water before we could use it safely.*
21. *The symbols on the cave walls are ambiguous; scientists have been debating their meaning for decades.*
22. *Despite the setbacks with the caterers, the Breedens managed to give a splendidly elegant party. (Eloquent means well-spoken.)*
23. *As someone committed to fairness in education, she could not accept the inequity. . . . (Iniquity is sin.)*

Lesson 12: Other Modifier Problems

Adjectives vs. Adverbs

Don't use an *adjective* to do the job of an *adverb*. *Adjectives* (like *green, generous,* and *gargantuan*) are words that modify *nouns*. *Adverbs* (like *gently, globally,* and *grossly*) are words that modify *verbs, adjectives,* or *other adverbs*.

Wrong: *I was impressed by how **cogent** his argument was presented.*

Although the *argument* was *cogent,* the modifier in this sentence is intended to answer the question *how was it **presented?*** Since it modifies a verb, it is an *adverb* and should take the *-ly* form.

Right: *I was impressed by how **cogently** his argument was presented.*

An *adverb* may also be used to modify the statement that a *whole sentence* makes.

Okay: *Clearly, the dust storm obscured the rider's vision.*

Some people claim that the adverb *clearly* must modify the verb *obscured,* and say that it's illogical for something to be *obscured clearly,* because *obscured* is the opposite of *clear.* However, *adverbs can be used to modify the statement as a whole* rather than the verb it contains. In this case, *Clearly* means *What follows is a clear and obvious statement,* but it's much more concise, wouldn't you agree?

Two common modifiers, *fast* and *well,* can be used as either adjectives or adverbs. *Fast* is an adjective in *The car is fast,* but it is an adverb in *He talks too fast,* describing how he *talks.* *Well* is an adjective meaning *healthy* in *I haven't been well lately,* but it is an adverb in *She sings very well,* describing how she *sings.*

Comparative Adjectives and Adverbs

Use the proper form when using comparative modifiers. *Comparative adjectives* take one of two forms: *fast* becomes comparative by adding *-er* to make *faster,* but *adorable* becomes

comparative by adding *more* to make *more adorable.* (*Adorabler* just doesn't sound right, does it?) *Comparative adverbs* almost always start with *more* as in *more rapidly,* but some irregular (that is, non "*-ly*") adverbs can take *-er,* as in *She runs **faster** than anyone else in the class.*

Wrong: *The briefcase feels **more light** than it did this morning.* (This is not the proper idiom.)

Right: *The briefcase feels **lighter** than it did this morning.*

Wrong: *Please try to hold the baby **gentler** next time.* (*Gentler* is a comparative adjective, not an adverb.)

Right: *Please try to hold the baby **more gently** next time.*

Some modifiers should not take the comparative form because they are *absolutes.* For instance, it is illogical for one thing to be *more unique* than another thing, because *unique* means *one of a kind,* and this shows an absolute quality.

Wrong: *The loss was made **more inevitable** by the injury to our starting pitcher.* (It's either *inevitable* or it's not!)

Right: *The loss was made **inevitable** by the injury to our starting pitcher.*

Eliminate Redundancy

A *redundancy* is an unnecessary repetition of an idea. *Eliminate all redundancies from your writing.* To check whether a word or phrase is redundant, reread the sentence without that word or phrase. If the meaning of the sentence remains unchanged, then the word or phrase is redundant.

Wrong: *With only seconds **remaining to go** in the game, Michael **sped quickly** down the court.*

Since *remaining* means roughly the same as *to go,* we don't need both. Also, to *speed* means to *move quickly,* so *sped quickly* is redundant.

Right: *With only seconds **remaining** in the game, Michael **sped** down the court.*

Concept Review 12: Other Modifier Problems

Give the comparative form of each adjective or adverb.

1. *gentle* _____

2. *precious* _____

3. *gently* _____

4. *lovely* _____

5. *quiet* _____

6. *sporty* _____

7. Circle the absolute modifiers in the list below.

wild	*impossible*	*sufficient*	*final*	*fatal*
complete	*inevitable*	*responsive*	*tolerable*	*willing*
entire	*effective*	*ideal*	*universal*	*unique*

8. What is the correct comparative form of an absolute modifier?

In each of the following sentences, circle the modifying words or phrases and label them *adjectives* (**ADJ**), *adverbs* (**ADV**), or *sentence modifiers* (**SMOD**).

9. *The music was overwhelmingly beautiful.*

10. *The other store is far less convenient than the one on the corner.*

11. *David unknowingly picked up the wrong bag.*

12. *Unfortunately, we could hardly see the band from our awful seats.*

13. *The best thing to do is to wait patiently.*

14. *Personally, I vastly prefer bison meat to beef.*

15. *Most likely, the lacrosse team left on the first bus.*

16. *I almost never watch television anymore.*

17. Cross out any redundant words or phrases in the paragraph below. (Hint: there are at least ten redundancies.)

When we refer back to past history, we can see that whenever a new innovation is introduced for the first time, people rarely accept the whole entire concept, at least not right away. If and when something threatens the ways of the past, people don't part easily with their old ways. Although not everyone necessarily needs to maintain the status quo, consistency and predictability make people feel comfortable. Even when technology comes up with a way to do things better, people often continue on with their older, less efficient ways. For instance, it's not uncommon for people to use e-mail while at the same time continuing to correspond via "snail mail." If they would quickly pause for a moment, they would see that they can communicate more effectively through the Internet—and save some trees!

Worksheet 12: Other Modifier Problems

Correct any modifier problems in the sentences below.

1. *The latest political commercials make their points stronger than previous ones.*

2. *My shirt smelled quite foully after rugby practice.*

3. *Recent technological advances have made it easier to extract minuscule chemical traces from geological samples.*

4. *We never usually get to go to such elegant restaurants.*

5. *Although both of my parents have pretty level heads, my father is the most patient.*

6. *The third graders weren't hardly interested in going to the museum after school.*

7. *I could always sing in front of a crowd easier than I could give a speech.*

8. *In many areas of the country, wind energy can be converted to electricity even more efficient than fossil energy.*

9. *I felt surprisingly well after Saturday's ten-mile run.*

10. *The microscopic size of the fracture made it more impossible to detect, even with special instruments.*

11. *The committee had never been so unanimous as they were on the most recent vote.*

12. *These measures won't barely address the state's deficit.*

13. *The teacher never told us about the test until the day before.*

14. *We weren't real sure that the plan would work.*

15. *Students never usually bother to examine the veracity of the "facts" they are supposed to memorize in history class.*

16. *Gena's guess was the most correct of anyone's in the class.*

Answer Key 12: Other Modifier Problems

Concept Review 12

1. *gentler*
2. *more precious*
3. *more gently*
4. *more lovely*
5. *quieter*
6. *sportier*
7. absolutes: *impossible, inevitable, ideal, complete, final, universal, entire, sufficient, fatal, unique*
8. Trick question! Of course, absolute modifiers are absolute *because* they have no comparative forms.
9. *overwhelmingly* (ADV modifying the ADJ *beautiful*); *beautiful* (ADJ)
10. *other* (ADJ); *far* (ADV modifying the ADJ *less convenient*); *less* (ADV modifying the ADJ *convenient*); *convenient* (ADJ); *on the corner* (ADJ prep phrase)
11. *unknowingly* (ADV); *wrong* (ADJ)
12. *unfortunately* (SMOD); *hardly* (ADV modifying the V *see*); *from our awful seats* (ADV prep phrase modifying V *see*); *awful* (ADJ)
13. *best* (ADJ); *to do* (ADJ infinitive); *patiently* (ADV)
14. *personally* (SMOD); *vastly* (ADV modifying V *prefer*); *to beef* (ADV prep phrase modifying V *prefer*)

15. *most* (ADV modifying ADJ *likely*); *likely* (ADJ); *lacrosse* (ADJ); *on the first bus* (ADV prep phrase modifying V *left*); *first* (ADJ)
16. *almost* (ADV modifying ADV *never*); *never* (ADV modifying V *watch*); *anymore* (ADV modifying V *watch*)
17. *When we refer to history, we can see that whenever an innovation is introduced, people rarely accept the entire concept, at least not right away. When something threatens the ways of the past, people don't part easily with their old ways. Although not everyone needs to maintain the status quo, consistency and predictability make people feel comfortable. Even when technology comes up with a way to do things better, people often continue with their older, less efficient ways. For instance, it's not uncommon for people to use e-mail while continuing to correspond via "snail mail." If they would pause for a moment, they would see that they can communicate more effectively through the Internet—and save some trees!*

Worksheet 12

1. *The latest political commercials make their points* <u>*more strongly*</u> *than previous ones.* (Use adverb, not adjective.)
2. *My shirt smelled quite* <u>*foul*</u> *after rugby practice.* (Here, the modifier is an adjective describing the shirt. The verb *smelled* is acting as a linking verb.)
3. *Recent technological advances have made it easier to extract minuscule chemical traces from geological samples.* (Correct)
4. *We* <u>*rarely*</u> *get to go to such elegant restaurants.* (The use of *never* is illogical.)
5. *Although both of my parents have pretty level heads, my father is the* <u>*more*</u> *patient.* (Use *more* when comparing two things.)
6. *The third graders* <u>*were hardly*</u> *interested in going to the museum after school.* (Double negative)
7. *I could always sing in front of a crowd* <u>*more easily*</u> *than I could give a speech.* (Use adverb, not adjective.)
8. *In many areas of the country, wind energy can be converted to electricity even* <u>*more efficiently*</u> *than fossil energy.*
9. *I felt surprisingly well after Saturday's ten-mile run.* (This is okay, but only if you mean that you

are *in a state of generally good health.* If, however, you mean to say that you don't feel fatigued or achy, it is better to use *good* rather than *well*.)
10. *The microscopic size of the fracture made it* <u>*impossible*</u> *to detect, even with special instruments.* (*Impossible* is an absolute adjective.)
11. *The committee had never been so* <u>*unified*</u> *as they were on the most recent vote.* (*Unanimous* is an absolute, but *unified* is not.)
12. *These measures* <u>*won't*</u> *address the state's deficit.* (Double negative)
13. *The teacher* <u>*didn't tell*</u> *us about the test until the day before.* (The use of *never* is illogical.)
14. *We weren't* <u>*really*</u> *sure that the plan would work.* (The modifier is an adverb modifying the adjective *sure*.)
15. *Students* <u>*rarely*</u> *bother to examine the veracity of the "facts" they are supposed to memorize in history class.* (*Never usually* is illogical.)
16. *Gena's guess was the most* <u>*nearly*</u> *correct of anyone's in the class.* (*Correct* is an absolute modifier, but guesses can *approach* correctness in varying degrees.)

Lesson 13: Irregular Verbs

Know Your Irregulars

When using the perfect tenses or using participial phrases, you must use the *past participle* of the verb rather than the *past tense* form of the verb. Don't mix them up!

For many verbs, the two forms are the same, as in *we **walked*** (past) and *we had **walked*** (past perfect), but for many "irregular" verbs, they are different, as in *we **ate*** (past) and *we had **eaten*** (past perfect). You should know the irregular forms of common verbs.

Infinitive	Past tense	Past participle
to arise	*arose*	*arisen*
to awake	*awoke*	*awoken*
to beat	*beat*	*beaten*
to begin	*began*	*begun*
to blow	*blew*	*blown*
to break	*broke*	*broken*
to burst	*burst*	*burst*
to cast	*cast*	*cast*
to come	*came*	*come*
to creep	*crept*	*crept*
to do	*did*	*done*
to draw	*drew*	*drawn*
to drink	*drank*	*drunk*
to drive	*drove*	*driven*
to forsake	*forsook*	*forsaken*
to get	*got*	*got, gotten*
to go	*went*	*gone*
to hurt	*hurt*	*hurt*
to kneel	*kneeled, knelt*	*knelt*
to know	*knew*	*known*
to lay (to put or place)	*laid*	*laid*
to lie (to recline)	*lay*	*lain*
to ride	*rode*	*ridden*
to run	*ran*	*run*
to shrink	*shrank*	*shrunk, shrunken*
to sink	*sank*	*sunk*
to speak	*spoke*	*spoken*
to spring	*sprang*	*sprung*
to take	*took*	*taken*
to tear	*tore*	*torn*
to write	*wrote*	*written*

Concept Review 13: Irregular Verbs

Complete the following sentences with the correct form of the verb:

1. *We would have _____ (to ride) even further if we had had the time.*

2. *Until now, that issue hasn't _____ (to arise).*

3. *Before we won last week's game, we hadn't _____ (to beat) the Cougars in ten years.*

4. *I would not have _____ (to drink) the punch if I had known that it had liquor in it.*

5. *We searched everywhere, but our friends had _____ (to go) out for the evening.*

6. *Had I never _____ (to know) about video games, I would have _____ (to get) perfect grades last semester.*

7. *At last night's concert, the band _____ (to sing) all of its greatest hits.*

8. *The Donnellys have _____ (to run) their corner store for over 20 years.*

9. *They had hardly _____ (to speak) about the incident until that night.*

10. *I can't believe you put my wool sweater in the dryer and _____ (to shrink) it.*

11. *His batting average has really _____ (to sink) ever since his injury.*

12. *She had _____ (to speak) for so long that the other speakers didn't have time to finish their presentations.*

13. *It seems as if the tulips _____ (to spring) out of the ground overnight.*

14. *We should have _____ (to take) that shortcut to work.*

15. *If we had jumped over that fence, the polar bear would have _____ (to tear) us to shreds.*

16. *I promise you that by next month I will have _____ (to write) the first four chapters of the book.*

Worksheet 13: Irregular Verbs

Circle the past participle(s) or past tense verbs in each sentence, and make any necessary corrections.

1. *Elisha could never have went to the state finals if I had not convinced her to join the team in the first place.*

2. *In retrospect, it seems I might have took too much time on the essay portion of the test.*

3. *While we played video games, Danny lay on the couch all afternoon.*

4. *Most people find it amazing that, millions of years ago, life sprung from a primordial swamp.*

5. *After we had placed our bets, we lay our cards on the table.*

6. *Carl would have tore his uniform if he had not stopped his slide at the last second.*

7. *The generals forsook their own troops to surrender and save their own lives.*

8. *When the temperature sunk below zero, the pipes bursted like water balloons.*

9. *The assets of the company were froze as soon as it declared bankruptcy.*

10. *Promptly at 6 o'clock, the assistant cook rung the bell for dinner, and the whole camp raced up the hill.*

11. *I was concerned about buying a cotton warm-up suit, and sure enough, it shrunk two sizes after the first wash.*

12. *By the time they pitched camp for the night, they had ridden over 30 miles.*

13. *George needed his friends more than ever, but they had forsook him.*

14. *We sung just about every song we knew, then we went to bed.*

15. *The senator could have spoke a lot longer, but she yielded the floor to her colleague.*

Answer Key 13: Irregular Verbs

Concept Review 13

1. We would have <u>ridden</u> even further if we had had the time.

2. Until now, that issue hasn't <u>arisen</u>.

3. Before we won last week's game, we hadn't <u>beaten</u> the Cougars in ten years.

4. I would not have <u>drunk</u> the punch if I had known that it had liquor in it.

5. We searched everywhere, but our friends had <u>gone</u> out for the evening.

6. Had I never <u>known</u> about video games, I would have <u>gotten</u> perfect grades last semester.

7. At last night's concert, the band <u>sang</u> all of its greatest hits.

8. The Donnellys have <u>run</u> their corner store for over 20 years.

9. They had hardly <u>spoken</u> about the incident until that night.

10. I can't believe you put my wool sweater in the dryer and <u>shrank</u> it.

11. His batting average has really <u>sunk</u> ever since his injury.

12. She had <u>spoken</u> for so long that the other speakers didn't have time to finish their presentations.

13. It seems as if the tulips <u>sprang</u> out of the ground overnight.

14. We should have <u>taken</u> that shortcut to work.

15. If we had jumped over that fence, the polar bear would have <u>torn</u> us to shreds.

16. I promise you that by next month I will have <u>written</u> the first four chapters of the book.

Worksheet 13

1. Elisha could never have <u>gone</u> to the state finals if I had not convinced her to join the team in the first place.

2. In retrospect, it seems I might have <u>taken</u> too much time on the essay portion of the test.

3. While we played video games, Danny lay on the couch all afternoon. (Correct)

4. Most people find it amazing that, millions of years ago, life <u>sprang</u> from a primordial swamp.

5. After we had placed our bets, we <u>laid</u> our cards on the table.

6. Carl would have <u>torn</u> his uniform if he had not stopped his slide at the last second.

7. The generals forsook their own troops to surrender and save their own lives. (Correct)

8. When the temperature <u>sank</u> below zero, the pipes <u>burst</u> like water balloons.

9. The assets of the company were <u>frozen</u> as soon as it declared bankruptcy.

10. Promptly at 6 o'clock, the assistant cook <u>rang</u> the bell for dinner, and the whole camp raced up the hill.

11. I was concerned about buying a cotton warm-up suit, and sure enough, it <u>shrank</u> two sizes after the first wash.

12. By the time they pitched camp for the night, they had ridden over 30 miles. (Correct)

13. George needed his friends more than ever, but they had <u>forsaken</u> him.

14. We <u>sang</u> just about every song we knew, then we went to bed.

15. The senator could have <u>spoken</u> a lot longer, but she yielded the floor to her colleague.

Lesson 14: The Subjunctive Mood

What is the "Mood" of a Verb?

The *mood* of a verb is its *factuality* or *urgency*. There are three moods of verbs in English.

Indicative mood: Most verbs are in the *indicative mood*, meaning they indicate something *real or factual*, as in *I am going to the park*.

Subjunctive mood: Verbs in the *subjunctive mood* indicate something *hypothetical, conditional, wishful, suggestive*, or *counter to fact*, as in *I wish **I were going** to the park*.

Imperative mood: Verbs in the *imperative mood* indicate a *direct command*, as in ***Go** to the park!*

> The only "tricky" mood in English is the *subjunctive mood*. Questions about the subjunctive mood are possible on the SAT, but they are not very common. You should recognize the common situations in which the subjunctive mood must be used, and know how to change the form of the verb accordingly.

> The subjunctive mood is usually indicated by *auxiliaries* like *would, should, might,* and *may,* or if the verb is *to be,* by the forms *were* and *be.*

He **would feel** better if only he would eat.	(Hypothetical)
If **I were** faster, I could play wide receiver.	(Hypothetical)
We thought that she **might win** the election, but she lost by a lot.	(Counter to fact)
He plays as though he **were** not even injured.	(Counter to fact)
I wish that he **would not act** so superior.	(Wishful)
I wish **I were** two inches taller.	(Wishful)
I truly doubt that she **would ever say** such a thing.	(Doubtful)
I think she **might be** in over her head.	(Doubtful)
She said that we **should practice** harder.	(Suggestion)
He asks that we **be** there at 6 o'clock sharp.	(Indirect command)

Don't Overdo It

> The subjunctive mood is slowly disappearing from the English language. Many subjunctive forms from the past now sound old-fashioned and are no longer "standard" English.

*Archaic: We must all respect the office of the presidency, no matter who **be** the current officeholder.*

*Better: We must all respect the office of the presidency, no matter who **is** the current officeholder.*

*Archaic: If that **be** so, we may see dramatic changes in the market.*

*Better: If that **is** so, we may see dramatic changes in the market.*

Watch Your Ifs

> One very common mistake is using the construction *if . . . would have . . .* as a past subjunctive form. The correct form is *if . . . had. . . .*

Wrong: *If he would have arrived a minute sooner, he would not have missed her.*

Right: *If he had arrived a minute sooner, he would not have missed her.*

Concept Review 14: The Subjunctive Mood

1. Name five auxiliaries that indicate the subjunctive mood.

2. What does the subjunctive mood indicate?

Circle the correct subjunctive verb form in each of the following sentences.

3. *If I (was/were) a little faster, I'd be able to anchor the relay team.*

4. *In fact, I (was/were) only 5 years old at the time.*

5. *He would feel better if only he (ate/would eat).*

6. *He asks that we (are/be) there at 6 o'clock sharp.*

7. *I wish that he (were/was) not so presumptuous about my motives.*

8. *If he (would have/had) caught the ball, the inning would be over now.*

9. *If I (was/were) a rock star, I'd tour all over Europe.*

10. *He plays as though he (was/were) not even injured.*

11. *I wish I (was/were) six inches taller.*

12. *I think she (might be/is) in over her head.*

13. *If she (would have/had) campaigned harder, she might have won the election.*

14. *I cannot tell whether he (is/be) friend or foe.*

Worksheet 14: The Subjunctive Mood

Circle the verb(s) in each sentence. If the verb mood is incorrect, cross it out and write in the correction.

1. We doubted that she will get enough votes to force a runoff, let alone win outright.   _____

2. If I was going to take the SAT tomorrow, I'd be sure to get plenty of sleep tonight.   _____

3. If I would have known that it would take this long, I'd have gone out for a snack.   _____

4. I would have liked to have been there just to see the panicked look on his face.   _____

5. The camp counselors asked that we were in our beds with lights out promptly at 10 o'clock.   _____

6. David ran as if he was carrying a refrigerator on his back.   _____

7. I wish that we would have paid the extra $50 a night to get a better room.   _____

8. Miss Hannigan demanded that we be silent unless spoken to and should always
    do what we're told.   _____

9. He spoke as if he was an expert in the field of international relations.   _____

10. I would have remembered to have left a generous tip, but I left my wallet at home.   _____

11. Had I known beforehand, I would not have mentioned her ex-boyfriend.   _____

12. If the rest of the class would have voted the way I did, we wouldn't be taking the test today.   _____

Answer Key 14: The Subjunctive Mood

Concept Review 14

1. *might, may, would, could, should*

2. that the verb indicates something hypothetical, conditional, suggestive, wishful, or counter to fact

3. *If I <u>were</u> a little faster, I'd be able to anchor the relay team.*

4. *In fact, I <u>was</u> only 5 years old at the time.*

5. *He would feel better if only he <u>would eat</u>.*

6. *He asks that we <u>be</u> there at 6 o'clock sharp.*

7. *I wish that he <u>were</u> not so presumptuous about my motives.*

8. *If he <u>had</u> caught the ball, the inning would be over now.*

9. *If I <u>were</u> a rock star, I'd tour all over Europe.*

10. *He plays as though he <u>were</u> not even injured.*

11. *I wish I <u>were</u> six inches taller.*

12. *I think she <u>might be</u> in over her head.*

13. *If she <u>had</u> campaigned harder, she might have won the election.* (Don't say *If she would have. . . .*)

14. *I cannot tell whether he <u>is</u> friend or foe.* (The form *be* is formally correct also, but such usage is now considered archaic.)

Worksheet 14

1. *We doubted that she <u>would</u> get enough votes to force a runoff, let alone win outright.*

2. *If I <u>were</u> going to take the SAT tomorrow, I'd be sure to get plenty of sleep tonight.*

3. *If I <u>had</u> known that it would take this long, I'd have gone out for a snack.*

4. *I would have liked to <u>be</u> there just to see the panicked look on his face.*

5. *The camp counselors asked that we <u>be</u> in our beds with lights out promptly at 10 o'clock.*

6. *David ran as if he <u>were</u> carrying a refrigerator on his back.*

7. *I wish that we <u>had</u> paid the extra $50 a night to get a better room.*

8. *Miss Hannigan demanded that we be silent unless spoken to and* (omit *should*) *always do what we're told.*

9. *He spoke as if he <u>were</u> an expert in the field of international relations.*

10. *I would have remembered to <u>leave</u> a generous tip, but I left my wallet at home.*

11. *Had I known beforehand, I would not have mentioned her ex-boyfriend.* (Correct)

12. *If the rest of the class <u>had</u> voted the way I did, we wouldn't be taking the test today.*

Lesson 15: Coordinating Ideas

Complex and Compound Sentences

Many sentences contain more than one complete idea, or *clause*. These are called *compound sentences* (if the individual clauses can stand alone as sentences) or *complex sentences* (if one or more of the individual clauses *cannot* stand alone as sentences). *The ideas in sentences must coordinate logically with each other.*

Example:

As we walked in the door, Bernie jumped all over us.

This is a *complex sentence* because the first clause, *As we walked in the door*, cannot stand alone as a sentence. This is called a *dependent clause*. The second clause, however, *Bernie jumped all over us*, is an *independent clause*, and can stand alone as a sentence.

He was very excited to see us: we had been away for nearly a full hour!

This is a *compound sentence* because the two clauses are *independent*.

Run-On Sentences

If *two independent clauses* are joined only by a comma, this is an error called a *run-on sentence* or a *comma splice*. (A run-on sentence isn't just a sentence that's too long!) To join two independent clauses in one sentence, you must use a *colon* (:), *a semicolon* (;), or a *conjunction like **but, or, yet, for, and, nor,** or **so.*** (Mnemonic: BOYFANS)

Wrong: *I have taken several science courses this year, my favorite was neuroscience.*

Two independent clauses are joined only by a comma, so the sentence is a run-on.

Right: *I have taken several science courses this year; my favorite was neuroscience.*

Because the two clauses are closely related, they can be joined with a semicolon.

Right: *I have taken several science courses this year, but my favorite was neuroscience.*

Here the two clauses are joined with the conjunction *but*. This changes the meaning slightly from the previous version; it emphasizes the contrast between the *group* of courses in the first clause and the *single* course in the second clause.

Wrong: *The ride was more harrowing than they expected, several times the car nearly skidded off the mountain.*

Right: *The ride was more harrowing than they expected: several times the car nearly skidded off the mountain.*

The colon is more appropriate than a semicolon here, because the second clause *explains* the first.

The Colon and Semicolon

The *semicolon* (;) is used primarily to join two closely related independent clauses in a single sentence. When using a semicolon to join clauses, make sure they are *independent*; that is, they can stand alone as sentences.

Wrong: *The test was unbelievably difficult; and hardly anyone finished it on time.*

A semicolon or a conjunction should be used to join the clauses, but not both.

Right: *The test was unbelievably difficult; hardly anyone finished it on time.*

The *colon* (:) is used in much the same way as a semicolon is used, but it also implies that an *explanation* will follow.

Unclear: *The meeting went well and everyone was impressed by my presentation.*

This sentence is a bit ambiguous: did the meeting go well *because* of the successful presentation, or for another reason?

Better: *The meeting went well: everyone was impressed by my presentation.*

This makes the relationship between the clauses clearer: the second explains the first.

Concept Review 15: Coordinating Ideas

1. When should a semicolon be used to join clauses?

2. When should a colon be used to join clauses?

3. What is a run-on sentence?

4. Name the seven conjunctions that can join independent clauses.

Write a sentence that logically and concisely incorporates the given clauses, with the first clause as the main clause.

5. Confederates in the Attic *has received widespread critical acclaim. It was written by Tony Horwitz. It portrays the legacy of the Civil War in the modern South. It is poignant and funny.*

_____

_____

_____

6. *Many of the rights given by the Constitution were bitterly contested by the Founding Fathers. Many people believe that the Founding Fathers agreed unanimously to safeguard those rights for us. The Constitution is much more a political compromise than a steadfast commitment to a set of ideals.*

_____

_____

_____

7. *The Sapir-Whorf hypothesis has been largely disproven. It claims that our thoughts are guided and limited by constraints on our language. Scientists now understand that having thoughts and expressing them are very different things.*

_____

_____

_____

8. *Corporations can effectively control the opinions of the people through the media. They can do this to a large degree because the people don't believe they are being manipulated. This happens in free and democratic societies. Unlike totalitarian societies, free and democratic societies do not use force to ensure popular compliance.*

_____

_____

_____

Worksheet 15: Coordinating Ideas

Make any necessary corrections to the following sentences to coordinate the clauses logically and concisely.

1. *Standardized test results can help measure the progress of individual students, and they are far less able to measure the effectiveness of entire school systems.*

   _____

   _____

2. *A consistent program of vigorous aerobic exercise maintains cardiovascular health, it also helps your brain to work more effectively.*

   _____

   _____

3. *If the Mets could just get some consistent relief pitching; they might be able to put a winning streak together.*

   _____

   _____

4. *We never should have bought the plane tickets, and it would have been much easier to drive.*

   _____

   _____

5. *The convention was not the success they had hoped it would be, their lead presenter came down with the flu; the salesman who had to fill in had never given a presentation in front of an audience.*

   _____

   _____

6. *Since 1998, the civil war in the Democratic Republic of Congo has been the deadliest since World War II, it has claimed over 3.3 million lives.*

   _____

   _____

7. *Mrs. Donovan seems to inspire every one of her students to achieve; she inspires them despite having to manage classes that sometimes number over 35 students.*

   _____

   _____

8. *The lab took us twice as long to complete as any of our other labs; but it was also the most worthwhile.*

   _____

   _____

Answer Key 15: Coordinating Ideas

Concept Review 15

1. when the two clauses are independent and are very closely related

2. when the two clauses are independent and the second clause explains the first

3. a sentence that joins two independent clauses without a colon, a semicolon, or a conjunction

4. BOYFANS: *but, or, yet, for, and, nor, so*

5. *Tony Horwitz's book* Confederates in the Attic, *a poignant and funny portrayal of the legacy of the Civil War in the modern South, has received widespread critical acclaim.*

6. *Although many people believe that the Founding Fathers agreed unanimously to safeguard our rights in the Constitution, many of those rights were bitterly contested by the Founding Fathers; in fact, the Constitution is much more a political compromise than a steadfast commitment to a set of ideals.*

7. *The Sapir-Whorf hypothesis, which claims that our thoughts are guided and limited by constraints on our language, has been largely disproven, and scientists now understand that having thoughts and expressing them are very different things.*

8. *Even in free and democratic societies, corporations can effectively control the opinions of the people not through force, as totalitarian societies do, but through the media, largely because the people don't believe they are being manipulated.*

Worksheet 15

1. *Standardized test results can help measure the progress of individual students, <u>but</u> they are far less able to measure the effectiveness of entire school systems.*

2. *A consistent program of vigorous aerobic exercise maintains cardiovascular health <u>and</u> helps your brain to work more effectively.*

3. *If the Mets could just get some consistent relief pitching, they might be able to put a winning streak together.*

4. *We never should have bought the plane tickets; it would have been much easier to drive.*

5. *The convention was not the success they had hoped it would be; their lead presenter came down with the flu, <u>and</u> the salesman who had to fill in had never given a presentation in front of an audience.*

6. *Since 1998, the civil war in the Democratic Republic of Congo has been the deadliest since World War II, <u>claiming</u> over 3.3 million lives.*

7. *<u>Despite having to manage classes that sometimes number over 35 students,</u> Mrs. Donovan seems to inspire every one of her students to achieve.*

8. *The lab took us twice as long to complete as any of our other labs, but it was also the most worthwhile.*

CHAPTER 16

PRACTICE TESTS WITH DETAILED ANSWER KEYS

PRACTICE TEST 1

ANSWER SHEET

Last Name:_____   First Name:_____

Date:_____   Testing Location:_____

Directions for Test

- Remove these answer sheets from the book and use them to record your answers to this test.
- This test will require 3 hours and 20 minutes to complete. Take this test in one sitting.
- The time allotment for each section is written clearly at the beginning of each section. This test contains six 25-minute sections, two 20-minute sections, and one 10-minute section.
- This test is 25 minutes shorter than the actual SAT, which will include a 25-minute "experimental" section that does not count toward your score. That section has been omitted from this test.
- You may take one short break during the test, of no more than 10 minutes in length.
- You may only work on one section at any given time.
- You must stop ALL work on a section when time is called.
- If you finish a section before the time has elapsed, check your work on that section. You may NOT work on any other section.
- Do not waste time on questions that seem too difficult for you.
- Use the test book for scratchwork, but you will receive credit only for answers that are marked on the answer sheets.
- You will receive one point for every correct answer.
- You will receive no points for an omitted question.
- For each wrong answer on any multiple-choice question, your score will be reduced by $\frac{1}{4}$ point.
- For each wrong answer on any "numerical grid-in" question, you will receive no deduction.

When you take the real SAT, you will be asked to fill in your personal information in grids as shown below.

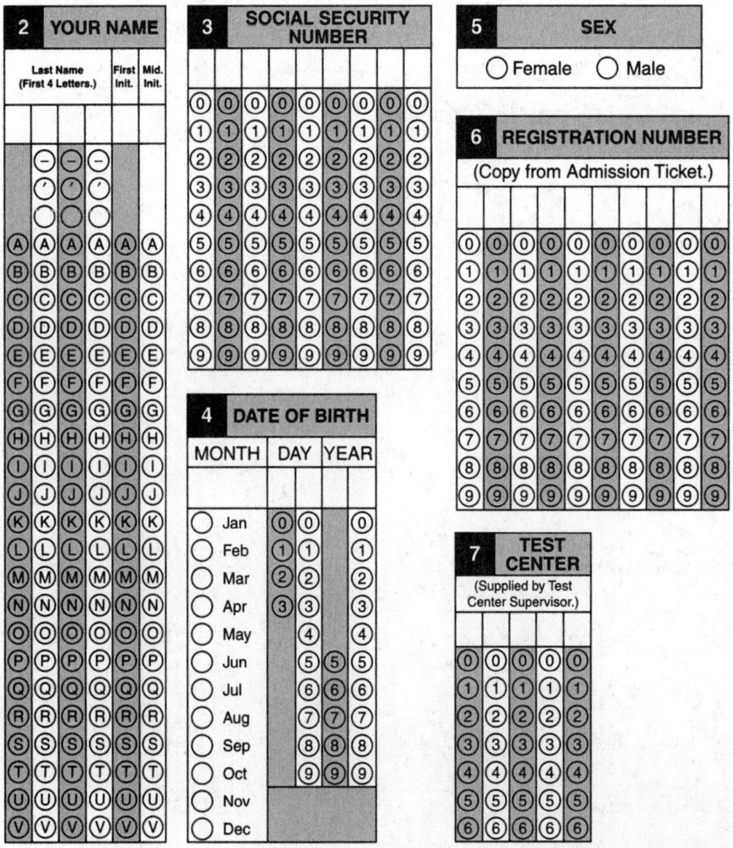

Start with number 1 for each new section. If a section has fewer questions than answer spaces, leave the extra answer spaces blank. Be sure to erase any errors or stray marks completely.

SECTION 2

1 A B C D E	11 A B C D E	21 A B C D E	31 A B C D E
2 A B C D E	12 A B C D E	22 A B C D E	32 A B C D E
3 A B C D E	13 A B C D E	23 A B C D E	33 A B C D E
4 A B C D E	14 A B C D E	24 A B C D E	34 A B C D E
5 A B C D E	15 A B C D E	25 A B C D E	35 A B C D E
6 A B C D E	16 A B C D E	26 A B C D E	36 A B C D E
7 A B C D E	17 A B C D E	27 A B C D E	37 A B C D E
8 A B C D E	18 A B C D E	28 A B C D E	38 A B C D E
9 A B C D E	19 A B C D E	29 A B C D E	39 A B C D E
10 A B C D E	20 A B C D E	30 A B C D E	40 A B C D E

SECTION 3

1 A B C D E	11 A B C D E	21 A B C D E	31 A B C D E
2 A B C D E	12 A B C D E	22 A B C D E	32 A B C D E
3 A B C D E	13 A B C D E	23 A B C D E	33 A B C D E
4 A B C D E	14 A B C D E	24 A B C D E	34 A B C D E
5 A B C D E	15 A B C D E	25 A B C D E	35 A B C D E
6 A B C D E	16 A B C D E	26 A B C D E	36 A B C D E
7 A B C D E	17 A B C D E	27 A B C D E	37 A B C D E
8 A B C D E	18 A B C D E	28 A B C D E	38 A B C D E
9 A B C D E	19 A B C D E	29 A B C D E	39 A B C D E
10 A B C D E	20 A B C D E	30 A B C D E	40 A B C D E

CAUTION   Use the answer spaces in the grids below for Section 2 or Section 3 only if you are told to do so in your test book.

Student-Produced Responses   ONLY ANSWERS ENTERED IN THE CIRCLES IN EACH GRID WILL BE SCORED. YOU WILL NOT RECEIVE CREDIT FOR ANYTHING WRITTEN IN THE BOXES ABOVE THE CIRCLES.

9   10   11   12   13

14   15   16   17   18

Start with number 1 for each new section. If a section has fewer questions than answer spaces, leave the extra answer spaces blank. Be sure to erase any errors or stray marks completely.

SECTION 4

1	A B C D E	11	A B C D E	21	A B C D E	31	A B C D E
2	A B C D E	12	A B C D E	22	A B C D E	32	A B C D E
3	A B C D E	13	A B C D E	23	A B C D E	33	A B C D E
4	A B C D E	14	A B C D E	24	A B C D E	34	A B C D E
5	A B C D E	15	A B C D E	25	A B C D E	35	A B C D E
6	A B C D E	16	A B C D E	26	A B C D E	36	A B C D E
7	A B C D E	17	A B C D E	27	A B C D E	37	A B C D E
8	A B C D E	18	A B C D E	28	A B C D E	38	A B C D E
9	A B C D E	19	A B C D E	29	A B C D E	39	A B C D E
10	A B C D E	20	A B C D E	30	A B C D E	40	A B C D E

SECTION 5

1	A B C D E	11	A B C D E	21	A B C D E	31	A B C D E
2	A B C D E	12	A B C D E	22	A B C D E	32	A B C D E
3	A B C D E	13	A B C D E	23	A B C D E	33	A B C D E
4	A B C D E	14	A B C D E	24	A B C D E	34	A B C D E
5	A B C D E	15	A B C D E	25	A B C D E	35	A B C D E
6	A B C D E	16	A B C D E	26	A B C D E	36	A B C D E
7	A B C D E	17	A B C D E	27	A B C D E	37	A B C D E
8	A B C D E	18	A B C D E	28	A B C D E	38	A B C D E
9	A B C D E	19	A B C D E	29	A B C D E	39	A B C D E
10	A B C D E	20	A B C D E	30	A B C D E	40	A B C D E

CAUTION Use the answer spaces in the grids below for Section 4 or Section 5 only if you are told to do so in your test book.

Student-Produced Responses

ONLY ANSWERS ENTERED IN THE CIRCLES IN EACH GRID WILL BE SCORED. YOU WILL NOT RECEIVE CREDIT FOR ANYTHING WRITTEN IN THE BOXES ABOVE THE CIRCLES.

9 10 11 12 13

14 15 16 17 18

Start with number 1 for each new section. If a section has fewer questions than answer spaces, leave the extra answer spaces blank. Be sure to erase any errors or stray marks completely.

SECTION 6

1	A B C D E	11	A B C D E	21	A B C D E	31	A B C D E
2	A B C D E	12	A B C D E	22	A B C D E	32	A B C D E
3	A B C D E	13	A B C D E	23	A B C D E	33	A B C D E
4	A B C D E	14	A B C D E	24	A B C D E	34	A B C D E
5	A B C D E	15	A B C D E	25	A B C D E	35	A B C D E
6	A B C D E	16	A B C D E	26	A B C D E	36	A B C D E
7	A B C D E	17	A B C D E	27	A B C D E	37	A B C D E
8	A B C D E	18	A B C D E	28	A B C D E	38	A B C D E
9	A B C D E	19	A B C D E	29	A B C D E	39	A B C D E
10	A B C D E	20	A B C D E	30	A B C D E	40	A B C D E

SECTION 7

1	A B C D E	11	A B C D E	21	A B C D E	31	A B C D E
2	A B C D E	12	A B C D E	22	A B C D E	32	A B C D E
3	A B C D E	13	A B C D E	23	A B C D E	33	A B C D E
4	A B C D E	14	A B C D E	24	A B C D E	34	A B C D E
5	A B C D E	15	A B C D E	25	A B C D E	35	A B C D E
6	A B C D E	16	A B C D E	26	A B C D E	36	A B C D E
7	A B C D E	17	A B C D E	27	A B C D E	37	A B C D E
8	A B C D E	18	A B C D E	28	A B C D E	38	A B C D E
9	A B C D E	19	A B C D E	29	A B C D E	39	A B C D E
10	A B C D E	20	A B C D E	30	A B C D E	40	A B C D E

CAUTION Use the answer spaces in the grids below for Section 6 or Section 7 only if you are told to do so in your test book.

Student-Produced Responses ONLY ANSWERS ENTERED IN THE CIRCLES IN EACH GRID WILL BE SCORED. YOU WILL NOT RECEIVE CREDIT FOR ANYTHING WRITTEN IN THE BOXES ABOVE THE CIRCLES.

9   10   11   12   13

14   15   16   17   18

PLEASE DO NOT WRITE IN THIS AREA

Start with number 1 for each new section. If a section has fewer questions than answer spaces, leave the extra answer spaces blank. Be sure to erase any errors or stray marks completely.

SECTION 8

1	(A) (B) (C) (D) (E)	11	(A) (B) (C) (D) (E)	21	(A) (B) (C) (D) (E)	31	(A) (B) (C) (D) (E)
2	(A) (B) (C) (D) (E)	12	(A) (B) (C) (D) (E)	22	(A) (B) (C) (D) (E)	32	(A) (B) (C) (D) (E)
3	(A) (B) (C) (D) (E)	13	(A) (B) (C) (D) (E)	23	(A) (B) (C) (D) (E)	33	(A) (B) (C) (D) (E)
4	(A) (B) (C) (D) (E)	14	(A) (B) (C) (D) (E)	24	(A) (B) (C) (D) (E)	34	(A) (B) (C) (D) (E)
5	(A) (B) (C) (D) (E)	15	(A) (B) (C) (D) (E)	25	(A) (B) (C) (D) (E)	35	(A) (B) (C) (D) (E)
6	(A) (B) (C) (D) (E)	16	(A) (B) (C) (D) (E)	26	(A) (B) (C) (D) (E)	36	(A) (B) (C) (D) (E)
7	(A) (B) (C) (D) (E)	17	(A) (B) (C) (D) (E)	27	(A) (B) (C) (D) (E)	37	(A) (B) (C) (D) (E)
8	(A) (B) (C) (D) (E)	18	(A) (B) (C) (D) (E)	28	(A) (B) (C) (D) (E)	38	(A) (B) (C) (D) (E)
9	(A) (B) (C) (D) (E)	19	(A) (B) (C) (D) (E)	29	(A) (B) (C) (D) (E)	39	(A) (B) (C) (D) (E)
10	(A) (B) (C) (D) (E)	20	(A) (B) (C) (D) (E)	30	(A) (B) (C) (D) (E)	40	(A) (B) (C) (D) (E)

SECTION 9

1	(A) (B) (C) (D) (E)	11	(A) (B) (C) (D) (E)	21	(A) (B) (C) (D) (E)	31	(A) (B) (C) (D) (E)
2	(A) (B) (C) (D) (E)	12	(A) (B) (C) (D) (E)	22	(A) (B) (C) (D) (E)	32	(A) (B) (C) (D) (E)
3	(A) (B) (C) (D) (E)	13	(A) (B) (C) (D) (E)	23	(A) (B) (C) (D) (E)	33	(A) (B) (C) (D) (E)
4	(A) (B) (C) (D) (E)	14	(A) (B) (C) (D) (E)	24	(A) (B) (C) (D) (E)	34	(A) (B) (C) (D) (E)
5	(A) (B) (C) (D) (E)	15	(A) (B) (C) (D) (E)	25	(A) (B) (C) (D) (E)	35	(A) (B) (C) (D) (E)
6	(A) (B) (C) (D) (E)	16	(A) (B) (C) (D) (E)	26	(A) (B) (C) (D) (E)	36	(A) (B) (C) (D) (E)
7	(A) (B) (C) (D) (E)	17	(A) (B) (C) (D) (E)	27	(A) (B) (C) (D) (E)	37	(A) (B) (C) (D) (E)
8	(A) (B) (C) (D) (E)	18	(A) (B) (C) (D) (E)	28	(A) (B) (C) (D) (E)	38	(A) (B) (C) (D) (E)
9	(A) (B) (C) (D) (E)	19	(A) (B) (C) (D) (E)	29	(A) (B) (C) (D) (E)	39	(A) (B) (C) (D) (E)
10	(A) (B) (C) (D) (E)	20	(A) (B) (C) (D) (E)	30	(A) (B) (C) (D) (E)	40	(A) (B) (C) (D) (E)

1   ESSAY   ESSAY   1

ESSAY
Time—25 minutes

Write your essay on separate sheets of standard lined paper.

The essay gives you an opportunity to show how effectively you can develop and express ideas. You should therefore take care to develop your point of view, present your ideas logically and clearly, and use language precisely.

Your essay must be written on the lines provided on your answer sheet—you will receive no other paper on which to write. You will have enough space if you write on every line, avoid wide margins, and keep your handwriting to a reasonable size. Remember that people who are not familiar with your handwriting will read what you write. Try to write or print so that what you are writing is legible to those readers.

Important reminders:

- **A pencil is required for the essay.** An essay written in ink will receive a score of zero.
- **Do not write your essay in your test book.** You will receive credit only for what you write on your answer sheet.
- **An off-topic essay will receive a score of zero.**

You have twenty-five minutes to write an essay on the topic assigned below.

Think carefully about the issue presented in the following excerpt and the assignment below.

> An entertainment-driven culture runs the risk of encouraging passivity among its citizens. If they can experience something vicariously through a movie, television show, or video game, why should they get involved with the activity itself? It's safer, after all, to watch someone scale a mountain than to do it yourself. The effect of this passivity, of course, is an apathetic frame of mind. We cease to care deeply about so many things because they are experienced, at best, second-hand.

Assignment: **Is apathy a problem in today's society?** Write an essay in which you answer this question and discuss your point of view on this issue. Support your position logically with examples from literature, the arts, history, politics, science and technology, current events, or your experience or observation.

If you finish before time is called, you may check your work on this section only.
Do not turn to any other section in the test.

SECTION 2
Time—25 minutes
20 questions

Turn to Section 2 of your answer sheet to answer the questions in this section.

Directions: For this section, solve each problem and decide which is the best of the choices given. Fill in the corresponding circle on the answer sheet. You may use any available space for scratchwork.

Notes

1. The use of a calculator is permitted.

2. All numbers used are real numbers.

3. Figures that accompany problems in this test are intended to provide information useful in solving the problems. They are drawn as accurately as possible EXCEPT when it is stated in a specific problem that the figure is not drawn to scale. All figures lie in a plane unless otherwise indicated.

4. Unless otherwise specified, the domain of any function f is assumed to be the set of all real numbers x for which $f(x)$ is a real number.

Reference Information

$A = \pi r^2$
$C = 2\pi r$

$A = \ell w$

$A = \frac{1}{2} bh$

$V = \ell wh$

$V = \pi r^2 h$

$c^2 = a^2 + b^2$

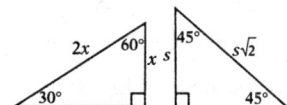

Special right triangles

The number of degrees of arc in a circle is 360.
The sum of the measures in degrees of the angles of a triangle is 180.

---

1. If $x = 3$ and $5x = 3x + y$, then $y =$

(A) 1.5
(B) 2
(C) 3
(D) 4
(E) 6

2. A store sells a package of 6 batteries for $4 and a package of 24 of the same batteries for $12. If you need to buy 48 of these batteries, how much money will you save by buying them in packages of 24 rather than packages of 6?

(A) $4
(B) $8
(C) $12
(D) $16
(E) $20

GO ON TO THE NEXT PAGE

2   **2**   **2**   **2**   **2**   **2**

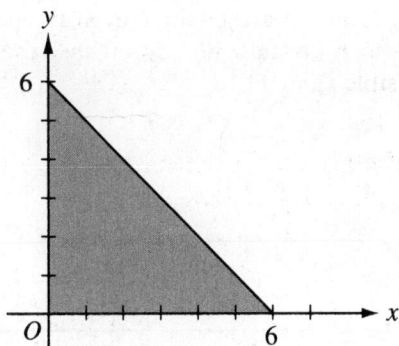

3. Which of the following points does NOT lie in the shaded region above?

(A) (1, 1)
(B) (1, 4)
(C) (2, 3)
(D) (4, 1)
(E) (5, 5)

4. If $\frac{1}{3}$ of $2x$ is 5, what is $\frac{2}{3}$ of $4x$?

(A) 5
(B) 10
(C) 15
(D) 20
(E) 25

5. If n is a positive integer that is divisible by 12 and 16, then n must also be divisible by

(A) 28
(B) 32
(C) 48
(D) 96
(E) 192

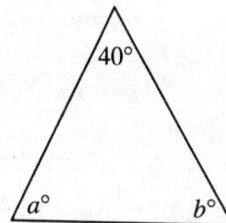

Note: Figure not drawn to scale.

6. In the figure above, if $a - b = 10$, then $a =$

(A) 60
(B) 65
(C) 70
(D) 75
(E) 80

7. If n is an integer, which of the following must be an even integer?

(A) $\frac{n}{2}$
(B) $n + 2$
(C) $2n + 1$
(D) n^2
(E) $n^2 + n$

8. Mike sold a total of 48 sodas at a snack stand. The stand sells only cola and root beer. If he sold twice as many colas as root beers, how many root beers did he sell?

(A) 32
(B) 24
(C) 18
(D) 16
(E) 8

9. If m and n are both squares of integers, which of the following is NOT necessarily the square of an integer?

(A) $9m$
(B) mn
(C) m^2
(D) $9mn$
(E) $9m - 9n$

GO ON TO THE NEXT PAGE

---

10. If $a + b = 9$, $a - c = 14$, and $a = 10$, then $c - b =$

(A) −5
(B) −3
(C)   3
(D)   5
(E) 23

---

11. If the average (arithmetic mean) of a, b, 4, and 10 is 8, what is the value of $a + b$?

(A)   4
(B)   6
(C)   9
(D) 15
(E) 18

0	1	2	3	4	5
1	2	4			
2					
3		x			
4					
5					

12. With the exception of the shaded squares, every square in the figure above contains the sum of the number in the square directly above it and the number in the square directly to its left. For example, the number 4 in the unshaded square above is the sum of the 2 in the square above it and the 2 in the square directly to its left. What is the value of x?

(A)   6
(B)   7
(C)   8
(D) 15
(E) 30

---

13. If a, b, and c are positive even integers such that $a < b < c$ and $a + b + c = 60$, then the greatest possible value of c is

(A) 36
(B) 40
(C) 42
(D) 54
(E) 57

---

14. The population of Bumpton increased by 10% from 1980 to 1990 and decreased by 10% from 1990 to 2000. What is the net percent change in the population of Bumpton from 1980 to 2000?

(A) −9%
(B) −1%
(C) +0%
(D) +1%
(E) +9%

---

x	$f(x)$
−2	−29
−1	−21
0	−13
1	−5
2	3
3	11
4	19

15. Several values of the function f are shown above. The function g is defined by $g(x) = 2f(x) - 1$. What is the value of $g(3)$?

(A) −21
(B) −13
(C)   3
(D) 11
(E) 21

GO ON TO THE NEXT PAGE

2   2   2   2   2   2

---

16. If $x > 0$ and $x = 5y$, then $\sqrt{x^2 - 2xy + y^2} =$

    (A) $2y$
    (B) $y\sqrt{6}$
    (C) $4y$
    (D) $16y$
    (E) $24y$

---

17. If $x > x^2$, which of the following must be true?

    　　I. $x < 1$
    　　II. $x > 0$
    　　III. $x^2 > 1$

    (A) I only
    (B) II only
    (C) I and II only
    (D) I and III only
    (E) I, II, and III

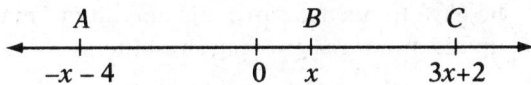

A   B   C
├────────┼──────┼────┼──────┼──────→
$-x-4$ 0 x $3x+2$

18. Which of the following represents the distance from the midpoint of $\overline{AB}$ to the midpoint of $\overline{BC}$ on the number line above?

    (A) $\dfrac{3x+2}{2}$

    (B) $2x - 1$

    (C) $2x + 3$

    (D) $3x + 1$

    (E) $4x$

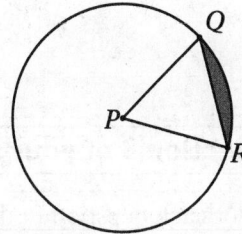

19. P is the center of the circle above and $PQ = QR$. If $\triangle PQR$ has an area of $9\sqrt{3}$, what is the area of the shaded region?

    (A) $36\pi - 9\sqrt{3}$

    (B) $24\pi - 9\sqrt{3}$

    (C) $18\pi - 9\sqrt{3}$

    (D) $9\pi - 9\sqrt{3}$

    (E) $6\pi - 9\sqrt{3}$

---

20. In a class of 160 seniors, the ratio of boys to girls is 3 to 5. In the junior class, the ratio of boys to girls is 3 to 2. When the two classes are combined, the ratio of boys to girls is 1 to 1. How many students are in the junior class?

    (A) 400
    (B) 360
    (C) 200
    (D) 180
    (E) 160

STOP

If you finish before time is called, you may check your work on this section only. Do not turn to any other section of the test.

Turn to Section 3 of your answer sheet to answer the questions in this section.

Directions: For each question in this section, select the best answer from among the choices given and fill in the corresponding circle on the answer sheet.

Each sentence below has one or two blanks, each blank indicating that something has been omitted. Beneath the sentence are five words or sets of words labeled A through E. Choose the word or set of words that, when inserted in the sentence, best fits the meaning of the sentence as a whole.

EXAMPLE:

Rather than accepting the theory unquestioningly, Deborah regarded it with ......

(A) mirth
(B) sadness
(C) responsibility
(D) ignorance
(E) skepticism

Ⓐ Ⓑ Ⓒ Ⓓ ●

---

1. Julia feared that her 6-month hiatus from playing the piano would cause her musical skills to -------.

   (A) atrophy
   (B) align
   (C) develop
   (D) reconcile
   (E) disseminate

2. Senator Harris is widely viewed as a ------- orator; his speeches are full of ------- commentary and domineering opinions.

   (A) vindictive . . pedantic
   (B) conciliatory . . treacherous
   (C) didactic . . moralizing
   (D) dogmatic . . meek
   (E) simplistic . . prosaic

3. Walter's ------- was beginning to annoy his co-workers; although they appreciated the thought he gave to his decisions, his inability to make up his mind was growing tiresome.

   (A) vacillation
   (B) solicitation
   (C) rejuvenation
   (D) admonishment
   (E) professionalism

4. To succeed as a writer, one needs a great deal of -------; successful writers are ------- even in the face of countless rejections.

   (A) affluence . . haughty
   (B) pertinacity . . apologetic
   (C) intimidation . . resilient
   (D) tenacity . . relentless
   (E) stoutness . . craven

GO ON TO THE NEXT PAGE

3 3 3 3 3 3

5. Although direct, forceful stances usually appeal to voters on the campaign trail, candidates usually resort to ------- during debates to avoid alienating any potential supporters.

(A) pontification
(B) circumlocution
(C) logic
(D) exaggeration
(E) brevity

6. Counselors in the prison rehabilitation program must have faith in the ------- of those who have committed felonies, yet be wary of -------; they must believe that criminals can change, but know that they can often return to their old habits.

(A) mutability . . astuteness
(B) variability . . consistency
(C) coarseness . . responsibility
(D) persuasion . . transcendence
(E) malleability . . relapse

7. Marullus' reference to "chimney-tops" during his monologue in *Julius Caesar* is considered by some historians -------, since such things are unlikely to have existed in Rome in the first century BC.

(A) a miscalculation
(B) an anachronism
(C) an idiom
(D) an interlocutor
(E) a mirage

8. The letter "h" at the end of Pittsburgh is ------- of American sentiments soon after World War I; it was added as part of a movement during that time to make the names of American cities sound less German.

(A) an inference
(B) an analogy
(C) a vestige
(D) an anomaly
(E) a quandary

The passages below are followed by questions based on their content. Answer the questions on the basis of what is <u>stated</u> or <u>implied</u> in the passage and in any introductory material that may be provided.

Questions 9 and 10 are based on the following passage.

Although countries can construct redoubtable stone barriers to separate "us" from "others," no barrier is stronger than language. We infer volumes from the language of another,
5 whether he is erudite or philistine, whether she is noble or mean. Our labels, too, can be impenetrable walls: we are "freedom fighters," they are "terrorists"; we are the "faithful," they are the "infidels." Those people who use such
10 wall-language are the Manichaeans,[1] those who refuse to see, or cannot see, shades of gray, the subtle truths of humanity. Their "truths" are the most dangerous weapons, wielded by the blind and the ignorant.

9. In this paragraph, language is characterized primarily as

(A) biased
(B) enlightening
(C) difficult to understand
(D) unifying
(E) changeable

10. In line 4, the word "volumes" most nearly means

(A) spaces
(B) editions
(C) measurements
(D) an abundance
(E) capacities

[1]Those who believe in absolute good and evil

GO ON TO THE NEXT PAGE ⇒

3 **3** **3** **3** **3** **3**

Questions 11 and 12 are based on the following passage.

It may be difficult for adults to learn not to interfere but rather to support the child's desire
for freedom and autonomy. For example, if
you watch a boy of three trying to tie his
shoes, you may see him work with extraordinary motivation even though the loops aren't
matched, and well over half the time as he
tries for the final knot, he ends up with two
separate laces, one in each hand. Then watch
his parents as they watch their children attempt a task like this. Too often the parent
will step in and take over, tie the shoes the
"right way" and defeat the child's growing
attempt at self-mastery. The same goes for
putting on boots, coats, and even playing with
toys. It is exceedingly easy to fall into the trap
of almost always responding negatively to a
child at this age. Commonly, a parent might
say no up to 200 times a day at this stage.
Such nagging not only is aversive in the
extreme, but also a constant reminder to the
child of his or her lack of self-control.

Line markers: 5, 10, 15, 20

11. The passage suggests that helping a boy to tie
his shoes the "right way" (line 13) can be

(A) necessary to his self-esteem
(B) important to his personal hygiene
(C) appropriate only if the boy has the neces-
sary fine motor skills
(D) essential to teaching him patience
(E) harmful to his autonomous development

12. The passage indicates that negative responses to
a child can lead to the child's

(A) rebellion
(B) feeling of helplessness
(C) persistence in the task
(D) mimicking of the negative behavior
(E) anger

Second passage: *Educational Psychology: A Developmental Approach*, Norman A. Sprinthall et al., McGraw-Hill, 1994, p. 149

Questions 13–18 are based on the following passage.

*The following is an essay about T. S. Eliot, an
American poet of the early 20th century, and the
Modernist movement, of which he was a part.*

Modernism is the most peculiar of all artistic
movements of the twentieth century and the
most difficult to pin down since people started
coming up with "movements" in the first
place. Modernism is the only thing that strikes
more fear into the heart of an English undergraduate than the idea of going to a lecture.
Critics and academics, not unwisely, prefer
their artistic movements to be readily comprehensible and clearly enough defined to make
some logical sense. Modernism, however, will
not be tamed. It is straggly, begins nowhere
and with no one in particular, and ends only
when its writers have started to baffle even
themselves. One treads carefully through its
key texts: James Joyce's *Ulysses*, T. S. Eliot's
The Waste Land (both 1922), and Virginia
Woolf's *Mrs. Dalloway* (1925). The authors of
these aberrations, these posturing, egotistical,
lunatic, kaleidoscopic works of blatant and
self-conscious genius, have laid literary landmines throughout their works. Joyce said of
Ulysses that "I've put in so many enigmas and
puzzles that it will keep the professors busy
for centuries arguing over what I meant, and
that's the only way of insuring one's immortality." This statement sums up the enigma of
modernism (if one can be said to sum up an
enigma) in that it contains arrogance min-
gling with modesty, cleverness tied up in self-
effacing humour, and above all absurdity with
a purpose. Plots, such as they exist at all in
modernist writing, are submerged beneath
wave upon wave of classical allusions,
archaisms, neologisms, foreign languages,
quotations, swear words and other hyper-
literary and meta-literary indulgences. If I
haven't made it clear already, it is hard not to
love modernism. It is hard to work out what
exactly it is.

Line markers: 5, 10, 15, 20, 25, 30, 35, 40

GO ON TO THE NEXT PAGE →

3   3   3   3   3   3

Recently, while browsing in an Oxford bookshop, a friend of mine picked up a copy of *Finnegans Wake*—James Joyce's final book—and read the first page. Between tears

45 of laughter, he managed to indicate to me that he couldn't understand a word of it. It is hard not to sympathise with the outsider's attitude so amply demonstrated by my friend's outburst of shock and wonder. To find one of

50 our most famous authors writing gibberish is rather heartening. Yet we remain outsiders to the work. *Finnegans Wake,* you see, is emblematic of all that is right and wrong with modernism. It took a spectacularly long time

55 to write and was finally published in 1939, seventeen years after its predecessor, *Ulysses.* That probably had something to do with the fact that over 40 different languages crept into its catalogue of portmanteau words

60 (ersatz words consisting of two or more real words or word elements, like those of Lewis Carroll in his poem "Jabberwocky"). The resulting book is uniquely inventive and at the same time uniquely confusing. In that sense,

65 it is the perfect example of a modernist text. It alienates its readers just as it tries to mimic how they think. The English modernist novel is a sociopath and a cad: dangerous and reprehensive but somehow roguishly

70 likeable.

13. In the first paragraph, the author characterizes Modernism as which of the following?

     I. self-centered
     II. ill-defined
     III. politically oriented

(A) I only
(B) II only
(C) I and II only
(D) II and III only
(E) I, II, and III

14. The passage suggests that critics and academics dislike artistic movements that are

(A) enigmatic
(B) comprehensible
(C) wide-ranging
(D) inventive
(E) socially conscious

15. The "landmines" in lines 21–22 are

(A) episodes in novels that refer to violence
(B) criticisms of the works of other novelists
(C) new methods of analyzing literature
(D) literary devices intended to baffle academics
(E) limitations that publishers place on an author's work

16. The reference to "wave upon wave" (line 34) suggests that, in Modernist fiction, plot is

(A) a powerfully moving element
(B) secondary to other considerations
(C) dominant over diction
(D) characterized by redundancy
(E) dangerous

17. The author's overall attitude toward Modernism can best be described as

(A) ambivalent
(B) reverential
(C) cynical
(D) indignant
(E) jocular

18. The final sentence of the passage employs each of the following EXCEPT

(A) simile
(B) juxtaposition
(C) personification
(D) contrast
(E) metaphor

Excerpted from *T. S. Eliot and the Elitism of Modernism,* by David Pinching, on http://www.bibliomania.com

GO ON TO THE NEXT PAGE ⟶

3   3   3   3   3   3

Questions 19–24 are based on the following passage.

The following is an excerpt from a book on genomics, the new science of gathering and using the information encoded in the genes of an organism.

Biology is being reborn as an information science, a progeny of the Information Age. As in-
Line formation scientists, biologists concern themselves with the messages that sustain life,
5   such as the intricate series of signals that tell a fertilized egg to develop into a full-grown organism, or the orchestrated response the immune system makes to an invading pathogen. Molecules convey information, and it is their
10 messages that are of paramount importance. Each molecule interacts with a set of other molecules and each set communicates with another set, such that all are interconnected. Networks of molecules give rise to cells; networks
15 of cells produce multicellular organisms; networks of people bring about cultures and societies; and networks of species encompass ecosystems. Life is a web and the web is life.
        Ironically, it was the euphoria for molecules
20 that touched off this scientific revolution. In the 1980s only a tiny percentage of the millions of different molecular components of living beings was known. In order to gain access to these molecules, a new science and even a
25 new industry had to be created. Genomics is the development and application of research tools that uncover and analyze thousands of different molecules at a time. This new approach to biology has been so successful that
30 universities have created entire departments devoted to it, and all major pharmaceutical companies now have large genomics divisions. Genomics has granted biologists unprecedented access to the molecules of life,
35 but this is more than just a technological revolution. Through genomics massive amounts of biological information can be converted into an electronic format. This directly links the life sciences to the information sciences,
40 thereby facilitating a dramatically new framework for understanding life.
        Information is a message, a bit of news. It may be encoded or decoded. It may be conveyed by smoke signals, pictures, sound
45 waves, electromagnetic waves, or innumerous other media, but the information itself is not made of anything. It has no mass. Furthermore, information always has a sender and an intended receiver. This implies an un-
50 derlying intent, meaning, or purpose. Information theory thus may seem unfit for the cold objectivism of science. The focus of the information sciences, however, is not so much on information content, but rather on
55 how messages are conveyed, processed, and stored.
        Advances in this area have been great and have helped to propel the remarkable development of the computer and telecommunication
60 industries. Could these forces be harnessed to better understand the human body and to improve human health?

19. The primary purpose of this passage is to

     (A) refute a theory
     (B) describe the origins of a misconception
     (C) analyze different perspectives on a phenomenon
     (D) describe a new trend in a field of study
     (E) suggest a new method of teaching

20. The passage mentions each of the following as an example of elements interrelating to form a larger whole EXCEPT

     (A) molecules forming a cell
     (B) organisms forming an ecosystem
     (C) pathogens forming the immune system
     (D) individuals forming a society
     (E) cells forming an organism

21. The passage mentions the "orchestrated response" (line 7) primarily as an example of

     (A) the coordinated efforts of scientists
     (B) molecules conveying information
     (C) the work being done to promote genomics
     (D) the similarity between cells and computers
     (E) an unrealized potential of the cell

Transducing the Genome, Gary Zweiger, McGraw-Hill, pp. xi–xii

GO ON TO THE NEXT PAGE

3   3   3   3   3   3

22. According to the passage, the "dramatically new framework" (lines 40–41) is one in which

(A) new university buildings are being built
(B) the immune system attacks a pathogen
(C) networks of molecules give rise to cells
(D) genomics research receives more federal funding
(E) biological data is translated into a new form

23. According to the passage, information theory "may seem unfit for the cold objectivism of science" (line 51–52) because

(A) it is better suited to commercial industry than to academic study
(B) it can be conveyed by sound waves
(C) it suggests that messages may have meaning or purpose
(D) it is not rigorously studied
(E) it analyzes biological information

24. Which of the following best describes the function of the final paragraph in relation to the rest of the passage?

(A) It modifies a theory presented earlier.
(B) It provides a solution to a problem mentioned earlier.
(C) It raises doubts about the value of genomics.
(D) It indicates actual and potential consequences of genomics.
(E) It mentions a viable alternative to genomics.

STOP

If you finish before time is called, you may check your work on this section only. Do not turn to any other section of the test.

4   **4**   **4**   **4**   **4**   **4**

SECTION 4
Time—25 minutes
35 questions

Turn to Section 4 of your answer sheet to answer the questions in this section.

Directions: For each question in this section, select the best answer from among the choices given and fill in the corresponding circle on the answer sheet.

The following sentences test correctness and effectiveness of expression. Part of each sentence or the entire sentence is underlined; beneath each sentence are five ways of phrasing the underlined material. Choice A repeats the original phrasing; the other four choices are different. Select the choice that completes the sentence most effectively.

In making your selection, follow the requirements of standard written English; that is, pay attention to grammar, choice of words, sentence construction, and punctuation. Your selection should result in the most effective sentence—clear and precise, without awkwardness or ambiguity.

EXAMPLE:

The children couldn't hardly believe their eyes.

(A) couldn't hardly believe their eyes
(B) could hardly believe their eyes
(C) would not hardly believe their eyes
(D) couldn't nearly believe their eyes
(E) couldn't hardly believe his or her eyes

Ⓐ ● Ⓒ Ⓓ Ⓔ

1. The controversial themes, which resonate with recent political events, explain why the book is selling at such a feverish pace.

(A) explain why the book is selling at such a feverish pace
(B) explains the feverish pace of the book
(C) explain the reason for the pace of the book's feverish sales
(D) explains why the book's selling pace is so feverish
(E) is why the book is selling well

2. One of the best features of the journalist's lifestyle is you never know what's next.

(A) you never know what's next
(B) it's so unpredictable
(C) that you never know what's next
(D) one can never predict what's next
(E) its unpredictability

3. Despite having an engaging personality and an outstanding education, Greg's search for a satisfying job was fruitless.

(A) Greg's search for a satisfying job was fruitless
(B) Greg searched fruitlessly for a satisfying job
(C) Greg's job search was fruitless because he insisted on a satisfying job
(D) the satisfying job that Greg sought was nowhere to be found
(E) Greg searched for a satisfying job, but it was fruitless

GO ON TO THE NEXT PAGE

4   4   4   4   4   4

4. The plot of the movie was neither plausible <u>and it was not even faithful to the novel</u>.

(A) and it was not even faithful to the novel
(B) nor was it faithful to the novel
(C) nor faithful to the novel
(D) and certainly not faithful to the novel
(E) yet hardly faithful to the novel

5. We were astonished that the package <u>had took so long to get</u> to its destination.

(A) had took so long to get
(B) had took so long getting
(C) had taken so long in its getting
(D) had taken so long to get
(E) had been so long getting

6. The committee agreed that the new principal should be able to inspire teachers, uphold tradition, and, above all, <u>he or she must maintain a scholarly atmosphere</u>.

(A) he or she must maintain a scholarly atmosphere
(B) they should maintain a scholarly atmosphere
(C) maintain a scholarly atmosphere
(D) keep things scholarly
(E) he or she should keep things scholarly

7. Although critics say that many have portrayed Othello with more passion than <u>he, they can't help but admire his acting</u>.

(A) he, they can't help but admire his acting
(B) him, they can't help but admire his acting
(C) he, they can't help but admire him acting
(D) him, they can't help but admire him acting
(E) him, they must only admire his acting

8. Neither <u>of the battling rams appeared to feel the pain of their wounds</u>.

(A) of the battling rams appeared to feel the pain of their wounds
(B) of the battling rams appeared to feel the pain of its wounds
(C) ram, that was battling, appeared to feel the pain of their wounds
(D) ram who were battling appeared to feel the pain of its wounds
(E) battling ram appeared as if to feel the pain of their wounds

9. Walking into her house after a hard day's work, <u>Liz's family surprised her with a warm, delicious meal and a clean house</u>.

(A) Liz's family surprised her with a warm, delicious meal and a clean house
(B) Liz was surprised to find a warm, delicious meal and a clean house, courtesy of her family
(C) Liz's family made her a warm, delicious meal and cleaned the house, surprising her
(D) Liz found a warm, delicious meal and a clean house surprising her from her family
(E) a warm, delicious meal and a clean house surprised Liz, courtesy of her family

10. An increasing number of students are coming to realize that an education at a public university can be <u>as good, if not better, than an elite private college</u>.

(A) as good, if not better, than an elite private college
(B) as good, if not better, as one at an elite private college
(C) as good as, if not better, than an elite private college education
(D) as good an education as, if not better, than one at an elite private college
(E) as good as, if not better than, one at an elite private college

GO ON TO THE NEXT PAGE ⟹

4   4   4   4   4   4

11. S. J. Perelman, whose hallmark of a grandilo-
     quent writing style is widely regarded as one of
     the finest American wits of all time.

     (A) S. J. Perelman, whose hallmark of a
          grandiloquent writing style is
     (B) Being that his hallmark is a grandilo-
          quent writing style, S. J. Perelman is
     (C) S. J. Perelman's grandiloquent writing
          style is his hallmark and is
     (D) S. J. Perelman and his hallmark of a
          grandiloquent writing style are
     (E) S. J. Perelman, whose hallmark is a
          grandiloquent writing style, is

The following sentences test your ability to
recognize grammar and usage errors. Each
sentence contains either a single error or no
error at all. No sentence contains more than
one error. The error, if there is one, is underlined and lettered. If the sentence contains an
error, select the one underlined part that must
be changed to make the sentence correct. If the
sentence is correct, select choice E. In choosing answers, follow the requirements of standard written English.

EXAMPLE:

By the time they reached the halfway point
                A
in the race, most of the runners hadn't hardly
        B   C   D
begun to hit their stride.   No error
                                 E

                              Ⓐ Ⓑ Ⓒ ● Ⓔ

---

12. The lack of progress

     in international relations reveals that
              A   B
     governments must study the art of
                      C
     diplomacy much closer.   No error
                D   E

13. Because Deborah has been a representative
                        A
     for over 20 years and also her popularity
                              B
     among her constituents, few are willing
             C
     to challenge her in an election.   No error
         D   E

14. Caravaggio demonstrated the great range
                    A
     of his artistic talent in such paintings as
           B   C
     "Bacchus" and "Basket of Fruit," painted in

     1593 and 1596, respectfully.   No error
                          D   E

15. Grizzly bears rarely show aggression toward
                    A
     humans, but they will protect their territory
            B
     from anyone whom they
          C
     would have considered to be a threat.
                    D
     No error
       E

GO ON TO THE NEXT PAGE ⇨

4   4   4   4   4   4

___

16. The choir's rendition of "America the

Beautiful" <u>was stirring</u>, particularly after the
        A

children <u>had finished</u> <u>their</u> presentation on
        B   C

<u>the meaning of</u> freedom.   <u>No error</u>
    D   E

17. Andre suggested <u>to the board</u> that both the
               A

fund deficit and the <u>disillusionment</u> of the
               B

investors were <u>a problem</u> that
         C

<u>had to be addressed</u> immediately.
    D

<u>No error</u>
  E

18. Because Phillips reasoned that either

<u>accepting</u> or rejecting the proposal <u>were</u>
  A   B

going to upset some <u>political faction</u>,
               C

he decided to delay the vote until

<u>after his reelection</u>.   <u>No error</u>
   D   E

19. The Attorney General <u>spoke at length</u> about
                A

the detrimental <u>effects</u> of having <u>less</u>
          B   C

defense attorneys <u>to serve</u> indigent
           D

defendants.   <u>No error</u>
          E

20. The service <u>at Centro</u> is much better than
          A

<u>the other restaurants</u> we frequent, so
  B

<u>we prefer</u> to go there when
  C

<u>we are entertaining</u> guests.   <u>No error</u>
   D   E

21. Before the curtain <u>rose</u>, Anthony wished
               A

that <u>he were</u> back in bed, only <u>dreaming</u>
    B   C

about performing in front of

<u>hundreds of strangers</u> rather than actually
        D

doing it.   <u>No error</u>
         E

22. James, like many parents, <u>believes</u> that if a
                 A

child can read <u>at a very young age</u>, <u>they</u> will
          B   C

grow to have <u>exceptional</u> literary talent.
         D

<u>No error</u>
  E

23. The <u>decline</u> of the Enlightenment
    A

<u>was hastened</u> not only by tyrants but also
  B

<u>because of</u> intellectual <u>opposition</u>.   <u>No error</u>
  C   D   E

GO ON TO THE NEXT PAGE

4   4   4   4   4   4

24. Although he pitched <u>professionally</u> for 3

                    A

decades, Nolan Ryan <u>never lost</u> any velocity

                   B

on his fastball, and few <u>maintained</u> such

                   C

<u>control over</u> so many pitches as he.

  D

<u>No error</u>

   E

25. The Senator and his <u>opponent</u>, Thomas

               A

Cowher, were running a very tight race until

<u>he</u> made a <u>racially insensitive</u> comment that

B   C

<u>offended</u> many voters.   <u>No error</u>

  D   E

26. Just when <u>those who</u> were observing

         A

the heart transplant procedure assumed

<u>the worst</u>, the surgeons themselves <u>are</u> <u>most</u>

  B   C D

confident.   <u>No error</u>

          E

27. <u>Although</u> testing <u>for unsafe</u> levels of

  A   B

asbestos particles is widely <u>advocated for</u>

                        C

houses <u>built before</u> 1950, many home

      D

owners ignore this suggestion.   <u>No error</u>

                           E

28. Between my brother <u>and I</u> <u>existed</u> a strong

                 A   B

bond that did not weaken even <u>when</u> he

                       C

chose to live <u>thousands of miles</u> away on a

          D

different continent.   <u>No error</u>

                E

29. <u>Writing about</u> the folk duo, one critic

    A

<u>has suggested</u> that <u>their</u> longevity is <u>due to</u>

    B   C   D

its ability to remain faithful to an honest

musical style while stretching the boundaries

of convention.   <u>No error</u>

             E

GO ON TO THE NEXT PAGE

4   4   4   4   4   4

Directions: The following passage is an early draft of an essay. Some parts of the passage need to be rewritten.

Read the passage and select the best answers for the questions that follow. Some questions are about particular sentences or parts of sentences and ask you to improve sentence structure or word choice. Other questions ask you to consider organization and development. In choosing answers, follow the requirements of standard written English.

Questions 30–35 refer to the following passage.

(1) For thousands of years, philosophers have debated whether humans discover mathematics or it is something that has been invented. **(2)** Plato believed that perceived mathematical objects like lines were only vague shadows of abstract "ideals" that exist outside of human experience. **(3)** Circular objects or circles drawn on paper aren't "really" circles. **(4)** Rather, they are just a flawed approximation of the perfect circular form. **(5)** So, in this sense, Plato believed that mathematics was something revealed imperfectly to humans, not invented by them. **(6)** Many students surely wish that mathematics had not been invented at all. **(7)** A position that opposes Plato's idealism is called mathematical intuitionism, which is the belief that all mathematics is the product of human minds.

(8) There is one good way to understand the difference between idealism and intuitionism. **(9)** Look at big numbers. **(10)** An idealist would say that all numbers, no matter how large, truly exist, even if no one has ever actually calculated them. **(11)** An intuitionist, on the other hand, might say that some numbers may be so big that they are physically impossible to calculate or express in a meaningful way, and so do not truly "exist."

(12) Another point of view that is different from these ones is one that says that it is a pointless thing to ask the question as to whether mathematical objects "really exist" or not. **(13)** This view simply regards mathematics as a tool for interpreting information from the world around us. **(14)** This view is essentially a compromise between idealism and intuitionism. **(15)** Although it acknowledges that mathematics reaches beyond the mind of a mathematician, it also denies that it has any meaning outside of the mind. **(16)** The concept of a circle is not a reflection of an abstract "ideal," and also it is not completely a human invention. **(17)** Instead it is a concept that we form in our minds after perceiving and thinking about many circular objects in the world around us.

30. Which of the following is the best revision of the underlined portion of sentence 1 (reproduced below)?

    For thousands of years, philosophers have debated whether <u>humans discover mathematics or it is something that has been invented</u>.

    (A) humans discover mathematics or invent it
    (B) humans so much discover mathematics as they do invent it
    (C) the discovery of mathematics is what humans do or the invention
    (D) humans discover mathematics or if it is invented
    (E) mathematics is something discovered or if humans invent it

31. In context, which of the following is the most logical revision of the underlined portion of sentence 3 (reproduced below)?

    <u>Circular objects</u> or circles drawn on paper aren't "really" circles.

    (A) Nevertheless, circular objects
    (B) According to his reasoning, circular objects
    (C) Furthermore, circular objects
    (D) Secondly, circular objects
    (E) All the while, circular objects

GO ON TO THE NEXT PAGE →

32. Which of the following is the best revision of sentence 4 (reproduced below)?

Rather, they are just a flawed approximation of the perfect circular form.

(A) But instead they are only a flawed approximation of the perfect circular form.

(B) Rather, they are only flawed approximations of the perfect circular form.

(C) Rather, their forms are merely an approximation of circular perfection alone.

(D) Instead, their approximation of the perfect circular form mentioned above is imperfect.

(E) Rather, their perfection as circular forms is only an approximation of it.

33. Which of the following sentences contributes least to the unity of the first paragraph?

(A) Sentence 3
(B) Sentence 4
(C) Sentence 5
(D) Sentence 6
(E) Sentence 7

34. Which of the following is the best way to combine sentences 8 and 9 (reproduced below)?

There is one good way to understand the difference between idealism and intuitionism. Look at big numbers.

(A) One good way to understand the difference between idealism and intuitionism is the following: look at large numbers.

(B) It is a good way to understand the difference between idealism and intuitionism in considering large numbers.

(C) The consideration of large numbers provides one good way toward the understanding of the difference between idealism and intuitionism.

(D) To consider large numbers is to have one good way of understanding the difference between idealism and intuitionism.

(E) One good way to understand the difference between idealism and intuitionism is to consider large numbers.

35. In context, which of the following is the best revision of sentence 12 (reproduced below)?

Another point of view that is different from these ones is one that says that it is a pointless thing to ask the question as to whether mathematical objects "really exist" or not.

(A) A third point of view regards it as pointless to ask whether mathematical objects "really exist."

(B) Another, completely different, point of view is the one that regards asking whether or not mathematical objects "really exist" as pointless.

(C) Asking whether mathematical objects "really exist" is pointless, according to another, third, different point of view.

(D) The asking of whether mathematical objects "really exist" is a pointless thing, says a third point of view.

(E) Another different point of view says it is pointless to ask about whether mathematical objects "really exist" or not.

STOP

If you finish before time is called, you may check your work on this section only. Do not turn to any other section of the test.

5   5   5   5   5   5

SECTION 5
Time—25 minutes
18 questions

Turn to Section 5 of your answer sheet to answer the questions in this section.

Directions: This section contains two types of questions. You have 25 minutes to complete both types. For questions 1–8, solve each problem and decide which is the best of the choices given. Fill in the corresponding circle on the answer sheet. You may use any available space for scratchwork.

Notes

1. The use of a calculator is permitted.

2. All numbers used are real numbers.

3. Figures that accompany problems in this test are intended to provide information useful in solving the problems. They are drawn as accurately as possible EXCEPT when it is stated in a specific problem that the figure is not drawn to scale. All figures lie in a plane unless otherwise indicated.

4. Unless otherwise specified, the domain of any function f is assumed to be the set of all real numbers x for which $f(x)$ is a real number.

Reference Information

$A = \pi r^2$ $A = \ell w$ $A = \frac{1}{2} bh$ $V = \ell wh$ $V = \pi r^2 h$ $c^2 = a^2 + b^2$ Special right triangles
$C = 2\pi r$

The number of degrees of arc in a circle is 360.
The sum of the measures in degrees of the angles of a triangle is 180.

---

1. If $2x = 10$ and $3y = 12$, then $4x + 6y =$

(A) 10
(B) 12
(C) 22
(D) 32
(E) 44

2. The average (arithmetic mean) of three numbers is 5. If one of the numbers is 4, what is the sum of the other two numbers?

(A) 8
(B) 9
(C) 10
(D) 11
(E) 12

GO ON TO THE NEXT PAGE

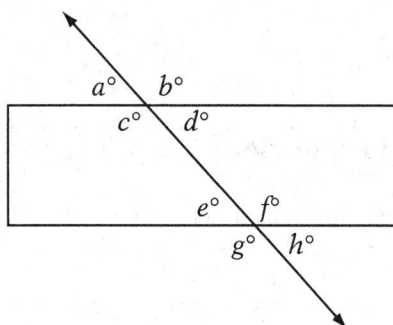

3. The figure above shows a rectangle intersected by a line. If $b = 2a$, then $d + e + g + h =$

(A) 120
(B) 240
(C) 300
(D) 320
(E) 360

4. For all real numbers x where $x \geq 1$, let $f(x) = \sqrt{\sqrt{x} - 1}$. What is the value of $f(100)$?

(A) 3
(B) 9
(C) 10
(D) 27
(E) 100

5. If $3^{k+m} = 243$ and $2^m = 8$, then what is the value of 2^k?

(A) 2
(B) 4
(C) 6
(D) 8
(E) 10

6. If b varies inversely as the square of c, and if $b = 8$ when $c = 3$, then what could be the value of c when $b = 2$?

(A) 2
(B) 5
(C) 6
(D) 25
(E) 36

7. In a certain soccer league, each of the five teams plays every other team in the league exactly three times each season. How many games are played in total in one season?

(A) 15
(B) 24
(C) 30
(D) 60
(E) 120

8. Pump A, working alone, can fill a tank in 3 hours, and pump B can fill the same tank in 2 hours. If the tank is empty to start and pump A is switched on for one hour, after which pump B is also switched on and the two work together, how many *minutes* will pump B have been working by the time the tank is filled?

(A) 48
(B) 50
(C) 54
(D) 60
(E) 64

GO ON TO THE NEXT PAGE

5   5   5   5   5   5

Directions: For student-produced response questions 9–18, use the grids at the bottom of the answer sheet page on which you have answered questions 1–8.

Each of the remaining ten questions requires you to solve the problem and enter your answer by marking the circles in the special grid, as shown in the examples below. You may use any available space for scratchwork.

Answer: $\frac{7}{12}$

Write answer in boxes.

Fraction line

Grid in result.

Answer: 2.5

Decimal point

Answer: 201
Either position is correct.

Note: You may start your answers in any column, space permitting. Columns not needed should be left blank.

- Mark no more than one circle in any column.

- Because the answer sheet will be machine-scored, **you will receive credit only if the circles are filled in correctly.**

- Although not required, it is suggested that you write your answer in the boxes at the top of the columns to help you fill in the circles accurately.

- Some problems may have more than one correct answer. In such cases, grid only one answer.

- No question has a negative answer.

- **Mixed numbers** such as $3\frac{1}{2}$ must be gridded as 3.5 or 7/2. (If [3 1 / 2] is gridded, it will be interpreted as , $\frac{31}{2}$ not $3\frac{1}{2}$.)

- **Decimal Answers:** If you obtain a decimal answer with more digits than the grid can accommodate, it may be either rounded or truncated, but it must fill the entire grid. For example, if you obtain an answer such as 0.6666..., you should record your result as .666 or .667. **A less accurate value such as .66 or .67 will be scored as incorrect.**

Acceptable ways to grid $^2/_3$ are:

GO ON TO THE NEXT PAGE →

9. If four times a certain number is decreased by 5, the result is 25. What is the number?

10. For every integer m greater than 1, let «m» be defined as the sum of the integers from 1 to m, inclusive. For instance,
«4» = 1 + 2 + 3 + 4 = 10.
What is the value of «7» − «5»?

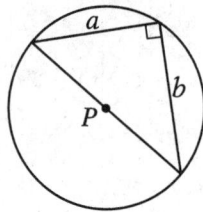

11. If the circumference of the circle above is 10π, then what is the value of $a^2 + b^2$?

A, B, C, D

12. How many different three-letter arrangements of the letters above are possible if no letter may be repeated? (An arrangement like ABC is distinct from an arrangement like BCA.)

13. If $96{,}878 \times x^2 = 10{,}200$, then $\dfrac{10{,}200}{5x^2 \times 96{,}878} =$

14. Every term in a certain sequence is one less than three times the previous term. If the fourth term of this sequence is 95, what is the first term of the sequence?

15. If $4 + \sqrt{b} = 7.2$, what is the value of $4 - \sqrt{b}$?

16. Admission to a museum is $10 for each adult and $5 for each child. If a group of 30 people pays a total of $175 in admission, how many adults are in the group?

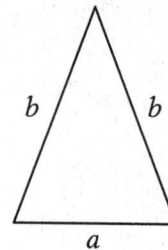

17. The perimeter of the isosceles triangle above is 24. If the ratio of a to b is 2 to 3, what is the value of b?

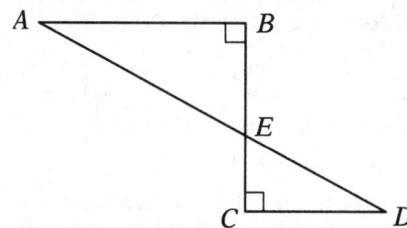

Note: Figure not drawn to scale.

18. In the figure above, $AB = 6$, $BC = 6$, and $CD = 2$. What is AD?

STOP

If you finish before time is called, you may check your work on this section only. Do not turn to any other section of the test.

6 6 6 6 6 6

SECTION 6
Time—25 minutes
24 questions

| **Turn to Section 6 of your answer sheet to answer the questions in this section.** |

Directions: For each question in this section, select the best answer from among the choices given and fill in the corresponding circle on the answer sheet.

Each sentence below has one or two blanks, each blank indicating that something has been omitted. Beneath the sentence are five words or sets of words labeled A through E. Choose the word or set of words that, when inserted in the sentence, best fits the meaning of the sentence as a whole.

EXAMPLE:

Rather than accepting the theory unquestioningly, Deborah regarded it with -----.

(A) mirth
(B) sadness
(C) responsibility
(D) ignorance
(E) skepticism

Ⓐ Ⓑ Ⓒ Ⓓ ●

1. The strange signal detected by the radio telescope, rather than being taken as evidence of a new cosmological phenomenon, was instead treated as merely ------- of the equipment itself.

(A) a malfunction
(B) a bulwark
(C) an anthology
(D) a mutation
(E) a transfer

2. The long-standing divisions among the indigenous ethnic groups in the region have created an ------- problem that may never be solved without international intervention.

(A) impotent
(B) intractable
(C) evanescent
(D) irate
(E) insipid

3. The ease with which the army's defenses were breached surprised the opposing general, who expected resistance to be far more ------- than it was.

(A) ephemeral
(B) compatible
(C) egregious
(D) tolerable
(E) imposing

4. Although dependence on electronic devices has ------- in recent years, the increased efficiency of common appliances has ------- the demand on the power grid.

(A) abated . . decreased
(B) surged . . attenuated
(C) increased . . compromised
(D) diminished . . reduced
(E) flourished . . elevated

GO ON TO THE NEXT PAGE ⟩

5. Although persecution at the hands of ------- landowners vanquished the will of many, it ------- the dreams of revolution among the hardier insurgents.

    (A) despotic . . squandered
    (B) cruel . . destroyed
    (C) amenable . . bore
    (D) celebrated . . initiated
    (E) ruthless . . forged

The passages below are followed by questions based on their content; questions following a pair of related passages may also be based on the relationship between the paired passages. Answer the questions on the basis of what is stated or implied in the passage and in any introductory material that may be provided.

Questions 6–9 are based on the following passages.

PASSAGE 1

The following is from a recent commentary on Jean-Jacques Rousseau (1712–1778), a French philosopher during the Enlightenment.

Taken as a whole, Rousseau's writings attacked the Age of Reason, gave impetus to the
Line Romantic movement by emphasizing feeling (leading Goethe to say that "feeling is all"),
5   revived religion even though he had doubts about some traditional teachings, provided a new direction for education (his book *Émile* was considered by some the best work on education since Plato's *Republic*), inspired the
10   French Revolution, made a unique impact on political philosophy, and, more than the writing of any of his contemporaries, influenced several subsequent philosophers, especially Immanuel Kant. On one occasion, Kant was
15   so absorbed in reading Rousseau's *Émile* that he forgot to take his celebrated daily walk. While Kant admitted that it was David Hume who awakened him from his dogmatic slumbers regarding the theory of knowledge, it was
20   Rousseau who showed him the way to a new

First passage: from "Rousseau: A Romantic in the Age of Reason," from *Socrates to Sartre*, McGraw-Hill, 1999, p. 278
Second passage: Copyright 2005 Christopher Black. All rights reserved.

theory of morality. So impressed was Kant by the insights of Rousseau that he hung a picture of him on the wall of his study, convinced that Rousseau was the Newton of the moral world.

PASSAGE 2

25   The roses we lay at Rousseau's feet for this theory of Natural Rights tend to overwhelm the less fragrant of his ideas. He persisted in believing in the nobility of the primitive state of nature, and that women's nature was to serve
30   men. His assertions about Natural Rights of Man laid the philosophical foundation of American independence, but his worship of emotion over reason and of "negative education" gave generations of parents permission to
35   ignore the need to discipline and teach their children.

6. Passage 1 suggests that Goethe

    (A) was at the forefront of the Age of Reason
    (B) was a traditionalist
    (C) was influenced by Rousseau
    (D) opposed the Romantic movement
    (E) inspired much of Rousseau's work

7. Passage 1 mentions Kant's "daily walk" (line 16) in order to emphasize

    (A) Kant's forgetfulness
    (B) Kant's commitment to healthful practices
    (C) the dogmatic nature of Rousseau's writings
    (D) the effect of Rousseau's philosophy on Kant
    (E) Kant's close friendship with Rousseau

8. Unlike Passage 1, Passage 2 characterizes Rousseau's emphasis on emotion as

    (A) insincere
    (B) innovative
    (C) harmful
    (D) temporary
    (E) necessary

GO ON TO THE NEXT PAGE

6   6   6   6   6   6

9. Both passages credit Rousseau with

(A) attacking the Age of Reason
(B) inspiring revolutionary thought
(C) encouraging discipline
(D) praising the primitive state of nature
(E) establishing the Romantic movement

Questions 10–16 are based on the following passage.

The following passage was written by an American essayist in 2003 about the status of capitalism.

In response to a journalist's question, "What do you think about Western civilization?"
Line Mahatma Gandhi is said to have replied, "It would be a good idea." Any honest person
5   who values the concept of the free market, who believes in the promise of open economic competition, would say the same thing about capitalism. We hear our politicians, and of course the corporate news and entertainment
10 media, speaking as if the United States were a model of free-market capitalism, as if anyone could start a business to create and sell a product or service without the obstruction of the government. The truth is quite different.
15 Those we hear saying such things are quite often voices that are bankrolled by large corporations, which themselves are often protected from competition by mutual agreement with the federal government.
20   The concept of free trade is simple: if Company A can produce and distribute a product more efficiently and at a higher quality than Company B, it should be allowed to do so, and to charge any price for it that free consumers
25 are willing to pay. Although Company B would likely suffer as a result, humanity would benefit from freer and cheaper access to high-quality goods. Sometimes free trade works nicely, as when Company A is in the United States and
30 Company B is in India. Then, agreements are signed to "open up" India to the cheaper goods made by Company A, even if doing so crushes Company B because, we say, consumers have a right to cheap, high-quality goods. But if Com-
35 pany A were in India and Company B were in the United States, the story would likely be very different.

This isn't an ideal example. India developed a pharmaceutical industry many years ago
40 that could produce drugs very cheaply that would have saved tens of thousands of lives each year. In a free-market economy, the Indian pharmaceutical industry would have been allowed to make drugs and get them to the
45 people who needed them. But that would mean that western pharmaceutical companies would make less profit. Of course, it's not that the American pharmaceutical companies don't care about Indian children dying
50 because they can't get drugs; it's just that their responsibility is to their stockholders. They must maximize profits. But the "free market" was getting in the way, so they simply changed the rules.
55   Thus, in 1994 India "agreed" (that is, gave in to Western pressure) to "liberalize" its pharmaceutical industry by allowing its largest drug companies to be sold to Western interests, thereby reducing competition.
60 Drug prices predictably shot up, putting them out of reach of people who needed them, but the Western corporations made more money. It was a big triumph for the "liberalization" of markets, but a great blow
65 to free markets.
        In a free economy, businesses are also expected to wager their own capital on success in the marketplace. The adventurous entrepreneur is a moral icon in the United States.
70 The American pharmaceutical industry, however, receives over half a billion dollars annually in federal tax dollars in the form of research grants to develop medications and vaccines that they can then patent and sell
75 back to consumers at monopolistic prices. The legislators who sponsor these grants know that their campaigns will likely receive reciprocal monetary benefit as a result. What is worse, most American voters accept this sys-
80 tem happily because they believe that they are simply helping to find cures for diseases. The reality, however, is very different: by discouraging the competition that leads to real progress, this system of protectionism is actually a huge
85 impediment to the elimination of disease.

GO ON TO THE NEXT PAGE ▷

6   6   6   6   6   6

10. The quotation from Mahatma Gandhi (lines 3–4) suggests that Gandhi believed that Western civilization was

(A) on the decline
(B) the beneficiary of unfair economic practices
(C) antithetical to progress in Asia
(D) a great triumph
(E) an unrealized concept

11. The "voices" mentioned in line 16 can be inferred to include all of the following EXCEPT

(A) American politicians
(B) leaders like Mahatma Gandhi
(C) television journalists
(D) some leaders of large corporations
(E) those who believe that the United States is faithful to the capitalist ideal

12. The primary function of the second paragraph (lines 20–37) is to

(A) illustrate a debate
(B) provide a statistical analysis
(C) explain a concept
(D) give historical background
(E) describe a popular viewpoint

13. By saying that "the story would likely be very different" (lines 36–37), the passage suggests that

(A) the rules of a free market are selectively applied
(B) trade laws favor smaller countries
(C) American companies produce the best products
(D) Asian countries are moving away from the free market
(E) American companies share the same interests as Indian companies

14. The quotation marks around particular words in the fourth paragraph (lines 55–65) serve primarily to indicate that those words are

(A) being used ironically
(B) technical economic terms
(C) adaptations of foreign words
(D) recently coined
(E) direct quotations from a document described earlier

15. The "triumph" described in line 63 is characterized as

(A) a rare success for free markets
(B) a legislative victory
(C) a breakthrough in the development of inexpensive drugs
(D) a tragic violation of the principle of free trade
(E) a success that was based on luck

16. The passage suggests that the "entrepreneur" (lines 68–69) differs from executives in the pharmaceutical industry in that the entrepreneur

(A) does not abide by free-market ideals
(B) risks his or her own money
(C) does not hire employees from overseas
(D) works more closely with representatives in Washington
(E) needs less money to start a typical business

GO ON TO THE NEXT PAGE ⟶

6   6   6   6   6   6

Questions 17–24 are based on the following passage.

The following passage is an excerpt from Mary Shelley's Frankenstein, *written in 1831.*

Natural philosophy, and particularly chemistry, became nearly my sole occupation.
Line I read with ardor those works, so full of genius and discrimination, that modern inquir-
5 ers have written on these subjects. I attended
the lectures and cultivated the acquaintance
of the men of science of the university. In
M. Waldman I found a true friend. His gentle-
ness was never tinged by dogmatism, and his
10 instructions were given with an air of frankness and good nature that banished every idea
of pedantry. In a thousand ways he smoothed
for me the path of knowledge and made the
most abstruse inquiries clear and facile to my
15 apprehension.
    As I applied so closely, it may be easily
conceived that my progress was rapid. My
ardor was indeed the astonishment of the
students, and my proficiency that of the mas-
20 ters. None but those who have experienced
them can conceive of the enticements of science. A mind of moderate capacity which
closely pursues one study must infallibly arrive at great proficiency in that study; and I,
25 who continually sought the attainment of
one object of pursuit and was solely wrapped
up in this, improved so rapidly that at the
end of two years I made some discoveries in
the improvement of some chemical instru-
30 ments, which procured me great esteem and
admiration at the university. When I had
arrived at this point and had become as well
acquainted with the theory and practice of
natural philosophy as depended on the
35 lessons of any of the professors at Ingolstadt,
my residence there being no longer conducive to my improvements, I thought of
returning to my friends and my native town,
when an incident happened that protracted
40 my stay.
    Whence, I often asked myself, did the prin-
ciple of life proceed? It was a bold question,
and one which has never been considered as a
mystery; yet with how many things are we
45 upon the brink of becoming acquainted, if

cowardice or carelessness did not restrain our
inquiries. I revolved these circumstances in
my mind and determined thenceforth to apply
myself more particularly to those branches of
50 natural philosophy which relate to physiology.
Unless I had been animated by an almost supernatural enthusiasm, my application to this
study would have been irksome and almost intolerable. To examine the causes of life, we
55 must first have recourse to death. I became
acquainted with the science of anatomy, but
this was not sufficient; I must also observe the
natural decay and corruption of the human
body. In my education my father had taken
60 the greatest precautions that my mind should
be impressed with no supernatural horrors. I
do not ever remember to have trembled at a
tale of superstition or to have feared the ap-
parition of a spirit. Darkness had no effect
65 upon my fancy, and a churchyard was to me
merely the receptacle of bodies deprived of
life, which, from being the seat of beauty and
strength, had become food for the worm. I
saw how the fine form of man was degraded
70 and wasted; I beheld the corruption of death
succeed to the blooming cheek of life; I saw
how the worm inherited the wonders of the
eye and brain. I paused, examining and analyzing all the minutiae of causation, as exem-
75 plified in the change from life to death, and
death to life, until from the midst of this darkness a sudden light broke in upon me—a light
so brilliant and wondrous, yet so simple, that
while I became dizzy with the immensity of
80 the prospect which it illustrated, I was surprised that among so many men of genius
who had directed their inquiries towards the
same science, that I alone should be reserved
to discover so astonishing a secret.

GO ON TO THE NEXT PAGE

17. In the first paragraph, the narrator indicates that the instruction given to him by M. Waldman was

(A) haughty
(B) challenging
(C) easily understood
(D) obscure
(E) expensive

18. In line 15, the word "apprehension" most nearly means

(A) fear
(B) reservation
(C) imprisonment
(D) understanding
(E) arrest

19. The narrator indicates that proficiency in an academic study requires which of the following?

    I. genius
    II. diligence
    III. financial resources

(A) I only
(B) II only
(C) I and II only
(D) II and III only
(E) I, II, and III

20. The narrator indicates that he considered leaving Ingolstadt because he

(A) had learned all he could from its instructors
(B) was acutely homesick
(C) was offered another job
(D) had a negative experience with a professor there
(E) had become ill

21. In saying that he was "animated by an almost supernatural enthusiasm" (lines 51–52), the narrator suggests that he

(A) was easily influenced by superstition
(B) loved lecturing at Ingolstadt
(C) was passionate about studying the physiology of life and death
(D) was excited about the prospect of returning home
(E) wanted to learn more about the origin of certain superstitions

22. The "seat of beauty and strength" (lines 67–68) is a reference to

(A) the churchyard
(B) the human body
(C) the worm
(D) the university at Ingolstadt
(E) the narrator's studies

23. In line 71, the phrase "succeed to" most nearly means

(A) inspire
(B) thrive
(C) replace
(D) proceed to
(E) promote

24. The final sentence of the passage suggests that the narrator feels

(A) intimidated by the enormous task before him
(B) grateful to those who instructed him
(C) anxious about the moral dilemma posed by his work
(D) baffled by particular scientific principles
(E) privileged to be on the verge of a momentous discovery

STOP

If you finish before time is called, you may check your work on this section only. Do not turn to any other section of the test.

7 7 7 7 7 7

SECTION 7
Time—20 minutes
16 questions

Turn to Section 7 of your answer sheet to answer the questions in this section.

Directions: For this section, solve each problem and decide which is the best of the choices given. Fill in the corresponding circle on the answer sheet. You may use any available space for scratchwork.

Notes

1. The use of a calculator is permitted.

2. All numbers used are real numbers.

3. Figures that accompany problems in this test are intended to provide information useful in solving the problems. They are drawn as accurately as possible EXCEPT when it is stated in a specific problem that the figure is not drawn to scale. All figures lie in a plane unless otherwise indicated.

4. Unless otherwise specified, the domain of any function f is assumed to be the set of all real numbers x for which $f(x)$ is a real number.

Reference Information

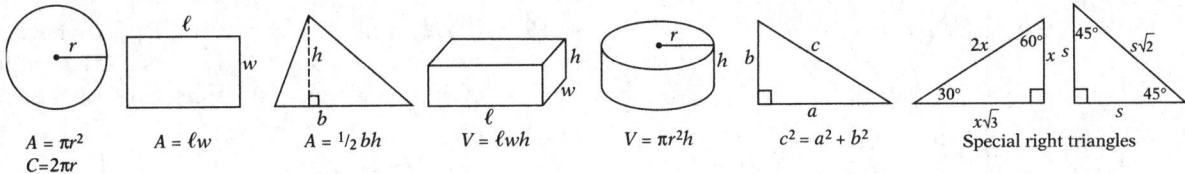

$A = \pi r^2$
$C = 2\pi r$

$A = \ell w$

$A = \frac{1}{2} bh$

$V = \ell wh$

$V = \pi r^2 h$

$c^2 = a^2 + b^2$

Special right triangles

The number of degrees of arc in a circle is 360.
The sum of the measures in degrees of the angles of a triangle is 180.

---

1. Which of the following integers is 2 greater than a multiple of 7?

   (A) 14
   (B) 15
   (C) 16
   (D) 17
   (E) 18

2. A store sells oranges for 20 cents each, but for every four oranges you buy, you may buy a fifth for only 5 cents. How many oranges can you buy from this store for $3.40?

   (A) 14
   (B) 17
   (C) 18
   (D) 19
   (E) 20

3. If r is a positive number and s is a negative number, all of the following must represent positive numbers EXCEPT.

   (A) $-r + s$

   (B) $r - s$

   (C) $\dfrac{r}{s^2}$

   (D) rs^2

   (E) $(rs)^2$

GO ON TO THE NEXT PAGE

4. Which of the following expresses the number that is 12 less than the product of 3 and $x + 1$?

(A) $x - 8$
(B) $x + 37$
(C) $3x - 11$
(D) $3x - 9$
(E) $3x + 15$

5. One bag of grass seed covers 5,000 square feet. If each bag costs $25, how much will it cost to buy enough grass seed to cover a square area that is 200 feet by 200 feet?

(A) $25
(B) $100
(C) $200
(D) $1,000
(E) $2,000

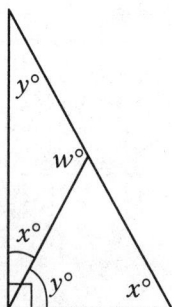

Note: Figure not drawn to scale.

6. In the right triangle above, what is the value of w?

(A)   30
(B)   60
(C)   90
(D) 120
(E) 150

7. Three integers have a sum of 7 and a product of 0. If the difference of the greatest number and the least number is 11, then the least of these numbers is

(A) −18
(B) −11
(C)   −9
(D)   −2
(E)   0

8. Four points lie on a circle. How many different triangles can be drawn with three of these points as vertices?

(A) 4
(B) 5
(C) 6
(D) 7
(E) 8

9. If a, b, and c are consecutive positive integers such that $a < b < c$ and abc is NOT a multiple of 4, then which of the following must be true?

(A) a is even
(B) b is even
(C) c is even
(D) $a + b + c$ is odd
(E) abc is odd

7   7   7   7   7   7

Questions 10–12 refer to the following graph.

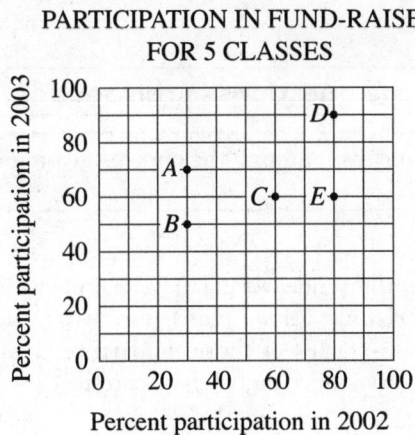

PARTICIPATION IN FUND-RAISER
FOR 5 CLASSES

10. For which class was the change in percent participation the greatest from 2002 to 2003?

(A) A   (B) B   (C) C
(D) D   (E) E

11. If class B and class E each had 100 students in 2002 and 2003, then, in total, how many more students participated in the fund-raiser from class E than from class B over the 2 years?

(A) 10   (B) 20   (C) 30
(D) 40   (E) 60

12. In 2002, the same number of students participated in the fund-raiser from class C as from class D. If class D contained 120 students in 2002, how many students were there in class C in 2002?

(A) 90   (B) 100   (C) 120
(D) 140   (E) 160

13. If $x = -1$ is a solution of the equation $x^2 = 4x + c$ where c is a constant, what is another value of x that satisfies the equation?

(A) −5   (B) −2   (C) 1
(D) 2   (E) 5

1, 2, 6, 7, 9

14. A three-digit integer is to be formed from the digits listed above. If the first digit must be odd, either the second or the third digit must be 2, and no digit may be repeated, how many such integers are possible?

(A) 6   (B) 9   (C) 18
(D) 24   (E) 30

15. If one pound of grain can feed five chickens or two pigs, then ten pounds of grain can feed 20 chickens and how many pigs?

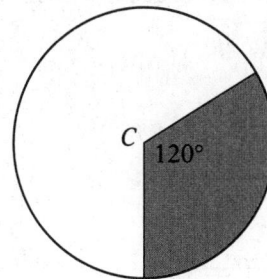

(A) 8   (B) 10   (C) 12
(D) 24   (E) 40

16. Point C is the center of the circle on the figure above. The shaded region has an area of 3π square centimeters. What is the *perimeter* of the shaded region in centimeters?

(A) $2\pi + 6$
(B) $2\pi + 9$
(C) $2\pi + 12$
(D) $3\pi + 6$
(E) $3\pi + 12$

STOP

If you finish before time is called, you may check your work on this section only. Do not turn to any other section of the test.

8   8   8   8   8   8

SECTION 8
Time—20 minutes
19 questions

Turn to Section 8 of your answer sheet to answer the questions in this section.

Directions: For each question in this section, select the best answer from among the choices given and fill in the corresponding circle on the answer sheet.

Each sentence below has one or two blanks, each blank indicating that something has been omitted. Beneath the sentence are five words or sets of words labeled A through E. Choose the word or set of words that, when inserted in the sentence, <u>best</u> fits the meaning of the sentence as a whole.

EXAMPLE:

Rather than accepting the theory unquestioningly, Deborah regarded it with ......

(A) mirth
(B) sadness
(C) responsibility
(D) ignorance
(E) skepticism

Ⓐ Ⓑ Ⓒ Ⓓ ●

---

1. The studio's most recent movies reflect a ------- of many different artistic visions rather than the ------- of a single director.

    (A) conglomeration . . insubordination
    (B) prudence . . unity
    (C) bastion . . despair
    (D) synthesis . . dominance
    (E) conspiracy . . retreat

2. Rather than endeavoring to write timeless fiction with lasting value, many novelists cater to the ------- tastes of those modern readers who read a book once and then discard it.

    (A) immoral
    (B) fleeting
    (C) valuable
    (D) solid
    (E) intellectual

3. Although many investors may tolerate short-term declines in the value of their securities, few will accept a ------- downturn in the stock market.

    (A) protracted
    (B) contemporaneous
    (C) transient
    (D) surreptitious
    (E) fickle

4. In most modern societies, athletes are ------- in the same way that successful warriors were celebrated by civilizations in years past.

    (A) invoked
    (B) repudiated
    (C) lionized
    (D) vilified
    (E) beguiled

GO ON TO THE NEXT PAGE ⟩

8   8   8   8   8   8

5. Dobson's overconfident and arrogant manner during press conferences was beginning to irritate his associates; there was no need to be ------- about the success of an endeavor that had yet to be launched.

(A) superficial
(B) capricious
(C) pious
(D) deferential
(E) supercilious

6. Although few literary critics approved of her criticism of the ------- society in which she lived, Virginia Woolf remained a ------- opponent of the male hegemony that hindered women's pursuit of professional and artistic success.

(A) matriarchal . . pugnacious
(B) patriarchal . . vociferous
(C) avuncular . . belligerent
(D) prejudiced . . rudimentary
(E) liberal . . negligent

The passages below are followed by questions based on their content. Answer the questions on the basis of what is stated or implied in the passage and in any introductory material that may be provided.

Questions 7–19 are based on the following passage.

The following are two essays on the American English spelling reform movement. Passage 1 was written in 1906 by the humorist Ellis Parker Butler. Passage 2 was written by a modern American writer in 2003.

PASSAGE 1

My own opinion of the spelling profession is that it has nothing to do with genius, except to
Line kill it. I know that Shakespeare was a promis-
cuous sort of speller, even as to his own name,
5   and no one can deny that he was a greater genius than Noah Webster. The reason America
so long lagged behind Europe in the production of genius is that America, for many
decades, was the slave of the spelling-book. No

10   man who devotes the fiery days of his youth to
learning to spell has time to be a genius.
Serena says, and I agree with her, that it is
the jealousy of a few college professors who
are trying to undermine the younger writers.
15   They know that it is excusable to spell incorrectly now, but they want this new phonetic
spelling brought into use so that there shall be
no excuse for bad spelling, and that then, Serena says, self-made authors like me, who
20   never can spell but who simply blaze with genius, will be hooted out of the magazines to
make room for a stupid sort of literature that
is spelled correctly. Serena looks upon the
whole thing as a direct, personal stab at me. I
25   look at it more philosophically.
To me it seems that the spelling reformers
are entirely on the wrong track. Their proposed changes are almost a revolution, and
we Americans do not like sudden changes. We
30   like our revolutions to come about gradually.
Think how gradually automobiles have come
to pass. If, in our horse age, the streets had
suddenly been covered with sixty horsepower
snorters going thirty miles an hour and
35   smelling like an eighteenth-century literary
debate, and killing people right and left, we
Americans would have arisen and destroyed
every vestige of the automobile. But the automobile came gradually—first the bicycle, then
40   the motorcycle, and so, by stages, to the present monsters. So slowly and progressively
did the automobile increase in size and number that it seemed a matter of course. We take
to being killed by the automobile quite natu-
45   rally now.
Of course, the silent letters in our words
are objectionable. They are lazy letters. We
want no idle class in America, whether tramp,
aristocrat, or silent letter, but we do not kill
50   the tramp and the aristocrat. We set them to
work, or we would like to. My theory of
spelling reform is to set the idle letters to
work.
Take that prime offender, *although*. *Altho*
55   does all the work, and *ugh* sits on the fence
and whittles. I would put *ugh* to work. *Ugh* is
a syllable in itself. I would have the *ugh* follow

GO ON TO THE NEXT PAGE ⟶

the pronounced *altho* as a third syllable.
60 Doubtless the asthmatic islanders who con-
cocted our English language actually pronounced it so.

    I propose to have some millionaire endow
my plan, and Serena and I will then form a so-
65 ciety for the reforming of English pronunciation. I will not punch out the *i* of any chief,
nor shall any one drag *me* from any programme, however dull. I will pronounce
programme as it should be pronounced—
70 *programmy*—and, as for *chief*, he shall be
pronounced *chy-ef*.

    The advantage of this plan is manifest. It is
so manifest that I am afraid it will never be
adopted.

    Serena's plan is, perhaps, less intellectual,
75 but more American. Serena's plan is to ignore
all words that contain superfluous letters. She
would simply boycott them. Serena would
have people get along with such words as are
already phonetically spelled. Why should peo-
80 ple write *although*, when they can write
notwithstanding that, and not have a silent letter in it? I have myself often written a phrase
twelve words long to stand instead of a single
word I did not know how to spell. In fact, I
85 abandoned my Platonic friendship for Serena,
and replaced it with ardent love, because I did
know how to spell *sweetheart*, but could not
remember whether she was my *friend* or
freind.

PASSAGE 2
90 For centuries, thinkers as notable as Ben-
jamin Franklin have registered the same complaint about English spelling: it is needlessly
complicated and inconsistent in pronunciation. Silent letters abound, and *ough* is pro-
95 nounced six different ways in the words
tough, bough, through, bought, although, and
cough. Franklin wanted to change the alpha-
bet and institute new spelling rules to make
English more sensible, more usable, and eas-
100 ier to learn. Such good ideas have been
around a long time, and we should put them
to rest for three good reasons.

    First, English, like most languages, has
dialects. In Boston, *Korea* and *career* are

105 homophones. In San Francisco, they are not.
To spell them the same way would be to impose a "preferred" dialect on all Americans,
forcing us all to talk like South Enders and vi-
olating our precious value of democracy over
110 elitism. Failure to do so would result in chaos.
Would a novelist from Alabama who was educated at Brown write in her native drawl, her
adopted New England dialect, or the homoge-
nized English of the educated elite? In a de-
115 mocratic society, isn't one of the great benefits
of a language-wide spelling system that it obscures those spoken dialects that are so often
used to stratify and separate us?

    Second, languages evolve, adopting words
120 from other languages, coining new ones, and
changing pronunciations over time. The silent
letters in the word *eight*, a bane of the "rational" speller, are the echoes of the German
acht, the Latin *octo*, the Greek *okto* and even
125 (faintly) the Sanskrit *asta*. The spelling may be
vexing to some, but it is a historical treasure
trove to others. Furthermore, this example
shows the folly of trying to standardize
spelling by linking it with pronunciation. The
130 words won't stand still.

    Third, languages are not influenced very
much by plan or reason; they develop by
evolving conventions of usage. They are cultural artifacts, not legislated standards.
135 Spelling is like football: there may be lots of
silly and illogical things in it, but that doesn't
mean you have a snowball's chance in hell of
replacing the rules.

GO ON TO THE NEXT PAGE ⟶

8   **8**   **8**   **8**   **8**   **8**

7. In the first paragraph of Passage 1, Noah Webster is mentioned as an example of

    (A) a genius who was a poor speller
    (B) one of the first spelling reformers
    (C) a man devoted to proper spelling
    (D) a famous playwright
    (E) one who shares the author's opinion

8. Serena regards phonetic spelling as a "personal stab" (line 24) at the author of Passage 1 because its proponents

    (A) have a history of vindictiveness
    (B) do not like hard work
    (C) are well educated
    (D) are wealthy
    (E) want to eliminate the author's excuse for poor spelling

9. The success of "Serena's plan" (line 74) depends on the ability of people to

    (A) change their habits of pronunciation
    (B) spell correctly
    (C) perfect their handwriting skills
    (D) learn an entirely new alphabet
    (E) change their writing habits

10. By saying that Serena's plan is "more American" (line 75), the author of Passage 1 implies that Americans

    (A) are good spellers
    (B) regard writers with disdain
    (C) are inclined to protest
    (D) do not read enough
    (E) can't take a joke

11. In Passage 1, the author's theory of spelling reform differs from that of Serena in that the author

    (A) wants to alter the pronunciation of words that Serena wants to ignore
    (B) regards Shakespeare as a genius but Serena does not
    (C) wants to change the alphabet but Serena does not
    (D) seeks to simplify spelling, while Serena does not
    (E) understands how to alter American habits but Serena does not

12. The author of Passage 1 claims to have fallen in love with Serena because

    (A) his spelling skills were weak
    (B) they agreed on a plan for phonetic spelling
    (C) she helped him to understand philosophy
    (D) they shared a distaste for automobiles
    (E) they were both writers

13. The "chaos" mentioned in line 110 refers to

    (A) the difficulty of spelling words with silent letters
    (B) the challenge of getting scholars to agree
    (C) the many ways of pronouncing *ough*
    (D) the possibility of many sets of spelling rules for different dialects
    (E) the disagreement among linguists regarding spelling reform

GO ON TO THE NEXT PAGE ⟶

14. According to Passage 2, "one of the great benefits of a language-wide spelling system" (lines 115–116) is that it

   (A) simplifies commonly misspelled words
   (B) discourages social distinctions implied by pronunciation
   (C) eliminates silent letters
   (D) makes it easier to translate words from English to other languages
   (E) imposes a preferred dialect

15. Passage 2 mentions the word "eight" (line 122) as an example of

   (A) a word with a spelling that is edifying to some
   (B) a commonly mispronounced word
   (C) a word with a spelling that the author believes should be simplified
   (D) a recently coined term
   (E) a word that has remained unchanged for centuries

16. The tone of the two passages differs in that Passage 1 is

   (A) jocular, whereas Passage 2 is logical
   (B) cynical, whereas Passage 2 is whimsical
   (C) analytical, whereas Passage 2 is lighthearted
   (D) scientific, whereas Passage 2 is satirical
   (E) strident, whereas Passage 2 is reflective

17. With which of the following statements would the authors of both passages most likely agree?

   (A) The rules of English spelling need to be changed.
   (B) Modern conventions of grammar are illogical.
   (C) Americans are lazy.
   (D) Conventions of language are not easily changed.
   (E) Writers should read widely to perfect their craft.

18. If the author of Passage 1 were serious about his plan for reforming English pronunciation, the author of Passage 2 would likely regard that plan as

   (A) a necessary addition to phonetic spelling
   (B) a logical alternative to the current system
   (C) inferior to the plan for phonetic spelling
   (D) unworkable because it disregards the way that conventions of language develop
   (E) a more plausible plan than Serena's

19. In both passages, the word "although" is regarded as

   (A) a word that is commonly mispronounced
   (B) a word that is difficult to spell
   (C) an example of an idiosyncrasy of English that some consider problematic
   (D) a word that reveals much about the development of the English language
   (E) a word that can easily be eliminated from the English language

STOP

If you finish before time is called, you may check your work on this section only. Do not turn to any other section of the test.

9   9   9   9   9   9

SECTION 9
Time—10 minutes
14 questions

Turn to Section 9 of your answer sheet to answer the questions in this section.

Directions: For each question in this section, select the best answer from among the choices given and fill in the corresponding circle on the answer sheet.

The following sentences test correctness and effectiveness of expression. Part of each sentence or the entire sentence is underlined; beneath each sentence are five ways of phrasing the underlined material. Choice A repeats the original phrasing; the other four choices are different. Select the choice that completes the sentence most effectively.

In making your selection, follow the requirements of standard written English; that is, pay attention to grammar, choice of words, sentence construction, and punctuation. Your selection should result in the most effective sentence—clear and precise, without awkwardness or ambiguity.

EXAMPLE:

The children <u>couldn't hardly believe their eyes</u>.

(A) couldn't hardly believe their eyes
(B) could hardly believe their eyes
(C) would not hardly believe their eyes
(D) couldn't nearly believe their eyes
(E) couldn't hardly believe his or her eyes

(A) ● (C) (D) (E)

1. <u>The chef's assistant cut the vegetables and laid them on the table, he</u> then started to prepare the meat.

   (A) The chef's assistant cut the vegetables and laid them on the table, he
   (B) The vegetables were cut and laid on the table by the chef's assistant when he
   (C) After cutting the vegetables and laying them on the table, the chef's assistant
   (D) The chef's assistant, having cut the vegetables and laying them on the table,
   (E) Laying on the table, the chef's assistant who cut the vegetables

2. Practicing their rebuttals ahead of time <u>helps the forensics team members to become a better debater</u>.

   (A) helps the forensics team member to become a better debater
   (B) helps forensic team members to become better debaters
   (C) helping the forensics team members to become better debaters
   (D) is helpful to the forensics team members who become better debaters
   (E) the forensics team member becomes a better debater

GO ON TO THE NEXT PAGE

3. *Billy the Bobcat,* <u>like other children's stories, have</u> elements that can only be fully appreciated by adults.

(A) like other children's stories have
(B) like other children's stories, has
(C) a children's story, like others, has
(D) is like other stories for children in that they have
(E) like that of other children's stories, has also

4. Ernest Rutherford, <u>a scientist when measuring the charge and mass of alpha particles,</u> discovered that they are virtually identical to the nuclei of helium atoms.

(A) a scientist when measuring the charge and mass of alpha particles
(B) a scientist who measured the charge and mass of alpha particles
(C) a scientist which measured the charge and mass of alpha particles
(D) measuring the charge and mass of alpha particles, was a scientist when he
(E) being the one who measured the mass and charge of alpha particles as a scientist

5. Oxytocin is the hormone that triggers uterine contractions during <u>labor, as well as</u> the preliminary contractions known as Braxton Hicks.

(A) labor, as well as
(B) labor, as well as being the hormone that triggers
(C) labor, causing as well
(D) labor; and also causes
(E) labor; also causing

6. During the Clinton presidency, <u>the U.S. enjoyed more than any time in its history peace and economic well being</u>.

(A) the U.S. enjoyed more than any time in its history peace and economic well being
(B) the U.S. enjoying more than any other time in its history peace and economic well being
(C) more peace and economic well being was enjoyed by the U.S. than any other time
(D) economic peace and well being was enjoyed by the U.S. more so than any other time in the country's history
(E) the U.S. enjoyed more peace and economic well being than at any other time in its history

7. The final three months of the year tend to be profitable for technology companies <u>because of increased consumer demand being around the holidays</u>.

(A) because of increased consumer demand being around the holidays
(B) because of increasing consumer demand occurs around the holidays
(C) an increased consumer demand around the holidays makes it so
(D) because consumer demand increases around the holidays
(E) because the increased consumer demand is what occurs around the holidays

8. As his moviemaking career began to wane, Jerry Lewis remained in the public eye by hosting both a variety show and <u>on an annual telethon with benefits for the Muscular Dystrophy Association</u>.

(A) on an annual telethon with benefits for the Muscular Dystrophy Association
(B) an annual telethon with benefits to the Muscular Dystrophy Association
(C) benefiting the Muscular Dystrophy Association with his annual telethon
(D) an annual telethon benefiting the Muscular Dystrophy Association
(E) the Muscular Dystrophy Association with an annual telethon

9. The development of bebop is attributed in large part to Dizzy Gillespie and also saxophonist Charlie Parker; <u>and their unique styles helped to contribute to and typified the bebop sound</u>.

(A) and their unique styles helped to contribute to and typified the bebop sound
(B) their unique styles contributed to and typified the bebop sound
(C) it was their unique styles that contributed to and were typifying the bebop sound
(D) but their unique styles helped contribute to the typical bebop sound
(E) the bebop sound was helped by the contributions of their unique styles and typified it

GO ON TO THE NEXT PAGE →

9   9   9   9   9   9

10. Many critics believe that video games <u>are harmful to children that contain violent imagery</u>.

    (A) are harmful to children that contain violent imagery
    (B) containing violent imagery are harmful to children
    (C) that contain violent imagery that harms children
    (D) containing violent imagery that are harmful to children
    (E) harmful to children containing violent imagery

11. Walking hand-in-hand along the boardwalk, <u>a vendor stopped the couple to try to sell them lemonade</u>.

    (A) a vendor stopped the couple to try to sell them lemonade
    (B) the couple was stopped by a vendor who tried to sell them lemonade
    (C) trying to sell them lemonade, a vendor stopped the couple
    (D) a vendor stopped the couple to try and sell them lemonade
    (E) the couple having been stopped by the vendor who tried to sell them lemonade

12. Professor Peterson had just stepped into the classroom <u>and that was when he discovered</u> that several lab manuals were missing.

    (A) and that was when he found out
    (B) and then he discovered
    (C) when he discovered
    (D) after which he discovered
    (E) discovering soon thereafter

13. Parents today spend more time working <u>than</u> 30 years ago.

    (A) than
    (B) than have
    (C) than of the parents of
    (D) than did parents
    (E) than of the parents

14. The anthropologists would have considered their research a success <u>if they would have found a language that shares lexical elements with the Borneans they were studying</u>.

    (A) if they would have found a language that shares lexical elements with the Borneans they were studying
    (B) had they found a language that shares lexical elements with that of the Borneans they were studying
    (C) if they found a language that shares lexical elements with the Borneans they were studying
    (D) if they had found a language that shares lexical elements with the Borneans they were studying
    (E) if they would have found a language that shares lexical elements with that of the Borneans they were studying

⬦ **STOP** ⬦

*If you finish before time is called, you may
check your work on this section only. Do not
turn to any other section of the test.*

ANSWER KEY

Critical Reading

Section 3

#	COR. ANS.	DIFF. LEV.	#	COR. ANS.	DIFF. LEV.
1.	A	2	13.	C	4
2.	C	2	14.	A	3
3.	A	3	15.	D	3
4.	D	3	16.	B	4
5.	B	3	17.	A	4
6.	E	3	18.	A	5
7.	B	4	19.	D	3
8.	C	5	20.	C	3
9.	A	5	21.	B	3
10.	D	3	22.	E	3
11.	E	3	23.	C	4
12.	B	4	24.	D	4

Number correct

Number incorrect

Section 6

#	COR. ANS.	DIFF. LEV.	#	COR. ANS.	DIFF. LEV.
1.	A	1	13.	A	3
2.	B	3	14.	A	4
3.	E	2	15.	D	3
4.	B	3	16.	B	4
5.	E	4	17.	C	3
6.	C	3	18.	D	5
7.	D	3	19.	B	4
8.	C	4	20.	A	3
9.	B	3	21.	C	2
10.	E	2	22.	B	3
11.	B	4	23.	C	4
12.	C	3	24.	E	4

Number correct

Number incorrect

Section 8

#	COR. ANS.	DIFF. LEV.	#	COR. ANS.	DIFF. LEV.
1.	D	2	11.	A	4
2.	B	2	12.	A	3
3.	A	2	13.	D	2
4.	C	3	14.	B	3
5.	E	4	15.	A	4
6.	B	5	16.	A	3
7.	C	2	17.	D	3
8.	E	4	18.	D	3
9.	E	4	19.	C	4
10.	C	3			

Number correct

Number incorrect

Math

Section 2

#	COR. ANS.	DIFF. LEV.	#	COR. ANS.	DIFF. LEV.
1.	E	1	11.	E	3
2.	B	2	12.	E	3
3.	E	2	13.	D	3
4.	D	2	14.	B	3
5.	C	3	15.	E	4
6.	D	2	16.	C	3
7.	E	3	17.	C	4
8.	D	3	18.	C	4
9.	E	3	19.	E	5
10.	B	3	20.	C	5

Number correct

Number incorrect

Section 5

Multiple-Choice Questions

#	COR. ANS.	DIFF. LEV.
1.	E	1
2.	D	2
3.	C	3
4.	A	4
5.	B	3
6.	C	3
7.	C	4
8.	A	5

Number correct

Number incorrect

Student-produced Response questions

#	COR. ANS.	DIFF. LEV.
9.	7.5	1
10.	13	2
11.	100	3
12.	24	3
13.	0.2 or 1/5	3
14.	4	4
15.	0.8	3
16.	5	4
17.	9	4
18.	10	5

Number correct (9–18)

Section 7

#	COR. ANS.	DIFF. LEV.	#	COR. ANS.	DIFF. LEV.
1.	C	1	9.	B	4
2.	E	2	10.	A	3
3.	A	2	11.	E	3
4.	D	2	12.	E	4
5.	C	2	13.	E	4
6.	C	3	14.	C	4
7.	D	4	15.	C	4
8.	A	3	16.	A	5

Number correct

Number incorrect

Writing

Section 4

#	COR. ANS.	DIFF. LEV.	#	COR. ANS.	DIFF. LEV.	#	COR. ANS.	DIFF. LEV.
1.	A	1	11.	E	4	21.	E	4
2.	E	1	12.	D	2	22.	C	3
3.	B	2	13.	B	1	23.	C	3
4.	C	3	14.	D	4	24.	E	3
5.	D	2	15.	D	3	25.	B	3
6.	C	2	16.	E	3	26.	C	3
7.	A	4	17.	C	2	27.	E	4
8.	B	5	18.	B	3	28.	A	3
9.	B	4	19.	C	3	29.	C	4
10.	E	4	20.	B	4	30.	A	3

#	COR. ANS.	DIFF. LEV.
31.	B	3
32.	B	4
33.	D	3
34.	E	3
35.	A	3

Number correct

Number incorrect

Section 9

#	COR. ANS.	DIFF. LEV.	#	COR. ANS.	DIFF. LEV.
1.	C	1	11.	B	3
2.	B	2	12.	C	3
3.	B	2	13.	D	4
4.	B	2	14.	B	4
5.	A	3			
6.	E	2			
7.	D	3			
8.	D	3			
9.	B	3			
10.	B	3			

Number correct

Number incorrect

NOTE: Difficulty levels are estimates of question difficulty that range from 1 (easiest) to 5 (hardest).

SCORE CONVERSION TABLE

How to score your test

Use the answer key on the previous page to determine your raw score on each section. **Your raw score on each section except Section 5 is simply the number of correct answers minus ¼ of the number of wrong answers. On Section 5, your raw score is the sum of the number of correct answers for questions 1–18 minus ¼ of the number of wrong answers for questions 1–8.** Next, add the raw scores from Sections 3, 6, and 8 to get your Critical Reading raw score, add the raw scores from Sections 2, 5, and 7 to get your Math raw score, and add the raw scores from Sections 4 and 9 to get your Writing raw score.

Raw Critical Reading score: _____   Raw Math score: _____   Raw Writing score: _____

Use the table below to convert these to scaled scores.

Scaled scores: Critical Reading: _____   Math: _____   Writing: _____

Raw Score	Critical Reading Scaled Score	Math Scaled Score	Writing Scaled Score	Raw Score	Critical Reading Scaled Score	Math Scaled Score	Writing Scaled Score
67	800			32	520	570	610
66	800			31	510	560	600
65	790			30	510	550	580
64	780			29	500	540	570
63	770			28	490	530	560
62	750			27	490	520	550
61	740			26	480	510	540
60	730			25	480	500	530
59	720			24	470	490	520
58	700			23	460	480	510
57	690			22	460	480	500
56	680			21	450	470	490
55	670			20	440	460	480
54	660	800		19	440	450	470
53	650	800		18	430	450	460
52	650	780		17	420	440	450
51	640	760		16	420	430	440
50	630	740		15	410	420	440
49	620	730	800	14	400	410	430
48	620	710	800	13	400	410	420
47	610	710	800	12	390	400	410
46	600	700	790	11	380	390	400
45	600	690	780	10	370	380	390
44	590	680	760	9	360	370	380
43	590	670	740	8	350	360	380
42	580	660	730	7	340	350	370
41	570	650	710	6	330	340	360
40	570	640	700	5	320	330	350
39	560	630	690	4	310	320	340
38	550	620	670	3	300	310	320
37	550	620	660	2	280	290	310
36	540	610	650	1	270	280	300
35	540	600	640	0	250	260	280
34	530	590	630	−1	230	240	270
33	520	580	620	−2 or less	210	220	250

SCORE CONVERSION TABLE FOR WRITING COMPOSITE
[ESSAY + MULTIPLE CHOICE]

Calculate your Writing raw score as you did on the previous page and grade your essay from a 1 to a 6 according to the standards that follow in the detailed answer key.

Essay score: _____   Raw Writing score: _____

Use the table below to convert these to scaled scores.

Scaled score: Writing: _____

Raw Score	Essay Score 0	Essay Score 1	Essay Score 2	Essay Score 3	Essay Score 4	Essay Score 5	Essay Score 6
−2 or less	200	230	250	280	310	340	370
−1	210	240	260	290	320	360	380
0	230	260	280	300	340	370	400
1	240	270	290	320	350	380	410
2	250	280	300	330	360	390	420
3	260	290	310	340	370	400	430
4	270	300	320	350	380	410	440
5	280	310	330	360	390	420	450
6	290	320	340	360	400	430	460
7	290	330	340	370	410	440	470
8	300	330	350	380	410	450	470
9	310	340	360	390	420	450	480
10	320	350	370	390	430	460	490
11	320	360	370	400	440	470	500
12	330	360	380	410	440	470	500
13	340	370	390	420	450	480	510
14	350	380	390	420	460	490	520
15	350	380	400	430	460	500	530
16	360	390	410	440	470	500	530
17	370	400	420	440	480	510	540
18	380	410	420	450	490	520	550
19	380	410	430	460	490	530	560
20	390	420	440	470	500	530	560
21	400	430	450	480	510	540	570
22	410	440	460	480	520	550	580
23	420	450	470	490	530	560	590
24	420	460	470	500	540	570	600
25	430	460	480	510	540	580	610
26	440	470	490	520	550	590	610
27	450	480	500	530	560	590	620
28	460	490	510	540	570	600	630
29	470	500	520	550	580	610	640
30	480	510	530	560	590	620	650
31	490	520	540	560	600	630	660
32	500	530	550	570	610	640	670
33	510	540	550	580	620	650	680
34	510	550	560	590	630	660	690
35	520	560	570	600	640	670	700
36	530	560	580	610	650	680	710
37	540	570	590	620	660	690	720
38	550	580	600	630	670	700	730
39	560	600	610	640	680	710	740
40	580	610	620	650	690	720	750
41	590	620	640	660	700	730	760
42	600	630	650	680	710	740	770
43	610	640	660	690	720	750	780
44	620	660	670	700	740	770	800
45	640	670	690	720	750	780	800
46	650	690	700	730	770	800	800
47	670	700	720	750	780	800	800
48	680	720	730	760	800	800	800
49	680	720	730	760	800	800	800

College Hill™ SAT Study Plan

See page 3A–5A for instructions.

Test # _____   RAW SCORES: CR _____ M _____ W _____ Essay _____

SCALED SCORES: CR _____ M _____ W _____ Essay _____

1. What were your test conditions?

2. What was your pre-test routine?

Goal	Attack	Get	CR pts	M pts	W pts
500	75%	50%	30	25	25
550	80%	60%	37	32	32
600	85%	67%	45	38	38
650	90%	80%	52	44	42
700	100%	90%	59	49	45
750	100%	95%	62	52	47
800	100%	100%	66	54	49

3. Did you attack all of the questions you needed to attack? (See the table above.)

4. Did you rush to complete any section?

5. How many more raw points do you need to make your score goal?   CR _____ M _____ W _____

6. Did you make educated guesses on any questions? If so, how many points did you pick up on these questions?

7. STUDY PLAN: Use the detailed answer key after the test to review the answers to the questions you missed. Below, list the lessons linked to the questions you missed, and list the tough words you missed from the test.

Lessons to Review   **Words to Review**

_____   _____

_____   _____

_____   _____

_____   _____

_____   _____

_____   _____

_____   _____

_____   _____

Detailed Answer Key

Section 1

Consider carefully the issue discussed in the following passage, then write an essay that answers the question posed in the assignment.

An entertainment-driven culture runs the risk of encouraging passivity among its citizens. If they can experience something vicariously through a movie, television show, or video game, why should they get involved with the activity itself? It's safer, after all, to watch someone scale a mountain than to do it yourself. The effect of this passivity, of course, is an apathetic frame of mind. We cease to care deeply about so many things because they are experienced, at best, second-hand.

Assignment: **Is apathy a problem in today's society?** Write an essay in which you answer this question and discuss your point of view on this issue. Support your position logically with examples from literature, the arts, history, politics, science and technology, current events, or your experience or observation.

The following essay received 6 points out of a possible 6, meaning that it demonstrates *clear and consistent competence* in that it

- develops an insightful point of view on the topic
- demonstrates exemplary critical thinking
- uses effective examples, reasons, and other evidence to support its thesis
- is consistently focused, coherent, and well organized
- demonstrates skillful and effective use of language and sentence structure
- is largely (but not necessarily completely) free of grammatical and usage errors

Every society seems to have platitudes about laziness, like "idle hands are the devil's workshop." This is because, to a society, the value of an individual is little more than his or her productivity. For many people, the worst kind of laziness is apathy, being too lazy to even care. But the fact is that we couldn't survive if we cared about everything that was worth caring about. We would go insane. Furthermore, those who complain about apathy are usually the great manipulators of the world, trying to blame others for their own failures.

Holden Caulfield seemed to be apathetic to his teachers at Pencey Prep. But he was far from apathetic; indeed, he probably cared too much. His brother's death and the suicide of a classmate affected him deeply, although he had trouble articulating his grief. He saw what the adults in his world seemed unable to see: the hypocrisy and meanness in the world. If he didn't get away from the things that the teachers and other adults wanted him to care about, he probably would have gone crazy. Indeed, those adults thought he was crazy, but to Holden, it was the hypocritical world that was mad. His desperation to protect himself

from the unbearable "phoniness" in the world led him, ironically, to often be phony himself. He hated his own hypocrisy, but he had to experience it to understand it. What others saw as apathy and cynicism was just his way of making it in the world.

Holden was quick to see that those who complained about his laziness and apathy were just the ones who wanted to control him because they couldn't control their own lives. Teachers too often assume that, if their students aren't "performing," they must be lazy and apathetic. "You're so smart. You would do well if you would just apply yourself." Teachers see this kind of comment as supporting, but it is supremely degrading, and it covers up the teachers' inability to inspire or even understand their students.

Some people even go so far as to assume that entire societies are lazy or apathetic, simply because they do not share their same sensibilities or "productivity," failing to see that productivity is often the product, not just of hard work, but of material and logistical advantage. I don't have to work as hard, for instance, to be "productive" as a teenager in rural China, because I have free access to a computer, the internet, a local library, and helpful adult professionals. The Chinese teenager might be far more intelligent, diligent and resourceful than I, but far less "productive."

Perhaps a sign of maturity and virtue in a society is the degree to which it values its citizens independently of their "productivity." Every human being desires to build a better world in his or her own way. Sometimes that way does not involve making more money, getting better grades, or doing what society has established as "productive."

The following essay received 4 points out of a possible 6, meaning that it demonstrates *adequate competence* in that it

- develops a point of view on the topic
- demonstrates some critical thinking, but perhaps not consistently
- uses some examples, reasons, and other evidence to support its thesis, but perhaps not adequately
- shows a general organization and focus but shows occasional lapses in this regard
- demonstrates adequate but occasionally inconsistent facility with language
- contains occasional errors in grammar, usage, and mechanics

---

The greatest danger to the modern world is not terrorists who have been indoctrinated into a twisted world view, but the masses of people who are indifferent to them, or even sympathize with them. "Live and let live," so many people say. "They have a right to their point of view that women are animals and that someone who speaks against their religion should have his tongue cut out. That is just their way of thinking." This apathy to the dangers of the world is even more dangerous than the terrorists themselves.

In Madrid, a band of Al Qaeda terrorists decided that it was a good idea, in March of 2004, to blow up 200 innocent commuters on a train so that they could influence the upcoming elections in Spain. They proclaimed that they love death more than westerners love life. They were hoping that the Spanish people would then be so frightened that they would elect a leader who would take Spain's troops out of Iraq, as Al Qaeda wished. And that is exactly what happened.

The people of Spain didn't care enough to realize that they were doing exactly what the terrorists were hoping they would do. The voters of Spain probably believed that they were making it less likely that the terrorists would strike again, but it was probably the exact opposite. The terrorists love to know that their violence scares people, and the Spanish people gave them what they wanted. Contrast this with the American response to terrorism: zero tolerance.

The worst evil occurs when good people do nothing. Millions of supposedly "good" German people sat on their hands as millions of "unwanted" Jews, gays and foreigners were slaughtered. Now, millions of people sit on their hands as religious fanatics look at the slaughter of innocent people as their ticket to paradise. It is unreasonable to believe that those with warped hatred of western cultures will stop their hatred and their evil deeds merely because they are appeased by weak governments.

The following essay received 2 points out of a possible 6, meaning that it demonstrates *some incompetence* in that it

- has a seriously limited point of view
- demonstrates weak critical thinking
- uses inappropriate or insufficient examples, reasons, and other evidence to support its thesis
- is poorly focused and organized and has serious problems with coherence
- demonstrates frequent problems with language and sentence structure
- contains errors in grammar and usage that seriously obscure the author's meaning

When people don't care about something, it's hard to get anything done. If a team has players that don't really want to play, for instance, it's almost impossible to get them to win a game, even if you're a master motivator. That's why it's so important to care about things and not have apathy.

If you don't care about something, also, it's just really difficult to be happy. You don't have anything to look forward to in life. Some people don't really care about school, and they just listen to their iPods and can't wait to hang out with their friends or play their XBoxes when they get home. College doesn't mean anything to them, and you can tell that they are miserable people. It's one thing to question your teachers and wonder whether the things you learn in school are relevant for your life, but it's entirely different to not even care about what you do in school even a little bit.

Research has shown that you can't really get anywhere without an education, so if you don't care about school you might as well not care about having any kind of successful life. If they would just find something important that they could care about, like a sport or a musical instrument or a job or something like that, then they might have something they could focus there life for, and have some positive purpose in life. Criminals probably come about because early on they didn't really learn to care about anything important, and that is the real tragedy. and foreigners were slaughtered. Now, millions of people sit on their hands as religious fanatics look at the slaughter of innocent people as their ticket to paradise. It is unreasonable to believe that those with warped hatred of western cultures will stop their hatred and their evil deeds merely because they are appeased by weak governments.

Detailed Answer Key

Section 2

1. **E** Just substitute 3 for x: $5x = 3x + y$
   Substitute: $5(3) = 3(3) + y$
   Simplify: $15 = 9 + y$
   Subtract 9: $6 = y$
   (Chapter 8, Lesson 1: Solving Equations)

2. **B** To buy 48 batteries in packages of 24, you will need two packages, which will cost 2($12) = $24. To buy them in packages of 6, you will need eight packages, which will cost 8($4) = $32. Buying in packages of 24 will save $32 − $24 = $8.
   (Chapter 9, Lesson 4: Rate Problems)

3. **E** You can probably solve this one best by quickly graphing each point and just inspecting. Clearly, (5, 5) lies outside the region.
   (Chapter 10, Lesson 4: Coordinate Geometry)

4. **D** Interpret the statement as an equation:
                              $(\frac{1}{3})(2x) = 5$
   Multiply by 2: $(\frac{2}{3})(2x) = 10$
   Multiply by 2: $(\frac{2}{3})(4x) = 20$
   (Chapter 8, Lesson 7: Word Problems)

5. **C** The smallest positive integer that is divisible by 12 and 16 is 48. If n is 48, the only factor among the choices is (C) 48.
   (Chapter 7, Lesson 7: Divisibility)
   (Chapter 8, Lesson 5: Factoring)

6. **D** The sum of the angles in a triangle is 180°, so
                              $a + b + 40 = 180$
   Subtract 40: $a + b = 140$
   Add the given equation: $\underline{+ (a - b) = 10}$
                              $2a = 150$
   Divide by 2: $a = 75$
   (Chapter 10, Lesson 2: Triangles)
   (Chapter 8, Lesson 2: Systems)

7. **E** Choose n = 1 as an example. Plugging this in to the choices gives answers of (A) ½ (B) 3 (C) 3 (D) 1 (E) 2. The only even number here is (E) 2.
   (Chapter 9, Lesson 3: Numerical Reasoning Problems)

8. **D** Let c be the number of colas that Mike sold and r be the number of root beers. Since the total sold is 48, $c + r = 48$. Since he sold twice as many colas as root beers, $c = 2r$. Substituting this into the first equation gives

                              $2r + r = 48$
   Simplify: $3r = 48$
   Divide by 3: $r = 16$
   (Chapter 8, Lesson 7: Word Problems)

9. **E** Pick two perfect squares for m and n, like 4 and 9. Plugging these in to the examples gives (A) 36 (B) 36 (C) 16 (D) 324 (E) −45. The only choice that is not a perfect square is (E) −45.
   (Chapter 8, Lesson 4: Working with Roots)

10. **B** One option is to solve each equation by plugging in 10 for a: $a + b = 10 + b = 9$
    Subtract 10: $b = -1$
    Second equation: $10 - c = 14$
    Subtract 10: $-c = 4$
    Divide by −1: $c = -4$
    So $c - b = -4 - (-1) = -4 + 1 = -3$
    (Chapter 7, Lesson 6: Negatives)

11. **E** Since the average of four numbers is 8, the sum of those four numbers must be $8 \times 4 = 32$. Therefore $a + b + 10 + 4 = 32$. Subtracting 14 from both sides gives $a + b = 18$.
    (Chapter 9, Lesson 2: Mean/Median/Mode Problems)

12. **E** Fill in the table above and to the left of the x by following the rule, like this:

0	1	2	3	4	5
1	2	4	7		
2	4	8	15		
3	7	15	x		
4					
5					

This shows that $x = 15 + 15 = 30$.
(Chapter 11, Lesson 5: Data Analysis)

13. **D** To maximize c you must minimize the value of $a + b$. Since the numbers must be positive and even, the least values that a and b can have are 2 and 4:
                              $a + b + c = 60$
    Plug in: $2 + 4 + c = 60$
    Simplify: $6 + c = 60$
    Subtract 6: $c = 54$
    (Chapter 9, Lesson 3: Numerical Reasoning Problems)

14. B It is easier to pick a simple value for the "starting" population in 1980, like 100. Since the population increased by 10% from 1980 to 1990, the 1990 population must have been $(100)(1.10) = 110$. Since it decreased by 10% from 1990 to 2000, the 2000 population must have been $(110)(0.90) = 99$. From 1980 to 2000, then, the percent change was $(99 - 100)/100 = -1/100 = -1\%$.
(Chapter 7, Lesson 5: Percents)

15. E According to the definition of g, $g(3) = 2f(3) - 1$. According to the table, $f(3) = 11$, so $g(3) = 2f(3) - 1 = 2(11) - 1 = 22 - 1 = 21$.
(Chapter 11, Lesson 2: Functions)

16. C Although you may substitute $5y$ for x as a first step, it's probably easier to simplify the expression first:

$$\sqrt{\left(x^2 - 2xy + y^2\right)}$$

Factor: $\sqrt{\left(x - y\right)^2}$

Simplify: $\left|x - y\right|$

Substitute: $\left|5y - y\right|$

Simplify: $\left|4y\right| = 4y$
(Chapter 8, Lesson 4: Working with Roots)
(Chapter 8, Lesson 5: Factoring)
(Chapter 8, Lesson 6: Inequalities, Absolute Values, and Plugging In)

17. C Think of numbers that are larger than their squares. This excludes negatives, because the squares of negatives are always positive. It also excludes numbers greater than 1, because the squares of these are bigger than the original numbers. Therefore, $0 < x < 1$. This means I and II are true, but not III.
(Chapter 9, Lesson 3: Numerical Reasoning Problems)

18. C Believe it or not, you don't need to find the two midpoints in order to answer this question. You need to know only that the distance between the two mid-points is half of the distance between the two endpoints. The distance between the endpoints is $(3x + 2) - (-x - 4) = 3x + 2 + x + 4 = 4x + 6$. Half of this is $2x + 3$.
(Chapter 10, Lesson 4: Coordinate Geometry)

19. E Since all radii of a triangle are equal, $PQ = PR$. Since $PQ = QR$ too, the triangle must be equilateral. Since its area is $9\sqrt{3}$, the lengths have the measures shown in the diagram. The circle has a radius of 6. The shaded region is equal to the area of the sector minus the area of the triangle. Since the central angle is 60°, the sector has an area that is ⅙ of the whole circle, or $(\frac{1}{6})(\pi(6)^2) = 6\pi$. Subtracting the area of the triangle gives $6\pi - 9\sqrt{3}$.

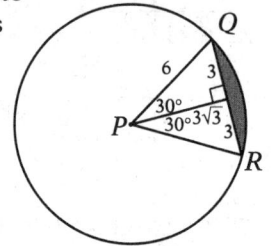

(Chapter 10, Lesson 3: The Pythagorean Theorem)
(Chapter 10, Lesson 5: Areas and Perimeters)
(Chapter 10, Lesson 8: Circles)

20. C If the ratio of boys to girls in a class is 3 to 5, then $3/(3 + 5) = ⅜$ of the class is boys and $5/(3 + 5) = ⅝$ of the class is girls. This means there are $(⅜)(160) = 60$ boys and $(⅝)(160) = 100$ girls in the senior class. Similarly, the fraction of boys in the junior class is ⅗ and the fraction of girls is ⅖. If there are x students in the junior class, then there are $(⅗)x$ boys and $(⅖)x$ girls in the junior class. If the ratio of boys to girls is 1:1 when the classes are combined, then

$$60 + (⅗)x = 100 + (⅖)x$$

Subtract 60 and $(⅖)x$: $(⅕)x = 40$
Multiply by 5: $x = 200$
(Chapter 8, Lesson 7: Word Problems)
(Chapter 7, Lesson 4: Ratios and Proportions)

Section 3

1. A A *six-month hiatus* (break) would cause her skills to *weaken*, something she might fear. *atrophy* = weaken from disuse; *align* = line up; *disseminate* = spread like seed

2. C *Domineering* opinions are overbearing and preachy. *vindictive* = inspired by revenge; *pedantic* = acting like a know-it-all; *conciliatory* = acting to bring people together; *treacherous* = betraying someone's confidence; *didactic* = preachy; *dogmatic* = condescendingly preachy; *prosaic* = ordinary

3. A The missing word must refer to Walter's *inability to make up his mind*. *vacillation* = inability to make up one's mind; *solicitation* = request for help; *rejuvenation* = restoration of one's youth; *admonishment* = mild reproof

4. **D** If a writer is *successful . . . even in the face of . . . rejections*, he or she must be very *persistent*. *affluence* = wealth; *haughty* = arrogant; *pertinacity* = strong persistence; *resilient* = able to endure hardship; *tenacity* = ability to hold fast; *relentless* = unwilling to give up; *stoutness* = courage or sturdiness; *craven* = cowardly

5. **B** The missing word must be in contrast to *direct, forceful stances*. *pontification* = haughty, self-important speech; *circumlocution* = indirect, evasive speech; *brevity* = conciseness

6. **E** The parallelism of the two clauses helps you to complete the sentence. If counselors *believe that criminals can change*, then they must *have faith in their changeability*. If they realize *that they can often return to their old habits*, they must by wary of *recidivism* (tendency to fall into old habits). *mutability* = changeability; *astuteness* = keen ability; *transcendence* = the quality of exceeding; *malleability* = ability to be bent; *relapse* = falling back into old ways

7. **B** If something is out of place in time, it is an *anachronism*. *anachronism* = something out of place in time; *idiom* = phrase with a meaning that is different from its literal meaning; *interlocutor* = someone who takes part in a conversation

8. **C** The sentence indicates that the "h" was evidence of an earlier time. *inference* = conclusion based on evidence; *analogy* = useful comparison; *vestige* = remaining trace; *anomaly* = unusual event; *quandary* = perplexing situation

9. **A** The passage states that language is used as *impenetrable walls* (line 7) between people, having biased connotations favoring one group over another.

10. **D** By saying that *we infer volumes* (lines 3–4), the author means that *we draw a lot of conclusions*.

11. **E** The passage states that instructing a child to tie shoes *the right way will defeat the child's growing attempt at self-mastery* (lines 12–14).

12. **B** The last sentence states that *nagging is a constant reminder to the child of his or her lack of self-control* (lines 21–22).

13. **C** The author states that Modernism is *egotistical* (line 19) and *self-conscious* (line 21) and also that it *begins nowhere and with no one in particular* (lines 12–13), suggesting that it is both *self-centered* and *ill-defined*, but the paragraph does not mention Modernism being *politically oriented*.

14. **A** The passage states that *Critics and academics . . . prefer their artistic movements to be readily comprehensible* (lines 8–10), so they do *not* like those that are hard to understand.

15. **D** The quotation from James Joyce in the next sentence describes these *landmines as enigmas and puzzles that . . . will keep the professors busy for centuries arguing over what I meant* (lines 21–25). In other words, they are literary devices placed in his novels to baffle professors.

16. **B** The passage states that *plots . . . are submerged beneath wave after wave of . . . hyper-literary and meta-literary indulgences* (lines 32–37), so it suggests that plot is not as important as other things.

17. **A** The author states that it is *hard not to love modernism* (lines 38–39) but also uses critical terms like *posturing aberrations* (line 19) to describe it. In the last two lines, he refers to modernism as *reprehensive but somehow roguishly likeable*. This is a very *ambivalent* characterization of modernism.

18. **A** The comparison is a *metaphor* but not a *simile* because it states that the *modernist novel* is *a sociopath*. *Juxtaposition* is the placement of two images one on top of the another, as in *a sociopath and a cad*. *Personification* is giving human qualities to something that is not human.

19. **D** The purpose of the passage is to introduce the reader to the new science of genomics.

20. **C** A *pathogen* (line 8) is not part of the *immune system* (lines 7–8) but rather what the immune system responds to.

21. **B** The *orchestrated response* of *the immune system* (lines 7–8) is mentioned as an example of how *molecules convey information* (line 9).

22. **E** The fact that *through genomics massive amounts of information can be converted into an electronic format* (lines 36–38) is what *facilitates a dramatically new framework for understanding life* (lines 40–41).

23. **C** The passage suggests that *information theory . . . may seem unfit for . . . science* (lines 50–52) because *information . . . implies an underlying intent* (lines 48–50).

24. **D** The final paragraph indicates that genomic advances *have helped to propel the remarkable development of the computer and telecommunication industries* (lines 58–60) and suggests that they may help to *improve human health* (lines 61–62). This discusses *actual and potential consequences*.

Section 4

1. **A** The sentence is correct.

2. **E** The underlined phrase should be a noun phrase that represents *one of the best features of the journalist's lifestyle*. Only (C) and (E) are noun phrases, and (E) is much clearer.
(Chapter 15, Lesson 4: Comparison Problems)

3. **B** The opening participial phrase modifies *Greg* and not *Greg's search*.
(Chapter 15, Lesson 7: Dangling and Misplaced Participles)

4. **C** Idiom requires *neither* to be followed by *nor*, and parallelism requires the *nor* to be followed by an adjective.
(Chapter 15, Lesson 10: Idiom Errors)

5. **D** The past participle of *to take* is *taken*, not *took*.
(Chapter 15, Lesson 13: Irregular Verbs)

6. **C** Although choice (D) is parallel in structure, its phrasing is nonstandard. The phrasing in (C) is both parallel and clear.
(Chapter 15, Lesson 3: Parallelism)

7. **A** The pronoun *he* is the subject of an implied verb, *he (did)*, so it is used correctly in the subjective form. Also, the phrase *admire his acting* is correct, because the object of the verb is *acting*, not *him*.
(Chapter 15, Lesson 6: Pronoun Case)

8. **B** *Neither* is the singular subject of the verb, so the verb should be *was*, not *were*. Also, the pronoun should be *its* because the subject is singular and a ram can only feel its own pain, not the pain of them both.
(Chapter 15, Lesson 1: Subject-Verb Disagreement)
(Chapter 15, Lesson 2: Trimming Sentences)
(Chapter 15, Lesson 5: Pronoun-Antecedent Disagreement)

9. **B** The participle *walking* modifies *Liz*, not *Liz's family*. Choice (D) makes this correction, but the modifiers are awkward and unclear.
(Chapter 15, Lesson 7: Dangling and Misplaced Participles)
(Chapter 15, Lesson 12: Other Modifier Problems)

10. **E** The phrase *if not better* is an interrupter, so the sentence should read well even if it is omitted. The only phrasing that meets this criterion is (E).
(Chapter 15, Lesson 2: Trimming Sentences)

11. **E** The original is not a sentence but a fragment.
(Chapter 15, Lesson 15: Coordinating Ideas)

12. **D** The phrase *much closer* modifies the verb *study* and so should be in adverbial form: *much more closely*.
(Chapter 15, Lesson 12: Other Modifier Problems)

13. **B** The two clauses must be parallel: *has been so popular* would make this clause parallel to the first.
(Chapter 15, Lesson 3: Parallelism)

14. **D** This is a diction error. *Respectfully* means full of respect, which makes no sense here. The word should be *respectively*.
(Chapter 15, Lesson 11: Diction Errors)

15. **D** The verb *would have considered* is in the wrong tense and mood. It should be *consider*.
(Chapter 15, Lesson 9: Tricky Tenses)
(Chapter 15, Lesson 14: The Subjunctive Mood)

16. **E** The sentence is correct.

17. **C** The *fund deficit and the disillusionment* are not a single problem, but two *problems*.
(Chapter 15, Lesson 4: Comparison Problems)

18. **B** The subject of the verb is *either accepting or rejecting*. If the subject of a verb is an *either . . . or* construction, the verb must agree with the noun after the *or*, which in this case is *rejecting*. Since this is a singular noun, the verb should be *was*.
(Chapter 15, Lesson 1: Subject-Verb Disagreement)

19. **C** Since *defense attorneys* can be counted, the correct comparative word is *fewer*, not *less*.
(Chapter 15, Lesson 4: Comparison Problems)

20. **B** It is illogical to compare *service* to *other restaurants*. The phrase should be *the service at the other restaurants*.
(Chapter 15, Lesson 3: Parallelism)

21. **E** The sentence is correct.

22. **C** This pronoun refers to *a child*, so it must be the singular *he or she*.
(Chapter 15, Lesson 5: Pronoun-Antecedent Disagreement)

23. **C** The phrase *not only A but also B* indicates a parallel structure. To make the structure parallel, the phrase should be replaced with *by*.
(Chapter 15, Lesson 3: Parallelism)

24. **E** The sentence is correct.

25. **B** The pronoun *he* is ambiguous. We are not certain which individual it is referring to. To correct the error, *he* should be changed to either Thomas Cowher or the Senator.
(Chapter 15, Lesson 5: Pronoun-Antecedent Disagreement)

26. **C** The sentence indicates that this occurred in the past by saying those who *were observing*. Therefore *are* should instead be *were*.
(Chapter 15, Lesson 1: Subject-Verb Disagreement)

27. **E** The sentence is correct.

28. **A** Between my brother and *I* should instead be between my brother and *me*. Subjective pronouns, such as *I*, should only be used as subjects. Objective pronouns, including *me*, can be used as objects of verbs or as objects of prepositions.
(Chapter 15, Lesson 6: Pronoun Case)

29. **C** The critic is writing about a *duo*, which is a singular subject. The *their* should therefore be replaced by *its*.
(Chapter 15, Lesson 5: Pronoun-Antecedent Disagreement)

30. **A** Choice (A) is the most concise and clear, and the phrasing is parallel.
(Chapter 15, Lesson 3: Parallelism)
(Chapter 15, Lesson 15: Coordinating Ideas)

31. **B** Sentence 3 presents an example of Plato's reasoning as described in sentence 2. Choice (C) may be tempting, but since the sentence does not extend the idea from sentence 2 but only provides an example, the word *furthermore* is inappropriate.
(Chapter 15, Lesson 15: Coordinating Ideas)

32. **B** The pronoun *they* and the noun *approximations* should agree in number. Choice (B) provides the most straightforward phrasing.
(Chapter 15, Lesson 5: Pronoun-Antecedent Disagreement)
(Chapter 15, Lesson 15: Coordinating Ideas)

33. **D** Sentence 6 does not fit because it shifts the discussion to what students dislike, rather than the nature of mathematical objects.

34. **E** Choice (E) provides the most logical, concise, and clear phrasing.

35. **A** Choice (A) provides the most logical, concise, and clear phrasing.

Section 5

1. **E** If $2x = 10$, then $4x = 20$, and if $3y = 12$, then $6y = 24$, so $4x + 6y = 20 + 24 = 44$.
(Chapter 6, Lesson 4: Simplifying Problems)

2. **D** Set up the equation: $(a + b + 4)/3 = 5$
Multiply by 3: $a + b + 4 = 15$
Subtract 4: $a + b = 11$
(Chapter 9, Lesson 2: Mean/Median/Mode Problems)

3. **C** If $b = 2a$, then $a + 2a = 180$, because the two angles form a linear pair. So $3a = 180$ and $a = 60$. Your diagram should now look like this:

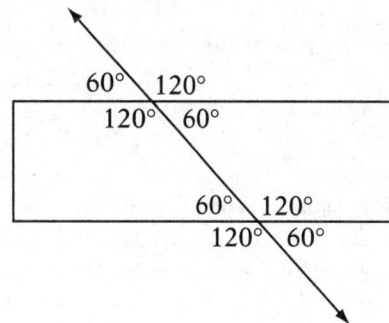

So $d + e + g + h = 60 + 60 + 120 + 60 = 300$.
(Chapter 10, Lesson 1: Lines and Angles)

4. **A** Substitute $x = 100$ into the function:
$$\sqrt{\sqrt{100} - 1} = \sqrt{10 - 1} = \sqrt{9} = 3$$
(Chapter 11, Lesson 2: Functions)

5. **B** If $2^m = 8$, then $m = 3$. So $3^{k+3} = 243$. Checking the powers of 3 shows that $k + 3 = 5$. Therefore, $k = 2$, so $2^k = 2^2 = 4$.
(Chapter 8, Lesson 3: Working with Exponentials)

6. **C** If b varies inversely as the square of c, then the equation that relates them is $b = k/c^2$ where k is some constant. To find the value of k, just plug in the given values for b and c:
$$8 = k/3^2$$
Multiply by 9: $72 = k$
Therefore, the specific equation relating b and c is $b = 72/c^2$. To find the value of c when $b = 2$, just substitute and solve:
$$2 = 72/c^2$$
Cross-multiply: $2c^2 = 72$
Divide by 2: $c^2 = 36$
Take the square root: $c = \pm 6$
(Chapter 11, Lesson 4: Variation)

7. **C** Each of the five teams must play four other teams three times apiece. In other words, each team must play in $4 \times 3 = 12$ games. Since there are five teams, it might seem at first that there are a total of $5 \times 12 = 60$ games, but since each game needs two teams, the total number of games is $60/2 = 30$.
(Chapter 9, Lesson 5: Counting Problems)

8. **A** If pump A can fill the tank in 3 hours, then it will fill ⅓ of the tank in 1 hour, leaving ⅔ of the tank to fill. Pump B can fill ½ of the tank in an hour, so working together, the two pumps can fill ½ + ⅓ = ⅚ of the tank per hour. To fill ⅔ of the tank working together, then, takes (⅔) ÷ (⅚) = ⅘ hour, which equals (⅘)(60) = 48 minutes.
(Chapter 9, Lesson 4: Rate Problems)

9. **7.5** Translate into an equation: $4x - 5 = 25$
    Add 5: $4x = 30$
    Divide by 4: $x = 7.5$
(Chapter 8, Lesson 7: Word Problems)

10. **13** «7» = 7 + 6 + 5 + 4 + 3 + 2 + 1
    «5» = 5 + 4 + 3 + 2 + 1
    So «7» − «5» = 7 + 6 = 13
(Chapter 9, Lesson 1: New Symbol or Term Problems)

11. **100** Circumference = πd, so you can find the diameter:

$$\pi d = 10\pi$$
    Divide by π: $d = 10$
This diameter is also the hypotenuse of a right triangle, so by the Pythagorean theorem, $a2 + b2 = d2 = 10^2 = 100$.
(Chapter 10, Lesson 3: The Pythagorean Theorem)
(Chapter 10, Lesson 8: Circles)

12. **24** This is a "counting" problem, so it helps to know the fundamental counting principle from Chapter 9, Lesson 5. Since you are making a three-letter arrangement, there are three decisions to be made. The number of choices for the first letter is four; then there are three letters left for the second spot, then two left for the third spot. This gives a total of $4 \times 3 \times 2 = 24$ possible arrangements.
(Chapter 9, Lesson 5: Counting Problems)

13. **0.2 or 1/5** This is a simple substitution. You can substitute 10,200 for $96,878 \times x^2$ because they are equal. So $10,200/(5 \times 96,878 \times x^2) = 10,200/(5 \times 10,200)$ = ⅕. Notice that the 10,200s "cancel."
(Chapter 6, Lesson 4: Simplifying Problems)

14. **4** If each term is 1 less than 3 times the *previous* term, then each term is also $1/3$ of the number that is

1 greater than the *successive* term. Since the fourth term is 95, the third term must be $1/3$ of 96, which is 32. Repeating this shows that the second term is 11 and the first term is 4. Check your work by confirming that the sequence satisfies the formula.
(Chapter 6, Lesson 7: Thinking Logically)
(Chapter 11, Lesson 1: Sequences)

15. **0.8** If $4 + \sqrt{b} = 7.2$ then $\sqrt{b} = 3.2$.

    So $4 - \sqrt{b} = 4 - 3.2 = 0.8$.
(Notice that you don't really have to deal with the root!)
(Chapter 8, Lesson 1: Solving Equations)

16. **5** If there are a adults, there must be $30 - a$ children, because the total number of people is 30.
    Therefore $10a + 5(30 - a) = 175$
    Distribute: $10a + 150 - 5a = 175$
    Simplify: $5a + 150 = 175$
    Subtract 150: $5a = 25$
    Divide by 5: $a = 5$
Now check: if there are 5 adults, there must be 25 children, and the tickets would cost $5(10) + 25(5) = 50 + 125 = 175$ (yes!).
(Chapter 8, Lesson 7: Word Problems)

17. **9** Since $a = (2/3)b$, the perimeter of the triangle is $b + b + (2/3)b = (8/3)b$. The perimeter is 24, so
                       $(8/3)b = 24$
    Multiply by 3/8: $b = 9$
(Chapter 10, Lesson 5: Areas and Perimeters)
(Chapter 7, Lesson 4: Ratios and Proportions)

18. **10**

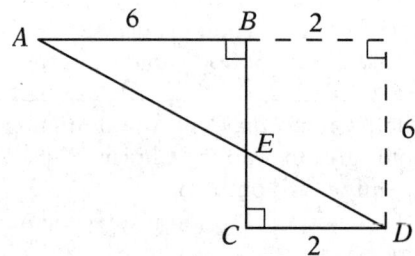

Mark the diagram with the given information. The dotted lines show that AD is the hypotenuse of a right triangle with legs of length 8 and 6. So to find it, just use the Pythagorean theorem: $6^2 + 8^2 = (AD)^2$
    Simplify: $100 = (AD)^2$
    Take the square root: $10 = AD$
(Chapter 10, Lesson 3: The Pythagorean Theorem)
(Chapter 10, Lesson 5: Areas and Perimeters)

Section 6

1. **A** Because the signal was *strange*, it was clearly not an expected result, but it was also not from outside of the telescope, so it was a *strange happening* from the telescope itself. *malfunction* = disruption of the normal workings; *bulwark* = defensive fortification; *anthology* = collection of literary works; *mutation* = change in form

2. **B** The problem is one that may never be solved, so it is *difficult* or *stubborn*. *impotent* = weak and ineffective; *intractable* = hard to manage, stubborn; *evanescent* = likely to vanish; *irate* = angry; *insipid* = dull, tasteless

3. **E** If the general was *surprised* at the ease with which the defenses were breached, he must have expected the resistance to be much *stronger*. *ephemeral* = short-lived; *compatible* = working well together; *egregious* = blatant or extreme; *imposing* = intimidating

4. **B** A *dependence on electronic devices* would be expected to *tax* the power grid, although *increased efficiency* of those devices would be expected to ease the burden. *abated* = decreased in intensity; *attenuated* = caused to be less intense; *compromised* = rendered vulnerable; *flourished* = thrived

5. **E** The word *although* indicates a contrast. Although the persecution *vanquished* (conquered) the will of some, it must have *strengthened* the will of others. *despotic* = tyrannical; *squandered* = wasted; *amenable* = obedient; *celebrated* = eminent; *ruthless* = merciless; *forged* = established

6. **C** The passage says that *Rousseau's writings* (line 1) were what led *Goethe to say that "feeling is all"* (line 4). Therefore, Goethe was influenced by Rousseau.

7. **D** The passage says that Kant *forgot to take his . . . daily walk* because he *was so absorbed in reading Rousseau's Émile* (lines 14–16).

8. **C** Passage 1 states that *"by emphasizing feeling"* (line 3) Rousseau inspired the Romantic movement and Goethe in particular, while Passage 2 criticizes Rousseau's *"worship of emotion"* (line 33) as encouraging poor parenting.

9. **B** Passage 1 states that Rousseau *"inspired the French Revolution"* (lines 9–10) and Passage 2 gives Rousseau credit for laying the *"philosophical foundation of American independence"* (lines 31–32).

10. **E** By saying *"It would be a good idea,"* Gandhi indicated that civilization in the West had not really been realized.

11. **B** The *voices* are those who are *bankrolled by large corporations* (lines 16–17) and who are *saying such things* (line 15) as that America is a *model of free-market capitalism* (line 11). This would certainly not include Mahatma Gandhi, but the passage indicates that it would include *politicians* and those in *corporate news and entertainment media* (lines 8–10).

12. **C** The second paragraph explains how *the concept of free trade* (line 20) works, so it is explaining a concept.

13. **A** The statement suggests that the rules of free trade would work differently if the parties involved were different, suggesting that the rules are selectively applied.

14. **A** This paragraph indicates that these words are being used ironically. It states that the Indians *(gave in to Western pressure)* (lines 55–56), so the agreement was not a completely free one. Also, the words "liberalize" and "liberalization" are used ironically because they refer to actions that in fact reduced competition and were *(a great blow to free markets)* (lines 64–65).

15. **D** The *triumph* was also described as *a great blow to free markets* (lines 63–65).

16. **B** The paragraph indicates that *businesses are . . . expected to wager their own capital on success in the marketplace* (lines 66–68) but that some pharmaceutical companies don't need to.

17. **C** In lines 14–15, the narrator describes the instruction as being "clear and facile to my apprehension," which means he found it easy to understand.

18. **D** The phrase *clear and facile to my apprehension* means *easy to understand*.

19. **B** The narrator says that *a mind of moderate capacity which closely pursues one study must infallibly arrive at great proficiency* (lines 22–24), thereby suggesting that only *diligence* is required for proficiency.

20. **A** The narrator was *as well acquainted with the theory and practice of natural philosophy as depended on the lessons of any of the professors at Ingolstadt* (lines 32–35), which means he had learned all he could from them.

21. **C** This *supernatural enthusiasm* describes the narrator's passion for his studies.

22. **B** The human bodies are described as changing from *the seat of beauty and strength* in life to *food for the worm* (line 68) in death.

23. **C** The rest of the sentence describes how the processes of death change a formerly living body. In saying that he *beheld the corruption of death succeed to the blooming cheek of life*, he is saying that death and decay have replaced or defeated life.

24. **E** The narrator reveals his sense of privilege in this discovery by stating that he is *alone* (line 83) among the *many men of genius* (line 81) who had studied this topic before.

Section 7

1. **C** 16 is equal to 2(7) + 2, so it is two more than a multiple of 7.
(Chapter 7, Lesson 7: Divisibility)

2. **E** Five oranges can be bought for 5¢ more than the price of four, which is 4(20¢) + 5¢ = 85¢. $3.40 is equivalent to 4(.85), so it will buy 4(5) = 20 oranges.
(Chapter 8, Lesson 7: Word Problems)

3. **A** If r is positive, then $-r$ is negative. If you add another negative, then the result will be even more negative.
(Chapter 7, Lesson 6: Negatives)

4. **D** Twelve less than the product of 3 and $x + 1$ can be represented as $3(x + 1) - 12$
Distribute: $3x + 3 - 12$
Simplify: $3x - 9$
(Chapter 8, Lesson 7: Word Problems)

5. **C** The square has an area of $200 \times 200 = 40,000$ square feet. $40,000 \div 5,000 = 8$, so this will require eight bags of seed at $25 apiece. $8 \times \$25 = \$200$.
(Chapter 10, Lesson 5: Areas and Perimeters)

6. **C** Analyzing the right angle shows that $x + y = 90$. Since the sum of the angles in a triangle is always 180°,
$$x + y + w = 180$$
Substitute $x + y = 90$: $90 + w = 180$
Subtract 90: $w = 90$
(Chapter 10, Lesson 2: Triangles)

7. **D** If the numbers have a product of 0, then at least one must equal 0. Call the numbers x, y, and 0. The problem also says that $x + y = 7$ and $x - y = 11$.
Add the equations:
$$x + y = 7$$
$$+ (x - y = 11)$$
$$2x = 18$$
Divide by 2: $x = 9$
Plug back in, solve for y: $9 + y = 7$
Subtract 9: $y = -2$
So the least of the numbers is –2.
(Chapter 8, Lesson 2: Systems)

8. **A** You can draw a diagram and see that there are only four possible triangles:

If you prefer to look at it as a "combination" problem, the number of triangles is the number of ways of choosing three things from a set of four, or $_4C_3 = 4$.

9. **B** The only way that abc would not be a multiple of 4 is if none of the three numbers is a multiple of 4 *and* no two of them are even (because the product of two evens is always a multiple of 4). One simple example is $a = 1$, $b = 2$, and $c = 3$. This example rules out choices (A), (C), (D), and (E).
(Chapter 9, Lesson 3: Numerical Reasoning Problems)

10. **A** A large percent change from 2002 to 2003 is represented by a point in which the y-coordinate is much greater than the x-coordinate. Point A represents a change from 30 in 2002 to 70 in 2003, which is a percent change of $(70 - 30)/30 \times 100\% = 133\%$.
(Chapter 7, Lesson 5: Percents)
(Chapter 11, Lesson 5: Data Analysis)

11. **E** If both classes have 100 students, then class B had 30 students participate in 2002 and 50 in 2003, for a total of 80. Class E had 80 in 2002 and 60 in 2003, for a total of 140. The difference, then, is $140 - 80 = 60$.
(Chapter 11, Lesson 5: Data Analysis)

12. **E** If class D has 120 students, then 80% of 120, or 96 students participated in 2002. If the same number participated from class C, then 96 is 60% of the number of students in class C. If the number of students in class C is x, then $.60x = 96$. Divide by .6: $x = 160$.
(Chapter 11, Lesson 5: Data Analysis)

13. **E** Substitute $x = -1$ into the equation to find c.
Simplify: $1 = -4 + c$
Add 4: $5 = c$
So the equation is $x^2 = 4x + 5$
Subtract $(4x + 5)$: $x^2 - 4x - 5 = 0$
Factor the quadratic (remember that since $x = -1$ is a solution, $(x + 1)$ must be a factor): $x^2 - 4x - 5 = (x + 1)(x - 5)$
Therefore $(x + 1)(x - 5) = 0$
So the solutions are $x = 1$ and $x = 5$
(Chapter 8, Lesson 5: Factoring)

14. **C** To create a three-digit number, three decisions must be made: you must choose the first digit, then choose where to put the two, then choose the final digit. Since the first digit must be odd, there are three options for the first digit. Since the two may be placed in either the second or the third slot, there are two options. Then there are three digits left to choose for the final slot. This means there are $3 \times 2 \times 3 = 18$ possibilities.
(Chapter 9, Lesson 5: Counting Problems)

15. **C** Since one pound feeds five chickens, four pounds are needed to feed 20 chickens. This leaves $10 - 4 = 6$ pounds of feed. Since each pound can feed two pigs, six pounds can feed $2 \times 6 = 12$ pigs.
(Chapter 6, Lesson 2: Analyzing Problems)
(Chapter 7, Lesson 4: Ratios and Proportions)

16. **A** Since 120° is 1/3 of 360°, the shaded region has 1/3 the area of the circle. Therefore, the circle has an area of $3(3\pi) = 9\pi$. Since $A = \pi r^2$, the radius is 3 centimeters. The circumference of the circle, then, is $2\pi r = 2\pi(3) = 6\pi$, and the arc of the shaded region has length $(1/3)(6\pi) = 2\pi$. The perimeter of the shaded region, then, is $3 + 3 + 2\pi = 2\pi + 6$.
(Chapter 10, Lesson 5: Areas and Perimeters)

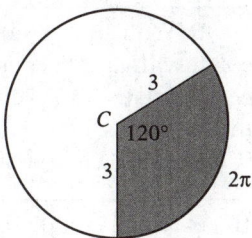

Section 8

1. **D** The word *rather* indicates the important contrast between the two ideas. The second word indicates something specific to a *single director* rather than *many visions. conglomeration* = collection; *insubordination* = disobedience; *prudence* = careful management; *bastion* = a well-fortified area; *synthesis* = a fusion of different elements; *conspiracy* = secret agreement to commit a crime

2. **B** The fact that modern readers *read a book once and then discard it* suggests that their interest in it is only *temporary*, rather than *timeless. immoral* = unethical; *fleeting* = short-lived

3. **A** *Although* indicates a contrast in ideas, so the missing word must mean *prolonged* rather than *short-term. protracted* = prolonged; *contemporaneous* = living or existing at the same time; *transient* = short-lived; *surreptitious* = secretive; *fickle* = tending to change one's mind often

4. **C** Since the sentence says that athletes are treated like successful warriors, you should look for a word like *celebrated. invoked* = called on or cited; *repudiated* = having its validity rejected; *lionized* = treated like a celebrity; *vilified* = defamed; *beguiled* = deceived by charm

5. **E** The word *although* indicates a contrast. Although the persecution *vanquished* (conquered) the will of some, it must have *strengthened* the will of others. *despotic* = tyrannical; *squandered* = wasted; *amenable* = obedient; *celebrated* = eminent; *ruthless* = merciless; *forged* = established

6. **B** If she was an *opponent of the male hegemony* (dominance of one group over another), she must have been an *outspoken* critic of the *male-dominated* society. *matriarchal* = female-dominated; *pugnacious* = belligerent; *patriarchal* = male-dominated; *vociferous* = outspoken; *avuncular* = like a good-natured uncle; *belligerent* = inclined to picking fights; *rudimentary* = basic; *liberal* = free-thinking

7. **C** The author begins by making the point that *the spelling profession* (line 1) kills genius. By saying that Shakespeare was not a good speller but was more of a genius than Noah Webster, he is reinforcing the point, thereby suggesting that Webster is someone in the "spelling profession."

8. **E** The previous two sentences discuss the fact that any attempt to make spelling easier would undermine the author's *excuse for bad spelling* (line 18).

9. **E** Serena's plan is to have people avoid spelling words with silent letters, but not change the way they pronounce words. This would require a change in writing habits.

10. **C** Serena's plan is to *boycott* (line 77) words with superfluous letters. Boycotting is a form of protest. By saying that her plan is more American than his, the author suggests that Americans are inclined to protest things.

11. **A** The author says he wants to *set the idle letters to work* (lines 50–51) by pronouncing them, while Serena plans to *ignore all words that contain superfluous letters* (lines 75–76).

12. **A** In the final paragraph of Passage 1, the author says that he *replaced* the *Platonic friendship* he had with Serena with *ardent love* (lines 85–86) because he didn't know how to spell the word *friend*.

13. **D** The *chaos* is mentioned as the result of failing to impose standards for spelling particular words and instead spelling a word in many different ways according to how it is pronounced in different dialects.

14. **B** Passage 2 says that standardized spelling *obscures those spoken dialects that are so often used to stratify and separate us* (lines 116–118).

15. **A** Passage 2 says that the silent letters in the word "eight" are *a treasure trove* (lines 126–127) to those who study the history of language.

16. **A** Passage 1 is clearly intended to be humorous, while Passage 2 is very systematic in discussing the problems with the spelling reform movement.

17. **D** Passage 1 says that *Americans do not like sudden changes* (line 29) to suggest the difficulty in enacting spelling reform. Similarly, Passage 2 says that *languages are not influenced very much by plan or reason* (lines 131–132).

18. **D** Because the final paragraph of Passage 2 discusses the problem of enacting a *plan* to change the conventions of language, the author of Passage 2 would likely regard such a plan as unworkable.

19. **C** The first passage discusses *although* as a word with too many silent letters, while Passage 2 discusses it because it contains a letter sequence that can be pronounced in many different ways.

Section 9

1. **C** The original sentence is a run-on sentence. Answer choice (C) properly coordinates the two ideas.
(Chapter 15, Lesson 15: Coordinating Ideas)

2. **B** In the original sentence, *a better debater* should instead be *better debaters*, the plural form. Answer choice (B) corrects this error.
(Chapter 15, Lesson 5: Pronoun-Antecedent Disagreement)

3. **B** *Billy the Bobcat* is a singular subject and the verb *have* is plural. It should instead be *has*.
(Chapter 15, Lesson 1: Subject-Verb Disagreement)

4. **B** The pronoun *when* should be used only to refer to a time. It should be replaced by *who*.
(Chapter 15, Lesson 5: Pronoun-Antecedent Disagreement)

5. **A** This sentence is correct as written.

6. **E** The original sentence is phrased awkwardly. As constructed it suggests that the U.S. enjoyed *peace and economic well being* more than *any time* did, which makes no sense. Answer choice (E) corrects this comparison error.
(Chapter 15, Lesson 4: Comparison Problems)

7. **D** The phrase *because of* is awkward. Answer choice (D) corrects the error in the most concise and logical fashion.
(Chapter 15, Lesson 10: Idiom Errors)

8. **D** The sentence requires parallel structure. Jerry Lewis hosted *a variety show* and *an annual telethon.* Answer choice (D) corrects the error.
(Chapter 15, Lesson 3: Parallelism)

9. **B** You should not begin the clause after a semicolon with *and* because it is supposed to be an *independent* clause. Answer choice (B) properly coordinates the two ideas.
(Chapter 15, Lesson 15: Coordinating Ideas)

10. **B** As originally constructed, the sentence suggests that the children themselves contain violent imagery, rather than the video games contain violent imagery. Answer choice (B) corrects this error.
(Chapter 15, Lesson 15: Coordinating Ideas)

11. **B** The opening participial phrase, *walking hand-in-hand* improperly modifies the *vendor* rather than *the couple.* Answer choice (B) corrects this error.
(Chapter 15, Lesson 7: Dangling and Misplaced Participles)

12. **C** The original sentence is awkward and wordy. The phrasing in answer choice (C) is the most concise and logical of the choices.
(Chapter 15, Lesson 2: Trimming Sentences)

13. **D** This question presents an illogical comparison. As written, the parents today spend more time working than 30 years ago did. The sentence is *trying* to say that parents today spend more time working than *parents did* 30 years ago. Answer choice (D) corrects the error.
(Chapter 15, Lesson 4: Comparison Problems)

14. **B** The phrase *if they would have* in (E) is incorrect subjunctive form, and the comparison between the *language* and the *Borneans* is illogical.
(Chapter 15, Lesson 14: The Subjunctive Mood)
(Chapter 15, Lesson 4: Comparison Problems)

PRACTICE TEST 2

ANSWER SHEET

Last Name:_____   First Name:_____

Date:_____   Testing Location:_____

Directions for Test

- Remove these answer sheets from the book and use them to record your answers to this test.
- This test will require 3 hours and 20 minutes to complete. Take this test in one sitting.
- The time allotment for each section is written clearly at the beginning of each section. This test contains six 25-minute sections, two 20-minute sections, and one 10-minute section.
- This test is 25 minutes shorter than the actual SAT, which will include a 25-minute "experimental" section that does not count toward your score. That section has been omitted from this test.
- You may take one short break during the test, of no more than 10 minutes in length.
- You may only work on one section at any given time.
- You must stop ALL work on a section when time is called.
- If you finish a section before the time has elapsed, check your work on that section. You may NOT work on any other section.
- Do not waste time on questions that seem too difficult for you.
- Use the test book for scratchwork, but you will receive credit only for answers that are marked on the answer sheets.
- You will receive one point for every correct answer.
- You will receive no points for an omitted question.
- For each wrong answer on any multiple-choice question, your score will be reduced by $\frac{1}{4}$ point.
- For each wrong answer on any "numerical grid-in" question, you will receive no deduction.

When you take the real SAT, you will be asked to fill in your personal information in grids as shown below.

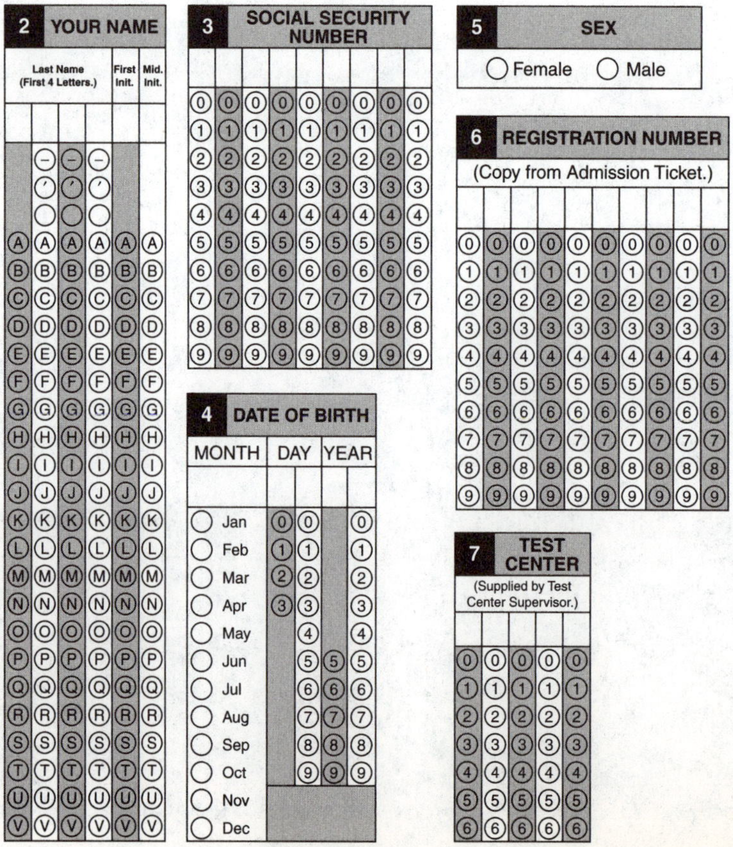

Start with number 1 for each new section. If a section has fewer questions than answer spaces, leave the extra answer spaces blank. Be sure to erase any errors or stray marks completely.

SECTION 2

1 Ⓐ Ⓑ Ⓒ Ⓓ Ⓔ	11 Ⓐ Ⓑ Ⓒ Ⓓ Ⓔ	21 Ⓐ Ⓑ Ⓒ Ⓓ Ⓔ	31 Ⓐ Ⓑ Ⓒ Ⓓ Ⓔ
2 Ⓐ Ⓑ Ⓒ Ⓓ Ⓔ	12 Ⓐ Ⓑ Ⓒ Ⓓ Ⓔ	22 Ⓐ Ⓑ Ⓒ Ⓓ Ⓔ	32 Ⓐ Ⓑ Ⓒ Ⓓ Ⓔ
3 Ⓐ Ⓑ Ⓒ Ⓓ Ⓔ	13 Ⓐ Ⓑ Ⓒ Ⓓ Ⓔ	23 Ⓐ Ⓑ Ⓒ Ⓓ Ⓔ	33 Ⓐ Ⓑ Ⓒ Ⓓ Ⓔ
4 Ⓐ Ⓑ Ⓒ Ⓓ Ⓔ	14 Ⓐ Ⓑ Ⓒ Ⓓ Ⓔ	24 Ⓐ Ⓑ Ⓒ Ⓓ Ⓔ	34 Ⓐ Ⓑ Ⓒ Ⓓ Ⓔ
5 Ⓐ Ⓑ Ⓒ Ⓓ Ⓔ	15 Ⓐ Ⓑ Ⓒ Ⓓ Ⓔ	25 Ⓐ Ⓑ Ⓒ Ⓓ Ⓔ	35 Ⓐ Ⓑ Ⓒ Ⓓ Ⓔ
6 Ⓐ Ⓑ Ⓒ Ⓓ Ⓔ	16 Ⓐ Ⓑ Ⓒ Ⓓ Ⓔ	26 Ⓐ Ⓑ Ⓒ Ⓓ Ⓔ	36 Ⓐ Ⓑ Ⓒ Ⓓ Ⓔ
7 Ⓐ Ⓑ Ⓒ Ⓓ Ⓔ	17 Ⓐ Ⓑ Ⓒ Ⓓ Ⓔ	27 Ⓐ Ⓑ Ⓒ Ⓓ Ⓔ	37 Ⓐ Ⓑ Ⓒ Ⓓ Ⓔ
8 Ⓐ Ⓑ Ⓒ Ⓓ Ⓔ	18 Ⓐ Ⓑ Ⓒ Ⓓ Ⓔ	28 Ⓐ Ⓑ Ⓒ Ⓓ Ⓔ	38 Ⓐ Ⓑ Ⓒ Ⓓ Ⓔ
9 Ⓐ Ⓑ Ⓒ Ⓓ Ⓔ	19 Ⓐ Ⓑ Ⓒ Ⓓ Ⓔ	29 Ⓐ Ⓑ Ⓒ Ⓓ Ⓔ	39 Ⓐ Ⓑ Ⓒ Ⓓ Ⓔ
10 Ⓐ Ⓑ Ⓒ Ⓓ Ⓔ	20 Ⓐ Ⓑ Ⓒ Ⓓ Ⓔ	30 Ⓐ Ⓑ Ⓒ Ⓓ Ⓔ	40 Ⓐ Ⓑ Ⓒ Ⓓ Ⓔ

SECTION 3

1 Ⓐ Ⓑ Ⓒ Ⓓ Ⓔ	11 Ⓐ Ⓑ Ⓒ Ⓓ Ⓔ	21 Ⓐ Ⓑ Ⓒ Ⓓ Ⓔ	31 Ⓐ Ⓑ Ⓒ Ⓓ Ⓔ
2 Ⓐ Ⓑ Ⓒ Ⓓ Ⓔ	12 Ⓐ Ⓑ Ⓒ Ⓓ Ⓔ	22 Ⓐ Ⓑ Ⓒ Ⓓ Ⓔ	32 Ⓐ Ⓑ Ⓒ Ⓓ Ⓔ
3 Ⓐ Ⓑ Ⓒ Ⓓ Ⓔ	13 Ⓐ Ⓑ Ⓒ Ⓓ Ⓔ	23 Ⓐ Ⓑ Ⓒ Ⓓ Ⓔ	33 Ⓐ Ⓑ Ⓒ Ⓓ Ⓔ
4 Ⓐ Ⓑ Ⓒ Ⓓ Ⓔ	14 Ⓐ Ⓑ Ⓒ Ⓓ Ⓔ	24 Ⓐ Ⓑ Ⓒ Ⓓ Ⓔ	34 Ⓐ Ⓑ Ⓒ Ⓓ Ⓔ
5 Ⓐ Ⓑ Ⓒ Ⓓ Ⓔ	15 Ⓐ Ⓑ Ⓒ Ⓓ Ⓔ	25 Ⓐ Ⓑ Ⓒ Ⓓ Ⓔ	35 Ⓐ Ⓑ Ⓒ Ⓓ Ⓔ
6 Ⓐ Ⓑ Ⓒ Ⓓ Ⓔ	16 Ⓐ Ⓑ Ⓒ Ⓓ Ⓔ	26 Ⓐ Ⓑ Ⓒ Ⓓ Ⓔ	36 Ⓐ Ⓑ Ⓒ Ⓓ Ⓔ
7 Ⓐ Ⓑ Ⓒ Ⓓ Ⓔ	17 Ⓐ Ⓑ Ⓒ Ⓓ Ⓔ	27 Ⓐ Ⓑ Ⓒ Ⓓ Ⓔ	37 Ⓐ Ⓑ Ⓒ Ⓓ Ⓔ
8 Ⓐ Ⓑ Ⓒ Ⓓ Ⓔ	18 Ⓐ Ⓑ Ⓒ Ⓓ Ⓔ	28 Ⓐ Ⓑ Ⓒ Ⓓ Ⓔ	38 Ⓐ Ⓑ Ⓒ Ⓓ Ⓔ
9 Ⓐ Ⓑ Ⓒ Ⓓ Ⓔ	19 Ⓐ Ⓑ Ⓒ Ⓓ Ⓔ	29 Ⓐ Ⓑ Ⓒ Ⓓ Ⓔ	39 Ⓐ Ⓑ Ⓒ Ⓓ Ⓔ
10 Ⓐ Ⓑ Ⓒ Ⓓ Ⓔ	20 Ⓐ Ⓑ Ⓒ Ⓓ Ⓔ	30 Ⓐ Ⓑ Ⓒ Ⓓ Ⓔ	40 Ⓐ Ⓑ Ⓒ Ⓓ Ⓔ

CAUTION Use the answer spaces in the grids below for Section 2 or Section 3 only if you are told to do so in your test book.

Student-Produced Responses ONLY ANSWERS ENTERED IN THE CIRCLES IN EACH GRID WILL BE SCORED. YOU WILL NOT RECEIVE CREDIT FOR ANYTHING WRITTEN IN THE BOXES ABOVE THE CIRCLES.

Start with number 1 for each new section. If a section has fewer questions than answer spaces, leave the extra answer spaces blank. Be sure to erase any errors or stray marks completely.

SECTION 4

1 Ⓐ Ⓑ Ⓒ Ⓓ Ⓔ	11 Ⓐ Ⓑ Ⓒ Ⓓ Ⓔ	21 Ⓐ Ⓑ Ⓒ Ⓓ Ⓔ	31 Ⓐ Ⓑ Ⓒ Ⓓ Ⓔ
2 Ⓐ Ⓑ Ⓒ Ⓓ Ⓔ	12 Ⓐ Ⓑ Ⓒ Ⓓ Ⓔ	22 Ⓐ Ⓑ Ⓒ Ⓓ Ⓔ	32 Ⓐ Ⓑ Ⓒ Ⓓ Ⓔ
3 Ⓐ Ⓑ Ⓒ Ⓓ Ⓔ	13 Ⓐ Ⓑ Ⓒ Ⓓ Ⓔ	23 Ⓐ Ⓑ Ⓒ Ⓓ Ⓔ	33 Ⓐ Ⓑ Ⓒ Ⓓ Ⓔ
4 Ⓐ Ⓑ Ⓒ Ⓓ Ⓔ	14 Ⓐ Ⓑ Ⓒ Ⓓ Ⓔ	24 Ⓐ Ⓑ Ⓒ Ⓓ Ⓔ	34 Ⓐ Ⓑ Ⓒ Ⓓ Ⓔ
5 Ⓐ Ⓑ Ⓒ Ⓓ Ⓔ	15 Ⓐ Ⓑ Ⓒ Ⓓ Ⓔ	25 Ⓐ Ⓑ Ⓒ Ⓓ Ⓔ	35 Ⓐ Ⓑ Ⓒ Ⓓ Ⓔ
6 Ⓐ Ⓑ Ⓒ Ⓓ Ⓔ	16 Ⓐ Ⓑ Ⓒ Ⓓ Ⓔ	26 Ⓐ Ⓑ Ⓒ Ⓓ Ⓔ	36 Ⓐ Ⓑ Ⓒ Ⓓ Ⓔ
7 Ⓐ Ⓑ Ⓒ Ⓓ Ⓔ	17 Ⓐ Ⓑ Ⓒ Ⓓ Ⓔ	27 Ⓐ Ⓑ Ⓒ Ⓓ Ⓔ	37 Ⓐ Ⓑ Ⓒ Ⓓ Ⓔ
8 Ⓐ Ⓑ Ⓒ Ⓓ Ⓔ	18 Ⓐ Ⓑ Ⓒ Ⓓ Ⓔ	28 Ⓐ Ⓑ Ⓒ Ⓓ Ⓔ	38 Ⓐ Ⓑ Ⓒ Ⓓ Ⓔ
9 Ⓐ Ⓑ Ⓒ Ⓓ Ⓔ	19 Ⓐ Ⓑ Ⓒ Ⓓ Ⓔ	29 Ⓐ Ⓑ Ⓒ Ⓓ Ⓔ	39 Ⓐ Ⓑ Ⓒ Ⓓ Ⓔ
10 Ⓐ Ⓑ Ⓒ Ⓓ Ⓔ	20 Ⓐ Ⓑ Ⓒ Ⓓ Ⓔ	30 Ⓐ Ⓑ Ⓒ Ⓓ Ⓔ	40 Ⓐ Ⓑ Ⓒ Ⓓ Ⓔ

SECTION 5

1 Ⓐ Ⓑ Ⓒ Ⓓ Ⓔ	11 Ⓐ Ⓑ Ⓒ Ⓓ Ⓔ	21 Ⓐ Ⓑ Ⓒ Ⓓ Ⓔ	31 Ⓐ Ⓑ Ⓒ Ⓓ Ⓔ
2 Ⓐ Ⓑ Ⓒ Ⓓ Ⓔ	12 Ⓐ Ⓑ Ⓒ Ⓓ Ⓔ	22 Ⓐ Ⓑ Ⓒ Ⓓ Ⓔ	32 Ⓐ Ⓑ Ⓒ Ⓓ Ⓔ
3 Ⓐ Ⓑ Ⓒ Ⓓ Ⓔ	13 Ⓐ Ⓑ Ⓒ Ⓓ Ⓔ	23 Ⓐ Ⓑ Ⓒ Ⓓ Ⓔ	33 Ⓐ Ⓑ Ⓒ Ⓓ Ⓔ
4 Ⓐ Ⓑ Ⓒ Ⓓ Ⓔ	14 Ⓐ Ⓑ Ⓒ Ⓓ Ⓔ	24 Ⓐ Ⓑ Ⓒ Ⓓ Ⓔ	34 Ⓐ Ⓑ Ⓒ Ⓓ Ⓔ
5 Ⓐ Ⓑ Ⓒ Ⓓ Ⓔ	15 Ⓐ Ⓑ Ⓒ Ⓓ Ⓔ	25 Ⓐ Ⓑ Ⓒ Ⓓ Ⓔ	35 Ⓐ Ⓑ Ⓒ Ⓓ Ⓔ
6 Ⓐ Ⓑ Ⓒ Ⓓ Ⓔ	16 Ⓐ Ⓑ Ⓒ Ⓓ Ⓔ	26 Ⓐ Ⓑ Ⓒ Ⓓ Ⓔ	36 Ⓐ Ⓑ Ⓒ Ⓓ Ⓔ
7 Ⓐ Ⓑ Ⓒ Ⓓ Ⓔ	17 Ⓐ Ⓑ Ⓒ Ⓓ Ⓔ	27 Ⓐ Ⓑ Ⓒ Ⓓ Ⓔ	37 Ⓐ Ⓑ Ⓒ Ⓓ Ⓔ
8 Ⓐ Ⓑ Ⓒ Ⓓ Ⓔ	18 Ⓐ Ⓑ Ⓒ Ⓓ Ⓔ	28 Ⓐ Ⓑ Ⓒ Ⓓ Ⓔ	38 Ⓐ Ⓑ Ⓒ Ⓓ Ⓔ
9 Ⓐ Ⓑ Ⓒ Ⓓ Ⓔ	19 Ⓐ Ⓑ Ⓒ Ⓓ Ⓔ	29 Ⓐ Ⓑ Ⓒ Ⓓ Ⓔ	39 Ⓐ Ⓑ Ⓒ Ⓓ Ⓔ
10 Ⓐ Ⓑ Ⓒ Ⓓ Ⓔ	20 Ⓐ Ⓑ Ⓒ Ⓓ Ⓔ	30 Ⓐ Ⓑ Ⓒ Ⓓ Ⓔ	40 Ⓐ Ⓑ Ⓒ Ⓓ Ⓔ

CAUTION Use the answer spaces in the grids below for Section 4 or Section 5 only if you are told to do so in your test book.

Student-Produced Responses ONLY ANSWERS ENTERED IN THE CIRCLES IN EACH GRID WILL BE SCORED. YOU WILL NOT RECEIVE CREDIT FOR ANYTHING WRITTEN IN THE BOXES ABOVE THE CIRCLES.

9   10   11   12   13

14   15   16   17   18

Start with number 1 for each new section. If a section has fewer questions than answer spaces, leave the extra answer spaces blank. Be sure to erase any errors or stray marks completely.

SECTION 6

1	Ⓐ Ⓑ Ⓒ Ⓓ Ⓔ	11	Ⓐ Ⓑ Ⓒ Ⓓ Ⓔ	21	Ⓐ Ⓑ Ⓒ Ⓓ Ⓔ	31	Ⓐ Ⓑ Ⓒ Ⓓ Ⓔ
2	Ⓐ Ⓑ Ⓒ Ⓓ Ⓔ	12	Ⓐ Ⓑ Ⓒ Ⓓ Ⓔ	22	Ⓐ Ⓑ Ⓒ Ⓓ Ⓔ	32	Ⓐ Ⓑ Ⓒ Ⓓ Ⓔ
3	Ⓐ Ⓑ Ⓒ Ⓓ Ⓔ	13	Ⓐ Ⓑ Ⓒ Ⓓ Ⓔ	23	Ⓐ Ⓑ Ⓒ Ⓓ Ⓔ	33	Ⓐ Ⓑ Ⓒ Ⓓ Ⓔ
4	Ⓐ Ⓑ Ⓒ Ⓓ Ⓔ	14	Ⓐ Ⓑ Ⓒ Ⓓ Ⓔ	24	Ⓐ Ⓑ Ⓒ Ⓓ Ⓔ	34	Ⓐ Ⓑ Ⓒ Ⓓ Ⓔ
5	Ⓐ Ⓑ Ⓒ Ⓓ Ⓔ	15	Ⓐ Ⓑ Ⓒ Ⓓ Ⓔ	25	Ⓐ Ⓑ Ⓒ Ⓓ Ⓔ	35	Ⓐ Ⓑ Ⓒ Ⓓ Ⓔ
6	Ⓐ Ⓑ Ⓒ Ⓓ Ⓔ	16	Ⓐ Ⓑ Ⓒ Ⓓ Ⓔ	26	Ⓐ Ⓑ Ⓒ Ⓓ Ⓔ	36	Ⓐ Ⓑ Ⓒ Ⓓ Ⓔ
7	Ⓐ Ⓑ Ⓒ Ⓓ Ⓔ	17	Ⓐ Ⓑ Ⓒ Ⓓ Ⓔ	27	Ⓐ Ⓑ Ⓒ Ⓓ Ⓔ	37	Ⓐ Ⓑ Ⓒ Ⓓ Ⓔ
8	Ⓐ Ⓑ Ⓒ Ⓓ Ⓔ	18	Ⓐ Ⓑ Ⓒ Ⓓ Ⓔ	28	Ⓐ Ⓑ Ⓒ Ⓓ Ⓔ	38	Ⓐ Ⓑ Ⓒ Ⓓ Ⓔ
9	Ⓐ Ⓑ Ⓒ Ⓓ Ⓔ	19	Ⓐ Ⓑ Ⓒ Ⓓ Ⓔ	29	Ⓐ Ⓑ Ⓒ Ⓓ Ⓔ	39	Ⓐ Ⓑ Ⓒ Ⓓ Ⓔ
10	Ⓐ Ⓑ Ⓒ Ⓓ Ⓔ	20	Ⓐ Ⓑ Ⓒ Ⓓ Ⓔ	30	Ⓐ Ⓑ Ⓒ Ⓓ Ⓔ	40	Ⓐ Ⓑ Ⓒ Ⓓ Ⓔ

SECTION 7

1	Ⓐ Ⓑ Ⓒ Ⓓ Ⓔ	11	Ⓐ Ⓑ Ⓒ Ⓓ Ⓔ	21	Ⓐ Ⓑ Ⓒ Ⓓ Ⓔ	31	Ⓐ Ⓑ Ⓒ Ⓓ Ⓔ
2	Ⓐ Ⓑ Ⓒ Ⓓ Ⓔ	12	Ⓐ Ⓑ Ⓒ Ⓓ Ⓔ	22	Ⓐ Ⓑ Ⓒ Ⓓ Ⓔ	32	Ⓐ Ⓑ Ⓒ Ⓓ Ⓔ
3	Ⓐ Ⓑ Ⓒ Ⓓ Ⓔ	13	Ⓐ Ⓑ Ⓒ Ⓓ Ⓔ	23	Ⓐ Ⓑ Ⓒ Ⓓ Ⓔ	33	Ⓐ Ⓑ Ⓒ Ⓓ Ⓔ
4	Ⓐ Ⓑ Ⓒ Ⓓ Ⓔ	14	Ⓐ Ⓑ Ⓒ Ⓓ Ⓔ	24	Ⓐ Ⓑ Ⓒ Ⓓ Ⓔ	34	Ⓐ Ⓑ Ⓒ Ⓓ Ⓔ
5	Ⓐ Ⓑ Ⓒ Ⓓ Ⓔ	15	Ⓐ Ⓑ Ⓒ Ⓓ Ⓔ	25	Ⓐ Ⓑ Ⓒ Ⓓ Ⓔ	35	Ⓐ Ⓑ Ⓒ Ⓓ Ⓔ
6	Ⓐ Ⓑ Ⓒ Ⓓ Ⓔ	16	Ⓐ Ⓑ Ⓒ Ⓓ Ⓔ	26	Ⓐ Ⓑ Ⓒ Ⓓ Ⓔ	36	Ⓐ Ⓑ Ⓒ Ⓓ Ⓔ
7	Ⓐ Ⓑ Ⓒ Ⓓ Ⓔ	17	Ⓐ Ⓑ Ⓒ Ⓓ Ⓔ	27	Ⓐ Ⓑ Ⓒ Ⓓ Ⓔ	37	Ⓐ Ⓑ Ⓒ Ⓓ Ⓔ
8	Ⓐ Ⓑ Ⓒ Ⓓ Ⓔ	18	Ⓐ Ⓑ Ⓒ Ⓓ Ⓔ	28	Ⓐ Ⓑ Ⓒ Ⓓ Ⓔ	38	Ⓐ Ⓑ Ⓒ Ⓓ Ⓔ
9	Ⓐ Ⓑ Ⓒ Ⓓ Ⓔ	19	Ⓐ Ⓑ Ⓒ Ⓓ Ⓔ	29	Ⓐ Ⓑ Ⓒ Ⓓ Ⓔ	39	Ⓐ Ⓑ Ⓒ Ⓓ Ⓔ
10	Ⓐ Ⓑ Ⓒ Ⓓ Ⓔ	20	Ⓐ Ⓑ Ⓒ Ⓓ Ⓔ	30	Ⓐ Ⓑ Ⓒ Ⓓ Ⓔ	40	Ⓐ Ⓑ Ⓒ Ⓓ Ⓔ

CAUTION Use the answer spaces in the grids below for Section 6 or Section 7 only if you are told to do so in your test book.

Student-Produced Responses ONLY ANSWERS ENTERED IN THE CIRCLES IN EACH GRID WILL BE SCORED. YOU WILL NOT RECEIVE CREDIT FOR ANYTHING WRITTEN IN THE BOXES ABOVE THE CIRCLES.

9 10 11 12 13

14 15 16 17 18

PLEASE DO NOT WRITE IN THIS AREA

Start with number 1 for each new section. If a section has fewer questions than answer spaces, leave the extra answer spaces blank. Be sure to erase any errors or stray marks completely.

SECTION 8

1 Ⓐ Ⓑ Ⓒ Ⓓ Ⓔ
2 Ⓐ Ⓑ Ⓒ Ⓓ Ⓔ
3 Ⓐ Ⓑ Ⓒ Ⓓ Ⓔ
4 Ⓐ Ⓑ Ⓒ Ⓓ Ⓔ
5 Ⓐ Ⓑ Ⓒ Ⓓ Ⓔ
6 Ⓐ Ⓑ Ⓒ Ⓓ Ⓔ
7 Ⓐ Ⓑ Ⓒ Ⓓ Ⓔ
8 Ⓐ Ⓑ Ⓒ Ⓓ Ⓔ
9 Ⓐ Ⓑ Ⓒ Ⓓ Ⓔ
10 Ⓐ Ⓑ Ⓒ Ⓓ Ⓔ

11 Ⓐ Ⓑ Ⓒ Ⓓ Ⓔ
12 Ⓐ Ⓑ Ⓒ Ⓓ Ⓔ
13 Ⓐ Ⓑ Ⓒ Ⓓ Ⓔ
14 Ⓐ Ⓑ Ⓒ Ⓓ Ⓔ
15 Ⓐ Ⓑ Ⓒ Ⓓ Ⓔ
16 Ⓐ Ⓑ Ⓒ Ⓓ Ⓔ
17 Ⓐ Ⓑ Ⓒ Ⓓ Ⓔ
18 Ⓐ Ⓑ Ⓒ Ⓓ Ⓔ
19 Ⓐ Ⓑ Ⓒ Ⓓ Ⓔ
20 Ⓐ Ⓑ Ⓒ Ⓓ Ⓔ

21 Ⓐ Ⓑ Ⓒ Ⓓ Ⓔ
22 Ⓐ Ⓑ Ⓒ Ⓓ Ⓔ
23 Ⓐ Ⓑ Ⓒ Ⓓ Ⓔ
24 Ⓐ Ⓑ Ⓒ Ⓓ Ⓔ
25 Ⓐ Ⓑ Ⓒ Ⓓ Ⓔ
26 Ⓐ Ⓑ Ⓒ Ⓓ Ⓔ
27 Ⓐ Ⓑ Ⓒ Ⓓ Ⓔ
28 Ⓐ Ⓑ Ⓒ Ⓓ Ⓔ
29 Ⓐ Ⓑ Ⓒ Ⓓ Ⓔ
30 Ⓐ Ⓑ Ⓒ Ⓓ Ⓔ

31 Ⓐ Ⓑ Ⓒ Ⓓ Ⓔ
32 Ⓐ Ⓑ Ⓒ Ⓓ Ⓔ
33 Ⓐ Ⓑ Ⓒ Ⓓ Ⓔ
34 Ⓐ Ⓑ Ⓒ Ⓓ Ⓔ
35 Ⓐ Ⓑ Ⓒ Ⓓ Ⓔ
36 Ⓐ Ⓑ Ⓒ Ⓓ Ⓔ
37 Ⓐ Ⓑ Ⓒ Ⓓ Ⓔ
38 Ⓐ Ⓑ Ⓒ Ⓓ Ⓔ
39 Ⓐ Ⓑ Ⓒ Ⓓ Ⓔ
40 Ⓐ Ⓑ Ⓒ Ⓓ Ⓔ

SECTION 9

1 Ⓐ Ⓑ Ⓒ Ⓓ Ⓔ
2 Ⓐ Ⓑ Ⓒ Ⓓ Ⓔ
3 Ⓐ Ⓑ Ⓒ Ⓓ Ⓔ
4 Ⓐ Ⓑ Ⓒ Ⓓ Ⓔ
5 Ⓐ Ⓑ Ⓒ Ⓓ Ⓔ
6 Ⓐ Ⓑ Ⓒ Ⓓ Ⓔ
7 Ⓐ Ⓑ Ⓒ Ⓓ Ⓔ
8 Ⓐ Ⓑ Ⓒ Ⓓ Ⓔ
9 Ⓐ Ⓑ Ⓒ Ⓓ Ⓔ
10 Ⓐ Ⓑ Ⓒ Ⓓ Ⓔ

11 Ⓐ Ⓑ Ⓒ Ⓓ Ⓔ
12 Ⓐ Ⓑ Ⓒ Ⓓ Ⓔ
13 Ⓐ Ⓑ Ⓒ Ⓓ Ⓔ
14 Ⓐ Ⓑ Ⓒ Ⓓ Ⓔ
15 Ⓐ Ⓑ Ⓒ Ⓓ Ⓔ
16 Ⓐ Ⓑ Ⓒ Ⓓ Ⓔ
17 Ⓐ Ⓑ Ⓒ Ⓓ Ⓔ
18 Ⓐ Ⓑ Ⓒ Ⓓ Ⓔ
19 Ⓐ Ⓑ Ⓒ Ⓓ Ⓔ
20 Ⓐ Ⓑ Ⓒ Ⓓ Ⓔ

21 Ⓐ Ⓑ Ⓒ Ⓓ Ⓔ
22 Ⓐ Ⓑ Ⓒ Ⓓ Ⓔ
23 Ⓐ Ⓑ Ⓒ Ⓓ Ⓔ
24 Ⓐ Ⓑ Ⓒ Ⓓ Ⓔ
25 Ⓐ Ⓑ Ⓒ Ⓓ Ⓔ
26 Ⓐ Ⓑ Ⓒ Ⓓ Ⓔ
27 Ⓐ Ⓑ Ⓒ Ⓓ Ⓔ
28 Ⓐ Ⓑ Ⓒ Ⓓ Ⓔ
29 Ⓐ Ⓑ Ⓒ Ⓓ Ⓔ
30 Ⓐ Ⓑ Ⓒ Ⓓ Ⓔ

31 Ⓐ Ⓑ Ⓒ Ⓓ Ⓔ
32 Ⓐ Ⓑ Ⓒ Ⓓ Ⓔ
33 Ⓐ Ⓑ Ⓒ Ⓓ Ⓔ
34 Ⓐ Ⓑ Ⓒ Ⓓ Ⓔ
35 Ⓐ Ⓑ Ⓒ Ⓓ Ⓔ
36 Ⓐ Ⓑ Ⓒ Ⓓ Ⓔ
37 Ⓐ Ⓑ Ⓒ Ⓓ Ⓔ
38 Ⓐ Ⓑ Ⓒ Ⓓ Ⓔ
39 Ⓐ Ⓑ Ⓒ Ⓓ Ⓔ
40 Ⓐ Ⓑ Ⓒ Ⓓ Ⓔ

1 ESSAY   ESSAY 1

ESSAY
Time—25 minutes

Write your essay on separate sheets of standard lined paper.

The essay gives you an opportunity to show how effectively you can develop and express ideas. You should therefore take care to develop your point of view, present your ideas logically and clearly, and use language precisely.

Your essay must be written on the lines provided on your answer sheet—you will receive no other paper on which to write. You will have enough space if you write on every line, avoid wide margins, and keep your handwriting to a reasonable size. Remember that people who are not familiar with your handwriting will read what you write. Try to write or print so that what you are writing is legible to those readers.

Important reminders:

- **A pencil is required for the essay.** An essay written in ink will receive a score of zero.
- **Do not write your essay in your test book.** You will receive credit only for what you write on your answer sheet.
- **An off-topic essay will receive a score of zero.**

You have twenty-five minutes to write an essay on the topic assigned below.

Consider carefully the issue discussed in the following passage, then write an essay that answers the question posed in the assignment.

> The best leaders are not those who seek power or have great political skill. Great leaders—and these are exceptionally rare, especially today—represent the best selves of the people they represent.

Assignment: **What are the most important qualities of a leader?** Write an essay in which you answer this question and discuss your point of view on this issue. Support your position logically with examples from literature, the arts, history, politics, science and technology, current events, or your experience or observation.

If you finish before time is called, you may check your work on this section only.
Do not turn to any other section in the test.

2   2   2   2   2   2

SECTION 2
Time—25 minutes
24 questions

Turn to Section 2 of your answer sheet to answer the questions in this section.

Directions: For each question in this section, select the best answer from among the choices given and fill in the corresponding circle on the answer sheet.

Each sentence below has one or two blanks, each blank indicating that something has been omitted. Beneath the sentence are five words or sets of words labeled A through E. Choose the word or set of words that, when inserted in the sentence, <u>best</u> fits the meaning of the sentence as a whole.

EXAMPLE:

Rather than accepting the theory unquestioningly, Deborah regarded it with ------.

(A) mirth
(B) sadness
(C) responsibility
(D) ignorance
(E) skepticism

Ⓐ Ⓑ Ⓒ Ⓓ ●

---

1. Even though Alisha had every reason to hold a grudge, she felt that ------- was not a healthful emotion.

   (A) resentment
   (B) fortitude
   (C) sarcasm
   (D) elation
   (E) fondness

2. Those who expected the governor to be inarticulate were surprised by his -------.

   (A) intolerance
   (B) fatigue
   (C) eloquence
   (D) endurance
   (E) violence

3. Before the Realist movement, novelists rarely utilized the ------- language of commoners, preferring the more ------- parlance of the upper classes.

   (A) normal . . ordinary
   (B) elite . . fancy
   (C) sympathetic . . wasteful
   (D) colloquial . . refined
   (E) effective . . utilitarian

4. Many college students are attracted to the ------- life of a journalist; the prospect of exploring the world is very appealing, even if the pay is not.

   (A) peripatetic
   (B) conventional
   (C) tolerant
   (D) coordinated
   (E) remunerative

5. A position that requires public speaking would be very difficult for one as ------- as he.

   (A) vivacious
   (B) garrulous
   (C) amiable
   (D) decent
   (E) reticent

GO ON TO THE NEXT PAGE ▷

2   2   2   2   2   2

6. One example of a ------- relationship is pro-
    vided by the tickbird, which gets protection
    and a free meal of ticks from the hippopota-
    mus and in turn supplies free pest removal
    services.

    (A) competitive
    (B) deteriorating
    (C) symbiotic
    (D) regressive
    (E) vacillating

7. Early philosophers used ------- alone to reach their
    conclusions; unlike modern scientists, they did
    not value the ------- information that comes only
    from close observation and experimentation.

    (A) reason . . empirical
    (B) coercion . . mathematical
    (C) deduction . . clerical
    (D) computation . . intuitive
    (E) compassion . . numerical

8. The ------- of many media companies under a
    single owner is troublesome to those who be-
    lieve that ------- is essential to the fair and bal-
    anced presentation of the news.

    (A) retraction . . differentiation
    (B) consolidation . . independence
    (C) collaboration . . sharing
    (D) unification . . dissemination
    (E) disintegration . . variety

The following passages are followed by questions based on their content. Answer the questions on the basis of what is <u>stated</u> or <u>implied</u>
in the passage and in any introductory mater-
ial that may be provided.

Questions 9–12 are based on the following passages.

PASSAGE 1

Education, then, beyond all other devices of
human origin, is the great equalizer of the con-
Line ditions of men—the balance-wheel of the social
machinery. It gives each man the independence
5   and the means by which he can resist the selfishness of other men. It does better than to dis-
arm the poor of their hostility toward the rich;
it prevents being poor. The spread of education,
by enlarging the cultivated class or caste, will
10 open a wider area over which the social feelings
will expand, and, if this education should be
universal and complete, it would do more than
all things else to obliterate factitious distinctions in society.

PASSAGE 2

15 For most students, the main product of
schooling is not education but the acceptance
of one's place in society and of the power of
that society to mete out the symbols of status.
Education is the acquisition of competence,
20 power, wisdom and discernment. These come
only from the unadulterated struggle for sense
in the world, and it is this struggle that is denied by schooling, which dictates experience
and then evaluates that experience as it
25 chooses. But only the experiencer can really
evaluate an experience.

9. Unlike Passage 1, Passage 2 focuses on the dis-
    tinction between

    (A) educating the poor and educating the
         wealthy
    (B) power and knowledge
    (C) teachers and students
    (D) educated people and uneducated people
    (E) schooling and education

First passage: Horace Mann, *The Case for Public Schools*, a
report to the Massachusetts Board of Education in 1848.
Second passage: Printed with the permission of its author,
Christopher Black, and College Hill Coaching. © 2005

GO ON TO THE NEXT PAGE

10. Passage 1 mentions each of the following as benefits of public education to the poor EXCEPT

(A) the diminishment of social distinctions
(B) the improvement of living standards
(C) better ability to counteract greed
(D) increased self-sufficiency
(E) the reduction of crime

11. Passage 1 suggests that the obliteration of "factitious distinctions" (lines 13–14) requires

(A) unlimited access to education
(B) a rigorous curriculum in civics
(C) hostility toward the rich
(D) dedicated teachers
(E) aggressive legislation

12. The author of Passage 2 characterizes the "struggle" (line 21) as

(A) regretful
(B) empowering
(C) illusionary
(D) unwinnable
(E) foreign

Questions 13–18 are based on the following passage.

The following is an essay from a textbook on the history of philosophy published in 1999.

The scientists of the Renaissance brought about the most fundamental alterations in the
Line world of thought, and they accomplished this feat by devising a new method for discovering
5 knowledge. Unlike the medieval thinkers, who proceeded for the most part by reading traditional texts, the early modern scientists laid greatest stress upon observation and the formation of temporary hypotheses. The
10 method of observation implied two things: namely, that traditional explanations of the behavior of nature should be empirically demonstrated, the new assumption being that such explanations could very well be wrong,
15 and that new information might be available to scientists if they could penetrate beyond the superficial appearances of things. People now began to look at the heavenly bodies with a new attitude, hoping not solely to find the
20 confirmation of Biblical statements about the firmament but, further, to discover the principles and laws that describe the movements of bodies. Observation was directed not only upon the stars but also in the opposite direc-
25 tion, toward the minutest constituents of physical substance.

To enhance the exactness of their observations, they invented various scientific instruments. Tippershey, a Dutchman, invented the
30 telescope in 1608, although Galileo was the first to make dramatic use of it. In 1590 the first compound microscope was created. The principle of the barometer was discovered by Galileo's pupil Torricelli. The air pump, which
35 was so important in creating a vacuum for the experiment that proved that all bodies regardless of their weight or size fall at the same rate when there is no air resistance, was invented by Otto von Guericke (1602–1686). With the
40 use of instruments and imaginative hypotheses, fresh knowledge began to unfold. Galileo discovered the moons around Jupiter, and Anton Leeuwenhoek (1632–1723) discovered spermatozoa, protozoa, and bacteria.
45 Whereas Nicolaus Copernicus (1473–1543) formed a new hypothesis of the revolution of the earth around the sun, Harvey (1578–1657) discovered the circulation of the blood. William Gilbert (1540–1603) wrote a major
50 work on the magnet, and Robert Boyle (1627–1691), the father of chemistry, formulated his famous law concerning the relation of temperature, volume, and pressure of

Excerpted from "The Renaissance Interlude," in *Socrates to Sartre*, by Samuel Enoch Stumpf, McGraw-Hill, New York, 1999. Reproduced with permission of The McGraw-Hill Companies.

GO ON TO THE NEXT PAGE →

2   2   2   2   2   2

gases. Added to these inventions and discover-
55 ies was the decisive advance made in mathematics, especially by Sir Isaac Newton and
Leibniz, who independently invented differen-
tial and integral calculus. The method of
observation and mathematical calculation
60 now became the hallmarks of modern science.
    The new scientific mode of thought in time
influenced philosophic thought in two important ways. First, the assumption that the basic
processes of nature are observable and capa-
65 ble of mathematical calculation and description had the effect of engendering another
assumption, namely, that everything consists
of bodies in motion, that everything conforms
to a mechanical model. The heavens above
70 and the smallest particles below all exhibit the
same laws of motion. Even human thought
was soon explained in mechanical terms, not
to mention the realm of human behavior,
which the earlier moralists described as the
75 product of free will.

13. Which of the following is the best title for this
passage?

(A) The Beginnings of the Scientific Method
(B) Scientific Instruments of the Renaissance
(C) The Art and Science of the Renaissance
(D) Biblical Influence on the Scientific Mode
     of Thought
(E) The Importance of Hypotheses in
     Scientific Thinking

14. As it is used in line 8, "stress" most nearly
means

(A) anxiety
(B) pressure
(C) emphasis
(D) desperation
(E) contortion

15. It can be inferred from the passage that if pre-
Renaissance scientists observed the motions
of heavenly bodies, they did so most likely in
order to

(A) confirm the formulas that describe the
     motions of the planets and stars
(B) distinguish the motions of various
     planets
(C) validate what the Bible says about those
     bodies
(D) demonstrate the utility of their newly
     invented instruments
(E) refute the hypotheses of their rival
     scientists

16. The passage indicates that Galileo did which
of the following?

    I.   invented an important optical
         instrument
    II. instructed another famous scientist
    III. made an important astronomical
         discovery

(A) II only
(B) III only
(C) I and II only
(D) II and III only
(E) I, II, and III

17. The passage indicates that, unlike the "earlier
moralists" (line 74), Renaissance scientists
began to perceive human behavior as

(A) a matter of free choice
(B) influenced by heavenly bodies
(C) controlled by a metaphysical spirit
(D) affected by animalistic impulses
(E) subject to the laws of physical motion

18. The primary function of the last paragraph
is to

(A) propose a solution to a problem
(B) identify those responsible for a discovery
(C) discuss the effects of a change
(D) refute a misconception
(E) address an objection to the author's thesis

GO ON TO THE NEXT PAGE

2   2   2   2   2   2

Questions 19–24 are based on the following passage.

The following passage is from a recent book on the history of warfare.

One of the high points of any production of Shakespeare's *Henry V* is the Saint Crispin's
Line Day speech at the Battle of Agincourt, in which the English king rhapsodizes over the
5   glorious plight of his vastly outnumbered army with the words "We few, we happy few, we band of brothers." What prompts this outpouring of fraternal emotion is the Earl of Westmoreland's complaint that if only they had
10 "ten thousand of those men in England that do no work today," they would at least have a fighting chance. But Henry will have none of that, and delivers his justly famous rejoinder:

> *If we are marked to die, we are enow*
15 > *To do our country loss; and if to live,*
> *The fewer men, the greater share of honor.*
> *God's will! I pray thee wish not one man more.*

This is usually assumed to be a show of stoic bravado that harks back to the prebattle
20 speeches recorded by ancient historians (notably Thucydides and Xenophon), speeches in which an outnumbered force cement their solidarity by reveling in their numerical disadvantage. "The fewer men, the greater the
25 honor" was by Shakespeare's time a well-known proverb, trotted out in many instances of the glorious, fighting few. In Froissart's account of the Battle of Poitiers in 1356, for example, the Prince of Wales harangues his men
30 prior to the battle in a speech that closely parallels Henry's. Shakespeare was undoubtedly familiar with it.

> *Now, my gallant fellows, what though we be a small body when compared to the army of our*
35 > *enemies; do not let us be cast down on that account, for victory does not always follow numbers, but where the Almighty God wishes to bestow it. If, through good fortune, the day shall be ours, we shall gain the greatest honor*
40 > *and glory in this world; if the contrary should happen, and we be slain, I have a father and beloved brethren alive, and you all have some relations, or good friends, who will be sure to revenge our deaths. I therefore entreat of you*
45 > *to exert yourselves, and combat manfully; for, if it please God and St. George, you shall see me this day act like a true knight.*

Of course the race does not always go to the swift nor the battle to the stronger in number.
50 Despite being outmanned, both King Henry and Prince Edward managed to prevail quite handily due to the incompetence of their opponents. In each instance, the French squandered their numerical advantage by charging
55 before they were ready, by bunching up, and by underestimating the range and accuracy of the English longbow. The numbers not only fail to tell the whole story, but they actually obscure it. Ten thousand more men might ac-
60 tually have hindered the English, whereas fewer men (and less overconfidence) might have saved the French. It seems that in fact, as these and many other examples show, strength is not always proportional to size.

19. The passage suggests that Henry V requests "not one man more" (line 17) because

(A) his strategy can work only with a small band of fighters
(B) he considers it more honorable to fight while outnumbered
(C) the opposing soldiers are unreliable
(D) no other fighters have the skills of the ones he has assembled
(E) he does not wish to be victorious

20. In line 26, the phrase "trotted out" most nearly means

(A) abused
(B) removed
(C) employed for rhetorical effect
(D) spared an indignity
(E) used flippantly

GO ON TO THE NEXT PAGE ➡

2   2   2   2   2   2

21. In line 34, the word "body" most nearly means

(A) stature
(B) strength
(C) corpse
(D) group
(E) anthology

22. In line 54, the word "charging" most nearly means

(A) accusing
(B) inspiring
(C) resting
(D) attacking
(E) prevailing

23. The passage indicates that the Battle of Agincourt and the Battle of Poitiers were similar in that in each case

    I. the victorious army was the smaller
    II. the French army was defeated
    III. one side committed tactical errors

(A) I only
(B) I and II only
(C) I and III only
(D) II and III only
(E) I, II, and III

24. The passage suggests that the "whole story" (line 58) should include the possibility that

(A) numerical supremacy would not have been an advantage to the British
(B) King Henry had more soldiers available than was previously believed
(C) the English longbow was not as accurate as the French soldiers believed it to be
(D) confidence aided the French more than the British
(E) the French did not really outman the British

STOP

If you finish before time is called, you may check your work on this section only. Do not turn to any other section of the test.

3 **3** **3** **3** **3** **3**

SECTION 3
Time—25 minutes
20 questions

Turn to Section 3 of your answer sheet to answer the questions in this section.

Directions: For this section, solve each problem and decide which is the best of the choices given. Fill in the corresponding circle on the answer sheet. You may use any available space for scratchwork.

Notes

1. The use of a calculator is permitted.

2. All numbers used are real numbers.

3. Figures that accompany problems in this test are intended to provide information useful in solving the problems. They are drawn as accurately as possible EXCEPT when it is stated in a specific problem that the figure is not drawn to scale. All figures lie in a plane unless otherwise indicated.

4. Unless otherwise specified, the domain of any function f is assumed to be the set of all real numbers x for which $f(x)$ is a real number.

Reference Information

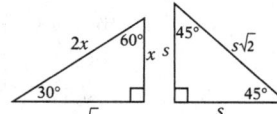

$A = \pi r^2$ $A = \ell w$ $A = \frac{1}{2}bh$ $V = \ell wh$ $V = \pi r^2 h$ $c^2 = a^2 + b^2$ Special right triangles
$C = 2\pi r$

The number of degrees of arc in a circle is 360.
The sum of the measures in degrees of the angles of a triangle is 180.

---

1. If n is 3 times an even number, then which of the following could be n?

(A) 14
(B) 15
(C) 16
(D) 17
(E) 18

---

2. A machine can produce 50 computer chips in 2 hours. At this rate, how many computer chips can the machine produce in 7 hours?

(A) 175
(B) 200
(C) 225
(D) 250
(E) 275

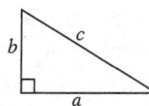

3. In the figure above, what is the value of x?

(A) 40
(B) 45
(C) 60
(D) 75
(E) 90

GO ON TO THE NEXT PAGE

3 3 3 3 3 3

4. Any positive integer that is divisible by 6 and 15 must also be divisible by

   (A) 12
   (B) 21
   (C) 30
   (D) 72
   (E) 90

5. If n percent of 20 is 4, what is n?

   (A) ⅕
   (B) 2
   (C) 5
   (D) 20
   (E) 500

6. If $f(x) = 3x + n$, where n is a constant, and $f(2) = 0$, then $f(0) =$

   (A) −6
   (B) −2
   (C) 0
   (D) 2
   (E) 6

7. A square has the same area as a right triangle with sides of lengths 6, 8, and 10. What is the length of one side of the square?

   (A) 4
   (B) $2\sqrt{3}$
   (C) $\sqrt{15}$
   (D) $2\sqrt{6}$
   (E) 12

8. If $12v = 3w$ and $v \neq 0$, then which of the following is equivalent to $2w - 8v$?

   (A) 0
   (B) $4w$
   (C) $-6w$
   (D) $2v$
   (E) $-2v$

9. If x is a negative number and $2|x| + 1 > 5$, then which of the following must be true?

   (A) $x < -3$
   (B) $x < -2.5$
   (C) $x < -2$
   (D) $x > -2$
   (E) $x > -5$

10. If $x = -2$, then $-x^2 - 8x - 5 =$

    (A) 3
    (B) 7
    (C) 15
    (D) 23
    (E) 25

11. If $\dfrac{5}{m} \leq \dfrac{2}{3}$, then what is the smallest possible positive value of m?

    (A) 6
    (B) 6.5
    (C) 7
    (D) 7.5
    (E) 8

12. Theo wants to buy a sweater that is priced at $60.00 before tax. The store charges a 6% sales tax on all purchases. If he gives the cashier $70.00 for the sweater, how much should he receive in change?

    (A) $3.60
    (B) $6.40
    (C) $7.40
    (D) $9.40
    (E) $66.40

GO ON TO THE NEXT PAGE

13. When m is subtracted from n, the result is r. Which of the following expresses the result when $2m$ is added to s?

(A) $s + 2n - 2r$
(B) $s + 2n + 2r$
(C) $2s + 2n - 2r$
(D) $2s + 2n + 2r$
(E) $s - 2n + 2r$

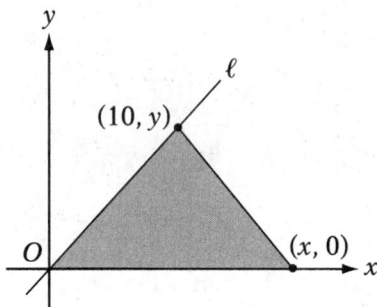

Note: Figure not drawn to scale.

14. In the figure above, the slope of line l is $\dfrac{3}{5}$ and the area of the triangle is 48 square units. What is the value of $x + y$?

(A)   13
(B)   14
(C)   19
(D)   22
(E)   96

15. Ellen takes a trip that is y miles long in total, where $y > 20$. She travels the first 15 miles at an average speed of 30 miles per hour and the rest of the trip at an average speed of 40 miles per hour. Which of the following represents the total time of the trip, in hours?

(A) $\dfrac{1}{2} + \dfrac{y - 15}{40}$

(B) $2 + \dfrac{y - 15}{40}$

(C) $\dfrac{1}{2} + 40y - 15$

(D) $2 + 40(y - 15)$

(E) $\dfrac{1}{2} + 40(y - 15)$

16. If y varies directly as m and inversely as the square of n, and if $y = 8$ when $m = 16$ and $n = 1$, then what is the value of y when $m = 8$ and $n = 4$?

(A)   0.125
(B)   0.25
(C)   0.5
(D)   1
(E)   2

17. If $a + b = s$ and $a - b = t$, then which of the following expresses the value of ab in terms of s and t?

(A) st

(B) $\dfrac{(s - t)}{2}$

(C) $\dfrac{(s + t)}{2}$

(D) $\dfrac{(s^2 - t^2)}{4}$

(E) $\dfrac{(s^2 - t^2)}{2}$

18. If $y = m^4 = n^3$ and y is greater than 1, then $mn =$

(A) $y^{1/12}$
(B) $y^{1/7}$
(C) $y^{7/12}$
(D) y^7
(E) y^{12}

GO ON TO THE NEXT PAGE

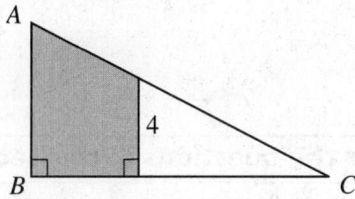

Note: Figure not drawn to scale.

19. In the figure above, if $AB = 6$ and $BC = 12$, what is the area of the shaded region?

(A) 20
(B) 22
(C) 24
(D) 26
(E) 28

20. Every car at a certain dealership is either a convertible, a sedan, or both. If one-fifth of the convertibles are also sedans and one-third of the sedans are also convertibles, which of the following could be the total number of cars at the dealership?

(A) 28
(B) 29
(C) 30
(D) 31
(E) 32

STOP

If you finish before time is called, you may check your work on this section only. Do not turn to any other section of the test.

4   **4**   **4**   **4**   **4**   **4**

SECTION 4
Time—25 minutes
18 questions

Turn to Section 4 of your answer sheet to answer the questions in this section.

Directions: This section contains two types of questions. You have 25 minutes to complete both types. For questions 1–8, solve each problem and decide which is the best of the choices given. Fill in the corresponding circle on the answer sheet. You may use any available space for scratchwork.

Notes

1. The use of a calculator is permitted.

2. All numbers used are real numbers.

3. Figures that accompany problems in this test are intended to provide information useful in solving the problems. They are drawn as accurately as possible EXCEPT when it is stated in a specific problem that the figure is not drawn to scale. All figures lie in a plane unless otherwise indicated.

4. Unless otherwise specified, the domain of any function f is assumed to be the set of all real numbers x for which $f(x)$ is a real number.

Reference Information

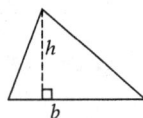 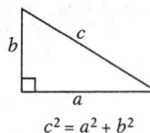 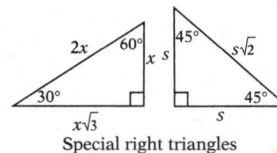

$A = \pi r^2$ $A = \ell w$ $A = \frac{1}{2}bh$ $V = \ell wh$ $V = \pi r^2 h$ $c^2 = a^2 + b^2$ Special right triangles

$C = 2\pi r$

The number of degrees of arc in a circle is 360.

The sum of the measures in degrees of the angles of a triangle is 180.

---

1. A square has a perimeter of 36 centimeters. What is its area in square centimeters?

(A) 24
(B) 36
(C) 49
(D) 64
(E) 81

2. If b is a positive integer less than 100, then how many integer pairs (a, b) satisfy the equation $\dfrac{a}{b} = \dfrac{1}{10}$?

(A) 7
(B) 8
(C) 9
(D) 10
(E) 11

GO ON TO THE NEXT PAGE ⟹

CLEANING COSTS IN THE McKENZIE OFFICE BUILDING

Room Type	Number of Rooms in the Building	Cost per Room to Clean
Bathrooms	10	$20
Offices	30	$15

3. According to the table above, how much will it cost, in dollars, to clean each bathroom twice and each office once in the McKenzie Office Building?

(A) 200
(B) 400
(C) 450
(D) 600
(E) 850

4. If $a^2 - b^2 = 10$ and $a - b = 2$, what is the value of $a + b$?

(A) 5
(B) 6
(C) 7
(D) 8
(E) 9

5. For all integers n greater than 1, let $f(n) = k$, where k is the sum of all the prime factors of n. What is the value of $f(14) - f(6)$?

(A) 4
(B) 5
(C) 6
(D) 9
(E) 14

6. The average (arithmetic mean) of four different positive integers is 20. What is the greatest possible value of any of these integers?

(A) 68
(B) 70
(C) 73
(D) 74
(E) 77

7. The radius of circle A is twice the radius of circle B. If the sum of their circumferences is 36π, then what is the radius of circle A?

(A) 9
(B) 12
(C) 14
(D) 16
(E) 18

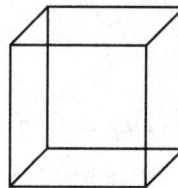

8. The figure above shows a cube. How many different planes can be drawn such that each contains *exactly* two edges of the cube?

(A) 4
(B) 5
(C) 6
(D) 7
(E) 8

GO ON TO THE NEXT PAGE

4　　**4**　　**4**　　**4**　　**4**　　**4**

Directions: For student-produced response questions 9–18, use the grids at the bottom of the answer sheet page on which you have answered questions 1–8.

Each of the remaining ten questions requires you to solve the problem and enter your answer by marking the circles in the special grid, as shown in the examples below. You may use any available space for scratchwork.

Answer: $\frac{7}{12}$

Write answer in boxes.

← Fraction line

Grid in result.

Answer: 2.5

← Decimal point

Answer: 201
Either position is correct.

<u>Note:</u> You may start your answers in any column, space permitting. Columns not needed should be left blank.

- Mark no more than one circle in any column.

- Because the answer sheet will be machine-scored, **you will receive credit only if the circles are filled in correctly.**

- Although not required, it is suggested that you write your answer in the boxes at the top of the columns to help you fill in the circles accurately.

- Some problems may have more than one correct answer. In such cases, grid only one answer.

- No question has a negative answer.

- **Mixed numbers** such as $3\frac{1}{2}$ must be gridded as 3.5 or 7/2. (If $3\ 1\ /\ 2$ is gridded, it will be interpreted as , $\frac{31}{2}$ not $3\frac{1}{2}$.)

- **Decimal Answers:** If you obtain a decimal answer with more digits than the grid can accommodate, it may be either rounded or truncated, but it must fill the entire grid. For example, if you obtain an answer such as 0.6666..., you should record your result as .666 or .667. **A less accurate value such as .66 or .67 will be scored as incorrect.**

Acceptable ways to grid $\frac{2}{3}$ are:

4   **4**   **4**   **4**   **4**   **4**

9. If 10 less than $2x$ is 22, then what is the value of x?

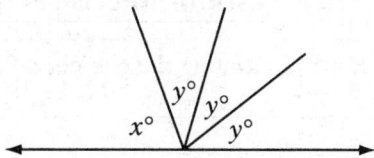

10. In the figure above, if $x = 2y$, then what is the value of y?

11. If $8x + 4y = 20$, then what is the value of $2x + y =$

12. In the xy-plane, the line $mx - 3y = 21$ passes through the point $(3, 5)$. What is the value of m?

13. The ratio of men to women in a room is 4:5. If the room contains three more women than men, how many women are in the room?

14. If, for some constant value b, the equation $y = |2x - b|$ is satisfied by the point $(5, 2)$, then what is one possible value of b?

15. A mixture of water and sucrose is 10% sucrose by weight. How many grams of pure sucrose must be added to a 200-gram sample of this mixture to produce a mixture that is 20% sucrose?

16. A runner runs a 16-mile race at an average speed of 8 miles per hour. By how many <u>minutes</u> can she improve her time in this race if she trains and increases her average speed by 25%?

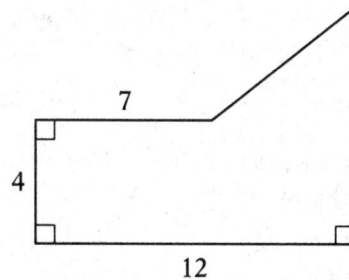

<u>Note:</u> Figure not drawn to scale.

17. The area of the figure above is 78. What is its perimeter?

18. Every sophomore at Hillside High School is required to study at least one language among Spanish, French, and Latin, but no one may study more than two. If 120 sophomores study Spanish, 80 study French, 75 study Latin, and 50 study two of the three languages, how many sophomores are there at Hillside High School?

STOP

If you finish before time is called, you may check your work on this section only. Do not turn to any other section of the test.

5   5   5   5   5   5

SECTION 5
Time—25 minutes
24 questions

Turn to Section 5 of your answer sheet to answer the questions in this section.

Directions: For each question in this section, select the best answer from among the choices given and fill in the corresponding circle on the answer sheet.

Each sentence below has one or two blanks, each blank indicating that something has been omitted. Beneath the sentence are five words or sets of words labeled A through E. Choose the word or set of words that, when inserted in the sentence, best fits the meaning of the sentence as a whole.

EXAMPLE:

Rather than accepting the theory unquestioningly, Deborah regarded it with ------.

(A) mirth
(B) sadness
(C) responsibility
(D) ignorance
(E) skepticism

Ⓐ Ⓑ Ⓒ Ⓓ ●

---

1. The ------- with which the advisor managed the funds forced his clients to seek more reliable advice regarding investment.

(A) skill
(B) caution
(C) ineptitude
(D) recognition
(E) bitterness

2. As an Armenian born in Iran and educated in Lebanon, Vartan Gregorian brought ------- flavor to the presidency of Brown University that was unprecedented in the Ivy League.

(A) a perpetual
(B) an authoritative
(C) a structured
(D) an artificial
(E) a cosmopolitan

3. The lawyers did not have time to consider the contract in great detail; rather, they were able to give it only a ------- reading before they had to make their presentation on its merits.

(A) verbatim
(B) meandering
(C) tormented
(D) cursory
(E) substantial

4. The ------- in many parts of the city has made the ------- of infectious diseases more rapid, because pathogens spread quickly in close quarters.

(A) overcrowding . . propagation
(B) squalor . . circulation
(C) poverty . . deterioration
(D) congestion . . elimination
(E) proximity . . resilience

GO ON TO THE NEXT PAGE ⟹

5   5   5   5   5   5

5. Much research in neuroscience today endeavors to ------- the mechanisms by which our brains turn the ------- data from our sense organs into coherent and understandable information.

   (A) enhance . . quality of
   (B) restore . . absence of
   (C) enlighten . . source of
   (D) attenuate . . dearth of
   (E) elucidate . . deluge of

The passages below are followed by questions based on their content. Answer the questions on the basis of what is <u>stated</u> or <u>implied</u> in the passage and in any introductory material that may be provided.

Questions 6 and 7 are based on the following passage.

Towards the middle and the end of the six-
teenth century there were many students and
Line   scholars possessing a great deal of erudition,
but very little means of subsistence. Nor were
5   their prospects very encouraging. They first
went through that bitter experience, which,
since then, so many have made after them—
that whoever seeks a home in the realm of intellect runs the risk of losing the solid ground
10   on which the fruits for maintaining human life
grow. The eye directed towards the Parnassus
is not the most apt to spy out the small tortu-
ous paths of daily gain. To get quick returns of
interest, even though it be small, from the capi-
15   tal of knowledge and learning has always been,
and still is, a question of difficult solution.

6. The "fruits" mentioned in line 10 represent

   (A) spiritual growth
   (B) artistic skill
   (C) technological progress
   (D) the means of acquiring food and shelter
   (E) scientific knowledge

7. The "question" in line 16 is whether

   (A) money can buy happiness
   (B) intellectuals can earn a good living
   (C) society can construct effective schools
   (D) old ideas are relevant to modern society
   (E) scholars are happier than merchants

Questions 8 and 9 are based on the following passage.

When there exists an inherited or instinctive
tendency to the performance of an action, or
Line   an inherited taste for certain kinds of food,
some degree of habit in the individual is often
5   or generally requisite. We find this in the
paces of the horse, and to a certain extent in
the pointing of dogs; although some young
dogs point excellently the first time they are
taken out, yet they often associate the proper
10   inherited attitude with a wrong odour, and
even with eyesight. I have heard it asserted
that if a calf be allowed to suck its mother
only once, it is much more difficult afterwards
to rear it by hand. Caterpillars which have
15   been fed on the leaves of one kind of tree,
have been known to perish from hunger
rather than to eat the leaves of another tree,
although this afforded them their proper food,
under a state of nature.

8. The "pointing of dogs" (line 7) is mentioned primarily as an example of

   (A) an innate habit
   (B) a behavior that humans find useful
   (C) a skill that is hard to learn
   (D) an ability that many other animals also have
   (E) a skill that helps animals to find food

First passage: Jacob Feis. *Shakespeare and Montaigne*, c. 1890. Public domain
Second passage: Charles Darwin. *The Expression of the Emotions in Man and Animals*. 1872. Public domain

GO ON TO THE NEXT PAGE

5   5   5   5   5   5

9. Which of the following best summarizes the main point of the paragraph?

(A) People will eat only what they are genetically determined to eat.
(B) All animal behavior is instinctive.
(C) Cows and other animals should not be fed by humans.
(D) Habits in animals are impossible to break.
(E) Inherited tendencies manifest themselves in behavioral habits.

Questions 10–16 are based on the following passage.

The following is an excerpt from an essay entitled Political Ideals, *written in 1917 by Bertrand Russell.*

It is not one ideal for all men, but a separate ideal for each separate man, that has to be real-
Line ized if possible. Every man has it in his being
to develop into something good or bad: there is
5   a best possible for him, and a worst possible.
His circumstances will determine whether his
capacities for good are developed or crushed,
and whether his bad impulses are strengthened
or gradually diverted into better channels.
10   But although we cannot set up in any detail
an ideal of character which is to be univer-
sally applicable—although we cannot say, for
instance, that all men ought to be industrious,
or self-sacrificing, or fond of music—there are
15   some broad principles which can be used to
guide our estimates as to what is possible or
desirable.
We may distinguish two sorts of goods,
and two corresponding sorts of impulses.
20   There are goods in regard to which individual
possession is possible, and there are goods in
which all can share alike. The food and clothing of one man is not the food and clothing of
another; if the supply is insufficient, what one
25   man has is obtained at the expense of some
other man. This applies to material goods generally, and therefore to the greater part of the
present economic life of the world. On the
other hand, mental and spiritual goods do not
30   belong to one man to the exclusion of another. If one man knows a science, that does
not prevent others from knowing it; on the

contrary, it helps them to acquire the knowledge. If one man is a great artist or poet, that
35   does not prevent others from painting pictures or writing poems, but helps to create the
atmosphere in which such things are possible.
If one man is full of good-will toward others,
that does not mean that there is less goodwill
40   to be shared among the rest; the more good-
will one man has, the more he is likely to
create among others.
In such matters there is no possession,
because there is not a definite amount to be
45   shared; any increase anywhere tends to
produce an increase everywhere.
There are two kinds of impulses, corresponding to the two kinds of goods. There are
possessive impulses, which aim at acquiring or
50   retaining private goods that cannot be shared;
these center in the impulse of property. And
there are creative or constructive impulses,
which aim at bringing into the world or making available for use the kind of goods in which
55   there is no privacy and no possession.
The best life is the one in which the creative impulses play the largest part and the
possessive impulses the smallest. This is no
new discovery. The Gospel says: "Take no
60   thought, saying, What shall we eat? or What
shall we drink? Or Wherewithal shall we be
clothed?" The thought we give to these things
is taken away from matters of more importance. And what is worse, the habit of mind
65   engendered by thinking of these things is a
bad one; it leads to competition, envy, domination, cruelty, and almost all the moral evils
that infest the world. In particular, it leads to
the predatory use of force. Material posses-
70   sions can be taken by force and enjoyed by the
robber. Spiritual possessions cannot be taken
in this way. You may kill an artist or a
thinker, but you cannot acquire his art or his
thought. You may put a man to death because
75   he loves his fellow-men, but you will not by so
doing acquire the love which made his happiness. Force is impotent in such matters; it is
only as regards material goods that it is effective. For this reason the men who believe in
80   force are the men whose thoughts and desires
are preoccupied with material goods.

GO ON TO THE NEXT PAGE ⟶

5   5   5   5   5   5

10. Which of the following best summarizes the main point of the passage?

   (A) People should strive harder to appreciate the arts.
   (B) Nothing can be possessed exclusively by one person.
   (C) Societies need strong laws against stealing.
   (D) Creativity is of higher value than possessiveness.
   (E) Scarce resources should be shared equally in a society.

11. The passage mentions "food and clothing" (lines 22–23) primarily as examples of things that

   (A) everyone needs to survive
   (B) create a positive atmosphere of sharing
   (C) many underdeveloped countries lack
   (D) cannot be shared as freely as other things
   (E) are hard to find

12. As it is used in line 43, "such matters" can be inferred to refer to situations in which

   (A) people must compete for ownership of goods
   (B) artists struggle to sell their works
   (C) people strive to be industrious
   (D) philosophers endeavor to define human ideals
   (E) possessing a good does not deny it to someone else

13. In line 51, the phrase "impulse of" most nearly means

   (A) reaction against
   (B) restriction of
   (C) sharing of
   (D) fear of
   (E) desire for

14. According to the author, "force is impotent in such matters" (line 77) because

   (A) violence cannot influence another person's thoughts
   (B) moral people do not engage in violence
   (C) spiritual things cannot be acquired coercively
   (D) a good person will always be protected by friends
   (E) reason is more powerful than physical force

15. In the last paragraph, the author indicates that his thesis is not

   (A) ancient
   (B) a matter of logic
   (C) relevant to those who are already happy
   (D) original
   (E) universal

16. Which of the following examples, if it existed, would most directly refute the main point of the author?

   (A) a person who finds a large sum of money and gives it to charity
   (B) an invention that benefits all of humankind even though it was created only to make money for its inventor
   (C) a tyrant who murders intellectuals in order to maintain his authority
   (D) a thief who steals in order to feed his starving family
   (E) an army that invades another country and plunders its wealth

GO ON TO THE NEXT PAGE

5   **5**   5   5   5   **5**

Questions 17–24 are based on the following passage.

The following passage was written for The Atlantic Monthly *in 1902 by Native American writer Zitkala-Sa, also known as Gertrude Simmons Bonnin.*

    The racial lines, which once were bitterly real, now serve nothing more than marking
Line out a living mosaic of human beings. And even here men of the same color are like the ivory
5 keys of one instrument where each represents all the rest, yet varies from them in pitch and quality of voice. Thus with a compassion for all echoes in human guise, I greet the solemn-faced "native preacher" whom I find awaiting
10 me. I listen with respect for God's creature, though he mouth most strangely the jangling phrases of a bigoted creed.

    As our tribe is one large family, where every person is related to all the others, he ad-
15 dressed me:

    "Cousin, I came from the morning church service to talk with you."

    "Yes," I said interrogatively, as he paused for some word from me.
20   Shifting uneasily about in the straight-backed chair he sat upon, he began: "Every holy day (Sunday) I look about our little God's house, and not seeing you there, I am disap-pointed. This is why I come today. Cousin, as
25 I watch you from afar, I see no unbecoming behavior and hear only good reports of you, which all the more burns me with the wish that you were a church member. Cousin, I was taught long years ago by kind missionar-
30 ies to read the holy book. These godly men taught me also the folly of our old beliefs.

    "There is one God who gives reward or pun-ishment to the race of dead men. In the upper region the Christian dead are gathered in un-
35 ceasing song and prayer. In the deep pit below, the sinful ones dance in torturing flames.

    "Think upon these things, my cousin, and choose now to avoid the after-doom of hell fire!" Then followed a long silence in which he
40 clasped tighter and unclasped again his inter-locked fingers.

    Like instantaneous lightning flashes came pictures of my own mother's making, for she, too, is now a follower of the new superstition.

45   "Knocking out the chinking of our log cabin, some evil hand thrust in a burning taper of braided dry grass, but failed of his in-tent, for the fire died out and the half burned brand fell inward to the floor. Directly above
50 it, on a shelf, lay the holy book. This is what we found after our return from a several days' visit. Surely some great power is hid in the sa-cred book!"

    Brushing away from my eyes many like pic-
55 tures, I offered midday meal to the converted Indian sitting wordless and with downcast face. No sooner had he risen from the table with "Cousin, I have relished it," than the church bell rang.

60   Thither he hurried forth with his afternoon sermon. I watched him as he hastened along, his eyes bent fast upon the dusty road till he disappeared at the end of a quarter of a mile.

    The little incident recalled to mind the copy
65 of a missionary paper brought to my notice a few days ago, in which a "Christian" pugilist[1] commented upon a recent article of mine, grossly perverting the spirit of my pen. Still I would not forget that the pale-faced mission-
70 ary and the aborigine are both God's creatures, though small indeed their own conceptions of Infinite Love. A wee child toddling in a wonder world, I prefer to their dogma my excursions into the natural gardens where the voice of the
75 Great Spirit is heard in the twittering of birds, the rippling of mighty waters, and the sweet breathing of flowers. If this is Paganism, then at present, at least, I am a Pagan.

17. The main purpose of the passage as a whole is to

(A) describe one person's perspective on an attempt at religious conversion

(B) compare Native American religious tradi-tion to European religious tradition

(C) analyze the rise of Christianity in Native American tribes

(D) refute a misconception about the nature of Paganism

(E) describe a conflict between the author and her mother

---

[1] One who fights for a cause; also, a prize fighter

GO ON TO THE NEXT PAGE ▷

5   5   5   5   5   5

18. The reference to "pitch and quality of voice" (lines 6–7) serves to emphasize

    (A) the variety in vocal quality of religious singers
    (B) the harshness with which many preachers rebuke their congregations
    (C) the sounds that the author hears in nature
    (D) the author's inability to understand what the native preacher is saying
    (E) the differences among members of the same race

19. In the first paragraph, the author characterizes the preacher primarily as

    (A) respectful
    (B) articulate
    (C) uneducated
    (D) intolerant
    (E) compassionate

20. According to the passage, the preacher addressed the author as "cousin" because

    (A) it is customary for preachers to refer to church members with that term
    (B) the tribe members are all related
    (C) the preacher's mother and the author's mother are sisters
    (D) the preacher had forgotten the author's name
    (E) the author refused to answer to her given name

21. According to the passage, the native preacher and the author's mother are alike in that they both

    (A) have experienced attempted arson
    (B) must travel a great deal
    (C) have similar religious beliefs
    (D) relish the midday meal
    (E) enjoy excursions into the natural gardens

22. In line 68, the word "spirit" most nearly means

    (A) apparition
    (B) lively nature
    (C) intent
    (D) fear
    (E) presence

23. In the final paragraph, the author characterizes herself primarily as

    (A) mature
    (B) creative
    (C) vengeful
    (D) repressed
    (E) awed

24. The author mentions "conceptions of Infinite Love" (lines 71–72) in order to emphasize which of the following characteristics of the "pale-faced missionary" (lines 69–70)?

    (A) small-mindedness
    (B) reluctance to persist in the attempt to convert the author to Christianity
    (C) generosity toward aborigines
    (D) sympathy for animals
    (E) high intelligence

STOP

If you finish before time is called, you may check your work on this section only. Do not turn to any other section of the test.

SECTION 6
Time—25 minutes
35 questions

Turn to Section 6 of your answer sheet to answer the questions in this section.

Directions: For each question in this section, select the best answer from among the choices given and fill in the corresponding circle on the answer sheet.

The following sentences test correctness and effectiveness of expression. Part of each sentence or the entire sentence is underlined; beneath each sentence are five ways of phrasing the underlined material. Choice A repeats the original phrasing; the other four choices are different. If you think the original phrasing produces a better sentence than any of the alternatives, select choice A; if not, select one of the other choices.

In making your selection, follow the requirements of standard written English; that is, pay attention to grammar, choice of words, sentence construction, and punctuation. Your selection should result in the most effective sentence—clear and precise, without awkwardness or ambiguity.

EXAMPLE:

The children couldn't hardly believe their eyes.

(A) couldn't hardly believe their eyes
(B) could hardly believe their eyes
(C) would not hardly believe their eyes
(D) couldn't nearly believe their eyes
(E) couldn't hardly believe his or her eyes

Ⓐ ● Ⓒ Ⓓ Ⓔ

1. Claims about harmful effects of the genetic alteration of vegetables <u>is more speculation than documented fact</u>.

   (A) is more speculation than documented fact
   (B) are more with speculation than of a documented fact
   (C) is more of a speculation than a documented fact
   (D) are more speculation than documented fact
   (E) are a matter of more speculation than documented fact

2. <u>Having passed</u> the test for certification, Mackenzie was looking forward to finding a challenging teaching position in her home town.

   (A) Having passed
   (B) Passing
   (C) Being that she passed
   (D) If she had passed
   (E) For her passing

3. Having once been a provincial schoolmaster, <u>Jean-Paul Sartre's writing was always oriented more towards clear instruction than pontification</u>.

   (A) Jean-Paul Sartre's writing was always oriented more towards clear instruction than pontification
   (B) Jean-Paul Sartre always wrote more to instruct than to pontificate
   (C) the writings of Jean-Paul Sartre were always oriented more toward instruction than pontification
   (D) Jean-Paul Sartre was oriented in his writing more toward instruction than pontification
   (E) Jean-Paul Sartre's writing was more to instruct than to pontificate

GO ON TO THE NEXT PAGE ▷

6   6   6   6   6   6

4. Adam Smith was a professor of philosophy, <u>a commissioner of customs, and founded the field of modern economics</u>.

    (A) a commissioner of customs, and founded the field of modern economics

    (B) worked as commissioner of customs, and founded the field of modern economics

    (C) a commissioner of customs, and the founder of the field of modern economics

    (D) commissioned customs, and was the founder of the field of modern economics

    (E) a commissioner of customs, and was the founder of the field of modern economics

5. John Locke was one of the first philosophers to attack the principle of <u>primogeniture, the practice of handing the monarchy down</u> to the king's first-born son.

    (A) primogeniture, the practice of handing the monarchy down

    (B) primogeniture; the practice of handing the monarchy down

    (C) primogeniture being the practice of handing the monarchy down

    (D) primogeniture that which handed down the monarchy

    (E) primogeniture this was the practice of handing the monarchy down

6. The nation's fledgling economy struggled <u>because the investment from other countries into its major industries was lacking from most of them</u>.

    (A) because the investment from other countries into its major industries was lacking from most of them

    (B) because few other countries were willing to invest in its major industries

    (C) due to the fact that few other countries would have invested in its major industries

    (D) because of the lack of investment from few other countries in its major industries

    (E) for the lack of investment in its major industries from other countries

7. The corporation began construction on the new building in January, but <u>there is still no completion</u>.

    (A) there is still no completion
    (B) they have yet to complete it
    (C) it has yet to complete the project
    (D) they have not still completed it yet
    (E) it isn't hardly done yet

8. Having spread more quickly than antibiotics could be distributed, <u>doctors were prevented from effectively treating the virulent disease</u>.

    (A) doctors were prevented from effectively treating the virulent disease

    (B) doctors could not effectively treat the virulent disease because it thwarted them

    (C) the doctors who were trying to treat it effectively were prevented by the virulent disease

    (D) the virulent disease prevented itself from its being treated effectively by the doctors

    (E) the virulent disease prevented the doctors from treating it effectively

9. Although psychologist B. F. <u>Skinner, who is best known as the man who popularized behaviorism, he</u> also wrote a utopian novel entitled *Walden Two*.

    (A) Skinner, who is best known as the man who popularized behaviorism, he

    (B) Skinner, who is best known as the man who popularized behaviorism,

    (C) Skinner is best known as the man who popularized behaviorism, he

    (D) Skinner popularized behaviorism, for which he is well known, nevertheless he

    (E) Skinner, who is best known as the man who popularized behaviorism, is the one who

GO ON TO THE NEXT PAGE →

10. <u>Singing for over two hours, Anita's hoarseness prevented her hitting the high notes</u>.

(A) Singing for over two hours, Anita's hoarseness prevented her hitting the high notes.
(B) Singing for over two hours, Anita was unable to hit the high notes because of her hoarseness.
(C) Having sung for over two hours, Anita's hoarseness prevented her from hitting the high notes.
(D) Having sung for over two hours, Anita was no longer able to hit the high notes because of her hoarseness.
(E) Having sung for over two hours, Anita's ability to hit the high notes was prevented by her hoarseness.

11. Some philosophers maintain that language is essential to formulating certain <u>thoughts; others, that</u> even the most complex thoughts are independent of words.

(A) thoughts; others, that
(B) thoughts, however, that others maintain that
(C) thoughts others suggest that
(D) thoughts and that others believe
(E) thoughts but others, however, that

12. Ellen turned around <u>quick</u> and noticed
                          A
<u>that the dog</u> that <u>had been following</u> her was
     B   C
now <u>gone</u>.   <u>No error</u>
       D   E

13. Marlena was honored not only for her

<u>initiative</u> in establishing the fund for war
     A
refugees but also <u>in devoting</u> so much
                       B
<u>of her own time</u> and money
     C
<u>to its success</u>.   <u>No error</u>
     D   E

14. The Medieval era in music <u>is considered</u>
                                    A
<u>by most</u> scholars <u>to begin</u> during the reign
     B   C
of Pope Gregory and to have ended

<u>around the middle of</u> the 15th century.
              D
<u>No error</u>
     E

15. Neither the artists <u>who were</u> at the vanguard
                              A
of the Expressionist movement <u>or even</u> the
                                   B
critics <u>of the era</u> could have foreseen
              C
<u>the impact</u> of this new mode on the general
     D
public.   <u>No error</u>
                E

GO ON TO THE NEXT PAGE ⟶

6   **6**   6   6   **6**   **6**

16. Several members <u>of the safety commission</u>
                            A

    <u>suggested</u> that lowering the speed limit
    B

    <u>on the road</u> would not necessarily result in
    C

    <u>less</u> accidents.   <u>No error</u>
    D   E

17. By the time the operation <u>was completed</u>,
                             A

    five surgeons <u>spent</u> over 20 hours <u>performing</u>
              B   C

    more than a dozen <u>procedures</u>.   <u>No error</u>
                    D   E

18. Not until the recent scandal <u>has</u> the
                         A

    newspapers published <u>anything</u> even
                   B

    vaguely <u>negative</u> about the company or
           C

    <u>its executives</u>.   <u>No error</u>
    D   E

19. <u>After falling asleep</u> on a horse-drawn bus in
    A

    Belgium in 1865, Friedrick Kekule had a

    <u>dream, it led</u> to <u>his discovery</u> of the structure
       B   C

    of the benzene molecule.   <u>No error</u>
             D   E

20. The movement <u>to establish</u> women's issues
                 A

    as important <u>subjects of study</u> <u>have had</u>
               B   C

    a profound impact on the curricula

    <u>offered in colleges</u> today.   <u>No error</u>
        D   E

21. Legends and folk stories inevitably become

    transformed and <u>exaggerated</u> as they are
                     A

    <u>passed down</u> through the generations, often
    B

    in order <u>to conform</u> to changing political
             C

    and <u>social standards</u>.   <u>No error</u>
         D   E

22. Although the remarks <u>were made</u> to the
                     A

    entire group, <u>everyone</u> at the meeting could
              B

    tell <u>that they were</u> particularly intended
        C

    <u>for Maria and I</u>.   <u>No error</u>
    D   E

23. By all accounts, the restructuring of the

    federal department was <u>successive</u>,
                     A

    <u>eliminating</u> unnecessary layers
    B

    <u>of bureaucracy</u> and dozens of
    C

    <u>wasteful procedures</u>.   <u>No error</u>
    D   E

24. The professor <u>suggested</u> that
                 A

    <u>those who wished</u> to attend the lecture next
    B

    week <u>be in the classroom</u> 10 minutes
        C

    <u>earlier than usual</u>.   <u>No error</u>
    D   E

GO ON TO THE NEXT PAGE ⟶

25. While in office a President <u>can usually</u>
                                                 A
pass more legislation, <u>and with fewer</u>
                                              B
procedural obstacles, when the Congress

and the administration are <u>underneath</u> the
                                                  C
<u>control of</u> the same political party.
         D
<u>No error</u>
     E

26. A quick <u>inspection</u> of Kurt's art collection
                     A
<u>would show clearly</u> that <u>he has</u> a discerning
              B   C
eye for <u>exemplary works</u> of art.   <u>No error</u>
                      D   E

27. <u>Surprisingly</u> absent from the debate <u>were</u>
           A   B
the vice president's arrogance <u>that</u> he
                                          C
typically displays <u>in such</u> forums.   <u>No error</u>
                          D   E

28. Of the numerous strains of *Streptococcus*

bacteria <u>that are known</u> to cause
               A
infections, type B is the <u>more</u> dangerous
                                  B
<u>for pregnant women</u> about <u>to give</u>
           C   D
birth.   <u>No error</u>
               E

29. Since 2001, the company <u>has spent</u>
                                            A
<u>more time on</u> employee training than
        B
<u>they did</u> in the previous 10 years <u>combined</u>.
     C   D
<u>No error</u>
     E

GO ON TO THE NEXT PAGE →

6   **6**   **6**   **6**   **6**   **6**

Directions: The following passage is an early draft of an essay. Some parts of the passage need to be rewritten.

Read the passage and select the best answers for the questions that follow. Some questions are about particular sentences or parts of sentences and ask you to improve sentence structure or word choice. Other questions ask you to consider organization and development. In choosing answers, follow the requirements of standard written English.

Questions 30–35 refer to the following passage.

(1) Most great scientists and artists are familiar with the so-called "eureka phenomenon." (2) This is the experience that a thinker has when, after they thought about a problem long and hard, they suddenly come upon a solution in a flash when they are no longer thinking about it. (3) The name of the phenomenon comes from the legend of Archimedes. (4) He had been thinking for days about a hard problem that had come from the king, King Hieron II. (5) The problem was how to determine whether the king's crown was pure gold without destroying it. (6) As he was bathing, the solution to the problem came to Archimedes in a flash and he ran naked through the streets of Syracuse shouting "Eureka!" meaning "I have found it!"

(7) Students should understand this also. (8) You have probably had the experience of thinking about a paper or a math problem for so long that it's like one's brain gets frozen. (9) When this happens, it is best to get away from the problem for a while rather than obsess about it. (10) Isaac Asimov, one of the most prolific writers of all time, used to go to the movies every time he got writer's block. (11) He claimed that he always came out of the movie knowing exactly how to get his story back on track.

(12) Unfortunately, many students today don't have time for that. (13) They feel so much pressure to get everything done—their homework, their jobs, their sports, their extracurricular activities—that they think that taking "time out" to relax their brains is just a costly waste of time. (14) This is really too bad because very often relaxation is more valuable to a student than just more hard work.

30. Which of the following is the best revision of the underlined portion of sentence 2 (reproduced below)?

This is the experience that a thinker has when, after they thought about a problem long and hard, they suddenly come upon a solution in a flash when they are no longer thinking about it.

(A) that a thinker has when, after they thought long and hard about a problem, their solution suddenly arises like a flash

(B) that thinkers have when a solution suddenly had arisen like a flash after they were thinking long and hard about a problem

(C) that a thinker has when, after having thought long and hard about a problem, they suddenly come upon a solution

(D) that thinkers have when, after having thought long and hard about a problem, they suddenly come upon a solution

(E) that thinkers have when, thinking long and hard about a problem, they suddenly come upon a solution in a flash

GO ON TO THE NEXT PAGE

31. Which of the following is the best way to combine sentences 3, 4, and 5?

(A) The name of the phenomenon comes from the legend of Archimedes, who had been thinking for days about how to determine whether King Hieron II's crown was pure gold without destroying it.

(B) Archimedes had been thinking for days about how to determine whether King Hieron II's crown was pure gold without destroying it, and this is where the name of the phenomenon comes from.

(C) The legend of Archimedes thinking about how to determine whether King Hieron II's crown was pure gold without destroying it is the origin of the name of the phenomenon.

(D) The phenomenon is named for Archimedes and his thinking for days about how to determine whether King Hieron II's crown was pure gold without destroying it.

(E) The name of the phenomenon was from Archimedes, and his thinking for days about how to determine without destroying it whether King Hieron II's crown was pure gold.

32. Which of the following revisions of sentence 7 most clearly and logically introduces the second paragraph?

(A) This historical episode is something that all students should learn about in school.

(B) Understanding this phenomenon may help students to improve their studies.

(C) Nevertheless, this episode is something that all students should know.

(D) Understanding this episode requires a more thorough understanding of its historical setting.

(E) Many have tried to understand this phenomenon, but few have succeeded.

33. Which of the following is the best revision of the underlined portion of sentence 8 (reproduced below)?

You have probably had the experience of thinking about a paper or a math problem for so long that it's like one's brain gets frozen.

(A) it seems that your brain gets frozen
(B) one's brain gets frozen
(C) your brain seems to freeze
(D) your brains seem to freeze
(E) one's brain seems to freeze

34. Where is the best place to insert the following sentence?

Perhaps if students could work such little excursions into their busy study schedules, they would have similar "eureka" experiences.

(A) after sentence 7
(B) after sentence 8
(C) after sentence 9
(D) after sentence 10
(E) after sentence 11 (as the last sentence of the second paragraph)

35. In context, which of the following revisions of the underlined portion of sentence 12 (reproduced below) is most effective at making it clearer and more specific?

Unfortunately, many students today don't have time for that.

(A) today have hardly even 1 hour for such things
(B) today, unlike those in Archimedes' time, don't have time to go to the movies
(C) today don't have time for such excursions
(D) of modern times lack sufficient time for the kinds of things explained above
(E) today lack sufficient time for things like this

STOP

If you finish before time is called, you may check your work on this section only. Do not turn to any other section of the test.

7 7 7 7 7 7

SECTION 7
Time—20 minutes
16 questions

Turn to Section 7 of your answer sheet to answer the questions in this section.

Directions: For this section, solve each problem and decide which is the best of the choices given. Fill in the corresponding circle on the answer sheet. You may use any available space for scratchwork.

Notes

1. The use of a calculator is permitted.

2. All numbers used are real numbers.

3. Figures that accompany problems in this test are intended to provide information useful in solving the problems. They are drawn as accurately as possible EXCEPT when it is stated in a specific problem that the figure is not drawn to scale. All figures lie in a plane unless otherwise indicated.

4. Unless otherwise specified, the domain of any function f is assumed to be the set of all real numbers x for which $f(x)$ is a real number.

Reference Information

$A = \pi r^2$
$C = 2\pi r$

$A = \ell w$

$A = \frac{1}{2}bh$

$V = \ell wh$

$V = \pi r^2 h$

$c^2 = a^2 + b^2$

Special right triangles

The number of degrees of arc in a circle is 360.
The sum of the measures in degrees of the angles of a triangle is 180.

---

1. If four apples cost 20 cents, then, at this rate, how much would ten apples cost?

(A) $.40
(B) $.50
(C) $.60
(D) $.70
(E) $.80

2. If $2^b = 8$, then $3^b =$

(A) 6
(B) 9
(C) 27
(D) 64
(E) 81

3. How much greater is the average (arithmetic mean) of a, b, and 18 than the average of a, b, and 12?

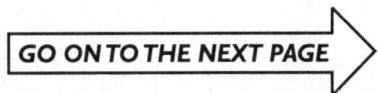

(A) 2
(B) 3
(C) 4
(D) 5
(E) 6

GO ON TO THE NEXT PAGE

4. The first day of a particular month is a Tuesday. What day of the week will it be on the 31st day of the month?

(A) Wednesday
(B) Thursday
(C) Friday
(D) Saturday
(E) Sunday

5. How many integer pairs (m, n) satisfy the statements $0 < m + n < 50$ and $\dfrac{m}{n} = 8$?

(A) 5
(B) 6
(C) 7
(D) 8
(E) more than 8

6. If $y\%$ of 50 is 32, then what is 200% of y?

(A) 16
(B) 32
(C) 64
(D) 128
(E) 256

7. For $x > 0$, the function $g(x)$ is defined by the equation $g(x) = x + x^{1/2}$. What is the value of $g(16)$?

(A) 16
(B) 20
(C) 24
(D) 64
(E) 272

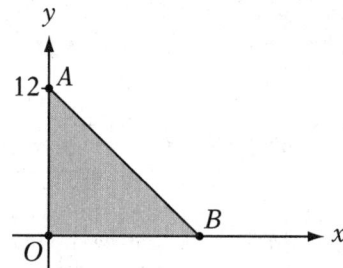

Note: Figure not drawn to scale.

8. In the figure above, if the slope of $\overline{AB}$ is $-\frac{3}{4}$, what is the area of $\triangle ABO$?

(A) 54
(B) 72
(C) 96
(D) 108
(E) 192

$$-1, 1, 2, -1, 1, 2, -1, 1, 2, \ldots$$

9. The sequence above continues according to the pattern shown. What is the sum of the first 25 terms of this sequence?

(A) 15
(B) 16
(C) 18
(D) 19
(E) 21

10. A jar contains only white and blue marbles of identical size and weight. The ratio of the number of white marbles to the number of blue marbles is 4 to b. If the probability of choosing a white marble from the jar at random is $\frac{1}{4}$, then what is the value of b?

(A) 1
(B) 2
(C) 6
(D) 12
(E) 16

GO ON TO THE NEXT PAGE

7   7   7   7   7   7

---

11. The area of a right triangle is 10 square centimeters. If the length of each leg, in centimeters, is a positive integer, then what is the *least* possible length, in centimeters, of the hypotenuse?

(A) $\sqrt{29}$

(B) $\sqrt{41}$

(C) $\sqrt{101}$

(D) $\sqrt{104}$

(E) $\sqrt{401}$

---

12. If y is a number less than 0 but greater than -1, which of the following expressions has the greatest value?

(A) $100y$

(B) y^2

(C) y^3

(D) y^4

(E) y^5

---

13.   If at least one wuzzle is grumpy, then some fuzzles are lumpy.

If the statement above is true, then which of the following must also be true?

(A) If all wuzzles are grumpy, then all fuzzles are lumpy.

(B) If no wuzzle is grumpy, then all fuzzles are lumpy.

(C) If all fuzzles are lumpy, then all wuzzles are grumpy.

(D) If no wuzzle is grumpy, then no fuzzle is lumpy.

(E) If no fuzzle is lumpy, then no wuzzle is grumpy.

---

14. Six buses are to carry 200 students on a field trip. If each bus must have no more than 40 students and no fewer than 30 students, then what is the greatest number of buses that can have 40 students?

(A) 6

(B) 5

(C) 4

(D) 3

(E) 2

---

15. The volume of right cylinder A is twice the volume of right cylinder B. If the height of cylinder B is twice the height of cylinder A, then what is the ratio of the radius of cylinder A to the radius of cylinder B?

(A) 1 to 2

(B) 1 to 1

(C) $\sqrt{2}$ to 1

(D) 2 to 1

(E) 4 to 1

---

16. In a garden that is divided into x rows of x squares each, w of the squares lie along the boundary of the garden. Which of the following is a possible value for w?

(A) 29

(B) 34

(C) 40

(D) 46

(E) 55

STOP

If you finish before time is called, you may check your work on this section only. Do not turn to any other section of the test.

8   8   8   8   8   8

SECTION 8
Time—20 minutes
19 questions

Turn to Section 8 of your answer sheet to answer the questions in this section.

Directions: For each question in this section, select the best answer from among the choices given and fill in the corresponding circle on the answer sheet.

Each sentence below has one or two blanks, each blank indicating that something has been omitted. Beneath the sentence are five words or sets of words labeled A through E. Choose the word or set of words that, when inserted in the sentence, <u>best</u> fits the meaning of the sentence as a whole.

EXAMPLE:

Rather than accepting the theory unquestioningly, Deborah regarded it with ......

(A) mirth
(B) sadness
(C) responsibility
(D) ignorance
(E) skepticism

Ⓐ Ⓑ Ⓒ Ⓓ ●

1. The evidence for ESP is ------- at best, so very few reputable scientists are willing to even ------- that the phenomenon exists.

   (A) meager . . regret
   (B) unconvincing . . suggest
   (C) plentiful . . admit
   (D) paltry . . deny
   (E) strong . . assume

2. The concept that the Earth is round was once ------- theory, but is now accepted as an inarguable truth.

   (A) an incontrovertible
   (B) a mellifluous
   (C) an admirable
   (D) a dubious
   (E) an accurate

3. The controversy within the party produced a ------- that broke it into several factions even before the matter could be fully discussed among the members.

   (A) unanimity
   (B) schism
   (C) caucus
   (D) commemoration
   (E) prognostication

4. Horace Mann, widely acknowledged as the father of American public schooling, ------- the Massachusetts legislature to institute a system for ------- universal access to education.

   (A) petitioned . . restricting
   (B) established . . denying
   (C) persuaded . . ensuring
   (D) tolerated . . requiring
   (E) discouraged . . vouchsafing

GO ON TO THE NEXT PAGE ⟹

8   8   8   8   8   8

5. The light from most stars takes millions of years to reach us, so not only is the present existence of these stars -------, but so are the very concepts of "the present" and "existence."

   (A) debatable
   (B) methodical
   (C) indecorous
   (D) imperious
   (E) profuse

6. Although many parents prefer to be ------- when their children broach sensitive personal subjects, others resort instead to ------- so as to make any potentially offensive matters seem less objectionable.

   (A) honest . . anachronism
   (B) intolerant . . laudation
   (C) clandestine . . obligation
   (D) candid . . euphemism
   (E) forthright . . coercion

The passages below are followed by questions based on their content; questions following a pair of related passages may also be based on the relationship between the paired passages. Answer the questions on the basis of what is <u>stated</u> or <u>implied</u> in the passage and in any introductory material that may be provided.

Questions 7–19 are based on the following passages.

The following two passages concern the use of "reinforcers," which are rewards or punishments used to encourage desired behaviors, and "contingencies," which are the arrangements of those reinforcers to shape behavior.

PASSAGE 1

"Avoid compulsion," said Plato in *The Republic*, "and let your children's lessons take the form
Line of play." Horace, among others, recommended rewarding a child with cakes. Eras-
5   mus tells of an English gentleman who tried to teach his son Greek and Latin without punishment. He taught the boy to use a bow and arrow and set up targets in the shape of Greek and Latin letters, rewarding each hit with a
10 cherry. He also fed the boy letters cut from

delicious biscuits. Privileges and favors are often suggested, and the teacher may be personally reinforcing as friend or entertainer. In industrial education students are paid for learning.
15 Certain explicit contrived reinforcers, such as marks, grades, and diplomas, are characteristic of education as an institution. (These suggest progress, but like progress they must be made reinforcing for other reasons.) Prizes
20 are intrinsically reinforcing. Honors and medals derive their power from prestige or esteem. This varies between cultures and epochs. In 1876 Oscar Wilde, then 22 years old and halfway toward his B.A. at Oxford, got
25 a "first in Mods." He wrote to a friend: ". . . I did not know what I had got till the next morning at 12 o'clock, breakfasting at the Mitre, I read it in the *Times*. Altogether I swaggered horribly but am really pleased with
30 myself. My poor mother is in great delight, and I was overwhelmed with telegrams on Thursday from everyone I knew." The contemporary student graduating *summa cum laude* is less widely acclaimed.
35   Although free of some of the by-products of aversive control, positive reinforcers of this sort are not without their problems. Many are effective only in certain states of deprivation which are not always easily arranged. Making
40 a student hungry in order to reinforce him with food would raise personal issues which are not entirely avoided with other kinds of reinforcers. We cannot all get prizes, and if some students get high grades, others must
45 get low.
       But the main problem again is the contingencies. Much of what the child is to do in school does not have the form of play, with its naturally reinforcing consequences, nor is
50 there any natural connection with food or a passing grade or a medal. Such contingencies must be arranged by the teacher, and the arrangement is often defective. The boy mentioned by Erasmus may have salivated slightly

First passage: B. F. Skinner, *The Technology of Teaching*,
   © 1968 Prentice-Hall.
Second passage: © 2004 Christopher Black. All rights reserved.
   Reprinted by permission of the author.

GO ON TO THE NEXT PAGE ⇒

55 upon seeing a Greek or Latin text, and he was
probably a better archer, but his knowledge of
Greek and Latin could not have been appre-
ciably improved. Grades are almost always
given long after the student has stopped be-
60 having as a student. We must know that such
contingencies are weak because we would
never use them to shape skilled behavior. In
industrial education pay is usually by the
hour—in other words, contingent mainly on
65 being present. Scholarships are contingent on
a general level of performance. All these contingencies could no doubt be improved, but
there is probably good reason why they remain defective.

PASSAGE 2

70   Even if they don't study it as a philosophical matter, all teachers must at some point
confront the issue of whether, when, and how
to punish or reward student behavior. Unless
a teacher is blessed with a class full of highly
75 motivated adult-pleasers, it is nearly impossible to avoid the need to nudge students in one
direction or another. Simple suggestion works
occasionally, but not frequently enough. Reasoning sometimes works, too, but explaining
80 the logical nuances of behavioral standards is
often time-consuming and too often falls on
deaf ears. So the practical question becomes:
the carrot or the stick?
         Most educators and psychologists agree
85 that reward is always better than punishment,
but a small yet vocal group of psychologists
have maintained since the 1960s that reward
is often just as harmful as punishment, if not
more so. Their arguments are subtle but very
90 persuasive. Educators like Alfie Kohn and psychologists like Edward Deci claim that careful
study has shown that the introduction of a reward system, like gold stars on an attendance
sheet or extra recess time for good behavior,
95 changes the nature of the desired behavior
completely, and not for the better. For instance, Deci conducted a study in which people were given a puzzle to solve. Some were
given money as a "reward" for solving the
100 puzzle and others were simply asked to solve
the puzzle. Afterwards, both groups were left
alone but watched carefully. Those who had
been paid stopped playing, but those who had

not been paid continued. Deci concluded that
105 the subjects who were paid probably construed the task as being manipulative: the experimenter was trying to get them to do
something through bribery. The unpaid subjects, however, were more likely to see the
110 task as fun and worth doing for its own sake.
         This study and many like it have profound
implications for the classroom. Several experiments have demonstrated that "pay-to-read"
programs, where students are given money or
115 certificates to read books, have surprisingly
negative effects on literacy. Such programs
usually get kids to "read" a lot more books,
but their reading skills and, far more importantly, their love of reading decline. Such pro-
120 grams, research suggests, turn reading into a
performance rather than a fulfilling personal
experience. They encourage students to read
books only superficially and only to get the
reward. What is worse, like Deci's puzzle-
125 solvers, the students don't want to continue
reading after the payments stop. Books have
become only enrichment for the pocket, not
enrichment for the mind.
         Of course, the human mind is an enor-
130 mously complex machine, and it would be a
mistake to use these few experiments to generalize that all rewards are bad. Certainly,
honest and mindful praise from a respected
teacher can do a great deal to encourage not
135 only good behavior but rigorous intellectual
curiosity. Parents and teachers, however, need
to be very aware of children's need to feel in
control of themselves.

7. It can be inferred that the "English gentleman"
(line 5) believed that good teaching utilized

(A) punishment
(B) well-written books
(C) reward
(D) humor
(E) careful grading

GO ON TO THE NEXT PAGE ▶

8. The parenthetical remark in lines 17–19 is intended to caution educators against

   (A) failing to make grades and diplomas meaningful to students
   (B) punishing students unnecessarily
   (C) employing dull lessons
   (D) emphasizing entertainment over rigor
   (E) using rewards as reinforcers

9. Passage 1 indicates that "cultures and epochs" (lines 22–23) vary in the ways that

   (A) universities choose from among their applicants
   (B) academic awards are effective as motivators
   (C) universities teach literature
   (D) students are paid money for learning
   (E) the media portray educational crises

10. The Wilde story in lines 23–32, "In 1876 . . . everyone I knew,'" is intended to illustrate

   (A) how the modern cultural perception of academic honors differs from that of a previous era
   (B) a particularly effective teaching strategy
   (C) how a famous author used rewards to teach his students
   (D) the dangerous effects of using academic rewards
   (E) the point that Plato makes in the first sentence

11. Passage 1 mentions which of the following as "problems" (line 37) inherent in the use of positive reinforcers in education?

   I. difficulties in scheduling the reinforcers
   II. limitations in the supply of reinforcers
   III. the fact that rewards encourage only superficial learning

   (A) I only
   (B) II only
   (C) I and II only
   (D) I and III only
   (E) I, II, and III

12. In the final paragraph of Passage 1, the author suggests that grades are problematic as reinforcers because they

   (A) cannot be given to every student
   (B) do not provide sensual gratification, as food does
   (C) are not publicized enough
   (D) are not given immediately after the desired behavior is exhibited
   (E) are not as useful to the student as money

13. The sentence that begins on line 78, "Reasoning sometimes works . . . on deaf ears," is intended to describe the interaction between

   (A) those who promote the use of punishments and those who oppose it
   (B) educators and philosophers
   (C) parents and teachers
   (D) teachers and administrators
   (E) teachers and students

14. In Passage 2, Alfie Kohn and Edward Deci (lines 90–91) are mentioned as examples of

   (A) teachers who use rewards as reinforcers
   (B) experts who question the effectiveness of rewards as reinforcers
   (C) scientists on opposite sides of a debate
   (D) educators who prefer negative reinforcers to positive reinforcers
   (E) educators who advocate a careful schedule of contingencies for students

GO ON TO THE NEXT PAGE

15. In saying that "the introduction of a reward system . . . changes the nature of the desired behavior" (lines 92–95), the author of Passage 2 indicates that

(A) many people object to the use of punishments in school
(B) teachers find it difficult to find the right kinds of rewards for student performance
(C) experts disagree about the effects of rewards on human behavior
(D) such systems tend to decrease student interest in the activity for its own sake
(E) not enough study has been done on the effectiveness of rewards in education

16. Deci's conclusion about the experiment described in Passage 2 (lines 96–110) assumes that the subjects in the study

(A) are well educated
(B) are highly proficient at solving puzzles
(C) have not participated in reward systems before
(D) can make inferences about the motives of the experimenter
(E) have some teaching experience

17. The author of Passage 2 mentions that "the human mind is an enormously complex machine" (lines 129–130) in order to suggest that

(A) a simplistic theory about the effectiveness of rewards is unwise
(B) people cannot be easily fooled
(C) many learning disabilities require special attention
(D) teachers often find it hard to teach certain subjects
(E) Deci's experiment was poorly constructed

18. The description of the "problems" (line 37) with positive reinforcers in Passage 1 would most likely be regarded by Edward Deci as

(A) thorough and fair
(B) presumptuous and incomplete
(C) unfair to educators
(D) erroneous in concluding that the methods of the "gentleman" were ineffective
(E) likely correct, but worthy of further study

19. Which of the following assumptions is shared by the authors of both passages?

(A) Rewards are ineffective as reinforcers of behavior.
(B) Honors and grades are necessary elements of institutional education.
(C) Good teaching is always focused on play.
(D) Negative feedback is not an effective teaching tool.
(E) If prizes are to be used in a classroom, there must be enough for all students.

STOP

If you finish before time is called, you may check your work on this section only. Do not turn to any other section of the test.

9   9   9   9   9   9

SECTION 9
Time—10 minutes
14 questions

Turn to Section 9 of your answer sheet to answer the questions in this section.

Directions: For each question in this section, select the best answer from among the choices given and fill in the corresponding circle on the answer sheet.

The following sentences test correctness and effectiveness of expression. Part of each sentence or the entire sentence is underlined; beneath each sentence are five ways of phrasing the underlined material. Choice A repeats the original phrasing; the other four choices are different. If you think the original phrasing produces a better sentence than any of the alternatives, select choice A; if not, select one of the other choices.

In making your selection, follow the requirements of standard written English; that is, pay attention to grammar, choice of words, sentence construction, and punctuation. Your selection should result in the most effective sentence—clear and precise, without awkwardness or ambiguity.

EXAMPLE:

The children <u>couldn't hardly believe their eyes</u>.

(A) couldn't hardly believe their eyes
(B) could hardly believe their eyes
(C) would not hardly believe their eyes
(D) couldn't nearly believe their eyes
(E) couldn't hardly believe his or her eyes

Ⓐ ● Ⓒ Ⓓ Ⓔ

---

1. <u>Choreographer Alvin Ailey's works, whose style is rooted in the techniques of modern dance, jazz dance and ballet, draw upon African American themes.</u>

   (A) Choreographer Alvin Ailey's works, whose style is rooted in the techniques of modern dance, jazz dance and ballet, draw upon African American themes.
   (B) Alvin Ailey has a style of a choreographer that is rooted in the techniques of modern dance, jazz dance and ballet of which also draws upon African American themes.
   (C) The works of choreographer Alvin Ailey, which draw upon African American themes, have a style that is rooted in the techniques of modern dance, jazz dance, and ballet.
   (D) Choreographer Alvin Ailey's works, which have a style that is rooted in the techniques of modern dance, jazz dance, and ballet, drawing upon African American themes.
   (E) Alvin Ailey's style, a choreographer, is rooted in the techniques of modern dance and jazz dance and ballet which also draws upon African American themes.

GO ON TO THE NEXT PAGE ⟶

9   9   9   9   9   9

2. The mountain climbers getting this far, they did not want to return without having reached the peak.

(A) The mountain climbers getting this far, they
(B) Having gotten this far, the mountain climbers
(C) To have gotten this far, the mountain climbers
(D) The mountain climbers having gotten so far that they
(E) Mountain climbers getting this far

3. Although usually even-tempered, Rachel's irritation with her supervisor caused her to become uncharacteristically cantankerous.

(A) Rachel's irritation with her supervisor caused her to become
(B) Rachel being irritated by her supervisor caused her to become
(C) Rachel was irritated by her supervisor, and so became
(D) her supervisor caused Rachel through irritation to become
(E) Rachel, due to her supervisor's irritation, caused her to become

4. Alberta had a high opinion of her own abilities, and so believed that her salary should be higher than the other agents in her firm.

(A) should be higher than
(B) should be higher than those of
(C) being higher than
(D) would have been highest of
(E) should have to be highest of

5. The police chief was hoping that by assigning an extra officer to the patrol he would decrease the amount of elicit behavior in the neighborhood.

(A) would decrease the amount of elicit
(B) would be able to decrease the elicit
(C) would decrease the amount of illicit
(D) might be able to lessen that of the illicit
(E) decreases the amount of illicit

6. Watching from the balcony, the paraders marched triumphantly through the streets below us.

(A) Watching from the balcony
(B) While watching from the balcony
(C) As we had been watching from the balcony
(D) As we watched from the balcony
(E) From the balcony, while watching

7. By the time we arrived at the campsite where the troop would be staying, the counselors set up all the tents.

(A) the counselors set up all the tents
(B) setting up all the tents were the counselors
(C) set up by the counselors are the tents
(D) the tents are set up by the counselors
(E) the counselors had set up all the tents

8. For the foreseeable future, neither Matt nor David are permitted to use the pool without first getting permission from a parent.

(A) neither Matt nor David are permitted to use the pool without
(B) Matt nor David can be permitted to use the pool without
(C) neither Matt nor David is permitted to use the pool without
(D) neither Matt or David is permitted for using the pool without
(E) neither Matt nor David is permitted to use the pool by

GO ON TO THE NEXT PAGE ⟶

9   9   9   9   9   9   9

9. An outstanding tennis player, Erica was con-
    cerned not only with working her way to the top
    of the national rankings, but <u>also wanted to
    compete with class and dignity</u>.

    (A) also wanted to compete with class and
         dignity
    (B) also with competing with class and
         dignity
    (C) also with wanting to have competed with
         class and dignity
    (D) she also wanted to compete with class
         and dignity
    (E) she was also wanting to compete with
         class and dignity

10. Roberto volunteered to be an usher, not wanting
    to be the one <u>that had to clean up the petals after
    the ceremony</u>.

    (A) that had to clean up the petals after the
         ceremony
    (B) which had to clean up the petals after the
         ceremony
    (C) who had to clean up the petals after the
         ceremony
    (D) that was cleaning the petals up after the
         ceremony
    (E) who was to be cleaning the petals after
         the ceremony

11. Rebecca liked to read <u>books, of which she found
    autobiographies being the most interesting</u>.

    (A) books, of which she found autobiogra-
         phies being the most interesting
    (B) books, the most fascinating of which to
         her she found the autobiographies
    (C) books, autobiographies being the most
         interesting she found
    (D) books; she found autobiographies to be
         the most interesting
    (E) books, to which autobiographies were
         the most interesting

12. Forced to live apart from his family and to move
    from place to place to avoid detection by the
    government's ubiquitous informers, <u>St. Pierre
    adopting a number of disguises</u>.

    (A) St. Pierre adopting a number of disguises
    (B) St. Pierre having adopted a number of
         disguises
    (C) had adopted for St. Pierre a number of
         disguises
    (D) a number of disguises by St. Pierre had
         adopted
    (E) St. Pierre had to adopt a number of
         disguises

13. The Santa Catalina <u>Mountains, forming twelve
    million years ago during a period when the West-
    ern North American Continent was stretching</u>,
    cracking into blocks bordered by steep faults.

    (A) Mountains, forming twelve million years
         ago during a period when the Western
         North American Continent was stretching
    (B) Mountains were formed twelve million
         years ago during a period when the
         Western North American Continent was
         being stretched
    (C) Mountains, having been formed twelve
         million years ago during a period when
         the Western North American Continent
         was stretching
    (D) Mountains was formed twelve million years
         ago during a period when the Western North
         American Continent was being stretched
    (E) Mountains had been formed during a
         period twelve million years ago when the
         Western North American Continent was
         stretching

14. The most challenging aspect of the project is <u>we
    have to coordinate our work carefully</u>.

    (A) we have to coordinate our work carefully
    (B) we must coordinate our work carefully
    (C) our coordination of our work carefully
    (D) coordinating our work carefully
    (E) in careful coordination of our work

STOP

*If you finish before time is called, you may
check your work on this section only. Do not
turn to any other section of the test.*

ANSWER KEY

Critical Reading

Section 2

	COR. ANS.	DIFF. LEV.		COR. ANS.	DIFF. LEV.
1.	A	1	13.	A	4
2.	C	2	14.	C	3
3.	D	3	15.	C	4
4.	A	4	16.	D	4
5.	E	4	17.	E	4
6.	C	3	18.	C	3
7.	A	4	19.	B	3
8.	B	3	20.	C	4
9.	E	3	21.	D	4
10.	E	2	22.	D	3
11.	A	3	23.	E	4
12.	B	4	24.	A	4

Number correct

Number incorrect

Section 5

	COR. ANS.	DIFF. LEV.		COR. ANS.	DIFF. LEV.
1.	C	2	13.	E	3
2.	E	3	14.	C	4
3.	D	3	15.	D	3
4.	A	4	16.	B	4
5.	E	4	17.	A	3
6.	D	3	18.	E	4
7.	B	4	19.	D	4
8.	A	3	20.	B	1
9.	E	4	21.	C	3
10.	D	4	22.	C	5
11.	D	5	23.	E	5
12.	E	4	24.	A	4

Number correct

Number incorrect

Section 8

	COR. ANS.	DIFF. LEV.		COR. ANS.	DIFF. LEV.
1.	B	2	11.	C	4
2.	D	3	12.	D	2
3.	B	2	13.	E	2
4.	C	3	14.	B	3
5.	A	4	15.	D	4
6.	D	5	16.	D	4
7.	C	1	17.	A	3
8.	A	3	18.	B	4
9.	B	4	19.	D	3
10.	A	3			

Number correct

Number incorrect

Math

Section 3

	COR. ANS.	DIFF. LEV.		COR. ANS.	DIFF. LEV.
1.	E	1	11.	D	3
2.	A	2	12.	B	3
3.	C	2	13.	A	3
4.	C	2	14.	D	3
5.	D	2	15.	A	4
6.	A	3	16.	B	3
7.	D	3	17.	D	4
8.	A	3	18.	C	4
9.	C	3	19.	A	4
10.	B	2	20.	A	5

Number correct

Number incorrect

Section 4

Multiple-Choice Questions

	COR. ANS.	DIFF. LEV.
1.	E	1
2.	C	3
3.	E	2
4.	A	3
5.	A	3
6.	D	3
7.	B	4
8.	C	4

Number correct

Number incorrect

Student-produced Response questions

	COR. ANS.	DIFF. LEV.
9.	16	1
10.	36	2
11.	5	2
12.	12	3
13.	15	3
14.	8 or 12	4
15.	25	4
16.	24	3
17.	52	4
18.	225	5

Number correct (9–18)

Section 7

	COR. ANS.	DIFF. LEV.		COR. ANS.	DIFF. LEV.
1.	B	2	9.	A	4
2.	C	2	10.	D	4
3.	A	3	11.	B	3
4.	B	3	12.	B	4
5.	A	3	13.	E	4
6.	D	3	14.	E	4
7.	B	4	15.	D	5
8.	C	3	16.	C	5

Number correct

Number incorrect

Writing

Section 6

	COR. ANS.	DIFF. LEV.		COR. ANS.	DIFF. LEV.		COR. ANS.	DIFF. LEV.		COR. ANS.	DIFF. LEV.
1.	D	1	11.	A	5	21.	E	4	31.	A	4
2.	A	1	12.	A	1	22.	D	3	32.	B	3
3.	B	2	13.	B	2	23.	A	3	33.	C	3
4.	C	2	14.	C	3	24.	E	4	34.	E	3
5.	A	2	15.	B	2	25.	C	4	35.	C	3
6.	B	3	16.	D	3	26.	E	3			
7.	C	3	17.	B	3	27.	B	3			
8.	E	3	18.	A	2	28.	B	3			
9.	C	4	19.	B	3	29.	C	5			
10.	D	4	20.	C	3	30.	D	3			

Number correct

Number incorrect

Section 9

	COR. ANS.	DIFF. LEV.		COR. ANS.	DIFF. LEV.
1.	C	2	11.	D	3
2.	B	2	12.	E	3
3.	C	2	13.	B	4
4.	B	4	14.	D	4
5.	C	4			
6.	D	3			
7.	E	3			
8.	C	4			
9.	B	3			
10.	C	3			

Number correct

Number incorrect

NOTE: Difficulty levels are estimates of question difficulty that range from 1 (easiest) to 5 (hardest).

SCORE CONVERSION TABLE

How to score your test

Use the answer key on the previous page to determine your raw score on each section. **Your raw score on each section except Section 4 is simply the number of correct answers minus ¼ of the number of wrong answers. On Section 4, your raw score is the sum of the number of correct answers for questions 1–18 minus ¼ of the number of wrong answers for questions 1–8.** Next, add the raw scores from Sections 2, 5, and 8 to get your Critical Reading raw score, add the raw scores from Sections 3, 4, and 7 to get your Math raw score, and add the raw scores from Sections 6 and 9 to get your Writing raw score. Write the three raw scores here:

Raw Critical Reading score: _____ Raw Math score: _____ Raw Writing score: _____

Use the table below to convert these to scaled scores.

Scaled scores: Critical Reading: _____ Math: _____ Writing: _____

Raw Score	Critical Reading Scaled Score	Math Scaled Score	Writing Scaled Score	Raw Score	Critical Reading Scaled Score	Math Scaled Score	Writing Scaled Score
67	800			32	520	570	610
66	800			31	510	560	600
65	790			30	510	550	580
64	780			29	500	540	570
63	770			28	490	530	560
62	750			27	490	520	550
61	740			26	480	510	540
60	730			25	480	500	530
59	720			24	470	490	520
58	700			23	460	480	510
57	690			22	460	480	500
56	680			21	450	470	490
55	670			20	440	460	480
54	660	800		19	440	450	470
53	650	800		18	430	450	460
52	650	780		17	420	440	450
51	640	760		16	420	430	440
50	630	740		15	410	420	440
49	620	730	800	14	400	410	430
48	620	710	800	13	400	410	420
47	610	710	800	12	390	400	410
46	600	700	790	11	380	390	400
45	600	690	780	10	370	380	390
44	590	680	760	9	360	370	380
43	590	670	740	8	350	360	380
42	580	660	730	7	340	350	370
41	570	650	710	6	330	340	360
40	570	640	700	5	320	330	350
39	560	630	690	4	310	320	340
38	550	620	670	3	300	310	320
37	550	620	660	2	280	290	310
36	540	610	650	1	270	280	300
35	540	600	640	0	250	260	280
34	530	590	630	−1	230	240	270
33	520	580	620	−2 or less	210	220	250

SCORE CONVERSION TABLE FOR WRITING COMPOSITE
[ESSAY + MULTIPLE CHOICE]

Calculate your Writing raw score as you did on the previous page and grade your essay from a 1 to a 6 according to the standards that follow in the detailed answer key.

Essay score: _____   Raw Writing score: _____

Use the table below to convert these to scaled scores.

Scaled score: Writing: _____

Raw Score	Essay Score 0	Essay Score 1	Essay Score 2	Essay Score 3	Essay Score 4	Essay Score 5	Essay Score 6
−2 or less	200	230	250	280	310	340	370
−1	210	240	260	290	320	360	380
0	230	260	280	300	340	370	400
1	240	270	290	320	350	380	410
2	250	280	300	330	360	390	420
3	260	290	310	340	370	400	430
4	270	300	320	350	380	410	440
5	280	310	330	360	390	420	450
6	290	320	340	360	400	430	460
7	290	330	340	370	410	440	470
8	300	330	350	380	410	450	470
9	310	340	360	390	420	450	480
10	320	350	370	390	430	460	490
11	320	360	370	400	440	470	500
12	330	360	380	410	440	470	500
13	340	370	390	420	450	480	510
14	350	380	390	420	460	490	520
15	350	380	400	430	460	500	530
16	360	390	410	440	470	500	530
17	370	400	420	440	480	510	540
18	380	410	420	450	490	520	550
19	380	410	430	460	490	530	560
20	390	420	440	470	500	530	560
21	400	430	450	480	510	540	570
22	410	440	460	480	520	550	580
23	420	450	470	490	530	560	590
24	420	460	470	500	540	570	600
25	430	460	480	510	540	580	610
26	440	470	490	520	550	590	610
27	450	480	500	530	560	590	620
28	460	490	510	540	570	600	630
29	470	500	520	550	580	610	640
30	480	510	530	560	590	620	650
31	490	520	540	560	600	630	660
32	500	530	550	570	610	640	670
33	510	540	550	580	620	650	680
34	510	550	560	590	630	660	690
35	520	560	570	600	640	670	700
36	530	560	580	610	650	680	710
37	540	570	590	620	660	690	720
38	550	580	600	630	670	700	730
39	560	600	610	640	680	710	740
40	580	610	620	650	690	720	750
41	590	620	640	660	700	730	760
42	600	630	650	680	710	740	770
43	610	640	660	690	720	750	780
44	620	660	670	700	740	770	800
45	640	670	690	720	750	780	800
46	650	690	700	730	770	800	800
47	670	700	720	750	780	800	800
48	680	720	730	760	800	800	800
49	680	720	730	760	800	800	800

College Hill™ SAT Study Plan

See page 3A–5A for instructions.

Test # _____   RAW SCORES: CR _____   M _____   W _____   Essay _____

SCALED SCORES: CR _____   M _____   W _____   Essay _____

---

1. What were your test conditions?

2. What was your pre-test routine?

Goal	Attack	Get	CR pts	M pts	W pts
500	75%	50%	30	25	25
550	80%	60%	37	32	32
600	85%	67%	45	38	38
650	90%	80%	52	44	42
700	100%	90%	59	49	45
750	100%	95%	62	52	47
800	100%	100%	66	54	49

---

3. Did you attack all of the questions you needed to attack? (See the table above.)

4. Did you rush to complete any section?

5. How many more raw points do you need to make your score goal?   CR _____   M _____   W _____

6. Did you make educated guesses on any questions? If so, how many points did you pick up on these questions?

7. STUDY PLAN: Use the detailed answer key after the test to review the answers to the questions you missed. Below, list the lessons linked to the questions you missed, and list the tough words you missed from the test.

Lessons to Review   **Words to Review**

_____   _____
_____   _____
_____   _____
_____   _____
_____   _____
_____   _____
_____   _____
_____   _____

Detailed Answer Key

Section 1

Consider carefully the issue discussed in the following passage, then write an essay that answers the question posed in the assignment.

> The best leaders are not those who seek power or have great political skill. Great leaders—and these are exceptionally rare, especially today—represent the best selves of the people they represent.

Assignment: **What are the most important qualities of a leader?** Write an essay in which you answer this question and discuss your point of view on this issue. Support your position logically with examples from literature, the arts, history, politics, science and technology, current events, or your experience or observation.

The following essay received 6 points out of a possible 6. This means that, according to the graders, it

- develops an insightful point of view on the topic
- demonstrates exemplary critical thinking
- uses effective examples, reasons, and other evidence to support its thesis
- is consistently focused, coherent, and well organized
- demonstrates skillful and effective use of language and sentence structure
- is largely (but not necessarily completely) free of grammatical and usage errors

---

There is no more important decision that a citizen can make than one's choice of a leader. I am inclined to agree with Thomas Hobbes, who believed that humans are hardly better than other mammals without a social contract that binds us to work together as a society. Artists could not survive in a society that does not provide a means of trading art for food. Great teachers cannot survive in a society without a means of trading wisdom for shelter. This requires a social order, a division of labor, and a group we call leaders. Yet we know that power corrupts, and absolute power corrupts absolutely. So how do we maintain a just society when we must bestow corrupting powers upon members of that society?

Those who seek power are too often not our best leaders, but rather our best politicians. George Bush, John F. Kennedy and Ronald Reagan came to power not so much because of their visionary leadership but because of their appeal to a television-viewing audience. The problems with democracy are well known. In order to become elected, most politicians must appeal to a broad range of citizens. To gain this appeal, they must pander to their constituents, and often take conflicting or equivocal stances on issues. Of course, the politicians claim that they are taking "forceful

stances" to "bring the people together." But it is far more likely that they are simply doing their best to make everyone happy without putting their feet in their mouths.

So why is democracy the best way of electing a leader? Because the alternatives are much worse. To gain power, one must either use force or pander to those who do. Which is a better alternative? A country is weak if its people do not support it, and, at the very least, a democracy can claim a good degree of public support. Even more importantly, only a democracy allows for the possibility of finding a reluctant leader with genuine leadership skills. It doesn't happen often enough, but when it does, it is breathtaking. Witness the phenomenon of Howard Dean's campaign for the 2004 Democratic nomination for president, or Ross Perot's run in 1992. Neither was ultimately successful, but both demonstrated the potential of motivated citizens to change their country.

Without democracy, there is no hope for an ordinary citizen to change his or her country. What makes America great is not that its policies are always correct. Indeed, they are often deeply flawed. What makes America great is that it is run by those who are not even seeking power: the citizens.

The following essay received 4 points out of a possible 6, meaning that it demonstrates *adequate competence* in that it

- develops a point of view on the topic
- demonstrates some critical thinking, but perhaps not consistently
- uses some examples, reasons, and other evidence to support its thesis, but perhaps not adequately
- shows a general organization and focus, but shows occasional lapses in this regard
- demonstrates adequate but occasionally inconsistent facility with language
- contains occasional errors in grammar, usage, and mechanics

---

Someone once said that great men don't seek greatness but have it thrust upon them. I think this is true, because those who have really changed the world were not slick politicians but rather people who had such great leadership skill and charisma that others forced them into leadership roles. Good examples of this are Jesus, Mahatma Gandhi, Mother Theresa and George Washington.

After his great victories in the American Revolutionary War against Great Britain, George Washington wanted to retire to his farm in Virginia and live out the rest of his days as a humble farmer. He did not want to become the political leader of a brand new country. But the Continental Congress looked to him for leadership, and sought him out to be the first President of the United States. Washington saw that his country needed him and answered the call.

Similarly, Mahatma Gandhi did not seek personal power, but only justice for his people. His humility and selflessness are what made him one of the great leaders of the twentieth century, and a model for the cause of nonviolent activism.

It is unfortunate that today only millionaires with big political connections seem to have any chance at being elected to national office. Maybe they have a shot at a local race, but the congress and the presidency seem to be off limits. The answer is to get more involved in politics yourself, as a voter, and avoid voting for candidates just because they are popular but instead because they have good souls.

The following essay received 2 points out of a possible 6, meaning that it demonstrates *some incompetence* in that it

- has a seriously limited point of view
- demonstrates weak critical thinking
- uses inappropriate or insufficient examples, reasons, and other evidence to support its thesis
- is poorly focused and organized and has serious problems with coherence
- demonstrates frequent problems with language and sentence structure
- contains errors in grammar and usage that seriously obscure the author's meaning

---

I'm not sure how it can be that you can be the best person to be in power if you don't want to be. In this country, at least, running for president or something like that takes a lot of effort, and I think you have to be a really hard worker in order to become president or senator.

An example of somebody who is a hard worker who got into office is former president Bill Clinton. Although many people think he had indiscretions in office, he came from a very poor family where he was only raised by his mother because his father left the family when he was young. He worked really hard and became a Rhodes scholar and was elected as governor at a very young age. He knew even when he was a very young kid that he wanted to become a great leader like John F. Kennedy.

Clinton was a good leader because he understood where a lot of people were coming from. He wasn't just a rich guy who got into office because he had rich relatives who got him there. I don't think you can say that the best leaders are the ones who don't want to be in office. If you didn't want to be in office, then you shouldn't run.

Section 2

1. A Alisha was holding a *grudge,* which is a feeling of resentment.
resentment = ill will; *fortitude* = strength of mind to endure; *sarcasm* = wit used to ridicule; *elation* = extreme joy

2. C There were people who expected the governor to be *inarticulate* (unable to speak clearly), so they would be surprised if he were *articulate. intolerance* = inability to put up with something; *fatigue* = tiredness; *eloquence* = persuasiveness in speech; *endurance* = ability to last, often through hard times

3. D The *language of commoners* would be logically described as *common.* But the novelists preferred another kind of *parlance* (speech): that of the *upper* classes. A word such as *elegant* would work nicely. *elite* = superior; *sympathetic* = compassionate; *colloquial* = characteristic of everyday language; *refined* = precise, elegant; *utilitarian* = practical, stressing utility

4. A The second half of this sentence presents a definition. The word in the blank should mean *"exploring the world." peripatetic* = walking from place to place; *conventional* = customary; *tolerant* = willing to put up with something; *coordinated* = well-matched; *remunerative* = profitable

5. E A position that requires public speaking would be *difficult* for a person who does not like to speak or is afraid of crowds. *vivacious* = full of life; *garrulous* = talkative; *amiable* = friendly; *reticent* = hesitant to share one's feelings or opinions with others

6. C The tickbird gets something from the hippopotamus, and the hippopotamus gets something from the tickbird; it's a *give-and-receive* relationship. *deteriorating* = diminishing in quality; *symbiotic* = of mutual benefit; *regressive* = going backwards; *vacillating* = going back and forth

7. A This sentence establishes a contrast between how *modern scientists* think and how *early philosophers* thought. The contrast shows that the early philosophers were not using experiments as much as their own minds to draw conclusions and that the modern scientists rely more on experimental data to draw their conclusions. *empirical* = relying on the observations made from experiments; *coercion* = pressure on someone to act; *deduction* = reaching a conclusion through the use of logic; *clerical* = relating to office work; *intuitive* = known innately

8. B The first blank should be a word like *merging* or *unification,* because many companies are under a *single owner.* This would be *troublesome* to those who value *independence. retraction* = taking something back; *differentiation* = finding a difference between two things; *consolidation* = combining of multiple things into one common entity; *collaboration* = working together on something; *dissemination* = the spread of something

9. E Passage 2 distinguishes between education and schooling. It states that the *main product of schooling is not education* (lines 15–16) and that the struggle that defines education *is denied by schooling* (lines 22–23). Passage 1 makes no such distinction, and speaks of education as if it is inseparable from the idea of schooling.

10. E The passage mentions that education would diminish social distinctions ("obliterate factitious distinctions in society" (lines 13–14)), improve living standards ("prevents being poor" (line 8)), provide the means to counteract greed ("resist the selfishness of other men" (lines 5–6)), and increase self-sufficiency ("gives each man the independence" (line 4)). It does not, however, mention anything about reducing crime.

11. A The passage suggests that education *is the great equalizer* and that *the spread of education will open a wider area over which the social feelings will expand.* It concludes by commenting that *if this education should be universal and complete* it would *obliterate factitious distinctions in society.*

12. B Passage 2 states that education, which is *the acquisition of competence, power, wisdom and discernment* (lines 19–20), is achieved only through the *struggle for sense in the world* (lines 21–22). Therefore, this struggle is empowering.

13. A "The Beginnings of the Scientific Method" is the best title, because this passage begins by discussing the scientists of the Renaissance and how they *brought about the most fundamental alterations in the world of thought . . . by devising a new method for discovering knowledge* (lines 1–5). This new method was the scientific method.

14. C Saying that *the early modern scientists laid greatest stress upon observation and the formation of temporary hypotheses* (lines 7–9) is like saying they *emphasized* observation and hypotheses.

15. C In lines 19–21 the passage suggests that earlier scientists were simply trying *to find the confirmation of Biblical statements about the firmament.*

16. D   Choice II is confirmed in lines 32–34: *The principle of the barometer was discovered by Galileo's **pupil*** (student) *Torricelli.* Choice III is confirmed in lines 41–42: *Galileo discovered the moons around Jupiter.*

17. E   The final paragraph states that Renaissance scientists believed *that everything consists of bodies in motion, that everything conforms to a mechanical model. The heavens above and the smallest particles below all exhibit the same laws of motion*—even, as it says in the next sentence, *human thought* (lines 67–71).

18. C   The final paragraph discusses how the scientific method changed the way science was done.

19. B   The passage mentions in lines 22–24 that many military leaders *cement their solidarity by reveling* (taking delight) *in their numerical disadvantage.* They considered it more honorable to fight with fewer men and beat a larger opponent.

20. C   Stating that *a well-known proverb* was ***trotted out** in many instances of the glorious, fighting few* (lines 25–27), in this context, is like saying that the proverb was *used for rhetorical effect* because it was used to persuade and inspire the troops.

21. D   When the prince says that *we be a small **body** when compared to the army of our enemies*, he is saying that they are a small army or group of men.

22. D   This sentence is discussing the tactical errors of the French in two different battles. The phrase *charging before they were ready* simply means *attacking before they were ready.*

23. E   All three of these facts are true and are mentioned in the passage.

24. A   The passage states in the final paragraph that *ten thousand more men might actually have hindered the English* (lines 59–60) and that *it seems that in fact . . . strength is not always proportional to size* (lines 62–64).

Section 3

1. E   Since *n* is equal to 3 times an even number, you can eliminate any answer choice that is not a multiple of 3 (A, C, and D). Answer choice (B): $15 = 3 \times 5$; 5 is an odd number, so this answer choice is out. Answer choice (E): $18 = 3 \times 6$; 6 is an even number.
(Chapter 9, Lesson 3: Numerical Reasoning Problems)

2. A   Set up a ratio: $\dfrac{50 \text{ chips}}{2 \text{ hours}} = \dfrac{x \text{ chips}}{7 \text{ hours}}$

Cross-multiply: $350 = 2x$
Divide by 2: $175 = x$
(Chapter 7, Lesson 4: Ratios and Proportions)

3. C   Angles that form a straight angle have a sum of 180°:

$$x + 2x = 180°$$
Combine like terms: $3x = 180°$
Divide by 3: $x = 60°$
(Chapter 10, Lesson 1: Lines and Angles)

4. C   Find the smallest number that is divisible by both 15 and 6 and see which answer choice works.
Multiples of 15: 15, **30**, 45, . . .
Multiples of 6:   6, 12, 18, 24, **30**, . . .
(Chapter 7, Lesson 7: Divisibility)

5. D   *n*% of 20 is 4

$$\frac{n}{100} \times 20 = 4$$
Simplify: $.20n = 4$
Divide by .20: $n = 20$
(Chapter 7, Lesson 5: Percents)

6. A $f(x) = 3x + n$
Plug in 2 for *x*: $f(2) = 3(2) + n = 0$
Simplify: $6 + n = 0$
Subtract 6: $n = -6$
Substitute for *n*: $f(x) = 3x - 6$
Plug in 0 for *x*: $f(0) = 3(0) - 6 = -6$
(Chapter 11, Lesson 2: Functions)

7. D   First find the area of the right triangle:

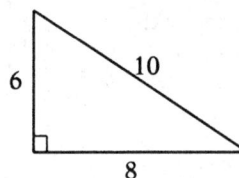

Area = ½(base)(height)
Area = ½(8)(6) = 24

Next, set up an equation for the area of a square.
                            Area = (side)²
Substitute 24 for area: $24 = (\text{side})^2$

Take the square root: $\sqrt{24} = \text{side}$

Simplify the radical: $2\sqrt{6} = \text{side}$

(Chapter 10, Lesson 5: Areas and Perimeters)

8. A   You are told that: $12v = 3w$
Divide by 3: $4v = w$
Multiply by 2: $8v = 2w$
The question asks for the value of: $2w - 8v$
Substitute for $2w$: $8v - 8v = 0$
Alternatively, you can try finding values for v and w that work, like 1 and 4, and plug them into $2w - 8v$ and into the choices and find the match.
(Chapter 8, Lesson 1: Solving Equations)

9. C $2|x| + 1 > 5$
Subtract 1: $2|x| > 4$
Divide by 2: $|x| > 2$
Interpret the absolute value: $x > 2$ OR $x < -2$
You are told that x is negative, so $x < -2$ is the answer.
(Chapter 8, Lesson 6: Inequalities, Absolute Values, and Plugging In)

10. B $-x^2 - 8x - 5$
Substitute -2 for x: $-(-2)^2 - 8(-2) - 5$
Square -2: $-(4) - 8(-2) - 5$
Simplify: $-4 + 16 - 5 = 7$
When evaluating $-x^2$, don't forget to square the value *before* taking its opposite!
(Chapter 8, Lesson 1: Solving Equations)

11. D $\dfrac{5}{m} \leq \dfrac{2}{3}$
Cross-multiply: $15 \leq 2m$
Divide by 2: $7.5 \leq m$
Since m is greater than *or equal to* 7.5, (D) is the answer.
(Chapter 8, Lesson 6: Inequalities, Absolute Values, and Plugging In)

12. B   First find the price after the 6% sales tax:
$60.00 × .06 = $3.60 tax
$60.00 + $3.60 = $63.60 price with tax
(A simpler way is just to multiply 60 by 1.06.)
Now find how much change Theo received:
$70.00 − $63.60 = $6.40 change
(Chapter 7, Lesson 5: Percents)

13. A   Write an equation for the first sentence.
$n - m = r$
Because none of the answer choices contain m, solve for m in terms of r and n: $n - m = r$
Add m: $n = r + m$
Subtract r: $n - r = m$
Now write an expression for what the question asks for:
$s + 2m$
Substitute for m: $s + 2(n - r)$
Distribute: $s + 2n - 2r$
Alternatively, you can substitute numbers for n, m, and r, making sure they "work," and get a numerical answer to the question.
(Chapter 8, Lesson 1: Solving Equations)

14. D   Two points on line l are $(0, 0)$ and $(10, y)$. Find the slope of the line:
$$m = \frac{y_2 - y_1}{x_2 - x_1} = \frac{y - 0}{10 - 0} = \frac{y}{10} = \frac{3}{5}$$
Cross-multiply: $5y = 30$
Divide by 5: $y = 6$
Since $y = 6$, the height of the triangle is 6. Find the area:
$A = \frac{1}{2}(\text{base})(\text{height})$
Substitute 48 for A: $48 = \frac{1}{2}(\text{base})(6)$
Simplify: $48 = 3(\text{base})$
Divide by 3: $16 = \text{base} = x$
Now find $x + y = 16 + 6 = 22$.
(Chapter 10, Lesson 4: Coordinate Geometry)

15. A   Ellen travels the first 15 miles at 30 miles per hour. Find out how much time that takes:
$$d = (rate)(time)$$
Plug in known values: $15 = 30t$
Divide by 30: $\frac{1}{2}$ hour $= t$
The rest of the trip, which is $(y - 15)$ miles long, she travels at an average speed of 40 miles per hour:
$$d = (rate)(time)$$
Plug in known values: $(y - 15) = 40t$
Divide by 40: $\dfrac{y - 15}{40} = t$
Add the two values together to find the total time:
$$\frac{1}{2} + \frac{y - 15}{40}$$
(Chapter 9, Lesson 4: Rate Problems)

16. B   Set up the relationship in equation form:
$$y = \frac{km}{n^2}$$
Plug in what you're given: $8 = \dfrac{k(16)}{(1)^2}$
Simplify: $8 = 16k$
Divide by 16: $\frac{1}{2} = k$
Write the new equation: $y = \dfrac{\frac{1}{2}(m)}{(n)^2}$
Plug in new values: $y = \dfrac{\frac{1}{2}(8)}{(4)^2} = \dfrac{4}{16} = \dfrac{1}{4}$
(Chapter 11, Lesson 4: Variation)

17. D

$$a + b = s$$
$$a - b = t$$

Add straight down: $2a = s + t$

Divide by 2: $a = \dfrac{s+t}{2}$

$$a + b = s$$
$$a - b = t$$

Subtract straight down: $2b = s - t$

Divide by 2: $b = \dfrac{s-t}{2}$

Find the product: $(a)(b) = \left(\dfrac{s+t}{2}\right)\left(\dfrac{s-t}{2}\right) = \left(\dfrac{s^2 - t^2}{4}\right)$

(Chapter 8, Lesson 2: Systems)

18. C $y = m^4 = n^3$

The answer is in terms of y alone, so find m and n in terms of y: $y = m^4$

Take the 4th root: $y^{1/4} = m$

$y = n^3$

Take the cube root: $y^{1/3} = n$

Find the product mn: $mn = (y^{1/4})(y^{1/3}) = y^{1/3 + 1/4}$

Add exponents: $mn = y^{7/12}$

(Chapter 11, Lesson 6: Negative and Fractional Exponents)

19. A   This question deals with similar triangles:

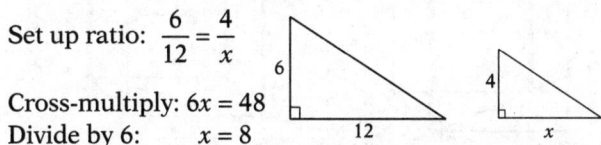

Set up ratio: $\dfrac{6}{12} = \dfrac{4}{x}$

Cross-multiply: $6x = 48$

Divide by 6: $x = 8$

Area of big triangle = ½(base)(height) = ½(12)(6) = 36
Area of small triangle = ½(base)(height) = ½(8)(4) = 16
Shaded area = area of big triangle – area of small triangle = 36 – 16 = 20

(Chapter 10, Lesson 6: Similar Figures)
(Chapter 10, Lesson 5: Areas and Perimeters)

20. A   Set up a Venn diagram to visualize the information.

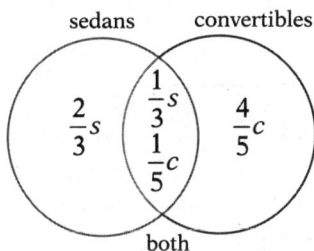

Notice that ⅓ the number of sedans must equal ⅕ the number of convertibles. Say the number of convertible sedans is x. If this is ⅓ the number of sedans, then there must be $3x$ sedans in total, and $3x - x = 2x$ of these are *not* convertibles. Similarly, if x is ⅕ the number of convertibles, then there must be $5x$ convertibles altogether, and $5x - x = 4x$ of these are *not* sedans. So now your diagram can look like this:

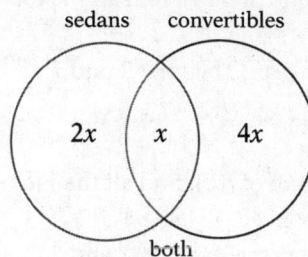

So there must be a total of $2x + x + 4x = 7x$ cars at the dealership. The only choice that is a multiple of 7 is (A): 28.

(Chapter 9, Lesson 5: Counting Problems)

Section 4

1. E

Perimeter of a square = $4s$

$36 = 4s$

Divide by 4: $9 = s$

Area of a square $= (s)^2$

Area $= (9)^2 = 81$

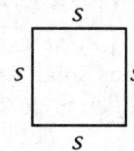

(Chapter 10, Lesson 5: Areas and Perimeters)

2. C

$$\dfrac{a}{b} = \dfrac{1}{10}$$

Cross-multiply: $b = 10a$

Try positive integer values of a to see how many work:

a	1	2	3	4	5	6	7	8	9
b	10	20	30	40	50	60	70	80	90

There are nine integer pairs that satisfy the equation.

(Chapter 9, Lesson 3: Numerical Reasoning Problems)

3. E   The ten bathrooms cost $20 each to clean:

Total cost = $20 × 10 = $200

To clean each bathroom twice would cost:

$200 × 2 = $400

There are 30 offices, and they cost $15 each to clean:

Total cost = $15 × 30 = $450

To clean each office once and each bathroom twice will cost: $400 + $450 = $850

(Chapter 11, Lesson 5: Data Analysis)

4. A Remember the "difference of squares" factoring formula: $a^2 - b^2 = (a - b)(a + b)$

Substitute: $10 = (2)(a + b)$

Divide by 2: $5 = a + b$

(Chapter 8, Lesson 5: Factoring)

---

5. A

To find the value of $f(14)$, find all the factors of 14:

$$1, \underline{2}, \underline{7}, 14$$

There are two prime factors, 2 and 7.

$$2 + 7 = 9$$
$$f(14) = 9$$

To find the value of $f(6)$, find all the factors of 6:

$$1, \underline{2}, \underline{3}, 6$$

There are two prime factors, 2 and 3.

$$2 + 3 = 5$$
$$f(6) = 5$$
$$f(14) - f(6) = 9 - 5 = 4$$

(Chapter 11, Lesson 2: Functions)

---

6. D First write an equation to find the average.

$$\frac{a + b + c + d}{4} = 20$$

Multiply by 4: $a + b + c + d = 80$

If you want a to be as large as possible, make b, c, and d as small as possible. You are told that they are all *different* positive integers: $a + b + c + d = 80$

Let $b = 1, c = 2, d = 3$: $a + 1 + 2 + 3 = 80$

Combine like terms: $a + 6 = 80$

Subtract 6: $a = 74$

(Chapter 9, Lesson 2: Mean/Median/Mode Problems)

---

7. B Let the radius of circle A $= a$ and the radius of circle B $= b$. It is given that $a = 2b$. The circumference of a circle can be found with the equation $C = 2\pi r$. The sum of their circumferences is 36π:

$$36\pi = 2\pi a + 2\pi b$$

Divide by π: $36 = 2a + 2b$

Substitute for a: $36 = 2(2b) + 2b$

Simplify: $36 = 4b + 2b$

Combine like terms: $36 = 6b$

Divide by 6: $6 = b$

Solve for a: $a = 2(b) = 2(6) = 12$

(Chapter 10, Lesson 5: Areas and Perimeters)

---

8. C This is a visualization problem. The six possible planes are illustrated below. Notice that the six faces of the cube "don't count," because each of those contains four edges of the cube.

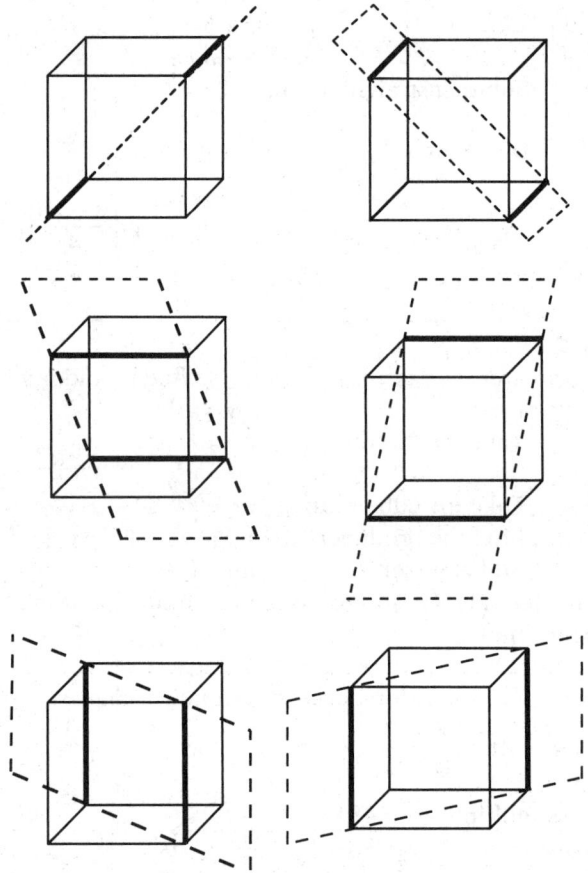

(Chapter 10, Lesson 7: Volumes and 3-D Geometry)

---

9. 16 Set up an equation: $2x - 10 = 22$

Add 10: $2x = 32$

Divide by 2: $x = 16$

(Chapter 8, Lesson 1: Solving Equations)

---

10. 36

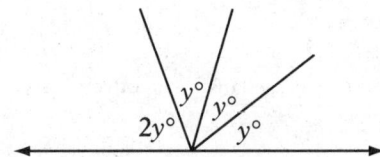

There are 180° on one side of a line:

$$2y + y + y + y = 180°$$

Combine like terms: $5y = 180°$

Divide by 5: $y = 36°$

(Chapter 10, Lesson 1: Lines and Angles)

11. **5**   Think simple: What's the simplest way to turn $8x + 4y$ into $2x + y$? Just divide by 4!

$$8x + 4y = 20$$
Divide by 4: $$2x + y = 5$$

(Chapter 8, Lesson 1: Solving Equations)
(Chapter 6, Lesson 4: Simplifying Problems)

12. **12**   Just substitute $x = 3$ and $y = 5$ into the equation and solve for m:

$$3m - 15 = 21$$
Add 15: $$3m = 36$$
Divide by 3: $$m = 12$$

(Chapter 8, Lesson 1: Solving Equations)
(Chapter 11, Lesson 2: Functions)

13. **15**   Ratios such as 4:5 can also be written as $4x$:$5x$. So the number of men m is $4x$ and the number of women w is $5x$.

Plug those values into the equation $w = m + 3$

$$5x = 4x + 3$$
Subtract $4x$: $$x = 3$$
Plug 3 in to $5x$: $$w = 5x = 5(3) = 15$$

(Chapter 7, Lesson 4: Ratios and Proportions)

14. **8 or 12**

	$y = \lvert 2x - b \rvert$
Plug in (5, 2):	$2 = \lvert 2(5) - b \rvert$
Simplify:	$2 = \lvert 10 - b \rvert$
	$(10 - b) = 2$ or $(10 - b) = -2$
Subtract 10:	$-b = -8$ or $-b = -12$
Multiply by -1:	$b = 8$ or $b = 12$

(Chapter 8, Lesson 6: Inequalities, Absolute Values, and Plugging In)

15. **25**   First calculate how many grams of sucrose there are in 200 grams of a 10% mixture.

$$(200 \text{ grams})(.10) = 20 \text{ grams of sucrose}$$

Since you will be adding x grams of sucrose, the total weight of sucrose will be $20 + x$ grams, and the total weight of the mixture will be $200 + x$ grams. Since the fraction that will be sucrose is 20%,

$$\frac{20 + x}{200 + x} = \frac{20}{100}$$

Cross-multiply: $(20 + x)(100) = 20(200 + x)$
Distribute: $2{,}000 + 100x = 4{,}000 + 20x$
Subtract 2,000: $100x = 2{,}000 + 20x$
Subtract $20x$: $80x = 2{,}000$
Divide by 80: $x = 25$

(Chapter 7, Lesson 5: Percents)
(Chapter 7, Lesson 4: Ratios and Proportions)

16. **24**   First calculate how long the race took.

$$distance = rate \times time$$
$$16 = (8)(time)$$
Divide by 8: $2 \text{ hours} = time = 120 \text{ minutes}$

Next, find the new rate that is 25% faster:

$$new\ rate = (8)(1.25) = 10 \text{ mph}$$

Calculate how long the new race would take:

$$distance = rate \times time$$
$$16 = (10)(time)$$
Divide by 10: $1.6 \text{ hours} = time = 96 \text{ minutes}$

So she can improve her time by $(120 - 96) = 24$ minutes.
(Chapter 9, Lesson 4: Rate Problems)

17. **52**

Break a shape like this into recognizable four-sided figures and triangles that are easier to deal with.

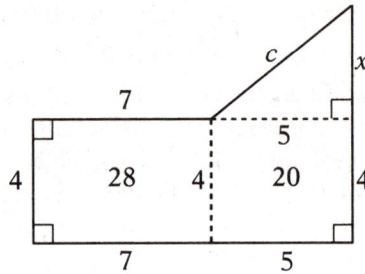

The area of the rectangle on the left is $7 \times 4 = 28$.

The area of the rectangle on the right is $5 \times 4 = 20$. The sum of those two areas is $28 + 20 = 48$. The area remaining for the triangle is the difference $78 - 48 = 30$. Set up an equation for the area of a triangle to solve for x:

$$\text{Area} = \tfrac{1}{2}(\text{base})(\text{height})$$
$$30 = \tfrac{1}{2}(5)(\text{height})$$

Divide by ½: $60 = 5(\text{height})$
Divide by 5: $12 = \text{height}$

To find the hypotenuse of the right triangle, set up the Pythagorean theorem and solve:

$$5^2 + 12^2 = c^2$$
$$25 + 144 = c^2$$
$$169 = c^2$$
$$c = 13$$

(Or just notice that it's a 5-12-13 triangle!)

To find the perimeter of the figure, add up all of the sides:

$$13 + 12 + 4 + 5 + 7 + 4 + 7 = 52$$

(Chapter 10, Lesson 5: Areas and Perimeters)
(Chapter 10, Lesson 3: The Pythagorean Theorem)

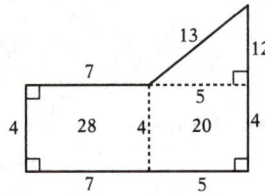

18. **225** Set up a three-circle Venn diagram to visualize this information.

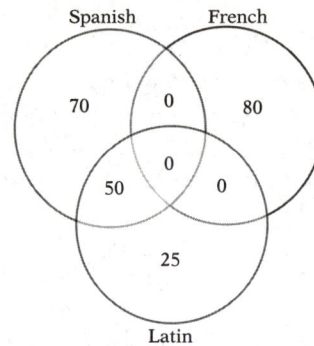

Fifty students study two of the three languages, so let's say that 50 students study both Spanish and Latin. (It doesn't matter *which* two languages those 50 students take; the result turns out the same.) This means that zero students study both Spanish and French, zero students study both French and Latin, and zero students study all three languages.

There are 120 Spanish students in all. There are therefore $120 - 50 = 70$ students who study Spanish alone. There are 80 French students in all, all of whom study just French, and there are 75 total Latin students including $75 - 50 = 25$ students who study only Latin.

This means that there are $70 + 50 + 80 + 25 = 225$ sophomores at Hillside High School.

(Chapter 9, Lesson 5: Counting Problems)

Section 5

1. **C** The clients were forced to seek more *reliable* investment advice, so the manager must have managed their funds badly. *ineptitude* = lack of skill

2. **E** Vartan is Armenian; he was born in Iran and educated in Lebanon and is now president of the American Brown University. He has a lot of *worldly* experience. *perpetual* = lasting forever; *authoritative* = showing authority; *cosmopolitan* = worldly

3. **D** They didn't consider it in great detail, so the reading must have been *without great care. verbatim* = word for word; *meandering* = wandering; *tormented* = feeling anguish or pain; *cursory* = quick and without care; *substantial* = of substance, quite large

4. A If the *pathogens* (infectious agents) spread more quickly in close quarters, the *crowding* would be a problem. This would cause the disease to *spread*. *propagation* = reproduction, increase in number; *squalor* = horrible or dirty conditions; *circulation* = moving of something around from place to place; *poverty* = state of being poor; *deterioration* = wearing down; *congestion* = crowdedness; *proximity* = closeness; *resilience* = ability to recover from a challenge

5. E The purpose of research is to find answers to questions of interest. Therefore, the research *endeavors* (attempts) to *determine* or *understand* the mechanisms by which our brains do things. If the data must be turned into *coherent and understandable information*, it must not have been coherent to begin with, but rather just a big rush of information. *enhance* = make better; *attenuate* = reduce in amount; *dearth* = scarcity, lack; *elucidate* = make clear; *deluge* = huge flood

6. D The *fruits* mentioned in line 10 refer to the means of acquiring food and shelter, because they are described as the *fruits for maintaining human life.*

7. B The question is whether one can *get quick returns of interest* (make money) *from the capital of knowledge and learning* (from one's education) (lines 13–15).

8. A The pointing of dogs is mentioned as an *instinctive tendency to the performance of an action* (lines 1–2).

9. E Inherited tendencies tend to show themselves in the behavior of an organism. The paragraph mentions the calf and the caterpillar as examples of organisms with instincts that show themselves in later behavior.

10. D The final paragraph begins with *The best life is the one in which the creative impulses play the largest part and the possessive impulses the smallest* (lines 56–58).

11. D Lines 22–26 say that *the food and clothing of one man is not the food and clothing of another; if the supply is insufficient, what one man has is obtained at the expense of some other man.* Therefore, food and clothing exist in finite amounts and can be used up.

12. E This section of the passage discusses matters such as *good-will* (line 38), *science* (line 31), and *painting pictures or writing poems* (lines 35–36) as things that are not denied to someone else when one person possesses them.

13. E This sentence discusses the *possessive impulses* (line 49) as distinct from the *creative impulses* discussed in the next sentence. The *impulse of property* in lines 51–52 is the *desire to possess property*.

14. C This statement echoes the point made in lines 71–72 that *spiritual possessions cannot be taken in this way*, that is, by force.

15. D Lines 58–59 say *This is no new discovery* and go on to cite the Gospel as a prior source expressing the same opinions as Russell's.

16. B The author's main point is that creativity is of higher value than possessiveness. The invention mentioned in answer choice (B) was created to make money for its inventor (a possessive and materialistic motive) but has the side effect of benefitting all of humankind.

17. A The passage discusses the perspective one Native American has on the appearance of the *new superstition* (line 44). It discusses how some villagers have taken to the new religion and also mentions one fellow tribe member's attempt to convert the main character.

18. E In saying that *men of the same color are like the ivory keys of one instrument where each represents all the rest, yet varies from them in pitch and quality of voice* (lines 4–7), the author is saying that people of the same race possess important differences.

19. D The author describes the preacher as *mouth[ing] most strangely the jangling phrases of a bigoted creed* (lines 11–12), indicating that she considers him to be an intolerant person. She describes herself as having *compassion* (line 7) and *respect* (line 10), but does not attribute these qualities to the preacher.

20. B Lines 13–14 say that *our tribe is one large family, where every person is related to all the others.*

21. C Both the preacher and the author's mother have become followers of *the new superstition* (line 44).

22. C In saying that a *pugilist commented upon a recent article of mine, grossly perverting the spirit of my pen* (lines 66–68), the author is saying that the pugilist distorted the author's words in a grotesque way.

23. E   The author characterizes herself as *a wee child toddling in a wonder world* (lines 72–73), indicating that she is in awe of the world around her. Although one might expect her to be vengeful in response to the *pugilist* (line 66) who *grossly pervert[ed] the spirit of [her] pen* (line 68), there is no indication in the paragraph that she is vengeful.

24. A   The author says in lines 68–72 that *still I would not forget that the pale-faced missionary and the aborigine are both God's creatures, though **small indeed in their own conceptions of Infinite Love.*** In other words, the author respects the missionary but believes he is small-minded.

Section 6

1. D   The verb must agree with the plural subject *claims.* Choice (D) is most concise and correct.

(Chapter 15, Lesson 1: Subject-Verb Disagreement)

2. A   The original sentence is best.

3. B   The participial phrase opening the sentence modifies Sartre himself, not his *writing.* This being the case, the phrase dangles.

(Chapter 15, Lesson 7: Dangling and Misplaced Participles)

4. C   Choice (C) best follows the law of parallelism.

(Chapter 15, Lesson 3: Parallelism)

5. A   The original sentence is best.

6. B   Choice (B) is the most concise, logical, and complete.

(Chapter 12, Lesson 9: Write Concisely)

7. C   The original phrasing contains an incomplete thought. Choice (C) is by far the most concise and direct.

(Chapter 15, Lesson 15: Coordinating Ideas)

8. E   The participle *having spread* modifies the *disease,* not the *doctors.*

(Chapter 15, Lesson 7: Dangling and Misplaced Participles)

9. C   The original phrasing contains an incomplete thought. Choice (C) is by far the most concise and direct.

(Chapter 15, Lesson 15: Coordinating Ideas)

10. D   The participle *singing* modifies *Anita,* not her hoarseness. Furthermore, the participle is in the wrong form; it should be in the perfect form *having sung,* because only the *previous* singing could have contributed to her hoarseness.

(Chapter 15, Lesson 7: Dangling and Misplaced Participles)

(Chapter 15, Lesson 9: Tricky Tenses)

11. A   The original sentence is best.

12. A   The word *quick* is an adjective and can thus modify only a noun. But since it modifies the verb *turned,* the adverb *quickly* is needed here.

(Chapter 15, Lesson 12: Other Modifier Problems)

13. B   This sentence violates the law of parallelism. If she is known *for her initiative,* she should also be known *for devoting her own time.*

(Chapter 15, Lesson 3: Parallelism)

14. C   Since the Medieval era is long past, its *beginning* is "completed" or, in grammar terms, "perfect." So this phrase should be the "perfect" form of the infinitive: *to have begun.*

(Chapter 15, Lesson 9: Tricky Tenses)

15. B   The word *neither* is almost always part of the phrase *neither of . . .* or *neither A nor B.* So choice (B) should read *nor even.*

(Chapter 15, Lesson 10: Idiom Errors)

16. D   The word *less* is used to compare only quantities that can't be counted. If the quantities are countable, as accidents are, the word should be *fewer.*

(Chapter 15, Lesson 4: Comparison Problems)

17. B   To convey the proper sequence of events, the perfect tense is required: *had spent.*

(Chapter 15, Lesson 9: Tricky Tenses)

18. A   The subject of the verb *has* is the plural noun *newspapers.* (The sentence is "inverted," because the subject follows the verb.) The proper form of the verb, then, is *have.*

(Chapter 15, Lesson 1: Subject-Verb Disagreement)

(Chapter 15, Lesson 2: Trimming Sentences)

19. B   The original sentence has a "comma splice" that incorrectly joins two sentences with only a comma. A better phrasing is *dream that led.*

(Chapter 15, Lesson 15: Coordinating Ideas)

20. **C**   The subject of the verb is the singular noun *movement*, so the proper verb form is *has led*.

(Chapter 15, Lesson 1: Subject-Verb Disagreement)
(Chapter 15, Lesson 2: Trimming Sentences)

21. **E**   The sentence is correct as written.

22. **D**   This is a prepositional phrase, so the pronoun is the object of the preposition and should be in the objective case. The correct phrasing is *for Maria and me.*

(Chapter 15, Lesson 6: Pronoun Case)

23. **A**   The word *successive* means *consecutive*, so it does not make sense in this context. The right word is *successful.*

(Chapter 15, Lesson 11: Diction Errors)

24. **E**   The sentence is correct as written.

25. **C**   The word *underneath* means that it is physically *below* something else. It should be changed to *under.*

(Chapter 15, Lesson 10: Idiom Errors)

26. **E**   The sentence is correct as written.

27. **B**   The subject of the verb *were* is *arrogance*, which is singular. It should instead be *was.*

(Chapter 15, Lesson 1: Subject-Verb Disagreement)

28. **B**   The sentence mentions there are *numerous* strains of the bacteria, which means that *more* should instead be *most.*

(Chapter 15, Lesson 4: Comparison Problems)

29. **C**   The subject *company* is singular. Therefore, *they* should instead be *it.*

(Chapter 15, Lesson 5: Pronoun-Antecedent Disagreement)

30. **D**   Choice (D) is most consistent, logical, and concise.

31. **A**   Choice (A) is most logical.

(Chapter 12, Lesson 7: Write Logically)

32. **B**   The first paragraph ends with the description of an idea. The second paragraph begins with an illustration of how students experience this idea in their daily lives and then goes on to explain how it can help them get through their *brain freezes.* Choice (B) is the best introduction to the paragraph, because it explains that a student using the phenomenon can improve his or her studies.

(Chapter 12, Lesson 7: Write Logically)

33. **C**   The sentence begins using the pronoun *you*, so that usage should be maintained throughout the sentence. Choice (D) is incorrect because a person has only one brain.

(Chapter 15, Lesson 5: Pronoun-Antecedent Disagreement)

34. **E**   Sentence 11 concludes a discussion of Isaac Asimov's "eureka" experience. The additional sentence expands upon that idea, relating it back to the lives of students.

(Chapter 12, Lesson 7: Write Logically)

35. **C**   Choice (C) is the most concise and logical revision.

(Chapter 12, Lesson 7: Write Logically)
(Chapter 12, Lesson 9: Write Concisely)

Section 7

1. **B**   Set up a ratio to solve this problem:

$$\frac{4 \text{ apples}}{20 \text{ cents}} = \frac{10 \text{ apples}}{x \text{ cents}}$$

Cross-multiply: $4x = 200$
Divide by 4: $x = 50$ cents

(Chapter 7, Lesson 4: Ratios and Proportions)

2. **C**   Solve for *b:* $2^b = 8$
$b = 3$
Plug in 3: $3^b = 3^3 = 27$

(Chapter 8, Lesson 3: Working with Exponentials)

3. **A**   The sum of *a*, *b*, and 18 is 6 greater than the sum of *a*, *b*, and 12. Since there are three terms in the group, it follows that the average of *a*, *b*, and 18 would be $6 \div 3 = 2$ greater than the average of *a*, *b*, and 12.

(Chapter 9, Lesson 2: Mean/Median/Mode Problems)

4. **B** If you have the patience, you can write out a quick calendar for yourself to track the days:

Su	M	T	W	**Th**	F	Sa
	1	2	3	4	5	
6	7	8	9	10	11	12
13	14	15	16	17	18	19
20	21	22	23	24	25	26
27	28	29	30	**31**		

Or you can use the simple fact that successive Tuesdays (like any other days) are always 7 days apart. Therefore, if the 1st of the month is a Tuesday, so are the 8th, the 15th, the 22nd, and the 29th. Therefore, the 30th is a Wednesday and the 31st is a Thursday.

(Chapter 9, Lesson 3: Numerical Reasoning Problems)

5. **A** From the given information:

$$m = 8n$$
$$0 < m + n < 50$$

Substitute for m: $0 < 8n + n < 50$
Combine like terms: $0 < 9n < 50$
Divide by 9: $0 < n < 5\frac{5}{9}$

Since n must be an integer, n can be 1, 2, 3, 4, or 5.

(Chapter 8, Lesson 6: Inequalities, Absolute Values, and Plugging In)

6. **D** First find the value of y: y% of 50 is 32.

Simplify: $\frac{y}{100} \times 50 = 32$
Cross-multiply: $50y = 3{,}200$
Divide by 50: $y = 64$

What is 200% of 64?
Interpret: $2.00 \times 64 = 128$

(Chapter 7, Lesson 5: Percents)

7. **B**

$$g(x) = x + x^{1/2}$$

Plug in 16 for x: $g(16) = 16 + 16^{1/2}$
Take square root of 16: $g(16) = 16 + 4$
Combine like terms: $g(16) = 20$

(Chapter 11, Lesson 2: Functions)

8. **C** The slope of the line is $-\frac{3}{4}$, so use the slope equation and the coordinates of point A (0, 12) to find the coordinates of point B (x, 0):

$$m = \frac{y_2 - y_1}{x_2 - x_1} = \frac{0 - 12}{x - 0} = \frac{-12}{x} = -\frac{3}{4}$$

Cross-multiply: $4(-12) = -3(x)$
Simplify: $-48 = -3x$
Divide by -3: $16 = x$

The base of the triangle is 16, and its height is 12.

Area = ½(base)(height)
Substitute: Area = ½(16)(12)
Simplify: Area = 96

(Chapter 10, Lesson 4: Coordinate Geometry)

9. **A** Find the sum of each repetition of the pattern:
$-1 + 1 + 2 = 2$

Next, determine how many times the pattern repeats in the first 25 terms: $25 \div 3 = 8$ with a remainder of 1.

Multiply the sum of the pattern by 8 to obtain the sum of the first 24 terms: $2 \times 8 = 16$

The 25th term is -1, which makes the sum $16 + -1 = 15$.
(Chapter 11, Lesson 1: Sequences)

10. **D** The ratio of white marbles to blue marbles is 4 to b. The probability of randomly selecting a white marble from the jar is ¼. This means that one out of every four marbles in the jar is white and three out of every four marbles are blue. If there are four white marbles, then there are $4 \times 3 = 12$ blue marbles.

(Chapter 7, Lesson 4: Ratios and Proportions)

11. **B** Area = ½(base)(height)
Substitute: $10 = ½(\text{base})(\text{height})$
Divide by ½: $20 = (\text{base})(\text{height})$

The base and the height are both integers. Find all the "factor pairs" of 20:   1, 20; 2, 10; and 4, 5

Plug each pair into the Pythagorean theorem to find the least possible length of the hypotenuse:

$$a^2 + b^2 = c^2$$
$$4^2 + 5^2 = c^2$$

Combine like terms: $41 = c^2$
Take square root: $\sqrt{41} = c$

$$a^2 + b^2 = c^2$$
$$2^2 + 10^2 = c^2$$

Combine like terms: $104 = c^2$
Take square root: $\sqrt{104} = c$

$$a^2 + b^2 = c^2$$
$$1^2 + 20^2 = c^2$$

Combine like terms: $401 = c^2$
Take square root: $\sqrt{401} = c$

$\sqrt{41}$ is the shortest possible hypotenuse.

(Chapter 10, Lesson 5: Areas and Perimeters)
(Chapter 10, Lesson 3: The Pythagorean Theorem)

12. **B** $-1 < y < 0$
This means that y is a negative decimal fraction. Answer choices (A), (C), and (E) will all be negative numbers. Answer choices (B) and (D) are positive numbers. When you raise a simple fraction to a positive number larger than 1, it gets smaller. $y^4 < y^2$, which makes (B) the greatest value. Pick a value like $y = -½$ and see.

(Chapter 9, Lesson 3: Numerical Reasoning Problems)

13. E   Any statement of the form *"If A is true, then B is true"* is logically equivalent to *"If B is not true, then A is not true."* Try this with some common-sense examples of such statements. For instance, saying *"If I am under 16 years old, then I am not allowed to drive"* is the same as saying *"If I am allowed to drive, then I must not be under 16 years old."* The statement in (E) is logically equivalent to the original.

(Chapter 6, Lesson 7: Thinking Logically)

14. E   If each bus contained only the minimum number of students, the buses would accommodate $6 \times 30 = 180$ students. But since you have 200 students to accommodate, you have 20 more students to place. To maximize the number of 40-student buses, place 10 more students in two of the buses. Therefore, a maximum of two buses can have 40 students.

(Chapter 9, Lesson 3: Numerical Reasoning Problems)

15. D   The volume of a cylinder is equal to $\pi r^2 h$. Let's say that the radius of cylinder A is a and the radius of cylinder B is b. Since the height of cylinder B is twice the height of cylinder A, if the height of cylinder A is h, then the height of cylinder B is $2h$. The volume of A is twice that of B:

	$\pi a^2 h = 2\pi b^2 (2h)$
Simplify:	$\pi a^2 h = 4\pi b^2 h$
Divide by π:	$a^2 h = 4b^2 h$
Divide by h:	$a^2 = 4b^2$
Take the square root of both sides:	$a = 2b$
Divide by b:	$\dfrac{a}{b} = \dfrac{2}{1}$

(Chapter 10, Lesson 7: Volumes and 3-D Geometry)

16. C   The key is to find a pattern among the many possible solutions. Pick some values for x to see if you can see a pattern. For instance, if $x = 3$, then the garden looks like this:

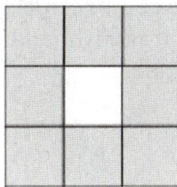

In this case $w = 8$. But if $x = 4$, the garden looks like this:

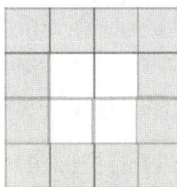

And here, $w = 12$. You might notice that the value of w has increased by 4. Does this pattern continue? Let's try $x = 5$ to check:

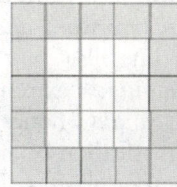

Sure enough, $w = 16$, and it seems that the pattern continues and w is always a multiple of 4. Only choice (C), 40, is a multiple of 4, so that must be the correct answer.

(Chapter 6, Lesson 3: Finding Patterns)

Section 8

1. B   A *reputable* scientist is well known and well respected. Saying *the evidence is ------- at best* indicates that there is not much evidence at all. It must be *flimsy*. Reputable scientists would not likely *admit* that a phenomenon exists if the evidence is weak. *meager* = scanty, deficient; *regret* = feel bad about an action, wish it hadn't happened; *paltry* = lacking worth

2. D   The concept that the Earth is round is *now accepted as an inarguable truth*. It can be inferred that it was at some point a fact that was thought to be wrong. *incontrovertible* = cannot be questioned; *mellifluous* = smooth flowing; *dubious* = doubtful

3. B   A profound break of a political party or religion into factions is a *schism*. (The Latin word *schisma* = split.) *unanimity* = full agreement; *schism* = division into factions; *caucus* = meeting of party members; *commemoration* = event that honors something or someone; *prognostication* = prediction

4. C   As the father of the American public school system, Horace Mann would *pressure* or *push* the Massachusetts legislature to institute a system for *ensuring* or *guaranteeing* universal access to eduction. *petitioned* = requested, lobbied for; *vouchsafing* = conceding, granting

5. A   Since the light from most stars takes millions of years to reach us, it is plausible to imagine that by the time we see the light the star might actually no longer be there. This would make the present existence of these stars *questionable*. *debatable* = disputable; *methodical* = systematic; *indecorous* = not proper; *imperious* = acting as if one is superior to another; *profuse* = abundant

6. D The *although* establishes a contrast. Something that makes *any potentially offensive matters seem less objectionable* is, by definition, a *euphemism*. The first blank should therefore be a word that contrasts with euphemism, like *straightforward*. *anachronism* = something out of place in time; *intolerant* = unable to put up with something; *laudation* = extreme praise; *clandestine* = secret, hidden; *candid* = honest, straightforward; *euphemism* = the substitution of an inoffensive term for an offensive one; *forthright* = honest; *coercion* = pressure on someone to act

7. C The English gentleman *tried to teach his son Greek and Latin without punishment, . . . rewarding his son with cherries and biscuits* (lines 5–11).

8. A In saying that *marks, grades, and diplomas . . . must be made reinforcing for other reasons* (lines 16–19), the author is saying that such things will not reinforce behavior by themselves but must be made to represent something more meaningful.

9. B The passage says that how *honors and medals derive their power from prestige or esteem* is what *varies between cultures and epochs* (lines 20–23). When Oscar Wilde got *a "first in Mods"* in 1876, he was the talk of the town. But the contemporary student graduating *summa cum laude* is *less widely acclaimed* (lines 33–34).

10. A The story follows the statement that how *honors and medals derive their power from prestige or esteem* is what *varies between cultures and epochs*. Therefore, the story is intended to illustrate that fact.

11. C Statement I is supported by lines 37–39, which say that certain kinds of reinforcements (like food) *are not always easily arranged*. Statement II is supported by line 43: *We cannot all get prizes*. The selection does not mention anything about rewards encouraging only superficial learning.

12. D In lines 58–60, the passage says that *grades are almost always given long after the student has stopped behaving as a student*. It then goes on to discuss how *such contingencies are weak* (lines 60–61).

13. E The paragraph as a whole discusses the need for teachers to address the issues of whether, when, and how to punish or reward student behavior, so it is about teacher-student interactions.

14. B Kohn and Deci are mentioned as examples of experts who believe *that reward is often just as harmful as punishment, if not more so* (lines 87–89).

15. D The second paragraph of Passage 2 goes on to argue that those who are doing a task without a reward continue to perform the task because they see it as being "fun," whereas those who do it for a reward stop playing because they are no longer being paid to continue. The activity's sole value comes from the payment they get for it, not from the enjoyment they get from participating.

16. D We are told that Deci concluded that the *subjects who were paid probably construed* (interpreted) *the task as being manipulative* (lines 105–106). In order to draw such conclusions, the subjects would have to make inferences about the motivations of the experimenter.

17. A The author follows that statement with *it would be a mistake to use these few experiments to generalize that all rewards are bad* (lines 130–132). These statements caution against an overly simplistic theory about the effectiveness of rewards.

18. B Deci's opinion is that the introduction of a reward system changes things for the worse. He would see the description of the *problems* mentioned in line 37 as presumptuous because they presume that the rewards actually have a positive effect and incomplete because they do not mention all of the problems that he sees in reward systems.

19. D Both authors agree that positive feedback is a more effective teaching mechanism than negative feedback. Passage 1 mentions the need of good educators to *teach . . . without punishment* (lines 6–7) and mentions the negative *by-products of aversive control* (control by punishment) (lines 35–36). Passage 2 mentions that *most educators and psychologists agree that reward is always better than punishment* (lines 84–85), and since the writer goes on to criticize even reward systems, he implies that punishment is most certainly a bad teaching technique.

Section 9

1. C The word *whose* should refer to Alvin Ailey, but the way the sentence is constructed, it is referring to Alvin Ailey's *works*. Answer choice (C) corrects this error in the most concise and logical fashion.

(Chapter 15, Lesson 2: Trimming Sentences)

2. B When a participle is used to indicate an action that is completed before another action, it should be *perfect*. *Getting* this far should instead be *Having gotten*.

(Chapter 15, Lesson 9: Tricky Tenses)

3. C The sentence is improperly describing Rachel's irritation as being even-tempered. In reality, it should be *Rachel* who is even-tempered. Answer choice (C) corrects this error.

(Chapter 15, Lesson 7: Dangling and Misplaced Participles)

4. B The original sentence contains an illogical comparison. Alberta's *salary* cannot logically be compared to *the other agents*, but rather must be compared to *the salaries of the other agents*. The only choice that makes a logical and idiomatic comparison is choice B.

(Chapter 15, Lesson 4: Comparison Problems)

5. C The word *elicit* means to call forth or draw out. The word should be *illicit*, which means unlawful.

(Chapter 15, Lesson 11: Diction Errors)

6. D The paraders were not watching from the balcony. The sentence needs to be changed so that the subjects represented by the final pronoun *us* are the ones watching from the balcony.

(Chapter 15, Lesson 7: Dangling and Misplaced Participles)

7. E The sentence contains two past tense verbs, and one event was completed before the other. The tents were set up before they arrived. So *set up* needs to be in the past perfect tense—*had set up*.

(Chapter 15, Lesson 9: Tricky Tenses)

8. C The subject *neither Matt nor David* is singular, because any *neither A nor B* noun phrase takes the same number as *B*, which in this case is the singular David. Therefore, the verb should be conjugated for a singular subject: *neither Matt nor David is permitted*.

(Chapter 15, Lesson 1: Subject-Verb Disagreement)

9. B When using not only A but also B, the words or phrases that replace A and B must be parallel. It should be replaced by not only *with working* but also *with wanting*.

(Chapter 15, Lesson 3: Parallelism)

10. C To correct this sentence, the word *that* should be replaced with *who*, since Roberto is a *person*.

(Chapter 15, Lesson 5: Pronoun-Antecedent Disagreement)

11. D Answer choice (D) connects the two clauses most effectively.

(Chapter 15, Lesson 15: Coordinating Ideas)

12. E When reading this sentence you should ask yourself: "who was forced to live apart from his family?" The answer to that question, St. Pierre, is what should immediately follow the comma after *informers*.

(Chapter 15, Lesson 7: Dangling and Misplaced Participles)

13. B The gerund form, *forming*, is not correct and needs to be changed to past tense *formed*. Choice (B) works best.

(Chapter 15, Lesson 9: Tricky Tenses)

14. D What follows the linking verb *is* must be a noun phrase representing *the most challenging aspect*, not an independent clause, as in the original. Choice (D) works best.

(Chapter 15, Lesson 15: Coordinating Ideas)

PRACTICE TEST 3

ANSWER SHEET

Last Name:_____   First Name:_____

Date:_____   Testing Location:_____

Directions for Test

- Remove these answer sheets from the book and use them to record your answers to this test.
- This test will require 3 hours and 20 minutes to complete. Take this test in one sitting.
- The time allotment for each section is written clearly at the beginning of each section. This test contains six 25-minute sections, two 20-minute sections, and one 10-minute section.
- This test is 25 minutes shorter than the actual SAT, which will include a 25-minute "experimental" section that does not count toward your score. That section has been omitted from this test.
- You may take one short break during the test, of no more than 10 minutes in length.
- You may only work on one section at any given time.
- You must stop ALL work on a section when time is called.
- If you finish a section before the time has elapsed, check your work on that section. You may NOT work on any other section.
- Do not waste time on questions that seem too difficult for you.
- Use the test book for scratchwork, but you will receive credit only for answers that are marked on the answer sheets.
- You will receive one point for every correct answer.
- You will receive no points for an omitted question.
- For each wrong answer on any multiple-choice question, your score will be reduced by ¼ point.
- For each wrong answer on any "numerical grid-in" question, you will receive no deduction.

When you take the real SAT, you will be asked to fill in your personal information in grids as shown below.

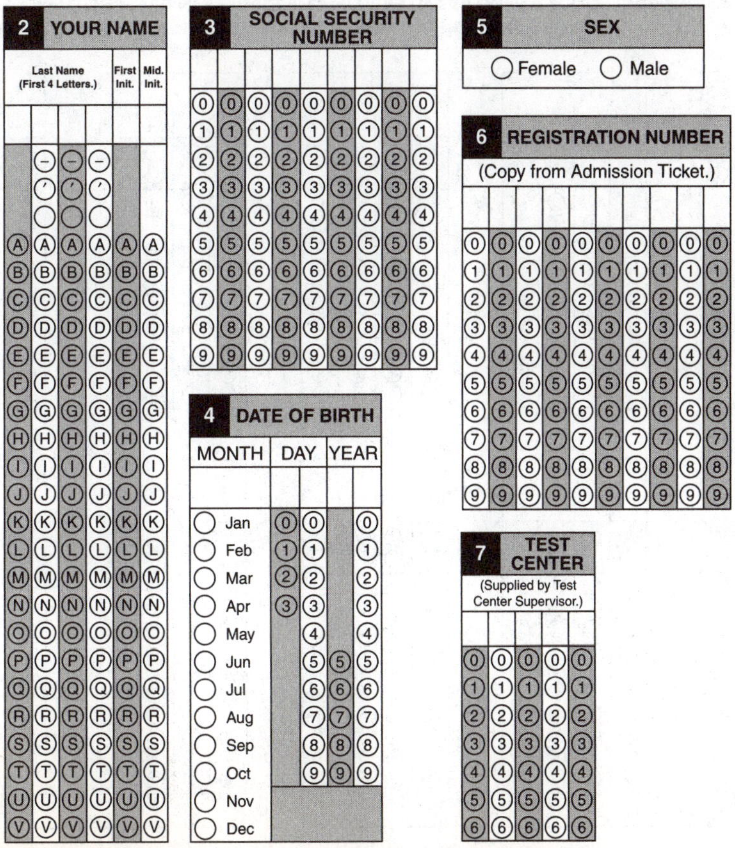

Start with number 1 for each new section. If a section has fewer questions than answer spaces, leave the extra answer spaces blank. Be sure to erase any errors or stray marks completely.

SECTION 2

1 A B C D E	11 A B C D E	21 A B C D E	31 A B C D E
2 A B C D E	12 A B C D E	22 A B C D E	32 A B C D E
3 A B C D E	13 A B C D E	23 A B C D E	33 A B C D E
4 A B C D E	14 A B C D E	24 A B C D E	34 A B C D E
5 A B C D E	15 A B C D E	25 A B C D E	35 A B C D E
6 A B C D E	16 A B C D E	26 A B C D E	36 A B C D E
7 A B C D E	17 A B C D E	27 A B C D E	37 A B C D E
8 A B C D E	18 A B C D E	28 A B C D E	38 A B C D E
9 A B C D E	19 A B C D E	29 A B C D E	39 A B C D E
10 A B C D E	20 A B C D E	30 A B C D E	40 A B C D E

SECTION 3

1 A B C D E	11 A B C D E	21 A B C D E	31 A B C D E
2 A B C D E	12 A B C D E	22 A B C D E	32 A B C D E
3 A B C D E	13 A B C D E	23 A B C D E	33 A B C D E
4 A B C D E	14 A B C D E	24 A B C D E	34 A B C D E
5 A B C D E	15 A B C D E	25 A B C D E	35 A B C D E
6 A B C D E	16 A B C D E	26 A B C D E	36 A B C D E
7 A B C D E	17 A B C D E	27 A B C D E	37 A B C D E
8 A B C D E	18 A B C D E	28 A B C D E	38 A B C D E
9 A B C D E	19 A B C D E	29 A B C D E	39 A B C D E
10 A B C D E	20 A B C D E	30 A B C D E	40 A B C D E

CAUTION   Use the answer spaces in the grids below for Section 2 or Section 3 only if you are told to do so in your test book.

Student-Produced Responses   ONLY ANSWERS ENTERED IN THE CIRCLES IN EACH GRID WILL BE SCORED. YOU WILL NOT RECEIVE CREDIT FOR ANYTHING WRITTEN IN THE BOXES ABOVE THE CIRCLES.

9   10   11   12   13

14   15   16   17   18

Start with number 1 for each new section. If a section has fewer questions than answer spaces, leave the extra answer spaces blank. Be sure to erase any errors or stray marks completely.

SECTION 4

1 A B C D E	11 A B C D E	21 A B C D E	31 A B C D E
2 A B C D E	12 A B C D E	22 A B C D E	32 A B C D E
3 A B C D E	13 A B C D E	23 A B C D E	33 A B C D E
4 A B C D E	14 A B C D E	24 A B C D E	34 A B C D E
5 A B C D E	15 A B C D E	25 A B C D E	35 A B C D E
6 A B C D E	16 A B C D E	26 A B C D E	36 A B C D E
7 A B C D E	17 A B C D E	27 A B C D E	37 A B C D E
8 A B C D E	18 A B C D E	28 A B C D E	38 A B C D E
9 A B C D E	19 A B C D E	29 A B C D E	39 A B C D E
10 A B C D E	20 A B C D E	30 A B C D E	40 A B C D E

SECTION 5

1 A B C D E	11 A B C D E	21 A B C D E	31 A B C D E
2 A B C D E	12 A B C D E	22 A B C D E	32 A B C D E
3 A B C D E	13 A B C D E	23 A B C D E	33 A B C D E
4 A B C D E	14 A B C D E	24 A B C D E	34 A B C D E
5 A B C D E	15 A B C D E	25 A B C D E	35 A B C D E
6 A B C D E	16 A B C D E	26 A B C D E	36 A B C D E
7 A B C D E	17 A B C D E	27 A B C D E	37 A B C D E
8 A B C D E	18 A B C D E	28 A B C D E	38 A B C D E
9 A B C D E	19 A B C D E	29 A B C D E	39 A B C D E
10 A B C D E	20 A B C D E	30 A B C D E	40 A B C D E

CAUTION Use the answer spaces in the grids below for Section 4 or Section 5 only if you are told to do so in your test book.

Student-Produced Responses ONLY ANSWERS ENTERED IN THE CIRCLES IN EACH GRID WILL BE SCORED. YOU WILL NOT RECEIVE CREDIT FOR ANYTHING WRITTEN IN THE BOXES ABOVE THE CIRCLES.

9   10   11   12   13

14   15   16   17   18

Start with number 1 for each new section. If a section has fewer questions than answer spaces, leave the extra answer spaces blank. Be sure to erase any errors or stray marks completely.

SECTION 6

1 (A) (B) (C) (D) (E)	11 (A) (B) (C) (D) (E)	21 (A) (B) (C) (D) (E)	31 (A) (B) (C) (D) (E)
2 (A) (B) (C) (D) (E)	12 (A) (B) (C) (D) (E)	22 (A) (B) (C) (D) (E)	32 (A) (B) (C) (D) (E)
3 (A) (B) (C) (D) (E)	13 (A) (B) (C) (D) (E)	23 (A) (B) (C) (D) (E)	33 (A) (B) (C) (D) (E)
4 (A) (B) (C) (D) (E)	14 (A) (B) (C) (D) (E)	24 (A) (B) (C) (D) (E)	34 (A) (B) (C) (D) (E)
5 (A) (B) (C) (D) (E)	15 (A) (B) (C) (D) (E)	25 (A) (B) (C) (D) (E)	35 (A) (B) (C) (D) (E)
6 (A) (B) (C) (D) (E)	16 (A) (B) (C) (D) (E)	26 (A) (B) (C) (D) (E)	36 (A) (B) (C) (D) (E)
7 (A) (B) (C) (D) (E)	17 (A) (B) (C) (D) (E)	27 (A) (B) (C) (D) (E)	37 (A) (B) (C) (D) (E)
8 (A) (B) (C) (D) (E)	18 (A) (B) (C) (D) (E)	28 (A) (B) (C) (D) (E)	38 (A) (B) (C) (D) (E)
9 (A) (B) (C) (D) (E)	19 (A) (B) (C) (D) (E)	29 (A) (B) (C) (D) (E)	39 (A) (B) (C) (D) (E)
10 (A) (B) (C) (D) (E)	20 (A) (B) (C) (D) (E)	30 (A) (B) (C) (D) (E)	40 (A) (B) (C) (D) (E)

SECTION 7

1 (A) (B) (C) (D) (E)	11 (A) (B) (C) (D) (E)	21 (A) (B) (C) (D) (E)	31 (A) (B) (C) (D) (E)
2 (A) (B) (C) (D) (E)	12 (A) (B) (C) (D) (E)	22 (A) (B) (C) (D) (E)	32 (A) (B) (C) (D) (E)
3 (A) (B) (C) (D) (E)	13 (A) (B) (C) (D) (E)	23 (A) (B) (C) (D) (E)	33 (A) (B) (C) (D) (E)
4 (A) (B) (C) (D) (E)	14 (A) (B) (C) (D) (E)	24 (A) (B) (C) (D) (E)	34 (A) (B) (C) (D) (E)
5 (A) (B) (C) (D) (E)	15 (A) (B) (C) (D) (E)	25 (A) (B) (C) (D) (E)	35 (A) (B) (C) (D) (E)
6 (A) (B) (C) (D) (E)	16 (A) (B) (C) (D) (E)	26 (A) (B) (C) (D) (E)	36 (A) (B) (C) (D) (E)
7 (A) (B) (C) (D) (E)	17 (A) (B) (C) (D) (E)	27 (A) (B) (C) (D) (E)	37 (A) (B) (C) (D) (E)
8 (A) (B) (C) (D) (E)	18 (A) (B) (C) (D) (E)	28 (A) (B) (C) (D) (E)	38 (A) (B) (C) (D) (E)
9 (A) (B) (C) (D) (E)	19 (A) (B) (C) (D) (E)	29 (A) (B) (C) (D) (E)	39 (A) (B) (C) (D) (E)
10 (A) (B) (C) (D) (E)	20 (A) (B) (C) (D) (E)	30 (A) (B) (C) (D) (E)	40 (A) (B) (C) (D) (E)

CAUTION Use the answer spaces in the grids below for Section 6 or Section 7 only if you are told to do so in your test book.

Student-Produced Responses

ONLY ANSWERS ENTERED IN THE CIRCLES IN EACH GRID WILL BE SCORED. YOU WILL NOT RECEIVE CREDIT FOR ANYTHING WRITTEN IN THE BOXES ABOVE THE CIRCLES.

PLEASE DO NOT WRITE IN THIS AREA

Start with number 1 for each new section. If a section has fewer questions than answer spaces, leave the extra answer spaces blank. Be sure to erase any errors or stray marks completely.

SECTION 8

1	Ⓐ Ⓑ Ⓒ Ⓓ Ⓔ	11	Ⓐ Ⓑ Ⓒ Ⓓ Ⓔ	21	Ⓐ Ⓑ Ⓒ Ⓓ Ⓔ	31	Ⓐ Ⓑ Ⓒ Ⓓ Ⓔ
2	Ⓐ Ⓑ Ⓒ Ⓓ Ⓔ	12	Ⓐ Ⓑ Ⓒ Ⓓ Ⓔ	22	Ⓐ Ⓑ Ⓒ Ⓓ Ⓔ	32	Ⓐ Ⓑ Ⓒ Ⓓ Ⓔ
3	Ⓐ Ⓑ Ⓒ Ⓓ Ⓔ	13	Ⓐ Ⓑ Ⓒ Ⓓ Ⓔ	23	Ⓐ Ⓑ Ⓒ Ⓓ Ⓔ	33	Ⓐ Ⓑ Ⓒ Ⓓ Ⓔ
4	Ⓐ Ⓑ Ⓒ Ⓓ Ⓔ	14	Ⓐ Ⓑ Ⓒ Ⓓ Ⓔ	24	Ⓐ Ⓑ Ⓒ Ⓓ Ⓔ	34	Ⓐ Ⓑ Ⓒ Ⓓ Ⓔ
5	Ⓐ Ⓑ Ⓒ Ⓓ Ⓔ	15	Ⓐ Ⓑ Ⓒ Ⓓ Ⓔ	25	Ⓐ Ⓑ Ⓒ Ⓓ Ⓔ	35	Ⓐ Ⓑ Ⓒ Ⓓ Ⓔ
6	Ⓐ Ⓑ Ⓒ Ⓓ Ⓔ	16	Ⓐ Ⓑ Ⓒ Ⓓ Ⓔ	26	Ⓐ Ⓑ Ⓒ Ⓓ Ⓔ	36	Ⓐ Ⓑ Ⓒ Ⓓ Ⓔ
7	Ⓐ Ⓑ Ⓒ Ⓓ Ⓔ	17	Ⓐ Ⓑ Ⓒ Ⓓ Ⓔ	27	Ⓐ Ⓑ Ⓒ Ⓓ Ⓔ	37	Ⓐ Ⓑ Ⓒ Ⓓ Ⓔ
8	Ⓐ Ⓑ Ⓒ Ⓓ Ⓔ	18	Ⓐ Ⓑ Ⓒ Ⓓ Ⓔ	28	Ⓐ Ⓑ Ⓒ Ⓓ Ⓔ	38	Ⓐ Ⓑ Ⓒ Ⓓ Ⓔ
9	Ⓐ Ⓑ Ⓒ Ⓓ Ⓔ	19	Ⓐ Ⓑ Ⓒ Ⓓ Ⓔ	29	Ⓐ Ⓑ Ⓒ Ⓓ Ⓔ	39	Ⓐ Ⓑ Ⓒ Ⓓ Ⓔ
10	Ⓐ Ⓑ Ⓒ Ⓓ Ⓔ	20	Ⓐ Ⓑ Ⓒ Ⓓ Ⓔ	30	Ⓐ Ⓑ Ⓒ Ⓓ Ⓔ	40	Ⓐ Ⓑ Ⓒ Ⓓ Ⓔ

SECTION 9

1	Ⓐ Ⓑ Ⓒ Ⓓ Ⓔ	11	Ⓐ Ⓑ Ⓒ Ⓓ Ⓔ	21	Ⓐ Ⓑ Ⓒ Ⓓ Ⓔ	31	Ⓐ Ⓑ Ⓒ Ⓓ Ⓔ
2	Ⓐ Ⓑ Ⓒ Ⓓ Ⓔ	12	Ⓐ Ⓑ Ⓒ Ⓓ Ⓔ	22	Ⓐ Ⓑ Ⓒ Ⓓ Ⓔ	32	Ⓐ Ⓑ Ⓒ Ⓓ Ⓔ
3	Ⓐ Ⓑ Ⓒ Ⓓ Ⓔ	13	Ⓐ Ⓑ Ⓒ Ⓓ Ⓔ	23	Ⓐ Ⓑ Ⓒ Ⓓ Ⓔ	33	Ⓐ Ⓑ Ⓒ Ⓓ Ⓔ
4	Ⓐ Ⓑ Ⓒ Ⓓ Ⓔ	14	Ⓐ Ⓑ Ⓒ Ⓓ Ⓔ	24	Ⓐ Ⓑ Ⓒ Ⓓ Ⓔ	34	Ⓐ Ⓑ Ⓒ Ⓓ Ⓔ
5	Ⓐ Ⓑ Ⓒ Ⓓ Ⓔ	15	Ⓐ Ⓑ Ⓒ Ⓓ Ⓔ	25	Ⓐ Ⓑ Ⓒ Ⓓ Ⓔ	35	Ⓐ Ⓑ Ⓒ Ⓓ Ⓔ
6	Ⓐ Ⓑ Ⓒ Ⓓ Ⓔ	16	Ⓐ Ⓑ Ⓒ Ⓓ Ⓔ	26	Ⓐ Ⓑ Ⓒ Ⓓ Ⓔ	36	Ⓐ Ⓑ Ⓒ Ⓓ Ⓔ
7	Ⓐ Ⓑ Ⓒ Ⓓ Ⓔ	17	Ⓐ Ⓑ Ⓒ Ⓓ Ⓔ	27	Ⓐ Ⓑ Ⓒ Ⓓ Ⓔ	37	Ⓐ Ⓑ Ⓒ Ⓓ Ⓔ
8	Ⓐ Ⓑ Ⓒ Ⓓ Ⓔ	18	Ⓐ Ⓑ Ⓒ Ⓓ Ⓔ	28	Ⓐ Ⓑ Ⓒ Ⓓ Ⓔ	38	Ⓐ Ⓑ Ⓒ Ⓓ Ⓔ
9	Ⓐ Ⓑ Ⓒ Ⓓ Ⓔ	19	Ⓐ Ⓑ Ⓒ Ⓓ Ⓔ	29	Ⓐ Ⓑ Ⓒ Ⓓ Ⓔ	39	Ⓐ Ⓑ Ⓒ Ⓓ Ⓔ
10	Ⓐ Ⓑ Ⓒ Ⓓ Ⓔ	20	Ⓐ Ⓑ Ⓒ Ⓓ Ⓔ	30	Ⓐ Ⓑ Ⓒ Ⓓ Ⓔ	40	Ⓐ Ⓑ Ⓒ Ⓓ Ⓔ

ESSAY   ESSAY

ESSAY
Time—25 minutes

Write your essay on separate sheets of standard lined paper.

The essay gives you an opportunity to show how effectively you can develop and express ideas. You should therefore take care to develop your point of view, present your ideas logically and clearly, and use language precisely.

Your essay must be written on the lines provided on your answer sheet—you will receive no other paper on which to write. You will have enough space if you write on every line, avoid wide margins, and keep your handwriting to a reasonable size. Remember that people who are not familiar with your handwriting will read what you write. Try to write or print so that what you are writing is legible to those readers.

Important reminders:

- **A pencil is required for the essay.** An essay written in ink will receive a score of zero.
- **Do not write your essay in your test book.** You will receive credit only for what you write on your answer sheet.
- **An off-topic essay will receive a score of zero.**

You have twenty-five minutes to write an essay on the topic assigned below.

Consider carefully the issue discussed in the following passage, then write an essay that answers the question posed in the assignment.

> Many among us like to blame violence and immorality in the media for a "decline in morals" in society. Yet these people seem to have lost touch with logic. Any objective examination shows that our society is far less violent or exploitative than virtually any society in the past. Early humans murdered and enslaved each other with astonishing regularity, without the help of gangsta rap or Jerry Bruckheimer films.

Assignment: **Do violence and immorality in the media make our society more dangerous and immoral?** Write an essay in which you answer this question and discuss your point of view on this issue. Support your position logically with examples from literature, the arts, history, politics, science and technology, current events, or your experience or observation.

If you finish before time is called, you may check your work on this section only.
Do not turn to any other section in the test.

2   2   2   2   2   2

SECTION 2
Time—25 minutes
20 questions

Turn to Section 2 of your answer sheet to answer the questions in this section.

Directions: For this section, solve each problem and decide which is the best of the choices given. Fill in the corresponding circle on the answer sheet. You may use any available space for scratchwork.

Notes

1. The use of a calculator is permitted.

2. All numbers used are real numbers.

3. Figures that accompany problems in this test are intended to provide information useful in solving the problems. They are drawn as accurately as possible EXCEPT when it is stated in a specific problem that the figure is not drawn to scale. All figures lie in a plane unless otherwise indicated.

4. Unless otherwise specified, the domain of any function f is assumed to be the set of all real numbers x for which $f(x)$ is a real number.

Reference Information

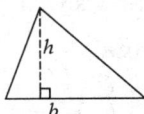

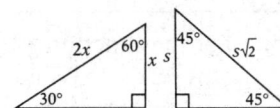

$A = \pi r^2$ $A = \ell w$ $A = \frac{1}{2} bh$ $V = \ell wh$ $V = \pi r^2 h$ $c^2 = a^2 + b^2$ Special right triangles
$C = 2\pi r$

The number of degrees of arc in a circle is 360.
The sum of the measures in degrees of the angles of a triangle is 180.

---

1. If $(x + 4) + 7 = 14$, what is the value of x?

   (A)   3
   (B)   7
   (C)   11
   (D)   17
   (E)   25

2. Erica spends $.95 each day for her newspaper subscriptions. She would like to determine the approximate amount she spends during the month of July, which has 31 days. Which of the following would provide her with the best estimate?

   (A) $.50 \times 30$
   (B) 1.00×30
   (C) 1.50×30
   (D) $.50 \times 35$
   (E) 1.00×35

GO ON TO THE NEXT PAGE

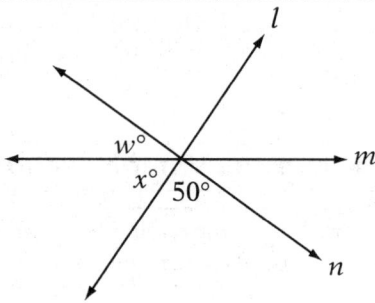

Note: Figure not drawn to scale.

3. In the figure above, lines l, m, and n intersect in a single point. What is the value of $w + x$?

    (A)   40
    (B)   70
    (C)   90
    (D)   130
    (E)   140

4. Let the function g be defined by the equation $g(x) = 3x + 4$. What is the value of $g(5)$?

    (A)   8
    (B)   11
    (C)   15
    (D)   19
    (E)   23

5. If $x > y$, which of the following equations expresses the fact that when the difference between x and y is multiplied by their sum, the product is 18?

    (A) $(x - y)^2 = 18$
    (B) $(x + y)^2 = 18$
    (C) $(x - y) \div (x + y) = 18$
    (D) $x^2 - y^2 = 18$
    (E) $x^2 + y^2 = 18$

6. If $3\sqrt{x} - 7 = 20$, what is the value of x?

    (A)   3
    (B)   9
    (C)   27
    (D)   36
    (E)   81

7. Chris buys a chocolate bar and a pack of gum for $1.75. If the chocolate bar costs $.25 more than the pack of gum, how much does the pack of gum cost?

    (A) $.25
    (B) $.50
    (C) $.75
    (D) $1.00
    (E) $1.50

8. 40% of 80 is what percent of 96?

    (A)   20%
    (B)   30%
    (C)   33⅓%
    (D)   50%
    (E)   66⅔%

9. If l, m, and n are positive integers greater than 1, $lm = 21$, and $mn = 39$, then which of the following must be true?

    (A) $n > l > m$
    (B) $m > n > l$
    (C) $m > l > n$
    (D) $l > n > m$
    (E) $n > m > l$

GO ON TO THE NEXT PAGE

2   **2**   **2**   **2**   **2**   **2**

ANNUAL PROFITS FOR ABC COMPANY
(IN THOUSANDS OF DOLLARS)

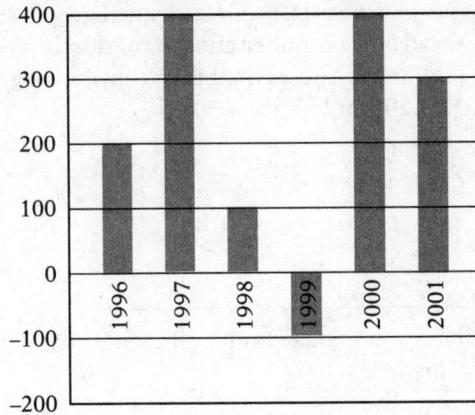

10. According to the graph above, ABC Company showed the greatest change in profits between which 2 years?

(A) 1996 and 1997
(B) 1997 and 1998
(C) 1998 and 1999
(D) 1999 and 2000
(E) 2000 and 2001

11. In a 9th-grade class, 12 students play soccer, 7 students play tennis, and 9 students play lacrosse. If 4 students play exactly two of the three sports and all other students play only one, how many students are in the class?

(A) 28
(B) 24
(C) 20
(D) 18
(E) 16

12. The point (14, 14) is the center of a circle, and (2, 9) is a point on the circle. What is the length of the diameter of the circle?

(A) 24
(B) 26
(C) 50
(D) 144π
(E) 169π

13. The population of Boomtown doubles every 18 months. In January of 2000, its population was exactly 12,000. At this rate, approximately when should the population reach 96,000?

(A) January 2003
(B) July 2004
(C) January 2006
(D) July 2007
(E) January 2012

14. In how many different ways can five students of different heights be arranged in a line if the tallest student cannot be on either end?

(A) 24
(B) 25
(C) 72
(D) 96
(E) 120

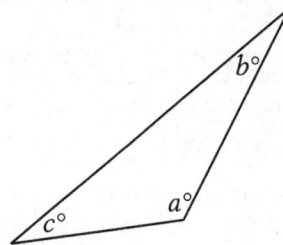

Note: Figure not drawn to scale.

15. In the figure above, $a > 90$ and $b = c + 3$. If a, b, and c are all integers, what is the greatest possible value of b?

(A) 43
(B) 46
(C) 60
(D) 86
(E) 89

GO ON TO THE NEXT PAGE ⟹

2 **2** **2** **2** **2** **2**

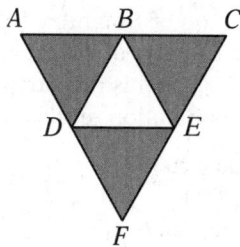

16. In the figure above, $\triangle ACF$ is equilateral, with sides of length 4. If B, D, and E are the midpoints of their respective sides, what is the sum of the areas of the shaded regions?

(A) $3\sqrt{2}$ (B) $3\sqrt{3}$ (C) $4\sqrt{2}$

(D) $4\sqrt{3}$ (E) $6\sqrt{3}$

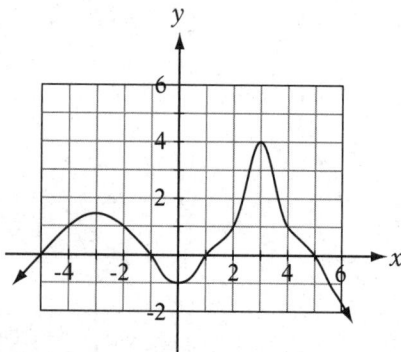

17. Given the graph of $y = f(x)$ above, which of the following sets represents all values of x for which $f(x) \geq 1$?

(A) all real numbers
(B) $x \geq 1$
(C) $-5 \leq x \leq -1; 1 \leq x \leq 5$
(D) $-4 \leq x \leq -2; 2 \leq x \leq 4$
(E) $x \leq -4; x \geq 4$

X: {2, 4, 6, 8, 10}

Y: {1, 3, 5, 7, 9}

18. If a is a number chosen randomly from set X and b is a number chosen randomly from set Y, what is the probability that ab is greater than 20 but less than 50?

(A) $\dfrac{1}{5}$ (B) $\dfrac{6}{5}$ (C) $\dfrac{7}{25}$

(D) $\dfrac{3}{5}$ (E) $\dfrac{18}{25}$

19. If $w^a \times w^5 = w^{15}$ and $(w^4)^b = w^{12}$, what is the value of $a + b$?

(A)   6
(B)   7
(C)   11
(D)   12
(E)   13

GO ON TO THE NEXT PAGE

2   2   2   2   2   2

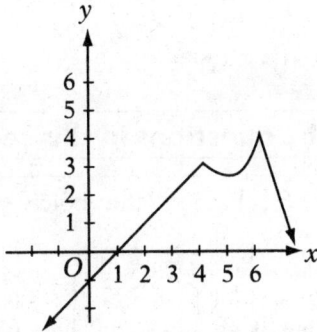

20. Given the graph of $y = f(x)$ above, which of the following represents the graph of $y = f(x - 2)$?

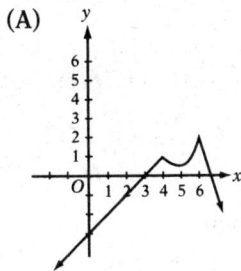

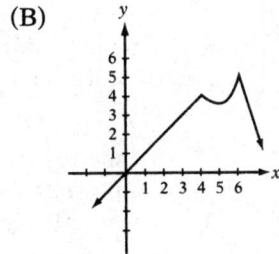

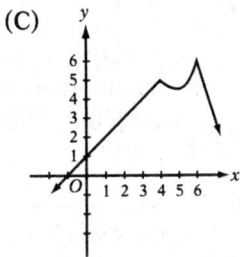

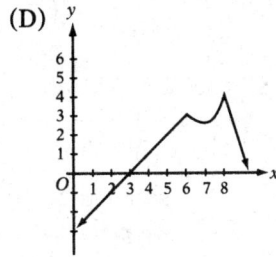

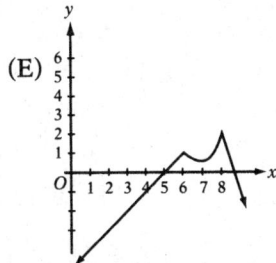

(A)

(B)

(C)

(D)

(E)

STOP

If you finish before time is called, you may check your work on this section only. Do not turn to any other section of the test.

3   **3**   **3**   **3**   **3**   **3**

SECTION 3
Time—25 minutes
24 questions

> ### Turn to Section 3 of your answer sheet to answer the questions in this section.

> **Directions:** For each question in this section, select the best answer from among the choices given and fill in the corresponding circle on the answer sheet.

Each sentence below has one or two blanks, each blank indicating that something has been omitted. Beneath the sentence are five words or sets of words labeled A through E. Choose the word or set of words that, when inserted in the sentence, <u>best</u> fits the meaning of the sentence as a whole.

EXAMPLE:

Rather than accepting the theory unquestioningly, Deborah regarded it with _____.

(A) mirth
(B) sadness
(C) responsibility
(D) ignorance
(E) skepticism

Ⓐ Ⓑ Ⓒ Ⓓ ●

---

1. Although he purchased his computer only 10 months ago, rapid improvements in technology have left Raúl with ------- machine.

   (A) an obsolete   (B) an adjunct
   (C) a novel   (D) an automated
   (E) an elusive

2. Only if the number of applicants continues to -------- can the admissions committee justify offering more scholarships in order to increase the number of applications.

   (A) mushroom   (B) expand   (C) plummet
   (D) satiate   (E) burgeon

3. My father is so ------- that he will never even consider another person's viewpoint to be valid if it is different from his own.

   (A) pragmatic   (B) dogmatic   (C) phlegmatic
   (D) cordial   (E) curt

4. J. K. Rowling's *Harry Potter* series is a collection of works that are ------- for children but are still ------- to adults.

   (A) penned . . prosaic
   (B) employed . . morose
   (C) censored . . incongruous
   (D) designed . . tedious
   (E) authored . . engaging

5. Julia approaches her homework assignments in such ------- way that it is very difficult to believe that she is at the top of her class.

   (A) an adept   (B) a diligent   (C) a fanatical
   (D) an extroverted   (E) a laggardly

6. The President was such a ------- orator that his opponents were always supremely cautious about agreeing to debate him.

   (A) redoubtable   (B) staid   (C) magnanimous
   (D) weak   (E) stoic

7. The newest clothing line revealed at the show was an eclectic mix that ranged from the modest and unadorned to the ------- and garish.

   (A) austere   (B) prophetic   (C) cordial
   (D) ostentatious   (E) solitary

> **GO ON TO THE NEXT PAGE** ⟩

3   3   3   3   3   3

8. Neil Campbell's textbook *Biology* is ------- and yet -------; it includes all of the essential information without ever being verbose.

   (A) compendious . . circumlocutory
   (B) reprehensible . . terse
   (C) comprehensive . . concise
   (D) praiseworthy . . grandiloquent
   (E) painstaking . . redundant

The passages below are followed by questions based on their content; questions following a pair of related passages may also be based on the relationship between the paired passages. Answer the questions on the basis of what is <u>stated</u> or <u>implied</u> in the passage and in any introductory material that may be provided.

Questions 9–12 are based on the following passages.

PASSAGE 1

The following is from President Bill Clinton's first inaugural address.

    Today, a generation raised in the shadows of the Cold War assumes new responsibilities in a
Line   world warmed by the sunshine of freedom, but threatened still by ancient hatreds and new
5   plagues. Raised in unrivaled prosperity, we inherit an economy that is still the world's strongest, but is weakened by business failures, stagnant wages, increasing inequality, and deep divisions among our own people. When
10   George Washington first took the oath I have just sworn to uphold, news traveled slowly across the land by horseback, and across the ocean by boat. Now the sights and sounds of this ceremony are broadcast instantaneously to
15   billions around the world. Communications and commerce are global. Investment is mobile. Technology is almost magical, and ambition for a better life is now universal.

PASSAGE 2

The following is a commentary on America written in 2005 by an American writer.

    The people of the world, save the majority
20   of our own citizens, are growing to appreciate the difference between America and the United States. America is the heart and mind of the world. It is an ideal to which all free-
25   thinking men and women aspire. It is the spirit of hope, freedom, vision and creativity. But the United States, at least since the turn of the century, has become something different. It constantly grasps at the cloak of America,
30   but this cloak fits our current leaders quite poorly. Our leaders have become dominated by fear and its value as a political tool. They speak incessantly of freedom but revel in repression. They speak of a "culture of life"
35   but revel in the culture of siege and war. The hope, freedom, vision and creativity of America have slipped through their fingers, and they have little hope of recapturing it. In America, that task is left to the people.

9. The word "unrivaled" in line 5 most nearly means

   (A) without enemies
   (B) supremely abundant
   (C) militarily superior
   (D) unimaginable
   (E) highly intelligent

10. Which of the following best describes the contrast between the "people" (line 9) as characterized in Passage 1 and the "citizens" (line 20) as characterized in Passage 2?

   (A) the "people" are ignorant, while the "citizens" are well educated
   (B) the "people" lack fortitude, while the "citizens" are courageous
   (C) the "people" are worldly, while the "citizens" are parochial
   (D) the "people" are proud of their leaders, while the "citizens" are not
   (E) the "people" lack unity, while the "citizens" lack awareness

GO ON TO THE NEXT PAGE ⇨

3   **3**   **3**   **3**   **3**   **3**

11. Passage 1 makes all of the following claims about the state of society EXCEPT that

   (A) an increasing number of people are happy with their lives
   (B) information is disseminated more rapidly than in the past
   (C) the current economy is strong
   (D) social inequities are deepening
   (E) workers' incomes are not increasing

12. Unlike the author of Passage 1, the author of Passage 2 does which of the following?

   (A) contrasts an ideal with a reality
   (B) explains a study
   (C) compares the past with the present
   (D) describes an injustice
   (E) acknowledges a responsibility

Questions 13–19 are based on the following passage.

The following passage is adapted from a short story published by a Russian author in the late 1970s.

What is all this? he thought, terrified. And yet . . . do I love her, or don't I? That is the
Line question!
       But she, now that the most important and
5 difficult thing had at last been said, breathed lightly and freely. She, too, stood up and, looking straight into Ognev Alexeyich's face, began to talk quickly, irrepressibly and ardently.
       Just as a man who is suddenly overwhelmed
10 by terror cannot afterwards remember the exact order of sounds accompanying the catastrophe which stuns him, Ognev could not remember Vera's words and phrases. His memory retained only the substance of her speech
15 itself and the sensation her speech produced in him. He remembered her voice, as though it were choked and slightly hoarse from excitement,

and the extraordinary music and passion of her intonation. Crying, laughing, the tears
20 glittering on her eyelashes, she was telling him that even from the first days of their acquaintance she had been struck by his originality, his intellect, his kind intelligent eyes, with the aims and objects of his life; that she had fallen pas-
25 sionately, madly and deeply in love with him; that whenever she had happened to come into the house from the garden that summer and had seen his coat in the vestibule or heard his voice in the distance, her heart had felt a cold
30 thrill of delight, a foretaste of happiness; that even the silliest jokes made her laugh helplessly, and in each figure of his copybook she could see something extraordinarily clever and grandiose; that his knotted walking stick
35 seemed to her more beautiful than the trees.
       The forest and the wisps of fog and the black ditches alongside the road seemed to fall silent, listening to her, but something bad and strange was taking place in Ognev's
40 heart. . . . Vera was enchantingly beautiful as she told him of her love, she spoke with eloquence and passion, but much as he wanted to, he could feel no joy, no fundamental happiness, but only compassion for Vera, and
45 pain and regret that a good human being should be suffering because of him. The Lord only knows whether it was his bookish mind that now began to speak, or whether he was affected by that irresistible habit of objectivity
50 which so often prevents people from living, but Vera's raptures and suffering seemed to him only cloying and trivial. At the same time he was outraged with himself and something whispered to him that what he was now see-
55 ing and hearing was, from the point of view of human nature and his personal happiness, more important than any statistics, books or philosophical truths . . . And he was annoyed and blamed himself even though he himself
60 did not understand why he was to blame.

GO ON TO THE NEXT PAGE

3   **3**   **3**   **3**   **3**   **3**

13. Which of the following best describes the characterization of the man and the woman in the first two paragraphs?

    (A) He is confused, while she is passionate.
    (B) He is angry, while she is jocular.
    (C) He is stoic, while she is serene.
    (D) He is ambivalent, while she is anxious.
    (E) He is disdainful, while she is whimsical.

14. The author suggests that one "who is suddenly overwhelmed by terror" (lines 9–10) is temporarily

    (A) vindictive
    (B) defensive
    (C) cautious
    (D) disoriented
    (E) resentful

15. The description of "the catastrophe" (lines 11–12) serves primarily to suggest that

    (A) the couple has endured a terrible accident
    (B) Ognev is devastated by Vera's harsh words
    (C) Ognev is deeply troubled by Vera's passionate expression of love
    (D) Ognev holds Vera responsible for a crime
    (E) Vera has told Ognev a horrible secret

16. In line 24, "objects" most nearly means

    (A) possessions
    (B) facts
    (C) decorations
    (D) goals
    (E) complaints

17. The passage suggests that the "bad and strange" (line 39) thing that was taking place in Ognev's heart was his

    (A) eagerness
    (B) sadism
    (C) jealousy
    (D) hatred
    (E) disaffection

18. In lines 57–58, "statistics, books or philosophical truths" are mentioned as examples of things that

    (A) Vera does not understand
    (B) Ognev and Vera share reluctantly
    (C) Ognev abandoned long ago
    (D) Vera loves passionately
    (E) Ognev inexplicably values more highly than passion

19. The primary function of the final paragraph is to show Ognev's

    (A) struggle to understand his own feelings
    (B) anger about Vera's misrepresentation of her feelings
    (C) frustration with the voices in his head
    (D) outrage with his inability to understand a philosophical concept
    (E) appreciation of Vera's beauty

GO ON TO THE NEXT PAGE ⟶

3   3   3   3   3   3

Questions 20–24 are based on the following passage.

The following is part of an introduction to the publication of a speech delivered by President Lyndon B. Johnson in the 1960s.

"Somehow you never forget what poverty
and hatred can do when you see its scars on
the hopeful face of a young child." So spoke
President Lyndon B. Johnson in the course of
5   one of the most deeply felt, and deeply moving, addresses ever delivered by an American
president. The date was March 15th, 1965; the
occasion was an extraordinary joint session at
night of the Senate and the House of Repre-
10   sentatives, televised across the nation. It was
the "time of Selma"—only a few days after the
historic mass demonstration in support of
voter registration in Alabama, in which many
of the peaceful marchers were physically at-
15   tacked and one of them, a white clergyman
from the north, was killed. The nation itself
was a shocked witness, via television, of much
of that unforgettable scene: the long rows of
marchers, a cross section of African Americans
20   and whites, Californians and New Yorkers,
resolutely striding, smiling, singing to hide
their exhaustion, trying not to see the hate-
twisted faces and shouting menace of the side-
walk crowd, trying not to fear the armored
25   troopers and police with their notorious supporting artillery of dogs, clubs, and cattle
prods.
This was the moment chosen by the President, himself a Southerner with a reputation
30   for compromise, to bear witness before the
nation, and to call upon his former associates
of Congress to stand up and be counted with
him—more specifically, to take action on a
bill which would correct the conspicuous
35   weakness of the 1964 Civil Rights Bill, its failure to protect the right of African Americans
to vote "when local officials are determined to
deny it." In forthright terms, President Johnson spelled out the full cruelty and ingenuity

40   of that discrimination, and crisply defined the
central issue involved: "There is no Constitu-
tional issue here. The command of the Constitution is plain. There is no moral issue. It is
wrong—deadly wrong—to deny any of your
45   fellow Americans the right to vote in this
country. There is no issue of state's rights or
national rights. There is only the struggle for
human rights."
The President spoke slowly, solemnly, with
50   unmistakable determination. His words and
his manner were perfectly synchronized; indeed he made the nationwide audience aware
of how deeply personal the issue of African
American rights was to him. He recalled his
55   own southern origins, and his shattering encounter with Mexican-American children as a
young schoolteacher ("They never seemed to
know why people disliked them, but they
knew it was so because I saw it in their eyes.")
60   He spoke more directly, more explicitly, and
more warmly of the human experience of
prejudice than any president before him. But
he also placed the problem of African American rights in a broader frame of reference—
65   that of poverty and ignorance, bigotry and
fear. "Their cause must be our cause too.
Because it is not just African Americans, but
really it's all of us, who must overcome the
crippling legacy of bigotry and injustice. And
70   we shall overcome."

GO ON TO THE NEXT PAGE

3   3   3   3   3   3

---

20. In the first paragraph, the marchers are characterized as

(A) ruthless
(B) gleeful
(C) intellectual
(D) stoic
(E) shocked

21. The passage indicates that the 1964 Civil Rights Act was deficient in that it did not

(A) sufficiently pressure local officials to extend voting privileges to all citizens
(B) provide enough funds to promote voter registration drives
(C) punish felons who committed hate crimes
(D) provide military protection for the Selma marchers
(E) invest in minority-owned businesses

22. In line 55, *shattering* most nearly means

(A) exploding
(B) disturbing
(C) fragmenting
(D) violent
(E) loud

23. The quotation in lines 57–59 ("They never seemed . . . in their eyes") indicates that Johnson

(A) understood the political process at a young age
(B) was unfamiliar with Mexican-American customs
(C) empathized strongly with his students
(D) was a victim of bigotry
(E) was unaware of the difficulties his students faced

24. The passage indicates that Johnson, unlike previous presidents, handled the issue of civil rights by

(A) successfully integrating the issue into his reelection campaign
(B) approaching the cause with objectivity and impartiality
(C) speaking clearly to reporters using terms they wanted to hear
(D) focusing primarily on the Mexican-American population
(E) directly addressing the public on the issue and describing it in personal terms

STOP

If you finish before time is called, you may check your work on this section only. Do not turn to any other section of the test.

SECTION 4
Time—25 minutes
35 questions

Turn to Section 4 of your answer sheet to answer the questions in this section.

Directions: For each question in this section, select the best answer from among the choices given and fill in the corresponding circle on the answer sheet.

The following sentences test correctness and effectiveness of expression. Part of each sentence or the entire sentence is underlined; beneath each sentence are five ways of phrasing the underlined material. Choice A repeats the original phrasing; the other four choices are different. If you think the original phrasing produces a better sentence than any of the alternatives, select choice A; if not, select one of the other choices.

In making your selection, follow the requirements of standard written English; that is, pay attention to grammar, choice of words, sentence construction, and punctuation. Your selection should result in the most effective sentence—clear and precise, without awkwardness or ambiguity.

EXAMPLE:

The children couldn't hardly believe their eyes.

(A) couldn't hardly believe their eyes
(B) could hardly believe their eyes
(C) would not hardly believe their eyes
(D) couldn't nearly believe their eyes
(E) couldn't hardly believe his or her eyes

Ⓐ ● Ⓒ Ⓓ Ⓔ

1. Exhausted from a day of hiking across steep, rain-soaked paths, the group of campers were relieved upon the final reaching of the car.

(A) group of campers were relieved upon the final reaching of the car
(B) camping group became relieved after they got to the car
(C) group of campers was relieved to finally reach the car
(D) campers were relieved after the car was finally reached
(E) group was relieved after the campers finally reached the car

2. Theodore Roosevelt's first term as President was marked by a ferocious battle between labor and management in Pennsylvania's coal mining industry.

(A) was marked by a ferocious battle between labor and management
(B) was marked by a ferocious battle of labor's and management's
(C) saw a ferocious battle: between labor and management
(D) was marked ferociously by labor and management's battle
(E) was marking a ferocious battle between labor and management

GO ON TO THE NEXT PAGE

4 4 4 4 4 4

3. Many great scientists and inventors of the past, such as Nikola Tesla, <u>has possessed the ability of extraordinary visualization skills</u> that enabled them to analyze the most minute details of complex machines before the devices were even constructed.

(A) has possessed the ability of extraordinary visualization skills
(B) have been able to possess extraordinary visualization skills
(C) possessed skills in visualization that was extraordinary
(D) possessed extraordinary visualization skills
(E) possessed skills of visualizing that was extraordinary

4. The Thracians, originally divided into numerous tribes, came together politically under King Teres in 500 BC, and <u>it enabled their resistance against</u> the many Roman invasions that would follow in the centuries to come.

(A) it enabled their resistance against
(B) this unity enabled them to resist
(C) enabling the ability to resist
(D) that enabled them to resist
(E) this unity gave them the ability of resisting

5. Disillusioned by American politics and culture, Ernest Hemingway <u>led an exodus of expatriate authors on an overseas journey</u> across the Atlantic following the World War I.

(A) led an exodus of expatriate authors on an overseas journey
(B) took an overseas journey leading an exodus of expatriate authors
(C) led an exodus of expatriate authors
(D) has led an exodus of expatriate authors
(E) leading an exodus of expatriate authors

6. Walter Cronkite was known for his honest presentation of the <u>news, plus the ability to be reassuring with his tone</u>.

(A) news, plus the ability to be reassuring with his tone
(B) news, plus his reassuring tone
(C) news plus the reassuring nature of his tone
(D) news and his tone that was reassuring
(E) news and his reassuring tone

7. Only half as many students study computer science <u>than they did</u> just a decade ago.

(A) than they did
(B) than was true
(C) as did
(D) when compared to
(E) than

8. Auto racing, often thought of as a regional phenomenon, <u>therefore is quite popular</u> throughout the nation.

(A) therefore is quite popular
(B) henceforth is quite popular
(C) is thus quite popular
(D) is actually quite popular
(E) in retrospect, is quite popular

GO ON TO THE NEXT PAGE ▷

9. The band decided to allow <u>downloading their songs for their fans free of charge</u>, in the hope of increasing its popularity.

   (A) downloading their songs for their fans free of charge
   (B) their fans downloading their songs free of charge
   (C) its fans to download its songs free of charge
   (D) free downloading of their songs to its fans
   (E) downloading of its songs to its fans, which were free of charge

10. The most likely reasons for the recent surge in legislation <u>is the fact that the voters agree on the issues and the political parties stopping</u> bickering.

   (A) is the fact that the voters agree on the issues and the political parties stopping
   (B) are because the voters agree on the issues and the political parties have stopped
   (C) are that the voters agree on the issues and that the political parties have stopped
   (D) is the voters agreeing on the issues and the political parties stopping
   (E) are the voters agreeing on the issues and the political parties have stopped

11. An untiring defender of the downtrodden, <u>Clarence Darrow's oratory could mesmerize his audiences and devastate his opponents</u>.

   (A) Clarence Darrow's oratory could mesmerize his audiences and devastate his opponents
   (B) Clarence Darrow could mesmerize his audiences and devastate his opponents with his oratory
   (C) the oratory of Clarence Darrow could mesmerize his audiences and devastate his opponents
   (D) Clarence Darrow's audiences could be mesmerized by his oratory and his opponents devastated by it
   (E) Clarence Darrow could mesmerize his audiences with his oratory, and his opponents could be devastated by it

The following sentences test your ability to recognize grammar and usage errors. Each sentence contains either a single error or no error at all. No sentence contains more than one error. The error, if there is one, is underlined and lettered. If the sentence contains an error, select the one underlined part that must be changed to make the sentence correct. If the sentence is correct, select choice E. In choosing answers, follow the requirements of standard written English.

EXAMPLE:

By the time <u>they reached</u> the halfway point
                A
in the race, <u>most of the runners</u> <u>hadn't hardly</u>
              B   C   D
begun to hit their stride.   <u>No error</u>
                                  E

Ⓐ Ⓑ Ⓒ ● Ⓔ

12. The local dairy company is <u>one of the most</u>
                                      A
<u>efficient</u> in the state, <u>so</u> it is surprising that
    B   C
the delivery of our milk products over the last

few days <u>have been</u> late.   <u>No error</u>
            D   E

13. Sea turtle hatchlings can find their way

<u>to the ocean</u> by sight alone, even at night, <u>because</u>
    A   B
they are capable <u>to distinguish</u> visually between
                      C
the bright reflections from the ocean surface <u>and</u>
                                                  D
the dark silhouettes of sand dunes and vegetation.

<u>No error</u>
    E

GO ON TO THE NEXT PAGE

4   4   4   4   4   4

14. This holiday season, several members of the
     A
    committee are sponsoring a dinner to raise
              B
    money for their efforts to encourage
                     C
    responsible driving.   No error
        D   E

15. The lavish photographs and fascinating

    diagrams in the biology textbook was so
                A   B
    engaging that I seriously considered
                              C
    becoming a zoologist.   No error
             D   E

16. Behavioral scientists believe that the way
                          A
    chimpanzees form friendships and alliances
                B
    is very similar to humans.   No error
       C   D   E

17. When the window was opened, the affects of
                     A   B
    the cool spring breeze were felt immediately
                                  C
    by the uncomfortable workers.   No error
            D   E

18. The probability of getting hit by lightning
                    A
    are fewer than the probability of winning
        B   C
    the lottery, although both are minuscule.
                     D
    No error
        E

19. According to the new editorial guidelines for
    A
    publication, before an author submits a
                                 B
    manuscript to the publisher, they must first
                                 C
    have the text reviewed by a qualified content
         D
    expert.   No error
                   E

20. In his book Night, Elie Wiesel employs a
    A
    disjointed style, frequently shifting point of view
                     B
    in order to capture the fragmented nature of
              C
    ghetto life in Germany in the time during
                            D
    the World War II.   No error
                             E

21. Although we had expected poor service at
    A
    the resort, we were more than satisfied at the
               B   C
    attention we received throughout our stay.
              D
    No error
        E

22. After we had ate a leisurely meal, we walked
            A
    down the street and discovered a jazz club
         B   C
    where a talented young trio was playing.
                                 D
    No error
        E

GO ON TO THE NEXT PAGE

23. Ancient Babylonian physicians <u>were</u> among
                                A

the first <u>to investigate</u> the character and
               B

course of diseases scientifically, <u>although</u>
                         C

they frequently attributed the causes of those

ailments <u>to the anger</u> of gods or demons.
              D

<u>No error</u>
  E

24. When <u>the filaments</u> of the angler fish
                A

<u>are stimulated</u>, its jaws, <u>armed</u> with bands of
  B   C

sharp inward-pointing teeth, <u>is</u> triggered to
                     D

snap shut. <u>No error</u>
      E

25. Some doctors <u>believe that</u> taking vitamins
                 A

<u>on a daily basis</u> <u>help</u> decrease a patient's
  B   C

susceptibility <u>to infection</u>. <u>No error</u>
                D   E

26. When my parents <u>went</u> out to dinner, they
                  A

left me <u>underneath</u> the <u>control of</u> our
              B   C

babysitter, <u>who lived</u> next door to us.
               D

<u>No error</u>
  E

27. Since 2001, the company <u>has spent</u> <u>more on</u>
                    A   B

employee training than <u>they did</u> in the
                   C

previous 10 years <u>combined</u>. <u>No error</u>
                D   E

28. <u>To create</u> a productive working relationship
  A

<u>with</u> high school students, <u>a teacher</u> should not
  B   C

only command respect, but <u>he or she should also</u>
                       D

develop a productive rapport. <u>No error</u>
                  E

29. After several trials, the chemists <u>discovered</u>
                    A

that the precipitates <u>could be</u> more effectively
                  B

separated <u>by</u> a high-speed centrifuge <u>and not</u>
              C   D

by a filtration system. <u>No error</u>
                E

GO ON TO THE NEXT PAGE ▷

4   4   4   4   4   4

Questions 30–35 refer to the following passage.

(1) While known when he was the President for his abundant energy and muscular build as an adult, Theodore Roosevelt's build as a child was actually quite puny. (2) Stricken with asthma, he was taught early that strenuous physical activity might be dangerous to his health and that, in fact, it might even be fatal. (3) Determined to overcome this obstacle, Roosevelt trained his body relentlessly and built his impressive girth through sheer grit and determination. (4) That these childhood passions stayed with him throughout his adult life should not be surprising. (5) Physical activities, though, were not the only childhood fascination to play a prominent role later in his life.

(6) A skilled hunter, Roosevelt spent much of his leisure time hunting various forms of game. (7) Beginning during his undergraduate days at Harvard, he spent significant time in snow-covered Maine forests as well as the arid deserts of the Dakota territory. (8) As a child, Theodore was so enraptured by birds, he would spend hours observing and writing about them, even phonetically spelling out their various calls and songs. (9) Upon reaching government office, Roosevelt became the first true conservationist, pushing for laws to protect wildlife and resources. (10) He cherished nature in all its forms, seeking to understand its variety through research and experience.

(11) By openly maintaining these passions while in political office, Roosevelt redefined the role of the American politician. (12) While his predecessors had often been aloof with regard to their own personal feelings, Roosevelt advertised his sense of morality by talking openly about it repeatedly with citizens and reporters in speeches and newspapers. (13) In the dawning of a new, industrialized age, Roosevelt chose to take on controversial issues, battling through the spoils system, disputes between management and labor, and the question of imperialism.

30. In context, which of the following is the best revision of sentence 1 (reproduced below)?

While known when he was the President for his abundant energy and muscular build as an adult, Theodore Roosevelt's build as a child was actually quite puny.

(A) While Theodore Roosevelt was known for his energy and muscular build, but the President was actually a quite puny child.

(B) Although known for his abundant energy and muscular build as an adult, President Theodore Roosevelt was actually quite puny as a child.

(C) While puny as a child, Theodore Roosevelt was known for his abundant energy and muscular build while being President.

(D) As President, Theodore Roosevelt was known for his abundant energy and muscular build, not for being puny as a child.

(E) Theodore Roosevelt was puny as a child and was known for his abundant energy and muscular build as President.

31. In context, which of the following is the best revision of the underlined portion of sentence 3 (reproduced below)?

Determined <u>to overcome this obstacle</u>, Roosevelt trained his body relentlessly and built his impressive girth through sheer grit and determination.

(A) (no revision needed)
(B) that this obstacle should be overcome
(C) to overcome such ideas that became obstacles
(D) not to allow this to become an obstacle standing in his way
(E) to take obstacles out of his way

GO ON TO THE NEXT PAGE ⟶

4   **4**   **4**   **4**   **4**   **4**

32. Where is the most appropriate place to move sentence 4?

  (A) Before sentence 1
  (B) Before sentence 2
  (C) Before sentence 6, to start the second paragraph
  (D) After sentence 10, to end the second paragraph
  (E) After sentence 13

33. Which of the following provides the most logical ordering of the sentences in paragraph 2?

  (A) 7, 9, 10, 6, 8
  (B) 8, 10, 7, 6, 9
  (C) 8, 10, 9, 6, 7
  (D) 9, 7, 8, 10, 6
  (E) 7, 10, 8, 6, 9

34. If the author wanted to make sentence 7 more specific, which of the following details would fit best in the context of the second paragraph?

  (A) Roosevelt's age
  (B) information about Roosevelt's course of study
  (C) details of Roosevelt's activities in the deserts and forests
  (D) an explanation of why the climate of Maine is so different from the climate of the Dakota territory
  (E) information about Roosevelt's political affiliation prior to these excursions

35. Where is the best place to insert the following sentence?

His brazen moves were often criticized, but Theodore Roosevelt will go down in the annals of history as a man who was always true to himself, whether as a private citizen or as President of the United States.

  (A) Before sentence 1
  (B) After sentence 1
  (C) After sentence 5
  (D) Before sentence 11
  (E) After sentence 13

STOP

If you finish before time is called, you may check your work on this section only. Do not turn to any other section of the test.

SECTION 5
Time—25 minutes
18 questions

Turn to Section 5 of your answer sheet to answer the questions in this section.

Directions: This section contains two types of questions. You have 25 minutes to complete both types. For questions 1–8, solve each problem and decide which is the best of the choices given. Fill in the corresponding circle on the answer sheet. You may use any available space for scratchwork.

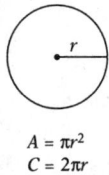

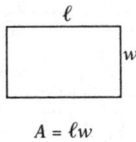

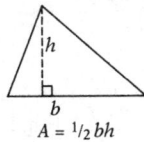

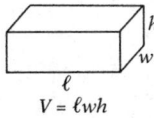

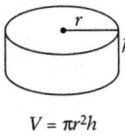

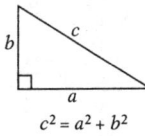

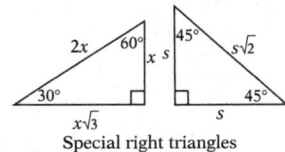

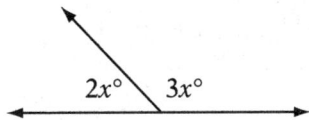

$2x°$ $3x°$

Note: Figure not drawn to scale.

1. In the figure above, what is the value of $2x$?

(A)   36
(B)   72
(C)   90
(D)   108
(E)   132

2. If $(x - 4)^2 = 36$, then x could be

(A)   −6
(B)   −2
(C)   0
(D)   4
(E)   6

GO ON TO THE NEXT PAGE

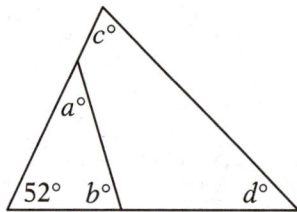

3. In the figure above, what is the value of $a + b + c + d$?

(A) 56
(B) 128
(C) 256
(D) 264
(E) 322

4. If $f(x) = x^2 - 4$, for what positive value of x does $f(x) = 32$?

(A) 5
(B) 6
(C) 7
(D) 8
(E) 9

5. A can of mixed nuts contains cashews, almonds, peanuts, and walnuts in the ratio of 2 to 4 to 5 to 7, respectively, by weight. What fraction of the mixture by weight is almonds?

(A) $\dfrac{1}{18}$

(B) $\dfrac{1}{9}$

(C) $\dfrac{2}{9}$

(D) $\dfrac{1}{4}$

(E) $\dfrac{5}{18}$

6. Twenty students in a chemistry class took a test on which the overall average score was 75. If the average score for 12 of those students was 83, what was the average score for the remaining members of the class?

(A) 60
(B) 61
(C) 62
(D) 63
(E) 64

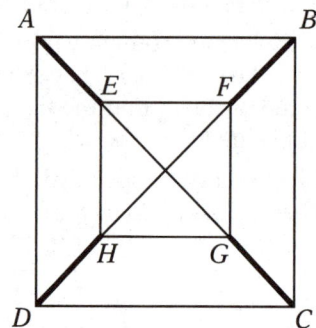

7. In the figure above, the vertices of square *EFGH* are on the diagonals of square *ABCD*. If $EF = 8\sqrt{2}$ and $AB = 14\sqrt{2}$, what is the sum of the lengths $AE + BF + CG + DH$ (heavier lines)?

(A) 24
(B) 28
(C) 32
(D) 36
(E) 38

$$\begin{array}{r} RS \\ + \underline{SR} \\ TR4 \end{array}$$

8. In the correctly worked addition problem above, each letter represents a different non-zero digit. What is the value of $2R + T$?

(A) 4
(B) 5
(C) 10
(D) 11
(E) 13

GO ON TO THE NEXT PAGE

5   5   5   5   5   5

Directions: For student-produced response questions 9–18, use the grids at the bottom of the answer sheet page on which you have answered questions 1–8.

Each of the remaining ten questions requires you to solve the problem and enter your answer by marking the circles in the special grid, as shown in the examples below. You may use any available space for scratchwork.

Answer: $\frac{7}{12}$

Answer: 2.5

Answer: 201
Either position is correct.

Write answer in boxes.

← Fraction line

← Decimal point

Grid in result.

Note: You may start your answers in any column, space permitting. Columns not needed should be left blank.

- Mark no more than one circle in any column.

- Because the answer sheet will be machine-scored, **you will receive credit only if the circles are filled in correctly.**

- Although not required, it is suggested that you write your answer in the boxes at the top of the columns to help you fill in the circles accurately.

- Some problems may have more than one correct answer. In such cases, grid only one answer.

- No question has a negative answer.

- **Mixed numbers** such as $3\frac{1}{2}$ must be gridded as

  3.5 or 7/2. (If $\boxed{3\ 1\ /\ 2}$ is gridded, it will be

  interpreted as $\frac{31}{2}$ not $3\frac{1}{2}$.)

- **Decimal Answers:** If you obtain a decimal answer with more digits than the grid can accommodate, it may be either rounded or truncated, but it must fill the entire grid. For example, if you obtain an answer such as 0.6666..., you should record your result as .666 or .667. **A less accurate value such as .66 or .67 will be scored as incorrect.**

Acceptable ways to grid $^2/_3$ are:

9. For all real numbers n, let $\boxed{n}$ be defined by $\boxed{n} = \frac{n^2}{16}$. What is the value of $\boxed{4}^2$?

10. The Civics Club earned 25% more at its bake sale in 2007 than it did in 2006. If it earned $600 at its bake sale in 2006, how much did it earn at its bake sale in 2007?

GO ON TO THE NEXT PAGE

11. If the sum of two numbers is 4 and their difference is 2, what is their product?

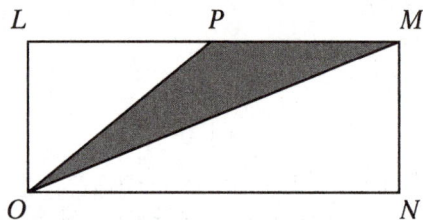

Note: Figure not drawn to scale.

12. In rectangle $LMNO$ above, P is the midpoint of side $\overline{LM}$. If the perimeter of the rectangle is 48 and side $\overline{LM}$ is twice the length of side $\overline{LO}$, what is the area of the shaded region?

13. If $64^3 = 4^x$, what is the value of x?

14. Points P, Q, R, and S lie on a line in that order. If $\overline{PS}$ is twice as long as $\overline{PR}$ and four times as long as $\overline{PQ}$, what is the value of $\dfrac{QS}{PQ}$?

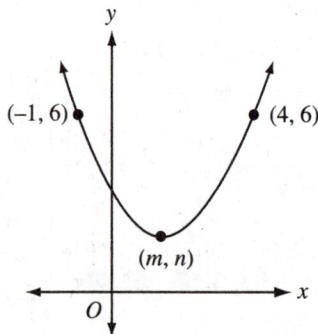

15. The figure above shows the graph in the xy-plane of a quadratic function with a vertex at (m, n). What is the value of m?

16. If the sum of five consecutive even integers is 110, what is the least of these integers?

NUMBER OF APPLICANTS TO COLLINS COLLEGE	
YEAR	APPLICANTS
1980	15,000
1985	18,000
1990	20,000
1995	24,000
2000	25,000

17. According to the data in the table above, by what percent did the number of applicants to Collins College increase from 1990 to 1995? (Disregard the % symbol when entering your answer into the grid. For instance, grid 50% as 50.)

18. A jar contains only black, white, and red marbles. If randomly choosing a black marble is four times as likely as randomly choosing a white marble, and randomly choosing a red marble is five times as likely as randomly choosing a black marble, then what is the smallest possible number of marbles in the jar?

STOP

If you finish before time is called, you may check your work on this section only. Do not turn to any other section of the test.

6   **6**   **6**   **6**   **6**   **6**

SECTION 6
Time—25 minutes
24 questions

Turn to Section 6 of your answer sheet to answer the questions in this section.

Directions: For each question in this section, select the best answer from among the choices given and fill in the corresponding circle on the answer sheet.

Each sentence below has one or two blanks, each blank indicating that something has been omitted. Beneath the sentence are five words or sets of words labeled A through E. Choose the word or set of words that, when inserted in the sentence, <u>best</u> fits the meaning of the sentence as a whole.

EXAMPLE:

Rather than accepting the theory unquestioningly, Deborah regarded it with _____.

(A) mirth
(B) sadness
(C) responsibility
(D) ignorance
(E) skepticism

Ⓐ Ⓑ Ⓒ Ⓓ ●

1. If John had not been there to ------- when tensions began to rise at the meeting, a fight would surely have ensued.

   (A) intervene
   (B) coalesce
   (C) harass
   (D) intermingle
   (E) exacerbate

2. The defendant hoped that the testimony of the surprise witness would corroborate his alibi and ------- him of the crime of which he had been accused.

   (A) convoke
   (B) synthesize
   (C) impeach
   (D) absolve
   (E) magnify

3. Rachel's ------- driving is not surprising, given that she spends ------- hours each day ensnarled in traffic delays.

   (A) antipathy for . . delightful
   (B) penchant for . . uncountable
   (C) predilection for . . dreary
   (D) proclivity for . . desperate
   (E) aversion to . . insufferable

4. Many medical practices once considered "state of the art" are now thought to be ------- by physicians who are often incredulous that such barbaric acts were once -------.

   (A) primitive . . sanctioned
   (B) ingenious . . approved
   (C) boorish . . censured
   (D) innovative . . endorsed
   (E) foolhardy . . condemned

5. The Prime Minister had vetoed the proposal several times in the past; thus, it came as a great surprise to the public when he ------- the same law in his most recent speech.

   (A) articulated
   (B) sanctioned
   (C) denounced
   (D) initiated
   (E) abbreviated

GO ON TO THE NEXT PAGE ⟩

6   **6**   6   6   **6**   **6**

The passages below are followed by questions based on the content. Answer the questions on the basis of what is <u>stated</u> or <u>implied</u> in the passage and in any introductory material that may be provided.

Questions 6 and 7 are based on the following passage.

The reverence for their goddess of protection accounts for the respect Navajos show to the
Line women of their tribe. The tradition is that a
man never lifts his hand against a woman,
5 although it is not an unusual thing for a
squaw to administer a sound thrashing to a
warrior husband who has offended her. All of
the sheep, which constitute the great wealth
of the tribe, are owned by the women, and in
10 the various families the line of descent is always on the side of the women. The Navajos
have little or no idea of a future existence but
are firm believers in the transmigration of
souls. For this reason they have great rever-
15 ence for different animals and birds, which
are supposed to be the re-embodiment of
departed spirits of Navajos.

6. Based on the information in the passage, with which of the following statements would the author most likely agree?

(A) Navajo warriors obey their wives obsequiously.
(B) Birds are a particularly vital food source for the Navajo.
(C) A Navajo man who disrespects a woman would likely face censure.
(D) The Navajo do not believe in reincarnation.
(E) In the winter, the Navajo migrate to warmer climates.

7. The word "administer" in line 6 most nearly means

(A) manage
(B) maintain
(C) govern
(D) rehearse
(E) dispense

Questions 8 and 9 are based on the following passage.

"Dying with dignity" is a topic that has inspired deep debate among the members of
Line the medical community. Should an individual
be allowed to determine when he or she wants
5 to die? Should a person who is merely receiving palliative care that provides no hope of a
cure be allowed to tell a doctor to stop all
treatment so she can die in peace? How can a
doctor know if a patient has the mental capac-
10 ity to decide for herself that the time has come
to stop fighting the disease? It is a challenging
and persistent debate.

8. As used in line 6, "palliative" most nearly means

(A) punitive
(B) remedial
(C) analgesic
(D) curative
(E) altruistic

9. The passage suggests that in cases of extreme illness, doctors may have difficulty in deter-mining their patients'

(A) state of mind
(B) prognosis
(C) quality of life
(D) tolerance of pain
(E) ability to remember facts

GO ON TO THE NEXT PAGE

6   6   6   6   6   6

Questions 10–16 are based on the following passage.

The following passage is excerpted from a recent book about seismology, the study of earthquakes.

In the 1970s, there was great optimism about earthquake prediction. A few so-called earth-
Line quake precursors had come to light, and there was even a theory (known as dilatancy) put
5   forth to explain many of the phenomena that come before a large earthquake. A series of foreshocks is an example of a precursor. How-ever, since foreshocks look just like any other earthquakes, they are not in themselves very
10 useful in prediction. From all points around the globe, there are numerous anecdotal re-ports about other precursors, earthquake folk-lore, if you will.
    Many widely reported earthquake precur-
15 sors are related to groundwater. A few hours before a large earthquake, marked changes have been reported in the level or flow of wells and springs. Groundwater has also reportedly changed temperature, become cloudy, or ac-
20 quired a bad taste. Occasionally, electrostatic phenomena such as earthquake lights (similar to St. Elmo's fire that appears on ships during electrical storms) and changes in the local magnetic field have been reported. Anecdotal
25 reports also persistently include the strange behavior of animals, which might be linked to electrostatic phenomena or foreshocks. Changes in strain and creep (silent tectonic motion, without accompanying earthquake)
30 along a fault normally locked by friction could also be considered precursors.
    In China in the 1970s, it became popular for people to predict earthquakes using "back-yard" measurements such as the monitoring
35 of well levels and observation of farm animals. At least one earthquake, the Haicheng quake in 1975, was successfully predicted and a

town evacuated, proving that, at least in some cases, earthquake prediction is possible. The
40 Haicheng earthquake had hundreds of fore-shocks, making it an easier-than-average earthquake to predict. Groundwater changes and anomalous animal behavior were also re-ported (for example, hibernating snakes sup-
45 posedly awoke and froze to death). In China, "evacuation" meant that compulsory outdoor movies were shown, so that when the quake did happen and the town was severely dam-aged, no one was killed. But Chinese seismol-
50 ogists missed predicting the catastrophic Tangshan earthquake, in which at least 250,000 reportedly perished.

10. Which of the following is the best title for this passage?

(A) The Effects of Earthquakes on Groundwater
(B) The Search for Earthquake Precursors
(C) A Novel Theory of the Origin of Earthquakes
(D) A History of Chinese Earthquakes
(E) How Animals Anticipate Earthquakes

11. The passage indicates that foreshocks are "not . . . very useful" (lines 9–10) in predicting earthquakes because they

(A) are exceptionally difficult to detect
(B) occur simultaneously with changes in groundwater
(C) are not part of the theory of dilatancy
(D) interfere with electrostatic phenomena
(E) are impossible to distinguish from earthquakes themselves

GO ON TO THE NEXT PAGE

6   **6**   *6*   *6*   **6**   **6**

12. According to the passage, which of the following features of groundwater have been reported to change immediately prior to an earthquake (lines 16–20)?

    I. density
    II. clarity
    III. flow

(A) II only
(B) III only
(C) I and II only
(D) II and III only
(E) I, II, and III

13. Which of the following could be considered a logical inconsistency in the passage?

(A) The passage states that foreshocks are not useful predictors of earthquakes but then cites foreshocks as instrumental to predicting an earthquake.
(B) The passage says that the Chinese are interested in predicting earthquakes but then says that they were devastated by the Tangshan earthquake.
(C) The passage reports that animals behaved strangely before an earthquake but then attributes this behavior to electrostatic phenomena.
(D) The passage states that the town of Haicheng was safely evacuated but then says that its citizens were forced to watch outdoor movies.
(E) The passage suggests that both strain and creep could be considered earthquake precursors.

14. Which of the following best describes the function of the third paragraph?

(A) to describe an application of a theory
(B) to provide an alternative perspective
(C) to recount a scientific experiment
(D) to summarize the ancient origins of a theory
(E) to demonstrate the difficulties of employing a technique

15. The passage suggests that the Tangshan earthquake

(A) was caused by strain and creep
(B) was preceded by changes in the groundwater
(C) caused more damage than the Haicheng earthquake did
(D) was preceded by several foreshocks
(E) was anticipated by the theory of dilatancy

16. In line 46, the word "evacuation" is placed in quotations in order to

(A) imply that an action was ineffective
(B) indicate that it is an archaic term
(C) emphasize the primitiveness of Chinese scientific methods
(D) suggest that a certain practice was unconventional
(E) underscore that an action was intended, but not implemented

6   **6**   6   6   6   **6**

Questions 17–24 are based on the following passage.

The following passage contains an excerpt taken from an anthology of autobiographies of American women.

On landing in America, a grievous dis-
appointment awaited us; my father did not
Line   meet us. He was in New Bedford, Massachusetts, nursing his grief and preparing to return
5   to England, for he had been told that the *John
Jacob Westervelt* had been lost at sea with every
soul on board. One of the missionaries who met
the ship took us under his wing and conducted
us to a little hotel, where we remained until
10   father had received his incredible news and
rushed to New York. He could hardly believe
that we were really restored to him; and even
now, through the mists of more than half a century, I can still see the expression in his wet eyes
15   as he picked me up and tossed me into the air.
I can see, too, the toys he brought me—
a little saw and a hatchet, which became the
dearest treasures of my childish days. They
were fatidical[1] gifts, that saw and hatchet; in
20   the years ahead of me I was to use tools as
well as my brothers did, as I proved when
I helped to build our frontier home.
We went to New Bedford with father, who
had found work there at his old trade; and
25   here I laid the foundations of my first childhood friendship, not with another child, but
with my next-door neighbor, a ship-builder.
Morning after morning, this man swung me
on his big shoulder and took me to his ship-
30   yard, where my hatchet and saw had violent
exercise as I imitated the workers around me.
Discovering that my tiny petticoats were in
my way, my new friends had a little boy's suit
made for me; and thus emancipated, at this
35   tender age, I worked unwearyingly at his side
all day long and day after day.
The move to Michigan meant a complete
upheaval in our lives. In Lawrence we had
around us the fine flower of New England

40   civilization. We children went to school; our
parents, though they were in very humble circumstances, were associated with the leading
spirits and the big movements of the day.
When we went to Michigan, we went to the
45   wilderness, to the wild pioneer life of those
times, and we were all old enough to keenly
feel the change.
Every detail of our journey through the
wilderness is clear in my mind. My brother
50   James met us at Grand Rapids with what, in
those days, was called a lumber-wagon, but
which had a horrible resemblance to a vehicle
from the health department. My sisters and I
gave it one cold look and turned from it; we
55   were so pained by its appearance that we refused to ride in it through the town. Instead,
we started off on foot, trying to look as if we
had no association with it, and we climbed
into the unwieldy vehicle only when the city
60   streets were far behind us.

17. Immediately upon arriving in America, the author was cared for by

(A)   John Jacob Westervelt
(B)   her father
(C)   a missionary
(D)   a childhood friend
(E)   a shipbuilder neighbor

18. In line 12, the word "restored" most nearly means

(A)   updated
(B)   refurbished
(C)   put into storage
(D)   deposited
(E)   returned

[1]Prophetic

Excerpted from "The Story of a Pioneer" by Anna Howard Shaw,
    in *Autobiographies of American Women: An Anthology*
    © 1992 by Jill Ker Conway, ed., pp. 475–477

GO ON TO THE NEXT PAGE ⟩

6   **6**   **6**   **6**   **6**   **6**

19. Which of the following best describes the relationship between the narrator and the men in her life?

    (A) She gladly provides for their needs.
    (B) She considers herself their equal.
    (C) She feels overly dependent on them.
    (D) She wishes to avoid them.
    (E) She believes that they suppress her wishes.

20. The author was "emancipated" (line 34) so that she might more easily

    (A) spend time with her father
    (B) play with her young friends
    (C) travel throughout New Bedford
    (D) work with tools
    (E) move to Michigan

21. In line 43, the word "movements" most nearly means

    (A) travels
    (B) cosmetic alterations
    (C) cultural changes
    (D) physical actions
    (E) mechanical workings

22. The author indicates that she regarded New England as superior to Michigan in that New England

      I. had humbler citizens
     II. was more culturally developed
    III. had finer gardens

    (A) II only
    (B) III only
    (C) I and II only
    (D) II and III only
    (E) I, II, and III

23. The author's attitude toward her move to Michigan is best described as

    (A) eager
    (B) awed
    (C) fearful
    (D) resentful
    (E) bewildered

24. The sisters refused to ride in the lumber wagon mainly because

    (A) they were embarrassed by its appearance
    (B) they felt it was unsafe
    (C) they had bad memories of it
    (D) it was cold
    (E) it lacked sufficient room for both of them

STOP

If you finish before time is called, you may check your work on this section only. Do not turn to any other section of the test.

7　　7　　7　　7　　7　　7

SECTION 7
Time—20 minutes
16 questions

Turn to Section 7 of your answer sheet to answer the questions in this section.

Directions: For this section, solve each problem and decide which is the best of the choices given. Fill in the corresponding circle on the answer sheet. You may use any available space for scratchwork.

Notes

1. The use of a calculator is permitted.

2. All numbers used are real numbers.

3. Figures that accompany problems in this test are intended to provide information useful in solving the problems. They are drawn as accurately as possible EXCEPT when it is stated in a specific problem that the figure is not drawn to scale. All figures lie in a plane unless otherwise indicated.

4. Unless otherwise specified, the domain of any function f is assumed to be the set of all real numbers x for which $f(x)$ is a real number.

Reference Information

$A = \pi r^2$ $A = \ell w$ $A = \frac{1}{2} bh$ $V = \ell wh$ $V = \pi r^2 h$ $c^2 = a^2 + b^2$ Special right triangles
$C = 2\pi r$

The number of degrees of arc in a circle is 360.
The sum of the measures in degrees of the angles of a triangle is 180.

---

1. If $4x + 5 = 20$, what is the value of $4x + 8$?

    (A)   3
    (B)   7
    (C)   16
    (D)   23
    (E)   30

2. If one serving of cereal is $\frac{1}{3}$ cup, how many servings are in 3 pints of cereal? (1 pint = 2 cups)

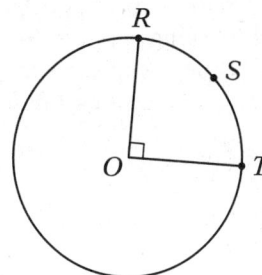

    (A)   3
    (B)   9
    (C)   18
    (D)   27
    (E)   36

3. If the radius of the circle with center O above is 4, what is the length of arc RST?

    (A) 2π
    (B) 4π
    (C) 8π
    (D) 12π
    (E) 16π

GO ON TO THE NEXT PAGE

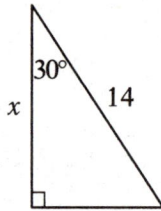

Note: Figure not drawn to scale.

4. In the triangle above, what is the value of x?

    (A)   7
    (B) $7\sqrt{2}$
    (C) $7\sqrt{3}$
    (D) $14\sqrt{3}$
    (E) $28\sqrt{3}$

5. For $x > 0$, let ∇x be defined by the equation $\nabla x = 3x - 3$. Which of the following is equivalent to $\dfrac{\nabla 7}{\nabla 3}$?

    (A) $\nabla 2$
    (B) $\nabla 3$
    (C) $\nabla 6$
    (D) $\nabla 8$
    (E) $\nabla 9$

6. Stephanie can clean a pool in 1 hour, and Mark can clean the same pool in 1.5 hours. If the rate at which they work together is the sum of their rates working separately, how many minutes should they need to clean the pool if they work together? (1 hour = 60 minutes)

    (A)   24 minutes
    (B)   36 minutes
    (C)   60 minutes
    (D)   72 minutes
    (E)   100 minutes

7. Which of the following has the greatest value?

    (A) $(100^3)^4$
    (B) $(100^5)(100^6)$
    (C) $(10{,}000)^4$
    (D) $(100^2 \times 100^2)^2$
    (E) $(1{,}000{,}000)^3$

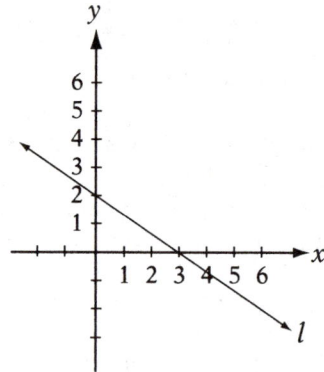

8. Line m (not shown) is the reflection of line l over the x-axis. What is the slope of line m?

    (A)   3/2
    (B)   2/3
    (C)   0
    (D)   −2/3
    (E)   −3/2

9. If $a^2 + b^2 = 4$ and $ab = 5$, what is the value of $(a + b)^2$?

    (A)   10
    (B)   12
    (C)   14
    (D)   16
    (E)   18

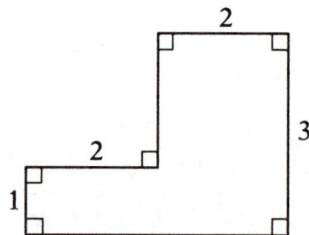

10. The figure above shows the dimensions, in feet, of a stone slab. How many of these slabs are required to construct a rectangular patio 24 feet long and 12 feet wide?

    (A)   18
    (B)   20
    (C)   24
    (D)   36
    (E)   48

GO ON TO THE NEXT PAGE

11. $12,000 in winnings for a golf tournament were distributed in the ratio of 7:2:1 to the first-, second-, and third-place finishers, respectively. How much money did the first-place finisher receive?

(A) $1,200
(B) $1,700
(C) $2,400
(D) $8,400
(E) $10,000

12. If $2x + 3y = 7$ and $4x - 5y = 12$, what is the value of $6x - 2y$?

(A) 5
(B) 8
(C) 15
(D) 17
(E) 19

13. If r and s are positive integers and $s + 1 = 2r$, which of the following must be true?

    I. s is odd
    II. r is even
    III. $\dfrac{s}{r} + \dfrac{1}{r}$ is an integer

(A) I only
(B) III only
(C) I and II only
(D) I and III only
(E) I, II, and III

14. A bag contains six chips, numbered 1 through 6. If two chips are chosen at random without replacement and the values on those two chips are multiplied, what is the probability that this product will be greater than 20?

(A) $\dfrac{1}{30}$ (B) $\dfrac{1}{15}$ (C) $\dfrac{2}{15}$

(D) $\dfrac{1}{5}$ (E) $\dfrac{13}{15}$

$$2, -4, -8, \ldots$$

15. In the sequence above, each term after the second is equal to the product of the two preceding terms. For example, the third term, −8, is the product of 2 and −4. How many of the first 100 terms of this sequence are negative?

(A) 33
(B) 34
(C) 50
(D) 66
(E) 67

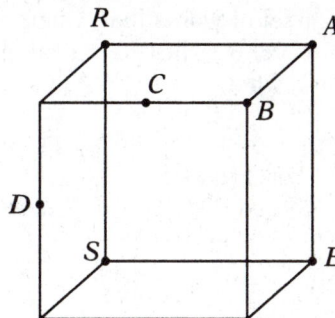

16. In the figure above, points C and D are midpoints of edges of a cube. A triangle is to be drawn with R and S as two of the vertices. Which of the following points should be the third vertex of the triangle if it is to have the largest possible perimeter?

(A) A
(B) B
(C) C
(D) D
(E) E

STOP

If you finish before time is called, you may check your work on this section only. Do not turn to any other section of the test.

8   **8**   **8**   **8**   **8**   **8**

SECTION 8
Time—20 minutes
19 questions

Turn to Section 8 of your answer sheet to answer the questions in this section.

Directions: For each question in this section, select the best answer from among the choices given and fill in the corresponding circle on the answer sheet.

Each sentence below has one or two blanks, each blank indicating that something has been omitted. Beneath the sentence are five words or sets of words labeled A through E. Choose the word or set of words that, when inserted in the sentence, best fits the meaning of the sentence as a whole.

EXAMPLE:

Rather than accepting the theory unquestioningly, Deborah regarded it with.......

(A) mirth
(B) sadness
(C) responsibility
(D) ignorance
(E) skepticism

Ⓐ Ⓑ Ⓒ Ⓓ ●

---

1. The latest review for the restaurant was -------, suggesting that the ------- cuisine came close to compensating for the insipid decor.

    (A) glowing . . indefatigable
    (B) banal . . mediocre
    (C) ambivalent . . sublime
    (D) severe . . piquant
    (E) antiquated . . tepid

2. As unexpected as the results of the experiment were, Dr. Thompson refused to characterize them as -------.

    (A) meticulous
    (B) belligerent
    (C) anomalous
    (D) convergent
    (E) warranted

3. The executives could only hope that the company's poor first-quarter performance was not ------- of the year to come.

    (A) an amalgam
    (B) a harbinger
    (C) an arbiter
    (D) a deception
    (E) a talisman

4. Around 1850, abolitionist and author Frederick Douglass sought to ------- those oppressed by slavery by facilitating the underground railroad, a widespread network of individuals and organizations that worked to transport former slaves out of bondage.

    (A) evaluate   (B) encumber   (C) unfetter
    (D) disorient   (E) forgo

5. Known for her ------- and decorative poetry, the author demonstrated her ------- by scribing a keenly analytical mystery novel.

    (A) flamboyant . . immutability
    (B) austere . . elegance
    (C) unadorned . . flexibility
    (D) florid . . versatility
    (E) grandiloquent . . insurgence

6. Because the mechanisms by which cancers attack the body are so -------, scientists have been ------- in their efforts to find a universal cure.

    (A) efficacious . . bilked
    (B) multifarious . . stymied
    (C) conspicuous . . thwarted
    (D) consistent . . hampered
    (E) lucid . . proscribed

GO ON TO THE NEXT PAGE ⟩

The passages below are followed by questions based on their content; questions following a pair of related passages may also be based on the relationship between the paired passages. Answer the questions on the basis of what is stated or implied in the passage and in any introductory material that may be provided.

Questions 7–19 are based on the following passages.

The following passages are excerpts from a recent debate between two well-known astronomers. The author of Passage 1 is a professor of geological sciences and the author of Passage 2 is a principal scientist in the Department of Space Studies in Boulder, Colorado.

PASSAGE 1

There is a cultural assumption that there are many alien civilizations. This stems in no
Line small way from the famous estimate by Frank Drake—known as the "Drake Equation"—that
5   was later amended by Drake and Carl Sagan. They arrived at an estimate that there are perhaps a million intelligent civilizations in the Milky Way Galaxy alone.

The Drake and Sagan estimate was based
10 on their best guess about the number of planets in the galaxy, the percentage of those that might harbor life, and the percentage of planets on which life not only could exist but could have advanced to culture. Since our
15 galaxy is but one of hundreds of billions of galaxies in the universe, the number of intelligent alien species would be numbered in the billions. Surely, if there are so many intelligent aliens out there, then the number of

20 planets with life must be truly astronomical. But what if the Drake and Sagan estimates are way off? If, as could be the reality, our civilization is unique in the galaxy, does that mean that there might be much less life in
25 general as well?

In my view, life in the form of microbes or their equivalents is very common in the universe, perhaps more common than even Drake and Sagan envisioned. However, complex life
30 is likely to be far more rare than commonly assumed. Life on earth evolved from single celled organisms to multi-cellular creatures with tissues and organs, climaxing in animals and higher plants. But is Earth's particular
35 history of life—one of increasing complexity to an animal grade of evolution—an inevitable result of evolution, or even a common one? Perhaps life is common, but complex life— anything that is multicellular—is not.

40 On Earth, evolution has undergone a progressive development of ever more complex and sophisticated forms leading ultimately to human intelligence. Complex life—and even intelligence—could conceivably arise faster
45 than it did on Earth. A planet could go from an abiotic state to a civilization in 100 million years, as compared to the nearly 4 billion years it took on Earth. Evolution on Earth has been affected by chance events, such as the
50 configuration of the continents produced by continental drift. Furthermore, I believe that the way the solar system was produced, with its characteristic number and planetary positions, may have had a great impact on the
55 history of life here.

It has always been assumed that attaining the evolutionary grade we call animals would be the final and decisive step. Once we are at this level of evolution, a long and continuous
60 progression toward intelligence should occur. However, recent research shows that while attaining the stage of animal life is one thing, maintaining that level is quite another. The geologic record has shown that once evolved,
65 complex life is subject to an unending succession of planetary disasters, creating what are known as "mass extinction" events. These rare

First passage: Peter Ward, "Great Debates Part I," *Astrobiology Magazine*, 2003
Second passage: David Grinspoon, "Great Debates Part III," *Astrobiology Magazine*, 2003

GO ON TO THE NEXT PAGE ➡

but devastating events can reset the evolutionary timetable and destroy complex life while
70 sparing simpler life forms. Such discoveries
suggest that the conditions allowing the rise
and existence of complex life are far more rigorous that are those for life's formation. On
some planets, then, life might arise and ani-
75 mals eventually evolve—only to be soon
destroyed by a global catastrophe.

PASSAGE 2

    It is always shaky when we generalize from
experiments with a sample size of one. So we
have to be a bit cautious when we fill the cos-
80 mos with creatures based on the time scales
of Earth history (it happened so fast here,
therefore it must be easy) and the resourceful-
ness of Earth life (they are everywhere where
there is water). This is one history, and one
85 example of life.
    I am not convinced that the Earth's
carbon-in-water example is the only way for
the universe to solve the life riddle. I am not
talking about silicon, which is a bad idea, but
90 systems of chemical complexity that we have
not thought of, which may not manifest themselves at room temperature in our oxygen atmosphere. The universe is constantly more
clever than we are, and we learn about com-
95 plex phenomena, like life, more through ex-
ploration than by theorizing and modeling.
I think there are probably forms of life out
there which use different chemical bases than
we, and which we will know about only when
100 we find them, or when they find us.
    An obvious rejoinder to this is, "But no one
has invented another system that works as
well as carbon-in-water." That is true. But to
this I would answer, "We did not invent
105 carbon-in-water!" We discovered it. I don't
believe that we are clever enough to have
thought of life based on nucleic acids and pro-
teins if we hadn't had this example handed to
us. This makes me wonder what else the uni-
110 verse might be using for its refined, evolving
complexity elsewhere, in other conditions that
seem hostile to life as we know it.
    I think it is a mistake to look at the many
specific peculiarities of Earth's biosphere and
115 how unlikely such a combination of characteristics seems, and to then conclude that

complex life is rare. This argument can only
be used to justify the conclusion that planets
exactly like Earth, with life exactly like Earth-
120 life, are rare.
    My cat, "Wookie" survived life as a near
starving alley cat and wound up as a beloved
house cat through an unlikely series of bio-
graphical accidents, which I won't take up
125 space describing but, trust me, given all of the
incredible things that had to happen in just
the right way, it is much more likely that there
would be no Wookie than Wookie. From this I
do not conclude that there are no other cats
130 (The Rare Cat Hypothesis), only that there are
no other cats exactly like Wookie.
    Life has evolved together with the Earth. Life
is opportunistic. The biosphere has taken advantage of the myriad of strange idiosyncrasies
135 that our planet has to offer. So it is easy to look
at our biosphere and conclude that this is the
best of all possible worlds; that only on such a
world could complex life evolve. My bet is that
140 many other worlds, with their own peculiar
characteristics and histories, co-evolve their
own biospheres. The complex creatures on
those worlds, upon first developing intelligence
and science, would observe how incredibly well
145 adapted life is to the many unique features of
their home world. They might naively assume
that these qualities, very different from Earth's,
are the only ones that can breed complexity.

7. The discussion of the Drake equation in the first
    paragraph indicates that the author holds which
    of the following assumptions?

    (A) The Drake equations are too complicated
        for most people to understand.
    (B) Mathematical formulas can influence
        public opinion.
    (C) Sagan did not substantially alter the
        Drake equation.
    (D) Mathematics tend to obscure scientific
        exploration.
    (E) Drake was not as reputable a scientist as
        Sagan was.

GO ON TO THE NEXT PAGE ⟶

8. Which of the following best describes the function of the third paragraph?

(A) It asks more questions similar to those posed in the second paragraph.
(B) It provides more background information on the debate discussed in the passage.
(C) It explains a comment made in the second paragraph.
(D) It defines an important term mentioned in the second paragraph.
(E) It presents an opinion contrary to one presented in the second paragraph.

9. In line 46, the word "abiotic" most nearly means

(A) resistant to bacteria
(B) devoid of life
(C) highly populated
(D) extremely advanced
(E) quick growing

10. Which of the following best summarizes the main idea of Passage 1?

(A) The conditions that support complex life may be much more difficult to maintain than is widely assumed.
(B) The Drake equation is not a valid predictor of life in the universe.
(C) Evolution on Earth has made it very unlikely that there would be complex life on other planets.
(D) The number of planets in the universe with complex life is astronomical.
(E) Conditions allowing for the existence of microbes are rare.

11. In line 57, "grade" most nearly means

(A) level
(B) slope
(C) evaluation
(D) life
(E) quantity

12. The author of Passage 1 makes all of the following claims in support of his argument EXCEPT

(A) Complex life on Earth was due in part to haphazard events.
(B) Higher life forms sometimes face the likelihood of extinction due to catastrophic events.
(C) The Earth's carbon-in-water example is probably not the only way for life to come into existence.
(D) Simple forms of life are far more common than highly evolved life forms.
(E) The evolution of life can be affected by the positions of planets around a star.

13. The "sample size of one" (line 78) refers to

(A) the Milky Way galaxy
(B) Drake and Sagan's data
(C) the planet Earth
(D) the Sun of our solar system
(E) mass extinction events

14. The quotations in lines 101–105 serve to

(A) show how the author would respond to someone who disagrees with him
(B) illustrate an argument for why there is no life on neighboring planets
(C) explain a theory the author has disagreed with his entire career
(D) describe a conversation the author had with a colleague
(E) illustrate the author's confusion about the origin of alternate life forms

15. The author includes the anecdote in lines 121–131 in order to

(A) compare his cat to the complex life forms in nearby galaxies
(B) give supporting evidence to the claim that life in the universe is unique to the Earth
(C) caution scientists about drawing premature conclusions from one specific occurrence
(D) mock scientists who believe that animals such as cats can live on other planets
(E) show the result of an evolutionary process

GO ON TO THE NEXT PAGE

8   **8**   **8**   **8**   **8**   **8**

16. In saying that "Life is opportunistic" (lines 132–133), the author of Passage 2 suggests that

(A) only the most cunning animals survive
(B) evolution takes advantage of the unique features of many different environments
(C) humans will likely always be the dominant species on Earth
(D) the theory of evolution is probably wrong
(E) all life forms seek to dominate others

17. The author of Passage 2 suggests that the "complex creatures" discussed in lines 142–148 are likely to believe that

(A) technological advancements are critical to their survival
(B) life is unique to planet Earth
(C) there is no life on other planets
(D) life on all planets originates in the same manner
(E) carbon is essential to the creation of life

18. The author of Passage 1 would most likely respond to the statement in Passage 2 that "The biosphere . . . offer" (lines 133–135) by saying that

(A) our planet also offers many dangers to the biosphere
(B) the biosphere is filled with far more complex life forms
(C) life on Earth has not evolved to such a high level
(D) our planet does not offer so many idiosyncrasies
(E) carbon is one of the most complex elements in the universe

19. The authors of both passages would most likely agree with which of the following statements?

(A) The estimates made by the Drake Equation are surprisingly accurate.
(B) Mass extinction events are not a factor in predicting the existence of extraterrestrial life.
(C) Mathematical models are the most helpful means of learning about the development of life in the universe.
(D) There is likely an abundance of life in the universe that has yet to be discovered.
(E) Complex life is very common in the universe.

◇ **STOP** ◇

If you finish before time is called, you may check your work on this section only. Do not turn to any other section of the test.

9   9   9   9   9   9

SECTION 9
Time—10 minutes
14 questions

Turn to Section 9 of your answer sheet to answer the questions in this section.

Directions: For each question in this section, select the best answer from among the choices given and fill in the corresponding circle on the answer sheet.

The following sentences test correctness and effectiveness of expression. Part of each sentence or the entire sentence is underlined; beneath each sentence are five ways of phrasing the underlined material. Choice A repeats the original phrasing; the other four choices are different. If you think the original phrasing produces a better sentence than any of the alternatives, select choice A; if not, select one of the other choices.

In making your selection, follow the requirements of standard written English; that is, pay attention to grammar, choice of words, sentence construction, and punctuation. Your selection should result in the most effective sentence—clear and precise, without awkwardness or ambiguity.

EXAMPLE:

The children <u>couldn't hardly believe their eyes</u>.

(A) couldn't hardly believe their eyes
(B) could hardly believe their eyes
(C) would not hardly believe their eyes
(D) couldn't nearly believe their eyes
(E) couldn't hardly believe his or her eyes

Ⓐ ● Ⓒ Ⓓ Ⓔ

1. His morning routine included eating an English muffin with grape jelly, <u>then to drink coffee from a styrofoam cup</u>, and sitting down to draw his daily comic strip.

   (A) then to drink coffee from a styrofoam cup
   (B) drinking coffee from a styrofoam cup
   (C) then drink coffee from a styrofoam cup
   (D) from a styrofoam cup he would drink coffee
   (E) he would drink coffee from a styrofoam cup

2. Pretending to have hurt his knee, <u>Mark's attempt to convince his coach to let him out of practice was a failure</u>.

   (A) Mark's attempt to convince his coach to let him out of practice was a failure
   (B) Mark's attempt to convince his coach failed to let him out of practice
   (C) Mark attempted to convince his coach to let him out of practice, but it was a failure
   (D) Mark attempted to convince his coach to let him out of practice, but failed
   (E) Mark attempted to convince his coach in letting him out of practice, but failed

3. The flier describing the details of the blood drive requested that we <u>are in the hospital lobby</u> promptly at 10 A.M.

   (A) are in the hospital lobby
   (B) should get at the hospital lobby
   (C) be in the hospital lobby
   (D) would be to the hospital lobby
   (E) should have been at the lobby of the hospital

GO ON TO THE NEXT PAGE >

4. Known for his temper, impatience, and how easily he can be irritated, Dr. McGee was not well liked by his patients.

(A) Known for his temper, impatience, and how easily he can be irritated
(B) Knowing his temper, impatience, and irritability
(C) Known for his temper, impatience, and irritability
(D) Known for his temper, impatience, and irritation
(E) Known for his temper, for his impatience, and his irritability

5. Winning the final match, Courtney gave a gracious speech thanking her competitor, the sponsors, and the spectators.

(A) Winning
(B) Having won
(C) Being that she won
(D) If she had won
(E) For her winning

6. Generally regarded as the most influential social science treatise of the 20th century, John Maynard Keynes wrote a book, *The General Theory of Employment Interest and Money* that forever changed the way scientists looked at the economy.

(A) John Maynard Keynes wrote a book, *The General Theory of Employment Interest and Money* that
(B) a book by John Maynard Keynes, *The General Theory of Employment Interest and Money,* that
(C) John Maynard Keynes' book *The General Theory of Employment Interest and Money* had already
(D) John Maynard Keynes wrote a book *The General Theory of Employment Interest and Money* having
(E) John Maynard Keynes' book *The General Theory of Employment Interest and Money*

7. Neither of the proposals remained in their original form by the time the legislature finished its deliberations.

(A) Neither of the proposals remained in their original form
(B) Neither proposal remained in its original form
(C) Both of the proposals did not remain in its original form
(D) With neither proposal remaining in its original form
(E) Neither proposal remained in their original forms

8. The Chief of Staff worked through the night to prepare the President's speech for the following day.

(A) to prepare
(B) in preparing
(C) in the preparation of
(D) for preparing
(E) in order for preparing

9. The storm waves crashed into the shore, inundating the stores along the boardwalk and many cars in the parking lot were swept away by them.

(A) boardwalk and many cars in the parking lot were swept away by them
(B) boardwalk with many cars in the parking lot being swept away
(C) boardwalk and sweeping away many cars in the parking lot
(D) boardwalk, and it swept away many cars in the parking lot
(E) boardwalk; sweeping away many cars in the parking lot

GO ON TO THE NEXT PAGE

9   9   9   9   9   9

10. The life of the ShinZanu, a tribe of the Australian Outback, have been realistically depicted in the books of Ronald Skinner.

   (A) The life of the ShinZanu, a tribe of the Australian Outback, have been realistically depicted in the books of Ronald Skinner.
   (B) The life of the ShinZanu tribe of the Australian Outback has been realistically depicted in the books of Ronald Skinner.
   (C) The ShinZanu, a tribe of the Australian Outback, has had its life realistically depicted with the books of Ronald Skinner.
   (D) Ronald Skinner has depicted the life of the ShinZanu realistically in his books; they are of the Australian Outback.
   (E) Depicting the lives of the ShinZanu tribe of the Australian Outback realistically, Ronald Skinner has done that in his books.

11. At the age of seven, my father took me to see my first baseball game.

   (A) At the age of seven, my father took me to see
   (B) My father took me, at the age of seven, to see
   (C) Being seven years old, my father took me to see
   (D) When I was seven years old, my father took me to see
   (E) I was taken by my father at seven years old, seeing

12. The President worked hard to implement legislation that would stimulate growth, curb inflation, and increase employment.

   (A) that would stimulate growth, curb inflation, and increase employment
   (B) stimulating growth, curbing inflation, and to increase employment
   (C) that stimulated growth, curbed inflation, and increasing employment
   (D) to stimulate growth, the curbing of inflation, and increasing employment
   (E) in order to stimulate growth, and for the purpose of curbing inflation and increasing employment

13. If anyone asks for a doctor, send them directly to the nurses' station for immediate assistance.

   (A) If anyone asks for a doctor, send them
   (B) Having asked for a doctor, send them
   (C) When anyone asks for a doctor, they should be sent
   (D) Had anyone asked for a doctor, send them
   (E) Send anyone who asks for a doctor

14. Even if they have been declawed as kittens, adult cats often run their paws along tall objects as if to sharpen their claws.

   (A) Even if they have been declawed as kittens
   (B) Even though they should have been declawed when being kittens
   (C) Even when being declawed as kittens
   (D) Declawed when kittens nevertheless
   (E) Declawed as kittens

STOP

If you finish before time is called, you may check your work on this section only. Do not turn to any other section of the test.

ANSWER KEY

Critical Reading

Section 3

	COR. ANS.	DIFF. LEV.			COR. ANS.	DIFF. LEV.
1.	A	1		13.	A	1
2.	C	2		14.	D	2
3.	B	3		15.	C	3
4.	E	3		16.	D	3
5.	E	3		17.	E	4
6.	A	4		18.	E	3
7.	D	4		19.	A	3
8.	C	4		20.	D	5
9.	B	3		21.	A	3
10.	E	1		22.	B	3
11.	A	4		23.	C	4
12.	A	3		24.	E	4

Number correct

Number incorrect

Section 6

	COR. ANS.	DIFF. LEV.			COR. ANS.	DIFF. LEV.
1.	A	1		13.	A	3
2.	D	3		14.	A	4
3.	E	3		15.	C	3
4.	A	4		16.	D	5
5.	B	5		17.	C	2
6.	C	3		18.	E	2
7.	E	4		19.	B	4
8.	C	3		20.	D	2
9.	A	1		21.	C	2
10.	B	2		22.	A	3
11.	E	3		23.	D	4
12.	D	4		24.	A	4

Number correct

Number incorrect

Section 8

	COR. ANS.	DIFF. LEV.			COR. ANS.	DIFF. LEV.
1.	C	3		11.	A	4
2.	C	2		12.	C	2
3.	B	3		13.	C	1
4.	C	4		14.	A	3
5.	D	4		15.	C	2
6.	B	5		16.	B	3
7.	B	4		17.	D	3
8.	E	3		18.	A	4
9.	B	2		19.	D	3
10.	A	3				

Number correct

Number incorrect

Math

Section 2

	COR. ANS.	DIFF. LEV.			COR. ANS.	DIFF. LEV.
1.	A	1		11.	B	4
2.	B	2		12.	B	3
3.	D	2		13.	B	3
4.	D	3		14.	C	4
5.	D	2		15.	B	4
6.	E	2		16.	B	3
7.	C	3		17.	D	5
8.	C	3		18.	C	4
9.	A	3		19.	E	4
10.	D	3		20.	D	5

Number correct

Number incorrect

Section 5

Multiple-Choice Questions

	COR. ANS.	DIFF. LEV.
1.	B	1
2.	B	3
3.	C	3
4.	B	3
5.	C	3
6.	D	4
7.	A	5
8.	D	5

Number correct

Number incorrect

Student-produced Response questions

	COR. ANS.	DIFF. LEV.
9.	1	2
10.	750	2
11.	3	2
12.	32	3
13.	9	3
14.	3	4
15.	1.5 or 3/2	4
16.	18	4
17.	20	4
18.	25	5

Number correct (9–18)

Section 7

	COR. ANS.	DIFF. LEV.			COR. ANS.	DIFF. LEV.
1.	D	2		9.	C	4
2.	C	2		10.	D	3
3.	A	2		11.	D	3
4.	C	3		12.	E	4
5.	A	3		13.	D	4
6.	B	3		14.	C	4
7.	A	3		15.	D	5
8.	B	4		16.	B	5

Number correct

Number incorrect

Writing

Section 4

	COR. ANS.	DIFF. LEV.			COR. ANS.	DIFF. LEV.			COR. ANS.	DIFF. LEV.			COR. ANS.	DIFF. LEV.
1.	C	1		10.	C	3		19.	C	3		28.	D	4
2.	A	1		11.	B	3		20.	D	3		29.	D	5
3.	D	2		12.	D	1		21.	C	3		30.	B	3
4.	B	2		13.	C	3		22.	A	3		31.	A	3
5.	C	3		14.	E	3		23.	E	4		32.	D	3
6.	E	2		15.	B	3		24.	D	4		33.	B	4
7.	C	3		16.	D	4		25.	C	4		34.	C	3
8.	D	3		17.	B	3		26.	B	3		35.	E	3
9.	C	4		18.	B	2		27.	C	4				

Number correct

Number incorrect

Section 9

	COR. ANS.	DIFF. LEV.			COR. ANS.	DIFF. LEV.
1.	B	1		8.	A	4
2.	D	2		9.	C	3
3.	C	2		10.	B	4
4.	C	3		11.	D	4
5.	B	4		12.	A	4
6.	C	3		13.	E	3
7.	B	5		14.	A	4

Number correct

Number incorrect

NOTE: Difficulty levels are estimates of question difficulty that range from 1 (easiest) to 5 (hardest).

SCORE CONVERSION TABLE

How to score your test

Use the answer key on the previous page to determine your raw score on each section. **Your raw score on each section except Section 5 is simply the number of correct answers minus ¼ of the number of wrong answers. On Section 5, your raw score is the sum of the number of correct answers for questions 1–18 minus ¼ of the number of wrong answers in questions 1–8.** Next, add the raw scores from Sections 3, 6, and 8 to get your Critical Reading raw score, add the raw scores from Sections 2, 5, and 7 to get your Math raw score, and add the raw scores from Sections 4 and 9 to get your Writing raw score. Write the three raw scores here:

Raw Critical Reading score: _____ Raw Math score: _____ Raw Writing score: _____

Use the table below to convert these to scaled scores.

Scaled scores: Critical Reading: _____ Math: _____ Writing: _____

Raw Score	Critical Reading Scaled Score	Math Scaled Score	Writing Scaled Score	Raw Score	Critical Reading Scaled Score	Math Scaled Score	Writing Scaled Score
67	800			32	520	570	610
66	800			31	510	560	600
65	790			30	510	550	580
64	780			29	500	540	570
63	770			28	490	530	560
62	750			27	490	520	550
61	740			26	480	510	540
60	730			25	480	500	530
59	720			24	470	490	520
58	700			23	460	480	510
57	690			22	460	480	500
56	680			21	450	470	490
55	670			20	440	460	480
54	660	800		19	440	450	470
53	650	800		18	430	450	460
52	650	780		17	420	440	450
51	640	760		16	420	430	440
50	630	740		15	410	420	440
49	620	730	800	14	400	410	430
48	620	710	800	13	400	410	420
47	610	710	800	12	390	400	410
46	600	700	790	11	380	390	400
45	600	690	780	10	370	380	390
44	590	680	760	9	360	370	380
43	590	670	740	8	350	360	380
42	580	660	730	7	340	350	370
41	570	650	710	6	330	340	360
40	570	640	700	5	320	330	350
39	560	630	690	4	310	320	340
38	550	620	670	3	300	310	320
37	550	620	660	2	280	290	310
36	540	610	650	1	270	280	300
35	540	600	640	0	250	260	280
34	530	590	630	−1	230	240	270
33	520	580	620	−2 or less	210	220	250

SCORE CONVERSION TABLE FOR WRITING COMPOSITE
[ESSAY + MULTIPLE CHOICE]

Calculate your Writing raw score as you did on the previous page and grade your essay from a 1 to a 6 according to the standards that follow in the detailed answer key.

Essay score: _____ Raw Writing score: _____

Use the table below to convert these to scaled scores.

Scaled score: Writing: _____

Raw Score	Essay Score 0	Essay Score 1	Essay Score 2	Essay Score 3	Essay Score 4	Essay Score 5	Essay Score 6
-2 or less	200	230	250	280	310	340	370
-1	210	240	260	290	320	360	380
0	230	260	280	300	340	370	400
1	240	270	290	320	350	380	410
2	250	280	300	330	360	390	420
3	260	290	310	340	370	400	430
4	270	300	320	350	380	410	440
5	280	310	330	360	390	420	450
6	290	320	340	360	400	430	460
7	290	330	340	370	410	440	470
8	300	330	350	380	410	450	470
9	310	340	360	390	420	450	480
10	320	350	370	390	430	460	490
11	320	360	370	400	440	470	500
12	330	360	380	410	440	470	500
13	340	370	390	420	450	480	510
14	350	380	390	420	460	490	520
15	350	380	400	430	460	500	530
16	360	390	410	440	470	500	530
17	370	400	420	440	480	510	540
18	380	410	420	450	490	520	550
19	380	410	430	460	490	530	560
20	390	420	440	470	500	530	560
21	400	430	450	480	510	540	570
22	410	440	460	480	520	550	580
23	420	450	470	490	530	560	590
24	420	460	470	500	540	570	600
25	430	460	480	510	540	580	610
26	440	470	490	520	550	590	610
27	450	480	500	530	560	590	620
28	460	490	510	540	570	600	630
29	470	500	520	550	580	610	640
30	480	510	530	560	590	620	650
31	490	520	540	560	600	630	660
32	500	530	550	570	610	640	670
33	510	540	550	580	620	650	680
34	510	550	560	590	630	660	690
35	520	560	570	600	640	670	700
36	530	560	580	610	650	680	710
37	540	570	590	620	660	690	720
38	550	580	600	630	670	700	730
39	560	600	610	640	680	710	740
40	580	610	620	650	690	720	750
41	590	620	640	660	700	730	760
42	600	630	650	680	710	740	770
43	610	640	660	690	720	750	780
44	620	660	670	700	740	770	800
45	640	670	690	720	750	780	800
46	650	690	700	730	770	800	800
47	670	700	720	750	780	800	800
48	680	720	730	760	800	800	800
49	680	720	730	760	800	800	800

College Hill™ SAT Study Plan

See page 3A–5A for instructions.

Test # _____	RAW SCORES:	CR _____ M _____ W _____ Essay _____
	SCALED SCORES:	CR _____ M _____ W _____ Essay _____

---

1. What were your test conditions?

2. What was your pre-test routine?

Goal	Attack	Get	CR pts	M pts	W pts
500	75%	50%	30	25	25
550	80%	60%	37	32	32
600	85%	67%	45	38	38
650	90%	80%	52	44	42
700	100%	90%	59	49	45
750	100%	95%	62	52	47
800	100%	100%	66	54	49

---

3. Did you attack all of the questions you needed to attack? (See the table above.)

4. Did you rush to complete any section?

5. How many more raw points do you need to make your score goal?   CR _____ M _____ W _____

6. Did you make educated guesses on any questions? If so, how many points did you pick up on these questions?

7. STUDY PLAN: Use the detailed answer key after the test to review the answers to the questions you missed. Below, list the lessons linked to the questions you missed, and list the tough words you missed from the test.

Lessons to Review   **Words to Review**

_____   _____
_____   _____
_____   _____
_____   _____
_____   _____
_____   _____
_____   _____

Detailed Answer Key

Section 1

Consider carefully the issue discussed in the following passage, then write an essay that answers the question posed in the assignment.

> Many among us like to blame violence and immorality in the media for a "decline in morals" in society. Yet these people seem to have lost touch with logic. Any objective examination shows that our society is far less violent or exploitative than virtually any society in the past. Early humans murdered and enslaved each other with astonishing regularity, without the help of gangsta rap or Jerry Bruckheimer films.

Assignment: **Do violence and immorality in the media make our society more dangerous and immoral?** Write an essay in which you answer this question and discuss your point of view on this issue. Support your position logically with examples from literature, the arts, history, politics, science and technology, current events, or your experience or observation.

The following essay received 6 points out of a possible 6. This means that, according to the graders, it

- develops an insightful point of view on the topic
- demonstrates exemplary critical thinking
- uses effective examples, reasons, and other evidence to support its thesis
- is consistently focused, coherent, and well organized
- demonstrates skillful and effective use of language and sentence structure
- is largely (but not necessarily completely) free of grammatical and usage errors

One of the most misguided notions of conventional wisdom is that depicting violence in the media makes our society more violent. A close examination shows that this claim is baseless. Societies with severe restrictions on violence in the media tend to be more, not less, violent than those with no such restrictions. Indeed, despite the popular myth of a more peaceful past, societies were far more violent before the advent of movies, television, and video games. Societies that restrict access to "immoral" western movies are the same ones that call their citizens to violent and irrational holy war.

As Michael Moore pointed out poignantly in the movie "Bowling for Columbine," Americans kill each other with firearms at a far greater rate than almost any other first-world nation. But he is quick to point out that our media is not more violent than those in Japan or Germany or even Canada, which have rates of violence that are a full order of magnitude lower than ours. Indeed, the killers among us are not likely to spend a lot of time listening to Marilyn Manson or playing Mortal Kombat on their PlayStations, despite what our more nearsighted and sanctimonious politicians and preachers would like us to believe. Ted Kaczynski, the Unabomber, lived in a one-room shack without electricity or running water, let alone cable. But even if murderers like Kaczynski were video game addicts, attributing their

motives to media violence would be missing the point entirely.

People who are habitually violent have adopted a "war mentality." They tend to see the world in black-and-white, us-against-them terms. Tragically, our leaders tend to have this very same mentality, but they couch it in "patriotism." Lobbing cruise missiles and landing marines in another country is not considered a horrible last resort, but a patriotic duty. If we wish to understand why Americans are more violent than the Japanese, violence in the media will hold no answers; Japanese kids watch just as much violence. Foreign policy is far more telling: which country has leaders who engage in violence against other countries at every opportunity, and constantly try to convince us that it's right?

If our pundits and politicians were truly concerned about making a safer world—and there are many reasons to believe they are not, since they profit the most from a fearful citizenry—they would begin by acknowledging that violence is almost a desperate grab for control from a person or people who believe they are being repressed. If we want a more peaceful and noble society, then we will stop coercing other countries with violence and economic oppression. As Franklin Roosevelt said, "We have nothing to fear but fear itself." We are the most fearful nation on the planet, and we are paying for it.

The following essay received 4 points out of a possible 6, meaning that it demonstrates *adequate competence* in that it

- develops a point of view on the topic
- demonstrates some critical thinking, but perhaps not consistently
- uses some examples, reasons, and other evidence to support its thesis, but perhaps not adequately
- shows a general organization and focus, but shows occasional lapses in this regard
- demonstrates adequate but occasionally inconsistent facility with language
- contains occasional errors in grammar, usage, and mechanics

People say that society today is much more violent due to all of the media portrayal of violence we see on a daily basis. The nightly news is often made up entirely of stories about murders, muggings, arson, and other gruesome crimes. The most successful shows on television are the investigative crime shows in which they solve disturbing murder mysteries. Movies like the Lord of the Rings contain gory fight scenes that show the death of hundreds of characters. It's hard even to find a video game anymore that doesn't somehow relate back to fighting.

Those who don't believe that violence breeds violence would argue that the United States murder rate had declined to its lowest level in 30 years and that this is proof that the violence in the media has not in fact made for a more violent society. But what they conveniently leave out is the fact that at the same time, youth gun killings were on the rise. This is who is being affected by the increased exposure to violence—the children. It is perhaps the video game violence and television/movie violence that can be held responsible.

Kids today are growing up in a society where violence is everywhere. It is difficult for a child to go through the day without witnessing some violent act on TV or hearing about a gruesome murder on the radio. A recent study we learned about in class concluded that because of what they see on television, children become immune to violence, accept it as something that is part of a "normal" life, and they often times will attempt to imitate what they see on television because it "looks fun."

Something needs to be done to reverse this trend of growing violence in our country and tighter regulation of the amount of violence on television, in music, and in the movies would be a great place to start. The youth of this country need to be reminded that violence is not an acceptable part of daily existence and that it should be avoided at all costs.

The following essay received 2 points out of a possible 6, meaning that it demonstrates *some incompetence* in that it

- has a seriously limited point of view
- demonstrates weak critical thinking
- uses inappropriate or insufficient examples, reasons, and other evidence to support its thesis
- is poorly focused and organized and has serious problems with coherence
- demonstrates frequent problems with language and sentence structure
- contains errors in grammar and usage that seriously obscure the author's meaning

Believing that the violence in the media has made the members of our society like violent murderers is an absurd notion. Sure, there are lots video games on the market that involve fighting ninjas and battling army troops. Yes, nightly television shows on the public television networks show many a violent episode. Sure, the nightly news is covered with violent crimes and such. For instance, the popular music of this era is full of violent references and foul language. But, no experiment or statistics that I have seen proves the above statement to be true. Just because a teenager kills over 500 fake people on his ninja fighting video-game, it does not mean that after he turns off the game console that he will run outside in his ninja costume and start attacking the people in his neighborhood.

It is absurd to say that violence is because of all the violence on video games television. Actually I think that video games make you better at eye-hand coordination which is a valuable skill. Hundreds of years before video games and movies and television, there were murder and violence. Human beings are violent people and the exposure to violence does not make us more violent than we already were. If we did not have all of these impressive technological advances such as radio, television and film, we would still be committing acts of violence. There will always be violent humans that are ready to hurt others to get what they want and eliminating violent references from our music and television shows might even make people madder.

Section 2

1. A
$$(x + 4) + 7 = 14$$
Subtract 7: $\quad x + 4 = 7$
Subtract 4: $\quad x = 3$
(Chapter 8, Lesson 1: Solving Equations)

2. B Write out a mathematical equation for how you would actually find the cost for the month: $.95 × 31. Answer choice B, $1.00 × 30, is closest to that amount.
(Chapter 7, Lesson 1: Numbers and Operations)

3. D A linear angle measures 180°. Write an equation:
$$w + x + 50 = 180°$$
Subtract 50°: $\quad w + x = 130°$
(Chapter 10, Lesson 1: Lines and Angles)

4. D
$$g(x) = 3x + 4$$
Substitute 5 for x: $\quad g(5) = 3(5) + 4$
Simplify: $\quad g(5) = 15 + 4 = 19$
(Chapter 11, Lesson 2: Functions)

5. D The difference between x and y is $(x - y)$.
The sum of x and y is $(x + y)$.
The product of those two is equal to 18:
$$(x - y)(x + y) = 18$$
FOIL: $\quad x^2 - xy + xy - y^2 = 18$
Combine like terms: $\quad x^2 - y^2 = 18$
(Chapter 8, Lesson 5: Factoring)

6. E
$$3\sqrt{x} - 7 = 20$$
Add 7: $\quad 3\sqrt{x} = 27$
Divide by 3: $\quad \sqrt{x} = 9$
Square both sides: $\quad x = 81$
(Chapter 8, Lesson 4: Working with Roots)

7. C Let b = cost of chocolate bar and g = cost of gum.
$$b + g = \$1.75$$
Chocolate bar is $.25 more: $\quad b = \$.25 + g$
Substitute for b: $\quad \$.25 + g + g = \$1.75$
Combine like terms: $\quad \$.25 + 2g = \$1.75$
Subtract $.25: $\quad 2g = \$1.50$
Divide by 2: $\quad g = \$.75$
(Chapter 8, Lesson 1: Solving Equations)

8. C First find 40% of 80: $.40 × 80 = 32$

Now find what percent of 96 is 32.

Translate: $\quad \dfrac{x}{100} × 96 = 32$

Multiply by 100: $\quad 96x = 3{,}200$
Divide by 96: $\quad x = 33\frac{1}{3}$
(Chapter 7, Lesson 5: Percents)

9. A If $lm = 21$ and both l and m are integers, then m must be either 1, 3, 7, or 21. If $mn = 39$, however, then m must also be a factor of 39, so it must be 3. Therefore, $l = 21/3 = 7$ and $n = 39/3 = 13$, so $n > l > m$. (Chapter 8, Lesson 6: Inequalities, Absolute Values, and Plugging In)

10. D There's no need to do a lot of calculation here. Look for the two adjacent bars with the greatest positive difference between them. Since 1999 shows the least profits of all the years on the graph and 2000 shows the greatest profits of any year on the graph, 1999–2000 must have the greatest change in profit. (Chapter 11, Lesson 5: Data Analysis)

11. B A Venn diagram can help you with this problem: Imagine that the 4 students who play two sports play soccer and tennis. (It doesn't matter which specific pair of sports they play.) This means that $12 - 4 = 8$ students play just soccer, $7 - 4 = 3$ students play just tennis, and 9 students play just lacrosse. This shows that there is a total of $9 + 8 + 4 + 3 = 24$ students. (Chapter 9, Lesson 5: Counting Problems)

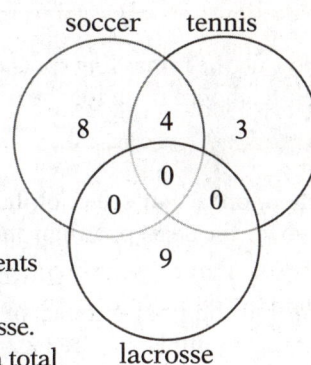

12. B To solve this problem, you need to find the distance between the center of the circle (14, 14) and the point on the circle (2, 9). To do this, you can use the distance formula.

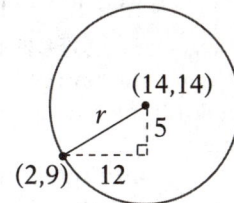

You can also draw a right triangle connecting the two points. It gives you a triangle with one leg of 5 and one leg of 12. Set up the Pythagorean theorem and solve for r.

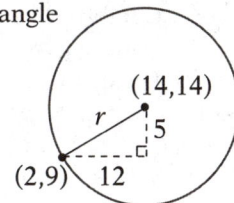

$$5^2 + 12^2 = r^2$$
Simplify: $\quad 25 + 144 = r^2$
Combine like terms: $\quad 169 = r^2$
Take square root: $\quad 13 = r$
The diameter is twice the radius = $2(r) = 2(13) = 26$.
(Chapter 10, Lesson 3: The Pythagorean Theorem)

13. B The population doubles every 18 months. Start with January of 2000 and start doubling.

	January 2000	12,000
18 months later:	July 2001	24,000
18 months later:	January 2003	48,000
18 months later:	July 2004	96,000

(Chapter 9, Lesson 3: Numerical Reasoning Problems)

14. C Use the Fundamental Counting Principle from Chapter 9, Lesson 5. To arrange these students, five choices must be made. First select the students for each end. Since one of the five (the tallest) cannot go on either end, you have four students to choose from for one end, and then, once that choice has been made, three students to choose from for the other end:

$$\underset{*}{\underline{4}} \ \underline{} \ \underline{} \ \underline{} \ \underset{*}{\underline{3}}$$

Now fill the remaining spots. There are three students left to choose from for the second spot:

$$\underset{*}{\underline{4}} \ \underline{3} \ \underline{} \ \underline{} \ \underset{*}{\underline{3}}$$

Then, once that selection has been made, there are two for the next spot, then one for the remaining spot:

$$\underline{4} \ \underline{3} \ \underline{2} \ \underline{1} \ \underline{3}$$

To find the total number of possible arrangements, simply multiply: $4 \times 3 \times 2 \times 1 \times 3 = 72$.
(Chapter 9, Lesson 5: Counting Problems)

15. B From the diagram, we know that $a + b + c = 180$, and we know that $b = c + 3$.

If you want b to be as large as possible, then you need to make the sum of a and c as small as possible. The smallest integer value of a possible is 91. So let's say that $a = 91$.

Substitute 91 for a:	$91 + b + c = 180$
Substitute $c + 3$ for b:	$91 + c + 3 + c = 180$
Combine like terms:	$94 + 2c = 180$
Subtract 94:	$2c = 86$
Divide by 2:	$c = 43$

So 43 is the largest possible value of c; this means that $43 + 3 = 46$ is the largest possible value of b.
(Chapter 10, Lesson 2: Triangles)

16. B Begin by finding the area of the big equilateral triangle. An equilateral triangle with sides of length 4 has a height of $2\sqrt{3}$, because the height divides the triangle into two 30°-60°-90° triangles.

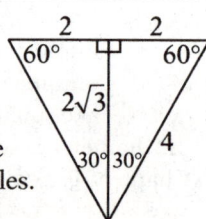

$$\text{Area} = \tfrac{1}{2}(\text{base})(\text{height}) = \tfrac{1}{2}(4)(2\sqrt{3}) = 4\sqrt{3}$$

The big triangle is divided into four equal parts, three of which are shaded, so the shaded area is ¾ of the total area.

$$\text{Shaded area} = \tfrac{3}{4}(4\sqrt{3}) = 3\sqrt{3}$$

(Chapter 10, Lesson 5: Areas and Perimeters)

17. D Just look at the graph and draw a line at $y = 1$.

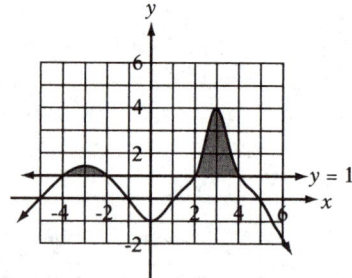

The y-values of the graph are at or above that line from $x = -4$ to $x = -2$ and from $x = 2$ to $x = 4$.
(Chapter 11, Lesson 2: Functions)

18. C This table shows all of the $5 \times 5 = 25$ possible values of ab:

x	2	4	6	8	10
1	2	4	6	8	10
3	6	12	18	24	30
5	10	20	30	40	50
7	14	28	42	56	70
9	18	36	54	72	90

Of those, only the seven shaded values are greater than 20 and less than 50, so the probability is 7/25.
(Chapter 9, Lesson 6: Probability Problems)

19. E

	$(w^a)(w^5) = w^{15}$
Simplify:	$w^{5+a} = w^{15}$
Equate the exponents:	$5 + a = 15$
Subtract 5:	$a = 10$
	$(w^4)^b = w^{12}$
Simplify:	$w^{4b} = w^{12}$
Equate the exponents:	$4b = 12$
Divide by 4:	$b = 3$

So $a + b = 10 + 3 = 13$.
(Chapter 8, Lesson 3: Working with Exponentials)

20. D The graph of $y = f(x - 2)$ is the graph of $y = f(x)$ shifted to the right two units without changing its shape. Therefore, the "peak" at point (6, 4) should shift to (8, 4).
(Chapter 11, Lesson 3: Transformations)

Section 3

1. A The word *although* indicates a contrast. Raúl purchased his computer only 10 months ago, but technology has been improving so fast that it is already *outdated*. *obsolete* = outdated; *adjunct* = auxiliary, or additional; *novel* = new, innovative; *elusive* = hard to catch

2. C The admissions committee is looking to justify offering more scholarships to increase the number of applications, so the number of applicants must be *decreasing*. *mushroom* = expand rapidly; *plummet* = decrease rapidly; *satiate* = satisfy; *burgeon* = grow

3. B If the father will not consider another person's viewpoint to be valid if it differs from his own, he must be pretty *stubborn* or *arrogant*. *pragmatic* = practical; *dogmatic* = arrogantly authoritative; *phlegmatic* = sluggish; *cordial* = polite; *curt* = abrupt and rude

4. E The books are written for children but are still *enjoyable* to adults. *penned* = written; *prosaic* = dull; *morose* = gloomy; *censored* = cleansed of profanity; *incongruous* = not compatible; *tedious* = boring, dull; *authored* = written; *engaging* = captivating, interesting

5. E Julia is at the top of her class, but if this is hard to believe, she must approach her work in a *lazy* or *irresponsible* way. *adept* = skilled; *diligent* = hardworking; *fanatical* = obsessive and crazy; *extroverted* = outgoing; *laggardly* = slow-moving, lagging behind

6. A The President's opponents were always cautious about debating him, so the President must be *highly skilled* or *intimidating* or *mean*. *redoubtable* = formidable, imposing; *staid* = calm, not outwardly emotional; *magnanimous* = generous; *stoic* = indifferent to pain or pleasure

7. D The new clothing line was described as being *eclectic* (containing much variety). It ranged from *modest* (not showy) and *unadorned* (undecorated) to -------- and *garish* (flashy). By parallelism, the missing word should be in opposition to the word *modest*. *austere* = severe, stern; *prophetic* = able to tell the future; *cordial* = polite; *ostentatious* = showy; *solitary* = alone

8. C The textbook *includes all of the essential information* but it is not *verbose* (wordy); the two missing words should be parallel to *containing lots of information* and *not verbose*. *compendious* = succinct; *circumlocutory* = talking around the subject, indirect; *reprehensible* = blameworthy; *terse* = concise; *comprehensive* = including a large amount of information; *concise* = brief and to the point; *grandiloquent* = speaking in a pompous manner; *painstaking* = done with great care; *redundant* = repetitive

9. B Saying that we were *raised in unrivaled prosperity* is like saying that the economy has been very strong and *abundant*.

10. E The "people" are plagued by *deep divisions* (line 9), and the *citizens* are the only ones who are not *growing to appreciate the difference between America and the United States* (lines 20–22). Therefore, the *people* lack unity, while the *citizens* lack awareness.

11. A Don't miss the word *EXCEPT* in the question. Choice (B) is supported in line 14, choice (C) in line 7, choice (D) in line 8, and choice (E) in line 8. The last lines say that *ambition for a better life is now universal*, implying that *not* everyone is happy with the status of their lives.

12. A Unlike Passage 1, Passage 2 discusses the difference between the ideal of America and the reality of the United States.

13. A The questions in the opening lines show the man's *confusion*, and the woman is said to talk *ardently* (passionately).

14. D The author says that one *who is suddenly overwhelmed by terror cannot afterwards remember the exact order of sounds accompanying the catastrophe which stuns him*—that is, he becomes disoriented.

15. C Line 11 suggests that Ognev is stunned by a *catastrophe*. The context of the passage makes it clear that this catastrophe is the expression of love from Vera, which Ognev has difficulty understanding.

16. D In saying that *she had been struck by . . . the aims and objects of his life* (lines 22–24), the author is saying that she was impressed with Ognev's *life goals*.

17. E In lines 42–44, the passage states that *much as he wanted to, he could feel no joy; no fundamental happiness*. In other words, the *bad and strange* thing was *disaffection*.

18. E In lines 51–52, the passage states that *Vera's raptures and suffering seemed to him* (Ognev) *to be only cloying* (excessively sweet) *and trivial* (of little significance). He felt her passion to be unimportant and was *outraged at himself* for feeling this way. To him, his *statistics, books or philosophical truths* were more important than this passion.

19. A The final sentence of the passage states that *he was annoyed and blamed himself even though he himself did not understand why he was to blame*. Ognev is confused and uncertain about how he *should* feel about Vera's passion. He feels indifference but thinks he should feel something different.

20. **D**   In lines 21–22 the marchers are described as *singing to hide their exhaustion* and then as *trying not to fear. . . .* This commitment to hiding emotion is *stoicism.*

21. **A**   Lines 35–38 criticize the bill's *failure to protect the right of African Americans to vote "when local officials are determined to deny it."* In other words, it did not sufficiently pressure local officials to extend voting rights to all citizens.

22. **B**   In context, saying that *his . . . encounter with Mexican-American children* was *shattering* is like saying that the encounter bothered the President and had a major impact on the way he approached civil rights issues later in his career.

23. **C**   Johnson indicates that he inferred, by looking into his students' eyes, that they knew that others disliked them. This indicates a strong empathy with his students, because he inferred it not from their words but from their expressions.

24. **E**   Lines 52–54 say that Johnson *made the nationwide audience aware of how deeply personal the issue of African American rights was to him* and lines 60–62 say that *he spoke more directly, more explicitly, and more warmly of the human experience of prejudice than any president before him.* In other words, he addressed it directly and in personal terms.

Section 4

1. **C**   The word *group* is the singular subject, so the verb should be *was.*
(Chapter 15, Lesson 1: Subject-Verb Disagreement)

2. **A**   The original sentence is best. Choice (B) is incorrect because the phrase *of labor's and management's* is redundant and unidiomatic. In choice (C), the use of the verb *saw* is non-standard, although idiomatic, and the colon is misused because it is not followed by a list or an explanatory independent clause. In choice (D), the phrase *marked ferociously* is illogical. In choice (E), both the tense and voice of the verb, *was marking,* are illogical.

3. **D**   The original sentence is awkward, and its verb *has possessed* does not agree with the plural subject, *scientists and inventors.* Choice (B) is incorrect because the verb *have been able to possess* is not logical. Choices (C) and (E) are incorrect because the verb *was* does not agree with the plural subject *skills.*
(Chapter 15, Lesson 1: Subject-Verb Disagreement)

4. **B**   In the original sentence, the pronoun *it* lacks a clear antecedent, as does the pronoun *that* in choice (D). Choice (C) is incorrect because it implies that the Thracians *enabled the ability*, which is illogical. In choice (E), the phrase *ability of resisting* is unidiomatic.
(Chapter 15, Lesson 5: Pronoun-Antecedent Disagreement)

5. **C**   The phrase *on an overseas journey* is redundant because the sentence also states that this journey was *across the Atlantic.* This redundancy is repeated in choice (B). Choice (D) uses an incorrect verb tense, and choice (E) produces a sentence fragment.
(Chapter 15, Lesson 12: Other Modifier Problems)

6. **E**   In the original sentence, the use of *plus* instead of *and* is non-standard, and the phrasing is not parallel. Only choice (E) avoids both problems.
(Chapter 15, Lesson 3: Parallelism)

7. **C**   The phrase *half as many . . . than* is unidiomatic. The correct idiom is *half as many as.* Only choice (C) is phrased idiomatically.
(Chapter 15, Lesson 10: Idiom Errors)

8. **D**   The use of *therefore* in the original phrasing is illogical, because the ideas in the sentence are related not as a cause and effect but rather as a contrast. The use of *actually* in choice (D) conveys the appropriate irony.
(Chapter 15, Lesson 15: Coordinating Ideas)
(Chapter 12, Lesson 7: Write Logically)

9. **C**   In the original sentence, the prepositional phrase *for their fans* is unidiomatic and awkward, and the pronoun *their* does not agree in number with its antecedent, *the band.* Choices (B) and (D) repeat the pronoun problem. Choice (E) is incorrect because it implies that the *fans* are free of charge, rather than the downloading.
(Chapter 15, Lesson 5: Pronoun-Antecedent Disagreement)

10. **C**   The plural subject *reasons* requires the plural verb *are,* so choices (A) and (D) are incorrect. Choice (B) is incorrect because the phrase *the reasons are because* is non-standard and illogical. Choice (E) is incorrect because the phrasing is not parallel.
(Chapter 15, Lesson 1: Subject-Verb Disagreement)

11. **B**   The appositive phrase *An untiring defender of the downtrodden* must be placed adjacent to the noun it modifies, which in this case is *Clarence Darrow.* Only choices (B) and (E) do this, but choice (E) is incorrect because it lacks parallel phrasing.
(Chapter 15, Lesson 8: Other Misplaced Modifiers)

12. **D**   The subject of this verb is *delivery*, which is singular, so the verb should be *has been*.
(Chapter 15, Lesson 1: Subject-Verb Disagreement)

13. **C**   The phrase *capable to distinguish* is unidiomatic. The correct phrasing is *capable of distinguishing*.
(Chapter 15, Lesson 10: Idiom Errors)

14. **E**   The sentence is correct.

15. **B**   The subject of this verb is *photographs . . . and diagrams*, which is plural, so the verb should be *were*.
(Chapter 15, Lesson 1: Subject-Verb Disagreement)

16. **D**   This is a comparison error. The *way in which chimpanzees form friendships* cannot logically be compared to *humans*. Instead, the phrase should be *to the way humans form friendships*.
(Chapter 15, Lesson 4: Comparison Problems)

17. **B**   As a noun, *affects* means *feelings or emotions*, so its use here is a diction error. The proper word is *effects*.
(Chapter 15, Lesson 11: Diction Errors)

18. **B**   There are two errors in this phrase. First, the subject *probability* is singular, so the verb should be *is*. Second, a probability can be *lower* than another, but not *fewer* than another.
(Chapter 15, Lesson 1: Subject-Verb Disagreement)
(Chapter 15, Lesson 4: Comparison Problems)

19. **C**   The pronoun *they* does not agree in number with its antecedent *an author*, and should be replaced with the phrase *he or she*.
(Chapter 15, Lesson 5: Pronoun-Antecedent Disagreement)

20. **D**   The phrase *in the time* is redundant because the word *during* conveys the same information. The entire phrase should be deleted.
(Chapter 15, Lesson 12: Other Modifier Problems)

21. **C**   People are satisfied *with* things, not *at* them.
(Chapter 15, Lesson 10: Idiom Errors)

22. **A**   The phrase *had ate* is an incorrect past perfect form. The correct form is *had eaten*. In this case, however, the word *after* conveys the time sequence, so the past perfect form isn't strictly necessary: *ate* (but not *had ate*) is an acceptable alternative.
(Chapter 15, Lesson 9: Tricky Tenses)

23. **E**   The sentence is correct as written.

24. **D**   The verb *is* does not agree in number with its plural subject, *jaws*, and should be changed to *are*.
(Chapter 15, Lesson 1: Subject-Verb Disagreement)

25. **C**   The subject of the verb *help* is *taking*, which is singular. Think of the subject as *it*. The word *help* should instead be *helps*.
(Chapter 15, Lesson 1: Subject-Verb Disagreement)

26. **B**   The word *underneath* means physically below something. The word should instead be *under*.
(Chapter 15, Lesson 10: Idiom Errors)

27. **C**   The subject *they* is referring to *the company*, which is singular. *They* should instead be *it*.
(Chapter 15, Lesson 1: Subject-Verb Disagreement)

28. **D**   The original phrasing is not parallel. When using the idiomatic phrase *not only A but also B*, the phrasing must be precise and the phrases in *A* and *B* must be parallel. Therefore, the phrase *he or she should* in choice D must be eliminated.
(Chapter 15, Lesson 3: Parallelism)

29. **D**   The comparison requires the idiomatic phrase *more A than B*. Therefore, the phrase *and not* should be replaced with *than*.
(Chapter 15, Lesson 4: Comparison Problems)

30. **B**   This phrasing is the most concise and logical of the choices.
(Chapter 12, Lesson 7: Write Logically)

31. **A**   The original phrasing is best.

32. **D**   Because the sentence refers to *these passions*, it is most logically placed after those passions are described. It also provides a logical transition to the third paragraph.
(Chapter 12, Lesson 7: Write Logically)

33. **B**   This order places the sentences in proper logical and chronological order: (8) identifies his childhood passion, (10) identifies his goals for this passion, (7) proceeds to his college years, (6) mentions where he pursued his passions, and (9) describes the connection between these passions and his later career.
(Chapter 12, Lesson 7: Write Logically)

34. **C**   The paragraph as a whole discusses Roosevelt's passion for nature, so details about his activities in these natural settings would be relevant.
(Chapter 12, Lesson 7: Write Logically)

35. **E**   This sentence would be a good conclusion to the passage because it gives historical perspective to the specific ideas in the passage.
(Chapter 12, Lesson 12: Finish with a Bang)

Section 5

1. B There are 180° on the side of a line.

$$2x + 3x = 180°$$
Combine like terms: $\quad 5x = 180°$
Divide by 5: $\quad x = 36°$
Multiply by 2: $\quad 2x = 72°$
(Chapter 10, Lesson 1: Lines and Angles)

2. B The equation states that some number, when squared, equals 36. That number can be either 6 or –6. Taking the square root of both sides of the equation gives:

$$x - 4 = \pm 6$$
Add 4: $\quad x = 10 \text{ or } -2$
Therefore, the answer is (B) –2.
(Chapter 8, Lesson 1: Solving Equations)

3. C There are 180° in a triangle. Set up equations for the two triangles in the figure.

$$a + b + 52 = 180$$
Subtract 52: $\quad a + b = 128$
$$c + d + 52 = 180$$
Subtract 52: $\quad c + d = 128$
$$a + b + c + d =$$
Substitute: $\quad 128 + 128 = 256$
(Chapter 10, Lesson 2: Triangles)

4. B

$$f(x) = x^2 - 4$$
Set $f(x)$ equal to 32: $\quad x^2 - 4 = 32$
Add 4: $\quad x^2 = 36$
Take positive square root: $\quad x = 6$
(Chapter 11, Lesson 2: Functions)

5. C The ratio of the nuts is a part-to-part-to-part-to-part ratio. Adding these numbers gives the total number of parts: $2 + 4 + 5 + 7 = 18$. Since four of these parts are almonds, the fraction of the mixture that is almonds is 4/18, or 2/9.
(Chapter 7, Lesson 4: Ratios and Proportions)

6. D If 20 students scored an average of 75 points, then the sum of their scores is $20 \times 75 = 1,500$ total points.

If 12 of those students scored an average of 83 points, then the sum of their scores is $12 \times 83 = 996$ points.

Therefore, the remaining 8 students scored $1,500 - 996 = 504$ points altogether, so their average score is $504 \div 8 = 63$ points.

(Chapter 9, Lesson 2: Mean/Median/Mode Problems)

7. A The sides of square $EFGH$ all have length $8\sqrt{2}$. A diagonal of this square can be found with the Pythagorean theorem: $(8\sqrt{2})^2 + (8\sqrt{2})^2 = \overline{EG}^2$.

Simplify: $\quad 128 + 128 = \overline{EG}^2$
$$256 = \overline{EG}^2$$
Take square root: $\quad 16 = \overline{EG}$

(Or, more simply, you can remember that the length of the diagonal of a 45°-45°-90° triangle is the length of the side times $\sqrt{2}$. So the diagonal is $8\sqrt{2} \times \sqrt{2} = 16$.) By the same reasoning, since the sides of square $ABCD$ all have length $14\sqrt{2}$: $\overline{AD} = 14\sqrt{2} \times \sqrt{2} = 28$.

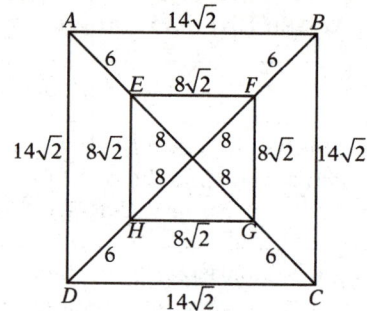

Notice that $\overline{AC} = \overline{AE} + \overline{EG} + \overline{CG}$; therefore, $28 = \overline{AE} + 16 + \overline{CG}$, so $\overline{AE} + \overline{CG} = 12$. By the same reasoning, $\overline{BF} + \overline{DH} = 12$, so $\overline{AE} + \overline{BF} + \overline{CG} + \overline{DH} = 24$.
(Chapter 10, Lesson 3: The Pythagorean Theorem)

8. D Although you were probably taught to add the "rightmost" digits first, here the "leftmost" digits provide more information about the number, so it's best to start there.

$$\begin{array}{r} RS \\ +SR \\ \hline TR4 \end{array}$$

The largest possible 3-digit number that can be formed by adding two 2-digit numbers is $99 + 99 = 198$. Therefore, T must be 1.

$$\begin{array}{r} RS \\ +SR \\ \hline 1R4 \end{array}$$

Therefore, there must be a "carry" of 1 from the addition of $R + S$ in the 10s column. Looking at the units column tells us that $S + R$ yields a units digit of 4, so $S + R = 14$. The addition in the 10s column tells us that $R + S + 1 = R + 10$. (The "+10" is needed for the carry into the 100s column.)

$$R + S + 1 = R + 10$$
Substitute $R + S = 14$: $\quad 14 + 1 = R + 10$
Subtract 10: $\quad 5 = R$
So $2R + T = 2(5) + 1 = 11$.
(Chapter 9, Lesson 3: Numerical Reasoning Problems)

9. 1

$$\boxed{n} = \frac{n^2}{16}$$

If it helps, you can think of this as $\quad f(n) = \dfrac{n^2}{16}$. Find the value of $(f(4))^2$

Plug in 4 for n: $\quad f(4) = \dfrac{4^2}{16} = \dfrac{16}{16} = 1$

Plug in 1 for $f(4)$: $\quad ((f(4))^2 = (1)^2 = 1$
(Chapter 9, Lesson 1: New Symbol or Term Problems)

10. **750** 25% of $600 is $150. Therefore, the club earned $150 more in 2007 than it did in 2006, or $600 + $150 = $750. Remember, also, that increasing any quantity by 25% is the same as multiplying that quantity by 1.25.
(Chapter 7, Lesson 5: Percents)

---

11. **3** Set up equations:

$$x + y = 4$$
$$\underline{x - y = 2}$$

Add straight down: $\quad 2x = 6$

Divide by 2: $\quad x = 3$

Plug in 3 for x: $\quad 3 + y = 4$

Subtract 3: $\quad y = 1$

Final product: $\quad (x)(y) = (3)(1) = 3$

(Chapter 8, Lesson 2: Systems)

---

12. **32** Let $LM = x$, and let $LO = y$. Since x is twice the length of y, $x = 2y$.

$$x + x + y + y = P$$

Substitute for x: $\quad 2y + 2y + y + y = P$

Combine terms: $\quad 6y = P$

Plug in 48 for P: $\quad 6y = 48$

Divide by 6: $\quad y = 8$

Solve for x: $\quad x = 2y = 2(8) = 16$

To find the area of the shaded region, you might notice that if PM is the base of the shaded triangle, then LO is the height, so area = ½(base)(height) = ½(8)(8) = 32.

If you don't notice this, you can find the shaded area by finding the area of the rectangle and subtracting the areas of the two unshaded triangles.

Area of rectangle = (length)(width)
Area of rectangle = $(x)(y) = (16)(8) = 128$

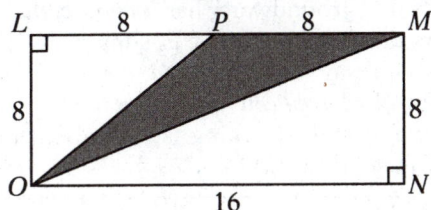

Area of triangle PLO = ½(base)(height)
Area of triangle PLO = ½(8)(8) = 32

Area of triangle MNO = ½(base)(height)
Area of triangle MNO = ½(16)(8) = 64

Area of triangle OPM = 128 − 64 − 32 = 32
(Chapter 10, Lesson 5: Areas and Perimeters)

---

13. **9**

$$64^3 = 4^x$$

Substitute 4^3 for 64: $\quad (4^3)^3 = 4^x$

Simplify: $\quad 4^9 = 4^x$

Equate the exponents: $\quad x = 9$

(Chapter 8, Lesson 3: Working with Exponentials)

---

14. **3** Draw a line with points P, Q, R, and S on the line in that order. You are given that $\overline{PS} = 2\overline{PR}$ and that $\overline{PS} = 4\overline{PQ}$, so choose values for those lengths, like $\overline{PS} = 12$, $\overline{PR} = 6$, and $\overline{PQ} = 3$.

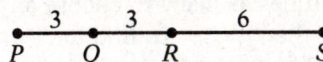

This means that $\overline{QS} = 9$, so $\overline{QS}/\overline{PQ} = 9/3 = 3$.
(Chapter 6, Lesson 2: Analyzing Problems)

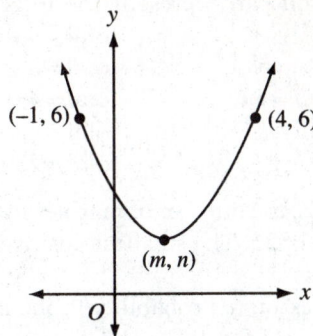

15. **1.5** Since the graph is a parabola, it has a vertical axis of symmetry through the vertex. The points (−1, 6) and (4, 6) have the same y-coordinate, so each one is the reflection of the other over the axis of symmetry. This axis, therefore, must be halfway between the two points. Since the average of −1 and 4 is (−1 + 4)/2 = 1.5, the axis of symmetry must be the line $x = 1.5$, and therefore $m = 1.5$.
(Chapter 11, Lesson 2: Functions)

---

16. **18** Since these numbers are "evenly spaced," their mean (average) is equal to their median (middle number). The average is easy to calculate: 110/5 = 22. Therefore, the middle number is 22, so the numbers are 18, 20, 22, 24, and 26.

Alternatively, you can set up an equation to find the sum of five consecutive unknown even integers, where x is the least of these:

$$x + (x + 2) + (x + 4) + (x + 6) + (x + 8) = 110$$

Combine like terms: $\quad 5x + 20 = 110$

Subtract 20: $\quad 5x = 90$

Divide by 5: $\quad x = 18$

So the five integers are 18, 20, 22, 24, and 26.
(Chapter 9, Lesson 2: Mean/Median/Mode Problems)

---

17. **20** Use the percent change formula:

$$\frac{\text{Final} - \text{Original}}{\text{Original}} \times (100\%)$$

$$\frac{24,000 - 20,000}{20,000} \times (100\%) = 20\%$$

(Chapter 7, Lesson 5: Percents)

18. **25** Let *b* = the number of black marbles, *w* = the number of white marbles, and *r* = the number of red marbles in the jar. If you are four times as likely to choose a black marble as a white one, then *b* = 4*w*. If you are five times as likely to choose a red marble as a black one, then *r* = 5*b*. To find the least possible number of marbles in the jar, imagine you have only one white marble. This would mean you have 4(1) = 4 black marbles and 5(4) = 20 red marbles, for a total of 1 + 4 + 20 = 25 marbles.

In general, you can represent the total number of marbles as

	total = *b* + *w* + *r*
Since *r* = 5*b*:	total = *b* + *w* + 5*b*
Since *b* = 4*w*:	total = 4*w* + *w* + 5(4*w*)
Simplify:	total = 4*w* + *w* + 20*w*
Simplify:	total = 25*w*

In other words, the number of marbles in the jar must be a multiple of 25. The smallest positive multiple of 25 is, of course, 25.
(Chapter 9, Lesson 6: Probability Problems)

Section 6

1. **A** If the fight did not ensue, John must have *intervened* to stop it. *intervene* = get in the way of something; *coalesce* = fuse together; *intermingle* = mix together; *exacerbate* = make worse

2. **D** The defendant hoped the testimony would *corroborate* (support) his alibi, which would *clear him of blame*. *convoke* = call together; *synthesize* = generate; *absolve* = free of blame; *impeach* = accuse

3. **E** Being *ensnarled* (tied up) in traffic is an unpleasant experience that Rachel would have an *aversion to* or *dislike for*. *antipathy* = feeling against; *penchant* = liking; *predilection* = liking; *proclivity* = tendency to do something; *aversion* = feeling of dislike; *insufferable* = intolerable

4. **A** If the practices are no longer considered *state of the art*, they must now be considered *outdated* or *unsophisticated*. The physicians are *incredulous* (not able to believe) that such barbaric acts were once *supported* or *condoned*. *primitive* = old, unsophisticated; *sanctioned* = approved; *ingenious* = incredible, brilliant; *boorish* = rude, *censured* = publicly condemned; *innovative* = new; *endorsed* = supported; *foolhardy* = recklessly bold; *condemned* = criticized

5. **B** The Prime Minister had vetoed the law in the past many times, so he didn't want it to pass. What would come *as a great surprise*? The Prime Minister's suddenly *supporting* the law. *articulated* = expressed

clearly; *championed* = defended; *denounced* = spoke out against; *initiated* = began; *abbreviated* = shortened

6. **C** Lines 3–4 state that the *tradition is that a man never lifts his hand against a woman*. Furthermore, if a man offends a woman, she is entitled to give him *a sound thrashing* (line 6). Therefore, a man who disrespected a woman would face *censure*.

7. **E** Saying that *it is not an unusual thing for a squaw to administer a sound thrashing to a warrior husband* (lines 5–7) is like saying that it is not unusual for her to *give* him a beating, or *dispense* it.

8. **C** Lines 5–6 say that *merely receiving palliative care . . . provides no hope of a cure*. Therefore, palliative care only reduces the discomfort of the symptoms, without curing the disease, as something *analgesic* does.

9. **A** Lines 8–11 ask, *How can a doctor know if a patient has the mental capacity to decide for herself that the time has come to stop fighting the disease?* This question indicates that there may be some difficulty in determining a patient's *state of mind*.

10. **B** The first sentence of the passage says *there was great optimism about earthquake prediction*. Each paragraph discusses potential *precursors*, or predictors, of earthquakes.

11. **E** Lines 8–10 say that because *foreshocks look just like any other earthquake*, they are not in themselves very useful in prediction.

12. **D** Support for choice II can be found in line 19, which says that groundwater has *become cloudy* prior to an earthquake. Choice III is supported in lines 16–18, which say that *before a large earthquake, marked changes have been reported in the level or flow of wells and springs*. Nothing is said about density changes in the groundwater.

13. **A** The passage says (lines 8–10) that *since foreshocks look just like any other earthquakes, they are not in themselves very useful in prediction* but later (lines 39–42) mentions that because *the Haicheng earthquake had hundreds of foreshocks*, it was *easier than average . . . to predict*, thereby suggesting that foreshocks are, in fact, useful in predicting earthquakes.

14. **A** This paragraph describes a particular application of the theory of earthquake prediction, described in the previous paragraphs, which led to scientists' predicting a large earthquake and saving many lives. Although this is said to have *prov[ed] that . . . earthquake prediction is possible* (lines 38–39), it was not a scientific experiment, as there was no control group.

15. C   Lines 49–50 mention that *seismologists missed predicting* the Tangshan earthquake and that over 250,000 people died. This was far worse than the Haicheng earthquake, which was *successfully predicted*, so that many lives were saved.

16. D   The word "evacuation" in line 46 is placed in quotations to indicate that it is not being used in the traditional sense. The task of evacuating a population from a natural disaster does not typically involve showing movies, so doing so is unconventional.

17. C   Lines 7–8 say that *one of the missionaries who met the ship took us under his wing.*

18. E   Saying that *he could hardly believe that we were really restored to him* is like saying he couldn't believe that we were returned to him.

19. B   The narrator states that she could *use tools as well as [her] brothers did* (lines 20–21), that her first childhood friendship was with a male ship-builder next door, and that she was eager and able to work with the ship-builders around her. Thus, she conveys a clear sense that she considers herself the equal of the males in her life.

20. D   The author was emancipated from her confining clothing so that she could work with tools, such as her hatchet, in the shipyard.

21. C   The *big movements of the day* refer to the changes in culture and *civilization* (line 43).

22. A   Choice II is supported by lines 38–40, which say that *we had around us the fine flower of New England civilization*, as opposed to Michigan, which the author characterizes as *the wilderness* (line 45). The passage does not suggest that New England had finer gardens or humbler citizens than Michigan had.

23. D   The author describes the move to Michigan as *a complete upheaval* (lines 37–38), and an unwelcome move from *the fine flower of New England civilization* (lines 39–40), thereby suggesting that she resents the move. She conveys no sign of bewilderment, fear, or awe in this passage, since she describes the move with insight and equanimity.

24. A   The passage says that the sisters *were so pained by* (the lumber wagon's) *appearance that we refused to ride in it* (lines 55–56) and that they wanted to *look as if we had no association with it* (lines 57–58).

Section 7

1. D

$$4x + 5 = 20$$

Add 3: $4x + 8 = 23$

(Chapter 8, Lesson 1: Solving Equations)

2. C   First find out how many cups are in 3 pints.

Set up a ratio: $\dfrac{1 \text{ pint}}{2 \text{ cups}} = \dfrac{3 \text{ pints}}{x \text{ cups}}$

Cross-multiply: $x = 6$ cups

Set up a ratio to solve for servings:

$$\dfrac{1 \text{ serving}}{\frac{1}{3} \text{ cups}} = \dfrac{x \text{ servings}}{6 \text{ cups}}$$

Cross-multiply: $\frac{1}{3}x = 6$

Divide by $\frac{1}{3}$: $x = 18$

(Chapter 7, Lesson 4: Ratios and Proportions)

3. A   Since the angle shown is a right angle, the arc represents ¼ of the circumference.

length of arc = $\frac{1}{4}(2\pi r)$

Substitute 4 for r: length of arc = $\frac{1}{4}(2\pi(4))$

Simplify: length of arc = 2π

(Chapter 10, Lesson 8: Circles)

4. C   This question tests your understanding of 30°-60°-90° triangles. The hypotenuse, which corresponds to $2x$, is 14. This means that the base is $x = 7$. The height is therefore $x\sqrt{3} = 7\sqrt{3}$.

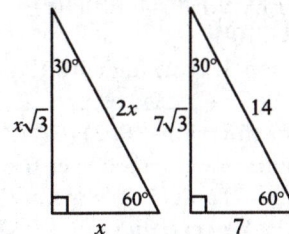

(Chapter 10, Lesson 5: Areas and Perimeters)
(Chapter 10, Lesson 3: The Pythagorean Theorem)

5. A   Given that $\nabla x = 3x - 3$, find $\nabla 7$.

$$\nabla 7 = 3x - 3$$

Plug in 7 for x: $3(7) - 3 = 18$

Find $\nabla 3$: $\nabla 3 = 3x - 3$

Plug in 3 for x: $3(3) - 3 = 6$

$$\dfrac{\nabla 7}{\nabla 3} = \dfrac{18}{6} = 3$$

Be careful not to pick answer choice (B) $\nabla 3$, because $\nabla 3 = 3(3) - 3 = 6$, not 3. Answer choice (A) $\nabla 2$ is correct, because $\nabla 2 = 3(2) - 3 = 3$.

(Chapter 9, Lesson 1: New Symbol or Term Problems)

6. B   A little common sense should tell you that they will not need a full hour to clean the pool, because Stephanie can clean it in an hour all by herself, but Mark is helping. Therefore, you should eliminate choices (C), (D), and (E) right away. You might also notice that it can't take less than 30 minutes, because that is how long it would take if they both cleaned one pool per hour (so that the two working together could clean it in half the time), but Mark is slower, so they can't clean it quite that fast. This eliminates choice (A) and leaves (B) as the only possibility.

But you should know how to solve this problem if it were not a multiple-choice question, as well:

Stephanie's rate for cleaning the pool is one pool per hour. Mark's rate for cleaning the pool is one pool ÷ 1.5 hours = $\frac{2}{3}$ pools per hour. Combined, they can clean $1 + \frac{2}{3} = \frac{5}{3}$ pools per hour. Set up a rate equation using this rate to determine how much time it would take to clean one pool:

$$1 \text{ pool} = (\tfrac{5}{3} \text{ pools per hour})(\text{time})$$

Divide by $\frac{5}{3}$: $\frac{3}{5}$ hours to clean the pool
Multiply by 60: $\frac{3}{5}(60) = 36$ minutes
(Chapter 9, Lesson 4: Rate Problems)

---

7. A   Change each expression to a base-10 exponential:
(A) $= ((10^2)^3)^4 = 10^{24}$
(B) $= ((10^2)^5)((10^2)^6) = (10^{10})(10^{12}) = 10^{22}$
(C) $= ((10^4)^4) = 10^{16}$
(D) $= (((10^2)^2)((10^2)^2))^2 = ((10^4)(10^4))^2 = (10^8)^2 = 10^{16}$
(E) $= (10^6)^3 = 10^{18}$
(Chapter 8, Lesson 3: Working with Exponentials)

---

8. B   Consider the points $(0, 2)$ and $(3, 0)$ on line l. When these points are reflected over the x-axis, $(0, 2)$ transforms to $(0, -2)$ and $(3, 0)$ stays at $(3, 0)$ because it is on the x-axis. You can then use the slope formula to find the slope of line m:

$$\frac{y_2 - y_1}{x_2 - x_1} = \frac{0 - (-2)}{3 - 0} = \frac{2}{3}$$

It's helpful to notice that whenever a line is reflected over the x-axis (or the y-axis, for that matter—try it), its slope becomes the opposite of the original slope. (Chapter 10, Lesson 4: Coordinate Geometry)

---

9. C

	$(a + b)^2 = (a + b)(a + b)$
FOIL:	$a^2 + ab + ab + b^2$
Combine like terms:	$a^2 + 2ab + b^2$
Plug in 5 for ab:	$a^2 + 2(5) + b^2$
Simplify:	$a^2 + b^2 + 10$
Plug in 4 for $a^2 + b^2$:	$4 + 10 = 14$

(Chapter 8, Lesson 5: Factoring)

---

10. D   The total area of the patio to be constructed is $24 \times 12 = 288$ ft². The slab shown in the figure has an area of 8 ft². Therefore, to fill the patio you will need $288 \div 8 = 36$ slabs.
(Chapter 10, Lesson 5: Areas and Perimeters)

---

11. D   The prize money ratio can also be written as $7x:2x:1x$. Because the total prize money is \$12,000,

$$7x + 2x + 1x = 12,000$$
Combine like terms: $10x = 12,000$
Divide by 10: $x = 1,200$
The first place prize is $7x = 7(1,200) = \$8,400$.
(Chapter 7, Lesson 4: Ratios and Proportions)

---

12. E   Always read the problem carefully and notice what it's asking for. Don't assume that you must solve for x and y here. Finding the value of $6x - 2y$ is much simpler than solving the entire system:

$$2x + 3y = 7$$
$$4x - 5y = 12$$
Add straight down: $6x - 2y = 19$
(Chapter 8, Lesson 2: Systems)

---

13. D   Think carefully about the given information and what it implies, then try to find counterexamples to disprove the given statements. For instance, try to disprove statement I by showing that s can be even. Imagine $s = 2$:

	$s + 1 = 2r$
Substitute 6 for s:	$6 + 1 = 2r$
Combine like terms:	$7 = 2r$
Divide by 2:	$3.5 = r$ (nope)

This doesn't work because r must be an integer. Why didn't it work? Because $2r$ must be even, but if s is even, then $s + 1$ must be odd and cannot equal an even number, so s must always be odd and statement I is true. (Eliminate choice (B).)

Statement II can be disproven with $r = 1$:

	$s + 1 = 2r$
Substitute 1 for r:	$s + 1 = 2(1)$
Subtract 1:	$s = 1$ (okay)

Since 1 is an integer, we've proven that r is not necessarily even, so II is false. (Eliminate choices (C) and (E).)

Since we still have two choices remaining, we have to check ugly old statement III. Try the values we used before. If $r = 1$ and $s = 1$, then $\frac{s}{r} + \frac{1}{r} = \frac{1}{1} + \frac{1}{1} = 2$, which is an integer. But is it always an integer? Plugging in more examples can't prove that it will ALWAYS be an integer, because we can never test all possible solutions. We can prove it easily with algebra, though. Since $s + 1 = 2r$:

Divide by r: $\dfrac{s + 1}{r} = 2$

Distribute: $\dfrac{s}{r} + \dfrac{1}{r} = 2$

Since 2 is an integer, statement III is necessarily true.
(Chapter 9, Lesson 3: Numerical Reasoning Problems)
(Chapter 6, Lesson 7: Thinking Logically)

---

14. **C**   Find all the possible products of the values on two chips: $(1)(2) = 2$; $(1)(3) = 3$; $(1)(4) = 4$; $(1)(5) = 5$; $(1)(6) = 6$; $(2)(3) = 6$; $(2)(4) = 8$; $(2)(5) = 10$; $(2)(6) = 12$; $(3)(4) = 12$; $(3)(5) = 15$; $(3)(6) = 18$; $(4)(5) = 20$; $(4)(6) = 24$; $(5)(6) = 30$. There are 15 different combinations of chips. Of these, only the last 2 yield products that are greater than 20. So the probability is 2/15.
(Chapter 9, Lesson 6: Probability Problems)

---

15. **D**   In this problem, only the signs of the terms matter. By following the rule of the sequence, you should see that the first six terms of the sequence are $+, -, -, +, -, -, \ldots$. The pattern $\{+, -, -\}$ repeats forever. In the first 100 terms, the pattern repeats $100 \div 3 = 33\frac{1}{3}$ times. Because each repetition contains two negative numbers, in 33 full repetitions there are $33 \times 2 = 66$ negative numbers. The 100th term is the first term of the next pattern, which is positive, so the total number of negative terms is 66.
(Chapter 11, Lesson 1: Sequences)

---

16. **B**   Draw the five triangles. The simplest way to solve this problem is to compare the choices one pair at a time. For instance, it should be clear just by inspection that $RB > RA$ and $SB > SA$, so we can eliminate A. Similarly, it should be clear that $RB > RC$ and $SB > SC$, so we can eliminate C. Likewise, since $RB > RD$ and $SB > SD$, we can eliminate D. Finally, we compare B with E. Since RB and RE are each a diagonal of one of the square faces, they must be equal. But SB is clearly longer than SE, because SB is the hypotenuse of triangle SEB, while SE is one of the legs.
(Chapter 10, Lesson 7: Volumes and 3-D Geometry)
(Chapter 6, Lesson 7: Thinking Logically)

Section 8

1. **C**   If the review suggested that the décor of the restaurant was insipid (tasteless), but that the cuisine came close to *compensating* for it, the review must have been part positive and part negative, that is, *ambivalent*. *indefatigable* = untiring; *banal* = lacking originality; *ambivalent* = characterized by conflicting feelings; *sublime* = supreme, impressive; *piquant* = spicy; *tepid* = lukewarm

---

2. **C**   The sentence suggests that Dr. Thompson should have characterized the results as unusual, but didn't. *meticulous* = concerned with detail; *belligerent* = prone to fighting; *anomalous* = deviating from the norm; *convergent* = coming together; *warranted* = appropriate to the situation

---

3. **B**   They would hope that bad news did not predict further bad news. *amalgam* = a combination of diverse elements; *harbinge* = omen; *arbiter* = judge; *talisman* = an object with magical power

---

4. **C**   To bring slaves *out of bondage* is to *free* or *unfetter* them. *encumber* = burden; *forgo* = relinquish

---

5. **D**   A writer who can produce both *decorative poetry* and a *keenly analytical mystery novel* is a *versatile* writer; that is, she is able to write in divergent styles. *flamboyant* = ornate; *immutability* = permanence, unchangeability; *austere* = plain; *florid* = ornate; *grandiloquent* = characterized by pompous language

---

6. **B**   The word *because* indicates that the sentence shows a cause-and-effect relationship. There are several ways to complete this sentence logically, but the only one among the choices is (B), because *multifarious* (widely varied) mechanisms would logically "stymie" (impede) scientists who are trying to investigate them. *efficacious* = capable of producing a desired effect; *bilked* = cheated; *conspicuous* = obvious; *thwarted* = prevented; *hampered* = hindered; *lucid* = clear; *proscribed* = forbidden

---

7. **B**   If the *cultural assumption that there are many alien civilizations . . . stems in no small way from . . . the "Drake Equation,"* then this equation has had quite an influence on public opinion.

---

8. **E**   The first two paragraphs discuss how the Drake Equation has led to the belief that there are many alien civilizations in the universe. The third paragraph discusses the author's contrasting view that there is indeed probably much simple life in the universe but very little if any other complex life.

---

9. **B**   The sentence states that *a planet could go from an abiotic state to a civilization in 100 million years* thereby implying that a *civilization* must, by definition, not be *abiotic*. Choice (B) is the only choice that necessarily cannot apply to a civilization.

---

10. **A**   The author states his thesis in lines 38–39: *perhaps life is common, but complex life is not,* and goes on to explain this thesis, stating in lines 61–67 that *research shows that while attaining the stage of animal life is one thing, maintaining that level is quite another. . . . Complex life is subject to an unending succession of planetary disasters, creating what are known as mass-extinction events.*

---

11. **A**   The phrase *the evolutionary grade we call animals* refers to the *level* of life form produced by evolution.

12. **C** Statement (A) is supported in lines 48–50, statement (B) is supported in lines 74–76, statement (D) is supported in lines 38–39, and statement (E) is supported in lines 51–55.

13. **C** The *sample size of one* refers to the uniqueness of *Earth history* (line 78).

14. **A** The first quotation in lines 101–103 is described as a *rejoinder*, or an opposing response, to the author's thoughts. The author then responds with his own quotation.

15. **C** The author says that he does not *conclude that there are no other cats (Rare Cat Hypothesis), only that there are no other cats exactly like Wookie* in order to convey the idea that one should not draw conclusions based on one occurrence.

16. **B** The author says that *life is opportunistic* to summarize the next statement that *the biosphere has taken advantage of the myriad of strange idiosyncrasies that our planet has to offer.*

17. **D** The passage says that these creatures *might naively assume that these qualities, very different from Earth's, are the only ones that can breed complexity,* that is, that all life evolved the same way.

18. **A** The author of Passage 1 believes that complex life, once evolved, faces numerous dangers that push it toward extinction. The author would point this fact out in response to the statement in lines 134–135 of Passage 2.

19. **D** The author of Passage 1 says in line 26, *In my view, life in the form of microbes or their equivalents is very common in the universe, perhaps more common than even Drake and Sagan envisioned.* The author of Passage 2 says in line 139, *My bet is that many other worlds, with their own peculiar characteristics and histories, co-evolve their own biospheres.* Both authors seem to agree that there is a lot of undiscovered life out there in the universe.

Section 9

1. **B** When you list items in a sentence, the items should have the same grammatical form. If the first item is in the gerund, they should all be in the gerund. Because the sentence says *Eating* an english muffin and *sitting* down, *drink coffee* should instead be *drinking coffee.*
(Chapter 15, Lesson 3: Parallelism)

2. **D** The sentence begins with a participial phrase, so the subject of the participle, *pretending*, must also be the subject of the main clause. Since Mark is the one pretending, the subject of the main clause should be *Mark*. Choice (C) is incorrect because the pronoun *it* lacks a proper antecedent and appears to refer, illogically, to the *practice*. Choice (E) is incorrect because it uses an unidiomatic phrase, *convince in letting*, rather than the proper idiom, *convince to let.*
(Chapter 15, Lesson 7: Dangling and Misplaced Participles)

3. **C** The verb *are* is the improper tense. It should be *be* as in answer choice (C).
(Chapter 15, Lesson 9: Tricky Tenses)

4. **C** When you list items in a sentence, the items should have the same grammatical form. If the first term is in the noun form, then they all should be in the noun form. Because the sentence says *his temper, impatience, how easily he can be irritated* should instead be *irritability.*
(Chapter 15, Lesson 3: Parallelism)

5. **B** Before she gave the *gracious speech*, she won the match. The verb *winning* should instead be in the past perfect form, *having won.*
(Chapter 15, Lesson 9: Tricky Tenses)

6. **C** The sentence begins by describing something that was the most influential science treatise of the 20th century. The pronoun to follow the comma should describe this treatise. Choice (C) corrects the error in the most logical and concise fashion.
(Chapter 15, Lesson 7: Dangling and Misplaced Participles)

7. B The pronoun *their* does not agree in number with its singular antecedent, *neither*. Choice (B) corrects this error concisely. Choices (C) and (E) are also guilty of pronoun-antecedent disagreement, and choice (D) produces a sentence fragment.
(Chapter 15, Lesson 5: Pronoun-Antecedent Disagreement)

8. A The original sentence is best. All other choices are unidiomatic.
(Chapter 15, Lesson 10: Idiom Errors)

9. C The sentence requires parallel phrasing of the two things that the storm waves did: *inundating* and *sweeping*. Choice (A) is not parallel and is needlessly wordy. Choice (B) is vague, since it does not explain what *swept away* the cars. In choice (D), the pronoun *it* does not agree in number with *storm waves*. Choice (E) misuses the semicolon, because the phrase that follows the semicolon is not an independent clause.
(Chapter 15, Lesson 3: Parallelism)

10. B In the original sentence, the verb *have been depicted* does not agree with its singular subject, *life*. In choice (C), the phrase *depicted with* is unidiomatic, and the verb *has had depicted* is illogical. In choice (D), the pronoun *they* lacks a clear and logical antecedent. The logic and phrasing in choice (E) is awkward.
(Chapter 15, Lesson 1: Subject-Verb Disagreement

11. D In the original sentence, the modifying phrase *at the age of seven* is misplaced, and incorrectly implies that the speaker's father, rather than the speaker himself, was seven. Choices (B), (C), and (E) commit the same error, but in slightly different ways.
(Chapter 15, Lesson 7: Dangling and Misplaced Participles)

12. A The original sentence is best, since it uses concise and logical parallel phrasing.
(Chapter 15, Lesson 3: Parallelism)

13. E The pronoun *them* refers to a plural subject. However, anyone is singular. Answer choice (E) clears up this pronoun-antecedent disagreement in the most concise and logical way.
(Chapter 15, Lesson 5: Pronoun-Antecedent Disagreement)

14. A Although the original phrasing is not the most concise option, it is the only one that logically coordinates the ideas in the sentence.

A right triangle has a leg of length 3 and a hypotenuse of length 4. What is the length of the other side?

If n is a positive real number, what is the simplest way to express $n^2 \times n^3$?

The average of 3 consecutive even integers is 80. What is the least of these integers?

Stephanie bought a sweater for $42.40, including a 6% sales tax. What was the price before tax?

If $5 - 2(x - 3) = 9$, then what is the value of x?

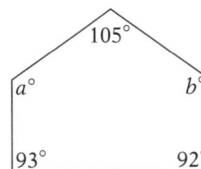

Note: Figure not drawn to scale

In the figure above, what is the value of $a + b$?

Formula/Concept:
When you multiply exponentials with the same base, you **add** the exponents.

Correct answer: n^5 $(n^2)(n^3) =$
Add the exponents: $(n^{2+3}) = n^5$

Common mistake: n^6
This is the result if you mistakenly multiply the exponents.

Formula/Concept:
The Pythagorean Theorem

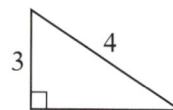

Correct answer: $\sqrt{7}$ $3^2 + x^2 = 4^2$
Subtract 9: $x^2 = 7$
Take square root: $x = \sqrt{7}$

Common mistake: 5
Don't assume it is a 3-4-5 triangle. In such a triangle, the 3-4 sides must both be **legs.**

Formula/Concept:
To find the price before a 6% tax, **divide** the final price by 1.06.

Correct answer: $40
$42.40 = (1.06)(x)$
Divide by 1.06: $40.00 = x$

Common mistake: $39.86
This is the result if you mistakenly deduct 6% of $42.40 (which is $2.54), from $42.40.

Formula/Concept:
If a set of numbers is "evenly" spaced, the average is the same as the middle number.

Correct answer: 78
If the average of consecutive even numbers is 80, then 80 must be the "middle" number in the set, so the numbers are 78, 80, 82.

Common mistake: 79
Don't overlook the fact that the numbers are **even.**

Formula/Concept:
$(n - 2)180°$ = the sum of the angles in an n-sided figure.

Correct answer: 250
The sum of the angles is $(5 - 2)(180°) = 540°$, so $105° + 93° + 92° + a + b = 540°$. Therefore, $a + b = 250°$.

Common mistake: 70
This is the result if you mistakenly think the sum is 360° instead of 540°.

Formula/Concept:
Distributing with negative numbers

Correct answer: 1 $5 - 2(x - 3) = 9$
Distribute: $5 - 2x + 6 = 9$
Combine like terms: $11 - 2x = 9$
Subtract 11: $-2x = -2$

Common mistake: −5
This results from improperly distributing the −2.

At the beginning of 1999, stock in ABC company cost $100 per share. It increased by 25% in 1999, decreased by 20% in 2000, decreased by 20% in 2001, and increased by 15% in 2002. What was the price at the end of 2002?

Shaquille O'Neal made 4 of his first 12 free throws. How many consecutive shots x must he hit for his free-throw percentage to reach 60%?

If the average of x, $x + 2$, and $2x + 8$ is 6, what is the value of x?

If a triangle has two sides of length 8 and 12, then what is the largest possible integer length of the third side?

A set consists of the integers from -12 to n. If the sum of the members of that set is 42, how many integers are in the set?

If 10 students in a class of 16 have an average score of 82 on a physics test and the remaining students have an average score of 90, what is the average score of the entire class?

Formula/Concept: Ratios and Proportions

Correct answer: $8 \qquad \dfrac{4+x}{12+x} = .6$

Cross-multiply: $(4 + x) = (12 + x)(.6)$
Distribute: $4 + x = 7.2 + .6x$
Subtract $.6x$: $4 + .4x = 7.2$
Subtract 4: $.4x = 3.2$
Divide by $.4$: $x = 8$

Common mistake: 4
This is the result if you forget to add the quantity x to the denominator as well as the numerator.

Formula/Concept: Percent change

e.g.   To *increase* a value by 20%, multiply by 1.20
To *decrease* a value by 10%, multiply by 0.90

Correct answer: 92   1999 = \$100
$(100)(1.25) = 125$ 2000 = \$125
$(125)(.8) = 100$ 2001 = \$100
$(100)(.8) = 80$ 2002 = \$80
$(80)(1.15) = 92$ 2003 = \$92

Common mistake: 100   This is result if you simply add up the percent changes instead of calculating the changes as above: 25 - 20 - 20 + 15 = 0.

Formula/Concept:
The Triangle Inequality:
$|B - A| < C < |B + A|$

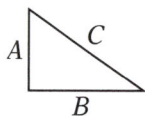

Correct answer: 19
$(B - A) < C < (B + A)$
Substitute for A and B: $(12 - 8) < C < (12 + 8)$
Simplify: $4 < C < 20$

Common mistake: 20
This is the common error that can be made if you mistakenly set $4 \leq C \leq 20$.

Formula/Concept: $\dfrac{sum}{\#} = average$
Average formula:

Correct answer: 2

$$\dfrac{x + (x+2) + (2x+8)}{3} = 6$$

Multiply by 3: $x + (x + 2) + (2x + 8) = 18$
Combine like terms: $4x + 10 = 18$
Subtract 10: $4x = 8$
Divide by 4: $x = 2$

Common mistake: 5
This is the result if you mistakenly think that there are 5 numbers instead of 3.

Formula/Concept: Weighted Averages
If two numbers being averaged have different "weights," you must remember to account for that when finding the average.

Correct answer: 85

$$\dfrac{10(82) + 6(90)}{16} = \dfrac{820 + 540}{16} = 85$$

Common mistake: 86
This is the result if you mistakenly take the "simple" average of the two scores, 82 and 90, rather than taking their *weighted* average.

Formula/Concept: Integer arithmetic

Correct answer: 28
Remember that the sum of the numbers from -12 to 12 is 0, because the negative integers "cancel" the positives. 13 + 14 + 15 = 42, so n must be 15. To find the number of integers in the set, just subtract the first from the last and add 1.

Common mistake: 27
This is the result if you forget that 0 is an integer or simply subtract the least from the greatest to count the integers in the set.

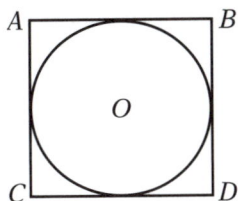

If the area of square ABCD in the figure above is 100 ft², then what is the circumference of inscribed circle O?

If the third Friday in January occurs on the 15th, what is the date of the fourth Wednesday in January?

In 1984, a share of stock in Black's Oil Trust cost $3. By 2000, it had increased to $15 per share. What is the percent increase in the price of the stock from 1984 to 2000?

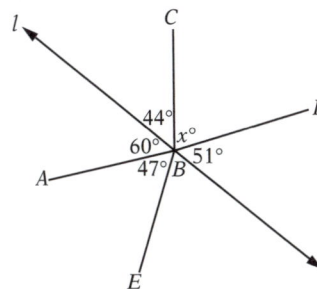

Note: Figure not drawn to scale.

In the figure above, line segments $\overline{AB}$, $\overline{EB}$ $\overline{CB}$, and $\overline{DB}$ intersect line l at point B. What is the value of x?

If $(x + 4)(x - 4) = 65$, then what is the value of x^2?

At a department store, all shirts are priced at s dollars, but if you buy one shirt at full price, you can buy any number of additional shirts at a $2 discount per shirt. What is the cost of buying x shirts at this sale?

Formula/Concept: Using Patterns
Correct answer: 27th
Make a calendar:

M	T	W	Th	F	Sa	Su
				1	2	3
4	5	**6**	7	8	9	10
11	12	**13**	**14**	**15**	16	17
18	19	**20**	21	22	23	24
25	26	**27**	28	29	30	31

Common mistake: **20th**
This is the result if you mistakenly assume, without drawing a calendar to confirm, that the third Wednesday occurs before the third Friday. In this particular month, the first Wednesday is after the first Friday.

Formula/Concept: Circumference $= 2\pi r = \pi d$
Correct answer: **10π**

Area of square $= (\text{side})^2$
Substitute 100 for area: $100 = (\text{side})^2$
Take square root: $10 = $ side of square diameter $d = $ side of square
Use circumference formula $C = \pi d = \pi(10) = 10\pi$

Common mistake: 25π
This is the result if you confuse the area formula with the circumference formula.

Formula/Concept: A linear angle measures 180°.

Correct answer: **85°**
$44° + x° + 51° = 180°$
Combine like terms: $95° + x° = 180°$
Subtract 95°: $x° = 85°$

Common mistake: **47°**
This is the result if you mistakenly think that angles CBD and ABE are vertical angles. But vertical angles must involve intersecting lines, not line segments. There are no vertical angles in this figure.

Formula/Concept:

$$\text{Percent change} = \frac{final - original}{original} \times 100\%$$

Correct answer: **400%**

$$\text{Percent change} = \frac{15-3}{3} \times 100\% = 400\%$$

Common mistake: **500%**
This is the result if you mistakenly find what percent 15 is of 3 instead of finding the percent **change** from 3 to 15.

Formula/Concept: Translating words into expressions

Correct answer: $s + (x - 1)(s - 2)$
The first shirt costs s dollars, and each additional shirt costs $(s - 2)$ dollars. Don't multiply the $(s - 2)$ by x, because this would account for the first shirt twice. Only $(x - 1)$ shirts are priced at $(s - 2)$ dollars.

Common mistake: $s + (x)(s - 2)$
This is the result if you forget that only $x - 1$ shirts are discounted, rather than all (x) shirts.

Formula/Concept: FOILing
$$(a + b)(a - b) = a^2 - ab + ab + b^2$$

Correct answer: **81**

$(x + 4)(x - 4) = 65$
FOIL: $x^2 - 4x + 4x - 16 = 65$
Combine like terms: $x^2 - 16 = 65$
Add 16: $x^2 = 81$

Common mistake: 9
This is result if you mistakenly solve for x instead of x^2.

If w divided by ¼ is equal to 32, then what is the value of w?

Point W is on line segment XY such that $\dfrac{XW}{WY} = \dfrac{3}{4}$. If $WY = 12$ then what is XY?

At Holston Hospital, a "team" consists of 1 resident and 2 medical students. If there are 4 residents and 5 medical students in the emergency department, how many different teams could be formed?

For all values of x, let $\boxed{x} = \dfrac{x-2}{4}$.

Which of the following is equal to $\boxed{34} - \boxed{10}$?

(A) $\boxed{6}$
(B) $\boxed{8}$
(C) $\boxed{14}$
(D) $\boxed{24}$
(E) $\boxed{26}$

If the average of 5, 6, 8, x, and 8 is 6, then what is the median of the set?

When 34 is divided by 6, the remainder is n. What is the remainder when n is divided by 2?

Formula/Concept: Ratios and Proportions

Correct answer: 21 $\dfrac{XW}{WY} = \dfrac{3}{4}$

Plug in 12 for WY: $\dfrac{XW}{12} = \dfrac{3}{4}$

Cross-multiply: $4XW = 36$
Divide by 4: $XW = 9$
Solve for XY: $XY = 9 + 12 = 21$

Common mistake: 9
This is the result if you solve for XW instead of XY.

Formula/Concept: To divide by a fraction, multiply by its reciprocal.

Correct answer: **8**
Write an equation: $w \div \frac{1}{4} = 32$
Multiply by the reciprocal: $w \times 4 = 32$
Divide by 4: $w = 8$

Common mistake: **128**
This is the result if you divide 32 by $\frac{1}{4}$ instead of multiplying it by $\frac{1}{4}$.

Formula/Concept: New Symbols/Functions
Correct answer: **E**

$\boxed{34} = \dfrac{34-2}{4} = \dfrac{32}{4} = 8$ $\boxed{10} = \dfrac{10-2}{4} = \dfrac{8}{4} = 2$

$\boxed{34} - 10 = 8 - 2 = 6$ $\boxed{26} = \dfrac{26-2}{4} = \dfrac{24}{4} = 6$

Common mistake: **A**
This is the result if you do not notice that the answer choices are also in boxes.

Formula/Concept: The Fundamental Counting Principle

Correct answer: $4 \times 5 \times 4 \div 2 = \mathbf{40}$
The number of options for choosing a resident is 4, since there are 4 residents. The number of different pairs of interns is 10, because there are 5 options for intern A and then 4 options for intern B, but since choosing AB is the same as choosing BA, we must divide this set by 2.

Common mistake: **100 or 80**
This is the result of $4 \times 5 \times 5$ or $4 \times 5 \times 4$.

Formula/Concept: Remainders
Correct answer: **0**

$6\overline{)34}\ ^{5R4}$ -30 4 $2\overline{)4}\ ^{2R0}$ -4 0

Common mistake: **2**
This is the result if you find the **quotient** rather than the remainder.

Formula/Concept: Median = middle number
Mean = average

Correct answer: 6 $\dfrac{5+6+8+x+8}{5} = 6$

Multiply by 5: $5 + 6 + 8 + x + 8 = 30$
Combine like terms: $27 + x = 30$
Subtract 27: $x = 3$
Find the median: $\cancel{3}, \cancel{5}, 6, \cancel{8}, \cancel{8}$
Common mistake: **8**
This is the result if you confuse **mode** with **median.**

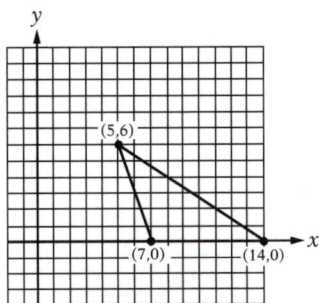

What is the area of the triangle in the figure above?

A printer can produce 50 pages in 3 minutes. At this rate, how many pages can it print in 300 minutes?

The slope of line *l* is −½. If two points on line *l* are (2, 4) and (*x*, −2), what is the value of *x*?

If $f(x) = (x - 2)^2$, what is the range of this function over the domain $-2 \leq x \leq 3$?

There are 25 students in Ms. Jamison's 4th-grade homeroom class. If 12 of her students have a cat, 19 have a dog, and every student has at least 1 pet, how many students have both a cat and a dog?

If *b* varies inversely as the square of *c* and directly as *a*, and *b* = 4 when *c* = 4 and *a* = 8, then what is the value of *b* when *a* = 18 and *c* = 6?

Formula/Concept: Ratios and Proportions

Correct answer: **5,000**

Set up a ratio: $\dfrac{50 \text{ pages}}{3 \text{ minutes}} = \dfrac{x \text{ pages}}{300 \text{ minutes}}$

Cross multiply: $15,000 = 3x$
Divide by 3: $5,000 = x$

Common mistake: 18
This is the result if you set up the ratio improperly.

$$\dfrac{50 \text{ pages}}{3 \text{ minutes}} = \dfrac{300 \text{ minutes}}{x \text{ pages}}$$

Formula/Concept: Area = ½(base)(height)

Correct answer: 21
The base of the triangle is the distance from $(7, 0)$ to $(14, 0)$, which is $14 - 7 = 7$. The height is the distance from the x-axis to $(5, 6)$, which is $6 - 0 = 6$.

$$\text{Area} = \tfrac{1}{2}(7)(6) = 21$$

Common mistake: 17.5
This is the common error that can be made if you use 5 as the height instead of 6.

Formula/Concept:
The range of a function is the set of all of the possible outputs, or "y-values."
Correct answer: $0 \leq y \leq 16$
Plug in the integer values of the domain and find the range:
$f(-2) = 16; f(-1) = 9; f(0) = 4;$
$f(1) = 1; f(2) = 0; f(3) = 1.$ This yields a range of $0 \leq y \leq 16$. Or you could graph it:

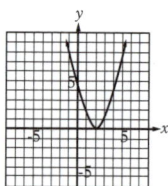

Common mistake: $1 \leq y \leq 16$
This results if you try to find the range by plugging in only the two domain endpoints, ignoring the points in between.

Formula/Concept: $slope = \dfrac{rise}{run} = \dfrac{y_2 - y_1}{x_2 - x_1}$

Correct answer: 14 $slope = \dfrac{y_2 - y_1}{x_2 - x_1} = \dfrac{-2 - 4}{x - 2} = \dfrac{-1}{2}$

Cross-multiply: $2(-6) = -1(x - 2)$
Simplify: $-12 = -x + 2$
Subtract 2: $-14 = -x$
Divide by −1: $14 = x$
Common mistake: −1
This is the result if you mistakenly calculate "run over rise" for the slope: $\dfrac{x_2 - x_1}{y_2 - y_1}$

Formula/Concept: Direct and Inverse Variation

Correct answer: 4
$$b = \dfrac{ka}{c^2} \qquad 4 = \dfrac{k(8)}{(4)^2}$$

Cross-multiply: $64 = 8k$
Divide by 8: $k = 8$
Set up new equation: $b = \dfrac{8a}{c^2} \qquad b = \dfrac{8(18)}{(6)^2} = \dfrac{144}{36} = 4$

Common mistake: ½
This is the result if you inversely relate b to the square **root** of c instead of relating it to the square of c.

Formula/Concept: Venn Diagrams
Correct answer: 6
Let x represent the number of students with both cats and dogs:

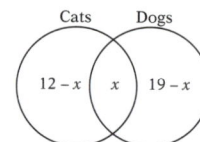

$$(12 - x) + (19 - x) + x = 25$$
Combine like terms: $31 - x = 25$
Subtract 31: $-x = -6$
Divide by −1: $x = 6$
Common mistake: 25 or 31
This is the result if you confuse "a cat and a dog" with "a cat **or** a dog."

If $-1 < w < 0$, then which of the following statements is true?

(A) $w < w^2 < w^3$
(B) $w^2 < w < w^3$
(C) $w < w^3 < w^2$
(D) $w^3 < w^2 < w$
(E) $w^3 < w < w^2$

If $5 - 2|x| > -9$, find the range of possible values for x.

$-2, 0, 2, -2, 0, 2, -2, 0, 2, \ldots$

The sequence above continues according to the pattern shown. What is the sum of the first 31 terms of this sequence?

A jar contains only red and white marbles. If the probability of randomly selecting a white marble from the jar is ¼ and there are 15 red marbles in the jar, how many white marbles are there?

The sum of a set of 7 integers is 67. If each of these numbers must be less than 14, what is the smallest possible value of any one number in the set?

Jim takes the same train to and from work each day. One winter day, during the morning commute, the train averaged 80 miles per hour. During the evening commute, due to ice on the track, the train averaged only 48 miles per hour. If Jim spent 2 hours in the train that day, how many miles is the train ride to work?

Formula/Concept: Powers of Fractions

Correct answer: **C**

Plug in a number for w:

Plug in $-\frac{1}{2}$ for w:

$$w = -\tfrac{1}{2}$$
$$w^2 = (-\tfrac{1}{2})^2 = \tfrac{1}{4}$$
$$w^3 = (-\tfrac{1}{2})^3 = -\tfrac{1}{8}$$

Rank the values of w, w^2, w^3: $-\tfrac{1}{2} < -\tfrac{1}{8} < \tfrac{1}{4}$

Common mistake: **A or E**

You might choose E if you forget that $-\tfrac{1}{8} > -\tfrac{1}{2}$. You might choose A if you forget that squaring any negative number will result in a positive number.

Formula/Concept:
Solving absolute value inequalities

Correct answer: **$-7 < x < 7$**

$$5 - 2|x| > -9$$

Subtract 5: $-2|x| > -14$

Divide by -2: (swap the inequality) $|x| < 7$

Take away absolute value: $-7 < x < 7$

Common mistake: **$x > 7$ or $x < -7$**

This is the common error that can be made if you forget to swap the inequality when dividing or multiplying by a negative number.

Formula/Concept: Ratios and Probability

Correct answer: **5**

If the probability of selecting a white marble is $\frac{1}{4}$, then the probability of selecting a red marble is $1 - \frac{1}{4} = \frac{3}{4}$.

Set up a ratio: $\dfrac{red}{total} = \dfrac{3}{4}$ $\dfrac{15}{total} = \dfrac{3}{4}$

Cross-multiply: $60 = 3(total)$

Divide by 3: $20 = total = white + red$

Solve for white: $20 = white + 15$

Subtract 15: $white = 5$ marbles

Common mistake: **20**

This is the result if you answer for the **total** number of marbles instead of the number of **white** marbles.

Formula/Concept:
Sequence problems: finding the sum of a random number of terms

Correct answer: **-2**

The pattern repeats every 3 digits, and the sum of each repetition is $-2 + 0 + 2 = 0$. The pattern occurs $31 \div 3 = 10\tfrac{1}{3}$ times, or 10 with remainder 1. The 10 full repetitions have a sum of $10(0) = 0$. Since the 31st term is -2, the sum is $0 + -2 = -2$.

Common mistake: **0**

This is the common error that can be made if you forget to add the 31st term after finding out that the pattern occurs $10\tfrac{1}{3}$ times.

Formula/Concept: Distance = Rate × Time

Correct answer: **60** (because he takes the same train, the distance is the same going in both directions.)

To work: $d = (80)(t)$

From work: $d = (48)(2 - t)$

Set them equal: $80t = 48(2 - t)$

Distribute: $80t = 96 - 48t$

Add 48t: $128t = 96$

Divide by 128: $t = .75$ hours

Plug in .75 for t: $d = 80(.75) = 60$ miles

Common mistake: **64**

This is the result if you average the two speeds, 80 and 48, and then using that speed of 64 to calculate a distance of 64 miles to work.

Formula/Concept: Numerical Reasoning

Correct answer: **-11**

$$a + b + c + d + e + f + g = 67$$

If you want g to be as **small** as possible, then make the sum of the other numbers as **large** as possible: Substitute 13 for a through f:

$$13 + 13 + 13 + 13 + 13 + 13 + g = 67$$

Combine like terms: $78 + g = 67$

Common mistake: **4**

This is the result if you assume the integers must be **different**: 13, 12, 11, 10, 9, and 8.

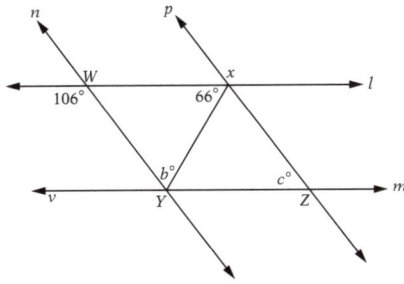

Note: <u>Figure not drawn to scale.</u>

In the figure above, if $l \parallel m$ and $n \parallel p$, what is the value of $b + c$?

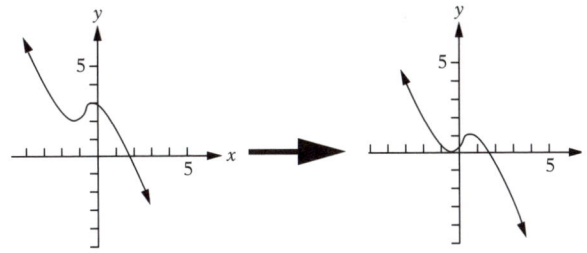

Given the graph of $y = f(x)$ shown above and the transformed graph on the right, what is the equation of the new function?

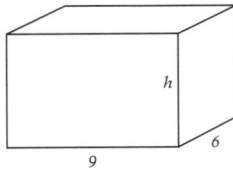

If the rectangular solid above has a volume of 162 cubic inches, what is the surface area of the solid?

Instructions for studying with Root Smart Cards

1st point: Define the word on the front of the card

2nd point: Give the meaning of the root in **bold.**

3rd point: List at least **three** words that contain the root.

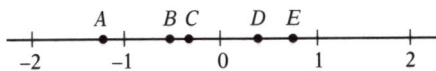

Which point corresponds to the result when the numbers corresponding to points E and B are multiplied?

magn**anim**ous

Formula/Concept: Transformations of Functions

Correct answer: $y = f(x - 1) - 2$
The graph is shifted **down** two units, which turns $y = f(x)$ into $y = f(x) - 2$. The graph is then shifted to the **right** one unit, which turns $y = f(x) - 2$ into $y = f(x - 1) - 2$.

Common mistake: $y = f(x - 2) - 1$
This is the result if you mistakenly reverse the vertical and horizontal shifts.

Formula/Concept:
Parallel lines and alternate interior, corresponding, and alternate exterior angles.

Correct answer: 114
Angle $ZYX = 66°$ and angle $ZYW = 106°$ because they form a "Z". $b = 40°$ because $106° - 66° = 40°$. Angle $VYW = 74°$ because $180 - 106 = 74°$. $c = 74°$ because of corresponding angles. $b + c = 40° + 74° = 114°$.

Mistake:
$80°$. If you think b and c are 40.

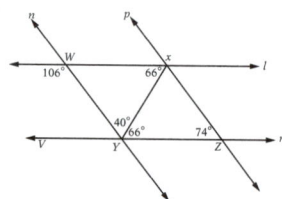

definition of the word

definition of the root

examples of words

Formula/Concept: Volume = lwh
Surface area (SA) = $2lw + 2lh + 2wh$

Correct answer: **198** volume = lwh
$162 = (9)(6)(h)$
Divide by 54: $3 = h$
$SA = 2lw + 2lh + 2wh$
Plug in and $SA = 2(9)(6) + 2(9)(3) + 2(6)(3)$
solve:
Simplify: $SA = 108 + 54 + 36 = 198$

Common mistake: **99**
This is the result if you forget to count the 3 unshown faces when calculating the surface area.

magn**anim**ous = generous

anima = life, spirit

anim**al**, **anim**ate, pusill**anim**ous, un**anim**ous, in**anim**ate

Formula/Concept: Numerical Reasoning

Correct answer: **C**
Assign approximate values to the points:
$A = -1.25; B = -0.50; C = -0.35; D = .35; E = .70$
$(E)(B) =$
Plug in values: $(0.70)(-0.50) = -0.35$

Common mistake: **D**
This is the result if you forget that $(.7)(-.5)$ is negative.

eloquent

peripatetic

immoral

propensity

sacro**sanct**

anthropology

peripatetic = wandering from place to place

peri = around

pericardium, **peri**stalsis, **per**ambulate,
periscope, **peri**pheral, **peri**od

eloquent = fluent in speech

loqu = to talk

loquacious, ventri**loqu**ist, e**locu**tion,
circum**locu**tion, inter**locu**tion

propensity = a tendency

pro = forward, forth

procrastinate, **pro**pagate, **pro**found,
provocative, **pro**lific, **pro**voke,
prophesy, **pro**phetic, **pro**ject, **pro**mote

immoral = lacking morals

im, in, ir = not

immodest, **im**material, **im**mature,
immeasurable, **im**perceptible,
irresponsible, **in**tractable, **im**pregnable

Caution: inflammable = easily ignited
invaluable = priceless
infamous = famous for bad deeds

anthropology = the study of humankind

anthropos = humankind

mis**anthrope**, phil**anthrop**ist,
anthropocentric, **anthrop**omorphic

sacro**sanct** = regarded as sacred

sanctus = holy

sanctimonious, **sanct**ion, **sanct**ify, **sanct**uary

abject

subconscious

Roots Smart Cards Roots Smart Cards
Smart Cards Roots Smart Cards Roots

anarchy

placid

Roots Smart Cards Roots Smart Cards
Smart Cards Roots Smart Cards Roots

tractable

theocracy

Roots Smart Cards Roots Smart Cards

subconscious = occuring in the mind but beyond conscious awareness

sub = under, secretly

subtle, **sub**cutaneous, **sub**liminal, **sub**lime, **sub**terfuge, **sub**sequent, **sub**servient, **sub**marine

abject = miserable

ab = away

abdicate, **ab**scond, **ab**duct, **ab**erration, **ab**solve, **ab**scess, **ab**omination

placid = calm

plac = to please

placate, **plac**ebo, com**plai**sant, com**plac**ent, dis**plea**se, **plea**

anarchy = absence of government

an = without

anecdote, **an**aerobic, **an**algesic, **an**emia, **an**esthetic, **an**onymous

theocracy = a government ruled by religious authority

theo = god

a**theist**, **theo**logy, en**thu**siasm, pan**theist**, mono**theism**

tractable = easily managed

tract = together

sub**tract**, abs**tract**, at**tract**, **tract**or, in**tract**able, dis**tract**, con**tract**, **tract**ion con**VOCA**tion

epitaph

tenacity

soliloquy

in**cite**

com**ple**ment

epitaph = an inscription on a tombstone

epi = upon

epicenter, **epi**demic, **ep**hemeral,
epilepsy, **epi**dermis, **epi**tome, **epi**logue

con**voca**tion = an assembly or meeting

vocare = to call

vocabulary, pro**voke**, con**voke**,
in**voke**, re**voke**, **voca**tion,
ad**voca**te, equi**voca**te

soliloquy = a speech to oneself

solus = alone

sole, **solo**, **soli**taire,
solitary, **soli**tude, **soli**psism

tenacity = persistence

tenere = to hold

sus**tain**, abs**tain**, con**tain**, de**tain**,
ob**tain**, enter**tain**, **ten**able, per**tain**,
per**tina**city, re**tain**

com**ple**ment = to complete the whole

plere = to fill

accom**pl**ish, re**ple**te,
de**ple**te, sup**ple**ment

in**cite** = to provoke

citare = to summon, to call

citation, ex**cite**, re**cite**, resus**cita**te, soli**cit**

pro**pon**ent

biology

Roots Smart Cards Roots Smart Cards
Smart Cards Roots Smart Cards Roots

eul**o**gy

apocryphal

Roots Smart Cards Roots Smart Cards
Smart Cards Roots Smart Cards Roots

circum**scribe**

etymo**logy**

biology = the study of life

bio = life

biogenesis, **bio**graphy, **bio**nics,
biopsy, **bio**sphere

pro**pon**ent = a supporter; an advocate

ponere = to place

im**pose,** inter**pose,**
op**pon**ent, op**po**site, ex**pon**ent,
ex**po**sition, ex**po**und, post**pone,** ap**po**sitive

apocryphal = of doubtful authenticity

apo = away from

apocalypse, **apho**rism, **apo**state,
apoplexy, **apo**stle, **apo**thecary,
apology

eulogy = praise; a praise-filled speech given at
someone's funeral

eu = good

euphemism, **eu**calyptus, **eu**charist,
eugenics, **eu**karyote, **eu**phoria, **eu**rhythmic

etymo**logy** = the study of the origin of words

logos = study of

astro**logy,** archaeo**logy,** geo**logy,**
onco**logy,** bio**logy,** paleonto**logy,**
psycho**logy,** etymo**logy,** theo**logy,**
patho**logy,** anthropo**logy**

circum**scribe** = to determine the
limits of; to draw a line around

scribe = to write

in**scribe,** con**scrip**tion, de**scrip**tion,
sub**scrip**tion, in**scrip**tion

paramount

levity

orthodox

in**cis**ive

equanimity

irre**ver**ent

levity = the state of being light, frivolity

levis = light in weight

elevator, relieve, levitate,
alleviate, elevate, oblivion

paramount = of extreme importance

para = beside, next to, beyond

paraphrase, parasite, paramedic,
paranoia, parallel, paradigm, paragon

incisive = clear in expression, penetrating

cis = cut

scissors, concise, schism,
precise, precision, decisive

orthodox = traditional

orthos = correct, straight

orthography, orthodontics, unorthodox,
orthopedic, orthodoxy

irreverent = disrespectful

vereri = respect
verus = truth

revere, reverent, reverend, veracity,
verify, verisimilitude, veritable

equanimity = calm, even-temperedness

equi = equal

equinox, equivalent, equalize,
equality, equipotential, inequality,
equitable, equator, equalize

denigrate

misanthrope

ob**sequi**ous

ex**culp**ate

im**pul**sive

antipathy

misanthrope = one who hates humankind

mis = bad, wretched, hatred

miser, **mis**ery, **mis**erly, **mis**erable,
miscarriage, **mis**chief, **mis**creant, **mis**direct,
miscue, **mis**demeanor, **mis**feasance,
misconduct

denigrate = to speak poorly of; to belittle

de = down, off

delineate, **de**scend, **de**mote,
decline, **de**moralize, **de**ride, **de**bate,
debrief, **de**bunk, **de**capitate, **de**ciduous,
decrepit, **de**cry, **de**ficient, **de**pict

ex**culp**ate = free from blame

culp = blame

dis**culp**ate, **culp**rit, **culp**able,
in**culp**ate, mea **culp**a

ob**sequi**ous = overly submissive

sequi = to follow

sequence, pro**secu**te, **segue**,
sub**seque**nt, pur**sue**, non **sequi**tur

antipathy = strong feeling against

anti = against

antisocial, **anti**biotic, **ant**onym,
antiseptic, **ant**agonist

im**pul**sive = acting on impulse without
much forethought

pel, pul = to push

com**pel**, im**pel**, ex**pel**, pro**pul**sion,
pro**pel**, re**pul**sive, pro**pel**ler

apathy

audible

"A stitch in time saves nine."

The statement above suggests that taking your time to do something well rather than rushing to get it done quickly will save time in the long run.

For 1 point each, generate a "furthermore," a "however," and a "for example" statement to this thesis.

"A bird in the hand is worth two in the bush."

The statement above suggests that it is better to opt for something certain than it is to try to achieve the impossible.

For 1 point each, generate a "furthermore," a "however," and a "for example" statement to this thesis.

"What's past is prologue."

The statement above suggests that it is important to remember the past because of the lessons it has for us all, but also that there is much to come in the future.

For 1 point each, generate a "furthermore," a "however," and a "for example" statement to this thesis.

"All that matters is that you try your best."

For 1 point each, generate an "I agree, because" and an "I disagree, because" thesis statement and a "for example" or a "nevertheless" statement for each point of view.

audible = able to be heard

aud = to hear

auditorium, **aud**ition, **aud**io,
audit, **aud**itory, in**aud**ible, **aud**ience

a**pathy** = lack of feeling

pathos = emotion

sym**pathy**, em**pathy**, anti**pathy**,
osteo**pathy**, **path**ogen, **path**etic, psycho**path**

Because there are so many possible answers to this question, we have not given specific examples for the point allocation. Ask a teacher, friend, parent, or tutor to score this card for you:

Give 1 point for each statement made by the student that is interesting, well thought out, and relevant to the given thesis.

Because there are so many possible answers to this question, we have not given specific examples for the point allocation. Ask a teacher, friend, parent, or tutor to score this card for you:

Give 1 point for each statement made by the student that is interesting, well thought out, and relevant to the given thesis.

Because there are so many possible answers to this question, we have not given specific examples for the point allocation. Ask a teacher, friend, parent, or tutor to score this card for you:

Give 1 point for each statement made by the student that is interesting, well thought out, and relevant to the given thesis.

Because there are so many possible answers to this question, we have not given specific examples for the point allocation. Ask a teacher, friend, parent, or tutor to score this card for you:

Give 1 point for each statement made by the student that is interesting, well thought out, and relevant to the given thesis.

"Everything you can imagine can become reality."

For 1 point each, generate a "furthermore," a "however," and a "for example" statement to this statement made by Pablo Picasso.

"All that glitters is not gold."

For 1 point each, generate a "furthermore," a "however," and a "for example" statement to this thesis.

"It is better to be safe than sorry."

For 1 point each, generate a "furthermore," a "however," and a "for example" statement to this thesis.

Is money the root of all evil?

For 1 point each, generate a "yes, because" and a "no, because" thesis statement and a "for example" or a "nevertheless" statement for each point of view.

"Too many cooks spoil the broth."

For 1 point each, generate a "furthermore," a "however," and a "for example" statement to this thesis.

Is ignorance bliss?

For 1 point each, generate a "yes, because" and a "no, because" thesis statement and a "for example" or a "nevertheless" statement for each point of view.

Because there are so many possible answers to this question, we have not given specific examples for the point allocation. Ask a teacher, friend, parent, or tutor to score this card for you:

Give 1 point for each statement made by the student that is interesting, well thought out, and relevant to the given thesis.

Because there are so many possible answers to this question, we have not given specific examples for the point allocation. Ask a teacher, friend, parent, or tutor to score this card for you:

Give 1 point for each statement made by the student that is interesting, well thought out, and relevant to the given thesis.

Because there are so many possible answers to this question, we have not given specific examples for the point allocation. Ask a teacher, friend, parent, or tutor to score this card for you:

Give 1 point for each statement made by the student that is interesting, well thought out, and relevant to the given thesis.

Because there are so many possible answers to this question, we have not given specific examples for the point allocation. Ask a teacher, friend, parent, or tutor to score this card for you:

Give 1 point for each statement made by the student that is interesting, well thought out, and relevant to the given thesis.

Because there are so many possible answers to this question, we have not given specific examples for the point allocation. Ask a teacher, friend, parent, or tutor to score this card for you:

Give 1 point for each statement made by the student that is interesting, well thought out, and relevant to the given thesis.

Because there are so many possible answers to this question, we have not given specific examples for the point allocation. Ask a teacher, friend, parent, or tutor to score this card for you:

Give 1 point for each statement made by the student that is interesting, well thought out, and relevant to the given thesis.

Is honesty the best policy?

For 1 point each, generate a "yes, because" and a "no, because" thesis statement and a "for example" or a "nevertheless" statement for each point of view.

Are women more constrained by society than men are?

For 1 point each, generate a "yes, because" and a "no, because" thesis statement and a "for example" or a "nevertheless" statement for each point of view.

Is the rapid advance of technology good or bad for humankind?

For 1 point each, generate a "yes, because" and a "no, because" thesis statement and a "for example" or a "nevertheless" statement for each point of view.

The most important thing for a leader to understand is history.

For 1 point each, generate an "I agree, because" and an "I disagree, because" thesis statement and a "for example" or a "nevertheless" statement for each point of view.

"There is a time and a place for censorship."

For 1 point each, generate a "yes, because" and a "no, because" thesis statement and a "for example" or a "nevertheless" statement for each point of view

For 1 point each, rewrite the sentences below to eliminate any wordiness, redundancy, clichés, or grammatical errors.

1. Veteran pitchers rely on past experience to know how to pitch to the best hitters.
2. It was clear that my son planned on asking me the question until I said yes.
3. In this day and age, too much emphasis is placed on how much annual income a person makes when trying to measure success.

Because there are so many possible answers to this question, we have not given specific examples for the point allocation. Ask a teacher, friend, parent, or tutor to score this card for you:

Give 1 point for each statement made by the student that is interesting, well thought out, and relevant to the given thesis.

Because there are so many possible answers to this question, we have not given specific examples for the point allocation. Ask a teacher, friend, parent, or tutor to score this card for you:

Give 1 point for each statement made by the student that is interesting, well thought out, and relevant to the given thesis.

Because there are so many possible answers to this question, we have not given specific examples for the point allocation. Ask a teacher, friend, parent, or tutor to score this card for you:

Give 1 point for each statement made by the student that is interesting, well thought out, and relevant to the given thesis.

Because there are so many possible answers to this question, we have not given specific examples for the point allocation. Ask a teacher, friend, parent, or tutor to score this card for you:

Give 1 point for each statement made by the student that is interesting, well thought out, and relevant to the given thesis.

1. **Redundancy:** Veteran pitchers rely on ~~past~~ experience to know how to pitch to the best hitters.

2. **Infinitive versus gerund:** It was clear that my son planned ~~on asking~~ **to ask** me the question until I said yes.

3. **Wordiness:** ~~In this day and age~~ **Today**, too much emphasis is placed on ~~how much~~ annual income ~~a person makes~~ when ~~trying to measure~~ **measuring** success.

Because there are so many possible answers to this question, we have not given specific examples for the point allocation. Ask a teacher, friend, parent, or tutor to score this card for you:

Give 1 point for each statement made by the student that is interesting, well thought out, and relevant to the given thesis.

"It is always good to follow authority."

For 1 point each, generate a "yes, because" and a "no, because" thesis statement and a "for example" or a "nevertheless" statement for each point of view.

For 1 point each, rewrite the sentences below to eliminate any wordiness, redundancy, clichés, or grammatical errors.

1. There are many reasons making it irresponsible to allow your children to do whatever they want every day after school simply because you are too busy at work to keep them in line.
2. When a bear is chasing you, one should not make loud noises and avoid sudden movements.
3. Put your pencils down; we are now at this time going to collect your test booklets.

For 1 point each, rewrite the sentences below to eliminate any wordiness, redundancy, clichés, or grammatical errors.

1. The company is looking to hire individuals who can think outside the box.
2. In the event that I am unable to make the wedding due to the fact that I am away on business, I hope that you are aware of the fact that I will be there in spirit.
3. We always give it 110% when we are on the field, and if we fail this year, we'll pick up the pieces and try again next year.

"Misfortune reveals your true friends."

For 1 point each, give 3 examples from literature, history, current events, or your own experiences that support this statement made by Aristotle.

For 1 point each, rewrite the sentences below to eliminate any wordiness, redundancy, clichés, or grammatical errors.

1. Ever since she was a young child, Ella has loved singing.
2. A diamond of perfect clarity is an object that is very difficult to find in the marketplace today.
3. Regardless of the fact that the best parts of the Star Wars trilogy have been combined together into one action-packed DVD, I still found it to be boring and uninteresting.

"Real integrity is doing the right thing, knowing that nobody's going to know whether you did it or not."

For 1 point each, give 3 examples from literature, history, current events, or your own experiences that support this statement made by Oprah Winfrey.

1. **Wordiness:** It is irresponsible to allow your children to do whatever they want after school simply because you are busy.

2. **Parallelism:** When a bear is chasing you, ~~one~~ **you** should ~~not~~ make **neither** loud noises ~~and avoid~~ **nor** sudden movements.

3. **Redundancy:** Put your pencils down; we are now ~~at this time~~ going to collect your test booklets.

Because there are so many possible answers to this question, we have not given specific examples for the point allocation. Ask a teacher, friend, parent, or tutor to score this card for you:

Give 1 point for each statement made by the student that is interesting, well thought out, and relevant to the given thesis.

Because there are so many possible answers to this question, we have not given specific examples for the point allocation. Ask a teacher, friend, parent, or tutor to score this card for you:

Give 1 point for each statement made by the student that is interesting, well thought out, and relevant to the given thesis.

1. **Jargony:** The company is looking to hire individuals who can think ~~outside the box~~ **creatively**.

2. **Wordiness:** ~~In the event that~~ **If** I am unable to make the wedding ~~due to the fact that~~ **because** I am away on business, I hope tha~~t you are aware of the~~ fact **know** that I will be there in spirit.

3. **Clichés:** We always ~~give it 100%~~ **try our hardest** ~~we are~~ on the field, and if we fail this year, we'll ~~pick up the pieces~~ **regroup** and try again next year.

Because there are so many possible answers to this question, we have not given specific examples for the point allocation. Ask a teacher, friend, parent, or tutor to score this card for you:

Give 1 point for each statement made by the student that is interesting, well thought out, and relevant to the given thesis.

1. **Unclear:** Ever since she was a young child, Ella has ~~loved~~ singing **to sing**. OR Ever since she was a young child, Ella has loved **listening to others sing**.

2. **Wordiness:** A diamond of perfect clarity is **rare.** ~~an object that is very difficult to find in the marketplace~~ today.

3. **Wordiness:** ~~Regardless of the fact that~~ **Although** the best parts of the Star Wars trilogy have been combined ~~together~~ into one action-packed DVD, **it was still dull.** ~~I still found it to be boring and uninteresting.~~

For 1 point each, rewrite the sentences below to eliminate any wordiness, redundancy, clichés, or grammatical errors.

1. Although the movie was different than its predecessor, it is nevertheless filled with similar themes and ideas.
2. Frustrated and tired, the struggling poet threw his notebook which hit the floor and let out a scream.
3. When Madonna's music was first introduced to the public, they had criticized it for being inappropriate and controversial.

"Knowledge is power."

For 1 point each, give 3 examples from literature, history, current events, or your own experiences that support this statement made by Sir Francis Bacon.

Who is your hero and why?

You will receive points for an answer that is thought-provoking, clear, and original. You will also receive a point for writing a strong concluding thought on heroism in general.

Give 3 examples from literature, history, current events, or your own experiences that demonstrate something meaningful about <u>courage</u>.

Does government-mandated testing affect education in a positive or a negative way?

For 1 point each, generate a "yes, because" and a "no, because" thesis statement and a "for example" or a "nevertheless" statement for each point of view.

Give 3 examples from literature, history, current events, or your own experiences that describe <u>an individual overcoming adversity</u>.

Because there are so many possible answers to this question, we have not given specific examples for the point allocation. Ask a teacher, friend, parent, or tutor to score this card for you:

Give 1 point for each statement made by the student that is interesting, well thought out, and relevant to the given thesis.

1. **Idiom error, tense error:** Although the movie was different ~~than~~ **from** its predecessor, it ~~is~~ **was** nevertheless ~~filled~~ **concerned** with similar themes and ideas.

2. **Coordination error:** Frustrated and tired, the struggling poet **let out a scream and** threw his notebook, which hit the floor. ~~and let out a scream.~~

3. **Redundancy/Tense error:** When Madonna's music was ~~first~~ introduced, ~~to the public, they~~ had criticized it for being inappropriate and controversial.

Because there are so many possible answers to this question, we have not given specific examples for the point allocation. Ask a teacher, friend, parent, or tutor to score this card for you:

Give 1 point for each reference made by the student that is interesting, well thought out, and relevant to the given thesis.

Because there are so many possible answers to this question, we have not given specific examples for the point allocation. Ask a teacher, friend, parent, or tutor to score this card for you:

1st point: for a response that is unique and thought-provoking.
2nd point: for a good "because" statement
3rd point: for a good concluding thought on heroism in general

Because there are so many possible answers to this question, we have not given specific examples for the point allocation. Ask a teacher, friend, parent, or tutor to score this card for you:

Give 1 point for each reference made by the student that is interesting, well thought out, and relevant to the given thesis.

Because there are so many possible answers to this question, we have not given specific examples for the point allocation. Ask a teacher, friend, parent, or tutor to score this card for you:

Give 1 point for each statement made by the student that is interesting, well thought out, and relevant to the given thesis.

Should criminal trials be televised?

For 1 point each, generate a "yes, because" and a "no, because" thesis statement and a "for example" or a "nevertheless" statement for each point of view.

Give 3 examples from literature, history, current events, or your own experiences that demonstrate something meaningful about <u>treachery</u>.

Give 3 examples from literature, history, current events, or your own experiences that say something meaningful about <u>devotion</u>.

One thing undervalued in today's society is. . . .

You will receive points for answers that are thought-provoking, clear, and original. Write 3 thesis statements that complete the phrase above.

Give 3 examples from literature, history, current events, or your own experiences that say something meaningful about <u>the power of knowledge</u>.

I have done many memorable things in my life, but the one moment I will never forget is. . .

You will receive points for an answer that is thought-provoking, clear, and original. You will also receive a point for writing a strong concluding thought on what makes a moment unforgettable.

Because there are so many possible answers to this question, we have not given specific examples for the point allocation. Ask a teacher, friend, parent, or tutor to score this card for you:

Give 1 point for each reference made by the student that is interesting, well thought out, and relevant to the given thesis.

Because there are so many possible answers to this question, we have not given specific examples for the point allocation. Ask a teacher, friend, parent, or tutor to score this card for you:

Give 1 point for each statement made by the student that is interesting, well thought out, and relevant to the given thesis.

Because there are so many possible answers to this question, we have not given specific examples for the point allocation. Ask a teacher, friend, parent, or tutor to score this card for you:

Give 1 point for each thesis written by the student that is interesting, well thought out, and relevant to the given phrase.

Because there are so many possible answers to this question, we have not given specific examples for the point allocation. Ask a teacher, friend, parent, or tutor to score this card for you:

Give 1 point for each reference made by the student that is interesting, well thought out, and relevant to the given thesis.

Because there are so many possible answers to this question, we have not given specific examples for the point allocation. Ask a teacher, friend, parent, or tutor to score this card for you:

1st point: for a response that is unique and thought-provoking.
2nd point: for a good "because" statement.
3rd point: for a good concluding thought on unforgettable moments.

Because there are so many possible answers to this question, we have not given specific examples for the point allocation. Ask a teacher, friend, parent, or tutor to score this card for you:

Give 1 point for each reference made by the student that is interesting, well thought out, and relevant to the given thesis.

Give 3 examples from literature, history, current events, or your own experiences that say something meaningful about <u>honesty</u>.

The greatest challenge I have faced in my life is. . . .

You will receive points for an answer that is thought-provoking, clear, and original. You will also receive a point for writing a strong concluding thought on what makes something challenging.

Is it better to change or maintain the status quo?

For 1 point each, generate a "yes, because" and a "no, because" thesis statement and a "for example" or a "nevertheless" statement for each point of view.

"A discovery is said to be an accident meeting a prepared mind."

For 1 point each, give three examples from literature, history, current events, or your own experiences that support this statement made by Albert Einstein.

Is jealousy always a bad thing?

For 1 point each, generate a "yes, because" and a "no, because" thesis statement and a "for example" or a "nevertheless" statement for each point of view.

Necessity is the mother of invention.

For 1 point each, generate a "furthermore," a "however," and a "for example" statement to this thesis.

Because there are so many possible answers to this question, we have not given specific examples for the point allocation. Ask a teacher, friend, parent, or tutor to score this card for you:

1st point: for a response that is unique and thought-provoking.
2nd point: for a good "because" statement.
3rd point: for a good concluding thought on unforgettable moments.

Because there are so many possible answers to this question, we have not given specific examples for the point allocation. Ask a teacher, friend, parent, or tutor to score this card for you:

Give 1 point for each reference made by the student that is interesting, well thought out, and relevant to the given thesis.

Because there are so many possible answers to this question, we have not given specific examples for the point allocation. Ask a teacher, friend, parent, or tutor to score this card for you:

Give 1 point for each example given by the student that is interesting, well thought out, and relevant to the given quotation.

Because there are so many possible answers to this question, we have not given specific examples for the point allocation. Ask a teacher, friend, parent, or tutor to score this card for you:

Give 1 point for each thesis written by the student that is interesting, well thought out, and relevant to the given question.

Because there are so many possible answers to this question, we have not given specific examples for the point allocation. Ask a teacher, friend, parent, or tutor to score this card for you:

Give 1 point for each thesis written by the student that is interesting, well thought out, and relevant to the given question.

Because there are so many possible answers to this question, we have not given specific examples for the point allocation. Ask a teacher, friend, parent, or tutor to score this card for you:

Give 1 point for each thesis written by the student that is interesting, well thought out, and relevant to the given question.